ANCIENT F

A companion volume to the highly successful *Ancient Greece: Social and Historical Documents from Archaic Times to the Death of Socrates*, this textbook is a valuable resource for students at all levels studying Ancient Rome. Lynda Garland and Matthew Dillon present an extensive range of material, from the Early Republic to the assassination of Julius Caesar. *Ancient Rome* includes:

- Source material on political developments in the Roman Republic (509–44 BC).
- Detailed chapters on social phenomena, such as Roman religion, slavery and freedmen, women and the family, and the public face of Rome.
- Clear, precise translations of documents taken not only from historical sources, but also from inscriptions, laws and decrees, epitaphs, graffiti, public speeches, poetry, private letters and drama.
- Concise up-to-date bibliographies and commentaries for each document and chapter.
- A definitive collection of source material on the Roman Republic.

Matthew Dillon is an Associate Professor in Classics, History and Religion at the University of New England, Australia. His research interests focus on the classical world, especially on Greek and Roman religion.

Lynda Garland is an Associate Professor in Classics, History and Religion at the University of New England, Australia. Her research interests cover the classical and Byzantine worlds.

ANCIENT ROME

From the Early Republic to the Assassination of Julius Caesar

Matthew Dillon

and

Lynda Garland

Routledge
Taylor & Francis Group

LONDON AND NEW YORK

First published 2005
by Routledge
2 Park Square, Milton Park, Abingdon, Oxon OX14 4RN

Simultaneously published in the USA and Canada
by Routledge
711 Third Avenue, New York, NY 10017

Routledge is an imprint of the Taylor & Francis Group

Typeset in Times New Roman by
Keystroke, Jacaranda Lodge, Wolverhampton
Printed and bound in Great Britain by
Antony Rowe Ltd, Chippenham, Wiltshire

British Library Cataloguing in Publication Data
A catalogue record for this book is available from the British Library

Library of Congress Cataloging in Publication Data
Garland, Lynda, 1955–
Ancient Rome : from the early Republic to the assassination of Julius Caesar /
Lynda Garland and Matthew Dillon.
p. cm.
Includes bibliographical references and index.
1. Rome—Civilization—Sources. I. Dillon, Matthew, 1963–
II. Title.
DG77.G37 2005
937′.6—dc22
2005013918

ISBN 978–0–415–22458–1 (hbk)
ISBN 978–0–415–22459–8 (pbk)

Contents

Preface

In 1994 the authors published a sourcebook entitled *Ancient Greece*, subsequently updated in a second edition in 2000. Our view at the time, reinforced by comments from colleagues and reviewers, was that a companion volume on the Roman Republic would be equally useful. Commitments of varying sorts have delayed its appearance until now, but we trust that the volume will prove of value to undergraduates and scholars in the current millennium.

As with *Ancient Greece, Ancient Rome* is a sourcebook aimed primarily at undergraduate students of Roman history at all levels, with some uses also as a research tool for the reader interested in further study. The period covered is that of the Roman Republic from its beginnings in 509 BC to the death of Julius Caesar in 44 BC, and the documents have been carefully chosen to reflect contemporary views of the main issues of political and social history within that period. Any sourcebook is naturally open to criticisms regarding the selection of material: the authors have attempted impartiality in their choice of topics and documents, but inevitably some imbalance of emphasis has probably occurred. Nevertheless the main areas of Roman Republican history have been covered in depth, with especial focus on social and political developments throughout the Republic. Beginning with a chapter on *Early Republican Rome*, which combines both social and political history for this period, the Republic's social history is represented by chapters on *Roman Religion, Slavery and Freedmen*, and *Women and the Family*, while we have tried to cover Roman concepts and values in a chapter entitled the *Public Face of Rome*, placed early in the volume to demonstrate the importance of an appreciation of the Romans' own perception of their world at this point in the course of study. The chapter on religion has also been placed near the beginning of the volume, because religious beliefs and practices determined so much of the Romans' approach to politics and conquest. The *Punic Wars, Rome's Mediterranean Empire*, the *Gracchi, Marius*, the *Social War, Sulla*, the *Collapse of the Republic*, and the *Civil War and Caesar's Dictatorship* have been given chapters to themselves to facilitate the study of what can be a complex and much-studied period. A survey of the ancient sources ends the volume. Throughout, the aim has been to give a wide range of material from contemporary sources, which will, if the authors' aim is achieved, be more than sufficient for a study of the Roman Republic at an undergraduate level.

A book covering so broad a subject must inevitably suffer from incompleteness in some areas, and we have had to limit not merely the topics covered, but the number of texts illustrating each section. We can only hope that our choice of material does not appear too arbitrary, and have tried to ensure that we have given references throughout to other useful passages which will direct the student to further documents of relevance in the area. We have also given suggestions for further reading on particular points of importance and envisage that the chapter bibliographies will enable students to pursue detailed research on particular topics. We have chosen to give detailed comments on most passages, with accompanying bibliographic references. Although this takes up space which could have been used to provide larger selections from the sources, we see little point in presenting lengthy passages from ancient sources which students cannot understand. Having taught ancient history for many years, we believe that it is better to take students through passage by passage with elucidating comments, rather than simply giving them large sections of translation from sources which are incomprehensible without adequate guidance. We also feel it is better to break long narratives up and to deal with them in small amounts rather than give students pages of text *en bloc*.

The bibliographies attached to each chapter are there for a particular reason: they are primarily for the use of the student. We hope that students, particularly those in second and third year university or college study, will choose to follow up particular points of detail. Even postgraduate students have commented on how useful the bibliographies in *Ancient Greece* have been and the authors intend that the bibliographies here will be equally valuable and serve as a bibliographic survey. Students are able to choose from a variety of bibliographical references to engage in further reading on broad topics such as the role of women in Roman religion, and on more detailed points such as modern discussions of Polybius' description of the recruitment procedure for the Roman army. References to older works have generally been avoided so as not to overwhelm the reader, and it is mainly the last three decades of scholarship on which we have concentrated.

In our translations we have followed the Latin and Greek of the ancient texts as closely as possible, even to punctuation, where this does not involve confusion, and poetry is as far as possible translated in lines following those of the original text. Present in our minds has been the thought that this would be a suitable text for use in a unit on 'ancient languages for historians', and to that end we have made comparisons of the translations with the original sources as easy as possible. For this reason we have carefully inserted all chapter and section numbers of the original sources in the text of our translations. For those students who do not as yet have the ancient languages, we can perhaps hope that this study of some of the more important documents of Roman history will inspire them to attempt to acquire either Greek or Latin. Titles of ancient sources are given in English, but references to the texts used in our translations can be found in the index of ancient sources.

The authors are currently working on a companion volume to *Ancient Rome*, to be entitled, *Republican Rome: an Introduction* which will contain a selection of points for discussion on the different topics, illustrations, maps, family trees, additional notes on the ancient authors and sources, and a variety of other aids for the student and lecturer.

PREFACE

As far as a dedication is concerned, we would like to offer this book, once again, with thanks, to our students in all areas of Ancient History, past, present, and future, as well as to *liberis nostris dilectissimis*, with assurances that the book on which we have been working for 'hundreds of years' has finally been completed.

Matthew Dillon and Lynda Garland
University of New England, Australia

1

Early Republican Rome: 507–264 BC

The city of Rome, halfway down the western coast of Italy and some fifteen kilometres inland, started its history as a few primitive huts on adjacent hills; the earliest archaeological remains belong to the foundations of dwellings on the Palatine dating to the middle of the eighth century BC. The city would eventually be built over and around the famous seven hills: the Aventine, Caelian, Capitoline, Esquiline, Palatine, Quirinal and Viminal. Tradition and myth gave the city a founder, Romulus, but nearly everything about him is probably fictitious. For the Romans, he was the first of seven kings, before the Republic came into being in 509 BC with the overthrow of the last king, the Etruscan Tarquinius Superbus 'the Proud'. Livy and Dionysius record much about these seven kings, who ruled over some 250 years, but the pre-regal and regal history of Rome is more or less lost except for the archaeological record. There was a tendency to ascribe Roman institutions and customs to these kings, as well as developments in the physical structure of the city (docs 1.1–2, 1.5, 2.3), though the idea of monarchy was hated throughout the Republic (doc. 1.10, 13.55).

By the sixth and fifth centuries BC Rome was part of the wider Mediterranean world: Herodotus knows of Agylla, 30 kilometres from Rome (Hdt. 1.167), and calls the defeat of Tarentum by the Iapygians in 473 BC the worst ever suffered by the Greeks (7.170), while Aristotle referred to the sack of Rome by the Gauls in the fourth century BC (Plutarch *Camillus* 22). The inscription of Sostratus found at Gravisca, the port of Etrurian Tarquinia, dated to c. 500 ('I am of Aeginetan Apollo. Sostratus . . .'; *LSAG²* p. 439), is evidence for Greeks trading on the Etruscan coast in the late sixth century, and this Sostratus is mentioned by Herodotus (4.152) as the archetypal profiteer: he may have been bringing Attic vases to Etruria. Athenian black-figure pottery dated to c. 570–560 BC has been found in the Roman forum, near the 'Black Stone' (lapis niger), on which there is an inscription in undecipherable Latin.

The standard abbreviation for the government of Rome was *SPQR*: 'senatus populusque Romanus' (the senate and people of Rome), and the state was known as *res publica*, literally 'public affairs', sometimes written as one word, *respublica*. The roles of the senate and people were seen as equally significant in the government of the city. As regards officials, Roman political life was highly competitive and underpinned by the principle of collegiality. From the expulsion of the kings, the tenure of magistracies was strictly annual, and supreme power was shared between two consuls (initially called praetors). It was the elected magistrates who convened the senate and assemblies, administered the law and finances, and commanded the armies and provinces. By the first century BC, the senior magistrates were the consuls, the supreme commanders of the army (docs 1.11–13) and the praetors, who were in charge of the administration of the law, but, like the consuls, able to lead an army and convene the centuriate assembly. These senior magistrates possessed the powers of imperium (military command) and auspicium (the right to take auspices: see docs 3.45–50). Junior magistrates consisted of the quaestors (whose duties were primarily financial) and the aediles (two curule and two plebeian), who were in charge of the infrastructure of Rome as a city and the holding of games. In times of crisis in early Rome a single dictator could be appointed for a limited period of time, usually six months (doc. 1.14), and two censors with an eighteen-month term of office were regularly elected to deal with the census (the registration of citizens) and carry out other duties (docs 1.15–17).

The senate was essentially an advisory body to the magistrates, as it had been to the kings, and prior to Sulla consisted of some 300 members (though in early Rome there were considerably less); the number was then raised by Sulla to 600, and by Julius Caesar to 900. The senate's numbers were kept up by the enrolment of elected magistrates, and hence, as a body of ex-officials, it possessed great influence over magistrates and people. However, the senate could not decide on war or peace, and it was the people which voted for legislation as the comitia tributa, 'tribal assembly' (in the comitium or forum), and for war and peace as the comitia centuriata, 'centuriate assembly', on the Campus Martius (doc. 1.58, cf. 1.19).

The people (the *populus Romanus*) had the constitutional rights of direct voting on legislation, electing magistrates, and making decisions on trials in the popular assembly (docs 1.19–21). Duties included military service (for those with the requisite economic status), paying the poll tax (up to 168 BC), and serving as jurors. Ten tribunes, who were also magistrates elected annually, represented the rights of the people and prevented them from exploitation (docs 1.22–23). Technically, therefore, the populus Romanus was sovereign, but of course only adult citizen males were members of assemblies (though these included freedmen). Polybius, writing in the mid-second century BC, saw the Roman constitution as a 'mixed' one and believed that the system of checks and balances between magistrates, senate and people was one of the factors in its successful working (doc. 1.58).

The forum was the centre of political life in Rome, as well as containing shops and businesses, while trials, gladiatorial and theatrical shows and the funeral orations of prominent citizens took place there. Political life revolved around the assemblies (held both in the forum and in the Campus Martius, the 'Field of Mars') and the senate house (the *curia*) in the forum, while important temples fronted onto the forum, where the residences of the pontifex maximus and Vestals were sited (docs 1.5–8).

Early Rome was dominated by two long-standing areas of conflict: the struggle between patricians and plebeians, the 'Conflict of the Orders', which lasted from 494 to 287 BC (docs 1.24–57), and Rome's drive to become the dominant state in Italy (docs 1.26–7, 60–73). The plebeians, those who were not patricians (members of specific clans originally with responsibility for religious rites), increasingly gained access to magistracies and the priesthoods (docs 1.47–55) and by 300 BC the wealthy plebeian families had joined Rome's political elite, while, as part of this conflict, the XII Tables were codified supposedly in response to popular agitation over the patricians' control of the law (docs 1.31–42, 44). Within Italy, Rome was engaged in continuous wars with its Italic neighbours from its foundation. The Etruscan city of Veii, some 15 kilometres north of Rome, was finally taken in 396 BC (doc. 1.60); Latium, the area inhabited by the Latins, was conquered by 300 BC (docs 1.26, 62–4); and the Samnites, though fierce enemies of Rome from 343 to 290 BC (and again in the Social War, 91–89 BC), were effectively neutralised, along with the Greek cities of southern Italy, by 272 BC: Rome's dominance over Italy was now complete.

Ancient sources: family history and heroic tales had a long oral tradition in early Rome; however there was also documentary evidence from the earliest period of the Republic, in the *Fasti* (the list of consuls for each year), and historians use, as their chronological framework, lists of the consuls, triumphs, military campaigns, alliances, colonies, public works, natural disasters and other such archival material. Cicero (*de orat.* 2.52) suggests that there was an official chronicle called the *Annales Maximi* (see doc. 14.2) kept by the pontifex maximus which listed all important events in a certain year and continued from the earliest times down to c. 120 BC (P. Mucius Scaevola). In addition state documents were kept in the temple of Saturn on the Capitol and pontifical colleges kept their own records.

Fragments of the *XII Tables*, the law-code compiled in 451/0, survive from quotations in later writers; while the XII Tables might have regulated existing legal practices (rather than reforming them) they are a very valuable source for law and society in the mid-fifth century and were later seen as the basis of all Roman law.

Antiquarians: Antiquarianism of language or customs became a popular study in the first century BC. M. Terentius Varro (116–27 BC) is said to have written 490 books (or more). Six of his 25 books *de lingua latina* (*On the Latin Language*) are extant; his *Antiquities* are lost but his work was highly significant as a source for later writers: Pliny the Elder, for example, in his 37 books of *Natural History* relied on his account. Another noted antiquarian was Dionysius of Halicarnassus, who is a very valuable source for the constitution and customs of early Rome. A Greek historian, he lived in Rome in the time of Augustus as a teacher of rhetoric and published his 20 books of *Roman Antiquities* (down to the beginning of the first Punic War) 22 years after Augustus' assumption of power. The first 11 books (to 441 BC) survive. As an outsider he describes much in Roman society which is otherwise not mentioned, but is concerned with showing Rome as essentially a Greek city and emphasising its intrinsic virtues, and his work is full of lengthy rhetorical speeches. Gellius' *Attic Nights* (Gellius was born c. AD 125) is a series of short notes which he put together for his children, which contain useful citations from earlier works now lost. Macrobius used him extensively: his *Saturnalia* is in the form of a series of dialogues which took place before and during the Saturnalia of perhaps AD 383 and contains nostalgic reminiscences of Rome's pagan past.

The main historian of early Rome is Titus Livius (59 BC–AD 17). His *ad urbe condita* (*From the Foundation of the City*) consisted of 142 books from Rome's origins to 9 BC. Only books 1–10 and 21–45 survive (with some fragments); books 11–20 are lost and this leaves a gap in the history for the period 293–264 BC. The *Epitome* of Livy (early third century AD) gives summaries of books 37–40, 48–55, and the *Periochae* (fourth century AD) summaries of all books except 136 and 137. Livy used literary sources almost exclusively, seldom bothering to consult archival records. In books 31–145 he mainly followed Polybius' account with a few additions from later writers such as Valerius Antias and Claudius Quadrigarius; he tended, though not exclusively, to follow one author for various sections of his work. Livy sees a grave moral decline in his own time, compared with the virtues that enabled Rome to defeat Hannibal and his aim in his writing is ostensibly a moral one (preface 10). From 318 Livy can be supplemented by Diodorus (down to 302) and the *Fasti*. Polybius (c. 200–c. 118), in Rome from 167 till 146 was a close companion of Scipio Aemilianus and wrote a history of Rome's speedy rise to power from the end of the First Punic War down to 167; his summary of Rome's constitution, supposedly at the time of the Second Punic War, is central to any discussion of Rome's early government.

On the sources for early Rome, see esp. Ogilvie and Drummond 1989; Cornell 1995: 1–30; for an introduction to early Rome, see especially Bloch 1960; Alföldi 1965; Palmer 1970; Heurgon 1973; Salmon 1982; Develin 1986; Mitchell 1986, 1990; Raaflaub 1986a; Cornell 1989, 1989a, 1989b, 1995; Drummond 1989, 1989a; Momigliano 1989.

GEOGRAPHY AND LOCATION

Despite Cicero's eulogy of Rome's location (doc. 1.4), the site certainly grew from small beginnings, and Strabo sees the Romans as having later made the best of the site's disadvantages (doc. 1.2). The Tiber, Italy's major river, begins in the Apennines, Italy's mountain 'backbone', and flows 400 kilometres to the sea. The river was navigable by sea-going vessels from its mouth to Rome (doc. 1.1), and the city increasingly relied upon it for supplies. It wanders through Rome as a lazy 's' and was known to flood; it flows around the Tiber island, where the sanctuary of Aesculapius was established in the third century (doc. 3.57). The Tiber was first crossed with a bridge (apparently very narrow), the Pons Sublicius, in the sixth century, which was sometimes destroyed by floods and replaced; it was a special concern of the priests (doc. 3.7).

The auspices were taken from the Capitol (the citadel) and here the great temple of Jupiter stood. The Forum Romanum, the political centre of Rome, lay at the foot of this hill, and shops were located in this forum and others (docs 2.7–10). The rich made the Palatine their home, while the Esquiline is perhaps best known as a burial area (doc. 3.75). The poorer citizens had their place in the Subura, between the Esquiline and Viminal hills. On the Aventine stood the temple of Juno Regina after her evocatio from Veii in 396 BC (doc. 1.33), as well as the temple of Ceres, Liber and Libera. The office of the plebeian aediles was also here, and Gaius Gracchus and his supporters seized the temple of Diana here in 121 (doc. 8.32).

Rome had an inaugurated boundary, the pomerium, consecrated by religion (docs 1.3, 3.15). There was a wall, ascribed to the sixth king, Servius Tullius (doc. 1.2), but actually dating to the fourth century, eleven kilometres in circumference, embracing all the hills except the Palatine, which had its own defences; the Servian Wall enclosed about 400 hectares but Rome quickly outgrew this and by the late Republican period the city sprawled significantly outside the wall, a testimony to Roman power and military confidence.

1.1 The Tiber

Dionysius of Halicarnassus *Roman Antiquities* 3.44.1–4

At 1.37.1–5 Dionysius praises the natural advantages of Italy in bearing crops, timber and raising cattle, as well as its climate. Tradition had it that Ancus Marcius (the fourth king of Rome: 640–617

BC) developed a trading post at the mouth of the Tiber at Ostia. No seventh-century remains have been discovered at Ostia, and the site is almost certainly no earlier than the fourth century BC, belonging to a period of development in Roman commerce and expansionism. There was no harbour as such there in the republican period and, as Dionysius notes, sea-going vessels went through the mouth of the Tiber at Ostia and were assisted on their way to Rome. In the late Republic, Roman aristocrats had villas here. Marius sacked Ostia in 87, and pirates destroyed a Roman fleet there in 67. Ostia: cf. Livy 1.33.9; Tiber: cf. Strabo 5.2.1; Pliny *Nat. Hist.* 3.53–5; McDonald 1966: 99–102.

1 The river Tiber, descending from the Apennine mountains and flowing close to Rome, discharges itself on harbourless and continuous shores which the Tyrrhenian sea has made, but it gave slight advantages to Rome, not worth mentioning, because of the lack of a trading-post (emporion) at its outlet, where goods brought by sea and down river from the interior could be received and exchanged with the merchants. However, as it was adequate for river boats of good size as far as its source, and as far as Rome itself for large sea-going merchant ships, Ancus Marcius decided to construct a sea-port at its outlet, making use of the river's mouth itself as a harbour. **2** For the Tiber broadens considerably when it unites with the sea and forms great bays, such as those of the greatest seaports; and, what anyone might marvel at, its mouth is not blocked by sandbanks heaped up by the sea, as happens to many of even the largest rivers . . . and it discharges itself through its one genuine mouth, repelling the ocean's breakers, despite the violence of the prevailing westerly wind. **3** As a result oared ships of any size and merchant ships of up to 3,000 measures (bushels) enter through the mouth of the river and are brought to Rome by rowing or by being dragged with towing-lines, while the larger ones ride at anchor off the mouth, where they are unloaded and loaded by river boats. **4** On the elbow of land between the river and the sea the king built a city, which he named 'Ostia' from its position, or as we should say 'thyra' or door, thus making Rome not only an inland city but a seaport and gave it a taste of good things from across the seas.

1.2 The city of Rome

Strabo *Geography* 5.3.7

Compare the eulogistic and idealised picture of Rome's situation given by Cicero (doc. 1.4). At 5.3.2 Strabo gives the story of Rhea Silvia, Romulus and Remus and the founding of the city. Strabo was born c. 64 BC, and wrote his geography (in 17 books) under the early emperors (he died after AD 21). He made several visits to Rome.

Fires will always have been a problem in a city like Rome, with buildings containing so much wood. Notable fires in the Republic include the Forum Boarium ('Cattle Market') in 213 BC, the Forum Romanum in 210 BC, and that of the temple of Jupiter on the Capitoline on 6 July 83 BC; there was also the deliberate burning of the senate-house for Clodius Pulcher's funeral pyre in 52 BC. Crassus owned 500 slaves who were architects and builders; he would buy houses that were on fire, and those adjacent (doc. 2.21), and rebuild them (nothing is said about putting the fires out). There was no organised fire-fighting system until Augustus: see Stambaugh 1988: 128, 348.

Titus Tatius was the Sabine king who attacked Rome after the 'rape of the Sabine women' and who afterwards formed a joint community with Romulus. 'Servius' wall' in fact dates to after the conquest of Veii (perhaps to 378 BC). In the second century BC the wall was raised from 8.5 metres in height to approximately 16 metres. The story of the Gallic sack in 390 BC suggests that Rome had no extensive defences prior to the 'Servian' wall, though the 'agger' (earthwork) with which Servius supposedly fortified the section between the Viminal and Esquiline may be sixth-century. On the walls of archaic Rome, see Ross Holloway 1994: 91–102; Cornell 1995: 198–204.

In the interior the first city above Ostia is Rome, and this is the only city which lies on the Tiber; concerning this city of Rome, I have already stated (5.3.2) that it was founded out of necessity, not choice, and I must add that those who later established certain additional districts could not, as masters, choose what was better, but had, like slaves, to fall into line with what was already there. The first founders walled the Capitol and Palatine and the Quirinal hill, which was so easy for outsiders to climb that Titus Tatius took it at his first attempt, in his attack when he came to avenge the insult of the abducted girls. Ancus Marcius added in Mount Caelium and Mount Aventine and the plain in between them, which were separated from each other and from the parts already walled, as a matter of necessity; for it was not a good idea to leave hills which were naturally strong outside the walls for those who wanted strongholds against the city, and he was not able to fill out the whole circle round to the Quirinal. Servius (Tullius) noticed the omission and filled it out, adding the Esquiline and the Viminal hills. It is easy, too, for outsiders to attack these, and therefore they dug a deep ditch, putting the earth on the inside, and extended the bank of earth about six stades on the inner side of the ditch, and placed on it a wall and towers from the Colline Gate to the Esquiline; below the centre of the mound there is a third gate, with the same name as the Viminal hill. This is what, then, the fortifications of the city are like, though it needs another set of fortifications. In my view the first founders had the same point of view both for themselves and their successors, that Romans ought to depend for their security and other welfare not on fortifications, but on arms and innate courage, believing that walls should not defend men, but men walls. So in the beginning, as the large and fertile country around them belonged to other people, and the site of the city was so open to attack, there was no good luck in their situation demanding congratulations; but when the land became their own, through their bravery and toil, there was a clear inrush of good things which surpassed any advantages of situation; it is because of this that, although the city has increased to such an extent, it has adequate supplies both of food and of wood and stones for building work, which goes on continuously because of collapses and fires and sales, these last being never-ending . . . To cater for this, the quantity of mines and timber and rivers for transport provide an amazing supply of materials, first the Anio which flows from Alba, the Latin city near the Marsi, through the plain below Alba to its junction with the Tiber, then the Nar and Teneas which flow through Ombrica to the same river, the Tiber, and the Clanis too, which runs through Etruria and the territory of Clusium.

1.3 The pomerium

Gellius *Attic Nights* 13.14.1–2

Cf. doc. 3.15; Livy 1.44.4–5; Tac. *Ann.* 12.24; Plut. *Rom.* 11.4. The actual inhabited area of Rome extended well beyond the pomerium, which was a religious boundary, the consecrated space within which the auspices connected with the city were taken (urban auspices, *auspicia urbana*, were not taken outside the boundary of the pomerium). The pomerium originally ended at the foot of the Palatine, was extended by Servius Tullius, and remained unchanged until Sulla enlarged it. It included all the hills of Rome, except for the Aventine, which was not included until Claudius' reign (Gell. 13.14.4, 7; Tac. *Ann.* 12.23, *CIL* VI.31538a–c). The pomerium was extended by Sulla, Caesar and Augustus (Gell. 13.14.4; Dio 43.50.1, 44.49.2; Tac. *Ann.* 12.23–4, cf. Cic. *Att.* 13.20.1): those who had added territory to the Roman state had the right to increase the extent of the pomerium (Tac. *Ann.* 12.24; Gordon 1983 no. 43); for the ritual involved, see doc. 3.12.

The temples of introduced deities not sanctioned by the state were not allowed within the pomerium: the Magna Mater had her temple on the Palatine within the pomerium because hers was a state sanctioned foreign cult. Burial was not permitted inside the area bounded by the pomerium but was permitted as a state honour, such as for Valerius Publicola (Patterson 2000: 265) and amongst the honours granted to Caesar in 44 BC was the right to be buried within it (Dio 44.7.1). Military imperium could not be exercised within the pomerium, and a holder of imperium could only enter the pomerium if — and on the day or days — he was celebrating his triumph. For the pomerium, see Platner-Ashby 392–6; Richardson *Top. Dict.* 293–6; Antaya 1980; Whittaker 1994: 21–5; *BNP* 1.177–81, 2.93–6; Patterson 2000: 264–5 (burials), 2000a: 88–9, 91–2.

1 'Pomerium' has been defined by the augurs of the Roman people who wrote the books *On the Auspices* in the following terms: 'The pomerium is the space inside what has been designated as the rural district around the circuit of the whole city outside the walls, marked by fixed boundary-lines and forming the limit of the city auspices.' **2** The most ancient pomerium, which was established by Romulus, ended at the foot of the Palatine hill. But that pomerium was extended a number of times, as the Republic grew, and enclosed many high hills.

1.4 Cicero on the site of Rome

Cicero *Republic* 2.10–11

Cicero here presents Scipio Aemilianus arguing that Romulus showed foresight in not founding Rome on the coast, because of the dangers of attack, and the moral degeneration suffered by maritime cities like Corinth and Carthage; for this passage, see Cornell 2001.

10 So how could Romulus have employed more divine wisdom in his making use of the advantages provided by the sea and in avoiding its disadvantages than by positioning his city on the bank of a broad river which flows constantly and unvaryingly down to the sea? This allows the city both to import from the sea what it needs and to export what it has in superfluity, and can also be used to convey items essential for life and civilisation not only from the sea, but also from inland — which suggests to me that Romulus must even in his day have foreseen that this city would one day be the centre and homeland of a vast empire, for hardly any city sited anywhere else in Italy could more easily have acquired the far-reaching sovereignty we currently possess.

11 As regards the city's own natural defences, is there anyone so blind that he does not have them clearly visualised and engraved on his mind? It was the wisdom first of Romulus and then of the kings who followed him which defined the line and course of its wall, so positioned on steep and precipitous hills that the only approach, lying between the Esquiline and the Quirinal hills, was surrounded by an immense defensive rampart and a huge ditch, and the citadel was so well defended by its precipitous situation and the rock which looks as if it has been cut away on all sides that even in those awful times when the Gauls arrived (390 BC) it remained unharmed and impregnable. Furthermore, he selected a site which enjoys plentiful springs and is healthy, despite the pestilential nature of the area, for there are hills which not only get the benefit of the breezes, but provide shade for the valleys.

THE FORUM

A forum (plural: fora) was the open area of a Roman town and city, around which clustered shops and which served as a market area. It was used for all forms of collective activity — trials, contiones (meetings; singular: contio), funeral orations, business, theatrical performances and gladiatorial shows. At Rome, the main forum was the Forum Romanum; other fora were the Forum Boarium and Forum Holitorium (for both see below). In 46 BC Caesar dedicated another, the Forum Caesaris (or Forum Julium); some of the emperors also built fora in Rome. In Republican sources, the Forum Romanum is always simply referred to as the forum, becoming known as the Forum Romanum in the imperial period. It was bounded by several hills: the Palatine and Capitoline hills faced onto and were approached from the forum, it was also bounded by the Velia and Quirinal hills. Runoff from these hills made the forum originally a marshy area (Ovid *Fasti* 6.40–8).

The forum was a crucial public space in Republican Rome. The popular assemblies met here from 145 BC, while judicial proceedings were conducted in the nearby comitium. When politics ground to a halt, the forum was deserted (doc. 1.8). The curia hostilia, senate house, stood adjacent to the comitium. The forum was also on the route of the triumph (docs 2.33–6) and the funeral eulogies of prominent men were delivered there (doc. 3.74). Gladiatorial contests were held in the forum from the third century BC until Statilius Taurus built an amphitheatre in 29 BC. The first reported gladiatorial contest in Rome was held in the Forum Boarium (in 264 BC: Val. Max. 2.4.7), but the funeral games of M. Aemilius Lepidus involving 22 pairs of gladiators, were held in the forum in 216 BC (Livy 23.30.15). These two shows were gladiatorial *munera*, 'gifts' and meaning, by extension, public shows, put on at the expense of the sons of the deceased. Temporary seating was erected around the area and tickets were sold: Gaius Gracchus in 122 forcibly removed the seats so that the poor could see the contests free of charge (Plut. *G. Gracchus* 12.5–6). Caesar in 46 BC covered the forum with awnings for his gladiatorial show to shade the spectators from the sun (Pliny *Nat. Hist.* 19.23). Theatrical performances could also be staged in the forum as part of the funeral games.

The temple of Concord at the foot of the Capitoline (built by Opimius in 121 and subsequently sometimes used for senate meetings) stood at the western end of the forum, Saturn's temple in the south-west, and the temple of Castor and Pollux in the south-east. The temple of Vesta and the Vestals' house was at the eastern end, with the domus publica, the residence of the pontifex maximus, nearby, together with the Regia, his headquarters. The Lacus Curtius was in the central area (according to legend a chasm closed by the self-sacrifice (devotio) into it of one M. Curtius in 362 BC); the 'Black Stone' (lapis niger) with its curious archaic inscription was near the comitium. The tabularium, records office, was built in 78 BC at the western end of the forum behind the Temple of Concord. The forum as such was a religious, political, administrative, judicial and mercantile centre. See for the forum: Platner-Ashby 230–6; Deman 1922; Nash 1.446–9; McDonald 1966: 108–17; Grant 1970; Mulryne 1977; Grimal 1983: 32–5; Wiseman 1990; Patterson 1992: 190–4; Richardson *Top. Dict.* 170–4; Purcell 1989, 1995; see also the various entries at Nash 1.154–9, 287–9, 362–4, 542–4, 2.21–3, 2.238, 264–7, 402; Richardson 42–5, 97–8, 133–4, 229–31, 267–8, 311, 328–9, 375–6, 376–7; Scott 1995, 1999.

1.5 The institution of the forum

Dionysius of Halicarnassus *Roman Antiquities* 3.67.4

Cf. 2.50.2; Livy 1.35.10. Tarquinius Priscus was the fifth king of Rome, 616–579 BC, who reputedly undertook drainage work in the forum, while the seventh king Tarquinius Superbus canalised the Cloaca Maxima stream which ran through it (Livy 1.38.6, 1.56.1). The Cloaca

Maxima ('Great Sewer') was not yet paved over; this seems to have occurred sometime in the first few decades of the second century BC. The forum, however, was always subject to inundation (Hor. *Odes* 1.2.13–16). Shops (tabernae) lined the Sacred Way (Sacra Via) which ran through the forum; these were the 'old shops' of Plautus *Curc.* 480 (doc. 1.6), as opposed to the new ones constructed in the northern forum at the front of the basilica Aemilia.

Tarquinius Priscus also adorned the forum, in which court cases are held, the assemblies meet and other political business is transacted, surrounding it with shops and colonnades.

1.6 The forum, as it really was

Plautus *Curculio* 467–84

Plautus' lively description of the Forum Romanum dating to the early second century BC reveals it as the centre of political and social life (for life in the forum, see also lines 280–98).

For homosexuality (482–3: 'who sell themselves, who either turn over or give others the chance to do so') and prostitutes, see docs 7.57–65. The temple of Venus Cloacina was a small shrine devoted to the deity (assimilated to Venus) of the stream which ran through the forum (Nash 1.262–3; Richardson *Top. Dict.* 92). In line 470 'perjurer' refers to the law courts and litigants (cf. Pliny *Nat. Hist.* 19.24).

> I will show you where you can easily find every type of person,
> So no one will have to work too hard if he wants to meet anyone
> Vicious or virtuous, worthy or worthless.
> 470 If he wants to meet a perjurer, he should go to the assembly (comitium);
> If a liar and braggart, to the temple of Venus Cloacina,
> While for rich, married spendthrifts, try the basilica.
> There too he'll find prostitutes past their prime and men who look for a bargain,
> While members of dining-clubs can be found at the fish-market.
> In the lower forum men of good repute and riches stroll around,
> In the middle forum near the canal you'll find the fellows who are just for show;
> Above the lake there's the bold, talkative, spiteful types,
> Who presumptuously slander other people for no reason
> And who could have plenty of home-truths said about themselves.
> 480 Under the old shops are those who lend and borrow at interest.
> Behind Castor's temple are those whom it would be unwise to trust too quickly.
> In the Tuscan quarter are the men who sell themselves,
> Who either turn over or give others the chance to do so.
> But there's a noise at the door: I must guard my tongue!

1.7 Life in the forum

Lucilius *Satires* 1145–51

Lucilius (180–102/1 BC) is here satirising life in the forum. It is not known from which book of satires this fragment comes; for his work, see Gruen 1992: 272–317. The comitium, the main place of public assembly, abutted onto the north-east of the forum and technically was not part of it; it was inaugurated space. The tribal assembly had traditionally met in the comitium, but in 145 BC C. Licinius Crassus as tribune was the first to bring the people into the forum for the passing of laws (Varro *Rust.* 1.2.9; Cic. *Amic.* 96; Nash 1.287–9; Richardson *Top. Dict.* 97–8).

Plautus (doc. 1.6), Dionysius (doc. 1.5) and Cicero (doc. 1.8) mention the law-courts in the forum; Cicero *Cat.* 4.2 calls it 'the forum, in which all justice is upheld'. It was to the forum that disputes were brought (Varro *Lat. Lang.* 5.145). Here, on platforms, trials took place, in public view in the open air. The praetor's tribunal and *quaestiones* (courts) were held in the outer forum by the first century BC (Purcell 1995: 332).

1145 But now from morning to night, whether holiday or working-day,
The entire people and senators in exactly the same way
All strut about in the forum and never leave it;
And they all give themselves to one and the same passion and skill —
To be able to cheat within the letter of the law, to fight craftily,
1150 To strive through the use of flattery, to pretend they're 'honest fellows', and
To set ambushes, as if they were all the enemies of all men.

1.8 The forum as the political centre of Rome

Cicero *Speech to the Senate on His Return from Exile* 6

In 57 BC, moves to have Cicero recalled were opposed by Clodius and his supporters, who through their violence effectively shut down the government of Rome; cf. docs 12.58–60. Cicero's picture might be overdrawn but he does clearly point to the forum (Romanum) as the centre of political life in Rome; cf. *Brut.* 311; docs 2.58–63, for the importance of oratory there. See Millar 1986, 1998 on the forum as the centre of political drama in the Republic with its contiones, legislative assemblies and trials (the comitia centuriata, however, met in the Campus Martius).

And so from this time on, citizens, you gave no responses to allies, or even kings; the juries gave no verdicts, the people gave no votes, this senate approved no measures; you looked upon a forum that was dumb, a senate-house without a tongue, a state that was silent and enfeebled.

SENATE AND MAGISTRACIES

The *lex Villia annalis* in 180 laid down regulations for the holding of office (Livy 40.44.1). Down to the mid-second century, holding the consulate twice in the space of 10 years was forbidden and the Genucian laws in 342 (doc. 1.49) had supposedly laid down that there had to be a ten-year interval between consulships: see Billows 1989 for a down-dating to c. 201, when this practice first appears. Subsequent legislation debarred a second consulship (although in practice exceptions were made, as in the case of Scipio Aemilianus), until in 81 Sulla restored the old rules, but raised the minimum age limits in the year of election from 36 to 42 (for consuls), from 33 to 39 (for praetors) and from 27 to 30 (for quaestors): Cic. *Phil.* 5.48; Astin 1958; Evans 1990, who lists 72 consuls who encountered delays between their praetorship and consulship, such as Marius. Many consuls were therefore older than the minimum age requirement, because of the intensity of the competition: hence Cicero's pride in his being elected 'suo anno', 'in his year', i.e., in the first possible year (doc. 2.40). Sulla also raised the number of magistrates elected every year: praetors from 6 to 8, and quaestors from 12 to 20 (earlier 2, in 447, 4 in 421, and 8 in 267). There was a rigid *cursus honorum* ('race of honour', or career path), for Roman magistrates from the early second century (Lintott 1999: 144–6): the praetorship could only be held by an ex-quaestor, and the consulship by an ex-praetor. As the number of consuls remained fixed at two per year there was clearly a 'pyramid' effect, leading to intense rivalry for the consulship. Prior to the holding of the quaestorship, cavalrymen were liable for 10 years' military service (Polyb. 6.19.2–4), and this was also a prerequisite for holding office as was the census-rating of an eques: Millar 1984: 11. On the cursus, see esp. Develin 1985: 89–96; Drummond 1989a: 186–97.

From Sulla the quaestorship involved automatic membership of the senate (prior to that most, but not all, quaestors would have become senators), and among the senators the most influential after the current consuls were the consulares (or ex-consuls). The presiding magistrate consulted members of the senate according to their seniority in descending order; the consulares first, according to their seniority, among whom was a princeps senatus (chief of the senate) appointed by the censors, when in office, who kept his position for life. Ex-magistrates dominated the senate; in addition, magistrates, senators and priests had exclusive control of public religious activity. The senate met in various locations, all of which were *templa* (consecrated spaces), the most important being the curia hostilia (alongside the comitium); the *senatus consultum* (senatorial decree) on the Bacchanalia in 186 BC prescribes a quorum of 100 (doc. 3.64).

On the senate: Wiseman 1971; Kunkel 1973: 19–20; Loewenstein 1973: 147–92; Shatzman 1975; Drummond 1989a: 178–86; Staveley 1989: 443–7; Lintott 1999: 65–88; Patterson 2000b: 21–8; on the constitution: Develin 1985: 17–42; on the princeps senatus: Tansey 2000.

1.9 The importance of traditions

Ennius *Annals* 467

Aug. *Civ. Dei* 2.12, citing Cic. *Rep*; *ROL* I.174l; Skutsch 1985: 84 (as line 156), commentary at 318. One of the most important concepts for the Romans was that of *mos maiorum* ('the custom of (our) ancestors'), the maintenance of the traditions and behaviour, such as frugality, austerity and courage, that had made Rome great. This line may have been spoken by Titus Manlius Torquatus (cos. 340), prior to his execution of his son in 337: cf. Livy 8.7.16; doc. 7.15.

On manners and men of olden times stands the Roman state.

1.10 The dangers of kingship

Ennius *Tragedies* FF402–3

(Cic. *Off.* 1.26; *ROL* I.370.) The first king of Rome was believed to have been Romulus, the founder of Rome (for his deification, see Enn. *Ann.* 1.114–15, 2.117–20). Of the others, one (Tullus Hostilius) was Latin, two (Numa and Ancus Marcius) were Sabine, and the two Tarquins Etruscan (the remaining king, Servius Tullius, was said to have been either Etruscan or Latin in origin). Though the chronology and number of the kings is disputed, the tradition that the last king, Tarquinius Superbus, was deposed by a group of aristocrats at the end of the sixth century is generally accepted, though the story of Tarquinius Superbus' son's rape in 509 BC of the noble Lucretia, her subsequent suicide, and the rebellion fomented by her husband L. Tarquinius Collatinus and L. Junius Brutus, who became the first two consuls, is clearly fictional: for Livy's emphasis on the role of Lucretia, see Moore 1993. The concept of kingship was viewed with horror by the senatorial aristocracy during the Republic, and it was a frequent accusation against political figures who were becoming too popular, such as Marcus Manlius Capitolinus (doc. 2.41) and the Gracchi (doc. 8.15, cf. 8.29). Julius Caesar avoided accepting the title 'rex': doc. 13.55. On the regal period, see Loewenstein 1973: 7–18; Scullard 1980: 42–77; Momigliano 1989: 87–112; Cornell 1995: 119–50, 215–26.

Various relics of monarchy survived under the Republic, notably the rex sacrorum (the 'king of the sacred rites'), the interrex, and the insignia of magistrates (such as the fasces and curule chair), as well as the triumph; for the Etruscans, see Athen. 12.517–18 (citing Theopompus).

To a king no association, no promise, is sacred.

1.11 The first consuls, 509 BC

Livy *History of Rome* 2.1.8–10

The first senior magistrates were initially called not consuls, but praetors (Livy 3.55.12). Consuls were originally military figures and possessed supreme power (imperium) in the field; from 367 to 88 BC it was customary for one or both consuls to be away from Rome on campaign. When both consuls went on campaign together it was usual for them each to take charge for a day at a time. Similarly the fasces (a bundle of rods tied with red thongs and containing an axe when outside of Rome) were carried by the 12 lictors before each consul on alternate months, signalling their precedence over the other for that period. The fasces were part of the Etruscan regalia which were retained by the consuls except for the embroidered robe and crown: Marshall 1984; Cornell 1995: 226–39; Lintott 1999: 94–109. The story is told of Brutus, the 'liberator', that he had his colleague Collatinus exiled because of his family relationship with Tarquin, and his two sons executed for attempting to restore Tarquin (doc. 7.14); for the first consuls, see *MRR* I.1–2.

8 The first consuls (Lucius Junius Brutus and Lucius Tarquinius Collatinus, Lucretia's husband) possessed all the rights and insignia of the kings, but care was taken in one respect, that twice the terror should not be inspired by their both having the fasces. Brutus, with his colleague's consent, was the first to have them, and he was no less zealous as a guard of liberty than he had been as its champion. **9** First of all, while the people were still covetous of their new freedom, in case, in the future, they should be swayed by the entreaties or presents of would-be kings, he made them swear an oath that they would never permit anyone to be king in Rome. **10** Next, in order that the numbers in the senate might give greater authority to that order, he made up the number of senators, which had been diminished by the king's murders, to the total of 300 by choosing the leading men of equestrian rank.

1.12 The magistracies

Cicero *On Duties* 1.124

Cicero dedicated this work to his son Marcus; it was completed in November 44. Due to the normal absence of the consuls from Rome, at least prior to the first century BC, the senate and lesser magistrates handled most day-to-day business and decisions.

It is especially the duty of a magistrate to bear in mind that he is the representative of the state and that he must uphold its dignity and honour, preserve its laws, apportion to all their constitutional rights, and remember that all this has been granted to him as a sacred trust...

1.13 The early magistracies and officials

Varro *On the Latin Language* 5.80–2, 87

Accius *Brutus* 41; Lucilius 1215. The secession here is that of 494 BC (doc. 1.24). Tribunus (tribune) is actually derived from tribus, man of the tribe. Varro, who died in 27 BC, wrote his work on the Latin language, addressed to Cicero, between 47 and 45 BC; only 6 of 25 books are extant. Lucius Accius was born in 170 BC at Pisaurum and wrote a number of tragedies at Rome, primarily on Greek models. There are also fragments of two *fabulae praetextae* (Roman tragedies), the *Brutus* and another on Decius Mus (see below, doc. 1.69). Accius' patron was D. Junius Brutus

Callaicus (doc. 5.48). On the technical terms for the different magistracies, see Stewart 1998: 114–16.

80 The consul was given this name because he had to consult the people and senate, unless it comes rather from the etymology which Accius uses in his *Brutus*:

'He who counsels rightly, let him be called consul.'

The praetor was so called because he should 'go before' (*praeire*) the law and the army; from which Lucilius says,

'So the role of the praetors is to go in front and before'.

81 The censor was so named as the one at whose *censio*, rating, that is his assessment, the people should be rated; the aedile, as the one to look after sacred and private *aedes*, buildings; the quaestors from *quaerere*, seek, as they have to seek into public moneys and wrong-doing, which the *triumviri capitales* now look into: from this name later on those who give judgement on the investigations were named *quaesitores*, investigators; the *tribuni militum*, military tribunes, because in the olden days three were sent to the army by the three tribes of Ramnes, Luceres and Tities; the *tribuni plebis*, tribunes of the plebs, because tribunes of the plebs were first created from the tribunes of the soldiers in the secession to Crustumerium with the role of defending the *plebs*, populace.

82 The dictator was so called, because he was named by the consul as one to whose *dictum*, order, all should listen; the *magister equitum*, master of the horse, because he has supreme power over the cavalry and reserves, just as the dictator has supreme power over the people, from which he is also called 'master' of the people. The remainder, because they are subordinate to these *magistri*, masters, are called *magistratus*, magistrates, derived in the same way as *albatus*, clothed in white, is derived from *albus*, white.

. . .

87 The *imperator*, commander, is named from the *imperium*, authority, of the people, as the one who subdued the enemies who had attacked it; the *legati*, legates, those who were officially *lecti*, chosen, whose aid or advice magistrates should use when away from Rome, or who should be messengers of the senate or people; the *exercitus*, army, because it is improved by *exercitando*, training; the *legio*, legion, because the soldiers *leguntur*, are gathered, in a levy.

1.14 The dictatorship

Dionysius of Halicarnassus *Roman Antiquities* 5.73.1–2

Dictators were extraordinary magistrates, usually nominated by a magistrate after approval by the senate (though they could be elected in the comitia centuriata: Livy 22.8), who were appointed to lead the army or hold elections. Dictatorships were relatively common in the fourth and third centuries down to 202 BC: the later dictatorships of Sulla and Caesar were simply so-called to disguise their autocracy. The maximum time-limit for a dictatorship was six months, though the office could be laid down earlier, and the dictator appointed as his second-in-command a master of horse (magister equitum); a dictator was preceded by 24 lictors. Titus Larcius Flavus was the first dictator (cf. Livy 2.18.4–8 who calls him Largius and puts the date of his dictatorship three years earlier in 501: *MRR* I.9); Spurius Cassius was his master of horse. Dionysius here links dictator with *dictare* (one who dictates) and *dictus* (named) and makes a comparison with the Greek 'aisymnetes', elected tyrant, like Pittacus of Mitylene. The first plebeian dictator was appointed in 356: see Drummond 1989a: 190–2; Lintott 1999: 109–113; cf. Gabba 1991: 141.

1 Larcius was the first man to be appointed sole ruler in Rome with absolute authority in war, peace, and all other matters. They call this person a dictator, either from his power of giving whatever orders he wishes and of laying down justice and right for the other citizens as he thinks best (for the Romans call commands and decrees regarding right and wrong edicts, '*edicta*'), or, as some record, from the form of election which was then brought in, since he was not to receive the magistracy from the people, according to ancestral custom, but was appointed by one man . . . **2** For the immensity of the power which the dictator holds is not at all indicated by his title; for the dictatorship is actually an elective tyranny.

1.15 The censorship (443 BC)

Livy *History of Rome* 4.8.2–5

Censors were senior magistrates, but without imperium, of whom two were elected for a period of 18 months. Generally ex-consuls, censors were appointed every four, later five years, though this could vary; censors wore purple togas (Polyb. 6.53.7). The censorship was instituted in 443 BC; initially both patrician, from 339 (under the leges Publiliae) one censor had to be a plebeian. The first plebeian censor was appointed in 351: Cram 1940 gives a definitive list of all censors up to 22 BC and reviews their activities; see Astin 1982 for the frequency of censorships, especially in the early period. Censors' duties included conducting the census and performing the *lustrum*, a ceremony of purification (no lustrum was completed or census held between 69 and 28 BC; Wiseman 1969 argues that conservative groups were blocking further Italian enrolment into the comitia centuriata: see docs 10.17, 24, 27), reviewing the tribes, senate and equites, the 'cavalry' (and expelling unsuitable members), introducing censorial laws and regulations, and supervising public building activities. The term censor implies 'assessor'; their initial duties would have been to register citizens for military duty (prior to Marius' reforms: docs 9.10–11) and for taxation (tributum was cancelled in 168: doc. 5.33). They were responsible for leasing public property, such as mines, and making contracts for public works and revenue collection. Prior to Sulla, censors were responsible for admitting members to the senate. Enrolment in the census was necessary for voting privileges in the comitia centuriata and involved making a sworn declaration of one's age, family and property: see Nicolet 1980: 48–88; cf. Drummond 1989a: 197–8; Lintott 1999: 115–20.

2 In this same year the censorship was inaugurated, an institution which started in a small way, but which later grew so immensely as to be responsible for regulating the morals and lifestyle of the Romans: the distribution of honour and dishonour to the senators and centuries of the equites was under the control of this magistracy along with jurisdiction over public and private places, while the revenues of the Roman people were entirely subject to its judgement. **3** The reason behind the institution was that the people had not been rated for a number of years and the census could not be postponed, but the consuls had no time for this duty, with wars against so many peoples hanging over them. **4** The matter was referred to the senate, on the grounds that so laborious a task, and one beneath the consuls' dignity, needed its own special magistrates, who should have a staff of clerks, the task of supervising the records, and the charge of regulating the form of the census. **5** Although it was a small matter, the senators were pleased to accept the suggestion, so that there might be more patrician magistrates in the government.

1.16 The censorship in Cicero's ideal state

Cicero *On the Laws* 3.3

Cicero here gives the censors their traditional duties; the prevention of celibacy was a concern of censors such as Metellus Macedonicus in 131 and Metellus Numidicus in 102: Livy *Per*. 59; Gell. 1.6.1–6; Lintott 1999: 228.

Censors shall record the age, offspring, household and property of the citizens; they shall be in charge of the city's temples, roads, water supply, treasury and revenues; they shall assign citizens into tribes, and also divide them according to wealth, age, and rank; they shall enrol the youth in the cavalry and infantry; they shall prohibit celibacy; they shall oversee public morality; they shall not allow anyone guilty of improper conduct to remain in the senate.

1.17 Cato the elder as censor

Plutarch *Life of Cato the Elder* 16.1–3

Livy 39.40–1. Cato was elected censor for 184 BC with his consular colleague of 195, L. Valerius Flaccus. Both had a programme of arresting moral decline and Cato, though opposed by seven other candidates, was elected by the people. Not only did he expel numerous senators and equites (including L. Quinctius Flamininus and a senator who had kissed his wife in daylight: docs 7.20, 58), but cut off illegal water pipes, removed buildings encroaching on public land, heavily taxed luxury goods, and reduced the cost of public works: see *MRR* I.374. His opponents got the senate to annul the payments for temples and public works he had authorised and mobilised the tribunes against him. The people however voted him a statue, inscribed 'when the Roman state was staggering to its fall, he was made censor, and by his helpful guidance, wise restraints, and sound teachings again restored it' (Plut. *Cato Mai.* 19.3); see Astin 1978; Scullard 1973: 153–65; for the competition at censorial elections: Develin 1985: 171–4.

1 Ten years after his consulship, Cato stood for the censorship. This magistracy was at the peak, as it were, of every office, and was, in a way, the culmination of a political career, as it had numerous powers including that of the examination of character and lifestyle. **2** They thought that neither marriage, nor procreation of children, nor daily life, nor entertainment of guests should be as each man should desire and choose, without investigation and examination, but rather, considering that these revealed the character of a man more than public and political actions, they appointed as guard, moderator and chastiser, so that no one for the sake of pleasure should turn aside and deviate from his native and customary lifestyle, one of the so-called patricians and one of the plebeians. **3** They named these 'censors', and they had the authority to demote an eques and expel from the senate anyone who lived in an unbridled and irregular fashion. They also reviewed property assessments and organised citizens in lists according to class and age, while the office also had other great powers.

THE ASSEMBLIES AND TRIBUNATE

The citizen in Rome — that is the adult male — had the rights of suffrage (the ability to vote), of standing for public office (provided he had been freeborn), of appeal (*provocatio*) and recourse to law, of inheritance, and of commercium (trade) and connubium (marriage) with other Roman citizens. Technically the populus Romanus was sovereign: but only adult citizen males were members of assemblies. Of the various assemblies, the oldest was the comitia curiata (consisting of divisions, curiae, of the three original tribes: docs 1.18, 20); it appears that by the second century this comitia had so fallen into disuse that the 30 curiae could be represented by lictors (Cic. *Leg. Agr.* 2.31). The latest known law passed in this assembly dated to 390 (the recall of M. Furius Camillus: Livy 5.46.10). By the first century BC this comitia only met for certain religious or legal matters, such as the inauguration of some priests, transfers of patricians to the plebs, like Clodius, or wills involving adoption.

The comitia centuriata was traditionally instituted by Servius Tullius, and based on field units in the army (the 193 *centuriae*, 'centuries'); even in the late Republic this comitia could only convene outside the pomerium because of its military significance, though by this time it had become primarily an electoral body. It was never an important legislative body: sources for the early Republic only mention five laws passed by this assembly which were not concerned with issues of peace and war, for example the ratification of the XII Tables; see Sandberg 2001: 126–7. The most noted example of a law passed in the comitia centuriata (after Sulla's reforms) was that recalling Cicero from exile (Millar 1998: 18). Higher magistrates (with imperium), the consuls and praetors, were elected in the comitia centuriata; the others (those without imperium) in the comitia tributa: M. Valerius Messalla (cos. 53) at Gell. 13.15.4.

The comitia tributa was based on the division of people into tribes (also ascribed to Servius Tullius). There were 4 urban tribes, while by 241 BC the rural tribes had gradually increased to 31, a total of 35 (Dion. Hal. 4.14–15). The normal way of legislating was by summoning the tribes; the comitia tributa comprised the whole citizen body under the direction of a curule magistrate; a further tribal assembly, the concilium plebis (supposedly established after the secessio of 494), was summoned by a tribune and only open to plebeians. Develin 1975, 1977, and Sandberg 2001: 105–13 argue that the tribal assembly of the whole Roman people is a modern assumption: that the concilium plebis was identical with the comitia tributa and that at least before Sulla it was exclusively plebeian and summoned only by the tribunes of the plebs (not accepted by Lintott 1999: 53–5). This tribal assembly could convene outside the pomerium and this is where it voted on military issues: increasingly, in the first century, the tribal assembly voted on the prorogation (extension) of military commands proposed by tribunes. The comitia tributa probably moved in 145 for legislation and trials from the comitium to the forum and to the Campus Martius, like the comitia centuriata, for elections: in Cicero's time the comitia tributa for elections were held in the Campus Martius, legislative comitia in the forum. It voted by majority, i.e., there were 35 votes, one for each tribe voting *en bloc*, and every citizen voted on an equal basis (i.e., it was not a timocracy) to decide all legislation and minor offices. This comitia's duties included voting on triumphs which might be in dispute, ratifying peace treaties, electing military tribunes and voting on issues of imperium; it also elected aediles and quaestors. The tribal assembly was heavily biased against the urban populace (including freedmen) which comprised only 4 or the 35 tribes.

The decision of Roman assemblies was determined not by the count of individuals but by that of groups. In the comitia centuriata elections were stacked in favour of the well-off voters; the 193 centuries were broken up as follows according to property qualifications (the seniores were men aged 46 and over, the iuniores men between 17 and 45):

Equites ('cavalry' or 'knights'): 18 centuries; First class: 40 centuries of seniores and 40 of iuniores; Second class: 10 centuries of seniores and 10 of iuniores; Third class: 10 centuries of seniores and 10 of iuniores; Fourth class: 10 centuries of seniores and 10 of iuniores; Fifth class: 15 centuries of seniores and 15 of iuniores; Trumpeters, horn-players and artisans: 4 centuries; Proletarii (those below the property qualification for the fifth class): 1 century.

The equites and first class thus comprised nearly half the voting units, and the centuries voted successively: when a majority had been reached, the voting was terminated (but see Dion. Hal. 4.21.3). On voting procedures, Hall 1964, 1998; Taylor 1966: 97–8; Staveley 1972: 179–81; Nicolet 1980: 246–85; Yacobsen 1995; Millar 1998: 209–10.

It has in the past been believed that Rome was controlled by a narrow oligarchy; that the better-off voters were privileged; that there existed stable long-term alliances amongst the elite which were able to direct elections and policies; and that nobles were able to influence voting through the power of their patronage (*clientela*): docs 2.49–57. Scholarship is now divided over the actual powers of the people, with Millar (esp. 1984, 1986, 1995) arguing strongly for their importance in decision-making. The *lex Gabinia* introduced the secret ballot in elections in 139; clients could then cast their votes without the knowledge of their patrons. Certainly only the assemblies could pass laws, elect magistrates, and (early in the Republic) hear major trials and declare wars, but their powers were often limited by patronage, political manipulation and bribery. In addition, their role was passive with no opportunities for debate — Roman democracy was non-participatory and assemblies had to be presided over by magistrates: see Taylor 1966; Staveley 1972, 1989: 436–43; Brunt 1988a–e: 281–502; Develin 1985: 17–30; Harris 1990; North 1990, 1990a; Yacobsen 1992, 1999: 20; cf. Kunkel 1973: 14–19.

It is also apparent that only a very small proportion of the populace actually used their right to vote, particularly in the rural tribes: Cicero (*Sest.* 109) states that some times only 5 people represented certain tribes or that men had to be drafted in from other tribes. Even the Saepta Julia (the voting enclosure on the Campus Martius, possibly begun by Julius Caesar) did not hold all the voters; Taylor 1966: 54 calculated that the Saepta could hold a maximum of 70,000 voters, revised by MacMullen 1980: 454 to 55,000, discussed by Mouritsen 2001: 27–36 (who calculates these to be some 12 per cent of the registered 910,000 voters in the first century BC); cf. Nicolet 1980: 289–97; Hall 1998: 27–8. Mouritsen (esp. 18–37) calculates that the comitium (used for voting until 145 BC) could hold a maximum of 4,800 voters, or 3,600 allowing for the enclosures and bridges, which would have been slightly more than 1 per cent of the citizens; the forum was larger and could hold a maximum of 15,000–20,000. According to Livy (45.35.8–36.6), when the army returned from Macedonia in 167, the soldiers filled the forum and their presence excluded anyone else from voting, while Gaius Gracchus (Plut. *G. Gracchus* 3.1) drew a crowd bigger than would fit into existing conditions in the Campus Martius.

The majority of the rural population would have been unable to vote and probably, on normal occasions, no more than 5–10 per cent of the possible voters took part in electing magistrates or passing laws (which would have made bribery more profitable and effective). Voting procedures were time-consuming and Sallust (*BJ* 73.6) highlights the fact that voting, or any involvement in politics, meant an economic sacrifice for the working class. While the plebs would have known election dates (before 153 BC consuls entered office on 15 March, after that date on 1 January), comitia otherwise had no fixed dates and could only be called by a magistrate, though notice of proposals had to be given three market days (17 days) in advance of the actual comitia, during which time informal discussions in the assembly (*contiones*, singular: *contio*) could be held. The people, unlike at Athens, also had to stand during speeches and debates; Cic. *Flacc.* 15–18. On assemblies, Kunkel 1973: 9–13; Loewenstein 1973: 91–146; Drummond 1989a: 198–204; Lintott 1999: 40–64; Patterson 2000b: 8–21.

1.18 The earliest tribes

Varro *On the Latin Language* 5.55–6

Ennius *Annals* 112–13; *ROL* I.38. The terms for the three tribes were non-Latin, hence Ennius' etymologies, according to Varro, are incorrect. These three tribes were divided into curiae, 10 for each tribe, which formed the basis for Rome's early military organisation and earliest assembly (the comitia curiata), which went back to the regal period: Ferenczy 1976: 29–30. Tatius Titius was the Sabine leader in the war between Romans and Sabines: after peace was made Romulus and Titius may have set up a double kingship in Rome. These three tribes were later replaced by a system of tribes based on places of residence (originally four under the king Servius Tullius) and the number of tribes was finally fixed at 35 (4 urban, 31 rural) in 241. Nothing is known of Volnius.

55 Roman territory (*ager*) was at first divided into three (*tris*) parts, from which came the term *tribe*, used of the Titienses, Ramnes and Luceres. They were named, as Ennius says, the Titienses from Tatius, the Ramnenses from Romulus, and the Luceres, according to Junius, from Lucumo; but all these words are Etruscan, as Volnius says, who wrote tragedies in Etruscan.

56 From this, four parts of the city were also used as the names of tribes, from the places — the Suburan, the Palatine, the Esquiline, the Colline (the four urban tribes); a fifth because it was 'under the walls of Rome', the Romilian (the first of the rural tribes); so also the other thirty for those reasons I wrote about in my *Book of the Tribes*.

1.19 Servius Tullius's reform of the comitia centuriata

Dionysius of Halicarnassus *Roman Antiquities* 4.20.1–5

Cf. Livy 1.42–3. It is generally held that Servius Tullius organised this assembly so that the votes of the poor (i.e., the proletarii who were confined to just one century) would be minimised. Dionysius is not describing the status quo in his own time and makes it clear that this early system later became 'more democratic' (4.21.3). The original system was clearly timocratic: Cic. *Rep.* 2.39 relates that Servius ensured that the voting was controlled by the rich, and the senators, equites and first property class comprised 98 of the 193 centuries. According to Livy (1.43.11) in the early period it was rare for the equites and first-class to disagree and the lower classes were therefore not often called on to vote: by the first century, however, the lower centuries could decide the issue in a close election: see Yacobsen 1999: 54–9. Dionysius and Livy essentially agree on the property qualifications for the different classes: 100,000 asses for the first class, 75,000 for the second, 50,000 for the third, 25,000 for the fourth, and 11,000 (or 12,500) for the fifth. Gell. 16.10.10 defines the proletarii (presumably the greater proportion of the citizens) as having a census less than 1,500, while those without any property (and hence no right to vote) were the capite censi (literally: counted by head), who had less than 375 asses. The proletarii and the capite censi may, however, have been members of the same final century; they were not usually recruited as soldiers until the time of Marius: see Rathbone 1993 for the census qualifications. Freedmen were perhaps assigned to the four non-armed centuries (artisans and musicians): Taylor 1966: 86, 155; Grieve 1985; Cornell 1995: 173–97 on Servius' reforms.

One major change was that, by the end of the third century, a century of the prima classis, the 'first class' (chosen by lot), not the equites, voted first. This *centuria praerogativa* could have a considerable impact on the voting: Millar 1998: 202–3. For the number of equites (initially the serving cavalry; technically 1,800 in number, but 5,000 in Augustan times), see Hill 1952; Henderson 1969; Wiseman 1970; Brunt 1988a. Lintott 1999: 55–61 discusses Cicero's picture (*Rep.* 2.39) of the comitia centuriata shortly before his own day: the centuries of equites and the first class (plus a century of carpenters) comprised 89 centuries, the others 104.

1 Having in this way placed on the rich the burden of danger and expense, he noticed that they were unhappy and relieved their dissatisfaction and mollified their anger in another way by giving them an advantage, through which they would become masters of the state, and excluding the poor from public affairs; and he achieved this without the plebeians noticing. This advantage concerned the assemblies, in which the most important matters were ratified by the people. **2** I have already mentioned earlier (2.14.3) that by the ancient laws the people was sovereign over the three most important and essential matters: they elected the magistrates both for the city and the army, ratified and repealed laws, and decided on matters of war and peace. Voting with regard to discussion and decision-making on these matters was carried out by curiae; and those who had the least property possessed an equal vote to those who had the most; but as there were few who were wealthy, as one might expect, when it came to voting the poor prevailed because of their far superior numbers. **3** Tullius saw this and transferred this voting power to the rich. For, whenever he thought it right to have magistrates elected or a law to be determined or war to be declared, he assembled the people by centuries rather than curiae. The first centuries he called on to give their vote were those with the highest property assessment, which consisted of the 18 centuries of equites and the 80 of infantry. **4** As these consisted of three more than all the rest put together, if they were of one mind they prevailed over the others and the decision was made; if they were not all of the same opinion, then he called on the 22 centuries of the second class. If the votes were still indecisive, he called on those of the third class; and fourthly those of the fourth class; and he kept doing this until 97 centuries voted alike. **5** If this had not happened after the fifth class was called, but the opinions of the 192 centuries were divided equally, then he called on the last century, which consisted of the mass of citizens who were poor and for that reason exempted from all military service and taxation; whichever side this century sided with, that side won. But this was rare and almost impossible. Most issues were determined by calling on the first class, and rarely got down as far as the fourth, and so the fifth and last class was superfluous.

1.20 The three popular assemblies

Gellius *Attic Nights* 15.27.5

It is also written in the same book (of Laelius Felix, *To Quintus Mucius*) that, 'Whenever voting is carried on according to people's families it is called a "curiate" assembly (*comitia curiata*), when by property and age a "centuriate" assembly (*comitia centuriata*), and when by regions and localities a "tribal" assembly (*comitia tributa*); moreover, it is against sacred law for a centuriate assembly to be held within the pomerium, because the army must be assembled outside the city, and it is unlawful for it to be assembled within the city. As a result, it was usual to hold the centuriate assembly on the Campus Martius (Field of Mars), and for the army to be summoned there for the purpose of protection while the people was occupied with casting votes.'

1.21 The assembly's judicial function

Polybius *Histories* 6.14.6–8

Crimes against the people were dealt with in assemblies with the case brought by a magistrate: generally a tribune, if a capital charge. In this way it was possible for the people to censor corrupt or incompetent magistrates after their term of office. The auspices were taken by a praetor; speeches for prosecution and defence were made at three contiones, each with a day between; after an interval of three market-days a vote in a formal assembly took place: Livy 26.3; Cic. *Dom.* 45; Lintott 1999: 150–7; cf. Lintott 1972: 257–8; Walbank I.682–7. Cic. *Laws* 3.11, 3.14 states that the XII Tables (9.1–2) laid down that cases involving a person or his right to citizenship had to be discussed at the comitia centuriata, which included all citizens (men tried on capital charges must have had the right of appeal to the comitia) because the whole people had to be involved in a capital charge. Generally, those likely to be convicted of a capital charge went into exile; the death-penalty was reserved for traitors; for the context of this passage: doc. 1.58.

6 It is the people, then, who frequently judge cases where the offence is punishable by a fine, and particularly when the accused have held the most distinguished offices; they alone can try a capital charge. **7** Regarding this they have a practice which is praiseworthy and should be mentioned. Custom allows those on trial for their lives, when they are being condemned, to depart openly, voluntarily sentencing themselves to exile, even if only one of the tribes which pronounce the verdict has not yet voted. **8** Such exiles find refuge in the territories of Naples, Praeneste, Tibur and other towns with whom treaties are in place.

1.22 The tribunes

Dionysius of Halicarnassus *Roman Antiquities* 8.87.6–8

The setting for this passage is 485 BC (cf. Livy 2.42), with the tribune Maenius attempting to prevent a further military levy; the consuls therefore enrolled troops outside the city to checkmate him. Macrob. 1.3.8: tribunes were not allowed to be absent from Rome for a whole day and night.

The first tribunes were apparently military tribunes who acted as spokespersons for the plebs in the 'First Secession' in 494 (doc. 1.24, cf. 1.13) and the original number of tribunes is given as two, four or five (see Cornell 1995: 256–65 for a synopsis of the debate). Cicero states that there were originally two, in opposition to the two consuls (*Rep.* 2.58), while Livy and Dionysius have them immediately co-opting three colleagues, the number being raised to ten in 457 (Livy 3.30.7). Their role was the protection of the plebeians (the *ius auxilii*); they were elected by the plebeian assembly and possessed inviolability (i.e., they were *sacrosanct*, possessing sacrosanctitas). Shortly after their inception they possessed the right to veto the act of any magistrate, other tribune, law or senatorial decree. The tribunate was originally revolutionary in character, though gradually tribunes were drawn from the same social class as other magistrates. From 133, the time of the Gracchi, they again became champions of people, challenging the senate. This was perceived by Sulla as dangerous and his reforms were directed against the tribunate (docs. 11.30, 32). Most of the laws in the later Republic were passed by tribunes, especially after the *lex Hortensia* of 287 (doc. 1.57), which made plebiscita, decrees of the tribal assembly, binding on the whole people, not merely the plebs; important measures like the leges Liciniae-Sextiae (Licinio-Sextian laws) were also associated with tribunes (doc. 1.47). Caesar's consulship in 59 is the first example of controversial social legislation being promoted by a consul (not a tribune): Miller 1998: 124. Sandberg 2001: esp. 94–6 argues for the historicity of these early tribunician laws and the primary role of tribunes in legislation in the period 367–88 BC, except that concerning war and foreign relations; for legislation brought by tribunes in the early period (362–217 BC), see Millar 1989: 145–6. Despite his innate conservatism, Cicero (*Laws* 3.24–5) sees the tribunate as an essential part of the constitution and its existence as the only way of controlling the populace. On the tribunes' right of veto (3.42) he states, 'Nothing is more beneficial than the maintenance of this custom, because it is better for a good measure to fail than a bad one to be allowed to pass'.

For *provocatio* (appeal to the community for protection against a magistrate) and *appellatio* (appeal to the tribunes), see Lintott 1972. The tribunician benches (their *subsellia*) was initially near the door of the curia so they could give help to anyone who requested it; by the mid-second century the tribunate qualified its holders to become members of the senate: Lintott 1999: 121–8. For the outbreak of civil war between Caesar and Pompey, see docs. 13.23–25.

6 The tribune who opposed the levy was no longer able to do anything. For those who possess tribunician power have no authority over anything outside the city; their jurisdiction is circumscribed by the city walls, and it is not lawful for them even to pass a night away from the city, except on a single occasion, when all the magistrates of the state ascend the Alban mount and make a common sacrifice to Jupiter on behalf of the Latin people. **7** This custom, of the tribunes possessing no authority over anything outside the city, continues to our own day; and indeed the motivating reason, among many others, of the civil war among the Romans which took place in my day and was greater than any war before it, which seemed of great importance and reason enough to divide the state, was this — that some of the tribunes, complaining that they had been forcibly driven out of the city by the general (Pompey) who was then in control of affairs in Italy, in order that they might no longer have any authority, fled to the general in command of the armies in Gaul (Caesar), as they had nowhere to turn to. **8** And the latter, making use of this pretext that he was coming with right and justice to the assistance of the sacrosanct magistracy of the people, deprived of its authority contrary to the oaths of their ancestors, himself entered the city in arms and restored the men to their magistracy.

1.23 Manipulation of tribunician power

Dionysius of Halicarnassus Roman Antiquities 9.1.4–5

Spurius Icilius, a tribune, opposed all legislation in 481 BC until a redistribution of land took place (*MRR* I.24); Livy 2.43–4 calls him Licinius. Sandberg 2001: 143 points out that the Licinio-Sextian laws in 367 (doc. 1.47) were only passed after a ten-year struggle: the patricians had perhaps learned how to make use of the tribunes' power of veto; cf. Livy 6.35.6, 4.48.6.

4 As the senate was at a loss and had no idea what to do, Appius Claudius proposed that they should consider how the other tribunes might be brought to disagree with Icilius, pointing out that when a tribune opposes and obstructs the senate's decrees, since he is sacrosanct and legally has the authority to do this, there is no other method of putting an end to his power, unless another of those of equal rank who possess the same power opposes him and orders the measures which the other is obstructing. **5** And he advised all consuls who succeeded him in this office to do this and to consider how they might always have some of the tribunes on their side as their friends, saying that the only way of destroying the power of their college was for them to fight among themselves.

THE BEGINNINGS OF THE 'CONFLICT OF THE ORDERS'

The traditional dates of the 'Conflict of the Orders', the struggle between patricians and plebeians, are from 494 to 287 BC. While patricians did not dominate the magistracies in the early Republic, they did have total control over the religious sphere; Cic. *Dom.* 14.38: 'if patrician magistrates are not elected, the auspices of the Roman peoples must perish.' The original concept of patres (the 'fathers') may in fact have been religious, with the patres being the priests, who, together with some selected non-patres, comprised the senatorial body ('qui patres, qui conscripti', 'some fathers, some conscripted': Livy 2.1.11). The term patrician is probably connected with patres (fathers), a term for patrician senators, and patricians, members of specific clans, monopolised certain positions: only a patrician could be an *interrex*, or hold a major priesthood (see Cic. *Dom.* 38; Palmer 1970: 300 for the names and dates of all interreges, who may have had to have been priests: Mitchell 1986: 143). Linderski 1986: 244–61 argues that a patrician form of marriage (confarreatio) developed to maintain this exclusive patrician status and guarantee religious purity: many 'plebeians' must have been the product of a mixed marriage of patrician and plebeian. Patricians, as part of their priestly status, controlled the calendar: Livy 6.1.10 states that when records of sacred laws were looked up after the Gallic invasion, the pontiffs kept them secret, 'so they could keep the minds of the people in subjection', and tradition stated that Gnaeus Flavius, c. 304, published the fasti (the days on which business could be conducted: Cic. *Mur.* 11.25; doc. 1.54.

Apparently, in the early Republic, plebeians were not excluded from magistracies; Cornell 1995: 253 lists 16 possible plebeian consuls in the fifth century, including Brutus himself, while the Cassii, Volumnii, Sempronii, Minucii, and Genucii were all plebeian gentes. However, the patricians increasingly gained control of such offices, until challenged by the plebeians in the fourth century: between 444 (the institution of the consular tribunate) and 367 plebeians were notably unsuccessful: Stewart 1998: 72–9 discusses this domination of political office by powerful gentes. From 367 plebeians were again eligible for the consulship and from 342 one of each pair of consuls supposedly had to be a plebeian (although until 172 one of each pair of consuls was always a patrician); the first plebeian dictator was appointed in 356; the first plebeian censor in 351; the first plebeian praetor in 337; and the first plebeian quaestor in 409. In 300, plebeians were admitted to the major priestly colleges. The main beneficiaries of the struggle were thus the wealthy plebeians who were thus enabled to share the privileges of office and power. On the conflict, see Loewenstein 1973: 19–40; Scullard 1980: 78–91; Develin 1985: 175–92; Raaflaub 1986, esp. 1986a; Mitchell 1986, 1990; Momigliano 1986; Drummond 1989a: 212–27; Cornell 1995: 242–71. For the tension between the populares (Cic. *Sest.* 96: politicians who legislated through the people) and the optimates (the 'best' men, nobles, who took their proposals to the senate), see Mackie 1992; Seager 1972, 1977; Lintott 1999: 173–4.

1.24 The first secession and creation of the tribunate, 494 BC

Livy *History of Rome* 2.31.7–33.3

Dion. Hal. 6.83–6. In this secession ('withdrawal') of the plebs, caused by the burden of debts, the plebeians withdrew outside the pomerium of the city, thus refusing their military service. It took place on the mons sacer, the Sacred Mount (or in another version the Aventine) and the plebs created their own assembly and officials. Aulus Verginius and Titus Veturius (or Vetusius) had been elected consuls for 494, but in this emergency Manius Valerius was appointed dictator. Initially the tribunes were granted the *ius auxilii* (to protect plebeians against the magistrates), then the *ius intercessionis* (veto) against senate, assemblies and magistrates (but not a dictator); they could thus prevent legislation or elections and the convening of the senate or raising of a levy. There were further secessions in 449 and 287.

31.7 Although a three-fold success (over the Sabines, Volsci and Aequi) had been won in the war, regarding the outcome of domestic matters both senators and plebeians were as anxious as ever, so great was the influence and cleverness with which the money-lenders had put things in train so as to frustrate not only the plebs but even the dictator himself. **8** For after the return of the consul (Titus) Vetusius, the first business which Valerius brought to the senate was on behalf of the victorious people, when he demanded that the senate should declare their policy about those bound over for debt. **9** When his proposal was rejected, he made the following statement: 'You do not approve of my being the instigator of harmony; you will very soon, I assure you, wish that the Roman plebs had spokespersons (patrons) like myself. For my part, I will neither disappoint my fellow citizens any further, nor will I be an ineffectual dictator. **10** Internal discord and foreign war have made this magistracy necessary for the state: peace has been made abroad, but hindered at home; I prefer to meet the revolt as a private citizen rather than as dictator.' With these words he left the senate-house and resigned his dictatorship. **11** It was clear to the people that the reason for his resignation was his indignation on their account. Accordingly, just as if he had fulfilled his promise, since it was not his fault that it had not been kept, they escorted him as he left for home with demonstrations of gratitude and praise.

32.1 The senators then began to be anxious that, if the army were disbanded, there would again be secret gatherings and conspiracies. As a result, although the levy had been ordered by the dictator, they considered the men still bound by their oath because they had been sworn in by the consuls, and, on the grounds that the Aequi had recommenced hostilities, instructed that the legions be led out of the city. **2** This brought matters to a head. Initially, it is said, there was talk of murdering the consuls, to release them from their oath; but when they were told that they could not be released from a sacred obligation by a crime, on the advice of one Sicinius, and without orders from the consuls, they withdrew to the Sacred Mount, across the river Anio, three miles from the city. **3** This version is more generally accepted than that related by Piso, in which their withdrawal was made to the Aventine. **4** There, without any leader, they fortified their camp with a rampart and ditch, and remained there peacefully for several days, taking only what they needed for subsistence, and neither receiving nor provoking hostility. **5** There was great panic at Rome, with all business ground to a halt due to the fear felt by everyone. The plebs, abandoned by their defenders, were afraid of violence by the senators; the senators were afraid of the plebeians who remained in the city, unsure whether they would rather see them stay or go. **6** Moreover, for how long would the mob which had seceded stay quiet? And what would happen if some foreign war should arise in the meantime? **7** Clearly there was no hope except in harmony between the citizens; by fair means or foul the state's harmony must be restored. **8** They therefore decided to send someone to speak to the people, Agrippa Menenius (Lanatus, cos. 503), a man of eloquence and dear to the plebs because he was one of them. Being admitted to the camp, he is said, in that time's antiquated and rough mode of speech, to have related the following tale: **9** 'At the time when all the parts of a man did not agree among themselves, as they do now, but each of them had its own will and voice, all the other parts were indignant that they should have the trouble and hard work and toil of providing everything for the stomach, while the stomach remained peacefully in their midst with nothing to do but enjoy the delights they gave it; **10** as a result they conspired together that the hands should not take any food to the mouth, nor should the mouth accept what it was given, nor the teeth chew up what they received. But, while in their anger they wanted to tame the stomach by hunger, the individual parts and the whole body were reduced to total weakness . . .' **12** Drawing a comparison from this to demonstrate how similar was the internal conflict within the body to the plebs' anger against the senators, he won the men over to his viewpoint. **33.1** They then began to work towards harmony, and an agreement was reached on condition that the plebs were to have magistrates, who would be sacrosanct, and who should have the right to protect the plebs against the consuls, while no patrician was to be allowed to take on this magistracy. **2** So two tribunes of the plebs were created, Gaius Licinius and Lucius Albinus. These appointed three other colleagues, amongst whom was Sicinius, the instigator of the revolt; there is less agreement about who the other two were. **3** There are those who say that only two tribunes were created on the Sacred Mount and that the law of their inviolability was passed there.

1.25 The inviolability of the tribunate

Dionysius of Halicarnassus *Roman Antiquities* 6.89.1–3

Tribunes were sacrosanct: physical violence could not be employed against them. They customarily entered office on December 10; fetials: doc. 3.12.

1 On the next day, Brutus and his fellows returned, after making the compact with the senate through the arbiters whom the Romans call 'fetials'. The people divided itself into the phratries of the time, or whatever one wishes to name the divisions which they call 'curiae', and appointed the following as their annual magistrates: Lucius Junius Brutus and Gaius Sicinnius Bellutus, whom they had had as their leaders up to then, and as well as these Gaius and Publius Licinius and Gaius Visellius Ruga. **2** These five were the first men to take on the tribunician power on the fourth day before the Ides of December (December 10), as has been the custom until our own time . . . Brutus called an assembly and advised the plebeians to make this magistracy sacred and inviolable, confirming its security by both a law and oath. **3** Everyone approved of this, and a law was drawn up by Brutus and his colleagues as follows: 'Let no one compel a tribune to do anything against his will, as if he were an ordinary citizen, let no one whip him, or command another to whip him, or kill him or command another to kill him. And if anyone should commit any of these prohibited acts, let him be accursed and his goods consecrated to Ceres, and whoever should kill any person who has committed such acts, let him be innocent of murder.'

ROME AND ITS ITALIAN NEIGHBOURS

For Rome's relations with the Latins and Italic peoples: Sherwin-White 1972: 23–40; Scullard 1980: 92–7; Cornell 1989: 243–94. The Latins inhabited ancient Latium, which was conquered by Rome by 300 BC. Rome is shown as dominant over Latium in the treaty between Rome and Carthage in 509 (doc. 4.1). Rebellion by the Latins led to a struggle which ended with the Latin defeat at the battle of Lake Regillus (499 or 496). Following the 'first secession' of the plebeians, Spurius Cassius Vecellinus in 493 signed a treaty and established a defensive military alliance between Rome and the Latin cities; this was extant in Cicero's time: *Balb.* 53; cf. Livy 2.33.4. Cassius is recorded in the fasti as having been consul in 502, 493 and 486, when he supposedly proposed an agrarian law and was condemned to death for tyrannical aims: *MRR* I.20; Cornell 1995: 271, 299–301. For wars against the Volsci and Aequi, see Alföldi 1965: 365–77.

1.26 The foedus Cassianum (the 'treaty of Cassius') 493 BC

Dionysius of Halicarnassus *Roman Antiquities* 6.95.1–3

1 At the same time a new treaty of peace and friendship was made on oath with all the Latin cities, since they had not tried to stir up trouble during the revolt, had been openly pleased at the people's return (from secession), and had appeared to be prompt in coming to the assistance of the Romans against the rebels. **2** The provisions of the treaty were as follows: 'Let there be peace between the Romans and all the Latin cities as long as heaven and earth remain in the same position; let them neither make war on each other, nor call in enemies from elsewhere, nor grant safe passage to those who make war, but let them assist the other, when attacked, with all their might, and let each have an equal share of the spoils and booty taken in their joint wars; let suits relating to private contracts be judged within ten days and in the place where the contract was made. And let it not be permitted to add anything to or take anything from this treaty except with the consent of both the Romans and all the Latins.' **3** This was the treaty which the Romans and the Latins made with each other, and which was confirmed by their oaths over sacrificial victims.

1.27 Treaty of alliance with the Aequi, 467 BC

Dionysius of Halicarnassus *Roman Antiquities* 9.59.3–5

Rome's alliance with the Latin cities had probably protected Latium from incursions by the Aequi and Volsci. According to Livy (6.12) the Aequi's numbers were small, but they had taken over the easternmost part of the Alban mount in the fifth century (Diod. 11.40), perhaps in 484 BC, and were not driven back until 431 at the Algidus (Livy 4.28–9), though Cincinnatus supposedly crushed them in 458 (cf. docs 2.13–14). They were defeated and Romanised at the end of the fourth century (Livy 9.45, 10.1.9). Fabius is Q. Fabius Vibulanus, the only member of his clan to avoid being killed at the river Cremera in 479 by the Veientines.

3 The Aequi sent ambassadors to Fabius to negotiate a reconciliation and friendship even before they were forced to do so by the destruction of their army or capture of their towns. **4** The consul exacted from them two months' supplies for his army, two tunics for each man, six months' pay, and anything else urgently needed, and concluded a truce with them till they could go to Rome and obtain peace terms from the senate. However, when the senate learnt of this, it gave Fabius full powers to make peace with the Aequi on whatever terms he should prefer. **5** After this, as a result of the consul's arbitration, the two people made an alliance, on these conditions: that the Aequi should be subject to the Romans while still possessing their cities and territories; and that they should not have to send anything to the Romans except troops, when ordered, to be maintained at their own expense.

THE ORIGINS OF THE TWELVE TABLES

In 451, supposedly due to popular agitation over the control of the law by patricians and priests, normal magistracies were suspended and ten patricians with consular powers (a *decemvirate*: board of ten men) were appointed to draw up legal statutes in writing. They were said to have sent to Athens to draw on the laws of Solon (archon 594/3 BC). Arguably, these statutes helped to consolidate patrician control rather than introduce legal reforms, and provisions appear to have been mostly drawn from existing private law, and to some extent from public and sacred law.

After this decemvirate had codified ten tables, a second decemvirate (said to have been half patrician, half plebeian) was appointed for 450 and compiled two more tables, including a ban on marriages between patricians and plebeians; though they attempted to remain in power for 449 they were deposed and normal government resumed. That plebeians formed a part of this second decemvirate is highly dubious and even the existence of a second decemvirate has been doubted; for the decemvirate, Cic. *Rep.* 2.36; Cornell 1995: 272–6; Ungern-Sternberg 1986; Drummond 1989: 113–18, 1989a: 227–34. For the XII Tables, see Kunkel 1973: 23–32; Watson 1975; Eder 1986; Westbrook 1988; Cornell 1995: 278–92. Augustine (*Civ. Dei* 21.11) cites Cicero as saying that the Tables contained eight types of punishment: fines, fetters, flogging, retaliation, disgrace, exile, death and slavery.

1.28 Dissatisfaction within Rome

Dionysius of Halicarnassus *Roman Antiquities* 10.1.1–4

1 Publius Volumnius and Servius Sulpicius Camerinus were elected as consuls at Rome (461 BC). They led out no army either to inflict punishment on those who had injured the Romans or their allies or to protect their possessions; they paid attention to evils within Rome, to prevent the people uniting against the senate and committing some horrendous deed. **2** For they were being roused up again by the tribunes and told that the best political institution for free men was equal rights, and they wanted private and public business to be administered according to laws. For there was not as yet among the Romans equality either of laws or of rights, nor had all their rules of justice been put in writing; but, initially, their kings had laid down judgements for those who asked for it, and whatever they decreed was law . . . **4** A few decisions were kept in sacred books, and had the force of laws, but only the patricians were aware of these because they spent their time in the city, while the majority of people were either merchants or farmers and came to the capital to the markets at intervals of many days, and were still unacquainted with them.

1.29 The creation of the decemvirate

Livy *History of Rome* 3.32.5–7

5 The next consuls were Gaius Menenius and Publius Sestius Capitolinus. In this year again (452 BC) there was no foreign war; disturbances, however, sprang up at home. **6** The legates had now returned with the Athenian laws. For that reason the tribunes demanded more insistently that a start should finally be made towards the codification of laws. It was decided to create decemvirs, subject to no appeal, and for there to be no other magistrates for that year. **7** Whether plebeians should be members of the decemvirate was a matter of dispute for some time; finally they gave in to the patricians, with the proviso that the Icilian law about the Aventine (i.e., the law establishing the tribunate: 2.33.1) and the other sacred laws should not be abolished.

1.30 The 'codification' of the law

Dionysius of Halicarnassus *Roman Antiquities* 10.55.4–5, 56.6–7

55.4 The motion carried was that of the consuls-designate, and was put forward by Appius Claudius who was the first to be called on: that ten of the most distinguished senators be elected; that these should govern for a year from the day of their appointment, having the same authority over everything to do with Rome as the consuls, and, before them, the kings had possessed; that all the other magistracies be abolished while the decemvirs were in charge of government; **5** that these men select out of ancestral customs and the Greek laws which the envoys brought back those best and appropriate for the Romans' city and codify them in the form of laws; that what was decided by the decemvirs, if the senate approved and the people ratified it, should be valid for all time, and all magistrates in the future should decide private contracts and administer public affairs in accordance with these laws. . . .

56.6 When they were satisfied with what they had drawn up, they first assembled the senate, and, when no new objection was made to the laws, had them pass a preliminary decree about them. They then summoned the people to the centuriate assembly (comitia centuriata), and once the pontiffs, augurs, and other priests present had conducted the rites according to custom, they distributed the votes to the centuries. **7** When the people too had ratified the laws, they had them inscribed on bronze tablets and placed them in sequence in the forum, selecting the most conspicuous spot.

THE XII TABLES

Crawford *Statutes* no. 40. The primary areas of concern in the XII Tables are family law, marriage and divorce; assault and injuries against person or property; inheritance and ownership; debt, slavery, and nexum (debt-slavery). The XII Tables are now only known from citations, but in the Republic the laws were learnt by heart by school-children; Cic. *Laws* 2. 59 states that as boys they used to learn the Twelve as an inescapable chant: a 'carmen necessarium'. Livy 3.34.6 calls the Tables 'the origin of all public and private law', though they became increasingly obsolete during the Republic. Tac. *Ann*. 3.27 sees the tables as the last piece of equitable legislation in the Republic. The angle brackets in the text give Crawford's proposed readings.

1.31 Rules for a trial

Table 1

In a trial the action began with the defendant being summoned to appear before the magistrate, by force if necessary. **1.1–3**: the rights and duties of the plaintiff against a defendant; **1.13–15**: penalties for 'iniuria', bodily harm or damage to property and theft. The XII Tables laid down monetary penalties for physical assault.

1.1 If he (anyone) summons (the defendant) to court, he shall go. If he does not go, he (the plaintiff) shall call a witness; then he shall take him. **2** If he (the defendant) delays or drags his feet, he (the plaintiff) shall lay hand on him. **3** If there is sickness or age, he (the plaintiff), shall provide a yoked beast of burden; if he does not wish to, he should not prepare a carriage. **7** If they do not agree, they are to present their case in the comitium or forum before midday. They are to finish bringing action together, both being present…

13 If he has maimed a part (of a body), unless he settles it with him, there is to be retaliation in kind. **14** If he has broken a bone of a free man, 300 (asses), if of a slave 150 are to be the penalty. **15** If he do (other) injury ?to another? (i.e., not as serious as the injury above), 25 (asses) are to be the penalty. **16** <If he has felled a productive tree, 25 (asses) are to be the penalty.> **17** If he committed theft by night and he killed him, he shall have been lawfully killed. **19** <If the theft is manifest, if he does not settle, he (the magistrate) shall flog him> and hand him over. <If a slave, he is to flog him and throw him from the (Tarpeian) rock. If underage, he is to flog him and the thief is to repair the damage.>

1.32 Debt law

Table 3.1–4, 3.6

Gell. 20.1.42: those judged liable for an unpaid debt had 30 days in which to find the money, during which no legal action could be taken. (The 30 days' delay might have applied to all kinds of cases, not just debt.) They were then summoned to the praetor's court and made over to the persons to whom they owed the money, who could bind them in chains. It appears that there was also the chance of compromising, presumably by the debtors choosing to become *nexi* ('bondsmen'; sing.: *nexus*) and pay off their debt by working for their creditor: if no compromise was reached at the end of this period (after the third market-day on which their debt was announced), they suffered capital punishment or were sold into slavery 'across the Tiber', i.e., in Etruscan territory (3.5); it appears that even at this period citizens could not be enslaved at Rome: Cornell 1995: 281. According to Roman writers (Gell. 20.1.48), if a man owed debts to several creditors, they were able to share out the body, though this probably referred to a division of his property or his value while he worked off his debt for one of his creditors (3.6): see Watson 1975: 111–24. Debt-slavery, or nexum, was obviously an important issue in the mid-fifth century: Varro *Lat. Lang.* 7.105 describes a nexus as a free person who has provided his labour in place of money he (or another member of his family) owes until the debt is paid. Nexi remained Roman citizens and continued to live at Rome; cf. Livy 2.23.1–15 where the debtor is not taken into service, but to prison; doc. 1.52 for sympathy for a handsome young man in debt-slavery, leading to the *lex Poetilia*: doc. 1.52.

3.1 In respect of an admitted sum (of debt) <and judgement>, thirty days (period of grace) shall be allowed. **2** After that there shall be laying on of a hand. **3** He (the plaintiff) shall bring him into court. Unless he does what has been judged, or someone acts as his protector in court, he (the plaintiff) shall take him with him. He is to bind him with rope or shackles for the feet. He shall bind him with not <more> than 15 pounds, or <less> if he wishes. **4** If he (the defendant) wishes, he is to live on his own. If he does not live on his own, he who shall have him bound shall give him a pound of spelt for each day; if he wishes he is to give more. **5** <On three successive market-days, he shall produce him in the comitium.> **6** <Unless he settles,> on the third market-day they (the creditors) shall cut (?his property?) into pieces. If they should have cut more or less, it shall be without penalty. **7** <If he (the plaintiff) wishes, he is to sell him abroad, beyond the Tiber.>

1.33 Family law

Table 4

According to Cic. *Laws* 3.19 the Tables laid down that a badly deformed child should be killed quickly (4.1); at 4.4 the Table stated that a child born 10 months after his father's death will not be allowed legal inheritance (a provision against adultery on the part of the mother). Children could be emancipated from patria potestas: Ulpian (*Tit.* 10.1) states that descendants are transferred as property and freed by emancipation, but that a son has to be transferred and manumitted three times. It appears here that a father could sell his son into slavery and, if freed by the buyer, the son was returned to patria potestas; this might be an old formula by which a son was emancipated by a pretend triple-sale; Watson 1975: 117–18, however, sees the son (or grandson) as sold into nexum a maximum of three times to provide the father with working capital or to pay off a debt; cf. Cornell 1995: 283.

4.1 <If he is born deformed, and he does not pick him up, it is without liability.>
4.2 If a father sells his son three times, the son shall be free from his father.

1.34 Guardianship and the status of women and lunatics

Table 5

Gaius *Inst*. 1.144–5. At 5.2 a woman's property could not be acquired by long possession (*usucapio*) unless delivered up by her with a guardian's sanction. At 5.6, where a guardian is not appointed by will, her agnates are her guardians: an agnate was a male kinsman by blood, tracing descent through the males of the family or by adoption back to a common ancestor. On incapacity and guardianship, see Watson 1975: 71–80. Plutarch *Numa* 10.3 ascribes the Vestals' freedom from tutelage to Numa; Vestals could also make wills: cf. Gell. 1.12.9. According to Ulpian (*Dig.* 27.10.1, *Tit*. 12.2) agnates or clansmen (*gentiles*) administered the property of a madman or spendthrift.

5.1 A Vestal Virgin <is to be free of guardianship (tutela).>
5.7 If there be a madman ?or spendthrift?, power in respect of him and his familia (estate) is to belong to his agnates and gentiles.

1.35 Inheritance

Table 5

These clauses concern intestate succession (i.e., where the deceased had not made a will): Watson 1975: 52–70; Crook 1986. Blood relations of both sexes would normally inherit if the head of a family died intestate, and a wife in her husband's control (in manu: 'in his hand') would rank equally with his sons and daughters. Debt bequeathed by inheritance was equally divided among the heirs (5.9); cf. doc. 7.1.

5.4 If he dies intestate and has no heir of his own (*suus heres*), the nearest agnate shall have possession of the estate (familia) ?and goods?
5.5 If there is no agnate, the clansmen (*gentiles*) shall have the estate ?and goods?

1.36 Freedmen and patrons

Table 5.8, 8.10

Guardianship of freedmen belonged to their patron (the ex-owner), like the right of inheritance if the freedman died intestate. Presumably otherwise freedmen had the right of making wills in favour of whomever they wished and clearly they could own property. **5.8**: Ulpian *Tit*. 29.1: the Law of the XII Tables makes the inheritance of a Roman citizen freedman over to his patron, if the freedmen has died intestate and without his own heir (*suus heres*). See Watson 1975: 81–97 on slaves and freedmen at this period, 98–110 on patrons.

5.8 If a freedman (dies intestate) . . . from that familia . . . to that familia.
8.10 If a patron shall have wronged his client, he must be forfeited (sacer).

1.37 Transfer of property and possession of land

Tables 6 and 7

The variation in the lapse of time within which title to possession could be established depended on the distinction between personal and immovable property. The term *res mancipi* included land, slaves and farm animals which could be broken in; mancipatio was a formal act of conveyance, requiring five witnesses and a formal weighing out of bronze: Watson 1975: 134–49; cf. doc. 7.4. Other items, *res nec mancipi*, were transferred by physical delivery (*traditio*). According to Gaius *Inst.* 2.42, the XII Tables laid down that usucapio of movable things could be completed in a year, but for an estate and buildings it took two years. The law of manumission by will was included in the laws of possession: usucapio was the right of ownership after a period of control or use, for example of a parcel of land. **6.5**: Guardianship of a woman could be transferred by usucapio, and a woman who remained married for a year was transferred by this year's ownership (usus) into the estate of her husband; to avoid coming into the manus (control) of her husband while married, a woman had to be absent for three nights a year (Gaius *Inst.* 1.111; cf. doc. 7.10); on manus and marriage in the Tables, see Watson 1975: 9–19. **6.6**: Ulpian *Dig.* 47.3.1 states that the law granted the right of action for double the cost of the damage against the person found guilty of having removed a beam from a neighbouring structure and having fixed it in his own building. **7.9**: Pomponius *Dig.* 43.27.2: if a tree on a neighbour's property should have been bent by the wind and lean over your farm, you may, by the Law of the XII Tables, take legal action for its removal; cf. Ulpian *Dig.* 43.27.1.8.

6.1 When he shall perform nexum (bond) and mancipium (formal purchase), as he has proclaimed by word of mouth, so shall it be legal. **1b** (Ulpian *Tit.* 2.4) A person who has been made a free man under this condition, that he should give 10,000 pieces to the heir, even if he has been legally transferred by the heir, shall achieve his liberty by giving the money to the purchaser; and the Law of the Twelve Tables lays this down. **3** For a piece of land right of possession (auctoritas) (is to be) two years <for other things it is to be one year>. **4** Against a foreigner right of possession <is to be> perpetual. **5** <If she is absent three nights in a year . . .> **6** He is not to detach from its joint a beam from a house or a vineyard . . . **7.9** <If a tree overhangs someone's land, he is to cut it back more than fifteen feet.>

1.38 Animal damage

8.2 If a quadruped <cause> loss, <unless he repair it he is to give it up for the damage.>

1.39 Slander, libel and witchcraft

Table 8

8.1: Cic. *Rep.* 4.12 states that the Tables laid down a capital penalty for anyone who 'sang or composed a song, such as caused dishonour or disgrace to another person'; singing or chanting of a song against someone (*occentare*) might imply witchcraft (cf. doc. 3.67).

8.1 Whoever casts an evil spell . . . <or whoever> sings <or> composes a spell . . .
8.4 Whoever has bewitched crops . . . or has enticed someone else's harvest . . .

1.40 Capital crimes: damaging crops, perjury, and arson

Table 8

Cic. *Tull.* F21.50: the XII Tables laid down that a thief could not be killed by day, unless he defended himself with a weapon; even if he resisted the victim must first call for help. At 8.15, a search for stolen property is to be carried out naked (so the searcher could not bring in any extraneous items and then pretend to find them), with only a loin-cloth and platter. If the thief was not caught in the act, the penalty was double damages (8.16).

8.5: Pliny *Nat. Hist.* 18.12 notes that the penalty for secretly treading down or cutting crops at night was more severe than that for murder (i.e., execution, with his property confiscated to Ceres). **8.6**: according to Gaius *Dig.* 47.9.9 anyone who deliberately burnt a building or a heap of corn placed next to a house was to be bound, flogged, and put to death by fire; if it was an accident, he was to repair the damage. A further capital crime was for a judge or arbiter to take a bribe (9.3). **8.13**: the penalty for unintentional homicide.

8.5 <If he has grazed or cut a crop by night, he is to be hanged for Ceres. If he is underage, he (the magistrate) is to flog (him) and he is to settle for double penalty.>
6 If he shall have burnt a building or a heap of corn placed near ?a house?, bound and beaten (he is to be killed) by fire. If by chance . . ., he is to repair the damage.
12 <If he shall have given false evidence, he (the magistrate) shall throw (him) from the (Tarpeian) rock.>
13 If a weapon has escaped his hand rather than that he has thrown it, <a ram is to be offered as a substitute.>

1.41 Money-lending and interest

Table 8

Tacitus (*Ann.* 6.16): 'Lending money at interest was a long-standing problem for the city and a very frequent cause of civil strife and unrest. For that reason it was checked even in the time of ancient and less corrupt (than now) morality. For the XII Tables were the first to establish that no one should practise usury at the rate of more than one-twelfth (i.e., 1 per cent a month), while before this it was carried on according to the desire of the rich.'

8.18 Our ancestors followed this (principle) and laid it down in their laws that a thief is condemned for double, the usurer for quadruple (the amount) (Cato *Agr.* pref.)

1.42 Sacred law

Table 10

Cic. *Laws* 2 cites sections from this table. No burial or cremation was allowed in the city (*Laws* 2.58) because of the danger of fire and pollution (cf. doc. 3.75); there were also sumptuary regulations about burials, concerning expenses and mourners. **10.7**: (*Laws* 2.60) it is clear that garlands to honour games winners or valour were allowed at funerals. Toher 1986: 302–3 n.7 believes that the shawls and tunic refer to the mourners (not the corpse). While generally classed as sumptuary legislation, these clauses appear not so much to be curbing the display of wealth by the aristocracy as regulating conduct at the funeral. **10.8**: *Laws* 2.60 explains that gold on the corpse is forbidden, 'but for him whose teeth are bound together with gold, if a person buries or burns him with that it shall be without penalty'.

10.1 He is not to bury or burn a dead man in the city. **2** He is not to do more than this; he is not to smooth the pyre with a trowel. **3** . . . <three shawls>, a small purple tunic . . . ten <flute-players> . . . **4** Women are not to tear their cheeks or hold a wake on account of the funeral. **5** He is not to collect the bones of a dead man to hold a funeral later (i.e., part of the dead body is not to be preserved for another ceremony). **7** Whoever wins a crown himself or his <family>, or it be given to him for courage, <and it is placed on him or his parent when dead, it is to be without liability>. **8** . . . nor is he to add gold, <but> whoever has teeth joined with gold, and if he should bury or burn it with him, it is without liability.

THE SUPPLEMENTARY TABLES

1.43 The creation of a second decemvirate, 450 BC

Dionysius of Halicarnassus *Roman Antiquities* 10.58.1–4, 60.5–6

Appius is Appius Claudius Crassinus Inregillensis Sabinus (cos. 471), head of the commission: *MRR* I.48. The fall of the decemvirate and the second secession was supposedly caused by Appius' attempted forcible seduction of the beautiful young girl Verginia (Livy 3.44–8; Dion. Hal. 12.24.2–4): the decemvirs thereupon committed suicide or went into exile.

58.1 Following a lengthy debate (in the senate), the view of those who preferred electing a decemvirate again to govern the state prevailed. For not only was their codification of laws clearly unfinished, in as much as it had been compiled in a short period, but in the case of the laws which had already been ratified a magistracy with absolute powers seemed essential so that, whether willingly or unwillingly, people should observe them. The main reason, however, which led them to choose the decemvirate was the disbanding of the tribunes, which they all desired more than anything . . .

3 On this occasion Appius, who was the leading member of the decemvirate, was greatly praised by everyone, and the whole mob of plebeians wanted to keep him in office, as they considered that no one else would govern better . . . **4** So he was again chosen in the centuriate assembly as a lawgiver, for the second time; chosen along with him were Quintus Fabius, surnamed Vibulanus, who had been three times consul and was a man without reproach up to that time and possessed of every good quality. From among the other patricians, whom Appius favoured, Marcus Cornelius, Marcus Sergius, Lucius Minucius, Titus Antonius and Manius Rabuleius, were elected, men of no particular distinction; and from among the plebeians, Quintus Poetelius, Caeso Duilius and Spurius Oppius. For these too were admitted by Appius as colleagues to flatter the plebeians, and he stated that since there was one magistracy governing everyone it was fair that the people should have some share in it . . .

60.5 Appius and his colleagues had the other laws inscribed on two tablets and added them to those published before. Among these new laws was this one, that it was not legal for the patricians to intermarry with the plebeians — a law, in my view, made simply to prevent the two orders from uniting in harmony once mingled by intermarriages and family connections. **6** And when the time for the election of magistrates came round, the decemvirs said goodbye to both the ancestral customs and the newly-written laws, and remained in the same magistracy without putting it to the vote by either senate or people.

1.44 A ban on intermarriage

Tables 11–12

In the supplementary laws of 449, intermarriage (connubium) between patricians and plebeians was disallowed and this was clearly an innovation. This was repealed shortly afterwards in 445 by the *lex Canuleia*. Cic. *Rep.* 2.63: 'When two tables of unjust laws had been added, they also laid down, by a very inhumane law, that intermarriage, which is even usually permitted between different peoples, should not be allowed between plebeians and patricians.' See Linderski 1986 for its significance; on conditions for marriage in the Tables, Watson 1975: 20–30. There were no limits to a master's power over his slaves; should a slave commit a crime, the action lay against his master; should a slave be injured, his master was compensated (doc. 1.31).

11.1 <There is not to be connubium> with the plebs.
12.2 If a slave commit theft or cause damage, <he is to be given for the damage>.

THE CONFLICT OF THE ORDERS CONTINUES

One of the most important issues in the Conflict of the Orders was the opening up of the important magistracies, especially the consulship, as well as the priesthoods to plebeians. Legislation concerning the consulship was passed (supposedly) in 367 (the leges Liciniae-Sextiae, laying down that one consul each year should be a plebeian: doc. 1.47) and in 342 (the leges Genuciae, which opened both consulships to plebeians: doc. 1.49); for the retrojected date, see Billows 1989, who argues that the leges Genuciae did not come into effect until c. 201 and that plebeians were not in fact eligible until 342; cf. Pinsent 1975: 64–7 for the anachronism here in Livy, as the first consular college of two plebeians was in 172. Pairs of patrician consuls are recorded in 355, 354, 353, 351, 349 and 343: Stewart 1998: 152. The disasters of the Second Punic War may have opened magistracies up to new plebeian families: 177 senators were added to the senate after the Trasimene disaster in 216 (Livy 23.23.7), many of whom were from new plebeian gentes. See Scullard 1980: 115–30; Cornell 1995: 327–44. Livy's account of the years 292–219 is lost.

1.45 The Valerio-Horatian laws, 449 BC

Livy *History of Rome* 3.55.1–7, 13–15

Cf. Dion. Hal. 11.45. The Valerio-Horatian laws were supposedly passed in response to dissatisfaction felt with the second decemvirate. Lucius Valerius Potitus and Marcus Horatius Barbatus were consuls in 449: *MRR* I.47. The law imposing plebiscites on the whole people was in fact the *lex Hortensia* of 287: this law may have validated plebiscites which had senatorial sanction, but the historicity of the Valerio-Horatian laws must remain in doubt: Ferenczy 1976: 47–72; Cornell 1995: 276–8.

1 They then, through an interrex, elected Lucius Valerius and Marcus Horatius as consuls, who at once took up their magistracies. Their consulship favoured the people's cause, without wronging the patricians in any way, although it still managed to offend them; **2** for whatever protected the liberty of the plebs was seen as detracting from their own powers. **3** First of all, since it was still an open question whether patricians were legally bound by plebiscites, they passed a law in the comitia centuriata that whatever the people should lay down in the tribal assembly should be binding on the people; this law furnished the tribunes' proposals (*rogationes*) with a very sharp weapon indeed. **4** Secondly, they not only restored a consular law about the appeal (*provocatio*), the unique safeguard of liberty which had been overturned by the power of the decemvirate, but even protected it for the future by enacting a new inviolable law, **5** that no one should appoint any magistrate without appeal; if anyone should do so, he might be put to death without violating law or religion, and this homicide would not be a capital crime. **6** And now they had fortified the plebs sufficiently through the right of appeal on the one hand and the tribunician help on the other, they also revived for the benefit of the tribunes themselves the consideration of their sacrosanct status, a matter that had come to be almost forgotten, by bringing back certain rites which had lapsed for a considerable period; **7** and they made them inviolate both on the grounds of religion and also by a law, which ordained that should any person harm the tribunes of the plebs, (plebeian) aediles or decemviral judges his head would be forfeit to Jupiter, and his household possessions be put up for sale at the temple of Ceres, Liber and Libera . . . **13** These were the consular laws. The same consuls also inaugurated the practice whereby senatorial decrees were handed over to the aediles of the plebs at the temple of Ceres, for previously these were often suppressed or falsified at the discretion of the consuls. **14** A tribune of the plebs, Marcus Duillius, then proposed to the plebs, and they decreed, that anyone who left the plebs without tribunes, and anyone who appointed a magistrate without appeal, should be scourged and beheaded. **15** None of these measures were opposed by the patricians (though they were not in favour of them), because as yet no one in particular was being targeted.

1.46 The Canuleian Laws, 445 BC

Livy *History of Rome* 4.1.1–3, 6.1–11

Cf. Dion. Hal. 11.53. Gaius Canuleius was tribune of the plebs in 445 (Cic. *Rep.* 2.63). His law repealed that of the second decemvirate which banned patrician-plebeian marriages: *MRR* I.52. This is the first recorded tribunician veto of a decree of the senate. Tribunes with consular powers remained until 367 (and were chosen 51 times). A contio was an official, non-voting assembly of the people, summoned by a magistrate or priest: see Pina Polo 1995; Mouritsen 2001: 38–62. Cicero speaks of daily contiones: *Sest.* 39. Bills were often introduced to the people in a contio, before voting took place, and they were used to display oratorical skills before the people; *senatus consulta*, edicts, and reports of battles were also communicated to the people at contiones. For those who attended the contiones (the *plebs contionalis*), see Vanderbroeck 1987: 161–5; Mouritsen 41–2 sees them as 'upper-class politically minded citizens' often in the forum.

1.1 Marcus Genucius and Gaius Curtius succeeded these (Titus Quinctius Capitolinus and Agrippa Furius) as consuls. It was a troubled year both at home and abroad. For, when it began, Gaius Canuleius, a tribune of the plebs, put forward a proposal concerning the intermarriage of patricians and plebeians, **2** which the patricians considered would contaminate their blood and mix up the proper classification of the gentes (clans), while a suggestion initially put forward hesitantly by the tribunes, that it should be permissible for one of the consuls to be a plebeian, later went so far that nine tribunes put forward a proposal **3** that the people should have the power to elect consuls of their choice, whether from the plebs or the patricians . . . **6.1** When the consuls had joined the meeting (contio) and formal speeches had been succeeded by bickering, the tribune asked why a plebeian should not be chosen as consul. **2** Curtius replied, perhaps truthfully, yet for the present not very profitably, 'Because no plebeian has the auspices, and that was the reason why the decemvirs prohibited intermarriage, in case the auspices be disturbed by the ill-defined status of the offspring of such intermarriage.' **3** At this the plebs blazed up with extreme indignation, at the suggestion that they were not allowed to take auspices, as if they were detestable to the immortal gods; nor did the controversy end — for the plebs had found a zealous promoter in the tribune, and rivalled him themselves in perseverance — until the patricians were finally overcome and allowed the law about intermarriage to be carried, **4** because they thought that the tribunes would either entirely abandon their struggle for plebeian consuls or put it aside until after the war, and that, in the meantime, the plebs would be satisfied with the right to intermarry and be prepared for the levy . . . **6** Since the consuls were unable to achieve anything through the senate while the tribunes interposed their veto, they privately held councils of their leading men. It was obvious that they would have to give in to being defeated by either the enemy or their own citizens. **7** Of all the consulars, Valerius and Horatius were the only ones who did not take part in these councils. Gaius Claudius' view was that they should arm the consuls against the tribunes; the Quinctii, both Cincinnatus and Capitolinus, were both averse to bloodshed and to harming those whom they had accepted as being sacrosanct in the treaty they had struck with the plebs. **8** The outcome of these deliberations was that they allowed military tribunes with consular powers to be elected indiscriminately from among the patricians and plebs, but made no alteration in the consular elections; with this, both tribunes and plebs were satisfied. **9** An election was called to elect three tribunes with consular powers . . . **11** The result of this election demonstrated how differently people behave when struggling for liberty and status, and when discord is put aside and their judgement unbiased; for the people elected all the (consular) tribunes from patricians, satisfied that the plebeians had been allowed to stand for election.

1.47 The Licinio-Sextian laws, 367 BC

Livy *History of Rome* 6.35.1–5

Lucius Sextius Sextinus Lateranus (cos. 366) and Gaius Licinius Stolo (cos. 364 or 361: *MRR* I.116 n.1) as tribunes in 367 are recorded as having passed a package of laws in the interests of the plebeians, many of whom had been reduced to debt-slavery: interest paid on a debt should be deducted from the principal; at least one of the consuls was to be chosen from the plebs, and a single praetor was to be elected; and individual holdings of ager publicus (state land) should be limited to 500 iugera (*MRR* I.114). A iugerum (pl.: iugera) is approximately 28,800 sq. feet, a little more than half an acre. The two tribunes had reputedly been in office since 376 and prevented the election of magistrates from 375 to 371, but the tradition is highly suspect. Billows 1989 argues for down-dating these laws to the early second century. A standard small-holding was seven iugera or less (500 iugera would have been a huge estate), and there would in any case have been little ager publicus in the fourth century (cf. doc. 8.6); Cornell, however, accepts that this might have been the maximum size of holdings (1995: 329–400), arguing that the Licinio-Sextian laws replaced the consular tribunate with the consulate and permitted plebeians to hold curule magistracies, with Lucius Sextius Lateranus as the first plebeian consul in 366. Stolo was said to have been prosecuted later for holding more land than his own law permitted and fined 10,000 asses: Livy 7.16.9; see Develin 1986; Cornell 1989a: 323–35; Münzer 1999: 12–27.

1 A chance for innovation was provided by the immense weight of debt, an evil which the plebs had no hope of lifting except by positioning their representatives in the highest magistracies: their view was that they had to get ready to plan for this; **2** with effort and toil the plebeians had got to the stage where, if they continued their struggles, they could reach the top and rival the patricians in honours as much as in merit. **3** For the moment, it was agreed that they should have tribunes of the plebs, through which office they might be able to open up a way to the other magistracies. **4** Gaius Licinius and Lucius Sextius were elected and proposed all their laws to the detriment of the patricians and for the advantage of the plebs — one concerning debt, that what had been paid back as interest should be deducted from the original, while the remainder should be paid back in equal instalments over three years. **5** Another limited the possession of land, forbidding anyone from holding more than 500 iugera. A third abolished the election of military tribunes and provided that one of the consuls, at least, should be elected from the plebs.

1.48 Election of the first plebeian consul, 367 BC

Livy *History of Rome* 6.42.9–14

Gell. 5.4.3. Sextius and Licinius had been tribunes 10 times: for 366 the plebeian Sextius was elected consul, as a 'new man'. According to Livy (7.1.4) the patricians purposely deferred all business to avoid anything being effected by a plebeian consul. When in 362 the first plebeian consul to lead an army under his own auspices, Genucius, was ambushed and killed by the Hernici, the patricians took this as a sign of divine displeasure and Appius who had opposed the election of plebeian consuls was made dictator. The year 367 is also noteworthy for the creation of new magistracies — one praetor and (two) curule aediles, responsible for the ludi Megalenses in April and the ludi Romani in September. The office of praetor urbanus (urban praetor) was opened to the plebs in 337 (8.15.9). 9: the Gallic threat was driven off by M. Furius Camillus, dictator for the fifth time in 350 and consul in 349.

9 Camillus had hardly put an end to the war when he was faced by even more violent conflict at home, and after immense struggles the dictator and senate were beaten, the tribunes' proposals adopted, and consular elections were held, against the wishes of the nobles, in which Lucius Sextius was made the first plebeian consul. **10** Not even this put an end to the disputes. The patricians refused to ratify the election, which almost brought about a secession of the plebs and threatened other terrible manifestations of civil strife, **11** when finally through the dictator the unrest was allayed by compromise: the nobles gave way to the plebs on the question of the plebeian consul, and the plebs conceded to the nobles that one praetor should be elected from the patricians to administer justice in the city. **12** So, after long rivalry, the orders were finally reconciled. The senate decided that this was a fitting occasion, and appropriate if ever any occasion was, to honour the immortal gods by a celebration of the Great Games, and an extra day was added to the normal three. **13** When the people's aediles refused this additional burden, the young patricians cried out that they would willingly take it on in honour of the gods. **14** They were thanked by the entire people, and the senate decreed that the dictator should propose the election of two aediles (later the curule aediles) from the patricians and that the senate should ratify all the elections of that year.

1.49 Further patrician concessions, the leges Genuciae, 342 BC

Livy *History of Rome* 7.42.1–3, 7

This legislation reputedly followed an army mutiny in 342 BC. The first year in which both consuls were plebeian was actually 172; possibly Lucius Genucius legislated as tribune that one of the consuls had to be plebeian. The provision that there should be a gap of ten years before holding the same magistracy again may have been retrojected from c. 201: Billows 1989; see Develin 1985: 184–5; *MRR* I.134; though Cornell 1995: 371 notes that this was in fact enforced over the next twenty years with one possible exception.

1 In addition to these events, I find in certain writers that Lucius Genucius, a tribune of the plebs, brought a proposal before the plebs that lending money at interest should not be permitted; **2** also that in other plebiscites it was laid down that no one should hold the same magistracy twice within ten years, nor two magistracies in the same year, and that it should be permissible for both consuls to be chosen from the plebs. If all these concessions were made to the plebs, it seems that the revolt had considerable impact. **3** It is recorded in other annals that Valerius (M. Valerius Maximus Corvus) was not made dictator, but that the whole affair was managed through the consuls, and that it was not before they came to Rome but at Rome itself that the enormous number of conspirators were frightened into taking up arms; .... **7** On no single point do ancient historians agree except on their having been a revolt and that it was settled.

1.50 A radical dictator, 339 BC

Livy *History of Rome* 8.12.14–17

Quintus Publilius Philo was consul in 339, 327, 320, 315; first plebeian praetor in 336 (doc. 1.51); censor in 332; and dictator in 339, after conflict between his consular colleague Aemilius Mamercinus and the senate. The proposal that plebiscites should be binding on the whole people duplicates the *lex Hortensia* of 287 and should probably not be accepted; for Publilius, see docs 1.51, 65; Develin 1985: 59–63; *MRR* I.137.

14 The dictatorship of Publilius was a popular one, both for his accusatory speeches against the senators and because he brought in three laws extremely favourable to the plebs and damaging to the nobility: **15** one, that plebiscites were to be binding on all the Quirites (Roman citizens); a second, that the senate should ratify measures proposed at the comitia centuriata before the beginning of voting; **16** and a third, that at least one censor should be chosen from the plebs, since they had already gone so far as to allow both to be plebeian. **17** The senators considered that the mischief done at home in that year by the consuls and dictator outweighed the increase in empire which resulted from their victory and management of campaigns away from home.

1.51 The first plebeian praetor, 336 BC

Livy *History of Rome* 8.15.9

Quintus Publilius Philo, the first plebeian praetor in 336, was opposed by the presiding consul, Gaius Sulpicius Longus, cos. 337, but not the senate.

In the same year Quintus Publilius Philo was made praetor, the first plebeian to be so, though Sulpicius the consul opposed his election and refused to receive votes for him. The senate, however, since it had failed in achieving this for the highest magistracies, was less stubborn with regard to the praetorship.

1.52 No imprisonment for debt, 326 BC

Livy *History of Rome* 8.28.1–2, 5–8

Dion. Hal. 16.5(9); cf. Val. Max. 6.1.9 who puts this after the Caudine forks disaster, in 321. Varro attributes the law to Poetelius' son, dictator in 313 (*Lat. Lang.* 7.105). In this episode a youth had given himself up to a usurer for his father's debt; his ill-treatment by his owner inflamed the people and the consuls were ordered to carry a proposal to the people that none should be confined in shackles or in the stocks except those who had been guilty of some crime: the *lex Poetelia de nexis* (Gaius Poetelius Libo Visolus was consul with Lucius Papirius Cursor in 326). From now on by law only a debtor's goods were distrainable, not his person: Crook 1967: 170–8, esp. 173.

1 In that year it was as if the liberty of the Roman plebs had a fresh start, for men were no longer to be imprisoned for debt; this change in the law was brought about by the equally outrageous lust and inhumanity of a single money-lender. **2** This was Lucius Papirius whose mind, when Gaius Publilius gave himself up to him as a debt-bondsman (nexus) for his father's debt, was inflamed to lust and outrage by his youth and beauty, though they might well have roused his compassion . . . **5** Lacerated with whip-marks, the youth rushed into the street, crying out against the money-lender's lust and inhumanity, **6** at which an immense mob of people, infuriated by compassion for his youth and anger at his treatment, as well as by consideration for their own status and that of their children, flocked into the forum and from there *en masse* into the senate house; **7** the consuls were compelled by this unexpected uproar to convene the senate, and the mob threw themselves at the feet of each of the senators as they entered the senate house, pointing to the youth's scourged back. **8** On that day, due to the unbridled wrong-doing of one man, the oppressive shackles of credit were overthrown, and the consuls were instructed to put a motion before the people that no one should be confined in shackles or fetters, apart from those who had been guilty of some offence and were awaiting punishment.

1.53 Appius Claudius refuses to retire as censor

Livy *History of Rome* 9.33.3–6, 34.26

Appius Claudius Caecus (the 'Blind) was censor in 312 (cos. 307 and 296, and praetor in 295). He commissioned, as censor, the construction of the via Appia and the aqua Appia (docs 2.4, 6). In 300 he opposed the inclusion of plebeians in the major priestly colleges. In this episode he refuses to resign after his 18 months as censor, though his colleague had retired: *MRR* I.160. For the Aemilian law of 434, see Livy 4.24.5; Ferenczy 1976: 120–200; on Appius, Develin 1985: 215–24; Cornell 1995: 373–7.

33.3 For many years now there had been no struggles between the patrician magistrates and the tribunes, when a dispute arose from that family which appeared destined to contend with the tribunes and plebs. **4** The censor, Appius Claudius, when the 18 months laid down by the Aemilian law as the term of the censorship had expired, and although his colleague Gaius Plautius had retired, could by no means be made to step down. **5** It was Publius Sempronius, a tribune of the plebs, who started proceedings to limit the censorship to its legal period, an action no less just than popular, and as welcome to every aristocrat as to the common people. **6** He repeatedly quoted the Aemilian law and praised its promoter, the dictator Mamercus Aemilius (434 BC: Livy 4.24.5–6), for restricting the censorship, which had until then been held for five years and was proving itself tyrannical on account of the long period its authority lasted, to a limit of a year and a half . . . **34.26** After making all these accusations, he ordered the censor to be seized and led off to prison. Six tribunes approved their colleague's action, while three protected Appius on his appeal, and he continued as sole censor despite his extreme unpopularity with all classes.

1.54 A novus homo in 304 BC

Livy *History of Rome* 9.46.1–9, 12–15

For this episode, cf. Pliny *Nat. Hist.* 33.17–19 and Gell. 7.9.5–6 (quoting Piso's *Annals*); *MRR* I.168. This passage demonstrates the possibility of social mobility in late fourth-century Rome and the general intransigence of nobles towards outsiders (see docs 2.40–1; 7.74). A paid bureaucrat (in this case an apparitor: a high-ranking salaried official attendant on magistrates) could not become a magistrate himself unless he resigned his post; for apparitors and other *scribae* (secretaries), see Badian 1989. The night watch, the tresviri capitales, was not regularly instituted until later (c. 290–87; see Livy *Per.* 11; Lintott 1999: 141–3). Censors, consuls, praetors and curule aediles were permitted to use the curule 'chair' (sella curulis) as a sign of office. The annalist Gaius Licinius Macer was tribune in 73 and praetor in 68; he was convicted of extortion in 66 and committed suicide (*MRR* II.110, 138; Alexander *Trials* no. 195). Both Livy and Dionysius used his work. The publication of the calendar (cf. docs 3.28–9) removed the need for consultation with the pontifices (pontiffs) before beginning a lawsuit.

1 In the same year Gnaeus Flavius, son of Gnaeus, a government clerk, who had been born in humble circumstances (his father being a freedman), but who was still a shrewd and eloquent man, was curule aedile. **2** I find in certain annals that when he was in attendance upon the aediles and saw that the tribes would elect him aedile, had not his candidature been unacceptable because he was acting as recorder, he put away his writing-tablet and swore that he would keep no record; **3** however, Licinius Macer alleges that he had ceased being a clerk some time before this, having already been a tribune and a triumvir, once on a commission in charge of the night watch and once in the foundation of a colony. **4** In any case, there is no argument about the obstinacy with which he battled with the nobles who despised his lowly birth; **5** he published the civil law, which had been put away in the secret archives of the pontiffs, and posted up the official calendar (the fasti) on white notice-boards around the forum for people to know when they could bring a legal action; **6** he dedicated a temple of Concord in the precinct of Vulcan, to the great resentment of the nobles; and Cornelius Barbatus, the pontifex maximus, was forced by the unanimous wish of the people to dictate the formula (of dedication) to him, although he insisted that by ancestral custom no one except a consul or imperator could dedicate a temple. **7** As a result, in accordance with a resolution of the senate, a measure was passed by the people that no one could dedicate a temple or altar without the authorisation of the senate or of a majority of the tribunes of the plebs. **8** I will relate an incident, not memorable in itself, except as evidence of the way the plebs asserted their liberty against the arrogance of the nobles. **9** Flavius had come to visit a colleague who was sick, and the young nobles who were sitting by the bed were united in their resolution not to rise to greet him, so he ordered his curule chair to be brought in and from his official seat gazed at his enemies who were overpowered with jealous resentment. . . .

12 So great was the indignation over the election of Flavius that many of the nobles put aside their gold rings and military decorations. **13** From that time the citizens were divided into two parties — the honest men, who supported and upheld right principles, had one point of view, and the rabble (factio) of the forum another, **14** until Quintus Fabius (Maximus Rullianus) and Publius Decius (Mus) became censors (304 BC) and Fabius, partly for the sake of harmony, partly so that the elections might not fall into the hands of the base-born element, separated out all the forum mob and threw it into four tribes, which he called the urban tribes. **15** It is said that this was so gratefully received that by this regulation of the orders he gained the surname of Maximus, which all his many victories had been insufficient to win him.

1.55 Priesthoods open to plebeians, 300 BC

Livy *History of Rome* 10.6.3–6, 9–11

Quintus Ogulnius Gallus, tribune in 300, was consul in 269; as tribune, with his brother Gnaeus, he carried a law that positions in the two major priestly colleges should be shared between patricians and plebeians: priesthoods were currently only open to patricians, and certain priesthoods, such as that of the Salii, remained a patrician prerogative. From this point four of the eight pontiffs and five of the nine augurs were plebeians. Appius Claudius Caecus strongly opposed the proposal; see Develin 1985: 66–70; Münzer 1999: 81–7 for the Ogulnii. The first plebeian pontifex maximus was in c. 254 (Livy *Per.* 18).

3 However, so that the tranquillity (caused by the sending out of colonies) might not be universal, dissension was stirred up among the leading citizens, patricians and plebeians, by the tribunes of the plebs Quintus and Gnaeus Ogulnius, **4** who had taken every opportunity of criticising the senators to the plebs, and, when all their other attempts had been frustrated, brought forward a course of action by which they would arouse not just the lowest of the plebeians but their very leaders — **5** those who had won consulships and triumphs, and who had lacked no official positions except the priesthoods, which were not yet open to everyone. **6** They therefore proposed that, since there were at that time four augurs and four pontiffs, and it was desired to increase the number of priests, four pontiffs and five augurs should be added to them, all taken from the plebs... **9** But since these were to be chosen from the plebs, the senators were as upset by the proposal as they had been when they saw the consulship thrown open. **10** They pretended that it was more the gods' concern than their own: that the gods would see to it that their rites were not polluted; for their part, they only hoped that no calamity should come upon the state. **11** But they put up little resistance, being now accustomed to being worsted in conflicts of this kind.

1.56 The final secession, 287 BC

Livy *Periochae* 11

Quintus Hortensius, a plebeian, was made dictator to solve the problem of the plebs' final secession to the Janiculum, caused by a debt crisis in 287. From this point plebiscites in the tribal assembly had the force of law: Cornell 1995: 377–80; *MRR* I.185.

The plebeians, after serious and lengthy dissension, seceded to the Janiculum Hill on account of their debts. They were brought back from there by the dictator Q. Hortensius, who died during his magistracy.

1.57 The Hortensian law, 287 BC

Gellius *Attic Nights* 15.27.4

In the same book of Laelius Felix (*To Quintus Mucius*), it is written: . . . 'Tribunes, however, do not summon the patricians or consult them on any question. And so, measures which are passed on the proposals of tribunes of the plebs are not properly called "laws" but "plebiscites", and these decrees were not binding on patricians until Quintus Hortensius as dictator brought in a law that whatever the plebs decided upon should be binding on all Quirites.'

POLYBIUS ON THE ROMAN CONSTITUTION AT ITS PRIME

Polybius sees Rome as a mixed constitution, blending monarchy, aristocracy and democracy. He has frequently been criticised for his attempt to analyse Roman institutions on the model of Greek ones and for misunderstanding the political situation at Rome: see North 1990. Millar 1984: 2, however, sees Polybius as right (and modern critics wrong) in his perception of Roman democracy. Polybius is here describing political institutions at their most perfect — supposedly, the time of the Second Punic War — though inevitably his depiction is coloured by practices of his own time: 'From the crossing of Xerxes into Greece . . . and for 30 years after that event it (the constitution) was continually modified detail by detail, being at its best and most perfect at the time of the Hannibalic war . . .' (6.11.1). Cf. 6.2.1–10: why he has left his discussion of Rome's political institutions till this point in his work; for Polybius' analysis, see Walbank I.675–92, 1972: 130–81; Alonso-Núñez 1999; Lintott 1999: 16–26.

1.58 Polybius and the Roman Constitution

Polybius *Histories* 6.12.1–16.5

(a) The consuls

12.1 The consuls, prior to leading out the legions, remain in Rome and have supreme authority over all public affairs. **2** All the other magistrates are subordinate to them and bound to obey them except the tribunes, and they present foreign embassies to the senate. **3** In addition to these duties, they refer urgent matters to the senate for discussion and carry out all the administrative details of the senate's decrees. **4** Also, as far as concerns all affairs of state administered by the people, it is their duty to supervise these and summon assemblies, bring forward measures, and preside over the execution of the people's decrees. **5** As regards preparation for war, and management of operations in the field generally, their authority is almost absolute. **6** They are permitted to make whatever demands on the allies they think appropriate, appoint military tribunes, and levy soldiers and select the most suitable. **7** In addition, they have the power to punish anyone they wish under their command while in the field; **8** and they have the authority to spend whatever amount they decide on from the public funds, being accompanied by a quaestor who readily carries out all their instructions. **9** So one could reasonably say, looking just at this part (of the constitution), that it is purely a monarchy or kingship.

(b) The senate

13.1 To pass on to the senate, first of all it has control of the treasury and regulates all revenue and expenditure. **2** For the quaestors are not allowed to disburse payments on any given projects without a decree of the senate, with the exception of payments made to the consuls; **3** the senate even controls the item of expenditure which is far more important and greater than all the others, that which the censors expend every five years on the restoration and construction of public works, and it makes a grant to the censors for this purpose. **4** Similarly, any crimes committed in Italy which require public investigation, such as treason, conspiracy, poisoning and assassination, are under the jurisdiction of the senate. **5** Furthermore, if any private person or community in Italy requires arbitration or censure or help or protection, the senate deals with all these matters. **6** Again, if any embassy has to be sent outside Italy to settle differences, or offer advice, or indeed impose demands, or receive submission, or declare war, this is also the responsibility of the senate. **7** Similarly, when embassies arrive in Rome, all the details of how they should be received and what answer should be given them are handled by the senate and are in no way the concern of the people. **8** As a result, to anyone residing in Rome in the absence of the consuls the constitution appears totally aristocratic; **9** this is the belief of many of the Greeks and also of the kings, as the senate handles almost all the business which concerns them.

(c) The people

14.1 After this one might reasonably inquire what part in the constitution is left for the people? ... **3** Nevertheless there is a role left for the people too, and a very important one. **4** For the people alone in the state has the power to award honours and punishments (the control of elections and the lawcourts), which alone hold together kingdoms and states and all human society generally ... **6** The people, then, frequently judge cases where the offence is punishable by a fine, and particularly when the accused have held the most distinguished offices; the people alone can try a capital charge ... **9** Furthermore it is the people who bestow offices on those who deserve them — the noblest reward for virtue in a state. **10** The people have the power to approve or reject laws, and, most important of all, it deliberates on matters of peace and war. **11** Again, in the case of alliances and the cessation of hostilities and treaties, it is the people who ratify each of these or the reverse. **12** So again one might reasonably say that the people has the greatest role in government and that the constitution is a democratic one.

(d) The senate as a check on the consuls

15.2 The consul, when he sets out with his army, possessed of the powers mentioned earlier, seems to possess absolute authority with regard to completing the task before him, **3** but in fact he needs the support of both the people and the senate, and without these he is unable to bring his operations to a conclusion. **4** For it is clear that the legions need constant supplies, and without the consent of the senate neither corn, nor clothing, nor pay can be provided, **5** so that a commander's plans are unworkable if the senate chooses to be negligent or obstructive. **6** It also rests with the senate as to whether a general's plans and designs can be carried to completion, since it has the authority to send out another general, when the former's term of office has expired, or to continue him in his command. **7** Moreover the senate has the power to celebrate generals' successes with pomp and magnify them or to obscure and belittle them; **8** for the processions they call triumphs, in which the spectacle of what the generals have achieved is brought before the citizens, cannot be properly organised, and in some cases not even held at all, unless the senate agrees and grants the necessary funds.

(e) The people as a check on the senate

16.1 The senate, again, though it has such great power, is obliged in the first place to pay attention to the people in public affairs and to respect its wishes, **2** while it is unable to carry out inquiries into the most serious and important crimes against the state, such as involve the death penalty, or take steps to exact punishment for them, unless the people ratifies the decree. **3** It is the same with regard to matters which concern the senate itself. For if anyone introduces a law, intended either to deprive the senate of some of its traditional authority or to abolish the senators' precedence and other distinctions or even to reduce their private property, in all these cases the people has the power to pass or reject them. **4** And, most important of all, if a single tribune interposes a veto, the senate is not only unable to reach a final decision on any matter, but may not even meet or sit in council. **5** The tribunes are always obliged to carry out the people's decrees and especially to respect its wishes — for all these reasons the senate is afraid of the masses and takes notice of the people.

1.59 How to override the system: the 'senatus consultum ultimum'

Sallust *Conspiracy of Catiline* 29.1–3

The term 'senatus consultum ultimum' ('final decree of the senate') is in fact a modern one, following Caesar *BC* 1.5 (doc. 13.24), where he describes the senate's resolution to suspend the constitution as 'that extreme and ultimate decree of the senate'. A declaration of emergency, the decree instructed the consuls to take measures to ensure 'that the state suffer no harm' and was first passed in 121 BC allowing the consul L. Opimius to take measures against Gaius Gracchus and M. Fulvius Flaccus; Flaccus was murdered and Gracchus committed suicide (docs 8.32–3). While the decree allowed the magistrates involved to override the constitution, the suspension of the laws and the legality of putting Roman citizens to death without a trial was questioned after the event: Opimius was prosecuted for his actions against Gaius Gracchus (doc. 8.34), Rabirius for his involvement in the killing of Saturninus and Glaucia (doc. 9.30), and Cicero went into exile because of his execution of the Catilinarian conspirators (docs 12.53–4). Cicero has here heard of Catiline's plot to murder him and of incitement to rebellion in Etruria: on 20 October 63 Cicero addressed the senate; see Lintott 1999: 89–93, 1999a: 213.

1 Cicero reported the matter, which had already been the subject of popular gossip, to the senate. **2** Thereupon, in accordance with its usual practice in dangerous crises, the senate decreed that 'the consuls should take measures that the state suffer no harm'. **3** The power thus conferred by the senate on a magistrate by Roman custom is supreme: they may raise an army, wage war, apply force by any means to allies and citizens, and exercise supreme command and jurisdiction at home and in the field; otherwise the consul has none of these privileges unless the people decrees it.

ROME'S STRUGGLE FOR ITALY

For Rome's early conquests in Italy, see Ferenczy 1976: 73–83; Alföldi 1965: 355–77; Scullard 1980: 92–114; Cornell 1989: 294–308, 1995: 293–326.

1.60 The sack of Veii, 396 BC

Livy *History of Rome* 5.21.10–13, 22.1, 8, 23.3

Veii, the most southerly Etruscan city, 15 kilometres north of Rome, was captured in 396 after a long-drawn out siege (supposedly lasting 10 years) by the dictator Marcus Furius Camillus; Rome had been engaged in intermittent conflict with Veii since the first Veientine War (483–474); for the evocatio of Juno, see doc. 3.55; Cornell 1995: 309–13, 320. The territory of Veii became part of the Roman ager publicus and increased it by some 562 square kilometres; four new tribes were created (Livy 6.5.8).

21.10 The mine, which was now filled with selected soldiers, suddenly discharged armed men into the temple of Juno, which was on Veii's citadel, of whom some attacked the enemies who had their backs to them on the walls, some tore down the bars on the gates, others set fires to stop the women and slaves throwing down rocks and tiles from the roofs. **11** Everywhere was filled with shouting — the varying cries of those who threatened and those who trembled, mixed with the lamentation of women and children. **12** In a moment the armed men were everywhere cast from the walls and the doors were thrown open, while some of the attackers rushed in *en masse*, others climbed the walls, and the city was overrun with enemies; fighting was everywhere; **13** then, after great slaughter, the fighting slowed and the dictator ordered heralds to declare that the unarmed would be spared . . . **22.1** On the next day the dictator sold the free inhabitants into slavery . . . **8** Such was the fall of Veii, the wealthiest city of the Etruscan people, which demonstrated its strength even in its final calamity, since after a siege of ten continuous summers and winters, in which it had inflicted far more disasters than it had received, when finally even fate turned against it, it was captured by siege-engines and not by force . . . **23.3** The senate decreed four days of supplications, a greater number of days than in any previous war.

1.61 The Gallic sack of Rome

Livy History of Rome 5.48.6–9

Traditionally dated to 390 BC, the Gallic sack of Rome took place c. 386 after the Romans were defeated at the river Allia, and the Gauls were paid a ransom in gold to withdraw. The Gauls were said to have been driven back from the Capitol by Marcus Manlius Capitolinus, who had been warned of their attack by Juno's sacred geese. This only temporarily halted Rome's policy of military expansion. See Cornell 1995: 313–18, suggesting that the Celts were mercenaries, interested only in moveable booty, en route to Sicily: Plut. *Cam.* 22.2–3.

6 Meanwhile the army on the Capitol was exhausted from picket and guard duty and, though they overcame all human evils, nature would not permit them to get the better of one, which was starvation. Day after day they looked to see if any help from the dictator was on its way, **7** but finally not only food, but hope too, began to fail them and when they went out on picket duty their bodies were nearly too weak to wear their armour, so they declared that they had either to surrender or ransom themselves on whatever terms they could, for the Gauls were throwing out clear hints that it would not take a very great price to persuade them to abandon the siege. **8** The senate then met and gave the military tribunes the task of negotiating terms. The matter was arranged at a conference between Quintus Sulpicius, the tribune, and Brennus, chieftain of the Gauls, with 1,000 pounds of gold as the price of a nation that was soon to rule the world. **9** This was an intense dishonour in itself, but a further insult was added: the weights brought by the Gauls were too heavy and, when the tribune objected, the insolent Gaul added his sword to the weight, with the words which Romans could not bear to hear, 'Woe to the conquered!' ('Vae victis!')

ROME AND THE LATINS

Following the establishment of the Republic the Latins revolted and formed an alliance (the 'Latin league'): after a battle at Lake Regillus (see doc. 2.67 for the intervention of Castor and Pollux), Rome and the Latins entered a defensive alliance in 493 negotiated by Spurius Cassius (cf. doc. 1.26) against their neighbours, the Aequi, Sabines and Volsci. Towards the end of the fifth century,

Rome began its conquest of southern Latium and southern Etruria, with the fall of the great Etruscan city of Veii in 396. In 341 the Latins again revolted, in the Great Latin War (in which they were allied with the Volsci, Campanians, Sidicini and Aurunci), after their request for a consulship and half the places in the senate was refused: Livy 8.5.5; *MRR* I.135. They were defeated and their territory settled by Rome: some Latin cities were given full Roman citizenship, others the status of allies. Confederations and leagues were dissolved and cities were bound directly to Rome and not allowed to have political relationships with each other: Alföldi 1965: 36–46, 377–419; Cornell 1989: 264–80, 1989b: 351–68, 1995: 347–52; Ferenczy 1976: 84–110; Salmon 1982: 40–56.

1.62 Brothers in blood, 340 BC

Livy *History of Rome* 8.6.15–16

Roman territorial expansion, such as the annexation of Tusculum in 381, was viewed with alarm by the Latins. Resorting to war in 341, they made demands on Rome, including the honour of one consulship. The crisis is depicted as grave and a time for strict military discipline (in one incident young Manlius Torquatus was killed by his father, the consul Titus Manlius Imperiosus Torquatus, before the battle at Veseris in 340 for breaking ranks and fighting a duel against the orders below: cf. doc. 7.15). Livy comments at 8.8.2 that this conflict resembled a civil war — so little did the Latins differ from the Romans in anything but in courage; for Roman expansion: Cornell 1995: 322–9.

15 Their anxiety was exacerbated by the fact that they had to make war against the Latins, who were similar to themselves in language, customs, type of arms, and above all in military institutions; soldiers had mixed with soldiers, centurions with centurions, tribunes with tribunes as equals and colleagues in the same garrisons, and often in the same maniples. **16** To prevent the men falling into some misjudgement because of this, the consuls proclaimed that no one was to leave his position to fight the enemy.

1.63 Defeat of the Latins, 340 BC

Livy *History of Rome* 8.11.11–16

Both of the consuls, Titus Manlius Torquatus and Publius Decius Mus, had a dream that a devotio (ritual dedication to the gods of the underworld) was required. It was agreed between them that whichever flank gave way, the consul commanding it would devote himself. Decius Mus did so (doc. 3.16); the Latins were defeated; and those who survived regrouped under Numisius with a new army raised from Latium and the Volsci. This new army was defeated on the Fenectane Plains (8.12.5) but there was continued unrest until the settlement of 338. Silver coins were probably first minted at Rome in 269 BC and the silver denarius was not actually struck until 211: Cornell 1995: 396.

11 The consul Torquatus met this force at Trifanum, a place between Sinuessa and Minternae. Without waiting to choose sites for their camps, both sides piled up their baggage and fought the battle that ended the war; **12** for the enemy suffered such great losses that, when the consul led his victorious army to plunder their lands, the Latins all surrendered and their surrender was followed by the Campanians. **13** Latium and Capua were deprived of their territory. The Latin territory, with the addition of that belonging to Privernum, and the Falernian territory as well (which had belonged to the Campanian people) as far as the river Volturnus was divided up amongst the Roman people. **14** The allocation was two iugera for each man in Latium supplemented by three-quarters of a iugerum from the land of Privernum or three iugera in Falernian territory with another quarter being added because of the distance involved. **15** The Laurentians and Campanian equites were exempted from the punishment of the Latins because they had not revolted. It was ordered that the treaty with the Laurentians be renewed, and it has been renewed every year from that time on the tenth day after the Latin festival. **16** Roman citizenship was granted to the Campanian equites, and in commemoration of this a bronze tablet was put up in the temple of Castor at Rome. In addition, the Campanian people — there were 1,600 of them — was ordered to pay per head an annual sum of 450 denarii.

1.64 Settlement with the Latins, 338 BC

Livy *History of Rome* 8.14.1–12

Lucius Furius Camillus and Gaius Maenius, as consuls in 338, put down Latium, which was still discontented; Camillus was awarded a triumph over Pedum and Tibur and his equestrian statue was erected in the forum; Maenius dedicated the 'beaks' (rostra) of the ships he captured at Antium under the speakers' platform in the forum, henceforth called the Rostra. Camillus has here been urging the senate to decide on a settlement.

1 The leading senators praised the motion of the consul (Camillus) on the policy to be followed, but said that, as the Latins were not all in the same position, his advice could best be carried out by the consuls' bringing forward proposals concerning the different peoples by name, so that a decision could be made on the merits of each. **2** Accordingly motions and decrees were taken on them individually. The city of Lanuvium was granted citizenship and their shrines restored to them, on condition that the temple and grove of Juno Sospita should be held in common by the townsfolk of Lanuvium and the Roman people. **3** The Aricini, Nomentani and Pedani were received as citizens on the same terms as the Lanuvini. **4** The Tusculans kept the citizenship they already had, and the charge of revolt was laid, not to the detriment of the community but against a few leaders. **5** The Veliterni, long-time Roman citizens, were severely penalised for having rebelled so many times: not only were their walls pulled down, but their senate was deported and ordered to live on the far side of the Tiber, **6** on the understanding that if any of them were caught on the near side his ransom should be no less than 1,000 pounds of bronze, nor should his captor release him from bondage until the money had been paid. **7** Colonists were sent to the senators' lands, and once they were enrolled Velitrae regained its former appearance of being well-populated. **8** A new colony was sent to Antium too, on the understanding that the Antiates, if they wished, should be permitted to enrol themselves as colonists; their warships were taken from them and their people were forbidden the sea and they were granted citizenship. **9** The Tiburtes and Praenestians were deprived of their territory, not only because of the latest charge of rebellion brought against them together with the other Latins, but also because they had once, in disgust at Roman rule, joined forces with the Gauls, a savage race. **10** The rest of the Latin peoples were deprived of their rights of intermarriage (connubium) and mutual trade (commercium) and of holding councils with each other. To show honour to their equites, because they had chosen not to revolt with the Latins, the Campanians were granted citizenship without the vote (*civitas sine suffragio*), as were the Fundani and Formiani, because they had always allowed a safe and peaceful passage through their territories. **11** It was resolved to give the people of Cumae and Suessula the same rights and terms as Capua. **12** Some of the ships from Antium were laid up in the dockyards at Rome, others were burnt, and it was resolved to use their prows (rostra) to adorn a platform constructed in the forum, and this sacred place was named the Rostra, or beaks.

THE SAMNITE WARS AND PYRRHUS

Samnium is situated in the central southern Apennines. The Romans fought three Samnite wars in all; the First (343–341 BC) gave Rome control over northern Campania (Salmon 1967: 187–213); the Second (326–321, 316–304) hindered Samnite expansion into Apulia, Lucania and southern Campania (Salmon 214–54); and despite defeat in the Third (298–290), the Samnites aided both Pyrrhus and Hannibal (Salmon 255–92), and at the beginning of the first century BC were one of Rome's most intractable enemies in the Social War (docs 10.10–11, 27–8).

Following the 'Latin War', further conquests and settlement of colonies led to increasing conflict with the Samnites; despite a decisive defeat at the Caudine Forks in 321 (doc. 1.66), Rome regained the offensive and began incursions into central Italy; its conquests were assisted by strategic alliances with the Marsi, Paeligni and other Italic peoples. An alliance of Samnites, Umbrians, Etruscans and Gauls was defeated at Sentinum in 295 (doc. 1.69). In an attempt to keep their independence Tarentum and other Greek cities of southern Italy invited Pyrrhus of Epirus to lead their defence in 280 (doc. 1.73); his defeat in 275 and the fall of Tarentum in 272 marked Rome's total dominance over the rest of Italy; for 'Magna Graecia', the Greek settlements in southern Italy and Sicily, see Lomas 1993: 19–57; for the Samnites, Heurgon 1973: 204–10; Scullard 1980: 131–9, 144–53; Salmon 1982: 57–72; Patterson 1987; Cornell 1989b: 351–91, 1995: 345–7, 352–63; for Pyrrhus: Plut. *Pyrrh.* esp. 14; Heurgon 1973: 213–16; Scullard 1980: 139–44; Franke 1989: 456–85; Cornell 1989b: 363–4; Lomas 1993: 50–7; on the organisation of Roman Italy: Torelli 1999: 1–13.

1.65 The causes of the Second Samnite War (326–304 BC)

Livy *History of Rome* 8.23.1–7

In 327 the Greek city of Palaepolis, not far from Naples, engaged in hostilities against Campania and Falerii. The senate decided for war against Palaepolis under one consul, Quintus Publilius Philo (docs 1.50-1), while the other, Lucius Cornelius Lentulus, was given command against the Samnites in case they should take the field. Fregellae in the Liris valley was established as a Latin colony in 328.

1 The senate was informed by both consuls that there was minimal hope of peace with the Samnites: Publilius reported that 2,000 soldiers from Nola and 4,000 Samnites had been taken into Palaepolis, rather under pressure from the Nolani than of the Greeks' own choice; **2** Cornelius that a levy had been called by the magistrates and that all Samnium was up in arms, while the neighbouring towns of Privernum, Fundi and Formiae were being openly invited to join them. **3** It was decided, for these reasons, to send legates to the Samnites before declaring war, and a defiant response was returned by the Samnites. **4** For their part, they accused the Romans of wrong-doing, while doing their best to clear themselves of the charges brought against them: **5** they stated that they were not assisting the Greeks with any public advice or support, nor had they invited Fundi or Formiae to join them; they were quite confident in their own forces, if they chose to fight. **6** However, they were unable to disguise the fact that the Samnite nation was angry that Fregellae, which they had captured from the Volsci and destroyed, should have been restored by the Roman people, and that they should have planted a colony in Samnite territory, which the colonists called Fregellae; **7** that was an insult and injury which, if those responsible for it did not undo it themselves, they would combat with all the force in their power.

1.66 Defeat by the Samnites at the Caudine Forks, 321 BC

Livy *History of Rome* 9.7.6–12

Livy 9.2–6: in 321 the Roman army was trapped in a narrow defile by the Samnite leader Gaius Pontius upon which it surrendered; the army was made to pass under the yoke. The Romans were shocked, not so much at the defeat as at the surrender; an interregnum was instituted, during which Quintus Publilius Philo and Lucius Papirius Cursor were elected consuls for 320: Salmon 1967: 218–22; Cornell 1995: 352–5, 371–2. The defeat was avenged in the following year, when Pontius was himself sent under the yoke at Luceria by Lucius Papirius Cursor, consul in 326, 320, 319, 315 and 313 and twice dictator, whom Livy compares to Alexander the Great (9.16.11–19; cf. doc. 5.3).

6 By this time Rome had also heard of its dishonourable defeat. The first report was that the army had been trapped; then came news which was even more melancholy on account of the shameful peace than on account of the danger they faced. **7** At the report of a blockade they had started holding a levy; they then, on hearing of so disgraceful a surrender, disbanded their preparations to send assistance, and at once, without any authorisation from the state, the whole people adopted every type of mourning. **8** The shops around the forum were closed, all public business in the forum was automatically suspended even before a public announcement; **9** tunics with broad purple stripes and golden rings were put away; and the citizenry was almost more depressed than the army itself — they were not only infuriated at the generals and those who had made and guaranteed the peace, but even detested the innocent soldiers and were unwilling to allow them into the city or their homes. **10** But the arrival of the army, which roused pity even in angry men, softened this general agitation. For they entered the city not like men returning home safely from a hopeless situation, but late in the day, with the appearance and bearing of captives, **11** with each man concealing himself in his own home, and on the next and subsequent days not one of them was prepared to look into the forum or out into the streets. **12** The consuls shut themselves up at home and transacted no public business, apart from the fact that a senatorial decree ordered them to name a dictator to preside over the elections. . . .

1.67 More colonies, 303 BC

Livy *History of Rome* 10.1.1–2

For fifth and early fourth-century Roman and Latin colonies, see Cornell 1995: 302–4; Torelli 1999: 14–42; for Latin colonies 334–263 BC, see Cornell 381–83 with map. The Hernici and Aequi were conquered overwhelmingly in 306–304, while their neighbours signed treaties of alliance with Rome. The colonies at Alba and Sora clearly had strategic aims regarding the consolidation of this region: unlike the earlier colonies of citizens, inhabitants were granted Latin rights, sharing the rights of intermarriage (connubium) and trade (commercium) with Romans: any who settled in Rome were granted citizenship.

1 In the consulship of Lucius Genucius and Servius Cornelius there was almost a complete rest from foreign wars. Colonies were sent out to Sora and Alba. 6,000 settlers were enrolled for Alba in the Aequian region: **2** Sora had belonged to Volscian territory, but the Samnites had occupied it; 4,000 men were sent there.

1.68 Epitaph of a conqueror of Italy

ILS 1

(*ILLRP* 309; *CIL* I2 6, 7; *ROL* IV.2.) Lucius Cornelius Scipio Barbatus ('Long-beard') was consul in 298 and censor perhaps in 280. He was probably the founder of the tomb of the Scipiones, on the Appian Way near the Porta Capena. The date of his epitaph has been disputed, but it now appears to have been written shortly after his death, perhaps c. 250: Millar 1989; van Sickle 1987: 41; Flower 1996: 159–76. In 298 the Romans were campaigning annually in Etruria and Umbria, while war against the Samnites was recommenced in 298. The victory over the Lucanians took place in 298; Livy only mentions Barbatus' successes in Etruria (Livy 10.11–12; cf. 10.14, 11.26; *MRR* 174).

Lucius Cornelius Scipio, son of Gnaeus.

Lucius Cornelius Scipio Barbatus,
Offspring of his father Gnaeus, a man brave and wise,
Whose looks well matched his courage,
Was consul, censor and aedile among you.
He took Taurasia and Cisauna from Samnium,
Totally subdued the Lucanian land and brought back hostages.

1.69 The devotio of Decius Mus, 295 BC

Livy *History of Rome* 10.28.12–18

The Third Samnite War broke out in 298 and in 296 a joint attack on Rome of Samnites, Etruscans, Umbrians and Gauls was planned: Quintus Fabius Maximus Rullianus and Publius Decius Mus (junior) were appointed consuls for 295, and they pursued the Samnites and Gauls over the Apennines: Decius had been consul in 312, 308, and 297 and was censor in 304. At the Battle of Sentinum in Umbria in 295 Decius sacrificed himself against the Gauls and Samnites as his father had done in 340 (doc. 3.16). When the left wing was scattered by Gallic chariots, Decius devoted himself and the hosts of the enemy to the powers below and was killed: the battle was saved and the enemy routed. Accius treated the subject in his play the *Aeneadae* or *Decius*: (14) Decius: 'Like my father I will dedicate myself and sacrifice my life to the enemy'.

12 Then, as he was powerless to stop their flight, he called on the name of his father Publius Decius: **13** 'Why do I delay longer,' he cried, 'to fulfil our house's destiny? Our family was granted the privilege of being sacrificed to avert our country's dangers. It is now my turn to offer up the legions of the enemy as victims to Earth and the gods of the underworld (*di manes*).'

14 With these words he ordered Marcus Livius, the pontifex, whom he had already told as he went into battle not to leave his side, to dictate the words with which he could devote himself and the legions of the enemy on behalf of the Roman people, the Quirites. **15** He was then devoted with the same form of prayer and the same dress as when his father Publius Decius had ordered himself to be devoted at Veseris in the Latin war. **16** Following the ritual prayers, he added that he was driving before him fear and rout, slaughter and bloodshed, **17** and the anger of the celestial and underworld gods, and would pollute with a deadly curse the standards, spears and arms of the enemy, while the same place would mark his own destruction and that of the Gauls and Samnites **18** — after uttering these curses upon himself and the enemy, he galloped his horse into the Gallic battle-lines, where he saw them thickest, and threw himself on the enemy's weapons to meet his death.

1.70 The Samnite wars continue

Livy *History of Rome* 10.31.10–15

The year is 295, after the victory at Sentinum, where the Romans were able to field an estimated 36,000 troops (Cornell 1995: 361); Livy 10.29.17–18 gives the figures of 8,700 Romans and 25,000 enemy killed. The Samnites were again overwhelmingly defeated at Aquilonia in 293; for the Samnite army, see Salmon 1967: 101–12.

10 There are still more Samnite wars to come, though we have been dealing with them continuously through four volumes over a period of 46 years, from the consulship of Marcus Valerius and Aulus Cornelius (343 BC), who were the first to bear arms in Samnium. **11** Without at this point going through the disasters suffered by both peoples over so many years and the hardships endured, by which nevertheless those brave hearts refused to be conquered, **12** in the past year the Samnites had fought in the territory of Sentinum, amongst the Paeligni, at Tifernum, in the Stellate plains, now by themselves, now with the addition of troops from other peoples, and had been cut to pieces by four armies under four Roman commanders; **13** they had lost their people's most distinguished general; they saw their allies in war, the Etruscans, Umbrians and Gauls, in the same plight as their own; **14** nor were they able to carry on, either with their own resources or outside support; but they would not abstain from war — so far were they from being tired of freedom, even though their defence of it had been unsuccessful, preferring to be defeated rather than not to try for victory. **15** Who then could begrudge the time spent on the reading and writing of wars when these did not weary those who fought them?

1.71 The Samnites' 'linen legion' remains undaunted, 293 BC

Livy *History of Rome* 10.38.2–4, 10–13

Cf. 9.39.5 where a similar selection process is used by the Etruscans to encourage bonding between the troops; for the 'linen legion', see Salmon 1967: 102–5, who notes that Livy's descriptions of Samnite weaponry conflict with the archaeological evidence; Livy 9.40.3 (308 BC) mentions that the Samnite soldiers wore linen (rather than enrolling under it); cf. Pliny *Nat. Hist.* 34.43.

2 The Samnites held a levy throughout all Samnium under a new law, **3** which stated that any man of military age who did not respond to the generals' proclamation or who left the army without orders would forfeit his life to Jupiter. **4** The entire army was then instructed to meet at Aquilonia. Some 40,000 soldiers, Samnium's fighting force, assembled . . . **10** Each man was then forced to swear an oath following a certain grim formula, invoking a curse on himself, his household and his family if he did not go into battle where his generals led or if he fled from the battle-line himself or saw someone else fleeing and did not immediately cut him down. **11** At first, there were some who refused to swear and they were beheaded in front of the altars; lying there amongst the piles of sacrificial victims they acted as a warning to others not to refuse to comply. **12** When the leading Samnites had bound themselves by this curse, ten of them were named by the general and each told to choose a man until their number had reached 16,000. This was called the 'linen legion' from the covering of the enclosure in which the nobles were sworn in; these were given distinguished armour and crested helmets to make them stand out among the others. **13** A little more than 20,000 men formed another force which was inferior to the linen legion in neither physical appearance, martial reputation or equipment. This was the number of men, their fighting force, which encamped at Aquilonia.

1.72 Colossal art in Rome from Samnite spoils

Pliny *Natural History* 34.43

Spurius Carvilius Maximus was consul in 293 and 272, as well as censor, probably in 289, and was awarded a triumph both for his victories against the Samnites in 293 and his defeat of Tarentum and the other Greek cities in 272. For Jupiter Latiaris and the Feriae Latinae celebrated each year on the Alban mount, see doc. 3.9.

Italy also used frequently to make colossal statues . . . After the Samnites were defeated after fighting under an inviolable oath (in 293 BC), Spurius Carvilius made the Jupiter, which stands in the Capitol, out of their breastplates, greaves and helmets. Its size is so great that it can be seen from the temple of Jupiter Latiaris (10 miles away on the Alban mount). Out of the left-over filings, he made a statue of himself, which stands at the feet of Jupiter's statue.

1.73 Pyrrhus of Epirus

Livy *Periochae* 12–14

Pyrrhus of Epirus (319–272 BC) was approached by Tarentum for help in their defence against Rome. Rome had begun interfering in the affairs of the Greek cities of southern Italy in 285: Lomas 1993: 39–51. According to Plut. *Pyrrh.* 14.3–5, Pyrrhus' aims included the conquest of Sicily and Carthage, as well as Italy, and his involvement gave rise to a simultaneous revolt of Samnites, Lucanians and Bruttians. Ennius *Annals* 178 refers to his arrival at Tarentum in 281: 'They found him a man of action, a Greek from a Greek father, and a king'. With 25,000 infantry, 20 elephants and 2,000 cavalry he defeated the Romans at Heraclea in 280, and, after an abortive march on Rome, again at Ausculum in 279. In 278 he fought the Carthaginians (Rome's allies: Polyb. 3.25.1–5) in Sicily, returning to Italy in 276. After a defeat at Beneventum, he returned to Epirus; his garrison at Tarentum was overcome by the Romans in 272. An attempt by Pyrrhus at negotiating a peace was foiled by a speech of Appius Claudius: Ferenczy 1976: 204–6.

12 A Roman fleet was seized by the Tarentines, the duumvir who commanded it was killed, and the envoys sent to them by the senate to complain about these injuries were driven away. On this account war was declared against them. The Samnites revolted. Several battles were successfully fought against them and the Lucanians, Brittii (Bruttians) and Etruscans by numerous generals. Pyrrhus, the Epirote king, came to Italy to aid the Tarentines. A Campanian legion led by Decius Vibellius sent to protect the people of Rhegium slaughtered the inhabitants and seized Rhegium. **13** The consul Valerius Laevinus (cos. 280) fought an unsuccessful battle against Pyrrhus, as the soldiers were extremely terrified by the unaccustomed sight of elephants… Cineas was sent by Pyrrhus to the senate as an envoy to request that the king be received into the city for the sake of arranging peace terms. It was resolved that this be referred to a more well-attended meeting of the senate and Appius Claudius (Caecus), who because of problems with his eyesight had for some time abstained from public business, entered the senate and won it over to his opinion that this be refused Pyrrhus . . . There was a second battle against Pyrrhus of which the result was indecisive . . . **14** Pyrrhus crossed over to Sicily . . . The consul Curius Dentatus (cos. 290, 275, 274) held a levy and was the first to sell the goods of anyone who did not answer when summoned; he also defeated Pyrrhus, who had returned from Sicily to Italy and drove him out of Italy. . . A Carthaginian fleet came to the aid of the Tarentines, which was a violation of the treaty by them. The book also deals with successful wars against the Lucanians, Bruttians and Samnites and the death of King Pyrrhus.

2

The Public Face of Rome

Even from the time of the kings, the city of Rome and especially its public works impressed visitors: as Strabo comments (doc. 2.1), the Romans concentrated on utilitarian projects rather than on aspects of beautification, and Rome was noted for its aqueducts and sewers (docs 2.1–4), while Rome's road-building (docs 2.5–8) was rivalled by no other ancient empire. Through it Rome signalled its territorial domination and control of the resources of the land through which the roads travelled, as well as aiding transport and movement throughout an increasing empire. The amenities of the city, too, whose inhabitants may have approached near to a million in the first century BC, were continually updated and designed to improve conditions for the growing urban population.

The Romans in general, and particularly the senatorial class, prided themselves on the traditions of austerity, frugality and common-sense that they had inherited from their earliest ancestors: heroes of renowned military campaigns like Cincinnatus and Curius Dentatus in early Rome were remembered for their pride in being simple farmers (docs 2.12–13), and this *persona* was revived by Cato the Elder who, though a 'new man' in the early second century BC, took pride in his parsimony and lack of interest in the expensive items which were introducing Romans of the mid-second century to luxury, gluttony and epicureanism (docs 2.14–17). Cato's instructions for the practical and profitable running of a country estate provide unrivalled details of the procedures and practices involved at this period on a small slave-run property (docs 2.15–16, cf. 6.31–3), while his prescriptions for the medicinal use of cabbage show that no item in the household was too trivial to escape his attention (doc. 2.17). Seneca the Younger similarly pays homage to the moral standards of olden days when he contrasts the baths thought appropriate for his own use by the great Scipio Africanus, conqueror of the Carthaginians, with those constructed in Seneca's own time (doc. 2.20).

Cato's adherence to traditional values was not, however, shared by the majority of the Roman upper-classes, particularly as immense wealth and resources became available with the second-century BC conquests of the Eastern and Western Mediterranean. Marcus Licinius Crassus in the first century BC may have been unusual in considering the term 'wealthy' to comprise the ability to keep a legion (some 4,200 men) on one's income, and he was also unusual in the way in which the bulk of his money had been acquired (from 'fire-sale' tactics: docs 6.3, 2.21). More common was the acquisition of wealth through conquest and administration of a province, and the lifestyle of L. Licinius

Lucullus shows to what degree of dilettantism this might lead (doc. 2.22); even official pontifical (priestly) banquets could have a menu that defies imagination, while by the late Republic delicacies such as peafowl and lampreys could be bred by aristocrats and command immense sums of money for consumption at banquets (docs 2.23–4).

Underpinning this lifestyle was a highly competitive, militaristic society, in which the ultimate goal was to attain the consulship, along with a provincial command which might lead to a triumph. It was seen as essential to live up to the virtues and achievements of one's ancestors and to acquire gloria (reputation) which would enhance the family's status and increase the number of imagines, masks of noble ancestors, in the house's vestibule (docs 2.25–28): the funeral oration for L. Caecilius Metellus demonstrates the achievements and status most sought after by a consular in the third century BC (doc. 2.29). These aims changed little, and desire for public office and political influence won by one's merits was a major virtue according to Cicero, who criticises his brother Quintus for possibly, by his conduct as governor of Asia, detracting from the family gloria won by Cicero himself in his consulship (docs 2.30–1).

The ultimate achievement was the celebration of a military triumph in Rome, which gave the triumphator the chance to display his captives, booty and dedicated soldiery (docs 2.32–5), and Cicero tried hard, but unsuccessfully, to persuade his political friends to award him a triumph for his governorship of Cilicia, which would have been the pinnacle of his career (docs 2.44, 13.20). As a result of this competitive culture, candidature for office was keenly contested: with only two consuls and a number of lesser magistrates per year, only a lucky few could hope to win the consulship. Largesse and bribery of the electorate were thus endemic to the process of canvassing, which could be an extremely costly business and which was expected to involve all one's friends and connections (docs 2.36–8). The electorate tended to prefer candidates of known ancestry, and even wealthy non-nobles, those without a consul in their ancestry, found it as outsiders difficult, though not of course impossible, to achieve the consulship: Cato the censor, Marius and Cicero were some of the exceptions, and such men were known as novi homines ('new men'; sing.: novus homo). Sallust sees such men as generally resented by the nobility and Cicero prides himself on the personal merits that have won him the prestigious position of consul (docs 2.39–40). New men were particularly disadvantaged by their lack of political friends (amici) and clients (clientes) who could help them in their candidature and canvassing. As Roman politics lacked formal political parties, unofficial political friendships (amicitiae) were invaluable in bringing together, even if only temporarily, men with common aims who could further each other's goals; Cicero gives numerous examples of how the system worked in practice (docs 2.42–5). New men in the political arena had to create their own amicitiae, and were also disadvantaged by their lack of clients, who were often inherited within the family and who could number several thousands: a politician's retinue of clients (his clientela) demonstrated his importance and prestige and was a significant aid in canvassing for office (docs 2.49–54). Generals and governors could also include entire provinces and foreign communities amongst their clientela (docs 2.55–7).

Even for well-known military figures, undertaking important prosecutions or defences in the law-courts was another way of winning clients and popularity generally. It was considered honourable to prosecute family enemies, though gratitude was especially won through a successful defence (docs 2.58–60). The ability to speak well in public was essential in Rome, not merely on the political stage but in the courts as well, and the training could be long and arduous (docs 2.61–2, 64). Included among the notably impressive speakers in the late Republic were the Gracchi (docs 8.3, 26–7) and Julius Caesar (doc. 2.63), as well, of course, as Cicero, whose career was built on his skill at forensic oratory (doc. 2.62).

It was naturally an important factor in success as a politician to have popular support, which could be gained by high birth, military achievements, and oratorical ability, but could also be attained by entertainment of the populace. The putting on of costly games was a common way for aediles to court the attention of the people with a view to their election later to the higher magistracies (docs 2.71–2), and gladiatorial shows, theatrical performances, wild-beast fights, and public banquets and other hand-outs were often aimed at canvassing support for current or potential candidates for office (docs 2.68–70, 73–4). Such expenditure, of course, made it even more desirable to achieve high office and the chance of the governorship of a profitable province afterwards to enable candidates to recoup their electioneering expenses.

Ancient sources: the evidence for the public face of Rome is scattered amongst the literary sources; the geographer Strabo, who wrote his vast work in the reigns of Augustus and Tiberius, and the antiquarian Dionysius of Halicarnassus in the early first century AD provide useful information on Rome's infrastructure and buildings, as does the work of Frontinus *On Aqueducts* (consul in 72 or 73, 98 and 100, and superintendent of aqueducts under Nerva in AD 97). Livy and Dionysius are the main sources for details of the history of early Rome, such as temples and dedications. Inscriptions also testify to specific contracts for public works such as roads and to traffic regulations in Rome (docs 2.7–8, cf. 10–11). Cato the Elder is the principal witness to the details of farming villa-estates in the mid-second century (docs 2.15–17) and to the accompanying traditional values. Cicero's 58 speeches and huge collection of letters to his friends, Atticus, and his brother Quintus are of course the main evidence for political concepts such as amicitia, gloria, clientela, and the novus homo, as well as for electioneering practices such as the prevalence of bribery and the importance of oratorical training, while aristocratic values are also evidenced by epitaphs of *nobiles* (such as docs 2.25–6). The *Lives* of Plutarch, especially *Pompey, Lucullus, Crassus* and *Cato the Elder* provide useful anecdotal information on the contrast between the supposed frugality of older times and the luxurious and wealthy lifestyle of first-century *nobiles* and the enormous power which such wealth and clientela gave them.

For a useful introduction to Roman political concepts and practices, see Adcock 1959; Earl 1967; Nicolet 1980; Brunt 1988b-e; Drummond 1989; Wallace-Hadrill 1989; Lintott 1999; on the aims and ideals of Roman politicians: Rosenstein 1992; Flower 1996; Kaster 1997; Patterson 2001: 29–52; Barton 2001.

THE INFRASTRUCTURE OF THE CITY

The main architectural features of Rome in the Republic were its aqueducts (doc. 2.4), sewers (docs 2.1–3), the buildings in the forum (such as the prison: doc. 12.22), and Jupiter's temple. As Rome's power grew, many new buildings, mainly temples, were constructed, often in fulfilment of vows made in war, or at the introduction of new cults (docs 3.57–64). Plans of the city survive, but from the imperial period, and much of what can be seen in Rome today dates from the building projects of the emperors. These projects, however, had republican antecedents, not just in Pompey's works (docs 2.68–9) and Caesar's (docs 13.54), but in the various buildings constructed in the forum and Campus Martius areas from the third century on. Rome's foundation in 753 BC was celebrated in the Republic and Imperial periods on 21 April.

For descriptions of the various monuments of Rome, see the entries in Platner-Ashby, Nash, and Richardson *Top. Dict.*; for a guide, Claridge 1998; MacAdam 1998; Rome as a city in the Republic: Stambaugh 1988: 1–47; a general survey of the city: Connolly & Dodge 1998: 105–217; sources: Dudley 1967; public order: Nippel 1995.

The standard figure for the population of Rome is generally given as c. 1,000,000 for the first century BC: Storey 1997, on analogy with Pompeii and Ostia, suggests 335,000 to 440,000; cf. Lo Cascio 1994 for the distribution of grain in Caesar's time to 320,000 adult males (Suet. *Jul.* 41.3) and Mouritsen 2001: 133 who argues that Rome was not a typical pre-industrial city, suggesting a population on grain distribution figures of over 800,000; cf. Jongman 2003: 106–9.

2.1 Engineering projects

Strabo *Geography* 5.3.8

Here Strabo, born c. 64 BC, who admired the physical infrastructure of the city of Rome, is describing Rome in the past. On the sewer dimensions, cf. Pliny *Nat. Hist.* 36.104–8. Houses were not individually connected to the sewers, the main purpose of which was to drain rainwater and the Cloaca stream. Sewers: Stambaugh 1988: 132–3; Gowers 1995; cf. Scobie 1986: 407–22 for urban sanitation (with Laurence 1997; Scheidel 2003).

The Greeks had the reputation for making good choices in their foundation of cities, because they aimed for beauty, defensibility, harbours and fertile soil, while the Romans were especially farsighted in matters to which the Greeks paid little attention, such as the construction of roads and aqueducts, and of sewers which could wash out the city's filth into the Tiber; and they have constructed roads throughout the country, adding the levelling of hills and the filling in of valleys, so that their wagons can carry boat-loads; and the sewers, vaulted with tightly-fitting stones, have enough room in some places for wagons loaded with hay to pass through. And such quantities of water are brought into the city by aqueducts that actual rivers flow through the city and the sewers, and almost every house has cisterns, service pipes, and plentiful fountains . . . In short, the ancient Romans paid little attention to the beauty of Rome because they were occupied with other, greater and more necessary, matters.

2.2 Rome's finest amenity — plumbing!

Dionysius of Halicarnassus *Roman Antiquities* 3.67.5

Livy and Dionysius follow a tradition that the fifth and seventh kings of Rome, the Tarquins, played a major part in the provision of public works, some built with forced plebeian labour (Dion. Hal. 4.44). Dionysius lists elsewhere Tarquinius Priscus' adornment of the forum (3.67.4), as well as the walls of the city, the sewers, the Circus Maximus and the temple of Jupiter, Juno and Minerva on the Capitoline Hill (3.68–9). The second Tarquin is also given the credit for the same works: cf. Livy 1.35.10, 1.38.6–7, 1.66.1–3; Cassius Hemina *HRR* I2 103 F15; Pliny *Nat. Hist.* 36.105–7. The temple of Diana on the Aventine and the pons Sublicius are also said to have dated from the time of the kings. The sewers clearly impressed later generations with the labour which must have been involved: the attribution to tyrannical kings and their use of forced labour was a natural conclusion. While the temple clearly is a sixth-century foundation, the sewers belong to a period of more intensive urbanisation, probably in the fourth and third centuries; the Tarquins and sewers: Cornell 1995: 128, 164–5. Acilius wrote a history of Rome in Greek in the second century BC (*FGrH* 813).

Tarquinius (Priscus) also began the digging of the sewers, through which all the water which flows off from the roads is diverted into the Tiber, thus constructing marvellous works which defy description. Indeed I would rate as the three most magnificent constructions of Rome, from which the greatness of her empire can particularly be seen, as the aqueducts, the paved roads, and the construction of the sewers. I say this not only with regard to the usefulness of the work, about which I shall speak in its proper place, but also to the size of the cost involved, which one can judge from a single example if one takes Gaius Acilius as his authority, who says that once, when the sewers had been neglected and no longer carried the water, the censors let out their cleaning and repair at the cost of a thousand talents.

2.3 Blocked sewers

Cicero *In Defence of Sestius* 77

Publius Sestius (tr. pl. 57) worked with Milo towards Cicero's restoration from exile; in the following year he was prosecuted for using armed force during his tribunate and was successfully defended by Cicero. Cicero is here referring to the bloodshed caused by the proposal of his recall in January 57, which was hotly opposed by Clodius. Appius Claudius Pulcher, as praetor, appears to have lent his brother Clodius a troop of gladiators he had amassed for funeral games. Appius Claudius was so unpopular that to avoid the hissing of the spectators at his own gladiatorial contests he made his way to them by the underground passages in the forum (perhaps constructed in the 70s in connection with stage appearances for theatrical performances) appearing as if he were an actor playing a suddenly appearing ghost (Cic. *Sest.* 126). The sewers and the Tiber were used for the disposal of the bodies of both the Gracchi and their supporters: Kyle 1998: 219–21.

Surely you remember, jurors, how the Tiber was then filled with the bodies of citizens, how the sewers were blocked, how the blood was wiped from the forum with sponges, so that everyone thought that such an immense band and magnificent display was not the work of a private citizen or plebeian, but of a patrician and praetor.

2.4 Aqueducts

Frontinus *Aqueducts* 1.5

Four aqueducts were introduced into Rome in the republican period: the aqua Appia (312 BC), anio Vetus (272 BC), aqua Marcia (144 BC) and the aqua Tepula (125 BC), each described by Frontinus Aqueducts 1–8. Frontinus notes that by 312 BC the city had outstripped the use of the Tiber, wells and springs as sources of water. This clearly indicates the growth of the urban population in the fourth century. The water of the appia and the Anio travelled mainly along underground channels; the familiar aqueduct structure came with the Marcia, with ten kilometres of arches immediately outside the city. Arriving in the city, water was diverted into settling tanks and then distributed to public fountains. The Appia was 16.5 kilometres in length and brought 75,700 cubic metres of water per day to the city, the Anio 64 kilometres (bringing 182,500 cubic metres), the Marcia nine kilometres (bringing 194,000 cubic metres), and the Tepula 18 kilometres (bringing 18,500 cubic metres). See Ashby 1935 with entries on these four; Morgan 1978; Grimal 1983: 72–6; Scobie 1986: 422–4; Stambaugh 1988: 128–31; Robinson 1992: 95–8; Evans 1994; Dodge 2000; Blackman 1979; Blackman & Hodge 2001; Kleijn 2001: 10–19; cf. O'Connor 1993: 150–62.

In the consulship of Marcus Valerius Maximus and Publius Decius Mus (312 BC), the thirtieth year after the start of the Samnite War, the Appian aqueduct was brought into the city by Appius Claudius Crassus, the censor, who was later given the surname Caecus ('the blind'); he was also responsible for the construction of the Appian Way from the Capena gate up to the city of Capua . . . The Appia draws water from the Lucullan estate on the Praenestine Way, between the seventh and eighth milestones, on a by-road, 780 paces to the left. From its intake to the Salinae, which is at the Trigemina gate, the length of the channel is 11,190 paces; of this 11,130 paces run underground, while 60 paces are supported above ground by substructures and, near the Capena gate, by arches.

COMMUNICATIONS AND PUBLIC WORKS

Roman roads were impressive and traversed Rome's empire. The first major road, the Via Appia, was constructed in 312 BC, and further roads were built in the Republic for communication and ease of military movement. In the third century BC, roads radiated out from Rome through central Italy and by the end of the second century major Roman roads linked the north, south, east, and west of Italy with the capital. Besides the Via Appia, other major roads were the Via Flaminia of 220 BC running north from Rome to the east coast, the Via Egnatia of around 130 which ran from the Adriatic to Byzantium and provided Rome with its main route to the east, and the Via Aurelia of 241 (extended in 109) which ran up the Italian north-west coast. These roads linked Rome with its colonies and major allies. Republican roads: Hindley 1971: 25–31; Wiseman 1987; Laurence 1999: 11–26; cf. Roman roads generally: Sitwell 1981; Chevallier 1989; O'Connor 1993: 7–15; Richardson *Top. Dict.* 413–20. For the letting out of contracts for public works and revenue collection: Polyb. 6.17.1–5; cf. doc. 2.7.

2.5 Procopius on the Appian Way

Procopius *History of the Wars* 5.14.6–11

Cf. Livy 9.29.9. The Via Appia built by Appius Claudius Caecus as censor in 312 BC extended some 210 kilometres from Rome to Capua, providing the Romans with their main route to southern Italy. Colonies of Roman citizens were sited along it, increasing the impression of Roman dominance and expansion. Later additions in the third century BC carried it further. The paving, in fact, was not carried out by Appius Claudius: the Via Appia within the city was paved in 295 BC (Livy 10.23.12: the Porta Capena was the gate in the Servian Walls through which the Via Appia issued), and it was presumably during Gaius Gracchus' road building programme (doc. 2.6), if not before, that the rest was sealed. Appius also built the Aqua Appia (doc. 2.5). Procopius in this passage is writing about Belisarius and his reconquest of Italy in the sixth century AD. See Hagen 1966: 15–30; Wiseman 1987: 134–7; O'Connor 1993: 9–11; Laurence 1999: 13–21; Robertson *Top. Dict.* 414.

6 Belisarius led his army by the Latin Way, leaving on their left the Appian Way, which the Romans' consul Appius built 900 years earlier and to which he gave his name. The Appian Way is five days' journey for an active man, for it extends from Rome to Capua. **7** The breadth of the road is such that two wagons going in opposite directions can pass each other, and it is one of the sights most worth seeing anywhere. **8** Appius quarried all the stone, which is millstone and naturally hard, from another place far away and brought it there, for it is not found anywhere in this region. **9** He worked the stones smooth and level, cut them square, and bound them to each other without putting gravel or anything else between them. **10** They were fixed together so securely, with the joints so tight, that they give the appearance, when you look at them, of not being fitted together but of having grown together. **11** And although so long a period has passed, and so many wagons and all kinds of animals have travelled over it each day, the stones have not separated at all at the joints, nor have any of them been worn out or become thinner — in fact they have not even lost any of their finish. Such, then, is the Appian Way.

2.6 Gaius Gracchus and communications within Italy

Plutarch *Life of Gaius Gracchus* 7.1–4

Cf. *G. Gracchus* 6.3; App. *BC* 1.23.98; docs. 8.28–9 for Gaius' other public works; see Wiseman 1987: 149, 155; Laurence 1999: 40, 49–51.

1 Gaius devoted particular attention to the construction of roads, bearing in mind both practical considerations as well as those relating to grace and beauty. His roads ran straight across the country without deviations, the surface consisting partly of dressed stone and partly of tight-packed sand. **2** Depressions were filled up, watercourses or ravines which crossed the road were bridged, and both sides of the road were of equal and corresponding height, so that the whole work presented a symmetrical and beautiful appearance. **3** In addition to this, he measured every road in miles (the mile is a little less than eight stades) and positioned stone pillars to mark the distances. **4** He set up other stones, too, at shorter intervals on both sides of the road, so that horsemen should be able to mount from these without assistance.

2.7 Contract for repairs to the Via Caecilia

ILS 5799

(*ILRRP* 465; *ROL* IV.180; *CIL* I2 808.) A tablet of stone, dating to approximately 90–80 BC, found in a wall at Rome, and recording a public document dealing with repairs to the (unidentified) Via Caecilia. 1,000 paces equals a Roman mile, or 1,480 metres. Note the city quaestor's responsibility for supervising road construction: Wiseman 1987: 138–41; Laurence 1999: 40.

... Works ... on the Via Caecilia [let out at contract]... out of [.... thousand sesterces.
A]t the thirty-fifth milestone a bridge over the river, [the s]um assigned, at the cost to the people of **5** [... sesterces]; Quintus Pamphilus, contractor, and workmen, with Titus Vibius T[e]mudinus, city quaestor, as [overseer] of roads; [the road] must be laid in [gr]avel from the [78th] milestone and pav[ed] through the [A]p[e]nnines for a distance of 20,[000 paces], the sum assigned, [at the **10** c]ost [to the people] of [1]50,[000] sesterces. Lucius Rufilius, freedman of Lucius and Lucius, [...] con[tr]actor, with Titus Vibius, [quaestor], as overseer of roads; [the road must be laid] from the 9[8]th milestone to the 11[... milestone ... turn-off t]o Interamnium u[p to the 1]20th milestone; the sum assi[gned, at the cost to the peop]le of 600,000(?) sesterces ...

15 Titus Sepunius O[. . .], son of Titus, [contractor], with Titus Vibius [T]em[udinus, city quaestor, as overseer of ro]ads . . . fallen [down] arch . . . [the sum assigned, at a cost to the people of . . . sesterces . . .; . . .] contractor, **20** [with Titus Vibius], city quaestor, [as overseer of roads] . . .

2.8 The lex Julia Municipalis

ILS 6085, 53–67

(*CIL* I1 206; Bruns 102; *FIRA* 140; *ARS* 113.) This is an extract from Julius Caesar's town-planning law of 44 BC; included here are the sections of his law which deal with roads: the grain-dole and the holding of political office in Italian communities were also covered. The regulations concerning roads were clearly an attempt to solve Rome's daytime traffic problems. For the procession for the games in the Circus Maximus (62), see doc. 2.65; (66) indicates that only a small proportion of excrement ended up in the sewers; many householders using chamber-pots must have had their excrement removed by collection. In Caesar's regulations, public streets are to be maintained by the owners of buildings along them; if they fail to do so, the job will be contracted out and they will be liable for the bill; special officials are to keep the streets clear of rubbish; traffic regulations limit day-time traffic; and no permanent structures are to be erected in public spaces or porticoes. Robinson 1992: 17, 59–62; on town-planning, see Crook 1967: 260–4.

53 Where a building adjoins an alleyway, the owner shall keep this alleyway properly paved along the entire face of the building with durable, whole stones to the satisfaction of the aedile in charge of roads in that district in accordance with this law . . .

56 Regarding the roads which are or shall be within the city of Rome or where there is continuous habitation, no one after the first day of January next shall in the daytime lead or drive a wagon on them after sunrise or before the tenth hour of the day, except for the purposes of transporting materials for the construction of the sacred temples of the immortal gods, or for the carrying out of public works, or for removing from the city materials from those places which are being demolished by public contract. For those cases it shall be permitted by this law for specified people to drive or lead wagons for the reasons specified.

62 On those days on which the Vestal Virgins, the rex sacrorum, and the flamines have to ride on wagons in the city for the sake of the public sacrifices of the Roman people, or wagons have to be led in a triumphal procession, on the day when someone celebrates a triumph, or wagons are needed for games publicly celebrated in Rome or within one mile of the city or for the procession for the games in the Circus Maximus, it is not the intention of this law to prevent the use of wagons in the city for these reasons and on those days.

66 It is not the intention of this law to prevent whatever ox wagons or donkey wagons have been driven into the city at night from leaving the city of Rome or within one mile of the city, empty or carrying excrement, between sunrise and the tenth hour of the day.

68 Regarding public places and public porticoes which are or shall be within the city of Rome or within one mile of the city of Rome, which are by law under the charge of aediles or of those magistrates who supervise the cleaning of roads and public places within the city of Rome or within one mile of the city of Rome, no one shall have anything built or erected in such places or porticoes, nor shall anyone acquire possession of any of these areas or porticoes nor shall anyone have any part of them enclosed or shut off to prevent the people from access to and use of such places and porticoes, except for those people to whom permission has been granted by laws, plebiscites and senatorial decrees.

2.9 The temple of Safety

Livy *History of Rome* 9.43.25

Salus was deified 'safety', or the welfare of the state. The Samnites were defeated and a peace made in 307/6 BC during the Second Samnite War: 30,000 Samnites had been killed. The terms were that they should provide corn for three months and a year's pay and tunic for each Roman soldier. Vowed in 311, the temple, on the Quirinal, was dedicated in 302 (Livy 10.1.9).

In the same year, the contract for the temple of Safety was let out by the censor Gaius Junius Bubulcus, which he had vowed, while consul, during the Samnite war. He and his colleague Marcus Valerius Maximus built roads throughout the countryside at the public expense.

2.10 Public amenities at Aletrium, c. 100 BC

ILS 5348

(*CIL* I² 1529; *ILLRP* 528; *ROL* IV.146.) On the front of a temple at Aletrium, 70 kilometres south-east of Rome. For Varus, see David 1996: 114; Varus spent a fortune on the town, as he restructured all of Aletrium on the lines of towns in the Greek East.

Lucius Betilienus Varus, son of Lucius, on the advice of the senate (of Aletrium), superintended the construction of the following works: all the streets **5** in the town, the colonnade leading to the citadel, a playing-field, a clock (*horologium*), a meat-market, the stuccoing of the basilica, the seats, the bathing pool; **10** he made a reservoir by the gate, with an aqueduct some 340 feet long bringing water to the town and citadel, and arches and sound water-pipes. On account of all this, they made him censor for the second time, and the senate ordered his son exempt from military service, **15** and the people gave him a statue and the title Censorinus (because he had been censor).

2.11 Amenities at Pompeii

ILS 5706

(*CIL* I² 1635; *ILLRP* 648; *ROL* IV.190.) This inscription dates to c. 90–80; see *CIL* I² 1679a & b (*ILLRP* 1142) for Ulius' election to office. The decurions are the members of the local senate.

Gaius Ulius, son of Gaius, and Publius Aninius, son of Gaius, Board of Two for pronouncing justice, let out a contract by decree of the decurions for the construction of a Spartan sweating-room and rub-down room and for repairs to porticoes and a wrestling-school **5** out of the money which they were required by law to expend on games or a memorial. They superintended and approved the completed work.

THE IDEOLOGY OF THE ROMAN SENATORIAL CLASS

Romans of the first century BC saw their ancestors as hard-working and frugal. Much of this perception is idealised by contrast with contemporary standards of living; however, there is evidence that prior to the conquests of the second-century BC many of the senatorial class were farmers on a small scale. According to Val. Max. 4.4.6, the consul Marcus Atilius Regulus, who in 256 won a victory in Africa (docs 4.12-13), was prorogued for the following year; he wrote back that as the manager of his seven-iugera (4.35 acre) farm had died and a hired worker had run off with livestock and equipment, his wife and children would starve if he was not allowed to return home. Lower down the social scale, the centurion Spurius Ligustinus in 171 had inherited one iugerum, less than an acre, of land, his wife was undowered, and he had to support eight children on this and his army service (doc. 5.9).

2.12 The mythology of the farmer-general

Cicero On Old Age 16.55–6

From 218 BC (the *lex Claudia*) senators were forbidden to engage in large-scale trade (Livy 21.63.4) and from then on they were mainly land-owners. Ownership of landed property worth a minimum of 400,000 sesterces was a prerequisite for equestrian rank and hence membership of the senate, which consisted of some 300 members prior to Sulla, and 600 afterward (900 under Caesar). Cato the Elder (or the Censor) is here speaking and is praising the fact that senators of olden times lived and worked on their own farms unless called on for public service. Of course this bears no relation to the reality of land-owning aristocrats in the later Republic, and encapsulates the tradition of old Roman frugality, austerity and unpretentiousness. Dentatus in 290 BC defeated the Samnites and in 276 Pyrrhus. Cincinnatus was dictator in 458: see Livy 3.26. According to Val. Max. 4.4.10, Cincinnatus' granddaughter Tuccia only brought her husband a dowry of 10,000 asses, which was thought to be large; Val. Max. 4.4.7: Cincinnatus only owned seven iugera of land of which he lost three as security for a friend.

55 I could relate at length all the various charms of country life, but I realise I have already spoken too much . . . Well, it was in this sort of life that Manius Curius Dentatus spent his remaining years after his triumphs over the Samnites, the Sabines and Pyrrhus; and whenever I look at his farm, which is not far from mine, I cannot admire enough the frugality of the man and the spirit of his generation. **56** When the Samnites brought Curius a great weight of gold, as he sat before the fire, he refused it; for he said that he thought the glory was not in possessing the gold, but in ruling those who had it. . . . In those times senators, that is *senes* (elders), lived on farms — if it is true that Lucius Quinctius Cincinnatus was ploughing his fields when he was told that he had been appointed dictator . . . Marcus Curius Dentatus and other elders were summoned from their farms to serve in the senate, which is why the messengers who were sent to summon them were called travellers (*viatores*). Surely then the old age of men such as these, who took pleasure in cultivating the soil, was not unhappy? Indeed, in my opinion, I think that nothing could be happier than a farmer's life, not only because of the service he performs, since agriculture benefits the whole human race, but also because of the pleasure, which I have mentioned earlier, and the plenty and abundance of all things which contribute to the sustenance of men and even to the worship of the gods.

2.13 Cincinnatus is made dictator, 458 BC

Dionysius of Halicarnassus *Roman Antiquities* 10.17.4–6

Livy 3.26.6–12. Suffect (substitute) consul in 460, Lucius Quinctius Cincinnatus was appointed dictator in 458 when a Roman army was besieged by the Aequi on Mt Algidus. Within 15 days, he raised an army, defeated the Aequi and returned to his plough: *MRR* I.39. Livy 3.26.8 places his four-iugera farm on the right bank of the Tiber and records his wife's name as Racilia. Cicero dates his leaving his plough for the dictatorship to the occasion when he was appointed for the second time in 439 (*Sen.* 56).

4 It happened that at that moment Quinctius was ploughing some ground for sowing, and was himself following the lean oxen that were breaking up the fallow, without a tunic and wearing a small loin-cloth and a cap on his head. When he saw a crowd of people coming into the field, he halted his plough and for some time was uncertain who they were or what they wanted with him; then, when one ran up to him and told him to make himself look more decent, he went into the cottage, dressed, and came out to meet them. **5** The men who were there to escort him all greeted him not by his name, but as consul, dressed him in the purple-bordered robe, placing in front of him the axes and other insignia of his magistracy, and asked him to follow them to the city. He paused for a moment and shed tears, only saying: 'So my field will be unsown this year, and we shall be in danger of not having enough food to support us.' Then he kissed his wife and, instructing her to look after things at home, went off to the city. **6** I am led to narrate these details for no other reason than make clear to everyone what type of men the leaders of Rome were at that time, that they worked with their own hands, led self-disciplined lives, did not complain about honourable poverty, and, far from pursuing positions of royal power, actually refused them when offered.

2.14 Cato the Elder as a model of the old-style Roman

Plutarch *Life of Cato the Elder* 3.1–2, 4.4–6

Marcus Porcius Cato, Cato the Elder, was consul in 195 and censor in 184. He was noted for his parsimony and adherence to traditional Roman values. He was against all unnecessary expenditure: Plut. *Cato Mai.* 5 (doc. 6.31) criticises Cato for his sale of elderly slaves, telling us (5.6) that he even left his campaign horse in Spain to save the city the cost of its transportation home; for Cato's views on the treatment of slaves, see docs 6.29–32.

3.1 There was a certain man of high birth and great influence at Rome, who was skilled at perceiving excellence in its early stages and well-disposed to cultivate it and bring it into repute, Valerius Flaccus. **2** He had a farm adjoining that of Cato, and, learning from Cato's servants of the way he farmed his own land and of his lifestyle, was amazed to hear them relate how Cato, early in the morning, walked to the market-place and pleaded the cases of all who wanted his aid, and then returned to his farm, where, clad in a sleeveless tunic in the winter, and stripped in summer, he worked with his servants, then sat down with them to eat the same bread and drink the same wine. . . .
   4.4 He tells us that he never wore clothing worth more than 100 drachmas; that, even when he was praetor or consul, he drank the same wine as his slaves and that, as for fish

and meat, he would buy for his dinner 30 asses worth from the market, and even this for the city's sake to strengthen his body for military service; **5** that he once inherited an embroidered Babylonian mantle, but sold it at once; that not a single one of his cottages was plastered; that he never paid more than 1,500 drachmas for a slave, as he wanted not the delicate or handsome types, but tough workmen like grooms and herdsmen . . . **6** In general, he said, he thought nothing cheap that one could do without, but that what a person did not need, even if it cost one cent (an *as*), was expensive; also that he acquired lands where crops were raised and cattle herded, not those where lawns were sprinkled and paths swept.

2.15 Cato and the good old ways: **running a vineyard**

Cato *On Farming* 11.1–5

The *de agri cultura* (*On Farming*) of c. 160 BC is the earliest extant piece of connected Latin prose and the only work of Cato which survives complete. In it Cato gives detailed advice to landowners of moderately sized slave-run estates producing wine and olive oil (the 'villa system' or estates of some 25 to 75 hectares). Cato had in §10 given the procedures for running a olive plantation of 240 iugera; he follows the vineyard with details of the pressing-room. 1 culleus holds 20 amphorae; directions for the actual wine-making are at 23.1–25.1. Varro *Rust.* 1.18.5–7 discusses Cato's figures here.

1 This is the equipment necessary for a vineyard of 100 iugera: an overseer, a house-keeper, 10 labourers, 1 oxherd, 1 donkey-driver, 1 willow-worker, 1 swineherd — a total of 16 persons; 2 oxen, 2 cart-donkeys, 1 donkey for the mill; 3 complete presses, jars to hold five harvests of a total of 800 cullei, 20 jars for holding grape- pulp, **2** 20 for grain, and the tops and covers for each jar, 6 pots made of broom, 4 amphorae of broom, 2 funnels, 3 wicker-work strainers, 3 strainers to remove the flower, 10 vessels for the unfermented juice; 2 carts, 2 ploughs, 1 wagon-yoke, 1 yoke for carrying wine (probably a manuscript error for ox harnesses), 1 donkey yoke, 1 bronze disk, 1 grinding-stone; a bronze vessel holding a culleus, 1 cover for a bronze vessel, 3 iron hooks, 1 cooking-pot holding a culleus, **3** 2 water pots, 1 watering-pot, 1 basin, 1 small pot, 1 slop-basin, 1 water bucket, 1 little dish, 1 ladle, 1 candlestick, 1 chamber-pot, 4 beds, 1 bench, 2 tables, 1 stone table, 1 clothes chest, 1 cupboard, 6 long benches, 1 well-wheel, 1 iron-tipped corn-measure, 1 half-measure, 1 wash-tub, 1 soaking-tub, 1 vat for lupines, 10 large jars; **4** ox-harnesses, donkey-harnesses, 3 rugs, 3 utensils, 3 strainers for wine-lees, 3 donkey-mills, 1 hand-mill; tools: 5 reed knives, 6 vine-dresser's knives, 3 pruning-hooks, 5 axes, 4 wedges, 2 ploughshares, 10 forks, 6 spades, 4 shovels, 2 four-toothed rakes, 4 manure-hampers, 1 manure-basket, 40 grape-harvesting hooks, 10 bill-hooks for cutting broom, 2 braziers, 2 pairs of fire-tongs, 1 fire-shovel; **5** 20 small Amerine baskets, 40 planting baskets or trays, 40 wooden spades, 2 treading vats, 4 mattresses, 4 coverlets, 6 cushions, 6 bed-covers, 3 towels, 6 patchwork cloaks for slaves.

2.16 The pan-Italian nature of early agriculture

Cato *On Farming* 135.1–3

Cato was born at Tusculum, though his family also owned property in Sabine country. His advice in this work is especially directed to farmers in Latium and Campania, districts he clearly knew well. Italian viticulture became particularly profitable in the mid to late second century BC and dominated the market in Rome and elsewhere in the empire. On Roman farming, see White 1970; Rossiter 1978.

1 At Rome buy tunics, togas, coats, patchwork cloaks, and boots; caps, iron tools, knives, spades, mattocks, axes, harness, bits, and small chains at Cales and Minturnae; spades at Venafrum; carts at Suessa and in Lucania; vats and tubs at Trebla, Alba and at Rome; **2** and tiles at Venafrum. Roman ploughs will be good for fertile soil, Campanian for blackish earth. Roman yokes will be the best. Detachable plough-shares will be the best. Olive-crushers at Pompeii, Nola and at the wall of Rufrium; locks and bolts at Rome; buckets, oil-urns, water-pitchers, wine-urns, and other bronze vessels at Capua and Nola; Campanian strainers will be found useful; **3** pulley-ropes and all goods made of broom at Capua; Roman strainers at Suessa and Casinum, but the best will be at Rome. Who makes press-ropes? Lucius Tunnius at Casinum, Gaius Mennius, son of Lucius, at Venafrum.

2.17 Cato and the uses of cabbage

Cato *On Farming* 156.1

Cato continues by giving recipes for, among other things, cleaning out the digestive tract, cures for colic, strangury, headaches and ulcers, and poultices (a cabbage poultice helps to heal a dislocation). The urine of those who eat cabbage can be used to bath babies and cure weak eyes: 157.10. His recipe for a purgative (158.1–2) includes ham, cabbage, beet, fern, fish, a scorpion, six snails, wine, and a handful of lentils. For Cato's negative views on Greek doctors, see Pliny *Nat. Hist.* 29.14–16 and Plut. *Cato Mai.* 23.3–4 (doc. 5.59), though he does make use of Greek theories. Pliny 20.78 comments that both Pythagoras and Cato believed in the efficacy of cabbage.

On cabbage and how it promotes digestion. It is the cabbage which surpasses all other vegetables. It may be eaten either cooked or raw. If you eat it raw, dip it in vinegar. It promotes digestion marvellously, makes a good laxative, and the urine is good for everything (i.e., medicinally). If you want to drink a good deal and dine freely at a dinner-party, before dinner eat as much raw cabbage, seasoned with vinegar, as you wish, and similarly after dinner eat some five leaves; it will make you feel as though you had not dined and you can drink as much as you want.

2.18 A Roman country farmer

[Cicero] *Letters to his Friends* 16.21.7

In 44 BC, in a letter to his father's freedman Tiro, who had bought a farm, Marcus Cicero junior jokes about his becoming a proper countryman, even to keeping the stones from dessert to sow them later. For Tiro, see docs 6.46–7; Cicero had manumitted him in 53 and 21 of Cicero's letters are addressed to him.

You're a land-owner! You'll have to drop all citified refinements — you've become a country Roman! How I picture you before my eyes right now, and a very pleasant sight it is! For I seem to see you buying country gear, talking to your bailiff, and saving up in your hem the fruit-stones from dessert.

2.19 Cato blamed for his mercantile activities

Plutarch *Life of Cato the Elder* 21.5–7

Though Cic. *Off.* 2.89 says Cato compared money-lending to murder, Cato engaged in it himself — though only at low risk. Note here that senators were not supposed to engage overtly in business, only in agriculture; compare the money-lending activities of Marcus Junius Brutus (doc. 5.69).

5 When he applied himself more seriously to making money, he considered agriculture more as an amusement than profitable, and he invested his capital in safe and certain ventures, buying ponds, hot springs, places given over to fullers, pitch works, land with natural pastures and woods — from which he acquired a great deal of money and which could not, as he used to say, 'be ruined by Jupiter'. **6** He also engaged in the most criticised type of money-lending, namely on ships, in the following way. He required the borrowers to form a large partnership; when there were 50 partners and as many ships, he acquired one share in this company himself through his freedman Quintio, who worked with the borrowers and sailed with them. **7** So the entire risk was not his, only a small part of it, and his profits were large.

2.20 The inadequacy of Scipio Africanus' baths

Seneca the Younger *Letters* 86.1, 4–6, 11–12

Seneca (died AD 65) paid a visit to the villa at Liternum (north of Cumae) which had belonged to Publius Cornelius Scipio Africanus, the victor over Hannibal, after his retirement: Livy 38.52. In describing the villa's baths he makes a point of contrasting modern luxury with antique austerity. For the excavation of a noble house (*domus*) on the Palatine (perhaps belonging to M. Aemilius Scaurus, praetor in 56), see Carandini 1988: 359–87: the basement provided sleeping quarters for 50 slaves; Cicero's town house on the Palatine (he had 8 country residences) cost him 3,500,000 sesterces: *Fam.* 5.6.2; for domestic space in Roman houses, see Wallace-Hadrill 1988; Nevett 1997; on baths, Yegül 1992.

1 I am writing this letter to you, while staying at the villa of Scipio Africanus himself . . . **4** I have looked at the house, which is built of squared stone . . . and at the narrow little bath, dark in keeping with ancient custom (for our ancestors thought that a bath should not be hot unless dark too). It was, therefore, a great delight to me to compare Scipio's habits with our own. **5** In this recess, the 'terror of Carthage', to whom Rome is indebted for having been captured only once (i.e., by the Gauls), used to bathe a body exhausted by farm work. For Scipio kept himself busy with hard work and even cultivated the land himself, as was the custom with the Romans of old. He stood under this mean roof, and this paltry floor bore his weight. **6** But who is there today who could bear to bathe like this? Everyone thinks himself poor and worthless unless his walls sparkle with large and costly decorations, unless marbles from Alexandria are set off by Numidian mosaics, unless their borders are covered on all sides with elaborate designs and multi-coloured like paintings, unless the vaulted roof is covered with glass, unless Thasian marble, once a rare sight even in a temple, lines our swimming pools . . . **11** Of what uncouthness some people nowadays condemn Scipio, because he did not let daylight into his caldarium through wide windows, because he did not cook himself in a sunlit room, and hang around before boiling in his bath. 'Wretched man!' they say. 'He didn't know how to live well. He did not bathe in unfiltered water — it was often dirty and after heavy rain was almost muddy!' But it didn't bother Scipio much if he had to bathe like that; he came to the baths to wash off sweat, not unguents. **12** And what do you suppose some people will comment? 'I don't envy Scipio; whoever had to bathe like that was really living in exile!' Actually, if you only knew, he didn't bathe every day. Those who have recorded the ancient customs say that they washed just their arms and legs every day, since those parts of the body gathered dirt from work, and only washed the rest once a week. Someone will say at this point, 'They must have been filthy chaps! Can you imagine how they smelled?' But they smelled of the army, hard work, and manliness!

CONSPICUOUS CONSUMPTION IN ROME

Despite the ideals of frugality, simplicity and adherence to traditional values, there was increasing dependence on luxury goods and lifestyles from the mid-second century BC: see also docs 5.51–63. The wealth of Roman aristocrats can be calculated partly from the dowries left to daughters: cf. doc. 7.70. Cicero's friend Atticus may not have been a typical equestrian, but some idea of inherited wealth in the first century BC can be seen from the fact that he inherited 2 million sesterces from his father and a further 10 million from his uncle who adopted him (Nepos *Atticus* 14.2, 5.1–2). The plebs, by contrast, largely lived a hand-to-mouth existence and mortality rates were high: Yavetz 1969; Scobie 1986; Cherry 1993; Laurence 1997; Storey 1997; Scheidel 2003.

2.21 The assets of Marcus Licinius Crassus

Plutarch *Life of Crassus* 2.1–7

Son of the consular P. Licinius Crassus (cos. 97), Marcus Crassus played the major part in defeating the slave rebellion of Spartacus, and was consul in 70 and 55 (both times with Pompey). He became enormously wealthy during Sulla's proscriptions (docs 11.19–25); cf. docs 6.3, 12.81. He died during his campaign against the Parthians in 53 BC (doc. 12.80).

1 The Romans say that this one vice, avarice, overshadowed Crassus' many virtues; it seems that this one became stronger in him than all other vices and obscured the rest. **2** The greatest proofs of his avarice are considered to be the way he made his money and the immensity of his wealth. **3** For, to begin with, he possessed no more than 300 talents, but during his consulship he dedicated a tenth to Hercules and provided a feast for all the people, as well as giving every Roman from his own purse enough grain to live on for three months, and yet, when he made a calculation of his assets before his Parthian expedition, he found he was worth 7,100 talents. **4** Most of this money, if the truth, though scandalous, must be told, he collected through fire and war, making his greatest profits from public misfortunes. For, when Sulla took over Rome and sold the property of the men he had proscribed, considering it and calling it spoils of war, he wanted to share the guilt with as many of the most influential men as possible, while Crassus refused neither to take nor to buy it from him. **5** In addition, when he saw what familiar and normal disasters at Rome fires were, and the collapse of buildings because of their weight and contiguity, he started buying slaves who were architects and builders. When he had more than 500 of these, he used to purchase houses that were on fire and ones next to those on fire, since because of their fear and uncertainty the owners would sell at a low price, and, as a result, the greater part of Rome came into his possession. . . . **7** And although he owned numerous silver mines and very valuable land with labourers on it, yet one might consider all this to be nothing in comparison with the value of his slaves, of whom he owned large numbers and who were highly qualified — readers, secretaries, silversmiths, stewards, waiters . . .

2.22 The luxurious lifestyle of Lucullus

Plutarch *Life of Lucullus* 39.2–5, 42.1–2

Lucius Licinius Lucullus was one of Sulla's supporters, and the only officer who backed his march on Rome in 88 BC. Consul in 74, he was given the command against Mithridates, which Pompey took over through the *lex Manilia* in 66. After attempts to frustrate ratification of Pompey's eastern settlements (doc. 12.34), he retired from politics to live in luxury: see Keaveney 1992: esp. 143–65 on his retirement. Cicero criticises his lifestyle at *Laws* 3.30. Gabinius, as tribune in 67, showed the people a picture of Lucullus' villa in the hope of undermining his reputation (Cic. *Sest.* 93).

39.2 I must assign to frivolity the extravagant buildings and covered walks and baths, and, still more, his paintings and statues and his devotion to these arts, which he collected at enormous expense, pouring lavishly into these the immense and splendid wealth which he had amassed during his commands — and even now when luxurious living has increased to such an extent, the gardens of Lucullus are numbered among the most extravagant of the imperial gardens. **3** As for his constructions on the seashore and near Naples, where he suspended hills over immense tunnels and circled his residences with rings of sea and streams for fish-breeding and built dwellings surrounded by sea, Tubero the Stoic on seeing them called him 'Xerxes in a toga'. **4** He also had country residences near Tusculum with belvederes commanding the view and complexes of open dining-rooms and walkways, where Pompey once criticised Lucullus for having organised his country residence in the best possible way for summer, but having made it uninhabitable in winter. **5** Lucullus just laughed at him and said, 'Do you suppose then that I have less sense than cranes and storks and fail to change abodes according to the seasons?' . . . **42.1** He collected many well-written books, his use of which reflected better on him than the way he acquired them, and his libraries were thrown open to everyone, as well as the colonnades around them and rooms for study, which were always open without restriction to the Greeks, who frequented them as if they were a lodging place of the Muses and spent the day there with each other, gladly escaping from their other occupations. **2** Lucullus often also spent time there with them, walking in the colonnades with their scholars and assisting their statesmen in whatever they wanted; and in general his house was a home and town hall (*prytaneion*) for any Greeks who came to Rome.

2.23 An extravagant pontifical banquet

Macrobius *Saturnalia* 3.13.10–12

Quintus Caecilius Metellus Pius was the son of Metellus Numidicus (for whom see docs 9.6–9, 28). A supporter of Sulla, he was made pontifex maximus and Sulla's colleague as consul in 80 BC. Feasts were a traditional part of the ritual of priestly colleges; the sacred grove of the Arval brothers included a cult dining-room. On this occasion of the installation of L. Cornelius Lentulus Niger as flamen of Mars (flamen Martialis) c. 69 BC (*MRR* II.135), the two youngest of the six Vestals were presumably left behind to perform the sacred duties. The Roman convivium, modelled on Etruscan practices, resembled the Greek symposium, except that women were allowed to be present (though not to recline). For this passage, see Gowers 1993: 73–4.

10 You must understand that extravagance was found among the most respectable dignitaries, for I would like to put before you the details of a very early pontifical banquet which is recorded in the fourth *Register* of the famous pontifex maximus Metellus, in the following words: **11** 'On the ninth day before the Kalends of September, the day on which Lentulus was installed as flamen of Mars, the house was decorated, the dining-room furnished with ivory couches, and the pontiffs reclined on two of the dining-couches: Quintus Catulus, Marcus Aemilius Lepidus, Decimus Silvanus, Gaius Caesar, ... the chief priest (*rex sacrorum*), Publius Scaevola, Sextus . . . Quintus Cornelius, Publius Volumnius, Publius Albinovanus and Lucius Julius Caesar, the augur who installed Lentulus. On the third dining-couch were Popilia, Perpennia, Licinia and Arruntia, the Vestal virgins, and Lentulus' wife Publicia the flaminica and Sempronia his mother-in-law.

12 This was the dinner: for the first course, sea urchins, raw oysters, as many as they wanted, giant mussels, cockles, thrushes on asparagus, fattened hens, a dish of oysters and mussels, shell-fish (both black and white); then came a course of cockles, shell-fish, sea-nettles, fig-peckers, haunches of goat and boar, fattened fowls in pastry, fig-peckers, murex and purple fish. For the main course, sow's udders, half-heads of boar, a dish of fish, a dish of sow's udders, ducks, boiled teal, hares, roast fattened fowls, creamed wheat and Picentine rolls.'

2.24 The farming of peafowl, dormice and lampreys

Varro *On Farming* 3.6.1, 6, 3.15.1–2, 17.2–3

Varro, born in 116 BC, began his *de re rustica* (*On Farming*), addressed to his wife Fundania who had just bought a farm, in his eightieth year. Hirrus (2.1.2) is the son-in-law of one of the speakers, Cossinius. Pliny *Nat. Hist.* 9.171 says that the lamprey loan took place at one of Caesar's triumphs as dictator: he speaks of 6,000 fish. Cic. *Att.* 2.1.7 laughs at such 'piscinarii', aristocrats concerned primarily about their fishponds, which were associated with aristocratic self-indulgence: see Higginbotham 1997; docs 12.35–6. Varro goes on to make fun of Hortensius for his care of his fish when sick (3.17.8); Hortensius, a great orator and one of Cicero's rivals in the courts, was consul in 69. Like L. Licinius Lucullus, he was given to a luxurious lifestyle and gourmandising.

6.1 (Lucius Cornelius) Merula said, 'As to peafowl, it is within our memory that flocks of them began to be kept and sold at high prices. Marcus Aufidius Lurco is said to pull in more than 60,000 sesterces a year from them (here follows detailed advice on how to keep them) . . . **6** It is said that Quintus Hortensius (cos. 69) was the first to serve these on the occasion of his inauguration as aedile, which was lauded rather by the dilettanti than by men of strict virtue. As many quickly followed his example, they raised the price to such an extent that their eggs now sell for five denarii each, the birds themselves easily for 50, and a flock of 100 easily brings in 40,000 sesterces — indeed, Abuccius used to say that if you wanted three chicks for every hen you could get as much as 60,000 . . .

15.1 The accommodation for dormice is built on a different design (than that for snails), the ground being surrounded not by water but by a wall; this is entirely covered on the inside by smooth stone or plaster, so that they cannot climb out. Inside it there should be small nut-bearing trees. When these do not bear fruit, acorns and chestnuts should be thrown inside the wall for them to fill up on. **2** They should have rather roomy holes made for them in which they can have their young; there should be little water as they don't use a great deal of it and prefer a dry spot. They are fattened up in large jars, which a lot of people even keep inside their villas, and which potters fashion in a very different shape from other jars, as they make channels along the sides and a hollow in which to put the food. In a jar like this people place acorns, walnuts or chestnuts. When a cover is placed over them the dormice grow fat in the dark . . .

17.2 There are two types of fish-ponds, fresh and salt, the one is open to ordinary people and not without profit, where the Nymphs provide water for our farm-house fish; the sea-water ponds of our nobles, however, for which Neptune has to provide the water and the fish, concern the eye more than the purse, and drain the owner's pocket rather than fill it. In the first place, they are constructed at great expense, secondly they are stocked at great expense, and thirdly they are maintained at great expense. **3** (Gaius Lucilius) Hirrus used to receive 12,000 sesterces from the buildings around his fish-ponds, but he spent all that income on the food he gave his fish. No wonder — I remember that on one occasion he lent Caesar 2,000 lampreys by weight, and that, on account of the great number of fish, his villa sold for 4,000,000 sesterces.

GLORIA

Aristocratic Rome was a highly competitive culture. It was important to be seen to live up to one's ancestors' achievements and fulfil family expectations, ideally by achieving the highest political office, the consulship. This gave a man, and his family, *dignitas* (prestige), *gloria* (renown) and *auctoritas* (influence and authoritative position). Even before Sulla increased the number of praetorships per year, many praetors had failed to become consul: Sallust *Cat.* 4.1 tells us that to retire after holding the praetorship left one open to charges of indolence and idleness — ambition for office was not, in itself, considered reprehensible. Cicero *Tusc. Disp.* 2.58: 'We naturally yearn after and hunger for honour, and when we have once glimpsed, as it were, some part of its radiance there is nothing we are not ready to endure and suffer in order to obtain it.' The successful consular candidate would then hope for a province where he could show his abilities, recoup his electioneering expenses, and, with luck, achieve a military triumph, the highest and most conspicuous honour. Roman values were those of a warrior culture (Barton 2001; 13) based on a cult of victory. For the 'dolor repulsae' ('grief at being beaten in an election') felt by Cato the Younger at his defeat in the consular elections for 51, see Caes. *BC* 1.4; cf. Broughton 1991; Konrad 1996; Flower 1996; Kaster 1997; Patterson 2000: 29–52.

With no professional politicians or bureaucrats, aristocratic competition underlay the Republic, and individual ambition provided the necessary officers of state on an annual basis

(Rosenstein 1993; cf. 1990a: 54–67 where Rosenstein argues that a track record of proven success was not necessary to ensure election in a crisis situation; observance of correct ritual and preservation of the 'pax deorum' (the 'peace of the gods') was considered sufficient to make a good consul; but cf. Tatum 1991). Attitudes towards aristocratic virtues can be seen in epitaphs, especially those of the Scipiones (docs 2.25–6) which stress their magistracies and military victories; those who died young have similar (potential) virtues, which they were unable to demonstrate in exploits (Lintott 1999: 169). The ideals of a Roman aristocrat comprised *dignitas*, *auctoritas*, *gloria*, *virtus* (courage, or the qualities of a man), *pietas* (piety to gods and family), and *gravitas* (dignity, austerity); see Adcock 1959: 13–17; Earl 1967: 20–43; MacMullen 1980.

2.25 Epitaph for Publius Cornelius Scipio

ILS 4

(*CIL* I² 10; *ILLRP* 311; *ROL* IV.4.) This inscription was found on the front of a sarcophagus, probably that of a son of Scipio Africanus who died c. 170 BC and who was the adoptive father of Scipio Aemilianus. Epitaphs conventionally praised the virtues of the dead and summarised their achievements, in this case the potential achievements of Scipio, who is presented here as young to emphasise the reason for his lack of public office — he was in fact an invalid for most of his life. He was known as an orator (Cic. *Brut.* 77 cites some of his speeches) and he became an augur in 180: *MRR* I.390. On this epitaph, see Flower 1996: 167–9; cf. van Sickle 1987.

You who have worn the distinguished cap of the flamen dialis,
Death caused all your qualities to be short-lived —
Your honour and reputation and courage, your glory and talents,
Through which, if you had been permitted to enjoy a long life,
You would easily have surpassed by your deeds the glory of your ancestors.
For which reason, Scipio, Earth joyfully receives you in her embrace,
Publius Cornelius, child of Publius.

2.26 A noble Roman

ILS 6

(*ILLRP* 316; *CIL* I² 15; *ROL* IV.8.) This Scipio was son of Scipio Hispallus (cos. 176 BC), and praetor peregrinus in 139 (Hispanus implies service in Spain); *MRR* I.482. This epitaph may date to c. 135 and he clearly died at about 40 years of age, after his praetorship but before he could stand for the consulship: Flower 1996: 169–70; cf. Bettini 1991: 182–3. His career is presented as following in the family traditions. For the decemvirs for judging lawsuits, see Cic. *Orat.* 156; the decemvirs for making sacrifices were the college of priests who preserved the Sibylline books: Livy 10.8; docs 3.36–7.

Gnaeus Cornelius Scipio Hispanus, son of Gnaeus, praetor, curule aedile,
quaestor, twice military tribune, member of the Board of Ten for judging lawsuits,
member of the Board of Ten for making sacrifices.

By my conduct I augmented the virtues of my family,
I had a family, I emulated the deeds of my father.
I upheld the praise of my ancestors, so that they are glad
I was created of their line; my magistracies have ennobled my lineage.

2.27 Ancestors inspire nobles to great deeds

Sallust *Jugurthine War* 4.5–6

Masks of ancestors (*imagines*) were carried in nobles' funeral processions, often by family members, and according to Polybius were kept in a prominent place in the house at other times (Polyb. 6.53.4–6: doc. 3.74). Men whose ancestors had held office as curule aedile, praetor, consul or censor had the right to keep such images of them, usually made of wax, in the atrium and have them carried in funeral processions. Sallust has Marius boast that, unlike his noble rivals, 'It is not possible for me . . . to show the masks or triumphs or consulships of my ancestors' (*BJ* 85.29); for these masks and their importance, see Flower 1996. Sallust is here presumably referring to the brothers Quintus Fabius Maximus Aemilianus and Publius Cornelius Scipio Aemilianus, the sons of L. Aemilius Paullus.

5 I have often heard that Quintus Maximus, Publius Scipio, and other distinguished men of our country were accustomed to declare that, whenever they looked on the masks of their ancestors, their hearts were set aflame in the pursuit of virtue. **6** Of course, they did not mean that the wax or the effigy had any such power over them, but that it is the memory of great achievements that kindles a flame in the breasts of eminent men that cannot be extinguished until their own excellence (*virtus*) has come to rival the reputation (*fama*) and glory (*gloria*) of their forefathers.

2.28 Family pride falsifies historical records

Livy *History of Rome* 8.40.3–5

Livy is here discussing the events of 322 BC and the dictatorship of Aulus Cornelius Cossus (cos. 343, 332): *MRR* I.149–50. For the importance of praise of one's ancestors, see Flower 1996: 128–58; on false genealogies, Wiseman 1974.

3 It is not easy to choose between the facts and the authorities. **4** The record has been falsified, I think, by funeral eulogies and lying inscriptions on portrait busts, each family trying to appropriate to itself by deception and falsification the fame of successes and dignities, **5** and this practice has led to confusion both in the achievements of individuals and the public records of events.

2.29 A consular's greatest aims — including elephants

Pliny *Natural History* 7.139–40

Cf. Dion. Hal. 2.66.4. Lucius Caecilius Metellus, consul in 251 and 247, magister equitum in 249, pontifex maximus from 243, and dictator in charge of holding elections in 224, had been a general in the First Punic War, winning a major victory over the Carthaginians at Panormus in Sicily in 250, which included the capture of numerous elephants: *MRR* I.213–14. His funeral speech was delivered by his son Quintus in 221 BC. He was supposedly blinded while rescuing the Trojan statue of Pallas, the *palladium*, from the burning temple of Vesta in 241 (and was then voted by the Roman people the right to ride in a chariot to senate meetings, the first to be granted this honour: Pliny *Nat. Hist.* 7.141). For the speech's emphasis on competitive achievements, see Wiseman 1985: 3–4. Funeral speeches were delivered in the forum from the rostra: Crawford 1941. Caecilius may not have been a nobilis: no Caecilius Metellus is definitely attested before him, though the consul of 284 (L. Caecilius Metellus Denter) *may* have been his father.

139 Quintus Metellus, in the oration which he gave at the final eulogy of his father the pontiff Lucius Metellus, twice consul, dictator, Master of the Horse, and land-commissioner, who was the first to lead elephants in his triumph from the First Punic War, left it in writing that his father had achieved the ten greatest and most glorious objects in the pursuit of which wise men pass their lives: **140** for he had aimed at being a first-class warrior, an outstanding orator, a brave and courageous general, at taking charge of events of the highest importance, enjoying the greatest honour, possessing exceptional wisdom, being considered the chief of all the senators, acquiring great wealth in a respectable way, leaving many children, and being the most distinguished person in the state; and stated that these had befallen his father and none other since the foundation of Rome.

2.30 The importance of ambition

Cicero *On Duties* 1.72–3

On Duties was written for Cicero's son Marcus in 44 BC. Cicero is here stressing the importance of undertaking a public role in government. Despite a rather 'wild youth', Marcus junior did become consul in 30 BC and then proconsul of Asia; cf. doc. 2.64.

72 Those to whom nature has given the qualities necessary for engaging in public affairs should cast aside all hesitation, strive for election to magistracies, and take part in government; for there is no other way that the state can be governed or greatness of mind be displayed. Those in charge of government, no less than philosophers, and perhaps even more so, need to possess that greatness of spirit and contempt for human affairs which I so often mention, together with peace of mind and freedom from care, if they are to avoid worry and live with dignity and consistency. **73** This is easier for philosophers, as, their lives being less subject to the blows of fortune, their wants are fewer, and, if any misfortune occurs, their fall is not so heavy. It is, therefore, not without reason that stronger emotions are aroused in those who engage in public life than in those who live quietly, as well as greater efforts to succeed; all the more, then, is their need to possess greatness of spirit and freedom from troubles.

Whoever enters government should take care to consider not only the honour involved, but also whether he has the capacity to succeed; at the same time, he should ensure that he does not despair prematurely through cowardice, nor be over-confident through ambition. In all such enterprises, before undertaking them, careful preparation is essential.

2.31 Gloria affects a man's nearest and dearest as well as himself

Cicero *Letter to his Brother Quintus* 1.1.43–4

This letter was written in 60 BC, when Quintus was propraetor of Asia: he had been aedile in 65 and praetor in 62 and governed Asia from 61 to 58. Marcus, his elder brother, is here presenting his own consulship of 63 BC as a benchmark which the family has to live up to. After much praise, he has just criticised Quintus for his outbursts of temper and advises that he control them. Quintus could be impetuous: Caesar criticises him, as his legate (54–51 BC), for his conduct at Aduatuca (*BG* 6.36–42), after having praised him earlier for his leadership skills against the Nervii

(5.38–52). For Quintus' service with Caesar in Gaul and Britain, see docs 12.84–6; Welch 1998: 94–8.

43 At the same time, bear in mind that we are not now working towards a glory we do not yet possess and which we hope for, but are striving for a glory already won, which, indeed, it was not so much our aim to win in the past, as it is now to defend in the present. And if anything I possess could be disassociated from you, I would desire nothing greater than the status I have already won. But now, indeed, the circumstances are such that, unless all your deeds and words over there accord with my achievements, I think that, great as have been my labours and achievements — all of which you have shared — they have gained me nothing at all. If, however, you have helped me more than anyone to acquire a splendid name, you will certainly work harder than others to ensure that I retain it. You should not only take into account the opinions and judgements of the men of today, but of those to come in the future; and their judgement will be the more accurate, being free from detraction and malice.

44 Finally, you also ought to recollect that you are not seeking glory for yourself alone; even if that were the case you would not be unmindful of it, especially as you have always wished to immortalise the memory of your name with the most splendid memorials, but that you have to share it with me and hand it on to our children.

THE ROMAN TRIUMPH

The celebration of a triumph was the ultimate goal for the Roman senatorial class. Victorious generals processed into Rome, via the triumphal gate (porta triumphalis: Richardson *Top. Dict.* 301), to the temple of Jupiter Capitolinus. The triumphator, the triumphing general, was dressed in the style supposed to have belonged to the old kings, with his face painted red in imitation of the red-painted face of the statue of Jupiter on the Capitoline, and was carried on a four-horse chariot preceded by his lictors, accompanied by his army, captives, spoils, freed prisoners of war, and the senate and magistrates. A prerequisite for the triumph was to have killed 5,000 of the enemy (Val. Max. 2.8.1). A slave rode in the chariot with the triumphator, reminding him as they went along that he was only a mortal. Triumphs were awarded by the senate; in the late Republic, troops could proclaim their general as imperator, as did Cicero's troops in Cilicia, and a triumph could follow on from this but not necessarily, as Cicero found out to his disappointment (doc. 13.20). A general might instead be awarded an oratio, or lesser triumph. The celebration of a triumph was the pinnacle of Roman military achievements. See Versnel 1970; Weinstock 1971: 64–76; Develin 1978; Nicolet 1980: 352–6; Stambaugh 1988: 238–9; Brennan 1994, 1996; Beacham 1999: 19–22; Flower 2004: 326–31; doc. 5.52 (Cn. Manlius Vulso); for awards worn in triumphs, see Maxfield 1981: 101–9.

2.32 The triumph and ovatio

Dionysius of Halicarnassus *Roman Antiquities* 5.47.1–3, 8.67.9

Cf. Livy 2.16.8–9 (Livy does not mention this war against the Sabines). Publius Postumius and Agrippa Menenius were consuls in 503 BC. Postumius is given the lesser triumph because he had previously been defeated and lost a large number of his men. Lucius Siccius Dentatus ('Sicinus' in Livy 2.41) was a plebeian military figure of the mid-fifth century BC. Licinius Macer was tribune in 73 and praetor in 68. Cf. Plut. *Marcell.* 22 for the difference between a triumph and an ovatio.

5.47.1 After achieving a brilliant victory, they returned home. **2** They were both honoured with triumphs by the senate, Menenius with the greater and more honourable type, entering the city in a royal chariot, and Postumius with the lesser and inferior type which they call *ouastes* (ovation), altering the name which is Greek to this meaningless form. For it was originally called *euastes*, from what actually took place, from what I conjecture and find recorded in many native histories, **3** and the senate, as Licinius (Macer) relates, introduced this type of triumph for the first time on this occasion. It differs from the other, firstly in that the general who celebrates the triumph called the ovation enters the city on foot, followed by his army, and not in a chariot like the other; and secondly because he does not wear the embroidered robe decorated with gold, with which the other is adorned, nor does he have the golden crown, but is dressed in a white toga bordered with purple, the native dress of the consuls and praetors, and wears a crown of laurel; he is also inferior to the other in not holding a sceptre, though everything else is the same.

8.67.9 Since Siccius seemed to have freed the state from the greater fear by his destruction of the insolent army of the Volscians and slaughter of their general, they voted him the greater triumph; he therefore drove into the city with the spoils, the prisoners, and the army that had fought under him, riding in a chariot drawn by horses with golden bridles and dressed in the royal robes, as is the custom in the greater triumphs. To Aquilius they granted the lesser triumph, which they call an ovation . . .

2.33 An early triumph against the Samnites

Livy *History of Rome* 10.46.2–6

Livy describes the triumph of Lucius Papirius Cursor, consul in 293, over the Samnites, whom he defeated at Aquilonia. His father had also defeated the Samnites in 320 at Luceria after the Caudine Forks (cf. docs 1.65–72). He was consul for the second time in 272. For crowns as military decorations, see doc. 5.7.

2 On his arrival at Rome Papirius was unanimously granted a triumph. He celebrated his triumph while still in office, in a style which was splendid for those times. **3** Infantry and cavalry marched or rode past adorned with their decorations; many civic crowns and crowns won by the first to climb a rampart or wall were to be seen; **4** the spoils won from the Samnites were examined and compared in splendour and beauty with those his father had won, which were well-known from being often used to decorate public places; a number of noble prisoners, distinguished for their own and their fathers' deeds, were led in the procession. **5** 2,533,000 pounds of heavy bronze were carried past; this bronze was said to have been acquired from the sale of prisoners; there were 1,830 pounds of silver which had been taken from the cities. All the bronze and silver was put in the treasury, with none of the booty being given to the soldiers; **6** the bad feeling to which this gave rise amongst the people was augmented by the collection of a war-tax to pay the soldiers, since, if he had forgone the glory of placing the captured money in the treasury, the soldiers could have been given a donative out of the booty, as well as providing for their pay.

2.34 Lucullus' triumph

Plutarch *Life of Lucullus* 37.3–6

Lucullus' triumph in 66 was blocked by his political opponents and he was accused of deliberately prolonging the war against Mithridates and appropriating money. He was initially refused a triumph, which was finally celebrated in 63; see Keaveney 1992: 129–36.

3 Lucullus exerted himself strongly against this, and the foremost and most influential men mingled with the tribes and, after much entreaty and hard work, eventually persuaded the people to allow him a triumph, but not, like some, a triumph which was astonishing and tumultuous from the length of the procession and the multitude of objects carried in it. Instead, he adorned the circus of Flaminius with the arms of the enemy, of which there was a immense number, and with the royal war-engines; and this was a great spectacle in itself which was hardly despicable. **4** Some of the mail-clad horsemen and ten of the scythe-bearing chariots took part in the procession, as well as 60 of the king's friends and generals, and 110 bronze-beaked war-ships were also carried in it, with a golden statue of Mithridates himself, six feet high, a shield decorated with jewels, 20 litters of silver vessels and 32 litters of gold cups, armour and coins. **5** These were carried by men; and there were 8 mules carrying golden couches, 56 with ingots of silver and 107 more with somewhat less than 2,700,000 pieces of silver coin. **6** There were also records on tablets of the money already paid by him to Pompey for the war against the pirates and to the public treasurers, and of the fact, too, that each of his soldiers had received 950 drachmas. Moreover, Lucullus gave a splendid feast to the city and the surrounding villages, which are called Vici.

2.35 Caesar's triumphs

Suetonius *Life of the Deified Julius* 37.1–39.4

Caesar celebrated triumphs over Gaul, Egypt, Pontus, Africa and Spain: triumphs could not be celebrated over Roman citizens. The Gallic, Egyptian, Pontic and African triumphs were actually celebrated between 20 September and 1 October 46; the Spanish one after the victory over the Pompeians at Munda in October 45 BC: App. *BC* 2.101–3, Plut. *Caes*. 55–6. 600 million sesterces from booty were displayed: Vell. 2.56.2; cf. App. *BC* 2.102.421.

37.1 With the wars over, Caesar celebrated five triumphs, four in the same month after defeating Scipio, with a few days' interval between them, and a fifth after overcoming Pompey's sons. The first and most splendid of his triumphs was the Gallic, after this came the Alexandrian, the Pontic, the African, and lastly the Spanish, each different in its splendour and staging. **2** On the day of his Gallic triumph, as he rode through the Velabrum, he was nearly thrown from his chariot when the axle broke, and he ascended to the Capital between forty elephants, in two lines on his right and left, carrying torches. In the Pontic triumph, among the procession's litters, one carried a sign of three words: 'I came, I saw, I conquered!' This referred not to the events of the war, like the others, but to the swiftness of the victory. **38.1** Every infantryman in Caesar's veteran legions received as booty 24,000 sesterces, in addition to the 2,000 sesterces paid them at the beginning of the civil war.

He also gave them all a farm, but not grouped together so as not to evict the possessors. To the ten modii of grain and ten pounds of oil given to every individual of the people, he added the 300 sesterces, which he had promised at first and now raised to 400, because of the delay. **2** He also remitted a year's rent at Rome to those who paid up to 2,000 sesterces, though in Italy not above 500 sesterces. He added a banquet and distribution of meat, and two dinners following his Spanish victory; for he considered that the first had not been sufficiently splendid and, five days later, served a second more magnificent one.

39.1 He put on spectacles of various kinds: a gladiatorial contest, plays for all districts of Rome with actors in all languages, chariot-races in the circus, athletic competitions, and a naval battle. At the contest in the forum, Furius Leptinus, of praetorian family, fought Quintus Calpenus, a former senator and lawyer. The sons of leaders of Asia and Bithynia danced the Pyrrhic sword dance. **2** In the plays, Decimus Laberius, a Roman eques, staged his own farce and, after being given 500,000 sesterces and his gold ring (the badge of equestrian rank), walked across from the stage through the orchestra to the equites' fourteen rows of seats. At the circus the track was lengthened at either end, and on the race-course, around which a trench had been dug, young aristocrats drove four-horse and two-horse chariots or rode pairs of horses, jumping from one to another. Two troops of older and younger boys performed the Troy game. **3** Wild-beast hunts were put on five days in a row, and ended with a battle between two forces comprised of 500 infantry, 20 elephants and 30 cavalry . . . The athletes competed over a three-day period in a temporary stadium built on the Campus Martius.

4 In the naval battle, on a lake dug in the Lesser Codeta, Tyrian and Egyptian fleets, with ships with two, three, or four banks of oars and a great number of combatants, engaged each other. Such huge numbers of spectators flocked to these shows from all directions that many visitors had to sleep in tents pitched along the streets or roads, and large numbers were crushed to death by the crowd, amongst them two senators.

CANDIDATURE FOR OFFICE (AMBITIO)

The term for canvassing for office was *petitio* (literally seeking or asking); *ambitio* was the pursuit of office, from ambire (to go around) implying the solicitation of votes; from the term ambitio comes *ambitus* (initially the acting of canvassing, but later meaning electoral malpractice or bribery), which was endemic to the Roman electoral system since there was intense competition for the consulship in most years, due to the workings of the 'pyramidical' cursus honorum. The introduction of the secret ballot by the *lex Gabinia* (which introduced it in 139 in electoral assemblies) made bribery more effective, with voters being able, unobserved, to sell their vote to the highest bidder. While, in theory, clients were obliged to vote for their patron (or at least make a choice between patrons), the widespread nature of bribery in the later Republic strongly suggests that the patronage system did not control most of the electorate. Another electioneering expense was that huge sums were expected to be spent on games and shows. Laws against bribery were passed in 181 and 159, though their provisions are uncertain but involved non-capital trials. According to Polybius (6.56.4) bribery was a capital offence, in practice meaning exile; however later Roman anti-bribery laws had non-capital penalties; the *lex Cornelia Baebia*, passed in 181, involved non-capital trials. By 116 a special court, *quaestio de ambitu*, had been introduced (Marius was tried before this: Plut. *Mar.* 5.4–5) and from the time of Sulla a praetor was in charge of this court. Sulla appears to have introduced legislation on bribery as dictator in 81, imposing as maximum penalty a ten-year exclusion from office (Cic. *Sull.* 17). The *lex Calpurnia* of 67, which unseated both consuls-elect for 65, laid down as a penalty expulsion from the senate, and Pompey's law of 52 probably laid down exile for life (doc. 13.5).

Candidates for office were of course supposed to engage in legitimate expenses in order to entertain or materially benefit sections of the electorate, particularly fellow-tribesmen and clients. Shows and feasts (in honour of deceased family members) apparently did not violate laws on bribery, though actual distributions of money did: Scipio Africanus obtained the aedileship because he was a giver of great gifts: Polyb. 10.5.6. Cicero himself, as consul in 63, carried a law forbidding the giving of gladiatorial shows during the two years before one was a candidate for office (Cic. *Vat.* 37); the giving of games earlier in one's career, specifically as aedile, was a good electioneering ploy for the future: cf. Caesar's games as aedile (doc. 2.71; 11.2 for Sulla). Cic. *Mur.* 70–2 tells us that candidates were not supposed to put on free shows for their fellow-tribesmen, but their friends could tacitly do so on their behalf. While canvassing for the consulship of 52, Milo put on extravagant games; Asconius 31 reports that he squandered three patrimonies (cf. Cic. *Mil.* 95) and that he had given each voter (presumably in the influential tribes) 1,000 asses (Asc. 33); cf. Yacobsen 1999: 31–3; he was, of course, later convicted of both murder (of Clodius) and bribery (Asc. 54).

Two candidates for the consulship of 53 were prepared to pay 10 million sesterces to the centuria praerogativa, the century that voted first and was supposed to set the trend of the election (Cic. *Quint.* 2.14.4). Not only the consulship was hotly contested: Cato in 54 was supposedly given on deposit 500,000 sesterces by each of the candidates for the tribunate, to be forfeited if they transgressed the legislation against bribery: Cic. *Quint.* 2.15.4, *Att.* 4.15.7–8, Plut. *Cato Min.* 44.7–11. Presumably candidates targeted critical sections of the electorate: banquets could entertain only a proportion of the populace (Crassus' in 70 was very large with 10,000 tables: Plut. *Crass.* 12.2).

Canvassers in Rome wore a specially whitened toga (the *toga candidata*: hence the term 'candidate'); they wore this without a tunic underneath. Candidates often used a slave nomenclator to help them remember the names of electors so they could address everyone personally: for the use of such nomenclatores, see Cic. *Mur.* 77 (their use was banned by the *lex Fabia*: Plut. *Cato Min.* 8.2). Candidates could also use divisores, officials whose job was to pass along patrons' gifts to members of their tribes, but who could also be used to distribute bribes. Antiochus Epiphanes aped Roman political behaviour when (at home in Antioch) he dressed in a white toga and walked around the agora grasping men's hands, embracing them and asking them for their votes (Polyb. 26.1, 5). For the *Commentariolum petitionis* (doubtfully attributed to Q. Cicero), a handbook on successful electioneering, see Richardson 1971: 436–42; Patterson 2000: 53–5.

For bribery, see Brunt 1988d: 425 (for laws against *ambitus*); Linderski 1985; Lintott 1990; Yacobsen 1992; 1999: 22–6; Wallinga 1994; candidates and electioneering: Evans 1991; Patterson 2000: 53–67; voting procedures: Taylor 1960; Hall 1964; Mouritsen 2001: 99–107; secret ballot: Yacobsen 1995, 1999: 124–47. See Lintott 1990: 11 for the irregularity of the verb 'to bribe' in the context of Roman politics: 'I take appropriate care of my friends, you are recklessly generous, he bribes.'

2.36 The toga without the tunic

Plutarch *Roman Questions* 49

See Plut. *Cor.* 14–15, where candidates for office walk about in the forum in a toga but without a tunic, either to emphasise their humility or to display their wounds: Coriolanus' wounds persuaded people to vote for him. Cato the Younger did the same, presumably to show his adherence to traditional customs and values (see Plut. *Cato Min.* 6, 44, 50; doc. 7.57). Cicero *Planc.* 12–13, 50 (in 54 BC) stresses that it was essential that candidates display humility in their canvassing, as if asking for favours, especially if their ancestors had already held public office. On entering office, the new consul also had to address the people thanking them for their support (see doc. 2.40).

Why was it the custom for those canvassing for a magistracy to do this in a toga but without a tunic, as Cato has recorded? Was it so they did not carry money in its folds and hand out bribes? Or was it, rather, because they used to judge those worthy of office not by their family, wealth, or reputation, but by their wounds and scars? So, to ensure that these were visible to anyone who met them, they used to go down to canvass without tunics. Or were they trying to curry popular favour through thus humiliating themselves by their lack of clothes, as they do by hand-shaking, appeals and subservience?

2.37 Liberality or bribery in 63?

Cicero *In Defence of Murena* 77

Cicero's *pro Murena* defends a consul-elect for 62 against the charge of *ambitus*: he argues that the populace had been won over by Murena's splendid games as praetor in 65 (38–9, 40) as well as by his 'traditional' feasts and shows during his campaign in 63 (72–3, 77); these may have infringed the *lex Capurnia de ambitu* (*Mur.* 67) by which Autronius and Sulla, consuls-elect for 65, had been condemned: Yacobsen 1999: 26–31, 91–6.

And so the Roman plebs should not be prevented from enjoying games, or gladiatorial contests, or banquets — all these our ancestors established — nor should candidates be restrained from showing that generosity which means liberality rather than bribery.

2.38 Electioneering notices

CIL I² 1641c, 1644a&c, 1656a&g, 1645a, 1665

(*ILS* 6398a–99; *ILLRP* 1128, 1131, 1133, 1137, 1140–1; *ROL* IV.286–8.) These notices supporting candidates for election were painted, in red, on walls at Pompeii around the time of Sulla: the 'colonists' would have been Sulla's veterans. Note the abbreviations used in what was obviously a frequently encountered phenomenon readily comprehensible to the passers-by: (i) reads L. Aqtium d. v. v. b. o. v. c.: duovirum, virum bonum, oro vos, coloni: 'as a member of the Board of Two, a fine man, I urge you, colonists (to elect him)'. See Jongman 1988: 27–329; cf. Franklin 1980: 17–26.

1641c Lucius Aqutius — a fine chap! Colonists, I appeal to you (to elect him) member of the Board of Two!
1644a Numerius Barcha — a fine chap! I appeal to you (to elect him) member of the Board of Two! So may Venus of Pompeii, holy, blessed (goddess) be kind to you.
1644c Numerius Veius Barcha — may you rot!
1656a Marcus Marius — I appeal to you to elect him aedile!
1656g Marcus Marius — a fine chap, I appeal to you, colonists!
1645c Quintus Caecilius — a generous man — for quaestor, I appeal to you!
1665 Quinctius. Anyone who votes against him should go and sit next to a donkey!

THE NOVUS HOMO

In Rome's competitive society, it was a struggle even for those of consular families (nobiles) to reach the consulship; for those without such a background, the task was far more difficult, though not impossible. Political power was generally in the hands of the nobiles, who stayed in power partly through their financial resources and partly through their ability to attract voters by using their clients and friends and the Romans' respect for family and lineage. According to Sallust, the nobles passed the consulship from hand to hand (doc. 9.6); for senatorial hostility towards new men, see Epstein 1987: 55–6; cf. Gruen 1996. However, the ruling elite was not a closed group, as the method of entry was by election, and the system did allow for the entry of new families into the oligarchy: while the Caecilii Metelli filled 15 consulships between 143 and 52, this was unusual. The term novus homo ('new man') is vague but could include both the first in a family to enter the senate and gain a magistracy, and a senator whose ancestors had never reached the consulship: for the son of a freedman who became curule aedile in 304 BC, see doc. 1.54. Cicero himself (*Mur.* 17) lists, as the 'new men' before him, M'. Curius (290 BC), Cato (195), Q. Pompeius (141), Marius (107), T. Didius (98) and C. Coelius Caldus (94) thus restricting the definition to total parvenus: other men of non-consular descent had been elected to the consulship but extreme examples of novi homines, equestrians who reached the consulship like Cicero, are rare. For nobilitas as meaning 'descent from a consul', see Gelzer 1969: 27–53; Shackleton Bailey 1986; Burckhardt 1990: 77–99, contra Brunt 1982; on novi ('new men'): Gelzer 1969: 27–53; Wiseman 1971; Brunt 1982 (who estimates c. 20 novi between 201 and 49); Shackleton Bailey 1986; Vanderbroeck 1986; Burckhardt 1990; Rosenstein 1992, who suggests that 194/5 out of 237/8 consuls between 179 and 49 were of probable consular descent.

New men, like Marius and Cicero, had to make their own connections and establish clientelae, but tended to accept the values of the senatorial order rather than to combat them. For the values of the nobilitas, see Lintott 1999: 144–70; doc. 2.29; for the tension between the populares (Cic. *Sest.* 96: politicians who legislated through the people, but who were often of consular ancestry) and the optimates (the 'best' men, nobles), see Mackie 1992; Seager 1972a, 1977; Lintott 1999: 173–4.

2.39 The jealousy of the nobility

Sallust *The Catilinarian Conspiracy* 23.5–6

Sallust states that it was the information that Catiline planned a conspiracy that gave rise to a general desire to give Cicero the consulship — implying that otherwise he might have been less successful in his candidature: cf. doc. 9.6; for Catiline, see docs 12.13–23.

5 It was this in particular that gave rise to general enthusiasm for bestowing the consulship on Marcus Tullius Cicero. **6** For, before this, most of the nobility were inflamed with jealousy and considered the consulship to be contaminated if a new man, however distinguished, acquired it. But at the approach of danger, jealousy and pride came to be of secondary importance.

2.40 Cicero on himself as novus homo

Cicero *On the Agrarian Law* 2.1–4

This was Cicero's first speech as consul to the people (at a contio preceding voting in the comitia tributa), made against the Rullan agricultural legislation (cf. doc. 12.13). In-coming consuls held a contio in which they traditionally thanked the citizens for electing them. Cicero makes great play of the fact that he is a novus homo, without consular lineage: the last 'new man' had been C. Coelius Caldus in 94 BC; Cicero as novus homo: Scullard 1964; cf. Smith 1966: 19–35, 83–104; Stockton 1971: 71–2; Rawson 1975: 29–59; Lacey 1978: 14-29. Cicero was made consul in 'his year', *suo anno* (the minimum age: 42 in the year of election for consuls by Sulla's legislation: doc. 11.30). For the importance of ancestors and imagines at the elections, see Flower 1996: 60–90. Bell 1997: 7 sees this speech as a lesson in how to appear popular when speaking against a popular measure.

1 It is a custom, Romans, instituted by our ancestors, that those who by your favour have acquired the right to images of their family should, in their first oration before the people (*contio*), combine thanks for your favour with praise of their own ancestors. In such speeches, some men are sometimes found to be worthy of their ancestors' rank, though the majority only manage to make clear that the debt owed to their ancestors is so great that something is still left over to be paid to their descendants. I myself, Romans, have no possibility of speaking of my ancestors before you, not that they were not such as you see us to be, begotten from their family and raised in their teaching, but because they lacked the people's praise and the light of the honour you granted. . . .

3 I am the first new man after a very long interval — nearly more remote than our times can remember — that you have made consul, and that rank, which the nobility kept secured by guards and entrenched in every way, you have broken open and shown that for the future it should be open to merit, with me taking the lead. And not only did you elect me consul, which is a glorious honour in itself, but did it in such a way in which few nobles have ever been made consuls in this city, and no new man before me.

For indeed, if you would be kind enough to consult your memory in regard to new men, you will find that those, who were made consuls without rejection, only became so after lengthy labour and at a favourable opportunity, becoming candidates many years after they had been praetors, and somewhat later than their age and the laws allowed, while those who became candidates in their own year (*suo anno*) were not elected without rejection; and that I am the only one of all the new men whom we can remember, who became a candidate for the consulship in the first year it was permitted and was made consul in my first candidacy, so that this honour granted by you, which I stood for as soon as I was allowed, does not appear to have been snatched on the occasion of the candidacy of an unsuitable person, nor to have been urgently requested with frequent petitions, but to have been obtained by merit. **4** It is a glorious honour, as I have just mentioned, Romans, that I was the first of the new men on whom, after so many years, you have bestowed this honour, that it was at my first candidacy, and that it was in my 'own year', and yet nothing can be more glorious or distinguished than the fact that at the comitia at which I was elected you did not hand in voting-tablets — their secrecy being the guarantee of freedom — but showed with unanimous voice your goodwill and attachment to me. Thus, it was not the last sorting of the votes, but your first rush to vote (i.e., he soon had a majority), not the individual voices of the heralds, but the unanimous voice of the Roman people which declared me consul.

AMICITIA

Political friends were *amici* (sing.: *amicus*), as opposed to personal friends (*familiares*: see docs 2.46–8). There were no political parties in Rome, and such *amicitiae* (friendships or political alliances) were unofficial, fluid and often changing, though regulated by ties of obligation and honour; political amici could also be inherited within a family. The features of such relationships were mutual assistance, a common political approach, and friendship through mutual respect, the key being an interchange of services (Brunt 1988c: 351–81; Lintott 1999: 170–3), and what friends called an 'amicitia' could easily be titled a 'factio' (faction) by political opponents (Sall. *BJ* 31.15). The term amici could include clients, not just social equals. The opposite of amici were inimici (personal or political enemies), such as Caesar's relationship with Bibulus and Cato the Younger (Caes. *BC* 3.16.3, 1.4.7). On Caesar as a personal friend, see Marchetti 2004.

For friends (amici) of the Roman people, see Marshall 1968, who argues that the status of amicus was diplomatic or political rather than allowing fiscal or judicial privileges: see esp. docs 10.25, 11.36 for the classing of individuals as amici (generally because of their loyalty to Rome). Amici of Rome were entered on a formal role and allowed to set up a bronze tablet on the Capitol and sacrifice to Roman state gods, as well as receiving public hospitality. Rome's relationship with foreign states was one of benefactors and recipients with obligations, hence a patron-client relationship: Badian *FC*; Edlund 1977; Brunt 1988d: 392–4.

Numerous letters of recommendation were sent by Cicero (*Fam.* book 13, with one exception, consists of such letters: 46–44 BC): in one to Valerius Orca, Cicero mentions a private symbol by which Orca could realise if it was a genuine 'commendatio' or simply a politeness (*Fam.* 13.6.2). Some 20 of these letters were to support a friend or client in a lawsuit; this was considered a perfectly respectable way of proceeding. In 46 Cicero sent 13 letters to one friend Servius Sulpicius Rufus, governor of Achaea, alone (Wallace-Hadrill 1989: 77). Personal connections could adversely affect decision-making: Cicero as governor of Cilicia refused the Salaminians' reasonable request because he did not wish to offend Brutus, his amicus (doc. 5.69).

2.41 Family fail to rally around the accused

Livy *History of Rome* 6.20.1–3

M. Manlius Capitolinus, consul in 392 and hero of the Gallic attack in 390, was supposedly brought to trial by his enemies for his courting of the populace (through a programme of cancellation of debts) and possible insurrectionist tendencies; he was executed in 385 (or 384). Not only family members, but friends and clients were expected to show their support in emergencies. The mourning toga, the *toga pulla*, was made of dark wool.

1 Manlius was committed for trial. The first effect of this was that the people was greatly disturbed, **2** especially when they saw the defendant dressed in mourning and unattended by any of the senators, or indeed by any of his relatives and connections, and not even by his brothers Aulus and Titus Manlius, for it had never happened before that day that a person's closest connections had not gone into mourning when he was threatened by such a crisis. **3** They recalled that, when Appius Claudius was imprisoned (cf. 3.58), his enemy Gaius Claudius and the entire Claudian family had gone into mourning, and they considered that there was a plot to put down the people's friend because he had been the first to abandon the patricians for the plebs.

2.42 Cicero on the changing nature of friendship

Cicero *On Friendship* 10.33–4

Cicero's *de amicitia* was probably written in 44 BC; it was set in 129 after the death of Scipio Aemilianus; Gaius Laelius, Scipio's close friend and consul in 140, is here talking to his sons-in-law about his relationship with Scipio.

33 Then listen, worthy gentlemen, to the points about friendship most often discussed between Scipio and myself (Laelius). He, indeed, used to say that nothing was more difficult than for a friendship to last to the last day of life: for it often used to happen, either that it might not be mutually advantageous, or that the parties did not share the same political views; he used to say, too, that men's characters frequently change, sometimes by adverse circumstances, at other times by the increasing burdens of old age. And then he would cite an example of this by analogy with adolescence, that boys' greatest attachments are often laid aside with the toga praetexta; **34** but if they continue to the mid-teens (*adulescentia*) they are sometimes broken off by rivalry, either over a marriage or some other advantage, in which both parties cannot be equally successful. If they should continue to be friends for a longer period, the friendship is often destroyed should a struggle for magisterial office take place; for, while for the majority of people there is no greater ruin to friendship than monetary greed, for the most worthy men (the *optimi*) it is the rivalry for official rank and glory from which have frequently arisen the greatest enmities between most devoted friends.

2.43 Cicero and the demands of amicitia

Cicero *In Defence of Murena* 7–10

In 63 BC, as outgoing consul, Cicero defended L. Licinius Murena, who had been elected consul for 62 but prosecuted for bribery by Servius Sulpicius Rufus, a loser in the same election and another friend of Cicero's, for whom Cicero had canvassed in the election. For this speech, see Craig 1981: 32–3; Brunt 1988c: 373–5, 1988d: 428–30. Cicero states that in defending Murena he will still bear in mind his friendship with Sulpicius (*Mur.* 10).

7 I admit, Servius Sulpicius, that in your canvass for the consulship I owed you all my energy and my support in view of our close relationship, and I think that I discharged my duty. When you were canvassing for the consulship, there was nothing additional on my part which could have been demanded either of a friend or of a supporter or of a consul. That time is past. The situation has changed. My view and conviction is this, that to prevent Murena's election I owed you as much as you dared ask me, but to prevent his acquittal I owe you nothing . . . **8** My friendship with Murena, jurors, is both great and of long duration and will accordingly not be destroyed by Servius Sulpicius in his prosecution of Murena on capital charges, simply because it was overcome in a contest for election with this same man. Even if this were not the case, either the public standing of this man or the greatness of the rank he has attained would have branded me with the worst reputation for pride and cruelty, if I had refused to take on the perilous case of a man so distinguished by his own honours and those of the Roman people . . . **10** I, jurors, would think myself despicable if I failed a friend, cruel if I failed a man in distress, arrogant if I failed a consul.

2.44 Cicero asks the consul C. Marcellus to support his supplicatio

Cicero *Letters to his Friends* 15.10

This letter was written at Tarsus, at the end of 51 BC, to the consul-elect for 50. Cicero is here recalling past services in order to induce C. Claudius Marcellus to have Cicero's governorship of Cilicia praised as highly as possible by the senate: a supplicatio (thanksgiving) was voted by the senate to betoken an important victory; for Cato's reply to a similar request by Cicero, see doc. 13.19. The phraseology is rather more tortuous than in most of Cicero's letters and Cicero may have felt some diffidence at making the request. The sense of the first sentence is that Marcellus' consulship is a good opportunity for him to show the devotion his family feels to Cicero.

Marcus Cicero, Imperator, to Gaius Marcellus, son of Gaius, consul, greetings.

1 Since it has happened, as I so greatly desired, that the devotion of all the Marcelli, and Marcellini too (for the goodwill always shown me by your family and those of your name is remarkable) — since, therefore, it has happened that the devotion of you all can be put into practice by your consulship, because in this consulship my achievements, and the praise and honour relating to them especially coincide, I am asking you — and it can be most easily done, for I am sure that the senate will not reject it — to see to it that the decree of the senate, after my dispatch has been read, be as complimentary as possible.

2 If I had been less closely associated with you than with all your family, I would commission those, by whom you know I am especially regarded, to present my case to you. Your father's services to me have been most splendid; no one can be said to be more supportive of my well-being or my honour. There is no man, I believe, who is unaware of how highly your cousin (Marcus Claudius Marcellus, cos. 51) values and has always valued me. In short, your whole family has always honoured me with the greatest favours of every kind. And, indeed, you have yielded to none of your family in your regard for me. Accordingly, may I ask especially that you desire me to win every possible honour through your doing, and that both in the matter of my being decreed a supplicatio, and in everything else, you consider my reputation as sufficiently committed into your hands?

2.45 Cicero recommends a friend to Memmius, 50 BC

Cicero *Letters to his Friends* 13.3

This is a typical, if short, letter of recommendation written by Cicero. It demonstrates the importance of testimonials in the Roman world, and Cicero's willingness to help his friends and increase his own influence and their obligations to him. Gaius Memmius (to whom Lucretius addressed his *de rerum natura*) was currently in Athens in exile after a charge of electioneering bribery in 54; he was praetor in 58 and propraetor in Bithynia in 57: nothing is known of Fufius.

Aulus Fufius, one of my most intimate friends, treats me with the greatest deference and devotion; a man of learning and great refinement, he is extremely worthy of your friendship. I would be glad, if you would behave towards him as you promised when we met. That would be more pleasing to me than anything else could be. Moreover you will bind the man himself to you for perpetuity by the strongest sense of obligation and regard.

2.46 Ennius on Servilius Geminus

Ennius *Annals* 210–27

(Gell. 12.4.4; *ROL* I.78–80; Skutsch 1985: 93–4 (as lines 268–86), commentary at 447–62.) Ennius is probably here referring to Gnaeus Servilius Geminus, consul in 217, who was killed at the battle of Cannae in 216 (or, less likely, to his father Publius Servilius Geminus, a hero of the time of the First Punic War). Geminus is portrayed as a noble and affable friend, and this passage demonstrates not clientship, but rather the friendly relationship possible between a cultivated intellectual and a Roman noble of good standing — the comrade has been suggested to have been Ennius himself (L. Aelius Stolo at Gellius 12.4.4) and Ennius may here be presenting his own view of his relationship with aristocrats such as the Scipiones and M. Fulvius Nobilior; see Gruen 1990: 111–3, cf. Badian 1984: 49–50; for literary and artistic patronage: Gold 1982; cf. White 1978.

210 Saying this he called to one with whom, willingly and gladly
His table, conversation, and personal affairs
He often courteously shared, when tired out
He had spent a great part of the day managing matters of utmost importance,
Through counsel given in the wide forum and sacred senate;
215 One to whom, without anxiety, he would boldly speak
Matters great and small and jests, and would burst forth and utter words
Good and bad, if he so wished, and place them in safe-keeping;
Who could share many pleasures and joys, both secretly and openly,
Whose nature no thought could persuade to do a wrong deed
220 Lightly or with evil intent; a learned, loyal,
Pleasant, eloquent man, content with his own, happy,
Shrewd, who spoke the right things at the right time, affable,
A man of few words, tenacious of many old ways created by that antiquity
Which is now buried, and of manners both old and new,
225 Holding to the ways of many of our elders, and the laws of gods and men,
Able, with discretion, both to speak and to keep silent.
This man, amongst the battles, Servilius thus addressed.

2.47 Caesar's pleasure in a friend's rescue

Caesar *Gallic War* 1.53.5–6

This passage is a notable exception to Caesar's generally objective tone in his narrative. The incident occurred in 58 BC, with the expulsion of Aristovistus, king of the Suebi, from Gaul; for Procillus, cf. *BG* 1.47.4.

5 In the flight, Gaius Valerius Procillus was being dragged along by his guards bound with three chains, when he fell in with Caesar himself who was pursuing the enemy with the cavalry. **6** This, indeed, delighted Caesar no less than the victory itself, for he saw the worthiest man in the whole province of Gaul, and his own *familiaris* (personal friend) and host, snatched from the hands of the enemy and restored to himself, nor did Fortune lessen any of the pleasure and rejoicing by Procillus' misfortune.

2.48 Catullus on the return of his friends

Catullus 9

Veranius is not known, but he has clearly returned from Spain and is mentioned in poems 12, 28 and 47 in company with Fabullus; they may have served together in Spain and then in Macedonia under L. Calpurnius Piso Caesoninus (cos. 58; proconsul 57–55).

Veranius, out of all of my friends
Superior in my view to three hundred thousand,
Have you come home to your household gods

And affectionate brothers and elderly mother?
You have come. O what joyful news!
I shall look upon you safe and sound and I shall hear you
Speaking of the places, history and tribes of the Hiberians,
In your accustomed way, and drawing your neck close to me
I shall kiss your beloved mouth and eyes.
Of all the world's most blessed men,
Who is more happy or blessed than I?

CLIENTELA AND PATROCINIUM

Early clientela ('patronage') was characterised by strict mutual obligations, supported by law; see XII Tables 8.10 (doc. 1.36), where a sacred obligation on the side of both patron and client is involved. By the later Republic, patronage and clientship played a large part in public and private life, with a patron-client relationship seen between generals and soldiers, founders and colonists, and conquerors and dependant foreign communities, as well, naturally, as between the large numbers of freedmen and their previous owners (duties for such freedmen were laid down and enforceable in law): The prestige, or dignitas, of nobles was publicly demonstrated by the number of their clients. Roman aristocrats could be hereditary patrons of foreign communities: see Badian *FC*, esp. 41–2, 68, who believes that Rome's friends and allies were in a position similar to that of clients; slightly modified by Gruen 1986, esp. 158–60; Braund 1984, 1989; Rich 1989; Burton 2003; cf. Nichols 1980.

However, the importance of political patronage has been overstated and confused with institutions such as amicitia and hospitium: see esp. Gelzer 1969: 139. There is a growing consensus that the importance of clientela as an informal contractual arrangement has been given too much weight. The poor were excluded from such relationships and in any case the urban population was too fluid to make large-scale patronage of the people practicable; at a higher level political alliances were often short-lived and there were no permanent factions in the sense of political 'parties' in Rome: Seager 1972; Develin 1985; Brunt 1988d; Wallace-Hadrill 1989; Mouritsen 2001: 73–4. Yacobsen 1999: 13–19 uses Marius' candidature for 107 to show the relative unimportance of the nobles' clientela in this election (cf. also 66–111).

The duties of a client could include the customary early-morning salutatio (greetings) at the residence of the patron (though this could also be a feature of amicitia or more general dependence), after which the clients could follow the patron into the forum and elsewhere; huge numbers could be involved — Sempronius Asellio, one of Scipio Aemilianus' military tribunes at Numantia stated, according to Gell. 2.13.4, that Tiberius Gracchus (tr. pl. 133), prior to his death, never left his house without the attendance of 3–4,000 supporters. Clients might also be expected to canvass and vote for their patron, or in his interests, though the introduction of the secret ballot made this less obligatory. In return the patron would give the client legal advice and representation in court, acting as a mediator between the client and the hierarchic order: Lintott 1999: 176–81; cf. Silverman 1965: esp. 176. Laurence 1994 stresses the clients' value as an information network (it was not until 59 that there was a publicly displayed written record of the actions of senate and people) and as an extension of personal canvassing.

Lacking clients, as a new man, Cicero used his forensic skill and rank as consul to become not only patron of his own home region (such as Arpinum, Reate, and Atella), but of the Sicilians, where he served as quaestor, of Cyprus, following his governorship of Cilicia, and of the publicani (tax-gatherers) generally (Brunt 1988d: 397). The Sicilians, grateful for his prosecution of Verres (doc. 5.65) contributed to the expenses of Cicero's election to the aedileship (Plut. *Cic.* 8). For Cicero as the heir and legatee of grateful clients, see Shatzman 1975: 409–12; cf. Dixon 1993 on gift-giving to strengthen such relationships; patrons and clients in general: Eisenstadt and Roniger 1984: 52–64.

2.49 Class divisions in early Rome

Dionysius of Halicarnassus *Roman Antiquities* 2.9.1–3

Clearly the situation described by Dionysius was not applicable in the late Republic and he has idealised the institution, placing its origins anachronistically back in the regal period, and stressing the good will and affections felt by both parties. Plut. *Rom.* 13.6 says it was later thought demeaning for nobles to take money from their clients (cf. the *lex Cincia* of 204 against the economic exploitation of clients: Livy 34.4.9). For the influential, clientship was in fact considered a humiliating status: see Plut. *Mar.* 4–5, where Marius, prosecuted for electoral bribery, is angry because Herennius refuses to give evidence against him on the grounds that Marius is his client. On Dionysius' picture of Roman clientship, see Brunt 1988d: 382–442; Wallace-Hadrill 1989; Drummond 1989.

1 After Romulus had distinguished the more powerful members of society from the less powerful, he then set up laws and established what things were to be done by each of the two groups. The patricians were to serve as priests, magistrates and judges, and were to aid him in the management of public business, devoting themselves to the city's affairs, while the plebeians were excused from these official duties because they were inexperienced in them and without leisure, because of their lack of means: they were to farm and breed cattle and practise trades that bring in a livelihood, so that they would not be seditious, as happens in other cities when either those in power maltreat the humble, or the common people and the poor are jealous of their superiors. **2** He gave the plebeians into the guardianship of the patricians, allowing each plebeian to choose the patron he wanted . . . **3** Romulus beautified the arrangement with an attractive title, calling this protection of the poor and humble 'patronage' (*clientela*), and laid down friendly duties for both, making their relationship a kindly one suited to fellow citizens.

2.50 Early rules for patrons and clients

Dionysius of Halicarnassus *Roman Antiquities* 2.10.1–4, 11.1–2

Dionysius considers clientela as one of the most important Roman institutions and as directly responsible for political stability. In his estimate of 630 years of harmony (down to 121 BC), he omits the murder of Tiberius Gracchus in 133.

10.1 The customs which Romulus then laid down concerning patronage, and which continued for a long time in use among the Romans, were as follows: it was the duty of patricians to explain to their clients the laws, of which they had no knowledge, and to take care of them in the same way whether they were present or absent, doing everything for them that fathers do for sons, with regard both to money and to contracts relating to money; to bring legal cases on behalf of clients who were wronged in any way to do with contracts, and to support them against those bringing charges against them; in short, to provide all the peace, both in private and state affairs, which they particularly needed. **2** It was the duty of clients to assist their patrons with raising dowries when their daughters were getting married, if the fathers lacked money, and to pay ransoms to enemies, if any of them or their children were taken prisoner; to pay out of their own funds their patrons' losses in private legal cases or fines that they owed to the state, not doing this as loans, but as a debt of gratitude; and to share with them the costs incurred in standing for magistracies and privileges and other public expenditures, just as if they were their relations. **3** For both alike, it was impious and unlawful to bring charges against the other in lawsuits, or act as a hostile witness, or vote in opposition, or be numbered amongst the other's enemies. If anyone was convicted of having done any of these things, he was guilty of treason by the law which Romulus had sanctioned, and it was lawful for anyone who wished to put him to death as a victim dedicated to infernal Jupiter — for it was a Roman custom to dedicate the bodies of those persons whom they wished to kill without incurring guilt to some god or other, and especially to the gods of the underworld; this was what Romulus now did. **4** Accordingly, the links between clients and patrons continued for many generations, and differed in no way from blood relationships, being handed down to their children's children, and it was a matter of great praise for men from distinguished families to have as many clients as possible and not only to preserve the continuation of the patronage they inherited, but to acquire others by their own merit.

11.1 It was not only in the city itself that the plebs were under the patricians' protection, but also every Roman colony and every city that was joined in alliance and friendship, as well as those conquered in war, had those protectors and patrons among the Romans that they wished. And the senate has frequently referred the controversies of these cities and peoples to their patrons, regarding their decisions as authoritative. **2** Indeed, so secure was the harmony which owed its beginning to the provisions of Romulus that they never came to bloodshed and mutual killing during 630 years, even though many great disputes concerning public affairs arose between the people and those in office, as is bound to happen in all cities, great and small.

2.51 *Hospitium*: the connections of Sextus Roscius

Cicero *In Defence of Sextus Roscius of Ameria* 5

In 80 BC Cicero, in his first criminal case, defended Roscius on a charge of parricide against the powerful members of Sulla's faction, notably Chrysogonus, one of Sulla's freedmen, who had Roscius' father entered on the proscription lists and bought his property (worth 6 million sesterces) for 2,000 sesterces; see docs. 11.24–5. *Hospitium* (the hospitable entertainment of those from outside Rome) was a hereditary relationship related to clientela in many ways; it was often exercised by Roman aristocrats over provincial families and communities. *Gratia* (obligation, gratitude) implied a favour done to others and the gratitude that this evinces; it also implies the influence that such a claim produces and the need to provide reciprocal services in return. When Roscius was proscribed he fled to Caecilia, daughter of Metellus Balearicus (cos. 123), who intervened on his behalf, and found Cicero to defend him: *Rosc. Am.* 27, 147, 149. Brunt 1988d: 396: under Sulla's dictatorship the Roscii left their old noble patrons for Chrysogonus (*Rosc. Am.* 106); on such hereditary hosts, see Wiseman 1971: 33–5; cf. D'Arms 1984.

Sextus Roscius, this man's father, was a citizen of the municipium of Ameria, and by his ancestry, noble birth, and wealth was easily the most prominent man, not only of his town, but also of the neighbourhood, while his reputation was enhanced by the esteem with which he was regarded by men of the highest rank and his relations of hospitality with them. For he was not only in a relation of hospitality with the Metelli, Servilii and Scipiones, but also enjoyed private intimacy and social intercourse with these families, whom, as is right, I mention with the respect due to their high character and consequence.

Well, of all these advantages, this is the only one he left to his son: for brigandly members of his family (Titus Roscius Capito and Magnus) have seized and possess his patrimony, while the reputation and life of the innocent son are being defended by the guests and friends of his father.

2.52 Cicero and ties of hospitality

Cicero *Letters to his Friends* 13.34

An example of one of Cicero's letters of recommendation (46 BC) on the basis of family ties of hospitality and his connections with Sicily; he wrote several to Acilius. Cicero had been quaestor of Lilybaeum in Sicily in 75 BC, and the Sicilians were his clients.

Cicero to Acilius, proconsul (in Sicily), greetings.
I am bound by ties of hospitality dating back to his grandfather's time with Lyso, son of Lyso, of Lilybaeum, who pays me great respect and whom I have found worthy of both his father and grandfather — for he comes from a very noble family. Accordingly, I commend him to you with more than ordinary urgency, as well as his household; and I beg of you very earnestly to ensure that he realises that my recommendation has been of the greatest assistance in your eyes, as well as a great compliment to him.

2.53 Cicero puts the hard word on Valerius Orca

Cicero *Letters to his Friends* 13.4.1, 4

Cicero is writing in autumn 45 BC to Valerius Orca, one of the commissioners responsible for carrying out Caesar's land grants to his veterans. Cicero had protected the people of Volaterrae in Etruria against the Rullan and Flavian land laws (docs 12.13, 34).

Marcus Tullius Cicero warmly greets Quintus Valerius Orca, son of Quintus, propraetorian legate.
1 I have the closest possible connection with the townsmen of Volaterrae. Having received great kindness from me, they have shown their gratitude in return most abundantly; for they have never been found wanting either in my times in office or in my troubles . . .
4 Were circumstances to give me at the present time power along the lines of the ability I used to have to protect the people of Volaterrae, as I have always looked after my own people, there is no act of service, no effort I would omit to be of service to them. But, as I am sure that my influence is no less with you at the present time than I have always possessed with everyone, I ask you in the name of our very close connection and our equal and mutual goodwill towards each other that you serve the people of Volaterrae in such a way that they think that the man who has been placed, as if by some divine plan, in charge of the land commission, is the very man on whom above all others I — their continual protector — am able to exert the greatest possible influence.

2.54 Cicero as patron of his home town

Cicero *Letters to his Friends* 13.11

Cicero is here writing in Rome some time in 46 to Marcus Junius Brutus as governor of Cisalpine Gaul. Arpinum, Cicero's home town, owned land in Gaul which paid rent to the township: cf. *Fam*.13.7 for a similar case (Atella in Campania). In a further letter (13.12) Cicero particularly recommends Q. Fufidius to Brutus' attention. Cicero, of course, has an axe to grind in proving his commitment to his home town: Arpinum was run by three aediles (one of whom managed the finances: *Att.* 15.15.1) and Cicero hopes, through his services to the community, to ensure the election as aediles of his son, nephew and friend.

1 Since I have always noticed that you are extremely careful to stay informed of all my concerns, I therefore have no doubt that you know not only which municipality I come from, but also how diligently I make it my habit to look after the interests of my fellow-townsmen, the inhabitants of Arpinum. Now, indeed, all their revenues and all their means of providing for the worship of the gods and for repairing their sacred dwellings and public buildings are comprised in the rents for the lands they hold in the province of Gaul. To inspect these, and to arrange for the payment of the money owed by the tenants and to investigate and administer the whole business, we have sent a commission of Roman equites, Quintus Fufidius, son of Quintus Fufidius, Marcus Faucius, son of Marcus, and Quintus Mamercus, son of Quintus.

2 I beg you more urgently than usual, in view of our close connection, to concern yourself with this matter and do what you can to see that the town's business is arranged as suitably and quickly as possible, and to treat the men themselves, whose names I have given you, with all possible courtesy and generosity in accordance with your natural disposition. **3** You will find that you have added some excellent men to your close connections and bound a most grateful municipality under obligation to you; indeed, I shall be even more grateful to you, as I have always been accustomed to look after the interests of my fellow-townsmen, and this year my attention and services are particularly appropriate because, in order to regulate the town's affairs, I have put my son up for aedile this year, as well as my brother's son and Marcus Caesius, a very intimate friend of mine — for aediles are the only magistrates we are in the habit of electing in our municipality; you will have done honour to them, and especially to me, if the affairs of the municipality are well managed thanks to your zeal and diligence — and this is what I earnestly ask you again and again to do.

2.55 Pompey as patron of the Eastern provinces

Plutarch *Life of Pompey* 45.1–5

This passage describes Pompey's triumph over Mithridates and the East in September 61 (doc. 12.28). All his conquests came into his clientela; note the oath supposedly sworn by Drusus' Italian supporters which would have given him unrivalled clientela in Italy: doc. 10.8.

1 The time was insufficient for the extent of Pompey's triumph, even though it was spread over two separate days, and many of the items prepared for it had to be left out of the spectacle — enough to dignify and adorn another triumph entirely. **2** The nations over which he was triumphing were displayed on posters which went in front. These were: Pontus, Armenia, Paphlagonia, Cappadocia, Media, Colchis, Iberia, Albania, Syria, Cilicia, Mesopotamia, Phoenicia and Palestine, Judaea, Arabia, and the entire piratical menace which had been overthrown by sea and on land. **3** In these campaigns, according to the posters, he had captured no less than 1,000 forts, nearly 900 cities, and 800 pirate ships, while founding 39 cities. **4** In addition to all this, the posters stated that while the public revenue from tax had been 50,000,000 drachmas, they were receiving from his acquisitions for Rome 85,000,000, and that he was bringing the public treasury 20,000 talents in coins and vessels of silver and gold, apart from what had been given to his soldiers, of which he who received the least share had 1,500 drachmas. **5** The prisoners led in the triumph were, apart from the pirate chiefs, the son of Tigranes of Armenia, with his wife and daughter, Zosime a wife of King Tigranes himself, Aristobulus, king of the Jews, a sister and five children of Mithridates . . .

2.56 Hispalis in Spain rebuked for ingratitude

[Caesar] *Spanish War* 42.1–3

Braund 1989: esp. 138–44. To Caesar's anger, Hispalis in Further Spain had supported the Pompeian forces in the civil war rather than Caesar's own, though Caesar had governed Further Spain as quaestor (69) and as propraetor (61). Cf. Plut. *Caes.* 5, 11–12, Suet *Jul.* 7–8, 18 for Caesar's service in Spain. Metellus Pius (cos. 80) presumably imposed taxes on Spain following the end of the rebellion of Sertorius (docs 12.2–3).

1 Caesar returned to Hispalis and on the following day summoned an assembly (contio) and reminded them of the following points: that at the start of his quaestorship he had made that province above all other provinces his own special concern, and had lavished on it whatever benefits were in his power at that time; **2** that subsequently, after acquiring the rank of praetor, he had requested the senate to rescind the taxes which Metellus had imposed and had freed the province from having to pay that money; that having once adopted the role of their patron he had undertaken its defence by facilitating the introduction of numerous deputations into the senate, as well as representing it in public and private legal actions through which he had incurred the enmity of many; **3** that similarly, during his consulship, he had in his absence granted the province all benefits that were in his power — and he was well aware that, in the current war and in the period preceding it, they were both forgetful of all these benefits and ungrateful for them towards both himself and the Roman people.

2.57 Caesar as patron of Roman political figures, 56 BC

Plutarch *Life of Pompey* 51.1–5

Sulla had raised the senate's numbers to 600; consuls and proconsuls each had 12 lictors carrying the fasces before them, praetors and propraetors (probably) six. Caesar here has a third of the senate and between 10 and 20 current magistrates and promagistrates requesting his patronage; cf. Suet. *Jul.* 24; docs 12.68–9.

1 In the meantime, his Gallic wars raised Caesar to eminence . . . . **3** By sending back to Rome gold and silver and the other booty and the rest of the wealth gained from his many wars, and enticing people with bribes and assisting with the expenses of aediles and praetors and consuls and their wives, he won the support of many. **4** Consequently, when he crossed the Alps and wintered at Luca, a great crowd of ordinary men and women collected there in haste, while 200 men of senatorial rank, among whom were Pompey and Crassus, and 120 fasces of proconsuls and praetors were to be seen at Caesar's door. **5** He satisfied all the rest with hopes and money, and sent them away; but between himself, Pompey and Crassus the following agreement was made . . .

LITIGATION AS A WAY OF LIFE

The Romans saw the XII Tables as the beginning of their legal history, though laws were attributed to the kings, such as Romulus: the XII Tables, though increasingly obsolete, were not superseded until the sixth century AD. Magistrates with imperium were the administrators of criminal justice. Trials could take place before the people or in court (*quaestio*; plural: *quaestiones*): perpetual quaestiones were set up in the second and first centuries. Quaestiones were under the direction of a presiding magistrate, with the prosecutor responsible for the production of evidence and the verdict dependent on the jury. Various forms of death penalty existed at the time of the XII Tables, but in practice in the later Republic the penalty could be avoided by voluntary exile prior to sentence. The key legal figure in Rome was the urban praetor, who at the beginning of his term of office published an edict setting out the way he intended to exercise his jurisdiction.

Court cases in Rome were a public spectacle, taking place in the forum in the open air, and could be viewed by any interested spectators: Crook 1967: 33–4. Appearance as prosecutor or defence counsel was an important way of bringing oneself and one's skills to public notice and acquiring a significant clientela: Crassus, for example, was always prepared to take on cases declined by others: Plut. *Crass*. 3.4 (cf. docs 12.40, 12.20). Counsel were not allowed to accept fees, although they could receive gifts for services rendered; for a study of the machinery of the law, see Crook 1967: 68–97; cf. Gruen 1968; Cloud 1994.

2.58 Prosecution: Roman 'pietas' at work

Plutarch *Life of Cato the Elder* 15.3–5

Cato the Elder was extremely litigious and known for a number of prosecutions during his career: particular targets were Scipio Africanus and his brother Lucius Cornelius Scipio Asiagenus (Plut. *Cato Mai*. 3.5–7; Scullard 1973: 290–303; Astin 1978: 60–3). According to Plutarch, Cato was himself prosecuted on numerous occasions. Enmities (inimicitiae) could be hereditary as were friendships (amicitiae). For litigation as a manifestation of inimicitiae in Roman society, see Epstein 1987: esp. 90–129; Gruen 1968; Brunt 1988c: 366–78.

3 It is said that a certain young man, who had got a verdict of loss of citizen rights against an enemy of his dead father, was passing through the forum on the conclusion of the case, when Cato met him and greeted him with the words: 'These are the offerings we should make to our parents — not lambs or kids, but the tears of their enemies and their condemnation.' **4** However, in his political life he was himself not unscathed, but, wherever he gave his enemies any handle, he was always being prosecuted and in danger of conviction. He is said to have defended nearly 50 cases, the last one when he was 86 years of age . . . **5** And even this one was not the end of his conflicts in the courts, as four years later, when he was 90, he brought a case against Servius Galba.

2.59 Prosecution as a good career move for a young man

Plutarch *Life of Lucullus* 1.1–3

Lucullus' grandfather, another Lucius Licinius Lucullus, had been consul in 151 and governor in Nearer Spain (see doc. 5.47); Lucullus was the nephew of Q. Caecilius Metellus Numidicus (docs 9.6–7). Gaius Servilius had succeeded Lucullus' father as governor of Sicily in 102 and his cousin Servilius 'the augur' brought a charge of extortion against the elder Lucullus for failing to put down the Second Sicilian slave war. Lucullus and his brother Marcus brought a charge against this Servilius, apparently of misappropriating public funds: Keaveney 1992: 4–7. Caesar, too, as a young man was noted for his prosecution of Cornelius Dolabella in 77 for extortion (Suet. *Jul*. 4.1); for the importance of oratorical skill in a young man's career, see Eyben 1993: 72–80.

1 In the case of Lucullus, his grandfather had been consul, and his uncle on his mother's side was Metellus, surnamed Numidicus. But, with regard to his parents, his father had been convicted of fraud and his mother, Caecilia, had a bad reputation as a woman of no discretion in her lifestyle. **2** Lucullus himself, while still a young man, before he had stood for any office or entered public life, made it his first task to prosecute his father's accuser, Servilius the Augur, whom he caught wronging the state. The Romans considered this a splendid achievement, and the case was talked of by everyone, like a great deed of prowess. **3** For, in fact, they thought the business of prosecution, in general and without special excuse, not a sordid action, but were very keen to see their young men clinging to wrong-doers like well-bred dogs to wild beasts. But great animosity was stirred up by the case, so that some people were even wounded and killed, and Servilius got off.

2.60 Cicero on prosecution and defence

Cicero *On Duties* 2.49–51

Cicero is here writing on moral duties to his son, Marcus. Lucius Licinius Crassus, the great orator (cos. 95), had at the age of 21 years successfully prosecuted Gaius Papirius Carbo, who committed suicide in 119 to escape condemnation: Cic. *Brut*. 158.

49 But while there are many kinds of occasion that require eloquence, and many young men in our Republic have won praise in speaking before the jurors, the people and the senate, it is the speeches in the courts which win the greatest admiration. Speeches in the courts fall into two categories. They are divided into speeches for the prosecution and for the defence; while, of these two, taking the side of the defence is the more praiseworthy, that for the prosecution has also frequently been considered honourable. A short while back I spoke of (Lucius Licinius) Crassus; Marcus Antonius (cos. 99), when a young man, had the same success. It was also a prosecution that brought the eloquence of Publius Sulpicius (tr. pl. 88) to public notice, when he brought an action against that seditious and dangerous citizen Gaius Norbanus (tr. pl. 103). **50** But this should not be done often, and only then for the sake of the state, as in the case of those I have mentioned, or to avenge wrongs, as in the case of the two Luculli, or to protect clients, as I did on behalf of the Sicilians, or as Julius did in prosecuting Albucius on behalf of the Sardinians. The diligence of Lucius Fufius in prosecuting Manius Aquillius (cos. 101) is also well-known. Prosecution may be undertaken, then, once or at any rate not often. But if it should have to be undertaken more often, it should be done as a service to the state, for taking vengeance on the state's enemies is not to be considered reprehensible; even then, however, there should be a limit. For it seems the characteristic of a hard-hearted man, or rather of one hardly human, to bring capital charges against many people. It is not only dangerous for the prosecutor himself, but damaging to his reputation to allow himself to be called a prosecutor; that happened to Marcus Brutus, who was born of the highest family, and the son of that Brutus who was one of the foremost authorities in civil law.

51 Furthermore, this rule of responsibility should be carefully observed, that you should never bring a capital charge against anyone who might be innocent; for there is no way one can do that without becoming a criminal. For what is so inhuman as to turn the eloquence given by nature for the safety and protection of mankind to the destruction and ruin of good men? Nevertheless, while we have to avoid this, we need have no scruples about defending a guilty person, as long as he is not notoriously wicked or impious; for the people expect it, custom allows it, even humanity accepts it. It is always the job of the judge in a trial to find the truth, and that of the defending counsel some-times to put forward an approximation to the truth, even if not entirely true; I would not dare to write this, especially when writing about philosophy, were it not also the view of Panaetius, that strictest of Stoics. Then, too, acting for the defence particularly wins one fame and gratitude, and the more so if you should happen to assist one who appears to be oppressed and harassed through the influence of someone in power, as I have done on a number of occasions, for example, when in my youth I defended Sextus Roscius of Ameria against the power of the tyrannical Lucius (Cornelius) Sulla — the speech, as you know, has been published.

THE IMPORTANCE OF ORATORY

Public speaking was an extremely important skill in Rome, whether to sway the assembly, the senate, or the jury (and listening public) in a law-court. Latin rhetoric was firmly based on Greek models and aristocratic Romans trained under Greek teachers and in the Greek language, upper-class Romans being fluent in Greek as well as Latin. Teachers of rhetoric are first mentioned in Rome in the second century BC, with instructional works in Latin, such as the *Rhetorica ad Herennium* and Cicero's *de inventione*, the stock early expositions of rhetorical practices, appearing in the 80s. On the importance of oratory and its place in the Roman educational system: see Clark 1957; Kennedy 1972; Eyben 1993: 128–59; Ulrichs 1994; Clarke 1996; Fantham 1997; Kirby 1997; Rawson 2003: 147–53.

2.61 An 'un-Roman' practice

Suetonius *On Rhetoricians* 1

The *senatus consultum* and edict of the censors on Latin philosophers and rhetoricians in 161 and 92 BC are given in doc. 5.57. Children probably transferred from their grammaticus (who taught language and poetry) to their rhetor, who taught rhetoric, at the age of 15 years. Preliminary exercises were followed by the teaching of the art of declamation through the practice of suasoriae (the presentation of historical or imaginary cases) and controversiae (court cases) and such stock exercises were practised in schools of rhetoric, in which the pupils were assigned a side of the case.

Gradually rhetoric itself came to appear useful and respectable, and many devoted themselves to it both in order to defend themselves and to acquire a fine reputation. Cicero used to declaim in both Greek and Latin up to the time of his praetorship, and in Latin even when comparatively elderly, and that in company with the future consuls Hirtius and Pansa (cos. 43 BC), whom he used to call his pupils and 'great big boys'. Some historians state that Gnaeus Pompey (Magnus) resumed the practice of declaiming just before the civil war to more easily argue against Gaius Curio, a very ready-witted young man who was taking up Caesar's cause; and that Mark Antony, and Augustus too, did not give it up even during the war at Mutina . . . Moreover many of the orators even published their declamations. As a result great enthusiasm was generally aroused and there was a huge influx of practitioners and teachers who prospered to such an extent that some of them advanced from the lowest status to senatorial rank and the highest offices.

But they did not all share the same teaching method and individuals varied in their practice, since each one trained his pupils in different ways. For they would expound speeches in detail with regard to their figures of speech, incidents and illustrations, now in one way and now in another, and compose narrations sometimes in a brief and summarised form, at other times with greater detail and more expansively; sometimes they would translate Greek works and praise or criticise illustrious men; they would demonstrate that some practices in everyday life were useful and essential, others dangerous and redundant; frequently they defended or attacked the credibility of myths, an exercise which the Greeks call 'destructive' and 'constructive' criticism; finally all these became obsolete, being succeeded by the debate (*controversia*).

2.62 Cicero's early career

Cicero *Brutus* 305–11, 314–16, 318–19

The *Brutus* was written in early 46 BC, before the battle of Thapsus, to justify Cicero's approach to oratory, which was now being questioned by the younger generation. This work is structured as a dialogue with Atticus and Brutus. Cicero tells us that nearly every day he heard the top speakers in the popular assemblies, whom he names as Quintus Varius (tr. pl. 90 BC), Publius Sulpicius Rufus (tr. pl. 88), Quintus Catulus (cos. 102), Marcus Antonius (cos. 99), and Gaius Julius Caesar Strabo (aed. 90). **314**: of course one of the main reasons for Cicero's leaving Rome after his defence of Roscius was in order to avoid reprisals from Sulla and Chrysogonus: doc. 11.25; for Apollonius Molo, see doc. 5.57.

305 The first disappointment inflicted on my passion for listening struck me when Cotta was exiled. I frequently listened to those who were left, and continued to write and read and declaim daily with intense diligence, but was not satisfied with just oratorical exercises. Then, in the following year, Quintus Varius went into exile, condemned by his own law; **306** I, however, for the study of civil law, spent much of my time with Quintus (Mucius) Scaevola, son of Quintus, who, although he was not given to teaching anyone, taught those who desired to hear him in his replies to those who consulted him.

The next year was that of the consulship of Sulla and Pompeius (88 BC). Publius Sulpicius was then tribune and I was able to get to know his whole style of speaking inside out as he addressed the popular assemblies on a daily basis; at that same time, when Philo, then head of the Academy, had fled from his home, along with the most reputable Athenians, because of the Mithridatic War and had come to Rome, I was ardently aroused to the study of philosophy and devoted myself to his wonderful teaching, in which I lingered the more attentively, not only because the variety and great magnitude of that subject captured me with its delight, but because it then seemed as if the whole justice system had disappeared for all time. **307** In that year Sulpicius had been killed and in the next year three orators of three different periods were most cruelly slain: Quintus Catulus, Marcus Antonius and Gaius Julius. In that same year too I devoted my time to study at Rome with Molo of Rhodes, a top-ranking advocate and teacher.

308 For a period of about three years . . .**309** I spent my nights and days in a study of all kinds of learning. I associated with Diodotus the Stoic, who made his home with me, and resided with me until a short time ago when he died at my house. By him, along with other subjects, I was diligently trained in dialectic, which can be thought of as a contracted or compressed form of eloquence . . . But while I devoted myself to his teaching and to the many varied arts he taught, I made sure that no day was spent without rhetorical exercises. **310** I prepared and gave declamations — as they are now called — often with Marcus Piso and Quintus Pompeius, or indeed with anyone, daily, and I used to do this often in Latin, but more frequently in Greek, both because Greek rhetoric, providing more opportunities for stylistic ornamentation, produced the habit of speaking similarly in Latin, and because the most outstanding teachers, being Greek, were unable to correct or teach me unless I spoke in Greek . . .

311 It was now for the first time that I began to take on both civil and criminal cases, my aim being not to learn in the forum, as most do, but as far as possible to come to the forum already trained. At the same time, I devoted my time to studying with Molo; for when Sulla was dictator Molo came as an envoy to Rome concerning the payments to the Rhodians. In this way, my first criminal case in defence of Sextus Roscius received such commendation that there was no case that appeared to be unworthy of my advocacy. There then followed a series of many others which I presented, carefully worked on as if laboured at through the midnight hours . . .

314 Since I had come to the conclusion that, with relaxation and improved control of my voice and an alteration in my style of speaking, I would be able to avoid risk to my health and deliver speeches with more moderation, the purpose of my leaving for Asia Minor was to change my habit of speaking. And so I left Rome, after having been engaged in cases for two years with my name already well-known in the forum. **315** When I arrived at Athens, I spent six months with Antiochus, the most celebrated and skilful philosopher of the old Academy, and I again took up the study of philosophy, in which I had engaged from my early youth and made increasing strides in and never completely abandoned, with the best guide and teacher. At the same time, however, I diligently continued with the practice of rhetoric, under the supervision of Demetrius the Syrian, a teacher of speaking of long-standing and not without reputation. Afterwards I travelled through the whole of Asia Minor, associating with the best orators there, who were generous in giving me the chance to practise with them; of these the leader was Menippus of Stratonicea, in my view the most eloquent man in all Asia at that time . . . **316** The person who associated with me most constantly was Dionysius of Magnesia; there were also Aeschylus of Cnidus and Xenocles of Adramattium. At that time these men were considered as the leading teachers of rhetoric in Asia. Not satisfied with these, I came to Rhodes and attached myself to Molo, whom I had heard in Rome, as he was an advocate in actual cases and an outstanding composer of speeches, as well as extremely skilful in perceiving and correcting mistakes and in his system of instruction and training. He dedicated his time to restraining, if it could be done, what was redundant and excessive in my style, with its youthful rashness and lack of control, and preventing it, as it were, from overflowing its banks. And so I returned two years later, not only with more training but almost transformed — my voice had ceased to be over-strained, my language had come off the boil, and my lungs had gained strength and my body weight. . . .

318 Accordingly, in the year after I returned from Asia (76 BC), I engaged in some notable cases, when I was standing for the quaestorship, Cotta for the consulship and Hortensius for the aedileship. In the meantime, the next year saw me as quaestor in Sicily, Cotta was sent to Gaul after his consulship, and Hortensius remained the leading advocate both in reality and reputation. When, however, a year later, I returned from Sicily, it was now clear that whatever I had in me was fully developed and had reached a certain maturity. I may seem to be saying too much about myself, especially as I am saying it myself; but the aim of all this part of my talk is for you to perceive not my talent or eloquence, which is far from my purpose, but my hard work and industry. **319** After, therefore, I had been involved in numerous cases with leading advocates for nearly five years, I then, as aedile-elect, engaged in a mighty struggle with Hortensius, the consul-elect, in defence of the province of Sicily (the prosecution of Verres in 70 BC).

2.63 Caesar as a public speaker

Suetonius *Life of the Deified Julius* 55.1–2

Cicero's letters to Cornelius Nepos were published in a collection of at least two books (Macrob. 2.1.14). For Gaius Gracchus' style of oratory, see docs 8.26–7.

1 In eloquence and military skill Caesar either equalled or surpassed the reputations of the most outstanding exponents. After his prosecution of Dolabella he was counted without hesitation amongst the foremost advocates. Certainly, Cicero, in his enumeration of orators in his *Brutus*, confessed that he had never seen anyone to whom Caesar should yield precedence, and describes his style of speaking as elegant and clear, even dignified and in a sense noble. He also wrote this to Cornelius Nepos about Caesar, **2** 'Well? What orator would you rank before him of those who have concentrated on nothing else? Is there anyone who makes such witty comments or so many of them? Or who uses such attractive and apposite vocabulary?' Caesar seems to have imitated his style, at any rate as a youth, on that of Caesar Strabo (Gaius Julius Caesar Strabo, aed. 90), some of whose speech *In Defence of the Sardinians* he borrowed word for word for use in one of his own trial orations. It is said that he pitched his voice high in speaking, and used impassioned movements and gestures which were not without charm.

2.64 The education of Marcus Tullius Cicero junior

Cicero Letters to his Friends 16.21.3, 5

In this, one of his many letters to Tiro, his father's freedman, the young Marcus in 44 BC, at the age of 21 or 22, discusses his education at Athens. His father had accused him of being extravagant and idle. Born in 65 BC, Marcus had gone to Cilicia with his father. A Pompeian, he was pardoned by Octavian and, despite his idleness as a young man (Pliny *Nat. Hist.* 14.147 accuses him of over-indulgence in alcohol) became consul in 30 BC and governor of Syria and Asia.

3 I should tell you that my close attachment to Cratippus (a philosopher of Mitylene) is not so much that of a pupil as that of a son. For not only do I enjoy attending his lectures, but I really find him extremely agreeable. I spend whole days with him, and often part of the night. I even beg him to dine with me as often as he can . . . **5** Besides this I have begun practising declamation in Greek with Cassius; but I like practising in Latin with Bruttius. I have as daily, intimate companions the people whom Cratippus brought with him from Mitylene, men of learning of whom he highly approves.

'BREAD AND CIRCUSES'

The ludi ('games') were intrinsic to Roman culture. Beast hunts (venationes) involving either the killing of animals by bestiarii, or of animals by other animals, are first heard at Rome in 186 BC as part of ludi vowed by M. Fulvius Nobilior during the Aetolian war: a hunt of lions and panthers was staged (Livy 39.22.2). In 169 BC venationes (involving bears, elephants and 'African animals') were put on by the aediles as part of the ludi circenses (Livy 44.18.8), and this became a regular annual practice; in 146 for the first time human beings were thrown to the beasts at Rome: Scipio Aemilianus punished non-Roman deserters from his army in this way (Val. Max. 2.7.13; cf. Livy *Per.* 51); in 167 Aemilius Paullus had non-Roman deserters from his army crushed to death by elephants in the games celebrated abroad after he defeated Perseus (Val. Max. 2.7.14). Cicero's difficulties in procuring panthers (doc. 2.72) show the importance of procuring exotic animals for the ludi, and the expansion of the Roman empire allowed for venationes involving elephants and African beasts, thus demonstrating the scope of Rome's power.

For criticism of lavish expenditure on public banquets, doles of meat, gladiatorial shows, magnificent games and wild-beast fights, see Cic. *Off.* 2.55–8; Cicero admits that even in the 'good old times' such expenditure was expected of an aedile, listing some of the more spectacular (e.g., Pompey's in his second consulship). Cic. *Mur.* 72; 'when was there ever a time when there was not the desire — whether from ambition or generosity — to provide seats in the circus or at the games for friends and fellow-tribesmen?'; cf. doc. 2.37; Nicolet 1980: 361–73; Cic. *Leg. Agr.* 2.71 for the people's enjoyment of games.

There were three types of ludi: the ludi circenses (doc. 2.65), the ludi scaenici (which involved theatrical performances: 2.68–70), and the combatant ludi, involving gladiators and wild beast displays (docs 2.72–4). Of the ludi scaenici, the Ludi Megalenses established in 191 honoured the arrival of the Magna Mater in Rome (docs 3.59–61). There were 57 days devoted to ludi by the end of the Republic, and they were held on fixed dates.

Gladiatorial contests (*munera*) are first mentioned in the third century BC and continued to grow in popularity, being always associated with funerals. They were first held in Rome in 264 BC by two brothers to honour their dead father (Marcus Junius Brutus Pera); three pairs of gladiators were involved (Val. Max. 2.4.7); this association of gladiatorial contests with funerals continued throughout the Republic and prior to Caesar's games in 46, gladiatorial shows under the Republic were restricted to funeral games, not public performances (docs 2.73–4). The number of gladiators soon escalated, and aristocratic rivalry must quickly have developed over the munera: from three pairs in 264, to 20 pairs at a funeral in 216, to 120 at a funeral in 183 accompanied by a huge feast, with banqueting tables set up through the entire forum (Livy 23.30.15, 39.46.3–4); Livy's history breaks off in 167 BC otherwise the proliferation could be traced over the next century to 65 BC when Caesar exhibited 320 pairs (see doc. 2.71). Already when Polybius wrote (31.28.6), a good gladiatorial exhibition cost 30 talents, so the aristocrats were investing large amounts of capital in these gladiatorial contests and would clearly look for remuneration in terms of popularity and social status.

Such munera usually took place in the forum, where the funeral procession had taken place and the eulogy been delivered, with the spectators on temporary wooden seating. There was opposition to the construction of theatres at Rome on the grounds that it would encourage idleness. C. Cassius Longinus and M. Valerius Messalla, censors of 154, began the construction of a permanent stone theatre at the Lupercal but were forced to dismantle it, when nearly completed, by Scipio Nasica who argued that it would damage public morals (App. *BC* 1.28; Livy *Per.* 48) and a *senatus consultum* banned seating at the ludi altogether in Rome and for a mile out of the city (Gruen 1992: 205–10, 221–2 argues this to have been a reassertion of aristocratic control over the theatre). The first permanent theatre was that of Pompey (docs 2.68–9) and the first permanent amphitheatre the wooden one of C. Trebonius Curio in 53 BC, with the first stone amphitheatre built in the Campus Martius in 29 BC. A stone amphitheatre had been built at Pompeii, however, by the Sullan colonists there in the 70s BC (*CIL* X.852; *ILS* 5627). For Republican amphitheatres: Sear 1989: 23–4; Welch 1991, 1994; Futrell 1997: 33–44; Bomgardner 2000: 32–60; cf. Coleman 1996; Holleran 2003. Temporary theatres could be magnificent: that of Marcus Aemilius Scaurus as aedile in 58, was three storeys high, the first with marble veneer, and supposedly held 80,000 spectators and 3,000 bronze statues: Pliny *Nat. Hist.* 36.113–15.

Cicero *Sest.* 106 notes that the opinion of the Roman people can be heard in three places: at a contio, in the comitium, and at ludi and gladiatorial contests (gladiatores). At ludi and gladiatorial shows politicians might be cheered or hissed: at one in 57 BC the spectators gave the tribune P. Sestius, working for Cicero's recall, thunderous applause (*Sest.* 124–7; cf. *Piso* 65). Cicero in 61 BC refers to himself receiving acclamations at such shows (*Att.* 1.16.11; cf. *Mur.* 38). In 59 the triumvirs were hissed at the 'gladiatores', and at the ludi Apollinares an actor attacked Pompey with the line, 'To our misery you are Great (magnus)' (*Att.* 2.19.3; doc. 12.50). The magnificent ludi and plays put on by L. Licinius Murena helped him win the consulship for 62 BC (Cic. *Mur.* 38).

For ludi, Wiedemann 1992: 1–3; Balsdon 1960; Scullard 1981: 41, 221; Morgan 1990; for the origins of gladiatorial competitions, whether Etruscan or Campanian, see Mouratidis 1996; Futrell 1997: 11–19; for the circus Maximus and chariot racing, see Humphrey 1986: esp. chap. 3; for plebeian culture, Horsfall 2003.

2.65 The ludi magni (Great Games)

Dionysius of Halicarnassus *Roman Antiquities* 7.72.1–73.4

Cf. Dion. Hal. 3.68. Livy 2.36 and Dion. 7.73.5 record the repeating of the ludi magni (Great Games, or Roman Games: Livy 1.35.8) in 491 BC due to the anger of the gods; Dionysius describes here the procession prior to these ludi in the Circus Maximus. The ludi magni were held in September, and were ludi circenses involving chariot racing, held in the Circus Maximus in the valley between the Palatine and Aventine (doc. 2.66).

72.1 Before starting the games, the most important magistrates conducted a procession in honour of the gods from the Capitol through the Forum to the Circus Maximus. The leaders of the procession were, first, their sons who were approaching manhood and of an age to take part in this ceremony, riding on horseback if their fathers had the property qualifications of equites, while those who would serve in the infantry went on foot; the former were in squadrons and troops, and the latter in divisions and companies, as if they were going to school; this was to show strangers the number and beauty of the state's youths who were near manhood. **2** They were followed by charioteers, some of whom drove four horses abreast, some pairs, and others rode unyoked horses; they were followed by the contestants in both the light and the heavy games, their bodies completely naked except for the covering around their waists . . . **5** The contestants were followed by numerous groups of dancers divided into three sections, the first of men, the second of youths, and the third of boys, and these were accompanied by flute-players, who played ancient, short flutes, as happens even to this day, and by lyre-players, who plucked ivory, seven-stringed lyres and instruments called *barbita*. The Greeks have stopped using these in my time, though their use was traditional, but they are still preserved by the Romans in all their ancient sacrificial ceremonies. **6** The dancers wore scarlet tunics girt with bronze belts with swords hanging at their sides, and carried shorter than average spears; the men also had bronze helmets adorned with conspicuous crests and plumes. Each group was led by one man who gave the others the figures of the dance and took the lead in expressing the warlike and rapid movements, usually in the proceleusmatic (i.e., four short syllables) rhythms . . . **10** After the groups of armed dancers, other groups of Satyric players took part in the procession enacting the Greek dance called *sicinnis*. The dress of those who represented Sileni consisted of fleecy tunics, which some people call *chortaioi*, and coverings of all sorts of flowers; and those dressed as satyrs had loin-cloths and goatskins, and manes that stood upright on their heads, with other similar things. These mocked and mimicked the serious movements of the others, turning them into more ridiculous performances. . . .

13 After these dancers came a crowd of lyre-players and numerous flute-players, and after them the persons carrying the censers in which perfumes and frankincense were burned along the whole route, as well as the men who carried the vessels made of silver and gold, both those sacred to the gods and those belonging to the state. Last of all in the procession came the images of the gods, borne on men's shoulders, showing the same likenesses as those made by the Greeks, and the same dress, symbols, and gifts which they are traditionally shown as inventing and bestowing on mankind: not only images of Jupiter, Juno, Minerva, Neptune and the rest whom the Greeks count among the twelve gods, but also of those still more ancient from whom, in legend, the twelve were sprung, namely Saturn, Ops, Themis, Latona, the Fates, Mnemosyne, and all the rest . . .

73.1 It now remains for me to describe briefly the games which the Romans performed after the procession. First was the race of four-horse chariots, two-horse chariots, and of unyoked horses . . . **3** After the chariot races were finished, those who contended in their own persons came on, the runners, wrestlers and boxers . . . **4** And, in the intervals between the contests, they observed a practice which was extremely Greek and the best of all customs, that of awarding crowns and proclaiming the honours with which they honoured their benefactors, just as was done at Athens during the festivals of Dionysus, and displaying to all who had assembled for the spectacle the booty they had taken in war.

2.66 The Circus Maximus, then and now

Dionysius of Halicarnassus *Roman Antiquities* 3.68.1–4

Cf. Livy 1.35.8–9. Traditionally the site of the Circus Maximus was established by Romulus, with stands for viewing built under the Tarquinii; the Tarquinius of this document is Tarquinius Priscus, the fifth king, 616–579. In 174 BC the *ova*, seven large wooden eggs, were set up, which were used to count the laps. Down the centre of the Circus Maximus ran the spina, around which barrier the chariots drawn by four horses turned. Caesar as dictator made substantial improvements to the Circus Maximus. He increased the length of the circus to 620 metres: horses racing seven laps, keeping to the inner side of the spina, would have run over three kilometres. There were two long sides and a semi-circle at each end. Seating for some 150,000 spectators was provided by Caesar, which must indicate that huge audiences had been viewing the races throughout the last century of the Republic; by contrast, the later imperial Flavian amphitheatre (the Colosseum) seated about 50,000. The Circus Maximus and horse racing: Livy 1.35.8, 1.56.2, 8.20.1, 41.27.6; Suet. *Jul.* 39; Pliny *Nat. Hist.* 36.102 (7.186 for the circus factions; Cameron 1976); Dio 49.43.2; Richardson *Top. Dict.* 84–7; Humphrey 1986: 56–77; Hyland 1990: 201–30; Rawson 1991; Coleman 2000: 211–17. There was also the Circus Flaminius of c. 221 BC in the Campus Martius but it lacked permanent seating arrangements and races were rarely held there; the booty for triumphs was exhibited here before the triumph itself, and *contiones* held there. A stade is approximately 600 Greek feet, a plethron 100 feet.

1 Tarquinius also constructed the largest of the hippodromes (the Circus Maximus) which lies between the Aventine and Palatine and was the first to place covered seats around it on scaffolding (for till then the spectators stood), with beams supporting the wooden stands; and dividing the places among the 30 curiae he assigned a section to each, so that every spectator was seated in his proper place. **2** This work was also to become in time one of the most beautiful and spectacular constructions in the city. For the length of the hippodrome is three and a half stades, and the width four plethra; around it on the two longer sides and one of the shorter ones a canal to take water has been dug, ten feet in depth and width. Behind the canal, porticoes three storeys high are built. The lowest of these has stone seats as in the theatres, gradually rising one above the other, and the upper ones have wooden seats. **3** The two longer porticoes are united and joined together into one by means of the shorter one, which has a crescent shape, so that the three of them form a single portico like an amphitheatre eight stades around and capable of holding 150,000 people. The other shorter side is left uncovered and has vaulted starting-places for the horses all opened together by a single machine. **4** Around the outside of the hippodrome there is another one-storey portico which has shops in it and dwellings over them, and through this portico via every shop there are entrances and ascents for those coming to be spectators, so that nothing obstructs the entrance and departure of so many tens of thousands.

2.67 The aid of Castor and Pollux continues to be celebrated

Dionysius of Halicarnassus *Roman Antiquities* 6.13.4–5

At the battle at Lake Regillus (499 or 496), Castor and Pollux were said to have appeared to help the Romans against the Latins in response to a vow by the dictator A. Postumius (cf. Livy 2.19–20). A procession in their honour was still celebrated in Dionysius' time, as well as annual sacrifices. At the time, a temple, one of the first monumental structures close to the forum, was erected where their apparitions had been seen and an adjacent fountain given their name.

4 But above all this there is the procession, which is held after the sacrifice by those who have a public horse who, arrayed by tribes and centuries, all ride in ranks on horseback, as if they came from battle, crowned with olive branches and dressed in the purple togas with stripes of scarlet which they call trabeae. They start from a certain temple of Mars built outside the walls, and, going through the rest of the city and the forum, pass by the temple of Castor and Pollux, sometimes numbering even as many as 5,000, wearing whatever rewards for valour they have received from their commanders in battle, a wonderful sight and one worthy of the immensity of the Roman empire. **5** These are the things I have learnt to be both related and performed by the Romans as a result of the epiphany of Castor and Pollux.

2.68 The dedication of Pompey's theatre

Cicero *Letters to his Friends* 7.1.2–3

Cf. Cic. *Piso* 65; Plut. *Pomp.* 62.5. Cicero is writing to his friend Marcus Marius who has decided to miss the shows put on by Pompey to celebrate the dedication of his new theatre in 55 BC, during his second consulship; this was the first permanent stone building for theatrical performances built in Rome and probably seated some 10,000 (40,000 according to Pliny *Nat. Hist.* 35.115). Five hundred lions were killed during the shows celebrating the dedication. There was also a display of 20 elephants: these were hunted down by African tribesmen brought to Rome for that purpose; the elephants attempted to escape and broke through to the spectators' seats, causing panic (Pliny *Nat. Hist.* 8.20–1).

Cicero, while criticising the games, had clearly attended and seen the same spectacles on previous occasions. He saw ludi which others marvelled at as a waste of time and was glad to get away from them (*Fam.* 7.1.3; *Att.* 2.1.1; Kyle 1998: 4; Lintott 1999: 41), but provided panthers for a friend (doc. 2.72). His attitude is atypical and most Romans — as he himself notes (*Sest.* 124) — enjoyed the gladiatorial exhibitions and venationes.

Beast hunts (venationes) were particularly popular in the late Republic. Terracotta plaques show these taking place in the Circus Maximus; the date of these representations is disputed: they are perhaps late republican or Augustan. These plaques depict bestiarii (animal fighters) with shield and sword fighting lions: in one plaque, almost certainly of republican date, a lion bites a gladiator's arm, another attacks a second gladiator's head; the crowd is shown looking on (Humphrey 1986: 180–6). Bestiarii and venationes: Coleman 1990; Wiedemann 1992: 56–67; Futrell 1997: 24–9; Beacham 1999: 11–13; Bomgardner 2000: 34–5. Pompey's theatre: Nash 2.423–8; Richardson *Top. Dict.* 383–5; Coleman 2000: 221–3.

2 To be sure, the games (should you want to know) were most splendid, but certainly not to your taste . . . They did not even have the charms which more modest games usually have. The sight of such a sumptuous production destroyed all enjoyment; I am sure you can endure having missed it with equanimity. What enjoyment is there in 600 mules in *Clytemnestra* or 3,000 mixing-bowls in the *Trojan Horse*, or a variety of infantry and cavalry equipment in some battle or other? These things which won the admiration of the common people would have brought you no enjoyment . . . **3** Or should I imagine that you regret missing the athletes, after scorning gladiators? Actually Pompey himself admits that he had wasted his time and money on them. That leaves the wild animal hunts, two a day for five days — magnificent, no one can deny it! But what pleasure can a civilised man get out of either a helpless man being torn to pieces by a powerful animal, or a magnificent animal being stabbed through with a hunting spear? Even if these were worth seeing, you have seen them often before, and we spectators saw nothing new. The last day was for the elephants. The mob showed great amazement, but no enjoyment; in fact, there was a certain sympathy, a feeling that the monsters had some kind of affinity with humans.

2.69 Criticism of Pompey's theatre

Tacitus *Annals* 14.20–1

Nero in AD 60 instituted four-yearly games at Rome on the Greek model: the reception was mixed, as with Pompey's theatre, and the emperor's suggestion that the games continue into the night, and that the upper class take part was greeted with horror, except by the people who approved the idea of more 'licence'. Prior to this wooden stages and (later) benches were temporarily erected, usually in the forum, for the occasion.

20 Indeed there were some who recalled the criticism of Pompey, too, by his elders for constructing a permanent theatre. For, previously, it had been usual to hold the shows with improvised seating and a stage put up for the occasion, or, if you go even further back, for the spectators to stand, in case, if they sat in the theatre, their idleness continue for days on end. . . .

21 The majority approved the licence, although they called it by more respectable names. Our ancestors, they said, did not shrink from such public entertainment as their resources permitted: actors (*histriones*) were brought from Etruria, horse-racing from Thurii; and, with the annexation of Greece and Asia, performances became more ambitious, nor had any respectably born Roman ever demeaned himself by taking to the stage, and 200 years had passed since the triumph of Lucius Mummius (cos. 146), who was the first to put on that kind of show in Rome. Moreover a permanent theatre was far more economical than one which was erected and pulled down every year at tremendous expense.

2.70 Problems faced by a dramatic producer

Terence *The Mother-in-law (Hecyra)* Prologue 20–40

This play was first performed at the ludi Megalenses of 165 and then at the funeral games of Aemilius Paullus in 160 (Polyb. 31.28.5–6). The prologue was spoken by the producer-actor Lucius Ambivius Turpio. According to the prologue, Terence has had to compete — unsuccessfully — with the attractions of boxers, tight-rope walkers, and gladiators; for this passage, see Gilula 1981. However, dramatic performances were only produced at ludi: Taylor 1937; cf. Gruen 1992: 210–18 who argues not the shortcomings of the audience, but that the prologue is ahistorical, designed to gain the audience's attention as the ludi scaenici and *munera* were fixed for performance on separate days and cannot have conflicted.

20   Now, for my sake, give my plea a fair hearing.
    Once again I am putting the *Hecyra* on before you, a play I have never been able
    to produce without interruption, so greatly has it been beset by misfortune.
    This misfortune your understanding
    Can lull, if you will be supportive of our efforts.
25   When I tried to produce it the first time, the report of boxers
    (joined to the belief that a tight-rope walker would appear),

the throng of their admirers, the shouting, and women's screaming
forced me off stage before the end.
I then decided to employ my usual approach on the new play
30   and try it out again; I put it on a second time.
The first act was going well; then rumour circulated
That a gladiatorial show was to be put on and the people flocked in,
Pushing and shouting, fighting for a place,
Leaving me unable to hold the stage.
35   Now there is no commotion: only peace and silence;
I now have a chance to put on the play, while you have the opportunity
To do honour to the stage.
Do not be responsible for allowing the dramatic art
To fall into the hands of a few; make sure that your influence
40   Supports and aids my own.

2.71 Caesar's games as aedile

Suetonius *Life of the Deified Julius* 10.1–2

The aediles were responsible for the ludi, financed by the state but with the aediles using their own money as well to provide magnificent celebrations which would be remembered: they used the opportunity to win political favour with the populace. Caesar was curule aedile in 65 BC (with Bibulus), producing ludi for which he supplemented the senatorial funds from his own purse, as well as putting on a huge gladiatorial show in honour of his deceased father with borrowed money.

Plutarch has Caesar putting on a show of 320 pairs of gladiators in single combat, as well as staging theatrical performances, processions and providing banquets (*Caes.* 5.8–9; Suet. *Jul.* 10.2; Pliny *Nat. Hist.* 33.53; Dio 37.8.1, mentioning specifically the ludi Romani and the ludi Megalenses). Aediles and ludi: Gelzer 1969: 110–11; Veyne 1990: 208–14. Cicero carried a law in 63 to prevent candidates for office giving gladiatorial games for two years prior to being a candidate, to overcome the popularity which such contests brought: Vatinius flouted the law prior to his candidature as praetor (*Sest.* 133–4).

Caesar's ludi as aedile were overshadowed by those accompanying his triumph of 46 BC (doc. 2.35): venationes, a naval battle on the Campus Martius (flooded for this purpose), and land battles in the Circus Maximus involving 40 mounted elephants, 1,000 soldiers and 400 cavalry (Suet. *Jul.* 39; Pliny *Nat. Hist.* 8.22; App. *BC* 2.102.423; Dio 43.22–3; Coleman 2000: 240, 2003: 62–5).

1 During his aedileship, Caesar decorated not only the comitium and forum with its basilicas, but even the Capitol, constructing temporary colonnades to display a large part of the equipment for his games. He put on wild-beast hunts and spectacles, sometimes with his colleague and sometimes on his own, the result being that he claimed all the credit for the shared expenditure too, so that his colleague, Marcus Bibulus, openly remarked, 'The same has happened to me as to Pollux: for just as the temple of the twin brothers in the forum is simply called Castor's, the joint liberality of myself and Caesar is just said to be Caesar's.' **2** Caesar also put on a gladiatorial show, but with far fewer pairs than he had intended; for the vast troop he had collected terrified his enemies, who passed legislation restricting the number of gladiators that anyone might keep in Rome.

2.72 Cicero tries to find some panthers

Cicero *Letters to his Friends* 2.11.2

Marcus Caelius Rufus (whom Cicero had earlier defended) was elected curule aedile for 50 and importuned Cicero as governor of Cilicia to send him some panthers for his games, as he only had 20; this is Cicero's reply. Caelius had previously asked Cicero to obtain him some as soon as he got word that he (Caelius) had been elected aedile (*Fam.* 8.2.2). Obviously it was important for Caelius' future career that he should put on a good show at the Circus Maximus: cf. doc. 13.14.

Regarding the panthers, the accustomed hunters are working diligently on my instructions. But there is a remarkable scarcity, and those that are left are said to be complaining because they are the only beings in my province for whom snares are set. Accordingly they are reported to have decided to leave my province for Caria. The matter, however, is receiving careful attention, especially from Patiscus. Whatever is found will be yours; but what that will come to I really don't know. I swear your aedileship is of great concern to me. The date itself reminds me of it, for I am writing this on the first day of the Ludi Megalenses (4 April).

2.73 Cicero on gladiators: 'with swords to the death'

Cicero *Tusculan Disputations* 2.41

Many gladiators were trained in Campania, especially at Capua, where the well-known revolt of Spartacus began in a gladiatorial school. Gladiators were generally slaves, and Spartacus' associates were largely slaves from Thrace and Gaul. Livy 28.21.2 refers to the lanistae (gladiator trainers) who bought up for gladiatorial contests slaves or free men (non-Romans) willing to sell themselves. Cicero notes the contempt felt for the gladiator who begs for mercy, but the desire of the crowd to save the one who had fought well (*Mil.* 92, cf. *Tusc. Disp.* 4.48–9).

The funerary associations of gladiatorial contests probably came from Etruria, where such contests had been part of funerals for warriors for some time, but this is debated; certainly noted gladiators were often Samnites. The first gladiatorial contests were held in Rome in 264 BC, after which the numbers involved increased and the contests became increasingly frequent. They were popular with all classes: 'the type of show which is frequented by great numbers of people from all classes, and in which the populace take particular pleasure' (Cic. *Sest.* 124). In 49 BC Caesar established a gladiatorial school which housed hundreds of gladiators (Cic. *Att.* 7.14.2), foreshadowing the large gladiatorial contests of the imperial age.

For an overview of interpretations of the contests as reflecting the martial interests of the Romans, or demonstrating the superiority of Romans over non-Romans, see Kyle 1998: 7–10. The games clearly appealed to Romans of all social classes and, while there was no ideology involved in venationes and gladiatorial munera, Romans of the imperial age, and probably earlier, saw the venationes and gladiatores as specifically Roman, articulating Roman identity, power, and Roman culture.

Most of the detailed ancient information about gladiators comes from the imperial period (see esp. Seneca *Letters* 7.3–5), while most modern literature concerns the imperial period, but for the Republic, see Grant 1967: 9–27; Hopkins 1983: 3–5, 14; Wiedemann 1992: 4–7; Auget 1994: 19-28; Futrell 1997: 29–44; Beacham 1999: 13–17; discussions of gladiators in general: Balsdon 1969: 288–301; Auget 1994; Hopkins 1–30; Grant 28–124; Stambaugh 1988: 233–5; Wiedemann 1992; Barton 1993, esp. 11–46; Plass 1995; Toner 1995: 34–52; Futrell 1997; Baker 2000; Köhne & Ewigleben 2000; see Kyle 1998 (cf. Potter 2001) on the disposal of human and animal corpses from the ludi.

In the street fights of the late Republic, gladiators were an important component of the gangs. Clodius used the gladiators his brother had for funeral games to disrupt the assembly voting on Cicero's return, killing many of the voters (docs 2.3, 12.58). When Clodius and Milo met on the Appian Way in 52 BC, the former had armed slaves and the latter gladiators, amongst them two well-known gladiatorial heroes: Eudamus and Birria (Asc. 31; Cic. *Vat.* 40, *Off.* 2.58, cf. *Mil.* 29; doc. 13.1). Gladiators served as body-guards (Lintott 1999: 84): C. Porcius Cato (tr. pl. 56; *MRR* II.209; not Cato the Younger) had a band of bestiarii as a bodyguard but couldn't afford to feed them and Milo, through a go-between, and without Cato's knowledge that he [Milo] was involved, made a successful offer to purchase them (Cic. *Quint.* 2.5.3). They could be seen as a threat: during Catiline's conspiracy the senate decreed that all gladiators be removed from Rome to Capua: Sall. *Cat.* 30.7; cf. Cic. *Sest.* 9.

What of gladiators, who are either ruined men or barbarians, see what blows they can put up with! See how those who have been well trained, prefer to receive a blow than to disgracefully avoid it! How often it is made clear that they prefer nothing more than giving satisfaction to their owner or to the populace! Even when they are exhausted by wounds, they send to their owners to ask their wishes — if they have given them satisfaction, they are happy to fall. What ordinary gladiator has ever given a groan or changed countenance? Who has disgraced himself, not only when standing, but even when he falls? Who, after he has fallen, has drawn in his neck when ordered to take the sword stroke? Such is the value of training, practice and habit. So, shall,

'The Samnite, low fellow, worthy of that sort of life and place',

have the ability to take this? Shall a man born to renown have any part of his soul so weak that he cannot strengthen it by practice and training? A gladiatorial show is often seen by some as cruel and inhumane, and I rather agree that it is so, in its present form: but, when criminals fought with swords to the death, there could be no better instruction against pain and death, for the eye at any rate, though for the ear there might perhaps be many.

2.74 Caesar buys popular support with gladiators

Suetonius *Life of the Deified Julius* 26.2–3

The concession 'being granted' was the right to stand for the consulship in absentia (doc. 13.7). The gladiatorial show (*munus*) for Julia was actually staged in 46 BC (Weinstock 1971: 88–90), along with Caesar's dedication of his forum and temple of Venus Genetrix. The contests were the first ever celebrated for a woman; the ludi he gave in the Circus Maximus involved prisoners of war and criminals condemned to death (Dio 43.22–3). Lentulus in 49 as consul offered Caesar's gladiators at Capua their freedom, was criticised by Capua's citizens, and distributed them into the custody of his (i.e., Lentulus') supporters at Capua (Caes. *BC* 1.14.4; Cic. *Att.* 7.14.2, 8.2.1: Caesar had written to Cicero about his gladiators, obviously concerned about them).

2 On this concession being granted, Caesar set his aims even higher and confidently omitted no kind of expenditure or granting of favours both as a candidate for office and as a private citizen. From his spoils, he began building a forum, and paid more than 100 million sesterces for the site. Then he announced a show and public banquet in memory of his daughter, which was quite unprecedented. To create as much anticipation as possible, he had the banquet, which was leased out to market contractors, also catered by his household. **3** He also proclaimed that any well-known gladiators, who might be fighting in front of a hostile audience, should be forcibly rescued and kept alive. He had new gladiators trained, not in the gladiatorial schools or by professional trainers (lanistae), but in private houses by Roman equites and even by senators, who had experience with weapons, and he begged these, as his letters demonstrate, to train these individually and personally instruct them in their practice. He doubled the legions' pay in perpetuity. Whenever there was an abundance of grain, he would give a distribution to them without measure and sometimes would give every man a slave from the spoils.

3

Religion in the Roman Republic

Most of what is known about Roman religion concerns the official state religion, organised and managed for the benefit of the state; less is known about the personal religion of the Romans as individuals. Politics and religion were intertwined because the Romans saw the gods as aiding and abetting their political success, and political action took place in religious space: the senate house (curia) was a templum, a piece of inaugurated ground, like the rostra in the assembly (for templum, see doc. 3.47, for the rostra, doc. 1.64). Roman religion was not an ethical system and Cicero is quite blunt on this topic: 'Did anyone ever give thanks to the gods because he was a good man? No, because he was rich, respected, safe and sound. The reason men call Jupiter "Best and Greatest" (Optimus Maximus) is not because he makes us just, temperate and wise, but safe, secure, rich and abundantly wealthy': Cicero *On the Nature of the Gods* 3.87. The gods, of course, did not condone wrongdoing, but this was not their principal concern: the Romans worshipped the gods to acquire specific benefits, such as the gods' continuing assistance or their help in some crisis.

The state religion was organised by the elite. Nowhere is this made clearer than in the well-known opening to Cicero's speech to the pontiffs, *On his House (de domo sua)*: 'Among the many divinely inspired expedients devised and instituted by our ancestors, pontiffs, there is nothing more noteworthy than that by which they desired the same individuals to be in charge of the worship of the immortal gods and the highest affairs of state, so that the most important and distinguished citizens might uphold religion by a good administration of the state, and the state by a wise interpretation of religion.' Priests were only drawn from patrician families prior to 300 BC (doc. 1.55), and it was the senate which outlawed the Bacchanalia (docs 3.63–4), and authorised the introduction of the new cults of Aesculapius (docs 3.57–8) and the Magna Mater (docs 3.59–61). When prodigies occurred, it was the senate that referred the matter to the Etruscan diviners known as haruspices (docs 3.4, 38) or instructed that the Sibylline Books be consulted (docs 3.36–7), and it decided which omens and prodigies of those reported warranted action.

The emphasis on the correct performance of ritual and the various rites which were performed for the state should not lead to the erroneous conclusion that the state religion lacked meaning for the ordinary citizen. The evidence indicates that in the Republic there was a vast array of traditional Roman festivals and cults which satisfied the religious requirements of the Romans as a people and as a state. At the same time, Rome, as its empire grew, naturally came into contact with new deities, and, as in any poly-theistic system, room could be made for new gods without compromising the old. New cults filled specific needs, such as that of the healing deity Aesculapius (docs 3.57–8), or, like the fetching of the Magna Mater (docs 3.59–61), were in response to a consul-tation of the Sibylline Books in an emergency situation. The introduction of new cults and gods into the religious pantheon was closely controlled by the state (that is, the senate) in the republican period, such as that of the Magna Mater. In contrast, the cult of Dionysus which spread to Rome without official sanction incurred the wrath of the senate (docs 3.63–4).

Religio was a sense of obligation, the relationship by which mortals — as individuals and a community — were bound (in the sense of the verb 'to bind', *religare*) to worship the gods. Cicero connects *religio* with the verb *relegere*, 'to go over again, to re-read': religious people (*religiosi*) were those who continually go over everything pertaining to the worship (*cultus*) of the gods (doc. 3.66). *Religio*, then, could be said to pertain to the rituals associated with the worship of the gods and the compulsory and bind-ing nature of this worship. The term for the maintenance of the correct relationship between the community of Rome and the gods was *pax deorum*, the 'peace of the gods' (Lucretius 5.1229; Livy 6.41, 7.2.2); it was the gods who guided the res publica (Cic. *Rab. Perd.* 5).

The 'decline' of religion in the late Republic is sometimes postulated (Goar 1972: 29–33 is a good example: in the late Republic; 'the official religion [was] more and more an empty formality'). There are several areas on which this assumption rests: Augustus' claim that he restored 82 temples (*Res Gestae* 20.4; Horace *Odes* 3.6.1–4; Ovid *Fasti* 2.59–66); the lack of a flamen dialis for several years from Murena's suicide in 87 until 11 BC; and the 'intellectual' approach to religion, best seen in Cicero's *On Divination*. The first is Augustan propaganda and should not be taken in a literal sense to mean that traditional religion had fallen into decay. The second points to the problems of the political organisation and its breakdown in this period, rather than to a religious decline; while the third is a sign of a new intellectual, rather than religious, climate in which Greek philosophical ideas could be discussed without destroying belief. While there are various examples of the blatant use of augury for political ends (doc. 3.73), this was not a new phenomenon, and Cicero expressed it as making use of the gods' assistance to avoid unsuitable legislation (*Laws* 3.27).

The gods themselves were worshipped through prayer (doc. 3.24), sacrifice (doc. 3.30), lectisternia (doc. 3.13) and other rituals presided over by priests. The major Roman gods were Jupiter, Juno and Mars, all of whom held important places in the state religion, with Jupiter *the* major deity of the Romans; he was also an Italian deity wor-shipped throughout the peninsula. At Rome, he was the supreme god of state presiding over the political activities of Rome through his role as the sender of *auspicia*, the auspices which were taken before elections, meetings of the assemblies, and any military action (docs 3.47–8); the first meeting of the senate each year took place in his temple on the Capitoline and on entering office the two consuls sacrificed an ox to Jupiter (Livy 41.14.7) His major temple on the Capitoline, that of Jupiter Optimus Maximus, also contained shrines to Juno Regina (Queen Juno) and Minerva; this triad (Jupiter, Juno and Minerva) is probably originally Etruscan. He was responsible for victories in war, and a huge statue was made of him in the third century BC from the bronze weapons taken from the Samnites (doc. 1.72). The ceremony of the triumph evoked his role as war-leader, with the general's face painted red, like that of Jupiter's statue and the procession ending at his Capitoline temple (docs 2.32–5). His priest was the flamen dialis (doc. 3.19), who presided over the Vinalia, the wine festival held in April in Jupiter's honour. He was invoked by and witnessed the rituals of the fetials (doc. 3.12), and the Feriae Latinae were celebrated in his honour (doc. 3.9).

Juno was also an Italian goddess, a guardian deity, and earned her cult title 'Moneta', she who warns, when her sacred geese gave warning of the Gauls secretly ascending the Capitol, or in another version, because at the time a voice was heard from her temple commanding that an expiatory sacrifice of a pregnant sow be made (geese: Plut. *Rom. Quest.* 98, *Cam.* 27.1–3; voice: Cic. *Div.* 1.101; cf. Ovid *Fasti* 6.183). Her cult as Juno Regina originated in the evocatio of this goddess from Veii (doc. 3.55). She was a goddess of women.

Vesta had a crucial role as the goddess of the hearth, and by extension as a deity of Rome: if her sacred fire in her temple in the forum went out, it was a sign of divine displeasure; prodigies and disasters could be interpreted as meaning that one or more of the Vestals had broken their vows of chastity, and expiation had to be made to correct the relationship between Rome and the gods. The Vestal Virgins (docs 7.86–92) were the only women cult personnel at Rome apart from the wife of the flamen dialis (doc. 3.19).

Mars' worship was marked by festivals in March and October, the beginning and end of the war season respectively (North 1989: 599–600). The Salii performed their rituals in this month to honour the god (doc. 3.11). Most famously the rite of the October horse (October 15) involved a two-horse chariot race: the right-hand horse of the victorious team was sacrificed to Mars: its head was cut off and the inhabitants of the Via Sacra and those of Subura fought for it; the tail was carried to the Regia and its blood sprinkled on the altar (Polyb. 12.4b1; Plut. *Rom. Quest.* 97). Rome was a militaristic state: the doors of the temple of Janus were closed only when Rome was at peace, and this occurred in the Republic only in 235 BC (Varro *Lat. Ling.* 5.165; Livy 1.19.2; Green 2000).

There were also personified concepts: Concord (concordia) had a temple on the lower Capitoline just above the forum, of uncertain foundation date (almost certainly not by M. Furius Camillus in 367 BC); it was famously rebuilt by Opimius on the orders of the senate in 121 after the assassination of Gaius Gracchus and the murder of his supporters (doc. 8.32). Fides, 'good faith' also had a temple, on the Capitoline. Traditional scholarship has placed a great deal of emphasis on the *numina* (spirits) and the gradual development of Roman religion away from numina to anthropomorphic deities. This model is now not accepted; clearly the Romans always had corporeal gods, chief amongst whom was Jupiter, and there were various minor deities as well as personifications of entities, often with quite specific roles, such as sowing and rust (docs 3.3, 71), as well as a variety of lesser agricultural deities (doc. 3.2).

Ancient sources: there were numerous sources on religion in the Republic that are now lost. The augurs kept records of their pronouncements (*decreta*) on prodigies, and also had books of augural lore (doc. 3.38), and several works on augury were written in the first century BC. The Etruscans had books of divination by entrail inspection (extispicy) and the pontiffs had books of prayers and rituals. In the late Republic Veranius wrote on augury and the pontifical colleges, and Granius Flaccus on the forms of words which the pontiffs used in calling on the gods, both now surviving only as fragments. Varro *Lat. Lang.* 6.86 (doc. 3.22) quotes from the *Censoriae Tabulae*, Censors' Records, when providing information about the lustrum held at the end of the census; Val. Max. 4.1.10 refers to the 'public tables' (publicae tabulae) with respect to the prayer recited by the censor at the lustrum (doc. 3.25).

In addition priests kept records (often of more importance to history as such than religion). The annales maximi, kept by the pontifex maximus, were an annual report posted each year on a whitened board near the Regia, which was wiped clean when the next yearly instalment was ready; the collected annales were published toward the end of the second century. They recorded the names of magistrates but also important events. As such the annals were a source for historians.

The main authors on Roman religion, Cicero and Varro, come late in the Republic. Cicero *On the Nature of the Gods* (*de natura deorum*) wrote on the nature and form of the gods; *On Divination* (*de divinatione*) is a discussion on the merits or otherwise of divination; *Laws* (*de legibus*) Book 2 discusses the religious system of his ideal state, analogous to that of the Roman state. In addition, Cicero's various works and letters contain numerous references to the practice of contemporary religion (e.g., docs 3.37–8, 40, 44, 51–2, 66, 78).

Varro: Varro's *Antiquitates rerum humanarum et divinarum* (*Human and Divine Antiquities*), in 41 books which appeared in 47 BC, had 25 books on Roman antiquities and 16 books (dedicated to Julius Caesar as pontifex maximus) on Roman religious themes: priesthoods, sacred places, festivals, rituals and gods. Some quotations from this work survive. He mentions various priestly records, such as the books of the Salii (*Lat. Lang.* 6.14). In his *On the Latin Language* (*de lingua Latina*) in dealing with the etymology of various words he reveals a great deal of information (docs 3.2, 15, 17, 22, 47).

Dionysius of Halicarnassus is next in importance after Varro and Cicero (docs 3.7–9, 11, 18, 30, 36, 65) and in his account *Roman Antiquities* preserves a mine of useful information on Roman religion. His account is based on his own observations and also on Roman literary sources, such as Varro's works on religion, which he notes at doc. 3.36. One of his concerns is to show that Roman religious practices are based on Greek models or that there are numerous similarities.

Historians such as Polybius and Livy provide information about Roman religion as part of their overall historical treatments. Livy is very interested in omens and religious events; amongst these are the condemnation of Vestal Virgins and human sacrifices (docs 4.38, 7.89), and his famous description of the Bacchanalia (doc. 3.63). Polybius in Book 6 writes about Roman funerary ritual (doc. 3.74) and makes a comment on the political use of religion at the time he is writing (doc. 3.73), but on the whole he does not deal with religious factors in his work.

Ovid's *Fasti* (docs 3.71, 7.77–81) is a month by month account — in poetry — of the Roman festival calendar. Unfortunately only half the year survives (January-June), and the other months may never have been written. Ovid (43 BC–AD 17) was writing outside of the Republican period but most of the festivals he describes belong to the Republic. Important details about dates, aetiological myths, and ritual practices are preserved.

Plutarch *Roman Questions* asks many (113) questions about Roman customs and practices and most of these questions concern religion. He cites several Roman authorities for his information. With his interest in delving into origins he is an important source for details about early Roman religion.

Julius Obsequens, of the fourth or early fifth century AD, in his *A Book of Prodigies* dealt with omens and prodigies from 249 to 11 BC, but only that part dealing with 190 to 11 BC survives.

Calendars: Over forty Roman religious calendars inscribed on stone or painted on walls have survived, sometimes extensively or as fragments, but only one from the republican period (doc. 3.28). These calendars vary in the information they supply, but all list festivals, and some provide information on the gods being honoured and temples whose anniversaries are being celebrated. Inscriptions provide evidence for dedications (e.g., docs 3.23, 53, 58).

For the ancient sources, consult North 1989: 573–82; Rawson 1985: 298–9, 302–3, 306; 1991a; cf. Beard 1994: 758–9, cf. 734–8; *BNP* 1.75–9, 115–17; sources on the priests: Szemler 1972: 10–20; Vangaard 1988: 123–69.

For an introduction to Roman religion, see Bailey 1932; Hus 1962: 99–127; Jocelyn 1966/7; Sharwood Smith 1975: 40–53; Goar 1972: 6–21; Wagenvoort 1980: 223–56; Wardman 1982: 1–21; Beard 1989, 1994; Kamm 1995: 76–101; Jones & Sidwell 1997: 172–9; Feeney 1998: 115–36; North 1989; Beard & Crawford 1999: 25–39; Rüpke 2004; useful full-length treatments: Warde Fowler 1911; Altheim 1938; Rose 1948; Ogilvie 1969; Dumézil 1970; Scullard 1981; North 2000; Turcan 2000. For conceptual issues, see esp. North 1995, 1997.

EARLY DEITIES AND CULTS

When the Republic was inaugurated in 509 BC, Roman religion had been exposed to Etruscan, and, to a lesser extent, Greek influence. The Romans in addition worshipped similiar gods and shared festivals with their Latin neighbours. The Romans attributed a large number of the features of their religion to Numa, the second king of Rome, following a standard ancient practice of attributing features of a political and religious structure to a particular reforming figure, such as Lycurgus in ancient Sparta. The first king of Rome, Romulus, was seen as founding the city and organising it, with the religious details then worked out by the next king, Numa (with additions and modifications by subsequent kings). It is clear that prior to the early Republic the basic features of Roman religion had already been established, and these survived throughout the period of the Republic, and in fact into the Imperial period.

It is, however, clear that by the first century of the Republic the Romans had forgotten the exact meaning of some of their rituals which they nevertheless continued to practice out of tradition and piety. The essentially Roman nature of religion in the early Republic is apparent from several of the following documents. Etruscan influence chiefly centres around the haruspices ('soothsayers'), while the major Greek influence is in fact later, not just with the introduction of Aesculapius (the Greek Asklepios) but in identifications of the Roman gods with the Greek (which, however, did not affect the rituals by which the Roman gods were worshipped). Yet despite Greek influences and the introduction of foreign deities such as the Magna Mater (docs 3.59–61) the penetration of the cult of Bacchus (docs 3.63–4), and the increasing prominence of the goddess Isis in the closing decades of the Republic (doc. 3.62), Roman religion in the Republic has a fundamentally *Roman* character: it was not a mish-mash of borrowings from neighbours, and in itself was clearly a 'well-rounded' religion. What is particularly striking from the beginnings of the Republic is the very developed and formal nature of civic Roman religion: the colleges of priests, manned by the elite, were fundamentally concerned with the relationship between the civic sphere and the gods (docs 3.17–20). In addition, another major emphasis was on agriculture, and agricultural festivals remained important to the very end of the Republic and beyond (docs 3.2–3, 10, 71).

For early Roman religion: Dumézil 1970: 18–31; Ferguson 1987: 750–1, 754–5; North 2000: 15; esp. *BNP* 1.1–72.

3.1 The divine council

Ennius Annals 60–1

(*ROL* I.22; Skutsch 1985: 91 (as lines 240–1), commentary at 424–6.) Ennius (c. 239–169 BC) here catalogues the twelve 'Olympian' Roman gods and goddesses, perhaps in connection with a lectisternium for all twelve great gods held in 217 BC: Jove is Jupiter.

Juno, Vesta, Minerva, Ceres, Diana, Venus, Mars,
Mercury, Jove, Neptune, Vulcan, Apollo.

3.2 The early deities

Varro On the Latin Language 5.74

Varro (116–27 BC) is here attempting to determine the linguistic origins of the names of deities. Some of these names are perfectly Roman. Novensides, 'new settlers', is apparently used in opposition to indigetes, 'native gods'; for Feronia: see doc. 3.8. Tatius was king of the Sabines at the time of the 'rape of the Sabine women'; he was said to have ruled Rome jointly with Romulus after the Sabine women captured by the Romans effected a reconciliation between them and to have jointly ruled Rome with Romulus.

Feronia, Minerva, the Novensides are from the Sabines. With minor changes, we say the following, also from the same people: Pales (goddess of shepherds), Vesta, Salus, Fortuna, Fons (god of springs), Fides. The altars too which were dedicated at Rome by the vow of King Tatius have the smell of the Sabine language; for, as the *Annals* tell us, he vowed altars to Ops, Flora, Vediovis and Saturn, Sun, Moon, Vulcan and Summanus (responsible for lightning), and likewise to Larunda (a nymph), Terminus, Quirinus, Vertumnus, the Lares, Diana and Lucina; some of these names have roots in either language.

3.3 Names of deities reflect their function

Servius On Vergil's Georgics 1.21

One Fabius Pictor wrote *On the Pontifical Law* (*HRR* I² 114–16 FF1–9); he is probably not the same individual as Fabius Pictor the historian, but rather an antiquarian of the mid-second century BC. The deities' names reflect their sphere of activity. Clearly, even at that point, the origin of these deities was obscure, but they were closely connected with agricultural activities with which much of early Roman religion was concerned.

It is quite obvious that names have been given to divine spirits in accordance with the function of the spirit. For example, Occator was so named after the word *occatio*, harrowing; Sarritor, after *sarritio*, hoeing; Sterculinus, after *stercoratio*, spreading manure; Sator, after *satio*, sowing. Fabius Pictor lists the following as deities whom the flamen of Ceres invokes when sacrificing to Mother Earth and Ceres: Vervactor (ploughing fallow), Reparator (replough), Imporcitor (make furrows), Insitor (sow), Obarator (plough up), Occator, Sarritor, Subruncinator (clear weeds), Messor (harvest), Convector (carry), Conditor (store), and Promitor (bring forth).

3.4 Rome's debt to the Etruscans

Diodorus Siculus *Library of History* 5.40.1–2

According to Livy 5.1.6, the Etruscans as a nation paid more attention than any other people to religious rites, all the more as they excelled in practising them. Etruscan practices (*Etrusca disciplina*) involved haruspices (priests who inspected the entrails of victims), the interpretation of thunder and lightning, and prescriptions for rituals involved in the founding of cities and other important events; see Cic. *Har. Resp.* 18, 25, 37, 53; Bloch 1960: 92–110; Rawson 1992c; Scullard 1980: 25–36, 56–62; van der Meer 1987.

Miniature fasces have been documented in an Etruscan seventh-century tomb, and the *sella curulis* (the ivory folding chair, perhaps originally an attribute of the kings) in numerous Etruscan tombs and paintings; see Cornell 1995: 159–72 on 'Etruscan' Rome.

1 The Etruscans also devised the majesty that surrounds rulers, granting them lictors, an ivory stool, and a toga with a band of purple, while with regard to houses they invented the peristyle, a very useful way of avoiding the confusion of crowds of attendants; the Romans copied most of these inventions, improved them and transferred them to their own nation. **2** The Etruscans also perfected literature and the teaching about nature and the gods, and they achieved more expertise than any other race in the art of divination by thunder and lightning, which is why, even up to this present day, the people who rule nearly the entire inhabited world show respect to these men and employ them as interpreters with regard to omens from heaven.

3.5 Numa Pompilius and early religious institutions

Ennius *Annals* 125–9

Varro *Lat. Lang.* 7.43–5; cf. 6.19; *ROL* I.42–4; Skutsch 1985: 79–80 (as lines 114–18), commentary at 266–70. Ennius here ascribes to Numa the introduction of several features of religious practice: Numa may not have been responsible but the ascription demonstrates the belief that the main features of Roman religion were pre-republican in origin and this view is probably correct. Varro explains the terms and comments that the deities mentioned here are obscure. Pancakes: the *liba*, offered at libations; bakers of offering cakes: the *fictores*, who made the liba; the shields refer to those carried by the Salii: doc. 3.11; rush-dummies: the *Argei* (see doc. 3.7); the *tutulati*, certain priests who wore a conical head-dress (the *tutulus*) at sacrifices.

Numa established the sacrificial banquets, as well as the shields,
and the sacrificial cakes, bakers of offering-cakes, rush-dummies, and the wearing
    of conical head-dresses.
The priests of Volturnus, Palatua, Furrina,
Flora, Falacer and Pomona were also instituted
By him.

3.6 Numa's arrangements for Roman religion

Livy *History of Rome* 1.20.1–7

Vestal Virgins: docs 7.86–92; Salii: doc. 3.11; flamen dialis: doc. 3.19. A feature of Roman religion was its written nature; here Numa sets down details about days for sacrifices, victims, and shrines, and in the Republic the priests had access to various books in which the precise nature of the rituals which they had to perform were prescribed.

1 Numa then turned his mind to the creation of priests, although he was accustomed to undertake many sacred duties himself, especially those which now pertain to the flamen dialis. **2** But since he thought that in a warlike society there would be more kings like Romulus than like Numa, and that they would take part in wars themselves, he appointed a flamen for Jupiter as his perpetual priest (the flamen dialis), so that the sacred duties of the royal office not be neglected, and equipped him with a special dress and a royal curule chair. To him he added two more flamens, one for Mars, another for Quirinus; **3** and he chose virgins for Vesta, a priesthood which originated in Alba and which was thus not unsuited to the race of its founder. So that they might be perpetual priests of the temple, he assigned them a salary from the public funds, and made them respected and holy through their virginity and other sacred observances. **4** He likewise chose 12 Salii for Mars Gradivus, and gave them the distinction of wearing an embroidered tunic and a bronze breastplate over the tunic, and instructed them to carry the divine shields, which are called *ancilia*, as they went through the city singing sacred songs to their rhythmic and solemn dance. **5** He then chose from the senators as pontifex (maximus) Numa Marcius, son of Marcus, and entrusted to him the sacred duties written out in full — with what victims, on what days, at what shrines rites should take place and from where money was to be expended to cover their costs. **6** All other public and private rites, too, he placed under the control of the decrees of the pontifex, that there might be someone whom the plebs could come to consult, so that there might be no confusion in divine law through the neglect of ancestral rites and the admission of foreign ones; **7** the pontifex was to teach not merely ceremonies to do with the gods in heaven, but correct funerary observances and the propitiation of the spirits of the dead, and what omens shown in lightning or other visible signs were to be dealt with and warded off.

3.7 Substitute human sacrifices?

Dionysius of Halicarnassus *Roman Antiquities* 1.38.2–3

Varro (*Lat. Lang.* 5.45, 7.44) gives the number of the effigies known as Argei as 27, while Dionysius has 30. The Argei were made of bulrushes, and the 30 given here would mean one for each curia. The bridge is the Pons Sublicius. A procession visited the shrines on March 16 and

17, and the Vestals threw the Argei into the Tiber on May 14, perhaps as a rite of purification (so Plut. *Rom. Quest.* 32, 86). The important point here is the presence of high-ranking religious personnel in a rite which by the end of the Republic was clearly not understood: the ritual was an ancient one which had to be performed as part of the overall relationship with the gods. For the Argei: Ovid *Fasti* 3.791–2, 5.621–62; Gell. 10.15.30; Cic. *Rosc. Am.* 100; Macrob. 1.11.46; Ogilvie 1969: 87; Dumézil 1970: 449–50; Harmon 1978: 1446–59; Scullard 1981: 90–1, 120–1; Gabba 1991: 106; Turcan 2000: 67, 70; Ziolkowski 1998/9: 210–18; Graf 2000; Wildfang 2001: 238–40.

2 It is said, too, that the men of old used to sacrifice human victims to Cronus (Saturn), as was done in Carthage while that city stood, and is still done to this day by the Gauls and some other western peoples, and that Hercules, wishing to put an end to the custom of this sacrifice, erected the altar on the Saturnian hill and began the sacrificial ceremony of unblemished victims burning on a pure fire; and, so that the people might not have any scruples about having neglected their ancestral sacrifices, he taught the natives to appease the wrath of the god by making effigies of the men whom they had bound hand and foot and thrown into the Tiber's stream and to dress these in the same manner and throw them into the river instead of the men, in order that any evil foreboding which remained in the minds of all might be removed, as the appearance of the ancient practice would still be retained. **3** The Romans have continued to do this every year right down to my own time, a little after the spring equinox in the month of May, on what they call the Ides, the day they wish to be the middle of the month; on this day the pontiffs, as they are called — the most important of the priests — offer preliminary sacrifices according to the laws and with them the virgins who guard the eternal fire, the praetors and those citizens who may lawfully be present at the rites throw 30 effigies made in the form of men from the sacred bridge into the stream of the Tiber; these they call Argei.

3.8 Early Sabine and Latin cult practices

Dionysius of Halicarnassus *Roman Antiquities* 3.32.1, 4

In the reign of Tullus Hostilius (672–641 BC), the Sabines, according to tradition, seized important Romans attending a festival, leading to a further Sabine-Roman war (see Livy 1.30.4–10). Dionysius here connects the Roman deities with Greek ones, and this is typical of his overall tendency to ascribe Greek origins to Roman religious practices or to stress similarities with Greek religion. Salii: see doc. 3.11 (Dion. Hal. 2.70.3–5 equates the Roman Salii with the Greek kouretes); Feronia: a Sabine goddess of uncertain function (for the establishment of her temple in the last quarter of the third century at Rome: Livy 22.1.18; Ziolkowski 1992: 25–8); the festival of Saturn referred to here is presumably the Saturnalia: doc. 3.69 (Accius *Annals* 2–7); the Opalia in December 19 celebrated the goddess Ops (Scullard 1981: 180). The interaction between the Romans and the religious life of Italy is worth noting. Tullus' vow (not surprisingly) brought success.

1 After this war another arose from the Sabine people against the Romans, of which the origin and cause was as follows: there is a sanctuary, honoured in common by both the Sabines and Latins and considered as extremely sacred, dedicated to a goddess named Feronia, whom some of those who translate the name into Greek call Anthophoros ('Flower-bearer'), some Philostephanos ('Lover of garlands'), and others

Persephone. People from the neighbouring towns used to gather at this sanctuary on the appointed festival days, many of them offering prayers and sacrifices to the goddess, and many with the purpose of doing business during the festival as merchants, craftsmen and farmers, and fairs more splendid than anywhere else in Italy were held here. Some distinguished Romans who had come to this festival were seized, bound and robbed of their money by some Sabines . . . (This led to war, at first with inconclusive results, but a battle was again fought at Eretum in the next year, 160 stades from Rome.)

4 When that battle continued equally balanced for a long period, Tullus, raising his hands to heaven, vowed to the gods that if he conquered the Sabines on that day he would institute public festivals in honour of Cronus and Rhea (Saturn and Ops: the Saturnalia and Opalia), which the Romans celebrate every year after they have gathered in all the fruits of the earth, and would double the number of the Salii as they are called. These are young men of noble family who, at appointed times, perform dances in full armour to the music of the flute and sing certain traditional hymns, as I have explained in the preceding book.

3.9 The Feriae Latinae

Dionysius of Halicarnassus *Roman Antiquities* 4.49.1–3

The consuls on entering office set the date for the Feriae Latinae (it was one of the festivals which did not have a fixed date in the calendar) and presided over the sacrifice during that festival on the Alban mount, to Jupiter Latiaris, identified with Latinus, eponymous ancestor of the Latin race. All the cities of Latium participated; Rome's chief organising role and the consuls' presiding role indicate that the festival reflected Rome's dominance of Latium, but also the cultural and historical links between it and Rome. Importance was attached to this festival by the Romans throughout the Republic. The Tarquinius here was the seventh king of Rome (534–510 BC). For Lavinium, another major religious centre of the Latins: *BNP* 1.323–4, 2.12–3.

See Livy 21.63.5, 8, 22.1.6 (217 BC); Cic. *Att.* 1.3.1; Alföldi 1965: 19–25, 29–34; Dumézil 1970: 1.204, 2.463; Scullard 1981: 39, 111–13; Cornell 1989: 264–74, 1995: 271; Turcan 2000: 61–2.

1 When Tarquinius had acquired sovereignty over the Latins, he sent envoys both to the cities of the Hernici and to those of the Volscians proposing that they too should enter into a treaty of friendship and alliance. All the Hernici voted to join the alliance, but only two cities of the Volscians, Ecetra and Antium, accepted the invitation. To ensure that the agreements with these cities should last for ever, Tarquinius decided to set up a place of worship in common for Romans, Latins, Hernici, and those Volscians who had joined the alliance, so that they should gather together each year at the designated place and jointly celebrate a festival, feast and partake in sacrifices in common. **2** When everyone welcomed the suggestion, he designated, as the place where they should gather, a high mountain lying almost in the middle of these nations and overlooking the Albans' city, on which, he laid down, a festival should be celebrated every year during which there should be a truce to all hostilities and sacrifices should be performed in common to Jupiter Latiaris, as he is called, and joint feasts held. He also assigned what each city was to contribute towards the sacrifices and the share each of them was to receive. Forty-seven cities took part in this festival and sacrifice. **3** The Romans celebrate these festivals and sacrifices to our own time, calling them the 'Latin festivals' (*feriae latinae*); and some of the cities that take part in them bring lambs, others cheeses, or a certain measure of milk, or something similar. One bull is sacrificed in common by all of them and each city receives its designated share of it. The sacrifices are made on behalf of them all and the Romans are in charge of the ceremonies.

EARLY HYMNS AND RITUALS

3.10 Hymn of the Arval Brothers

ILS 5039

(*CIL* VI.2104; cf. *CIL* VI.2033–119, 32338–98, 37164f (inscriptions of the members of the priesthood and its ceremonies); Diehl 138; *ILLRP* 4; Gordon *Album* vol. 3, no 476; Gordon 1983: no 75; *ROL* IV.250–3.)

The song of the twelve Arval brothers, a college of priests, perhaps dates to as early as the sixth century BC; the hymn was recorded in AD 218 on an inscribed marble tablet, found at Rome in AD 1778. Varro's (doc. 3.17) is the only mention of the Arval brothers in the Republic, but the Hymn of the Arval Brothers has archaic language (such as Lases for Lares) and the Arvals were clearly a Republican institution of some antiquity; Augustus revived it. At a grove eight kilometres from Rome they maintained the cult of Dea Dia (apparently a goddess of agricultural fertility). At her main festival in May the Arvals sang the hymn now known as the *carmen arvale* (arval hymn).

The hymn invokes the Lares and Mars (Marmar, Marmor), who was originally an agricultural deity and protector of farmland (and so repelled invaders; for Mars in agriculture, see doc. 3.21). The Lares were protective deities of the household and crossroads. Leaping here is imitative magic to make crops grow; arva is the Latin word for fields. According to Gellius the Arvales originated with Romulus, their insignia being a garland of wheat ears and white fillets (Gell. 7.7.8; cf. Pliny *Nat. Hist.* 18.6); see Dumézil 1970: 1.228–30; Beard 1985; Syme 1982; *BNP* 1.194–6, 2.87–88, 151–2.

Then the priests closed the doors, tucked up their robes, took the books in hand, divided into groups, and danced in three-step rhythm singing in the following words:

Oh help us, Lares! Oh help us, Lares! Oh help us, Lares!

Do not let plague or ruin, O Marmar, assail more people.

Do not let plague or ruin, O Marmar, assail more people.

Do not let plague or ruin, O Marmar, assail more people.

Be satisfied, fierce Mars, leap the threshold! Stop! Burn (?)! Be satisfied, fierce Mars, leap the threshold! Stop! Burn (?)! Be satisfied, fierce Mars, leap the threshold! Stop! Burn (?)!

In turn invoke all the gods of sowing. In turn invoke all the gods of sowing. In turn invoke all the gods of sowing.

Oh help us, O Marmor! Oh help us, O Marmor! Oh help us, O Marmor!

Triumph! Triumph! Triumph, triumph, triumph!

After the triple-rhythmed dance, at a given signal, the public slaves then came in and took the books.

3.11 The leaping of the Salii

Dionysius of Halicarnassus *Roman Antiquities* 2.70.1–5

Varro *Lat. Lang.* 7.26; cf. Plut. *Numa* 12.4; docs 3.6, 8; cf. doc. 3.49 for the sacred staff. Dionysius has clearly seen the Salii in action. The Salii ('leapers') were two groups (the Palatini and the Agonales) of 12 priests; they were formed according to tradition by Numa with King Tullus Hostilius later adding a second group (doc. 3.8). They were devoted to Mars and sang and danced in his honour, wearing military dress and carrying shields, in March and October: the first ritual dance took place on March 1. They danced through Rome, including in the Forum and on the Capitoline, and their name suggests that the dancing involved leaping. The original ancile (shield) was said to have fallen from heaven in Numa's reign and Rome's safety was thought to depend on it. Numa had 11 more shields made (Dion. Hal. 2.71; cf. Tac. *Hist.* 1.89). Dionysius refers to 'martial gods', who must be Mars and Quirinus. Quintilian (*Education of an Orator* 1.6.41: late first century AD): 'The language of the hymn of the Salii . . . is now hardly understood by its own priests. But religion forbids those words to be altered, and we must treat them as holy objects.' See for the Salii: Bloch 1960: 134–41; Ogilvie 1969: 79–80, 1970: 98–9; Dumézil 1970: 1.146–7, 276–7; Scullard 1981: 85–6; *BNP* 2.126–8; Turcan 2000: 66.

1 Numa himself appointed the Salii from the patricians, selecting the 12 best-looking young men. Their sacred objects are kept on the Palatine hill, and they themselves are called the *Palatini*. For the (Salii called the) *Agonales* . . . who have their repository of sacred objects on the Quirinal hill, were appointed by King Hostilius after Numa's reign, fulfilling a vow which he had made in the war fought against the Sabines. All these Salii are a kind of dancers and hymn-singers in honour of the martial gods. **2** The festival takes place . . . in the month of Martius (March). It is celebrated for many days, at public expense, during which time the *Salii* dance through the city to the Forum and the Capitoline Hill, and to many other places, public and private. They are attired in embroidered tunics fastened with belts of bronze, and robes with scarlet stripes and a purple border fastened with brooches. These robes are known as *trabeae*, a peculiarly Roman dress and a mark of the greatest honour. On their heads they wear apices, high caps tapering into a cone shape. . . . **3** Each of the Salii has a sword hung from their belt, and in his right hand a spear or staff or some such thing, and in his left a Thracian shield, an oblong shield which looks like a lozenge, with the sides drawn in to form hollows (i.e., a 'figure of eight shield'). . . . **5** They make rhythmic movements in their armour to the sound of the flute, sometimes all together, sometimes in turns; and while they dance they sing various traditional hymns.

3.12 The origin of the fetials

Livy *History of Rome* 1.32.5–14

Here Livy records a formula for the declaration of war established by the fourth king of Rome, Ancus Marcius (640–617 BC). The 20 fetials (*fetiales*) were responsible for the rituals associated with the declaration of war and also the making of treaties (Livy 1.24 has the fetials responsible for treaties in an incident under the third king, Tullus Hostilius, 672–641 BC). The ascription to Ancus Marcius may well be fictitious, and the formula here perhaps reflects later practice or was an antiquarian reconstruction (North 1989: 587), but clearly the fetials were of ancient origin and the formula reflected procedures regarding wars with neighbouring states prior to the Mediterranean expansion. When the enemy territory was no longer in proximity to Rome, the ritual spear throwing occurred at Rome itself, near the temple of Bellona. The fetials as an institution existed amongst the Latin states generally. The phrase 'just and righteous' at (12) indicates the Roman desire to have divine backing for their wars; it does not mean that the Romans were pacifists who went to war only when they had a 'water-tight' case for doing so: they wanted to declare a 'just war' (*bellum iustum*); Livy in particular in his history of Rome was at pains to show that the Romans only became involved in such just wars. The fetials could be consulted by the senate on the proper procedures for declaring war.

See doc. 3.17; Livy 1.24.4–9; Plut. *Numa* 12.4 (fetials and *Salii* established by Numa); Dion. Hal. 2.72 (a detailed account); Ogilvie 1970: 127–36; Garlan 1975: 48–50; Rich 1976: 104–7; Brunt 1990: 175–8; Wiedemann 1986; Penella 1987; North 1989: 587–8; Rawson 1991b: 90–3; Watson 1993, esp. 1–9, 58; *BNP* 1.132–4, 2.132; Turcan 2000: 94–6.

5 In order that, just as Numa had established religious practices in time of peace, he (Ancus Marcius) might give war its own ceremonial and wars should not only be fought but also declared with some formality, he copied from the ancient tribe of the Aequicolae the law which the fetials now possess, by which redress is sought. **6** When the envoy arrives at the boundary of the people from which redress is sought, he covers his head with a fillet (the covering is woollen) and says, 'Hear, Jupiter! Hear, boundaries of — naming whichever nation's they are! Let righteousness hear! I am the public messenger of the Roman people; I come rightly and religiously commissioned and let trust be placed in my words.' He then goes through his demands. **7** Then he calls Jupiter to witness: 'If I demand contrary to justice and religion that these men or goods be surrendered to me, then never allow me to share in my country.' **8** He makes this statement, with only a few changes in the formula of the oath, when he crosses the frontier, when the first man encounters him, when he passes through the town's gate, and when he has entered the forum. **9** If those he demands are not surrendered, after 33 days — the established number — he declares war in the following words: **10** 'Hear, Jupiter; and you, Janus Quirinus; and hear, all you gods in heaven, and you on earth and you under the earth. I call you to witness that this people — naming whichever one it is — is unjust and does not make due restitution. But concerning these things we will consult the elders in our country, as to how we may obtain our right.' Then the messenger returns to Rome for consultation. The king would immediately consult the senators (patres) in words like these: **11** 'Regarding the things, cases, causes about which the pater patratus (fetial priest) of the Roman people of the Quirites has made demands on the pater patratus of the Ancient Latins and the men of the Ancient Latins, which things they have not handed over, fulfilled or done, which they ought to have handed over, fulfilled and done, speak,' he would say to the man whose opinion he was accustomed to ask first, 'what is your view?' **12** He would then reply, 'I consider that they ought to be sought in just and righteous warfare and thus I agree and vote.' Then the others would be asked in order; and when the majority of those who were there sided with the same view, war had been agreed. It was usual for the fetial to bear to their opponents' boundary a spear with a head of iron or wood hardened in the fire, and in the presence of not less than three adult men proclaim: **13** 'Whereas the peoples of the Ancient Latins and the men of the Ancient Latins have acted and committed offences against the Roman people of the Quirites, and whereas the Roman people of the Quirites has ordered that there be war with the Ancient Latins, and the senate of the Roman people of the Quirites has approved, agreed and voted that there be war with the Ancient Latins, accordingly

I and the Roman people hereby declare and make war on the peoples of the Ancient Latins and the men of the Ancient Latins.' After proclaiming this, he would hurl the spear into their territory. **14** It was in this way that redress was sought from the Latins and war declared, and later generations adopted the same custom.

3.13 The introduction of the lectisternium to Rome, 399 BC

Livy *History of Rome* 5.13.4–8

The rite of the lectisternium (plural: lectisternia) was introduced in 399 BC when the Sibylline Books were consulted (for which, see doc. 3.36). It was a banquet of the gods, in which they were provided with couches, and has clear affinities with Greek ritual. However, the practice was not wholly alien: there was the traditional rite of the *epulum Iovis* celebrated in September and November in which Jupiter was invited to dine on a couch, and Juno and Minerva on chairs (Val. Max. 2.1.2; Scullard 1981: 186–7). Lectisternia were held to propitiate the gods, such as when plague struck (as in this example and Livy 7.27.1–2), after the defeats of 218 BC (doc. 3.31), and after the military disaster of Trasimene (Livy 22.1.18, 22.9.11, 22.10.9: 217 BC). (A different approach was taken after Cannae when human sacrifice was performed: doc. 4.38.) A lectisternium was also held when the cult of the Magna Mater was introduced in 205 BC (doc. 3.59). The duumvirs ('two men') were at this time in charge of the Sibylline Books: doc. 3.36. See Warde Fowler 1911: 263–6; Toynbee 1965: II.377; Dumézil 1970: 2.567–8; Ogilvie 1970: 655–8; Scullard 1981: 20–1; Orlin 1997; 92–5; Turcan 2000: 88–9.

4 The severe winter was followed — whether because of the sudden change from such an inclement season to the exact opposite or from some other reason — by a summer that was oppressive and unhealthy to all living creatures. **5** Since nothing could be found to explain the origins of this incurable pestilence or put an end to it, on the senate's advice the Sibylline books were consulted. **6** The duumvirs in charge of the sacred rites then, for the first time in Rome's history, held a lectisternium and for a period of eight days appeased Apollo, Latona and Diana, and Hercules, Mercury and Neptune by spreading three couches for them with all the abundance possible at that time. **7** They also celebrated this same sacred rite at their homes. Throughout the whole city, doors were left open, all kinds of goods were placed out in the open for general consumption, strangers were generally welcomed whether known or not, and men spoke courteously and companionably even to their enemies. People refrained from arguments and law-suits; **8** chains were even removed from prisoners during that period; and they later felt it wrong to imprison those to whom the gods had given this assistance.

3.14 The development of drama to placate the gods

Livy *History of Rome* 7.2.1–7

A lectisternium failed to alleviate a plague in 365–364 BC, and a new form of placatory ritual was therefore introduced. The term fescennine entertainments was probably derived from Fescennia in Etruria, or from fascinum, a phallus-shaped amulet (Hor. *Ep.* 2.1.145). Livius Andronicus of Tarentum was to compose the first Latin comedy, adapted from Greek, performed in Rome in 240 BC (cf. doc. 7.83). This ritual also failed and an older one was remembered in which a dictator had hammered a nail into a temple to end a plague (Livy 7.3.1–8), so affixing it and ending its effects; see Turcan 2000: 89.

1 The plague lasted during both this and the subsequent year, the consulship of Gaius Sulpicius Petico and Gaius Licinius Stolo (cos. 364). **2** Nothing worth remembering was done in that year, except that a lectisternium was held for the third time since the foundation of the city, in the hope of entreating the goodwill of the gods. **3** And when the force of the plague was alleviated by neither human counsel or divine aid, the Romans' minds were overcome by superstition and, amongst other practices intended to placate the gods' anger, they are said to have instituted scenic entertainments, a new departure for a warlike people, for their only public spectacle had been that of the Circus. **4** These indeed began in a modest way, as most things do, and were in fact imported from abroad. Without any singing, without any miming of song, players brought in from Etruria danced to the sounds of the flute and performed graceful movements in the Etruscan style. **5** Then the young Romans began to copy them, at the same time exchanging jokes in rude verses, their movements harmonising with the words. **6** Thus the entertainment was accepted and established by frequent usage. The native actors were called *histriones*, because *ister* is the Etruscan word for actor; **7** they no longer, as before, threw at each other rude, improvised lines, like Fescennine verses, but performed *saturae* (medleys), accompanied by music, with the singing properly arranged to fit the flute-playing and with appropriate movements.

3.15 Etruscan ritual in founding a town

Varro *On the Latin Language* 5.143

Many people employed the Etruscan ritual when they were founding a town in Latium — that is, using a team of cattle, a bull with a cow on the inside, they would run a furrow around it with a plough (for religious reasons they would do this on an auspicious day), so they might be defended by a ditch and wall. The place where they ploughed up the earth, they called a 'ditch' (fossa), and the earth thrown inside it a 'wall' (murus). The 'circle' (orbis) which was made behind this was the beginning of the 'city' (urbs); because it was 'behind the wall' (post murum), they called this the postmoerium (pomerium) which is the outside limit for auspices taken for the city. Markers of the pomerium stand around both Aricia and Rome.

3.16 The devotio of Decius Mus, senior

Livy *History of Rome* 8.9.4–8, 10.11–11.1

The *devotio* of Decius Mus in 340 BC was the most famous in the Republic but was not a unique example of the ritual, which his own son (doc. 1.69), and grandson were also later said to have performed (Cic. *Tusc. Disp.* I.89, *Fin.* 2.61; Dio X in Zonaras VIII.5): it is only specifically attested as a battle-field ritual for these three generations. At the time of the Gallic invasion half a century earlier than Decius senior, the old men who had held curule office dressed themselves in their state robes and seated themselves in their houses and devoted themselves to death on behalf of the state (Livy 5.41.1–3, 9).

In 340 the consuls T. Manlius Torquatus and P. Decius Mus were about to engage the Latins in battle near Mt Vesuvius. The consuls offered sacrifice and the haruspex informed Decius that the lobe of the liver of Decius' sacrifice was ill-omened. Decius was on the left wing, which was pushed back, and he undertook the devotio ritual, which involved the general devoting himself and the enemy to the 'Gods of the underworld (the divine *manes*) and to Earth'. The sacrifice before battle sought the good-will of the gods, who here gave a warning and indicated that Decius must consecrate and sacrifice himself to win the battle; for his conduct as military tribune, see doc. 5.8.

The *cinctus gabinus* was a particular way of wearing the toga, described here by Livy, for some ceremonial rites; it left the arms free (the weight of a toga had to be supported in the crook of the left arm: cf. Serv. *Aen.* 7.612). For *devotio*: Versnel 1976, 1980: 131–43, 148–63; North 1989: 593; *BNP* 1.35–6; Turcan 2000: 96–7; for the devotio of Marcus Curtius after an earthquake in 362, see Livy 7.6.3–5.

9.4 In this moment of confusion the consul Decius cried out to Marcus Valerius in a loud voice: 'Marcus Valerius, we need the gods' help; you are a state pontiff of the Roman people — come, dictate the words with which I may devote myself to save the legions.' **5** The pontiff told him to put on his purple-edged toga, and, with his head veiled and with one hand protruding from his toga and touching his chin, stand on a spear laid under his feet and repeat as follows: **6** 'Janus, Jupiter, Father Mars, Quirinus, Bellona, Lares, New Gods (divi novensiles), Native Gods (di indigetes), Gods, in whose power are we and our enemies, and you Gods of the underworld (di manes), **7** I supplicate and revere you, I seek your favour and entreat you, that you prosper the might and victory of the Roman people, the Quirites, and afflict the enemies of the Roman people, the Quirites, with terror, fear and death. **8** As I have pronounced the words, so on behalf of the Republic of the Roman people, the Quirites, and on behalf of the army, the legions and the auxiliaries of the Roman people, the Quirites, do I devote myself and with me the legions and auxiliaries of the enemy to the Gods of the underworld and to Earth.' . . . .

10.11 It seems appropriate to add here that when a consul, dictator or praetor devotes the legions of the enemy, he need not devote himself but may pick any citizen he wishes from an enlisted Roman legion; **12** if the man who has been devoted dies, it is considered that all is well; if he does not die, then an effigy of him is buried seven feet or more under the ground and a propitiatory sacrifice slaughtered; it is not lawful for Roman magistrates to climb the mound where that effigy has been buried. **13** But if someone chooses to devote himself, as Decius did, and does not die, he cannot perform any religious act either for himself or the people without desecrating it, whether a sacrifice or anything else he chooses. He who has devoted himself has the right to dedicate his arms to Vulcan or to any other god he chooses; **14** it is not lawful for the spear on which the consul has stood and prayed to fall into the hands of the enemy; if it should, a propitiatory sacrifice must be made to Mars with a pig, sheep and bull (a *suovetaurilia*). **11.1** These details, although the memory of every divine and human practice has been erased by men's preference for the new and foreign in place of what is ancient and traditional, I have considered it not inappropriate to repeat in the very words in which they were handed down and publicly pronounced.

PRIESTHOODS

The basic unit of organised Roman religion was the priesthood. Priests were drawn from the elite; when plebeians became eligible, plebeian priests came from the elite plebeian families, and great social distinction applied to holding a priesthood: Cicero was augur (Cic. *Fam.* 6.6.7, 15.4.13; probably elected in 53) and Caesar pontifex maximus (doc. 3.20). Cicero could state that the same individuals were 'in charge of the worship of the immortal gods and the highest affairs of state', and that this was the will of the gods (*Dom.* 1). Novi homines are rarely found among the members of priesthoods: only one novus homo (out of 81) is known to have been pontifex maximus, and only two (Marius and Cicero) are among the known augurs (Szemler 1986: 2317–18). The known names of those who held priestly office show that three-quarters of the priests of the four main colleges held the consulship (Szemler 2326–31). Priests were male; the main exception were the Vestal Virgins and the wife of the flamen dialis. From 180 to 47 BC it was normal to hold only one priestly office; Caesar's election as augur and quindecimvir in 47 BC when he was already pontifex maximus was the first time more than a single priesthood had been held by one individual (Gordon 1990: 182). Roman priests belonged to specific colleges charged with various responsibilities in the maintenance of the state's rites and cults. Though the number of individual priests was increased over time, the only new priesthood formed during the Republic was the college of three *epulones* introduced in 196 BC, and increased to seven by Sulla. There were four major colleges of priests: the *pontifices, augures, quindecimviri sacris faciundis*, and *epulones*.

The pontifex maximus was the head of the college of pontifices (pontiffs) and his main role was to address the senate on behalf of the pontifices. He also disciplined the pontifices and the Vestal Virgins (doc. 7.88). There were eight pontifices from 300 BC (under the *lex Ogulnia*; doc. 1.55), four were plebeian and four patrician; access to priesthoods had been one of the aims of the plebeians in the 'Conflict of the Orders'. Sulla increased their number to fifteen (cf. doc. 11.28). Also belonging to the college of pontifices were the six Vestal Virgins, the rex sacrorum ('king of the sacrifices', performing the religious duties of the old kings), and fifteen flamines (singular: *flamen*; priest). Each flamen worshipped a single deity, and the three most important *flamines* were the *flamen dialis* (Jupiter: doc. 3.19), *martialis* (Mars) and *quirinalis* (Quirinus). The pontifices as a college were largely concerned with the *sacra* (sacred rites), on which they could be called upon to advise the senate. There was also a pontifical scribe, who read out the prayers for magistrates to repeat after him (doc. 3.24); or in the case of a vow described by Livy, the consul repeated the words after the pontifex (docs 3.16, 54).

The second major college was that of the augures, augurs, or diviners. There were nine members (five plebeian) under the *lex Ogulnia*, increased to 15 by Sulla. Their main duty lay with the interpretation of the auspices. There were originally two officials (the *duumviri sacris faciundis*, and then ten (decemviri) from 376 and 15 (quindecimviri) under Sulla. They had charge of the Sibylline Books but consulted these only at the direction of the senate. The epulones organised the epulum Iovis, a feast for Jupiter held at the ludi. Other groups of priests included the fetials, haruspices, Luperci, Fratres Arvales (Arval brothers) and Salii (docs 3.4, 10–12, 17, 7.76).

For Roman priesthoods, see Cowell 1964: 179–86; Taylor 1949: 90–7; Ogilvie 1969: 106–11; Dumézil 1970: 576–93; Szemler 1972 (esp. 21–46), 1986; Goar 1972: 6–11; Ferguson 1987: 753–4; Vanggaard 1988; Beard 1988, 1990, 1994: 731, 742–3; Gordon 1990: 179–82; Scheid 1993; Cornell 1995: 232–6; *BNP* 1.18–30, 99–108, 2.194–202; North 1989: 582–90, 2000: 22–8; Turcan 2000: 52–8; diagrams setting out the priesthoods: Beard 1990: 20–1; North 2000: 23–4.

3.17 The priesthoods

Varro *On the Latin Language* 5.83–6

Rome's priesthoods were remarkably stable from the early Republic, with little innovation. Varro's explanation of the etymology of the term pontiffs (pontifices) is to be preferred to Scaevola's: there will have been sacred rites associated with the bridge crossing the Tiber, including that of the Argei; doc. 3.7 (cf. Hallett 1970).

83: Quintus Scaevola was consul 95 BC and pontifex maximus c. 89–82 BC (*MRR* II.37); *facere*, to do: here in the sense of 'to make sacrifices'. For the Sublicius pons (bridge), built by Ancus Marcius, the oldest bridge on the Tiber in Rome, see Livy 1.33.7, 2.10 (the story of Horatius Cocles' heroic defence of Rome at the bridge); doc. 3.7. The thirty curiae were the earliest divisions of the Roman people (docs 1.18, 20) and the basis for political and military organisation. **84**: For the flamines: Vangaard 1988, esp. 24–9; for Furrina and her festival, obscure even in Varro's time, see doc. 3.5. Falacer was also obscure, perhaps an old Italian hero.

83 The *sacerdotes*, priests, were collectively so named from the *sacra*, sacred rites. The *pontiffs*, high-priests, according to Quintus Scaevola the pontifex maximus, were named from *posse*, to be able, and *facere*, to do, as though *pontentifices*. I actually think the term comes from *pons*, bridge: for it was by them that the wooden bridge on piles (the Sublicius) was first made and frequently repaired, since in this connection sacred rites are performed on both sides of the Tiber with great ceremony. The *curiones*, priests of the curiae, were named from the *curiae*; they are created for the purpose of conducting sacred rites in the *curiae*.

84 The *flamines*, flamens, because in Latium they always had their heads covered and bound with a *filum*, woollen fillet, were called *filamines*. Individually they have their cognomens from the god whose rites they perform: but some are clear and other obscure: clear like Martialis and Volcanalis; obscure like Dialis and Furinalis, since Dialis is from Jupiter (for he is also Diovis), and Furinalis from Furrina, who even has a Furinal festival in the calendar, and the flamen Falacer, too, from the divine father Falacer.

85 The Salii were named from *salitare*, to dance, because they had the custom and duty of dancing every year in the places of assembly in their sacred rites. The Luperci were named, because they make offerings in the Lupercal at the Lupercalia festival. The Arval brothers were so called as they perform public rites to make *arva*, plough-land, bring forth crops . . . **86** The *fetiales*, fetial priests, because they were in charge of the state's word of honour between peoples; for it was through them that a war that was declared should be a just war, and through them it was ended so that by a *foedus*, treaty, the *fides*, good faith, of the peace might be established. Some of them were sent before war was declared, to demand restitution, and even now it is through them that the *foedus*, treaty, is made, which Ennius writes was pronounced *fidus*.

3.18 The duties of Roman priests

Dionysius of Halicarnassus *Roman Antiquities* 2.73.1–2

Dionysius sketches the main duties of the pontifices (pontiffs), the most important of the four major colleges of priests.

1 The pontiffs have authority over the matters of greatest importance. **2** They serve as judges in all religious cases concerning private citizens or magistrates or those who minister to the gods, and make laws concerning religious rites which have no written record or established tradition, which they consider appropriate to be sanctioned by law and custom; they inquire into all the magistracies which have duties involving any sacrifice or religious duty as well as all the priesthoods, and ensure that their servants and attendants whom they use in the rituals commit no error in regard to the sacred laws; to the private citizens who are not knowledgeable about religious matters concerning the gods and divine spirits, the pontiffs are expounders and interpreters; and if they learn that some people are not obeying their instructions, they punish them, examining each of the charges. They themselves are not liable to any prosecution or punishment, nor are they accountable to the senate or people, at any rate concerning religious matters.

3.19 The flamen dialis

Aulus Gellius *Attic Nights* 10.15.1–30

Cf. Plut. *Rom. Quest.* 44. This Fabius Pictor was the author of *On the Pontifical Law* (not the historian). The flamen dialis was the priest of Jupiter; the origins and meaning of the various taboos affecting this priest are unclear, and were probably so to Romans by the end of the Republic. This priesthood almost eliminated any possibility of a military career, as this flamen could not even see the army. The best known flamen dialis was L. Cornelius Merula, flamen dialis, elected consul suffectus (substitute) in place of Cinna when the latter was expelled from Rome in 87; on Cinna's return he was put on trial, so Merula committed suicide in Jupiter's temple, polluting the altar and cult statue with his blood. Julius Caesar had been designated for this priesthood in 87 or 86 under Marius and Cinna, but Sulla cancelled all their appointments when Rome fell to him (Suet. *Jul.* 1.1) and this priesthood was not filled between 87 and 11 BC (sources: *MRR* II.47; Tac. *Ann.* 3.58; Vangaard 1988: 87). This is sometimes explained as owing to a general unwilling- ness to take on an office with so many restrictions, and as a decline in 'traditional' religion. However, in this long break, the pontiffs performed the rituals which this flamen would otherwise have (Tac. *Ann.* 3.58), so it was not a lack of religiosity which was the problem here, but one of organising who would hold the position (Beard 1994: 742; *BNP* 1.131).

The flamen dialis was married to his wife by the sacred marriage ceremony, confarreatio (doc. 7.10), which involved a sacrifice to Jupiter. Varro *Divine Antiquities* (at Gell.10.15.32), notes that the flamen dialis wore a white cap. The *rex sacrificulus* (or rex sacrorum) succeeded the kings in presiding over sacrifices, but essentially he was not important, though nominally outranking the pontifex maximus and the flamen dialis. The wife of the flamen dialis was the flaminica dialis, and she too was subject to various restrictions. Her role was passive: she wove the ritual garment which her husband as flamen dialis had to wear (the *laena*); she could not divorce her husband.

For the flamen dialis, see Ogilvie 1969: 109; Dumézil 1970: 1.151–4; Szemler 1972: 95–9; Goodman & Holladay 1986: 162–3; Vangaard 1988: 83–4, 108; Beard 1990: 24–5; Scheid 1992: 400–3; *BNP* 1.130–2; Turcan 2000: 52–3.

1 Numerous ceremonies are imposed upon the flamen dialis and also many restraints, about which we read in the books written *On the Public Priests* and which are also recorded in the first book of Fabius Pictor. **2** Of these I remember in general the following points: **3** it is unlawful for the flamen dialis to ride a horse; **4** it is likewise unlawful for him to see the 'classes arrayed' outside the pomerium, that is, the army in battle order; for this reason the flamen dialis is rarely made a consul, since wars were entrusted to the consuls. **5** It is likewise unlawful for him ever to take an oath; **6** it is likewise unlawful for him to wear a ring, unless it is perforated and without a stone. **7** It is also against the law to carry out fire from the flaminia (the flamen dialis' dwelling) except for a sacred ritual; **8** if a prisoner in chains enters his house he must be released and the chains must be drawn up through the impluvium ('rainhole') onto the roof-tiles and let down from there into the street. **9** He must have no knot in his cap or girdle or any other part of his clothes; **10** if anyone is being led away to be flogged and falls at his feet as a suppliant, it is unlawful for him to be flogged that day. **11** The hair of the dialis may not be cut except by a free man. **12** It is customary for the flamen neither to touch nor even to name a female goat, or uncooked meat, ivy or beans.

 13 He must not walk underneath a trellis for vines. **14** The feet of the bed on which he lies must have a thin coating of clay, and he must not be away from the bed for three nights in a row, nor is it lawful for anyone else to sleep in that bed. At the foot of his bed there must be a box containing a little pile of sacrificial cakes and offering-cakes. **15** The clippings of the dialis' nails and hair must be buried in the ground beneath a fruitful tree. **16** Every day is a holy day for the dialis. **17** He must not go outdoors without his cap; that he is now allowed to do this indoors, was only recently decided by the pontiffs, **18** as Masurius Sabinus wrote, and it is also said that some of the other ceremonies have been remitted and he has been excused from them.

19 It is not lawful for him to touch bread made with yeast. **20** He does not take off his inner tunic except in covered places, so he may not be naked under the open sky, as it were under the eye of Jove. **21** No one else reclines above him at a banquet except the rex sacrificulus (the rex sacrorum). **22** If he loses his wife he resigns from the flaminate. **23** The marriage of the flamen may not be dissolved except by death. **24** He never enters a place where bodies are buried, and he never touches a corpse; **25** however, he is not forbidden to attend a funeral.

26 The flaminica dialis has almost the same ceremonies; **27** they say that she observes certain other different ones, for example, that she wears a dyed robe, **28** and that she has a twig from a fruitful tree tucked in her veil, and that it is forbidden for her to go up more than three rungs of a ladder **29** (except what the Greeks call ladders), and also that, **30** when she goes to the Argei, she neither combs her head nor arranges her hair.

3.20 Caesar buys his priesthood

Suetonius *Life of the Deified Julius* 13

Note also Plut. *Caes.* 7.3: 'Today, mother, you will see your son either as high priest or as an exile' (cf. Sall. *Cat.* 49.2; Vell. 2.43.3). When in 63 BC Titus Labienus successfully proposed to restore the right of the tribal assembly to elect pontiffs, first granted in Ahenobarbus' tribunate in 104 (Cic. *Laws* 2.18–19), Caesar supported him (Dio 37.37.13). This (as well as the bribery) must help explain Caesar's election in 63, against two other prominent candidates, P. Servilius Isauricus (cos. 79) and Q. Lutatius Catulus (cos. 78); he received more votes in the tribes of the other candidates than they received in all of the tribes, though, at 37 years, he had not yet been praetor. See Taylor 1949: 92–3, 1966: 82; *MRR* II.168, 171; Meier 1995: 160–2.

After abandoning his ambition of governing the province (Egypt), Caesar stood for the office of pontifex maximus, using the most lavish bribery. It is said that, working out the enormous debts he had contracted, when he went to the comitia that morning he told his mother, as she kissed him, that if he would not return unless as pontifex maximus. However, he defeated his two most influential rivals, both of whom were much older and more distinguished, and he won more votes from their own tribes than either won in the entire election.

ROMAN PURIFICATORY RITUALS

3.21 A purificatory ritual

Cato the Elder *On Farming* 141.2–4

The Ambarvalia was celebrated in May, both as a public agricultural festival, designed to purify all fields, and as a private rite, here described by Cato. The Ambarvalia was a *lustratio* (lustration), the performance of a *lustrum*, a purificatory rite to avert harm and evil in general; it was a 'movable' festival and so its date does not appear in the calendars. A *lustratio* involved a procession finishing at its starting point, invoking divine assistance to keep harm from the area being traversed, and a *suovetaurilia* (the sacrifice of a pig, sheep and bull; *sus, ovis,* and *taurus* respectively); cf. docs 3.16, 25. The private suovetaurilia used young beasts, the public ones a full grown male pig, ram and bull. The principal lustration was that at the end of the census: doc. 3.22. There could also be a *lustratio* of an army (Livy 23.35.5) and fleet (App. *BC* 5.97.401). See for the lustratio: Dumézil 1970: 238–9; *BNP* 1.178. Manius, here, is a generic name.

Note the agricultural role of Mars, as in the hymn of the Arval brothers (doc. 3.10): Mars here is the protector of boundaries; Janus is routinely invoked at the beginnings of prayer. The prayer itself was probably in the form of a hymn (carmen: Courtney *ALP* 47, 63). The *strues* and *fertum* are sacrificial cakes: the strues was a heap of little offering-cakes, shaped rather like fingers joined together; the fertum was an oblation-cake. Ambarvalia: Ogilvie 1969: 88–9; Dumézil 1970: 230; Scullard 1981: 124–5; Versnel 1993: 300; Courtney *ALP* 63–7.

1 This is the formula to be used for purifying the land. Bid the suovetaurilia to be led around with the words, 'So that, with the good will of the gods, our efforts may be successful, take care, Manius, to purify my farm, land, and ground with this suove-taurilia, however you think it best for them to be driven or carried around.' **2** First invoke Janus and Jupiter with an offering of wine, then say: 'Father Mars, I pray and entreat you to be kindly and well-disposed towards me and our home and household. For this reason I have ordered a pig-sheep-bull procession to be driven around my field, land and farm, so that you will prevent, ward off and turn away diseases, seen and unseen, barrenness and fruitlessness, disasters and storms; and so that you will allow fruits, grains, vines, and saplings to grow and achieve fruition; **3** and so that you will protect the shepherds and the flocks and give safety and good health to me and our home and household. For these reasons, therefore, and for the consecration of my farm, land, and field, and the offering of a sacrifice for purification, as I have said, accept the sacrifice of the suckling pig-sheep-bull.' Repeat: 'Therefore, Father Mars, accept the suckling pig-sheep-bull sacrifice.'

4 Do it with a knife. Have the *strues* and *fertum* at hand, then make the offering. As you slaughter the pig, lamb and calf, you must say: 'Therefore, accept the sacrifice of the pig-sheep-bull.' Mars must not be named, nor the lamb and calf. If all the offerings are not favourable, say as follows: 'Father Mars, if anything in the suckling pig-sheep-bull sacrifice was not satisfactory to you, I offer this new pig-sheep-bull sacrifice as atonement.' If there is doubt about only one or two, say as follows: 'Father Mars, since that piglet was not satisfactory to you, I offer this piglet as atonement.'

3.22 Preparation for the lustrum at the completion of a census

Varro *On the Latin Language* 6.86–7

See also Varro *Lat. Lang.* 6.93, *Rust.* 2.1.10; Livy 1.44.1–2; Dion. Hal. 4.22.1–2; Val. Max. 4.1.10. Varro relates that he has taken this extract from the *Censors' Records*; he deals with the various meanings of templum at 7.6–7.

A *lustrum* (purification) of the assembly was performed by one of the censors after the census was complete; the act was known as *lustrum condere*, and it took place in the Campus Martius with the citizens drawn up in their centuries. The chief feature of the ceremony, as with any lustrum, was the suovetaurilia. The rite indicates the close connection between religion and civic politics: the citizen body — in the form of its military assembly — was purified and protected from harm by a religious rite. One of the censors was chosen to perform the actual lustrum, and he recited a prayer that the gods increase the size of Rome's dominions (Val. Max. 4.1.10; doc. 3.25).

The lustrum is shown on the so-called 'altar of Domitius Ahenobarbus' of the late second century BC, or perhaps showing the census of 97 BC. A fully grown pig, ram and bull are led before an altar by attendants. Behind the altar stands Mars, waiting for the sacrifice. The figure with toga and wreath about to pour a libation at the altar must be the censor, who has led the purification carrying the vexillum (standard, like a flag: Varro *Lat. Lang.* 6.93) but which is now carried by another figure (contra Gruen). Behind Mars stand a singer and a musician; for the 'altar', see Torelli 1982: 1–25, esp. 11–13; Henig 1983: 72–3; Gruen 1992: 147–50, pl. 3; Boardman 1993: 231–2. See, for the lustrum at the census: Ogilvie 1969: 89; Scullard 1981: 232–3; Hopkins 1991: 491; Wiseman 1994: 327–9.

86 Now, first, I will put down from the *Censors' Records*: When at night the censor has gone into the sacred enclosure (templum) to take the auspices, and a message has come from the sky, he shall command the herald to call the men: 'May this be good, fortunate, happy and advantageous to the Roman people, the Quirites, and to the government of the Roman people, the Quirites, and to me and my colleague, to our good faith and our magistracy: All the citizen soldiers in arms, and private citizens, spokespersons of all the tribes, pronounce an *inlicium* (invitation to a special assembly) in case anyone wishes a reckoning (i.e., a protest against his censor's rating) to be given for himself or for another.'

87 The herald calls it first in the sacred enclosure, afterwards likewise from the walls. When it becomes light, the censors, secretaries, and magistrates are anointed with myrrh and ointments. When the praetors and the tribunes of the people and those who have been called to the *inlicium* have come, the censors shall take lots between them to see which shall perform the purification. When the sacred enclosure (in the Campus Martius) has been fixed, then the one who is going to perform the purification holds the assembly.

RITUAL UTTERANCES

The Romans placed a great deal of importance on the correct performance of rituals. There were tabellae, records, of the prayers to be used by magistrates, and these were read rather than recited by heart so that no mistakes were made. The term *religio* in fact embraces the correct performance of religious ritual. Numa's written texts: doc. 3.6; *religio*: Szemler 1986: 2320–23; Turcan 2000: 1; North 2000: 82; Scheid 2003: 22–3; Rüpke 2004: 179.

3.23 The importance of correct ritual utterances

ILS 3124

(*CIL* I² 365; *ILLRP* 238; *ROL* IV.80.) This bronze tablet at Falerii (modern Cività Castellana) was dedicated to Minerva. The inscription is in five lines, read from right to left; the language is a mixture of Faliscan and Latin. The senate was involved in the making of the dedication, illustrating the close connection between the state and the gods. That the dedication was made in the correct way, presumably following ritual norms, is recorded.

Sacred to Minerva. Lars Cotena, son of Lars, praetor, by the vote of the senate gave this as a votive gift. When it was given, it was dedicated in the prescribed manner.

3.24 The importance of ritual prayers

Pliny the Elder *Natural History* 28.10–11

While Pliny wrote in the imperial period, his comments are also valid for the Republic, and his is the fullest statement of the principle of correct ritual observance. The flute drowned out any ill-omened noises so that the efficacy of the prayer was not affected; for flute players at sacrifices, see also doc. 3.70, cf. 3.8, 11. Cicero records that the ludi Megalenses in honour of the Magna Mater might have to be repeated, if the dancer stopped dancing, the flute-player stopped playing, or the aedile made an error in reciting the formula or in handling the libation bowl (*Har. Resp.* 23).

10 Of all the remedies which man has discovered, the first gives rise to a most important question, which is always unanswered: do words and ritual incantations have any effect? If they do, it would be right and fitting to give man the credit, but individually all our wisest men reject belief in them, although in general the public unconsciously believes in them all the time. Indeed, the sacrifice of victims or due consultation of the gods is thought to have no effect if unaccompanied by a prayer. **11** Furthermore, there is one form of words for seeking favourable omens, another for warding off evil, and another for requesting protection. We also notice that our highest magistrates have adopted set prayers, and, so that no word is omitted or spoken in the wrong place, one attendant reads the prayer from a written text, another is assigned to check it, and a third is put in charge to ensure silence, while a flautist plays so only the prayer can be heard. There are remarkable cases recorded where the sound of unfavourable omens has ruined the ritual or an error has been made in the prayer, when suddenly the head of the liver or the heart has been missing from the entrails or have been doubled, while the victim was still standing.

3.25 Scipio Aemilianus changes the formula of prayer

Valerius Maximus *On Memorable Deeds and Sayings*
(Of Self-confidence) 4.1.10

Valerius Maximus, in describing the lustrum performed by Scipio Aemilianus as censor in 142 to conclude the census, refers to the scribe reciting the prayer from the records, which Scipio then repeated after him. The incident as recorded is perhaps unhistorical.

When as censor, the younger Africanus was concluding the census, during the suove-taurilia (solitaurilia) the scribe recited in front of him from the public tablets the formula of prayer in which the immortal gods were requested to make the state of the Roman people better and greater. 'It is good and great enough,' stated Scipio, 'So I pray that they keep it safe in perpetuity'. And he thereupon ordered that the formula in the public tablets be emended accordingly. From that time on the censors have employed this modest form of prayer in concluding the census.

3.26 Ritual for ensuring an unknown god is not offended

Cato the Elder *On Farming* 139

Cato advises that a farmer placate the deity of a grove before clearing it. Many Greek sacred laws concern the protection of a grove dedicated to a particular god; for Rome: Bloch 1960: 126–7. There were several sacred groves in the city: Gaius Gracchus committed suicide in the grove of the Furies (Plut. *G. Gracchus* 17.3); for a grove of Faunus and Picus below the Aventine: Ovid *Fasti* 3.295–6.

To clear a grove you must use the Roman rite, as follows. Make an expiatory sacrifice of a pig, and say these words: 'Whatever god or whatever goddess you may be to whom this grove is sacred, as it is right to make an expiatory sacrifice of a pig to you for taking this sacred grove, in respect of this, whether I do it or someone else at my orders, may it be rightly done. Therefore, in offering this expiatory sacrifice of a pig to you, I entreat with humble prayers that you will be kindly and propitious to me, my house and household and my children; and so accept this expiatory sacrifice of a pig.'

3.27 Even forgotten cults maintained

ILS 4015

(*CIL* I² 801; *ILLRP* 291; *ROL* IV.88.) On an altar at Rome, c. 90–80 BC. Sextius Calvinus may have been the son of the consul of 124 (C. Sextius Calvinus).

Whether sacred to god or to goddess, Gaius Sextius Calvinus, son of Gaius, praetor, restored this on a vote of the senate.

A RELIGIOUS CALENDAR

Roman religious calendars provide a wealth of information about the dates of festivals. There is only one from the Republic, which includes only brief notices about the deity being honoured; imperial examples often have comments about the nature of the festival, and historical anniversaries. Not all festivals are marked: some were 'movable festivals' with the date, literally, 'to be announced' by the rex sacrorum. See for religious calendars: Macrob. 1.16.2–6; Taylor 1949: 78; Ogilvie 1969: 71–3; Dumézil 1970: 559–65; Scullard 1981: 41–9; Ferguson 1987: 755–6; Beard 1991: 54–5; Gordon 1990: 184–91; Dupont 1992: 188–218; Scheid 1992a: 119–21; *BNP* 1.5–6, 2.60–77; cf. Salzman 1990: 5–8; for a list of the festivals of the Roman year: North 2000: 48–9. Varro *Lat. Lang.* 6.27–31 (cf. Plut. *Rom. Quest.* 24) explains various calendar terms.

3.28 A pre-Julian calendar (*tabula fastorum*) for the month Sextilis

Inscriptiones Italiae XIII.2, pp. 1–28

(*ROL* IV.450–65.) This calendar, written on a wall at Antium (Anzio), a Roman colony south of Rome, and probably of the first century BC, is the only surviving Roman calendar prior to Caesar's calendar reforms. It measures 1.16 by 2.5 metres and was meant to be visible and public. There is an eight-day week (listed here as A–H) and it covers the twelve months of the year, as well as the intercalated month, each month having its own column. It adds up to a normal republican year of 355 days. At the base of the column, the number of days in each month are given. The names of the months are abbreviated. July is called Quin[tilis] (the original fifth month), but it was later renamed after Caesar to honour him (hence July). Similarly, August is called Sex[tilis] (i.e., originally the sixth month): it was renamed after Augustus in his reign. Letters indicated the status of the day with regard to public business. An 'N' after a day indicated *nefastus* (plural: *nefasti*), a day when the assemblies and courts could not be convened; 'F' indicated *fastus* (plural: *fasti*) when courts could convene and business was permitted; 'C' (*comitialis*) when assemblies could be held; 'EN' (*endotercisus*) showed that the day was split between a religious festival and public business, such as day F in the third week. The aim of the calendar seems primarily to ensure that profane business did not occur on days set aside for the gods. The calendar notes the kalends (as K, the first day, the new moon) and the ides (as EID, the middle day of month, the thirteenth or fifteenth day; full moon), as well as the nones (as NON, the first quarter of the moon), the fifth or seventh day of a month. On the nones the rex sacrorum announced the dates of any movable festivals to be celebrated in that month. Some of the readings in the calendar are uncertain, hence the question marks (?). For this calendar, see North 1989: 574–5; esp. *BNP* 2.61–4.

A   Kalends of Sextilis [August]. To Hope; to the Two Victories.
B   Business in court.
C   Business in Assembly (?).
D   Business in Assembly (?).
E   Nones. No business. Public holiday. To Safety.
F   Business in court.
G   Business in Assembly.
H   Business in Assembly.

A   Business in court (?).
B   Business in Assembly (?).
C   Business in Assembly.
D   Business in Assembly.
E   Ides. No business. Public holiday. To Diana, Vortumnus, Fortune, Horsewoman, Hercules the Conqueror, Castor, Pollux, Camenae (the Muses).
F   Business in court.
G   Business in Assembly.
H   Business in Assembly.

A   Festival, of God of the Harbour (Portunus). No business. Public holiday (?).
B   Business in Assembly (?).
C   Festival, of Vintage. Business in court in the morning. To Venus.
D   Business in Assembly (?).
E   Festival, of Consus (god of fertility). No business. Public holiday.
F   Midsplit (i.e., nefastus in the morning, fastus for the rest of the day).
G   Festival, of Vulcan. No business. Public holiday. To Vulcan, Hora, Quirinus (or Hora, wife of Quirinus), Maia above the Comitium.
H   Business in Assembly.

A   Festival, of Goddess of Sowing (Ops Consiva). No business. Public holiday (?).
B   Business in Assembly (?).
C   Festival, of Volturnus. No business. Public holiday.
D   Business in Assembly (?).
E   Business in Assembly (?).

3.29 Caesar's calendar reforms, 46 BC

Suetonius *Life of the Deified Julius* 40.1–2

Originally, the Roman year consisted of ten months, March to December (part of winter was presumably not represented in the calendar); hence September (= seven, 'septem') was the seventh month, October ('octo', the eighth) and so on. January and February were added later, but it was not until 153 BC that January 1 became the first day of the year, when the consuls entered office (previously it was March 15). The year had 355 days and, to bring it up to a rough solar year of 365 days, an extra month was inserted (intercalated) after February, which was shortened to 23–24 days. The pontiffs were in charge of the process but by 46 BC the calendar was three months ahead of the actual solar year. Caesar, in his role as pontifex maximus, reformed the calendar in 46 BC: the shorter months were lengthened to bring the total of calendar days to 365, and every fourth year an extra day was added between 23–24 February. To have 45 BC start on the correct solar date, 46 BC was lengthened to 445 days. The agricultural festivals, as held on their calendar dates, were now in tune with the seasons. This Julian calendar was modified by Pope Gregory XIII, and the 'Gregorian' calendar came into use in 1582 in Catholic Europe (in 1752 in Britain), and remains the western calendar; see Scullard 1981: 42.

1 Turning then to domestic reorganisation, Caesar first corrected the calendar which was in a total mess because of the pontiffs' habit of arbitrary insertions, so that the harvest festival no longer coincided with summer or the vintage festival with autumn; he adjusted the year to the course of the sun by making it 365 days, removing the short intercalary month and adding one day every fourth year. **2** Furthermore, so that the correct reckoning should start with the next Kalends of January, he inserted two months between November and December, so that that year, when these changes were made, had fifteen months, including the intercalary one which customarily fell in that year.

SACRIFICE

Sacrifice was *the* most important feature of Roman religion. The participants and the sacrificial victim — always a domestic beast — were purified, and then a procession led the victim, which had to be willing, to the sacrificial altar. The magistrate presiding over the sacrifice wore the *cinctus gabinus* (see doc. 3.16). Sacrifices took place outside, in the open air, both due to the 'mess' involved in sacrifice and the need to cook the beast once it was killed. Wine and incense were offered to the gods on a *foculus*, a 'portable' hearth placed next to the altar. The *immolatio* was the next stage: the animal's back was sprinkled with *mola salsa* (salted meal (flour), from which the term *immolatio* derives), and a prayer (*precatio*) recited giving the beast to the divinity receiving the sacrifice. Making the *mola salsa* for sacrifices was one of the chief duties of the Vestal Virgins.

The beast was then killed, not by the presiding magistrates or priests, but by *victimarii* or *popae*, who also butchered the carcass. At this stage the entrails (*exta*) were read by a haruspex: if the entrails were perfect, i.e., auspicious, then the ceremony had drawn to a successful conclusion (*litatio*). If there was something wrong with them this meant that the sacrifice was not acceptable to the god and had to be repeated. Imperfect entrails presaged disasters. Before his death, Caesar presided over two sacrifices: at one the victim had no heart, at the second the liver lacked its head (Cic. *Div.* 1.119). The animals usually sacrificed were cattle, sheep and pigs. Jupiter and Juno preferred white beasts, the *di Manes* black ones; pregnant cows were sacrificed to Tellus (Earth) at the Fordicidia in April for the fertility of the fields (Scullard 1981: 102). See Cic. *Laws* 2.20: 'the priests shall give attention to the victims which are proper and acceptable to each god'.

The entrails were cooked: those of bovines were boiled, while those of pigs and sheep were put on spits and cooked; in 176 BC news that a liver liquefied while being boiled at a sacrifice terrified the senate (Livy 41.15.1–4). The entrails (unlike in Greek religion in which the participants ate them) were then offered to the god, being burnt on the altar along with wine and more mola salsa. The rest was eaten by the participants. Sacrifices could also be non-animal, consisting of cakes, but the animal sacrifice was the more important and the one used for purposes of state. The only depiction of sacrificial procedure dating from the Republic is the altar of Domitius Ahenobarbus, which shows the procession and victims, and the altar with the presiding magistrate about to perform a purifying libation. Most of the information concerning Roman sacrifice comes from a late source, the Christian Arnobius' work *Against the Gentiles*, which gives numerous details. But there are enough comments in sources such as Livy and Dionysius for the overall picture for the Republic to be known (doc. 3.30 is the fullest pagan description of a Roman sacrifice; cf. doc. 3.71).

Roman rituals were accompanied by specific prayers which had to be recited precisely as they were written down (docs 3.16, 24–5), following an established and unalterable form several hundred years old by the end of the Republic: 'Prayers to the immortal gods, which are made according to Roman ritual, are set down in the books of the priests of the Roman people and in many ancient works' (Gell. 13.23.1). Sacrifice was held to be of no efficacy without accompanying prayer (doc. 3.24) which took place before the beast was killed (doc. 3.30). Flutes were played while the prayer was recited, so that 'only the prayer can be heard': cf. doc. 3.24. Prayers are found in numerous ritual contexts (see docs 3.16, 3.24–5, 3.47–8, 7.88) and were offered up by officials before taking up office.

For Roman sacrifice, see Warde Fowler 1911: 179–91; Ogilvie 1969: 41–52; Bloch 1960: 131–2; Dumézil 1970: 557–9; Scullard 1981: 22–5; North 1988, 2000: 44–5; *BNP* 1.35–7; Turcan 2000: 8–10.

3.30 Roman sacrificial practices

Dionysius of Halicarnassus *Roman Antiquities* 7.72.15, 18

Dionysius at 7.70–3 is describing the ludi magni (Great Games) of 490 BC (ludi magni: see also 7.68–9; Livy 2.36–7; Plut. *Cor.* 24–5), commenting on the procession which took place in the circus and the subsequent sacrifice. An important theme of his work is to show that Roman religion was Greek in origin, but, while there were similarities between Greek and Roman sacrifice, Roman sacrifice was not in any sense derivative and the features described above do not all apply to Greek sacrifice. There are several features to note in Dionysius' description: the procession, the fact that the consuls preside over the games, the involvement of the priests in sacrifice, the purifications, and the libations. Dionysius was an eye-witness of the ceremonies but also cites Fabius Pictor as his authority on the ludi (7.71.1; *FGrH* 809 F13b); see Gabba 1991: 89, 106, 134–5; North 2000: 44.

15 When the procession was over, the consuls and those of the priests whose duty it was immediately sacrificed oxen, and the way in which the sacrifices were performed was the same as our own. For, after washing their hands and purifying the victims with clean water, they sprinkled the fruits of Demeter on their heads, offered up a prayer, and gave the assistants orders to sacrifice them. Some of these struck the victim on the temples with a club while it was still standing, others placed the sacrificial knives beneath it as it fell. They then flayed and dismembered it and took portions from each organ and every limb as first-fruits, which they sprinkled with grains of barley and took in baskets to the sacrificing priests, who placed them on the altars, lit a fire beneath them, and poured a libation of wine over them while they were being consumed. . . . **18** I know of these ceremonies from having seen the Romans performing them in their sacrifices even in my own time; and satisfied with this single piece of evidence I am sure that the founders of Rome were not barbarians but Greeks who assembled from many different places.

3.31 Panic over portents calmed by public sacrifices (218 BC)

Livy *History of Rome* 21.62.1–11

Prodigies were considered to indicate that something was amiss between the gods and mortals; expiations would set matters right. The historical context of this passage is the winter of 218 BC, after the disastrous defeat at Trebia, though Livy is sceptical of some incidents. More expiations were required after the disaster of Trasimene in spring 217 brought forth new prodigies: the Sibylline Books were consulted and as a result temples were vowed to Venus Erycina and Mens (Mens Bona: 'Good Sense), and a 'sacred spring' vowed (Livy 22.9.7–11). A sacred spring (*ver sacrum*) involved sacrificing to Jupiter all the offspring of domestic flocks born in that season of spring, and is described by Livy (22.10.1–6). In 216, after the disaster at Cannae, human sacrifice was again resorted to as in 228 and 113 (doc. 4.38).

6–8: For the decemviri and the Sibylline books, see docs 3.36–7; for the lectisternium and the couches employed in this ceremony, see doc. 3.13. **9:** Hercules had several places of worship but that of Hercules Invictus ('the Unconquered') at the Ara Maxima in the Forum Boarium was the most important and is presumably meant here. Originally an introduced deity (Greek Herakles), his rites were celebrated with a Greek style of ritual (*graeco ritu*: Scheid 1995, esp. 20); Ara Maxima: esp. Ziolkowski 1992: 46–50; cf. Platner-Ashby 254; Richardson *Top. Dict.* 186–7. **10:** The genius of the Roman people was the deified entity of the Roman people. Vows were frequently made to the gods promising to do something in return for a specific outcome. Here the praetor is instructed to make a vow in return for ten years' stability (it is not specified exactly what is vowed). Generals going into battle might make such vows, sometimes of temples, if they were victorious (if they were defeated, the vow, of course, did not need to be fulfilled). **11:** The purpose of the expiations was to appease the gods but they also created confidence that the correct relationship had been established between the gods and mortals; for the expiations of 218 BC, see Toynbee 1965: II.379–80.

1 In Rome and the area around the city many queer prodigies occurred that winter, or, as tends to happen when men's minds once turn towards religion, many were said to have happened and were too easily believed. **2** Amongst these were a free-born baby of six months of age, who had shouted "Triumph!" in the vegetable market, **3** while in the Forum Boarium an ox had climbed, of its own accord, up to the third storey, and then, frightened by the screaming of the occupants, thrown itself out of the window; **4** shapes like ships had shone in the sky; the temple of Hope in the vegetable market was struck by lightning; at Lanuvium a sacrificial victim had moved all on its own, and a raven had flown down into the temple of Juno and perched on Juno's couch; **5** in the region of Amiternum apparitions of men, dressed in white, had been seen at a distance in many places, but they did not approach anyone; in Picenum it had rained stones; at Caere the divination tablets (*sortes*) had shrunk; and in Gaul a wolf had pulled a sentry's sword from its sheath and run off with it.

6 For other prodigies the decemvirs were instructed to consult the (Sibylline) *Books*, but for the rain of stones at Picenum, a nine-day period of sacrifice was proclaimed. Then almost all the citizens took part in expiation of the other portents. **7** First of all, the city was purified, and greater sacrificial victims (i.e., cattle) were offered to the gods designated in the *Books*. **8** A gift of gold, 40 pounds in weight, was carried to Lanuvium for Juno, and the matrons dedicated a bronze statue to Juno on the Aventine; a lectisternium was ordered at Caere, where the divination tablets had shrunk, and a supplicatio (expiation ceremony) to Fortune on Mount Algidus; **9** at Rome, too, another lectisternium was ordered to be made in honour of Youth (Juventas), as well as a supplicatio at the temple of Hercules, first by named individuals, then by the whole people before all the couches; **10** five greater victims were sacrificed to the Genius of the Roman people; and Gaius Atilius Serranus, the praetor, was commanded to make vows, 'if during the next ten years the state should remain unchanged'. **11** These purifications and vows, prescribed by the *Sibylline Books*, went far to relieve men's minds from their superstitious dread.

3.32 Cato's recipe for the libum

Cato the Elder On Farming 75

Libum was a cake often offered to the gods, especially on one's birthday. For other recipes, see Ovid *Fasti* 4.743–4 (millet); Athen. 125f (milk, honey and biscuit).

Make libum in this way: crush two pounds of cheese in a mortar. When it is thoroughly crushed, add one pound of wheat flour or, if you wish it to be lighter, half a pound of fine flour and mix it well with the cheese. Add one egg and mix together well. Then make it into a loaf, place it on leaves and bake slowly on a hot pan under an earthenware pot.

3.33 Pre-harvest sacrifice

Cato the Elder On Farming 134.1–4

See also Gell. 4.6.9–11. Before the harvest the *porca praecidanea* (the pre-harvest piglet) was sacrificed: Gell. 4.6.8. The entrails were used for divination and then burnt. The rest of the pig was eaten by the participants. Ovid *Fasti* 1.349–54: Ceres rejoiced in the sacrifice of a pig that had damaged her crops; for Ceres: Spaeth 1996. Varro *Rust.* 1.1.4–6 lists as the especial patrons of farming, Jupiter 'the Father', Tellus (Mother Earth), Sol (Sun), Luna (Moon), Ceres, Liber, Robigus (Robigo), Flora, Minerva, Venus, Lympha (Moisture), and Bonus Eventus ('Good Issue').

1 Before you harvest, the sacrifice of the *porca praecidanea* should be made in this way. Offer a piglet, as porca praecidanea, to Ceres before spelt, wheat, barley, beans, or rape seed are harvested. Make a prayer with incense and wine to Janus, Jupiter and Juno, before you kill the piglet. **2** Present an offering-cake (strues) to Janus in these words: 'Father Janus, in offering these cakes I entreat with good prayers that you will be kindly and propitious to me, my children, my house and my household.' Make an offering of an oblation-cake (fertum) to Jupiter with these words: 'Jupiter, in offering this cake I entreat with good prayers that, accepting this cake, you will be kindly and propitious to me, my children, my house and my household.' **3** Then give wine to Janus in these words: 'Father Janus, as I prayed with good prayers in offering the cakes, in the same way accept the wine offered to you.' And then pray to Jupiter in these words:

'Jupiter, accept this cake, accept the wine offered to you.' Then sacrifice the porca praecidanea. **4** When the entrails have been cut out, offer and present an offering-cake (strues) to Janus, making the offering in the same way as before, and offer and present a cake (fertum) to Jupiter, making the offering in the same way as before. In the same way give wine to Janus and give wine to Jupiter as you did before on account of the offering of the strues and the offering of the fertum. Afterwards give the entrails and wine to Ceres.

3.34 Druids and human sacrifice in Gaul

Caesar *Gallic War* 6.14, 16–17, 19

The Romans, despite their gladiatorial competitions and the formal 'sacrifice' of Greeks and Gauls in times of crisis (doc. 4.38), did not believe in (regular) human sacrifice, and they banned those of the Gauls; see for Druids, *BNP* 1.234.

14.1 The Druids do not take part in warfare and do not pay taxes like the other Gauls; they are exempt from military service and other such duties . . . **5** Among their teachings they place particular stress on the belief that the soul does not die but passes from one to another after death, and they think that this is the greatest incentive to courage, as it removes fear of death. **6** Furthermore, they hold discussions about the stars and their movements, about the size of the universe and earth, the physical constitution of the world, and the strength and power of the immortal gods and instruct their young men in these subjects. . . .

16.1 As a nation all the Gauls are extremely superstitious, and as a result **2** those suffering from severe illnesses, as well as those exposed to dangers and battles, offer, or vow that they will offer, human sacrifices, employing druids to perform these. **3** For they believe that, unless in place of a man's life another life is offered up, they cannot appease the might of the immortal gods, and they hold regular public sacrifices of the same kind. **4** Some of them have gigantic images, made of wickerwork, the limbs of which they fill with living men; these are set on fire and the men burnt to death. **5** They think that sacrifices of those caught in the act of theft or brigandage or guilty of some other offence are preferred by the immortal gods, but if the supply of these runs short they move on to the sacrifice of innocent people. **17.1** The god they reverence most is Mercury. They have numerous images of him, and consider him the inventor of all arts, the guide of roads and journeys, and as having the most power in matters of money-making and trade. **2** After him they reverence Apollo, Mars, Jupiter and Minerva . . .

19.3 Husbands have power of life and death over their wives, as over their children; and when the head of a noble family dies, his relatives convene and, if the circumstances of his death are suspicious, they examine his wives as we do slaves and should guilt be established they are put to death by fire and other tortures.

DIVINATION

The Romans sought the guidance of the gods in various ways. Augurs took the auspices prior to undertaking military campaigns and before public meetings (docs 3.45–50, 72). At other times, such as at elections and assemblies, the augurs advised magistrates who presided over the auspices, interpreting the flight of birds, or lightning and thunder to ascertain what needed to be done to overcome (expiate), by means of rituals, the displeasure of the gods. When the state was confronted by crisis (docs 3.13, 4.38), the religious action to be undertaken could be sought through consultation of the Sibylline Books, while in the case of prodigies, the Books or, more frequently, the haruspices could be consulted. The consuls made lists of prodigies that had been observed and passed this on to the senate, which could in turn consult the pontifices, the haruspices or quindecimviri (keepers of the Sibylline Books) for advice on the action to be taken. Livy 43.13.6 notes that two portents in 169 were designated as not being relevant, and it must often have occurred that the senate used its discretion in deciding which portents should be of public concern (MacBain 1982: 25–33).

Haruspices (sing.: haruspex) were diviners (sometimes the term is translated as 'soothsayers'), members of the Etruscan aristocracy, particularly concerned with examining the entrails of animals when they had been sacrificed and foretelling the future from these; they also interpreted thunderbolts as well as 'out of the way events', such as the noise outside Rome in 56 BC (see doc. 12.60). The senate could call upon them and take their advice, but they were not an official college of priests as such. Entrail divination was an Etruscan speciality (Cic. *Div.* 1.93; there is a discussion on haruspices and entrail divination at *Div.* 2.26–53). Cicero mentions a senatorial decree, perhaps of the second century, that a set number of Etruscan youths be trained in the art of haruspicy in order to keep it alive (*Div.* 1.92; Val. Max. 1.1.3). While the elder Cato could remark, 'It's amazing that a haruspex doesn't laugh when he sees another haruspex' (*Div.* 2.51), the state clearly took them seriously.

A bronze sheep's liver dating to the first century BC from Piacenza in Etruria is marked by lines into 42 sections, each with an Etruscan inscription; clearly it was used as a guide in entrail interpretation (Dumézil 1970: 650–4; Pallottino 1975: 138–47; van der Meer 1987; see the photograph at North 1990: 68 fig. 6; *BNP* 2.177). For haruspices: Ogilvie 1969: 65; MacBain 1982: 43–59; North 1990: 67–8, 2000: 45; *BNP* 1.19–20, 101–2, 2.175–8; Turcan 2000: 57, 87.

3.35 Cicero on Roman divination

Cicero *On Divination* 1.1

Cicero's *On Divination* is imbued with Greek philosophical ideas, and many of the arguments of Quintus in the first book in favour of divination are based on those of Posidonius the Stoic; Quintus attempts to reconcile divination with philosophy. The work takes the form of a dialogue between Cicero and his brother Quintus at Tusculum. At 1.58 Quintus states that he does not recognise fortune-tellers (sortilegi), those who prophesy for money, or necromancers. In the second book, Cicero ridicules divination: he was himself an augur and is presenting a philosophical position rather than his own beliefs, and the discussion must reflect ideas that were current amongst the Roman aristocracy of the time (North 2000: 79; cf. Beard 1994: 756–7); for Plato, see Plato *Phaedrus* 244c (*mania*); for Cicero and divination, see Goar 1972: 96–104; Beard 1986; Schofield 1986.

There is an ancient belief, handed down to us right from the times of the heroes, and confirmed by the agreement both of the Roman people and of all other nations, that some kind of divination exists among mankind, which the Greeks call *mantike* — that is, the foresight and knowledge of future events. This is indeed a splendid and beneficial thing, if only it really exists, by which mortal nature can approach very closely to the power of the gods. And just as we have done many things better than the Greeks, so we have given this most extraordinary faculty a name (*divinatio*) derived from *divi* (gods), while the Greeks, as Plato interpreted it, derived their term from *furor* (frenzy).

3.36 The Sibylline books

Dionysius of Halicarnassus *Roman Antiquities* 4.62.4–6

Cf. Gell. 1.19.1–11; Val. Max. 1.1.13. Dionysius 4.62.1–3 relates the story that Tarquinius Priscus (fifth king of Rome) was offered the Sibylline books (nine in total): after rejecting them the first time, the woman selling them burned three of them, then offered the remaining six; he refused to buy and she burnt another three; he consulted the augurs who advised him to buy the remaining three at the same price as the original nine. Two men chosen to care for them later became ten (the decemviri sacris facundis), and under Sulla were increased to fifteen (the quindecimviri sacris faciundis), who had to be proficient in the Greek language. Tarquin's punishment for religious crimes such as impiety later became standard for parricide: docs 7.19, cf. 2.52.

The Sibylline oracles (ritual texts and prophecies) were written in Greek hexameters, and those thought genuine were composed as acrostics, the initial letters spelling out the words of the first verse or verses. One extant example is preserved by Phlegon of Tralles: *FGrH* 257 (*BNP* 2.179–80; North 2000a: 102–4); the last known consultation was in AD 363: Amm. Marc. 23.1.7. The senate's use of these Books indicated not so much a debt to Greek religion but rather an ability to master these oracles and use them for the Roman state's own ends. Nothing is known of how the Books were consulted or a relevant oracle chosen and interpreted.

See Warde Fowler 1911: 255–7; Cowell 1964: 179–83; Ogilvie 1969: 62–3; North 1976: 9; 2000: 54–5; Parke 1988: 76–8, 136–45, 190–215; Scheid 1995: 25; Orlin 1997: 76–115; *BNP* 1.62–3, 2.179–81; Turcan 2000: 54–5.

4 Tarquinius chose from the citizens two distinguished men, with two public slaves to assist them, to whom he handed over the guardianship of the books, and when one of the two, Marcus Atilius, appeared to have betrayed his trust and was informed upon by one of the public slaves, he had him sewn up in a leather bag and thrown into the sea. **5** After the expulsion of the kings the commonwealth took upon itself the protection of the oracles, appointing two extremely distinguished men as their guardians, who hold this office for life and are exempt from military service and all other state duties, with public slaves assigned to assist them, and without these being present the men are not allowed to consult the oracles. In short, there is nothing, either sacred or profane, which the Romans guard so carefully as the Sibylline oracles. They consult them, whenever the senate decrees, if the state is overcome by discord, or a great misfortune has befallen them in war, or great portents and apparitions, difficult of interpretation, have been seen, as has often happened. Until the time of the Marsian war, as it was called (the Social War), these oracles remained underground in the temple of Jupiter Capitolinus in a stone chest, guarded by ten men. **6** After the one hundred and seventy-third Olympiad (83 BC) the temple was burnt down, either deliberately, as some think, or by accident, and these oracles were destroyed by fire together with the other dedications to the god. Those now in existence have been collected from many places, some brought from the cities of Italy, others from Erythrai in Isaia, where by the senate's vote three envoys were dispatched to copy them; others were brought from other cities, transcribed by private persons. Of these some are found to be interpolations among the Sibylline oracles, which are recognised by means of the so-called acrostics. My account is based on what (Marcus) Terentius Varro has recorded in his work on religion.

3.37 Cicero on the Sibyl

Cicero *On Divination* 2.110

Cicero's *On Divination* (*de divinatione*) follows on from his *On the Nature of the Gods* (*de natura deorum*); it was completed after the assassination of Caesar. Here Cicero is countering his brother Quintus' arguments in favour of divination: cf. docs 3.35, 40. The man described as 'king in face' was Caesar. The Sibylline Books were housed in the temple of Jupiter and consulted only when the senate authorised this.

We Romans venerate the verses of the Sibyl who is said to have uttered them while in a frenzy. Recently there was a rumour, which was believed at the time, but turned out to be false, that one of the interpreters of those verses was going to declare in the senate, that, for our safety, the man whom we had as 'king in face' should be made king also in name. If this is in the books, to what man and to what time does it refer? For it was clever in the author to take care that whatever happened should appear foretold because all reference to persons or time had been omitted. He also employed a maze of obscurity so that the same verses might be adapted to different situations at different times. Moreover, that this poem is not the work of frenzy is quite evident from the quality of its composition (for it exhibits artistic care rather than emotional excitement), and is especially evident from the fact that it is written in what are termed 'acrostics', wherein the initial letters of each verse taken in order convey a meaning . . . That surely is the work of concentrated thought and not of a frenzied brain. And in the Sibylline Books, throughout the entire work, each prophecy is embellished with an acrostic, so that the initial letters of each of the lines give the subject of that particular prophecy. Such a work comes from a writer who is not frenzied, who is painstaking, not crazy. Therefore let us keep the Sibyl under lock and key, so that in accordance with the ordinances of our forefathers her books may not even be read without permission of the senate and may be more effective in banishing than encouraging superstitious ideas.

3.38 The 'divinely inspired' art of the haruspices

Cicero *On the Nature of the Gods* 2.10–12

Tiberius Gracchus (father of Tiberius Gracchus, tr. pl. 133) as consul was presiding in 163 BC over the elections for the consuls for 162. Gracchus was an augur himself, as he mentions, but it was as a magistrate that he took the auspices. As the pomerium was an inaugurated area (docs 1.3, 3.15), he had to take the auspices again when he crossed the pomerium back to where the election was taking place (in the Campus Martius). The books Tiberius read must be collections of augural lore. Cicero notes that the Etruscans had books on interpreting entrails, thunder and lightning, and there were also Roman augural books (Cic. *Div.* 1.72; Szemler 1972: 25). For this incident: Taylor 1949: 84; Scullard 1973: 226–7; Harris 1989: 171; Linderski 1986: 2168–73; *BNP* 2.171–2.

In 56 BC, a rumbling noise was heard near Rome in the ager Latiniensis; the senate called in the haruspices who gave their interpretation that there must be an expiation because of various religious infringements. In his *On the Response of the Haruspices* (doc. 12.60), Cicero argued that Clodius had profaned the games of the Magna Mater (by having his gangs of slaves in the audience), as well as the rites of the Bona Dea (docs 7.84–5), and had thus created the need for the expiation.

10 Why, in the consulship of Publius Scipio and Gaius Figulus actual fact proved the correctness of the teaching of our augurs and the Etruscan haruspices; when Tiberius Gracchus, consul for the second time, was holding their election, the first polling-officer suddenly fell dead just as he was reporting their names. Gracchus, none the less, carried on with the election and, as he noticed that that event had aroused the religious scruples of the people, brought the matter before the senate. The senate decided that it be referred to 'the customary people'. Haruspices were brought forward who proclaimed that the polling-officer for the elections had not been in proper order. **11** Gracchus thereupon fell into a rage, as my father used to tell me: 'What is this? Was I not in proper order, I who put it to the vote as consul, augur, and after taking the auspices? Do you, Etruscan barbarians, know the Roman people's laws of auspices? Can you be the interpreters of augury for our elections?' And so he then told them to leave; later on, however, he sent a dispatch from his province to the college, that, while he was reading the books, he had recollected an irregularity in the auspices when he had chosen Scipio's gardens as the site for his tent, because after this he had crossed the pomerium to hold a meeting of the senate and when he had crossed the pomerium on his return he had forgotten to take the auspices; therefore there was an irregularity in their election as consuls. The augurs referred the matter to the senate; the senate decided the consuls should resign; they resigned. What more important instances can we look for? A man of the greatest wisdom and, perhaps, supreme distinction, preferred to admit his error that could have been concealed, rather than allow the impiety to cling to the commonwealth; the consuls preferred to lay down the highest state office immediately rather than to hold it for a moment of time in violation of religion. **12** The authority of augurs is immense; and surely the art of haruspices is also divinely inspired?

3.39 Portents in Livy's history

Livy *History of Rome* 43.13.1–4, 7–8

Livy routinely includes the prodigies for each year in his history. The year in question is 169 BC (during the Third Macedonian War); only about half of his list has been included here.

1 I am not unaware that, owing to the same disrespect because of which men generally believe in this day and age that the gods foretell nothing, no portents at all are publicly reported or recorded in our histories. **2** But, as I write of ancient matters, not only does my mind in some way become old-fashioned, but certain religious scruples prevent me from regarding what those very wise men considered worthy of public concern as unworthy of being recorded in my history. **3** At Anagnia two portents were reported in that year, a shooting star was seen in the sky, and a cow which spoke; she was being kept at public expense. Also at Minturnae during those same days the sky appeared to be on fire. **4** There was a shower of stones at Reate. At Cumae the Apollo on the citadel shed tears for three days and nights . . . **7** Because of the public portents, the Books were approached by the decemvirs, who proclaimed the gods to whom the consuls should sacrifice 40 larger victims, **8** that a day of prayer (supplicatio) should be held, that all the magistrates should sacrifice larger victims at all the couches of the gods, and that the people should wear wreaths. All this was carried out as the decemvirs prescribed.

3.40 Chance remarks as omens

Cicero *On Divination* 1.103–4

See also Val. Max. 1.5.3–4; Plut. *Aem.* 10.3–4. L. Aemilius Paullus, as consul in 168, defeated Perseus of Macedon at Pydna (see docs 5.32–33); Tertia ('third') Aemilia was presumably his third daughter. Flaccus is probably L. Valerius Flaccus, praetor in 63. On the maternal aunt's role in taking nuptial omens for her niece, see Bettini 1991: 88–9. At 2.83 Marcus in his reply to Quintus ridicules taking such chance remarks as omens.

103 I will now give you some well-known examples of omens: when Lucius Paullus was consul for the second time, and it had fallen to his lot to wage war against King Perseus, he returned home in the evening on that very same day and noticed when he kissed his little daughter Tertia, who was still very small, that she looked rather sad. 'What's the matter, Tertia my dear?' he asked, 'Why are you unhappy?' 'Oh, Daddy,' she replied, 'Persa has died.' He then embraced her even more closely and said, 'Daughter, I accept the omen.' It was actually a puppy by that name that had died. **104** I heard Lucius Flaccus, the flamen of Mars, tell the story of Caecilia, daughter of Metellus, who wanted to arrange the marriage of her sister's daughter and went to a small sanctuary to receive an omen, according to ancient custom. For a long time, while the girl was standing and Caecilia was sitting on a stool, no word was spoken. The girl then grew tired and asked her aunt to let her sit on her stool for a little while. 'Certainly,' replied Caecilia, 'I will let you have my place.' And this was a omen of what followed; she died in a short time and the girl married Caecilia's husband. I realise of course that these omens can be made light of and even laughed at, but to make light of the signs sent by the gods is nothing less than to disbelieve in the gods' existence.

3.41 The omens prior to Caesar's death

Suetonius *Life of the Deified Julius* 81.1–3

Cic. *Div.*1.118–19 discusses the sacrificial omens before Caesar's death; cf. doc. 13.64; on dreams as divination: Kragelund 2001 (Calpurnia: 55–6).

1 Caesar's death was proclaimed beforehand by unmistakable omens. A few months earlier, the colonists sent to colonise Capua under the Julian law were breaking up old tombs to construct their houses — the more eagerly because they discovered a large number of ancient vases — and came across a bronze tablet in a tomb, in which Capys, the founder of Capua, was said to have been buried, which was inscribed in Greek letters and words to the effect that: 'when the bones of Capys are found, his descendant will be murdered by the hand of kinsmen and quickly avenged with great disasters to Italy.' **2** No one should think this fictional or fraudulent, because the authority is Cornelius Balbus (cos. 40), an intimate friend of Caesar's. Shortly afterwards, Caesar learnt that herds of horses, which he had dedicated on crossing the river Rubicon and allowed to wander unguarded, were stubbornly failing to graze and were weeping copiously. Also, while he was performing a sacrifice, the haruspex Spurinna warned him to 'beware the danger, which will not come later than the Ides of March'. **3** On the day before the Ides, a 'king' bird, with a sprig of laurel, flew into the hall of Pompey pursued by various birds from a nearby grove, which tore it to pieces there. And on that night, on which dawned the day of his murder, he seemed to himself in a dream to be flying above the clouds and to shake hands with Jupiter, while his wife Calpurnia dreamt that the gable ornament of the house collapsed and her husband lay stabbed in her embrace; suddenly the doors of the bedroom opened of their own accord.

3.42 Oracular responses (1)

CIL I² 2173–89

(*ILLRP* 1072–87a; *ROL* IV.246.) Cicero deprecates the use of the sortes, 'lots', at Praeneste (modern Palestrina), which were written on oak and drawn as a form of divination, commenting that only the common people (*vulgus*) of Praeneste use them and that everywhere else they had gone out of fashion (*Div.* 2.85–87; cf. doc. 3.31). There is no evidence that the Romans themselves used this form of divination. For the Praenestine sortes: Rawson 1985: 306; Harris 1989: 171; Beard 1991: 52. What follows below are sortes, inscribed on bronze, generally in hexameters, apparently dating to the first century BC. Their place of origin is unknown.

2173 Believe that what has been made crooked can hardly now be made straight.
2174 Do you believe what they say? Things are not so. Don't be foolish.
2175 If you are wise about what is uncertain, take care that things don't become certain.
2176 Don't let lies arise from truth by being a false judge.
2177 That horse is very beautiful, but you can't ride him.
2178 It's an uphill road; you are not allowed to follow by the road you want.
2179 He is afraid of everyone; it is better to follow what he fears.
2180 Many men are [liars]. Don't believe them.
2181 An untrustworthy enemy (will arise from) a trustworthy man, unless you take care.
2182 I command it; and if he does it for him he will rejoice for ever.
2183 Seek joyfully and willingly, and you will rejoice for ever because it will be granted.
2184 We sortes ('lots') are not the liars you said; you consult like a fool.
2185 Now do you ask me? Now do you consult? The time has now passed.
2186 I help very many; when I have helped, no one thanks me.
2187 After all your hopes have collapsed, do you consult me?
2188 Do not despise what you run away from, what you throw away, what is granted you.
2189 Why do you seek advice after the event? What you ask does not exist.

3.43 Oracular responses (2)

CIL XI.1129 a, c

(*ILLRP* 1071; *ROL* IV.248.) Oracular replies on a bronze tablet, written in prose, found at Forum Novum; they apparently date to the first century BC.

(a) [Why] do you ask advice now? Be at peace and [enj]oy your li[fe].

... You have death far from you ... It is not possible for death to be fastened on you before your fate comes.

... An illness is revealed ...

(c) She who was previously barren will give birth.

3.44 Astrology gains ground

Cicero *On Divination* 2.98–9

Astrology was not part of traditional Roman beliefs but Chaldaean astrologers from the east were expelled from Rome in 139 BC (Val. Max. 1.3.3), and Cato the Elder advised his bailiff not to consult them (*Agr.* 5.4); Ennius, in Cic. *Div.* 1.132, 'didn't give a toss' for astrologers, preferring good old-fashioned Roman divination, which he describes (doc. 3.45). In the first century BC a slave from the east, Manilius Antiochus, was 'the founder of astronomy' at Rome (doc. 6.12). Cicero ridiculed astrologers' predictions but they continued to gain ground. Astrology in the Republic: Cramer 1951: 14–17, 1954: 44–80; Rawson 1985: 307; Barton 1994: 147–54, 1994a: 33–9; for the Parilia (21 April) at 98: Beard 1987.

98 And if it matters under what aspect of the sky or composition of stars every living thing is born, then necessarily the same conditions affect inanimate things; can any statement be more absurd than that? Indeed, Lucius Tarutius of Firmum, our good friend, who was excessively learned in Chaldaean computations, calculating from the fact that our city's birthday was on the Parilia, the date when we are told it was founded by Romulus, asserted that Rome was born when the moon was in Libra, and from this did not hesitate to prophecy Rome's destiny. What incredible power delusion has! ... **99** But why say more? They are refuted daily. I remember numerous prophecies which the Chaldaeans made to Pompey, to Crassus, even to the late Caesar, saying that none of them would die except in old age, at home, and with great renown!

AUGURY

There were three augurs (augures, singular: augur) in the early Republic; under the *lex Ogulnia* of 300 BC the college grew to nine members, four patricians and five plebeians; Sulla increased their number to fifteen. Cicero (himself an augur) considers them the most important authority in the state, able with the pronouncement that the auspices were unpropitious to adjourn assemblies or declare their acts null and void, postpone business and force the consuls to resign (*Laws* 2.12, cf. 2.21). Auspices were temporarily binding and could be taken again on the next day.

Magistrates took the auspices, with an augur present as an advisor (*BNP* 1.22). The taking of the auspices ('auspicia') was not a means of divining the future but of finding out the will of the gods in relation to a particular activity or event. The auspices were of two main types: those deliberately watched for and those accidentally encountered or discovered. They were derived from five categories: from the sky (lightning, thunder, hailstorms and the like), from the movements of birds (flight, cries and number, as in doc. 3.45), from the sacred chickens (docs 3.50–2), from four-legged animals (any unusual behaviour thereof) and also from unusual events. The auspices were taken for all state activities, in particular the elections. For augury and augurs, see also Cic. *Laws* 2.20–1, *Div.* 2.76–7; Plut. *Rom. Quest.* 99; esp. Linderski 1986; also Warde Fowler 1911: 292–313; Cowell 1964: 183–5; Ogilvie 1969: 56–7; Dumézil 1970: 595–9; Liebeschuetz 1979: 11–15; Beard 1990: 39–40, 1994: 744; North 1989: 584–5, 1990: 51, 54, 2000: 23, 25; *BNP* 1.21–3, 110–11; Turcan 2000: 85–7; Cohee 2001; Vaahtera 2001; for the college of augurs, see esp. Linderski 1986: 2151–225; Vaahtera 2001: 136–43; for divination, see Dumézil 1970: 594–610; North 1990.

3.45 'A most glorious omen, a bird flying on the left'

Ennius *Annals* 80–100

Cic. *Div.* 1.107–8; *ROL* I.28–30; Skutsch 1985: 76–7 (as lines 72–91), commentary at 223–38. According to legend (Livy 1.3.10–4.7; Dion. Hal. 1.76.1–79.8), Rhea Silvia (or Ilia), a Vestal Virgin of Alba Longa who was beloved of Mars, gave birth to twins, Romulus and Remus, who were raised by a she-wolf. Here Romulus, standing on the Aventine, and Remus, on the Remuria, take the auspices at dawn to see who should rule the city and have it named after one of them. The number of the birds, their direction and that they headed towards 'places of favourable and fine omen' are all relevant. This was the most famous, if mythical, example of divination, relevant to divination in the Republic. For further auguries in Ennius, see 150–3 (eagle on the left), and 454 (thunder on the left).

According to Cic. *Rep.* 2.9, Romulus 'followed the auspices absolutely, as we still do today to the great safety of our state. For he not only took the auspices himself when he founded the city — an act that was the beginning of our state — but also, before the performance of any public act, selected augurs to help him in taking the auspices, one from each tribe.'

80   Then carefully — with great care — both eager
     For rule, they concentrate on divination and augury;
     . . . on a hill . . .
     Remus dedicates himself to divination and on his own
     Keeps watch for a favourable bird. But handsome Romulus on high
85   Aventine searches, and watches out for the high-flying breed.
     They are contesting whether they should call the city Roma or Remora.
     All men are filled with care as to which should be the ruler:
     Just as when the consul intends to give the signal
     All men wait, eagerly watching the race's starting-gate to see
90   How soon he will dispatch the chariots from the painted mouth:
     Thus the people waited and held their tongues, to learn
     Who should be granted the victory of great kingship.
     Meanwhile the white sun withdrew into the depths of night.
     Then bright light, irradiated, beaming forth —
95   Just then from the height came a most glorious omen,
     A bird flying on the left, just as the golden sun was rising.
     Three times four sacred forms of birds left the sky,
     Taking themselves to places of favourable and fine omen.
     Thence Romulus sees that to him, in due form,
100 By divination, had been granted a kingdom's stable throne and land.

3.46 The taking of auspices begins with Romulus

Dionysius of Halicarnassus *Roman Antiquities* 2.5.1–6.2

Romulus insisted on consulting the auspices when the people wished to grant him sovereignty: his kingship was confirmed by a flash of lightning from the left to the right, a favourable direction. It became the practice from this that the gods had to sanction any king or magistrate. Lightning was only considered unfavourable during elections: Cicero attacked Vatinius, '. . . (if you had been elected augur), were you intending to decree, as all augurs since Romulus have decreed, that, when Jupiter sends a flash of lightning, it is sacrilegious to bring proposals before the assembly, or, because you had always brought them under those conditions, were you intending as augur to do away with auspices altogether?' (Cic. *Vat.* 8.20; cf. *Div.* 2.42–3).

5.1 As the people approved, he proclaimed a day on which he would consult the auspices about the kingship, and when the time came he rose at daybreak and left his tent. After taking his stand under the open sky in a clear space and offering the customary preliminary sacrifice, he prayed to King Jupiter and the other gods whom he had taken as the leaders of his colony that, if they wished him to be king of the city, favourable signs would appear in the sky. **2** After his prayer lightning flashed across the sky from left to right . . . **6.1** This custom relating to the auspices long continued to be observed by the Romans, not only while the city was a monarchy, but also after the overthrow of the monarchy in the election of consuls and praetors and other legal magistrates. **2** It has, however, ceased in our own day, except for a certain semblance of it which remains for form's sake. For those who are about to take up office spend the night outside and rising at dawn offer certain prayers under the open sky, and some of the augurs present state that they have seen lightning from the left — which was not there.

3.47 An old formula for taking the auspices

Varro On the Latin Language 7.8

Varro is quoting from the augural books (Linderski 1986: 2241–56). Here the trees are set as boundaries and the four quarters for the auspices set within them. The term templum (plural: templa) is a complex one which is not exactly conveyed by the modern word 'temple'. A templum was a rectangular area in the sky marked out by the taker of the auspices, an augur or magistrate, in which he would look for auspices from birds (see doc. 3.48). A templum could also be an area of ground so marked out, as here described by Varro. Important templa were the curia, rostra, and comitium, as places where political decisions were made. The augurs' view had to be unobstructed: 'when the augurs were planning to take observations from the citadel they ordered Tiberius Claudius Centumalus, owner of a house upon the Caelian Hill, to pull down the parts of the building that obstructed the taking of the auspices because of their height (99 BC)' (Cic. *Off.* 3.66; cf. Val. Max. 8.2.1). For templum, see Linderski 1986: 2261–79; Beard 1990: 39–40; *BNP* 1.22, 2.86–7; cf. Ziolkowski 1992: 209–14; for the auguraculum, the place from which the augurs presided over the observation of the auspices, see Vitruvius 2.1.5; Platner-Ashby 61; Linderski 1986: 2257; Nash 163; Richardson *Top. Dict.* 45; cf. Vaahtera 2001: 99–100.

On the earth *templum* is the name given to a place used for the sake of augury or the taking of auspices and restricted by certain formulaic words. The form of words is not the same everywhere; on the citadel (on the Capitoline hill) it is as follows:

> Temples and wild lands be mine in this way, up to where I have named them rightly with my tongue.
> Of whatever kind that truthful tree is, which I consider that I have mentioned, temple and wild land be mine on the left.
> Of whatever kind that truthful tree is, which I consider that I have mentioned, temple and wild land be mine on the right.
> Between these points, temples and wild lands be mine for direction, observation and interpretation, just as I consider that I have named them rightly.

3.48 The augur marks off the heavens

Livy *History of Rome* 1.18.6–10, 20.7

The lituus, the 'crooked staff without a knot', was a badge of office for augurs; the term probably derived from an Etruscan word for 'crooked' (doc. 3.49). It is shown on some of Sulla's coins to indicate that he was an augur (doc. 11.47). Jupiter was the god of auspices (Cic. *Laws* 2.20) and so the augur here calls upon him (the auspices here are taken from the Capitoline, Jupiter's major cult centre); he was Elicius because the signs were elicited, 'drawn', from Jupiter (Ovid *Fasti* 3.327–8). See, for this passage, Dumézil 1970: 597; Linderski 1986: 2256–96; Vaahtera 2001: 104–5.

18.6 Summoned to Rome, Numa Pompilius instructed that the gods should be consulted in his case, just as for Romulus, who at the founding of Rome had assumed power after taking auguries. He was therefore conducted by an augur, to whom as a mark of honour a permanent state priesthood was granted from then on, to the citadel, where he sat on a stone facing south. **7** The augur with veiled head took his seat on Numa's left, holding in his right hand the crooked staff without a knot, which they call the *lituus*. Then, looking out over the city and the country beyond, he prayed to the gods and marked off the heavens from east to west, declaring the southward side to be 'right' and the northward side 'left'. **8** He fixed in his mind a point straight in front of him as far away as his eyes could reach, changed the staff to his left hand, placed his right upon Numa's head and prayed in the following words: **9** 'Father Jupiter, if it is Heaven's will that this man, Numa Pompilius, whose head I touch, should be king of Rome, make clear to us specific signs within those limits I have set.' **10** Then he described the auspices that he wished to be sent. When they were sent, Numa was proclaimed king and went down from the augural site (templum). . . . **20.7** Numa consecrated an altar on the Aventine to Jupiter Elicius, whom he consulted by augury as to what signs from heaven it should be proper to regard.

3.49 The sacred staff

Cicero *On Divination* 1.30–1

The temple of the Salii was burnt in the Gallic attack traditionally dated to 390 BC; see Livy 5.41; Val. Max. 1.8.11. Attus Navius was the augur of Tarquinius Priscus, the fifth king of Rome.

30 From where did you augurs inherit that staff which is the most conspicuous mark of the office of augurs? It is indeed the one with which Romulus marked out the boundary-lines for observing omens when he founded the city. Now this staff of Romulus is a curved wand, slightly bent at the top, which derives its name from its resemblance to the curved trumpet which gives the signal from battle. It was placed in the temple of the Salii on the Palatine, and when the temple was burnt down it was found intact. **31** What historian of antiquity fails to mention that many years after Romulus, in the reign of Tarquinius Priscus, the boundary lines for observations were marked out with this staff by Attus Navius?

3.50 Patrician control of augury

Livy *History of Rome* 6.41.4–10

In 367 BC the tribunes Sextius and Licinius as part of their programme of reform successfully proposed that half of the board of ten in charge of the Sibylline Books (*decemviri sacris faciundis*) should be plebeians; Lucius Sextius Sextinus Lateranus was also to be the first plebeian consul: see docs 1.47–8. This is an extract from Livy's version of the speech made by Appius Claudius Crassus against the tribunes when they sought re-election for the tenth time; cf. *MRR* I.114; Cornell 1995: 332–40; doc. 1.55.

4 What am I to say about religious observances and auspices, disregard and insult of which involve the immortal gods? This city was founded under auspices, and who is unaware that all its measures are carried out under auspices, whether in war or peace, at home or on the battlefield? **5** Who then controls the auspices by ancestral tradition? Why, the patricians, for no plebeian magistrate is elected under auspices; **6** and the auspices are ours to such an extent that not only do the patrician magistrates elected by the people have to be elected under auspices, but we can ourselves, without the people's vote, take auspices and appoint an interrex. In fact, we can take them in our capacity as private citizens, which plebeians cannot do even when in office. **7** So whoever by creating plebeians as consuls removes auspices from the patricians — who alone can take them — deprives the state of auspices. **8** They can laugh now, if they like, at religious scruples: 'So what does it matter if the chickens will not feed, if they are slow to come out of their hencoop, if a bird squawks an unlucky omen?' These are trivial matters, but it was by not despising these trivial matters that your ancestors built up this great Republic — **9** and now we, as if we no longer had any need of the gods' goodwill, are defiling all the sacred rites. So, let pontiffs, augurs, and kings of the sacrifices (the rex sacrorum) be chosen from the common people; let us place the flamen dialis' head-dress on anyone's head, as long as he is a man; and hand over the shields, shrines, gods, and the gods' service to those whom divine law excludes; **10** let laws be proposed, and magistrates elected, without taking of the auspices; let neither the centuriate or curiate assemblies be sanctioned by patricians.

THE SACRED CHICKENS

Employing haruspicy or taking the auspices was not always convenient for the commander in battle. Chickens, kept in a cage, provided a mobile divination kit: when they were fed, it was an auspicious omen if they ate greedily and the pellets fell from their beaks; if they did not eat, it was a bad omen. Before a battle with the Samnites in 293 BC the sacred chickens refused to feed, but the sacred-chicken keeper (*pullarius*, pl. *pullarii*) lied to the consul and reported a good omen. Next day, an argument between the pullarii about the auspices was reported to the consul. He reacted by placing them in the front line of battle; the lying pullarius was struck by an enemy javelin. The consul declared that the gods had punished the transgressor and the Romans went on to win (Livy 10.40.2–3, cf. Livy 6.41.8).

Sacred chickens are depicted on an *aes signatum* (bronze ingot), minted at Rome, c. 260–242 BC: two chickens face each other, eating, and so giving a favourable omen. On the obverse are two tridents, one on the left and one on the right, both pointing into the middle of the ingot, with two dolphins, their tails curved around the right hand trident (Crawford *RRC* 12.1; Scullard 1981: pl. 6). See for the sacred chickens: Ogilvie 1969: 57; Dumézil 1970: 599; Scheid 2003: 115–16.

3.51 It doesn't pay to ignore the chickens!

Cicero On the Nature of the Gods *2.7–8*

Publius Claudius Pulcher as consul in 249 BC lost his fleet at Drepanum; having ignored the unfavourable auspices of the chickens (they were presumably too sea-sick to eat), he was held responsible for the defeat and charged with *perduellio* (treason) and fined. The other consul L. Junius Pullus also ignored unfavourable omens. Polyb. 1.49–51 does not mention the incident of the sacred chickens in the First Punic War, but this does not mean that it is a late invention (*pace* Walbank I.113–4); Polybius rarely draws attention to religious matters and it is mentioned by several sources: see *MRR* I.214. The use of sacred chickens was widespread and the temptation to ignore unfavourable omens must have been strong when battle was about to be joined. At 1.77 Quintus relates the incident where Flaminius ignored the advice of the keeper of the chickens and was defeated by Hannibal at Lake Trasimene in 217 (doc. 4.32): cf. *Div.* 2.21; doc. 5.48 (for C. Hostilius Mancinus). Note the connection which Cicero makes in this passage between *religio* and the success of the Roman empire.

7 Shall we not be moved by the temerity of Publius Claudius in the First Punic War? He was laughing at the gods in jest, when the chickens were removed from their cage and would not feed, ordering them to be thrown into the water to drink, as they didn't want to eat. But the joke, when the fleet was defeated, brought many tears to him and a great catastrophe to the Roman people. And did not his colleague Junius in that same war lose a fleet in a storm, when he did not obey the auspices? As a consequence, Claudius was condemned by the people and Junius committed suicide. **8** Caelius writes that Gaius Flaminius, after neglecting the dictates of religion (*religio*) fell at the battle of Trasimene, which gave our state a great blow. The fate of these men demonstrates that our empire was extended by commanders who obeyed the dictates of religion. And if we want to compare our national characteristics with those of others, we shall find that, while in all other respects we are either their equals or even their inferiors, yet in our sense of religion, that is, in reverence for the gods, we are greatly superior.

3.52 Chickens and 'forced augury'

Cicero On Divination *1.27*

Quintus Cicero is complaining here that the chickens are left hungry and then fed in such a way that a favourable omen was inevitable: cf. 2.72–3. There was a proverb quoted by Cato the Elder 'between the mouth and the pellet' (i.e., cup and lip): Gell. 13.18.1.

Among us Romans the magistrates make use of auspices which are 'forced'; for, when the pellets are thrown bits have to fall from the chicken's beak as it is eating. But according to what you augurs have written, if anything falls to the ground, a favourable omen (tripudium) has taken place, and what I spoke of as a 'forced' augury you call the most favourable of omens (*tripudium solistimum*). And so many auguries and auspices, as Cato the Wise complains, have been entirely lost and abandoned by the carelessness of the college.

DEDICATIONS AND VOWS

Dedications were a means of thanking the gods for 'services rendered'. Often such dedications were vowed in moments of crisis and the vow fulfilled if the crisis passed successfully: dedications could range from small inscribed tablets to temples and monuments. For other dedications, see esp. doc. 3.58 (healing); docs 4.33, 46, 5.32, 41–2 (victory); doc. 6.50 (manumission); docs 7.75, 82–3 (by Roman women).

3.53 A dedication at Furfo, 58 BC

ILS 4906

(*CIL* I² 756; *CIL* IX.3513; *ILLRP* 508; Bruns 105; *FIRA* 3.225; Gordon no.19; Courtney *ALP* 112–17.) Furfo is 60 miles east of Rome. 13 July 58 BC would actually, because of the disarray of the calendar (see doc. 3.28), have been 13 April, a better season for flowers (Gordon p. 95). A special provision allows iron into the temple: 'Most religious ceremonies have roots that predate the Iron Age, so iron is generally not admitted into the sacral surroundings' (Courtney *ALP* 115). Here provision is made that dedications in the temple can be sold, but for the temple's benefit; see Glinister 2000: 68.

Lucius Aienus, son of Lucius, and Quintus Baebatius, son of Sextus, dedicated the temple of Jupiter Liber at Furfo on 13 July in the consulship of Lucius (Calpurnius) Piso and Aulus Gabinius (58 BC), in the month of Flowers, laying down these regulations and these boundaries, that the lowest foundations are to be constructed of stone for the purpose of this temple, **5** and that towards that temple and the staircase, constructed of stone columns on this side of the staircase leading towards the temple, and the posts and beams of this temple are to stand; that it be permissible under human and divine law to touch, repair, cover, remove, drive in, clean out, use iron, push forward and realign. If any gift be given, presented, or dedicated to that temple, that it be permitted to use or sell it; when it has been sold, it is to be secular. Let the sale or lease be in the hands of whomever **10** the village of Furfo has elected as aedile, so that they feel that they are selling or leasing that object without crime or impiety; no-one else is to have this power. Whatever money is received, that money may be used to buy, lend, put out at interest or give, so that the temple may be improved and more handsome. Any money used for those purposes is to be secular, as there is no fraud involved. Any objects bought with the money, bronze or silver, given for purchase, those things should be subject to the same regulations as if they had been dedicated. **15** If anyone here steals a sacred object, his fining is the responsibility of the aedile, whatever amount he wishes; and if the village of Furfo by majority vote wishes either to acquit or condemn, this is to be allowed. If anyone sacrifices at this temple to Jupiter Liber or to the Genius of Jupiter, the skins and hides are to belong to the shrine.

3.54 A public vow to Jupiter

Livy *History of Rome* 36.2.1–5

The consuls of 191 BC drew lots for their provinces: Acilius drew Greece, which had been invaded in 192 by Antiochus, king of Syria (docs 5.27–30). The senate decreed that there be a supplicatio to invoke the aid of the gods for the forthcoming war. A supplicatio (plural: *supplicationes*) could be held as an expiation ceremony, or as in this case described by Livy, in connection with a vow, as a thanks-giving. Statues of the gods were placed on couches (*pulvinaria*), the temples were opened, and the populace called upon to worship the gods. A supplicatio traditionally lasted for one day (as in the lengthy description of the one of 207 BC held to expiate various prodigies: Livy 27.37). Pompey and Caesar were voted much longer ones for their great victories: docs 12.30, 66, 89. The consul here repeats the words after the pontifex maximus, as part of the procedure to ensure that the exact ritual formulas were used (see doc. 3.24).

1 To Acilius fell Greece, to Cornelius Italy. **2** With the casting of lots determined, the senate passed a decree that, since the Roman people had at that time ordered there to be a war with King Antiochus and those under his authority, the consuls should proclaim a period of prayer (*supplicatio*) for its success and that the consul Manius Acilius should vow great games to Jupiter and gifts at all the couches of the gods (*pulvinaria*). **3** The consul made this vow, repeating it after the pontifex maximus, Publius Licinius, in the following words: 'If the war which the people has ordered to be undertaken with King Antiochus shall be brought to a conclusion deemed satisfactory by the senate and people, **4** then the people will hold in your honour, Jupiter, great games for ten consecutive days, and will offer gifts at the couches of the gods of whatever value the senate shall decide. **5** Whatever magistrate shall hold these games, at whatever time and place, let these games be duly celebrated and these gifts be duly offered.' Then the period of prayer, to last for two days, was proclaimed by both consuls.

THE INTRODUCTION OF NEW GODS

Cicero's own ideal religious laws included the following: 'no one shall have gods separately, whether new gods or alien gods, unless recognised by the state; privately they shall worship those gods whose worship they have duly received from their forefathers . . . They shall worship as gods both those who have always been thought to dwell in heaven, and also those whose merits have admitted them to heaven: Hercules, Liber, Aesculapius, Castor, Pollux, Quirinus' (*Laws* 2.19).

The Romans were not on principle opposed to the introduction of new gods, as their acceptance of Aesculapius, the Magna Mater and their practice of 'calling out' the gods of states they were at war with indicates. But the Roman state as represented by the senate had a clear sense of what was appropriate within a Roman context. It was the senate (and certainly never the people) which decided which foreign gods gained legitimacy and worship within the formal apparatus of the state religion. The state's interest was active, as can be seen in the Bacchanalia, when the senate took steps to persecute its adherents. Isis began to be popular at Rome in the closing decades of the Republic but the senate destroyed her temples on more than one occasion in the 50s and 40s BC. For the question of Roman religious tolerance, see North 1976, 1979, 1980; Garnsey 1984: 6–12; cf. Watson 1992: 58–62.

3.55 The *evocatio* of Juno from Veii, 396 BC

Livy *History of Rome* 5.21.1–3, 22.3–7

Cf. Livy 5.19–23; Plut. *Cam.* 5–8; Dion Hal. *Rom. Ant.* 12.14–15, 13.3; Pliny *Nat. Hist.* 28.418; see doc. 1.60 on the sack of Veii. *Evocatio* was the procedure by which the Romans would call out the main god of an enemy city, promising it a cult at Rome, and sometimes a temple. The enemy would thus be deprived of divine support. The general in command would undertake the evocatio: in this case the dictator Camillus (*MRR* I.87–8), who did so without having previously consulted the senate. After the defeat of Veii, Juno's temple was built at Rome on the Aventine Hill in 392 BC; it housed the wooden statue brought from Veii (Platner-Ashby: 290; Richardson

Top. Dict. 215–17; Ziolkowski 1992: 238–40; Orlin 1997: 15, 53–4). In 218 BC Roman women dedicated a bronze statue in Juno's temple (Livy 21.62.8), and in 207 her temple was struck by lightning while the Roman matrons were learning a song in the temple of Jupiter to expiate the prodigy of the birth of a hermaphroditic child: the haruspices divined that the matrons and the lightning were connected, and all Rome's women were summoned and an offering and sacrifice made to Juno Regina (Livy 27.37: doc. 7.83). Camillus' vow to Apollo was sent to Delphi (Livy 5.28.1–5).

An *evocatio* is recorded by a late source for Juno at Carthage in 146 BC (Serv. *Aen.* 12.841) and Macrob. 3.9 has Scipio Aemilianus in 146 calling out whichever god or goddess protected Carthage and promising it a temple at Rome, though none was ever built (see doc. 3.56). It is possible that there is an example from 75 BC (*BNP* 2.248), but otherwise the practice of *evocatio* resulting in a temple built at Rome belongs solely to the fourth and third centuries, with the evocatio of Vortumnus, a deity of the city of the Volsinians, with his temple built on the Aventine in 264 BC, as the last example (Richardson *Top. Dict.* 433). For *evocatio*: Bloch 1960: 129; Dumézil 1970: 424–7; Ogilvie 1970: 673–5; *BNP* 1.132–4; Turcan 2000: 97–9.

21.1 A great multitude came out and filled the camp. After taking the auspices, the dictator then went out and commanded the troops to arm themselves: **2** 'Under your leadership,' he declared, 'Pythian Apollo, and inspired by your divine guidance, I proceed to the destruction of the city of Veii and to you I vow a tenth part of its spoils. **3** And at the same time, Queen Juno (Juno Regina), who dwells now in Veii, I pray that you come with us, the victors, to our — soon to be your — city, where a shrine worthy of your greatness will receive you'. . . .

22.3 Now that all the wealth belonging to the human residents had been carried out of Veii, they started to remove the gifts to the gods and even the gods themselves, but more in the fashion of worshippers than of looters. **4** For young men were selected from the whole army who washed themselves clean and put on white garments and these were assigned the task of carrying Queen Juno to Rome. They entered her shrine with reverence and at first were awe-struck at the thought of approaching her with their hands, **5** because the statue by Etruscan custom was only to be touched by a priest of a specific family. Then one of them, whether touched by divine inspiration or a youthful sense of humour, said, 'Do you wish, Juno, to go to Rome?' and the others shouted together that the goddess had nodded yes. **6** It was later added to the tale that her voice had also been heard saying she was willing; at any rate, we are told that she was moved from her station by machines of little power as if she went with them of her own accord and was light and easy to handle during the transfer, and reached the Aventine safe and sound, **7** the eternal home to which the vows of the Roman dictator had summoned her, where Camillus afterwards dedicated to her the temple he had vowed.

3.56 Carthaginian cults transferred to Rome in 146 BC

Macrobius *Saturnalia* 3.9.6–9

(Courtney *ALP* 107–12.) For a discussion, see Rawson 1991b: 95–9; cf. *CIL* I.2954 (Courtney 109). Serenus Sammonicus was an antiquary killed in AD 211; Furius is thought to be L. Furius Philus, cos. 136 BC, a friend of Scipio Aemilianus. Nevertheless the formulae seem reliable and of the correct date and would have been spoken by Scipio, the besieging general: Macrob. 3.9.4. For calling gods from a besieged city, see Livy 1.55.4 (Terminus); doc. 3.55 (Veii). Macrob. 3.9.3 states that this practice explains why the Romans were careful not to reveal the name of the tutelary god of Rome or the Latin name of the city (cf. Plut. *Rom. Quest.* 61).

6 We must be careful to make a distinction, unlike some who have incorrectly supposed that a single formula (carmen) is used both to call the gods out of a city and to devote the city itself to destruction. I have found both formulas in the fifth Book of the *Secret World (Res Reconditae)* of Sammonicus Serenus, who stated that he had come across them in an extremely ancient book by one Furius.

7 The formula to call the gods out of a city encircled by a siege is as follows: 'Whether god or goddess, under whose protection are the people and state of Carthage, and to you especially who have been charged with the protection of this city and people, I pray and do reverence and ask a favour of you all, that you abandon the people and state of Carthage, forsake their places, temples, shrines, and city, **8** and depart from these; and that you bring fear, terror and bewilderment upon that people and state; and that, once you have abandoned them, you come to Rome, to me and to mine; and that our places, temples, shrines, and city may be more acceptable and pleasing to you; and that you take me and the Roman people and my soldiers under your charge that we may know and understand this. If you shall so have done, I vow to you that I shall construct temples and celebrate games.'

9 With these words victims should be sacrificed, and the authority of the entrails examined to see if they predict these events for the future.

3.57 Aesculapius, 292 BC

(a) Livy *History of Rome* 10.47.6–7

Cf. Livy 29.11.1, 40.37.2–3 (gilded statues made to Apollo, Aesculapius and Salus (the Roman equivalent of the Greek Hygieia (Health) daughter of Aesculapius) in 180, on the order of the senate after a consultation of the Sibylline books when several important Romans died in quick succession); Ovid. *Metam.* 15.622–744; Suet. *Claud.* 25.2. In 292 BC one of Aesculapius' sacred serpents was brought to Rome by ship and his healing cult established on the island in the Tiber, chosen by the snake itself; there is still a hospital, of St Bartolomeo (Bartholomew), on the island and the stone bows of a ship, with Aesculapius' snake, can still be seen there, commemorating Aesculapius' arrival. Healing was by incubation: sick individuals slept overnight in the temple hoping that the god would appear to them in a dream and heal them. Cured individuals had to thank the god for the cure (doc. 3.58): Dumézil 1970: 2.443–4; Scullard 1981: 54–6; Parke 1988: 194–5; Edelstein & Edelstein I.324, 435–41; *BNP* 1.69–70, 2.43; for healing sanctuaries in central Italy, see North 1989: 580.

The year (293 BC) had in many ways been a happy one, but this served as insufficient consolation for one disaster, a plague which raged through both town and country-side; the calamity was considered a portent, and the (Sibylline) Books were consulted to find what limit or remedy the gods proposed for this misfortune. It was discovered in the books that Aesculapius should be summoned from Epidaurus to Rome; nothing, however, could be done in that year, as the consuls were occupied with the war, except that a one-day supplication was held for Aesculapius.

(b) Livy *Periochae* 11

When the state was suffering under a plague, the envoys, who had been sent to fetch the statue of Aesculapius over from Epidaurus to Rome, brought with them a serpent, which came on board their ship of its own accord and in which it was believed that the divinity himself dwelt. When it went ashore on the island in the Tiber, a temple to Aesculapius was built there.

3.58 Early dedications to Aesculapius

ILS 3833, 3834

(*CIL* I² 26, 28; *ILLRP* 35–6; *ROL* IV.68.) These dedications were discovered in the river Tiber. The first (26) dates to the third century BC, the second is a little later. Republican dedications to Aesculapius in the Tiber: Scullard 1981: 55.

26 To Aesculapius: a gift dedicated by Lucius Albanius, son of Kaeso.

28 To Aesculapius: a gift given willingly and deservedly by Marcus Populicius, son of Marcus.

3.59 The Magna Mater comes to Rome, 204 BC

Livy *History of Rome* 29.14.10–14

The Magna Mater, 'Great Mother', was also known as Cybele or the Idaean goddess (from Mount Ida). See also for her introduction to Rome: Ovid. *Fasti* 4.179–372; Cic. *Har. Resp.* 2.25; Dion. Hal. 2.19.4–5. Livy comments (25.1.6–8) that in 213 BC an increasing number of foreign cults appeared in Rome; he points mainly at women but his account makes clear that men were also involved, suggesting that the war against Hannibal, with its uncertainties, was leading to the popularity of foreign cults. The senate took action and ruled that 'no one was to conduct a sacrifice in a public or sacred place according to a strange or foreign rite' (Livy 25.1.12), and games (ludi Romani and ludi plebeii) were held, presumably to divert attention away from the foreign rites (Toynbee 1965: II.383; Scullard 1973: 23).

Frequent showers of stones in 205 led to a consultation of the Sibylline Books: an oracle was found that said, 'If ever a foreign enemy invaded the soil of Italy, he could be driven out of Italy and vanquished, if the Idaean Mother were brought from Pessinus to Rome' (Livy 29.10.5). A delegation was sent to Pessinus in Phrygia to obtain the black meteoric stone of the Idaean Mother, the Magna Mater or Cybele (that it was a statue is an invention of Ovid).

Publius Cornelius Scipio Nasica (praetor in 194 and cousin of Scipio Africanus) was chosen by the senate as the 'best' of the Romans by the senate and ordered to go to Ostia to meet the goddess (Livy 29.14.6–9). She was carried into Rome on 4 April 204 with all due ceremony. Claudia Quinta's reputation for virtue was in doubt, but when the ship stuck on a sandbank at the mouth of the Tiber, soothsayers announced that it could only be moved by a virtuous matron. Claudia pulled the ship off, proving her innocence (doc. 7.30; for her statue: Val. Max. 1.8.11).

The Megalesia in the Magna Mater's honour was first held in 204 BC and became at some stage an annual event (ludi Megalenses), probably from 191 BC when the temple of Magna Mater was dedicated on the Palatine (Livy 29.14.14, 36.36). Clodius Pulcher's slaves were to cause a riot there: Cic. *Har. Resp.* 22–4.

Introduction of Magna Mater, and her cult in the Republican period: Toynbee 1965: II.384–7; Vermaseren 1977: 38–41; Harmon 1978: 592–3; Wiseman 1979: 94–9 (Claudia Quinta); Scullard 1981: 97–100; Wardman 1982: 108–12; Thomas 1984: 1502–8; Bremmer 1987; Parke 1988: 195; Stehle 1989: 153–6; Gruen 1990: 5–33, 1992: 118–19; Beard 1994a: 164–80; Burton 1996; Turcan 1996: 35–43, 2000: 109–17; *BNP* 1.164–5, 2.43–6.

10 Publius Cornelius Scipio was instructed to go to Ostia with all the matrons to meet the goddess; he was to receive her himself from the ship and then hand her, once she was on land, to be carried by the matrons. **11** When the ship arrived at the mouth of the river Tiber, he did as he had been ordered, rowing out to sea, receiving the goddess from her priests, and bringing her to land. **12** The foremost matrons of the city, among whom the name of Claudia Quinta alone is illustrious, received her. Claudia's reputation, which, it is recorded, had before been uncertain, made her virtue, shown by her attendance on the goddess, more noteworthy to posterity. **13** The matrons carried the goddess, passing her from hand to hand one after another; the whole city poured out to meet her, and incense burners were placed in front of the doorways along the route, with people praying, as they lit the incense, that the goddess would enter the city of Rome graciously and propitiously. **14** They carried the goddess into the temple of Victory, which is on the Palatine, on 4 April, and that day was declared a festival. Crowds of people brought gifts to the goddess on the Palatine, and a lectisternium was held and games called the Megalesia.

3.60 The Galli of the Magna Mater

Lucretius *On the Nature of the Universe* 2.610–32

The activities of Cybele's priests and the rites in her honour were considered to be most un-Roman and emotional, especially the self-mutilation (castration) of the priests; here Lucretius (94–55/51 BC) describes a procession in honour of the Magna Mater. The cult was placed under the jurisdiction of the keepers of the Sibylline books and no Roman citizens were allowed to become priests, or Galli. No Roman was permitted to take part in the procession or worship the goddess in the Phrygian way; for the 'figures and pectorals' worn by the Galli, priests of Cybele, see Polyb. 21.6.7, 21.37.5; for Lucretius and the Magna Mater: Summers 1996.

610   Various nations, according to the ancient tradition of her rites, call her
        Idaean mother and assign her bands of Phrygians
        As her attendants, because it was that region first, they say,
        Out of all the earth, which began to produce crops.
        They give her Galli as attendants, to show that those who violate their mother's will
615   And treat their fathers with ingratitude,
        Should be thought unworthy
        Of producing living descendants in the sunlit world.
        Tightly-stretched drums thunder out, struck by palms, and curved cymbals,
        And horns threaten with their hoarse-sounding blare,
620   While the hollow flute inspires the heart with Phrygian tunes.
        They carry weapons before her as symbols of violent frenzy,
        That the ungrateful minds and impious hearts of the crowd
        May be terror-struck with fear of the goddess' power.
        So, when she is first carried into a large city
625   And silently bestows wordless blessings on mankind,
        People strew her path along the entire route
        With lavish gifts of copper and silver, with a snow-shower of roses

Shadowing the Mother and her bands of attendants.
Next armed group of attendants, called by the Greeks
630   Phrygian Curetes, hold mock battles
And dance in rhythm, delighted by the bloodshed,
Shaking, with a nod, the terrifying crests upon their heads.

3.61 Vengeance on a mocker of the Great Mother's priest (102 BC)

Diodorus Siculus *Library of History* 36.13.1–3

See also Plut. *Mar.* 17.5–6 (the senate vote a temple for the goddess in Rome). Aulus Pompeius,
tr. pl. 102: *MRR* I.568. Battaces, priest of Great Mother of the gods, arrived from Pessinus in 102
BC to state that rites of purification were needed; the context is the ongoing wars with the Cimbri
and Teutones, successfully concluded in 101: Rawson 1991: 157–8.

1 A certain man called Battaces, who was a priest of the Great Mother of the gods,
arrived from Pessinus in Phrygia. He stated that he had come on the orders of the goddess, and obtained an audience with the consuls and senate, where he said that the temple
of the goddess had been polluted and that rites of purification had to be publicly
performed to her at Rome. He wore a robe which, like the rest of his dress, was exotic
and totally alien to Roman custom; he had a huge golden crown and a brightly-coloured
cape interwoven with gold, denoting royal rank. **2** He made a speech to the people from
the rostra and inculcated in the populace a feeling of religious awe, and was thought
worthy of state lodgings and hospitality. He was, however, forbidden to wear his crown
by Aulus Pompeius, one of the tribunes. Brought back to the rostra by another of the
tribunes and asked about the purification of the temple, he gave answers which imparted
religious awe. When he was attacked on factional grounds by Pompeius and sent back
with insults to his lodgings, he did not appear in public again, saying that not only had
he been outrageously and impiously treated, but the goddess as well. **3** Pompeius was
immediately struck with a burning fever, after which he lost his voice and was seized
with quinsy, dying on the third day, and it seemed to the populace that his death was
divinely inspired to avenge his actions against the priest and goddess, for the Romans
are very much given to religious awe. Accordingly, Battaces was allowed to wear his
costume and sacred robe, was honoured with noteworthy gifts, and was escorted by a
large crowd of both men and women when he set out on his journey home from Rome.

3.62 Opposition to the cult of Isis

Valerius Maximus *Memorable Doings and Sayings*
(Of Superstitions) 1.3.4

The goddess Isis first made an appearance in Rome in the 50s BC and her worship encountered
the opposition of the senate, but became entrenched in the early empire. Isis was worshipped
particularly by women, but the personal soteriology of the cult also attracted men. In 90 BC a
sistrum (an Egyptian sacred rattle) appears as a control mark on a denarius of the moneyer C.
Vibius Pansa (Crawford *RRC* 342, p. 349). Catullus, who died in 59–54 BC, refers to the temple
of Serapis in Rome (Cat. 10.26). In 59 BC the senate destroyed the altars of the Egyptian deities
Serapis, Anubis and Harpocrates (Horus), but their ardent worshippers soon rebuilt them, and on
1 January 58 BC, a crowd interrupted one of the consuls as he examined the entrails from the

sacrifice to Jupiter Capitolinus and heckled him because he was doing nothing supportive about the worship of Isis and Serapis (Varro in Tertull. *Apol.* 6, *Nat.* 1.10.17–18; Arnob. 2.73). In 53 BC the senate had the temples of Isis and Serapis, built by private individuals, demolished (Dio 40.47.3). Again, in 50 BC the senate once more ordered that the temples of Isis and Serapis, which had clearly been rebuilt, be destroyed: the workmen refused, so L. Aemilius Paullus (cos. 50) smashed an axe against the doors. In 48 BC after a series of prodigies, the augurs had the shrines of Egyptian gods on the Capitoline destroyed (*CIL* VI.2247). Octavian in 28 BC forbade Egyptian cults inside the pomerium (Dio 53.2.4, cf. 54.6.6), but under subsequent emperors the goddess had great popularity throughout the Roman empire, including at Rome (see esp. Apuleius *Metamorphoses* 11).

Isis in the Republic: Roullet 1972: 2; Takács 1995: 27–70; Turcan 1996: 85–7, 2000: 120–1; for Isis in the Roman world generally: Heyob 1975: 14–19; Solmsen 1979: 68; Burkert 1987: 40, 99; Versnel 1990: 39–52; Hayne 1992; Kraemer 1992: 71–79; Witt 1997: 70–88; Richardson *Top. Dict.* 211–13.

When the senate decreed that the temples of Isis and Serapis be destroyed, and none of the workmen dared to touch them, the consul Lucius Aemilius (Lepidus) Paullus (cos. 50) took off his toga praetexta, grabbed an axe, and smashed it against the door of that temple.

THE BACCHANALIA OF 186 BC

Full narrative at Livy 39.8–19; see also doc. 7.16; Cic. *Laws* 2.15.37; Val. Max. 1.3.1, 6.3.7.

The Greek cult of Bacchus (Dionysus) and its rites spread from southern Italy to Rome. Plautus' plays show that he and his audience were familiar with the cult, and that in the popular imagination it involved secret meetings and ritual floggings, as well as rumours of human sacrifice (Gruen 1990: 150–2 with references, esp. Plaut. *Aul.* 408–9, *Amph.* 703–4, *Bacch.* 371–2). As the cult had been at Rome for some time, Livy's account of the consuls' and senate's sudden 'discovery' of the cult are clearly wrong, but it was in 186 BC that, for whatever reason, the senate took action. Possibly the practice of the cult was becoming simply too public (note the women going to the Tiber with torches) and the patience of the elite exhausted.

The account of the *senatus consultum* and the action which the senate took is straightforward (see Nippel 1984: 24–5). Livy's account of how the cult came to the attention of one of the consuls, Postumius, is rather dramatic and not entirely credible (39.9.2–14.3; see Walsh 1996; doc. 7.63 for the role of the prostitute Hispala Faecenia), but the details of the senate's treatment of the cult must be correct.

The holding of the Bacchic rites at night in the presence of both sexes could easily have led to the accusations of promiscuous sexuality (both homoerotic and heterosexual). These elements were missing from the Greek cult; the severe penalty visited upon those involved seems to indicate that the senate and many Romans were convinced that 'vices' were being practised in the rites. Factors behind this persecution, the first in the Roman state, were the cult's popularity and the emergence for the first time of a group of readily identifiable devotees formed into an association. The senate did not react against the cult merely because it was foreign — after all, it was less than 20 years since the Magna Mater had been officially welcomed from the east — but because of the secret nature of the cult, its reputedly unacceptable practices, and the involvement of women.

According to Livy, 7,000 men and women were involved (39.17.6); many committed suicide, and others tried unsuccessfully to escape from Rome; participants were rounded up and put in chains, while those convicted of debauchery or murder were put to death; women were handed over to their family councils for punishment if the death penalty was required (doc. 7.16). The cult was strictly controlled from that date, not only in Rome but throughout Roman Italy (doc. 3.64).

See Warde Fowler 1911: 344–9; Toynbee 1965: II.391–400; North 1979: 86–98, 2000: 63–6; Garnsey 1984: 8–9; Scafuro 1989; Bauman 1990, 1992: 35–7; Gruen 1990: 34–78, 150–2; Scheid 1992: 398–400; Turcan 1996: 300–6, 2000: 117–19; Walsh 1996; *BNP* 1.92–6; Takács 2000.

3.63 'A wicked conspiracy including all crime and lust'

Livy *History of Rome* 39.8.3–18.8

8.3 Both consuls were assigned the duty of investigating secret conspiracies. It started when an obscure Greek arrived in Etruria, not with any of those arts which that most learned of all races brought to us in great numbers to cultivate our minds and bodies, but a dealer in sacrifices and soothsaying; **4** nor was he one who imbues minds with falsehood by practising his rites in public and openly proclaiming his profession and doctrine, but a celebrant of secret, nocturnal ceremonies. **5** There were mysteries which were at first only divulged to a few, but which then began to be widely disseminated among men and women. The delights of wine and feasting were added to the religious rites, to allure more people into joining. **6** When their minds were inflamed with wine, and night, and the mingling of men and women, young and old, had annihilated all sense of decorum, all kinds of vice first came into being, since all had at hand the chance to indulge in the pleasure to which nature most inclined them. **7** There was not just one kind of depravity, promiscuous debauchery between free men and women, but false witnesses, forged seals and wills, and perjured informants were all the product of this same workshop, **8** as well as poisonings and murders so secret that sometimes the bodies were not even available for burial. Much was dared by cunning, and more by violence. The violence was concealed because amid the wailing and the crashing of kettle-drums (tympana) and cymbals no sound of shrieks could be heard from this scene of debauchery and murders. **9.1** This evil, with all its virulence, spread from Etruria to Rome like the contagion of a plague. At first the size of the city with its greater capacity and tolerance for such evils concealed them: finally information reached the consul (Spurius) Postumius (Albinus). . . .

13.8 Hispala then disclosed the origin of the mysteries. At first, she said, it was a rite for women and it was a rule that no man be admitted to it. Three days had been set aside each year on which, during the day, initiations into the Bacchic rites were conducted; it was customary for the matrons to be made priests in turn. **9** Paculla Annia, a Campanian, when priest, had altered all this, supposedly at the god's behest: for she had been the first to initiate men, her sons Minius and Herennius Cerrinius; she had held the mysteries by night rather than by day, and instead of three days a year had made five days in each month into days of initiation. **10** From the time that the mysteries were held indiscriminately, and with men mixing with women, and with the licence of night-time added as well no crime or depravity had been omitted. There was more debauchery among men with one another than among women. **11** Any of them, who were less tolerant of submitting to outrage or more reluctant to commit crime, were sacrificed as victims. To consider nothing to be impious was the highest type of religious belief amongst them. **12** Men, as if out of their minds, would make prophecies, throwing their bodies about violently as if under divine inspiration; matrons, dressed as Bacchantes, would run, with their hair unkempt, down to the Tiber carrying flaming torches, plunge the torches into the water and (because they contained a mixture of live sulphur and calcium) pull them out with the flame still alight. **13** People were said to have been snatched away by the gods (in fact they were bound to a machine and carried off out of sight to hidden caves): they were the ones who had refused either to join in conspiracies or take part in crimes or suffer sexual violation. **14** The number of adherents was immense, almost amounting to a second nation; amongst them were some men and women of the nobility. Within the last two years it had been laid down that no one over the age of twenty should be initiated: they sought out young people of this age who would engage in both wickedness and debauchery . . .

14.3 When both witnesses were secured in this way, Postumius brought the matter before the senate, setting out all the points in order, first what had been reported, then what he had himself discovered. **4** The senators were seized with great alarm, both for the public, in case these conspiracies and assemblies might be harbouring some secret treachery or danger, and privately each for himself, in case any connection of their family might be involved in the evil . . .

17.6 More than 7,000 men and women were said to have been involved in the conspiracy. However, it was evident that the ring-leaders of the conspiracy had been Marcus and Gaius Atinius of the Roman plebs and the Faliscan Lucius Opicernius and the Campanian Minius Cerrinius: **7** all the crimes and wickedness had sprung from them, and they were the high priests and founders of the cult. Care was taken that they were arrested at the earliest opportunity. They were brought before the consuls and confessed, asking for no delay in being brought to trial . . .

18.3 Those who had simply been initiated and who had repeated at the priest's dictation, in accordance with the ritual formula, the prayers which contained the impious conspiracy to commit every crime and lust, but had not been involved in any of those deeds against either themselves or others which they had bound themselves on oath to commit, were left in prison; **4** those who had dishonoured themselves by debauchery or murder, who had been polluted by false witness, forged seals, the substitution of wills and other kinds of fraud, suffered capital punishment. **5** More were killed than thrown into prison. There was an immense number of men and women in both categories. **6** Convicted women were handed over to their family, or to those whose authority they were under, so that these could punish them privately: if there was no appropriate person to exact the punishment, it was inflicted by the state. **7** The consuls were then given the task of destroying all forms of Bacchic worship, first in Rome and then through the whole of Italy, except for places where an ancient altar or statue had been consecrated. **8** The senate then decreed that for the future there should be no Bacchanalia in Rome or in Italy.

3.64 The senate's resolution over Bacchanalian 'orgies', 186 BC

ILS 18

(*CIL* I² 581; *CIL* X.104; *ILLRP* 511; *FIRA* 1.30; Bruns 36; *ARS* 28; Gordon no. 8; Courtney *ALP* 93–101; *ROL* IV.254–9.) Livy mentions three decrees: 39.14.5, 18.7, 18.8. This document is a letter of the consuls of 186, including the actual *senatus consultum*, written to the people of the Ager Teuranus in Bruttium; it was found on a tablet of brass at Tiriolo in Bruttian territory (and is now in Vienna). This tablet was presumably a copy of the letter made to be publicly displayed and is the oldest extant surviving *senatus consultum* (Gordon p. 83). Clearly the senate assumes that it has the right to interfere in the internal affairs of allied states. **§30**: 'anything sacred' might include an ancient altar or statue: Livy 39.18.7 (doc. 3.63).

The consuls (Quintus) Marcius (Philippus), son of Lucius, and Spurius Postumius, son of Lucius, consulted the senate on the Nones (7th) of October in the temple of Bellona. Present as witnesses to the record were Marcus Claudius, son of Marcus, Lucius Valerius, son of Publius, and Quintus Minucius, son of Gaius. Regarding the Bacchanalia, they resolved that the following decree be made known to Rome's allies:

'Let none of them be minded to maintain a place devoted to [B]acchus; if there are any people who say that it is necessary for them to maintain a place devoted to Bacchus, they must come to the praetor urbanus at Rome, **5** and, when their w[o]r[d]s have been heard, our senate shall decide concerning these matters, provided that not less than 100 senators are present [when t]he matter is discussed. Let no man, whether Roman citizen or Latin by name or any of the allies, be minded to attend a meeting of Bacchant women, unless they have first approached the praetor urbanus and he has given them authorisation through a vote of the senate, provided that not less than 100 senators were present when the matter is discussed.' Passed.

10 'Let no man be a priest; let not any man or woman be a master (magister, i.e., administrator); nor let anyone be mi[nd]ed to [k]eep a commo[n] fund; nor let anyone be minded to make any man [or wo]man a master or vice-master; nor henceforward let anyone be minded to swear togeth[er], [no]r vow together, nor make mutual promises, nor pledge to others, nor be minded to plight faith to each other. **15** Let no one be minded to hold sacred rites in secret, whether in public or privately, nor be minded to hold rites outside the city, unless he has first approached the praetor urbanus, and he has given them authorisation through a vote of the senate, provided that not less than 100 senators were present when the matter is discussed.' Passed.

'Let no one in a group of more than five, men and women together, **20** be minded to hold sacred rites, and let not more than two men and not more than three women be minded to attend there, unless with the agreement of the praetor urbanus and senate as written above'.

You are to proclaim this in a public meeting (contio) for a period of no less than three market-days (seventeen days), and so that you may be acquainted with the vote of the senate, this vote was as follows: 'Should there be any, who act contrary to what has been recorded above, **25** the senate resolves that proceedings for a capital crime should be taken against them; and the senate thought it right that you shall inscribe this on a bronze tablet and you shall order it to be put up where it can most easily be seen; and that you ensure that those places devoted to Bacchus which exist be dissolved as recorded above, **30** unless there be anything sacred there, within ten days of the receipt of this letter.'

In the Ager Teuranus.

3.65 The decorous nature of Roman worship

Dionysius of Halicarnassus *Roman Antiquities* 2.19.2–5

Dionysius here compares Roman ritual practices with Greek. Behaviour in Roman religion was more controlled than in Greek with fewer avenues for spontaneous religious expression. Dionysius' point about the Romans' non-acceptance of foreign cults, or their transformation of them, is born out by his example of the Magna Mater, whom he refers to as the Idaean goddess (docs 3.59–61).

2 No festival is observed by the Romans by the wearing of black or as a day of mourning with women beating their breasts and lamenting over the disappearance of gods, as the Greeks do over the abduction of Persephone or the misfortunes of Dionysus and other such events; nor may one see amongst them, even though their customs have now been corrupted, any instances of divine possession, Corybantic frenzies, religious begging rituals, Bacchic rites and secret mysteries, all-night vigils of men and women together in temples or any other trickery of this kind, but there is a reverence in all their words and actions in respect of the gods, which is not seen among either Greeks or barbarians; **3** and the thing that I have marvelled at most of all is that, although the city has attracted tens of thousands of peoples who are compelled to worship their native gods according to the customs of their homelands, it has never publicly adopted any of these foreign practices, as many other cities have done, but, even when she has followed oracles which instructed her to introduce certain rites, she celebrates these according to her own customs after banishing all mythical nonsense, as in the case of the rites of the Idaean goddess. **4** For the praetors perform sacrifices and games for this goddess every year according to Roman customs, but her priest and priestess are Phrygians and they process through the city, begging for alms as is their custom, and wearing images on their breasts and striking their kettle-drums, to the accompaniment of their followers playing songs to the goddess on their flutes; **5** no native-born Roman, however, either ritually begs for alms or processes through the city accompanied by flute-players wearing a multi-coloured robe, or worships the goddess with the Phrygian rites — a law and decree of the senate has prohibited this. The city is extremely cautious with respect to religious customs which are not native to Rome and regards as inauspicious all pomp and ceremony which lacks decorous behaviour.

CURSE TABLETS AND SYMPATHETIC MAGIC

Magic was known to the Romans as early as the XII Tables, where the phrases 'whoever shall have bewitched the crops' and 'whoever shall have cast an evil spell' occur (doc. 1.49; Pliny *Nat. Hist.* 28.18). Through incantations people and things (such as crops) could be harmed. Beneficent magic was also used, as for cures like that in which Cato uses common spell techniques: incomprehensible nonsense words, and ingredients (here the reed), which are handled and chanted over (doc. 3.68). Through the use of the spell he aims to influence the natural world (here the dislocation of a limb). Pliny (*Nat. Hist.* 28.59) reports that ancient Romans forbade anyone to cross their legs during official meetings (or sacred ceremonies) because it hindered the transaction of business. Magic — good and bad — was coercive, and differed from the relationship between the gods and Romans which was meant to be reciprocal, though religion did, of course, seek to bind the gods to the people and state, but in a different way. Similarly, the difference between *superstitio* and *religio* was clear to Cicero (doc. 3.66). Curse tablets aimed to gain power over a person, generally for malevolent purposes (as in doc. 3.67), and invoked the deities of the underworld, here the Roman goddess Proserpina (equivalent to the Greek Persephone), wife of Pluto, god of the underworld.

While magic had always clearly been practised in the Roman Republic, its last half century saw a shift of focus and a new interest, foreshadowing its more prominent place in the imperial period. Magical practices outside the Roman experience are referred to, and Cicero's accusations against Vatinius (that he called up the spirits of the dead and appeased them with the entrails of boys: Cic. *Vat.* 14) indicate that a new array of magical practices was entering Rome (Beard 1994: 759–61; cf. North 1980: 186); Vatinius foreshadows Horace's description of magical practices in *Epodes* 5.

3.66 Superstitio versus religio

Cicero *On the Nature of the Gods* 2.71–2

Cicero carefully distinguishes between *superstitio* and *religio*. *Religio* entailed rituals handed-down over generations and concerned primarily the worship (cultus) of the gods. At *Div.* 2.149 Cicero, listing arguments against divination, describes *superstitio* as listening to a prophet or omen, sacrificing, watching the flight of birds, consulting astrologers or soothsayers, and noting thunder and lightning and prodigies. *Superstitio*: North 2000: 82; Scheid 2003: 23.

71 *Religio* has been distinguished from *superstitio* not only by philosophers but also by our forebears. **72** People who passed entire days in prayer and sacrifice so that their children would outlive them were called *superstitious* (from *superstes*: survivor), and the word later came to have a wider meaning. Those, however, who diligently reviewed and retraced everything pertaining to the *cultus* (worship) of the gods were known as *religious*, from *relegere* (to retrace, or re-read).

3.67 Curses

CIL I² 1614, 1615, 2520

(*ILS* 8746; *ILLRP* 1146, 1149; *ROL* IV.280–5.) These three inscriptions are curse tablets (defixiones). No. 1614 is a round tablet of lead (an uncommon type), supposedly found at Cumae, and written in a mixture of Latin and Oscan; no. 1615 is small bronze plate, discovered in a tomb at Cumae.

CIL I² 2520 comprises the inscribed curses of five thin plates of lead, discovered at Rome. Each plate is wrapped around a nail, and each curses a single person, in the example given an individual named Plotius; each of the five follows the same wording, so that gaps in the curse against Plotius can be filled in from the other plates (the restorations in no. 2520 are not marked here). They date to the first century BC (between about 80 and 40 BC). These five curses are all inscribed by the one hand, in the month of February, suggesting the work of someone well-versed in cursing. Note the importance of addressing the deity by the right names, the need to list specifically all body parts to be affected, and the anonymity preserved by the curser to avoid retaliation; see Gordon 1999: 270–4. The meaning of *fancua* is unknown.

For curses, cf. *CIL* I² 1012, 1013, 2541; X.8214 (*ILLRP* 1147). Large numbers of curse tables survive from the imperial period from Rome and throughout the empire: for an introduction, see Gager 1992: 3–41.

1614 Lucius Harines, son of Herius Maturus, Gaius Eburius, Pomponius, Marcus Caedicius son of Marcus, Numerius Andripius, son of Numerius. May the *fancua* of them all stand straight up! May their breath be dry!

1615 To face judgement (among the dead): Naevia Secunda, freedwoman of Lucius, or whatever name she goes under.

2520 Good and beautiful Proserpina, wife of Pluto, unless I ought to call you Salvia ('Saviour'), may you tear from Plotius health, body, colour, strength, vigour. May you deliver him over to Pluto your husband. May he not be able to avoid this by his own devices. May you deliver him to the fourth-day, the third-day, the every-day fever (i.e., malaria), and may they wrestle and struggle it out with him; may they vanquish and overcome him until they tear away his life. Wherefore **10** I deliver this victim to you Proserpina, unless, Proserpina, I ought to call you Acherousia (i.e., goddess of the underworld). May you send, I pray, someone to summon the three-headed dog to tear out Plotius' heart. Promise that you will give him three victims, dates, dried figs, a black pig, if he should have finished before the month of March. These things, Proserpina Salvia, I will give you when you have gratified my wish. I give you the head of Plotius, (slave) of Avonia, **20** Proserpina Salvia, I give you Plotius' forehead, Proserpina Salvia, I give you Plotius' eyebrows, Proserpina Salvia, I give you Plotius' eyelids, Proserpina Salvia, I give you Plotius' pupils, Proserpina Salvia, I give you Plotius' nostrils, lips, ears, nose, tongue, teeth, so Plotius may not be able to say what pains him; his neck, shoulders, arms, fingers, so he may not be able to help himself in any way; **30** his chest, liver, heart, lungs, so he may not be able to feel what gives him pain; his intestines, stomach, navel, sides, so he may not be able to sleep; his shoulder-blades, so he may not be able to sleep soundly; his testicles, so he may not be able to urinate; his buttocks, anus, thighs, knees, shanks, shins, feet, ankles, soles, toes, nails, so he may not be able to stand by his own strength. Should there have been written, **40** whether great or small, any curse, in whatever way Plotius has properly (i.e., according to the laws of magic) written anything (i.e., against me) and committed it, thus I deliver Plotius to you, and commit him that you may deliver and commit that fellow in the month of February. Damn him!, to hell with him!, damn him utterly! May you commit him, may you hand him over, so he may not be able to see, look on or regard any month further!

3.68 Ritual nonsense performs a cure

Cato the Elder *On Farming* 160

See Varro *Rust.* 1.2.27 for a similar cure for gout. Pliny *Nat. Hist.* 28.20 refers to magical prayers with 'foreign unpronounceable words'. The alternative spellings for the incomprehensible words in Cato's spell are given this way in different manuscripts.

In case of dislocation it may be cured by the following spell. Take a green reed four or five feet long and split it down the middle, and let two men hold it to their hips. Begin to chant, 'motas vaeta daries dardares astataries dissunapiter' and continue until the pieces meet (another manuscript has 'motas vaeta daries dardaries asiadarides una petes'). Brandish a knife over the pieces and when they meet so that one touches the other, grasp with the hand and cut at right and left. Bind it to the dislocation or fracture and it will heal. And meanwhile chant every day in the following way in the case of a dislocation, 'huat haut haut istasis tarsis ardannabou dannaustra' (another manuscript has 'huat haut haut ista pista sista dannabo dannaustra').

FESTIVALS

Calendars recorded the dates of festivals and the deities so honoured. The range of gods honoured by festivals took in the whole array of the Roman pantheon, from the mighty Jupiter himself, to the deity of rust. For the festivals, see Ovid's *Fasti*; and the various descriptions in Scullard 1981; for women's festivals, see also docs 7.75–82.

3.69 The origins of the Saturnalia

Accius *Annals* 2–7

(*ROL* II.590–2.) Lucius Accius was born in 170 BC at Pisaurum in Umbria; as well as tragedies he wrote the *Annals* dealing with religious festivals. Here Accius states that the annual Roman festival of the Saturnalia began in Greece pointing to a hellenising tendency apparent in the third and second century BC in Roman religion. Dionysius apparently dates the festival to the seventh century (doc. 3.8) and Livy 2.21.2 to 496 BC. Dionysius is closer to the mark: Saturn is an Italian and Roman deity, his name deriving from *satus*: sowing (Varro *Lat. Lang.* 5.64). His festival commenced on 17 December, and lasted for several days. Cicero (*Att.* 5.20.5) mentions the Saturnalia as a 'merry' occasion (celebrated by him and his men in Cilicia), and at *Att.*13.52.1 writes, 'the less elegant freedmen and slaves lacked nothing. I entertained the more elegant ones with style'. Catullus (14.15) described the festival as 'the best of days', and even the parsimonious Cato the Elder issued extra rations to his farm personnel for the festival (doc. 6.32). It is one of the festivals listed in the Antium calendar under December (cf. doc. 3.28). For the Saturnalia, see: Ogilvie 1969: 98; Dumézil 1970: 271; Scullard 1981: 205–7; Versnel 1993: 136–227, 1993a; *BNP* 2.124, 173; Turcan 2000: 35–6.

Most of the Greeks, and especially Athens, celebrate a festival
In honour of Saturn, which by them is known as the Cronia;
In celebration of this day, through all the fields and cities,
They joyfully hold feasts, and each man waits upon
His own slaves; that same custom has been handed down from there to us,
So that here, too, slaves feast with their masters.

3.70 The secession of the flute-players

Livy *History of Rome* 9.30.5–10

This incident took place in 311 BC; Rome was at risk from the Etruscans and was finishing a war with Samnites. For the role of flute-players at sacrifices, particularly during the recitation of prayers, see doc. 3.24. The 'period of three days a year' was the festival of the flute players celebrated each year on 13–15 June. Strike and festival: Ovid *Fasti* 6.651–710; Plut. *Rom. Quest.* 55; Val. Max. 2.5.4; Scullard 1981: 152–3. The censors of 312 were Appius Claudius Caecus and Gaius Plautius.

5 I would have passed over an incident of the same year as being hardly worthy of mention, had it not seemed to concern religion (*religio*). The flute-players, annoyed at having been forbidden by the last censors to hold their feast in the temple of Jupiter according to ancient custom, headed off in a body to Tibur, with the result that there was no one in the city to play at sacrifices. **6** Concerned by the religious implications of the incident, the senate sent delegates to Tibur requesting them to try to return the men to Rome. **7** The Tiburtines courteously promised to do so, summoned them to the senate-house and urged them to return; when they were unable to persuade them, they handled them with a measure not inappropriate to their natural disposition. **8** On a public holiday various people invited some of them home on the pretext of celebrating the feast with music, loaded them with wine (to which that type of men is generally well-disposed) and got them off to sleep. **9** In this condition they threw them into carts, still fast asleep, and carried them off to Rome. The carts were left in the forum and the players knew nothing about it until daylight found them there — still inebriated. **10** The people then gathered round and prevailed with them to stay, and they were permitted to wander the city in festive dress for a period of three days a year, making music and enjoying the licence which is now customary, while those who played at sacrifices were given back the right of feasting in the temple. This happened at a time of anxiety over two serious wars.

3.71 A dog sacrifice keeps Mildew away

Ovid *Fasti* 4.905–42

The Robigalia (from Robigus or Robigo, the deity of mildew or grain rust) was celebrated on April 25. In Ovid's description several typical features of the sacrifice can be noted: the procession to the grove of the god, the wine and incense, and the burning of the entrails of the sheep and dog. Prayer accompanied all sacrifices and here the flamen Quirinalis in a typical ritual pattern seeks to propitiate the malevolent force of Robigus by making a prayer, naming the god he is invoking, and then presiding over the sacrifice. The festival took place on the via Claudia, at the fifth milestone; the dog star is Sirius.

Dogs were also sacrificed at other ceremonies. Red bitches were sacrificed at the *augurium canarium* prior to the grain emerging from the sheath, red equating with the colour of rust (Pliny *Nat. Hist.* 18.14). Plutarch *Rom. Quest.* 52 records that the Romans sacrifice a bitch to the birth goddess Geneta Mana, while the Luperci sacrifice a dog (doc. 7.76). See Varro *Lat. Lang.* 6.16; Pliny *Nat. Hist.* 18.15 (quoting from the libri pontificales); Columella 10.342–4; Scullard 1981: 108–10; North 1995: 140–1; Turcan 2000: 39–40, 69; for the Cerealia, see Ovid *Fasti* 4.679–82, 703–12; Spaeth 1996: 36.

905 On that day, as I was returning to Rome from Nomentum,
　　　　A crowd of people in white robes blocked the middle of the road.
　　　　A flamen was going to the grove of ancient Mildew,
　　　　To give to the flames the entrails of a dog and a sheep.
　　　　I immediately went closer to learn about the ritual.
910 Your flamen, Quirinus, pronounced these words:
　　　　'Harsh Mildew, spare the sprouting grain,
　　　　And let their smooth tips quiver on the surface of the ground.
　　　　Allow the crops, nurtured by the stars of a propitious sky,
　　　　To grow until they become ready for the sickles.
　　　　Your power is not slight: the corn, which you have marked,
　　　　The farmer sadly gives up as lost.
　　　　Neither winds, nor rain storms harm the corn,
　　　　Nor the marble-like frost which whitens the brown grain,
　　　　As much as does the sun when it warms the wet stalks:
920 Then is the time, dread deity, for you to show your anger.
　　　　Spare, I pray, and keep your scabby hands off our harvests.

Do not harm our fields: it is enough that you have the power to do so.
Grasp not tender crops, but hard iron.
First destroy anything which can destroy others.
You will more profitably devour swords and harmful weapons:
There is no need of them — the world is at peace.
Let the hoes and hard mattock and the curved ploughshare,
The farm equipment, shine brightly: but let rust stain weapons,
And when someone tries to pull a sword from its sheath,
930   Let him feel it stick from long disuse.
But do not pollute the corn, and may the farmer always
Be able to offer prayers to you in your absence.'
Thus he spoke: from his right hand hung a loosely woven napkin
And he had a bowl of wine and a casket of incense.
On the fire he placed the incense, wine, sheep's entrails,
And the foul guts of a disgusting dog — we saw him.
Then to me he said: 'Do you ask why these rites are assigned an unusual victim?'
I had asked that. 'Learn the reason,' said the flamen.
'There is a Dog, which they call the Icarian dog, and when that star rises
940   The earth is scorched and dry, and the crops ripen too early.
This dog is put on the altar in place of the starry dog,
And the only reason for this is his name.'

RELIGION AND POLITICS

State religion was dominated by the elite; Polybius offers an assessment that religion could be manipulated to keep the 'masses' in check (doc. 3.73). The most frequently manipulated area of religion was divination, because an unfavourable declaration of omens by the presiding magistrate could terminate meetings of the assembly and could stop elections in the comitia centuriata. Omens could also be used to block the activities of tribunes and the proposing of laws which were opposed by the senate. Cicero writes concerning the auspices: 'The taking of auspices (is granted) so that there may be credible excuses for postponing many unprofitable meetings of the assembly; for the immortal gods have often used auspices to restrain the people's unreasonable ardour' (*Laws* 3.27); after all, the auspices were meant to be of utility to the state (*Laws* 2.32). This was the procedure followed by Bibulus in 59 BC when Caesar's agrarian legislation was opposed by the senate (doc. 3.72). Similarly, thunder was 'heard' during the voting for Saturninus' land legislation, but he threatened hail against those who heard it (*Vir. Illust.* 73.7). The announcing of adverse omens was *obnuntiatio*: see docs 12.41, 52.

Another ploy was to 'discover' that a ritual had been incorrectly performed and needed repeating. This would mean that days which had been available for meetings of the assembly (comitial days) became earmarked for a religious celebration and no public business could be transacted. In addition, laws which had been passed could be annulled by the senate as having been passed 'against the auspices' (*contra auspicia*); this occurred in 91 BC with Drusus' citizenship law for the Italians (Asc. 68–9; there was also a procedural issue involved). For manipulation of religion for political purposes, see esp. Taylor 1949: 76–97; also Liebeschuetz 1979: 14–15; Beard 1994: 739–40.

3.72 Pompey's manipulation of the auspices in 55 BC

Plutarch *Life of Cato the Younger* 42.1, 4–5

Pompey as consul in 55 BC, when presiding over the elections of praetors for 54, obstructed the election of Cato by hearing thunder: Plut. *Cat. Min.* 42, *Pomp.* 52.3; *MRR* II.214. Similarly, M. Calpurnius Bibulus as consul in 59 BC had attempted to obstruct the other consul, Julius Caesar, through the manipulation of omens, proclaiming them unfavourable. This meant that the assembly could not be held; any decisions it reached were void. Such a manipulation of the omens had been employed successfully before, but not on such a scale. Clodius later attempted to repeal Caesar's agrarian legislation of 59 on the grounds that it had been passed *contra auspicia* (Cic. *Dom.* 39–41, *Har. Resp.* 48; Taylor 1949: 95; Lintott 1999: 135).

1 Cato would not back down, but came forward as a candidate for the praetorship, wanting to have a base of operations for his conflicts against them (Pompey and Crassus) . . . **4** When the first tribe called forward voted for him, Pompey suddenly lied and proclaimed that he heard thunder and then disgracefully dissolved the assembly (since they were accustomed to consider such things as inauspicious and not to ratify anything after a divine sign had occurred). **5** They then resorted again to immense bribery, drove the best citizens from the assembly, and so, by force, got Vatinius elected praetor instead of Cato.

3.73 The political uses of religion

Polybius *Histories* 6.56.6–12

The Roman aristocrats themselves probably did not see their religion in quite the same blunt, cynical fashion as Polybius below. While they may have entertained no scruples in manipulating the auspices, religion was crucial not for keeping the common people under control, but for the state's survival. The Romans' relations with the gods as expressed in sacrifices and festivals, and the expiation of prodigies, assured the support of the gods for Rome's supremacy: no-one, not even in the closing decades of the Republic, doubted this support was dependent on the gods. Polybius' word 'superstition', *deisidaimonia*, is not strictly correct here, as the Romans would not have seen their religious practices, their *religio*, as superstitious or as being a collection of superstitions. Despite Polybius' stress here on the importance of religion in Roman public life, religious factors are generally absent from his narrative (Vaahtera 2000). The most conspicuous way in which the Roman aristocracy used religion against the people, namely the auspices, are not mentioned. For this passage: Walbank I.741–2; Vaahtera 2000: 252–3.

6 But it is in religious belief that the Roman commonwealth seems to me to be vastly superior (to other states). **7** I believe that what is an object of derision among other peoples, namely superstition, is actually the element that holds the state together; **8** for these matters are treated with such pomp, and introduced to such an extent into both public and private life, that they have a place of pre-eminence. This may seem remarkable to many people. **9** My view is that this practice has been adopted for the sake of the common people. **10** If it had been possible to form a state composed of wise men, this approach might not have been necessary; **11** but since the common people is always easily swayed and full of lawless desires, unreasoning anger, and violent passions, the only course is to restrain the masses through vague terrors and suchlike dramatisations. **12** For this reason I believe that the ancients were not acting at random or haphazardly when they introduced to the masses notions about the gods and beliefs in the underworld — rather people nowadays are acting at random and foolishly in throwing them out.

FUNERARY PRACTICES

See doc. 1.52 for funerary regulations in the XII Tables. The Romans of the Republic believed that those who died joined the *di manes*, the shades of the deceased, and had no particular 'existence' after death. They were honoured at the Parentalia festival, while at the Lemuria festival the unburied dead were placated. The bodies of the dead and burial places were considered polluting; the flamen dialis could not go to a cemetery or touch a corpse but was allowed to attend funerals (doc. 3.19).

There are few tombs surviving from the Republic: only in the first century BC did the aristocracy begin constructing grandiose ones. From the first half of the third century BC the Cornelii Scipiones were buried in an extensive but plainly decorated tomb which had niches for burials in sarcophagi (Nash 2.352; Toynbee 1971: 103–4). The best-known piece of funerary art in the Republic is in fact the sarcophagus of L. Cornelius Scipio Barbatus from this tomb (doc. 1.68). In the final years of the Republic, tombs of slaves and freedmen begin to appear (Toynbee 117; Nash 349–51; docs. 6.55–60).

Varro at the end of the Republic refers to inhumation burial in mass graves — large pits known as *puticuli* — and mentions those in the public burial ground near the Esquiline Hill at Rome, which have been excavated (Varro *Lat. Lang.* 5.25; Bodel 1986 [1994] 38–54; Kyle 1998: 164–6; Hope 2000: 110–12; cf. Morris 1992: 42, Bodel 2000). Cremation became increasingly common as the Republic progressed: in the third century BC the practice of cremation, placing the bones and ashes in urns and burying them in tombs, begins amongst the aristocracy (though not among the Cornelii Scipiones), and by the first century BC cremation was quite normal at Rome; Tacitus writing of the reign of Nero has cremation as 'the Roman custom' (*Ann.* 16.6). It was unusual that Sulla in 78 BC was the first of the Cornelii to be cremated (Cic. *Laws* 2.57; Pliny *Nat. Hist.* 7.187). The pattern then reversed itself from the first century AD to the third century, with inhumation becoming more and more prevalent (Morris 1992: 42–69).

For death, funerals and the afterlife, see Cumont 1922, esp. 1–43; Dumézil 1970: 363–9; Toynbee 1971: 33–64; Nicolet 1980: 346–52; North 1988a; Ochs 1993: 84–103; Lindsay 2000: 161–6; Noy 2000, 2000a.

3.74 Funerary practices as a unifying political factor

Polybius *Histories* 6.53.1–54.3

The public funeral procession was the preserve of the *nobiles*. It celebrated the deeds of the deceased and his ancestors, reminding the public of his services to the state. It was a visual experience: those impersonating the ancestors wore colourful togas, rode in chariots with the insignia of the offices the ancestors had worn, and finally sat on 'seats of ivory', displaying themselves to the assembled crowd, which would hear the ancestors' virtues extolled by the eulogist. Polybius refers to the deceased being in an upright position, presumably meaning that the corpse was seated as it was carried in procession; wax substitutes are attested later but the practice here was to display the actual corpse (Walbank I.737).

Dionysius also refers to the funeral oration as an ancient Roman custom (5.17.3). For Caesar's eulogies of his aunt Julia and wife Cornelia from the rostra in 69 BC, see doc. 7.35; for funeral orations, see Ochs 1993: 105–11. The masks (imagines) of the ancestors had a 'conspicuous place' in the house. They were made of wax and each was kept in its own wooden cupboard in the atrium of the house (Pliny *Nat. Hist.* 35.6; cf. doc. 2.27). The masks were intended to be as lifelike as possible (cf. Pliny *Nat. Hist.* 35.4–7; Gruen 1992: 153–5 and 155–82 for realistic portraiture in general and its stylised portrayal of 'grim resolve' as a feature of the Roman magisterial class). Those who wore the masks of the ancestors of the deceased, 'men who seem to most resemble the original', are usually interpreted to be actors (or perhaps family members). The masks enabled the actors to represent the ancestors at the height of their importance (as praetor, consul or censor), and to be recognisable as such: the masks are therefore not death masks but actual portraits; for masks, see Toynbee 1971: 47; Flower 1996: esp. 59, 91–127; docs 2.27. Togas served to designate the most important achievements of the ancestors: consul or praetor (toga with purple border, the toga praetexta), the toga of the censor (purple toga: toga purpurea) or triumphator (purple with gold embroidery: toga picta); for togas: Stone 1994, esp. 13.

The setting of the forum, the use of the rostra (from which political speeches were delivered) and the presence of the people underlined the connection between the state (the deceased are shown as office bearers with their insignia) and the community. The young men, argues Polybius, are inspired 'for the common good'; for Polybius' description, see the commentary at Walbank I.737–40; Toynbee 1971: 47; Flower 1996: 36–8, 110, T61; cf. Flower 2004: 331–7.

53.1 Whenever one of their distinguished men dies, as part of his funeral procession he is carried with all honour into the Forum to the so-called Rostra, sometimes conspicuous in an upright position, or, more rarely, reclining. **2** With the whole people standing around, his son, if he has one of adult age to follow him and who happens to be present, or, if not, some other relative, mounts the Rostra and discourses on the virtues of the deceased and his successful achievements during his lifetime. **3** As a result, the populace, when such facts are recalled to their minds and brought before their eyes — not only those who played a part in these achievements, but also those who did not — feel such deep sympathy that the loss seems not to be confined to the mourners, but to be a public one which affects the whole people. **4** Next, after burying the body and performing the usual ceremonies, they place the image of the deceased in the most conspicuous place in the house, enclosed in a wooden shrine. **5** This image is a mask fashioned into a remarkable likeness in both its modelling and its painting. **6** On the occasion of public sacrifices, they display these masks and carefully decorate them, and when any distinguished member of the family dies they take them to the funeral, where they are worn by men who seem to most resemble the original in both height and general bearing. **7** These men also wear togas with purple borders, if the deceased had been a consul or praetor, a purple one, if a censor, and a purple one embroidered with gold, if he had celebrated a triumph or performed a similar achievement. **8** They all ride in chariots with the fasces, axes and other insignia appropriate to the dignity of the offices held by each in his lifetime carried before them, and when they arrive at the Rostra **9** they all seat themselves in a row on chairs of ivory. There could be no more edifying sight for a young man who aspires to fame and virtue; **10** for who would not be moved by the sight of the images of men renowned for their excellence, all together as if alive and breathing? What spectacle could be more glorious than this?

54.1 Moreover, the speaker over the man about to be buried, when he has finished his address on the subject of the deceased, goes on to speak of the successes and achievements of each of the others whose images are present, beginning with the oldest. **2** Through this practice, this constant renewal of the fame of brave men, the glory of those who performed some noble deed is made immortal, while the renown of those who served their country well becomes common knowledge and a heritage for those to come. **3** But the most important consequence is that young men are inspired to endure everything for the common good for the sake of winning the glory which accompanies brave men.

3.75 Regulations against cremations

ILS 6082

(*CIL* I² 591; *ROL* IV.252.) This inscription, on a pillar, dating probably to c. 150–120 BC, is a *senatus consultum* concerning 'the hill village' and was found on the Esquiline hill in Rome; an area outside the Esquiline Gate was used as a cemetery for paupers, who were informally dumped (without burning) into pits: Varro *Lat. Lang.* 5.25 reports that one derivation of *puticuli* (pits) was from the word *putrescere*, 'to rot'. The *senatus consultum* effectively bars cremations from this area and so reserved it for dumping of the bodies of the poor (citizen paupers, slaves, the bodies of executed criminals, and the like). On the area, note Horace *Serm.* 1.18.14–16 that walking along the city walls one could see the area's mass grave (*commune sepulchrum*) and the whitened bones. As with *CIL* I² 591, the edict of the praetor L. Sentius and his three boundary stones (cippi) at the end of the Republic delimited an area where crematoria could not be built, stercus (excrement) dumped or corpses abandoned (*CIL* I² 838–9, VI.31614–15; *ILS* 8208, 2981). Here the *ustrinae* are permanent crematoria, the *foci ustrinae causa* temporary burning sites, i.e., pyres for a single corpse. See esp. Bodel 1986 [1994] 47–50; cf. Jongman 2003: 107.

Senatus consultum concerning the hill village:

. . . and that they should take care and guard it on the decision of the aediles of the plebs, whosoever they might be; and that there shall be no burning-grounds (ustrinae) for corpses on those sites or in the vicinity, nor hearths (foci ustrinae causa) **5** for burning the dead, nor shall those who have rented these sites from the mountain village choose to make dung-heaps or throw dirt within those sites, and if anyone shall have made dung-heaps or thrown dirt in these sites, there shall be (a fine of) . . . sesterces, his property shall be confiscated and pledges taken.

3.76 Presentation of burial sites (except for gladiators)

CIL 1² 2123

(*ILLRP* 662; *ROL* IV.50.) A stone tablet found at Sassina in Umbria. Burial sites of a specified size could be chosen while one was still alive; descendants could use the plot.

. . . . Horatius Balbus, son of . . ., to his fellow townsmen and other residents, at his own expense gives burial sites, except for gladiators and those who strangled themselves with their own hand and those who **10** followed an unclean profession: to each a site 10 feet in front and 10 feet in depth between the bridge over the Sapis and the upper monument which is on the edge of the Fangonian estate. In those places where no one has been buried, anyone who wishes shall make a tomb for himself while still alive. In those places where someone has been buried, **20** it will only be permitted to have a monument for him who has been buried there and his descendants.

3.77 Funerary feast for a father, c. 60 BC

CIL I² 1578

(*ILLRP* 667; ROL IV.48.) Lucius Papius Pollio set up this inscription, found at Carinola, as a memorial for his father. Board of Two: though in Italian towns there could be praetors or consuls, it was normal for there to be a *duoviri iure dicundo*, a 'Board of Two for pronouncing justice' at the head of the community, with two more junior magistrates (the *duoviri aediles* or *duoviri aedilicia potestate*; see doc. 2.60). Gladiatorial shows given at funerals were the origins of gladiatorial competitions: see docs 2.78–9.

Lucius Papius Pollio, son of Lucius, of the Teretine tribe, member of the Board of Two, in honour of his father Lucius Papius, son of Lucius, of the Falernian tribe, gave a feast of mead and pastry to all the colonists of Sinuessa and Caedex, and a gladiatorial show and a dinner to the colonists at Sinuessa and the Papii. He set up a memorial at the cost of 12,000 sesterces **5** by the will and testament (of his father) and with the approval of Lucius Novercinius Pollis, of the Pupinian tribe, son of Lucius.

3.78 Inhumation practices

Cicero *On the Laws* 2.57

'The same fate' which Cicero refers to here is Sulla's scattering of the remains of Marius in the river Anio (*Laws* 2.56). Prior to Sulla, the Cornelii had been inhumed. On funerary practices, 'It is unnecessary for me to explain when the period of family mourning is ended, what sort of a sacrifice of wethers is offered to the Lar, in what manner the severed bone is buried in the earth, what are the rules in regard to the obligation to sacrifice a sow, or when the grave first takes on the character of a grave and comes under the protection of religion' (Cic. *Laws* 2.22); cf. Varro *Lat. Lang.* 5.23.

Maybe it was because he was afraid that the same fate might happen to his body that Sulla, for the first time among the patrician Cornelii, instructed that he be cremated. For Ennius says about Africanus, 'Here he is laid.' And correctly; for 'laid' is used of those who are buried. But their place of burial is not a grave until the proper rites are performed and the pig slaughtered. And the term now in general use for all who are buried, that they are interred, was then restricted to those bodies where earth was thrown on and covered them, and pontifical law confirms this custom. For until a clod of earth is thrown onto the bones, the place where a body is cremated has no religious character; when the clod is thrown on, the burial has taken place and it is called a grave, and from that point many sacred laws protect it. And so, in the case of a person who has died on a ship and has then been thrown into the sea, Publius Mucius (Scaevola) proclaimed his family free from pollution, because none of the bones lay above the earth; but his heir had to provide the sow, and a holiday of three days had to be kept.

3.79 Temple of Jupiter Capitolinus; denarius of 78 BC

Crawford *RRC* 385.1

Grueber I.388; Sydenham 774; Carson *PCRR* 152; Hill *MAR* no. 27. The coin depicts the temple of Jupiter Capitolinus; which had burned down in Sulla's capture of the city in 83 BC.

Obverse: Head of Jupiter, facing right, with laurel wreath.
Reverse: Temple of Jupiter Capitolinus. The temple is shown with three closed doors between four columns; Jupiter's thunderbolt is shown in the temple's pediment. The three doors are the entrances to the three cellas (chambers), each devoted to one to the Capitoline triad: Jupiter, Juno, and Minerva.

4

The Punic Wars: Rome against Carthage

Rome fought three great wars against the Phoenician city of Carthage in Africa: the First Punic War (264–241 BC), the Second (218–201 BC), and the Third (149–146 BC) which ended with the total destruction of Carthage and the enslavement of its inhabitants in 146 BC, the same year as the Roman destruction of Corinth. The Carthaginians were Phoenicians, Poeni, hence the term 'Punic' Wars.

The outbreak of the First Punic War in 264 BC marks the beginning of the Middle Republic. This is because the First Punic War was a watershed in Roman history, and dramatically altered Rome. Before the war, Rome dominated Italy, but had no overseas possessions: the intervention in Sicily was in fact the first time that the Romans had sent an army overseas. By the end of the Punic Wars, a century later, Rome had possessions in the Mediterranean and was embarked on a round of conquests that continued unabated to the end of the Republic. The First Punic War began the process of territorial expansion; by 146 Rome's chief rival was destroyed, and the Romans had possession of Sicily, Sardinia, Corsica, Carthaginian Africa, parts of Spain, and, through activities in the eastern Mediterranean, Illyria, Macedonia and Epirus, with *de facto* control of Greece. Rome was transformed from the dominant city in Italy to the main Mediterranean power, while in the first century BC it would go on to conquer the Greek east.

Carthage was a colony of Tyre, founded about 814 BC, in modern Tunisia, near the city of Tunis. Phoenician ships had been cruising the Mediterranean since about 1000 BC, trading wherever they could. Legend has it that the Libyans offered Elissa, or Dido, the amount of land which an ox-hide could cover: she cut it into very thin strips to encompass more land than the Libyans had bargained for. Carthage was ideally positioned: an eastern peninsula of hills protected its two harbours. Being strategically situated, it prospered, and it in turn sent out its own colonies; by 246 BC Carthage controlled the north African coastline from Cyrene, a Greek colony, to the Atlantic, and western Sicily, Sardinia and Corsica. In the sixth century, in Sicily, the Carthaginians and the Greek colonies in cities, which had been established since the eighth century, became rivals; Sardinia and Corsica (in neither of which the Greeks had an interest) became Carthaginian. Southern Spain was dominated by Carthage by around 500 BC, and after the First Punic War the Carthaginians extended and tightened their control there. The Carthaginian colonies were primarily established for trade, but often involved, as at Carthage, the political and economic domination of the neighbouring indigenous inhabitants. Tribute was levied from the peoples the Carthaginians dominated, and this was a marked difference between Carthage and Rome, though the Romans did levy troops from the Latin allies. The Carthaginian army was made up of their Libyan subjects and mercenaries, again in contrast to Rome; despite this, these troops were generally loyal and in Spain and in Italy proved a match for the Romans. At the beginning of the First Punic War, the Carthaginians had both ships and elephants; the Romans had neither but soon had a navy that eclipsed that of the Carthaginians who were primarily a maritime power, unlike the Romans who had previously had no experience on the sea.

The three Punic Wars were not a struggle between different cultures and societies. If Rome had not won, Carthage would probably have dominated the Mediterranean. Its imperial system was no better or worse than the Roman; its culture was in significant respects materially richer and it had its own literature, which has not survived. Rome won and the Mediterranean's history went one way rather than the other. If Hannibal had won, whether that history under Carthage would have been any worse, or less successful — or even less blood-thirsty — will never be known.

Ancient sources: it can be no coincidence that it was in the period of the Punic Wars that the Romans began to write their history: there was clearly a sense that Rome's achievements were worth recording. The basic sources for the Punic Wars are Polybius and Livy, who drew on him. Other sources used by Polybius such as Philinus and Fabius Pictor (see docs 4.4–5, 21) have not survived.

For the First Punic War, the basic narrative is Polybius Book 1. There are also the fragments of Diodorus 22–4, and Dio 9–11, also fragmentary. Livy's account survives only in the *Periochae* 12–19. Philinus of Acragas (Latin: Agrigentum; modern Agrigento) in Sicily wrote a history, which does not survive, of the First Punic War in Greek, and appears to have been a contemporary witness of it. He favoured the Carthaginians, understandably given the Roman treatment of his own city. Polybius clearly had access to his account (see doc. 4.4). Naevius' Latin epic *The Song of the Punic War* (*Carmen belli Poenici*; doc. 4.18) on the First Punic War is mainly lost; he served at the close of the war.

The main surviving accounts of the Second Punic War are those of Polybius Books 3–4, 7–15 and Livy 21–30 (Books 11–20 are lost): note Ridley 2000. Diodorus 25.15–27.18 and Appian *Wars in Spain* (*Iberike*) 1–37, *Hannibalic War*, and *Punic Wars* (*Libyka*) 1–66 are also relevant. Various other histories no longer survive: the Romans Fabius Pictor and L. Cincius Alimentus both wrote in Greek, and were contemporaries of the second Punic War; Polybius drew on Fabius but tended to be critical of his work (see doc. 4.21). Cato in his lost *Origines* dealt with the Second Punic War (incidentally the first history of Rome to be written in Latin), concerning which one sentence survives (Astin 1978: 211–39). Quintus Ennius (239–169 BC) in his poetic *Annals* covered the foundation of Rome down to his own day; Parts 7–9 of the *Annals* dealt with the Second Punic War. He stressed the role of the gods in Rome's constant expansion. Cornelius Nepos (c. 110–24 BC) also wrote biographies (which survive) of Hannibal and Hamilcar, and Plutarch of Fabius Maximus and Marcellus.

Two Greek authors, Sosylus of Sparta and Silenus of Caleacte, both accompanied Hannibal on campaign (Nepos *Hannibal* 13.3), and presumably had a pro-Carthaginian viewpoint. They were stigmatised by Polybius as not historical, but as retailing the gossip of the barber's shop (3.20.5; *FGrH* 176 & 177). It is a great loss, as with Philinus' history of the First Punic War, not to have these perspectives. For other references in the ancient sources to these lost accounts, see Walbank I.64–5, 333; Rich 1996: 3–14; Lancell 1998: 25–8; Daly 2002: 17–25.

For the Third Punic War, Polybius was an eyewitness to the destruction of Carthage, but unfortunately his narrative of this event is largely lost (36.1–8, 16; 38.19–22). In addition nothing of major substance survives from Diodorus and Dio, and Livy's account survives only in the *Periochae* (47–51). Appian *Punic Wars* (*Libyka*) 74–135 is therefore a crucial account (doc. 4.62), especially as he probably used Polybius' lost eye-witness account. Cato the Elder's role is narrated by Plutarch *Cato the Elder (Cato Mai.)* 26–7 (doc. 4.61).

On the whole, then, the sources are written from the Roman point of view: the Punic side of events is lost. While Polybius could be critical of individual Romans, his perspective is nonetheless a Roman one. But his account is credible and reliable, and certainly lacks the enthusiastic pro-Roman stance of Livy. For Polybius as a source for the wars: Walbank I.27–9; Lazenby 1996: 2–6; Goldsworthy 2000: 19–23.

This chapter is not a narrative history (which is detailed and complex) of the Punic Wars nor a discussion of internal politics at Rome in this period. Students need to read a basic outline, such as that of Scullard 1980: 157–239. Of the three wars, most scholarly attention is directed to the Second Punic War, but Lazenby 1996 deals with the first. See Starr 1953: 35–9; Dorey & Dudley 1971; Errington 1972: 12–29, 49–130; Caven 1980; Scullard 1989, 1989a; Briscoe 1989; Harris 1989: 142–62; Bagnall 1990, 2002; Goldsworthy 2000; Lazenby 2004; politics at Rome in the Second Punic War: Scullard 1973: 39–88.

For Rome and Carthage at the time of the First and Second Punic Wars, in military and political terms, including Carthaginian culture, see: Picard 1964: 96–118; Picard & Picard 1968: 108–15, 171–81; Scullard 1980: 157–64 (note the unnecessarily hostile tone at 163), 1989: 486–517; Picard & Picard 1987: 15–35; Bagnall 1990: 3–34; Lancell 1995, esp. 1–34; Lazenby 1996: 11–30; Goldsworthy 2000: 25–62. For the city of Carthage, note Warmington 1969 (esp. 128–53); Picard 1964; Picard & Picard 1961, 1968, 1987; Khader & Soren 1987; Raven 1993: 17–32; Lancell 1995; Hoyos 2003: 21–33; Roman and Carthaginian relations to 264 BC: Palmer 1997: 15–30.

ROME'S TREATIES WITH CARTHAGE: 508, 348, 279 BC

Polybius gives the details of three treaties between Rome and Carthage: one from the year of the first consuls (509/8), and from 348 and 279 BC. These treaties safeguarded Carthaginian interests and in them Rome appears to be the junior partner. In signing these treaties Rome indicated that its interests were land-bound in the Italian peninsula, and that there was an absence of a Mediterranean focus or any conception of sea-power at Rome. In these treaties it is clear that trading interests were crucial to the Carthaginians.

4.1 The treaty of 508 BC

Polybius *Histories* 3.22.1–23.6

This treaty of 'friendship between the Romans and the Romans' allies and between the Carthaginians and the Carthaginians' allies' is not mentioned by Livy who sees the second treaty mentioned by Polybius (doc. 4.2) as the first treaty (Livy 7.27.2; cf. Diod. 16.69.1). The authenticity of this first treaty is guaranteed by Polybius' reference to the text being in an 'ancient' form of Latin and difficult to understand. The kings were expelled in 509/8, which dates the treaty. The newly inaugurated republic may well have been renewing a treaty which had existed between the kings and Carthage, or the fledgling state may have felt it needed friends. Certainly at this stage Carthage was the more powerful. The differences in the interests of the two states are clear: Carthage regulates Roman trading within the Carthaginian sphere of interest, and in turn Rome receives a guarantee that Carthage will not interfere with Latin towns. See Walbank I.339–45; Scullard 1989: 517–26; Bagnall 1990: 39–40; Lancell 1995: 86–8; Lazenby 1996: 31; Goldsworthy 2000: 69.

22.1 The first treaty between Rome and Carthage dates to the consulship of Lucius Junius Brutus and Marcus Horatius, the first consuls instituted after the expulsion of the kings, and by whom the temple of Jupiter Capitolinus was founded. **2** This was 28 years before Xerxes' crossing to Greece. **3** I have recorded below as accurate an interpretation as I can. For the difference between the ancient language and that of the Romans today is such that only some of it can be made out by the most intelligent men through careful examination. **4** The treaty is basically as follows: 'On these terms there is to be friendship between the Romans and the Romans' allies and between the Carthaginians and the Carthaginians' allies: **5** the Romans and the Romans' allies are not to sail with long ships beyond the Fair Promontory, **6** unless forced by storm or by enemies; if anyone should be forcibly carried beyond it, he is not permitted either to buy or to take anything except for the repair of the ship or for sacrifice, **7** and shall leave within five days. **8** Those coming for trade shall do no business except in the presence of a herald or official secretary. **9** The price of whatever is sold in their presence shall be owed to the seller by the guarantee of the state, if sold in Libya or Sardinia. **10** If any Roman comes to the part of Sicily, which is under Carthaginian control, he shall enjoy equal rights. **11** The Carthaginians shall do no wrong to the peoples of Ardea, Antium, Laurentium, Circeii, Terracina or any other of the Latins who are (Roman) subjects; **12** as to those who are not subjects, they shall keep their hands off their cities; if they take one, they shall hand it over undamaged to the Romans. **13** They shall not build a fort in Latium. If they enter the country as enemies, they shall not spend the night in the country.'

23.1 The Fair Promontory is the one which lies in front of Carthage to the north; . . . **5** From the phrasing of the treaty they show that they consider Sardinia and Libya as their own; concerning Sicily they distinctly express themselves otherwise, mentioning in the treaty only the parts of Sicily which are under Carthaginian rule. **6** Similarly the Romans only include Latium in the treaty and do not mention the rest of Italy, because it was not under their authority.

4.2 The treaty of 348 BC

Polybius *Histories* 3.24.1–15

This treaty of friendship is not dated by Polybius, but is probably the same as the one which Livy and Diodorus date to 348, and which they incorrectly regarded as the first treaty (see esp. Walbank I.346). As in the treaty of 508 the Carthaginian sphere of interest is clear. Sicily is still only partly in Carthaginian hands, while Carthaginian territory in Libya has increased. But largely it confirms the previous treaty. Mastia and Tarseum do not refer to Spain, as sometimes thought, but to places near Carthage itself; Rome — and its allies — was being excluded from the western Mediterranean. Rome's expansion in the Italian peninsula was not checked, but Carthage was certainly guarding its existing interests. See Walbank I.345–9; Scullard 1989: 526–30; Bagnall 1990: 40; Lazenby 1996: 31–2; Goldsworthy 2000: 69.

1 Later on they made another treaty, in which the Carthaginians include the Tyrians and the people of Utica. **2** It also includes Mastia and Tarseum, in addition to the Fair Promontory, as places beyond which the Romans may not either plunder or found a city. **3** The treaty is basically as follows: 'There is to be friendship on the following terms between the Romans and the Romans' allies, and the Carthaginians, Tyrians and Uticans and their allies. **4** The Romans shall neither plunder or trade nor found a city beyond the Fair Promontory, Mastia and Tarseum. **5** If the Carthaginians capture any city in Latium which is not subject to the Romans, they may keep the property and captives, but shall give up the city. **6** If any Carthaginian captures anyone who is a member of a city with a written treaty of peace with Rome, but which is not subject to them, he may not bring him into Roman harbours; if one should be brought in and a Roman take hold of him (i.e., makes him his slave), he shall be set free. **7** Likewise, the Romans shall not do this. **8** If a Roman takes water or provisions from any country which the Carthaginians control, he shall not use these provisions to wrong anyone whose people has a treaty of peace or friendship with the Carthaginians. **9** Likewise, the Carthaginians shall not do this. **10** If they do so, the person shall not punish them privately; if anyone does this his wrongdoing shall be public. **11** No Roman shall trade or found a city in Sardinia or Libya . . . (nor remain there) except to take on provisions or repair his ship. If a storm take him there, he shall leave within five days. **12** In the part of Sicily controlled by the Carthaginians and at Carthage he may do and sell anything which is permitted to a citizen. **13** A Carthaginian in Rome may do likewise.' **14** Again in the treaty they lay stress on Libya and Sardinia as their own possessions and close all means of approach to the Romans, **15** but concerning Sicily they clearly state the opposite, mentioning the part subject to them.

4.3 The treaty of 279 BC

Polybius *Histories* 3.25.1–5

Polybius does not date this treaty, but it is clearly the one referred to by Livy (*Per.* 13; Diod. 22.7.5) as being in 279/8 BC, as the reference to Pyrrhus also indicates. Each side was to support the other against Pyrrhus of Epirus, in western Greece. The Carthaginians did not want Rome making peace with Pyrrhus, who was a principal enemy of Carthage in Sicily, for he would then be free to assist the Greek cities in Sicily against Carthage (see doc. 1.73). Roman negotiations with Pyrrhus had commenced after the Roman defeat at Ausculum in 279 BC. The Carthaginians are therefore generous in this treaty, which is no longer concerned only with excluding the Romans from the Carthaginian sphere of interest, but in the new clauses given by Polybius offers the use of the Carthaginian navy. Roman seapower was clearly negligible. There were later treaties in 241 and 238 BC: Polyb. 3.27–8 (doc. 4.17). See Walbank I.349–55; Scullard 1980: 164, 1989: 530–7; Bagnall 1990: 40–1; Lazenby 1996: 32–4; Goldsworthy 2000: 69–70.

1 The Romans made another final treaty at the time of the invasion of Pyrrhus, before the Carthaginians had started the war for Sicily; **2** in this they maintain everything in the existing agreements, and add the following: **3** 'If they make an alliance with Pyrrhus, both shall make it a written condition that there shall be provision that they shall go to the assistance of each other in the country which is under attack; **4** whichever has the need for help, the Carthaginians shall provide the ships for transport and attack, but each shall provide the pay for their own men. **5** The Carthaginians shall aid the Romans by sea, if necessary. But no one shall force the crews to land against their will.'

4.4 Historical methodology at its worst

Polybius *Histories* 3.26.1–7

Polybius rejects Philinus' treaty of 306 BC (3.26.3), which could well have been a fabrication to put the Romans in the wrong, on the basis of hard evidence: he has seen the treaties between Rome and Carthage on bronze tablets, and Philinus' treaty is not one of them. The location of the quaestors' treasury is unknown, but the tablets presumably hung on a wall there. Philinus' treaty: Walbank I.353–5; Hoyos 1985; Lazenby 1996: 32–3; Goldsworthy 2000: 69–70; Philinus as a source: see Lazenby 1996: 2–3; Walbank I.27.

1 Since the treaties were such, and preserved as they are even today on bronze tablets near the temple of Jupiter Capitolinus in the quaestors' treasury, **2** who cannot reasonably be amazed at Philinus the historian, not because he is ignorant of them — for that is not remarkable, since even in my day the oldest of the Romans and Carthaginians, and even those who particularly seemed to be conversant with public affairs, were ignorant of them — **3** but how and on what grounds did he think to write the exact opposite, that there was a treaty between Rome and Carthage through which the Romans had to keep away from the whole of Sicily and the Carthaginians from the whole of Italy, **4** and that the Romans broke the treaty and their oath when they made their first crossing to Sicily? There is not and never has been such a document at all. **5** But he states this in his second book quite explicitly . . . **6** Of course, if anyone wants to criticise the Romans for their crossing to Sicily, because they accepted the Mamertines into their friendship and afterwards helped them in their need when they had broken their treaty not only with Messana, but also with Rhegium, his disapproval would be only reasonable. **7** But if anyone considers that they made their crossing in violation of the treaty and their oath he is clearly ignorant of the truth.

THE FIRST PUNIC WAR: SICILY

In doc. 4.4, Polybius indicates that the Roman crossing into Sicily to help the Mamertines (doc. 4.7) caused the First Punic War (264–241 BC). This was the first Roman military expedition outside Italy and it was to have enormous implications for Roman history. The treaties between Rome and Carthage proved inadequate to deal with the situation. The Romans had no real pretext for interfering in Sicily, except perhaps for fears that Carthage might then use an extended control of Sicily to acquire a position in Italy. Once the Romans invaded, they quickly made up their mind to conquer the whole island and in 23 years succeeded in securing control of it.

The main source for the First Punic War is the Greek historian Polybius, Book 1.13–64, and 65–88 for the mercenary war that broke out in Carthage immediately afterwards. The relevant books of Livy are lost. For the First Punic War, see Walbank I.63–150; Frank 1928; Picard & Picard 1968: 182–201; Warmington 1969: 154–85; Dorey & Dudley 1971: 1–28; Errington 1972: 12–29; Caven 1980: 1–66; Scullard 1980: 157–78, 1989: 537–69; Caven 1980: 5–66; Bagnall 1990: 49–107; Bernstein 1994: 68–74; Lazenby 1996; Roth 1999: 158–9; Goldsworthy 2000: 65–140.

4.5 Polybius' reasons for focusing on the First Punic War

Polybius *Histories* 1.14.1–6

Polybius here sets out his historical methodology, imputing bias to the Greek historian Philinus and the Latin Fabius Pictor as being pro-Carthaginian and pro-Roman respectively. Elsewhere he makes clear his attraction to the Punic Wars as a theme for historical writing: he can speak to and question those who participated in the events, and he himself lived through some of them (4.2.2, 12.4c.2–5, 12.25e). Polybius is critical of both Philinus and Pictor; while he drew on other sources these were the most important (other sources: Walbank I.27–35). Fabius Pictor was the first Roman historian and wrote in Greek, recording a history of Rome from its beginnings down to his own time; he went on an embassy to Delphi in 216 BC; for Pictor, see Lazenby 1996: 3; Walbank I.64–5; Mellor 1999: 15–18; historical sources for the First Punic War: Lazenby 1996: 1–9.

1 I have been persuaded to concentrate on this war by a factor equally important to those already mentioned, namely that the historians considered to be the greatest authorities on it, Philinus and Fabius (Pictor), have failed in my view to record the truth as they should have done. **2** I do not want to imply that these men have intentionally lied, judging from their lives and principles; but they do seem to me to have been something in the position of people in love. **3** For, through his convictions and partisan stance, Philinus considers that the Carthaginians acted wisely, well and courageously in every case, and the Romans in the opposite way, while Fabius takes a completely different view. **4** In other spheres of life one should perhaps not rule out such favouritism, for a good man ought to love his friends and his country and share his friends' hatred of their enemies and their love of their friends; **5** but, when a person takes on the role of a historian, he has to forget everything of this sort, and often speak well of his enemies and award them the highest praises when their actions demand this, while criticising and severely censuring his closest friends, should their errors of conduct demand this. **6** For, just as a living creature deprived of its eyes is totally incapacitated, so, when history is deprived of truth, nothing is left but an unprofitable tale.

4.6 The differences between Rome and Carthage

Polybius *Histories* 6.51.1–8. 52.1–6, 56.1–4

This passage is from Polybius' discussion of the Roman constitution in Book 6 (6.11–18, 6.43–58), with an important section on Rome's army (6.19–42; see docs 1.58, 5.12–16); at 6.51–6 Rome and Carthage are compared.

51.1–8: Polybius sees the oligarchic senate as the mainstay of Roman dominance, but the increasing influence of the people at Carthage as a weakness (6.51–8). The 'kings' of Carthage Polybius refers to were two annual officials known as *suffetes*. The Carthaginian senate (*gerontion*) consisted of 300, with a sub-council within it of thirty which included the two suffetes. There were also 104 judges (see Aristotle *Politics* 1272–3). Polybius writes below (6.56.2): 'nothing is disgraceful [there] which leads to profit'. Carthage had a mixed constitution (as at Rome and Sparta, Polybius notes), but the 'popular element' was becoming more important, referring to the rise of the Barca family and its popular support (Walbank I.736). Arist. *Pol.* 1273a35–9 notes that at Carthage the highest offices, such as king and general, are for sale, resulting in wealth being of more account than merit, and causing the whole state to be focussed on making money. Despite Polybius, the constitution itself was not probably as instrumental to Carthaginian defeat as he imagines: what happened on the battlefield and the nature of the two groups' military systems is more relevant. 'Although they were totally defeated' (51.8) refers to Cannae in 216 BC. Carthage's constitution is discussed by: Picard & Picard 1968: 125–71, 222–29; Warmington 1969: 138–44; Scullard 1980: 161–2; Bagnall 1990: 12–14; Hoyos 1994; Lancell 1995: 110–20; Lazenby 1996: 21, 23; Goldsworthy 2000: 30; Polybius on Carthage's mixed constitution: Alonso-Núñez 1999: 14–15.

52.1–6: Carthage was a sea-power, Rome a land-power; for Rome's naval build-up in the First Punic War, see discussion at docs 4.8–10. At 1.37.6–10 Polybius criticises the Romans' reliance on force on all occasions, which leads to victories by land, but disasters in sea battles. The Roman army had at its core for the Punic wars one basic unit: the legion. The Roman navy was quite undeveloped. For the Roman army, see docs 5.11–21.

Carthage had only a small citizen body, and the citizens served mainly in the navy, fighting as infantry only when necessary, as at Zama (doc. 4.53). Infantry came from 'foreign and mercenary troops', which Polybius 6.52.4 contrasts here with the Romans' use of natives and citizens. They fought in their groups with their native armour; they were probably organised along the lines of the Greek phalanx when they went into battle. Cavalry was recruited from the Libyans. Mercenaries were paid for, other troops were meeting their treaty obligations. Despite this, the Carthaginian army was formidable as indicated by Trasimene (217 BC) and Cannae (216 BC), and their activities in Spain. Against Polybius, it must be said that the Carthaginian employment of mercenaries and foreign troops did not play a significant part in Carthage's defeats and they fought well (Bagnall 1990: 10–11; Lazenby 1996: 29–30). Livy is incorrect at 30.35.6 in calling them 'men mingled from the dregs of all races, who were held not by loyalty but by pay'.

For Carthage's military system at this time: Picard & Picard 1961: 192–204; Bagnall 1990: 8–12; Lancell 1995: 114–19; Lazenby 1996: 26–7; Goldsworthy 2000: 30–6; the Roman army during the Punic Wars: Bagnall 1990: 22–6; Lazenby 1996: 12–14; Goldsworthy 2000: 44–54, cf. 54–62, 2000a: 55–75; note Adcock 1940; Watson 1969; Sabin 2000; Polybius on the Roman army: Walbank I.697–723; Fuller 1954: 116–17; Lazenby 1996: 14; Gilliver 1999: 16, 18, 26–7, 38–40, 63, 68–9, 115–16.

56.1–4: Polybius' comments about bribe-taking at Rome should be compared to those of Sallust: docs 9.3, 9.7.

51.1 The Carthaginian constitution appears to me to have been originally well designed in its general features. **2** For there were kings, and the *gerontion* (senate) had aristocratic powers, while the people were supreme in their own sphere; the arrangement of the whole system was similar to that of the Romans and Spartans. **3** But at this time, when the Hannibalic war commenced, that of the Carthaginians was worse and that of the Romans better . . . **5** For, just as Carthage had previously been stronger and more prosperous than Rome, by the same degree Carthage had now begun to decline and Rome was at its peak in its system of government. **6** As a result the people in Carthage had already taken over most of the power of decision-making, while at Rome the senate still possessed this. **7** It was for this reason, with the people making decisions on one side, and the most distinguished men on the other, that the Romans' deliberations on public affairs were superior. **8** And although they were totally defeated, they were finally victorious over the Carthaginians in the war through their wise decision-making.

52.1 To pass to the details, such as the conduct of war to start with, the Carthaginians are superior at sea, as is natural, both in training and equipment because from olden times this practice has been their national pastime and they have had much more to do with the sea than any other people, **2** while the Romans are much better exponents of warfare on land than the Carthaginians. **3** For the Romans devote themselves to this entirely, while the Carthaginians completely neglect their infantry, though they do pay some small attention to their cavalry. **4** The reason for this is that they employ foreign and mercenary troops, while the Romans use natives and citizens. **5** So in this respect, too, it must be admitted that Rome's constitution is better than that of Carthage; for Carthage has always to place her hopes of freedom on the valour of mercenaries, but the Romans on their own courage and the support of their allies. **6** As a result, if the Romans are defeated at the outset, they always retrieve their defeat, but the Carthaginians the opposite . . .

56.1 The customs and laws regarding money-making are also better at Rome than at Carthage, **2** for at Carthage nothing is disgraceful which leads to profit, while at Rome nothing is more disgraceful than accepting bribes and making dishonest gains; **3** the Romans' approval of money-making in an honest way is no stronger than their disapproval of profit by forbidden means. **4** Proof of this is that at Carthage they win magistracies by open bribery, but at Rome the penalty for this is death.

4.7 The Romans help the Mamertines

Polybius *Histories* 1.10.1–11.5

Carthage had controlled parts of Sicily for centuries, contesting control with the Greek cities there; its chief rival was the great city of Syracuse, the third largest Greek city after Athens and Corinth. Agathocles, tyrant of Syracuse, had from 310 to 289 BC fought with the Carthaginians for control of Sicily and had expanded his kingdom. He had employed mercenaries from Campania in Italy; after his death they lacked employment, and when hospitably received into the Sicilian city of Messana slaughtered the male citizens, and took their wives and property as their own. They called themselves the Mamertines (Latin: Mamertini) after the Italian god of war, Mamers (Roman Mars).

Messana is a key city in Sicily, near its northern tip and opposite the city of Rhegium on the toe of Italy; the Straits of Messana divide Italy from Sicily. Rhegium was allied to Rome and had asked for a garrison against Pyrrhus. It was sent a body of 4,000 Campanians. Seeing the example of their fellow Campanians in Messana, they took over Rhegium, and supported the Mamertines across the straits of Messana; in 271 BC the Romans sent an army and captured the city (300 of the survivors were beheaded at Rome). A new tyrant at Syracuse, Hiero, defeated the Mamertines some time before 265. The Mamertines sent to both Carthage and Rome for help and the Carthaginians sent a small garrison. The Romans had no previous problems with the Carthaginian presence in Sicily, as the treaties at docs 4.1–3 indicate. But now Carthage looked as if it could control all of Sicily. Moreover, Roman control of Italy now extended to its very south, to Rhegium, and, if Messana and then Syracuse fell, Rome and Carthage would have a common border. Polybius presents the reason for Roman involvement as fear of Carthaginian expansion into Italy if Messana became Carthaginian. He has been criticised for exaggerating the danger from Carthage and the importance of Messana. But whether Carthage would have gained control of all Sicily and whether this would have threatened Roman Italy are not in themselves important: rather, it is that Rome felt threatened and viewed Carthage as expansionist.

By 'the people' Polybius must mean the comitia centuriata, as the consuls make the proposal, and it relates to war. Here the wealthiest voted first, and, if they came to an agreement, the other voters in the comitia centuriata were not called upon (cf. doc. 1.19). Polybius (11.2) writes of the 'gains' that would accrue to the Romans; by this he means the booty and plunder, including (as it turned out) profits from the sale of the 25,000 inhabitants of Agrigentum as slaves, and the ransoming or enslavement of the 27,000 people of Panormus (see doc. 6.9). The wealthier citizens who voted for war in the comitia centuriata (to help the Mamertines, not as a vote of war against Carthage) clearly hoped to gain from the enterprise.

At 11.2, Polybius uses the Greek word for generals, but must mean consuls, whom he has urging the people to war. One of these, Appius Claudius Caudex (cos. 264), was given the command in Sicily. (The other consul, M. Fulvius Flaccus may already have left for his campaign against the Volsinii in Etruria; *MRR* I.202–3.) Claudius' own personal motives presumably included *gloria*; he would be the first Roman to lead an expedition overseas. For the Mamertines and the origins of the conflict, Livy 30.31.4, *Per.* 16; Diod. 22.1.1–3, 13.1.1–23.1.3; Walbank I.57–62; Caven 1980: 5–21; Scullard 1980: 164–7, 1989: 537–45; Hoyos 1989; Bagnall 1990: 42–5; Lazenby 1996: 36–42; Goldsworthy 2000: 65–75.

10.1 The Mamertines, who had previously lost their support from Rhegium, as I stated above, had now suffered a total defeat on their home territory for the reasons I have just mentioned, and some of them had recourse to the Carthaginians, offering to put themselves and the citadel under their protection, **2** while others sent an embassy to Rome, offering to hand over the city and begging them as a people of the same race to give them assistance. **3** The Romans for a long time were undecided because of the obvious illogicality of giving them assistance. **4** Only a short while earlier, the Mamertines' fellow-citizens had suffered the ultimate penalty for breaking their treaty with the people of Rhegium, and now to try to help the Mamertines, who had done exactly the same not only at Messana, but at Rhegium as well, was an injustice which it was hard to excuse. **5** The Romans were not unaware of this, but they saw that the Carthaginians had subjugated not only Libya, but also large parts of Spain, and that they possessed all the islands in the Sardinian and Tyrrhenian Seas, **6** and were worried that, if they also gained control of Sicily, they might be very difficult and formidable neighbours, encircling them on every side and threatening every part of Italy. **7** It seemed evident that they would soon be in control of Sicily unless the Mamertines received assistance. For, once Messana was in their hands, **8** they would shortly conquer Syracuse, as they were masters of nearly all the rest of Sicily. **9** As the Romans foresaw this and considered it necessary not to abandon Messana and allow the Carthaginians, as it were, to build a bridge for crossing to Italy, they debated the question for a considerable time, **11.1** and the senate even in the end did not authorise the proposal for the reasons just stated. They considered that the illogicality of helping the Mamertines was equally balanced by the advantages of assisting them. **2** The people, however, were worn out by recent wars and in need of all kinds of restorative, and, when the generals pointed out that the war would be for the general good for the reasons just stated and the obvious and enormous gains which each of them would privately incur, resolved to send assistance. **3** When the measure had been authorised by the people, they appointed one of the consuls, Appius Claudius, as commander and ordered him to cross with assistance to Messana. **4** The Mamertines threw out the Carthaginian general who already held the citadel, partly by threats and partly by deception; they welcomed Appius, and placed the city in his hands. **5** The Carthaginians crucified their general, thinking that he lacked both judgement and courage in abandoning the citadel.

4.8 The Romans build a fleet, 264 BC

Polybius *Histories* 1.20.9–21.3

A major problem for the Romans in their invasion of Sicily was the lack of a fleet to transport soldiers to Sicily and keep them supplied. Appius Claudius sent a small initial force under C. Claudius to Messana, and then moved his two consular legions using ships from Rhegium and other cities. The office of *duovir navalis* (one of two officials in charge of the navy) had lapsed in Rome, which was unprepared for naval warfare.

Hiero, tyrant of Syracuse, agreed to aid the Carthaginians against the Romans. Appius Claudius negotiated unsuccessfully with both Hiero and the Carthaginian commander Hanno; he then met them both in battle and defeated them (Polyb. 1.11.7–12.4, 15). Hiero came over to the Roman side and remained a loyal ally; most of the cities revolted from Syracuse and Carthage and joined Rome (Polyb. 1.16). But the war against Hanno and the Carthaginians was to go on until 241 BC. Though the Mamertines had been 'saved' (Polyb. 1.20.1) and the Carthaginians decisively defeated at Agrigentum in 261, Roman aims now expanded to the expulsion of the Carthaginians from Sicily. In 261 BC, failing to capture several coastal towns, the Romans decided to build a fleet.

The trireme was the Greek warship *par excellence*, consisting of three levels of rowers, while quinqueremes were differently organised, with five men rowing at each oar. Penteconters were 50-oared ships, with 25 rowers on either side; penteconters had been in use by the Greeks since at least the seventh century. **1.21.3**: 'practising for a short time': 60 days according to Pliny *Nat. Hist.* 16.192. At 6.19.3 (doc. 5.12) Polybius records that citizens with less than 400 asses of property (the proletarii) were employed in naval service (as the rowers); the marines may also have been proletarii, but men from the legions could be used (Polyb. 1.49.5, 1.61.3; Lazenby 1996: 66; Goldsworthy 2000: 105). Some consider the account of the copying of the captured ship as legendary colouring, and that there would have been quinqueremes available for copying amongst the Greek states of southern Italy. Polybius, however, mentions the penteconters and triremes borrowed from the Greeks (1.20.14), and the Romans would have had to have built their quinqueremes on the basis of a Carthaginian model.

See Walbank I.73–6; Tarn 1907; Adcock 1940: 33–5; Thiel 1954: 66–100; Scullard 1980: 169; Caven 1980: 27–8; Bagnall 1990: 60; Lazenby 1996: 62–6; Goldsworthy 2000: 96–103; for Carthaginian warships, see esp. Lancell 1995: 125–33.

20.9 Observing how the war was dragging on, the Romans then for the first time undertook the building of ships, 100 quinqueremes and 20 triremes. **10** As the shipwrights were entirely inexperienced in building quinqueremes, since none of the communities of Italy used such ships at that time, the enterprise caused them much difficulty. **11** From this, anyone might see the spirited and reckless nature of the Romans' determination. **12** For it was not that they had reasonable resources for it, but no resources at all, nor had they ever given any thought to the sea, but once they first had the idea they undertook it so boldly that, before they had any experience at all of the matter, they at once undertook a naval battle against the Carthaginians who had held undisputed command of the sea from their ancestors' time. **13** Evidence for the truth of what I am saying and for their unbelievable daring is this: that when they first undertook to send their forces across to Messana, not only did they not have a single decked ship, but no warship at all, not even a single boat, **14** but they borrowed penteconters and triremes from the Tarentines and Locrians, and also from the Eleans and Neapolitans, and transported their troops across in them at considerable risk. **15** On this occasion the Carthaginians put to sea to attack them as they were crossing the straits, and one of the decked ships (quinqueremes) advanced too far in its eagerness and as a result ran aground, falling into the Romans' hands. They then used this as a model, constructing their whole fleet along these lines, **16** so that, if this had not happened, it is clear that they would in the end have been prevented from carrying out their plan from lack of experience. **21.1** Thereupon, those who were charged with constructing the fleet were busy with preparation of the ships, while those who collected the crews were teaching them to row on land in the following way. **2** Seating the men on their benches on dry land, in the same order as on their seats on the ships themselves, and stationing the boatswain in the middle, they got them all used to falling back together bringing their hands back, and again to bending forward pushing out their hands and to beginning and stopping these movements at the boatswain's orders. **3** When they had been trained, they launched the ships as soon as they were finished, and, after practising for a short time at sea, they sailed along the coast of Italy as their general had commanded.

4.9 The invention of the 'raven'

Polybius *Histories* 1.22.1–11

Gnaeus Cornelius Scipio Asina (cos. 260) went from Messana with 17 ships to Lipara, the main island in the Lipari group, off north-east Sicily; he had received an offer to betray the island. The Carthaginians arrived, and trapped Scipio's fleet in the harbour; he surrendered (Polyb. 1.21.8). Despite receiving the nickname 'Asina' ('donkey') he went on to another consulship in 254 BC. The main Roman fleet had been ordered by him to Messana. As the Battle of Mylae was to prove (doc. 4.10), the Carthaginians did not know at this stage how to deal with the raven (corvus, plural: corvi), which gave the Romans the advantage of boarding enemy ships without damaging their own. As Polybius makes clear (1.22.9), the corvi were not stationary but could pivot; this made them very effective in close encounters with enemy ships. The corvus enabled the Romans to overcome the advantage of experience which the Carthaginians had in naval warfare; it was used only in the First Punic War. For the raven ('corvus', a translation of Polybius' corax (plural: corakes); also translated as 'crows'), see Thiel 1946: 432–47, 1954: 101–28; Wallinga 1956; Scullard 1980: 170, 1989: 550 (line drawing at 551); Bagnall 1990: 61–2; Lazenby 1996: 28–9, 68–71, 92, 95 (line drawing at 69); Goldsworthy 2000: 106–8; Steinby 2000. The consuls of 260 (Gnaeus Asina and Duilius): *MRR* I.205.

1 After this the Romans approached the Sicilian coastline and, when they learnt of the disaster that had happened to Gnaeus, they immediately sent a message to Gaius Duilius (the other consul for 260 BC), the commander of the land force, and awaited his arrival, **2** while at the same time, hearing that the enemy's fleet was not far away, they began to prepare to fight at sea. **3** As their ships were poorly constructed and hard to manoeuvre, someone suggested to them the machines which later came to be called 'ravens' as an aid in battle. Their construction was as follows: **4** on the prow stood a round pole four fathoms in length and in width three palms in diameter. **5** This had a pulley at the top and round it was put a gangway with cross planks nailed to it, four feet in width and six fathoms in length. **6** In the gangway was an oblong hole, and it went round the pole at a distance of two fathoms from its near end. The gangway also had a railing on each of its long sides to the height of a knee. **7** At its end was fastened a piece of iron like a pestle with a point on it with a ring at the other end, so that the whole thing resembled machines for making bread. **8** To this ring was tied a rope with which, when they rammed other ships, they raised the ravens by using the pulley on the pole and let them down on the deck of the enemy ship, sometimes on the prow and sometimes bringing them round when the ships collided side on. **9** Once the ravens were fixed in the planks of the deck, connecting the ships together, if they were broadside on, they boarded from all directions, but, if on the prow, they attacked by passing over the raven itself two abreast; **10** the leaders covered the front by holding up their shields, and those who followed secured the two flanks by resting the rims of their shields on the top of the railing. **11** So, after adopting this device, they looked out for the opportunity to fight at sea.

4.10 Gaius Duilius, consul 260 BC

ILS 65

(*CIL* I² 25; *ILLRP* 319; *ROL* IV.128.) In 260, with the Roman ships equipped with the ravens, Duilius gave command of the army to the military tribunes and took control of the fleet (Polyb. 1.23.1; Scipio had been taken prisoner). With the enemy ravaging Mylae on the north coast of Sicily, Duilius sailed against them; the Carthaginians, commanded by Hannibal (not *the* Hannibal of the Second Punic War) sighted their fleet and 'contemptuous of the inexperience of the Romans' joined battle (1.23.3). The Romans boarded the Carthaginian ships, and it became 'like a land-battle' (1.23.7). The Carthaginians surrendered or were slaughtered, other ships fled the battle, and Hannibal escaped. The Romans became twice as determined to prosecute the war (1.24.1). They had won their first naval battle, but the bulk of the Carthaginian fleet was still intact. Duilius then lifted the siege at Segesta and captured Macela. For Mylae, Polyb. 1.23; Diod. 23.10.1; Walbank I.79; Scullard 1980: 170, 1989: 551–3; Caven 1980: 28–30; Bagnall 1990: 62–4; Lazenby 1996: 67–8, 70–3; Goldsworthy 2000: 107–9.

Duilius celebrated Rome's first naval triumph. To commemorate his victory, he erected a *columna rostrata* in the forum: a column decorated with the bronze rams of captured ships, with an inscription commemorating his deeds. The inscription is now in the Capitoline Museum. Letters are missing and the monetary sums would have been much greater than the figures below; the self-important tone of the inscription is evident; for the inscription: Walbank I.76, 79; Bagnall 1990: 67–8; Palmer 1997: 57–8; Goldsworthy 2000: 108–9.

[. . . and the Segest]aeans . . . he delivered [from siege]; [and all the Carthaginian] legions and [their mi]ghty le[a]der (Hamilcar) [after nine days] fled their camp [in broad d]aylight; and he took [their town] Mace[la **5** b]y storm. And, in the same com[mand] as consul, he h[ad a suc]cess with ships at sea, the first to do so, and he was the first to equip and t[rain] naval [crews and f]leets; and with these ships [he defeated in bat]tle on the high seas the Punic fleets and [likewise all the mig]htiest forces of the Carthaginians in the presenc[e of Hannibal] **10** their commander. And, by f[or]ce, [he captu]red shi[ps] with their crews: namely, one septir[eme, thirty quinquerem]es and triremes, and [sank thirteen]. Captured [go]ld: 3,600. . . . pieces. Captured [silv]er, together with booty: 100,000 . . . pieces. **15** [Total] sum taken in Roman money 2,100,000 . . . He was [al]so the fir[st to give] the people booty from a naval battle, [and the first] to l[ead free]-born Carthagi[ni]ans [in triumph] . . .

4.11 The Romans decide to invade Africa

Polybius *Histories* 1.26.1–3

The Romans proved unable to press home an advantage in Sicily (Polyb. 1.24–5; Diod. 23.11–12). They resolved to defeat the Carthaginians on their home territory, while the Carthaginians were determined to stop the Romans getting to Africa, and a great naval battle was fought at Ecnomus off eastern Sicily in 256. Roman victory, again using the ravens, meant that the invasion, the first of the Roman invasions of Carthaginian Africa, could go ahead that year. Ecnomus: Polyb. 1.26–8; Thiel 1954: 116–20; Walbank I.85–8; Caven 1980: 32–5; Bagnall 1990: 66–9; Lazenby 1996: 81–96; Goldsworthy 2000: 109–15.

1 The intention of the Romans was to sail to Libya and divert the war there, so that the Carthaginians might find not Sicily, but themselves and their country in danger. **2** The Carthaginians were resolving on doing exactly the opposite, for, knowing that Libya was easily accessible and that all the people in the country would be easily overcome by anyone who once invaded it, they were not able to allow this, **3** but were eager to run the risk of fighting a naval battle.

4.12 The Romans face an unusual problem in Africa

Livy *History of Rome* F10

(Val. Max. 1.8. ext.190) The incident of the giant serpent is a curious story which does not appear in Polybius. M. Atilius Regulus, suffect-consul, was sent to Africa in 256 (L. Manlius Vulso was the other consul). After initial success in laying waste to Carthaginian territory, Vulso was recalled to Rome, leaving Regulus with 40 ships, 15,000 infantry and 500 cavalry; he continued the campaign into 255. For Regulus, see Mix 1970.

Let me also mention the serpent described equally carefully and elegantly by Titus Livius. For he states that in Africa at the Bagradas river there was a snake of such size that it prevented the army of Atilius Regulus from using the river; many of the soldiers were seized in its huge mouth and large numbers of them crushed by the coils of its tail, nor could it be pierced by weapons hurled at it, but, finally, when it was attacked on all sides by missiles from catapults it collapsed under the frequent, heavy blows from the stones and seemed to everyone, both allied troops and legions, to be more frightful than Carthage itself. With the waters stained with its blood and the area around polluted with the noxious smell of its dead body, it drove the Roman camp away from there. He also says that the beast's skin, which measured 120 feet, was sent to Rome.

4.13 The Carthaginians employ a Spartan general, 256–255 BC

Appian *Roman History (The Punic Wars)* 1.3–4

Polybius (1.32–34, cf. 35) gives a longer and different account of this battle in 255, stressing the role of the elephants which trampled a large part of the Roman army: 'most of the Romans were trampled by the immense strength of the animals, while the rest were shot down in their ranks by the numerous cavalry' (1.34.7; Carthaginian use of elephants in the Punic Wars: Scullard 1974: 146–77). The Romans also appear to have been defeated by the superior generalship of the Spartan Xanthippus and his outflanking tactics. But Appian's references to 'heat, thirst and fatigue' are also credible. Polyb. 1.36.2 states that Xanthippus himself decided to return home, but hints (36.4) at another story, perhaps the one recorded by Appian here. Regulus was captured, and later in 250 was sent on an embassy to Rome, keeping his word that he would return to Carthage whatever the outcome; for the story of his horrible death in Carthaginian captivity, see Val. Max. 9.2. ext.1; cf. 1.1.14; Diod. 23.16; Gell. 7.4.1–3; while sources tend to expatiate on Carthaginian cruelty, this episode may have been invented or expanded to offset the tale of his widow and sons' torturing of two Carthaginian prisoners after his death: Diod. 24.12; Gell. 7.4.4.

The Romans had not expected defeat in Africa and, after manning a fleet in 255 BC, defeated the Carthaginian navy and captured 114 ships, rescuing the Romans still in Libya (1.36.5–12). Back in Sicily, a huge storm off Camarina left only 80 Roman ships out of 364 undamaged; the commanders had refused to listen to the advice of their captains about the course and time of year, when such storms were prevalent (1.37; the Romans lost another 150 ships to storm in 253: 1.39.6). For Regulus and the battle of 255: Thiel 1954: 206–41; Walbank I.91–4; Caven 1980: 37–9; Scullard 1989: 554–7; Bagnall 1990: 70–8; Lancell 1995: 367–70; Lazenby 1996: 97–110; Goldsworthy 2000: 84–92.

3 Events began with the Sicilian war when the Romans attacked Libya with 350 ships, took several towns, and left Atilius Regulus in command (256 BC), who captured another 200 towns, which handed themselves over to him through hatred of the Carthaginians, and advanced ravaging the countryside. The Carthaginians requested a general from the Spartans, thinking that their misfortunes were due to lack of a leader. They sent them Xanthippus, and Atilius, camped beside a lake in the season of burning heat, marched round it against the enemy, his soldiers suffering severely from the weight of their weapons, heat, thirst and fatigue, and under attack from missiles from the heights above them. As he approached towards evening a river separated them, and he immediately crossed the river in order to terrify Xanthippus, but Xanthippus drew up his forces and sent them from his camp hoping to overcome an enemy which was exhausted and in such distress and thinking that night would be on the side of the conquerors. Xanthippus was not disappointed in his hope; for, of the 30,000 men led by Atilius, only a few with difficulty escaped to the city of Aspis, while all the rest were killed or taken prisoner. Amongst the prisoners was the general Atilius, the consul.

4 Not long afterwards (250 BC), the Carthaginians, tired of fighting, sent Regulus together with their own ambassadors to Rome, to obtain peace for them or return without it; Atilius Regulus secretly urged the Roman magistrates to continue the war with all their strength, and returned to certain torture, for the Carthaginians killed him by shutting him up in a cage full of spikes. Xanthippus' success was the beginning of his misfortunes; the Carthaginians, in order that the credit for the victory might not seem due to the Spartans, pretended to honour him with numerous gifts and escorted him with galleys to Sparta, but instructed the captains to throw him overboard with his Spartan companions. In this way he paid the penalty for his success.

4.14 Beware of elephants

Polybius *Histories* 1.39.10–12

After the great success of the elephants in 255, the Carthaginians took them to Sicily: Hasdrubal, after the destruction of Roman fleet, crossed to Lilybaeum with 140 beasts (Polyb. 1.38.2). Operations in western, Carthaginian, Sicily continued; the Romans built a new fleet of about 200 ships. They successfully took Panormus, modern Palermo, the most important Carthaginian possession in Sicily, in 254 (1.38.7–10), and the Carthaginians were confined to a small part of western Sicily. A Roman expedition in 253 to Libya was spectacularly unsuccessful with the Romans simply raiding Carthaginian territory. Returning to Sicily, the fleet was largely wrecked by storm, and the Romans decided not to build a new fleet, and to rely instead on the army (1.39.1–7).

10 The Carthaginians now possessed the secure control of the sea as the Romans had withdrawn from it, and had great hopes of their land forces. **11** This was not unreasonable; for the Romans, when the report got round about the battle in Libya of how the beasts had broken their ranks and killed most of their men, **12** were so terrified of the elephants for the next two years following this period, that even though they were often drawn up in the district of Lilybaeum or that of Selinus five or six stades from their enemy, they were never bold enough to begin a battle and would never come down to level ground at all, through fear of the charge of the elephants.

4.15 The Carthaginians look for help elsewhere, 252 BC

Appian *Roman History (Of Sicily and the Other Islands)* F1

In 252 the Romans controlled most of Sicily, and had invaded Africa in 256 and 253.

The Romans and Carthaginians were both at a loss for money, and the Romans were no longer able to build ships, being exhausted by taxes, though they raised an infantry force and sent it to Libya and Sicily year after year, while the Carthaginians sent an embassy to Ptolemy, son of Lagus, king of Egypt, asking to borrow 2,000 talents. He was on friendly terms with both Romans and Carthaginians, and tried to reconcile them. Being unable to do so, he said that one should help friends against enemies, but not against friends.

THE LAST YEARS

By 252–251 BC both sides were exhausted. In 250 Hasdrubal, commander of the Carthaginian forces, attacked Panormus with his elephants, but many were wounded by projectiles thrown from the walls and Rome held the city (Polyb. 1.40). The Romans then besieged Lilybaeum, a Carthaginian stronghold well-planned to withstand a siege, which it did from 251–240 (holding out beyond the treaty of 241). According to Polybius both sides realised that if the Romans took Lilybaeum 'it would be easy to transfer the war to Libya' (1.41.4–5). Himilco was the Carthaginian general at Lilybaeum.

The Romans suffered their only naval defeat in the First Punic War, under the consul for 249 BC, P. Claudius Pulcher. He decided to attack the Carthaginian fleet at Drepana, setting out at night in an (unsuccessful) attempt to avoid detection. The Romans no longer used the corvus: the Carthaginians had learned how to reduce its effectiveness, and it affected the ship's handling

(Bagnall 1990: 86). The Carthaginian commander Adhurbal saw the fleet approaching and sailed out of the harbour without the Romans knowing. The Roman fleet began to sail into the harbour, but, realising the Carthaginian fleet wasn't there, the order was given to leave, resulting in great confusion amongst the ships. Evenly balanced at first, the Carthaginians gained the upper hand: Adhurbal had command of the open sea, better and faster ships and better crews. Thirty Roman ships, including Claudius' escaped; 93 were captured. Back at Rome, he was fined: 'Publius . . . was greatly attacked for having acted thoughtlessly and without a plan, and for having single-handedly placed Rome in great danger' (Polyb.1.52.2: several sources, but not Polybius, record that the sacred chickens had refused to eat before the battle, a bad omen, so Claudius had them thrown into the sea: see doc. 3.51).

The other consul, L. Junius Pullus, took charge of the fleet, which was then destroyed by a storm. The Romans abandoned naval warfare now for several years: they had lost several fleets, with hundreds of ships and thousands of sailors, to storms and now 93 ships and crews had been captured. They put their hopes in the siege at Lilybaeum and breaking the Carthaginians on land. The siege of Lilybaeum: Polyb. 1.41–8, 55–8; Claudius and the Battle of Drepana: 49–52; for both: Thiel 1954: 255–93; Walbank I.103–23; Scullard 1980: 174–7; Caven 1980: 45–62; Bagnall 1990: 79–99; Lazenby 1996: 123–41; Goldsworthy 2000: 118–21 (useful diagram of the battle at Drepana: 119).

4.16 The final gamble, 243/2 BC

Polybius *Histories* 1.58.9–59.8

Under their overall commander Hamilcar, the Carthaginians had from 249 BC kept the Romans at bay, effectively destroying their naval power at the battle of Drepana in 249 and maintaining control of both Drepana and of Lilybaeum despite the Roman sieges. In 243 BC the Romans decided to return to naval warfare and built another fleet.

58.9. The Romans and the Carthaginians were worn out with the hard work of coping with a succession of crises and at length began to despair, with their strength paralysed and drained by taxes and expenses continuing over many years. **59.1** Nevertheless, the Romans, as if fighting for their lives, although for nearly five years they had entirely withdrawn from naval operations because of the disasters they had suffered, and because of their belief that they could win the war through their land forces alone, **2** when they saw that their work was not progressing as they had calculated due especially to the audacity of the Carthaginian general (Hamilcar), decided for the third time to place their hopes on naval forces, **3** considering that this plan, if they could strike an opportune blow, was the only way of putting a successful end to the war. And this they finally achieved. **4** On the first occasion they had withdrawn from the sea yielding to the blows of fortune, on the second it was because of their defeat at the battle of Drepana; **5** now they made their third attempt (at Aegusa), through which they won a victory and shut off the Carthaginian legions at Eryx from their supply-line by sea, making a final end to the whole war. **6** It was rather a struggle for existence than an attack. There was no money in the treasury for the purpose; yet through the patriotism and generosity of the leading citizens funds were found to carry it out. **7** By ones, twos and threes, according to their means, they undertook to provide a fully equipped quinquereme, on the understanding that they would be repaid if all went well. **8** In this way 200 quinqueremes were swiftly fitted out, all of them constructed on the model of the 'Rhodian' ship. The Romans then appointed Gaius Lutatius (Catulus) as commander and sent him out at the beginning of the summer.

ROMAN SUCCESS

4.17 The peace treaty of 241 BC

Polybius Histories 1.61.8–63.3; 3.27.1–10

In 241, C. Lutatius Catulus (cos. 242) besieged Drepana, as the Carthaginian fleet had returned to Carthage. Hearing of his activities, the fleet returned to Sicily, and battle was joined off Lilybaeum at the Aegates Islands. The Carthaginian ships were bringing supplies to Drepana, and were not in battle condition with untrained crews, while the new Roman fleet was in peak condition (1.59.8–60). Fifty Carthaginian ships were sunk and 70 captured. The war in Sicily was over. Twenty-three years previously the Romans did not have a navy; by 241 they had defeated the Mediterranean's greatest maritime people. All of Sicily was now Roman, and they had acquired their first overseas territory. The peace treaty gave Rome Sicily and the adjacent islands, and the Carthaginians paid a huge war-indemnity. For the battle of the Aegates Islands: Polyb. 1.60–1; Diod. 24.11; Thiel 1954: 305–16; Walbank I.103–23; Scullard 1980: 177; Bagnall 1990: 96; Lancell 1995: 370–2; Lazenby 1996: 155–7; Goldsworthy 2000: 122–6.

Carthage's mercenaries revolted when they were not paid on their return home, and Rome seized Sardinia in 238 while Carthage was distracted by this revolt. The Carthaginians bitterly resented this and were to refer to it at the outbreak of the Second Punic War: see Polyb. 1.65–88; docs 4.17, 21–3, 27, cf. 64; loss of Sardinia: Lancell 1998: 10–12, 22–4. Rome took Corsica in 231, after an earlier expedition in 259.

Reasons for the Roman victory: Lazenby argues the following (1996: 161–70; cf. Goldsworthy 2000: 129–33): Rome had greater resources, rebuilding fleets wrecked by storm, though with great financial hardship (doc. 4.16). It also had more manpower, because of her allies, who served both in the army and in the fleet as naval allies (*socii navales*). Roman losses were huge: the census figures for before the war were 292,234 adult males, as against 241,212 in 247/6 BC. Naval losses in particular were enormous. Roman quinqueremes had crews of 300, with about 40 marines: Polybius records that the Romans lost 700 of these (1.63.4). Rome decided that to win it needed a navy, and that it had to take Carthaginian cities in Sicily one by one (according to Polyb. 1.20.1–2 the Romans decided to conquer all of Sicily after their capture of Agrigentum in 261). Their greatest failure was the lack of success of their African expeditions, which were undermanned and suffered from a lack of objective. The Carthaginians were worthy opponents, but they lacked initiative, and tended to respond to Roman offensives rather than develop their own strategies. Their defeat was only partial, and related only to Sicily, followed by Sardinia and Corsica, and they still held Africa and part of south-western Spain. The potential for future conflict remained. All of Sicily except for Hiero's Syracuse came under Roman administration in 241, and when the city was captured by the Romans in 211 all Sicily became a province.

1.61.8 The Roman general (Lutatius) sailed away to Lilybaeum and the legions and occupied himself with the arrangements for the captured ships and men — a tremendous task, as the prisoners captured alive in the engagement were not many less than 10,000. **62.1** After this unexpected defeat, the Carthaginians were still prepared to continue the war under the influence of their passions and ambition, but were at a loss with regard to reasoned argument. **2** They were no longer able to provision their forces in Sicily with the enemy in control of the sea; and if they gave these up and, as it were, became their betrayers, they had no other men or leaders whom they could use to continue the war. **3** For this reason they quickly sent to (Hamilcar) Barca giving him full powers. He acted like an extremely good and sensible leader. **4** While there had been some reasonable hope in events, he had omitted nothing however reckless or dangerous, but put to the test every hope of success in war, if ever any general ever did. **5** But with fortunes reversed, and no reasonable hope left of saving the troops under his command, he showed his intelligence and good sense in yielding to events and sending envoys to negotiate for peace terms. **6** For a general ought to be able to tell both when he is victorious, **7** and when defeated. Lutatius gladly accepted the proposals, as he was aware that his side was already worn out and exhausted by the war, and he succeeded in putting an end to the conflict in a treaty in which the terms were basically as follows: **8** 'On the following terms there shall be friendship between the Carthaginians and Romans, if approved by the Roman people. The Carthaginians are to withdraw from the whole of Sicily and not make war on Hiero or bear arms against the Syracusans or the Syracusans' allies. **9** The Carthaginians are to hand over to the Romans all prisoners without ransom. The Carthaginians shall pay the Romans over twenty years 2,200 Euboic talents.' **63.1** When these conditions were referred to Rome, the people did not accept the treaty, but sent ten men to investigate matters. **2** On their arrival, they made no great changes to the conditions, but imposed slightly more severe terms on the Carthaginians. **3** They reduced the term of payment by half, and added 1,000 talents to the sum, and demanded that the Carthaginians withdraw from all the islands lying between Italy and Sicily.

4 This was how the war between Romans and Carthaginians over Sicily ended and these were the peace terms, the war having lasted for 24 years continuously, **5** which is the longest, most continuous and greatest of any I have ever heard of. In it, apart from the rest of the battles and equipment, on one occasion, as I said earlier on, more that 500 quinqueremes in total and on another close to 700 were engaged in conflict with each other. **6** The Romans also lost about 700 quinqueremes in this war, including those destroyed in shipwrecks, and the Carthaginians about 500.

3.27.1 At the end of the war for Sicily, they made another treaty, with the following conditions: **2** 'The Carthaginians are to withdraw from all the islands which lie between Italy and Sicily. **3** The allies of each are to be secure from attack by the other. **4** Neither is allowed to impose contributions, construct public buildings, or enlist soldiers in the others' territory, nor to make alliances with the allies of the other. **5** The Carthaginians are to pay 2,200 talents within ten years, and 1,000 immediately. **6** The Carthaginians are to hand over to the Romans all prisoners without ransom.' **7** Later, at the end of the Libyan war (238 BC) when the Romans had passed a decree declaring war on the Carthaginians, they added an additional clause to the treaty: **8** 'The Carthaginians are to withdraw from Sardinia and pay another 1,200 talents', as I said above. **9** In addition to these, the last agreement was made with Hasdrubal in Spain (226 BC), 'That the Carthaginians are not to cross the river Ebro in arms.' **10** These were the official contracts between Romans and Carthaginians from the beginning up to the time of Hannibal.

4.18 The first national epic

Naevius *The Song of the Punic War*

(*ROL* II.60, 64.) Naevius was a Roman citizen, born c. 270 BC, who served in the First Punic War, and began to produce plays in Rome in 235, mostly *fabulae palliatae* (Greek comedies) or *togatae* (Roman comedies), and then the new *fabula praetexta*, soon after 222, a historical Roman play, dealing with the victory won against the Gauls at Clastidium by M. Marcellus in 222. In his plays he attacked famous statesmen, including Scipio Africanus and the Caecilii Metelli: eventually he was thrown into prison: note esp. his comment 'the Metelli are made consuls at Rome by Fate'

(*Satire* 2), perhaps on Q. Caecilius Metellus, cos. 206. Later exiled, he died in north Africa, perhaps in 201. His *Song of the Punic War* greatly influenced Ennius and Virgil. Cicero praises it, despite Ennius' criticism (*Brutus* 75–6). Little is known of Regulus' activities in Malta (Lazenby 1996: 78); at 6.39 the reference is perhaps to Hamilcar on Mount Eryx, between Panormus and Drepana, a scene of tussles between the two sides (Polyb. 1.55.6–58.7). 7.41–3 refers to the provisional peace of 241 arranged between C. Lutatius Catulus and Hamilcar.

4.31–2   The Roman crosses over to Malta, an island undamaged;
He burns, ravages, lays waste, and puts an end to the enemy's occupation.

6.39   Proudly and disdainfully he wears out the legions.

7.41–3   This also they agree, that their fortifications shall be such
As to conciliate Lutatius; while he agrees
To return the numerous prisoners held as hostages.

THE SECOND PUNIC WAR

Between the First and Second Punic Wars Rome faced conflict with the Gauls, as well as activity in Illyria, in north Greece along the Adriatic; Rome had only just concluded campaigns in Illyria against Demetrius of Pharus when Saguntum fell to Hannibal (Polyb. 2.2–12, 14–35, 3.16–19).

Modern scholarship has focussed on the Second Punic War: the combination of elephants, Hannibal, and Rome's struggle for survival has been irresistible, much to the detriment of the equally fascinating First Punic War. An initial reading list is: Baker 1929; Hallward 1930, 1930a, 1930b; Picard & Picard 1968: 230–71; Warmington 1969: 186–222; de Beer 1969; Scullard 1980: 203–39; Caven 1980: 85–248; Hoyos 1983; Lazenby 1978; Bradford 1981; Briscoe 1989; Bagnall 1990: 155–299; Cornell 1996; Peddie 1997; Lancell 1998; Roth 1999: 159–61; Goldsworthy 2000: 143–328; as well as the novel by Cottrell 1960.

4.19 Roman manpower in the census of 225 BC

Polybius *Histories* 2.24.2–17

The figures given by Polybius here may derive from Fabius Pictor's account, which probably came from official Roman lists provided by the various communities of Italy (see Walbank I.196–203; Brunt *IM* 44–60; Baronowski 1993; Rosenstein 2002). Polybius' figures actually add up to 768,300. The context is a survey of Italian manpower carried out in 225 BC to ascertain available forces, when Italy was threatened by a Gallic invasion.

1 To make it clear from the facts how great were the resources that Hannibal dared to attack, and how great was the Romans' empire which he boldly confronted, and on which he so nearly achieved his aim of inflicting major disasters, **2** I must state what resources and number of troops was available to them at that time. **3** Both of the consuls commanded four legions of Roman citizens, each consisting of 5,200 infantry and 300 cavalry. **4** The allied troops in each consular army totalled 30,000 infantry and 2,000 cavalry. **5** The Sabines and Etruscans, who had temporarily come to Rome's assistance, had 4,000 cavalry and more than 50,000 infantry. **6** The Romans massed these troops and stationed them on the border of Etruria, under the command of a praetor. **7** The Umbrians and Sarsinates, who lived in the Apennines, totalled around 20,000, and there were 20,000 Veneti and Cenomani . . . **9** In Rome itself there was a reserve force prepared for all contingencies of war, of 20,000 Roman infantry and 1,500 cavalry, and 30,000 allied infantry and 2,000 cavalry. **10** The lists of men able to fight that were sent back were as follows: Latins, 80,000 infantry and 5,000 cavalry; Samnites, 70,000 infantry and 7,000 cavalry; **11** Iapygians and Messapians, 50,000 infantry and 16,000 cavalry; **12** Lucanians, 30,000 infantry and 3,000 cavalry; Marsi, Marrucini, Frentani and Vestini, 20,000 infantry and 4,000 cavalry. **13** In Sicily and Tarentum there were two reserve legions, each consisting of about 4,200 infantry and 200 cavalry. **14** The total for Romans and Campanians came to 250,000 infantry and 23,000 cavalry; . . . **16** so the total number of Romans and allies able to bear arms was more than 700,000 infantry and 70,000 cavalry, **17** while Hannibal invaded Italy with less than 20,000 men.

4.20 Roman manpower in 217 BC

Livy *History of Rome* 22.36.1–4

Livy was clearly frustrated in his attempt to ascertain the precise numbers of combatants following the Battle of Trasimene in 217 (Brunt *IM* 419, 648). The Romans and their allies were able to field huge numbers of men. In 218 there were six legions, and five more were raised before Trasimene in 217, bringing the total to 11. The loss of two legions at Trasimene was immediately made up. By Cannae there were 13 legions in service. The men lost at Cannae (and the two legions annihilated in Gaul in the same year) were replaced by enough men for five more legions, so that even after Cannae Rome could field 14 legions, one more than before Cannae. The number peaked in 212 and 211 with 25 legions in the field: the numerical strength of individual legions did vary, from 4,500–5,500 men. For the number of legions: Brunt 418; Peddie 1997: 47, 122; Wise & Healy 1999: 76. But there were huge losses; Livy records a census figure of 137,108 citizens for 208 BC, well down on the census figures for the period of the First Punic War (Livy 27.36.7).

1 The armies were also increased; the size of the forces added to the infantry and to the cavalry I should hardly venture to say for certain, so greatly do authors differ both on the number and type of forces. **2** Some say 10,000 new troops were conscripted as replacements, others that four new legions were raised so that they took the field with eight; **3** some say that the number of infantry and cavalry in the legions were increased by 1,000 infantry and 100 cavalry, **4** so that each was composed of 5,000 infantry and 300 cavalry, and that the allies gave double the number of cavalry but the same number of infantry and that at the time of the battle of Cannae, there were 87,200 men under arms.

4.21 The causes of the Second Punic War

Polybius *Histories* 3.6.1–8, 9.6–10.6

Compare Livy 21.1.1–4.1; App. *Iber.* 5–13, *Hann.* 1–3, *Pun.* 6; Dio F55; Diod. 25.15–16. Polybius, who provides the most extensive account of the causes of the second war, notes that the historians of the war provide two reasons (the Carthaginian siege of Saguntum, and the crossing of the Ebro, the latter breaking the treaty of 226 BC). He argues that these were the beginnings of the war, but not its causes and differentiates between origins and initial incidents, much as Thucydides saw that the pretexts for the Spartans declaring war on the Athenians were not the 'truest cause' (Thuc. 1.23.4–6).

At 3.8.1–11 Polybius takes Fabius Pictor ('a contemporary and Roman senator': 3.9.4) to task for asserting that, as well as Saguntum, a cause of the war was Hasdrubal's ambition, and

Hannibal's emulation of Hasdrubal in defiance of Carthaginian opinion. For Polybius, the most important Carthaginian was Hamilcar Barca, father of Hannibal. Hamilcar had negotiated the treaty with Rome (1.62), and both he and the Carthaginians realised the difficulty of continuing the war after the defeat at the Aegates islands. But he clearly felt cheated by the peace (the first cause), to which was added the anger of the Carthaginians (the second cause), and the success of Carthage in Spain (the third cause). Certainly that the Carthaginians wanted revenge for the loss of Sicily and Carthage is not inexplicable.

Polybius argues that Carthage was justified in going to war because of its loss of Sardinia, but that Rome could put Hannibal in the wrong because he had attacked Saguntum (Rich 1996: 6–14). He probably does not place enough stress on disagreements both at Carthage and Rome about foreign policy, which are revealed in the debate at Rome about whether to go to war (Livy 21.16; Polyb. 3.20.1–5 unreasonably denies that any such debate occurred), and Hanno's opposition to Hannibal (doc. 4.29). Polybius' account is, however, largely valid: there was genuine anger at Carthage over the loss of their possessions.

Rome decided to make the issue of Saguntum a reason for war. At 3.9.9, 'civil disturbances' refers to the mercenaries' revolt at Carthage (237–229 BC). For the causes of the Second Punic War, especially Saguntum, see Salmon 1960: 134–6; Astin 1967; Errington 1970: 26–32, 41–5, 1972: 49–61; Dorey & Dudley 1971: 29–37; Sumner 1968: 232–46, 1972; Lazenby 1978: 22–8; Harris 1979: 200–5; Caven 1980: 85–97; Scullard 1980: 198–202, 1989a: 32–43; Rich 1996; Lancell 1998: 46–51; Goldsworthy 2000: 143–50; Hoyos 2003: 87–97; on Livy's account of the causes, esp. Ridley 2000: 18–23. For the Carthaginians in Spain, and the foundation of New Carthage on the south-west coast, basically a Barca family enterprise, see Schulten 1928; Picard & Picard 1968: 202–29; Lazenby 1978: 21–2; Scullard 1980: 195–8, 1989a: 17–31; Caven 1980: 73–84; Richardson 1986: 17–20; Bagnall 1990: 142–51; Lancell 1995: 376–80, 1998: 28–46; Goldsworthy 2000: 136–8; Hoyos 2003: 55–72.

6.1 Some of those who have written the history of Hannibal and his times, as they wanted to show us the causes that led to this war between Rome and Carthage, put forward as its first cause the Carthaginians' siege of Saguntum, **2** and as its second their crossing of the river called by the locals the Iber (Ebro), contrary to treaty. **3** I could agree that these might be called the beginnings of the war, but I can by no means concede that they were its causes. **4** You could just as well say that Alexander's crossing to Asia was the cause of his war against Persia and Antiochus' landing at Demetrias the cause of his against the Romans, neither of which is either plausible or true . . .

9.6 But to return to the war between Rome and Carthage, from which this digression has taken us, we must consider its first cause as being the anger of Hamilcar, surnamed Barca, the father of Hannibal. **7** His spirit was unconquered by the war for Sicily, since he thought that he had kept the army at Eryx under his command with its energies unimpaired, and that he had only made peace through force of circumstances after the defeat of the Carthaginians in the naval battle (at the Aegates islands), and he maintained his resolve, watching for a chance to strike. **8** If the mercenaries' mutiny against the Carthaginians had not occurred, he would soon have found another opportunity and resources, as far as was in his power. **9** He was, however, fully occupied with these civil disturbances which took all his attention. **10.1** After the Carthaginians had put down this mutiny, the Romans declared war against them, and the Carthaginians were at first willing to negotiate on all points, thinking that as right was on their side they would win . . . **3** But, as the Romans took no notice, they yielded to circumstances. Though deeply resentful, they were powerless to prevent it, and withdrew from Sardinia as well as agreeing to pay another 1,200 talents in addition to the previous sum, to avoid being forced into another war at that time. **4** This, then, should be taken to be the second and most important cause of the war which followed. **5** Hamilcar added the anger felt by his fellow-citizens at this to his own rage, and, as soon as he had put down the mutiny of the mercenaries and secured the safety of his country, at once threw all his resolution into the conquest of Spain, with the design of using these resources for the war against the Romans. **6** The success of the Carthaginian project in Spain must be considered as the third cause of the war, for this additional strength caused them to enter into it with confidence.

HANNIBAL

4.22 Was Hannibal's hatred for Rome inherited?

Livy *History of Rome* 21.1.3–5

Here Livy's comment on the hatred felt by the Carthaginians ties in with Polybius' first and second causes of the war. Livy 21.2.1–2 argues that, if Hamilcar had lived, he would have invaded Italy, and that the war in Spain was a prelude to this. In this case, the Carthaginians had planned to attack Rome for many years and, if so, the Romans were relieved of the responsibility for the war. Polybius 3.11.5–7 tells the same story of Hannibal's oath, which lends credibility to it. He has the sacrifice made to Zeus, but the actual Carthaginian deity involved will have been Ba'al Shaman, Zeus' equivalent. The oath was religious in nature, and binding. The Carthaginians' most notable religious habit was the sacrifice and burning of infants to Ba'al Shaman; this practice continued until the city's destruction (doc. 3.7; Lancell 1995: 227–56).

3 The hatred, too, with which they fought was almost greater than their strength, for the Romans were angry that the conquered should of their own accord be attacking their conquerors, while the Carthaginians believed that the conquered had been treated with arrogance and greed. **4** There is also a story that, when Hannibal was about nine years old, in a childish way he coaxed his father Hamilcar, who had finished the African war and was sacrificing prior to leading the army to Spain, to take him with him. Hamilcar led the boy to the altar and made him swear an oath, touching the offerings, that as soon as he could he would be the enemy of the Roman people. **5** The loss of Sicily and Sardinia tormented Hamilcar's proud spirit; for he believed that Sicily had been surrendered in premature despair and that Sardinia had been wrongly snatched by the Romans during the African revolt with an indemnity imposed on them to make matters worse.

4.23 Hannibal interferes with Saguntum, 220/19 BC

Polybius *Histories* 3.14.9–15.13

Hamilcar spent nine years in Spain (237–229) and on his death in 229 was succeeded by his son-in-law Hasdrubal; on Hasdrubal's assassination in 221 BC, Hannibal succeeded as Carthaginian commander of military operations in Spain. Livy has the Barca *factio* dominant at Carthage from 237. Hamilcar and Hasdrubal had incorporated the Spanish tribes into the Carthaginian empire (Polyb. 2.1.5–9; Livy 21.2.1–6; Bagnall 1990: 142–51; Rich 1996: 14–18; Picard & Picard 1968: 202–29). The Carthaginians acquired great wealth, not just from the booty of war but, like the Romans after them, from exploiting the Spanish silver mines. The need to pay back the indemnity to Rome, and to make up for the financial loss of western Sicily and Sardinia, will have been foremost in the Spanish undertaking (Dio F48). Neither Hamilcar nor Hasdrubal had antagonised the Romans: in 226 BC, the peace treaty of 241 was renewed by Hasdrubal, except that now it took Spain into consideration, indicating a Roman concern with Carthaginian expansion there (docs 4.27–8).

Polybius does not see Hannibal as a cause of the war, preferring to look further back, to Hamilcar and 241 BC. But Hannibal must be taken into consideration: he attacked Saguntum, with the blessing of Carthage, despite the Roman request that he not do so; without him, there might never have been a Second Punic War. At 3.15.7, Hannibal refers to the civil dissension that had broken out in 221 BC at Saguntum, in which some of the Saguntines had appealed to Rome against another faction. Roman ambassadors to Saguntum had organised the execution of the leaders of the other, pro-Carthaginian, group. Hannibal made this a ground of complaint against Rome, and, to their demand that he keep his hands off the city, made no promises. The Roman envoys saw war as inevitable, and sailed to Carthage.

Livy's account is intended to put Roman actions in the best possible light, and has Saguntum besieged before the envoys left Rome. Hannibal refuses to see the embassy, which highlights his bellicosity, and serves the purpose of showing that the Romans attempted to do something while Saguntum was under siege, while in truth they did nothing for eight months (Rich 1996: 5). Polybius has the Roman embassy arriving at New Carthage before Hannibal attacked the city and this version is earlier and perhaps preferable, as it does not seek to justify Roman actions.

The independence of Saguntum, which was 150 kilometres south of the Ebro, had been guaranteed in the treaty of 226 BC (docs 4.27–8); Livy 21.16.2 refers to the Saguntines as allies (socii), and Hanno at Carthage tells his countrymen that the treaty forbids them from approaching the city (21.10.6). Polybius has the Romans saying that Saguntum was under their protection (3.15.3), and that the Saguntines relied on their alliance (*symmachia*) with Rome (3.15.8). This must mean that there was a formal alliance between Rome and Saguntum and that the guarantee of Saguntine independence meant independence from Carthage. Carthage could have no involvement north of the Ebro, but this did not cancel out the Roman alliance with Saguntum, made several years before Hannibal took command in Spain. When Hannibal attacked Saguntum, Rome had every right to feel that the treaty of 226 had been broken. In 219 Hannibal deliberately courted war, reflecting Polybius' third cause: Carthaginian success in Spain, without which there would have been no conflict. According to Livy, the Romans feared that Hannibal would cross the Ebro, bringing the Spanish tribes with him, rouse the Celts to revolt, and that there would be war in Italy and 'under the walls of Rome' (21.17.6). He writes with hindsight, and Polybius makes it clear that the Romans in fact thought the fight would be around Saguntum: the battle with Carthage was envisaged as taking place away from Italy and far from Rome.

The siege of Saguntum began in April or May of 219 BC and went on for eight months during which time the city received *no* assistance from the Romans. Rome was pre-occupied with Demetrius of Pharus (Illyria): he and his pirates were extending their power into territory protected by Rome, and both consuls for 219 were thereby occupied when Hannibal besieged Saguntum (Polyb. 3.16–20). Roman preparations for war occurred only after Saguntum had fallen, and by then the field of military operations in Illyria was closed. **3.15.8**: 'were behaving unjustly towards some of the people who were subject to Carthage' refers to Saguntine attacks against the Turdenti, allies of the Carthaginians.

14.9 Following their defeat none of the peoples south of the Ebro river ventured to face the Carthaginians lightly, except the Saguntines. **10** As far as he could Hannibal tried to keep his hands off this city, as he wished to give the Romans no acknowledged excuse for war, until he had secured possession of the rest of the country, following his father Hamilcar's suggestions and advice.

15.1 But the Saguntines kept sending to Rome, partly because they were anxious on their own account and foresaw what was going to happen, and partly because they wished that the Romans not be taken by surprise by the Carthaginians' growing power in Spain. **2** The Romans, who had frequently disregarded them, on this occasion sent envoys to investigate the situation. **3** Hannibal at the same time had subdued the tribes he intended and returned with his forces to winter at New Carthage, which was in a way the showpiece and capital of the Carthaginians in Spain. **4** He found there the embassy from Rome, and gave them an audience, listening to what they had to say.

5 The Romans affirmed that he should keep away from Saguntum, which lay under their protection, and not cross the river Ebro in accordance with the treaty made in Hasdrubal's time. **6** Hannibal, who was young and full of martial energy, successful in his plans, and encouraged by his long-time hatred of the Romans, **7** replied to them that he was protecting the interests of the Saguntines, and accused the Romans of having unjustly executed some of the leading men, when a short time previously civil conflict had broken out and they were called in as arbiters. The Carthaginians, he said, would not overlook this violation of good faith; for it was an ancestral tradition of theirs to ignore no victim of injustice; **8** and he sent to Carthage asking what action he should take, as the Saguntines, relying on their alliance with Rome, were behaving unjustly towards some of the people who were subject to Carthage. **9** He was wholly influenced by his unreasoning and violent anger, and so did not give the true reasons, but took refuge in groundless pretexts, as people generally do when they disregard their duty under the influence of a pre-existing passion. **10** How much better it would have been if he had demanded that the Romans restore Sardinia, and at the same time the indemnity which they had unjustly exacted, taking advantage of Carthage's misfortunes, and, if this was rejected, to threaten her with war!

11 But now, by keeping silent about the real cause and inventing a non-existent one about the Saguntines, he appeared to be embarking on the war not only without reason, but even without justice. **12** The Roman envoys, seeing clearly that war was unavoidable, sailed to Carthage wishing to make a similar appeal to them; **13** of course they never expected that there would be war in Italy, but in Spain, using Saguntum as a base for war.

4.24 Did Hannibal start the war on his own initiative?

Polybius *Histories* 3.8.1–8, 11

Polybius records Fabius Pictor's view that Hannibal started the war on his own initiative; cf. Livy 21.5.1–3, who seems to accept this view. Polybius, however, makes it clear that Hannibal sent to Carthage for advice on what to do concerning Saguntum (doc. 4.23).

1 Fabius, the Roman historian, says that, besides the injury done to the Saguntines, one of the causes of the Hannibalic war was Hasdrubal's arrogance and love of power. **2** He tells us how, having acquired great power in Spain, he arrived in Africa and tried to dissolve the laws of Carthage and change the constitution into a monarchy. **3** The leading statesmen, however, foresaw his plan and united to oppose him, **4** whereupon Hasdrubal, mistrusting them, left Africa and for the future governed Spain along his own lines, paying no attention to the Carthaginian senate. **5** Hannibal from boyhood had shared and admired Hasdrubal's policy, and, when he succeeded to the command of Spain, he had used the same approach to dealing with affairs as Hasdrubal. **6** As a result, he now began this war against the Romans on his own initiative and against Carthaginian opinion, **7** with not one of the leading men in Carthage approving Hannibal's conduct towards Saguntum. **8** After saying this, Fabius tells us that after the capture of this city, the Romans demanded that the Carthaginians should either hand over Hannibal to them or accept war . . . **11** But they were so far from doing any of this, that they carried on the war continuously for 17 years in accordance with Hannibal's policy, and did not abandon the war until they had finally lost every hope because of the danger threatening their country and its inhabitants.

4.25 Hannibal the man, 221 BC

Livy *History of Rome* 21.4.1–10

Hannibal went to Spain as a boy of nine years with his father Hamilcar in 237. There was clearly interest in Hannibal's character, and what made him 'tick'. For Livy on Hannibal: Ridley 2000: 32–3.

1 Hannibal was sent to Spain, where immediately on his arrival the whole army received him with enthusiasm; **2** the old soldiers believed that Hamilcar himself had returned to them, as he was when he was young, seeing in Hannibal the same force of expression and energy of glance, the same countenance and features. But soon he brought it about that his likeness to his father was the least consideration in gaining him support; **3** never was the same nature more adaptable to the most diverse things — obeying and commanding. As a result you could not easily tell whether he was dearer to the general or the army; **4** there was no one Hasdrubal preferred more when anything bold or difficult was to be done, nor did the men show more confidence and daring under any other leader. **5** To recklessness in incurring danger he added the greatest judgement when in the midst of the dangers themselves; his body could not be exhausted or his mind overcome by any hard work; **6** he was equally tolerant of cold and heat; his manner of eating and drinking was regulated by natural desire not pleasure; his times of waking and sleeping were not delineated by day and night; **7** what remained when his work was done was given to rest, which he summoned not with a soft bed or silence, but was often seen by many lying on the ground wrapped up in a military cloak among the sentinels and pickets. **8** His clothes were no different from those of his fellows, though his arms and horse did stand out. He was undoubtedly the best of horsemen and infantry; the first to enter battle, and the last to leave once the fighting had begun. **9** These excellent qualities were equalled by his great vices: inhuman cruelty, perfidy more than Punic, no regard for truth or the divine, no fear of the gods, no reverence for an oath, no religious scruples. **10** With this disposition for virtues and vices he served for three years under Hasdrubal's command, omitting nothing that should be done or seen by one who was to become a great commander.

4.26 Hannibal's greed

Polybius *Histories* 9.25.1–4

All of Polyb. 9.22–6 is taken up with a discussion of Hannibal's character. The Carthaginian sources may have been individuals Polybius had met, in Greece or Italy.

1 Hannibal does seem to have been exceptionally fond of money, as was his friend Mago who commanded in Bruttium. **2** I obtained this account both from the Carthaginians themselves **3** (for locals know not only in which direction the wind lies, as the proverb says, but also the character of their compatriots), **4** and in more detail from Masinissa, who dwelt at length on the love of money as a characteristic of all Carthaginians, and especially of Hannibal and Mago who was known as the Samnite.

WHOSE FAULT: ROME OR CARTHAGE?

4.27 Rome and Carthage both at fault

Polybius *Histories* 3.30.1–4

Polybius argues that the Carthaginians had 'good cause' to go to war, but that if the cause was the destruction of Saguntum, then the Carthaginians were in the wrong for having broken the treaty.

1 It is an undisputed fact that the Saguntines many years before Hannibal's time had placed themselves under Rome's protection. **2** The greatest evidence for this, and one accepted by the Carthaginians themselves, is that when political conflict broke out in Saguntum, they did not turn to the Carthaginians, although they were close at hand and were already involved in affairs in Spain, but to the Romans, and with their help restored the political situation. **3** So, if one were to regard the destruction of Saguntum as the cause of the Hannibalic War, it must be admitted that the Carthaginians were in the wrong in beginning the war, both from the point of view of the treaty of Lutatius, in which the allies of each power were to be secure from attack by the other, and from that of the agreement with Hasdrubal, in which the Carthaginians were not to cross the Ebro in arms. **4** But if we take th2e cause of the war to have been the annexation of Sardinia and the additional indemnity, then it must certainly be agreed that the Carthaginians had good reason to enter on the Hannibalic war, for, after yielding to circumstances, they were now retaliating with the help of circumstances against those who had wronged them.

4.28 Livy's version of the Ebro Treaty, 226 BC

Livy *History of Rome* 21.2.7

The background to the treaty, signed in 226 BC, is sometimes seen as the threat to Rome and Italy from the Gauls, but it is clear that the Romans had become concerned about Carthaginian expansion in Spain. Saguntum was within the area, south of the Ebro river, in which by the treaty of 226 the Carthaginians could operate, but the treaty clearly envisaged the continuing independence of the city. That the treaty was signed by Hasdrubal rather than the Carthaginian state gave the Carthaginians grounds for arguing that they need not necessarily observe it (doc. 4.29).

Here Livy has the Ebro as a buffer zone between the two empires, though the nearest Roman territory was some distance away on the Italian side of the Alps. The treaty as mentioned by Polybius has the Carthaginians not able to cross the Ebro, but does not mention the Romans. This makes it much more favourable to the Romans, as one would expect of a treaty between Rome and a city which had been severely defeated in 241; cf. Polyb. 2.13.7: the Carthaginians were not to cross the river under arms.

It was with Hasdrubal, because of his amazing skill in encouraging the Spanish tribes to join the Carthaginian empire, that the Roman people had renewed their treaty (i.e., that of 241 BC), laying down that the river Ebro should be the boundary for each empire, while the Saguntines, situated between the two empires, should preserve their independence.

4.29 Q. Fabius Maximus, envoy at Carthage, 218 BC

Livy *History of Rome* 21.18.1–19.5

Cf. Polyb. 3.20.6–21.10, 33.1–3. The first Roman embassy to Carthage had met Hannibal to no avail at New Carthage and then sailed to Carthage, where Hanno 'the Great', commander in the First Punic War, was the lone Carthaginian voice for peace and for observing the treaty (of 226 BC). He argued for the surrender of Hannibal and for abandoning the siege of Saguntum, but the Carthaginian council supported Hannibal and his actions in Spain (Livy 21.10.1–11.2). When the Roman embassy returned home, news came that Saguntum had fallen, and the senate, 'ashamed' at not helping the city, prepared for war, though, according to Livy, they did not undertake war lightly, recognising the skill of their enemy (21.16). Before declaring war, a second embassy was sent to Carthage; for Roman ceremonies for declaring war, see doc. 3.12.

The speeches have no historical validity, but do reflect core historical truths, that there was an embassy and a debate, and perhaps the broad lines of the arguments used. Speeches as a historical device are found in Herodotus and Thucydides; they add 'flavour' and a touch of reality, for most negotiation was carried on in this way. **2.18.1**: M. Livius Salinator and L. Aemilius Paullus had been the consuls for 219; **2.18.13**: the story of the toga is also in Polyb. 3.33.2–3.

18.1 When these arrangements had been made, to make sure they observed all the due ceremonies before making war, the Romans sent to Africa an embassy of older men, Quintus Fabius, Marcus Livius, Lucius Aemilius, Gaius Licinius and Quintus Baebius, to put to the Carthaginians the question whether Hannibal had attacked Saguntum on the orders of the state; **2** and if, as seemed to be likely, they admitted the act and defended it as state policy, to declare war on the Carthaginian people. **3** After the Romans had arrived at Carthage and the senate granted them a hearing, Fabius put only the single question which they had been instructed to ask. One of the Carthaginians replied: **4** 'Even your previous embassy, Romans, when you demanded that we hand over Hannibal for besieging Saguntum on his own initiative, was somewhat rash; but your present embassy, though expressed up till now more mildly, is in fact more harsh. **5** On that occasion Hannibal was accused and his surrender demanded; now you are trying to extort from us a confession of guilt and immediate reparation as if we had already confessed. **6** Now, in my view, you should be asking not whether Saguntum was attacked on the state's orders or on the decision of an individual, but whether justly or unjustly;

7 the inquiry into the acts of one of our citizens, whether he acted on our authority or his own, and his punishment, is up to us; with you we have only one point for discussion — whether what he did was permissible under the treaty. **8** Therefore, since you want there to be a distinction between what commanders do on orders from the state and what they do on their own initiative, consider the treaty made between us and you by Gaius Lutatius, your consul, in which the allies of both sides were protected, but nothing was stipulated about the Saguntines, since they were not as yet your allies. **9** But you will perhaps say that in the treaty which Hasdrubal made the Saguntines are especially mentioned. To which I will only say the answer learnt from you. **10** For you have denied that you were bound by the treaty which the consul Gaius Lutatius originally made with us, because it had been made neither on the senate's authority or the people's command; and so an entirely new treaty was made with the state's approval. **11** If you are not bound by your treaties unless they are made by your authority and command, then neither is Hasdrubal's treaty, which he made without our knowledge, binding on us. **12** So say no more about Saguntum and the Ebro, and produce the thought that has long been developing inside your mind!' **13** At this, the Roman, gathering his toga into a fold, replied, 'Here we bring you peace and war: take which you will!' With his words, they cried out no less aggressively that he might give them what he wished; **14** when he shook out the fold again and said that he gave them war, they all replied that they accepted it and that they would fight in the same spirit in which they accepted it.

THE FIRST STAGES OF THE WAR IN ITALY

At the Roman declaration of war in 218 BC, Hannibal had not yet crossed the Ebro river. The Romans thought they had the advantage. They appointed one of the consuls of 218, P. Cornelius Scipio, to a command in Spain, with 24,000 men and 60 ships, while the other consul, Ti. Sempronius Longus, was sent to Africa, with 26,000 men and 160 ships. Rome was in a sense dividing its efforts, but the strategy was clear: deal with Hannibal in Spain, and keep the Carthaginians busy in Africa. But as doc. 4.31 indicates, Hannibal was one step ahead. For a good synopsis of the Second Punic War in Italy, see Errington 1972: 62–97; Briscoe 1989: 47–56; Bernstein 1994: 77–82.

4.30 The beginning of the Second Punic War

Ennius Annals 256–7

(Skutsch 1985: 91 (as lines 236–7), commentary at 417–19; *ROL* I.94.) Parts 7–9 of Ennius' *Annals* dealt with the Second Punic War. These lines here graphically describe Hannibal's advance from New Carthage, in spring 218.

> Finally with great force the four-footed horses and riders and elephants
> Hurl themselves forward.

4.31 Was Hannibal wise to cross the Alps?

Polybius Histories 3.47.6–9, 48.10–12

Cf. Livy 21.30–7. The crossing of the Alps by Hannibal, with infantry, horses and even elephants, has captured the imagination of both modern and ancient writers: too much so on the part of the latter, according to Polybius. His judgement on Livy would have been very similar.

Polybius refers to the native guides who knew their way through the passes and Polybius himself made the crossing (cf. Livy 21.38.6–9). His references to eyewitnesses are important: they were one of his main sources for the war. Exactly where Hannibal crossed the Alps into Italy is uncertain, perhaps a pass somewhere between the Little St Bernard and Mt Genèvre; the Mont Cenis pass was used by Napoleon in 1800 and could have been Hannibal's route. Hannibal's crossing took about 15 days. For the crossing of the Alps, probably in early November 218, see Walbank I.381–3, Torr 1935; de Beer 1955, 1967: 120–82; Walbank 1956; Dorey & Dudley 1971: 38–45; Proctor 1971; Lazenby 1978: 45–8; Scullard 1980: 204–5; Caven 1980: 104–6; Bradford 1981: 58–65; Bagnall 1990: 165–7; Peddie 1997: 9–32; Goldsworthy 2000: 163–6; Hoyos 2003: 111–12. For Hannibal's elephants: Polyb. 3.55, 74; de Beer 1955, 1967; Scullard 1948, 1970, 1974: 154–73; Scullard & Gowers 1950; Shean 1996: 174–5; Peddie 1997: 206–16 (with references to Livy); Edwards 2001.

The Carthaginians had made use of elephants in Spain, and it was not surprising that Hannibal would attempt to use them again, given their success against the Romans in Sicily (except at the Carthaginian siege of Palermo in 250 BC). Hannibal took 37 elephants with him when he crossed the Rhône, and presumably the same number across the Alps. They were present at the battle of Trebia (modern Trebbia); only one survived by 217, which Hannibal rode through the marshes of Arretium, where he lost the sight of an eye through infection (Livy 22.2.10–11). Reinforcements of elephants reached him in 215 BC, and they were present at Nola (215 BC), Capua (210 BC), Lucania (210 BC and again in 207) and Apulia (209 BC): their military value appears in fact to have been slight. Neither Polybius nor Livy record that they carried howdahs on their backs (structures in which soldiers could be carried: Pliny *Nat. Hist.* 8.27) or crews (Peddie 1997: 206–16). The Carthaginian fleet had not really recovered from the defeat at the Aegates islands in 241, but there were sufficient ships for Hannibal to have had his army transported by sea. However, much of the coast along the way was in Roman hands, and this route might have meant a confrontation with Scipio's fleet (Rankov 1996: 52–5).

According to Polybius, Hannibal arrived in Italy with 12,000 African and 8,000 Spanish infantry, and about 6,000 cavalry: in 205 BC he set up a bronze pillar with an inscription in Punic and Greek in the temple of Hera at Lacinium, near Croton on the south Italian coast, recording his achievements in Italy (Livy 28.46.16) and from this inscription Polybius took the numbers (3.56.4: at 3.33.9–16 he cites the same inscription for the numbers of troops left in Spain and those sent to Africa: Walbank I.364, 366).

At the crossing of the Rhône Hannibal had 38,000 infantry and 8,000 cavalry (Polyb. 3.60.5), which meant he lost 18,000 men from the crossing of the Rhône to the descent from the Alps. Livy 21.38.3–5 has L. Cincius Alimentus, taken prisoner by the Carthaginians, told by Hannibal that he had lost 36,000 men after crossing the Rhône. Polybius, however, disparages writers exaggerating the difficulties Hannibal faced in crossing the Alps: while Hannibal lost many men (Polyb. 3.56.2), Livy's numbers for the losses are unrealistic, particularly given that Hannibal had native guides, that he had ascertained how rich the countryside was into which he would descend, and that the inhabitants were opposed to the Romans; they were to supply warm clothing and footgear and food to the Carthaginian army (3.48.10–12, 49.10–13). After being joined by Gauls from northern Italy, Hannibal had 40,000 infantry and 10,000 cavalry at Cannae (Livy 22.46.6–7).

47.6 Some of those who have written about this crossing, because they wanted to astonish their readers with their marvellous tales about these places already mentioned, have, unnoticed, fallen into the two vices most alien to all writing of history — for they are forced into the making of false statements and self-contradiction. **7** On the one hand they describe Hannibal as a general unrivalled in courage and foresight, but at the same time present him to us as totally without judgement, **8** and are unable to find a solution or way out of their falsehood except by introducing gods and the children of gods into a pragmatic history. **9** For they show the impassability and rugged character of the Alps to be such that not only horses and troops accompanied by elephants, but even active infantrymen would have difficulty in crossing them, while at the same time they describe to us the desolation of the country as being such that unless some god or hero had met Hannibal and shown him the way, his whole army would have been lost and utterly perished, unquestionably falling into both the above mentioned vices. . . .

48.10 Of course Hannibal did not act as these writers suggest, but conducted his enterprise with great common sense. **11** For he had clearly ascertained the natural wealth of the country into which he planned to descend and the resentment of its people towards the Romans, and to deal with the difficulties of his route he employed native guides and scouts who were going to share his aims. **12** I can speak with confidence on such matters because I made inquiry about what happened from men who were present on these occasions, and have inspected the country and crossed the Alps to see and learn for myself.

CATASTROPHE IN ITALY

Hannibal had avoided Scipio, crossing the Rhône a mere three days before Scipio arrived. Scipio decided not to pursue Hannibal by land. He left the army with his brother Gnaeus in command to proceed to Spain, and himself went by sea to northern Italy (Polyb. 3.49.1–4; Livy 21.32.1–5). Hannibal arrived in Italy, took Taurini (Turin), and began besieging cities in Cisalpine Gaul. Scipio and two legions crossed the Po river, taking Hannibal by surprise: the consul had crossed 1,000 miles of sea and land. Rome was astir: talk of the sack of Saguntum had only just ended and Hannibal was already in Italy, attacking cities. Tiberius Sempronius Longus, the other consul, who had got as far as Lilybaeum in Sicily on his expedition to Africa, was recalled (Polyb. 3.61.1–12; Livy 21.38.6–6). The stage was set for the first confrontation.

In November 218 the armies met at Ticinus and Hannibal was victorious, Scipio was wounded, but saved by his son (doc. 4.51). This was less of a battle than a skirmish; the first real battle came in December, at the river Trebia which flows into the Po. The Romans suffered a major defeat under the other consul, Longus, and most of the army was annihilated. Hannibal now dominated northern Italy.

For Ticinus, Trebia and Trasimene, see Polyb. 3.60–87.5; Livy 21.39–22.7; de Beer 1969: 184–97; Dorey & Dudley 1971: 47–54; Errington 1972: 67–70; Lazenby 1978: 55–67; Scullard 1980: 206–8; Caven 1980: 98–132; Bradford 1981: 72–92; Briscoe 1989: 49–50; Bagnall 1990: 173–82; Peddie 1997: 55–72; Wise & Healy 1999: 92–105; Goldsworthy 2000: 169–90.

4.32 Trasimene, 21 June 217 BC

Polybius *Histories* 3.83.1–84.7

In 217, the consuls Gaius Flaminius and Gnaeus Servilius Geminus were sent to guard the Apennines (Italy's mountainous backbone). In June 217, the Romans under Flaminius, who was killed in battle, were defeated again, losing 15,000 men in an ambush at Lake Trasimene, 140 kilometres north of Rome; the defeat was put down to Flaminius' neglect of the auspices (as a novus homo): Livy 21.63.5–14, 22.3.11–14; cf. Polyb. 3.79.3; Cic. *Div.* 1.77, 2.21; cf. doc. 3.51. Polybius and Livy disagree about the actual site of the battle. Hannibal could now move freely in central Italy.

83.1 The road led through a level defile with high hills on each side all along its length, while in front crossways was a steep ridge, difficult to climb, while behind was the lake with only a narrow access to the defile between the lake and the hillside. **2** Hannibal skirted the lake and passed through the defile, occupying the ridge in front and encamping on it with his Spaniards and Libyans, **3** while he brought his slingers and pikemen round to the front and stationed them in an extended line under the hills lying to the right of the defile. **4** Similarly, taking his cavalry and Celts in a circle round the hills on the left, he deployed them in a continuous line, so that the last of them were at the entrance to the defile, which lay between the lake and the hillside. **5** After making these preparations in the night and surrounding the defile with troops in ambush, Hannibal stayed quiet. **6** Flaminius followed behind him, eager to engage with him; **7** he had encamped on the previous day at a very late hour close to the lake itself, and on the next day, as soon as it was dawn, he led his vanguard beside the lake into the above-mentioned defile, wanting to keep in touch with the enemy. **84.1** It was an unusually misty morning, and Hannibal, as soon as the greater part of the enemy's column had entered the defile and the vanguard had already made contact with him, gave the signal for battle and sent messages to the men waiting in ambush, attacking the enemy simultaneously from all sides. **2** Their sudden appearance took Flaminius totally by surprise, and, as the condition of the air made it still very difficult to see clearly, and the enemy were charging at and attacking them from above in many different places, the Romans' centurions and military tribunes were not only unable to do anything necessary to help the situation, but could not even understand what was going on. **3** They were being attacked simultaneously from the front, from the rear, and from the sides, **4** and, as a result, most of them were cut down in marching order, not able to protect themselves, and as if betrayed by their commander's lack of judgement. **5** For while they were still considering what they ought to do, they were being killed without knowing how. **6** It was at this point that some of the Celts attacked and killed Flaminius himself, who was in the greatest distress and difficulty. **7** So in the defile nearly 15,000 Romans fell, unable either to yield to circumstances or to do anything, but considering it their most important duty to adhere to their tradition of not fleeing or leaving their ranks.

4.33 Marcus Minucius, Dictator

ILS 11

(*CIL* I² 607; *ILLRP* 118; *ROL* IV.76.) This inscribed dedication is on the side of an altar found at Rome. The disaster at Trasimene led to the appointment by the comitia centuriata of a dictator, Q. Fabius Maximus; they also appointed as his master of horse M. Minucius Rufus (cos. 221). Fabius normally would have appointed his own master; that he was chosen for him might indicate a desire to keep a rein on the dictator. It is possible that the people, with the 'people's consul' Flaminius dead, appointed Minucius (Scullard 1973: 46; cf. Ridley 2000: 29–32). The relationship between Fabius and Minucius was strained. Minucius attacked the enemy — against Fabius' delaying strategy — at Geronium in Apulia, winning a minor victory there which so excited the demoralised Romans that they made him equal with the dictator (Polyb. 3.103.4). Another attack was less successful, with Minucius only saved by Fabius. Minucius was killed in battle at Cannae in the next year (Polyb. 3.100–105; Livy 22.18.5–10, 23.9–29.6; Plut. *Fab.* 8–13; App. *Hann.* 15–16). Scholars who feel that Minucius was not appointed co-dictator on equal terms with Fabius argue that the dictatorship referred to here is one for the holding of elections, perhaps in 220, rather than a military dictatorship (Walbank I.434, but see Scullard 1973: 48).

Marcus Minucius, dictator, son of Gaius, vowed this dedication to Hercules.

4.34 Ennius on Fabius Maximus 'Cunctator'

Ennius *Annals* 360–2

(Skutsch 1985: 102 (as lines 363–5), commentary at 529–32.) 'Cunctator' means the delayer. Upon appointment as dictator in 217 after the disaster at Trasimene, Fabius carried out extensive religious rites, and restored confidence at Rome. His policy was to avoid pitched battle, in which Hannibal clearly had the upper hand; the latter bypassed Rome and moved into prosperous Campania. So far, no cities had deserted Rome. Fabius' policy of allowing the Carthaginians to pillage and loot Roman and Latin territory and property was unpopular. In 216 consuls were elected as usual: L. Aemilius Paullus (cos. 219) and the *novus homo* C. Terentius Varro. Fabius: Polyb. 3.100–5; Livy 22.8.7–8, 10.10–12.12, 15.1–18.10, 23.1.1–30.10, 31.8–11; App. *Hann.* 12–16; Plut. *Fab.* 4–13; *MRR* I.243; Baker 1929: 105–25; de Beer 1969: 200–9; Dorey & Dudley 1971; Lazenby 1978: 67–73; Scullard 1980: 209; Caven 1980: 124–32; Bagnall 1990: 183–9; Erdkamp 1992; Peddie 1997: 73–4, 76–7; Goldsworthy 2000: 193–6, 199–200. Cicero (*Off.* 1.84) quotes these lines by Ennius in praise of Fabius.

One man by his delays restored our state for us.

He put no rumours before our safety;

Therefore in after times — even today — this hero's glory shines forth, more than once it did.

4.35 Cannae, 216 BC

Polybius *Histories* 3.113.1–118.5

See Polyb. 3.107–18 passim; Livy 22.44–52; App. *Hann.* 19–26; Plut. *Fab.* 15–16, *Marcell.* 9; Diod. 25.19.1. The Romans refused to adhere to Fabius' delaying strategy and confronted Hannibal at Cannae; the result vindicated Fabius. In 216 Hannibal had captured the hill-top town, in Apulia in eastern Italy, which the Romans had used as a supply depot (Polyb. 3.4). The battle was an outstanding military disaster of the first order for the Romans: one consul, L. Aemilius Paullus died, while the other escaped (C. Terentius Varro), 70,000 Romans were killed, and 10,000 captured. This was probably the greatest casualty rate in a day for any European army in history. Hannibal lost 6,700 men. But the loss of the men was not Rome's greatest problem, for, with its allies, it could and did make up this loss, and refused to ransom its surviving defeated soldiers (doc. 4.36): rather, the defection of allies and loss of territory was the greatest blow.

The Roman army of eight legions and an additional 40,000 allied troops (80,000 men all told) was commanded on alternate days by each of the two consuls. Hannibal with about 40,000 foot and 10,000 cavalry was clearly outnumbered (the force he had arrived with had been augmented by Gauls in northern Italy); for Roman and Carthaginian manpower at Cannae, see esp. Daly 2002: 25–32. On the day of battle it was Varro's turn to command, and when the battle was lost he fled, for which Polybius criticises him (3.116.13). The sources have Aemilius Paullus trying to persuade Varro not to join battle with Hannibal (Polyb. 3.110.2–8, cf. 112.2; Livy 22.44). Polybius' hostility was possibly because, as a novus homo consul, Terentius reflected the populares' side of politics rather than the senatorial. But Varro was not disgraced: he was proconsul in 215–13 in Picenum, and held *imperium pro praetore* in 208/7 in Etruria (Walbank III.448 with references). Clearly he was not held responsible for Cannae at the time: Hannibal's superior generalship had won. As is clear from Polybius' description, Hannibal used outflanking tactics to defeat the Romans, and the level plain on which the battle was fought was ideally suited to Hannibal's cavalry.

For Cannae: Baker 1929: 132–49; de Beer 1969: 209–22; Dorey & Dudley 1971: 63–7; Errington 1972: 74; Lazenby 1978: 77–85; Scullard 1980: 210–11; Caven 1980: 133–47; Bradford

1981: 108–16; Briscoe 1989: 51; Bagnall 1990: 190–5; Samuels 1990; Hanson 1995: 48–9; Shean 1996; Peddie 1997: 89–96; Wise & Healy 1999: 115–42; Goldsworthy 2000: 197–21, 2001; Daly 2002, esp. 156–202. For Hannibal's battle disposition, see Lazenby 1996: 40–1; Goldsworthy 2001: 95–113; Daly 2002: 156–66; for armour, equipment and dress of the Roman and Carthaginian forces, see Daly 2002: 48–112, and for colour reconstructions of these: Wise & Healy 1999: 29–36; for the Celts, Spaniards and Samnites, see esp. Rawlings 1996; for their fighting naked at 3.114.4, cf. 2.28.7–8; Livy 22.46.6; Daly 103. See Sabin 1996 (cf. 2000) for how the Romans fought in their early defeats.

113.1 On the very next day it was Gaius (Terentius Varro's) turn to take command and at the first sign of sunrise he moved his troops out of each encampment, **2** crossing the river with those from the larger camp, whom he drew up at once in battle-order, while he stationed those from the other camp alongside them in the same line, all facing south. **3** The Romans' cavalry he positioned near the river on the right wing, and the infantry next to them in the same line, placing the maniples more closely together than had been done before, and making the depth of the maniples many times greater than the front; **4** he drew up the allied cavalry on the left wing; and in front of the whole army and some distance away he drew up the light-armed troops. **5** Counting the allies, there were 80,000 infantry and a little more than 6,000 cavalry. **6** At the same time, Hannibal sent his slingers and pikemen across the river and placed them in the front of his army, while he led the rest of his troops out of camp, crossing the river in two places and drawing them up facing the enemy. **7** On his left, near the river, he put his Spanish and Celtic cavalry opposite the Roman cavalry, and alongside these half of his heavy-armed Libyans, then his Spaniards and Celts. Beside these he positioned the other half of his Libyans, and put his Numidian cavalry on the right wing. **8** When he had drawn up his whole army in a straight line, he took the middle companies of the Spaniards and Celts and brought them forward, keeping the rest in contact with these, but making the front crescent-shaped and thinning the line of battle, intending to have his Libyans as a reserve-force in the battle, and let the Spaniards and Celts bear the brunt.

114.1 The Libyans were armed in the Roman style, as Hannibal had equipped them all with selected spoils from earlier battles; **2** the Spaniards' and Celts' shields were similar, but their swords totally different; **3** the thrust of the Spaniards' swords was no less effective than their cut, but the Gallic sword was only able to cut and not at close-quarters. **4** With their companies drawn up alternately, the Celts naked and the Spaniards in their national costume, short tunics edged with purple, they were a strange and awe-inspiring sight. **5** Altogether the Carthaginian cavalry numbered about 10,000 and their infantry, including the Celts, not much more than 40,000. **6** Aemilius commanded the Romans' right wing, Gaius (Terentius) the left, and Marcus (Atilius) and Gnaeus (Servilius Geminus), the previous year's consuls, the centre. **7** Hasdrubal commanded the Carthaginian left, Hanno the right; Hannibal himself the centre, with his brother Mago. **8** As the Roman line looked south, as I said before, and the Carthaginians north, neither was troubled by the rising sun.

115.1 The advance guards were the first to engage, and at first, with only the light-armed troops involved, the conflict was even, but, as soon as the Spanish and Celtic cavalry on the left met the Romans, the conflict was truly barbaric; **3** for there were none of the customary wheeling movements, but having once engaged they dismounted and fought hand to hand. **4** When the Carthaginians prevailed and killed most of the enemy in the engagement, with all the Romans fighting with great bravery, they started driving the rest along the river, slaughtering them without mercy, and then the heavy infantry took over from the light-armed troops and fell on each other. **5** For a short time, the ranks of the Spaniards and Celts stayed firm and fought bravely with the Romans; then, under the pressure, they gave way and fell back, losing the crescent-shape. **6** The Romans' maniples bravely pursued them and easily cut through the enemy's line, as the Celts were drawn up thinly, while the Romans had crowded together from the wings to the middle where the action was; **7** for the wings and the centres did not engage simultaneously, but the centres first, as the Celts were drawn up in a crescent-shape, a long way in advance of their wings, with the convex front of the crescent facing the enemy. **8** The Romans, pursuing these and putting pressure on the centre and that part of the enemy's line that was giving way, pushed so far forward that on each side of their flanks they now had the Libyans in their heavy armour; **9** of these, those on the right wing faced left, and charged the enemy flank from the right, **10** while those on the left faced right and reforming did the same from the left, the situation making it clear how to act. **11** As a result, as Hannibal had planned, the Romans, in their pursuit of the Celts, were caught in the middle of the Libyans. **12** They no longer kept formation, but turned either singly or in companies and fought the enemy who were attacking their flanks . . .

116.7 At this point Hasdrubal seems to have acted with great skill and common sense; seeing that the Numidians were very numerous and most skilful and formidable against a fleeing enemy, he allowed them to deal with those in flight (i.e., the Roman cavalry), and led his men to the conflict between the infantry, eager to assist the Libyans. **8** Falling on the Roman legions from the rear and making successive attacks with his companies simultaneously from various points, he encouraged the Libyans and subdued and terrified the spirits of the Romans. **9** It was at this point that Lucius Aemilius, after several severe wounds, lost his life in hand-to-hand combat, a man who did his duty to his country, if ever anyone did, both during the whole course of his life and on this final occasion. **10** As long as the Romans could turn and present a front to the enemy that surrounded them they held out; **11** but while the outer ranks kept falling and they were increasingly hemmed in, they were all finally killed, including Marcus and Gnaeus, the previous year's consuls, who in this conflict had acted like brave men worthy of Rome.

117.1 This was the outcome of the battle between the Romans and Carthaginians at Cannae, a battle which had the bravest men as both victors and vanquished. **2** This was clear from events. For, of the 6,000 cavalry, 70 escaped to Venusia with Terentius, and around 300 of the allied horse found safety in the cities in scattered groups; **3** of the infantry some 10,000 were captured fighting, but not in the battle itself, and perhaps only 3,000 escaped from the conflict to the neighbouring cities. **4** All the rest, some 70,000, died bravely, the main contribution to the Carthaginians' victory, both on this occasion and formerly, being the number of their cavalry . . . **6** Of Hannibal's army, about 4,000 Celts fell, 1,500 Spaniards and Africans, and 200 cavalry . . .

118.2 The Carthaginians, through this action, came into immediate control of nearly all the rest of the coast; **3** the Tarentines at once surrendered, while the Argyrippans and some Campanian towns invited Hannibal to them, while all the rest now looked towards the Carthaginians. **4** These had great hopes of becoming masters of Rome itself at the first attempt; **5** the Romans at once gave up hopes of keeping their supremacy in Italy because of this defeat, and were in great fear and danger on their own account and that of their ancestral city, expecting Hannibal to arrive at any moment.

4.36 Conquer or die!

Polybius *Histories* 6.58.2–13

Cf. Livy 22.58–61; Cic. *Off.* 3.113; Walbank I.746. Following the defeat, the senate refused to ransom the 8,000 men who had been guarding the Roman camp, even though it was not their fault that they had not engaged in the battle and had no chance against Hannibal's troops; it preferred to enrol slaves in the army (doc. 6.1). The reason was partly to avoid giving Hannibal monetary resources with which to carry on the war (Livy 22.26.1–2), but at the same time they were upholding the doctrine of 'no surrender' on any terms. Hannibal therefore sold the prisoners into slavery; the 2,000 who were still enslaved in Greece in 194 BC were freed by Flamininus: Livy 34.50.5–6, Val. Max. 5.2.6.

2 When, after his victory at Cannae, the 8,000 men who were guarding the camp came into Hannibal's hands, he took them all prisoner and allowed them to send a deputation home on the subject of ransom and release. **3** They chose ten of their most distinguished men and he sent them off, after making them swear an oath that they would return to him. **4** One of the men selected, as he was going out of the camp's palisade, said he had forgotten something and went back, leaving again after collecting what he had left behind, and thinking that by his return he had kept his faith and absolved himself of the oath. **5** When they arrived in Rome, they begged and entreated the senate not to begrudge the prisoners their release, but allow each of them to pay three minas and return to their families; for Hannibal, they said, had allowed this; **6** they were worthy of release: for they had not been guilty of cowardice in the battle, nor done anything unworthy of Rome, but had been left behind to guard the camp, and when all the others had been killed in the battle had been forced by circumstances to surrender to the enemy. **7** But the Romans, despite having encountered serious defeats in their battles, and having now, so to speak, lost all their allies, and despite the fact that they were expecting Rome itself to be threatened any day, **8** listened to what they said but neither disregarded their dignity under the pressure of disasters, nor neglected any necessary step in their consideration, **9** but seeing that Hannibal's purpose was, through this action, both to obtain funds and deprive the men opposed to him in battle of their high spirit, by showing that if defeated they might still hope for safety, **10** were so far from agreeing to this request that they took no account either of pity for their relatives nor of the future value which these men would be to them, **11** but thwarted Hannibal's calculations and the hopes he had placed in them, and refused to ransom the men, while they imposed a law on their troops that, when they fought, they must either conquer or die, as there was no hope of safety for them if they were defeated. **12** Consequently, after deciding this, they sent away the nine envoys who returned willingly according to their oath, while they put the man, who had tried to trick his way out of the oath, into chains and returned him to the enemy, **13** so that Hannibal's pleasure at his victory in the battle was not so great as his disappointment, when he saw with amazement the steadfastness and high spirit of the Romans in their resolutions.

4.37 Ennius on Cannae

Ennius *Annals* 276–7

(Skutsch 1985: 91 (as lines 234–5), commentary at 414–16.) Propertius 3.3.9–10: 'and (Ennius) sang . . . of the victorious delays of Fabius, and the unlucky battle at Cannae, and the gods being turned (to hear) our pious prayers.' Hannibal's African and Spanish mercenaries were remarkable for their loyalty and discipline; here Hannibal is offering his troops Carthaginian citizenship.

He who will strike an enemy, I promise, will be a Carthaginian,
Whoever he may be, whatever country he comes from . . .

4.38 Emergency measures

Livy *History of Rome* 22.57.2–6, 9–12

Polyb. 3.112.8–9 comments on the religious activity at Rome just before Cannae, and notes that the Romans considered no rites unseemly or undignified which would propitiate the gods. In 228, 216 and 113 BC a Gallic couple and a Greek couple were buried alive in the Forum Boarium at Rome after a consultation of the Sibylline Books recommended this course of action. In 216 and 113 the burials occurred after Vestal Virgins were convicted of unchastity. Fear of military defeat and disasters in battle prompted the burial of the Gauls and Greeks and the punishment of the Vestals, and the burials must be seen as expiatory (Eckstein 1982). Livy specifically uses the word *sacrificia*. He mentions at 22.57.6 the previous occurrence, in 228 (Plut. *Marcell.* 3.5–6; Dio F47); for 113: Plut. *Rom. Quest.* 83. Human sacrifice was banned by senatorial decree only in 97 BC (Pliny *Nat. Hist.* 30.3.12). In 359–358 BC, 307 captured Roman soldiers were sacrificed by the Etruscans of Tarquinii, but the Romans avenged them (Livy 7.15.10, 7.17. 7.19). Toynbee 1965: II.381 has the Gauls and Greeks as representing the Gallic conquerors of Rome (390 BC) and the Greek conquerors of Troy (Rome's mythical ancestors), but most scholars are puzzled by the inclusions of Greeks (whereas the Gauls invaded Italy prior to all three occasions which might explain why they were chosen as victims). See also Ogilvie 1969: 87; Dumézil 1970: 449–50; Rawson 1991: 156; Beard 1994: 733–4; *BNP* 1.81, 2.158.

On this occasion in 216 two Vestal Virgins, Opimia and Floronia, had been convicted of unchastity, which was considered a great pollution. Their conviction was not unusual as a response to Roman disasters (cf. doc 7.91). The slaves in the army were eventually freed by their commander Gracchus (grandfather of the Gracchi). On his death they deserted, but were re-enlisted (Livy 24.16.17, 25.20.4, 22.3). In 214 slaves were again enlisted, as sailors, but not freed: they remained the slaves of their original owners (Livy 24.11.7–9).

2 The Romans were terrified, moreover, not only by these immense disasters, but also by numerous prodigies, and in particular because two Vestals in that year, Opimia and Floronia, had been convicted of fornication, and one of them had been buried alive, as the custom is, near the Colline Gate, while the other had committed suicide; **3** Lucius Cantilius, a pontifical secretary (one of those who are now called lesser pontiffs), who had slept with Floronia, was scourged so harshly in the comitium by the pontifex maximus that he died under the lashes. **4** Since this impious crime, being in the midst of so many disasters was, as often happens, converted into a portent, the decemvirs were ordered to consult the (Sibylline) Books, **5** and Quintus Fabius Pictor was sent to Delphi to ask the oracle what prayers and supplications they should use so as to appease the gods and what the end of these immense disasters would be. **6** Meanwhile, on the instructions of the Books of Fate, some extraordinary sacrifices (*sacrificia*) were made, amongst which a Gallic man and woman and a Greek man and woman were buried alive in the Forum Boarium in a place enclosed with stone, which had even on an earlier occasion been saturated with the blood of human victims, a rite most untypical of Roman practice . . . **9** On the senate's authority a dictator, Marcus Junius (Pera), was appointed with Tiberius Sempronius (Gracchus) as his master of horse, and after proclaiming a levy they enlisted young men over the age of seventeen and some still wearing the toga praetexta. **10** From these they made up four legions and a thousand horsemen. They also sent to the allies and the Latins to supply their soldiers according to agreement. They ordered that armour, weapons and other things be prepared and took down old enemy spoils from the temples and porticoes. **11** The levy had a novel appearance owing to the scarcity of free men and the crisis: they bought with state money 8,000 young, strong slaves, and armed them, asking each first if he were willing to serve. **12** They preferred these as soldiers, though at less expense they could have redeemed the prisoners of war.

4.39 Hannibal does not march on Rome

Livy *History of Rome* 22.51.1–4

The story of Maharbal (son of Himilco), commander of the Libyan cavalry, urging Hannibal on the battlefield of Cannae to march on Rome, is not found in Polybius. It is possibly an invention of Livy or one of his sources in order to express amazement that after such a spectacular victory Hannibal did not march on the city (Polyb. 3.118.5 has Rome in 'great fear' that he would come). If Hannibal had marched on and defeated Rome, the outcome of the war might have been markedly different.

Lazenby advances several reasons why Hannibal did not march on Rome: Rome was 400 kilometres away, and there were two legions in the city to defend it (Livy 23.14.2), as well as the male members of the population; Rome still had troops and could raise others; whether Hannibal could take Rome quickly was uncertain and a siege could drag on; also Hannibal's aims were to detach the Latin and Italian allies from Rome (Livy 34.60.3). Hannibal did not want a war to the death with Rome; the war was about *dignitas* and *imperium* (Livy 22.58.3), and he proposed peace, though his ambassador to Rome, Carthalo, was turned back by the orders of Marcus Junius Pera, dictator for 216 (Livy 22.58.7–9): Lazenby 1978: 85–6; 1996a: 39–47; cf. Hoyos 2000.

While it is sometimes stated that he had no siege equipment and did not construct any in Italy (Hoyos 1983: 176–7), Hannibal did besiege cities (Livy 23.18.8: siege sheds (and mines) at Casilinum 216 BC; 23.37.2: a massive wooden tower at Cumae, 215 BC; 25.11.10: siege machines 'of every kind' at Tarentum in 212 BC; 29.7.4–5: ladders and 'other assault gear' constructed against Locri, 205 BC). See Shean 1996: 161–7 for Hannibal's siege capabilities, arguing that Hannibal had constant supply problems and probably could not have provisioned his force if encamped outside Rome (184–5). Hannibal did march on Rome in 211 to draw off Roman forces from their siege of Capua (Polyb. 9.3.1–9.10; Livy 26.7.3–11.7), but did not settle down to besiege the city.

1 While the other officers had crowded round Hannibal, congratulating him on his victory and counselling him, now that he had brought so great a war to an end, to rest himself and allow it to his exhausted soldiers for what remained of that day and the following night, **2** Maharbal, the cavalry commander, considered that now was least of all the time for inactivity: 'On the contrary,' he said, 'that you may understand what has been achieved in this battle, on the fifth day you will banquet, as victor, in the Capitol! Follow — I will go on ahead with the cavalry so the Romans may know that you have arrived before they know you are coming.' **3** The suggestion seemed to Hannibal too delightful and immense for his mind to be able to grasp it all at once. So he said that he praised Maharbal's goodwill, but needed time to think about his advice. **4** To which Maharbal replied, 'Truly, the gods do not give the same man all their gifts: you know how to win battles, Hannibal, but you do not know how to use victory.' That day's delay is generally believed to have saved Rome and the empire.

4.40 Rome appeals to businessmen and contractors, 215 BC

Livy *History of Rome* 23.48.4–49.3

In this emergency situation, businessmen, especially those who had profited from the business of war, were asked in 215 to make loans to the state, with deferred repayment, and to supply the army. The composition of the senate was now altered by the war. Numerous senators had died in the conflict, as well as magistrates. Nevertheless, Spurius Carvilius' proposal to enrol two Latins from each Latin people as senators met with outright opposition (Livy 23.22.4–9). M. Fabius Buteo (cos. 245 and censor in 241) was appointed dictator to co-opt members into the senate; he chose 177, firstly from those who had held a curule office but had not yet been enrolled in the senate, then from those who had been aediles, military tribunes or quaestors, then from those who had not held public office, who had spoils from the enemy fixed to their houses or who had received the civic crown (Livy 23.22.10–23.8). Roman finances: Briscoe 1989: 74–5; for a scandal in 213 over contracts to supply the Roman army: Livy 25.3.8–5.2; for the events in Spain, see Livy 22.22, 23.26–34.

48.4 At the end of summer, a letter came from Publius and Gnaeus Scipio, reporting the extent and success of their campaign in Spain, but that the army needed money for pay, clothing, and grain, while allies in the navy were in need of everything. **5** With regard to the pay they would, if the treasury was empty, find some way of obtaining it from the Spaniards; the rest had certainly to be sent out from Rome or else neither the army nor the province could be kept. **6** When the letter was read out, there was no one among them all who did not admit that the statements were true and the demands reasonable . . . **9** Therefore, the senate came to the conclusion that unless the state could be supported by credit, its assets were insufficient to keep it going. **10** They decided that the praetor, Fulvius, should appear before the assembly, inform the people of these public needs, and urge those who had increased their family property through state contracts, to allow the state, from which they had acquired their wealth, **11** time to make payment and to contract to supply what was needed for the army in Spain, on condition that they be the first to be paid when there was money in the treasury. **12** The praetor put this to the assembly, and named a day on which he would let the contracts for providing clothing and grain to the Spanish army and whatever else was needed for the allies in the navy. **49.1** When that day came, three companies of nineteen men came forward to take up the contracts, but they had two demands: **2** one, that they should be exempt from military service while they were engaged in this public business, the other, that the cargoes on their ships should be at the risk of the state as regards the threats of enemies or storms. **3** When both these demands were agreed to, they took up the contracts, and the state was carried on with private money.

THE IMPACT ON THE ALLIES

4.41 Hannibal and the allies, 218–217 BC

Polybius *Histories* 3.77.3–7

Hannibal's attempt to stir up revolt and 'free' the Italians after the battles of Trebia (218 BC) and Trasimene (217) had not led to any defections, perhaps due to the length of time many of the Italian peoples had been allies of Rome, and their military obligations and loyalties. Moreover, the outcome of the contest was not yet clear. But even after Cannae the Latin allies remained firm, despite the fact that Hannibal let the allied troops return home without ransom, as he had after Trebia and Trasimene (Livy 22.58.1–2; Polyb. 3.77), clearly in order to win over their communities. He told the captured allies after Trebia and Trasimene that he had come not to fight them but to free them: he was in Italy fighting for (not against) the Italians (Polyb. 3.77, 3.85.4; note Erskine 1993). Capua took up his offer, but emphasised its independence of the Carthaginians (doc. 4.42).

Livy 34.60.3 reports that Hannibal had assumed that Italy would provide supplies and soldiers to a foreign enemy and expected the allies' support. This partly explains why he had brought a relatively small army into Italy, hoping not only that the allies would desert Rome but that they would fight for him. In this he was ignorant of the close links (but certainly not equality) that had been forged between Rome and the allies.

For Capua, de Beer 1969: 218–22; Lazenby 1978: 90, 112–15, 120–1; Scullard 1980: 222–3; Caven 1980: 169–74; Bagnall 1990: 237–8, 249–54; Goldsworthy 2000: 233–5; for the allies in general: Briscoe 1989: 75–8; Lazenby 1996a: 44–5; Hoyos 2003: 122–33.

3 Hannibal, while wintering in Cisalpine Gaul, kept the Romans whom he had captured in battle imprisoned, giving them just enough to eat, **4** but he continued to show great kindness to those from the allies and later called them to a meeting and spoke to them, stating that he had not come to make war on them, but on the Romans on their behalf. **5** So, if they were sensible, they should accept his friendship, **6** for he had come primarily to restore the freedom of the Italian people, as well as to help them recover the cities and territory which had been taken from each of them by the Romans. **7** Having spoken in this way, he sent them all to their homes without ransom, as he wished by doing so to win over the inhabitants of Italy to his side and at the same time to turn their loyalties against Rome, while inciting to revolt those who thought their cities or harbours had suffered decline under Roman rule.

4.42 The secession of Capua, 216 BC

Livy History of Rome 23.4.6–8, 6.5–8, 7.1–3

Following Cannae, the situation in Campania changed. Its chief city, Capua, was an Oscan city with Etruscan influence; in 338 BC the equites of Campania had been granted Roman citizenship, following an unsuccessful demand in 340 that one of the consuls be from Latium (Livy 8.5.5, 7; doc. 1.64). But in 216, it went over to Hannibal. **23.4.8**: the horsemen had been demanded by the Romans (hostages in effect) directly after Cannae.

Capua was the most spectacular of the revolts against Rome, which Livy lists: the Campanians, Atellani, Calatini, Hirpini, some of the Apulians, the Samnites, Bruttians, Lucanians, Uzentini, and almost all the Greek coastal cities, as well as Tarentum, Metapontum, Croton, Locri and the Cisalpine Gauls (Livy 22.61.11–15, cf. Polyb. 3.118; see the map at Wise & Healy 1999: 135). But Cannae, and these defections, did not make the Romans think of peace (Livy 22.61.13).

However, given that allies made up about 50 per cent of Roman manpower, these revolts were a major concern (Lazenby 1996a: 44n.27). Hannibal had gained more allies, but he had also acquired responsibilities including the need to protect these cities, especially Capua, which tied him down in southern Italy for several years. Capua was recovered by Rome in 211 (doc. 4.44); Tarentum in 209; Locri in 205; Croton in 203.

While the proposal to enrol Latins as senators was dismissed, partly because the senate doubted their loyalty (Livy 23.22.8), the Latin allies were staunchly loyal. However, in 209, twelve Latin colonies refused to meet their military obligations, though the rest remained supportive: Livy 27.9.7–10.10.

4.6 To the Campanians' contempt for the laws, magistrates and senate, there was now added, after the disaster at Cannae, scorn too for the power of Rome, for which they used to have some respect. **7** The only thing which held them back from immediate secession was that the ancient right of connubium (intermarriage) linked many distinguished and powerful families with the Romans, **8** and the strongest bond was that 300 horsemen, the most noble of the Campanians, were serving in the Roman army, chosen by the Romans and sent to garrison Sicilian cities . . .

6.5 Finally the majority view prevailed that the same envoys who had gone to the Roman consul should be sent to Hannibal. **6** Before they went and before the plan to secede was settled, I find in some annals that envoys were sent to Rome by the Campanians, with the demand that one of the consuls should be a Campanian, if they wished them to aid the Roman state; **7** anger was aroused and they were ordered to be removed from the senate house, and a lictor was sent to lead them from the city and order them stay for the rest of that day outside Roman territory. **8** There was once a very similar demand made by the Latins, and because Coelius and other writers have with some reason omitted it I have been afraid to set this down as certain.

7.1 The envoys came to Hannibal, and made peace on these conditions: that no Carthaginian general or magistrate should have any jurisdiction over a Campanian citizen and no Campanian citizen should be forced to serve in the army or perform any other service; **2** that Capua was to have its own laws and magistrates; that the Carthaginians should give the Campanians 300 of their Roman prisoners, whom the Campanians were to choose, with whom there would be an exchange for the Campanian cavalry who were serving in Sicily. **3** These were the terms; in addition to this agreement, the Campanians committed the following crimes: for the populace suddenly seized prefects of the allies and other Roman citizens, some of them on military duty, others engaged in private business, and ordered them all to be shut up in the baths, as if under guard, where they might die in a terrible way, suffocated by the extreme heat.

4.43 Hannibal and the Locrians, 215 BC

Livy *History of Rome* 24.1.13

Livy includes amongst the defectors Locri and the other Greek cities, but these cities initially opposed Hannibal in 216: Hannibal attacked the Greek cities in alliance with the Bruttians, so they stayed firm in the Roman alliance (Livy 24.1.1). The Locrians surrendered to Hannibal in 215 but allowed the Roman garrison to leave secretly; for the Roman peace settlement with Locri in 204, see Livy 29.19.6–8. These defections gave Hannibal control of much of southern Italy. Rhegium, prominent in the First Punic War, was attacked to no avail and remained loyal to Rome (Livy 24.1.2).

By Hannibal's order, the Locrians were given peace: they were to live in freedom under their own laws, their city should be open to the Carthaginians, their harbour was to be in the control of the Locrians, and the alliance was to stand on the condition that the Carthaginians should help the Locrians and the Locrians the Carthaginians in peace and war.

4.44 Capua brought back into the fold, 211 BC

Livy *History of Rome* 26.16.5–10, 13

In 215, Rome's activities in Spain prevented reinforcements reaching Hannibal; the Carthaginian attempt to win back Sardinia came to nothing when Hasdrubal's army was defeated by T. Manlius Torquatus (cos. 235, 224) and a rebellion in Africa necessitated Hasdrubal's recall to Africa. The Romans hemmed Hannibal into southern Italy with some success. In 214, the consuls M. Claudius Marcellus and Q. Fabius Maximus 'Cunctator' (also consul in 215, and his son in 213) pushed Hannibal further south. But 213 saw several Greek cities go over to Hannibal, including Tarentum which was recaptured in 209. The year 212 saw preparations for the recapture of Capua, which occurred in the following year; Syracuse was also retaken in 211, despite a Carthaginian attempt under Bomilcar to relieve the city. For the treatment of Capua, Livy 31.31.10–15; fifty-three Capuan senators were beheaded (because as Roman citizens they were traitors): 26.14.9–15.9.

The Scipio brothers, Gnaeus and Publius, had successfully campaigned in Spain against Hasdrubal since 218 and 217. By 212 three Carthaginian armies, under Mago, Hasdrubal (Barca), and Hasdrubal son of Gisgo, were tied up in Spain, denying Hannibal much needed re-inforcements. Moreover, a rebellion by Syphax of Numidia in 214–213 meant that some Carthaginian troops had been withdrawn from Spain to deal with this. In 212 the Scipios captured Saguntum, but in 211 they died in battle, while the surviving Roman forces fell back behind the Ebro river. This was to be the lowest ebb in Roman fortunes in Spain. The years 212–211, in hindsight, with the Roman recovery of Sicily and Capua, were in fact the beginning of the end for Hannibal in Italy. The younger Scipio drove the Carthaginians from Spain in 206 BC, at the battle of Ilipa. The Romans in Spain to 206 BC: Richardson 1986: 20–61; Keay 1988: 27–9; Curchin 1991: 24–8; cf. Badian *FC* 116–25.

5 From Cales the Romans returned to Capua and the surrender of Atella and Calatia was received. There too punishment fell on the leaders responsible. **6** Thus some 70 leading senators were executed, while approximately 300 Campanian nobles who were imprisoned, and others who were sent under guard to cities of the Latin allies, died in various ways: the rest of the citizens of Capua were sold. **7** Discussion continued about the city and the remaining land, some being of the opinion that a city so powerful, so close and so unfriendly ought to be destroyed. But present advantage triumphed; on account of the land, which was well-known to be the most fertile of any in Italy, the city was saved so there might be a home for the farmers. **8** To populate the city, the foreign residents, freedmen and retailers and craftsmen were allowed to stay: all the land and buildings became the public property of the Roman people. **9** But it was decided that Capua should remain a city only in the sense of a place of habitation, and it was to have no political body — no senate, no assembly of the people, no magistrates: **10** without a public council, without military authority they thought the mob, having nothing in common with each other, would be incapable of agreement; a praetor would be sent each year from Rome to administer justice . . . **13** The enemy had to admit what power the Romans possessed to exact punishment from disloyal allies and how helpless Hannibal was to guard those whom he had taken under his protection.

THE TIDE TURNS

4.45 The alliance between Hannibal and Philip of Macedon, 215 BC

Polybius *Histories* 7.9.1–17

Cf. Livy 23.33.10–12; App. *Mac.* 1. Philip V of Macedon approached Hannibal after Cannae for this alliance; Rome knew of the alliance through capturing Xenophanes, Philip's ambassador who was returning to Philip with the treaty (this may be the source of Polybius' copy). Philip is of interest because of the part he plays later in the First and Second Macedonian Wars (215–205, 200–196 BC; cf. doc. 5.23). The Romans had intervened in Illyria, near Macedon, over Demetrius of Pharos, and Philip seems to have been uneasy about their intervention. The alliance brought Hannibal no material value, but its psychological effect and propaganda value in Sicily and southern Italy amongst the Greek cities which had rebelled might have been important. The First Macedonian War was not an undue tax on Rome's resources and never assumed the importance of a major sphere of operations, opening with a small fleet of 50 ships under the praetor M. Valerius Laevinus in 215 BC (as consul in 210 he recaptured Agrigentum in Sicily; in 205 he was the leader of the embassy to Phrygia that returned to Rome with the cult of the Magna Mater: see doc. 3.59). While it was a mutual alliance, it does not specifically state that either party would come to the military assistance of the other: at any rate, neither did.

It is clear that there was no Carthaginian intention to destroy Rome, but certainly to limit its power. Carthaginian activity in Sardinia and Sicily, their successes in Spain, the alliance with Philip, and Hannibal's presence in Italy were meant to divide Roman resources. To an extent this was the case, but the Romans found the requisite resources and were to keep Sicily and Sardinia, conquer Spain, and deal with Philip. For the treaty, Walbank II.42–56; Baker 1929: 160–3; Lazenby 1978: 159–60; Bagnall 1990: 199–200; Goldsworthy 2000: 255–60; for the deities of the oath and their Carthaginian equivalents, see Lancell 1995: 208–9.

1 The sworn treaty made between Hannibal the general, Mago, Myrcan, Barmocar, and all the Carthaginian senators with him and all the Carthaginians serving under him, and Xenophanes the Athenian, son of Cleomachus, the envoy whom King Philip, son of Demetrius, sent to us on behalf of himself, the Macedonians and the allies.

2 In the presence of Zeus, Hera and Apollo; in the presence of the god of Carthage, Heracles, and Iolaus; in the presence of Ares, Triton and Poseidon; in the presence of the gods who battle for us and of the sun, moon and earth; in the presence of rivers, harbours and waters; **3** in the presence of all the gods who possess Carthage; in the presence of all the gods who possess Macedonia and the rest of Greece; in the presence of all the gods of the army who preside over this oath.

4 Hannibal the general, and all the Carthaginian senators with him, and all the Carthaginians serving under him, propose that in respect of what seems good to you and to us, we should make this sworn treaty of friendship and goodwill to be friends, kinsmen and brothers, **5** on the following conditions:

That King Philip and the Macedonians and the rest of the Greeks who are their allies shall protect the Carthaginians, the sovereign people, and Hannibal their general and those with him and those subject to the Carthaginians who have the same laws; also the people of Utica, and all cities and peoples subject to the Carthaginians, and our soldiers and allies; **6** also all cities and peoples in Italy, Gaul and Liguria, which whom we are in alliance and those in this country with whom we may hereafter be in alliance;

7 That King Philip and the Macedonians and the other Greeks who are their allies shall be protected and guarded by the Carthaginians who are serving with us, by the people of Utica, and by all cities and peoples that are subject to Carthage, by our allies and soldiers, and by all peoples and cities in Italy, Gaul and Liguria, who are our allies and such other as may hereafter become our allies in Italy and the neighbouring regions;

8 That we shall make no plots against each other, nor set ambushes against one another, but with all zeal and goodwill, without guile or treachery, we will be enemies of those who make war against the Carthaginians, excepting the kings, cities and harbours with whom we have sworn treaties and friendships;

9 That we shall also be the enemies of those who make war against King Philip, excepting the kings, cities and peoples with whom we have sworn treaties and friendships;

10 That you will be our allies in the war which we now wage against the Romans, until the gods grant victory to us and to you, **11** and you will give us such help as we need or as we agree on;

12 That when the gods have granted us victory in the war against the Romans and their allies, if the Romans ask us to make terms of peace, we shall make such an agreement that shall include you also, **13** on the following conditions:

That the Romans shall never be permitted to make war on you; that the Romans shall no longer have authority over Corcyra, Apollonia, Epidamnus, Pharos, Dimale, Parthini, or Atintania; **14** and that they shall hand back to Demetrius of Pharos all those of his friends who are in Roman territory;

15 That if the Romans should make war on you or on us, we shall help each other in the war, as may be required by either side; **16** that we shall do the same if any others do so, excepting the kings, cities and peoples, with whom we have sworn treaties and friendships; **17** that if we decide to withdraw from or add to this sworn treaty, we will withdraw or add such conditions as are agreed by both.

4.46 Marcus Claudius Marcellus in Sicily

ILS 12, 13

(*CIL* I² 608, 609; *ILLRP* 218, 295; *ROL* IV.76.) Below are two dedications found at Rome, dated to 211 BC; at 13, *vovit*, vowed, was originally inscribed and replaced by *dedit*, gave, when the vow was fulfilled. M. Claudius Marcellus (271–208 BC) was victorious in Sicily between 214 and 212; he had served in the First Punic War. Consul for the first time in 222 BC, at 46 years of age, when campaigning against the Insubrian Gauls he was challenged to single combat by the Gallic chief Viridomarus, whom he defeated and so won the *spolia opima*: the right to dedicate the enemy spoils. His force defeated the Gauls and captured their capital Mediolanum (Milan) in Cisalpine Gaul, and he celebrated a triumph (Plut. *Marcell.* 6–8; Flower 2000). For single combat between Romans and their enemies: Polyb. 6.54.3–4; Oakley 1985 (Marcellus at p. 395). Naevius' *Clastidium*, the first Roman historical play, celebrated Marcellus' victory over Viridomarus (cf. doc. 4.18).

Marcellus worked well with his colleague Fabius and in 214 they captured Casilinum. In the same year (214) Marcellus took up the command against Syracuse which had revolted on the death of Hiero, Rome's ally of the First Punic war, and conquered the city in 211 BC, celebrating an *ovatio* (*Marcell.* 13–19). The return of this city was crucial to Roman control of Sicily: most cities on the island now joined Rome with the notable exception of Agrigentum, which was taken in 210.

Back in Italy, in 208 BC Marcellus quieted Etruria which was ready to revolt, and made his way to Locri with the aim of defeating Hannibal in a decisive battle; he, his son, and his fellow consul (T. Quinctius Crispinus) were mortally ambushed at Venusia, the first time two consuls had fallen in a single action (Plut. *Marcell.* 29.18). Consul five times (222, 215, when he had to step down due to a peal of thunder during the election, 214, 210, and 208), his career has been overshadowed by that of Scipio Africanus; *MRR* I.232, 254, 259, 277, 289. Syracuse and the Carthaginian loss of Sicily: Baker 1929: 173–95; de Beer 1969: 237–43; Dorey & Dudley 1971: 119–33; Lazenby 1978: 115–19; Caven 1980: 162–5, 175–8; Scullard 1980: 216–19; Bradford 1981: 139–43; Briscoe 1989: 61–2; Bagnall 1990: 220–5; Lancell 1998: 124–7; Goldsworthy 2000: 260–7.

12 Marcus Claudius, son of Marcus, consul, took this (as booty) from Enna (in Sicily).

13 To Mars, Marcus Claudius, son of Marcus, consul, gave this.

4.47 Marcus Claudius Marcellus and Greek art

Plutarch *Life of Marcellus* 30.6–9

Archimedes, the great mathematician, was killed in the capture of Syracuse to Marcellus' regret; his many inventions had aided the defence of the walls: Livy 24.34.2–14; Plut. *Marcell.* 14.7, 14.12–18.1. Plut. 21.1–6 tells how Marcellus (unlike Fabius) brought Syracuse's works of art to Rome, to adorn the capital, the first massive influx of Greek art into Rome: Livy 25.40.1–3; Polyb. 9.10.2–13; Cic. *Verr.* 4.120–1; Lintott 1972; Rawson 1989: 432–3; Gruen 1992: 94–101; cf. docs 5.51–63.

6 The monuments which Marcellus dedicated, besides those in Rome, were a gymnasium at Catana in Sicily, and statues and tablets from Syracuse in the temple of the gods named the Cabiri in Samothrace and in the temple of Athena at Lindos. **7** On his statue there, as Posidonius tells us, the following epigram was inscribed:

8 This man, stranger, was the great star of his country, Rome,
Claudius Marcellus, of distinguished ancestors,
Seven times consul he protected her in warfare
Through which he launched plentiful death at the enemy.

9 The rank of pro-consul, which he held twice, the writer of the epigram has counted with his five consulates.

4.48 Q. Fabius Maximus 'Cunctator' recaptures Tarentum, 209 BC

Plutarch *Life of Fabius Maximus* 22.5–6, 23.1

The Romans had lost Tarentum in 213 through the revolt of the aristocrats (Polyb. 8.23–4; Livy 25.7.10–11.20). According to Plutarch, Fabius took the city by treachery with the help of a Bruttian contingent (whom he then slaughtered); Livy 27.16 says that the Bruttians were killed because of a feud with Rome.

22.5 At that point Fabius' love of honour appears to have taken a nose dive: he ordered his men to kill the Bruttians first, to hide the fact that he took the city by treachery;

however, he failed to win credit for this, and incurred a charge of bad faith and savagery. **6** Many of the Tarentines were slaughtered too, 30,000 were sold as slaves, and the city was sacked by the Roman army, while 3,000 talents found their way into the treasury ... **23.1** It is said that Hannibal had arrived within only 40 stades of the city, and in public remarked, 'The Romans have another Hannibal; we have lost the city of Tarentum as we took it,' though in private he then told his friends for the first time that he had seen for a long time that it would be difficult for them to conquer Italy with their existing forces, and now he saw it was impossible.

THE METAURUS, 22 JUNE 207 BC

Hannibal had relied on the peoples of Italy joining him against Rome, and had had some limited success. The Carthaginians had other military commitments in Spain and Sicily, and briefly in Sardinia (215), and, while Bomilcar in 215 had managed to land a small party of reinforcements at Locri in southern Italy, Hannibal had to manage with the force he brought in 218 and Italian additions. Mago Barca's contingent intended for Italy had been deployed instead in Spain because of Roman activities there.

The Massiliotes (from modern Marseilles, France) informed the Romans that Hasdrubal, son of Hamilcar Barca and Hannibal's brother, left in command of Spain by Hannibal in 218 BC, was on his way with reinforcements, and he crossed the Alps and entered Italy in 207 BC. For the Romans, the challenge was to prevent his joining forces with his brother Hannibal. Hannibal moved north to Grumentum, held by the consul C. Claudius Nero with four legions, and the brothers planned to join forces in Umbria; the Romans captured Hasdrubal's letter to this effect. Taking 6,000 infantry and 1,000 cavalry Nero marched north and joined the other consul M. Livius Salinator at the Metaurus river. Here the battle was evenly disposed until Nero took his right wing around behind the left of the Roman army and fell on the Carthaginian rear. Polybius gives 10,000 Carthaginian and Gauls and 2,000 Roman dead (11.3.3); Livy expands this to 56,000 enemy dead, and 8,000 Romans and allies, and makes it a second Cannae, this time for the Carthaginians. Hannibal could now expect no more reinforcements and was bogged down in Italy. For the Metaurus: Polyb. 11.1.1–3.6; Livy 27.43–9; Baker 1929: 236–7; Fuller 1954: 134–7; de Beer 1969: 264–8; Dorey & Dudley 1971: 85–6; Lazenby 1978: 182–90; Caven 1980: 208–16; Scullard 1980: 230–1; Bradford 1981: 169–77; Bagnall 1990: 263–6; Lancell 1998: 144–9; Goldsworthy 2000: 238–43.

4.49 Hasdrubal fails to reinforce Hannibal

Polybius *Histories* 11.1.1–3, 3.3–6

1 Hasdrubal's arrival in Italy was much easier and swifter than Hannibal's had been. Rome had never before been so expectant and terrified, awaiting the outcome ... **2** None of this pleased Hasdrubal, but with circumstances no longer permitting delay, since he saw the enemy advancing in battle formation, he was forced to draw up his Spaniards and the Gauls who were with him. **3** Positioning his elephants, who were ten in number, at the front, he increased the depth of his line, making his whole army very narrow, and then taking up his position in the centre of the line of battle behind the elephants he made his onslaught on the enemy's left, having resolved that in this crisis he had either to conquer or die ...

3.3 Not less than 10,000 Carthaginians and Gauls were killed in the battle, and about 2,000 Romans. Some distinguished Carthaginians were captured alive, and the rest were slain. **4** When the news reached Rome, they did not believe it at first, because they had so badly wanted to see this happen; **5** when more messengers came, not only reporting the event but giving exact details, the city was full of surpassing joy, and every shrine was decorated, every temple full of offerings and sacrificial victims, **6** and they generally became so confident and bold that everyone thought that Hannibal, whom they had been so terrified of earlier, was now not even in Italy.

4.50 Hasdrubal's head

Livy *History of Rome* 27.51.11–12

It was common for Romans to behead traitors, such as the Capuan senators who had allied the city with Hannibal (doc. 4.44). The Gauls were head-hunters: after the battle of Ticinus, some Gallic troops deserted Scipio, and brought Hannibal the heads of the Roman soldiers who had been camped near them (Polyb. 3.67). Postumius, consul-elect for 215, was ambushed and killed in Gaul in 216 by the Boii: they gilded his skull and used it as a sacred vessel for pouring libations at festivals (Livy 23.24.12).

11 After the consul, Gaius Claudius (Nero), had returned to his camp, he ordered that the head of Hasdrubal, which he had carefully kept and brought with him, be thrown in front of the enemy's outposts and that captured Africans be displayed, just as they were, in chains . . . **12** Hannibal, under the impact of so great an affliction, both public and private, is reported to have said that he could see the fate of Carthage.

SCIPIO AFRICANUS

The Scipio brothers had perished in Spain in 211. With the capture of Capua (211), the senate and people could concentrate on Spain (Livy 26.18.2: 'At Rome, once Capua had been recovered, the senate and people were no longer more worried about Italy than about Spain'). According to Livy none of the leading men put themselves forward for the command, when Publius Cornelius Scipio, 24 years old, suddenly did so (Livy 26.18). Duly appointed commander by the people, the younger Scipio continued the war, sent out as a private citizen, *privatus*, invested with *imperium pro consule* (Livy 26.18.4–11, 19.10–11), the first *privatus* to be so invested. In late 210 he arrived in Spain. Instead of continuing a war of attrition such as his father and uncle had fought, he decided to go for the jugular of Carthaginian Spain: New Carthage, where the Carthaginians kept huge amounts of supplies. All of the three Carthaginian generals, Hasdrubal Barca, Hasdrubal son of Gisgo, and Mago, were at least a march of a week or two away and none of them were on speaking terms. In 209, Scipio attacked the city frontally; a force sent across a shallow lagoon, the depth of which decreased in the afternoon, overwhelmed the defenders who were concentrating on the frontal attack; Scipio had promised the men that Neptune would come to their aid (Polyb. 10.8.1–20.8, Livy 26.42.2–46.10).

In 208, Hasdrubal Barca and Scipio fought at the Battle of Baecula; Scipio won through an outflanking tactic (Polyb. 10.34–40; Livy 27.17–20) and Hasdrubal Barca left with his remaining forces for Italy, to bring reinforcements to Hannibal (see doc. 4.49). The following year, 207, saw further Roman successes in Spain, and in 206 Hasdrubal son of Gisgo and Mago risked all — unsuccessfully — in battle with Scipio at Ilipa, near modern Seville (Polyb. 11.20–24.9; Livy 28.12.10–16.15). Carthaginian control of Spain ended in the same year, with no sizeable Carthaginian forces remaining after this battle. Scipio had, in a matter of a few years, captured Carthage's main overseas possession. Two Roman provinces were created in Spain in 197 BC; further wars followed and it was not until 19 BC that all of Spain was in Roman hands.

For the war in Spain, see Baker 1929: 211–16, 222–7; de Beer 1969: 252–5; Scullard 1970: 1–107 (New Carthage: 39–67), 1980: 225–9; Dorey & Dudley 1971: 95–118; Errington 1972: 80–92; Lazenby 1978: 125–56; Develin 1980; Caven 1980: 193–207; Briscoe 1989: 56–61; Lancell 1995: 392–5, 1998: 149–51; Kern 1999: 256–74; Goldsworthy 2000: 269–85; Scipio's command in Spain, and Africa: Vishnia 1996: 64–9, and 69–73. Book treatments of Scipio: Liddell Hart 1926; Haywood 1933; Scullard 1930, 1970.

4.51 The character of Scipio Africanus

Polybius *Histories* 10.3.1–7

The battle near the Po River was the battle of Ticinus in 218 (see Polyb. 3.64); according to Livy, Publius was 'just approaching manhood' at the time: 21.46.7. Laelius was an important source on Scipio for Polybius (10.3.2).

1 It is widely agreed that he (Scipio) was beneficent and magnanimous, but that he was also shrewd and discreet, with a mind always concentrated on the object in view, would only be admitted by those who had been closely associated with him and who had scrutinised his character, as it were, by the light of day. **2** One of these was Gaius Laelius (cos. 190), who from his boyhood until the end of his life had shared in his every word and deed, and who has produced this belief in me because his account seemed probable and in agreement with Scipio's actual achievements. **3** He says that Publius' first distinguished act was during the cavalry battle between his father and Hannibal near the river called the Po. **4** At the time he was 17 years of age and, this being his first campaign, his father had put him in command of a troop of picked cavalry to keep him safe and sound, but when he saw his father in danger, surrounded by the enemy with only two or three horsemen and badly wounded, he at first tried to urge his companions to assist his father, **5** and, when they hung back for a while because of the large numbers of enemy surrounding them, he is said to have recklessly and audaciously charged on his own against those encircling them. **6** Thereupon the others were also compelled to attack, and the enemy broke up in terror, while Publius, so unexpectedly saved, was the first to address his son as his preserver in the hearing of everyone. **7** Having won a universally acknowledged reputation for bravery through this service, for the future he seldom exposed himself to danger when the hopes of his entire country depended on him — which is a characteristic not of a leader who relies on luck, but of one who possesses intelligence.

4.52 Fabius Maximus disapproves of the young Scipio's methods

Plutarch *Life of Fabius Maximus* 25.1–4, 26.2–3, 27.1

Once elected to the consulship for 205 BC, Scipio requested Africa as his allocated province. Fabius opposed this, probably on the grounds discussed by Scullard: Fabius' outlook was wholly Italian, and his priority was to secure Italy, while Scipio, with his experience in Spain, had a wider Mediterranean perspective. In military terms, Fabius wanted to drive Hannibal from Italy, Scipio to defeat both Hannibal and Carthage (Scullard 1973: 75–6, 1980: 233). Scipio's initiative in putting himself forward for the Spanish command was reflected in the desire to go to Africa. Something of a compromise was effected in the allocation of troops to him: the two legions in Sicily, comprising the men who had survived Cannae and been sent to the island, more or less as a disciplinary measure. Scipio also raised volunteers, and his force was to prove very effective in Africa.

The Numidian prince Masinissa joined Scipio, who had negotiated with him from Spain, but the Numidian chief Syphax, king of the Masaesylii who had revolted from Carthage in 214, was now on Carthage's side, having married Sophonisba (Saphanba'al), daughter of Hasdrubal son of Gisgo; when Masinissa and C. Laelius defeated Syphax near Cirta in 203 she committed suicide (Livy 30.11–15).

The Roman siege of Utica occupied 204–203; it was an important port (included in the treaties: docs 4.2, 4.45). Two large Carthaginian camps were established nearby (Hasdrubal's camp with 30,000 foot and 3,000 horse; and the Numidian camp under Syphax, with 50,000 and 10,000 horse), and Scipio sent out insincere peace feelers while his envoys gathered intelligence information about the camps. These were made up of huts of brushwood, reed matting and the like and Scipio managed to set both camps on fire, killing most of the troops (Polyb. 14.5.7–11). Scipio's forces pursued those who escaped and Carthaginian hopes of containing the Romans in the area of Utica were shattered.

Hasdrubal escaped and with Syphax assembled a force of 20,000 men at the Great Plains 75 miles from Utica. When Scipio learned of this, he took a force in 'light marching order' (Polyb. 14.8.1) and destroyed the force in battle. Next, he took Tunis, a mere 10 kilometres from Carthage; the garrison had bolted. The capture of Syphax led the Carthaginians to sue for peace and the treaty was ratified at Rome. Before news came of Roman acceptance, a Roman supply fleet of 230 ships arriving from Sicily ran into a storm; Hasdrubal collected the ships and brought them to Carthage (Livy 34.24; some of Polybius' narrative is missing at this point; it resumes with Scipio's protest about the seizing of the ships: 15.1). Scipio sent ambassadors to protest, but the Carthaginians were clearly no longer interested in peace: Hannibal was on his way home. The Roman ambassadors were ambushed at sea on the way back to Scipio but escaped with their lives. When the Roman and Carthaginian ambassadors arrived back from Rome, Scipio informed them of what had happened; the peace was off. The scene was set for Zama in 202 BC.

The recall of Hannibal in 202 BC meant the end of his plan to capture Italy; for several years since 216 he had really only been active in southern Italy and was eventually more or less confined to Bruttium and the Lacinian promontory: 'They all knew well that Hannibal and his forces had, for two years now, withdrawn from the whole of Italy into the area around the Lacinian promontory, and, confined there and all but besieged, they had with difficulty saved themselves and left for (Africa)' (Polyb. 15.1.11).

For Scipio in Africa, including Zama and the consequent peace-treaty, see Polyb. 14.1–10, 15.19; Livy 29–30 (with Smith 1993); Baker 1929: 48–76; Picard & Picard 1968: 263–5; Warmington 1969: 211–22; Dorey & Dudley 1971: 134–52; Errington 1972: 257–69; Scullard 1970: 116–61, 1980: 232–9; Caven 1980: 230–58; Bradford 1981: 185–202; Briscoe 1989: 62–5; Bagnall 1990: 267–99; Raven 1993: 41–5; Lancell 1995: 396–404; Peddie 1997: 183–8; Goldsworthy 2000: 286–309; Hoyos 2003: 152–78; more detailed on Zama: Scullard 1970: 140–61; Lazenby 1978: 218–32; Lancell 1998: 158–85; for Scipio's earlier African campaigns, Scullard 116–39; Lazenby 193–217. Diagram of the battle of Zama: Baker 269; Goldsworthy 301; map of Scipio's operations at Utica and Tunis: Lancell 1998: 166.

25.1 Cornelius Scipio had been sent to Spain, defeating the Carthaginians in numerous battles and driving them from the country, as well as winning for the Romans the support of many tribes, large cities, and splendid victories. When he returned to Rome, he possessed more good-will and a better reputation than anyone ever before, and was elected consul (205 BC). Recognising that the people demanded and expected a great exploit from him, he decided that the strategy of engaging with Hannibal in Italy was quite out of date and overcautious, and resolved to immediately pour troops and armies into Libya and ravage Carthage herself, so transferring the war scene from Italy to Africa, and he encouraged the people to support this plan with all his enthusiasm. **2** Fabius, however, did his best to spread fear through the city, on the grounds that they were being led into extreme risks by a thoughtless young man, and spared neither words nor deeds which he thought might deter his fellow-citizens. He convinced the senate, but the people thought that he was jealous of Scipio's success and afraid that, if Scipio achieved some great and splendid success and either completely ended the war or took it out of Italy, he himself might appear to be lazy and cowardly for having let the war drag on for so long. **3** It seems likely that originally Fabius' drive to oppose Scipio was due to his great caution and foresight, fearing the risks, which were indeed great, while his effort to prevent Scipio's increasing influence made him more violent and extreme, and brought in an element of rivalry and competition. He even tried to persuade (P. Licinius) Crassus, Scipio's fellow consul, not to hand over the army but to lead it across himself, if the resolution was taken, and did not allow Scipio to be given money for the war. **4** Scipio was therefore forced to find the money himself, and raised it privately from the cities in Etruria, as they were personally devoted to him; Crassus was kept at home partly by his nature, as he was not quarrelsome, but mild, and partly on religious grounds, as he held the highest priesthood . . .

26.2 Fabius managed to frighten the Romans, and they voted that Scipio should use only the troops already in Sicily, and take with him 300 of the men who had served him loyally in Spain. Fabius appears to have followed this policy through his innate caution. **3** But when Scipio crossed to Libya (204 BC), news of wonderful achievements and victories, splendid in both size and glory, immediately reached Rome, and immense booty followed as proof of these reports, including the King of Numidia as a prisoner, and the burning and destruction of two enemy camps together with numerous men, weapons and horses, and envoys were sent to Hannibal by the Carthaginians, asking and begging him to leave his fruitless hopes in Italy and come to help them at home . . .

27.1 Not long afterwards, Scipio defeated Hannibal in a pitched battle (Zama), overthrowing fallen Carthage's pride and trampling it underfoot, thus giving his fellow-citizens a joy greater than any they had hoped for and restoring their supremacy.

4.53 The battle of Zama, 202 BC

Polybius *Histories* 15.14.1–9

See Polyb. 15.5.3–10 for the background to the battle and the battle itself; Livy 30.29–35 (other sources given at Walbank II.446).

Scipio had marched his troops out to the Great Plains and Hannibal encamped nearby at Zama, about 160 kilometres south-west of Carthage. Scipio and Hannibal, at Hannibal's request, met for a conference, both having moved camps: Scipio to the (unknown) town of Margaron (Livy's Naragarra), Hannibal to within 30 stades. Hannibal argued for peace, but Scipio replied that the Carthaginians had already rejected one peace offer (Polyb. 15.5–8; Livy 30.30–1). Scipio had the upper hand: after a string of successes in Spain and Africa, he was up against a Hannibal who had won no major battle since 216. They then proceeded to battle. Polyb. 15.9.2: 'On the next morning, at dawn, both sides led out their forces and joined battle, the Carthaginians for their own safety and control of Libya and the Romans for the empire and domination of the world'. The battle did not actually take place at Zama, where Hannibal was no longer encamped, but this is the name the battle has been given (Walbank II.446).

Forces: Hannibal had 36,000 infantry, 4,000 cavalry, and 80 elephants, outnumbering Scipio's 29,000 infantry and 6,000 cavalry. Hannibal drew up his 80 elephants, more than he had ever used in battle, in front, but Scipio had left gaps in the Roman line through which some of them passed (Polyb. 15.12.3–4; Livy 30.33.5). Some of the elephants in fact charged the Numidian cavalry supporting the Carthaginians on the left, which Masinissa then attacked and routed. Laelius' cavalry attacked the right wing of the Carthaginian cavalry. The infantry advanced on each other, the Roman infantry in three lines, under Scipio: hastati, principes, and the triarii (see commentary to doc. 5.11). Hannibal also had three lines, the first of mercenaries, the second of Libyans and Carthaginians, and the third of the troops he had brought with him from Italy, separated out by a space from the first two lines (Livy 30.35.6–9 has an inaccurate account of Hannibal's dispositions). The Romans eventually prevailed against the first two lines. There was so much carnage that Scipio reformed his troops and the battle proceeded as Polybius describes below. On the arrival of the cavalry of Masinissa and Laelius 'in the nick of time' at 30.14.7–8, it is not melodramatic to state: 'the cavalry had arrived in time to decide the course, not only of the battle, but of the world's history' (Scullard 1980: 237).

1 The space between the remaining armies was full of blood, slaughter, and corpses, and this obstacle to his pursuit of the enemy put the Roman general in a great quandary; **2** for the slippery nature of the corpses, which were covered in blood and had fallen in heaps, and the piles of arms, which had been thrown away at random along with the bodies, would make it difficult for his men to remain in their ranks while crossing the ground. **3** Nevertheless, after moving the wounded to the rear of the army and calling back by trumpet those of the hastati who were pursuing the enemy, he placed these in the front of the battle opposite the enemy's centre, **4** and, getting the principes and triarii to close their ranks on each wing, ordered them to advance through the dead. **5** When these had got across and were in a line with the hastati, the phalanxes engaged with each other with the greatest eagerness and enthusiasm. **6** As both sides were a good match in numbers, spirit, courage and armour, the battle was for a long time undecided, with men falling honourably where they stood, **7** until Masinissa and Laelius returned from pursuing the cavalry and joined battle fortuitously at the right moment. **8** When they fell on Hannibal's men from the rear, most of them were cut down in their ranks, while few of those who fled managed to escape, as the cavalry were nearby and the region was level. **9** More than 1,500 Romans fell, and more than 20,000 Carthaginians, with nearly as many being taken prisoner. **15.1** This was the outcome of the final battle between the two afore-mentioned commanders, the one which decided everything in the Romans' favour.

4.54 Livy's praise for Hannibal at Zama

Livy *History of Rome* 30.35.3–5, 37.13

35.4: Hadrumentum was Hannibal's base (Livy 30.29.1). **35.10**: Hannibal was nine years old when he left Carthage for Spain. **37.13**: Hannibal was elected as one of the two suffetes in 196. He did not leave Carthage until 195, driven into exile by enemies at home who accused him of intriguing with Antiochus III; he spent several years with Antiochus (doc. 5.29), then from 187–183 with King Prusias of Bithynia. He committed suicide in 183 when Prusias decided to surrender him to Flamininus. For this latter part of his career: Baker 1929: 277–309; Bradford 1981: 203–9; Lancell 1995: 401–4, 1998: 186–224; cf. Scullard 1983: 284. The fact that Scipio defended Hannibal in the Roman senate in 196 and that Rome tolerated Hannibal's presence in Carthage from 201 to 196 is interesting.

35.3 Over 20,000 of the Carthaginians and their allies were killed on that day; about the same number were captured, with 132 military standards and 11 elephants; about 1,500 of the victors fell. **4** In the commotion Hannibal escaped with a few of his cavalry and fled to Hadrumentum. He had tried everything possible both before the battle and during it before he left the fighting, **5** and even by Scipio's admission and that of all the military experts he deserved praise for having drawn up his battle-line that day with remarkable skill . . .

10 After performing this as his last act of military skill, Hannibal fled to Hadrumentum, but was summoned from there to Carthage, returning in the thirty-sixth year since he had left it as a boy. **11** In the senate house he admitted that he had not only been conquered in the battle but in the war, and that there was no hope of safety except in treating for peace . . . **37.13** Some authors relate that Hannibal went straight from the battle to the coast, and then, on a ship prepared for him, sailed immediately to King Antiochus, and that when Scipio demanded that Hannibal be surrendered to him before everything else, the answer was that Hannibal was not in Africa.

4.55 Lucilius on Hannibal

Lucilius *Satires* 29.3.952–3

(*ROL* III.306.) This quotation probably concerns Hannibal's defeat at Zama, 202, when Scipio's tactics neutralised Hannibal's elephants.

. . . that in this way, I say, that old fox, that old wolf
Hannibal was taken in.

4.56 Scipio Africanus the hero

Ennius *Scipio* 1–6

(*ROL* I.398–400.) Ennius devoted a whole poem to the African campaigns of his friend Scipio, who was given the cognomen 'Africanus' for his victories there. This was the highpoint of his career: he was censor in 199, consul again in 194, with minor campaigns in northern Italy, envoy to Masinissa and Carthage in 193, and legate to Asia in 190. In 187 BC he was attacked in the senate and his brother Lucius was put on trial; Scipio himself was indicted for trial in 184, but went into self-exile in Campania, dying in 183. For the trials of the Scipios, see Polybius 23.14.1–11; Livy 38.50.4–60; Scullard 1970, 210–24, 1973: 290–303, 1980: 336–7; for the divine descent of Scipio, see Livy 26.19.6–8; for Ennius' *Scipio*, see Skutsch 1985: 3.

From the rising sun above the marshes of Maiotis
There is no one able to match his deeds . . .
If it is right for anyone to ascend to the regions of the gods
To me alone heaven's great gate lies open . . .
Here lies that man to whom no citizen or enemy
Will be able to render a recompense befitting his services.

4.57 Satires on the Roman commanders

Naevius *Unassigned Fragment from Comedy (fabula togata)* 1–3

(*ROL* II.138.) Naevius was less generous than Ennius, and appears to have retailed scandal about Scipio; for Scipio's hellenising dress (the *pallium*), see doc. 5.51; for his amatory adventures, see Polyb. 10.19.3–7; Plut. *Mor.* 196b; Gell. 7.8.5; Val. Max. 6.7.1; Scullard 1973: 253–4; Jocelyn 1969: 38–9; Gruen 1990: 93–102, esp. 100–2.

Even he, who often with his hand gloriously achieved great exploits,
Whose deeds now live and flourish, pre-eminent among all nations,
He, with just a single cloak (pallium), was dragged by his father from his mistress.

PEACE TERMS

The peace treaty came into effect in 201 BC. After Zama, the defeat of all their forces and of their last hope, Hannibal, the Carthaginians had to surrender, or else endure a long siege. Hannibal was instrumental in arguing for peace (Polyb. 15.19.1–9, Livy 30.37.7–10). The Second Punic War was over; for the effects it had on Italy: Brunt *IM* 269–77; Cornell 1996; and (generally) Toynbee 1965.

4.58 Peace terms offered to Carthage

Polybius *Histories* 15.18.1–8

See Livy 30.37 for the same terms. Compare the previous conditions that Rome had proposed in 203, which were a little more lenient: Livy 30.16. The terms were crushing, but Carthage would survive.

1 The main points of the terms proposed were as follows: Carthage was to retain all the cities she had earlier possessed in Africa before entering on the last war against the Romans, and all her former territory, all flocks and herds, slaves and other property; **2** from that day onward the Carthaginians were to suffer no further injury, they were to be governed by their own laws and customs and not have a garrison. **3** These were the lenient conditions; the others of an opposite nature were as follows: the Carthaginians were to pay reparation to the Romans for all acts of injustice during the truce; prisoners of war and deserters who had come into their hands at any time were to be handed over; all ships of war, with the exception of ten triremes were to be handed over, **4** as were all elephants; they were not to make war on any people outside Libya at all, and on none in Libya without the Romans' consent; **5** they were to restore to King Masinissa all the houses, territory, cities and other property which had belonged to him or to his ancestors within the boundaries which were to be assigned to him; **6** they were to provide the Roman army with corn for three months and with pay until a reply should be received from Rome concerning the treaty; **7** they were to pay an indemnity of 10,000 talents of silver over a period of 50 years in instalments of 200 Euboic talents each year; **8** and they were to hand over as a guarantee of good faith 100 hostages, to be chosen by the Roman commander from the young men between the ages of fourteen and thirty.

4.59 Scipio's triumph, 201 BC

Livy *History of Rome* 30.45.1–7

No real details are given in Polybius 16.23; the most descriptive account is App. *Pun.* 66; cf. Val. Max. 6.2.3. This is the first time Livy mentions Polybius (cf. 33.10.10 where a statement of his — 'a not unknown author' — is preferred). Scipio celebrated his triumph over Hannibal, the Poeni (Carthaginians) and Syphax. (Scipio had not been given a triumph for his Spanish success because he was a *privatus* at that time.) Culleo was a senator, captured in Africa. This is the end of Livy's ten books on the war against Hannibal.

1 With peace made by land and sea, and his army embarked on ships, Scipio crossed to Lilybaeum in Sicily. **2** After sending a large proportion of his soldiers on shipboard, he made his way to Rome through Italy, which was enjoying peace just as much as the victory, while not only cities poured out to honour him, but crowds of countryfolk also blocked the roads, and on his arrival he rode into the city in the most distinguished of all triumphs. **3** He brought into the treasury 123,000 pounds of silver in weight. To his soldiers he distributed 400 asses each from the booty. **4** Syphax by his death was removed rather from the sight of the spectators than from the glory of the triumphing general; he had died not long before at Tibur, where he had been taken from Alba. However his death attracted general notice because he was given a state funeral. **5** Polybius states that this king was led in the triumph, and he is an authority not to be lightly dismissed. Following Scipio as he triumphed was Quintus Terentius Culleo, wearing a liberty cap, who for the rest of his life, as was proper, honoured Scipio as the author of his freedom. **6** Whether his popularity with the soldiers or the favour of the people first gave him the honorific surname of Africanus, just like Felix for Sulla and Magnus for Pompey in our fathers' time, I cannot say. **7** He was certainly the first general to be distinguished by the name of a nation conquered by him; later, following his example, men who were in no way his equals in victory won eminent superscriptions for their masks and glorious surnames for their families.

4.60 War bonds, 200 BC

Livy *History of Rome* 31.13.1–9

In 210, businessmen had loaned money to the state to enable Rome to continue the war against Hannibal (Livy 26.28.8), and an arrangement was made in 204 that this loan should be repaid in three instalments, payable every two years. The third instalment of this loan by businessmen to the state, due in 200, was not actually repaid until 196 to those who preferred not to take up the option offered in this passage (33.42.3): even though the Punic War was over, Rome was still involved in war against Philip of Macedon.

1 When the consuls were ready to set off to their provinces, **2** a number of private citizens, who were owed this year the third instalment of repayment on the loans made in the consulship of Marcus Valerius (Laevinus) and Marcus Claudius (Marcellus), appealed to the senate, **3** as the consuls had stated that, because the treasury had hardly enough funds for the new war, which was to be waged with a great fleet and great armies, there was no money at present to make them this payment. **4** The senate could not withstand their complaints: if the state wanted to use for the Macedonian War the money lent for the Punic War, with one war arising after another, what would happen except that in return for their generosity, their money would be confiscated, as if it had been a crime?

5 Since these private citizens were making a reasonable request, but the state was nevertheless unable to pay back the loan, **6** the senate decided on a middle course halfway between justice and expediency: that, because many of the creditors said there was land for sale everywhere, land which they would like to buy, they should be given the opportunity to receive public land within the fiftieth milestone from the city. **7** The consuls were to give a valuation on the land and impose a rent of one *as* per iugerum to show that it was still public land; **8** when the state was able to pay its debts, if any of them preferred to have the money, rather than the land, he could give the land back to the people. **9** The private citizens happily accepted this arrangement.

THE THIRD PUNIC WAR, 151–146 BC

Rome and Carthage made peace in 201 BC. Carthage made a quick economic recovery, and by the 150s was once again prosperous. Its main problem was with Masinissa king of Numidia (c. 238–148 BC), Scipio Africanus' ally of the Second Punic War, who by the peace was granted all his ancestral lands. He took this to mean that he could continually encroach on Carthaginian territory. The Carthaginians complained to Rome in 153 about Masinissa, and an embassy, including Cato, was sent from Rome, which saw how prosperous and populous Carthage had become (App. *Pun.* 69). Upon his return, therefore, Cato ended every senatorial speech with 'Delenda est Carthago': 'Carthage must be destroyed' (doc. 4.61). In this policy, Cato was opposed by Scipio Nasica (censor 159) who unsuccessfully advocated a more lenient policy towards Carthage, according to the ancient sources on the grounds that Rome needed a rival to keep Rome warlike: see Livy *Per.* 49; App. 69; cf. Diod. 32.5 (Polyb. F99); Astin 1967: 276–80; Harris 1979: 234–40; Scullard 1980: 309.

The Carthaginians eventually declared war on Masinissa (violating the terms of their peace with Rome) in 151/50 BC; the Carthaginians gave in when Masinissa besieged their army camp (App. 70–3). Polybius considers that the Romans had been looking for an excuse to make war against Carthage, preferring to fight 'just' wars (36.2.1–3; cf. doc. 3.12), and the Carthaginian campaign against Masinissa in 151 (despite being a failure) provided one (App. 74). War was declared in 149 BC just before a Carthaginian embassy arrived in Rome. Finding war declared, the embassy surrendered Carthage 'to the faith of Rome' (Polyb. 36.3.9; explained at 35.4.1–3: *deditio in fidem*: complete and utter surrender of all territory, cities, people and possessions to Rome). The senate accepted this but demanded that 300 hostages be sent to Lilybaeum in Sicily and obedience to the orders of the consuls (which were not specified). The hostages were duly handed over.

Cato's opinion that the senate should adhere to its declaration of war prevailed (Livy *Per.* 49). Manius Manilius and the other consul for 149, L. Marcius Censorinus, were sent to Africa, and demanded that the Carthaginians hand over all their arms: 200,000 sets of arms and 2,000 catapults were surrendered (Livy *Per.* 48, in pro-Roman fashion, has them specifically made for use not against Masinissa, but against Rome). The Carthaginians, however, refused to accede to the consuls' request that they abandon their city, and settle at least ten (Roman) miles from the sea, and the consuls began the war, with limited success.

The war dragged on into 148, with the Romans under the consul L. Calpurnius Piso Caesoninus making little progress. P. Cornelius Scipio Aemilianus, the second son of L. Aemilius Paullus, but adopted by P. Cornelius Scipio, the son of *the* Scipio (victor of 201 BC), was then elected to the consulship for 147 BC, though he had not held the aedileship or praetorship; he was also several years under age. In fact he was standing for the aedileship when elected consul! The age limit was set aside for one year to allow his election (App. 112; Livy *Per.* 50). His reputation (won in Greece, Spain and Africa), general impatience with the ongoing war, and popular support secured him the consulship and he restored discipline and morale in the Roman army in Africa and campaigned energetically (App. 115–17) as he did later in 134 at Numantia (docs 5.49–50). For his command against Carthage: Astin 1967: 48–80, 270–87; see *MRR* I.459, 462, 463, 490.

The Third Punic War saw the deaths or enslavement of thousands of Carthaginians and the destruction of a city with a long history and vibrant culture; it was almost certainly unnecessary and counts as one of the great tragedies of Mediterranean history. But Scipio won his *gloria*, a great triumph was celebrated, and Rome moved on to its next round of conquests. For the Third Punic War, for which there is no separate book treatment in English, see Walbank III.653–58, 677–8 (with Baronowski 1993); Hallworth & Charlesworth 1930; Picard 1964: 119–51; Astin 1967: 48–80, 270–87; Picard & Picard 1968: 285–98; Warmington 1969: 223–42; Dorey & Dudley 1971: 153–74; Errington 1972: 260–8; Bagnall 1990: 313–20; Caven 1980: 273–94; Scullard 1980: 306–17; Badian *FC* 125–40; Raven 1993: 45–8; Baronowski 1995; Lancell 1998: 404–27; Gilliver 1999: 158–9; Goldsworthy 2000: 331–56; Cato and Carthage: Astin 1978: 125–30, 283–8.

4.61 Carthage must be destroyed!

Plutarch *Life of Cato the Elder* 26.1–27.5

Carthage was of course usually much more than three days by sea from Rome; Cato's fig will probably have come from his own estates or have been purchased by Cato on his way to the senate from a vendor in the forum. Cato was a decisive influence in the declaration of war but whether he was the foremost articulator of senatorial fears or actually moulded senatorial policy is unclear. He died in 149 BC.

26.1 The last of Cato's public services is said to have been the destruction of Carthage. It was actually Scipio the Younger who completed the work, but the war was undertaken mainly on the counsel and advice of Cato, in the following way. **2** Cato was sent to the Carthaginians and Masinissa the Numidian who were at war with each other, to inquire into the reasons for their conflict. Masinissa had been a friend of the Roman people from the beginning, and the Carthaginians had entered into a treaty with Rome after their defeat by Scipio (Africanus), which deprived them of their empire and imposed a heavy monetary indemnity. **3** Finding, however, that the city was not, as the Romans thought, in a poor and unprosperous state, but well-populated with good fighting men, teeming with immense wealth, full of all kinds of arms and provisions for war, and not a little proud of this, Cato thought that it was not the time for the Romans to be organising the affairs of the Numidians and Masinissa; rather, if they did not now put a stop to the city which had always been their most hostile enemy and was now grown to so unbelievable an extent, they would once more be in danger as great as before. **4** So he quickly returned to Rome and advised the senate that the former defeats and disasters of the Carthaginians had lessened not so much their power as their foolishness, and that these were likely to make them in the end not weaker, but more skilful in warfare, while their conflict with the Numidians was a prelude to conflict with the Romans, and peace and treaty were just names for a war which was waiting for a suitable opportunity to arise . . . **27.1** In addition to this, it is reported that Cato arranged to drop a Libyan fig in the senate when he shook out the folds of his toga. To the senators who admired its size and beauty, he remarked that the country where it grew was only three days' sail from Rome. **2** And in one respect he was even more violent, in that whenever he gave his vote on any issue whatever he would add the words: 'In my view Carthage must be destroyed!' . . . **5** In this way Cato is said to have brought about the third and last war against the Carthaginians.

4.62 The destruction of Carthage

Appian *Roman History (Punic Wars)* 8.128–30 (610–17, 620)

Appian has the most detailed account of the physical destruction of the city: *Pun.* 127–32; it is he who refers to Polybius' presence with Scipio at the sack (*Pun.* 132.629; cf. Polyb. 36.12.2 (the fragmentary book about the Third Punic War): 'I (Polybius) was much involved in the events I am about to record'. Hasdrubal, the Carthaginian commander, when everywhere was lost except the inaccessible temple of Asclepius, surrendered to Scipio in person, but his wife reproached him, calling to him from the temple, slew their two boys, threw them into the burning temple, and then immolated herself: 'so did the wife of Hasdrubal die, as Hasdrubal ought to have' (App. *Pun.* 131.625–7). For the 'calling out' of the Carthaginian gods from the city by Scipio Aemilianus, see doc. 3.56; for Scipio's tears as Carthage was destroyed, and his musing on the rise and fall of empires, quoting Homer *Iliad* 6.448–9, see App. 132.629–30; Astin 1967: 282–7.

What was left of Carthage was destroyed on the senate's orders; would-be settlers were cursed, but not the ground itself. Archaeology has shown that massive ruins nevertheless survived, especially of the six-storey buildings Appian describes. Scipio did not have the ruins ploughed nor the earth salted, and the first mention in literature of the sowing of the earth of Carthage with salt is modern: Hallward & Charlesworth 1930: 484; Visonà 1988; Lancell 1995: 428. The Gracchan colony there was abandoned after supposedly bad omens (doc. 8.30; App. *Pun.* 136); Julius Caesar's colonisation plan came to nothing but Augustus acted upon it. The new foundation, which prospered, was the capital of the province of Africa; for Roman Carthage: Lancell 1995: 430; cf. Raven 1993: 54–121; Miles 2003; for Roman involvement in Africa after 146 BC, see esp. docs 9.6–13.

610 Scipio's energies were directed towards an attack on Byrsa; this was the most strongly fortified part of the city, and most of the inhabitants had taken refuge there. There were three streets leading up to it, with densely packed, six-storey houses on all sides, from which the Romans were targeted, but they captured the first houses and from them attacked those on the neighbouring houses. **611** When they had taken these over, they placed planks and boards over the narrow passages between and crossed as if on bridges. **612** While one battle was taking place up on the roofs, another was going on in the streets as opponents met each other. Everywhere was full of groaning, shrieks, cries and all kinds of suffering; some were killed hand-to-hand, others were thrown alive down from the roofs to the pavement, some falling onto the points of spears, or other sharp points, or swords. **613** No one as yet began lighting fires until Scipio had reached Byrsa; then he set fire to the three streets altogether, and ordered that the burning streets be made passable so that the troops as they moved position might pass through freely. **614** After this came new horrific scenes, as the fire consumed and ravaged everything, with the soldiers destroying the houses not little by little, but demolishing them all at once. **615** The crashing became much louder, and with the stones fell heaps of corpses. Others were still living, especially old men and children and women, who had hidden in the recesses of houses, some wounded, others half-burnt, uttering hideous cries. **616** Still others, being hurled and falling from so great a height along with stones, and timbers and fire, were torn into various horrible shapes, smashed and broken. **617** Nor was this the end of their sufferings; for the stone-movers who were removing the rubbish with axes, mattocks and poles and clearing the streets to make them passable, removed the dead and those still living into holes in the ground, some with axes and mattocks, others with the hooks on their poles, sweeping them like timber or stones, or turning them over with iron tools — and humans were used for filling up ditches . . .

620 Six days and nights were spend in such labours, with the soldiers working in rotation so they might not be worn out with sleeplessness, toil, slaughter and hideous sights.

4.63 The site of Carthage and its destruction by Scipio Aemilianus

Strabo *Geography* 17.3.14–15

Most of these details are taken from App. *Pun.* 13–14. Ten ships, not twelve, were mentioned in the Second Punic War treaty. Strabo here refers to the numbers of arms surrendered at the demand of the consuls for 149 BC.

14 Carthage, too, is situated on a kind of peninsula, which comprises a circuit of 360 stades, this circuit having a wall, while 60 stades of its length are taken up by the neck itself from sea to sea, which is where the Carthaginians had their elephant-stalls and is a spacious place. Near the centre of the city was the acropolis, which they called Byrsa, a fairly steep hill inhabited all around, with at the top the temple of Asclepius, which the wife of Hasdrubal burnt during the sack, along with herself. The harbours lie below the acropolis, as does Cothon, a circular island surrounded by a strait which has ship-sheds all around on both sides.

15 . . . The Carthaginians' power should appear evident from the last war, in which they were defeated by Scipio Aemilianus and their city utterly destroyed. For when they began to wage this war, they possessed 300 cities in Libya, and had 700,000 people in the city, and, when they were under siege and compelled to turn to surrender, they gave up 200,000 suits of armour and 3,000 catapults, on the understanding that there would not be a war again; but when they decided to recommence the war, they suddenly organised weapons manufacture, and each day produced 140 fitted shields, 300 swords, 500 spears and 1,000 catapult missiles, and the women slaves provided the hair for the catapults. Moreover, though they only had 12 ships for 50 years earlier in accordance with the treaty made in the second war, they then, although they had already fled for refuge into the Byrsa, constructed 120 decked ships in two months, and, since the mouth of Cothon was being guarded, they dug another mouth, from which the fleet unexpectedly sailed out; for old timber had been stored away and a large number of craftsmen were in waiting and maintained at public expense. But despite all this, Carthage was still captured and razed to the ground.

4.64 Carthaginians continue in Sardinia

CIL I² 2225

(*ILLRP* 158; *ROL* IV.84.) A marble pedestal inscribed in both Latin and Punic, found on Sardinia, dating to not earlier than the time of Sulla; for Carthaginian religious and linguistic 'survivals', see Picard 1964: 152, 169–80; Lancell 1995; 430–8.

To Himilco, son of Idnibal, who superintended the construction of this temple by the state's decree, his son Himilco set up this statue.

5

Rome's Mediterranean Empire

Rome's first encounter with Macedon (The First Macedonian War) took place following Philip V's alliance with Hannibal in 215 BC (doc. 4.45); Philip hoped to force the
Romans to withdraw from the Illyrian coast. It was in this context that the Romans
sent envoys to Greek states hostile to Macedon, and Marcus Valerius Laevinus made
a treaty with the Aetolians against Philip in 212/11 BC (doc. 5.22). This was Rome's
first alliance in the Eastern Mediterranean.

Prior to 205 Antiochus III of Syria (223–187) was occupied with restoring Seleucid
control of Armenia and Iran (Polyb. 11.39.11–16), after which he adopted the title of
Great King and attempted to regain control of western Asia Minor. He then took
advantage of the death of Ptolemy Philopator of Egypt in 204 to invade Coele Syria
and seize the Egyptian possessions of Phoenicia and Palestine. The peace of Phoenice
was made between Philip and Rome in 205, but from 203 Philip, after some incursions
into Illyria, continued his expansion in the Aegean, defeating Rhodes, capturing Miletus
and attacking Pergamum. In 201 Rhodes and Attalus, king of Pergamum, requested
Roman aid (Livy 31.2.1–3). Envoys were sent to Philip demanding that he make war
against no Greek states and pay compensation to Attalus (Polyb. 16.27.2–3); the envoys
then proceeded to Egypt to request Ptolemy's support, should war eventuate against
Philip (Livy 31.2.3–4; cf. Polyb. 16.34.2–3). Rome decided on war, despite an initial
vote against it in the assembly (which suggests that it was less popular with the people
than with the magisterial class), to be under the command of Publius Sulpicius Galba,
one of the consuls for 200, who received Macedonia as his province (Livy 31.6.1–8.2);
Philip meanwhile was ravaging Attica, and besieging Abydus to gain control of the
Hellespont. The Aetolians again joined Rome in 199, and in 198 the Achaean league
broke its alliance with Macedon and defected to Rome. Flamininus, consul in 198,
promoted the image of Rome as liberator of Philip's Greek possessions from Macedon
and won the support of southern and central Greece by early 197. Philip was defeated
at the battle of Cynoscephalae in 197 and agreed to withdraw from Greece, including
the 'Three Fetters' of Greece: Demetrias, Chalcis and Acrocorinth (doc. 5.23). In 196,
at the Isthmian Games, Flamininus proclaimed the unrestricted freedom of the Greeks
(doc. 5.24), and in 194 all Roman troops were finally withdrawn.

Antiochus III had taken advantage of Rome's war against Philip to recover coastal
territories in Asia Minor in 197, attacking Smyrna and Lampsacus in the winter or spring
of 196 and crossing to Europe where he rebuilt the town of Lysimachia on the Thracian

coast. Hannibal fled from Carthage to Antiochus in 195, which intensified Rome's concern. Envoys were sent to Antiochus at Lysimachia to demand that he leave the autonomous cities of Asia Minor alone and withdraw from those that had belonged to Ptolemy; if he did not withdraw from Europe Rome would interfere on behalf of the freedom of the Greeks in Asia (Polyb. 18.49.3–51.10). Antiochus continued military activities in Thrace in 193 and 192; meanwhile the disgruntled Aetolians captured Demetrias, but failed to take Sparta and Chalcis (Livy 35.31–9). At their invitation Antiochus crossed to Demetrias in the autumn of 192, thus provoking war with Rome. In spring 191, the consul Manius Acilius Glabrio took charge with 20,000 men. With little support from within Greece, Antiochus decided to make a stand at Thermopylae and his army was totally defeated. Lucius Scipio (brother of Africanus) and Gaius Laelius were elected consuls for 190; after arranging a truce with the Aetolians the Scipio brothers led the first Roman army into Asia in autumn 190, where Antiochus was defeated at Magnesia. He agreed to the Romans' terms at the peace of Apamea, signed in 188 (doc. 5.29).

In 184 or 183 Philip was instructed to withdraw his garrisons from Thracian cities claimed by Eumenes of Pergamum (Polyb. 22.13.1–2, 23.1.1–4, 3.1–3; Livy 39.33.1–34.1, 46.6–9, 53.10). Demetrius, Philip's younger son, who had been a hostage in Rome, returned in 183 and was murdered in 180 for supposedly plotting with the Romans to seize the throne: Livy 40.20.3–6, 24.1–8, 54.1–55.8. Following Philip's death in 179, his son Perseus tried to reassert Macedon's position against the background of increasing intransigence from Rome. When Eumenes of Pergamum brought charges against Perseus in 172, Perseus was declared an enemy and the war (the Third Macedonian War) was entrusted to the consuls of 171 (Livy 42.11.1–13.12, 18.1–5). After some Macedonian successes, Perseus was finally manoeuvred by Lucius Aemilius Paullus, cos. 182 and 168, into giving battle at Pydna (Livy 44.41.1–42.9); his army was defeated. He later surrendered at Samothrace and featured in Paullus' triumph.

Rome was involved in new theatres of war in the 150s, such as Dalmatia c. 155 (according to Polybius to check the effeminacy at Rome caused by twelve years of peace: 32.13.6–8; Livy Per. 46–7); Spain from 154 to 133; Macedonia, where a pretender, Andriscus, had initial successes in 149, but was captured in 148 (Polyb. 36.10.2–7; Livy Per. 49–52); and Carthage and mainland Greece in 146, when Corinth was sacked and enslaved by the consul Lucius Mummius (doc. 5.40). The destruction of Carthage by Scipio Aemilianus ended the long tension between Rome and Carthage (docs 4.61–3), while the sack of Corinth saw Greece, with Macedonia, become a Roman province. Asia Minor was to follow, with the death of Attalus III in 134/3 (doc. 5.44).

In the West, from 201 to 190 one or both consuls had been assigned to the Gallic region to reconquer the tribes that had regained their freedom with the arrival of Hannibal. These were finally subdued by Publius Scipio Nasica as consul in 191. The Latin colonies of Cremona and Placentia (both established in 218) were resettled in 206 and reinforced in 190 (Livy 37.46.9–47.2), with further colonies such as Bononia, Forum Livii, Regium Lepidum, Parma and Mutina, and Aquileia established in the 180s. Spain, at the beginning of the second century, consisted of cities of Punic or Greek character on the coast with numerous independent peoples in the interior. The Romans initially became involved in Spain to drive out the Carthaginians. Following Scipio Africanus' victory at Ilipa, two Spanish provinces (Hispania Ulterior, 'Further', and Citerior, 'Nearer') were created, signifying that control and conquest of Spain had become governmental policy (Livy 32.28.11). In 198 two new praetorships were created for these Spanish provinces (Livy 32.27.6). Cato was to serve in Spain as consul in 195 (doc. 5.45), while both Tiberius Sempronius Gracchus (the elder) and Lucius Aemilius Paullus governed one of the Spanish provinces. Roman misgovernment led to escalating warfare from the middle of the century (docs 5.47–8), until the last real stronghold of Spanish resistance, Numantia, was finally destroyed by Scipio Aemilianus in 133 (docs 5.49–50).

Ancient sources: most valuable is the extensive epigraphic evidence, from the Hellenistic East and elsewhere recording treaties (docs 5.22), edicts (docs 5.25, 46), dedications by victorious commanders (docs 5.32, 41–2) and *senatus consulta* and letters (docs 5.28, 31, 43, 44). Of literary sources, Polybius (c. 200–c. 118 BC) is the earliest: he was a Greek historian concerned with chronicling Rome's rapid rise to power between 220 and 167 (he later continued the work down to 146) and contemporary with much of the material about which he writes: he was an eye-witness of certain important events, such as the sack of Carthage in 146. He consulted all types of sources, was well-travelled, and spoke with eye-witnesses and is often critical of other more 'slip-shod' historians. He is biased towards Scipio Aemilianus and his family and, as an Achaean, against the Aetolian league, but attempts to discover the facts and interpret them scientifically. He frequently quotes or paraphrases treaties (docs 5.23, 27, 29–30, 37). Only books 1–5 of the 40 books of his *Histories* remain intact; others are represented by excerpts made by later writers, or are extensively used by Livy. Books 21–45 of Livy's *Ab urbe condita* cover the period 218–167 BC, with book 31 beginning the account of Rome's domination of the Greek East and focussing through to book 45 on the conflicts with Philip V of Macedon, Antiochus and Perseus. Livy relies on literary sources, and from book 31 onwards he clearly used Polybius as his main source, though he also looked at the works of the first-century writers Q. Claudius Quadrigarius, Valerius Antias and L. Coelius Antipater and perhaps others; for missing books of Livy there are the *Periochae*, fourth-century AD summaries of the text (see doc. 5.48), which may not always reflect entirely accurately the contents of Livy's books. His account generally tends to be pro-Roman. On the Roman army, Livy gives a description of the army c. 340 BC, while Polybius records detailed information (docs 5.7, 11–20) on the army and its practices in his own day. Appian of Alexandria was writing in the second century AD; his book on the *Spanish Wars* preserves valuable material for the Roman conquest of Spain (docs 5.45, 47, 49–50), especially because many of the sources he used (Polybius was one of them) are now lost. Pausanias (c. AD 150) wrote a *Description of Greece*, concentrating particularly on monuments and monumental art prior to 150 BC; his account of the sack of Corinth (doc. 5.40) is a useful supplement to Polybius.

Plutarch's *Lives* have been used minimally in this chapter, though his biographies of Flamininus, Philopoemen, and Aemilius Paullus help to flesh out portrayals of some of the main characters of the time; Plutarch's primary aim, however, is a moralising one. His *Life of Titus* (Flamininus) preserves a hymn to Flamininus sung at his festival on Chalcis (doc. 5.26). The twenty books of Aulus Gellius, the *Attic Nights*, written in the second century AD, are particularly concerned with matters of Latin grammar and expression; his discussion of usages often includes valuable citations of passages of text otherwise lost (e.g., doc. 5.36).

For an introduction to Roman imperialism, see Badian 1968; Harris 1979; Derow 1989; Errington 1989, 1989a; Gruen 1984; Yavetz 1991.

THE IDEOLOGY OF ROMAN MILITARY SUPREMACY

Military glory was always the highest form of prestige in Rome — after all, the Romans believed that they were descended from the god Mars himself (doc. 5.6). The greatest honour for any Roman magistrate was the victorious command of an army and the award of a triumph (docs 2.32–5); military virtues were seen as those most essential for any Roman; and it was considered that Rome's destiny was to rule the inhabited world. For Rome as a warrior state, see Bernstein 1994; cf. Habicht 1989: 382–7.

5.1 Valour as the highest Roman virtue

Plutarch *Life of Coriolanus* 1.6

Gnaeus Marcius Coriolanus (Gaius in Plutarch and Dion. Hal. 6.92.3) supposedly received his surname for taking Corioli from the Volsci in 493 BC. He was later exiled for tyrannical behaviour and defected to the Volsci, inflicting severe defeats on Rome. Plutarch contrasts the Greek terms *arete*, virtue, and *andreia* (from *aner*: the qualities belonging to a man, hence bravery). The Latin *virtus* (from *vir*, man) means manliness, or the excellences of a man, particularly that of bravery in combat. Cicero accepts the definition of virtus as the ideal of manliness at *Tusc. Disp.* 2.43. On virtus as an aristocratic Roman concept (comprising military success and the holding of office), see Badian 1968: 12–15; a good example is the epitaph of L. Cornelius Scipio Barbatus: doc. 1.68.

In those days Rome honoured most highly that aspect of virtue concerned with war-like and military achievements, and proof of this can be seen by the fact that the Romans only have one word for virtue, which is *virtus* (valour), and use the specific virtue of valour to stand for virtue in general.

5.2 The army is Rome

Livy *History of Rome* 9.4.10–14

When the Romans were trapped at the Caudine Forks by the Samnites in 321, the consuls were in despair at the proposal that the Roman army should pass under the yoke. This passage is part of the speech put into the mouth of Lucius Lentulus (cos. 328) by Livy on this occasion; for the great humiliation suffered by the Roman soldiers, see Livy 9.6.11–13: Rome went into mourning at the news of this disgrace (doc. 1.66); for the concept of 'victory or death', see doc. 4.36.

10 Indeed I confess that death on behalf of one's country is a glorious thing, and I am ready either to devote myself on behalf of the Roman people and legions or to throw myself into the midst of the enemy; **11** but it is here I see my country, here are all Rome's legions, and unless they choose to rush upon death for their own sakes, what have they to save by dying? **12** 'The roofs and walls of the city,' someone might say, 'and the multitude by whom the city is inhabited.' But, by Hercules, all these are betrayed, not saved, once this army is annihilated! **13** For who will protect them then? The common folk, unwarlike and unarmed, I suppose! — just as it preserved them from the

Gallic attack . . . **14** Here are all our hopes and resources, and if we save these we save our country, whereas if we give them up to death we abandon and betray it.'

5.3 Papirius Cursor makes a joke!

Livy *History of Rome* 9.16.16

Papirius Cursor (*MRR* I.152, 154) routed the Samnites in 319 and made them pass under the yoke in revenge for the Roman defeat at the Caudine Forks (cf. docs 1.66, 2.33). Being himself very tough ('cursor' was supposed to prove his swiftness, though in fact the name belonged to his grandfather and father), no general was harder on his men.

Indeed, a story is told how his cavalrymen once dared to ask him to let them off some task in return for a job well done, and that he replied to them, 'So you won't be able to say that I don't let you off anything, I excuse you from patting your horses' backs when you dismount'.

5.4 Rome's invincibility

Lucilius *Satires* 26.708–11

One of Lucilius' earliest books of satire, perhaps written c. 131. For Viriathus, see docs 5.47–8.

> . . . the Roman people has often been defeated by force and overcome in many battles
> But never in an actual war, on which everything depends —
> No, we do not know the disgrace of being defeated in war by a barbarian
> Viriathus or Hannibal.

5.5 Military excellence supersedes all other forms of virtue

Cicero *In Defence of Murena* 22

Cf. Cic. *Rep.* 3.35–7: Rome's imperium is just and natural, for superior peoples should govern inferiors to the latter's advantage: cf. *Rhet. ad Herenn.* 4.13. The fact that L. Licinius Murena had served with Lucullus in Asia and been propraetor of Transalpine Gaul in 64 of course slants Cicero's argument here in his praise of military excellence.

Excellence in military service outranks all other forms of excellence. It is this that has won the Roman people its fame, that has won this city its ever-lasting glory; it is this that has made the whole world obey this government; all the activities within this city, all these glorious pursuits of ours, the applause and the labours here in the forum, all lie under the care and protection of excellence in warfare.

5.6 Rome's great destiny

Virgil *Aeneid* 1.275–88

Jupiter here prophesies to the goddess Venus, mother of Aeneas, 'ancestor' of Julius Caesar and Augustus (here called 'Julius'), the future military success of Rome, including the conquest of Greece. Mars was the father of Romulus and Remus; the house of Assaracus means the Trojans and their Roman descendants; Julus, son of Aeneas, was supposedly the ancestor of the Julian gens. For Rome's conquest of Greece in 146, see docs 5.40–2; for the development of the Trojan legend, see Gruen 1992: 6–51; for Roman concepts of empire, Gruen 1986: 273–87.

275 Then, joyful in the tawny skin of the she-wolf, his nurse,
Romulus will inherit the line and found the walls of Mars,
Calling his people 'Romans' after his own name.
For these I limit their empire by no boundaries or periods of time;
I have granted them dominion without end. Yes, even fierce Juno,
280 Who now with fear wearies both sea and earth and sky,
Shall turn to better counsels, and with me cherish
The Romans, masters of the world, nation of the toga.
This is my decree. As the years slip by, an age will come
When the house of Assaracus shall crush with servitude
285 Phthia and famed Mycenae and hold dominion over conquered Argos.
From this glorious line shall be born the Trojan Caesar,
To make Ocean his limit of empire, the stars the limit of his fame,
A Julius, his name descended from great Julus.

THE IDEOLOGY OF THE MILITARY HERO

Nicolet 1980: 89–109 on citizens as soldiers; probably 1/10 of the adult males in Italy were under arms at any one time (Nicolet 112). Citizens were by definition soldiers and liable for service from the age of 17 to 46 (at 46 men joined the *seniores*). Citizens were called up by the *dilectus* (levy), for which the consuls, as commanders, were responsible; the maximum number of annual campaigns was probably between 16 and 20, while the equites only needed to serve 10. For examples of military discipline, see Val. Max. 2.7.1–15; docs 7.14–15, cf. 7.59. Discipline was all-important: Q. Fabius Rullianus, magister equitum to the dictator Papirius Cursor in 325, was nearly executed for fighting a battle contrary to orders: *MRR* I.148.

5.7 Awards for valour

Polybius *Histories* 6.39.1–10

Decorations for wounding or killing the enemy were awarded only for courage above and beyond the call of duty. The most important awards were the *corona graminea* (grass crown), also known as the *corona obsidionalis* (siege crown) granted for the raising of a siege on a Roman position; the *corona muralis* or *vallaris* (wall or rampart crown) for the first soldier to scale the wall of a besieged town; the *corona civica* (civic crown) made of oak leaves for saving a fellow-soldier's life in battle; the *corona navalis* (or *rostrata*) for bravery in naval engagements; and the *corona aurea*, gold crown, awarded for other acts of bravery (cf. doc. 7.59). For crowns, see Maxfield 1981: 61, 67–100; Rawson 1991: 47–8; Walbank I.721–2; for other ornaments (the torque, armilla or phalerae), see Maxfield 86–91; Linderski 2001; for triumphal ornaments, see docs 2.32–5. The ceremonial spear (the *hasta pura*) could also be awarded as a military decoration. Besides the awards Polybius describes here, other inducements to fight well were booty, and the money distributed to soldiers at triumphs (Brunt *IM* 394). The armour of a killed enemy commander — known as the *spolia opima* — was dedicated on the Capitol (Rich 1996; Flower 2000).

1 The Romans also have an excellent way of encouraging the young soldiers to face danger. **2** Whenever some of them distinguish themselves in action, the general summons the army to an assembly, brings forward those whom he considers to have conducted themselves with conspicuous excellence, and first makes a speech in praise of the courageous actions of each one, and of anything else in their conduct worthy of commendation, **3** and then hands out the following rewards: to the man who has wounded an enemy, a javelin; and to the man who has killed and despoiled an enemy, a cup, if he is in the infantry, and horse-trappings, if in the cavalry — although originally the reward was only a spear. **4** These rewards are not given to men who have wounded or stripped enemies in a pitched battle or the capture of a city, but only to those who have done so in skirmishes or other similar situations, in which there was no need to hazard themselves in single combat, but who threw themselves into this voluntarily and by their own choice.

5 When a city is stormed, the first man to scale the wall is awarded a crown of gold. **6** In the same way, those who have shielded and saved any of the citizens or allies receive honorary gifts from the consul, and those whom they saved present them of their own free will with a crown; if not, the tribunes who judge the case compel them to do so. **7** A man preserved in this way also reveres his preserver like a father for the rest of his life and must treat him in every way like a parent. **8** By such incentives, they incite to emulation and rivalry in times of danger not only those who are present and witness what takes place, but those who stay at home as well; **9** for the recipients of such gifts, apart from their prestige in the army and their fame soon afterwards at home, are especially distinguished in religious processions after their return to their native land, for in these no one is allowed to wear decorations except those honoured for their bravery by the consuls, **10** and they hang up the spoils they have won in the most conspicuous places in their homes, considering them as the tokens and evidence of their valour.

5.8 The grass crown

Livy *History of Rome* 7.37.1–3

Livy is describing the conflict against the Samnites in 345/3 BC. During the battle, the military tribune Publius Decius Mus (later consul in 340) took and held a hilltop; in the Roman victory 30,000 Samnites were killed. Both consuls celebrated a triumph over the Samnites with Decius given a place of honour in the procession (Livy 7.38.3). For the grass crown (the *corona graminea*) see Pliny *Nat. Hist.* 22.6–13; he records eight recipients (the last being Augustus).

1 After the engagement had terminated in this way, the consul called an assembly (contio) and not only completed the praises of Publius Decius he had begun before, but recounted those due to his recent deeds of bravery, and besides other military gifts he gave him a golden crown and a hundred oxen, plus one exceptionally fine fat white one with gilded horns. **2** The soldiers in his troop with him were granted a double ration of grain for life, and for the time being an ox each and two tunics. Following the consul's presentation, the legions placed on Decius' head the wreath of grass for delivering them from a siege, accompanying the gift with cheering; another wreath, a mark of the same honour, was put on him by his own troops. **3** Wearing these insignia, he sacrificed the fine ox to Mars and gave the other hundred to the soldiers who had been with him on the expedition. To these same soldiers the legions contributed a pound of spelt and a pint (a *sextarius*) of wine each; all this was done with great enthusiasm, the soldiers' cheering demonstrating unanimous approval.

5.9 Spurius Ligustinus, the ideal Republican soldier

Livy *History of Rome* 42.34.5–14

This incident takes place in 171 BC, when there was dissatisfaction because some Romans who had previously served as centurions were drafted as common soldiers. Ligustinus, being over 46, was enlisting voluntarily. He had been on campaign for 22 of the last 30 years, though he had a small farm and eight children.

Roman soldiers were conscripts in that they had to serve for minimum lengths of time and present themselves for recruitment when eligible. Until Marius, it was those with property who served. Evading military service led to flogging, fines, confiscation of property, imprisonment, or even enslavement (Cic. *Caec.* 99; Dion. Hal. 8.87.5; Brunt *IM* 391). There were sometimes problems with recruiting, and tribunes of the plebs might oppose recruitment in times of economic hardship or after long periods of military conflict. Recruitment in 151 BC for Spain was difficult because the young men were terrified at reports of the numerous battles, the great casualties suffered, and the bravery of the Celtiberians, but, when Scipio Aemilianus volunteered for service, recruits put themselves forward enthusiastically (Polyb. 35.4.1–14; cf. doc. 5.49). For difficulties in recruitment: see Brunt *IM* 391–3, 396–7. Ligustinus: Smith 1958: 5; Brunt 395; Nicolet 1980: 126–8; Webster 1985: 16–17; Hanson 1995: 45; cf. Keppie 1984: 53–4.

5 I became a soldier in the consulship of Publius Sulpicius and Gaius Aurelius (200 BC). I spent two years as a common soldier in the army which was taken to Macedonia against King Philip; in the third year, because of my bravery, Titus Quinctius Flamininus made me centurion of the tenth maniple of hastati. **6** After Philip and the Macedonians had been defeated, and we were brought back to Italy and discharged, I immediately set out for Spain as a volunteer soldier with the consul Marcus Porcius (Cato, in 195). **7** Those who have had experience of him and other commanders through long service know that of all the generals now alive none was a keener observer and judge of bravery. This general judged me worthy to be made centurion of the first century of the hastati. **8** I became a volunteer soldier again for the third time in the army which was sent against the Aetolians and King Antiochus (191). Manius Acilius made me centurion of the first century of the principes. **9** When King Antiochus had been driven out and the Aetolians beaten, we were brought back to Italy; twice after that I served in campaigns where the legions served for a year. I then campaigned twice in Spain, once when Quintus Fulvius Flaccus was praetor (181) and again when Tiberius Sempronius Gracchus was praetor (180). **10** I was brought back by Flaccus to appear with him along with others whom he brought back from the province for his triumph because of their valour; I went back to the province because Tiberius Gracchus asked me. **11** Four times within a few years I was chief centurion; thirty-four times I was rewarded by my generals for valour; I have received six civic crowns. I have served twenty-two years in the army and I am over fifty years old. . . . **13** For myself, as long as anyone who is enrolling armies considers me a suitable soldier, I will never try to be excused from service. **14** Of whatever rank the military tribunes think me fit, that is their decision; I shall make sure that no one in the army surpasses me in bravery; and, that I have always done so, both my generals and those soldiers who served with me are my witnesses.

5.10 The most courageous Roman of them all

Pliny the Elder *Natural History* 7.101–6

Pliny is here discussing the Roman who most demonstrated outstanding courage. He also mentions M. Manlius Capitolinus, who repelled the Gauls from the Capitol in 390, but in Pliny's view his attempt at kingship negated his achievements. For Dentatus, see Dion. Hal. 10.36–39, 44–47; Gell. 2.11.1; Livy 3.31.7–8; *MRR* I.43; Sergius: *MRR* I.333; for single combat, see Oakley 1985; cf. Flower 2000.

101 Lucius Siccius Dentatus, who was tribune of the plebs in the consulship of Spurius Tarpeius and Aulus Aternius (454 BC), not long after the kings had been expelled, gets an extremely large number of votes for having fought in 120 battles, been the victor in 8 challenges to single combat, and having the distinction of 45 scars in front and none on his back. **102** He also captured spoils 34 times, was given 18 spear-shafts, 25 badges of honour, 83 torques, 160 armlets, 26 crowns (including 14 civic crowns, 8 of gold, 3 for being the first to scale the walls, and one for rescuing others from a siege), a bag of money, 10 prisoners and with them 20 cows, followed in the triumph of 9 generals whose victories were primarily due to him, and furthermore (which I think to be the finest of his achievements) **103** had one of his generals, Titus Romilius, at the end of his consulship, convicted of maladministration. . . .

104 In these cases, indeed, there are great achievements of courage, but even more of fortune: while no one, in my view at any rate, can justly rank any man above Marcus Sergius, even though his great-grandson Catiline lowers his name's fair repute. In his second campaign Sergius lost his right hand, and in two campaigns he was wounded 23 times, with the result that he was disabled in both hands and both feet, with only his spirit unwounded; although crippled, he served afterwards in numerous campaigns. He was twice taken prisoner by Hannibal — he was engaged not just with any old enemy — and twice escaped from Hannibal's incarceration, although he was kept in chains or fetters every single day for twenty months. He fought four times with his left hand alone, and two horses he was mounted on were cut from under him. **105** He had a right hand of iron made for himself, and, going into battle with it tied on, raised the siege of Cremona, saved Placentia, took twelve enemy camps in Gaul, all of which are known from his speech during his praetorship when he was barred by his colleagues from the sacrifices as disabled — a man who with a different enemy would have heaped up piles of crowns! . . . **106** Others have indeed conquered men, but Sergius conquered Fortune too.

THE ROMAN ARMY

The army was a crucial component of Roman culture and civilisation. The Roman ability to wage war successfully allowed their city-state to emerge from the status of just another community in Italy to become master of the Mediterranean world. The Roman army was complex, made up of legions with a highly structured organisation, the main developments being from a phalanx to an army structured around maniples and later cohorts. The art of war was never more successfully practised in the ancient world than by the Romans and Polybius' *Histories* were written to explain Rome's rise as the major power, with a long discussion on the Roman army.

Polybius (at 6.19–42) gives the earliest contemporary description of the Roman army, that of the second century BC (docs 5.12–16), including the equipment of the soldiers of his day (doc.

5.15), while Livy provides a description of the army of the fourth century BC (doc. 5.11). Cato the Elder wrote a *de re militari*, which has not survived, which was drawn upon (along with other sources) by Vegetius in his late imperial manual *Epitoma rei militaris* (cf. Campbell 1987; for Cato's *de re militari*, see: Astin 1978: 184–5, 204–5).

Another important source is the 'Altar of Domitius Ahenobarbus' dating to the late second or early first century BC which depicts soldiers: in one section, two Roman soldiers with shields, plumed helmets, and armour stand back to back (the dagger of one is visible), while two other soldiers, face to face, are similarly attired (their daggers not visible) standing in front of a soldier with dagger and plumed helmet, with a horse (presumably an eques, hence an officer); all the soldiers are barefoot (see Boardman 1993: 231).

The maniple formation (*manipulus*) came into use in the fourth century BC when it replaced the phalanx (see doc. 5.11). The pilum also came into use in the fourth century: this was a spear to be thrown and so more space was needed between individual soldiers and the tight packed phalanx went out of use. The legion, first with its maniples and later cohorts, was flexible and manoeuvrable, as opposed to the Greek phalanx with its emphasis on a fixed line. The size of the legion in 340 BC was 5,000 infantry with 300 cavalry (doc. 5.11), while its size varied between 4,200 or 5,000 infantry in the middle Republic (doc. 5.13). The army generally comprised four legions, two assigned to each consul. Within the legions described by Polybius there were different types of legionary soldier. They served in four main lines: first the hastati, then principes, then triarii, with the velites skirmishing in front of the hastati. Livy's earlier legion has the hastati, principes and triarii, but also another two groups, the rorarii and accensi, superseded by Polybius' time. The Romans and their allies were organised into different units, and only Roman citizens could serve in the legions.

The velites (sing.: veles) were light-armed soldiers, first heard of towards the end of the third century BC (Livy 26.4.4–7: 211 BC). A few years previous to this the property qualification for army service had been reduced, and the velites will have been the poorer soldiers who could not afford full armour. 1,200 velites were then assigned to each of the legions; they acted as skirmishers before the three legionary lines of hastati, principes, and triarii respectively. After skirmishing, they withdrew through the ranks of the other three lines.

The cohors (cohort) became the standard way of organising Roman soldiers into legions by the end of the second century BC and it was perhaps Marius who engineered this change (see doc. 9.22). The cohors had its origin in the early Republic: the allied contingents provided for the Romans under treaty arrangements were grouped into a cohors (plural: cohortes), commanded by a Roman or allied officer known as a *praefectus*.

Rome's allies — the Latins and Italians — provided Rome with troops; this in fact was their main obligation to Rome. Their numbers, armour and organisation are not as well known as for the Romans. Cavalry does not appear often in the sources; it seems mainly to have been provided by the allies and it fought in Sicily and in Africa. As well as their allies from Italy, the Romans made use of forces — auxilia — drawn from outside of Italy itself, such as Scipio's use of Masinissa's cavalry at the battle of Zama in 202 BC (doc. 4.53). A further development was the use of foreign units in campaigns away from their country of origin. Jugurtha (Masinissa's grandson) served with Numidian units at Numantia in Spain under P. Cornelius Scipio Aemilianus, patron of Numidia, in 133 BC.

For the hastati, principes and triarii and how they operated in turn during battle: doc. 5.11; Walbank I.702; Parker 1958: 14–17; Connolly 1981: 140–2; Webster 1985: 5–6; Watson 1987: 79–80; Hanson 1995: 45–6; Gilliver 1999: 15–18; Goldsworthy 2000: 49–52; velites: Bell 1965: 419–22; allies and auxilia: Keppie 1984: 21–3; Gilliver 1999: 22–6; cavalry: Connolly 1981: 133–4; Hyland 1990: 66–197; McColl 2002. There are numerous works on the Roman army in general; for the Republic see: Adcock 1940; Smith 1958; Parker 1958: 9–71; Bell 1965; Fuller 1965: 74–96; Gabba 1976: 1–69; Nicolet 1980: 89–148; Keppie 1984: 1–102, 1989; Webster 1985: 1–27; Connolly 1989, 1989a; Warry 1989: 100–73; Wise & Healey 1999: 75–91; Goldsworthy 1996, 2000: 1–106; Watson 1969: 21–2, 1987; Hanson 1995, 1995a: 50–7; Potter 2004; cf. Holden 1973; Wilkes 1972; Grant 1974; Connolly 1975; Hodge 1977; Graham 1981; Carrié 1993; Dando-Collins 2002; supplies and logistics: Erdkamp 1998, esp. 27–45; Roth 1999:

158–65, 224–35; Adams 2001; military intelligence in the Republic: Austin & Rankov 1995: 87–108; duration of battles and casualties: Sabin 2000; training: Stephenson 1997.

5.11 Early army organisation, 340 BC

Livy *History of Rome* 8.8.3–14

Livy here notes the change in types of shield: the *clipeus* (plural: *clipei*) was round and made of bronze; the *scutum* (plural: *scuta*) was oval (oblong) and made of wood covered with bull's hide. He describes the various ranks of the Roman army and how they operated in the mid-fourth century BC. The first two lines of the battle formation were the hastati and principes, each having 15 maniples. Livy divides the third last line into the triarii, rorarii and accensi. The rorarii and accensi do not appear in Polybius' account, indicating that the army had changed by that time; the rorarii seem to have been subsumed into the velites. The 15 maniples of the hastati included 20 light-armed men with the rest of the maniple being more heavily armed with body armour and the scutum, which had replaced the smaller clipeus; the 15 maniples of the principes were all heavily and better armed. These 30 maniples were the antepilani. Behind them, the structure became more complicated. Here there were 15 companies (*ordines*, sing: *ordo*; Livy does not use the word maniples in describing them), each company having three parts (*vexilla*); the names of the three parts were the triarii, rorarii and accensi, placed in that order within the companies (there were thus 15 ordines, each made up of three vexilla). Livy does not indicate the size of the maniple in 340 BC, but from his description of the ordines, they must have had 60 to 70 men each.

Livy notes the change from the phalanx to maniples ('handfuls'): see Keppie 1984: 19; Webster 1985: 5; Connolly 1989; Hanson 1995: 45–6; Gilliver 1999: 15–18; the maniples in turn gave way to cohorts (doc. 9.22); for Livy's description of the Roman army: Connolly 1981: 126–8; Webster 1985: 5–7; Watson 1987: 76–8; Rawson 1991: 51–7; Gilliver 1999: 17.

3 The Romans had earlier used round shields (clipei), but, after they began to serve for pay, they made oblong shields (scuta) instead of round ones; and what had earlier been a phalanx, like the Macedonian ones, afterwards began to be a battleline formed in maniples, **4** the troops in the rear being drawn up in a number of companies (ordines). **5** The first line, the hastati, consisted of 15 maniples, stationed a short distance apart; the maniple included 20 light-armed soldiers, the remainder carrying oblong shields — those who were called light-armed carried only a spear and javelins. **6** This front line of the battle-order contained the pick of the young men, who had reached the age for military service. Behind these came a similar number of maniples made up of men of more mature age, who were called the principes, all with oblong shields and especially splendid arms. **7** This body of 30 maniples was called the antepilani, because right behind the standards were positioned another 15 companies, each of which had three sections, the first section of each being named the pilus; **8** a company consisted of three vexilla (standards), a vexillum having 60 soldiers and two centurions, with one standard-bearer (vexillarius), making 186 men altogether. The first standard led the triarii, veteran soldiers of proven courage, the second the rorarii, younger and less experienced men, the third the accensi, the least reliable group, who were for that reason assigned to the line furthest back.

9 When an army had been drawn up in this order, the hastati were the first of all to open the battle. If the hastati were unable to overcome the enemy, they slowly retreated and were received through the gaps between the principes. The fighting was then the job of the principes with the hastati following them. **10** The triarii knelt under their standards with the left leg in front, shields resting against their shoulders, holding their spears fixed in the ground with the point facing upwards, just as if the battleline was bristling with a protective fortification. **11** If the principes were also unsuccessful in their fighting, they fell back slowly from the front line to the triarii (from which comes the proverb when things are going badly, 'to have reached the triarii'). **12** The triarii, rising up when they had allowed the principes and hastati to pass through the gaps in their lines, would at once compress their ranks, just as if they were blocking the pathways, and in one unbroken body, with no more reserves behind, would fall upon the enemy; **13** this was especially disconcerting for the enemy, who had followed up those they thought defeated only to see a new line suddenly rising up with increased numbers. **14** There were generally about four legions enlisted, each with 5,000 foot-soldiers and 300 horse to each legion.

POLYBIUS ON ROME'S MILITARY SYSTEM

Polybius' description of the Roman army falls into two overall sections: (a) 6.19–26 on the army itself and its various features, such as the enrolment of troops (doc. 5.13), length of service (doc. 5.12), pay (doc. 5.14), and equipment (doc. 5.15) and (b) 27–42 on the Roman camp (docs 5.16, 18). These details apply to the time at which Polybius was writing, and the army he describes is generally thought to be that which had come about as a result of the Second Punic War. The organisation of the camp will presumably not have changed for the rest of the Republic, but Marius' reforms introduced significant reforms in weaponry and recruitment (docs 9.21–3). For Polybius and the Roman army: Walbank I.697–723; Toynbee 1965: 1.506–9, 516–17; Connolly 1981: 129–42, 1989a; Keppie 1984: 33–40; Webster 1985: 10–15; Rawson 1991: 35–48; Miller & de Voto 1994; Gilliver 1999: 16–18.

5.12 Length of service

Polybius *Histories* 6.19.1–5

Roman citizens who were 17 years old were eligible for military duty. The length of time required for military service before political office could be sought indicates the martial character of Roman society and its political institutions. Slaves were not enrolled except in the emergency of the Second Punic War (Nicolet 1980: 95; docs 4.36, 6.1); the Romans did not generally employ mercenaries, making efficient use of their allies to supply additional manpower (Krasilnikoff 1996: 12–18). In this document, the military tribunes should not be confused with the plebeian tribunes (for which, see docs 1.22–3). Polybius' Greek for the years of service of the infantry is corrupt, and is usually emended by editors to read 16 years, though six years seems more probable. Under Augustus the term of service was 16 years, but this reflects a period when long service in the armies of the civil war and the professionalisation of the army had taken place (later 20: Dio 54.25.6, 55.23.1; see Keppie 1983: 35–6). App. *Iber.* 6.78.334 has six years' service as the norm in 140 BC, though service could be longer (doc. 5.9) and ten years service was a prerequisite for a Roman pursuing a political career. Military service took place between the ages of 17 to 46 (Cic. *Sen.* 60); length of service: Walbank I.698; Smith 1958: 6–7, 28–43.

1 After electing the consuls, they appoint military tribunes, 14 from those who have served for five years, **2** and ten from those who have served for ten. With regard to the rest, a cavalryman must complete ten years' service and an infantryman six before reaching the age of 46, **3** except for those whose property was assessed at less than 400 drachmae; all these are assigned to naval service. In the case of a pressing emergency,

4 the infantry are obliged to serve for 20 years. No one is able to hold political office **5** before he has completed ten years' service.

5.13 Enlistment of troops

Polybius *Histories* 6.19.5–21.4

Enlistment took place on the Capitol at Rome. While Polybius refers to an initial day for recruitment it is clear that enlistment might take several days, which would be understandable given the numbers involved (Livy 43.15.1: 11 days in 161 BC). The tribunes mentioned here are the military tribunes, of whom there were 24, and Polybius might well have taken his information from *commentarii* (diaries) of military tribunes. Enlistment: Walbank I.698–701; Smith 1958: 4–5; Brunt *IM* 625–34; Nicolet 1980: 96–102; Rawson 1991: 37–9 (Walbank and Brunt see some difficulties with Polybius' account, but Rawson counters their points and Polybius' account is acceptable).

19.5 When the consuls are about to enrol soldiers they announce at a meeting of the assembly the day on which all Roman citizens of military age must present themselves. **6** They do this annually. On the appointed day, when those liable for service have arrived in Rome **7** and assembled on the Capitoline Hill, the junior military tribunes divide themselves into four groups, in the order in which they have been appointed by the people or consuls, as the main and original division of the Roman forces was into four legions. **8** The four first appointed are allocated to the first legion, the next three to the second, the next four to the third, and the last three to the fourth. **9** Of the senior tribunes the first two are assigned to the first legion, the next three to the second, the next two to the third, and the last three to the fourth.

    20.1 Once the division and appointment of the tribunes has been made so that each legion has the same number of officers, **2** those of each legion take their seats apart and draw lots for the tribes one by one, summoning each in the order of the lottery. **3** From each tribe they select four youths, who resemble each other as far as possible in age and physique. **4** When these are brought forward, the officers of the first legion have the first choice, those of the second legion second choice, those of the third third, and those of the fourth last. **5** When the next batch of four are brought forward the officers of the second legion have first choice and so on, with those of the first legion last. **6** Then when another batch of four are brought forward the officers of the third legion have first choice and those of the second last. **7** By giving each legion the first choice in turn, every legion gets men of roughly the same standard. **8** When they have chosen the required number, that is, when each legion has 4,200 infantry, or 5,000 in times of especial danger, **9** they then used in earlier times to choose the cavalrymen after the 4,200, but now they choose them first, the censor selecting them on the basis of their wealth, and 300 are assigned to each legion.

    21.1 When the enrolment has been completed in this way, those tribunes whose duty it is in each legion collect the enrolled soldiers, and picking out of them all one who seems the most suitable **2** make him take the oath that he will obey his officers and carry out their commands to the best of his ability. **3** Then the others come forward and each in turn swears that he will do the same as the first man. **4** At the same time the consuls send orders to the allied cities in Italy which they wish to contribute allied troops, stating the number required and the day and place at which those selected should present themselves. The cities select the men and administer the oath in a manner similar to the one described and send them off, after appointing a commander and paymaster.

5.14 Army pay

Polybius *Histories* 6.39.12–15

The army was at first a volunteer one, but Rome's continual wars meant that pay had to be introduced for Roman legionaries by the middle Republic. Polybius, writing in Greek, gives the pay of the Roman soldier in Greek currency: there were six obols to a drachma, and a drachma was roughly equivalent to the Roman denarius, both the drachma and denarius were silver coins. Note that, at this stage, deductions for expenses were taken from the pay, offset by the fact that a cavalryman's pay was higher to cover the costs of keeping a horse. Caesar doubled army pay (Suet. *Jul.* 26.3). Allies were not paid by the Roman state but received a food allowance. For pay, see Watson 1958, 1987: 84–5; Garlan 1975: 114; Nicolet 1980: 115–22; Keppie 1984: 33–4; Alston 1994: 113–14; allies: Roth 1999: 16–17; rations: Forbes & Foxhall 1982: 86–8; Erdkamp 1998: 27–45.

12 As their pay the infantrymen each receive two obols a day, centurions twice this, and cavalrymen a drachma. **13** The infantry are each allowed about two-thirds of an Attic medimnus of wheat a month, and the cavalry seven medimni of barley and two of wheat. **14** Of the allies, the infantry get the same, and the cavalry one and one-third medimni of wheat and five of barley. **15** These are provided free to the allies, but in the case of the Romans the quaestor deducts from their pay the price fixed for the grain and their clothes and any additional arms they might need.

5.15 Army equipment

Polybius *Histories* 6.22.1–23.15

The Spanish sword — *gladius Hispaniensis* — was a short weapon used for chopping and stabbing at close range, and adopted from the Spanish; the surviving example is 76 mm long (Bishop & Coulston 1993: 53–4; Quesada Sanz 1997). Most modern authorities give a figure of 60 mms as standard (Goldsworthy 2000: 44). It differs, as Polybius 3.114.2–3 notes, from the long Gallic sword which was used for slashing and needed room to do so. In addition, not mentioned by Polybius, was the dagger carried by the legionaries and adopted apparently also from the Spanish. While the Roman soldier made use of the *pilum* in the initial stages of a battle, he was primarily a swordsman (Goldsworthy 2000: 43; cf. Zhmodikov 2000). The *pilum* (plural: *pila*), was to be adapted by Marius (doc. 9.23), but had long been standard equipment of the Roman soldier. Polybius records that each of the hastati had two pila. Soldier's equipment in the Republic: Hanson 1995: 45; Connolly 1981: 130–3, 1997; Bishop & Coulston: 48–64; Keppie 1984: 19, 35; Webster 1985: 6–8; Connolly 1997; Coulston 1998: 168–70.

22.1 The youngest soldiers, the velites, are ordered to carry a sword, javelins and shield (*parma*). **2** The shield is strongly constructed and of sufficient size for protection; it is circular and three feet in diameter. **3** They also wear a plain helmet (i.e., with no crest), sometimes covered with a wolf's skin or something of that sort, both for protection and as a distinguishing mark by which their officers can recognise them and observe whether or not they show bravery in battle. **4** The wooden shaft of the javelin measures about two cubits in length and a finger's breadth in thickness, and the head is a span long and is so thinly hammered out and finely sharpened that it is necessarily bent by the first impact and the enemy are unable to hurl it back; otherwise the weapon could be used by both sides.

23.1 The next in seniority, who are called hastati, are ordered to wear a full set of armour (panoply). **2** The Roman panoply consists, first, of a shield, the convex surface of which measures two and a half feet (5 hemipodia) in width and four feet in length, **3** with the depth at its rim being the width of a palm, which is made by gluing two planks together and covering the outer surface first with canvas and then with calf-skin. **4** Its upper and lower edges have a shield-rim which helps it to ward off descending sword-blows and protects it when fixed in the ground. **5** An iron boss is also attached to it which protects it from violent blows from stones, pikes and heavy weapons generally. **6** Besides the shield they also carry a sword which is worn on the right thigh and called a Spanish sword. **7** This has a sharp point and an effective cutting-edge on both sides as the blade is very strong and firm. **8** In addition they have two throwing-spears (*pila*), a bronze helmet and greaves. **9** Some of the pila are thick, others thin. Of the thicker kind, some are round and a palm's breadth in diameter, others a palm square. The thin type that they carry in addition to the others are like moderate-sized hunting-spears, **10** the length of the wooden shaft of all of these being about three cubits. Each is fitted with an iron head which is barbed and of the same length as the shaft; **11** this is fastened securely by attaching it right along the shaft up to the middle and fixing it with numerous rivets, so that in battle the iron will break rather than the fastening come loose, although its thickness at the bottom, where it touches the wood, is the width of one and a half fingers — they take such great care to attach it securely. **12** Finally they wear as an ornament a circle of feathers with three upright black or purple feathers, **13** about a cubit in height. With these placed on the helmet on top of the rest of the armour, every man looks twice his real height and it gives him a fine appearance which strikes terror in the enemy. **14** The common soldiers also wear in addition a bronze breast-plate a span square, which is placed over the heart and called a heart-protector, which completes their armaments, **15** but those who are rated above 10,000 drachmas wear a coat of chain-mail instead of this heart-protector. 16 The principes and triarii are armed in the same way except that instead of pila the triarii carry thrusting-spears (*hastae*).

MILITARY TECHNOLOGY

5.16 The Roman camp

Polybius *Histories* 6.27.1–3, 6.31.10–14, 6.34.1–6

This is an extract from a lengthy discussion of the camp (Polyb. 6.27–42). Polybius describes a two-legion camp, half of the larger camp when the two consular armies (i.e., 4 legions) were together (see esp. 6.32.6–8); that is, each two-legion consular army had its own camp, but shared one side of it with the other army (Walbank I.711). The Roman army would encamp each night. Such camps were generally temporary, occupied for that night alone, or for longer periods if outside a besieged town or city. The camp epitomised the 'discipline and organization of the Roman army' (Gilliver 1999: 63). It protected the army from surprise attack and provided a sense of security; it made posting sentries easier (see 6.34.7–37.6). Those found guilty of cowardice had to camp outside the camp itself (doc. 5.20). The camp had the appearance of a town, as Polybius notes, with several streets, including the via principalis ('main street') along which was the praetorium (general's tent), quaestorium (quaestor's quarters) and the forum. The camp, rebuilt each day when on the move, was 'a soldier's second fatherland' (Livy 44.39.5). The remains of a camp near Numantia are probably to be associated with the various Roman attempts, finally successful in 133 BC, to capture the town (doc. 5.50). Otherwise, remains of camps, especially those found in Britain, are largely imperial in date. From the camp, the army would march out each day in a fixed order of march (depending on whether it expected to be attacked or not), described by Polybius 6.40.1–14; Sall. *Jug.* 46, 100; Caesar *BG* 2.19; see Webster 1985: 14–15; Gilliver 1999: 38–40. The camp: Walbank I.709–23; Fabricius 1932; Luttwak 1976: 55–7; Keppie 1984: 36–8, 46–7; Webster 1985: 12–13; Watson 1987: 82–3; Peddie 1994: 59–79; Goldsworthy 1996: 111–13; Gilliver 1999: 63–88, esp. 63–5; booty: Shatzman 1972; Garlan 1975: 74–77; Keppie 1983: 38–41.

27.1 Their method of laying out a camp is as follows. Once the site for the camp has been chosen, the position in it most suitable for obtaining a general view and issuing orders is allocated to the general's tent (praetorium). **2** They plant a standard on the spot where they intend to pitch the tent and measure off around the standard a square plot, each side of which is 100 feet from the standard, so that the whole area measures four plethra (one plethron = 10,000 square feet). **3** Along one side of this square, in the direction which seems to offer the best facilities for watering and foraging, the Roman legions are stationed . . .

31.10 The result of these arrangements is that the whole camp forms a square, and its division into streets and its general plan gives it the appearance of a town. **11** The rampart is dug on all sides at a distance of 200 feet from the tents, and this empty space serves a number of important uses. **12** To begin with, it provides the suitable facilities necessary for marching the troops in and out; for they all march out into this space via their own streets, rather than converging into one street en masse and jostling and trampling each other. **13** It is here, too, that they collect any cattle brought into camp and booty taken from the enemy and guard them safely during the night. **14** But most important of all is that in night attacks neither fire nor weapons can reach them, apart from a very few, which are almost harmless due to the distance and the space left in front of the tents . . .

34.1 As regards the construction of the ditch and stockade, the two sides along which their two wings are quartered are the responsibility of the allies, the other two being that of the Romans, one for each legion. **2** Each side is divided into sections, one for each maniple, and the centurions stand by and supervise each section, with two of the military tribunes superintending the work as a whole on each side. **3** They also supervise all other work to do with the camp; they divide themselves into pairs, drawing lots for their turn, and each pair is on duty for two months out of every six, supervising all field operations. **4** The prefects of the allies use the same procedure in dividing their duties. **5** At dawn all the cavalry officers and centurions parade at the tents of the tribunes, and the tribunes report to the consul. He gives the necessary orders to the tribunes, **6** and the tribunes pass them on to the cavalry officers and centurions, and they convey them to the soldiers when the proper time comes.

5.17 Roman siege works against the Aduatuci (57 BC)

Caesar *Gallic War* 2.30–1

Caesar is here engaged in campaigns in Gaul: the Aduatuci were coming to the aid of the Nervii, but on hearing of their defeat returned home and collected together in a town of great strength on high rocks with a double wall and only one approach. For Marius' canal at the river Rhone, see doc. 9.23; construction of roads: docs 2.5–8.

30 On the arrival of our army, they made frequent sorties from the fortress and engaged with our troops in minor skirmishes; later, when they were enclosed by a rampart 12 feet high, 15,000 feet in circumference, and with forts at frequent intervals, they stayed inside the town. When the mantlets had been pushed forward and a ramp constructed, and they saw a siege-tower being erected at some distance, they first made fun of us from the wall and loudly criticised us for having set up so great a machine at such a distance: by what handiwork and what strength, they cried, could men of such short stature (for our stature, short when compared to their own gigantic build, is generally despised by the Gauls) expect to place so heavy a tower on the wall? **31** When, however, they saw the tower moving and approaching the walls, they were dismayed at such a novel and unusual sight and sent envoys to speak to Caesar about peace, in the following way: they considered, they said, that the Romans did not make war without divine assistance, as they could move forward with such speed machines of such height: they therefore submitted themselves and all their possessions to the Romans' power.

MILITARY DISCIPLINE

Roman military discipline was severe and uncompromising. There was no appeal against standard punishments to be inflicted for various offences. But to balance the discipline was the system of rewards (see docs 5.7–10), and the fact that soldiers could not be arbitrarily punished. The punishments for delinquency on the night-watch are clearly understandable: this sort of laxness endangered the safety of the camp and the lives of all the men within it. Discipline: Nicolet 1980: 105–09; Webster 1985: 13–14.

5.18 The watchword

Polybius *Histories* 6.34.7–12

7 The way they ensure the safe passing round of the watchword for the night is as follows: **8** from the tenth maniple of every class of cavalry and infantry, the maniple which is encamped at the lower end of the street, a man is selected who is relieved from guard duty and who presents himself every day at sunset at the tent of the tribune. He receives the watchword — that is, a wooden tablet with the word inscribed on it — and takes his leave. **9** When he returns to his maniple he hands over the tablet and watchword, in the presence of witnesses, to the commander of the next maniple, who in turn passes it on to the one next to him. **10** All in turn do the same until it reaches the first maniples, the ones near the tents of the tribunes. These men have to return the tablet to the tribunes while it is still light. **11** If all the tablets issued are returned, he knows that the watchword has been given to all the maniples and has passed through them all on the way back to him; **12** if one is missing, he makes inquiry immediately, being able to tell from the inscription from what quarter the tablet has not returned. The person responsible for the hold-up meets with the punishment he deserves.

5.19 Punishment for delinquency on the night-watch

Polybius *Histories* 6.37.1–3, 6

Polybius here discusses the punishment for deliquency on the night-watch. Death by beating with cudgels and stoning (the *fustuarium*) was also the punishment for those who stole in camp, gave false evidence, were homosexuals (doc. 7.59), and for anyone punished for the same offence three times (6.37.9): Walbank I.719–20.

1 A court-martial composed of the tribunes immediately meets to try him, and if found guilty he is punished by being beaten to death. This is carried out as follows: **2** the tribune takes a cudgel and just touches the condemned man with it, **3** whereupon all those in camp strike him with clubs and stones, usually killing him in the camp itself. **4** But even those able to escape have no hope of safety — how could they? They are not allowed to return to their homes and no relative would dare to receive such a man in his house. So those who have once fallen into this misfortune are utterly ruined . . . **6** Consequently, due to the severity of this inescapable penalty, the night-watches of the Roman army are kept impeccably.

5.20 'Decimation'

Polybius *Histories* 6.38.1–4

Dion. Hal. 9.50.7 notes that decimation was the 'traditional penalty amongst the Romans for those deserting the ranks or abandoning the standards'; Crassus imposed this penalty on the army defeated by Spartacus (doc. 6.45). Death was by the *fustuarium* (see above). Walbank I.721; Watson 1969: 119–20; Keppie 1984: 38; Webster 1985: 14. The standards: Dusanic & Petkovic 2003.

1 If it ever happens that a large body of men behave in the same way (i.e., run away or throw away their weapons) and whole maniples leave their posts under heavy pressure, they reject the possibility of beating to death or executing all who are guilty, but find a solution to the problem which is both effective and terrifying. **2** The tribune assembles the legion and brings out to the front those who left the ranks, reprimands them severely and finally chooses by lot sometimes five, sometimes eight, sometimes twenty of the offenders, calculating the number so that it represents as far as possible a tenth of those guilty of cowardice. **3** Those who are chosen by lot are mercilessly beaten to death in the manner described above, and the rest are given rations of barley instead of wheat and are ordered to make their quarters outside the safety of the rampart. **4** The danger and the fear of drawing the lot threatens everyone equally, as there is no knowing on whom it might fall, and as the shame of receiving rations of barley falls on all alike the practice adopted is the one best adapted to inspire fear and correct such faults.

5.21 Military oaths

Aulus Gellius *Attic Nights* 16.4.2–4

Cincius: *HRR* I² civ; Huschke F13; Courtney *ALP* 103–5; cf. Polyb. 6.19.1–6. Laelius and Lucius Cornelius Scipio Asiaticus were consuls in 190 BC, cf. Livy 37.2.2–4. The oaths taken by their soldiers are summarised by Polyb. 6.33.2, 6.26.2–4; see Walbank I.701; Nicolet 1980: 102–05; Rawson 1991: 39–40. At 10.16.2–17.5 Polybius describes the procedure for collecting and sharing booty from a captured city: no more than half the total force was sent to collect it, the rest remaining on the alert, and after it was sold it was the responsibility of the military tribunes to ensure that it was equitably distributed.

2 Also in the fifth book of the same Cincius' *On Military Science* there is written: 'When a levy was made in ancient times and soldiers were enrolled, the military tribune compelled them to take an oath in these words: "In the army of the consul of Gaius Laelius, son of Gaius, and the consul Lucius Cornelius, son of Publius, and for ten miles around, you will not commit a theft with malice aforethought, either alone or with others, of greater value than a silver sesterce on any one day; and except for a spear, spear-shaft, firewood, fruit, fodder, wineskin, sack and torch, if you find or carry off anything there which is not yours, which is worth more than one silver sesterce, you will bring it to the consul Gaius Laelius, son of Gaius, or Lucius Cornelius, son of Publius, or to whomsoever either of them should order, or within the next three days you will reveal whatever you have found or carried off by malice aforethought, or you will return it to its owner, whomever you think that to be, as you wish to do what is right."
3 'When the soldiers had been enrolled, a day was appointed on which they should appear and answer the consul's summons; then an oath was taken that they should be present, **4** with the following exceptions added: "Unless there be any of the following reasons: a family funeral or days of purification (but not if they have been appointed for that day in order that he might not appear on that day), or a serious disease, or an omen which could not be passed by without expiation, or an anniversary sacrifice which could not be properly celebrated unless he himself were there on that day, or violence or enemies, or a stated and appointed day with a guest; if anyone shall have any of these reasons, then on the day following that for which he is excused for these reasons, he shall come and serve the one who made that district, village or town subject to levy." '

ROME'S CONQUEST OF THE MEDITERRANEAN

5.22 Treaty between Rome and the Aetolian league, 212 or 211 BC

SEG 13.382, lines 5–20

(*ARS* 14a.) This treaty made by Marcus Valerius Laevinus (*MRR* I.269) with the Aetolians against Philip in 212/11 was Rome's first alliance in the eastern Mediterranean. This is the earliest extant Roman official document found in Greek: Harris 1979: 205–8.
This formal bilateral agreement sets out arrangements for conducting the war, the division of booty and the terms of peace. The Aetolians were to wage war on Philip by land, while Rome was to provide at least 25 quinqueremes; any towns south of Corcyra that were taken by the Romans were to belong to the Aetolians, with movable property to belong to Rome; cities conquered by

the Romans and Aetolians acting in concert were to belong to the Aetolians, but their movable property was to be shared; cities which came over voluntarily could under certain circumstances join the Aetolian league; and the Romans were to help Aetolia to conquer Acarnania, an ally of Philip. If peace was made by one of the allies, it was only valid if Philip did not wage war on the other party. The treaty was not ratified for two years because the senate was unhappy about the unfavourable terms made by Laevinus. The Aetolians' aim was to extend their influence at the cost of Philip's allies; the Romans wanted to gain booty and recoup their costs. Aegina was captured by the allies in 209, and sold by the Aetolians for 30 talents to Attalus of Pergamum. An Aetolian peace with Philip was probably made in autumn 206, while Rome made peace in 205: see Eckstein 2002; after the Second Macedonian War the Aetolians believed that they were still allied to Rome on the same conditions: Flamininus, however, told them that their separate peace in 206 had abrogated this agreement; Livy 26.24.8–14, 29.12.1–4, 33.31.1–9; Polyb. 18.38.1–9; see Balsdon 1967: 184–5; Badian 1970: 49–53, 1984: 56–8; Harris 1979: 207; Errington 1989: 94–106, esp. 99–101; for treaties of alliance in the third century: Eckstein 1999.

5 If the Romans take by force any cities of these peoples, as far as the Roman people are concerned the Aetolian people shall be permitted to keep these cities and their territories; anything else, apart from the cities and territories, that **10** the Romans take the Romans shall keep. If the Romans and the Aetolians in concert capture some of these cities, as far as the Roman people are concerned the Aetolians shall be permitted to keep those cities and their territories; anything they take apart from the cities shall belong jointly **15** to both. If any of these cities submits or surrenders to the Romans or the Aetolians, as far as the Roman people are concerned the Aetolian people shall be permitted to take these people and their cities and territories **20** into their league . . .

5.23 Peace settlement with Philip after Cynoscephalae, 196 BC

Polybius *Histories* 18.44.1–7

The Second Macedonian War ended with Philip's defeat at Cynoscephalae in 197: for Ennius' account, see *Annals* 333–41; for the battle itself, Hammond 1988. The peoples named in the treaty had been part of Philip's empire in Greece; cf. Livy 33.31.1–32.9. Livy follows Polybius' account, though including the amounts of indemnity given by Valerius Antias (4,000 pounds of silver annually for ten years) and Claudius (4,200 pounds annually for 30 years and 20,000 pounds immediately), and has two additional clauses, that Philip should have no more than 5,000 soldiers and no elephants, and that he should wage no war outside Macedonia without the senate's permission: Walbank II.609–12; Scullard 1973: 92–7, 1980: 251–8; Harris 1979: 140–1, 212–18; Badian *FC* 62–72; Sherwin-White 1984: 18–19; Errington 1989a: 248–74; Walsh 1996: 354–6; for Flamininus' career, Balsdon 1967; Badian 1970: 28–57; *MRR* I.330, 334, 336. On sources for the period, see Astin 1989a: 1–16.

1 At this time the ten commissioners came from Rome to deal with affairs in Greece, bringing with them the senate's decree about peace with Philip. **2** The decree's main points were as follows: all the rest of the Greeks in Asia and Europe were to be free and subject to their own laws; **3** Philip was to hand over to the Romans all Greeks under his rule and all towns with garrisons before the start of the Isthmian games (June 196 BC); **4** he was to leave free, after withdrawing his garrisons from them, the towns of Euromus, Pedasa, Bargylia and the town of Iasus, as well as Abydus, Thasus, Myrina and Perinthus; **5** in accordance with the senate's decree Titus (Flamininus) was to write to Prusias (of Bithynia) about the liberation of the Ciani; **6** Philip was to restore to the

Romans all prisoners of war and deserters within the same time period, and all his decked ships, with the exception of five light vessels and his ship with 16 banks of oars; **7** he was to pay them 1,000 talents, half immediately and half by instalments over ten years.

5.24 The 'liberation' of Greece by Flamininus

Polybius *Histories* 18.46.1–47.2

Cf. Plut. *Flam.* 10.4; Livy 33.32.5; App. *Mac.* 9.2; Val. Max. 4.8.5. Titus Quinctius Flamininus was less than 30 years of age as consul in 198 BC, having held neither the curule aedileship nor the praetorship; two tribunes attempted to prevent his election (Livy 32.7.8–12; Scullard 1973: 97–100) and legislation was introduced that the praetorship was to be a prerequisite for consular candidates; two new praetorships were also created (Livy 32.27.6; Astin 1989: 176). Flamininus was fluent in Greek (Plut. *Flam.* 5.5), perhaps from the time he had spent stationed at Tarentum during the Second Punic War, and wrote Greek verses for a dedication at Delphi: Plut. 12.6–7, though Rawson 1989: 440 believes Plutarch did not intend to imply that Flamininus wrote these himself. This universal declaration of freedom for Greeks included Greeks in Asia Minor, doubtless with a view to curbing Antiochus' activities there; the motive was not 'philhellenism' but rather the wish to weaken Macedon, without committing Rome to administering new territory: Scullard 1973: 106–9; Badian 1970: 3–27, *FC* 72–5; Rawson 1989: 439. Walsh 1996 sees the propaganda as initiated by Flamininus himself; cf. Gruen 1986: 132–57. Many Greek cities honoured Flamininus as a benefactor (e.g., *IG* XII.9.931, Chalcis), while, according to Plutarch, he was granted divine honours at Chalcis and Argos (the cult of the 'Titeia'): Plut. *Flam.* 16 (doc. 5.26); Gruen 1986: 167. His three-day triumph in 194 included magnificent treasures: Livy 34.52.4–8; Cic. *Verr.* 2.4.129.

46.1 With the Isthmian games now approaching, and the most distinguished men from nearly the whole world gathered there owing to their expectation of what would take place, many different rumours were current during the whole festival, **2** with some saying that it was impossible for the Romans to withdraw from certain places and cities, while others declared that they would withdraw from the places considered to be famous, but would keep those which had less appeal but which were equally useful to them. **3** They even named these on the spot out of their own heads and competed with each other in their ingenious guesswork. **4** This was everyone's current concern, and, when the crowd had gathered in the stadium to watch the games, the herald came forward and, after silencing the crowds with his trumpeter, made the following announcement: **5** 'The senate of Rome, and Titus Quinctius (Flamininus) the proconsul, having overcome King Philip and the Macedonians, leave free, without garrisons, subject to no tribute, and governed by their ancestral laws, the Corinthians, Phocians, Locrians, Euboeans, Achaeans, Magnesians, Thessalians, and Perrhaebians.' **6** At the very start an incredible shout immediately went up, with some people not having heard the announcement, while others wanted to hear it again. **7** The great majority of the audience, unable to believe it and thinking that they heard the words as if in a dream because of the unexpected nature of the event, **8** each moved by a different impulse shouted to the herald and trumpeter to come forward into the middle of the stadium and repeat the proclamation, wishing, I think, not only to hear the speaker but to see him due to the unbelievable nature of his announcement. **9** When the herald came forward into the middle and silenced the uproar with his trumpeter, once more reading out the same proclamation as before, such a tremendous outburst of cheering arose that those who hear of the event today cannot easily conceive it. **10** When the noise finally died down, no one took any further account of the athletes, but all talked away, some to each other, some to themselves, as if quite out of their senses. **11** Indeed, after the festival was over, they were so grateful that they almost killed Titus through their excessive joy; **12** some of them wanted to look him in the face and call him their saviour, others were anxious to take his hand, and most people threw garlands and fillets on him, so he was almost torn in pieces. **13** But however extravagant their gratitude was, one may say with confidence that it was far inferior to the importance of the event. **14** It was remarkable that the Romans and their general Titus should be there for this purpose, and incur every expense and danger for the sake of the Greeks' freedom; it was also a great thing that they employed a force adequate to realise their purpose; **15** but greatest of all was that no mischance occurred to oppose their design, with everything leading to that one moment when, by a single announcement, all Greeks living in Asia and Europe were free, without garrisons, subject to no tribute, and governed by their ancestral laws.

47.1 When the festival was over, the commissioners first gave an audience to the envoys from Antiochus, instructing him with regard to the cities in Asia to keep his hands off those which were autonomous and make war on none of them, and to withdraw from those he had just captured which had been subject to Ptolemy and Philip. **2** In addition they declared that he should not cross with an army to Europe; for none of the Greeks was now being made war on by anyone or subject to anyone.

5.25 Flamininus to the people of Chyretiae, 194 BC

*SIG*³ 593

(*RDGE* 33.) Flamininus' command in Greece was prorogued (extended) until 194 and much of his time between 196 and 194 was taken up with organising the internal affairs of the Greek city-states. This document concerning the people of Chyretiae in Thessaly demonstrates the kind of settlement made by Flamininus before the Romans' departure and his wish to ensure Greek support or neutrality for Rome's forthcoming confrontation with Antiochus III; cf. Livy 34.48.3–49.11 for his farewell speech at Corinth.

'Persons who are not accustomed to act according to the highest standards of behaviour' are the Aetolians who had sacked Chyretiae in 199 (Livy 31.41.5) and who were aggrieved that the terms of their alliance with Rome in 212 were not still in force, insisting that Rome would never abandon key positions in Greece (Polyb. 18.38.6–9, 45.1–9; Livy 33.13.7–13); for Polybius' unfavourable view of the Aetolians (Polybius was an Achaean), see Polyb. 30.11.1–6. Flamininus in this document returns Chyretian property currently in Rome's possession, which had been taken by the Aetolians. The Chyretians were grateful: when Perseus invaded Perrhaebia in 171 Chyretiae held out for a day (Livy 42.53.9). See Armstrong & Walsh 1986: 34–6 for Flamininus' fluent command of colloquial Greek in this document (*pace* Rawson 1989: 440), who suggest a date of 194 (42); Erskine 1994: 83. The tagoi are Flamininus' newly appointed magistrates.

Titus Quinctius, consul of the Romans, to the magistrates (tagoi) and people of Chyretiae, greetings.

Just as in all other matters also I have made clear my personal policy and that of the Roman people, which we have towards you in general, I have decided **5** in the following matters also to demonstrate in every respect our support for what is honourable, so that not even in these matters can persons who are not accustomed to act according to the highest standards of behaviour have the opportunity to criticise us.

For any of your possessions, in land or buildings, that may still be in the possession of the treasury **10** of Rome, I grant them all to your city, that you may recognise our magnanimity in this respect too and to show we have no desire for financial profit in any matter at all, since we value good will and a good reputation above all else. If any do not recover what belongs to them, **15** if they prove to you and appear to you to be speaking reasonably, as long as you adhere to the decisions given by me in writing, I consider that these should in justice be restored to them. Farewell.

5.26 The girls of Chalcis honour Flamininus

Plutarch *Life of Flamininus* 16.7

This paean was sung by the girls of Chalcis in Euboea in 191 BC to honour Flamininus and Roman *fides* (Greek *pistis*, 'good faith'); cf. Gruen 1982. Chalcis was one of the 'three fetters of Greece', which were to retain Roman garrisons after 196. In 194, at Corinth, Flamininus announced that these would be withdrawn (Livy 34.49–51). Flamininus protected the city against M'. Acilius Glabrio (cos. 191), who wanted to punish Chalcis for having been Antiochus' headquarters in 192/1: Antiochus, while there, had married a Chalcidian wife. Flamininus was to be honoured as Chalcis' patron, and his cult, the Titeia, was established with an elected priest. Plutarch here cites the last lines of the long cult hymn of praise. This is the earliest extant hymn which mentions the goddess Roma (see doc. 5.34); 'Great Zeus' may be an attempt in Greek to reproduce Jupiter Optimus Maximus.

> We revere the fides of the Romans,
> Which we have solemnly sworn to cherish;
> So celebrate, girls, in song and dance
> Great Zeus, and Roma, and Titus and the Romans'
> Fides; hail, all hail,
> Titus our saviour.

ANTIOCHUS III 'THE GREAT'

Antiochus III of Syria (223–187 BC) was defeated by Rome at Thermopylae: Livy 36.19.11–12; Polyb. 20.8.6; App. *Syr.* 18; for Cato's role as military tribune in the engagement: Plut. *Cato Mai.* 13–14; for Magnesia: Livy 37.39–44.2; App. *Syr.* 30–5; for Rome's motives for taking an army into Asia Minor: Harris 1979: 219–23; Badian *FC* 75–83.

5.27 The peace treaty with the Aetolian League, 189 BC

Polybius *Histories* 21.32.1–15

See also Livy 38.11.1–9; Badian *FC* 84–7; Gruen 1986: 456–62, 479–80; Walbank III.131–6. En route through Greece in 190 the Scipio brothers had arranged a six-month truce for the Aetolians, Antiochus' main supporters in Greece. In 189 consul M. Fulvius Nobilior (*MRR* I.360) marched against them and they surrendered. The terms were that they should pay 500 talents over six years and restrict the membership of the league. The terms were not reciprocal and the Aetolians had to agree to 'uphold the empire and sovereignty of the Roman people', and so the treaty was an 'inequitable one' (*foedus iniquum*); Gruen 1986: 29–30; cf. Cic. *Balb.* 35 for similar phraseology in a treaty between Rome and Cadiz. The sections in square brackets are supplied from Livy.

1 When the senate had passed a decree and the people had voted in favour of it, the peace was ratified. The detailed conditions of the treaty were as follows: **2** 'The Aetolian people [shall uphold in good faith] the empire and sovereignty of the Romans. **3** They shall not permit any enemies making war against the Romans or their allies or friends to pass through their country, nor shall they provide any supplies by public consent. **4** [They shall have the same enemies as the Roman people] and if the Romans make war on anyone, the people of Aetolia shall make war likewise. **5** The Aetolians shall surrender all deserters, fugitives and prisoners belonging to the Romans and their allies, **6** excepting those who were taken in war, returned to their own country and again captured, and excepting those who were enemies of the Romans at the time when the Aetolians were fighting in alliance with Rome. All of these are to be surrendered within 100 days of the peace being sworn, to the magistrate on Corcyra; **7** if any are not found before that date, they shall be surrendered without fraud when they are discovered; and they are not to return to Aetolia after the peace is sworn. **8** The Aetolians are to hand over at once to the consul in Greece 200 Euboic talents, in silver not inferior to Attic money, paying a third of the sum in gold, if they wish, at the rate of one gold mina for ten silver minae, **9** and, for the first six years after the swearing of the peace, 50 talents a year; the money is to be brought to Rome. **10** The Aetolians are to give the consul forty hostages, not younger than twelve years of age or older than forty, for six years, whom the Romans are to choose, none of them being a general, hipparch, public secretary or one of those previously a hostage in Rome. These hostages are to be brought to Rome: **11** if any of the hostages dies they are to replace him with another. **12** Cephallenia is not to be included in the treaty. **13** Of the villages, cities and people previously subject to the Aetolians, who were captured or became friends of the Romans in or after the consulship of Lucius Quinctius (Flamininus) and Gnaeus Domitius Ahenobarbus (192 BC), none of these cities or their inhabitants is to be annexed by the Aetolians. **14** The city and territory of Oeniadae is to belong to Acarnania.' **15** When the oaths were taken, peace was finalised on these conditions. This was the settlement of affairs in Aetolia and Greece generally.

5.28 Letter and decree on Delphian privileges, 189 BC

*SIG*³ 612

(*ARS* 25; *RDGE* 1.) This inscription suggests that envoys from Delphi had sent to discuss their rights of asylum and to request immunity from tribute, or more likely (as no tribute was imposed at this time) exemption from military requisitions by Rome, during the war against Antiochus III. Spurius Postumius was the urban praetor in 189 BC: Livy 37.47.8; *MRR* I.361.

A ... concerning the freedom of the city and the right of sanctuary for the temple ...

B Spurius Postumius, son of Lucius, praetor of the Romans, to the Delphian League, greetings.

The envoys sent by you, Boulon, Thrasycles and Orestas, have discussed with us the question of sanctuary for your temple and city, omitting no mark of respect, and made a request concerning freedom and exemption from tribute, so that the city and territory of Delphi may be autonomous and immune from taxation. Know then that the senate has resolved that the temple of Apollo and the city shall have the right of sanctuary, **5** that the city and territory of Delphi shall be exempt from taxation, and that its citizens shall be autonomous in every respect . . . being free, administering their own government by themselves and being responsible for the temple and its precinct, as has been their ancestral right from of old. For your information, I am sending you a copy.

C May 4. Spurius Postumius, son of Lucius, praetor, consulted the senate in the comitium . . . Gaius Atinius, son of Gaius, Tiberius Claudius, and . . . assisted in the drafting. Whereas the Delphians spoke about the right of sanctuary for the temple, the freedom of the city, the exemption of its territory from taxation, and autonomy, regarding this matter the senators **5** resolved as follows: 'Whereas it was the decision of Manius Acilius (Glabrio) that Delphi should possess those privileges which had earlier been hers, it was resolved to abide by this decision.'

5.29 The treaty of Apamea, 188 BC

Polybius *Histories* 21.41.6, 9–43.1–3

The Romans initially demanded that Antiochus evacuate all of Asia Minor and pay the full cost of the war. Negotiations failed and Antiochus was defeated near Magnesia, probably in December 190 or January 189; the Scipios' terms were later approved by the senate: Antiochus had already made a payment of 3,000 talents; a further indemnity of 12,000 Euboic talents was imposed (as well as 540,000 modii of grain), and Antiochus was to surrender most of his fleet and elephants, hand over Hannibal (who went to Bithynia), pay compensation to Pergamum, and evacuate all Asia north and west of the Taurus mountains. Antiochus agreed to these terms at Apamea.

Gnaeus Manlius Vulso, cos. 189, succeeded L. Cornelius Scipio in the command of the war in Asia and conquered the Galatians, Antiochus' allies (for Vulso's triumph, which was contested by his political opponents, see Livy 38.43.1–50.3; doc. 5.52); his command was prorogued for 188: *MRR* I.360, 366. The treaty between Rome and Antiochus was sworn at Apamea and Antiochus was confined to Syria (his empire still stretched from the Taurus Mountains to Eastern Iran); cf. Livy 38.38.1–18; Diod. 29.10; App. *Syr.* 38–9; Scullard 1973: 139, 1980: 270–3; Sherwin-White 1984: 20–7; Evans 1993; Grainger 1995; *ARS* 27; Walbank III.154–6. Eumenes II Soter, Rome's ally, was king of Pergamum (197–160/59). On Eumenes II, see Hansen 1971: 70–129; Sherwin-White 1984: 36–40; Gruen 1986: 550–63; Habicht 1989: 324–34. The section in square brackets is supplied from Livy.

41.6 The ten commissioners and King Eumenes reached Ephesus by sea in early summer; they rested there for two days after their journey and went up country to Apamea . . . **9** On arriving at Apamea and meeting Eumenes and the ten commissioners, Manlius Vulso took counsel with them about the situation. **10** They decided first of all to ratify the sworn treaty with Antiochus, about the conditions of which I need say no more, but will give the document itself. **42.1** The conditions in detail were as follows: 'There is to be friendship between Antiochus and the Romans for all time, if he keeps to the conditions of the treaty. **2** King Antiochus and his subjects shall not permit the passage through their territory of any enemies making war against the Romans and their allies, nor provide any supplies for them; **3** the Romans and their allies shall undertake to do likewise towards Antiochus and his subjects. **4** Antiochus is not to make war on the inhabitants of the islands **5** nor on those of Europe. **6** He is to withdraw from all cities, villages, [lands and forts on this side of Taurus as far as the river Halys, and all between the valley of Taurus and the mountain ridges that descend to Lycaonia]; he is to take away nothing except the arms carried by his soldiers; if anything should be carried away it is to be restored to the same city. **7** He is not to receive soldiers or anyone else from the kingdom of Eumenes. **8** If any men in the army of Antiochus are from the cities which the Romans take over, they shall be brought to Apamea. **9** If there are any men from the kingdom of Antiochus with the Romans and their allies, they are permitted to stay or leave as they wish. **10** Antiochus and his subjects are to hand over the slaves of the Romans and of their allies, both those who were captured in war and those who deserted, and any prisoners they may have taken. **11** Antiochus is to give up, if it is in his power, Hannibal son of Hamilcar the Carthaginian, Mnasilochus the Acarnanian, Thoas the Aetolian, Eubulidas and Philo the Chalcidians, and all Aetolians who have held public office, **12** as well as all the elephants now in Apamea, nor is he to have any for the future. **13** He is to give up his long ships and their equipment and fittings, and is not to have more than ten decked ships for the future; nor is he to have any galley rowed by more than 30 oars, nor a ship with one bank of oars for any war in which he is the aggressor. **14** His fleet is not to sail beyond the Calycadnus and the Sarpedonian promontory, unless carrying tribute, envoys or hostages. **15** Antiochus is not to be permitted to hire mercenaries from territory subject to the Romans or to receive fugitives. **16** All houses of the Rhodians or their allies in the territory subject to Antiochus shall belong to the Rhodians, as they did before he began the war. **17** If any money is owed to them, it shall likewise be recoverable; and if anything has been taken away from them, it may be sought and handed back. Goods meant for Rhodes are to be free of duty, as before the war. **18** If Antiochus has given to others any of the cities which he has to hand over, he is to remove the garrisons and men from these as well. And if any later wish to desert (to him) he is not to receive them. **19** Antiochus is to pay to the Romans 12,000 talents of the best Attic silver over twelve years, paying 1,000 talents per year, the talents weighing not less than 80 Roman pounds, and 540,000 modii of corn. **20** He is to pay to King Eumenes 350 talents in the next five years, 70 a year, at the time appointed for his payments to the Romans, **21** and in place of the corn, as King Antiochus estimated it, 127 talents and 1,208 drachmas, which Eumenes has agreed to receive as an acceptable payment. **22** Antiochus is to give 20 hostages not younger than 18 years of age and not older than 45 and send others in exchange every three years. **23** If there is any discrepancy in his payments of money, he shall hand it over in the following year. **24** If any of the cities or nations, against whom Antiochus is forbidden to make war, should first make war on him, he is allowed to make war. **25** He is not to have sovereignty over these cities or nations or bring them into his alliance. **26** Any wrongs committed by one party against another are to be taken to court. **27** If both parties wish to add clauses to this treaty or remove them by mutual decree, they may do so.'

43.1 When this was sworn to, the proconsul immediately sent Quintus Minucius Thermus and his brother Lucius, who had just brought the money from Oroanda, **2** to Syria, with instructions to receive the king's oath and ensure that each detail of the treaty was carried out. **3** He sent letter-carriers to Quintus Fabius (Labeo), the commander of the fleet, ordering him to sail back to Patara, seize the ships there, and burn them.

5.30 The final settlement of Asia Minor

Polybius *Histories* 21.45.1–3, 9–11

Cf. Livy 38.39.1–17. The Romans' settlement of Antiochus' Asia Minor possessions laid down that, of the non-Greek territories vacated by Antiochus, Lycia and Caria were to belong to Rhodes, the rest to Eumenes II of Pergamum; Greek cities which joined Rome before the battle of Magnesia were to be free, the others were to be divided between Rhodes and Eumenes depending on their geographical position. The Romans at this point did not claim territory in Asia Minor: Pergamum now separated the empires of Syria and Macedonia. For the Taurus line (Cape Sarpedon on the coast to the river Tanais), see McDonald 1967; McDonald & Walbank 1969; for the commissioners: *MRR* I.363.

1 At Apamea the ten (commissioners) and Gnaeus (Manlius Vulso) the Roman proconsul listened to all those who presented themselves, and, where the dispute was about land, money or something else, assigned cities which both parties were agreed upon where they could settle the matters under dispute. The general settlement that they made was as follows. **2** All autonomous towns which had formerly paid tribute to Antiochus, but had then remained loyal to Rome, they freed from tribute; all that paid contributions to Attalus were instructed to give the same sum as tribute to Eumenes. **3** If any had withdrawn from the Roman alliance and fought with Antiochus, they ordered them to give to Eumenes the tribute imposed on them by Antiochus . . . **9** Regarding King Eumenes and his brothers they had made all possible provision for them in the treaty with Antiochus and they now added, in Europe, the Chersonese, Lysimachia and the adjoining forts and territory, which Antiochus had ruled, **10** and, in Asia, Hellespontic Phrygia, Greater Phrygia, the part of Mysia which Prusias had earlier taken from Eumenes, Lycaonia, the Milyas, Lydia, Tralles, Ephesus and Termessus. **11** These were the gifts they gave Eumenes; regarding Pamphylia, as Eumenes declared it was on this side of the Taurus, and Antiochus' envoys said it was on the other, they were unable to reach a decision and referred the question to the senate.

ROME AS MASTER OF THE MEDITERRANEAN

For Perseus' attempt in the 170s to strengthen Macedon's position vis-à-vis Rome, see Scullard 1973: 175–6, 198–200; Gruen 1986: 403–19. Rome's conduct of the Third Macedonian War was not totally straightforward: envoys under Q. Marcius Philippus arranged a truce, ostensibly so Perseus could present his case to Rome (Livy 42.43.1–3, 47.1–3; Polyb. 27.5.7), but in fact to give the Romans a chance to prepare for war. Perseus' defeat of a Roman army at Callinicus led to Greek defections (Polyb. 27.9.1–10.5), while the behaviour of Roman commanders was such (sacking and attacking allied towns) that the senate sent envoys to announce that orders to give support to Roman generals had to be accompanied by official senatorial decrees (*senatus consulta*): Livy 43.17.2–3; Polyb. 28.3.3. See Harris 1979: 227–33; Scullard 1980: 274–83; Gruen 1986: 505–14; for sources for relations between Rome and Greece from 188 to 146 BC: Derow 1989: 290 n.1.

From the late third century Roman policy became increasingly aggressive and was determined by political considerations (Habicht 1989: 382–7). Rome's attitudes towards her allies and conquests also became increasingly autocratic; for Rome as 'the cloud looming in the West', see Polyb. 5.140. On Rome's policies towards annexation of her conquests, see Harris 1979: 131–54; the norm was to send out a commission of ten legati (legates) to arrange any necessary settlements. For Polybius' depiction of Rome's consciousness of its military might and his view of it as a 'monarchical' force, see Richardson 1979; cf. Derow 1979. Badian 1968: 80 is worth citing: 'the Romans had raised an astonishing structure founded on ambition, greed and lust for power, bringing out the worst that had perhaps been implicit in the Roman way of life.'

From 182, Rome is seen in honorific inscriptions as the 'common benefactor' of the Greeks, with Rome being considered the superior power even when Rome is not directly the subject of the inscriptions: Erskine 1994; for the cult of Roma, see Mellor 1975: esp. 111–33; Gruen 1986: 178–9, 187.

On treaties and their terminology, see Sherwin-White 1984: 58–79; on *deditio*, see Badian *FC* 4–7; Eckstein 1995. At Polybius 20.9.1–10.17, *deditio in fidem* appears to imply unconditional surrender (Glabrio and the Aetolians in 191), though Gruen 1982 argues this to have been an exceptional event; cf. 36.4.2; Livy 1.38.1–2. However, see Polyb. 35.4.1–3, 36.3.9 for the terms of the surrender of Carthage in 146.

5.31 Edict or letter of the Romans to Delphi, 171 BC

*SIG*³ 643

This edict or letter presents Roman charges against Perseus made before the Amphictyons at Delphi after Rome had declared war on Perseus of Macedon in 171, to encourage them to assist Rome. Macedonian agents had supposedly attempted to assassinate Eumenes II of Pergamum at Delphi: Livy 42.15.3–16.9; *ARS* 29. Derow 1989: 307 n. 23 sees this document almost certainly as an official Roman communication on the eve of the war against Perseus.

Though responsible for the declaration of war against Perseus, Eumenes II lost Rome's support after Perseus' defeat (supposedly for trying to negotiate with Perseus: Polyb. 29.6.1–9.12; Livy 44.24.1–25.12) and was not allowed to visit Rome to state his case: Polyb. 30.19.1–14; Livy 45.19.1–20.3; *RDGE* 40. For Abrupolis, see Polyb. 22.18.2; Livy 42.13.5. The Gauls attacked Delphi in 279 BC (§2).

1 . . . you shall administer, as it concerns Perseus, who in violation of what is fitting came to Delphi with an army in the truce of the Pythian games; it was not at all right to allow him either to come forward or to share in the oracle or the sacrifices or the games or the Amphictyonic Council, in which all the Greeks participate. **2** For he **(10)** brought barbarians, who dwell beyond the Danube and who, once before, gathered for nothing good but for the enslavement of all Greeks, and invaded Greece and marched against the Temple of Pythian Apollo at Delphi intending to plunder or destroy it, but met with fitting punishment from the god, and most of them perished. **3** He also broke the oaths, made by us to his father, and the treaty, which he himself had renewed. **4 (15)** He also made war against the Thracians, our friends and allies, and made them homeless. **5** Abrupolis, whom we included as our friend and ally in a treaty with him, he expelled from his kingdom. **6** Envoys sent from the Greeks and the kings to Rome about an alliance with the Thebans he drowned and others in other ways he attempted to put out of the way. **7** He also reached such a degree of folly that he had it in mind to kill our council by poisons. **8** The Dolopians **(20)** were deprived of freedom though his attacks. **9** In Aetolia he planned both war and slaughter and brought their whole people into upheavals and discord. **10** Also against all Greece he continues to do the worst things, both by devising other evils and receiving fugitives from cities. **11** Also, by destroying the leading men and at the same time courting the masses, he both promised cancellations of debts and brought about revolutions, making clear his policy towards both the Greeks and the **(25)** Romans. **12** As a result, it has happened that the Perrhaebians and the

Thessalians and the Aetolians fell into incurable misfortunes and the barbarians have become still more terrible to the Greeks. **13** Desiring war against us for a long time, that he might catch us without aid, when no one was opposing him, and enslave all the Greek cities, **14** he bribed Genthius the Illyrian and set him against us. **15** He plotted to kill King Eumenes, our friend and ally, by means of Evander, **(30)** at the time when Eumenes was going to Delphi to pay a vow, without considering at all the safe-conduct given by the god to all who come to him and without taking into account that the sanctity and inviolability of the city of Delphi, for both Greeks and barbarians, acknowledged by all men, has existed for all time . . .

5.32 Lucius Aemilius Paullus, victor in 168 BC

ILS 8884

(*CIL* I² 622; *ILLRP* 323; *ROL* IV.78.) After the battle of Pydna in 168 BC, Aemilius toured Greece and at Delphi replaced Perseus' statue on a monument under construction with one of himself on horseback (Polyb. 30.10.2; Plut. *Aem.* 28.2; Livy 45.27.7). The frieze recorded scenes from the battle of Pydna: Kähler 1965: esp. 7–23; Gruen 1992: 141–5, 246–7, pl. 1. Significantly the inscription was in Latin, not Greek. Polybius relates that Paullus gave all Perseus' wealth to the state, except for his library: 18.35.4–5, 31.22.1–4; Plut. *Aem.* 28.6, 10–11; Rawson 1989: 464 discusses what it might have contained. He later brought to Rome, for the temple of Fortuna, Pheidias' statue of Olympian Zeus: Pliny *Nat. Hist.* 34.54; Polyb. 30.10.6.

Lucius Aemilius, son of Lucius, imperator, took this (as booty) from King Perseus and the Macedonians.

5.33 Booty from Epirus, 167 BC

Livy *History of Rome* 45.33.1, 5–7, 34.1–6

Cf. Polyb. 30.15 (doc. 6.9). The Molossians had taken the side of Perseus: following a senatorial decree, 70 towns in Epirus, mostly Molossian, were sacked to provide booty for the army and as an object lesson. The cities, which had supported Perseus, had surrendered to the praetor Anicius in 168; the punishment was perhaps on the persuasion of Charops, a pro-Roman Epirote, who was put in charge following the sack: Polyb. 27.15.1–16, 30.12, 30.32.12. Strabo 7.327 notes that over 100 years later the area was still a desert. See Plut. *Aem.* 29.3; Livy 44.45.3–4 for the booty distributed to the troops (not as much as they expected). Paullus paid so much into treasury that all citizens were relieved from the annual *tributum*, or land tax (Valerius Antias at Livy 45.40.1 gives the sum as 120 million sesterces, Vell. 1.9.6 as 210 million sesterces, Pliny *Nat. Hist.* 33.56 as 300 million sesterces); for the tributum, see Nicolet 1980: 149–69. Paullus also gave 100 denarii to each infantryman at his triumph; for Paullus' entertainment and banquets at Amphipolis, see Livy 45.32.

For Paullus, see Scullard 1973: 207–19; Reiter 1988: 69–80; Rawson 1989: 462–3; *MRR* I.427, 433–4; for a more human side: doc. 3.40. Even Plutarch, whose portrait of Paullus is eulogistic, states that this devastation was against Paullus' character: *Aem.* 30.1. Macedon was eradicated and Macedonia, like Illyria, was formed into four separate republics without the rights of intermarriage or trade. On the partitioning of Macedonia and Illyricum, see Scullard 1973: 212–13; Badian *FC* 96–7; Gruen 1986: 425–35; cf. Harris 1979: 158–62. Perseus died in prison, following Paullus' triumph: Livy 45.40.1–42.5; Plut. *Aem.* 32–4; Diod. 31.8.12–9.7; Reiter 1988: 134–42.

33.1 After the public games had been held (at Amphipolis) and the bronze shields had been piled onto the ships, the rest of the arms of all kinds were heaped into a huge pile, and the general, after praying to Mars, Minerva, Mother Lua, and the rest of the gods to whom it is right and lawful to dedicate the spoils of the enemy, personally used a torch to kindle it . . . **5** The gaze of the crowd which came was no more drawn to the stage spectacle, the athletic contests or the chariot races, than to all the booty of Macedonia which was put on show — statues, paintings, textiles, vessels of gold, silver, bronze and ivory made with great pains in the palace (at Pella), **6** not only for immediate show, like the things with which the palace at Alexandria was filled, but for constant use. **7** These were loaded onto the fleet and given to Gnaeus Octavius to transport to Rome . . . **34.1** Paullus sent despatches to Anicius so that there should be no disturbance over what was going to take place, saying that the senate had granted to his army the booty from the cities of Epirus which had defected to Perseus, **2** and sent centurions to the individual cities, to say that they had come to remove the garrisons so that the people of Epirus might be free like the Macedonians. He also summoned ten leading men from each city and told these to have all the gold and silver brought into the public square, while cohorts were sent to all the cities. **3** Those to the cities further away were sent before those to the nearer ones, so that they would all arrive on the same day. **4** The tribunes and centurions had been instructed as to what to do. Early in the morning all the gold and silver was collected; at the fourth hour the soldiers were given the signal to plunder the town; **5** there was so much booty that a distribution was made of 400 denarii to each of the cavalry and 200 to the infantry, and 150,000 people were led into slavery. **6** Then the walls of the plundered cities were torn down; there were about 70 communities. All the booty was sold and from this the amounts given above were paid to the army.

5.34 Melinno 'of Lesbos' on the might of Rome

Stobaeus 3.7.12 (Melinno F1)

See, for discussion, Bowra 1957: 21–8; Mellor 1975: 121–4; Plant 2004: 99–100. Roma, Rome, is here portrayed as a warrior goddess, whose rule is both eternal and unique. Melinno's date and origins are not known, but the poem is generally now dated to the early second century BC and was possibly written for performance at a local festival, perhaps on Lesbos, in honour of Roma.

> Hail, Roma, daughter of Ares,
> Golden-crowned warrior queen
> You who live on earth on holy Olympus,
> For ever indestructible.

> 5   To you alone, most revered one, has Fate
> Granted royal glory of unbreakable dominion,
> So that, with your sovereign power,
> You might lead the way.

Under your yoke of strong leather straps,
10   The chests of earth and grey sea
Are tightly bound together; with firm hand you govern
The cities of your peoples.

The longest eternity, which overthrows everything
And shapes the course of life first in this way, then in that,
15   For you alone does not change the wind
Which fills the sails of empire.

Indeed, out of all, you alone give birth to
Strong men, wielders of spears,
Sending forth a well-aiming crop of men
20   Like the fruits of Demeter.

ROME'S IMPERIALIST STANCE

5.35 Rome the arbiter of peace and war, 168 BC

Polybius *Histories* 29.26.1, 27.1–11

Cf. Livy 44.19.13–14, 45.12.1–7; Diod. 31.2.1–2; Val. Max. 6.4.3. In this episode, Gaius Popillius Laenas (cos. 172) prevented Antiochus IV Epiphanes from making war on Ptolemy VI Philometor, even though this was not contrary to the Treaty of Apamea; see Scullard 1973: 210–11; Badian *FC* 107; Sherwin-White 1984: 46–9; Gruen 1986: 657–60; Habicht 1989: 344; Walbank III.402–6. Antiochus, brother of the assassinated Seleucus IV, took the throne in 175; when Egypt, under Ptolemy VI Philometor, began a war to recover Southern Syria and Palestine (the Sixth Syrian War), which had been lost to Antiochus III, Antiochus IV occupied Cyprus and invaded Egypt and in early 168 was close to capturing Alexandria. An Egyptian embassy to Rome led to direct Roman intervention: a Roman commission, led by the blunt Gaius Popillius Laenas, met Antiochus at Eleusis outside Alexandria, and threatened that whichever king failed to withdraw from the war would lose Rome's friendship, demanding an instant response; for Popillius Laenas, see Livy 45.10.8, 12.5; *MRR* I.410–11, 430.

26.1 Forgetting all that he had written and said, Antiochus was preparing for war against Ptolemy . . . **27.1** As Antiochus was approaching Ptolemy in order to occupy Pelusium, **2** Popillius, the Roman commander, when greeted from a distance by the king who held out his right hand, gave him the tablet which he had ready containing the decree of the senate, and ordered Antiochus to read it first, not thinking it right, **3** it seems to me, to give this usual mark of friendship before he knew whether the intentions of the person greeting him were friendly or hostile. **4** When the king had read it, he said that he wanted to consult his friends about this information, but Popillius, on hearing this, acted in a manner thought to be harsh and extremely arrogant; **5** he had with him a staff cut from a vine, with which he drew a circle round Antiochus and ordered him to give his decision about the letter while still inside the circle. **6** The king was startled at this assumption of authority, but, after a few moments of doubt, said he would do all that the Romans demanded. Popillius and his entourage then all took his hand and greeted him warmly.

7 The letter told him to cease his war against Ptolemy immediately. **8** As a result, since a specific number of days were granted him, he led his forces back to Syria, unhappily and with complaints, but giving way to circumstances for the present. **9** Popillius arranged matters in Alexandria and instructed the Egyptian kings to agree, telling them to send Polyaratus to Rome, and then sailed to Cyprus, wanting to use all expedition in expelling the troops there from the island. **10** When he arrived and found that Ptolemy's generals had been defeated in battle and that things in Cyprus were generally all upside down, he soon made the (Syrian) army withdraw from the country and stayed there until the troops had sailed to Syria. **11** In this way the Romans saved Ptolemy's kingdom, or at least as much of it as had not already been reduced . . .

5.36 Cato's speech in support of the Rhodians, 167 BC

Aulus Gellius *Attic Nights* 6.3.16, 38, 48–50

(*ORF* [4] FF164, 168, 169; Courtney *ALP* 78–85.) For Rhodes' relationship with Rome and the debate on Rhodes' future, see Polyb. 30.4.1–9; Livy 45.21.1–4, 25.1–4; Diod. 31.5.3; Scullard 1973: 216–17; Sherwin-White 1984: 30–6; Badian *FC* 100–2; Gruen 1986: 563–72; Habicht 1989: 334–8. For its part in the defeat of Antiochus III, Rhodes gained control of Caria and Lycia. When Rhodes' economy suffered during the Third Macedonian War against Perseus, the consul of 169 Marcius Philippus seems to have suggested that Rhodes attempt to negotiate between Perseus and Rome: Polyb. 28.17.1–15, 29.10.1–4; Livy 45.3.3–8, 20.4–9. Unfortunately the Rhodian envoys only arrived at Rome after Perseus' defeat and were almost declared an enemy of Rome at the instigation of the praetor M'. Juventius Thalna (Polyb. 30.4–5; Livy 45.21.1–25.10; *MRR* I.433). War against Rhodes was averted by a speech from Cato (censor 184), and Rhodes finally entered into a formal alliance with Rome in 164/3 (Polyb. 30.21.1, 23.2–4, 31.17–20; Livy *Per.* 46), while the senate declared Caria and Lycia 'free', as well as ordering the Rhodians to withdraw from Caunus and Stratoniceia when these rebelled (Polyb. 30.5.11–16, 21.3–5, 31.4–12; Livy 45.25.6). Delos was given to Athens in 166 on condition it be a free port, though Sherwin-White argues (1984: 32–5) that this was not a measure deliberately designed to ruin Rhodes economically (cf. Polyb. 30.20.7; Strabo 10.5.2–4).

This speech was subsequently introduced into Cato's *History* (*Origines: HRR* I[2] 84–8 F95). Gellius is here disagreeing with Tiro, Cicero's freedman, who wrote a letter to Quintus Axius criticising this speech of Cato's.

16 And Tiro gives Cato's own words as follows: 'And I really think that the Rhodians did not want us to put an end to the war as we did, or conquer King Perseus. But the Rhodians were not the only people who felt like that: in fact I believe many peoples and many nations felt the same. I rather think that some of them did not desire our success, not for the sake of making us look small, but because they were afraid that, if there was no one whom we feared, we would do whatever we liked. I think that they held that opinion for the sake of their own liberty, so they would not be entirely subject to our empire and in servitude to us. Also, the Rhodians never publicly aided Perses. Consider how much more cautiously *we* deal with each other as individuals. For each of us, if he thinks anything is being done against his interests, tries as hard as he can to prevent it; they however let it happen.'. . . . **38** Later on Cato continues: 'But if it is not right for honour to be won because someone says that he wanted to do well, but did not do so, shall the Rhodians suffer not because they did wrong, but because they are said to have wanted to do wrong?' . . .

48 The charge of arrogance, which was particularly brought at that time against the Rhodians in the senate, he evades and disposes of it in a brilliant and almost divinely inspired reply. **49** I will give Cato's actual words, since Tiro has omitted them: **50** 'They say the Rhodians are arrogant, accusing them of something which I should certainly not want to have brought against me or my children. Suppose they are arrogant? What is that to do with us? Are you going to be angry, just because someone is more arrogant than we are?'

5.37 Decree of the senate on Achaean exiles, c. 165 BC

Polybius *Histories* 30.32.6–12

Cf. Paus. 7.10.12; cf. Polyb. 30.29.1, 30.30.1, 32.3.14–17, 33.1.3–8, 33.3.1–2, 33.14. After Perseus' defeat, 1,000 'pro-Macedonian' Achaeans were deported to Italy and 550 leading Aetolians were murdered and others exiled (Livy 45.28.7). The 1,000 were sent to Italy as hostages where they remained for 17 years; one of these was Polybius, who was lucky enough to win the friendship of Scipio Aemilianus. This is one of the occasions the exiles' return was requested and refused, in case their return might upset the pro-Roman government, that of Callicrates, in Achaea; for a similar request in 155 BC, see Polyb. 33.1.3. Charops was in charge of a pro-Roman government in Epirus, while Callicrates had been responsible for the deportation of the 1,000 Achaeans in the first instance. The issue was finally settled in 150 when Scipio Aemilianus enlisted Cato's support; at this point only 300 of the exiles were still alive (Polyb. 35.6.1–3; Plut. *Cato Mai.* 9); see Walbank III.461–2; Badian *FC* 90–1, 97–8; Gruen 1986: 518–20.

6 The senate listened to what the envoys said in accordance with their instructions, and found it difficult to make a decision, as they were met by objections on every side; **7** they did not think it was their duty to pronounce judgement, while setting the men free without trial would, they considered, involve the certain destruction of their friends; **8** so under force of circumstances and with the intention of entirely dispelling the hope of the populace for the restoration of those in detention, in order to make them obey in silence the party of Callicrates in Achaea and in the other states thought to be friends of Rome, they wrote the following answer: **9** 'We are not of the opinion that it is in the interests either of the Romans or of your peoples that these men shall return home'. **10** When this reply was delivered, not only did utter despair and helplessness fall upon those who had been summoned to Italy, but all the Greeks went, as it were, into mourning, as the reply seemed to deprive **11** the poor men of all hope of restoration. And when the reply given about the accused to the Achaeans was announced in Greece, the people's spirit was crushed and a kind of hopelessness came over everyone, **12** while the supporters of Charops and Callicrates and all the defenders of their policy were again in high spirits.

5.38 The partitioning of Egypt, 163–162 BC

Polybius *Histories* 31.10.1–3, 6–10

When in 164 Ptolemy VI Philometor was expelled from Egypt by his brother Ptolemy VIII Euergetes II (or Physcon: 'pot-bellied'), he went to Rome and the commission in the East led by Gnaeus Octavius was asked to settle the quarrel. As Euergetes' reign was unpopular, the brothers agreed that Philometor should have Egypt and Cyprus and Euergetes should have Cyrene. In 162, however, Euergetes came to Rome and asked for Cyprus, which was granted to him. In 154, after making a will in 155 which left his kingdom to Rome should he die without heirs (*SEG* 9.7), presumably to make it pointless for his brother to have him killed, Euergetes came to Rome to accuse his brother of an assassination attempt against him. His testament was not implemented as he had a son after he succeeded to the Egyptian throne: for his will see esp. Braund 1984: 129–31. The senate refused to listen to a counter embassy from Philometor and five commissioners were sent to restore Euergetes in Cyprus. Nothing eventuated and Euergetes made his own attempt to capture Cyprus, unsuccessfully, but was restored by his brother to Cyrene: cf. Polyb. 17.1–19.4, 33.11.1–7, 39.7.1–6; Diod. 31.33, 32.9c, 33.6–6a, 33.13; Walbank III.474–7; Badian *FC* 109–10. One of these Ptolemies, presumably Euergetes, was said to have offered marriage to Cornelia, mother of the Gracchi: doc. 8.1; see Scullard 1973: 230–1, 236–7; Sherwin-White 1984: 45, 262–3; Badian *FC* 108–10; Gruen 1986: 692–708.

1 After the two Ptolemies had partitioned the kingdom, the younger Ptolemy (Euergetes) arrived in Rome, as he wanted to cancel the division which had been effected between himself and his brother, **2** stating that it was not of his own free will, but by compulsion and under pressure of circumstances that he had done what he had been ordered to. **3** He therefore begged the senate to assign him Cyprus, for, even with this, his share would still be greatly inferior to his brother's . . . **6** As the senate saw that the divisions had been quite [unjust], and as it wanted to partition the kingdom in an effective way, with themselves responsible for the partition, they agreed to the requests of the younger brother as this coincided with their own interests. **7** For, nowadays, many of the Romans' decrees are of this kind, and they effectively increase and build up their own empire through the mistakes of their neighbours, simultaneously granting a favour and appearing to confer benefits on those who commit the mistakes. **8** Accordingly, since they perceived the importance of Egypt's kingdom and were afraid that, if it should acquire a protector, he might think more highly of himself than he should, **9** they appointed Titus Torquatus and Gnaeus Merula to accompany Ptolemy as envoys to Cyprus and put his plan and their own into execution. **10** They immediately dispatched them, with instructions to reconcile the brothers and establish the younger brother in Cyprus without warfare.

5.39 Treaty with the Jews, 161 BC

1 Maccabees 8.17–32

In 162 the Seleucid ruler Demetrius (I Soter), son of Seleucus IV and nephew of Antiochus IV Epiphanes (175–164), who had spent some 16 years in Rome as a hostage, escaped to Syria with the help of Polybius (31.11.1–15.10) and took the throne. Rome allowed him to rule and hold the title of 'king', but later supported opposition against him: Polyb. 31.33.1–5, 32.3.13, 33.18.5–14. The Jews had rebelled under Antiochus IV and, after defeating Demetrius' army in 161, Judas Maccabaeus sent an embassy to Rome to secure an alliance which was granted by the senate; cf. Joseph. *Ant.* 12.10.6; *ARS* 35. No practical help resulted: Demetrius' army again attacked Judaea and Judas was killed (1 Macc. 9.17–32; Joseph. *Ant.* 12.11.1–2); Rome was to send no actual aid for fifty years after this 'alliance', which was renewed in 142, 139 and 132 (1 Macc. 12.1–4, 14.24; Joseph. 13.5.8, 13.7.3, 13.9.2); see Habicht 1989: 346–50, 356–8; cf. Gruen 1986: 748–51; Sherwin-White 1984: 70–9, who considers, despite the wording, that a formal treaty was not signed; on treaties and their terminology, see *ibid.* 58–79.

17 And Judas chose Eupolemus, son of John, son of Accus, and Jason, son of Eleazar, and sent them to Rome to establish friendship and alliance with the Romans, **18** and to request that they would take the yoke from them, for they saw that the kingdom of the Greeks was reducing the Jews to slavery. **19** And they went to Rome, a very great journey, and came into the senate where they spoke and said, 'Judas Maccabaeus and his brothers and the people of the Jews have sent us to you to establish with you an alliance and peace, and for us to be enrolled as your allies and friends.' And the speech pleased the senate. **22** And this is the copy of the letter which the senate wrote in reply on bronze tablets and sent to Jerusalem to be for them there a memorial of peace and alliance: **23** 'May it be well for the Romans and the nation of the Jews by sea and land forever, and may the sword and enemy be far from them. **24** But if war comes first upon Rome or any of their allies in all their dominion, **25** the nation of the Jews will fight alongside them with all their heart, as the occasion prescribes for them. **26** To those making war they shall not give or supply grain, arms, money, or ships, as seems good to the Romans; and they shall keep their covenants without receiving anything for them. **27** In the same way, if war is made on the nation of the Jews first, the Romans shall fight alongside them wholeheartedly, as the occasion prescribes. **28** And grain, arms, money, or ships shall not be given to those fighting against them, as seems good to Rome; and they shall keep their covenants and that without deceit.

29 'According to these words the Romans have made a covenant with the people of the Jews. **30** And if after these words one side or the other should wish to add or subtract anything, they shall do so as they choose, and whatever they add or take away shall be ratified. **31** And concerning the wrongs that King Demetrius is committing against them, we have written to him saying, "Why have you made your yoke heavy on our friends and allies the Jews? **32** If, therefore, they appeal any more against you, we shall give the decision for them and shall make war against you by sea and land"'.

ROME'S CONQUEST OF GREECE

The Achaean exiles returned in 150 BC to find that Sparta was again on bad terms with the rest of the Achaean league. When Sparta seceded, Achaea was determined to force her back, ignoring the advice of Roman embassies and of Quintus Caecilius Metellus, the Roman commander in Macedonia. The winter of 147/6 was spent by the Achaeans in preparing for war against Sparta and at the assembly of the Achaean league war was declared (Polyb. 38.13.6). Lucius Mummius, cos. 146, was already on his way with an army to prevent the attack on Sparta, while Metellus marched south from Macedonia where he had remained after dealing with Andriscus. The Achaean forces were routed and Corinth was sacked, while a senatorial decree ordered that it was to be burnt and its property sold. Macedonia, which included southern Greece, became a Roman province and all confederacies were dissolved: Harris 1979: 146–7, 240–4; Badian *FC* 112–13; Derow 1989: 320–1.

5.40 The sack of Corinth, 146 BC

Pausanias *Description of Greece* 7.16.1, 7–10

Mummius has gained a reputation as a complete philistine: Polybius himself was present at the sack of Corinth, and tells us (39.2.1–2) that Mummius' soldiers played dice on masterpieces of Greek art; cf. Vell. 1.13.4 (any ancient works lost *en route* had to be replaced with new ones).

Gruen 1992: 123–8 argues that this is a distortion: Paus. 7.16.8 records that Mummius kept the best works of art for Rome, leaving the less distinguished for Attalus II of Pergamum, and clearly the majority of artworks ended up at Rome. For himself he kept no booty: Polyb. 39.6. The philhellene A. Postumius Albinus was his legate: Polyb. 39.1.11. According to Pliny (*Nat. Hist.* 35.24, cf. 35.99, 37.12; cf. Strabo 8.6.23) Aristides' picture of Dionysus which went to the temple of Ceres on the Aventine (though Attalus was willing to pay 100 talents for it) was the first picture from abroad to become Roman property, but foreign art had in fact been brought to Rome since Marcellus' capture of Syracuse in 211 BC (docs 4.46–7). For Mummius' magnificent triumph in 145, see Livy *Per.* 52; though a novus homo, he gained the censorship in 142: *MRR* I.465–6, 474.

1 Mummius brought with him Orestes, who had earlier been sent to deal with the conflict between the Spartans and the Achaeans, and reached the Roman army at dawn. After sending Metellus to Macedonia, he waited at the Isthmus for his whole force to assemble. 3,500 cavalry arrived, while the infantry numbered 23,000; then came Cretan archers and Philopoemen, who led troops from Attalus, sent from Pergamum on the Caicus . . . **7** At nightfall, the Achaeans, who had taken refuge in Corinth after the battle, escaped from the city; most of the Corinthians escaped with them as well. Mummius at first held back from entering Corinth, though the gates were open, suspecting that an ambush had been set inside the walls; however, on the third day after the battle, he took Corinth by storm and burnt it. **8** The Romans slaughtered most of those they captured, but Mummius sold the women and children as slaves; he also sold all the slaves who had been set free and who had fought on the Achaean side who had not immediately fallen on the battlefield. Mummius carried off the dedications which were especially admired, as well as other works of art, while he gave the lesser ones to Philopoemen, the general sent by Attalus; in my time there was still Corinthian booty at Pergamum. **9** Mummius razed the walls of all the cities that had fought against Rome, and seized their arms, even before commissioners were sent from Rome; when these arrived to act with him, he began to put down democracies and establish governments where magistrates were chosen for their property qualifications; tribute was imposed on Greece and those with property were forbidden to acquire property abroad; all confederacies based on race, whether Achaeans, Phocians, Boeotians or any other Greeks, were all put down in the same way. **10** A few years later, the Romans began to feel sorry for Greece, and restored the various ancient racial confederacies, the right to acquire property abroad, and removed the penalties Mummius had imposed; for he had ordered the Boeotians to pay 100 talents to the people of Heraclea and Euboea, and the Achaeans 200 to the Spartans. Although these impositions on the Greeks were removed by the Romans, a governor was sent out even down to my time; the Romans call him governor not of Greece, but of Achaea, because they subjugated Greece on account of the Achaeans, the leaders at that time of the Greek world.

5.41 Lucius Mummius (1)

ILS 20

(*CIL* I² 626; *ILLRP* 122; *ROL* IV.84.) Lucius Mummius (Achaicus) destroyed Corinth as consul in 146; this tablet was found at Rome on the Mons Caelius and was dedicated in 142. Mummius also left dedications at Delphi, Olympia and many other sites (*ILLRP* 327–31); see Polyb. 39.6.1–2; Paus. 5.10.5, 5.24.4; Strabo 8.6.23.

1 Lucius Mummius, son of Lucius, consul.

Under his leadership, auspices, and command, Achaea was captured and Corinth **5** destroyed and he returned to Rome for a triumph. On account of these successful achievements, this temple and statue of Hercules the Conqueror (Victor), which he had vowed during the war, **10** he dedicates as imperator.

5.42 Lucius Mummius (2)

ILS 21d

(*CIL* I² 630; *ILLRP* 331; *ROL* IV.86.) Here Mummius makes a dedication at Italica in Spain for the capture of Corinth. He had been praetor in Hispania Ulterior (Further Spain) in 153 (App. *Iber*. 6.56–8.236–43).

[Lucius Mumm]ius, son of Lucius, imperator, [gave this] on the capture of [Co]rinth [to the town of Ital]ica.

5.43 Letter of Q. Fabius Maximus to the people of Dymae

SIG³ 684

(*ARS* 40; *RDGE* 43.) Mummius settled Greece with the help of a commission of ten; democracy was no longer to be the normal form of government. According to Pausanias (doc. 5.40) governments were based on a census qualification. Reactionaries in Achaean Dymae revolted later, with the aim of cancelling debts, perhaps caused by tribute to Rome (public records were burnt), and the pro-Romans appealed to the proconsul Quintus Fabius Maximus. Clearly the Greeks and Romans differed over the meaning of 'freedom'. The few restorations are not marked. See Erskine 1994: 83–4 (dating it 'most probably' to 115; if so, the proconsul was Q. Fabius Maximus Eburnus, cos. 116: *MRR* I.530); App. *Mithr*. 58; Crawford 1977: 45–6; Gruen 1986: 524.

1 In the priesthood of Leon, when Stratocles was secretary of the council. Quintus Fabius Maximus, son of Quintus, proconsul of the Romans, to the magistrates, councillors and city of Dymae, greetings.

Since the councillors, led by **5** Cyllanius, have notified me of the crimes committed in your city, that is, the burning and the destruction of the archives and the public records, in which the leader of the entire disturbance was Sosus, son of Tauromenes, who also drafted the laws in opposition **10** to the constitution given to the Achaeans by the Romans, which I have already discussed in detail with my advisory council at Patrae; since, therefore, in committing these actions they seem to me to be devising a condition of the worst kind of political disorder and upheaval for all the Greeks, not only by disaffection towards one another and by cancellation of private debts, **15** but also by acting contrary to the freedom granted to the Greeks in common and our policy; and since the accusers have provided genuine proofs, I judge Sosus, the leader in what was done and the framer of the law for the abolition of the constitution granted by us, **20** to be liable to the death penalty, and similarly Phormiscus, son of Echesthenes, one of the demiurgi, who co-operated with those who burned the archives and the public records, as he himself confessed.

But since Timotheus, son of Nicias, who drafted the legislation with Sosus, seems less guilty, **25** I have ordered him to proceed to Rome and have exacted an oath that he shall be there on September 1 and I have informed the praetor peregrinus that he shall not be allowed to return home until . . .

5.44 A senatorial decree on the acts of Attalus III of Pergamum

OGIS 435

(*ARS* 42; *RDGE* 11.) Strabo 13.4.2; Polyb. 33.18.2–4. Attalus III, the son of Eumenes II of Pergamum, probably died in September 134. An unusual ruler, he had marked scientific interests: Diod. 34.3; Hansen 1971: 142–50. Although Ptolemy Euergetes (like Nicomedes IV of Bithynia in 75/4) had left his kingdom and wealth to Rome in default of heirs (*SEG* 9.7), Attalus' bequest seems to have surprised Rome: Attalus was only in his mid-30s: for the will, see Braund 1984: 130–3. *OGIS* 338 records the grant of freedom to Pergamum by Attalus' will, and all the Greek cities were to have autonomy: Livy *Per.* 58; Strabo 13.4.2; for the ratification of Attalus' acts, see Plut. *Ti. Gracch.* 14.1–2: doc. 8.14.

Gruen 1984: 603–4 dates this inscription and *OGIS* 436 (another copy) to 129 BC. A committee of five legati, with the pontifex maximus Scipio Nasica in charge, went out to settle affairs in 133/132. Scipio died after his arrival in Pergamum and a pretender to the throne, Aristonicus (perhaps an illegitimate son of Eumenes II), proclaimed himself Eumenes III: see Habicht 1989: 378–80, esp. n.208 for references; Magie 1950: 147–58; Hansen 1971: 150–59; Sherwin-White 1984: 84–8; Gruen 1986: 595–604. The consul Publius Licinius Crassus Mucianus arrived with an army in the summer of 131; on his death he was succeeded by M. Perperna, cos. 130, and the pretender was defeated and sent to Rome (Val. Max. 3.2.12; Strabo 14.1.38; see doc. 10.1). The war was ended by the consul Manius Aquillius, in 129, who with ten envoys created the Roman province of Asia (for Gaius Gracchus and Aquillius, see doc. 8.23). The extent of the province was reduced by granting much of Greater Phrygia and all Lycaonia to Pontus and Cappadocia (App. *Mithr.* 57; Justin 37.1.2). This inscription appears to confirm an earlier senatorial decree, with governors being instructed to adhere to the proposals of the earlier commissioners, and tacitly abolishes anything done in the name of the rebel Aristonicus: Harris 1979: 147–9; Sherwin-White 1984: 80–4; Gruen 1986: 603–8.

Decree of the senate. The praetor Gaius Popillius, son of Gaius, consulted the senate . . . on the . . . **5** of . . . ember.

Whereas there was a discussion about affairs in Pergamum as to what instructions should be given to the praetors being dispatched to Asia regarding whether the regulations, gifts, concessions, and fines that had been made by the kings in Asia up to the death of Attalus **10** should remain in force, the senate resolved as follows in regard to this affair: 'Concerning the matters brought up by the praetor Gaius Popillius, son of Gaius, the senators resolved as follows in regard to this affair: any regulations and fines or gifts and concessions which were made by King Attalus and the other kings, **15** and which took place at least one day before the death of Attalus, shall be valid, and the praetors dispatched to Asia shall alter nothing without good reason, but shall allow these to remain in force in accordance with the senate's decree.'

20 Public Servilius . . . assisted in drafting the decree.

THE WESTERN MEDITERRANEAN

Cato the Elder, as consul in 195, was sent to Hispania Citerior (Hither Spain) because of the deteriorating situation: the proconsul Gaius Sempronius Tuditanus had been killed in battle there in 196 (Livy 33.25.8–9, 33.43.1–2). Cato took with him two legions, supported by 15,000 allies,

800 cavalry and 20 warships. Between 197 and 180 there seems to have been little systematic conquest, rather 'a random hunt for peoples to fight and booty to take home': Richardson 1986: 56.

Tiberius Sempronius Gracchus (the Elder) was governor of Nearer Spain from late 180, returning in 178 with 40,000 pounds of silver (Livy 40.40.14–15, 47.1–50.5, 41.7.1–3; *MRR* I.388, 393, 395–6). He was long remembered for his integrity: for his treaties, see Polyb. 35.2.15, Plut. *Ti. Gracchus* 5.2; App. *Iber.* 6.43.179; Livy 40.50.5. The Roman offensive then halted for some 20 years, while the Romans were engaged primarily in the East. In 171, several peoples from both Spanish provinces sent delegates to Rome to complain of the misconduct of governors (Livy 43.2.1–12). Spain was a profitable possession for Rome: by this point there was a fixed tax (*stipendium*) and a 5 per cent levy on grain (Richardson 1976a: 139–40, 1986: 70–5; Curchin 1991: 60–1). Polyb. 34.9.8–9 (Strabo 3.2.10) states that there were 40,000 slaves in the silver mines at New Carthage (originally organised by Cato: Livy 34.21.7), bringing in 25,000 denarii a day in revenue for the Roman people, which implies a large group of merchants and entrepreneurs also; see doc. 6.26; Badian 1972: 31–5, *FC* 116–24; Richardson 1986: 120–3; Keay 1988: 63–6; Harris 1989: 118–42; Curchin 1991: 136–8; for Roman cultural influence on Spain: Keay 2001.

5.45 Cato the Elder in Spain

Appian *The Spanish Wars* 6.40–1 (161–70)

Cato's only active army command was during his time as consul in Spain in 195 (he had been praetor in Sardinia in 198): Livy 29.25.10, 32.8.5; Livy's account was presumably taken from Cato's own *Origines* or his *Speech on his Consulship*. Cato himself boasted that he had captured more towns in Spain than he had spent days there, and he was awarded three days of public thanksgiving (a supplicatio) and a triumph: Plut. *Cato Mai* 10.3; Livy 34.21.8, 42.1, 46.2. The senate made the mistake of disbanding his army, presumably because of Cato's representation of his victories, as conflict in Spain was by no means resolved: Livy 35.1.1–3; Astin 1978: 28–50, 302–7; Richardson 1986: 95; Harris 1989: 123–4. Ennius had been brought by Cato, when quaestor, to Rome from Sardinia in 204 (Nepos *Cato* 1.4): for their relationship and Ennius' praise of Cato later in his *Annals*, see Gruen 1990a: 107–8; Cato was however critical of generals, like Fulvius Nobilior, who took poets with them on campaign to celebrate their deeds: Cic. *Tusc. Disp.* 1.3 (Ennius accompanied Fulvius to the East and wrote the *Ambracia* to celebrate his capture of this city: cf. doc. 5.52). In the *Annals* (353–6) Ennius speaks of Cato's fighting in Spain, perhaps near Emporium in 195: 'Then the shields resounded and the iron spear-points whistled'. See Curchin 1991: 29–31; Richardson 1986: 79–94, 1996: 52–4; *MRR* I.339; cf. Livy 34.17.5–12 for the disarmament: one city, Segestica, refused, and was taken by storm.

161 When Cato sailed to Spain and arrived at the place called Emporion, the enemy gathered against him from all sides to the number of 40,000. **162** He quickly trained his army and, when he was about to engage in battle, he sent away the ships that he possessed to Marseilles and told the army: 'Do not be afraid that the enemy will overwhelm us with their numbers — for a brave spirit will always overcome superior numbers — but because we have no ships, unless we win, we have nothing — not even safety . . .' **165** When he saw that the centre of his forces were in particular difficulties, he rushed amongst them, putting himself at risk, and threw the enemy into confusion by his deeds and cries, and was the first to begin the victory. **166** He pursued them all that night, capturing their camp and killing many of them. On his return, the soldiers embraced him and celebrated with him as leader of the victory. After this he rested the army and sold the booty.

167 When all sent embassies to him, he demanded more hostages and sent sealed letters to each, telling all those who carried them to hand them over on the same day; he fixed the day by estimating when the letters would reach the furthermost town. **168** The message instructed all the magistrates of the towns to destroy their walls on the same day, that on which they received the letters; if they postponed the day, he threatened them with enslavement. **169** Having recently been defeated in a great battle, and being ignorant whether these orders had been given to them alone or to everyone, they were afraid that, if they were the only ones, that they would be powerless, and, if they were with others, that they would be the only ones to delay, and, as they had no time to send round to each other and were wary of the soldiers who had come with the letters and were standing right in front of them, they all considered their own safety to be of prime importance and hastily dismantled their walls. Once they decided to obey, they competed against each other to complete the task quickly. **170** And in this way the towns along the river Ebro themselves destroyed their own walls on a single day, as the result of just one stratagem, and, because the Romans could easily attack them, they remained mostly at peace.

5.46 L. Aemilius Paullus in Spain, 189 BC

ILS 15

(*ILLRP* 514; *CIL* 1² 64; *ARS* 22.) Paullus was in charge of Further Spain as propraetor 191–189 BC, defeating the Lusitanians in 189: Livy 37.46.7; *MRR* I.353, 357, 362. This decree on a bronze plate frees the serfs of the city of Hasta and allows them to retain the lands they worked, presumably an attempt to weaken Hasta economically and territorially by establishing them as a separate community. Hasta was again fighting the Romans in 186, when it was taken: Livy 39.21.1–4; Richardson 1986: 118; Reiter 1988: 110–11; Harris 1989: 124; Gabba 1989: 229; Curchin 1991: 31–2.

1 Lucius Aemilius, son of Lucius, commander-in-chief, decreed that the serfs of the people of Hasta, who live in the tower of Lascuta, are to be free; he ordered that the land and town **5** which they possessed at that time they are to possess and hold as long as this is the wish of the Roman people and senate. Enacted in camp, 19th day of January.

5.47 Massacre in Spain, 151–150 BC

Appian *The Spanish Wars* 6.51–2, 59–60 (215–20, 247–55)

In 154 the Lusitanians in Further Spain, who were still independent, invaded Roman territory and defeated two praetors (App. *Iber.* 6.56–7.234–40), even crossing to North Africa. Rome, under the consul Q. Fulvius Nobilior, was also seriously defeated by the Celtiberians in 153 (Polyb. 35.1.1: the 'fiery war'). Though M. Claudius Marcellus, consul for the third time in 152, was successful in Spain and urged that peace be made, the senate wanted military triumphs and continued the war (Polyb. 35.2.1–3.9, App. 6.49.206–8). Marcellus, however, did arrange a peace on the surrender of some tribes. His successor, L. Licinius Lucullus, cos. 151, without authority, attacked the Vaccaei, a Celtiberian tribe, despite the fact that they were not at war with Rome. After an initial engagement in which his troops killed some 3,000 of the inhabitants, he ordered the killing of 20,000 men at the Vaccaenan city of Cauca in 151, though they had surrendered; see Scullard 1980: 300–3; Richardson 1986: 60–4; Harris 1989: 133–4, 137; cf. Badian *FC* 124–5.

In Lusitania, Sulpicius Galba, praetor in Hispania Ulterior in 151 and prorogued for 150, defeated and accepted the surrender of 8,000 Lusitanians, who were then butchered. The avaricious Galba was brought to trial for his misconduct in Spain but still became consul in 144: Cato published his speech against Galba in book 7 of his *Origines* (Gell. 13.25.15). Shortly after this a tribune, Lucius Calpurnius Piso Frugi, passed in 149 a law setting up a permanent court of senators to deal with extortion (*quaestio de rebus repetundis*) through the Lex Calpurnia (*MRR* I.459; Cic. *Brut.* 106). Appian portrays both L. Licinius Lucullus and Galba as greedy (6.51.215, 54.230, 60.255), and condemns the 'glory-seekers' in the senate (80.349).

Viriathus survived Galba's massacre and was to become the hero of the resistance to the Romans, being finally assassinated by treachery in 139: Livy *Per.* 52; Dio F73; Diod. 33.1.1–5, 21; Richardson 1986: 126–49; Curchin 1991: 33–6.

215 The war against the Belli, Titthi and Arevaci had in this way come to an end before Lucullus' time, but Lucullus, who was eager for glory and needed money because of his poverty, attacked the Vaccaei, another Celtiberian tribe, neighbours of the Aravaci, though no vote on this had taken place, nor had the Vaccaei made war on the Romans or wronged Lucullus himself in any way. **216** He crossed the river called the Tagus and arrived at the town of Cauca and made camp beside it . . . **218** On the next day the elders, wearing crowns and carrying olive-branches, again asked Lucullus what they should do to be friends. He demanded that they give hostages and 100 talents of silver and ordered that their cavalry fight on his side. **219** When he had received all this, he demanded that a garrison enter the town. The Caucaei accepted this too, and he led in 2,000 men, chosen for their courage, whom he told to take up positions on the walls once they were inside. When the 2,000 had taken the walls, Lucullus led in the rest of the army and with a trumpet blast signalled that they should kill all the Caucaei of age. **220** The Caucaei, calling on their guarantees and the gods as witnesses of their oaths, and cursing the Romans for their bad faith, were savagely slaughtered, with only a few of the 20,000 men escaping through difficult passages; Lucullus sacked the town and brought the Romans into disrepute . . .

247 Lucullus had made war without authority on the Vaccaei and was at that point wintering in Turditania. Learning that the Lusitanians were making attacks on the neighbouring regions, he sent out his best commanders and killed about 4,000 of them. **248** He also killed about 1,500 others as they were crossing the straits near Cadiz, and, when the remainder took refuge on a hill, he fenced them off with a ditch and captured a vast number of them. He also invaded Lusitania and ravaged it bit by bit. **249** Galba also ravaged it on the other side. When some of their envoys came to Galba, wanting to confirm the treaty they had made with Atilius, the previous general, and then broken, he received them and made a truce, pretending to feel sympathy with them because they were compelled by poverty to plunder, make war and break treaties. **250** 'For,' he said, 'the poverty of your soil and your penniless condition force you to do these things; I will divide you into three and give you, my poor friends, good land, settling you in fertile country.'

251 Expecting this to happen, they left their own country and gathered at the place Galba had appointed; he divided them into three groups, and showed each a certain plain, commanding them to remain on this plain until he came and told them where to settle. **252** When he came to the first division, he instructed them as friends to put down their arms, and, when they had done so, he fenced them off with a ditch and sent in men with swords who slaughtered them all, as they lamented and called on the names of the gods and their guarantees of good faith. **253** In the same way he rushed to the second and third divisions and slaughtered them, while they were still ignorant of what had happened to the first, repaying treachery with treachery and imitating barbarians in a way not worthy of the Romans. **254** A few of them escaped, among them Viriathus, who not long afterwards became leader of the Lusitanians, killing many Romans and achieving great successes. But I shall speak later of these subsequent events. **255** Galba, who was more avaricious than Lucullus, then distributed a small amount of the booty to his troops, and a little to his friends, but kept the rest for himself although he was already one of the wealthiest of the Romans; but they say that even in peace he did not stop lying and breaking his word for the sake of gain. Although hated and brought to court, he escaped because of his wealth.

5.48 Rome repudiates treaties

Livy *Periochae* 54–6

From 144 Celtiberian revolt centred around the town of Numantia. Revolt was exacerbated by the Romans' constant repudiation of peace agreements.

54: the treaty made by Pompeius, consul in 141, was not ratified by the senate: App. *Iber.* 6.79.338–44; Harris 1989: 135 n. 146 emends the text to 'because of his weakness', not 'repudiated by the Roman people'. Quintus Fabius is probably Q. Fabius Maximus Aemilianus (cos. 145) not Fabius Servilianus his brother by adoption (cos. 142): App. 6.69.293–4; *MRR* I.480. Viriathus defeated at least four Roman armies and from 145 consuls were sent against him. In 141/0 he surrounded a Roman army and terms were made. Fabius' treaty was ratified (App. 6.69.294), but then disowned at the instigation of Q. Servilius Caepio, new governor of Hispania Ulterior and consul in 140, who was sent out to resurrect the war. The assassins, Audax, Minurus and Ditalco had been sent by Viriathus in 139 to negotiate with Servilius, who bribed them, but later refused them their rewards: App. 6.75.319 states that Viriathus' resistance lasted 8 years (i.e., from 147), not 14. Marcus Popillius Laenas was consul in 139 and serving in Spain as proconsul; the treaty broken was that made earlier by Pompeius.

C. Hostilius Mancinus, consul in 137, in attempting to withdraw from Numantia by night, was trapped and surrounded; terms made by the quaestor Ti. Sempronius Gracchus (tr. pl. 133) saved the lives of the 20,000 Romans, but were repudiated by the senate: Plut. *Ti. Gracch.* 5 (doc. 8.7); App. 6.79–80.345–8. Mancinus was handed over to the Numantines by the senate, to honour its good faith, naked and in chains, but the offer was not taken up: remarkably he was elected to a second praetorship and commissioned a statue of himself being handed over to the Numantines: Pliny *Nat. Hist.* 34.18; Rosenstein 1990: 148–9; Gruen 1992: 119–20; *MRR* I.484, 486. D. Junius Brutus ('Callaicus', for his victory over the Gallaeci), cos. 138, reconquered tribes in 137–136; his Gallaeci campaign in north-west Spain was in 134. His gift of land was perhaps to soldiers, i.e., veterans, who had fought *against* Viriathus, not under him (Harris 1989: 140; but see Richardson 1986: 147, 161; Keaveney 1998: 66–73, 87 for the dates of his campaigns). Aemilius Lepidus Porcina undertook his campaign on his own initiative and was fined by the senate after his return: App. 6.80–83, 85. Appian comments on Porcina (6.80.349) 'some took their governorships not for the benefit of the state, but for fame, material rewards, or the honour of a triumph'; see Harris 1989: 131–5; Richardson 1986: 66–8.

54 The consul Quintus Pompeius conquered the Termestini in Spain (141 BC). He made a peace-treaty with them and the Numantines, which was repudiated by the Roman people . . . Quintus Fabius, as proconsul, won successes in Spain but spoiled his record by making peace with Viriathus on equal terms (140 BC). Viriathus was assassinated by traitors at the instigation of Servilius Caepio and was greatly mourned by his army and given a noble burial. He was a great man and a great leader and, in the 14 years in which he waged war against the Romans, he got the better of them more often than not. **55** The consul Junius Brutus in Spain gave those who had served under Viriathus land and a town, called Valentia. Marcus Popillius, after a peace treaty with the Numantines had been repudiated by the senate, was routed and put to flight by them together with his army. When the consul Gaius Hostilius Mancinus was sacrificing, the chickens flew out of their enclosure; later when he was going on board his ship to set out for Spain, the cry, 'Stay, Mancinus', was heard; that these omens were unfavourable was proved by the outcome. For he was both defeated by the Numantines and his camp despoiled, and, when there was no hope of saving his army, he made a ignominious peace with them, which the senate refused to ratify. 40,000 Romans were defeated by 4,000 Numantines. Decimus Junius totally subdued Lusitania, by storming its cities right up to the Atlantic Ocean. **56** Decimus Junius Brutus waged a successful campaign in Further Spain against the Gallaeci. A different outcome resulted when the proconsul Marcus Aemilius Lepidus made war on the Vaccaei, and he suffered a similar disaster to that at Numantia. To release the Roman people from the sanctity of the Numantine treaty, for which he was responsible, Mancinus was handed over to the Numantines, who would not accept him.

5.49 Scipio Aemilianus ejects army camp-followers

Appian *The Spanish Wars* 6.84–5 (363–70)

By 134 only the northern peoples of Spain (in the mountains parallel to the north coast) and the Aravaci of the Numantia region remained unsubdued. To deal with the situation — recruitment for Spain had become very unpopular — Scipio Aemilianus was elected consul for 134, despite a law forbidding second consulships, and raised a force of volunteers. Appian's detailed account may derive from the work of Rutilius Rufus (*HRR* 1² 187–90) who served as military tribune under Scipio at Numantia (App. 6.88.382).

Scipio tightened up discipline in the Spanish troops and evicted all unnecessary camp-followers and equipment: Livy *Per.* 57: 2,000 prostitutes; Val. Max. 2.7.1; Astin 1967: 135–6. Lucilius was a close friend of Scipio Aemilianus and in his entourage at Numantia, though Gruen 1992: 280–9 argues against Lucilius dedicating one book of satires to Scipio and against Scipio as Lucilius' literary patron. Many of the satires contain allusions to the Spanish campaign: Lucilius *Satires* 11.430–1, 'In response to this, our praetor (said): 'What a dirty face he has, because all those people to a man/ He has expelled out of the camp, like shit thrown out of doors'; cf. 438–9, which mentions the Spaniards' war-cloaks, trousers and torques (heavy metal collars); Vell. 2.9.3.

Similarly Metellus Numidicus during the Jugurthan campaign evicted the camp-followers (lixae), did not allow bread or cooked food to be sold in the camp, and forbade soldiers slaves or mules; Marius continued this practice (Sall. *BJ* 45.2, Plut. *Mar.* 13). Camp-followers, however, could play useful military roles on occasions: see Gilliver 1999: 29–31; cf. MacMullen 1984: 444–5.

363 In Rome the people, tired of the Numantine issue, as the war had been much longer and more difficult than they had expected, chose Cornelius Scipio, the conqueror of Carthage, to be consul for a second time, as the only person able to overcome the Numantines. **364** Even at that point he was still younger than the age-limit for consuls, and so the senate, just as when he was elected to fight against the Carthaginians, once more decreed that the tribunes should repeal the law about the age-limit and bring it in again the next year . . . **367** When he arrived, he drove out all the merchants, prostitutes, diviners, and fortune-tellers, whom the soldiers constantly consulted in their anxiety over their lack of success; and, for the future, he prohibited the importation of anything superfluous, not even a victim prepared for divination. **368** He also ordered that the wagons and the superfluous items loaded on them, and the draft animals, except for those he exempted, be sold. Furthermore, no one was permitted to have any equipment for cooking, except a spit, a bronze pot, and one drinking-cup. Their food was restricted to boiled and roast meat. **369** He forbade them to have beds, and was the first to lie down to rest on a straw mattress. He also forbade them to ride on mules while marching: 'For what can be expected in war,' he said, 'from a man unable to walk on foot?' When they rubbed themselves with oil and when they were in the baths, they put on their own oil, as Scipio joked that it was those, like mules, who had no hands, that needed others to rub them down. **370** In this way he converted them all to self-restraint, and got them used to respect and fear, as it was difficult to get access to him and he was averse to granting favours, especially those against regulations.

5.50 The end of Numantia, 133 BC

Appian *The Spanish Wars* 6.97–8 (419–24)

Scipio surrounded Numantia with seven camps and a massive stone wall nine kilometres in length and some three metres high, starving it out in 133 BC after a siege of 8 months (Marius (doc. 9.22), Jugurtha (doc. 9.3), Polybius, the poet Lucilius, and Gaius Gracchus were all there). The populace, which had resorted to cannibalism, were sold as slaves, but he allowed a day in which those who wished could commit suicide. The city was destroyed and the senate dispatched 10 legati to organise its territory and that conquered by Callaicus: Astin 1967: 137–60; Scullard 1980: 303–6; Keay 1988: 38–42; Harris 1989: 135–6; doc. 5.48).

419 Such was the love of freedom and of courage in a city that was both barbarian and small in size. In peace time there were only about 8,000 inhabitants, yet they inflicted such numerous great defeats on the Romans, made such treaties with them on terms of complete equality (though the Romans never agreed to make such treaties with anyone), and frequently challenged in battle such a great general, the last to be sent against them, who surrounded them with 60,000 men. **420** He was, of course, a better general than they were, and would not come to grips with wild beasts, but exhausted them through starvation, an evil which cannot be fought, through which alone it was possible to take the Numantines and through which alone they were taken. **421** This is what I have to say about the Numantines, looking at their small numbers, their ability to bear hardship, their many achievements, and the length of time they held out; **422** first of all, those who wished killed themselves, each in his own way; the rest came out on the third day to the appointed spot, an appalling sight and a completely inhuman one, with their bodies unwashed, full of hair, nails and filth, smelling dreadfully, with their clothes foul and stinking no less than they did. **423** To their enemies, this made them seem pitiable, but their expressions made them terrifying; for they looked at the Romans in a way that displayed their anger, their grief, their suffering, and their consciousness of their cannibalism. **424** Scipio chose 50 of them for his triumph, sold the rest and destroyed the city.

THE IMPACT OF GREEK CULTURE ON ROME

Between 211 (Marcellus' capture of Syracuse) and 146 BC (Mummius' sack of Corinth and Scipio Aemilianus' sack of Carthage), Rome was flooded with the spoils of war; this included Greek art, as well as goods such as precious metals, gems, money and slaves. Vast sums were acquired through conquests in both the East and West. The drive to acquire religious statues and works of art had gained momentum during the Second Punic War: Harris 1979: 261–2; Gruen 1992: 86–93. For rules for plundering and division of booty, see Polyb. 10.16.2–9. Generals had the right to distribute booty (Shatzman 1972: 177–205) and could retain a substantial share for themselves: this could be used for the building of temples, monuments or other public purposes, to advertise the general's successes. Mummius, for example, used his share of booty from Corinth to beautify Italy and the provinces and Cicero praises Aemilius Paullus, Scipio Aemilianus and Lucius Memmius for retaining little wealth for themselves: Cic. *Off.* 2.76; cf. Polyb. 39.6.1; docs 5.41–2. Generally allied and citizen soldiers received the same share of booty: when Gaius Claudius Pulcher, cos. 177, only gave the allied soldiers half shares, they marched in silence at his triumph to show their displeasure (Livy 41.13.8; Harris 1984: 97).

Secular works could be kept as private property, but dedications and votive offerings won as booty were usually placed publicly in Roman temples, often with an inscription celebrating the victor. Marcellus, for example, seized many religious statues in his capture of Syracuse, which he dedicated in his temple of Honour and Virtue (only keeping one object for himself): docs 4.46–7; Livy 25.40.1–3; Polyb. 9.10.2–13; Gruen 1992: 94–101; Rawson 1989: 432–3. See Pollitt 1978: 157–8, 170–4 for a list of Rome's holdings of major works of art; cf. MacMullen 1991: 424–6; Morel 1989: 493–4.

A provincial governorship could be extremely profitable: Licinius Lucullus and Galba in Spain made war for plunder (doc. 5.47); Verres as governor in Sicily extorted 40 million sesterces in 3 years (Cic. *Verr.* 1.56; Harris 1979: 78; see doc. 5.65). Aemilius Paullus, who was 'not well off' for a Roman noble, left more than 60 talents (Plut. *Aem.* 39, Polyb. 31.28.3); Scipio Aemilianus, who was a man of moderate property 'for a Roman', gave two daughters dowries of 50 talents each: Polyb. 18.35.10; 31.27.2; doc. 7.70. Such rewards for victory were all the more valuable, as the Lex Claudia of 218 limited ways in which Roman senators or their sons might engage in trade, and they were prohibited from owning sea-going ships of a capacity of more than 300 amphorae: Livy 21.63.4, 'since money-making was considered undignified in a senator'; cf. Cic. *Verr.* 2.2.18; Yavetz 1962; Rawson 1989: 424; Vishnia 1996: 34–42.

Successful warfare also generated prestige (*dignitas*) and popularity (as well as personal wealth). According to Cicero (when defending a military man), true gloria was only won in war (doc. 5.5) and was the attribute most desired by Roman nobles. A general's military success was signalled by the senate's award of a triumph, in which the commander was able to show off booty and captives; see Gruen 1990a: 130–3 on the 'scramble' for triumphs after the Hannibalic War (esp. 200–180 BC). Such perceptions naturally added to the intense rivalry for office among the very competitive magisterial class (Polyb. 6.57.5–6). It was an honour to be awarded an extra cognomen from the site of a splendid victory: L. Mummius (Achaicus), Q. Caecilius Metellus (Macedonicus), L. Cornelius Scipio (Asiagenus), P. Cornelius Scipio (Africanus and Numantinus) and Q. Caecilius Metellus (Numidicus).

The treasury, and hence the Roman people, won great economic gains from their generals' victories: Flamininus, for example, in 194 returned with 18,270 pounds of silver, 84,000 tetradrachms (silver coins worth four drachmas), 3,714 pounds of gold, 14,514 gold coins and numerous works of art; 250 asses were given to each of the infantry, 500 to centurions, 750 to equites (Livy 34.52.4–11, Plut. *Flam.* 14). This was not used to recoup the costs of the war: Roman policy insisted that the costs of war should be reimbursed by the defeated enemy; according to Livy's figures between 200 and 167 BC 250,000,000 silver denarii or the equivalent was acquired by the state through indemnities and booty, and according to Pliny the treasury in 157 had a vast surplus of over 100 million sesterces (Pliny *Nat. Hist.* 33.55–6; Sherwin-White 1984: 15; cf. Badian 1972: 30; Gruen 1984; Yavetz 1991). Rome's Italian allies also received extensive economic benefits from Rome's conquests: Harris 1984: esp. 100–2. Vast numbers of slaves were acquired in conquest, like the 150,000 Epirotes acquired in 167 (docs 5.33, 6.9); for estimates of numbers, see Harris 1979: 80–3; once Delos was set up as a free port after 167, it could handle the sale of 10,000 slaves a day: Strabo 14.668 (referring to 142–137 BC). This, of course, had a great impact on agriculture in Italy and Sicily and the growth of slave-run landed estates. Not all slaves were captives in war: freelance slave traders made a significant contribution to the slave market, and there were numerous Syrians and Cilicians active in the Sicilian slave wars (docs 6.43–4); see Crawford 1977: 42–52 for the economic consequences of Rome's exploitation of the Greek East. Even slaves captured in war were not transferred to Italy *en masse*, but sold on the spot, reaching Italy via the medium of the slave trade: Millar 1984: 10; Bradley 1994: 33–6.

A high proportion of Roman adult males had the chance to come into contact with other cultures: perhaps more than half the Roman male adult population fought at some time in the army: Hopkins 1978: 35; Rawson 1989: 435; Roman senators were regularly sent on embassies to foreign states; and some Romans also experienced temporary slavery in the East: Plut. *Flam.* 13.4–5 mentions 1,200 Romans captured during the Second Punic War who served as slaves in Greece and were later ransomed by Flamininus (doc. 4.36), while in 189 Q. Fabius Labeo was awarded a naval triumph for rescuing 4,000 Roman and Italian slaves from the Cretans (Livy 37.60.5–6, citing Valerius Antias).

5.51 Scipio Africanus goes Hellenic in Syracuse

Livy *History of Rome* 29.19.10–13

Cf. Val. Max. 3.6.1; Plut. *Cato Mai.* 3.5–7. Fabius Maximus and other senators attacked Scipio for his conduct while he was preparing for war in Africa. In addition, the Locrians had complained of the behaviour of his legate Pleminius and other Roman troops under Scipio's command after the recapture of Locri in 205 BC (Livy 29.16.4–18.20). Scipio is here criticised not for his interest in Greek activities *per se*, but because he pursues them so openly; he is not behaving in a manner befitting a Roman commander on duty. Scipio was a lover of Greek culture and was granted honours by Greek communities; his son composed a history of Rome in Greek (Cic. *Brut.* 77; cf. *Sen.* 35); Scullard 1973: 132; Gruen 1992: 242–3. Naevius supposedly attacked Scipio in his poems, for being dragged away from his mistress by his father, wearing only a pallium (a Greek garment): doc. 4.57. A statue of Africanus' brother Lucius, set up after the defeat of Antiochus in 189, caused comment because Lucius was shown dressed (in Greek fashion) in sandals and chlamys (a short cloak): Cic. *Rab. Post.* 10.27; he also took the title Asiagenus, though was later known as Asiaticus: Livy 39.44.1; Diod. 34.33.1; Rawson 1989: 440 comments that Asiagenus, rather than the more correct 'Asiaticus', shows an ignorance of Greek.

The antagonism between Scipio and Cato is presented by Plutarch as originating at this time, when Cato as quaestor in 204 served with Scipio in Sicily (Plut. *Cato Mai.* 3.5–7 has Cato criticise Scipio for pandering to his troops and spending too much time in the palaestra ('wrestling ground') and theatre; Scullard 1973: 112); this could be a throwback from their later quarrels: Rawson 434; cf. Plut. 3.7, Astin 1978: 14. For the expensive festival paraphernalia of Scipio's wife Aemilia, see doc. 7.70.

10 Not all the senators' opinions could be asked on that day because of the party spirit which was inflamed for and against Scipio. **11** In addition to the crime of Pleminius and the disastrous situation of the Locrians, even the general's appearance was the subject of attack, not only as un-Roman, but even as unsoldierly: **12** he was said to stroll about in the gymnasium in Greek mantle (*pallium*) and sandals; to give his attention to books and exercising in the palaestra; his entire staff was enjoying the amenities of Syracuse in idleness and relaxation; **13** Carthage and Hannibal had been entirely forgotten; and the whole army was being spoiled by lack of discipline, just as had happened at Sucro in Spain and currently at Locri, and was more to be feared by allies than by the enemy.

5.52 The triumph of Gnaeus Manlius Vulso, 186 BC

Livy *History of Rome* 39.6.3–7.5

Cf. Polyb. 21.34.1–37.9; Livy 38.12–27: Vulso (cos. 189) as proconsul took 40,000 prisoners from the Galatians of central Asia Minor at Mt Olympus (who were sold to neighbouring tribes: App. *Syr.* 42) and levied large sums from different cities for Rome's 'friendship'. He celebrated a triumph over the Galatians, whom he defeated in two battles (*MRR* I.366, 369); for arguments against the belief that Vulso's campaign had mainly been for plunder, see Grainger 1995, esp. 41–2. For the luxuries imported from the East, see Pliny *Nat. Hist.* 34.14 (where the list is derived from L. Calpurnius Piso), 34.34, 37.12. Political attacks on Vulso at the time tried to block his triumph (Livy 38.44.1–50.3), but allegations criticising his introduction of luxury are later (Pliny 34.34), as with those against L. Scipio Asiagenus: Pliny *Nat. Hist.* 33.148; cf. Vell. 2.1–2; Polyb. 6.57.5–7, dating the introduction of luxury to 146; cf. Levick 1982. Attacks on captured art objects as a source of moral decline date to later in the Republic with no connection to imports of artefacts from the East or Greece, while Sallust blames Sulla for the demoralisation of the army in the 80s in 'voluptuous' Asia (*Cat.* 11.5–6). Vulso's booty was used to reimburse citizens for their war loans, probably including those made during the Second Punic War: Buraselis 1996: esp. 165–6.

Similarly M'. Acilius Glabrio (cos. 191) was attacked by Cato regarding items captured in his campaign against Antiochus which never appeared in his triumph or in the treasury: Livy 37.57.10–58.2; *ORF*⁴ F66; Astin 1989: 179 points out that both Cato and Glabrio were rivals for the censorship; cf. Scullard 1973: 137; Shatzman 1972: 191–4; Gruen 1992: 111; Vishnia 1996: 128–9. M. Fulvius Nobilior (cos. 189), after ending the Aetolian War in 187, was accused by the Ambraciotes of extortion and of despoiling every temple, an attack engineered by his political rivals. He brought many artists to Rome (Livy 39.22.2), as did Scipio Asiagenus (39.22.10), and took Ennius with him on campaign (Cic. *Tusc. Disp.* 1.3). For Pyrrhus' palace at Ambracia: Livy 38.9.13; Scullard 1973: 181–4; Harris 1979: 224–5. Cistophoroi were Asiatic coins worth approximately four drachmas; philippei were Macedonian gold coins worth twenty drachmas.

6.3 At the end of the year, when the magistrates had already been elected, on the third day before the Nones of March, Gnaeus Manlius Vulso triumphed over the Gauls (i.e., the Galatians) who live in Asia. **4** The reason for his leaving the celebration of his triumph so late was to avoid making his defence under the lex Petillia before the praetor Quintus Terentius Culleo and being consumed in the flames of another's trial, where Lucius Scipio had been condemned, **5** in as much as the jurors were far more hostile to him than to Scipio, because rumour stated that he, as Scipio's successor, by allowing all kinds of licence, had ruined the military discipline which Scipio had strictly preserved. **6** Nor was this the only grounds on which he was criticised — hearsay accounts of what had occurred in his province far out of sight — but more damning was the evidence seen daily in the conduct of his soldiers. **7** For the army which returned from Asia introduced the beginnings of foreign luxury into the city. They brought to Rome, for the first time, bronze couches, valuable robes as coverings, tapestries and other textiles, and — what was at that time considered to be splendid pieces of furniture — tables with one foot and ornate sideboards. **8** Female lute-players and harpists and other entertaining acts became a feature of banquets; moreover, the banquets themselves began to be prepared with both greater care and expense. **9** It was then that the cook — to the men of olden times the most worthless of slaves in both monetary valuation and practical value — began to be worth something, and what had been merely an occupation now came to be seen as an art-form. But even these imports, which were then seen as remarkable, were hardly even the seeds of the luxury which was to follow.

7.1 In his triumph, Gnaeus Manlius bore 212 golden crowns, 220,000 pounds of silver, 2,103 pounds of gold, 127,000 Attic four-drachma pieces, 250,000 cistophori, and 16,320 gold philippei, **2** as well as arms and many Gallic spoils carried in wagons, while 52 enemy leaders were led before his chariot. He gave the soldiers 42 denarii each, twice that to each centurion, three times that to each eques, and doubled their pay; **3** many soldiers of all ranks, who had been given military awards, followed his chariot. Songs which were sung by the soldiers about their general clearly showed that they were sung about an indulgent commander who courted their goodwill, and that the triumph was conspicuous more by the applause of the soldiers than that of civilians. **4** But Manlius' friends were able to win popularity with the people as well; **5** at their urging, the senate passed a decree that the arrears of the tax contributed by the people into the treasury should be paid out of the money which had been carried in the triumph. The city quaestors scrupulously paid 25 and one half asses for every thousand asses.

5.53 Tiberius Sempronius Gracchus dedicates a painting, 174 BC

Livy *History of Rome* 41.28.8–10

Tiberius Sempronius Gracchus (the Elder) commissioned a huge painting, including a map, as a memorial of his victory in Sardinia, which was placed in the temple of Mater Matuta at Rome and dedicated to Jupiter; for his promagistracy in Sardinia: *MRR* I.397–8, 401–2.

The family name of Fabius Pictor (aristocrat, historian and diplomat) was said to have been acquired by an ancestor who painted frescoes in the temple of Salus in 303: Pliny *Nat. Hist.* 35.19; Val. Max. 8.14.6 (a 'vulgar occupation'). The poet Pacuvius also executed a painting for the temple of Hercules in the Forum Boarium: Pliny 35.19. By the late Republic, however, such occupations were the preserve of professional artisans and artists (Pliny 35.20). Quintus Hortensius paid 36,000 denarii for just one picture: Pliny 35.130; he also left 10,000 jars of Chian wine in his will (Pliny 14.95).

8 In the same year a tablet was placed in the temple of Mater Matuta with the following inscription: 'Under the command and auspices of the consul Tiberius Sempronius Gracchus, the legion and army of the Roman people conquered Sardinia. In that province more than 80,000 of the enemy were killed or captured. **9** After the state had been successfully organised, the allies freed, and the revenues restored, he brought the army back home safe and unimpaired and loaded with booty; for the second time he entered the city of Rome in triumph. To commemorate this he dedicated this tablet to Jupiter.' **10** It had the shape of the island of Sardinia and on it depictions of the battles were painted.

5.54 Dilettantism among young aristocrats

Diodorus Siculus *Library of History* 37.3.1–6

Diodorus is here referring specifically to the period following the Third Macedonian War (171–168 BC). Paullus brought home after Pydna and his Greek tour huge amounts of spoils, as well as an artist, Metrodorus, to decorate his triumph: Livy 45.32.8–33.7; Plut. *Aem.* 6.5; Pliny *Nat. Hist.* 35.135; Macrob. 3.16.1 on young nobles wearing perfumes, drinking with prostitutes and going only reluctantly and late in the day to the comitium. The criticism here is especially directed against extravagance and epicureanism (qualities very much opposed to the Romans' traditional view of their own ancestral frugality and self-control). For Cato's remark, cf. Diod. 31.24; Cato *(ORF*[4] F96) also criticised the erection of statues to the cooks Ochus and Dionysodorus.

For the symposium as the 'most concentrated manifestation of "civilisation" of which the Romans had experience', see MacMullen 1991: 431–3. Note Scipio Aemilianus' disapproval of long-sleeved tunics in his speech against Sulpicius Gallus: doc. 7.57.

1 In olden days the Romans, by employing the best laws and customs, gradually increased their power to such an extent that they gained the greatest and most glorious empire within memory. In more recent times, when most nations had been subjugated and peace was of long duration, love of ancient custom at Rome turned to perdition. **2** For, with the end of warfare, the youth turned to luxury and licentiousness, using their wealth to obtain their desires. Extravagance was preferred throughout the city to frugality, leisure to the practice of warlike deeds; the man considered blessed by the populace was not the man who was ornamented by his excellences, but the man who spent his whole life enjoying the most enticing pleasures. **3** Accordingly, elaborate dishes at expensive dinner-parties became fashionable, and the perfumes of wondrous unguents, the provision of costly, coloured draperies and the construction of dining-couches from ivory and silver and the other most expensive materials by the most skilful artisans. With wines, one that only moderately delighted the palate was rejected, while Falernian, Chian and every wine which gave similar pleasure to these were consumed without restraint, as were those fish and other delicacies which were most highly prized for enjoyment. **4** In line with this, the young men would wear garments of incredible softness in the Forum, so fine as to be transparent, something similar to women's clothes. And since they were providing themselves with everything relating to pleasure and ruinous ostentation, they soon raised the price of these commodities to unbelievable heights. **5** A jar of wine sold for 100 drachmas, a jar of Pontic preserved fish for 400 drachmas, chefs especially gifted in the arts of cookery for four talents, and male catamites of exceptional beauty for many talents . . . **6** Marcus Cato, a prudent man distinguished for his good conduct, denounced in the senate the prevalence of luxury at Rome, saying that only in this city were jars of Pontic preserved fish worth more than men who drove a yoke of oxen, and pretty boys more than farmland.

5.55 The social impact of conquest on Rome

Polybius *Histories* 31.25.2–8

Polybius is here praising Scipio Aemilianus, his friend and patron; Scipio was 18 years old at the time to which this passage refers (c. 167/6). With the wealth in money and slaves that poured into

Rome in the first half of the second century, many upper-class Romans acquired a taste for Greek pursuits, artefacts and extravagance: Walbank III.499–502; Wardman 1976: 25–60; Balsdon 1979: 30–58. Appreciation of Greek culture was not necessarily seen as conflicting with Roman standards, and it is incorrect to label Romans as 'philhellene' or 'antihellene': Gruen 1992: 223–71; Rawson 1989: 448–63. Cato's speech against the repeal of the *lex Oppia* (Livy 34.2.1–4.20; cf. doc. 7.67) as presented by Livy bemoans the use of statues and ornaments but is anachronistic (a reflection of Augustan policy: Pollitt 1978: 158–60). Similarly the 'Scipionic circle' (whether political or cultural) is something of a misnomer: Saunders 1944; Astin 1967: 294–306; Gruen 1992: 226. Polybius here is unusual in linking Rome's moral failure with the aftermath of the Third Macedonian War, and the impact of Greek lack of discipline: accusations of enjoyment of luxuries are not generally linked with hellenism (Gruen 1992: 260) and there was usually a distinction made between the public man and his private interests (MacMullen 1991: 430, 438).

Scipio was fond of Xenophon's *Cyropaedia*, and had Panaetius, a Stoic philosopher, live with him, but retained his 'Roman' principles; cf. Cic. *Tusc. Disp.* 1.81, 2.62; Astin 1967: esp. 12–25. Laelius, in Cic. *Rep.* 1.34, says Scipio frequently discussed the best form of state with Panaetius in the presence of Polybius. According to Plutarch, Aemilius Paullus gave his children a liberal education, including training in sculpture and drawing, and while in Greece, after Pydna, had Scipio taught hunting and gave him and his brother Perseus' library (Plut. *Aem.* 6.5, 28.6, 10–11; cf. Polyb. 18.35.4–5); for Scipio's return to Sicily of art plundered by the Carthaginians, see Cic. *Verr.* 2.2.86.

As censor in 142, Scipio attacked Sulpicius Gallus for homosexuality (doc. 7.57) and Tiberius Claudius Asellus for wasting a third of his patrimony and spending more on a prostitute than he had reported for the census as the value of all the equipment of his Sabine estate: Gell. 6.11.9; Astin 1967: 90–1, 115–24; *MRR* I.474–5.

2 The first object of Scipio's desire to lead a good life was to win a reputation for temperance and in this respect to surpass all the young men of his age. **3** This is a great prize and one difficult to attain, but was one easy to win in Rome at this time because of the tendency of most of the young men towards vice. **4** For some of them had given themselves up to homosexual relationships with boys, or to affairs with courtesans, many to musical entertainments and drinking-parties and the extravagance these involve, having swiftly become attached to the Greeks' laxity during the war against Perseus. **5** So unbridled was the licence that the youth had fallen into in such matters that many paid a talent for a favourite boy, and many 300 drachmas for a jar of Pontic pickled fish. Marcus (Cato), indignant at this, once said in a speech to the people that the best sign that the state was degenerating was when lovely boys fetched more than fields and jars of pickled fish more than ploughmen. **6** It was at the time we are speaking of that the current tendency became obvious, first of all because, after the Macedonian kingdom fell, they thought that their universal sovereignty was uncontested, **7** and next because, after the wealth of Macedonia had been brought to Rome, there was a great parade of riches both in private life and in public. **8** Only Scipio set out to follow the opposite lifestyle, combating all his desires and shaping his life to be in all respects uniform and harmonious, gaining in about the first five years a universal reputation for self-discipline and temperance.

5.56 The lex Fannia and sumptuary legislation, 161 BC

Aulus Gellius *Attic Nights* 2.24.2–4

(Lucilius 1172.) At the Megalesia nobles gave dinner-parties to each other on 4 April; the ludi Romani (in Cicero's time) lasted from 5 to 19 September; the plebeian games from 4 to 17 November; the Saturnalia, originally on 17 December, later lasted for seven days.

The *lex Orchia* in 182 had limited the number of dinner guests: Macrob. 3.17.2; Scullard 1973: 265–6; Cato may have spoken against an attempt to abrogate it (*ORF*⁴ FF139–46). According to Athenaeus (6.274c) the *lex Fannia* in 161 (sponsored by the consul C. Fannius Strabo) prohibited the private entertainment of more than three people outside of the family, or five on nundinae (market-days), while laying down the maximum expenditures for daily purchases and limits on annual outlays (e.g., on smoked meat); Macrob. 3.17.3–5; Pliny *Nat. Hist.* 10.139 tells us that poultry dishes were banned, except for one chicken per meal, as long as it had not been artificially fattened. A *senatus consultum* earlier in the year had limited expenditure on food items and the use of silverware: Sulla's ancestor, P. Cornelius Rufinus, an ex-consul, had supposedly been expelled from the senate in 275 because he possessed 10 pounds of silver tableware: *MRR* I.196 (doc. 11.1).

Eighteen years later the *lex Didia* of 143 encompassed all Italy (Macrob. 3.17.6); the *lex Licinia*, later in the second century, repeated the provisions of the *lex Fannia* with maximum weights set for dried meat and fish (Macrob. 3.17.7–10; Gell. 2.24.7–10); the *lex Aemilia* in 115 regulated specific foods (Pliny *Nat. Hist.* 8.223, 36.4; Gell. 2.24.12). The proliferation of sumptuary laws clearly meant that they were not enforced, and perhaps were not intended to be. Gruen 1990a: 170–4 sees such laws as a 'symbolic resistance to Greek morals and manners' effecting the public character, and clearly prodigal spending is disapproved of as undermining Roman standards: Astin 1989: 184–5. The rhetorician decree (doc. 5.57) was also passed in the same year as the *lex Fannia*. MacMullen 1991: 428 (following a discussion of Greek loan words in Plautus' comedies): 'of the Roman aristocracy . . . we can indeed assert that they were surrounded by . . . a sea of products and artefacts and daily usages that had originated in the east.'

2 Just recently I read in Ateius Capito's *Miscellanies* an old senatorial decree passed in the consulship of Gaius Fannius and Marcus Valerius Messala, in which the leading citizens, who by ancestral custom 'interchanged' at the Megalesian games — that is, hosted banquets for each other in turn — were instructed to take an oath in front of the consuls in set terms: that they would spend no more on each dinner than 120 asses, excepting vegetables, bread and wine; that they would not serve foreign wine, but only that produced locally; and that at a banquet they would not use more than 100 pounds of silverware. **3** But, following that senatorial decree, the lex Fannia was introduced, which allowed 100 *asses* a day to be spent at the Roman games, plebeian games, Saturnalia, and, on other specific days, 30 *asses* a day on ten further days in each month, and only ten on all other days. **4** It is this law to which the poet Lucilius refers, when he says, 'Fannius' miserable 100 asses'.

5.57 Edicts on Latin philosophers and rhetoricians, 161 and 92 BC

Aulus Gellius *Attic Nights* 15.11.1–2

Cf. Suet. *Rhet.* 1 (doc. 2.61). Following the Third Macedonian War many Greek intellectuals were imported to Rome (Plut. *Aem.* 33.3), and the lectures given by the Greek philosopher Carneades in Rome in 155 were to prove highly popular (to Cato's dismay; doc. 5.58). As most rhetoricians and philosophers would have been part of private households, this edict was primarily symbolic, intended to reassert Roman native traditions, in the same way as the senate's banishment of two Epicureans from Rome in 173 or 154 and the sumptuary legislation of this period.

The edict of 92 also aimed at moral censure, rather than the closing of schools of Latin rhetoric; possibly increased tribunician activity had led to a demand for 'quick' training in Roman oratory, but primarily the censors were defending the principles of Greek rhetoric and showing their disapproval of those who would cheapen the training by short-cuts: Gruen 1990a: 179–92. See Suet. *Rhet.* 2.1 for advice to Cicero as young man to be trained not in Latin rhetoric (by Lucius Plotius) but in Greek. In Cicero's *de orat.* 3.93–5, Crassus defends his edict by praising the wisdom of the Greeks; Crassus was himself notably fluent in Greek: Cic. *de orat.* 2.2.

The first speech recorded as given by a Greek ambassador to the senate in Greek without an interpreter was that of Apollonius Molo, Cicero's tutor, in 82 or 81: Val. Max. 2.2.3. It was customary for translators to be employed (as for the embassy in doc. 5.57, and for Scipio and Hannibal's meeting before Zama, though both knew Greek: Livy 30.30.1). Cicero was criticised for addressing the Syracusan senate in Greek (*Verr.* 2.4.147); this was seen as demeaning because official business should generally be conducted in Latin, even though all educated Romans understood Greek (one of Cicero's accusations against Verres was that he did not know Greek: *Verr.* 2.4.127): Gruen 1992: 235–41; Wallace-Hadrill 1998: 80–83; Rawson 2003: 147–53.

1 In the consulship of Gaius Fannius Strabo and Marcus Valerius Messala, this decree of the senate was passed concerning Latin-speaking philosophers and rhetoricians: 'The praetor Marcus Pomponius put a motion before the senate. Following a discussion about philosophers and rhetoricians, they resolved as follows, that Marcus Pomponius, the praetor, should take heed and ensure in whatever way seemed to him to be in the interests of the state and the dignity of his office that they should not remain in Rome.'

2 Then some years after that senatorial decree Gnaeus Domitius Ahenobarbus and Lucius Licinius Crassus, the censors, proclaimed the following edict for repressing Latin rhetoricians: 'It has been reported to us that there are men who have introduced a new kind of training, whose schools the youth frequent; that these men have adopted for themselves the title of Latin rhetoricians; that young men sit idle there for whole days. Our ancestors laid down what they desired their children to learn and to what schools they wished them to go. These innovations, that are contrary to our ancestors' customs and principles, neither please us or appear proper. Wherefore, it appears to be our duty that we should declare our opinion, both to those who hold these schools and to those who are in the habit of attending them, that they displease us.'

5.58 Cato and the Greeks

Plutarch *Life of Cato the Elder* 2.5–6, 22.1–23.6

Cato was consul in 195, censor in 184; he posed as a champion of austerity and old Roman standards. Nevertheless, Cato was in no way totally opposed to hellenic culture. On his ability to speak Greek and knowledge of Greek texts early in life, see Plut. *Cato Mai.* 12.4–5; Astin 1978: 159–81; Gruen 1992: 56–60. Cato's own *Origines* were written on the Greek model. While Cato criticised Aulus Postumius Albinus for apologising for writing his history in Greek, the point was not that a Roman should write in Latin, but that Postumius should not have written in Greek if he couldn't do it well: Polyb. 39.1.4–9. While there grew up a later tradition that Cato was hostile to all things Greek (Pliny *Nat. Hist.* 7.113: that he wanted all Greeks expelled from Italy; Plut. *Cato Mai.* 23.1), he was not a simple hellenophobe; he served in Sicily and south Italy in the Second Punic War, and was in Greece in 191 when he spent some time at Athens and fought at Thermopylae. He supposedly learnt Pythagoreanism from Nearchus in 209: Cic. *Sen.* 39, 41;

Plut. *Cato Mai.* 2.3; Rawson 1989: 451–62. However, while Greek art was prized, the typical contemporary Greek was not: for the stereotypical Greek in Roman eyes, see Wardman 1976: 1–24. In his *Origines*, Cato compares a Roman tribune to Leonidas, suggesting that a Roman junior officer could be as great as a Spartan king (Gell. 3.7.18–19).

For a similar portrait of Marius (who could, however, quote Pindar: Plut. *Mar.* 29.3; cf. 2.2), see docs 9.1–2; Gruen 1992: 268–9; the point is that neither would use Greek for 'serious' matters; Cato, for example, addressed the Athenians in Latin, through an interpreter, though capable of speaking Greek himself: Plut. *Cato Mai.* 12.4.

For Cato's opposition to the philosophic embassy of 155, see Pliny *Nat. Hist.* 7.112; Cic. *Rep.* 3.9; Plut. *Cato Mai.* 22.1–7; Gruen 1992: 53. Cato heard Carneades' speeches in Rome. Athens had suffered a damaging judgement in her dispute with Oropus (which was heard by Sicyon, which imposed a fine of 500 talents). Athens appealed to the senate, using as spokespersons the heads of three major philosophical schools, who also offered public lectures. These were extremely popular and their popular appeal and disregard of 'truth' were Cato's major concern, and he encouraged the senate to hasten its decision so the philosophers could leave Rome: Gruen 1990a: 174–7; Erskine 1990: 188–92. The fine was reduced to 100 talents: Paus. 7.11.5. Significantly, the senate had to be addressed in Latin; the senator Gaius Acilius acted as interpreter: Gell. 6.14.9; Plut. *Cato Mai.* 22.5. For Cato's antipathy to Greek doctors and preference for Roman customs, see Astin 1978: 170–2; Gruen 1992: 54–5, 75–80, who sees Cato not as an enemy of Greece, but as an advocate of Rome and Rome's dignity; Rawson 1989: 430 for Greek medicine arriving in Rome; 455 on this passage; for Cato's belief in the medicinal uses of cabbage: doc. 2.17.

In 154 (probably: the other possible date is 173) two Epicureans were expelled from Rome, doubtless a token protest at their philosophy of pleasure: Athen. 12.547a; Gruen 1990a: 171–9; Gruen 1992: 259–60. This year was also notable as that in which P. Scipio Nasica Corculum (cos. 155) prevented the completion of the construction of a permanent theatre in Rome on the grounds that this was associated with decadence and idleness: App. *BC* 1.28; Livy *Per.* 48, Vell. 1.15.3; Val. Max. 2.4.2; Rawson 1989: 470.

2.5 It is said that he did not learn Greek until later in life, and was quite old when he took to reading Greek books, when his oratory benefited a little from Thucydides, but more from Demosthenes. **6** However, his writings are fairly well adorned with Greek opinions and stories, and many literal translations from Greek can be found in his maxims and proverbs . . .

22.1 When he was already an old man, Carneades the Academic and Diogenes the Stoic philosopher came as envoys from Athens to Rome (155 BC) to request the reversal of a judgement against the Athenian people . . . **2** The most scholarly of Rome's young men immediately thronged to them, and became their admiring audience . . . **4** This delighted the other Romans, and they were pleased to see their young men acquiring Greek culture and associating with such remarkable men; **5** but Cato, from the time when this zeal for eloquence had poured into the city, was unhappy, fearing that the young men, through turning their ambition in this direction, would come to desire a reputation for speaking more than one based on exploits and campaigns. And when the philosophers' fame rose even higher in the city and their first speeches to the senate were interpreted by that distinguished man Gaius Acilius, at his own desire and request, Cato resolved to have all these philosophers removed from the city on a decent pretext. **6** So, in the senate, he criticised the magistrates for detaining for so long an embassy of men who could easily achieve through persuasion anything they wished; **7** they ought to make a decision and vote on the embassy as quickly as possible, so that they could return to their schools and lecture to the young men of Greece, and the youth of Rome could listen to their laws and magistrates as before.

23.2 . . . In an attempt to prejudice his son against Greek culture, he employs a dictum too bold for an old man, stating like a prophet or visionary that the Romans will lose their empire once they are infected with Greek learning. **3** But time has shown these words of evil omen to be groundless, for when the city was at its peak of empire she adopted every type of Greek learning and culture. He not only hated Greek philosophers, but was also suspicious of Greeks who practised medicine at Rome. **4** It would seem that he had heard of Hippocrates' answer, who told the Great King, when asked for his services for a fee of many talents, that he would never work for barbarians who were enemies of Greece. Cato said all Greek doctors had taken a similar oath, and urged his son to beware of all of them; **5** he had himself written a book of medical notes, which he used in treating and regulating the diet of any of his household who were sick. He never prescribed fasting for anyone, but fed them on vegetables, or bits of duck, pigeon or hare; **6** this diet was light and suitable for invalids, except for often causing dreams in its eaters, and by employing such treatment and diet he was in good health himself and kept his family healthy.

5.59 Cato to his son Marcus

Pliny *Natural History* 29.14

Pliny here cites an extract from a work supposedly addressed by Cato to his son, though it was perhaps a collection of axioms for a wider audience: Gruen 1992: 77–8.

Polybius was acquainted with Cato: Polyb. 35.6.1–4; Plut. *Cato Mai.* 9.2–3; for Cato's learned Greek slave Chilon, see Plut. 20.5 (Chilon taught all the children in Cato's household except Cato's son). Clearly Cato was well enough informed about Greek literature to pass a judgement, but believed that such study should not replace Roman norms (contra MacMullen 1991: 435–6 who sees Cato as condemning all Greek literature). The Romans may well have felt themselves culturally inferior to the Greeks: on the term Opici, see Dubuisson 1983: 522–45. In another critical perception of the Romans, Plautus identifies Romans as porridge-eaters, 'pultiphagi' (Plaut. *Mostell.* 828; *Poen.* 54). On Greek assumptions of cultural superiority, see Crawford 1978: 195–7; for attitudes towards Rome generally, see Gruen 1986: 316–56; Erskine 1990: 181–204.

I shall speak about those Greek fellows in their proper place, Marcus, my son, making clear what I learnt at Athens and convincing you what good comes of looking at their literature, but without thoroughly studying it. They are a totally good-for-nothing and incorrigible race of people — take my words as prophetic! When that race gives us its literature it will corrupt everything — and still worse, if it sends us its doctors! They have conspired among themselves to murder all 'barbarians' with their drugs, and, what's more, do this for a fee, to gain our confidence and easily dispose of us. Moreover, they keep calling us barbarians and bespatter us even more obscenely than others by giving us by the nickname of 'Opici' (Oscans).

5.60 Nudity and pederasty

Cicero *Tusculan Disputations* 4.70–1

(Ennius F407.) Cicero is here referring not to homosexuality *per se*, but to pederasty practised with citizens youths. Homosexuality in itself was not alien to Roman culture, and there was no moral stigma about relationships with young male prostitutes and slaves, though it was considered shameful to be the passive partner. One of the main issues involved in the Bacchanalia was the seduction of young freeborn male adults (*stuprum*): MacMullen 1991: 429–30, 434–5. Similarly, homosexual relationships in the army were severely dealt with (because between citizens): Polyb. 6.37.9; Dion. Hal. 16.4.1–3; Val. Max. 6.1.10–12; doc. 7.59. Gaius Gracchus, on his return from Sardinia where he had been quaestor in 125 (doc. 8.22), made a point of stressing that he had solicited no slave boys and treated young men in his retinue with respect; for homosexuality in Rome, see docs 7.57–61. Plutarch *Rom. Quest.* 101 suggests that the bulla, the amulet worn by free children, was intended to mark free from slave when naked, and thus prevent free children from molestation, as slaves would naturally be the object of ancient Roman pederasty (Preston 2001: 114); see Williams 1999: esp. 92–95, updating MacMullen 1982.

The Romans saw nakedness between citizens as improper: Cato even refused to bathe with his son (Plut. *Cato Mai.* 20.7–8) blaming Roman nudity on the Greeks; cf. Cic. *Off.* 1.129; Val. Max. 2.1.7. Bettini 1991: 10–3 sees this as a mechanism of shame which 'blocked the establishment of excessively close relations between sons and fathers'. Laius was a character in a lost play of Euripides, *Chrysippus*.

70 Why is it that no one is ever in love with an unsightly youth or a handsome old man? My view is that this custom appears to have grown up in the gymnasia of the Greeks, in which such loves were free and permissible; it was well said by Ennius,

Nudity amongst citizens is the beginning of disgrace.

Even when such relationships are, as I see they can be, within the bounds of propriety, they cause uneasiness and anxiety — all the more because they are a law unto themselves and are subject to no outside control. **71** Again, leaving aside love for women, to which nature has allowed greater license, who can either doubt the poets' meaning in the tale of the rape of Ganymede, or fail to understand Laius' speeches and desires in Euripides' play?

5.61 Roman athleticism

Plutarch *Roman Questions* 40 (*Moralia* 274de)

This passage gives the Romans' view rather than Plutarch's, though he continues: 'It is hard work when men strip in the open air to escape these consequences'. He is here discussing why the flamen dialis was forbidden to anoint himself with oil in the open air (doc. 3.19); cf. Preston 2001: 114–15. Williams 1999: 69 notes that the emphasis is on the self-indulgent method of training; cf. Plut *Cato Mai.* 20.6 (doc. 7.21) for Roman exercises and training (throwing the javelin, fighting in armour, horse-riding, boxing, swimming); note Scipio Aemilianus' criticisms of current trends in education: doc. 8.20.

The Romans used to be very suspicious of rubbing themselves down with oil, and they believe that nothing has been more responsible for the enslavement and effeminacy of the Greeks as their gymnasia and wrestling-schools, which give rise to much idleness and waste of time in their cities, as well as bad practices and pederasty and the ruin of the bodies of the young men by a regimen of sleeping, walking, rhythmical movements, and strict diet. Through these practices they have unconsciously left off the practice of arms, and have become happy to be called nimble, beautiful athletes instead of excellent foot-soldiers and horsemen.

5.62 Cicero's defence of Roman native qualities

Cicero *Tusculan Disputations* 1.1–3

In his *Tusculan Disputations*, written in 45, Cicero is trying to make Greek philosophy accessible to the general reader. Preston 2001 notes that Cicero here stresses the limited nature of Greek influence on Roman culture: areas of study may be Greek, but virtues and morals are Roman and the Romans have improved on what they have borrowed. Livius Andronicus, a Greek, came from Tarentum, Naevius from Campania, Ennius from Calabria; Livius was commissioned by the government in 240 to adapt Greek drama to celebrate the end of the First Punic War; his hymn for a procession of maidens in 207 (doc. 7.83), which was also publicly commissioned, resulted in public approval for the guild of writers and dramatic artists. He also turned the *Odyssey* into Latin and Suetonius (*Gram.* 1.2) says he was the first to teach literature in Rome: Rawson 1989: 430–1; Gruen 1990a: 80–92. According to Plutarch (*Rom. Quest.* 59) a freedman of Spurius Carvilius, c. 230, was supposedly the first to set up a school for learning letters (with education previously being within the family).

As a schoolboy, Cicero still learnt the *XII Tables* by heart: *Laws* 2.59. His later education in rhetoric was based on Greek models: writing to his brother as governor of Asia (*Quint.* 1.1.28), advising him to remember he is governing a civilised race, he states; 'All that I have attained, I owe to the studies and disciplines handed down to us by the literature and teachings of Greece' (cf. doc. 2.62 for his early career). Cicero's commentary on his own consulship was in Greek: *Att.* 1.19.10, 20.6 (cf. doc. 12.26). But, in addressing a jury, Cicero is careful to protest that he knows little of Greek art: *Verr.* 2.4.94.

1 I have always been convinced that our fellow countrymen have in every field shown themselves to be wiser than the Greeks, whether in what they have discovered for themselves or in the ways they have improved upon what they had taken over from the Greeks, at any rate in those areas which they considered worthy of their exertions. **2** For we undoubtedly uphold standards of morality, regulate our lives, and run our families and households in a much better and more honourable fashion, while our forefathers organised government with better practices and laws than anyone else. What shall I say about the science of warfare? In this our countrymen have shown their superiority, not only through their excellence, but even more by their disciplined practice. As for those qualities which are attained by nature, not through books, they cannot be compared with those of the Greek or any other race. For where has such dignity, such firmness of character, such greatness of spirit, such integrity, such trustworthiness — where has such pre-eminent excellence in every respect been found in any races which could bear comparison with that of our ancestors? **3** Greece was superior to us in learning and all kinds of literature, and it was easy for them to win with no competition. For, while, among the Greeks, the most ancient learned class is that of the poets, since Homer and Hesiod lived before the founding of Rome and Archilochus in the reign of Romulus, we acquired poetry at a later date. About 510 years after the foundation of Rome Livius (Andronicus) produced a play in the consulship of Gaius Claudius, son of Caecus, and Marcus Tuditanus, in the year before Ennius was born, who was older than Plautus and Naevius.

5.63 Varro on the decline of Roman standards

Varro *On Farming* 2.1.1–3

Varro here demonstrates the degree to which Romans could adopt Greek habits and architecture within their private villas: Wallace-Hadrill 1998: 86–91; on Scipio Africanus' baths, see doc. 2.20. The ninth-days refer to the market-days (nundinae) on the last day of the eight-day week.

1 Not without reason did those great men, our ancestors, put those Romans who lived in the country before those who lived in the city. For, as in the country, those who live in the villas are lazier than those who are engaged in doing work on the land, so those who reside in town they thought to be more slothful than those who dwelt in the country. As a result, they divided up their year in such a way that they only saw to their city affairs on the ninth-days, and dwelt in the country for the remaining seven. **2** As long as they kept up this practice they achieved both objects — keeping their fields extremely productive through cultivation, and themselves fitter in health and not in need of the city gymnasia of the Greeks. Nowadays one gymnasium is hardly enough, nor do people consider they have a villa unless it resounds with many Greek terms for individual locations called procoetion (ante-room), palaestra (exercise-room), apodyterion (dressing-room), peristylon (colonnade), ornithonon (aviary), peripteros (veranda), and oporotheca (fruit-room). **3** As, therefore, almost all heads of families have nowadays crept inside the walls, abandoning the sickle and plough, and prefer to employ their hands in the theatre and circus than in the wheat-fields and vineyards, we hire a man to bring us grain from Africa and Sardinia so our stomachs can be filled, and the vintage we store up comes in ships from the islands of Cos and Chios.

ROME AND THE PROVINCES

The term 'province' originally implied the area in which a magistrate functioned: by the second century provinces had come to mean overseas territories permanently administered by the Romans. The first was Sicily, mostly acquired in 241 BC, following the First Punic War, which became a unified province in 211, followed by Sardinia and Corsica in 227, and then in 198/7 by the two Spanish provinces. Macedonia was annexed in 146, Asia in 129, Transalpine and Cisalpine Gaul after 100, Cilicia c. 80, and Bithynia and Pontus, Crete, Cyprus and Syria in the 70s, 60s and 50s. Initially allocated to magistrates and promagistrates by the senate and then by lot, in 123 Gaius Gracchus legislated that the senate was to decide, before the consular elections (and hence before the election results were known), which provinces would be consular (i.e., would be held by the successful consular candidates as promagistrates after their year of office): doc. 8.28; praetorian provinces were still assigned by lot. Major wars and the increasing number of provinces led to long tenures of office, such as that of Lucullus and then Pompey in the East.

Promagistrates were often motivated by personal gain (the expenses of election were immense) and the desire for *gloria* (and possibly a triumph). As generals with imperium, they possessed total control over non-citizens in the province. Accompanied by one or more quaestors, and with a staff of officers, attendants and troops as necessary, the governor appointed his own consilium (advisory council). While he could nominate a judge, he was entitled to try cases and decide upon them himself, both with regard to Roman citizens and the locals: Cic. *Verr.* 2.2.26, 'Verres put in the plaintiff, Verres ordered his appearance, Verres heard the case, Verres gave the judgement'. Governors could be subject to prosecution on their return to Rome, especially for extortion (repetundae), but in practice convictions were rare. Note Gaius Gracchus' fulminations on the misconduct of Roman magistrates, docs 8.22, 24. For an introduction to Roman provincial administration, see Richardson 1976: 27–58.

5.64 The unpopularity of Roman imperium

Cicero *On the Agrarian Law* 2.45

Cicero as consul in 63 is speaking against Rullus' proposal of a commission of ten who would be given powers to sell state lands and purchase land for distribution in Italy: doc. 12.13. Free embassies were undertaken by senators wishing to visit provinces.

Foreign nations can hardly stand our ambassadors, men with slight authority, who go on free embassies for the sake of their own private affairs. For the name of imperium is oppressive and feared even when its possessor is insignificant, because it is your name, not their own, that they abuse when they have left Rome.

5.65 The iniquities of a Sicilian governor

Cicero *Against Verres* 2.3.66, 120–1, 2.4.1–2

Praetor urbanus in 74, Verres had been made pro-praetorian governor of Sicily and his term extended to 71: *MRR* II.102, 112. His governorship is a fine illustration of the abuses perpetrated by many Roman governors; from Rome's annexation of Sicily in 241 Rome had adopted Hiero of Syracuse's fair system of taxation, but Verres did not adhere to this. Cicero had served as quaestor in Sicily and had connections and clients there, hence his taking the side of the prosecution against Verres. See Plut. *Cic.* 7–8 on the way in which Cicero compressed his speech and evidence to the only day available (Verres' friends wanted to delay the hearing until 69 when the presiding judge would be friendly and Verres' counsel, Hortensius, would be consul): the full literary account was written up after the event. The fine was accessed at 750,000 denarii (a low assessment: Plut. *Cic.* 8.1) and Verres went into exile at Marseilles. Verres' governorship was contemporaneous with the revolt of Spartacus.

3.66 You observe, jurors, how great a blaze swept at the tax-gatherers' approach not only through the farmers' fields but even through their remaining possessions, and not only through their possessions, but even through their rights as free men and citizens, with Verres as governor. You could see some of the farmers hanging from trees, others being beaten and flogged, still more held as prisoners, others made to remain standing through banquets, others being convicted by the governor's personal doctor and herald; the goods of all of them being meanwhile despoiled and swept away from their farms. What does all this mean? Is this the government of Rome? Are these the laws a governor administers? Are these the courts that judge our loyal allies, our closest province? . . . **120** How then can all this be proven? By this fact, most of all, that the tax-paying lands of the province of Sicily were deserted owing to his greed. It was not merely that those who did stay on their land continued farming on a much smaller scale, but that a great many wealthy men, important and diligent farmers, abandoned their broad and fertile properties and left their entire farms derelict. The fact can easily be made clear from the communities' public records, since by a law of Hiero a return of the number of farmers is officially made to the magistrates every year. Read out now the total of farmers in the Leotini district when Verres arrived in the province: 84. The number who made a return in his third year: 32. So we see that 52 farmers were thrown out in such a way that no one even came in to take their places. How many farmers were there in the Mutyca district while you were en route to Sicily? Let us see from the public records: 187. Well now, in your third year? 86. Owing to his iniquities, a single district feels the lack of 101 farmers — indeed, our own nation, since the revenues are those of the Roman people, feels the lack of all these men and their families and demands their restitution. The district of Herbita in his first year had 252 farmers, 120 in his third; 132 of its householders were driven from their homes and fled elsewhere. The Agyrium district — what fine, well-regarded, substantial inhabitants! — had 250 farmers in the first year of your governorship. And now? How many in your third year? 130, as you have heard, jurors, from representatives of Agyrium who read it from their public records. **121** Immortal gods! If you had driven out 170 farmers from the whole of Sicily, could you be acquitted by a serious court? It is this single district of Agyrium which is emptier by 170 farmers — can you not then, jurors, hazard a guess regarding Sicily as a whole?

4.1 I come now to what he himself calls his favourite occupation, his friends a foolish obsession, and the Sicilians highway robbery; what name I should give it, I do not know. I will place the facts before you, and you can judge it by its nature not its name. First, listen to its general characteristics, jurors, after which you will, perhaps, have no difficulty in deciding what you think it should be called. I maintain that in the whole of Sicily, such a wealthy, ancient province, in all its towns, in all its very substantial households, there was not one vessel of silver, not one of Corinthian or Delian bronze, no precious stone or pearl, nothing made of gold or ivory, no bronze, marble or ivory statue, no painting or embroidered textile that he did not seek out, examine, and, if he liked it, appropriate . . . **2** In no man's house, even though he be his host, in no public place, even though it be a sacred shrine, in the possession of no man, whether Sicilian, or even Roman citizen, nowhere, to be brief, has he left anything which struck his eyes or taste, whether private or public property, belonging to men or gods, in the whole of Sicily.

5.66 Corruption and arrogance as the norm in the provinces

Cicero *Letters to his Brother Quintus* 1.1.8, 13, 22

Part of a lengthy letter of advice written by Cicero to his younger brother Quintus in 60 or early 59 BC, when Quintus was governing Asia as propraetor (he had been praetor in 62 and governed Asia 61–58). Cicero is here clearly concerned with subordinates (and perhaps slaves: see his concerns as to their influence at 1.1.17) accepting bribes to influence the governor's judgement; cf. doc. 6.48 on his concerns over the behaviour of Quintus' freedman Statius in the province. This is part of a long letter of advice on the behaviour of a governor from Marcus to Quintus; for Quintus, see Wiseman 1966.

8 It is a mark of great distinction that you have been two years in Asia in supreme command and that no statue, picture, dish, garment, slave, beautiful face, or offer of money — all of which that province has in abundance — has caused you to deviate from the highest integrity and moderation. What can be found so outstanding or desirable as that your virtue, self-restraint, and self-control should not lie hidden and out of sight in shadow, but be displayed to the light of Asia, to the eyes of that most illustrious province, and to the ears of all races and nations? That these men are not terrified by your official visits? That they are not exhausted by your expenditure? That they are not anxious at your approach? That, wherever you arrive, there is the greatest public and private happiness, since it appears that their city has received a protector, not a tyrant, the home a guest, not a despoiler? . . .

13 Finally let it be public knowledge that you will be severely displeased not only with those who have taken a bribe, but with those who have given one, if you come to know of it. Nor indeed will anyone give a bribe, when it is made perfectly clear that nothing can be got out of you by those people who pretend to have great influence with you . . .

22 If such courtesy is welcome at Rome, where there is so much arrogance, such unrestricted freedom, such infinite licence generally, and in short so many magistrates, so many sources of aid, such popular power, such senatorial authority, how welcome then must the courteousness of a praetor be in Asia, where so great a multitude of citizens and allies, so many cities, so many states watch for the nod of a single man? Where there is no legal help, no chance to complain, no senate, no assembly? It must therefore always be the role of a great man, and one not only controlled by his own nature but also by the knowledge and study of the finest of the arts, so to conduct himself in a position of such power that the existence of no other power may be desired by those over whom he rules.

5.67 The problems of being a governor

Cicero *Letters to his Brother Quintus* 1.1.32–3

One of the main problems for governors involved the demands of the publicani on the provincials: G. Gracchus had arranged for the indirect taxes of Asia to be sold to publicani on five-year contracts, and their rapacity led to the rebellion in Asia of 88 BC, followed by Sulla's imposition of an indemnity of 20,000 talents, which with interest shortly grew to 120,000 talents (docs 11.8–10). In this case, the syndicate of publicani had obviously overbid on the contract and demanded a cancellation of it (cf. *Att.* 1.17.9; doc. 12.33).

32 To all your goodwill and diligence the publicani present a serious problem; if we oppose them, we will alienate both from ourselves and from the government a class which has deserved the best from us and which has, through our efforts, been brought into association with the government; if, however, we give in to them in every situation, we will be permitting the total ruin of those people whose safety and advantage we are bound to consider. If we want to consider the matter truthfully, this is the one problem in your whole administration. For as to being temperate, controlling your passions, keeping your staff in check, maintaining a fair system of justice, showing yourself to be courteous in investigating cases and in listening to and giving audiences to men — all this is rather a matter of splendour than difficult. For it depends not on any hard work, but on making up your mind and willingness to carry it out. **33** How much bitterness this question of the publicani causes among our allies we have appreciated from our own citizens, who recently, when harbour-dues were abolished in Italy, complained not so much of the tax as of certain offences by the collectors. I am therefore aware of what happens to our allies in far-off lands when I hear such complaints from citizens in Italy.

And for you to behave in such a way that you satisfy the publicani, especially when their contract for tax collection has proved unprofitable, yet not allow our allies to be ruined, seems to require a certain divine excellence — such as you possess, of course.

5.68 The desperate state of Cilicia

Cicero *Letters to Atticus* 5.16.2

Cicero wrote this letter to Atticus on his arrival in his province of Cilicia in 51, en route between Synnada and Philomelium. Provincial communities were frequently forced to borrow from Roman businessmen in order to pay their poll tax or war indemnities. On his arrival Cicero heard numerous complaints about his predecessor Appius Claudius Pulcher who had supported the publicani against the provincials: *MRR* II.229.

I must tell you that on 31 July I made my eagerly awaited arrival in this desperate and, in fact, totally and permanently ruined province . . . I have heard about nothing but inability to pay the mandatory poll tax, the universal sale of taxes, the groans and laments from the communities, monstrous deeds, as of some savage beast, not of a human being. In short, these people are absolutely weary of life.

5.69 The (ig)noblest Roman of them all

Cicero *Letters to Atticus* 6.1.5–6

Cicero as governor of Cilicia in 51–50 BC discovered that not only publicani were exploiting the locals: M. Junius Brutus (Cicero's friend and later one of Caesar's assassins), under cover of two agents Scaptius and Matinius, was loaning money to the people of Salamis on Cyprus at a rate of 48 per cent per annum, having made sure that his money was protected by a decree of the senate (Cicero as governor had set interest rates at 12 per cent, 1% per month: *Att.* 5.21). Cyprus was under the control of the governor of Cilicia, having been annexed by Cato in 58–56 BC (docs 12.55–7), when Brutus had accompanied him. In fact, not wanting to anger Brutus because of their close connection, Cicero left the problem to his successor and ignored the Salaminians' difficulties, though he clearly sympathised with them.

5 Now let me tell you about the Salaminians: I see that it came as a surprise to you as much as it did to me. I never heard him (Brutus) say that the money was his; in fact, I even have a memorandum of his in which it is stated: 'The Salaminians owe money to Marcus Scaptius and Publius Matinius, friends of mine.' He recommends them to me; he even adds, as an extra spur to me, that he had gone surety for them for a large sum of money. I had arranged that the Salaminians should pay off their debt at 1 per cent a month, with interest to be added annually. But Scaptius demanded 4 per cent. I feared, if he got it, that I would lose your regard; for I would have had to renege on my own edict and totally ruin a community under the patronage of Cato and Brutus himself, and one on which I had bestowed favours.

6 And at this very moment Scaptius hands me a letter from Brutus stating that he, Brutus, was the person concerned, a fact which Brutus had never told me or you, and requesting that I give Scaptius a prefecture. But I had already told him, through you, that one would not be given to a businessman: even if I did, it would surely not be to him. He had been prefect under Appius (Cicero's predecessor) and had cavalry squadrons with which he locked the senate of Salamis in their senate house and besieged them, so that five senators died from starvation! And so, on the very day on which I reached my province . . . I sent a letter ordering the cavalry to leave the island immediately. For these reasons, I suppose, Scaptius has written Brutus some injurious remarks about me. However, this is what I have decided: if Brutus is going to think that I ought to have imposed 4 per cent interest, even though I recognised 1 per cent throughout the whole province and had stated this in my edict, with the approval of even the most grasping moneylenders; if he is going to complain because I refused a prefecture to a business-man; . . . if he is going to be annoyed because I ordered the cavalry recalled, I shall be sorry, of course, to have angered him, but much sorrier that he is not the man I thought he was.

5.70 The duties of a provincial governor

Cicero *Letters to his Friends* 15.4.2–4

Cicero is here writing to Cato the Younger in January 50 BC, from Tarsus during his governorship of Cilicia. As governor he achieved some successes against the Parthians and kept allied potentates well-disposed; clearly Cicero felt he deserved a triumph and is here asking for Cato's support, initially requesting that a supplicatio be granted, and to this end giving Cato a detailed account of how he had conducted himself in the province; cf. doc. 2.44 to Marcellus; for Cato's reply, see doc. 13.19.

2 When I arrived at my province on the last day of July and saw that on account of the time of year I should join my army as quickly as possible, I spent two days in Laodicea, then four days at Apamea, three days at Synnada, and the same number at Philomelium. I held large courts of law in these towns and freed many communities from excessively harsh taxation, exorbitant interest payments and false claims of debt. As the army had been scattered, before my arrival, by a near mutiny, and five cohorts, without a legate, without a military tribune, and even without a single centurion, had encamped at Philomelium, while the rest of the army was in Lycaonia, I ordered my legate Marcus Anneius to bring those five cohorts to join the rest of the army, and after the army was assembled in one spot to make camp at Iconium in Lycaonia. **3** When all this had been diligently carried out, I arrived at the camp on 24 August, having in the meantime, in the preceding days, in accordance with the decree of the senate, collected a trustworthy band of veterans, a quite sufficient cavalry corps, and volunteer auxiliaries from the free peoples and allied kings. Meanwhile, after I had reviewed the army and begun the march into Cilicia, some envoys sent to me by the king of Commagene reported on 28 August in a state of panic, but not untruthfully, that the Parthians had crossed into Syria. **4** On hearing this, I was seriously concerned about Syria as well as my province and in fact about the whole of Asia . . . I therefore made camp on the border on Cappadocia, not far from Mt Taurus at the town Cybistra, in order to protect Cilicia and by holding Cappadocia to prevent any new schemes on the part of our neighbours.

5.71 An inflammatory governor

Diodorus Siculus *Library of History* 38.11

Cf. Cic. *Verr.* 2.1.70; Livy *Per.* 86; Val. Max. 9.10.2; *MRR* II.69. C. Fabius Hadrianus, governor of Africa since 84, was so unpopular that the Roman citizens in Utica burned his headquarters with him inside it in 82 because of his greed and cruelty; cf. Cic. *Verr.* 2.5.92–5. Roman officials must often have inflamed local sensibilities: at some time between 60 and 56 BC Diodorus was present when an Egyptian mob lynched a visiting Roman official for killing a cat, presumably accidentally (Diod. 1.83.8–9).

Hadrianus, the propraetor governing Utica, was burnt alive by the Uticans. Although the deed was terrible, no charges were brought because of the wickedness of the victim.

6

Slaves and Freedmen

Slavery was a social institution in Rome from the earliest times and slaves are included in the lawcode of the XII Tables (doc. 1.54, cf. 1.42), though slaves and the institution of slavery as such are not defined in the Republic; such definitions were to be the work of the imperial jurists. To the Romans of the Republic, a slave was a piece of property and slavery an institution in which human beings owned by others fulfilled labour requirements for their owners. Slaves, whether acquired as booty in warfare or raised within the household, were items of property, *res mancipi*, a term applied to other types of property such as land and animals, and so wholly in the ownership of their masters who had the power of life and death over them. Slaves were not considered fully competent beings: a master could be sued for his slave's wrongs. Slave status depended on that of the mother: if the mother was a slave so was the child, even if one of the citizen males of the household was the father.

Rome became a true 'slave-owning society' only in the second century BC when slaves, both in the mines and, especially, on the latifundia (large landed estates), became a vital aspect of Roman production. Rome can be said to have become reliant on slave labour from this time on. The crucial factor was not simply the acquisition of large numbers of slaves through conquest, but the control of land by an aristocratic elite which could afford to buy large numbers of slaves to work that land: Sicily, in particular, came to be dominated by the latifundia of this elite in the second century BC. Agriculture became a major absorber of slaves, displacing peasant farmers, with social, political and military consequences (see docs 8.5–9). In this sense, Roman slavery best approximates to that other major historical slave-owning society, the slave-owning states of the United States of America. But while agriculture in both of these societies provided the bulk of employment for slaves, their uses in ancient Rome were widespread. Slaves are found in a variety of domestic situations (doc. 6.14–22), with Greek slaves employed as secretaries and in other educated roles within the household (docs 6.12, 46, 53), and it was these slaves, in close contact with their masters and having the possibility of reward for their service and loyalty, who stood the most chance of being manumitted. Slaves also carried out a wide variety of tasks in manufacturing and industrial concerns such as the silver mines (docs 6.24–26) and on the landed estates (docs 6.31–6). The 'entertainment industry' also made use of slaves, as actors and mimes (docs 6.27–9), while the great playwright Terence himself, born in Carthage, came to

Rome as a slave (doc. 6.54). Gladiators were also slaves, and Spartacus' slave revolt began in the gladiators' barracks in Capua (doc. 6.45).

As in all slave societies, there were important variables in how slaves were treated in republican Rome; the most important of these were their occupations and the character of their masters. The Roman slave system in the Republic allowed for slaves on the latifundia to work in chain gangs and those in the Spanish silver mines to be brutally treated by their overseers (doc. 6.26) — on the other hand Cicero could free his trusted slave Tiro, who continued in Cicero's employment, and gladly address him as 'my dear' (doc. 6.46–7). Cato the Elder, in contrast, advised selling off old and useless slaves along with other equipment past its prime (doc. 6.31). Slaves could be and were tortured for evidence in judicial cases (docs 6.38–9) and if Cicero is to be believed sometimes with shocking results, even by Roman 'standards' (doc. 6.39).

Slaves could resist their enslavement in various ways, by disobedience and laziness, much caricatured by Plautus but probably reflecting slaves' tendency, if they could, to work slowly and inefficiently as a means of resisting their status and ameliorating it (doc. 6.21). Another method was to run away but such slaves could be recaptured (docs 6.41–2). Those with a tendency to run off were provided with a slave collar (doc. 6.40). The slave rebellions which broke out in Sicily and Italy are clearly indicative of the problems associated with slavery (docs 6.43–5). In all three cases, the slaves that rebelled seemed largely to have been free men who had been enslaved in Rome's wars of conquests and who did not accept their servile status. These rebellions took the Roman authorities some time to suppress but led to no reflection on the nature of slavery or any improvement in the treatment of slaves, despite their appeal in modern times: Spartacus' rebellion and the film based on his activities has almost made him a modern household name.

There is little actual information about Roman attitudes to slavery in the Republic. There were certainly none of the discussions, such as those that occurred in the Greek world of the fourth century BC, about the institution of slavery and whether it was legal or moral. For Cicero, the human booty of war was simply a welcome addition to his work force (doc. 6.11). An understanding of Roman slavery during the Republic is inhibited by a lack of legal sources for this period, with much of the best evidence for Roman slavery coming from the imperial period. More importantly, a freed slave such as Tiro has left behind no autobiographical information about life as a slave — all the sources accept the system, and 'contain at most only minimal sensitivity to the servile perspective of events' (Bradley 1994: 7). Publilius Syrus (doc. 6.20) proves perhaps a partial exception, though his maxims depend on the role being played by the character that speaks them in his mimes. What is most missing is, of course, accounts of enslavement and the resulting servile experience from the point of view of the slaves themselves — men, women and children — who were captured by the Romans in the extra-Italian conflicts of the third to first centuries BC, though epitaphs by freedpersons show the relief and gratitude of those who had managed to escape the system and acquire Roman citizenship (docs 6.55–60, 7.33).

The economic effects of slavery are difficult to assess. While not essential to the development of the latifundia, the available numbers of slaves not only squeezed out the labour of the native citizenry, but ensured that the owners of the land received higher profits: Brunt 1958: 168. For some of the methodological issues involved in the study of slavery, and historical approaches to Roman slavery, see Finley 1980; 11–66, 69; Yavetz 1988: 115–62; Bradley 1994: 8–9.

Ancient sources: for the history of the Sicilian slave revolts (135–132, 104–100 BC), there is the narrative of Diodorus, which depends greatly on Posidonius (c. 135–51 BC; *FGrH* 87): Diodorus definitely used Posidonius for the first slave revolt and probably did for the second. Unfortunately, Diodorus' account of the first revolt does not survive intact, but in two summaries, one by the ninth-century Byzantine patriarch Photius and the second by the tenth-century Byzantine emperor Constantine VII Porphyrogenitus. That of Constantine is longer and more detailed. Both accounts agree that it was the cruelty and arrogance of the masters that caused the revolt. For the revolt of Spartacus, the narrative of Appian *Civil Wars* 1.116–20 is particularly important (see doc. 6.45).

While ancient Greek authors, especially philosophers, wrote about slavery, there is no body of similar writings for Roman slavery. While some legal material about Roman slavery in the Republic survives, as in the XII Tables and in scattered literary sources, the main body of legislation about Roman slavery comes from the imperial period. The evidence for slavery is scattered amongst the literary sources. The playwrights give an indication of popular opinions about slaves in general (docs 6.21–2), while Cicero makes clear how the relationship between a master and slave could be close (docs 6.46–7). However, while slave characters speak in plays, the genuine 'voice' of a slave and their feelings is never heard in Republican Rome: it is the masters who record their feelings about slavery and slaves.

Most modern treatments of slavery and freedpersons generally combine evidence from both the Republic and empire; for background reading on Roman slavery, see Carcopino 1941: 69–74; Raymer 1940/1: 17–21; Brunt 1965: 169–81; Balsdon 1979: 77–81; Harris 1980; Grant 1992: 100–11; Dupont 1992: 56–69; Thébert 1993; Bradley 1985, 1994: 1–9; cf. Toynbee 1965: I.313–31; the main modern works are those of Bradley 1987, 1989, 1992, 1994. See also the general Greco-Roman treatments of Finley 1987; Wiedemann 1981, 1997.

SLAVE NUMBERS IN REPUBLICAN ROME

The XII Tables include a number of laws pertaining to the institution of slavery, and slavery was obviously an accepted institution in the fifth century BC, though Rome was not yet a slave-owning society on a large scale. When conquering communities in Italy, such as the city of Veii, large scale enslavements such as were later practised do not seem to have taken place (despite Livy 5.22.1; doc. 1.60) and awards of citizenship were Roman policy (Livy 6.4.4); see Watson 1975: 83. Slave numbers did not assume significant proportions until Rome entered upon its wars of conquest outside of the Italian peninsula. Slaves as significant in the growth of the city of Rome's population in the second and first centuries BC: Jongman 2003, esp. 116–21.

6.1 Slaves used in war in times of crisis

Valerius Maximus *Memorable Deeds and Sayings (Of Necessity)* 7.6.1a

Valerius refers to the property qualification for serving in the Roman army, which excluded free but property-less citizens: the Roman state, in its desperation after the disastrous defeat at Cannae in 216 BC (docs 4.35–6), enrolled slaves. Like the Greeks, the Romans preferred free men who would fight with unquestioned loyalty and could afford their own equipment. The Tiberius Gracchus here is the consul of 215 BC, great-uncle of the Tiberius Gracchus who was tribune in 133. Livy 22.57 has the number of purchased slaves at 8,000; the slaves were to serve in legions for two years and then be freed; their masters were reimbursed (Livy 24.14.1–8, 24.18.12). With an army which included these slaves Gracchus raised the siege of Cumae, and captured the envoys of Philip V of Macedon to Hannibal. According to Livy (10.21.4) freedmen were called up for military service in 296 during the Third Samnite War. Pompey the Great's son Gnaeus recruited 800 of his slaves and shepherds for the war against Caesar (Caesar *BC* 3.4.4). Slaves — who remained slaves — were used by the Romans as rowers in the Second Punic War (Polyb. 10.17.11–13; Livy 24.11.7–9), but only because of manpower shortages; free crews were used in 191 BC against Antiochus (Libourel 1973: 118–19).

During the Second Punic War, when the Roman youth of military age had been reduced by a number of unfavourable battles, the senate, on a motion of the consul Tiberius Gracchus, decreed that slaves should be bought out of public moneys for use in war and in repulsing the enemy. After a bill about this was put to the people by the tribunes of the plebs and passed, three commissioners were appointed to purchase 24,000 slaves. These were bound by an oath that they would give strenuous and courageous service and that they would bear arms as long as the Carthaginians were in Italy, and were sent to camp. In addition, from Apulia, from the Paediculi, 270 slaves were bought as replacements for the cavalry . . . . The city which up to this time had scorned to have as soldiers even free men without property (the *capite censi*) added to its army as its main support persons taken from slave quarters and slaves gathered from shepherd huts.

6.2 Slave numbers of 'traditional' Romans

Athenaeus *Deipnosophistae* 6.272de, 273ab

The setting for this discussion about slavery is Alexandria, c. AD 200. In the Republic, important Romans did not own large numbers of slaves simply for the purposes of ostentatious show, although Aemilia, wife of Scipio Africanus, appears to have been accompanied by a large slave retinue at religious festivals: doc. 7.70. Scipio Aemilianus was sent by the senate to the east in 140 BC: Broughton, *MRR* I.418; Polybius F76 (Walbank III.749–50); Posidonius *FGrH* 87 F59, cf. F35. Cotta (*HRR* II.45 F1) wrote in Latin; Larensius, the speaker, is Roman, hence his remark 'in our native language'.

272d But every Roman (as you know very well, my dear Masurius) **272e** owns the greatest number of slaves he can; in fact numerous people own 10,000, 20,000 or even more, not for the sake of income, like the extremely wealthy Greek Nicias — the majority of Romans keep the largest numbers to accompany them when they go out . . . **273a** The Romans of olden days were moderate and superior in every respect. Scipio Africanus (Aemilianus), for example, when sent by the senate to organise all the kingdoms of the world so that they would submit to their rightful rulers, only took five slaves with him, as Polybius and Posidonius tell us, **273b** and, when one of them died on the trip, he wrote to his relatives telling them to buy and send him out another one in his place. Julius Caesar, the first of all men to cross over to the British Isles, had a thousand ships but only took with him three slaves, as Cotta, who was serving under him, relates in his work on the *Roman Constitution* in our native language.

6.3 Total slave numbers?

Pliny *Natural History* 33.47

For the Republic, it is difficult to estimate the numbers of slaves any individual Roman might have owned. Gaius in the second century AD (*Inst.* 1.43) envisages that it was possible for an individual to own more than 500 slaves, but this is for the imperial period. That elite Romans owned dozens if not hundreds of slaves in the last decades of the Republic does not seem improbable. For Italy in 28 BC, a citizen population of 3,500,000 and 2,000,000 slaves has seemed reasonable to scholars for some time. Isidorus: Brunt 1958: 165; Treggiari 1969: 109; Bradley 1994: 11. Appian (*BC* 1.7.29–30: doc. 8.5) sees the slave class as reproducing itself in the second half of the second century.

A 5 per cent manumission tax was introduced in 357 BC (Livy 7.16.7), and from then to 209 BC the tax brought in 4,000 pounds of gold (Livy 27.10.11; Westermann 1955: 71; Brunt *IM* 549–50; Bradley 1987: 149–50; Alföldy 1988: 38). But calculations based on the amount of this tax in the treasury at any one time are hazardous: Treggiari 1969: 31–2; Brunt 549. This tax indicates that manumissions were reasonably frequent, but it need not be seen as an attempt to discourage manumissions (which it apparently did not).

Marcus Crassus (cos. 70, 55) used to say that nobody was rich unless he could maintain a legion on his annual income. He owned property worth 200,000,000 sesterces — being the richest citizen after Sulla . . . In later times we have seen many freed slaves who were even richer — three equally so, quite recently, during Claudius' reign: Callistus, Pallas and Narcissus. And, to leave these aside, as if they were still in power, there was the case of Gaius Caecilius Isidorus, freedman of Gaius, who, in the consulship of Gaius Asinius Gallus and Gaius Marcius Censorinus (8 BC), stated in his will dated 27 January that in spite of great losses in the civil war, he left 4,116 slaves, 3,600 pairs of oxen, 257,000 other cattle, and 60,000,000 sesterces in money, and he ordered 1,100,000 to be spent on his funeral.

6.4 Urban poverty and self-sufficiency

Lucilius *Satires* 6.2.278–81

(*ROL* III.86.) Gaius Lucilius (c. 180–102/1 BC) was from a senatorial family and served with Scipio Aemilianus at Numantia (134/3 BC). His poetry was satirical and often attacked political figures.

He who has no beast of burden, slave, or any companion
Keeps with him his purse and any coins he might have;
He eats, sleeps and washes with his purse; the man's whole property
Is in the one purse; this purse is tied onto his upper arm.

6.5 A well-equipped household

Lucilius *Satires* 30.3.1053–4, 1055–6

(*ROL* III.342.) The varied use of slaves within the household is made clear in this passage. Obviously even in the late second century BC, when Lucilius was writing, there were households (presumably well-off) with numerous specialist slaves.

Take care that there are at home
A weaver, maidservants, slave-boys, a belt-maker, a wool-weaver.
If you should have enough money, you should add
A large-sided female baker who knows about all sorts of Syrian breads.

6.6 Top slave prices

Pliny *Natural History* 7.128

Pliny writing in the first century AD contrasts these Republican prices with the 50,000,000 sesterces Clutorius Priscus paid for Sejanus' eunuch Paezon. The price-tag of 700,000 (below) was considerable. M. Aemilius Scaurus was consul in 115 BC; see Treggiari 1969: 113. Slave prices in the Republic are elusive (Westermann 1955: 71); Cato the Elder would pay at most 1,500 *denarii* for a slave (doc. 6.34). Most slaves in the later Republican period cost in the range of 1,200–1,500 sesterces. Slaves were not cheap, despite the large numbers gained through warfare, and ordinary Romans are not to be imagined as owning slaves (many poor Romans could hardly feed themselves, judging from the free and subsidised grain distributions at Rome, let alone support a slave). For the actor Roscius, see doc. 6.29, where Panurgus, a slave trained by Roscius, is estimated by Cicero as worth 4,000 sesterces before his training (but as more than 100,000 with it).

The highest price paid up till now for a man born in slavery, as far as I have been able to ascertain, was when Attius of Pesaurum was selling the grammarian Daphnis and the princeps senatus, Marcus Scaurus, offered 700,000 sesterces. In our own time this figure has been exceeded — and quite considerably — by actors buying their freedom with their earnings; even in the days of our ancestors the actor Roscius is said to have earned 500,000 sesterces a year.

SOURCES OF SLAVES

In the Republic, the greatest source of slaves was from warfare. From the third century BC on, Rome's wars of expansion resulted in large numbers of enslaved persons, but even in the fourth century wars in Italy provided significant numbers of slaves (doc. 6.7). The 150,000 persons enslaved by the Romans when they captured Epirus (doc. 6.9) shows how war easily outweighed all other sources. People could also be enslaved for economic reasons and free-lance slave traders contributed previously free persons to the slave market, as with the numerous Syrians and Cilicians active in the Sicilian slave wars; according to Plutarch, Sulla's settlement of Asia was so harsh that people had to sell their children into slavery, and may have caused an oversupply of Asian slaves (doc. 11.10; cf. Treggiari 1969: 2), while Nicomedes of Bithynia told Marius, in 104, that most Bithynians had been taken by tax farmers and were now in slavery in Roman provinces; though doubtless an exaggeration, the Roman senate did issue a decree that all citizens of allied states now in slavery should be liberated: 800 were released in Sicily, until pressure from the wealthy ensured no more action was taken; Diod. 36.3.1; Westermann 1955: 66; Crawford 1977: 49; Balsdon 1979: 78; Rubinsohn 1982: 445.

Pompey's suppression of piracy in 67 BC must have closed an important source of slaves (see doc. 6.13 for Julius Caesar's capture by pirates). The evidence of large late Republican coin hoards in Romania suggests that the Black Sea area, known to Polybius as a source of slaves (4.38.4–5), then became an important supplier (Crawford 1977). See Treggiari 1969: 1–11, who notes that by the first century BC slaves came from East and West: Syrians, Cilicians, Phrygians, Jews, Asians, Greeks, Thracians, Gauls, Spaniards, and Britons were all to be found in Rome; for enslavement: Watson 1967: 159–72.

6.7 Italians enslaved in 307 BC

Livy *History of Rome* 9.42.7–8

In 307 BC, during the Second Samnite War, the Romans enslaved the allies of the Samnites after Q. Fabius Maximus (cos. 308) confined the Samnite army in its camp near Allifae.

7 The next day, before it was properly light, they started to surrender and the Samnites amongst them asked to be allowed to go in just their tunics; they were all sent under the yoke. **8** The allies of the Samnites were protected by no guarantee and 7,000 of them were sold into slavery.

6.8 Compassionate treatment for slaves captured in war

Polybius *Histories* 10.17.6–15

Captives could be distributed to troops and sold by them to dealers, or all the captives sold *en bloc* to dealers and the proceeds divided amongst the soldiers. Here at Scipio's capture of New Carthage in Spain, in 210, some of the prisoners became state property but with the prospect of manumission (Walbank II.217–18; Westermann 1955: 70–1). Compare his behaviour in 202 when, because of the Carthaginians' treachery, Scipio sold into slavery the inhabitants of even those towns who surrendered (Polyb. 15.4.1). Polyb. 10.16.2–17.5 discusses the division of booty amongst soldiers in the Roman army.

6 While the military tribunes were organising the collection and distribution of booty, the Roman general, when the crowd of prisoners, numbering a little less than 10,000, had been collected, ordered first the citizens with their wives and children to be set apart, and next the craftsmen. **7** When this had been done, he called on the citizens to be favourably disposed to the Romans and remember how well they had been treated and dismissed them to their own houses. **8** Simultaneously weeping and rejoicing at the unexpectedness of their deliverance, they prostrated themselves before the general and departed. **9** He told the craftsmen that, for the present, they were public slaves of Rome, but, if they showed good will and hard work in their various crafts, he promised them freedom if the war against Carthage proceeded successfully. **10** He ordered them to enrol themselves with the quaestor and appointed a Roman supervisor for every group of thirty; their total number was about 2,000. **11** From the other prisoners he chose the strongest, best looking and youngest and mixed them in with his crews, **12** thus acquiring half as many sailors again as he had before and manning the captured ships. In this way the crews of the ships were a little under double what they had been — **13** there were 18 captured ships and he originally had 35. **14** He promised these men too their freedom if they showed good will and hard work, once they had won the war against Carthage. **15** By this treatment of the prisoners he made the citizens well-disposed and loyal both to himself and to Rome, and the craftsmen hard-working in the hope of being set free.

6.9 Aemilius Paullus takes 150,000 slaves

Polybius *Histories* 30.15 (Strabo 7.7.3)

This is perhaps the most famous passage dealing with the acquisition of slaves in warfare, and reflects the huge influx of slaves into Roman Italy in the second century BC. Aemilius Paullus was the victor in the Third Macedonian war in 168 BC against Perseus (see docs 5.32–3; Livy 45.33.8–34.7; Plut. *Aem.* 29); from the booty for himself he only kept Perseus' library. Epirus was given over to the Roman army for booty: it was sacked, looted and enslaved and remained a desert 100 years later (Strabo 7.327; Walbank III.438–39). Numbers of slaves taken elsewhere underline the figure of 150,000: Agrigentum: 25,000 (262 BC, Diod. 23.9.11), Panormus: 13,000 (254 BC, Diod. 23.18.5), Tarentum: 30,000 (209 BC, Livy 27.16.7), Africa: 8,000 (204 BC, Livy 29.29.3) Histria: 5,632 (177 BC, Livy 41.11.8); Sardinia 40,000 (174 BC, Livy 41.28.8), Carthage: 50,000 (146 BC, App. *Pun.* 130): Alföldy 1988: 39, 56; cf. Westermann 1955: 60, 62; Hopkins 1978: 8–14, 102–5; Bradley 1989: 21. In 189, Cn. Manlius Vulso sold 40,000 Galatians to neighbouring tribes; at the sack of Corinth, Mummius sold all the women and children into slavery; Scipio Aemilianus also sold all the Numantines, except 50 kept for his triumph (docs 5.40, 50, 52). Ziolkowski 1986 argues that the enslavement of Epirus was due to a shortage of slaves at that time. Cf. Diod. 23.18: when the Romans captured Palermo in 259, they ransomed the inhabitants for 2 minae each; enough money was found in the city for 14,000; the other 13,000 were sold as booty.

Polybius says that after his defeat of Perseus and the Macedonians, Aemilius Paullus destroyed 70 cities in Epirus, most of these belonging to the Molossians, and sold 150,000 people into slavery.

6.10 A job lot in Gaul

Caesar *Gallic War* 2.33.1–7

In 57 BC, after the defeat of the Nervii, the Aduatuci retreated to their stronghold; they took part in negotiations, but then broke the truce. Caesar clearly handed the inhabitants over to the slave-dealers who followed the armies. He occasionally awarded a Gaul as a slave to each of his soldiers: Suet. *Jul.* 26.3.

1 Towards evening Caesar ordered the gates to be closed and the soldiers to leave the town so that the inhabitants might receive no injury at night at the hands of the soldiers. **2** The townsfolk, it appeared, had formed a plan, believing that following the surrender our troops would leave their posts or at least man them less carefully . . . In the third watch they suddenly sallied out with all their forces, on the side where the ascent to our defences seemed less steep. **3** The signal was swiftly given by flares, as Caesar had instructed beforehand, and troops from the nearest forts rushed there. **4** The enemy fought bravely, as might have been expected of brave men in a crisis, when all hope of deliverance lay in bravery alone, fighting on unfavourable terrain against troops who could hurl weapons at them from rampart and towers. **5** About 4,000 men were killed and the rest were driven back into the town. **6** On the next day, the gates were smashed open, for there were now no more defenders, and, after our soldiers had been sent in, Caesar sold the whole town as one lot at auction. **7** The purchasers informed him that the number of persons was 53,000.

6.11 Slaves from Gaul for Cicero

Cicero *Letter to his brother Quintus* 3.9.4

Cicero is writing from Rome to Quintus in Gaul in December 54. What is particularly interesting in this passage is that there is no moral or ethical consideration on Cicero's part of these slaves as human beings who are to be transported against their will to an alien culture: Cicero simply appreciates the offer of more hands; see Bradley 1994: 7.

I thank you most gratefully for the slaves, which you promise me; I am indeed, as you say in your letter, short-handed both at Rome and on my estates. But take care, my dear brother, that you do not consider doing anything for my convenience, unless it is entirely convenient for you and totally within your means.

6.12 Roman imports of educated slaves

Pliny *Natural History* 35.199–200

Pliny is here discussing different medicinal earths. The proscriptions referred to are those of Sulla in 82 BC (docs 11.19–25) and of the 'Second Triumvirate' in 43 BC. Menas was Sextus Pompey's admiral c. 40 BC, who deserted twice to Octavian; for Publilius, see doc. 6.20. Many educated slaves were eventually freed, and their names were well-known in Rome: see Westermann 1955: 79–80; Treggiari 1969: 110–42. Imperial references to slave feet marked by chalk: Ovid *Amores* 1.8.64; Juv. 1.111; Propertius 4.5.52.

199 There is another kind of chalk called 'silversmith's' because used for polishing silver, but the cheapest kind is that which our ancestors set the custom of using to denote the victory-line in the circus and mark the feet of slaves brought from overseas when up for sale; examples are Publilius (Syrus) from Antioch, the founder of the mimic stage, and his cousin Manilius Antiochus the founder of astronomy, and Staberius Eros the first grammarian — all of whom our great-grandfathers could see arrive on the same ship. **200** But why mention these men, recommended as they are by their literary honours? Other examples they saw up for public sale were Sulla's Chrysogonus, Quintus Catulus' Amphion, Lucius Lucullus' Hector, Pompey's Demetrius, Demetrius' Auge (although she was also believed to have belonged to Pompey), Mark Antony's Hipparchus, and Menas and Menecrates who belonged to Sextus Pompey — as well as a list of others whom this is not the occasion to enumerate, who enriched themselves by the bloodshed of Roman citizens and the licence permitted by proscriptions.

6.13 Caesar and the pirates

Suetonius *Life of the Deified* Julius 4.1–2

Piracy in the eastern Mediterranean provided another major source of slaves. Pirates' activities became so notorious that Pompey was empowered under the *lex Gabinia* of 67 BC to deal with them (see docs 12.8–9). Those from Cilicia were especially responsible for kidnapping free people for enslavement: Strabo describes this as profitable and the victims as 'easily captured'. The clearing-market for the slaves was the Aegean island of Delos and the customers were Romans who 'employed many slaves' after the destruction of Carthage and Corinth (both in 146 BC). According to Strabo, who is perhaps exaggerating, c. 142–37 BC 10,000 slaves could arrive and be dispatched from there every day; Delos was an immense slave clearing-house (Strabo 14.5.2, cf. 14.3.2; see Westermann 1955: 61, 65; Bradley 1989: 22; 1994: 37). Delos was sacked in 88 BC by one of Mithridates' generals, bringing an end to its slave trade, but piracy was a problem until 67 BC.

Plutarch's version (*Caes.* 2) of Caesar's capture by pirates varies considerably from that of Suetonius: the pirates ask for 20 talents, and Caesar raises the sum to 50; the ransom is brought from Miletus; the pirates are put into prison at Pergamum and, when the governor fails to act immediately, Caesar takes the pirates and crucifies them; for Caesar and the pirates: Westermann 1955: 65; Treggiari 1969: 3; Ward 1975, 1977.

1 After Lepidus' revolt had been suppressed, Caesar brought a charge of extortion against Cornelius Dolabella (cos. 81), an ex-consul who had held a triumph; when he was found not guilty, Caesar decided to withdraw to Rhodes, both so the ill-feeling would have time to die down and so he could, while at leisure, study under Apollonius Molo, the most distinguished teacher of rhetoric at that time. The winter months had already arrived while he was on his way to Rhodes, and he was captured by pirates near the island of Pharmacussa. He remained with them, not without the greatest indignation, for nearly 40 days, accompanied by only a doctor and two valets. **2** For he had at once sent off his companions and other slaves to procure the money by which he might be ransomed. Once the 50 talents had been paid and he was left on the shore, he raised a fleet without delay and went off in pursuit of them. Once they were in his power he put them to death, as he had often threatened to do to them in jest.

DOMESTIC SLAVES

Slaves were used in a wide variety of contexts: mining, domestic service, education, and as secretaries to officials; for slave occupations: Westermann 1955: 73–4; Vogt 1974: 109–120; Bradley 1994: 58–64. In terms of societal occupations, slaves were only barred from political office and army service, though slaves could be enrolled as soldiers and rowers in a crisis (doc. 6.1).

6.14 Kitchen slaves on a bronze casket, c. 250 BC

CIL I² 560

(*ROL* IV.198.) The casket, dated to c. 250–235 BC, on which this inscription appears depicts a countrified kitchen scene and shows two or more slave cooks having an animated discussion while preparing a meal. The inscriptions run partly from right to left. Some of the meanings are obscure.

> A: Prepare the fish (shown cutting up a fish).
> B: I have collected the garlic (taking down part of a pig).
> B: I have prepared it (holding dish and knife).
> A: Beat it some more (holding dish out to B).
> B: Boil for me properly (addressing a cauldron).
> A: Mix well (stirring the cauldron and holding a plate).
> B: I'm here, coming (walking away).

6.15 Slaves and the Latin language

Varro *On the Latin Language* 8.6, 10, 21, 83

For the ease of naming a single slave, see doc. 6.16, where 'Marcipor' is the slave ('puer') of Marcus. Romanus as a slave name: Livy 4.61.10. Roman masters chose not to use the original name of the slave, both for ease of pronunciation, and because a new name was a means of asserting ownership; for names of slaves, see Treggiari 1969: 7.

6 For example, those who have recently been bought as slaves in a large household quickly learn to inflect the names of all their fellow-slaves in the oblique cases, when they have only heard the nominative . . .

10 In those matters in which usage was simple, the inflection of the name was also simple, just as in a house with only one slave there is only need for one slave name, but in a house with numerous slaves there is need of numerous names . . .

21 There are two kinds of word-derivation, voluntary and natural; voluntary derivation is when an individual of his own accord chooses a word-derivation. So, when three men have brought a slave each at Ephesus, one sometimes derives his name from that of the seller Artemidorus, and calls his Artemas, another names his slave from the region where he bought him, so Ion from Ionia, and the third calls him Ephesius because he bought him at Ephesus. In this way each derives the name from a different cause, as he chooses . . .

83 Most freedmen set free by a town (municipium) have their names from the town, though in this matter the slaves of associations and temples have not observed the rule in a similar way, and the freedmen of the Romans ought to be called Romanus, like Faventinus from Faventia and Reatinus from Reate. In this way freedmen whose fathers were public slaves would be named Romanus if they had been manumitted before they began to take the names of the magistrates who set them free.

6.16 'Marcipors and Lucipors'

Pliny *Natural History* 33.26

Pliny is here talking about the increasing need to use seal-rings to protect possessions. Marcipor and Lucipor mean 'Marcus' boy' and 'Lucius' boy' — an easy way of denoting a single slave. Marcipores and Lucipores are plurals, respectively, of 'slave of Marcus' and 'slave of Lucius'. Pliny recalls the Republic when individual masters had far fewer slaves, whereas in his time a nomenclator, a slave whose special job was that of remembering names, needs to be employed. He is perhaps exaggerating, as Varro in doc. 6.15 clearly envisages several slaves in a republican household, but household slave retinues *were* larger in the imperial period.

To think what life was like in olden days, and what innocence there was when nothing was sealed! Nowadays even articles of food and wine have to be protected from theft by a ring. This has been brought about by our legions of slaves, the crowd of outsiders in our homes, and the fact that we have to employ a nomenclator even to tell us the names of our own slaves! In times of old things were different — there were just single slaves, Marcipors and Lucipors, part of their masters' families, who took all their meals in common with the family, and there was no need to keep a watch in the house over the household slaves.

6.17 Slave women and Juno Caprotina

Macrobius *Saturnalia* 1.11.36–40

On slave women, their dedication to their households, and their festival day of Juno Caprotina, see Plut. *Rom.* 29.6, *Cam.* 33.4. Caproficus is a wild fig tree.

36 It is well-known that the Nones of July is the festival of female slaves, and both the origin and the reason for the celebration is common knowledge. For on that day free women and female slaves both sacrifice to Juno Caprotina under a wild fig tree in commemoration of the generous spirit which was displayed by female slaves in preserving Rome's public honour. **37** For, after the city had been captured, and the Gallic onslaught had subsided, the state was reduced to such weakness that her neighbours were on the watch for the chance to attack Rome; they appointed as their leader Postumius Livius, the chief magistrate of Fidenae, and he sent instructions to the senate demanding that, if they wished the remnants of their state to survive, they should hand over to him their married women and unmarried girls: **38** when the senators were wavering in anxious debate, a female slave named Tutela, or Philotis, promised that she and the other slaves would go to the enemy under the names of their mistresses, and in the dress of married women and girls they were handed over to the enemy with the tears of those accompanying them as proof of their grief. **39** When they had been allocated in the camp by Livius, they tempted the men with copious wine, pretending it was a festival day at Rome, and after making them drowsy, they gave a signal to the Romans from a wild fig tree near the camp. **40** These were victorious in their sudden attack, and the senate, grateful for the service, ordered all the female slaves to be manumitted, gave them dowries from the treasury and permitted them to wear the type of dress they had assumed. The senate named the day itself 'Nonae Caprotinae', after the wild fig tree from which the signal leading to victory was received, and it resolved that there should be an annual festival and sacrifice, when the juice of the wild fig tree should be offered in commemoration of this deed I have narrated.

6.18 A lucky doorkeeper

Suetonius *On Rhetoricians* 27

Slave doorkeepers served in chains so that they were unable to run away. Voltacilius is another example of a slave manumitted because it was felt that his talents warranted this. From a mere doorkeeper, he became an historian, though Suetonius' comment 'is said to have been' might indicate his disbelief in this background. He may be the same person as the M. Voltacilius Pitholaus at Macrob. 2.2.13; see Treggiari 1969: 118.

Lucius Voltacilius Pilutus is said to have been a slave and even to have served as a doorkeeper in chains, according to ancient custom, until he was manumitted for his talents and interest in literature, and helped his patron prepare for his work as prosecutor. Then he became a teacher of rhetoric and taught Pompey the Great, and wrote a history of his father's achievements, as well as those of Pompey himself, in numerous volumes; in the view of Cornelius Nepos he was the first freedman who undertook the writing of history, which up to that time had always been written by men of the highest rank.

6.19 A favourite slave

Lucilius *Satires* 22.624–5

(*ROL* III.196.) Books 22–25 of Lucilius apparently consisted mainly of epigrams and epitaphs on his slaves and freedmen in their own dialects; for the 'faithful slave': see Vogt 1974: 122–45 (Metrophanes at 131).

> A slave neither unfaithful to his master nor useless in any respect.
> A little pillar of Lucilius' household lies here — Metrophanes.

6.20 Publilius Syrus: maxims on slavery

Publilius *Syrus Maxims* 414, 489, 596, 616

Publilius was from Syria, brought to Rome from Antioch as a slave in the late 80s BC; on the same ship was his cousin who went on to become the astronomer Manilius (doc. 6.12). Educated by his purchaser, Publilius became a composer of mimes, a dramatic genre common to Italy. He performed at Caesar's invitation at the games (ludi) of 46 BC and defeated his free-born opponent Laberius (doc. 2.35; Pliny *Nat. Hist.* 35.199; Macrob. 2.7.6–10; Suet. *Jul.* 39; Cic. *Fam.* 12.18.2). Pithy sayings (apophthegms) by his characters were collected together in the first century AD, and many of these concern slaves and slavery. Despite line 489, he also saw the role of a slave as involving duty and loyalty; cf. Treggiari 1969: 12, 242.

414 There are less risks in being tame, but it makes you a slave.
489 It is glorious to die instead of being degraded as a slave.
596 If you serve wisely you will have a share in the master's role.
616 If you don't like being a slave, you will be miserable; but you won't stop being a slave.

6.21 Treatment of household slaves

Plautus *Pseudolus* 133–70

Plautus was writing between c. 205 and 184 BC. Here Ballio, a relatively well-off if uncultured householder, is giving instructions to his slaves. Cic. *Off.* 1.41 believes that masters have an obligation to treat their slaves properly, as if they were hired workmen ('the lowest station and fortune is that of slaves, and those who tell us to treat them like hired workers are quite right to do so: work must be exacted, their dues paid'). In this passage the whippings are made an object of comedy: the slaves are so hardened that the owner hurts himself more than the slave when he undertakes to flog them. But beneath the humour lies the ugly reality of the whipped and beaten slave, ordered, bullied and threatened by the master, all over a meal designed to impress. Note in particular the stock complaints of masters about their slaves, the main one here in the *Pseudolus* being that of servile idleness, which was probably an important form of passive servile resistance to slavery. The passage makes clear that the master had physical control of the slave; cf. Westermann 1955: 75; Watson 1967: 173–5; Hopkins 1978: 118–20.

  Plautus is an important source for slavery: Roman stereotypes about slaves, slaves' resistance to work, how they were beaten, their *peculium* (personal fund) and manumission, and the existence of slave families within the elite household or farm, are all in evidence in his work. Slave women are found in a variety of roles in Plautus, as singers, wardrobe keepers, doorkeepers, nurses, obstetricians, attendants, hairdressers and clothes-folders, and men slaves as masseurs, jewellery attendants, messengers, pages, and grooms; the household could also have a male chaperone of the children (*paedagogus*), as well as a male cook; for Plautus and slavery, see Bradley 1987: 28–9, 38–9, 146–7, 1989: 27–30, 36–7; Thalmann 1996; Rei 1998; McCarthy 2000.

In addition to this negative portrait there was also the slave who showed loyalty (*fides*) and obedience (*obsequium*) toward the master. Tyndarus in the *Captivi*, for example, is the loyal slave, and implicit in Plautus are ideals about the faithful slave (cf. Vogt 1974: 131; Parker 1998, for *exempla* of faithful slaves).

Ballio: Get out, come on, out with you, you lazy things, kept at a loss and bought at a loss,

None of you ever thinks at all of doing anything right;

I can't get any use out of you, unless I try this treatment!

I've never seen any men more like donkeys, your ribs are so hardened with blows!

If you flog any of them you hurt yourself the most — they actually wear out the whip,

And all they think of when they get the chance is to rob, steal, pinch, loot, drink, eat and run away: this

140   Is their idea of work, and you'd rather leave wolves in charge of sheep,

Than these in charge at home.

I will say that when you look them over they don't seem too bad:

It's their work which is no good.

Now — unless you all pay attention to this pronouncement,

Unless you get that sleep and laziness out of your chests and eyes,

I'll whip your sides till they're really colourful,

They'll have more colours that Campanian coverings

Or clipped Alexandrian tapestries with their embroidered beasts.

I gave you all your orders and 'assigned your provinces' yesterday,

But you're so good at being cunning and worthless,

150   I must remind you of your duties with a good thrashing.

True, that's the way you're made: your toughness is too much for me — and this!

Look at that, will you? They're not even paying attention! Attend to this, concentrate on this,

Turn your ears here to what I'm saying, you race of men born to be flogged!

By Pollux! Your hide will never be tougher than my rawhide here.

Now what? Does it hurt? That's for a slave who ignores his master.

All line up in front of me and pay attention to what I tell you.

You there, with the pitcher, fetch the water, and make sure the cook's pot is filled.

You with the axe, I appoint you to the province of wood-chopping.

Slave: But the axe is blunt.

Ballio: Well, what if it is? You're all blunted with thrashings, too:

160   But is that any reason why I shouldn't get work out of you all?

Now you — I order you to make the house shine. You've got your job, hurry up, go on in!

You, put the couches straight. You, clean the silver, and put it away.

Now, when I come back from the forum, make sure I find everything ready :
Swept, sprinkled, polished, smoothed, cleaned and all as it should be.
Today's my birthday and you all ought to celebrate it.
Make sure the ham, skin, sweetbreads and udder are put to soak in water, do
    you hear?
I want to entertain some classy gentlemen in high style so they think I've got
    money.
Get indoors and hurry along with all this quickly, so there's no delay when
    the cook comes;
I'm off to market to see what sort of fish I can buy.
170   Boy, you go on in front: we must take care no one cuts a hole in my purse.

6.22 A sensible slave

Plautus *The Two Menaechmuses* 966–84

A household slave, Messenio, is soliloquising; his master (Menaechmus Sosicles) is one of the twin brothers of the play's title.

This is the proof of a good slave, who looks after his master's business,
Sees to it, gives it his care, and thinks about it,
That when his master is away he cares for his master's business diligently,
Just as if he were present, or even more so.
970   His back rather than his appetite, his legs than his stomach,
Ought to concern a fellow whose heart is in the right place.
He should remember what good-for-nothings
Get from their masters — lazy, worthless fellows:
Whippings, fetters,
The mill, weariness, hunger, bitter cold—
These are the rewards of laziness.
That's what I'm really afraid of; that's why it's better to be good than be bad.
I can much more easily stand a telling-off; but I hate floggings,
And I'd much rather eat the meal than do the grinding.
980   That's why I follow master's orders, carry them out properly and quietly;
And I find it pays.
Others can do as they think proper; I'll be just where I should be:
Let me keep a sense of fear, and avoid making mistakes, so I'll always be
    there when master wants me.
I shan't have much to fear. Master will soon reward me for my service.

6.23 Slaves indistinguishable from their masters

Appian *Civil Wars* 2.120 (505)

Appian is here stressing the 'degeneration' of the plebs at Rome in the context of Caesar's assassination and the speeches of the 'tyrannicides'. According to Dio 48.34 a slave nearly became a quaestor in 39 BC but was recognised by his master; in the same year another runaway slave was found to be one of the praetors and thrown from the Tarpeian Rock, after being manumitted so he could suffer the punishment suitable to a free man. While there was no special slave clothing, clearly it would be simple and probably much-worn: Bradley 1994: 87–9, 95–7.

The plebs is now very much intermingled with alien blood, while a freedman has the same citizen rights as a citizen has, and a man who is still a slave wears the same clothes as his master; for, except for the senatorial class, the dress of the rest of the citizens is the same as that of the slaves.

SLAVES IN INDUSTRY AND MANUFACTURE

Slaves were employed widely in Italian agriculture. The degree, however, to which they were employed in industry and manufacture is unclear. Republican Rome was hardly a consumer society: most free people were simply too poor to provide a market for anything but the most essential items for daily life. Slavery may have obstructed technological development because of the ease of employing a servile workforce, but there was no mass market of consumers, and production and consumption of manufactured items was largely limited to functional, everyday items.

6.24 Early inscriptions denoting slave or freedman manufacture

CIL I² 412, 416, 2487

(*ILS* 8567; *ILLRP* 1214, 1217–18; *ROL* IV.202.) Inscriptions by slaves on pottery items made prior to 220 BC at Cales, north of Naples; Cales was known for its pottery, which has been found in various parts of Italy. In (i) and (ii) 'slave' may mean ex-slave, i.e., freedman. Pottery was the ancient equivalent of modern plastic; a patera is a shallow dish.

(i) I, Retus Gabinius, slave of Gaius, made you at Cales (on a patera found at Tarquinii).
(ii) Kaeso Serponius made this at Cales in the Esquiline quarter. A slave of Gaius (on a patera).
(iii) Marcus, at Cales. A household slave (verna) (on a clay vessel).

6.25 'Tesserae consulares'

CIL I² 889–90, 2663a

(*ILS* 5161c, d; *ILLRP* 1001–3; *ROL* IV.214.) These pieces of bone or ivory (sing.: tessera) with a handle or hole for attachment to some item give a slave or freedman's name, his master or patron, the word *spectavit*, 'inspected' (or an abbreviation thereof), and date by day, month and consulship. They have been argued to record the official checking of coins for weight and genuineness as opposed to counterfeit. Each *tessera* showed that a particular cashier had inspected a batch of coins, the tessera being attached to that money-basket. Alternatively, an older, less likely, view was that each tessera recorded the date of discharge of a gladiator (the day on which he 'became a spectator'). These particular tesserae date to the 90s.

(i) Inspected by Capito, slave of Memmius, in November in the consulship of Gnaeus Domitius and Gaius Cassius (cos. 96).
(ii) Inspected by Menophilus, slave of Lucius Abius, in the consulship of Gaius Valerius and Marcus Herennius (cos. 93).

(iii)   Inspected by Philoxenus, servant of the association of iron-smiths, on the Nones (5th) of April in the consulship of Gaius Coelius and Lucius Domitius (cos. 94).

6.26 Slaves in Spanish mines

Diodorus Siculus *Library of History* 5.36.3–4, 38.1

The silver mines in Spain were owned by the Roman state, but worked by individual operators who turned over a proportion of the profits to the state (Richardson 1976). Slaves were used in the mining and conditions were clearly inhumane with the precious metal worth more than the lives of the slaves. Polybius writes that there were 40,000 workers involved in the mines outside New Carthage (34.9.9); not all of these would have worked in the shafts and some would have been employed in subsidiary tasks such as washing the ore and smelting it; Diodorus is here citing the Stoic philosopher Posidonius (*FGrH* 87 F117). For the silver mines, see also Strabo 3.147–8 = Polyb. 34.9.8–11 (Walbank III.605–7), cf. Strabo 12.3.40; for conditions in the mines: Burford 1972: 73–5; Hopkins 1978: 119; Bradley 1987: 77; Yavetz 1988: 159.

36.3 Initially any individuals who came along used to work the mines, and these acquired great wealth because the silver-bearing earth was accessible and abundant; later, when the Romans took control of Spain, a large number of Italians took over the mines and acquired great wealth through their love of profit. **4** They purchase a large number of slaves and hand them over to the overseers of the mining operations, who open shafts in numerous places and dig deep into the ground in search of its seams rich in silver and gold; they go not only a long way into the ground, but extend their digging to the depth of many stades with galleries twisting and turning in all directions, thus bringing from the depths the ore which provides their profits. . . .

38.1 The men engaged in the mining operations procure unbelievably large revenues for their masters, but through their excavations under the earth both by day and by night they wear out their own bodies, many of them dying because of the exceptional hardships; they are not allowed any relaxation or rest, but are compelled by the beatings of their supervisors to endure these terrible evils and throw away their lives in this wretched manner, although some of them who can endure it suffer their misery for a long time because of their bodily strength or sheer will-power; but they prefer dying to surviving because of the extent of their suffering.

SLAVES AND THE ENTERTAINMENT INDUSTRY

The entertainment 'industry' was an important one at Rome, and slaves were prominent in it. There were slave actors and mimes, slave-gladiators and slave prostitutes. Some actors were quite valuable. Unlike the freedman of Lucius (doc. 6.28), Protogenes (clearly a Greek) had apparently not been freed (doc. 6.27), nor had Panurgus (doc. 6.29) due presumably to the value of these slaves. Some eleven republican actresses, the majority of them slaves, are known by name: see docs 7.62–5.

6.27 An entertaining slave

ILS 5221

(*CIL* I² 1861; *ILLRP* 804; *ROL* IV.10.) Found in a wall at Preturo, near Amiternum, perhaps dating to c. 165–160 BC. The inscription is clearly not the work of a professional.

Here is laid the delightful mimic actor Protogenes, slave of Clulius,
Who gave great enjoyment to people through his jesting.

6.28 An entertaining freedman

CIL I² 1378

(*ROL* IV.42.) A first-century BC epitaph from a grave at Rome.

For . . . freedman of Lucius, a professional jester (*scurra*),
A most respectable and excellent
Freedman of utmost trustworthiness,
His patron made this.

6.29 A comedian's market-value

Cicero *In Defence of Quintus Roscius the Comedian* 28–9

Quintus Roscius, the famous actor, and Gaius Fannius Chaerea jointly owned a slave, Panurgus, whom Roscius was training as a comic actor (*histrio*). When Panurgus was murdered by a certain Q. Flavius, Roscius accepted a farm in lieu of his half of the slave; at the time of the speech the farm was worth 100,000 sesterces. However Fannius brought an action that half the farm ought to be his in compensation for his part-ownership of Panurgus. Cicero argues that the value of the slave was owing to his training by Roscius; for Roscius, see doc. 6.6 (his annual earnings); doc. 11.39 (his friendship with Sulla); Macrob. 3.14.3 (his free birth and status as an eques); Cic. *de orat*. 3.102 (his range of comic and tragic parts); his death was 'recent' in 62 BC (Cic. *Arch*. 17).

28 You state, Saturius, that Panurgus was the property of Fannius. But I maintain that he belonged entirely to Roscius. For what part of him belonged to Fannius? His body. What part belonged to Roscius? His training. It was not his appearance but his skill that was worth money. The part that belonged to Fannius was worth no more than 4,000 sesterces; the part that belonged to Roscius was worth more than 100,000 sesterces, for no one judged him by his bodily physique, but valued him by his skill as a comedian. His limbs by themselves could not earn more than 12 asses, but his training, received from this man, brought in no less than 100,000 sesterces . . . . **29** The hopes and expectations, the devotion and favour that Panurgus won on the stage were because he was the pupil of Roscius! Those who loved Roscius supported him, those who admired Roscius approved of him — in short those who had heard Roscius' name considered Panurgus excellent and accomplished.

6.30 A satire on gladiators

Lucilius *Satires* 4.2.172–81

(*ROL* III.56–8; Cic. *Tusc. Disp*. 4.48.) This is a satire on a famous gladiatorial fight. Anyone who fought in the arena was either a slave or a free man who gave up his rights as a free person; for gladiators, see docs 2.74–5. Slaves and gladiators were also often employed in armed gangs: both Milo and Clodius used armed slaves in their electioneering and political campaigns and both were accompanied by slave bodyguards (Milo's included well-known gladiators) at their meeting on the Appian way in January 52 which led to Clodius' murder: doc. 13.1, 2.3; cf. Cic. *Att*. 4.3.2.

In the gladiatorial show put on by the Flacci
Was a certain Aeserninus, a Samnite, a vile chap, worthy of that life and station.
He was matched with Pacideianus, best by far
Of all gladiators since the birth of mankind.

Pacideianus speaks:

'Indeed I'll kill him and win, if that's what you want,' he said.
'But I think it will happen like this: first I'll take it on my face,
Then I'll fix my sword in that blockhead's stomach and lungs.
I hate the fellow, I'll fight in a temper, and we'll wait no longer
Than it takes each of us to adjust our sword to our right-hand —
So furiously am I carried away by my passion, anger and hatred for him.'

FARM SLAVES: THEIR OCCUPATIONS AND TRAINING

Slaves had been used in large numbers on landed estates, such as the latifundia, since the second century BC (doc. 8.6), and their presence there had been an important factor in the Gracchan land reforms. As is clear from both Cato the Elder and Varro's agricultural treatises slaves were important in farming, carrying out a wide variety of tasks, and were in fact the 'backbone' of agriculture.

6.31 Slave duties on an old-fashioned farm

Cato the Elder *On Farming* 2.2–4, 7

Even in antiquity, Cato was viewed as a hard master. His manual, written for the farming gentry c. 160 BC, provided advice on how to make a profit from farming; Varro in the Republic and Columella in the imperial period wrote similar agricultural treatises and all three of them took slavery to be the backbone of farming: Brunt 1988: 242; Bradley 1994: 15, cf. Jones 1960: 8, 10. Cato's advice to sell old slaves is well-known (cf. doc. 6.34; Wiedemann 1981: 202, 210; 1985: 167). Clearly agricultural slaves, even when they grew old, did not expect manumission. Few would have had any personal contact with their masters, especially those kept in chains, and obviously there were runaways. For Cato and his slaves: Astin 1978: 244–5, 261–6; Westermann 1955: 76; Jones 1960: 8; Bradley 1987: 28–9; 1989: 27, 30, 45, 51; Grant 1992: 101–2; on the role of the slaves on the farm: Rathbone 1981: 12–15; for a translation and notes to Cato's *On Farming*, see Dalby 1998; also Astin 1978: 189–203, 240–66.

2 If the amount of work does not seem to the master to be sufficient, but the overseer says that he has been industrious, but the slaves have not been well, the weather has been bad, slaves have run away, he has had public work to do — when he has given these and many other reasons, call the overseer back to the calculation of the work and workmen. **3** If the weather has been rainy, mention the work which could have been done during rain: washing out the wine vats, pitching them, cleaning the farmhouse, moving grain, carrying out manure, making a manure-pit, cleaning seed, mending ropes and making new ones; and that the slaves ought to have mended their rag-coverings and hoods. **4** On festivals, too, old ditches might have been cleaned out, road work done, brambles cut back, garden dug, meadows cleared, wood bundled, thorns weeded, grain husked, and cleaning-up done. When the slaves were sick, such large rations ought not to have been issued . . . **7** Inspect the livestock and hold a sale: sell the oil, if the price is right, and sell surplus wine and grain; sell old oxen, defective cattle, defective sheep, wool, hides, an old cart, old tools, an elderly slave, a sickly slave, and anything else superfluous. The paterfamilias (master of the household) ought to be fond of selling, not of buying.

6.32 Rations for slaves

Cato *On Farming* 56–9

The slave diet consisted mainly of bread and wine with some relishes. The rations are clearly daily amounts, and are sufficient for daily needs (Brunt 1965: 176: 'as much wheat as the soldier got'; Rowland 1970: 229; cf. Bradley 1994: 82; Forbes and Foxhall 1982: esp. 63–4, 88 on grain as a staple food). A hemina is half a sextarius, and a congius is six sextarii or approximately six pints (three litres). A modius is a measure of corn (16 sextarii); a quadrantal a liquid measure (eight congii). Cato's 'pound' (libra) is actually 13 ounces or 0.325 kg. **56**: The slaves shackled together receive their ration as bread rather than as grain: being shackled, they cannot make their own bread from grain, unlike the other slaves; for chain gangs, see Columella 1.8.16. **57**: The Saturnalia involved a degree of license on the part of slaves, both in drinking and in a relaxed attitude toward their masters. The Saturnalia in Cicero's time was five days but perhaps shorter in Cato's (see doc. 3.69). The Compitalia was in honour of the Lares Compitales, the lares of the cross-roads. Both festivals were at the turn of the year. Three litres were allowed for each slave for both festivals. Holidays for slaves: Bradley 1979, 1987: 40–3. **59**: At doc. 2.16 Cato advises that tunics and shoes be purchased at Rome.

56 Rations for the slaves. For the workers four modii of wheat through winter and four and a half through summer; for the overseer, housekeeper, superintendent and shepherd three modii; for the slaves shackled together four pounds of bread through the winter, five from when they begin to dig the vineyard until the figs come, then return to four. **57** Wine ration for the slaves. For three months after the harvest let them drink after-wine; in the fourth month give them a hemina (half a pint) a day, that is two and a half congii a month; in the fifth, sixth, seventh and eighth month a sextarius (a pint) a day, that is five congii a month; in the ninth, tenth, eleventh and twelfth month three heminae a day, that is an amphora a month; in addition give out a congius per person for the Saturnalia and Compitalia: total of wine for each person per year . . . . For the shackled slaves issue an additional amount in proportion to their work; it is not too much for them to drink ten quadrantals of wine each year. **58** Relish for the slaves. Conserve as many windfall olives as possible. Later conserve the ripe olives from which you will get the least oil and be sparing with them, so they will last as long as possible. When the olives are eaten up, give out fish-paste and vinegar. Issue each person with a pint of oil a month. A modius of salt per person per year is sufficient. **59** Clothing for the slaves. A tunic three and a half feet long, and a coat every other year. Whenever you give out a tunic or coat to anyone, first take the old one and make rag-coverings of it. You should issue heavy boots every other year.

6.33 Instructions on supervising the housekeeper

Cato *On Farming* 143.1–3

Cato here instructs the slave overseer on the role of the slave housekeeper. Plautus *Merc.* 396–9: 'Our housekeeper has almost nothing to do — only weaving, making flour, chopping wood, spinning, sweeping up, getting slapped in the face, and, naturally, preparing all the household meals every day.' Must is new wine boiled thick.

1 Take care that the housekeeper performs her duties. If the master has given her to you as your wife, be satisfied with her. Ensure that she respects you. Make sure she is not too extravagant. She should visit the neighbouring and other women as little as possible and not invite them to the house or her part of it. She should not go out to meals or be fond of going out. She should not take part in religious worship or get others to do it on her behalf without the orders of the master or mistress: she should remember that the master sees to religious worship for the whole household. **2** She should be clean; and she should keep the whole farmhouse clean; she should sweep the hearth every day before she goes to bed. On the Kalends, Ides and Nones — whenever there is a holy day — she should place a garland on the hearth, and on those days she should pray to the household gods as much as she is able. She should take care to have cooked food available for you and the household. **3** She should keep many hens and eggs. She should have stores of dried pears, sorbs (berries), figs, dried grapes, sorbs in must, pears, grapes and sparrow-quinces preserved in jars, raisins preserved in grape pulp and in pots buried in the ground, as well as fresh Praenestine nuts buried in a pot in the ground. She should keep Scantian apples in jars and other fruits that are usually preserved, as well as crab-apples. All these she should make sure she has stored away diligently every year. She should also know how to make good flour and fine spelt.

6.34 Was Cato a typical slave owner?

Plutarch *Life of Cato the Elder* 4.5–5.2, 21.1–3. 7–8

Huge numbers of slaves were imported from the third century BC to the end of the Republic but it is also clear that the slave population reproduced itself to some degree, as Cato's and Varro's comments about allowing sexual relationships between slaves makes clear.

4.5 He tells us that he never paid more than 1,500 drachmas for a slave, as he wanted not the delicate or handsome types, but tough workmen like grooms and herdsmen; and, when they got older, he thought that he ought to sell them and not feed useless workers. **6** On the whole, he considered nothing was cheap if you didn't need it, and what a man didn't need was expensive even if it only cost an *as*; and that you should buy land for tilling and grazing, rather than for watering and sweeping. **5.1** Some people put this down to stinginess on his part, while others accepted that he kept within his means to make others mend their ways and learn some moderation. For myself, I consider his conduct towards his slaves in getting full use out of them like pack-animals, and then, when they got old, driving them off and selling them, as the mark of a thoroughly inflexible character, unable to recognise any dealings between man and man except necessity . . . . **2** A good man will take care of his horses even when age has worn them out, and look after his dogs not only when they are puppies, but when they need care in their old age . . . .

21.1 Cato acquired a great many slaves whom he bought as prisoners of war, particularly the young ones, who could still be raised and trained, like pups and colts. None of these ever entered into another person's house unless sent there by Cato himself or his wife. If anyone of them were asked what Cato was doing, he answered only that he did not know. **2** At home, a slave either had to be doing his work or asleep, and Cato greatly preferred the sleepy ones, thinking them to be more mild-tempered than those who were wakeful, and better workers at anything when they had enjoyed a sleep than those who had not. **3** Considering also that the greatest reason for misconduct in slaves was their sexual passions, he arranged at a fixed price for them to sleep with the females, and none of them was allowed to associate with a woman outside the household . . . **7** He also lent money to those of his slaves who wished it; they would buy boys and, when they had trained and taught them at Cato's expense, would sell them again after a year. **8** Cato kept many of these for himself, accounting to the trainer the highest price offered. To encourage his son to such practices, he used to say that lessening the value of an estate was not the mark of a man, but of a widow woman.

6.35 Varro on slave labour

Varro *On Farming* 1.17.3–7

Varro emphasises rewards, rather than punishments, and encourages loyalty amongst the slaves. At 1.17.3 he suggests that labourers should be not less than 22 years. At 1.16.4 he explains that rich landlords prefer to have specialist slaves (e.g., smiths and other essential craftsmen) in their household so that they have their services at any time. Varro makes clear that slave-breeding occurred and that he and other owners provided for women to follow the herdsmen, while Cato allowed the male slaves to purchase sexual gratification as a means of keeping the slaves under control. From these sexual unions, slaves were born, belonging to the master. Slave families thus came into existence, though legally slaves could not marry, and therefore their families had no legal status. For Varro and slave intercourse: Bradley 1987: 50–1, 1989: 26; already by the end of the second century BC the slave class was reproducing itself to some degree (App. *BC* 1.7) but continued importation of slaves was necessary. Children born of slaves were the property of the mother's master and were known as vernae (sing. verna); if the mother was a slave, so was the child (the father's status was not taken into consideration). See Westermann 1955: 76–7.

3 Slaves ought to be neither timid nor high-spirited. **4** They ought to have men over them who have had some training in letters and a degree of education, who are honest, and older than the labourers I have mentioned . . . **5** They are not to be allowed to control the men with whips instead of words, as long as you can achieve the same result. You should not acquire too many slaves of the same nation; for that is the strongest cause of domestic hatreds. The foremen are to be made more eager by rewards and care must be taken that they have some property of their own and are mated to fellow-slaves, from whom they can have children, for from such treatment they become steadier and more attached to the estate. It is on account of such relationships that slave households from Epirus are more highly regarded and more expensive than others. **6** The good will of the foremen should be acquired by showing them some consideration, and those of the labourers who are superior to the others should also be spoken to about the work to be done, since, when this is done, they are less inclined to think that the master despises them, and believe that he holds them in some regard. **7** They are made to take more interest in their work by being treated more liberally either in regard to food, or more clothing, or exemption from work, or by being allowed to graze some livestock of their own on the estate, or something of the same kind, so that, if some punishment or heavier labour than usual is imposed on them, their good will and friendliness towards their master may be restored by the consolation derived from such concessions.

6.36 Varro on herdsmen and their acquisition

Varro On Farming 2.10.2–8

Varro refers to six different ways in which possession of slaves can be legally obtained. Mancipium was a formal purchase, and cession was when someone 'ceded' the ownership of an item to another; the other four ways were inheritance, possession (usus), war-booty and purchase at a public sale (Westermann 1955: 70). The reference to war-booty can be compared to Cicero's request for slaves from his brother campaigning in Gaul (doc. 6.11): obviously this was still an important source of slaves in the first century BC. Note the reference to the slave's peculium which was transferable with the slave; for the peculium, Westermann 1955: 83; Watson 1965: 188–9, 1967: 178–81 (several references to the fund in Plautus' plays), 1987: 90–101; Treggiari 1969: 12.

Varro does not mention the exposure of children as a source of slaves. In both Plautus (*Casina*) and Terence (*Heautontimorumenos*) exposed children are brought up as slaves, but they are still nevertheless free, as recognised by Roman law. Like the case of Gnipho (doc. 6.53) they indicate that exposure might well be a source of slaves (Watson 1967: 172; cf. Brunt 1958: 167; Watson 1965: 46–7; Treggiari 1969: 2; Bradley 1994: 43). Cossinius is speaking in this passage.

2 The herdsmen should be made to stay on the pasture-land the whole day and feed the herds together, but on the other hand each should spend the night with his own herd . . . **3** The type of men selected for this should be those that are tough and swift, nimble, with supple limbs, who are not only able to follow the herd but protect it from wild beasts and robbers, who can lift loads onto pack animals, run with speed, and throw the javelin. **4** Not every race is fitted for herding duties, and neither a Bastulan nor a Turdulan (from southern Spain) is suitable, while Gauls are ideal, especially for draught animals. In purchasing them there are some six ways of acquiring legitimate ownership: by legal inheritance; by receiving them, in proper form, through mancipium from one who had a legal right to do so; by legal cession, from one who had the right to give them up, and at the proper time; by right of possession (usus); by purchase from war-booty; or at a public sale among other property or confiscated property. **5** In the purchase of slaves it is usual for the peculium to go with the slave, unless specifically excepted, and for a guarantee to be given that he is sound and has not committed theft or damage; or, if mancipium is not granted, double the amount is guaranteed, or, if agreed on, just the purchase price. They should have their food apart during the day, each with his own flock, but in the evening all those under one supervisor should eat together . . .

6 Regarding the breeding of herdsmen, it is easy in the case of those who stay all the time on the farm, because they have a female fellow-slave in the farmhouse and the pastoral Venus looks no further than this. But, for those who tend the flocks in mountain-valleys and wooded country and escape rain-storms not in the farmhouse but in hastily-constructed sheds, many have thought it advisable to send them women to follow the herds, prepare victuals for them and make them harder-working. **7** But these women have to be tough and not ugly, and in many ways they are as good as the men in their work, as can be seen generally in Illyricum, for they can tend the herd, carry the firewood and cook the food, or look after the equipment in the huts. **8** As to nursing their babies, I say only this, that generally they can feed them as well as bear them. At the same time turning to me, he said, 'I have heard you say that when you were in Liburnia you saw mothers carrying firewood and children whom they were nursing at the same time, sometimes one, sometimes two, showing that our mothers who lie for days under their mosquito-nets after giving birth are weak and contemptible'.

SLAVES AND THE LAW

The slave was a *res mancipi* in the ownership of his master and in the Republic there were no constraints on how masters treated slaves (Watson 1967: 173, cf. 1983: 53–6). Slaves were routinely tortured in law-suits in Rome (as in Greece). The rationale was that slaves could not be trusted to tell the truth in any other circumstances; see Robinson 1981: 223–7; Watson 1983: 56–9; Bradley 1994: 165–70.

Slavery is not defined in the XII Tables, though manumission is mentioned in Table 5.8. Table 12.2 (doc. 1.44) points to the legal incapacities of slaves: a slave was without rights, and only a person with rights (*sui iuris*) could be party to a legal action (*legis actio*). Therefore slaves themselves could not be sued for any actions they committed or damage they caused. The master had to pay the prescribed penalty for his slave's wrongdoing, or hand the slave over for punishment to the wronged party: Gaius *Inst.* 4.75; Watson 1975: 85–6; the XII Tables and slavery: Watson 1975: 81–97; Grant 1992: 114–15; Cornell 1995: 280–3; on Gaius: Tellegen-Couperus 1993: 100–1, 104; Roman law on slavery: Buckland 1908; Watson 1987 (mainly imperial); Robinson 1995: 32–5.

6.37 The legal position of slaves

Gaius *Institutes* 1.52

The legal codified definitions of slavery come from the imperial period, sometimes, but not usually, drawing on republican sources. Writing in the second century AD, Gaius records details which are nevertheless true for the Republic. The slave-owner had *dominium* over his slave, including the power of life and death. Gaius and laws on slavery: Finley 1980: 99–100; Bradley 1987: 100, 1994: 10–11, 43, 86, 123.

Slaves are in the potestas of their masters, and this potestas is acknowledged by the laws of all nations, for we know that in all nations alike the master has the power of life and death over his slaves, and whatever a slave acquires is acquired by his master.

6.38 Roscius' slaves prevented from giving evidence

Cicero *In Defence of Roscius of Ameria* 77–8

Roscius was accused in 80 BC of parricide by family members supported by Sulla's freedman Chrysogonus: this was Cicero's first criminal case. Roscius had an impregnable alibi. Roscius' advocates may have been P. Cornelius Scipio Nasica, praetor 94 or 93, and M. Metellus, praetor 69. In this case, the accusers have decided that to submit the slaves of Roscius to torture is too risky as they will not go along with false charges, whereas in doc. 6.39 the accuser depends on the slaves breaking down under torture and agreeing to false charges; cf. docs 6.49, 7.89.

77 There remains the possibility that he committed the crime using the agency of slaves. O ye immortal gods! What a wretched and calamitous affair! That which in an accusation of such a kind is generally the salvation of innocent men — that they should offer their slaves up for examination — is not permitted to Sextus Roscius! You, the accusers of this man, have all his slaves; not a single boy out of so large a household has been left to see to his daily meals. I appeal to you now, Publius Scipio, and you Metellus, when you were counselling him and acting on his behalf, Sextus Roscius several times demanded two of his father's slaves from his opponents for examination; do you not remember that Titus Roscius refused? Well? Where are those slaves? Jurors, they are part of the household of Chrysogonus, by whom they are honoured and valued . . . **78** Jurors, everything in this case is lamentable and scandalous, but nothing more severe or unjust than this can be pronounced — that a son should not be allowed to examine his father's slaves about his father's death!

6.39 Slaves remain firm under torture

Cicero *In Defence of Cluentius* 175–8

Cluentius was charged with having poisoned his step-father Oppianicus, who had married his mother Sassia: according to Cicero, who defended him at his trial in 66 BC, Sassia had tried several years earlier to force slaves to incriminate her son Cluentius. Two of the slaves were hers, but the third had belonged to the deceased Oppianicus, now in the possession of his son, the young Oppianicus (176). Despite two separate days of the 'severest tortures' (177) the slaves would not incriminate Cluentius. A further third torture of two of the slaves (Strato and Nicostratus) occurred some three years after these tortures and Strato was crucified after his tongue was torn out (182–7). What arouses Cicero's condemnation is that the slaves were tortured with the intention of providing false evidence: the use of torture on slaves as such is not condemned. But in *Sull*. 78, Cicero criticised the value of evidence arrived at by torture, noting that different individuals have varying resistance to pain. For Cicero on Cluentius' case, see Bradley 1994: 165–6; at §175, Oppianicus is a 'vagrant', exiled under Sulla.

175 While wandering from place to place as a vagrant and exile, everywhere rejected, Oppianicus took himself to Lucius Quinctius in Falernian territory, where he first fell sick and remained seriously ill for some time. Sassia was with him, and was more intimate with a certain tenant-farmer called Sextus Albius, a fine healthy fellow, than even the most dissolute husband could tolerate while his own fortunes were intact. She thought that the requirements that a marriage be chaste and lawful no longer applied now her husband had been convicted. It is said that a trusty slave-lad of Oppianicus' called Nicostratus, who was inquisitive and totally truthful, used to report much of this to his master. Meanwhile Oppianicus, who was beginning to recover and was unable to put up with the Falernian tenant's misbehaviour any more, set off for Rome — he used to rent somewhere to stay outside the city gate — but is said to have fallen from his horse and, being already unwell, hurt his side seriously; he arrived at Rome with a fever, and died a few days later. The manner of his death, jurymen, is such as to admit no suspicion; if any should be admitted, it has to be confined to the household within those four walls.

176 After his death that wicked woman Sassia immediately began to plot against her son, and decided to hold an investigation into her husband's death. She bought a slave called Strato from Aulus Rupilius, who Oppianicus had employed as a doctor, as if intending to do the same as Habitus when he bought Diogenes. She said that she was going to interrogate this Strato and one of her own slaves called Ascla. Furthermore she demanded that young Oppianicus here should hand over for interrogation the slave Nicostratus, who, she thought, had been too talkative and loyal to his master. Since he was a boy at the time, and the investigation was supposedly being held to inquire into his father's death, he did not dare refuse, although he believed that this slave was well-intentioned towards himself just as he had been towards his father. Many friends and associates both of Oppianicus and of the woman herself were summoned, respectable men distinguished in every way. The interrogation was carried out extremely rigorously with every form of torture. The slaves were tempted with both promises and threats to make them say something under interrogation, but encouraged, I believe, by the high rank of those summoned to witness the inquiry and the violence of the tortures they stood by the truth and said they knew nothing.

177 The interrogation ceased for that day on the advice of the friends. Some considerable time later they were summoned again. The interrogation was held over again: the severest tortures were vigorously employed. The witnesses objected, unable to bear it any longer, while the cruel and savage woman was furious that her schemes were not proceeding as she had hoped. When the torturer and even his instruments of torture were exhausted and she still did not want to bring proceedings to a close, one of the witnesses, a man of eminent public rank and the highest character proclaimed that he considered that the purpose of the proceedings was not to find the truth, but to force the slaves to say something false. The others agreed and it was the view of them all that the interrogation had gone far enough.

178 Nicostratus was returned to Oppianicus, while Sassia went to Larinum with her people, grieving over the thought that her son would now certainly be safe, since not only no true accusation, but not even a fabricated suspicion could touch him, and not only his enemies' open hostility, but even his mother's secret plots had been unable to harm him. When she got to Larinum, although she had pretended that she was convinced by the story that her husband had earlier been poisoned by Strato, she immediately gave him a well set-up and fully stocked shop at Larinum so that he could practise medicine.

RUNAWAYS AND FUGITIVES

There were three basic forms of slave action against their servitude, though not all slaves engaged even in passive resistance: deliberate destruction of property and obstruction of whatever work had to be undertaken; flight; and, thirdly, the most radical option, revolt against their masters, as in Sicily and with Spartacus. Columella in the imperial period mentions various forms of obstruction (1.7.6–7). Nothing similar survives from the Republican period, but Cato's instructions to keep the slaves busy hints at slaves avoiding work or pretending sickness. Cato's comment that if the work is not completed because of sick slaves then they should have received fewer rations might hint at this form of non-compliance, especially given the lack of regular holidays; sickly slaves were to be sold off: doc. 6.31.

The treatment of slaves varied from master to master and from occupation to occupation. Slavery was implicit in Roman society, and that slaves had to be forced to work was accepted (doc.

6.21; cf. Cic. *Rep.* 37). Running away was one way of rejecting servile status, but masters took steps to recover their property (doc. 6.42) and the state took an interest as well (doc. 6.41). The *triumviri capitales*, established in 290–287 BC, had the power of *coercitio* over slaves, whom they could imprison, flog and return to their masters if found out and about at night (Livy *Per.* 11; Plaut. *Amphitryo* 155; Lintott 1999: 102). Running away was especially common in times of disturbance: in 40 BC, when Octavian (Augustus) was at war with Sextus Pompey, so many slaves decamped from Italy that the Vestal Virgins publicly prayed that these desertions stop: Dio 48.19.4. Augustus later claimed to have returned 30,000 slaves to their masters after defeating Sextus; those whose masters could not be found were impaled: *Res Gestae* 4.25; Dio 49.12. For various means of resisting slavery, see Bradley 1994: 107–31, but most of the evidence is imperial.

6.40 A collar and chain

Lucilius 29.917–8

(*ROL* III.296.) Slave-collars with the name of a slave, the owner, and address to which to return the slave and the promise of a reward are well-evidenced in the imperial period; cf. Plaut. *Capt.* 357. See Thompson 2003: 238–40.

. . . when I bring him back home like a runaway in manacles and a dog-chain and dog-collar.

6.41 Runaway slaves recovered as a public duty

ILS 23

(*CIL* I^2 638; *ILLRP* 454; *Inscr. Ital.* 3.1, 272; *ROL* IV.150.) The following document is a road milestone near Forum Popillii in Lucania recording the achievements either of Publius Popillius Laenas (cos. 132) or of T. Annius Rufus (cos. 128 and propraetor in 131). The Via Popillia (or Via Annia) continues the Via Appia from Capua to Rhegium. The milestone records actions combating the serious slave-rising which began in 135: 'the men from Italy' were perhaps resident in Sicily. See, for the inscription, Laurence 1999: 30; Shaw 2001: no. 23.

I made the road from Rhegium to Capua and on that road I positioned all the bridges, milestones and signposts. From here there are 51 miles to Nuceria, 84 to Capua, **5** 74 to Muranum, 123 to Consentia, 180 to Valentia, 231 to the strait at the statue (at the straits of Messina), 237 to Rhegium: total from Capua to Rhegium 321. Also as praetor in **10** Sicily I sought out the runaways belonging to men from Italy and returned 917 people. I was also the first to cause cattle-breeders to retire from public state land in favour of ploughmen. **15** Here I put up a market and public buildings.

6.42 One of Cicero's slaves decamps

Cicero *Letters to Friends* 13.77.3

Cicero wrote this letter to P. Sulpicius Rufus in Illyricum in 46 BC. The first part of the letter assures Sulpicius that Cicero will vote for a supplicatio in his honour, and recommends Marcus Bolanus to his notice. It seemed credible to Marcus Bolanus and others that Cicero had manumitted his slave Dionysius, when in fact he had not done so (he was still at large in 44 BC: Treggiari 1969: 253; cf. Finley 1980: 112; Bradley 1989: 32–4, runaways in general: 32–8). In a similar episode, Cicero (*Quint.* 1.2.14) refers to a runaway slave of Aesopus the tragic actor, posing as a freedman, and now in prison at Ephesus: Cicero requests Quintus to see that he gets returned to his master.

Cato the Elder also had problems with runaway slaves (doc. 6.31). Despite doc. 6.41, it is quite clear from Cicero's account that there was no actual state apparatus for helping owners to recover their runaway slaves. The professional slave-catcher (fugitivarius, plural: fugitivarii) appeared in the late Republic to help slave-owners recover their property.

I beg of you with more urgency than usual, in view of our friendship and your continual devotion to me, that you particularly exert yourself in the following matter: my slave Dionysius, who had charge of my library which is worth a great deal of money, stole a large number of books and, believing he would not get away with it unpunished, ran away. He is in your province. Both my friend Marcus Bolanus and many others saw him at Narona, but they believed him when he asserted that I had manumitted him. If you should see to returning him to me, I can't tell you how grateful I would be. It is a small thing in itself, but has made me very upset. Bolanus will tell you where he is and what can be done. If I should receive the fellow back through your agency I shall consider that you have done me a very great favour.

SLAVE REVOLTS

Individual slaves could run away and desert their masters, but there was another phenomenon in the Roman world, not evident in classical Greece, and that was the slave revolt, when large numbers of slaves rose up against their masters. The most famous rebellion was that of Spartacus (73–71 BC), but there were revolts on a considerable scale in Sicily (135–132, 104–100 BC). Slave revolts, and other passive means of defying enslavement, underline the struggle at the heart of slavery: the slaves' attempts to 'protest' at their slavery through laziness, sabotage and wilful damage, and various degrees of disobedience including outright revolt, and the attempts of their owners to induce them to work productively while denying them basic human rights.

There were isolated slave revolts in Italy prior to the 130s, with causes similar to those of the later great revolts (Bosworth 1968; Bradley 1989: 41–3). All three major revolts, the two in Sicily and that of Spartacus were crushed ruthlessly but did not lead the Romans into a consideration of how to avoid such disasters in future, and no alleviation of the plight of slaves occurred. Punishment of slaves and severity towards them was seen as the best defence against revolt (Cic. *Verr.* 2.5.7–8).

General background on the slave revolts: Brunt 1958: 169; Alföldy 1988: 39; Grant 1992: 102–3; Lintott 1994: 25–7. Detailed discussions: Vogt 1974: 39–102; Bradley 1989: 18–101; Scullard *GN* 13–14; Thompson 2003: 245–66; slaves in the Catilinarian conspiracy: Bradley 1978; for the general lack of slave revolts in the imperial age, see Bradley 1987: 31; Thompson 2003: 264–6.

6.43 Slaves revolt in Sicily, 135–132 BC

Diodorus Siculus *Library of History* 34.2.1–23

Sicily was finally unified as a Roman province in 211 BC and its ability to feed Rome immediately recognised: Livy 26.40.15–16, 27.5.2–5. Historians have seen major problems with the similarity of Diodorus' accounts of the two Sicilian slave revolts and the emphasis which he lays on pastoralism rather than agriculture in Sicily (see for example: Verbrugghe 1975). But the accounts can be broadly accepted, and it is clear that pastoralism was important in this period, perhaps more so with the vast increase in the number of slaves available (Rathbone 1983: 161; Bradley 1987: 47–8).

Constantine VII Porphyrogenitus' account gives some details not found in Photius' below: Damophilus of Enna had a retinue of armed slaves with which he inspected his land, and large numbers of handsome slave boys (sexual exploitation is not mentioned), and his wife treated her women slaves cruelly. He branded his slaves and tattooed their bodies; some had leg irons and were kept in slave barracks and were not fed or clothed adequately. In particular, Constantine notes that the slaves who rebelled had been free men; he is more hostile to the land-owners than Photius and places the blame for the revolt on them, which may reflect Diodorus-Posidonius' account.

When the slaves from country estates attacked the nearby city of Enna, they were joined by slaves from the city. Diodorus gives their numbers as 200,000; other sources have 60–70,000 which given the population of Sicily at the time is more probable (Bradley 1989: 64). The Romans found it difficult to quell the revolt: it commenced in 135 (in fact, perhaps earlier) and was finally squashed in 132, after the Romans had suffered some notable defeats; Rupilius, the consul who terminated the revolt, was the third consecutive consul sent out to deal with it (*MRR* I.497–8). For the method of government used by the slaves and its similarities to hellenistic kingship, see: Green 1961: 21–4; Vogt 1974: 51–4; Bradley 1983, 1989: 117–19. As with the Spartacus revolt, the slaves in Sicily were aiming at freedom; they were not the precursors of proletarian uprisings or social revolution, they wanted to be free again and no longer subject to brutalisation. They failed. Rupilius the Roman consul who defeated them produced the lex Rupilia on Sicily's administration, but it did not address the condition of the slaves (contra to some modern accounts it did not deal with the size of the latifundia, and certainly did not improve slave working conditions); cf. Bradley 1989: 71. For the first slave revolt, see Westermann 1945: 8–9; Green 1961: 10–29; Forrest & Stinton 1962: 87–92; Vogt 1974: 46–8; esp. Bradley 1989: 46–65, and for the full accounts of Photius and Constantine, see Shaw's translation, 2001: 87–94, with Livy's summary and other minor sources: 95–106.

The second slave revolt followed the same pattern: large numbers of the newly enslaved, and harsh working conditions, led the slaves to revolt. Photius and Constantine each preserve a summary of Diodorus' account of this second rebellion; for a translation of the sources: Shaw: 2001: 107–29; the best discussion is Bradley 1989: 66–82; see also Finley 1968: 137–47; Vogt 1974: 48–9, 56–9; Verbrugghe 1972: 540–1, 544–5, 552–8, 1974; Rubinsohn 1982: 436–51. For longer extracts on the Sicilian revolts, see Yavetz 1988: 15–44, 67–112.

1 When Sicily, after the Carthaginian collapse, had enjoyed 60 years of prosperity in every respect, the slave war arose for the following reason: the Sicilians had become so prosperous and acquired such great wealth that they began purchasing a great number of slaves, on whose bodies they put identifying marks and brands when they had dragged them home in herds from the slave-depots. **2** They used the young men as herdsmen, and the others in whatever way they happened to be useful. But they treated them harshly in their service, and thought that they deserved only the very slightest care in terms of food and clothing. As a result, most of them made a living from robbery, and there was bloodshed everywhere as the robbers were like scattered armies. **3** The praetors tried to stop them, but did not dare to punish them because of the power and influence of the masters who owned the robbers, and were forced to overlook the plundering of the province . . . **4** The slaves, oppressed by their hardships and often quite unreasonably mistreated by beatings, could not endure it. When opportunity offered they got together and discussed the subject of revolt, until they put their plan into action. **5** There was a certain Syrian slave (Eunus), belonging to Antigenes of Enna, from Apamea by birth, and given to magic and wonder-working. He claimed to foretell the future through commands from the gods in his sleep, and deceived many by his skill in this direction. Going on from there, he prophesied not only through dreams but even pretended to see visions of the gods and hear the future from them while awake . . .

10 There was a certain Damophilus of Enna, a man of great wealth and property, but very arrogant in his behaviour. He maltreated his slaves to excess, and his wife Megallis closely rivalled her husband in her punishments and other inhumanity towards the slaves. Reduced by this savage treatment to the level of animals, they agreed to revolt and kill their owners. Going to Eunus, they asked him if their decision was approved by the gods. With his usual marvels he promised the gods' approval and persuaded them to engage in the undertaking at once. **11** They immediately, therefore, gathered together 400 of their fellow-slaves and, having armed themselves as opportunity presented, fell upon the city of Enna with Eunus leading them and working his miracle with flames of fire for their benefit. They broke into the houses and committed great bloodshed, sparing not even breast-feeding babies. **12** Instead they tore them from the breast and dashed them to the ground; I am unable to say how they insulted and outraged the women — and this with their husbands watching. They were joined by a great number of slaves from the city, who first did their worst to their masters and then turned to the slaughter of others. (Damophilus and his wife are captured, but their daughter spared because of the humanity she had shown. Damophilus was killed in the theatre.)

14 After that Eunus was chosen as king, not because of his courage or military leadership, but only because of his marvels and because he had started the revolt, as well as for his name which seemed to suggest the favourable omen that he would bear 'good will' towards his subjects. **15** Established as master of the rebels in all respects, he summoned an assembly and put to death all the citizens of Enna who had been captured, except for those skilled in manufacturing weapons, and these he put to work in chains. He gave Megallis to the female slaves to deal with as they wished; they tortured her and then threw her over a cliff. He himself put to death his own owners Antigenes and Python. **16** He wore a diadem and adorned himself with all the other attributes of royalty, proclaimed the woman living with him as queen — she was a Syrian and from the same city as himself — and appointed as counsellors men who seemed to be especially gifted with intelligence, one of whom was Achaeus (Achaeus by name and an Achaean by birth), a man exceptionally gifted both in planning and in action. In three days Eunus had armed, as best he could, more than 6,000 men as well as leading others who had single and double-edged axes, slings, sickles, fire-hardened stakes, or even cooking-spits. He went about plundering the whole countryside, and since he kept being joined by a countless number of slaves he even ventured to do battle against Roman generals, and in the engagements frequently overcame them by weight of numbers, as he already had more than 10,000 soldiers.

17 Meanwhile a man named Cleon, a Cilician, began a revolt of other slaves. Everyone was buoyed up with hopes that the two groups of revolutionaries would come into conflict with each other and that the rebels would liberate Sicily from strife by destroying themselves, but against expectations they joined forces, with Cleon subordinating himself to Eunus merely at his command and carrying out the duties of a general towards his king. His personal following consisted of 5,000 soldiers; it was now about 30 days since the beginning of the revolt. **18** Shortly afterwards they engaged in battle with a praetor, Lucius Hypsaeus, who had arrived from Rome and commanded 8,000 Sicilian soldiers, and the rebels were victorious, being now 20,000 in number. In a short time their total reached 200,000 and in many battles against the Romans they acquitted themselves well and were seldom beaten. **19** As this news spread, a revolt of a band of 150 slaves flared up in Rome, and of more than 1,000 in Attica, and of others on Delos and in many other places; due to the speed with which forces were brought against them and the severity of the punishments inflicted, the magistrates of the communities in each case quickly put an end to the rebels and brought to their senses anyone on the point of revolting. **20** In Sicily, however, the situation continued to deteriorate, and cities were captured with all their inhabitants and many armies cut to pieces by the rebels, until Rupilius (cos. 132 BC), the Roman commander, recovered Tauromenium for the Romans, after besieging it severely and confining the rebels under conditions of unspeakable hardship and starvation, which resulted in their beginning by eating their children and progressing to their womenfolk, and finally not entirely abstaining from eating each other; it was on this occasion that Rupilius captured Comanus, Cleon's brother, as he was trying to escape from the besieged city. **21** In the end, after Sarapion, a Syrian, had betrayed the citadel, the general seized all the runaways in the city, whom he tortured and threw over a cliff. From there he went to Enna and besieged it in much the same way, bringing the rebels into extreme hardship and dashing their hopes. Their leader, Cleon, came out from the city and fought heroically with a few men until Rupilius displayed him dead covered with wounds, and took this city too by betrayal, since it was impregnable to force of arms because of its strength. **22** Eunus took his bodyguard of 1,000 men and fled in a cowardly fashion to a precipitous region. The men with him, however, realised that their fate was unavoidable, for the general Rupilius was already marching against them, and killed each other with their swords by beheading. Eunus, the wonder-worker and king, who had through cowardice taken refuge in certain caves, was dragged out with four others, a cook, a baker, the man who massaged him in his bath, and a fourth who used to entertain him when he was drinking. **23** Placed in prison, his body disintegrated into a mass of lice and he died at Morgantina by a death appropriate to his villainy. Thereupon Rupilius marched throughout Sicily with a few picked men and liberated it from every band of robbers sooner than anyone expected.

6.44 The suppression of the Second Sicilian Slave Revolt

Crawford *RRC* 401.1

A denarius of 71 BC. (Grueber 1.3364; Sydenham *CRR* 798; Carson *PCRR* 163; Burnett *CRW* pl. 5.29; Shaw 2001: 116 fig. 6.)

Obverse: Bust of Virtus wearing helmet; legend on right rim: 'Virtus'.
Reverse: Standing soldier, with shield in left hand; with right hand he raises up a prostrate kneeling woman. Legend below: 'SICIL'; on right rim of denarius: 'MN AQUIL'; on left: 'MN F MN N'. The reference is to Manius Aquillius and his successful suppression of the second slave revolt in Sicily as consul in 101 BC and proconsul in 100; the coin was issued by the consul's grandson (as indicated by the left and right legends). The soldier may be taken to represent the consul himself. Issued after the suppression of Spartacus' revolt, the coin reminded the public of the achievements of Aquillius' grandfather in a previous slave insurrection.

6.45 Spartacus and the gladiators' revolt, 73–71 BC

Appian *Civil Wars* 1.116–20 (539–59)

It is the Spartacus revolt which has captured both the scholarly and popular imaginations, due to the combination of a heroic figure, the involvement of gladiators, and the spectacular mass crucifixions of slaves. It is also Spartacus with whom the Marxist historians engaged in their treatment of ancient slavery.

Other sources besides Appian are translated in Shaw 2001: 131–65; the most important are Sallust *Histories* Book 3 FF90–94, 96–102, 106, Book 4, FF22–3, 25, 30–3, 37, 40–1; Plut. *Crass.* 8–11, *Pomp.* 21 (all in Shaw; also in Yavetz 1988: 83–112); cf. doc. 12.4. Discussions in Baldwin 1966/7; Vogt 1974: 59–61; Kamienik 1976; Korzheva 1976; Bodor 1981; Bradley 1989; Seager 1994: 221–3; cf. Rubinsohn 1971.

116: Spartacus had been a free man before he became a slave-gladiator; he and the other escaping gladiators preferred to 'endanger their lives in pursuit of freedom' rather than in the 'public spectacle' of the arena. One specialist occupation of slaves was as gladiators (Cic. *Dom.* 6: amongst the slaves of Milo's gangs were gladiators: cf. docs 2.3, 6.30, 13.1; Cic. *Att.* 4.3.2). However, gladiatorial contests had not yet entered the era of regular, mass public entertainment as in the imperial period. Only 25 gladiatorial exhibitions are known at Rome from 94 to 44 (and not all of these are certain: Bradley 1989: 84). Capua was the major gladiatorial training centre for Rome.

Spartacus attempted to leave Italy through the Alps: he was initially aiming to leave Italy. He was clearly not leading a proletarian uprising to reshape the world order: Marxist historians have traditionally overlooked this (Vogt 1974: 83–91, cf. 175–8; Konstan 1975; Grant 1992: 137–9; see also Vogt 1974: 175–8; Finley 1980: 40–3, 45–6, 57–8; Yavetz 1988: 123–30). But the Marxist conception that slavery was fundamental to ancient society cannot be overlooked. Plutarch and Appian confuse the names of the praetors involved: see *MRR* II.109–10.

117: Spartacus' decision not to march on Rome, like Hannibal's, was perhaps a grave error. **118**: The Roman response was slow and Spartacus scored notable successes against praetors and then the two consuls of 72 BC, whose initial success soon turned to defeat. Crassus, probably praetor in 73 (*MRR* II.110), was given proconsular imperium and was successful in driving Spartacus into the toe of Italy where the rebels aimed to cross into Sicily. Crassus' execution of one in ten of the legionaries was the *decimatio* (see doc. 5.20), aimed at instilling bravery and fear of defeat in the remaining troops ('applying after the passage of much time an ancestral punishment to the soldiers': Plut. *Crass.* 10.4); on the nature of Crassus' command: Marshall 1973.

119: Crassus clearly had the situation in hand but in 71 the senate also appointed Pompey to the command; he had just returned from Spain (where he had defeated Sertorius and Perperna), while M. Terentius Varro Lucullus (cos. 73) had returned from Macedonia (at 557, Appian confuses him with L. Licinius Lucullus, cos. 74: *MRR* II.109); Crassus hastened to finish off Spartacus in order not to share the gloria with Pompey. The war against Sertorius in Spain was going on at the same time as the Spartacus revolt.

120: Crassus defeated the main contingent of slaves; Pompey overcame 5,000 slaves fleeing from the battle and informed the senate that, while Crassus had defeated the gladiators, he (Pompey) had rooted out the slave revolt (Plut. *Pomp.* 21.4, *Crass.* 11.11). But in the late 60s groups of renegade slaves were still being dealt with in southern Italy by Roman forces (Suet. *Aug.* 3: the father of Octavian (Augustus) wiped out a band at Thurii). Plut. *Crass.* 11.9 has the dramatic detail of Spartacus killing his horse so that he would have to fight to the bitter end and not be able to flee the battle. On the issue of possible negotiations between Spartacus and the Romans: Doi 1984.

Pompey received a triumph for his success against Sertorius in Spain; but Crassus had fought against slaves (considered by the Romans to be a lesser enemy) and was entitled only to an *ovatio* (Gell. 5.6.20–3; Marshall 1972; doc. 2.32). For Crassus, Pompey, and the slave revolt: Marshall 1973, 1976: 25–48; Ward 1977a: 83–98; Greenhalgh 1980: 58–71; Seager 1994: 221–3, 2002:

36. For the best-known film about this revolt, *Spartacus*, with Kirk Douglas as director and in the leading role, produced in 1960, see Shaw 2001: 186.

539 At the same time (as the murder of Sertorius, and Perperna's conquest by Pompey) there were in Italy some gladiators who were being trained at Capua to appear in public shows. Spartacus, a Thracian, who had at one time served with the Roman army but who had become one of the gladiators after being imprisoned and sold, persuaded about 70 of them to endanger their lives in pursuit of freedom rather than in a public spectacle and with them he overcame the guards and escaped; **540** they armed themselves with clubs and daggers belonging to some travellers and fled to Mount Vesuvius, where, after being joined by many runaway slaves and some free men from the fields, he plundered the neighbouring region, having as his subordinates gladiators named Oenomaus and Crixus. **541** As he divided up the plunder equitably he soon had plenty of men; Varinius Glaber (actually the praetor Gaius Claudius Glaber) was the first sent against him, and after him Publius Valerius (actually the praetor Publius Varinius), but not with regular armies, just any men they could gather quickly on their route (for the Romans did not yet consider this a war, but a raid similar to banditry), and when they attacked they were defeated. Spartacus himself even captured Varinius' horse — so close did the Roman general himself come to being a gladiator's prisoner. **542** After this even more people rushed to join Spartacus, until his army totalled 70,000 and he was making weapons and gathering equipment, when the Romans sent out the consuls with two legions.

543 Crixus, leading 30,000 men, was defeated by one of the consuls near Mount Garganus, and both he and two-thirds of his army perished; **544** Spartacus was making haste through the Apennines to the Alps and the Gauls beyond, but one of the consuls got ahead of him and cut off his chance of flight, while the other pursued him. He turned on them one after another and successively defeated them. **545** They retreated from there in disorder, and Spartacus sacrificed 300 Roman prisoners to Crixus and marched on Rome with 120,000 foot-soldiers, after burning any useless equipment, killing all his prisoners and butchering his pack-animals so he could move unhindered; many deserters approached him but he refused to accept any of them. **546** The consuls met him again in the region of Picenum and there was another great conflict and another great defeat, too, for the Romans.

547 Spartacus changed his mind about marching on Rome, on the grounds that he was not yet powerful enough for that and his whole army was not properly armed (for no city had joined him, only slaves and deserters and rabble), but he occupied the mountains around Thurii and took the city itself, and prohibited merchants from bringing in gold or silver and the possession of these by his men, but they bought a great deal of iron and bronze and did no harm to those who imported them. **548** Supplied in this way with abundant material they prepared themselves well and went out frequently on plundering expeditions. When they next engaged with the Roman forces they were again victorious and returned laden with booty.

549 This war was now in its third year and terrible for the Romans, though ridiculed and despised at first because it was against gladiators. When it was time for the election of new praetors everyone was overcome by cowardice and no one stood, apart from

Licinius Crassus, distinguished among the Romans by birth and wealth, who accepted the command and marched against Spartacus with six legions; when he reached the front he also took over the two legions of the consuls. **550** Of these he immediately chose by lot and executed one man out of every ten for having been so often defeated. Some say instead that, after engaging in battle with his whole army and having himself been defeated too, he chose by lot and executed a tenth, about 4,000, of them, undeterred by the number involved. **551** Whatever he did, after demonstrating to the army that he was more to be feared than defeat by the enemy, he overcame 10,000 of the Spartacans who were encamped by themselves, killed two-thirds of them, and marched contemptuously against Spartacus himself. He won a glorious victory over him and pursued him as he fled to the sea where he intended to sail to Sicily; catching up with him he hemmed him in with ditch, wall and palisade.

552 Spartacus tried to break out and get into Samnite territory, but Crassus killed about 6,000 of his men in the morning and about the same number towards nightfall, with only three of the Roman army being killed and seven wounded — so great a change in their confidence of victory had come about as a result of their punishment. **553** Spartacus, who was expecting cavalry to join him from somewhere, no longer went into battle with his whole army, but frequently harassed the besiegers from different sides with sudden and continuous attacks, throwing bundles of wood into the ditch and setting light to them and making their job difficult. He also crucified a Roman prisoner in the area between the two armies, to show his own men the sight of what they would suffer if they did not win. **554** When the Romans in the city learnt of the siege they thought it would be disgraceful if the war against gladiators went on any longer and appointed Pompey too, who had just arrived from Spain, to the command, as they believed that the task of confronting Spartacus was still a great and formidable one.

555 As a result of this vote Crassus tried in every way to come to grips with Spartacus, so that the glory of the war might not be Pompey's, and Spartacus, wanting to anticipate Pompey's arrival, invited Crassus to come to terms with him. **556** When this was scornfully rejected he decided to risk a battle and, since his cavalry had now arrived, he broke out through the besieging wall with all his army and fled to Brundisium with Crassus pursuing him. **557** When Spartacus learnt that Lucullus too had just arrived at Brundisium after his victory over Mithridates he despaired of everything as hopeless and engaged his forces, which were even then very numerous, against Crassus; there was a long and hard-fought battle, to be expected of tens of thousands of desperate men, and Spartacus, wounded in his thigh with a spear, fell onto his knee and fought against his attackers holding his shield in front of him until both he and the great number of those with him were surrounded and killed. **558** The rest of his army broke ranks and were cut down in crowds, the slaughter being so great that no one could count them; the Romans lost about 1,000 men, and the body of Spartacus was not found. **559** A large number of his men fled from the battle to the mountains, where Crassus went after them. They divided themselves into four parts and kept fighting until all perished except for about 6,000, who were captured and crucified along the whole road (the Via Appia) from Capua to Rome.

THE MANUMISSION OF SLAVES

In 214 BC, Philip V of Macedon in writing to the city of Larissa in Thessaly noted the Roman attitude to manumission: 'The Romans even admit slaves to citizenship when they manumit them, and give them a share in the offices of the state': *IG* IX.517 (*SIG*[3] 543; *ILS* 8763); cf. Westermann 1955: 75. Actually a Roman freedman could not hold office at Rome, but his descendants could, and the Roman attitude to manumission and to freedmen was more generous than the Greek.

The XII Tables in the fifth century BC do not specifically deal with manumission (Watson 1975: 86–7; Cornell 1995: 280–1). A master could manumit one of his slaves by one of three methods: *vindicta*, *censu*, and by will. *Manumissio vindicta* involved a master having a friend claim in the presence of a magistrate that the slave was free; if the master did not deny the charge, the magistrate pronounced the slave free. *Manumissio censu* involved the consent of the master in enrolling the slave amongst the citizens at the census. The slaves themselves could not initiate any of the three types of manumission; for these, see Daube 1946; Watson 1967: 185–200, 1975: 86–92; Treggiari 1969: 20–31; Bradley 1994: 154–65.

If a slave was manumitted in a will with the proviso that he pay a certain sum to the heir before obtaining his freedom, the slave even if sold by the heir could purchase his freedom by paying the stipulated sum to the purchaser. This refers to the peculium, the money which slaves could own and use for purchasing their freedom (only of course at their master's discretion). Freed slaves retained obligations toward their ex-master, and in this way owners did not lose complete control of their property. The ex-slave was now the client of his master.

Slaves who were manumitted joined one of the four urban tribes (Dion. Hal. 4.22.4; cf. Livy 9.46.10–14). Freedmen were ineligible for magistracies, and could not be senators or equestrians. Priesthoods were closed to them, as were magistracies in the municipalities; for restrictions on freedmen, see Treggiari 1969: 162–207. However, these disabilities did not carry through into the second generation: sons of freedmen could even become a senator, and Appius Claudius Caecus, censor in 312, enrolled sons of freedmen in the senate; for an early example, see doc. 1.54. Various restrictions on manumission were introduced by Augustus, suggesting that manumission was a largely unrestricted process until then; for general background on manumission: Treggiari 1969: 11–31; Balsdon 1979: 86–8; Wiedemann 1985: 165–7; Grant 1992: 114–16; cf. Brunt 1958: 164–5; Badian 1982: 168.

Slaves were generally freed because of services they had rendered to their masters, or because of an associated feeling that a slave was too talented to be enslaved, rather than any idea that the institution of slavery was immoral: Treggiari 1969: 11–20; for other motives, see doc. 6.51. The free slave was known by two designations: *libertus* (plural: *liberti*, used to express the relationship between an ex-slave and master) and libertinus (plural: *libertini*, expressing the relationship with the community at large). The freedman was distinct from the man who was born free (an *ingenuus*; plural: *ingenui*, the freeborn). The ex-slave became a Roman citizen; his sons, if born after their father's manumission, were ingenui; for freedmen, see esp. Treggiari 1969: passim; generally: Burford 1972: 38–9; Alföldy 1988: 51–2; Grant 1992: 112–22; Dupont 1992: 65–6; Millar 1995. In the first century AD freedmen enjoyed significant political power through the patronage of the emperors.

6.46 Cicero's favourite slave freed

Quintus in [Cicero] *Letters to Friends* 16.16.1–2

In this letter from Quintus Cicero to his brother Marcus in 54 or 53 BC Quintus expresses his joy that Cicero has freed his trusted slave secretary Tiro, who is a classic example of a valued slave in the household, loyal and dependable; for Tiro, see Treggiari 1969: 259–63 (cf. 252–8); McDermott 1972; Dupont 1992: 67–8; Bradley 1994; 1, 158. Two of Cicero's other freedmen deserted his son, clearly breaking their client obligations to their patron, and Cicero accordingly hoped to have their manumission annulled (Cic. *Att.* 7.2.80); for the obligations of freedmen towards their former masters: Treggiari 1969: 68–81.

1 With regard to Tiro, my dear Marcus, as surely as I hope to see you and my son Cicero and my darling Tullia and your son, you have done what gave me the very greatest pleasure when you preferred that he, who did not deserve his bad fortune, should be our friend rather than our slave. Believe me, when I had read your letter and his, I jumped for joy. I both thank you and congratulate you. **2** For if Statius' faithful service is such a source of great pleasure to me, how valuable should such qualities be in Tiro, especially when we take into account his literary skills, his conversational powers, and his refinement, which outweigh even the personal services he can perform.

6.47 Cicero writes to Tiro

Cicero *Letters to Friends* 16.18.1, 3

For the first time in this letter (written after October 47) Cicero addresses Tiro as an equal, using the address 'Tullius Tironi': only familiars were addressed without the praenomen (i.e., Marcus). Later Cicero is to go a step further and address Tiro as 'dear': 'Tullius Tironi suo'. In *Fam.* 16.27 (where Tiro is so addressed) Cicero talks of giving him ardent kisses. All medical terms are in Greek. Tiro was not an isolated case of a valued slave: Cicero wrote to Atticus in January 61 that 'my reader, Sositheus, a charming boy, has died, and it has upset me more than the death of a slave perhaps should' (*Att.* 1.12.4).

1 Well, what about it? Isn't it quite right? I certainly think it is — and even that I ought to add 'dear'. But, as you wish it, let criticism be avoided — although I have often treated it with contempt. I'm pleased that perspiring has done you good. But if my place at Tusculum has helped, merciful gods!, how much more charming I will find it! But, as you love me — as indeed you either do or make a good pretence of it, in which, it is true, you succeed very well — however that may be, look after your health which, indeed, you have not sufficiently seen to up to now because you have been devoting yourself to me. You are not unaware of what it demands — good digestion, proper rest, moderate walking, massage and proper movement of the bowels. Make sure you return in good health — and I will love not only you, but also my place at Tusculum . . .

3 I will send you the sun-dial and books, if we have nice weather. But about yourself, do you have no light reading with you? Or are you composing something Sophoclean? Show me what you've been working on. Aulus Ligurius, Caesar's friend, is dead, an excellent man and a friend of mine. Make sure I know when to expect you. Look after yourself carefully. Goodbye.

6.48 An overbearing slave and freedman

Cicero *Letter to Quintus* 1.2.3

This letter was written by Cicero in late 59 BC advising Quintus not to leave any incriminating records behind in his province. Quintus Cicero's freedman and secretary Statius was considered somewhat overbearing. Cf. Cic. *Quint.* 1.1.13: magistrates appointed their own freedmen as their secretaries.

But what used to irritate me most was when I kept on being told that he had more influence over you than was called for by the weight of your years and your experience in government — how many people do you think have pleaded with me to recommend them to Statius? How many times when talking to me has he naively used terms like, 'I didn't agree with that', 'I warned him', 'I urged him', 'I discouraged him'? Although all this demonstrates the highest loyalty (and I quite believe it, since that is what you think), nevertheless the very appearance of a freedman or slave enjoying such favour is totally undignified — and indeed I maintain (for I should neither speak rashly nor keep anything back designedly) that all the subject-matter of the gossip of those who wish to denigrate you has been provided by Statius; previously nothing could be understood but that some people were angry with you for your severity; now, with his manumission, those who were angry have plenty to talk about.

6.49 Milo frees his slaves to avoid interrogation

Cicero *In Defence of Milo* 57–8

Milo was put on trial in 52 for the murder of Publius Clodius Pulcher, and was defended by Cicero (docs 13.1–5). Milo manumitted all his slaves before the trial, and it was clearly thought that he was worried about what they would reveal under torture. Cicero counters with the idea that Milo was rewarding his slaves, which must have been a normal enough reason for manumission for Cicero to suggest it. Milo was convicted and went into exile. See Treggiari 1969: 18; for the torture of slaves, docs 6.38–9.

57 Then why did Milo manumit them? Of course, it was because he feared they might incriminate him, that they might be unable to endure the pain, that they might be compelled by torture to confess that Publius Clodius was murdered on the Appian Way by Milo's slaves. Why would you need a torturer? What fact are you looking for? Whether he killed him? He did kill him. Was it justified or not? That is nothing to do with a torturer. . . . **58** What reward can be great enough for slaves so devoted, so brave, and so loyal, who saved their master's life? . . . Had he not manumitted them, they were to be handed over to torture — the saviours of their master, the avengers of crime, the averters of death. Indeed, amidst all his misfortunes, there is nothing which Milo views with more pleasure than the fact that, whatever may befall him, these have been given a well-deserved reward.

6.50 A freedman pays his vow

ILS 3491

(*CIL* I² 972; *ILLRP* 56; *ROL* IV.92.) On an altar at Rome, dating to before 80 BC. Slaves might make a vow and fulfil it, once free. See Bradley 1987: 82 for other examples.

Quintus Mucius Trypho, freedman of Quintus, vowed this as a slave and paid it willingly and deservedly when free; sacred to the Good Goddess.

SLAVES AND FREEDMEN

6.51 Freedmen and manumission in Rome — then and now

Dionysius of Halicarnassus Roman Antiquities 4.24.1–6

Here Dionysius comments on slavery under Servius Tullius, though his remarks on warfare as the most important method of obtaining slaves are obviously relevant to his own time. He then comments on manumission and the peculium in his own day, giving various reasons why slaves might be manumitted, particularly because the ex-slaves could receive and give their ex-masters the grain dole for which they would now be eligible (since Gaius Gracchus' reforms of 122 BC): Treggiari 1969: 16; Hopkins 1978: 117; Badian 1982: 168; Alföldy 1988: 51–2; Grant 1992: 116. Dio 39.24 refers to the many slaves freed when Pompey was placed in charge of the grain supply in 57 BC (see docs 12.61–3). Note his mention of the liberty cap worn by freedpersons. Bradley 1987: 90 sees Dionysius' complaints as part of a literary topos about the decline of standards.

1 As I have come to this section of my narrative, I think that I ought to give the details of the customs of the Romans of that time with regard to their slaves, to prevent anyone blaming either the king who was the first to undertake to make citizens of those who had been slaves, or those who accepted the law, for rashly casting aside traditions. **2** The Romans acquired their slaves by the fairest means: they either bought them from the state under the spear (i.e., at an auction) from the spoils of war, or the general allowed them to keep the prisoners they had taken as well as the rest of the booty, or they obtained the slaves by purchasing them from others who had acquired them by these same means. **3** Neither Tullius who established the custom, nor those who accepted it and kept it up, thought that they were doing anything shameful or harmful to the public interest if those who had lost their country and their freedom in war and who had served well those who had enslaved them, or those who had purchased them from these people, were granted country and freedom by their masters. **4** Most of them received their liberty as a free gift for their good conduct, and this was the best method of discharge from their masters, but a few paid a ransom which they had collected by lawful and honest labour.

In our day, however, this is not the case, but affairs have come to such a state of confusion, and the traditions of the Roman commonwealth have become so dishonoured and sordid, that some buy their freedom with money acquired from robbery, house-breaking, prostitution and every other corrupt means and are Romans on the spot; **5** others who have been their masters' collaborators and accomplices in poisonings, murders, and crimes against the gods or state receive from them their freedom as their reward. Some are freed so that, when they receive every month the corn given at public expense and any other liberality donated by the powerful to the poorer citizens, they can bring it to those who granted them their freedom; and others owe it to the light-mindedness of their master and his thirst for popularity. **6** At any rate I know of some who have allowed all their slaves to be freed after their deaths, so that, when dead, they might be called good men and many people with felt skullcaps (i.e., liberty caps) on their heads might follow their funeral biers; some of those taking part in these processions, as could be heard from those in the know, were criminals, just released from prison, who had committed crimes deserving ten thousand deaths. But most people are unhappy when they look on these stains that can hardly be washed away from the city, and condemn the custom, considering it not appropriate for a pre-eminent city, which thinks itself fit to rule the whole world, to make such people citizens.

332

THE OCCUPATIONS OF FREEDMEN

Educated slaves, and those that had served their masters well in other professional capacities or in domestic service, might very well be manumitted and follow the same occupations after manumission (as did Tiro). Many freedpersons, by necessity and due to the demands of the patron-client system and manumission obligations, will have remained in their master's employ. As noted, agricultural and mining slaves were not usually manumitted and did not become freedmen (libertini). Many of the craftsmen and shopkeepers at Rome were freedmen; for freedwomen prostitutes and actresses, docs 7.62–5; for the occupations of freedmen, see Treggiari 1969: 33, 87–161.

6.52 An association of Greek actors

CIL I^2 2519

(*ILLRP* 771; *ROL* IV.46.) This is from a tablet of stone dedicated by a society of Greek actors, who put on Greek shows. It was discovered in a tomb near the Praenestine gate. The second part of the inscription was added when the tomb was later restored by Philo.

Belonging to the association of Greek actors who are in this company (synodos), out of their common fund. Maecenas Mal . . ., son of Decimus, master of ceremonies and patron of the company approved it. Marcus Vac[ci]us Theophilus, freedman of Marcus, and Quintus Vibius Simus, freedman of Quintus, chairman of the company of D[ec]umiani, **5** superintended the purchase of a site for the tomb and its construction.

Lucius Aurelius Philo, freedman of Lucius, chairman for the seventh time of the company of the association of Greek singers and those who are members of this association, superintended the restora[t]ion from his own funds.

6.53 Freedmen as teachers and literary figures

Suetonius *On Grammarians* 7, 10, 13, 15

Educated Greek slaves were an indispensable component of elite family households, where they served as teachers, doctors, readers, secretaries and even astrologers. A recurring theme is manumission on the basis of talent. Staberius was able to purchase his own freedom through his peculium at a public sale (13), but slaves could not purchase their own freedom without their master's consent, even if the peculium was of sufficient value. Roman education, with its strong Greek flavour, required slaves from that country. For M. Antonius Gnipho, see Treggiari 1969: 114–15 (cf. Watson 1967; 171); Staberius: 115–16; Lucius Ateius Philologus: 121–2; 110–42; for freedmen in the professions and arts: Westermann 1955: 79; Vogt 1974: 122–8; Balsdon 1979: 30–58.

7 Marcus Antonius Gnipho was born free in Gaul but disowned; he was manumitted by his foster-father and educated (in Alexandria, according to some, and in close association with Dionysius Scytobrachion; but I am unable to believe this for reasons of chronology). He is said to have been a man of great talent, of unexampled memory, and educated in Greek no less than in Latin; moreover his character was affable and good-natured, never stipulating any fees, with the result that he received all the more from the generosity of his pupils. He first taught in the house of the Deified Julius (Caesar) when the latter was still a boy, and then in his own home. He taught rhetoric too, and gave instruction in the art of speaking every day, but in declamation only on market-days (i.e., once a week). It is said that distinguished men also attended his school, amongst them Marcus Cicero, even when he was holding office as praetor.

10 Lucius Ateius Philologus was a freedman born at Athens. The well-known jurist Ateius Capito calls him 'a rhetorician among grammarians, and a grammarian among rhetoricians'. Asinius Pollio, in the book in which he criticises the writings of Sallust for being flawed by a striving after archaisms, writes as follows: 'In this he was especially encouraged by Ateius Praetextatus, a famous Latin grammarian, later a critic and teacher of declamation, who finally styled himself Philologus.' He himself wrote to Laelius Hermas that he had made great progress in Greek literature and some in Latin, had been a pupil of Antonius Gnipho, and then a teacher; also that he had instructed many eminent young men, among them the brothers Appius and Claudius Pulcher, whom he had also accompanied to their province. He appears to have assumed the name Philologus ('lover of literature') because like Eratosthenes, who was the first to claim the surname, he considered himself a man of extensive and varied learning. This is certainly evident from his commentaries, although very few survive; he gives some idea of their number in another letter to Hermas: ' Remember to recommend my *Hyle* to others, in which, as you know, I collected all kinds of material in 800 books.' He was afterwards a great friend of Gaius Sallustius (Sallust) and, after his death, of Asinius Pollio, and when they began writing history he provided one with a summary of all Roman history from which he could select what he wished, the other with rules on the art of writing.

13 Staberius Eros was purchased by his own savings at a public sale and manumitted because of his commitment to literature; he taught Brutus and Cassius amongst others. Some people say that he was so generous that in the times of Sulla he admitted the children of the proscribed to his school free and without any fees.

15 Lenaeus, freedman of Pompey the Great and his companion on nearly all his campaigns, on the death of Pompey and his sons supported himself by a school, teaching in the Carinae, near the temple of Tellus, the quarter where the Pompeys' house had been, and was so devoted to his patron's memory that he tore the historian Sallust to pieces in a savage satire because he had described Pompey as being of honest face but shameless character . . . It is also said that when he was still a boy he was stolen from Athens, but escaped and returned to his homeland, and, after acquiring a liberal education, offered the price of his freedom to his former master, but was manumitted for free on account of his talents and learning.

6.54 Terence: a success story

Suetonius *Life of Terence* 1–5

Publius Terentius Afer was born at Carthage, according to Suetonius, and came to Rome as a slave of Terentius Lucanus (though there may be a misunderstanding based on his cognomen Afer, i.e., 'the African'). He was the author of six comedies in the 160s BC and was supported in his work by his patrons Scipio Aemilianus (cos. 147, 134) and his friends C. Laelius (cos. 140) and L. Furius Philus (cos. 136). Note that there are various versions of his death given here: clearly no one actually knew where he retired; for his servile status: Westermann 1955: 79; Treggiari 1969: 112–13, 241; Finley 1980: 117; Gruen 1992: 218–20.

1 Publius Terentius Afer, born at Carthage, was the slave at Rome of the senator Terentius Lucanus, by whom, on account of his talent and appearance, he was not only given a liberal education, but quickly manumitted. Some think that he was captured in war, but Fenestella shows that this cannot possibly have been the case, since Terence was born and died between the end of the second Punic war (201 BC) and the beginning of the third (149 BC); and if he had been captured by the Numidians and Gaetulians he would not have been able to come into the hands of a Roman commander, as commerce between the Italians and Africans did not begin until after the destruction of Carthage. He lived on familiar terms with many men of the nobility, and particularly with Scipio Africanus and Gaius Laelius. It is even thought that he won their favour through his appearance, which Fenestella also denies, arguing that he was older than both, although Nepos records that they were all of the same age and Porcius raises a suspicions of love affairs with these words:

> 'While he sought the lusts of noble men and their false praises,
> While he drank in the divine voice of Africanus with greedy ears,
> While he thought it glorious to dine constantly with Furius and Laelius,
> While he was often taken to the villa at Alba for his youthful charms,
> Later he found he had lost everything and was in total penury.
> So he withdrew from the sight of all to the furthest part of Greece,
> Dying at Stymphalus, a town in Arcadia. Neither Publius
> Scipio, nor Laelius, nor Furius benefited him,
> The three most comfortably well-off nobles of that time.
> He did not even have with their assistance a rented house,
> Where at least his little slave could announce his master's death.'

2 He wrote six comedies, and when he offered the first of these, the *Andria*, to the aediles, he was told to read it to Caecilius. When he arrived, he found Caecilius at dinner, and it is said that because of his humble dress he read the beginning of the play sitting on a bench near Caecilius' dining couch, but after a few lines he was invited to recline at table, and later went through the rest of the play to Caecilius' great admiration. Furthermore this play and the other five delighted the people equally . . . The *Eunuch* was even acted twice in the same day and earned more than any previous comedy of this type had ever done, that is 8,000 sesterces; the sum is even included on the title-page . . .

4 After publishing these comedies before he had passed his twenty-fifth year, either to avoid the gossip about his publishing other people's work as his own, or to study Greek manners and customs, in case he had not depicted them quite successfully in his writings, he left Rome and never returned. Concerning his death, Vulcacius writes as follows:

> 'But when Afer had presented six comedies,
> He journeyed from here to Asia, and from the time
> He went on board, he was never seen again; thus he vanished from life.'

5 Quintus Cosconius writes that he died at sea while returning from Greece with 108 plays adapted from Menander. The others record that he died at Stymphalus in Arcadia or at Leucadia in the consulship of Gnaeus Cornelius Dolabella and Marcus Fulvius Nobilior (159 BC), after becoming ill from grief and irritation when his luggage was lost, which he had sent on in advance by ship, and with it the new plays he had written. He is said to have been of medium height, slender figure and dark complexion. He left a daughter, who afterwards married a Roman eques; also gardens of 20 iugera on the Appian Way near the villa of Mars.

FREEDMEN'S FUNERARY INSCRIPTIONS

While the vast majority of inscriptions and funerary reliefs relating to freedpersons (and slaves) in the city of Rome come from the imperial period, there are examples from the late Republic (Treggiari 1969: 32 n.4). These funerary inscriptions (epitaphs) are invaluable both in attesting to individual manumissions, and also the occupations of the manumitted slaves and their family relationships. Their assimilation into society was complete upon their death when, like other Romans who could afford such luxuries, they were buried in tombs with funerary inscriptions.

In fact, the evidence seems to suggest that more freedpersons and their families had tombs and inscriptions than free people (the *libertini* outnumber *ingenui* three to one). This does not necessarily reflect actual population ratios. It could well be because the freedpersons involved were prosperous and many of the free born too poor to afford inscriptions and tombs (Treggiari 1969: 33). It is also possible that libertini were proud to display on their tombs the three names (*tria nomina*) of the citizens which they had become, and hence placed a priority on funerary monuments (Taylor 1961: 129–30). At any rate, it is clear that there was a high frequency of manumission at Rome, and that freedpersons constituted a sizeable proportion of the population in the first century BC. The open attitude to citizenship via manumission distinguished the Romans from other ancient peoples, as Philip of Macedon recognised, and ensured that by the end of the Republic, if not earlier, large numbers of the citizen residents of Rome were ex-slaves or descended from slaves: Scipio Aemilianus in the second century BC described the urban plebs as having Italy only as a step-mother (Vell. 2.4.4; Val. Max. 6.2.3).

6.55 A doctor's family in Rome

ILS 8341

(*CIL* 1² 1319; *ILLRP* 798; *ROL* IV.42.) The doctor freedman of this inscription had clearly been successful enough to afford a tomb large enough to contain so many occupants (it was common to include in the inscription the tomb's dimensions). The marital relationships mentioned are important: it was often the case that freedmen married freedwomen (often, but not always, from the same household), and included other freedpersons in their tomb. For these epitaphs and their value as evidence, see Treggiari 1969: 32–3, 215–16.

Gaius Hostius Pamphilus, a doctor, freedman of Gaius, bought this memorial for himself and for Nelpia Hymnis, freedwoman of Marcus, and for all their freedmen and freedwomen **5** and their descendants. This is our home for evermore, this our farm, this our gardens, this our memorial. Frontage 13 feet, depth 24 feet.

6.56 Quintus the butcher

ILS 7642

(*CIL* 1² 1604; *ILLRP* 784, from Capua; *ROL* IV.46.) Another freedman butcher: doc. 7.33.

Here lie the bones of Quintus Tiburtius Menolavus, freedman of Quintus, who slaughtered animals for sacrifice.

6.57 Farewell, be well

ILS 8417

(*CIL* I² 2273; *ILLRP* 981; *ROL* IV.32.) From New Carthage in Spain (probably first century BC). This memorial is her reward for her good conduct ('how she behaved').

Here lies Plotia (often called Phryne), freedwoman of Lucius and Fufia. This memorial shows how she behaved towards her patron and patroness, her father, and her husband. 5 Farewell, be well.

6.58 Aulus the auctioneer

ILS 1932

(*CIL* I² 1210; *ILLRP* 808; *ROL* IV.20.) From Rome, dating to c. 100 BC.

    This silent stone asks you, stranger, to stop
    While it reveals to you what he, whose shade it covers, entrusted it to reveal.
    The bones of a man of honour and great trustworthiness,
    Aulus Granius, the auctioneer, lie here.
5   That is all. He wanted you to know this. Farewell.
    Aulus Granius Stabilio, freedman of Marcus, auctioneer.

6.59 Two inseparable slaves

ILS 8432

(*CIL* VI.22355a, found at Rome on the Appian Way.)

For Aulus Memmius Clarus.
Dedicated by Aulus Memmius Urbanus to his fellow freedman and his dearest companion.
    5 I cannot remember, my most honoured fellow freedman, there having been any quarrel between us. By this epitaph, I call the gods of heaven and of the underworld as witnesses that 10 together we stood on the slave-dealer's platform, that in the same household we were made freedmen, and that nothing ever separated us until this your fatal day.

6.60 Grave of a freedwoman

CIL I² 1570

(*ILLRP* 977; *ROL* IV.52.) Larcia Horaea was freed by Publius Larcius Nicia and Saufeia, both of whom were themselves freedpersons (libertini), and became the wife of Publius Larcius Brocchus, their son. While it was unusual for free persons to marry freedpersons, here the servile origin of the husband's parents (he himself is not designated as a freedman) overcame social norms. This inscription was found at Traiectum (on the Liris) and may date to c. 45 BC: Treggiari 1969: 16, 213. Compare the epitaphs of the couple Aurelia Philematium and Aurelius Hermia: doc. 7.33.

Publius Larcius Nicia, freedman of Publius; Saufeia Thalea, freedwoman of a matron; Lucius Larcius Rufus, son of Publius; Publius Larcius Brocchus, son of Publius; Publia Horaea, freedwoman of Publius and his wife.

> I was respected by the good and hated by no honourable woman.
> I was obedient to my aged master and mistress, but to him I was dutiful,
> For they gave me my freedom and he married me.
> From when I was a girl I supervised the house for twenty years —
> The whole of it. My final day gave its judgement,
> And death took my spirit, but did not remove the splendour of my life.

7

Women and the Family

The Roman family was typically an extended one, under the authority of the eldest male (the *paterfamilias*, or 'father of the family'), and included all descendants, except those that had been emancipated (given their independence by the paterfamilias). Hence the family might comprise not only the head of the household, but children and grand-children, the wives of married sons and grandsons, adopted children, and slaves (doc. 7.1). The paterfamilias had almost total control over all members of the household, and was the only one to own property, unless he had specifically allowed any of his sons a peculium, or fund, of their own or to enter into legal contracts. This authority over family members was called *patria potestas* (doc. 7.2). While he had total power to kill slaves as and when he chose, it appears that his power of 'life or death' over his children was tempered by the custom of consulting a family council beforehand: should the advice of the council be in favour, then the offending family member would be put to death with no guilt incurred by the father (docs 7.12, 14–15, 17). Should the paterfamilias wish, he could emancipate any of his children, and a son would then be a paterfamilias in his own right, just as if his father had died (doc. 7.4).

The status of wives varied and, while women needed a male guardian (doc. 7.5), they could either be in the power (*manus*, or 'hand') of their husband, or remain members of their original family and in the control of their father or brother. If married by *coemptio* (a pretend sale), the wife, together with her property, came into the manus of their husband, giving her the status of one of her husband's daughters. However, if married by *usus*, or cohabitation, the wife could avoid coming into her husband's manus if she absented herself from his household for three nights in the year, and in this case her property remained entirely separate from that of her husband and she was not considered a member of his family for inheritance purposes should her husband die intestate (docs 7.10–11). This form of marriage was referred to in the XII Tables in the fifth century BC, and by the first century at least it seems to have been the most common form of marriage. Where a wife was not 'in manu' to her husband, it was the duty of the wife's own relatives, not her husband, to exact punishment if she were found guilty of criminal behaviour, as with those women initiated in the Bacchanalia (docs 7.16–7). Divorce in Rome, except for those married by confarreatio, the religious form of marriage restricted to patricians, was easy for both parties, though the wife's dowry had to be returned (with certain deductions for children or misconduct: doc. 7.13).

In being financially independent of her husband, and in possessing far greater freedom within the household than the citizen women of ancient Athens (doc. 7.28), the *materfamilias* ('mother of the family') had a significant role in the upbringing of children and grandchildren and in the running of the home generally, and women were not excluded from meeting men outside their own families (docs 7.22–23). Stereotypical descriptions of the 'ideal' wife, especially in funeral eulogies and epitaphs, do not disguise the great respect often felt for wives or mothers, and their influence over their children (docs 7.30–7). The relationship between parents and daughters could be extremely close and indicative of great affection and respect on either side (docs 7.24–7). Anecdotes regarding marital disagreements, as with Cicero's brother Quintus and his wife Pomponia, suggest that many women also felt free to express their views (docs 7.38–41), and their freedom of movement and active social life is confirmed by the evidence of numerous adulterous liaisons engaged in by upper-class Roman women, as well as by their involvement in outlawed or non-mainstream religious rites (docs 7.42–6, 52).

While adultery on the part of the wife was clear grounds for divorce (doc. 7.18), Roman men were free to engage in heterosexual love affairs, as long as they steered clear of citizen women (docs 7.47–56), and there was no stigma involved in visiting prostitutes (docs 7.62–4). Following the successful conquests of the second century BC, many young men engaged in a luxurious and dilettantist life-style and the cost and availability of high-class prostitutes rose accordingly, as did that of handsome young boys: while passive homosexuality degraded a citizen and made him, at best, an object of ridicule (doc. 7.60), it was considered normal that Romans should use young male slaves or prostitutes as passive sexual objects (docs 7.57–61), and the best known love poet of the Republic, Catullus, not only chronicled his supposed affair with the faithless 'Lesbia', but eulogised the attractions of certain young boys (docs 7.47–9, 51, 61).

In the early Republic women were given both a praenomen (first name) of their own and the family nomen; by the middle Republic women are only distinguished by the female form of their father's nomen (e.g., Tullia, daughter of Marcus Tullius Cicero). Where there were numerous daughters they could be identified by numerals, such as Claudia Quinta ('fifth') and Aemilia Tertia ('third'): docs 3.40, 7.30. But by the late Republic women could also adopt the female form of their father's cognomen and were beginning to be noticed by historians as individuals, worthy of comment or criticism in their own right (as with Sempronia: doc. 7.44).

Indeed, by the late Republic, women ere well-documented as owners of property, and, while their interests could be trivialised by historians in the stress on women's desire for ornaments and cosmetics (docs 7.66–8), it is clear not only that these ornaments were frequently used in a religious context, to display their status and that of their husband in festivals and processions (doc. 7.70), but that women could have great importance as consumers and, like Cicero's wife Terentia, *de facto* control over considerable financial investments (docs 7.69, 71–2, 74). Roman women also played an extremely significant role in the worship of the gods, with numerous festivals restricted to women-only participation, including the important cult of the 'Bona Dea' (docs 7.84–5). Many of these cults were primarily concerned with child-birth and fertility (docs 7.76–9, 81), while others involved not only citizen women but prostitutes (docs

7.80). Women could also play an important role in making supplication on behalf of the state in times of crisis (docs 7.82–3). The six Vestal Virgins not only guarded the 'sacred things' in the temple of Vesta and prepared the mola salsa (meal) for sacrifices, but took part in various state religious ceremonies (docs 7.86, 88); the welfare of the state was bound up with the preservation of their chastity, and should a Vestal break her vows it was seen as threatening the security of Rome itself (docs 7.87–9, 91).

Ancient sources: it is the jurists of the imperial period, such as Gaius, Ulpian and Pomponius, who give definitions of the Roman family and the status of the persons within it (docs 7.1–7, 9–10, 13). Otherwise, information on Roman families and their lifestyles has to be gleaned from a variety of literary and historical sources: Livy and Dionysius for early Rome; Plutarch and Valerius Maximus for anecdotal evidence for family life and the position of women, while Cicero's *Letters* reveal the relationships within his own family; epitaphs (docs 7.23–5, 31–3, 37) for wives and daughters and the ways in which they were valued; comic dramatists (docs 7.38, 7.68) for humorous depictions of married life; Catullus (docs 7.46–51) on heterosexual love in first-century Rome; and the *Fasti* of Ovid (43 BC – AD 17) for a survey of women's religious festivals in the first half of the year (docs 7.77–81).

For an introduction to the family in Rome, see Crook 1967; Saller 1984, 1986; Lacey 1986; Rawson 1986; Bradley 1991; Corbier 1991a; Dixon 1992; Gardner 1998; Treggiari 2002; for Roman women: Balsdon 1974; Clark 1981; Gardner 1986; Dixon 2001. The following older works on women can still be useful: Adcock 1945; Smethurst 1950; Balsdon 1959; Best 1969/70.

FAMILY LAW

In early Rome *gentes* (sing.: *gens*), or clans were formed by a number of related families who possessed a common name and shared a common family cult (such as the Julian gens or Claudian gens). In the absence of closer family members, the XII Tables laid down rules on guardianship and intestate inheritance within such gentes (doc. 1.34).

Should a paterfamilias (plural: *patres familiarum*) die intestate, the order of inheritance was, firstly, direct heirs, such as children, grandchildren, and his wife (if 'in manu'); then the closest agnate, or family member in the male line of succession, who was linked to the deceased through males (siblings and paternal uncles); finally *gentiles*, or clansmen, of the same name: Crook 1967a: 118–28, 1986; Watson 1975. The XII Tables made provision for written wills (doc. 1.36; Saller 1991a). In the first century BC cognates were increasingly recognised, so the order of inheritance then became children, husband and wife.

Endogamy: while parallel-cousin marriages were not common, there were no restrictions on the marriage of first cousins or more distant kin: Shaw & Saller 1984; Treggiari 1991a: 103–4; cf. Plut. *Rom. Quest.* 108.

7.1 The definition of a Roman family

In theory the paterfamilias (plural: patres familiarum) possessed unlimited power over all his household until he either died or emancipated his children; until then, whatever the age of his children or grandchildren, he was the only one with the right to own property, although he could allow them to have control of a fund called a peculium, and incur financial obligations: for the son's peculium, Crook 1967a: 110–11. After his death his descendants (should there be no other direct male ancestor living) became *sui iuris* (independent) and the sons were in their own turn patres familiarum. On the paterfamilias, see Watson 1975: 40–51; Gardner 1986: 5–11; Saller 1984; Treggiari 1996: 118–19; the Roman concept of the family: Saller 1984; Bradley 1991; Dixon 1992, Martin 1996.

(a) *Digest* 50.16.195 (Ulpian)

1 Let us see how the word 'familia' should be understood, for it is understood in various ways, as it refers to both property and persons; to property, as in a Law of the XII Tables where it is said, 'Let the nearest agnate (the next of kin on the father's side) have the estate (familia)'. The term 'familia' also refers to persons, as when the same law referring to a patron and his freedman says, 'from this familia into that familia.' In this instance, it is understood that the law refers to persons.

2 The term 'familia' also refers to a collection of persons, connected either by their own legal rights vis-à-vis each other, or by a more general kinship relationship. We say that a family is connected by its own legal bond when several persons are either by nature or by law subjected to the potestas of one person — for example, the paterfamilias, materfamilias, and son and daughter under paternal control, as well as their descendants, such as grandsons, granddaughters, and their successors. The person who has authority over the household is designated the paterfamilias, and he is properly called so even if he has no son, for we do not merely designate him as a person, but also his legal right. We even style a minor the paterfamilias, when his father dies, and each of the persons who were under the father's control begins to have a separate household and take on the title of paterfamilias. The same thing happens in the case of a son who is emancipated, for he also begins to have his own familia when he becomes independent (sui iuris). We also use the term 'familia' of all the agnates, because even though the paterfamilias may have died and each of them have a separate familia, still all who were under the potestas of this one man can properly be said to belong to the same familia, as they have sprung from the same house and gens (clan).

3 We are also accustomed to use the term familia for groups of slaves . . . In the interdict 'On violence' the term familia includes not only all the slaves but the children as well. **4** Again the term familia is used of all those persons who are descended by blood from a single ancestor (as we speak of the Julian family), referring as it were to persons derived from a single remembered origin. **5** A woman, however, is the beginning and end of her own familia.

(b) Gaius *Institutes* 1.196 (*On the Provincial Edict* XVI)

The head of the family is himself included in the term 'familia.' It is clear that children do not belong to the wife's family, because anyone who is born to a father does not belong to his mother's family.

7.2 Patria potestas

Gaius *Institutes* 1.48–9, 52, 55

While technically the paterfamilias had the right of 'life and death' over members of his household, in practice, a paterfamilias would not exercise the right of life and death over his sons without consultation with a family council (consilium); for the consilium, see Lacey 1986: 137–9.

However, a paterfamilias was quite free to disinherit his children (though, in general, feelings were against this): Crook 1967: 120–1. Patria potestas was however limited by the late age at which most Roman males married, generally in their late twenties, and only a small proportion of adult males would have had a father still living: Saller 1987 suggests only 30 per cent of 25 year olds and 19 per cent of 30 year olds; most adult males were therefore sui iuris at the time of their marriage and independent long before they were of magisterial age. From 180 BC, a young man could not start on the cursus honorum until he was 27, or 30 after Sulla, though he assumed the toga virilis (man's toga) at about 15 years. In Servius Tullius' reforms (cf. doc. 1.19), men were pueri (boys) until 17, *iuniores* (youths) up to 46, then *seniores* (elders). Patriapotestas: Pomeroy 1975: 150–1; Rawson 1986a: 15–18; Lacey 1986; Crook 1967a: 107–11, 1967b; Dixon 1988: 61–2; Saller 1986, 1991; Harris 1986; Bettini 1991: 1–13; Treggiari 1991: 15–16.

48 Some persons are legally independent (*sui iuris*), others are subject to another person (*alieni iuris*). **49** Of those subject to another person, some are in potestas, and others in manus to a husband. **52** Slaves are in the potestas of their masters . . . **55** Similarly, any of our children, whom we have begotten in lawful marriage, are in our potestas. This right is peculiar to Roman citizens, for there are almost no other peoples who have such power over their children as we have . . .

7.3 Adoption

Gaius *Institutes* 1.97–107

The law distinguished between the transfer of a son by his natural father to a new family and *adrogatio*, where a person *sui iuris* placed himself under another's potestas. Both required public ratification; testamentary adoption, however, was a purely private practice; for the adoption of Scipio Aemilianus and his brother Q. Fabius Maximus Aemilianus, see Polyb. 31.26.1–4; Livy 44.44.1–3; Plut. *Aem.* 5.3–4; the families of P. Scipio Africanus and Q. Fabius Maximus would otherwise had died out in a generation had they not adopted two of the sons of L. Aemilius Paullus and Papiria. In October 58, from Thessalonica, Cicero wrote to his friend Atticus, now Quintus Caecilius Pomponianus Atticus, congratulating him on his adoption by his uncle Caecilius in his will and on being left heir to his fortune (*Att.* 3.20). See Gell. 5.19.10 on women not being adopted by adrogatio; for adoption: Crook 1967a: 111–13; Corbier 1991: 142–3; Gardner 1999.

97 Not only, as we have stated, are natural children in our potestas, but also those whom we adopt. **98** Adoption takes place in two ways: either by the authority of the people, or by the imperium of a magistrate, as, for instance, a prætor.

99 We adopt, by the authority of the people, those who are their own masters, and this kind of adoption is called 'arrogation', for the reason that he who does the adopting is asked, that is to say 'arrogated', whether he desires to have the person whom he intends to adopt as his lawful son; and he who is adopted is asked whether he is willing for this to take place; and the assembled people are asked whether they direct this to take place. By the command of the magistrate we adopt those who are under the potestas of their parents, whether they are in the first degree of descendants, like a son or a daughter, or whether they belong to an inferior degree, like a grandson or a granddaughter, a great-grandson or a great-granddaughter.

100 Adoption by the authority of the people can only take place at Rome, while the other method generally takes place in the provinces before the provincial governors. **101** The prevailing view is that women cannot be adopted by the authority of the people; but women may be adopted in the tribunal of the prætor at Rome, or in the provinces in the tribunal of the proconsul or legate . . .

103 It is a rule common to both kinds of adoption that persons who are incapable of begetting children, like eunuchs, can adopt. **104** Women, however, cannot adopt other persons in any way, because they do not have potestas even over their natural children. **105** Similarly, if anyone adopts another person, either by the vote of the people, or by the consent of the prætor or provincial governor, he can give the son he has adopted in adoption to another. **106** It is debatable, however, with reference to both forms of adoption, whether a person can adopt someone who is older than himself.

107 It is peculiar to that kind of adoption which takes place by the vote of the people, that, if he who gives himself to be adopted has children under his control, he will not only himself be subject to the authority of the adopter, but his children will also be under the latter's authority, as grandchildren.

7.4 Emancipation of family members

Gaius *Institutes* 1.116–20

On emancipation: Crook 1967a: 109–13; Gaius *Inst.* 1.132. Sons could be disadvantaged by emancipation: if their father died intestate they would lose their chance of inheritance.

116 We now have to explain which persons are subject to mancipation (*in mancipio*).

117 All children, whether male or female, who are under the potestas of their father, can be mancipated by him in the same way as slaves.

118 The same rule of law applies to anyone who is in the control of another, and they can be mancipated in the same way by those to whom they have been sold, just as children may be mancipated by their father; also, while a woman who is married to the purchaser may only occupy the place of his daughter, even if she should not be married to him, and not occupy the position of his daughter, she can still be mancipated by him.

118a In general, mancipation takes place either by parents or by those who obtain possession by coemptio, when the parents and the so-called 'purchasers' wish to free the persons from their authority, as will appear more clearly below.

119 Mancipation, as stated above, is a kind of fictitious sale, and the law governing it is peculiar to Roman citizens. The ceremony is as follows: not less than five witnesses (who must be Roman citizens above the age of puberty) are assembled, plus another person of the same status who holds a brass balance in his hand and is styled the 'balance-holder.' The so-called 'purchaser', holding a piece of bronze in his hands, then states: 'I declare that this man belongs to me by my right as a Roman citizen. Let him be purchased by me with this piece of bronze, and bronze balance.' Then he strikes the scales with the piece of bronze, and gives it to the so-called 'seller' as purchase money.

120 In this way both slaves and free persons are mancipated, as well as any animals that are subject to sale, including oxen, horses, mules, and donkeys, and also urban and country estates.

7.5 Guardianship

Ulpian *Rules* 11.1, 27

All women had a tutor, if they had no father living or were not in manu to a husband; freedwomen had their patron as their guardian; on guardianship of women and minors up to 25 years, Crook 1967a: 113–18; Watson 1967: 146–50, 1971: 40, 1975: 71–80; Eyben 1981; 329–31; Saller 1991a: 38–44. Even widows could not have potestas over their children and the children needed a tutor. On widows, see Rawson 1986a: 31–2; Harlow & Laurence 2002: 88–90, 100–02. Women who were *sui iuris* could inherit and receive legacies and, while in early Rome women were unable to make a will, later they could do so with their guardian's consent; by the time of Polybius it was considered normal for women of the propertied class: Dixon 1985a: 170; Saller 1991a; for the will of Hispala, a freedwoman, see doc. 7.63.

1 Guardians are appointed for both males and females: only for males who have not yet reached the age of puberty, because of their infirmity of age, but for females both before and after puberty because of the weakness of their sex, as well as their ignorance of business matters.

27 A woman needs the approval of her guardian in transactions of this kind, that is if she wishes to bring a legal action; if she accepts a legal or financial obligation; if she permits a freedwoman of hers to cohabit with another's slave; or if she wishes to alienate property transferable by mancipation. The guardian's approval is also required by wards for the alienation of property which is not transferable by mancipation.

7.6 Second-class citizens

Digest 50.17.2 (Ulpian *On Sabinus*)

Women are excluded from all civil and public offices; as a result they cannot sit on juries or perform the duties of magistrates, or bring actions in court, or be guarantors for others, or act as advocates. Similarly children should not hold any public office.

THE FORMALITIES OF MARRIAGE

The reason for matrimony was, in legal terms, in order to have children: adult males were asked by the censors, 'to the best of your knowledge and belief, have you a wife?': Gell. 4.20.3; Cicero *Off.* 1.54 considered marriage the 'seedbed' (seminarium) of the city.

There were three types of marriage in Rome: confarreatio, according to Dion. Hal. 2.25.1, was established by Romulus: no divorce was possible and it was the only religious marriage performed. It involved a sacrifice to Jupiter Farreus of bread made of spelt, plus fruits of the earth and mola salsa; and the pontifex maximus and flamen dialis had to be present, as well as ten witnesses. Certain priests such as the rex sacrorum and flamen dialis had to be married by confarreatio (as did their parents), and confarreatio was presumably restricted to patricians: Linderski 1986.

Coemptio was a fictitious sale of a girl to her husband which brought the wife into manus, giving her the status in her new family of a daughter, subject to her husband's potestas (see doc. 7.10, cf. 7.4). In usus, the normal form of marriage in the late Republic, manus was acquired after cohabitation for a year. The wife could however avoid passing into her husband's manus if she stayed away for three nights during the year (a possibility laid down by the XII Tables: doc. 1.37): Gardner 1986: 31–65; Treggiari 1991: 15–36 on the wife's status within marriage types; Rawson 1974 on concubinage, a form of marriage not based on any ceremony, but consisting of cohabitation between eligible partners (280). See Treggiari 1991: 17–21 (usus), 21–24 (confarreatio), 25–28 (coemptio).

On the formalities accompanying the wedding ceremony, see Williams 1958; Gardner 1986: 44–50; Rawson 1986: 250–1 for a bibliography; Treggiari 1991: 161–70; Thomsen 2002 (for Catullus' wedding poems); Harlow & Laurence 2002: 60–4, 79–91 on the changes marriage entailed for girls. Plutarch *Roman Questions*, gives numerous details: the bride touching fire and water (1), the torches of fire (2), the bride being lifted over the threshold (29), her saying 'where you are Gaius, there am I Gaia' (30), the singing of 'talassio' (31), the husband's approach to his bride in darkness (65), the parting of her hair with a spear (87), the fact that girls did not marry on public holidays, though widows did (105). The bride, having put away her toga praetexta, had her hair parted into six locks tied with woollen fillets; she wore a straight white tunic and a flame-coloured veil and shoes. After a ceremony of consent in her father's house and a sacrifice, the contract was signed and she was escorted to her new home. The bride walked separately in the wedding procession, accompanied by three boys, the one preceding her carrying a torch lit at her hearth. At the groom's house she was greeted with water and another torch; when she entered the house after anointing the doorposts she had to 'touch fire and water'. During the procession, the guests sang obscene 'fescinnine' songs. On the following morning the new wife sacrificed at the family hearth.

A respectable citizen married woman was distinguished by her long stola (over-garment) and the headbands covering her hair; on the bride's costume, see Sebesta 1994: 48; La Follette 1994; on the married woman, Sebesta 48–50.

Marriage alliances among the upper-classes, which often took place earlier than was otherwise usual, were frequently intended to cement political alliances, or end political dissension. Julius Caesar married his daughter Julia (born c. 73) to Pompey in April 59: Pompey, born in 106, was thus 33 years older than his new wife. Julia was at this point engaged to Servilius Caepio. At the same time Caesar himself married Calpurnia, daughter of Calpurnius Piso, who gained Caesar's support for his consular candidature for 58. Cato at this protested that the government was being prostituted by marriage alliances (doc. 12.43; cf. App. *BC* 2.14). The political value of marriage can also be seen in the earlier marriage of Pompey and Aemilia, step-daughter of Sulla, who was pregnant at the time and died in childbirth; the mother of Pompey's divorced wife, Antistia, whose father had been killed for being a supporter of Pompey, committed suicide (Plut. *Pomp.* 9.1–4; Haley 1985).

7.7 Betrothal

Digest 23.1.4, 12 (Ulpian *On Sabinus*)

The minimum legal age at marriage for girls was 12 and boys 14 years (perhaps formally laid down by Augustus: *CJ* 5.4.24, cf. Dio 54.16.7: the twelfth and fourteenth year), and betrothals could take place at any age, though the majority of betrothals seem to have taken place not long before the marriage. Though many aristocratic girls may have married young (between 12 and 15), those outside the elite seem to have married considerably later. Cicero's daughter Tullia, born between 79 and 76/5, was married by 63, but betrothed considerably earlier in 67 (Cic. *Att.* 1.3.3). Men were generally 9–10 years older than their wives; on men's age at marriage, see Saller 1987, who suggests that outside the upper-classes 25 years or over was usual. On the age at which girls married, see Hopkins 1964/5; ages revised upwards by Shaw 1987; Treggiari 1991: 39–43; Harlow & Laurence 2002: 95–104; for girls' transition to adulthood: Harlow & Laurence 54–64; for the father's role in matchmaking: Treggiari 1991a: 94–6; criteria for choosing a daughter or son-in-law: Dixon 1985b; Treggiari 1991a; Corbier 1991: 136–42; betrothal procedures: Gardner 1986: 45–7; Treggiari 1991: 138–60: verbal consent between the parties and patres familiarum was all that was necessary, though a written contract and dowry arrangements might be formalised.

4 Mere consent is sufficient in contracting a betrothal. It is laid down that parties who are absent can be betrothed, and this takes place every day.

12 A girl who does not obviously resist the will of her father is understood to give her consent. A daughter is only allowed to refuse her consent to her father's wishes where he selects someone for her husband who is unworthy because of his habits or because he is of infamous character.

7.8 A materfamilias is affronted

Livy *History of Rome* 38.57.5–8

Cornelia, younger daughter of Scipio Africanus and Aemilia (daughter of L. Aemilius Paullus who died at Cannae), was betrothed to Ti. Gracchus the elder in 187; as the story is here told by Livy a wife expected to be consulted on the selection of a husband for her daughter; cf. Plut. *Ti. Gracchus* 4.3–4, where a similar story is told of Tiberius Gracchus the younger and his betrothal to the daughter of Appius Claudia and Antistia; see Dixon 1983: 107. While the consent of the paterfamilias was necessary in arranging a marriage (as in Cato's refusal to allow his nieces to marry Pompey and his son: Plut. *Cato Min.* 30, *Pomp.* 44), the wife also played a part in the decision. Indeed, during Cicero's absence in Cilicia in 50, his wife Terentia and Tullia arranged Tullia's (third) marriage to Dolabella, even though Cicero had another candidate (Tiberius Nero) in mind and Dolabella was prosecuting Cicero's friend Appius Claudius at the time: *Fam.* 8.6.2, 3.12, *Att.* 6.6.1. Dixon 1984: 88–91 (on Tullia's dowry payments), 1986: 102–11; Treggiari 1991: 127–34.

5 The story goes that the senate, which had happened to dine that day on the Capitoline hill, rose up and begged that during the banquet Africanus should betroth his daughter to Gracchus. **6** When the betrothal contract had been duly made on this public occasion, Scipio returned home and told his wife Aemilia that he had betrothed their younger daughter. **7** She, indignant as any woman would naturally be at not being consulted about their daughter, who was hers as well as his, added that the mother ought to be consulted on the matter, even if his choice were Tiberius Gracchus. **8** Scipio, pleased that they agreed on this, replied that it was to Gracchus that he had betrothed her.

7.9 The dowry

Digest 23.3.6 (Pomponius *On Sabinus*)

While the husband (or his paterfamilias) became the owner of the wife's dowry, it was returnable on death or divorce. Deductions could be made from the dowry for the wife's misconduct (i.e., 1/6 for adultery, or 1/8 for less serious offences) or to provide for children (1/6 for each child up to one half of the total). While the dowry could be used to help underwrite some household expenses, it remained the wife's, and any non-dotal property the wife inherited or received remained under her own control if she was not 'in manu': Gardner 1986: 71–7; cf. Pomeroy 1976; Dixon 1984, 1986. Dowry: Crook 1967a: 104–5; Dixon 1984: 95, 1985b, 1986; Gardner 1985, 1986: 97–116; Evans 1991: 53–71; Treggiari 1991: 323–64. Dowries were usual but not essential, especially among the poorer classes: cf. Spurius Ligustinus in 171 who had an undowered wife (doc. 5.9); in Varro *Rust.* 3.16.2 Appius Claudius Pulcher (cos. 54, brother of Clodius) admits that he betrothed his sister Clodia to L. Licinius Lucullus without a dowry because of the family's poverty; Lucullus later divorced Clodia for adultery (cf. docs 7.85, 12.67).

Scipio Africanus gave each of his daughters a dowry of 50 talents: doc. 7.70; the dowry of Terentia, Cicero's wife, was 400,000 sesterces (Terentia's half-sister Fabia was a Vestal Virgin which implies they were from an aristocratic family) and that of his second wife Publilia, his ward, considerably more (Plut. *Cic.* 8.3, 41.4–5; doc. 7.40).

Relief is granted to the father by law, for, when he has lost his daughter, he is entitled to the return of the dowry which he provided, and this is done for his consolation, so he may not suffer the loss of both his daughter and the money.

7.10 Forms of marriage with and without manus

Gaius *Institutes* 1.108–15b, 136–7a

The paterfamilias' power over his wife and daughter(s)-in-law was called manus. For a Roman girl, marriage 'in manu' meant a change of status; she was no longer in the power of her father, but became part of her husband's family with rights equivalent to those of his daughters (i.e., if he died intestate she succeeded as if she were an agnate). Everything she owned belonged to her husband, being counted as dowry (Cic. *Top.* 4.23), but her property was distinguishable and recoverable; any property, together with her dowry, had to be returned on divorce or the husband's death. If a wife was under her husband's manus, he could in his will appoint a tutor for her or allow her to choose one for herself. If there were children, the property was divided between widow and children equally. However, if they were married by free marriage the wife did not inherit unless specific provisions were made in the will, though he could make her a legacy no larger than that to his heir. Her property remained entirely separate and a wife not in manu looked to her father to supply her living expenses, and managed her own business through agents: Dixon 1984. Manus: Crook 1967a: 103; Watson 1975: 9–19; Pomeroy 1975: 155–7; Gardner 1986: 11–14; Treggiari 1991: 16–17, 28–32; on inheritance within the family: Crook 1967a: 98–138, 1986: 58–82; Gardner 1986: 163–203; Dixon 1988: 44–60; Treggiari 1991: 379–96.

108 Let us now consider persons who are in manus, which is another right peculiar to Roman citizens. **109** While both males and females are found in potestas, only females can come into manus. **110** In olden days, women passed into manus in three ways, by usus, confarreatio, and coemptio. **111** A woman used to pass into her husband's manus by usus if she cohabited with him continuously for a year, the rationale being that she, as it were, had been acquired by usucapio through possession during one year and so passed into her husband's family where she occupied the place of a daughter. Accordingly it was provided by the law of the XII Tables that any woman who did not wish to come into her husband's manus in this way should absent herself from him for three nights in each year and thus interrupt the usus during each year. But the whole of this institution has been abolished partly by statutes and partly by disuse.

112 Women come into the manus of their husbands by confarreatio, through a kind of sacrifice made to Jupiter Farreus, in which the spelt cake (*far*) is employed, from which the ceremony obtains its name. Additionally, in the course of the ceremony, many other rituals are performed and enacted, accompanied with special formal words, in the presence of ten witnesses. This institution is still in existence today, for the major flamens, that is those of Jupiter, Mars, and Quirinus, as well as the rex sacrorum, can be selected only from persons born of marriages celebrated by confarreatio. Further, these persons themselves cannot serve as priests unless they are married by confarreatio.

113 When women come into the manus of their husbands by coemptio, it takes the form of a mancipation, that is a sort of fictitious sale, in which the man purchases the woman who comes into his manus in the presence of not less than five witnesses, who must be Roman citizens over the age of puberty, and also of a balance-holder.

114 Through this act of sale a woman cannot only perform a coemptio with her husband but also with a stranger: that is to say, the coemptio takes place for the purpose of either marriage or a trust. A woman who disposes of herself in this way to her husband for the purpose of occupying the place of his daughter is said to have performed a coemptio for matrimonial purposes; but where she does this for some other purpose, either with a husband or with a stranger, for instance in order to avoid a guardianship, she is said to have made a coemptio for fiduciary purposes.

115 What takes place is as follows: if a woman wishes to get rid of her existing guardians and obtain another, she makes this coemptio of herself with their authority; her purchaser then sells her again to the person she chooses as her guardian, and he manumits her by the ceremony of the prætor, and by this means becomes her guardian. He is designated a fiduciary guardian, as shown below. **115a** Formerly fiduciary coemptio was performed for the purpose of acquiring power to make a will, for women, with certain exceptions, did not then have the right to make a will unless they had made a coemptio and been resold and manumitted... **115b** Even if a woman makes a fiduciary coemptio with her husband, she still occupies the place of his daughter; for if a wife comes into the manus of her husband for any reason whatsoever, it is accepted that she acquires the rights of a daughter.

136 A woman placed in the manus of her husband by confarreatio is not, for this reason, currently released from paternal potestas unless coemptio has been performed ... However, a woman placed in the manus of her husband by coemptio is freed from her father's potestas; and it is the same whether she is placed in the manus of her husband, or that of a stranger, although only those who are in the manus of their husbands are considered to occupy the place of daughters.

137 Women placed in the manus of their husbands by coemptio cease to be subject to this authority in the same way as daughters under their father's potestas; that is, either through the death of the person in whose power they are, or because he has been forbidden water and fire (i.e., exiled).

137a They also cease to be in the manus of their husbands by a single mancipation; and if emancipated by a sale they become independent (*sui iuris*). A woman who has concluded a coemptio with a stranger can compel him to sell her again to anyone whom she chooses, but a woman who has been sold to her husband, in whose manus she is, cannot compel him to do so, any more than a daughter can compel her father, even if adopted. A woman, however, can, by serving notice of divorce, force her husband to release her, just as if she had never been married to him.

7.11 A wife and her property

Aulus Gellius Attic Nights 17.6.1, 9–10

(Jordan p. 54, 5.) Cato here, in his support for the Voconian law (169 BC, doc. 7.69), thunders at the increasing economic power held by wives in his time, who are clearly not married in manu: they bring a large dowry, and also retain large sums of money as their own separate property, which they then lend to their husbands. Cicero, for example, while in exile was unhappy that Terentia was spending her personal fortune in efforts to help his return: *Fam.* 14.2.3, 14.1.5. The wife and husband's fortunes were entirely separate and the husband was not responsible for his wife's debts if she was not 'in manu'. Like Terentia, a wife sui iuris could manage her own business through agents; for Terentia's separate property, see Dixon 1984: 78–87.

1 Marcus Cato, when supporting the Voconian law, spoke as follows: 'To start with, the woman brings a large dowry; then she retains a large sum of money, which she doesn't entrust to her husband's control, but lends it to him instead. Then later on, when she is angry with him, she orders a slave of her own to follow him around and hound him for the money back . . .' **9** So, from that property of her own, which she retained after the dowry was given, she lent her husband money. **10** When she happens to be angry with her husband, she appoints to dun him for it a slave of her own, that is a slave in her possession whom she had kept back with the rest of the money and not given as part of her dowry, but retained; for it would be inappropriate for the woman to give such an order to her husband's slave, but only to her own.

7.12 Authority over women and children

Dionysius of Halicarnassus *Roman Antiquities* 2.25.6–27.1

For Carvilius Ruga, see Gell. 4.3.2, who states that Carvilius loved his wife but preferred to honour his oath to the censors to marry for the sake of begetting children. Carvilius' was not of course the first divorce, but it appears that this, in 231 BC, was the first legal case in Rome over the return of a wife's dowry; for the selling of sons into slavery in ancient Rome, see doc. 1.33.

25.6 These offences (of a wife) were judged by her relatives together with her husband: among them were adultery and, what would seem to the Greeks to be the least of all faults, if a wife was found to have drunk wine. For Romulus allowed them to punish both these offences with death, as the worst crimes women could commit, considering adultery the beginning of madness and drunkenness of adultery. **7** And both these continued for a long time to be met by the Romans with implacable wrath. The length of time is witness to the excellence of the law concerning women. For it is agreed that during 520 years no marriage was dissolved at Rome; and in the 137th Olympiad, when Marcus Pomponius and Gaius Papirius were consuls (231 BC), the first man to divorce his wife was Spurius Carvilius, a man of distinction, who was compelled by the censors to swear that he had married his wife for the sake of children (his wife was barren), and who was hated for this deed by the people for ever after, although it was done out of necessity.

26.1 These, then are the excellent laws which Romulus brought in regarding women, by which he made them behave better towards their husbands, but those which he introduced with regard to the respectful and dutiful behaviour of children, so that they should honour their parents by doing and saying whatever they might order them to do, were even more honourable and dignified than these and greatly superior to our own laws . . . **4** The Romans' lawgiver granted the Roman father almost total power over his son, valid through the whole of his life, whether he chose to imprison him, to whip him, to put him in chains to work in the fields, or even to kill him, even if the son was already involved in public affairs, counted among the highest magistrates, and lauded for his zeal towards the state . . . **27.1** And the Romans' lawgiver did not even stop the father's power at that point, but allowed the father to sell his son, without worrying whether this permission might be considered as cruel and harsher than natural affection would warrant. And — what anyone who has been educated in the relaxed customs of the

Greeks would marvel at as savage and tyrannical — he even permitted the father to make a profit by selling his son up to three times, thus giving more power to a father over his son than to a master over his slaves.

7.13 Divorce

Digest 17.24.1, 2, 10

It appears that in the early Republic divorce was only permitted in specific cases (Dion. Hal. 2.25.7: doc. 7.12). According to Plutarch (*Rom.* 22.3), in early Rome a wife could be divorced only for poisoning her children (perhaps abortion), counterfeiting the keys, or adultery; divorce for any other reason involved half the husband's property going to his wife and half being consecrated to Ceres. On abortion, which was seen not as a crime against society but against the husband, see Hopkins 1965; Dickison 1973; Watts 1973; Eyben 1980/1; Harris 1994; Riddle 1992; Rawson 2003: 114–15; infanticide was not illegal until AD 374. The XII Tables (4.3) recognised divorce, but there is no evidence on what grounds. Those sui iuris could terminate their own marriage; those in potestas needed the consent of their paterfamilias. A paterfamilias could bring about a son's divorce, even against his son's wishes; see Crook 1967a: 105–6; Watson 1975: 31–4; McDonnell 1983; Rawson 1986a: 32–7; Treggiari 1991: 435–82, 1991b; Harlow & Laurence 2002: 85–8; for a list of attested divorces in the Republic: Treggiari 1991: 516–17.

The wife's position was protected by the need for the husband to return her dowry on divorce, and the frequency of divorce amongst the nobility was probably not replicated elsewhere in Roman society; situations like that of the younger Cato divorcing his wife Marcia so Hortensius, a friend of his, could marry her are unexampled and bizarre, as was his remarriage to Marcia (now a rich widow) after Hortensius' death: Plut. *Cato Min.* 25.1–12.

(a) Paulus *On the Edict* 35

Marriage is dissolved by divorce, death, captivity, or by any other kind of servitude which may happen to be imposed upon either of the parties.

(b) Gaius *On the Provincial Edict* 11

The word divorce is derived either from difference of opinion, or because those who dissolve their marriage go different ways. **1** In cases of repudiation, that is to say, in renunciation of marriage, the following words are employed: 'keep your property' or 'keep the management of your property.' **2** For the purpose of dissolving betrothals, it is certain that a renunciation must be made, in which case the following words are used, namely: 'I will not accept your conditions.' **3** It makes no difference whether the renunciation takes place in the presence or in the absence of the person under whose control one of the parties may be, or of him who is under that control.

(c) Modestinus *Rules* 1

A freedwoman, who has married her patron, cannot divorce herself from him without his consent, unless she has been manumitted under the terms of a trust, and then she can do so even though she is his freedwoman.

OLD-FASHIONED FAMILIES

7.14 Traditional fathers: 509 and 485 BC

Valerius Maximus *Memorable Deeds and Sayings (Of Fathers'
Severity towards their Children)* 5.8.1–2

L. Junius Brutus was one of the Republic's first consuls, in 509 BC; Spurius Cassius was father of Sp. Cassius Vicellinus, consul (not tribune) in 486 (also in 502 and 493): Livy 2.41. Brutus, an example of parental severity, executes his son as consul, not as father, hence without consulting a family consilium; see Livy 2.5.5. Dion. Hal. 8.77–80 knows two versions of Cassius' execution, in one of which he is prosecuted for treason by two quaestors, and in the other the father's condemnation is approved by the senate; cf. Livy 2.41.10–12; Cic. *Rep.* 2.35.60; Pliny *Nat. Hist.* 34.15. See Harris 1986 who stresses the rarity of the killing of adult sons, and certainly, in the case of Brutus, the father acts as the ideal magistrate, above all family emotions. In other examples, A. Postumius Tubertus as dictator in 431 put his son to death for desertion (Livy 4.29.6; Val. Max. 2.7.6); T. Manlius Torquatus, as consul in 340, put his son to death for disobeying orders (Livy 8.7.19–22; Val. Max. 2.7.6); and the latest republican case in which a father exercised his right of life and death over a son, was that of the senator A. Fulvius, who killed his son for joining Catiline in 63 or 62 (Dio 37.36.4; Sall. *Cat.* 39.5; Val. Max. 5.8.5).

1 Lucius Brutus' glory is equal to that of Romulus, since the latter founded the city, while the former established its freedom. While he held supreme authority, his sons attempted to restore the rule of Tarquin, which he had himself driven out — he ordered that they be arrested, beaten with rods in front of the tribunal, tied to a stake, and beheaded with an axe. He divested himself of the role of father to take on that of consul, and chose to live childless rather than to fail to exact public retribution. **2** Cassius emulated his example. When his son, Spurius Cassius, who, as tribune of the plebs, had been the first to propose agrarian legislation and gain popular support in many other ways, laid down his office, Cassius summoned a council of relatives and friends and condemned him in his house on the charge of aiming at kingship. He ordered him to be flogged and executed and dedicated his property to Ceres.

7.15 An imperious paterfamilias: Lucius Manlius Imperiosus

Livy *History of Rome* 7.4.4–7

Cf. Val. Max. 5.8.3, 10.1. Manlius, dictator in 363 BC, was put on trial in 362 by the tribune Marcus Pomponius; Manlius was hated by the people for the severity of his levy against the Hernici and his cruel disposition. In fact, his son, whom he has so badly treated, threatened the tribune, had the charge withdrawn and grew up to be the famous Titus Manlius 'Torquatus', who as consul put his own son to death for disobeying orders in 340 (Livy 8.7.19; Val. Max. 2.7.6). Note how this incident is later used as an exemplum of old-fashioned austerity or *gravitas*: Livy 8.34.2, 35.9; Bettini 1991: 6–9.

Sons who committed suicide because they had been banished from their fathers' sight for disgracing the family included D. Junius Silanus (praetor in 141) for peculation in his propraetorship (he hanged himself), and Aemilius Scaurus, son of the consul of 115, for cowardice against the Cimbri: MacMullen 1980: 3–4; Harris 1986: 85–6.

4 Amongst other charges, the tribune brought up Manlius' treatment of his son, who, though found guilty of no misconduct, had been banished from his city, home and household gods, from the forum, public view, and the company of his equals, and consigned to servile labour, all but in a prison or penitentiary, **5** where this young man of the highest rank and son of a dictator could learn by daily misery how truly 'imperious' his father was. And what was his fault? **6** That he was not sufficiently quick with words and not ready with his tongue! Should his father not have tried to help this natural infirmity, if he had any humanity in him, rather than chastising it and making it conspicuous by his persecution? . . . **7** But Lucius Manlius aggravated his son's difficulties by adding to them, putting heavier pressure on his natural backwardness, and, if there were any spark of natural ability in him, quenching it by his uncultivated lifestyle and rustic upbringing among cows and sheep.

7.16 Women and the Bacchanalia, 186 BC

Livy *History of Rome* 39.17.5–6, 18.5–6

For a full narrative see Livy 39.8–19 (doc. 3.63).

17.5 The names of many suspects were reported to the authorities, and some of these, both men and women, committed suicide. **6** More than 7,000 men and women were said to have been involved in the conspiracy . . . **18.5** More were killed than thrown into prison. There was an immense number of men and women in both categories. **6** Convicted women were handed over to their family, or to those whose authority they were under, so that these could punish them privately: if there was no appropriate person to exact the punishment, it was inflicted by the state.

7.17 Wife-beating

Valerius Maximus *Memorable Doings and Sayings*
(On Severity) 6.3.8–9

Livy *Per.* 48. Both Publicia and Licinia were supposed to have poisoned their husbands and, in punishment, were put to death by their own relatives. This took place c. 154–150 BC. As in the case of the Bacchanalia, it appears that husbands had no right to kill their wives without the consent of their blood relatives, even if they were in manu: Watson 1975: 37–8. For Egnatius Mecennius (supposedly in the time of Romulus), see Pliny *Nat. Hist.* 14.89. Wine-drinking by women was thought to lead to adultery (docs 7.12, 18) and Pliny (14.89) also cites Fabius Pictor's *Annals* for the case of an unnamed materfamilias who was starved to death by her relatives because she had broken open the casket containing the keys to the wine-cellar. In the women-only Bona Dea ritual, wine was consumed by the women, but called 'milk' and its container a 'honey-pot' (Macrob. *Sat.* 1.12.15; docs 7.84–5). However, the archaeological record indicates that women in the archaic period did take part in banquets and wine-drinking, as at Livy 1.57.9; see Pomeroy 1975: 217; Russell 2003.

8 Publicia, who had poisoned her husband, the consul Postumius Albinus (cos. 154), and Licinia, who had done the same to her husband Claudius Asellus, were strangled by the decree of their relatives: for those men of severity did not think that in so obvious a crime they should wait for a lengthy public enquiry. And so they made haste to punish the guilty, whom they would have defended had they been innocent. **9** Their severity was aroused to exact punishment by a great crime, that of Egnatius Mecennius, for a far slighter reason. He beat his wife to death with a cudgel because she had drunk some wine, and his action found no one to prosecute or even criticise it, for all the best men considered that the penalty she had paid to injured sobriety was a good precedent. For assuredly any woman who desires to drink wine without moderation closes the door to all virtues and opens it to all vices.

7.18 The punishment for adultery and alcohol

Aulus Gellius *Attic Nights* 10.23.1–5

(*ORF* [4] Cato FF 221–2, *On the Dowry*.) This passage cites a speech of Marcus Porcius Cato the Elder. For adulterous wives and their punishments, see docs 7.42–6; Cato here highlights the double standards of morality which pervaded Roman life.

1 Those who have written about the life and culture of the Roman people say that the women of Rome and Latium 'lived an abstemious life,' that is, that they always abstained from wine, which in the early language was called *temetum*, and that it was customary for them to kiss their relations for the purpose of detection, so that, if they had been drinking, the smell would give this away. **2** But they say that the women were accustomed to drink the second pressing, raisin wine, myrrhed wine and other drinks of that kind which taste sweet. **3** Indeed, these things are related in those books which I have mentioned, but Marcus Cato states that women were not only censured but also punished by a judge no less severely if they had drunk wine than if they had committed a heinous act like adultery. **4** I have copied the words of Marcus Cato from his speech *On the Dowry*, in which it is also stated that husbands had the right to kill wives caught in adultery: 'When a husband,' he says, 'divorces his wife, he judges the woman as a censor does, and has full powers if she has committed any wrong or disgraceful act; she is punished if she has drunk wine; if she has done wrong with another man, she is condemned to death.' **5** However, regarding the right to put her to death he wrote as follows: 'If you should catch your wife in adultery, you may with impunity put her to death without a trial; but, if *you* should commit adultery or indecent acts, she should not dare to lay a finger on you, nor is it lawful.'

7.19 The parricide's punishment

Livy *Periochae* 68

The summary of Livy is presumably referring to the first historical occasion (in 101 BC) on which this punishment was inflicted; Tarquinius Superbus used this punishment for crimes against religion, according to Dion. Hal. 4.62 (doc. 3.36) and Val. Max. 1.1.13. The murder of a parent carried deep pollution for the criminal and the state. Cicero in 80 defended Sextus Roscius of Ameria on the charge of murdering his father. The law laid down an awful penalty for parricide — to be sewn alive in a sack with a dog, cock, ape and viper and thrown in the river: Cic. *Rosc. Am.* 69–73. A letter Cicero wrote to his brother Quintus as propraetor in Asia in 59 refers to Quintus having sewn up two Mysians in a sack at Smyrna — obviously a punishment for parricide or matricide; Quintus also wished to do the same to Zeuxis of Blaudus who murdered his mother (*Quint.* 1.2.5).

Publicius Malleolus, who had killed his mother, was the first to be sewn up in a sack and thrown into the sea.

FAMILY RELATIONSHIPS

Lucretius 3.894–9 describes a young father returning home and being welcomed by his wife and children; according to Gell. 1.23 in the early Republic boys were taken by their fathers to the senate to learn its workings. Cato the Elder certainly believed in close interaction with his son (doc. 7.21). On family relationships generally, Rawson 1986a: 15–31, 2003: 210–68; on parents and children, Rawson 2003: 220–39; Dixon 1988: 13–40, 104–40 (on mothers and young children); Hallett 1984 (fathers and daughters); Dixon 1988: 210–232 (mothers and daughters). On mothers' duty to look after their children's interests: Dixon 1988: 61–5; for the mother's honourable role within the household, Saller 1998; on stepmothers, Gray-Fow 1988.

Child mortality in the first week of life was very high: girls were not named until their eighth day, boys on their ninth, prior to which they were 'more like a plant than an animal' (Plut. *Rom. Quest.* 102). Garnsey 1991: 51–4 estimates that 28 per cent of those born alive died in their first year and 50 per cent before they were 10 years old. Legally children under 12 months were not to be mourned.

On attitudes to children, see Golden 1988, 1992; on exposure, Boswell 1984; Eyben 1980/1: esp. 12–19; Engels 1980; Harris 1982, 1994; Garnsey 1991; Corbier 2001; Rawson 2003: 116–19. The XII Tables laid down that an especially deformed child was to be quickly killed (Cic. *Laws* 3.8.19; doc. 1.33); Dion. Hal 2.15.2 states, no doubt anachronistically, that Romulus required that all male children and first-born females be reared. The poor were often constrained by poverty to abandon children: see App. *BC* 1.10.40 (doc. 8.10) for the poor before 133 BC being unable to raise their children. It was the father's decision whether to keep or abandon the new baby: Cic. *Att.* 11.9.3; Saller 1991a: 39–40; Shaw 2001. It is important to remember that exposure did not equal infanticide: there was a strong presumption by parents that their child would be taken over, by slave dealers or childless couples, at least in the later Republic, and whenever there was a high demand for slaves. Exposure also had the advantage of allowing parents to choose their children's sex.

7.20 Cato the Elder and his wife

Plutarch *Life of Cato the Elder* 17.7, 20.1–3

This provides an interesting side-light on the austere Cato. Cato lived between 234 and 149: a reactionary, even for his time, he represented old Roman virtues and respect for traditional practices. His wife was Licinia; for Cato's regulation of public morals as censor, cf. doc. 7.58.

17.7 Cato expelled another person from the senate who was thought to have a good chance of winning the consulship, Manilius, because he kissed his wife in daytime with his daughter watching. For his own part, he said, he never kissed his wife except during loud thunder; and it was a joke of his to say that he was a happy man when it thundered.

20.1 He was also a good father, a kindly husband, and a manager not easily to be despised, nor did he give only a subsidiary attention to this, as a matter of little or no importance. So I think I should recount appropriate episodes of his conduct in such matters. **2** He married a wife who was more well-born than rich, considering that, although both alike may possess dignity and pride, the high-born in their fear of disgrace are more obedient to their husbands in all that is honourable. **3** He used to say that the man who struck his wife or child laid hands on the most sacred of objects. He also used to say that he thought it was more praiseworthy to be a good husband than a great senator; and that there was nothing else to admire in Socrates in olden times except that he always treated his bad-tempered wife and stupid sons with kindness and gentleness.

7.21 Cato's education of his son

Plutarch *Life of Cato the Elder* 20.4–7

For breast-feeding in aristocratic Rome, see Bradley 1986; Garnsey 1991; 59–62; for education, Rawson 1986: 248–9 (with bibliography); Eyben 1993: 128–31; Harlow & Laurence 2002: 34–53.

4 Once his son was born, Cato considered no business so urgent, except government duties, as to prevent him from being there while his wife was bathing and swaddling the baby. **5** She nursed it with her own milk, and often gave her breast to her slaves' infants, so that from this common nurture they should develop good-will towards her son. And when the child was old enough to learn, Cato himself took him in hand and taught him to read, even though he had an accomplished slave, called Chilon, who was a teacher and had taught many boys; **6** Cato, however, did not think it right, as he himself says, for his son to be told off by a slave, or to have his ears pulled when he was slow at learning, or to owe so priceless a thing as his education to a slave. Therefore, he was himself his reading teacher, his law teacher, his athletics coach, teaching his son not only to hurl a javelin, fight in armour, and ride a horse, but also to box, endure both heat and cold, and swim strongly through the eddies and surges of the river. **7** He also says that he wrote his *History* with his own hand and in large letters so his son might have the chance to become acquainted at home with Rome's ancestral traditions; and he states that he was careful to avoid indecent language no less in his son's presence than in that of the holy virgins who are called Vestals.

7.22 Women's role as educators

Cicero *Brutus* 210–11

See doc. 8.25, for fragments of a letter attributed to Cornelia; for Cornelia's education of her sons, see Plut. *Ti. Gracchus* 1.6–7 (doc. 8.1); for mothers' role in educating young children: Rawson 2003: 157–8; for the education of girls: Rawson: 197–209. Laelia must be the daughter of Gaius Laelius, friend of Scipio Aemilianus and consul in 140; she married Q. Mucius Scaevola 'the Augur', cos. 117; one of her daughters, the Muciae, married M'. Acilius Glabrio, the other Lucius Licinius Crassus, the great orator who was consul in 95; one of her granddaughters, the Liciniae, married P. Cornelius Scipio Nasica, and was the mother of Q. Caecilius Metellus Pius Scipio, cos. 52.

Cornelia was granted the honour of a seated statue which stood in the colonnade of Metellus (Pliny *Nat. Hist.* 34.31), the first statue of a non-religious woman set up in a public place in her lifetime; for Cornelia, see docs 8.1–2, 9, 33; Barnard 1990; for other statues of named women in the Republic, see Fantham 1994: 220; Rawson 2003: 25–6.

210 It makes a great difference what kind of speakers one hears at home every day, the people whom one has been talking with from childhood, and the way in which fathers, tutors and even mothers speak. **211** I have read the letters of Cornelia, mother of the Gracchi; it is clear that her sons were not so much raised at her breast as through her conversation. I have often frequently heard Laelia, daughter of Gaius, speak; clearly her speech was coloured by her father's refinement, and I have also heard her daughters, both Muciae, whose speech I knew well, and her granddaughters the Liciniae, one of whom, the wife of Scipio, I expect you, Brutus, have also sometimes heard speak. 'Yes, with pleasure,' replied Brutus, 'and the more so, as she was Lucius Crassus' daughter.'

7.23 A perfect mother: the Eulogy for Murdia

ILS 8394

(*CIL* VI.10230.) This first-century BC marble tablet in honour of Murdia (the 'laudatio Murdiae') records a funerary eulogy by the son of her first marriage. She had children from two marriages; on her death she left her money to her second husband but ensured that her son by her first husband received the money she had inherited from his father and that all her sons were equally treated in her will: Hallett 1984: 43; Crook 1986: 74; Dixon 1988: 48–9. For the standard catalogue of domestic virtues, as in the case of Claudia (doc. 7.31), see Forbis 1990: 493–4.

She made all her sons equal heirs, and gave her daughter a share. Her maternal love was demonstrated by her care for her children and their sharing equally. She left a specified sum to her husband so that the dowry, which was his right, should be increased by the acknowledgement of her good opinion. Recalling the memory of my father, and following the advice of that and her own trustworthiness, she left me a legacy after a valuation had been made, not to show preference for me over my brothers **10** and insult them, but because, mindful of my father's generosity, she thought what she had, at her husband's discretion, received from my patrimony ought to be returned to me, so that, after preserving it in her *usus*, she might restore it to my ownership.

This was typical of her behaviour; she was married by her parents to worthy men; she safeguarded her marriages by her obedience and probity; as a wife, she was the more welcome for her merits, the more beloved for her fidelity, and left the more honoured for her discretion. After her death, she was unanimously praised by the citizens for the division of her property, which demonstrated her gratitude and trustworthiness towards her husbands, her fairness towards her children, and her genuine love of justice.

20 Eulogies of all good women are generally straightforward and similar to each other, because the innate merits women safeguard require very little variety of expression, and it is enough that all of them have behaved in the same way deserving of good repute. As it would be a hard task to discover new praises for a wife, since her life is troubled by less diversity, stock phrases have necessarily to be employed, in case any of the proper maxims be left out and discredit all the rest.

My mother, who was dearer to me than anything, deserved all the more praise for being the equal of all respectable women with regard to her modesty, probity, chastity, obedience, skill at wool-working, diligence and trustworthiness, nor was she second to anyone when her virtue, **30** industry and wisdom were put to the test, showing herself to be outstanding. . . .

7.24 A beloved daughter

CIL I² 1837

(*ILLRP* 971; *ROL* IV.20–2.) This epitaph was discovered at Monteleone in Sabine territory. It is unclear whether the daughter was born before or after the mother was freed: if before she may have purchased her daughter's freedom. For attitudes towards daughters, see Hallett 1984: esp. 62–149; doc. 3.40 for Aemilius Paullus and Tertia.

Posilla Senenia, daughter of Quartus, and Quarta Senenia, freedwoman of Gaius.
Stranger, stop and at the [same] time rea[d] through what is written here:
A mother wa[s] not permitted to enjoy her [on]ly daughter,
On whom some god [or other], I believe, cast an evil eye.
Since it [was] not permitted for her to be adorned by her mother while she was
    [a]live,
She did this after her death, as was ri[gh]t, at the end of her time,
And honoured with a monument the girl whom she had loved.

7.25 A beloved daughter (2)

CIL I² 1222

(*ROL* IV.28.) A marble tablet found at Rome.

If anyone has a grief to add to mine,
Let him stand here and weep with not a few tears.
A sorrowful parent has [here laid to rest] his only daughter,
Nymphe, whom he cherished and enjoyed with tender love,
[While the shortened] time of the Fates [allowed] it.
She, so dear to her family, [has now been snatched] from her home and is covered
    with earth.
Her [lovely fa]ce and figure praised as lovely
Are [all no]w [insubstantial shadow] and her bones just a little ash.

7.26 A letter of condolence

[Cicero] *Letters to his Friends* 4.5.1, 4–6

Tullia, Cicero's only daughter and eldest child, born between 79 and 76/5, was married to Gaius
Calpurnius Piso Frugi between 63 and 58, then to Furius Crassipes in 56 (divorced in 51), and
then to Publius Cornelius Dolabella in 50. Here Servius Sulpicius Rufus (governor of Greece at
the time: *MRR* II.302) writes a letter of condolence from Athens in mid-March 45 to Cicero, on
the death of Tullia after the birth of her second son to Dolabella: both boys died. Her death
devastated Cicero. On Tullia, see Collins 1951/2; Dixon 1984, 1986; Clark 1991; Treggiari 2002:
49–73, esp. 67–8. For Cicero's affection for her: he is willing to attend games Tullia wanted to
see (*Att.* 2.8.2); on her welcome at his return to Brundisium (4.1: doc. 12.59); his desire to build
a shrine to honour her memory (12.12.1, 18.1, 19.1, 36.1).

Servius to Cicero, greetings.

1 After the news about the death of your daughter Tullia reached me, I was really,
as I ought to have been, deeply and painfully sorry, and I felt that this calamity had
struck us both. If I had been in Rome, I would have been with you and shown my grief
to you in person. . . .

4 Recently, so many distinguished men died at the same time, so great a weakening
of the power of the Roman state occurred, all our provinces were shaken to their depths;
can you be moved so deeply by the loss of the poor soul of one poor woman? Even if
she had not died now, she must nevertheless have died in a few years because she was

mortal. **5** You too must remove your mind and your thought from these things and dwell instead on matters which are worthy of your character: that she lived as long as was good for her, that is, she lived while there was a Republic; she saw you, her father, praetor, consul, and augur; she was married to young men from noble families; she enjoyed almost all of life's blessings; and when the Republic died, she left life. How then, can you or she quarrel with Fortune on this account? . . .

6 There is no grief which the passage of time does not lessen or soften. It is unworthy of you to wait for the time to pass rather than anticipating it with your own good sense. If any consciousness remains in those below, her love for you and her dutiful devotion to all her family were such that she certainly does not wish you to act like this. Yield to your dead daughter, yield to others, your friends and family, who are distressed because of your grief, yield to your country so that, if need arises, it can use your service and counsel.

7.27 Tullia's death

Cicero *Letters to Atticus* 12.46 (Lanuvium, 15 May 45 BC)

Tullia died at Cicero's villa at Tusculum in mid-February 45, a month after giving birth to her second son; in his grief, Cicero retreated to Atticus' house at Rome, leaving for his place at Lanuvium in early March, where he wrote his well-known *Consolation* (now lost: *Att.* 12.14.3) and resumed his correspondence with friends.

I think I shall overcome my feelings and go from Lanuvium to Tusculum. For I must either give up my property there forever (since my sorrow will remain the same, although it may be better hidden), or else realise that it doesn't matter in the slightest whether I go there now or in ten years. Certainly it will not possibly remind me of her any more than do the thoughts that consume me perpetually, day and night. You will ask, 'Is there no help in books?' In this case, I am afraid, they actually make it worse; perhaps I would have been tougher without. For in an educated mind there is nothing rough or unfeeling.

WIVES AND THEIR ROLE

As with Murdia (doc. 7.23), stereotypes of women's epitaphs include the terms: old-fashioned, domestic, chaste, obedient, charming, not extravagant or given to ornamentation, religious, and devoted to household work. The term 'univira' (married to only one man) was especially a point of honour: Treggiari 1991: 231–61, esp. 231–7. On the proscriptions of 43, following Caesar's death, Vell. 2.67.2 states of the proscribed that: the 'utmost loyalty was shown by their wives, great loyalty by their freedmen, a little by their slaves, and none at all by their sons'; cf. Parker 1998 for exempla of loyal wives.

7.28 Roman versus Greek women

Cornelius Nepos *Great Generals of Foreign Nations* Preface 6–7

While the Roman matron might spend much of her time at home, she was not secluded there or kept from the sight of visitors; for public and private areas in Roman houses, see Treggiari 1991: 415–16; Wallace-Hadrill 1996; George 1997; Ellis 2000; Harlow & Laurence 2002: 20–33; Rawson 2003: 211–15; for wives' place within their families: Hallett 1984: 211–62; Saller 1999.

On the duties and occupations of aristocratic women, see Clark 1981; Treggiari 1991: 423–7; Evans 1991: 101–65, 210–18.

6 Much of what we consider to be respectable the Greeks think to be disgraceful. What Roman, for example, would be embarrassed at taking his wife to a dinner-party? What wife (materfamilias) does not hold the place of honour in her house and circulate in full public view? **7** Things are very different in Greece; there women are not admitted to dinner-parties, except for ones with just family members, and she stays in the more retired part of the house called the 'women's apartments', to which no man has access unless he is a close relative.

7.29 Aemilia turns a blind eye

Valerius Maximus *Memorable Deeds and Sayings (On the Fidelity of Wives towards their Husbands)* 6.7.1

A 'good' wife obviously considered it beneath her to comment on her husband's love-affairs within the household (whether with male or female slaves); Aemilia is here unusual, not in the fact that she ignores the liaison, but that she rewards the girl of her own accord. Africanus died in 183. In contrast, Cato the Elder's son and daughter-in-law were scandalised at his living openly with a slave girl; their disapproval led to his second marriage: Plut. *Cato Mai.* 24.2–7.

To touch on wifely fidelity too, Tertia Aemilia, wife of the elder Africanus and mother of Cornelia of the Gracchi, was so accommodating and forbearing that, although she knew that one of her slave girls was having an affair with her husband, she pretended not to know of it, so that she, a woman, should not accuse the great hero, conqueror of the world, of lack of self-control. And she was so little interested in revenge, that, after Africanus' death, she freed the slave-girl and married her to one of her own freedmen.

7.30 Selecting the best

Pliny *Natural History* 7.120

Sulpicia was chosen, c. 215 BC, as the chastest woman in Rome to dedicate a statue of Venus Verticordia 'changer of hearts', to be erected to improve female morals; the festival day was 1 April: Val. Max. 8.15.12; Pliny *Nat. Hist.* 7.120; Pomeroy 1975: 208; Evans 1991: 27–8. The death rate among adult males during the Second Punic War had obviously left many women unsupported, and some may have had to turn to illicit liaisons or prostitution (cf. the prosecutions for immorality in 213: Livy 25.2.9). Claudia Quinta was later accused of unchastity: in 204 a ship carrying the black stone of Cybele (the Magna Mater) from Pessinus to Rome was grounded; the soothsayers announced that only a chaste woman could move it and Claudia pulled it free (Livy 29.14; Val. Max. 1.8.11; doc. 3.59).

The first time a woman was judged the most chaste by the vote of all the matrons was Sulpicia, daughter of Paterculus and wife of Fulvius Flaccus, who was selected from a previously chosen 100 to dedicate the statue of Venus in accordance with the Sibylline Books; and on another occasion, in a test of her piety, Claudia, when the Mother of the Gods was being brought to Rome.

7.31 The Perfect Wife (1)

ILS 8403

(*CIL* I² 1211; *ILLRP* 973; *ROL* IV.12.) This epitaph is now lost, but it probably dates to c. 135–120 BC. Claudia is here shown as the epitome of all the traditional wifely virtues: Forbis 1990; Treggiari 1991: 243, 1996: 116; Wallace-Hadrill 1996.

Stranger, my message is short; stand by and read it through.
This is the unlovely tomb of a lovely woman.
Her parents gave her the name of Claudia.
She loved her husband with her whole heart.
She had two sons, of whom one
She leaves on earth, the other she has placed under the earth.
Her conversation was charming, yet her bearing correct.
She kept the house, she made wool. I have spoken. Depart.

7.32 The Perfect Wife (2)

ILS 8398

(*CIL* VI.26192; *ROL* IV.16.) Found at Rome, dating to the first century BC.

Here lies the renowned, dutiful, virtuous, chaste
And modest Sempronia Moschis,
To whom thanks for her merits
Are here returned by her husband.

7.33 The Perfect Wife (3)

ILS 7472

(*CIL* I² 1221; *ILLRP* 793; *ROL* IV.22–4.) A stone slab now in the British Museum, found at Rome near the Via Nomentana. It dates to c. 80 BC; both man and wife are Greek ex-slaves who served the same family; Treggiari 1996: 121–2.

[Lucius Au]relius [H]ermia, freedman of Lucius, a [bu]tcher on the Viminal Hill. [S]he who preceded me in death, my only [w]ife, chaste in body, a loving woman possessed of my heart, lived faithful to her [f]aithful husband. Equal in devotion, she never in bitter times shrank from her duties.
Aurelia, freedwoman of Lucius.

Aurelia Philematium ('Little Kiss'), freedwoman of Lucius.
In life I was called Aurelia Philematium,
Chaste and modest, not knowing the crowd, faithful to my husband.
My husband was a fellow-freedman, whom I've now lost alas!,
And was in real truth more than a father to me.
He took me to his bosom when I was seven years old,
And at the age of forty I am in death's power.
He always flourished through my constant care. . . .

7.34 Calvus and Quintilia

Catullus 96

Gaius Licinius Calvus, an orator and poet, and son of the historian Licinius Macer, was a friend of Catullus and a colleague of Cicero (Cic. *Fam.* 15.21.4): Tacitus (*Dial.* 21.2, cf. 34.7) stated that Calvus' speeches against Vatinius were still read by every student of rhetoric. Calvus wrote an elegy on the death of his young wife (Propertius 2.34.89–90; Ovid *Trist.* 2.431–2) and Catullus here acknowledges the poem. Poems 14 and 50 are also addressed to Calvus, while in poem 53 Catullus laughs at his stature.

> If anything welcome or acceptable from our grief
> Is able to reach the dumb grave, Calvus,
> By the longing with which we renew our old loves
> And weep for friendships lost in times past,
> Surely Quintilia does not grieve so much for her premature death
> As much as she rejoices in your love.

7.35 Eulogies for Caesar's women: Julia and Cornelia

Plutarch *Life of Julius Caesar* 5.1–5

Caesar had previously refused to divorce his first wife Cornelia, daughter of Cinna, despite Sulla's orders. Both his aunt (the widow of Marius; doc. 9.5) and his wife died in 69. Suet. *Jul.* 6 relates that while eulogising his aunt Julia's ancestry he emphasised that of the Caesars as a whole — Julia's mother being descended from kings, and her father from gods. The first person to deliver a eulogy for a woman was Q. Lutatius Catulus, cos. 102, for his mother Popilia (Cic. *de orat.* 2.44); the next were for Caesar's wife and aunt. In 42, Atticus gave a eulogy for his 90 year old mother Caecilia, in which he stated that he had never had a disagreement with his mother, nor quarrelled with his sister (Pomponia, wife of Quintus Cicero): Nepos *Atticus* 17.1.

1 The first proof Caesar received of the people's goodwill towards him was when he competed for the post of military tribune against Gaius Popilius and was elected (for 71 BC). **2** A second and much clearer proof was when, after the death of his aunt Julia, the wife of Marius, he delivered a brilliant eulogy of her in the forum, and was daring enough to bring out in the funeral procession images of Marius, which were then seen for the first time since Sulla's regime, when the Marians had been declared public enemies. **3** Some people cried out against Caesar for this, but the populace answered them enthusiastically, welcomed Caesar with applause, and admired him for having brought back into the city after so long, as if from the dead, the honours due to Marius.

4 It was an ancient Roman tradition to give funeral orations for older women, but it was not customary for young women, and Caesar was the first to make a funeral oration when his own wife died. **5** This also brought him popular favour and gained the sympathies of the populace, who loved him as a tender-hearted man, full of feeling.

7.36 Cicero to Terentia

Cicero *Letters to his Friends* 14.1.1 (mid-November 58 BC)

Cicero divorced Terentia for extravagance and dishonesty in 46 after a marriage lasting some 33 years. This letter was written to her after he was exiled in November 58 and shows his affection for Terentia and their daughter Tullia (he speaks of wanting to die in Terentia's arms, *Fam.* 14.4, and of weeping at the thought of her face: 14.3); numerous affectionate letters are addressed to her during this period: Dixon 1984: 78–87 on her financial independence and commercial dealings during his absence; Treggiari 1991: 253–5 on their correspondence in 58; cf. Hales 2000. Cicero blames himself for not accepting Caesar's offer of a *legatio* in 59, which would have protected him from Clodius' hostility: doc. 12.44.

Many people's letters and everyone's conversation tell me about your amazing courage and fortitude, and that you are not exhausted by your hardships of mind and body. Woe is me! that you, with such courage, loyalty, probity, and generosity, should have fallen into such great tribulations on my account! And that our darling Tullia should receive such grief from a father in whom she used to take such delight! . . . .

7.37 A strong-minded daughter and wife: the Laudatio 'Turiae'

ILS 8393

(*CIL* VI.1527, 31670.) An inscription discovered in Rome, which records an oration in a deceased wife's honour, which was probably delivered over the grave (2.22, 67); Cicero tells us that families preserved funeral orations, as they did ancestral masks (imagines): *Brut.* 61. Events in the first paragraph refer to 49 BC; the woman is conventionally known as 'Turia' because of a conjectured identification with the wife of Quintus Lucretius Vespillo (perhaps consul in 19 BC): at Val. Max. 6.7.2 Vespillo's wife Turia is said to have hidden him in her bedroom above the rafters during the proscriptions of 42 (cf. App. *BC* 4.44). Here the husband lists his wife's domestic virtues, and stresses his horror at her suggestion that because they were childless that he should remarry; their marriage had lasted 41 years (1.28). The wife here is clear evidence for women's involvement in legal and political issues: her father and mother had been murdered in 49, when her future husband was overseas. She brought the killers to justice and secured her inheritance. Her husband was a republican and in 42 she saved him in the proscription of Octavian and Mark Anthony, receiving physical violence at the hands of Lepidus. Her financial independence is shown by the fact that she gave dowries to her young cousins and nieces. See Wistrand 1976; Gordon 1977; Horsfall 1983; Rawson 1986a: 29–30; Crook 1986: 74; Ramage 1994; Hemelrijk 2004; with general agreement against the husband being identified with Vespillo.

I.3 You were suddenly orphaned before the day of our marriage, when both your parents were murdered together in a lonely part of the countryside. It was mainly through you, since I was on my way to Macedonia, and your sister's husband Gaius Cluvius on his way to the province of Africa, that the death of your parents did not go unavenged. You put so much hard work into this act of piety in asking questions and demanding punishment, that we would not have been able to do any more, even had we been there. The credit is due to you and that most pious lady your sister.

10 While you were involved in this and the guilty had been punished, you left your father's house in order to protect your virtue and took yourself to my mother's house, where you awaited my arrival. **13** You were then pressured to state that your father's will, in which we were the heirs, had been invalidated, since he had married his wife by coemptio, which would have made it necessary for you, with all your father's property, to pass into the guardianship of those who were bringing the case. Your sister would have got nothing, because she had passed into the manus of Cluvius, and, although I was not there, I heard about the courage with which you heard their proposals and the presence of mind with which you resisted them.

18 You defended our common interests by the truth: that the will had not been invalidated, and in order that we both be the heirs, rather than you alone possessing the entire property, you were determined to **20** uphold your father's actions, in the same way that, if you had not won your point, you intended to share with your sister and were not going to let yourself pass into the guardianship of someone who had no legal right over you, and for whom no relationship of gens with your own family could be proved, which might force you to do that. For even if your father's will had been invalidated, nevertheless that right did not belong to those who claimed it, since they did not belong to the same gens. Because of your persistence they gave up, and did not take the case any further; by this deed of reverence towards your father, piety towards your sister, and loyalty to me, you single-handedly succeeded in the defence you had undertaken.

27 Few marriages of such length are ended by death and not broken by divorce. In our case our marriage lasted for forty-one years, without a disagreement. Would that the final ending had come about through me instead, since it would have been fairer for me, as the elder, to yield to fate! . . .

30 Why should I mention your personal virtues — your modesty, obedience, kindliness, good nature, dedication to wool-making, piety without superstition, inconspicuous adornment and understated elegance. Why speak about your affection for your relatives, your piety towards your family, for you looked after my mother just like you did your own parents and gave her the same care? Why speak of the innumerable other qualities which you share with all matrons of respectability? The ones which I claim for you are peculiar to you and few people have possessed similar qualities or demonstrated them in practice: the destiny of humankind shows us how rare they are . . .

II.41 You were unhappy about your barrenness and grieved because of my lack of children, lest by remaining married to you I would lose the hope of having children and be miserable for that reason; you spoke of divorce and suggested handing over your household to another woman who was fertile, and that you would yourself find and arrange for me someone worthy of our well-known love; you declared that you would treat future children as your own and would not divide up our inheritance, which until now had been joint: it would remain, if I wanted, under my control. You would not detach or separate yourself from me, you would from now on carry out the duties and role of my sister or my mother-in-law. **50** I have to admit that I was so infuriated that I lost my mind and was so horrified by your suggestions that I could hardly regain control of myself. How could you consider a separation before it was dictated by fate! How could your mind even conceive any reason that you, while still alive, should cease to be my wife — you who had remained so loyally with me when I was in exile, almost exiled from life itself! How could the desire or need for children be so great that I would break faith with you, that I would change certainties for doubts! But what else can I say? You stayed with me; for I could not have given in to you without my own dishonour and our joint misery . . .

77 The conclusion of my oration is this: you have deserved all, and I will never be able to repay you fully. I have always considered your commands as my law. I will continue to do for you whatever else I still can. I pray that your Manes (spirits of the dead) give you, and protect, your rest.

MARITAL DISCORD

According to Gellius (1.6.1–6) Metellus Numidicus during his censorship in 102–101 BC urged men to wed: 'If we were able to exist without wives, fellow Romans, we would all be free from that troublesome matter; but since nature has so ordained that it is impossible to live very comfortably with them, and utterly impossible to live without them, we must consider our long-term welfare rather than our short-term pleasure'; see McDonnell 1987, arguing that Numidicus is not here a mistake for his uncle Macedonicus (censor in 131–130); cf. Suet. *Aug.* 89.2.

Spurius Carvilius Ruga was supposedly the first to divorce his wife (for childlessness) c. 231: Gell. 4.3.1–2; Val Max 2.1.4; Dion. Hal 2.25.6–7 (doc. 7.12). This was not the first divorce in Rome, but a new kind of divorce with the return of the dowry and without laying criminal blame on the wife; his defence was that he felt bound by his oath to the censor that he had married to produce children. On the importance of child-bearing in marriage, see Treggiari 1991: 11–13; Rawson 2003: 95–6. Val. Max. 6.3.10 (cf. Plut. *Rom. Quest.* 14) also mentions the divorces of C. Sulpicius Galus (cos. 166; *MRR* I.437) because his wife went about with head uncovered, Q. Antistius Vetus because he had seen his wife talking with a freedwoman (i.e., a prostitute), and P. Sempronius Sophus (perhaps cos. 268) because his wife had attended the games without his knowledge.

Unhappy marriages are attested, such as that of Scipio Aemilianus and Sempronia, who was suspected of complicity in his murder (doc. 8.21). Jokes about wives were common: L. Scipio Nasica, when asked by Cato as censor, whether on his conscience, he was sure he had a wife, replied, 'Certainly, but not one to my taste'; Cato is said to have disenfranchised him for this joke. Cicero cites a further example: a Sicilian was lamenting to a friend that his wife had hanged herself on a fig-tree; the friend replied, 'Do please let me have some cuttings of that tree to plant' (Cic. *de orat.* 2.64.260, 2.69.278; Gell. 4.20.4–5); for satire against women, see Rudd 1986: 193–225.

7.38 A domineering wife

Caecilius Statius Plocium 136–8, 141–4, 151–5

(Gell. 2.23.10, 13; *ROL* I.520–2.) Caecilius was a Gaul brought to Rome, possibly from Milan, between 200 and 194, presumably as a slave of a certain Caecilius; he died in 168. A friend of Ennius, he took to writing comedies from Greek models (fabulae palliatae). While using Menander as a model, as with the *Plocium* (*Little Necklace*) he was very free with his source. This extract shows us the extent to which Roman audiences appreciated marital discord in comic stage-presentations, even if the original was Greek. At line 156 one of the husbands comments about his wife, 'I got really fond of her after she was dead'. The satirist Lucilius wrote (27.1.747; *ROL* III.242), perhaps on a 'perfect' wife, 'let her cut wood, spin her weight of wool, sweep the house and take a flogging'.

A. Indeed, he is a wretch who doesn't know how to hide his misery
Out of doors; for my wife, even if I keep quiet, gives the game away by her looks
and actions —

My wife, who has everything you don't want — except a dowry. Anyone who's
 wise will learn from me . . .
While I long for her death, I live as a corpse among the living.
She says that I secretly consorted with my maidservant; that's what she charges
 me with,
And so by begging, and pleading, and threatening, and scolding she forced me
To sell her.

B.   But tell me, is your wife bad-tempered?
A.   Well, what a question!
B.   Well, how then?
A.   It upsets me just talking about it.
      Whenever I come home and sit beside her, the first thing she does
      Is give me a kiss with that awful breath of hers.
B.   She makes no mistake with that kiss —
      She wants you to vomit up what you've been drinking outside.

7.39 A quarrelsome wife

Cicero *Letters to Atticus* 5.1.3–4 (Minturnae, 5/6 May 51 BC)

Pomponia, sister of Cicero's friend Atticus, was married to Cicero's brother Quintus, primarily
to strengthen Marcus' connections with Atticus. The couple had a son Quintus. When this letter
was written in 51 BC the couple were clearly experiencing difficulties (as they were as early as
November 68: *Att.* 1.5.2); expenditure seems to have been an issue, as well as Quintus' dependence
on his freedman Statius (see docs 5.66, 6.46, 6.48). They later divorced, but the marriage had lasted
from 69 to 44. Quintus decided against a second marriage, commenting in April 44 that (*Att.*
14.13.5–6) there was nothing more pleasant than a single bed. For the disagreements in Pomponia
and Quintus' marriage, see Dixon 1997: 154–61; Harlow & Laurence 2002: 82–4; Marchetti
2004: 283–4. Pomponia seems to have been at least forty at the time of the marriage, so Quintus
was probably her second husband.

3 Now I come to the line written crossways at the end of your letter, in which you
mention your sister. These are the facts of the case. When I reached Arpinum, and my
brother met me, we first had a long talk about you. I then brought the conversation round
to the discussion you and I had about your sister at Tusculum. I have never seen anything
gentler or kinder than my brother's behaviour at that time towards your sister, which was
such that, if there was any quarrel about expenditure, there were no signs of it. So passed
that day. On the next day we left Arpinum. Quintus had to stay at Arcanum for a festival,
while I went to Aquinum, but we lunched at Arcanum. You know his property there.
When we arrived, Quintus said most politely, 'Pomponia, you invite the women and I'll
ask the men.' Nothing, as far as I could see, could have been gentler than his words or
his intention and expression. But she, in everyone's hearing, said, 'Oh, but I'm just a
stranger here!' I suppose because Statius had been sent ahead to see to the arrangements
for our lunch. Then Quintus said to me, 'There! I have to put up with that every day!'
   4 You will say, 'So, what's wrong with that?' A lot! She really upset me, she
answered with such unnecessary rudeness in word and look. I hid my annoyance and

we all took our places except her. Quintus sent her some food from the table: she refused it. In short, it seemed to me that nothing could have been more tolerant than my brother and nothing more rude than your sister; and I have passed over many incidents that upset me more than they did Quintus. I then went on to Aquinum. Quintus stayed at Arcanum and met me the next morning and told me that she had refused to sleep with him and that, when she was leaving, she was as bad-tempered as when I had seen her. Actually, you may tell her that in my opinion she behaved with a total lack of courtesy that day.

7.40 Cicero's last letter to Terentia

Cicero *Letters to his Friends* 14.20 (October 47 BC)

This is Cicero's last extant letter to Terentia, written in October 47. Its curtness shows the breakdown in the relationship. Terentia had apparently been fraudulent in her handling of finances during his absence: Dixon 1984: 88–90, 96, 1986; Verboven 2001 suggests that she refused to use a loan she had recovered to provide for his travelling expenses when he left to join the republicans in 49 (cf. *Fam.* 4.14.3; *Att.* 8.7.3, 10.4.12); for her strong-mindedness, see doc. 7.84. Cicero found it very difficult to repay Terentia's dowry (if he did): *Att.* 16.15.5; for Quintus' trouble in repaying Pomponia's: *Att.* 14.13.5. Shortly after his divorce in 45 Cicero married his ward Publilia, mainly because he needed her money for his creditors and the repayment of Terentia's dowry (according to Tiro): Plut. *Cic.* 41.3–4. He had been married for 33 years and was 60 years of age; he divorced her the next year, because she showed little grief at Tullia's death. The tub (labrum) was a large container in which the bathers washed before immersing themselves.

I think I shall arrive at the Tuscan estate either on the Nones (the 7th) or the day after. See that everything is got ready. I will perhaps have several others with me and I expect that we shall stay there for a considerable time. If there is no tub in the bath, see that there is one — the same regarding everything else necessary for life and health. Goodbye. 1 October, Venusia.

7.41 A ritual consultation for marital harmony

Valerius Maximus *Memorable Deeds and Sayings*
(Of Ancient Institutions) 2.1.6

Whenever there was some little argument between husband and wife, they used to go to the shrine of the goddess Viriplaca on the Palatine hill. There each in turn stated what they wanted; and, after they had put aside their quarrelsome feelings, they went back home in harmony. The goddess is said to have obtained this name because of her power to placate husbands; she certainly deserves to be venerated and honoured with some outstanding and exceptional sacrifices as the guardian of peace in everyday and household affairs, who by her very title grants the respect owed by wives to the superior rank of husband within the yoke of equal affection.

ADULTERY, CONSPIRACY AND SORCERY

The husband, or the wife's father, was allowed to kill the wife if caught in the act of adultery: doc. 7.18; Val. Max. 6.1.13 gives examples of specific punishments inflicted on the adulterer (whipping, castration, rape); according to Horace (*Sat.* 1.2.37–46) an adulterer caught in the act could be beaten to death, raped by the husband's slaves, castrated or fined, either by the woman's husband or her father; the husband was entitled to retain some of the adulterous wife's dowry. When Gellius Publicola, censor in 70 BC, was informed that his son had committed adultery with his stepmother he planned to murder him, but instead referred the matter to the senate who acquitted the young man (Val. Max. 5.9.1).

Normally the seduction of wives and daughters was the concern of the family, though a number of public trials are recorded, presumably where there were no male relatives to take action: Treggiari 1991: 275–7. Republican attitudes to adultery: Fantham 1991: 270–1; Treggiari 1991: 299–309. Treggiari 1991: 507 lists allegations of adultery in the Republic; on female sexualities: Dixon 2001: 32–44. Clearly adultery was not just the bugbear of traditional husbands or the fabrication of prejudiced sources: Caelius was able to write to Cicero in April 50 BC that Servius Ocella had been caught twice in adultery within three days ([Cic.] *Fam.* 8.7.2).

7.42 Sorceresses anonymous

Livy *History of Rome* 8.18.2–11

This story, which Livy affects to disbelieve, took place in the context of a bad plague in 331 BC. As with the Bacchanalia women are shown as 'out of control'. There were a number of group prosecutions against women in the middle Republic (such as the Bacchanalia and the poisoners of 154: docs 7.16–17). Only those who had no kinsfolk were punished by the state, under the aegis of the aedile. While this story is probably apocryphal, adultery and poisoning were linked in the Roman mind: Fantham 1991: 282–3.

2 One thing, however, I should be glad to believe has been falsely handed down — and not all the authorities mention it — namely that those whose deaths made the year notorious for the plague were in fact killed by poison; **3** still, I must set down the story as it has been handed down, lest I destroy confidence in any of my sources. **4** When leading citizens were suffering from the same kind of disease which ended in nearly every case with their death, a certain maidservant came to Quintus Fabius Maximus, the curule aedile, and declared that she would reveal the cause of this general pestilence if she were given a promise by him that her evidence would not injure her. **5** Fabius immediately referred the matter to the consuls and they to the senate and with its agreement the promise was made to the informer. **6** She then disclosed that the city was suffering from the crimes of its women, and that these poisons were being prepared by married women who could be caught in the act if they were willing to follow her at once. **7** They followed the informer and found certain women brewing poisons and others that were stored away. **8** These were brought to the forum and some twenty matrons in whose houses they had been found were summoned there by an apparitor. Two of these, Cornelia and Sergia, both from patrician families, asserted that they were salutary medicines, but when the informer refuted this and told them to drink and prove her wrong in the sight of all, **9** they took time to confer and when the crowd had been sent away referred the question to the rest; finding that like themselves they would not refuse to drink, they swallowed down the poison and all perished by their own evil practices. **10** Their attendants were immediately arrested and informed against a large number of married women, of whom 170 were found guilty. **11** Before that day there had never been a trial for poison in Rome.

7.43 Adulteresses on trial

Livy *History of Rome* 10.31.9

295 BC saw the great defeat of the Gauls and Samnites (docs 1.69–70), as well as prodigies (many in Appius' army were struck by lightning, and the Sibylline Books were consulted). Gurges here was presumably aedile: he had been military tribune in 297 and was consul in 292 (10.47.5; *MRR* I.181). This Venus was worshipped as Venus Obsequens (Servius *Aen.* 1.720). Fantham 1991: 282 suggests that these women were not noblewomen, but rather that a clean-up of prostitution was taking place, as in 213 under the aediles Tapulus and Fundulus, where the women concerned were driven into exile (cf. doc. 7.30).

In this year (295 BC) Quintus Fabius Gurges, son of the consul (Q. Fabius Maximus Rullianus), exacted fines from a number of married women convicted of adultery before the people; with the money from these fines he built the temple of Venus which is near the Circus.

7.44 A unconventional woman

Sallust *The Catilinarian Conspiracy* 24.3–25.5

Sempronia, wife of Decimus Junius Brutus (cos. 77), is an example of an educated aristocratic woman in the first century BC and was one of Catiline's adherents in 63. This passage is useful for the mobility, ruthlessness and independence open to noble women. Sempronia is seen by Dixon (2001: 18) as a character in a literary-political narrative, demonised perhaps in much the same way as Lesbia is shown prowling the alleys for pick-ups: Catullus 58.4–5 (doc. 7.51). Fantham 1994: 280–5, however, sees such women as Sempronia as representative of a 'new pattern of female behaviour'; cf. Hillard 1993: 47–8.

Catiline's conspiracy was revealed by Fulvia who had learnt it from her lover Quintus Curius (who had been expelled from the senate by the censors in 70) and who was to act as a go-between between Cicero and Curius (Sall. *Cat.* 23.3–4, 26.3, 28.2; doc. 12.15): this is not the same Fulvia who was wife of Clodius, Curio and Mark Antony, who, with Pompey's ex-wife Mucia, was said to have been present at a 'brothel party' in honour of Q. Metellus Pius Scipio (cos. 52): Val. Max. 9.1.8.

A love of learning and music was not necessarily linked with immorality: Cornelia, wife first of Publius Crassus, who was killed at Carrhae, and then of Pompey, was widely read, proficient at geometry, fond of philosophical discussions, played the lyre, and yet was 'not unattractive' (Plut. *Pomp.* 55.2; Haley 1985). For the connotations of dancing, see doc. 8.20.

24.3 At that time (the news that Cicero and Antonius were to be consuls for 63) Catiline is said to have gained numerous supporters of every class, and even of some women who had at first supported their excessive extravagance by prostitution, and then, when their age put an end to their income, though not their luxurious tastes, had piled up huge debts. **4** With their help, Catiline believed, he would be able to rouse the city slaves to his side and set fire to the city, and either get their husbands to join him or murder them.

25.1 Now among their number was Sempronia, a woman who had often committed many crimes of masculine daring. **2** In birth and beauty, as well as in her husband and children, the woman had been well gifted by fortune. Well-educated in Greek and Latin literature, she was more skilled at playing the lyre and dancing than a respectable women need be, having many other accomplishments which minister to extravagant tastes. **3** But there was nothing that she valued less than decency and chastity; you would find it difficult to say whether she was less sparing of her money or her reputation; her desires were so ardent that she more often made advances to men than they did to her. **4** Even before this she had often broken her word, repudiated debts on oath, and been an accessory to murder; extravagance and poverty combined had sent her headlong. **5** Nevertheless, her talents were not negligible; she could write poetry, crack jokes, and converse with modesty, tender feeling or wantonness; in fact she possessed great wit and considerable charm.

7.45 Caesar's love-life

Suetonius *Life of the Deified Julius* 50.1–2

Suetonius also relates Caesar's affairs in Gaul and the queens who had been his mistresses; Eunoe, wife of Bogudes, and Cleopatra (52.1). Servilia, wife first of M. Junius Brutus and then of D. Junius Silanus (cos. 62), was Cato the Younger's older half-sister and mother of M. Junius Brutus. She is frequently mentioned in Cicero's correspondence: see esp. *Att.* 15.11.1–2, 15.12.1, 15.13a.4; Bauman 1992: 73–6. Aegisthus was the lover of Clytemnestra, wife of Agamemnon.

1 It is generally believed that Caesar was much disposed to love affairs and to extravagant behaviour within these affairs, and that he seduced a great many well-born women, among them Postumia, wife of Servius Sulpicius, Lollia, wife of Aulus Gabinius, Tertulla, wife of Marcus Crassus, and even Gnaeus Pompey's wife Mucia. Certainly Pompey was reproached by both Curio the Elder and Curio the Younger and many others for having married Caesar's daughter for political gain, when it was on Caesar's account, whom Pompey had often named in his laments as 'Aegisthus', that he divorced his wife after she had born him three children.

2 But above all others he loved Marcus Brutus' mother Servilia the best, and in his first consulship he bought her a pearl worth 6,000,000 sesterces, and gave her many presents during the civil war, as well as letting her buy certain lavish estates at auction for a trifle; when many wondered at the low price, Cicero quipped: 'It was an even better bargain than you think, because a third (*tertia*) was discounted' — Servilia, you see, was also thought at the time to be prostituting her daughter Tertia to Caesar.

7.46 A front-door tells all

Catullus 67

A dialogue with the front door of a house in Verona reveals the gossip relating to the household, especially the fact that the new bride, after earlier indiscretions, was no virgin and had been seduced by her father-in-law: Wray 2001: 138–43. It is unlikely that Caecilius is the poet and friend of Catullus (cf. poem 35), or that Cornelius is the same person as Cornelius Nepos, in poem 1.

Catullus

> Dear to a beloved husband and pleasing to his father,
> Greetings, and may Jupiter preserve you with kindly help,

House-door, whom they say used once to do kind service to Balbus,
When the old man himself owned the house,
And which they say since then has been doing evil service to his son,
Now the old man's been laid out and you've become the door of married people.
Come, tell us why you're said to have changed
And abandoned your old loyalty to your master.

House-door

It is not (so may I please Caecilius, to whom I've been handed over)
10   My fault, though it is said to be mine,
Nor can anyone speak of any wrong done by me:
But people will say that the door does it;
Whenever any ill deed is discovered
They all shout at me, 'Door — it's your fault!'

Catullus

It's not enough for you to say it with a single word,
But to do it so that anyone may know and see it.

House-door

How can I? No one asks or is concerned to know.

Catullus

I want to know: don't hesitate to tell me.

House-door

First then, that she was handed over to us a virgin as is said
20   Is a lie. It was not her husband who was the first to touch her
Whose 'little dagger' hangs more listless than a young beetroot
And never erects itself to mid-tunic.
Instead his father is said to have dishonoured his son's bed
And polluted the wretched house;
Either because his impious mind burned with blind lust,
Or because the son was impotent, with barren seed
So they had to find one more vigorous
Who could unloose her maiden tie.

Catullus

You speak of a father distinguished by remarkable affection,
30   Who comes in the lap of his own son.

House-door

And yet Brixia under the cliffs of Cycnea,
Brixia, which golden Melo runs through with its soft stream,
Brixia, beloved mother of my own Verona,
Says he isn't the only one known to have had her;
But she tells about Postumius and the love of Cornelius,
With whom she was involved in wicked adultery.

Catullus

Here someone might say, 'What? How do you, door, know all this?
You who are never allowed to be away from your master's threshold,
Nor to listen to the people, but fixed under this lintel

40   Are only accustomed to close and open the house?
House-door

> I have often heard her talking in a secretive voice
> Alone with her maids about these crimes of hers,
> Speaking by name of those of whom I spoke, as if
> She thought that I had neither tongue nor ear.
> Moreover she added someone, whom I don't want to mention
> By name, lest he should raise his red eyebrows.
> He is a tall man, once troubled by a great lawsuit
> About a false womb and a lying pregnancy.

HETEROSEXUAL LOVE: CATULLUS AND LESBIA

'Lesbia' has generally been supposed to have been the pseudonym of Clodia Metelli, one of the three sisters of the tribune P. Clodius Pulcher: the identification was made by Apuleius (*Apologia* 10: AD 158); see, for example, Skinner 1983; Wiseman 1985; Treggiari 1991: 304. This Claudia (Clodia) was married to Quintus Caecilius Metellus Celer, cos. 60. Metellus died in March 59 and shortly afterwards Clodia is supposed to have begun an affair with M. Caelius Rufus (Catullus 58 and 100 may be addressed to him), whom she later accused of attempted poisoning. In April 56 Clodia Metelli was in court as a witness against Caelius, whom she claimed owed her money. Cicero, who defended him, concentrates on a character assassination of Clodia as an ageing prostitute, who might have poisoned her husband, and who had an incestuous relationship with her brother (59–60; Pompey's supporters shouted obscene chants about Clodius and Clodia: doc. 12.67). Catullus is an inventive and elegant poet, full of allusions and well-schooled in hellenistic poetry, and we should not take his poems as reflecting a love-affair with a single woman — scholarship now refuses to accept the poems as the chronicle of a genuine relationship, seeing Lesbia as a poetic construct; Dixon 2001: 142 considers Lesbia an applied composite of hostile stereotypes of Roman women — frivolous, luxurious, ambitious, killer of her husband, and unchaste. It has even been suggested that Cicero invented the intimate relationship between Caelius and Clodia to aid his defence: Holzberg 2000: 30. On the portrayal of Clodia/Lesbia, see Hillard 1993: 48–53; Fantham 1994: 280–4; Holzberg 2000; Wray 2001: 64–112; Dixon 2001: 135–56; cf. Bauman 1992: 69–73. Scholars no longer see Clodia as a political manoeuverer (Hillard 1989, 1993: 48–52; Wiseman 1985) and 'Lesbia' is indeed pictured not as a lady of senatorial rank but as an hetaera (a cultured prostitute), a familiar literary character. While the name Lesbia might reflect that of Sappho of Lesbos (whose famous poem Catullus adapts in poem 51), it could also refer to the Greek verb *lesbiazein* (Latin: fellare; to perform oral sex): Wirshbo 1980; Holzberg 33–34, who argues that Sappho, being seen as shameless in Roman eyes, is a good model for the Lesbia portrayed by Catullus.

Thirteen of Catullus' 116 poems refer to Lesbia, moving from passion to disillusionment; 12 others are addressed to an unspecified girl (puella) and poem 32 to Ipsitilla (though this could be a misreading for ipsicilla, i.e., domina or lady: Gratwick 1991: 547; Holzberg 2000: 32). Other love poems, however, are written to young boys such as Camerius and Juventius (doc. 7.61) and it would be unwise to see Catullus as inflamed by a single grand passion, but rather as a skilful poet adapting and refining hellenistic models of love poetry.

7.47 An idyllic relationship

Catullus 7

Compare poem 5; Wray 2001: 145–54 (with references at note 78) notes that this picture of Catullus would have been, in Roman eyes, uncontrolled and effeminate and that the poem is deliberately intended to shock. Holzberg 2000 sees a role reversal in this and the rest of the corpus, with Lesbia in the dominant male role, and Catullus as the unmanly passive partner, unable to do anything except kiss.

> You ask how many kissings of you,
> Lesbia, will be enough and to spare.
> As great a number as the grains of Libyan sand
> That lie on silphium-bearing Cyrene,
> 5   Between the desert oracle of Jupiter Ammon
> And the sacred tomb of legendary Battus,
> Or as many as are the stars, in the silent night,
> That see men's clandestine loves —
> To kiss you with so many kisses
> 10   Is enough and to spare for your infatuated Catullus,
> Which busybodies could not count up
> Nor an evil tongue bewitch.

7.48 Love and hate

Catullus 85

> I hate and love. Why I do so, perhaps you will ask.
> I do not know, but I feel it to be so, and I am in torment.

7.49 A less than gallant address

Catullus 43

Catullus also addresses Mamurra's girl-friend, Amaena, in poem 41, where she propositions him for the price of 10,000 sesterces. Clearly the poem is yet another attack on Caesar's architect Mamurra: cf. poems 29 and 57 (doc. 12.87), and 105 (where he is called 'prick'); Wray 2001: 70–2, 172–7. Compare Catullus 86 where Quintia, who is fair, tall and upright, but without grace, is compared to the 'beautiful' Lesbia who has stolen all the graces from other women: Papanghelis 1991.

> Greetings, girl without a tiny nose
> Without a pretty foot or black eyes
> Or long fingers or a dry mouth,
> Not to mention, in truth, a tongue of minimal refinement,
> 5   Lady-friend of the bankrupt of Formiae (Mamurra).
> Are you beautiful, as the province (Cisalpine Gaul) declares?
> Is our Lesbia compared with you?
> O what a world! So stupid! So undiscriminating!

7.50 Septimius and Acme: a love idyll

Catullus 45

Septimius is not known; the name Acme suggests a Greek freedwoman. In Roman divination the left was the fortunate side (Cic. *Div.* 2.82), in Greek the right; for Roman divination, see docs 3.35–52.

> Septimius, holding his love Acme in his arms, says, 'My Acme,
> If I do not love you desperately and if I am not prepared to go on loving you
>   everlastingly all my years
> 5 As much as the most devoted of lovers ever could, may I in Libya or parched
>   India
> Encounter on my own a green-eyed lion. As he said this Love, on the left, as
>   before
> On the right, sneezed approbation. Then Acme, slightly tilting her head
> 11 And kissing the love-drunk eyes of her sweet boy with those rosy lips,
> Says, 'As I hope, my life, my dear Septimius, that we may to the end serve this
>   one master,
> 15 The passion that burns in my tender marrow is far greater and fiercer than in
>   yours.'
> As she said this, Love, as before on the left, sneezed approbation on the right.
> Now starting with a good omen they love and are loved with interchanged hearts.
> 21 Poor love-sick Septimius prefers Acme to any Syria or Britain:
> In Septimius alone his faithful Acme takes her pleasure and desires.
> Who ever saw people more blessed? Who ever saw a more auspicious love?

7.51 Disenchantment

Catullus 58

Many of Catullus' poems to Lesbia are in fact works of invective, accusing her of deceit and shameful affairs with others: cf. poems 11, 36 (where Lesbia 'my girl' wants him to stop writing invective against her), and 37; for a reconciliation see poem 107.

> Caelius, my Lesbia, well-known Lesbia,
> Lesbia whom Catullus alone loved
> More than himself and all his own,
> Now in the street-corners and alley-ways
> Performs oral sex with the descendants of high-minded Romulus.

7.52 Lesbia by another name

Cicero *In Defence of Caelius* 32–5, 47–9

Clodia, widowed in 59 when Metellus Celer died as proconsul designate of Transalpine Gaul, was, according to Cicero, one of the forces behind Calpurnius Bestia's prosecution of Marcus Caelius Rufus on a charge of attempted murder and robbery in 56; **49**: Lucius Herennius Balbus was one of the prosecutors. Caelius is presented by Cicero as having been her former lover and his approach is to show Caelius as a naïve, pleasure-loving young man and Clodia as a seductress and quasi-prostitute. Appius Claudius Caecus, her ancestor, was censor in 312, and consul in 307 and 296. Baiae was a fashionable resort and spa near Cumae. See Harlow & Laurence 2002: 71–2 on Caelius' youth.

32 And indeed I never thought I should have to engage in quarrels with women, especially with one whom all have generally considered to be a 'friend' to everyone rather than anyone's enemy. **33** But first I will ask her whether she prefers me to deal with her severely, solemnly and in an old-fashioned way, or indulgently, mildly, and politely. If in that serious traditional fashion I will have to raise up from the dead one of those bearded men of old, not with a little trimmed beard such as she takes delight in, but with one of those rough ones as seen on old statues and busts, who can rebuke the woman and speak on my behalf, so she may perhaps not be enraged with me. Let me conjure up, therefore, some member of her own family, and particularly the venerable Appius Claudius the Blind (Caecus) — for he will feel less sorrow than anyone else because he will not be able to see her. **34** If he should appear, this is certainly how he would speak and what he would say: 'Woman, what business have you with Caelius, who is a young man and unrelated to you? Why have you been so friendly with him that you lend him gold, or so hostile that you are afraid of poison? Have you not seen that your father, have you not heard that your uncle, your grandfather, your great-grandfather, your great-great-grandfather and your great-great-great-grandfather were consuls? Finally, did you not know that you were recently married to Q. Metellus, an illustrious and courageous man, totally committed to his country, who had only to set foot out of doors to surpass almost all his fellow-citizens in excellence, reputation and rank? When you had married from a house of the greatest importance into a most illustrious family, why was Caelius so closely linked with you? Was he a blood-relative? A marriage connection? A close friend of your husband? He was none of these things. What therefore could it have been except some uncontrollable passion? . . . .'

35 As for you, woman (for now it is I and not a fictional person who is addressing you), if you plan to prove the truth of what you did, said, asserted, designed and alleged, you will need to account for and explain the reason for such familiarity, such intimacy, such a close friendship. Indeed, the prosecutors are hurling at us the words debauchery, love-affairs, adultery, Baiae, beach resorts, dinner-parties, revels, singing, music, boat-trips, and at the same time tell us that all this is said with your approval. And since in some kind of mad and reckless frame of mind you have wanted all these matters to be brought into the forum and the court, you must either disprove them and demonstrate them to be untrue, or admit that neither your accusation nor your evidence is to be believed . . .

47 So, does that well-known neighbourhood not put us on the scent? Does general rumour, does Baiae itself tell us nothing? Baiae not only tells us something, it even resounds with the news that the passions of one woman are so degraded that she not only does not seek privacy and darkness and such veils for disgraceful deeds, but rejoices in her shameless activities in well-frequented gatherings and broadest daylight . . . **49** If a woman without a husband opens her house to the desires of all men and openly conducts herself like a prostitute, if she is in the habit of taking part in dinner-parties with men totally unconnected with her, if she does this in the city, in the gardens, in those crowds at Baiae, if, finally, she so behaves that not only her walk, her dress, and her companions, not only the ardour of her glances and the freedom of her speech, but even her embraces, kisses, days at the beach, sailing trips, and dinner-parties show her to be not only a prostitute but one who is wanton and shameless — if a young man should happen to consort with her, would you, Lucius Herennius, consider him an adulterer or a lover? Would you think that he wanted to storm her chastity or satisfy his passion?

7.53 Sulpicia on her lover

[Tibullus] 3.13 (4.7)

The daughter or granddaughter of Servius Sulpicius Rufus (who prosecuted Murena when defeated by him for the consulship in 62 BC and was finally consul in 51) and niece of Marcus Valerius Messalla Corvinus (cos. 31), Sulpicia belonged to the group of poets associated with Messalla. Her elaborately constructed poems, addressed to a young man whom she calls Cerinthus, have been preserved in the collection of Tibullus. While clearly exploiting conventional elegiac themes, as an educated aristocratic woman she is highly unusual in thus publicly appearing to publish poetry relating her personal emotional experience. See Santirocco 1979; Hinds 1987; Lowe 1988; esp. 203–5; Snyder 1989: 130–6; Parker 1994; Plant 2004: 106–11; Rawson 2003: 200–1; James 2003: 220. Treggiari 1991a: 107 sees Sulpicia as presenting the preliminaries to an eligible marriage in the guise of a romantic affair.

> At last love has come, of a kind which to conceal through modesty
> Would be more of a scandal than to bare it to anyone.
> Cytherea, won over by my poetic Muses,
> Has brought him and placed him in my arms.
> 5 Venus has fulfilled her promises: let those talk about my joy,
> Who, it is said, have none of their own.
> I would not choose to entrust anything to sealed tablets,
> So that no one could read it before my lover did —
> I delight in offending, and to wear a mask for scandal's sake
> 10 Bores me: let me declare that I, a worthy woman, am linked with a worthy man.

7.54 A lover's graffiti

CIL I² 2540a, c

(*ILLRP* 1125; *ROL* IV.288–90.) These graffiti were scratched in the same hand on a wall of the smaller theatre at Pompeii, c. 90–80 BC. (a) may be a quotation from a poem; (c) is unfinished; 'da veniam ut veniam' (give me leave to come) is a clever play on words.

(a) ['What's the matte]r? After your eyes have forcibly drawn me into the fire. . . .
with your copiously flowing cheeks'.
['But] tears cannot put out the flame;
[lo]ok, they burn the face and waste away the heart.'
The composition of Tiburtinus.

(c) If you know how strong love is, if you know that you are human,
take pity on me, give me leave to come.
May Venus' flower (be given) to me . . .

7.55 The folly of romantic love

Lucretius *On the Nature of the Universe* 4.1121–40, 1278–87

Lucretius (c. 94–c. 55 BC) is here condemning romantic love from the Epicurean standpoint (to Epicureans tranquillity was the greatest goal): in lines 1052–4 he allows the love object to be either a woman or 'a boy with womanish limbs', but his examples are purely heterosexual. He derides lovers for turning their mistresses' defects into charms in their imagination (1155–70), though the final lines of the book imply that habit and judicious behaviour on the part of a woman can bring about love.

1121 Add to this that they consume their strength and perish under the strain;
　　 Add to this that their time is passed at the whim of another.
　　 Meanwhile their wealth slips away and is converted into Babylonian brocades,
　　 Duties are neglected and reputation wavers and sickens.
　　 Fine perfumes and Sicyonian slippers smile on his lady's feet;
　　 Yes, huge emeralds flashing with green light
　　 Are clasped in gold, and sea-coloured garments are worn away
　　 With constant use in which they absorb Venus' perspiration;
　　 The hard-won wealth of his father's turns into head-bands and turbans,
1130 Or perhaps into a robe and garments from Alinda and Ceos.
　　 Banquets with magnificent trappings and food, entertainments,
　　 Wine in abundance, perfumes, garlands, wreaths of flowers are got ready —
　　 In vain, since from the middle of the fountain of delights
　　 Rises a taste of bitterness that causes torment amongst the very flowers,
　　 Either when a guilty conscience happens to sting the lover with the thought
　　 That youth is being spent in sloth and perishing in debauchery,
　　 Or perhaps she has let fly and left rankling a word of doubtful import,
　　 Which fixes in his passionate heart and glows there like fire,
　　 Or because he thinks that she is making eyes and gazing at another man,
1140 While he sees the traces of mockery in her face.

1278 Nor is it due to divine intervention or the arrows of Venus
　　 When a woman deficient in beauty happens to be beloved;
　　 For the woman herself sometimes manages by her own conduct,
　　 By her compliant manners and by keeping herself fresh and neat,
　　 To make it easy for a man to get used to spending his life with her.
　　 Furthermore, it is habit that produces love;
　　 For whatever is struck by frequent blows, however light,
1285 Yields in the long run and gives way.
　　 Do you not see that even drops of water falling on a stone
　　 In the long run wear the stone through?

7.56 The idealisation of noble women

Lucilius *Satires* 17.1.567–73

(*ROL* III.178.) The satirist Gaius Lucilius served with Scipio Aemilianus at Numantia (doc. 5.50); his sister was grandmother of Pompey the Great. Here he parodies epic stereotypes of characterisation; Alcmena was the wife of Amphitryon, prince of Tiryns and leader of the Thebans; Zeus was enamoured of her and she gave birth to twins, Heracles (Hercules) to Zeus and Iphicles to Amphitryon: Homer *Iliad* 14.323–4; *Odyssey* 11.266–8. Helen of Troy was, of course, a whore or adulteress because she ran away with Paris, abandoning husband and daughter.

> Surely you don't believe that any 'lovely-locked', 'lovely-ankled' girl
> Can't possibly have her breasts touching her stomach and navel,
> Or that Amphitryon's wife Alcmena couldn't have been knock-kneed or bow-legged,
> And that others, even Helen herself could not have been — I can't say it;
> See to it yourself and choose any two-syllable word you like —
> That a daughter of a noble sire could not have had some distinguishing mark,
> A wart, mole, mark, one slightly projecting tooth?

HOMOSEXUALITY

It was normal for adult male Romans to penetrate both women and young boys: Cato the Elder fulminates on the prices of young boys after the Third Macedonian War (docs 5.54–5) and Catullus writes love poems interchangeably to women and boys (see poems 24, 48, 81, 99: to Juventius (doc. 7.61); 55: to Camerius; cf. 15, 21) as well as pitying a hypothetical young slave boy, abandoned on his master's marriage (Cat. 61.121–41); several of Plautus' plays, esp. the *Casina*, present a homosexual relationship between master and slave (Lilja 1982); Q. Lutatius Catulus (cos. 102) addressed a poem to a certain Theotimus: Gell. 19.9.10–4. Sulla's relationship with the female impersonator Metrobius (docs 11.1, 32) is unusual primarily in that it continued throughout Metrobius' career, not only while he was a youth. However, there was great shame attached to passive homosexuality (passive objects should be young slaves or male prostitutes) and Cicero uses such accusations to tarnish the reputations of Catiline (doc. 2.18) and Clodius (*Har. Resp.* 42).

Gell. 9.12.7 states that Cato the Elder aligned male prostitutes with slaves, in that both could be beaten, unlike other free citizens: to allow oneself to be sexually penetrated was to put yourself into the position of a slave. It was a grave criminal offence to attempt to seduce a free-born youth: Plut. *Marcell.* 2.3–4, Val. Max. 6.1.7. The lex Poetelia in 326 was said to have resulted from a freeborn youth's attempted seduction by his father's creditor: doc. 1.52. Valerius Valentinus lost his case against Gaius Cosconius when a poem of his about the seduction of an underage boy and a free girl (presumably a literary *morceau* or joke) was read out in court (Val. Max. 8.1 abs. 8); see also docs 5.60–1.

Homosexuality was particularly outlawed in the army: Marius honoured the soldier who killed an officer who attempted to seduce him: doc. 7.59; Cicero (*Mil.* 4.9) also records the tale of a young man who killed a military tribune for propositioning him. See Williams 1999; Eyben 1993: 241–6; McMullen 1982, 1991; Richlin 1993; Parker 1997; for expressions of love for boys, see Richlin 1992a: 34–44; on the 'cinaedus', or pathic (originally a male dancer), see Richlin 1993; Parker 1997; docs 7.57, 8.20.

7.57 Scipio Aemilianus' views on P. Sulpicius Gallus

Aulus Gellius *Attic Nights* 6.12.1–7

(*ORF*⁴ I, Scipio Aemilianus F17; Courtney *ALP* 119–20.) This speech was delivered against P. Sulpicius Gallus when Scipio was censor in 142, as part of his *recognitio equitum*, the yearly review of the equites. He employs stereotypical insults, commenting on Gallus' depilation, use of mirrors, tunics with sleeves, perfumes, and plucking of eyebrows; see Fantham 1991: 288; Richlin 1992: 96, 1993: 556–7; Williams 1999: 23; for increasing dandyism among the young, see Eyben 1993: 98–102. Cicero portrays the worst category of Catiline's supporters (*Cat.* 2.22) as glistening with carefully arranged hair, either without beards, or with long ones, and cloaked in sails not togas, while he attacks Clodius for wearing a tunic with sleeves to the wrist (*In Clodium et Curionem* 22). Traditional Romans wore a toga without a tunic, or with a sleeveless tunic; Cato the Elder wore a sleeveless tunic in winter (Plut. *Cato Mai.* 3.2); on Cato the Younger's old-fashioned practice of wearing a toga without tunic or shoes, even as praetor, see Plut. *Cato Min.* 6, 44, 50; cf. doc. 2.36. Caesar was unusual in wearing a tunic with fringed wrist-length sleeves: doc. 13.56.

1 For a man to wear tunics coming below the elbow, right up to the wrist and nearly to the fingers, was considered inappropriate in Rome and all Latium. **2** Our countrymen called these tunics by the Greek name 'chiriotae' (long-sleeved) and considered that a long and flowing robe was suitable only for women, in that it protected their arms and legs from sight. **3** Roman men, however, at first wore just the toga without tunics; later on, they had tight, short tunics ending at the shoulder, which the Greeks call 'exomides' (sleeveless). **4** Accustomed to this traditional practice, Publius Africanus, son of Paullus, a man endowed with all great arts and every excellence, rebuked Publius Sulpicius Gallus, a man addicted to luxury, with the accusation that, among many other things, he wore tunics which completely covered his hands. **5** These are Scipio's words: 'For one who daily perfumes himself and dresses in front of a mirror, whose eyebrows are plucked, who walks around with his beard pulled out and smooth thighs, who, though a young man, has reclined on the inner side of a couch in a long-sleeved tunic with a lover, who is not only a wine-lover but a man-lover too, does anyone doubt that he acts as pathics generally act?'

7.58 A shameful relationship

Plutarch *Life of Cato the Elder* 17.1–5

Titus Quinctius Flamininus conquered Philip at Cynoscephalae in 198 BC (cf. doc. 5.23); his brother Lucius was praetor urbanus in 199 and Titus' legate in charge of the navy (198–194); Lucius became consul in 192, but was expelled from the senate during the censorship of Cato the Elder and Valerius Flaccus in 184 for the incident described below. Livy 39.42.8 calls the boy Philippus, a Carthaginian male prostitute whom Lucius, when consul, had taken to Liguria with him; he also cites Valerius Antias (39.43.1) for another version in which the butchery took place at Placentia to please a woman of local notoriety of whom Lucius was enamoured, a tradition followed by Val. Max. 2.9.3; cf. Cic. *Sen.* 42; Plut. *Flam.* 18; for this episode, see Fantham 1991: 287–8, who suggests that the young Carthaginian boy had been enslaved at Carthage's defeat in 202 and subsequently gone freelance; McGinn 1998: 43; Williams 1999: 44–6. The outrage is inspired not by the prostitute's sex but by the inapposite use of *imperium* at a banquet while under the influence of alcohol.

1 Cato named Lucius Valerius Flaccus, his colleague and friend, princeps senatus, and expelled many others from the senate, including Lucius Quinctius, who had been consul seven years earlier, and, what contributed more to his reputation than his consulship, was brother of the Titus Flamininus, who defeated Philip. **2** The reason for his expulsion was as follows: Lucius kept a youth who, ever since his boyhood, had been Lucius' favourite, keeping him with him and taking him on campaigns with greater honour and influence than any of Lucius' closest friends and relatives. **3** While he was administering his consular province, at a certain banquet the lad, as was his custom, reclined beside him and started flattering a man who was easily led when under the influence of wine, saying he loved him so much that 'when there was a gladiatorial show back at Rome, something I had never seen, I rushed away to join you, though I really desired to see a man killed'. **4** Lucius responded affectionately, 'Well, don't lie there distressed with me over that, for I can put that right'. And after ordering that one of the men sentenced to death be brought to the banquet and that a lictor with an axe stand beside him, he asked his beloved again if he wanted to see the man struck dead. When he said he did, Lucius ordered the man's head to be cut off.

5 This is the version which most writers narrate, and so Cicero has represented Cato himself as recounting in his dialogue *On Old Age*. But Livy says the man killed was a Gallic deserter, and that Lucius did not have the man slain by a lictor, but did it with his own hand, and that this is the version in a speech of Cato's.

7.59 Marius' nephew killed for seduction

Plutarch *Life of Marius* 14.4–8

Val. Max. 6.1.12; Cic. *Mil.* 9. Marius, during his campaign against the Cimbri, excused the homicide of his own nephew by a soldier whom he had propositioned; freeborn youths were closely protected against homosexual seduction or rape, while homosexual relationships were strictly forbidden in the army, offenders being clubbed to death (the *fustuarium*): Polyb. 6.37.9; cf. Val. Max. 6.1.10–11; docs 5.19–20.

4 Gaius Luscius, Marius' nephew, had been assigned an army command under him, and, while in all other respects he was a man of good repute, he had a weakness for good-looking boys. **5** He was attracted by one of the young men who served under him, called Trebonius, and had often unsuccessfully attempted to seduce him; at length he sent a servant at night to summon Trebonius. **6** The youth being unable to disobey a summons went, but when he was conducted into the tent and found himself the object of Luscius' violence he drew his sword and killed him. **7** This took place in Marius' absence, but on his return he brought Trebonius to trial. **8** As there were many accusers, but no one speaking in his defence, Trebonius boldly took the stand and recounted what had happened, bringing witnesses to show that he had frequently refused Luscius' solicitations and that he had never prostituted his body to anyone, despite offers of expensive gifts. Marius in admiration and delight ordered the traditional crown for bravery to be brought and himself crowned Trebonius with it, declaring that in a time that was in need of noble examples he had performed the noblest deed of all.

7.60 Caesar and Nicomedes

Suetonius *Life of the Deified Julius* 49.1–2, 4

Caesar, while serving as a young man in Asia, was sent to Nicomedes IV of Bithynia in 81 to acquire ships for the siege of Mitylene: his success was rumoured to have been gained through a homosexual relationship with the elderly king. Dio comments (43.20.4) that Caesar welcomed all his soldiers' jokes except for these allusions to Nicomedes; cf. Suet. *Jul.* 22.2; Catullus 57; cf. 29, 54, 93; Richlin 1992a: 96; Williams 1999: 165. The charges of passive homosexuality were damaging to Caesar in a way that rumours of his affairs with married women could never be: see doc. 7.45. The orator and poet Gaius Licinius Calvus was a close friend of Catullus: doc. 7.34.

1 The only charge that damaged his reputation for virtue was that of his intimacy with Nicomedes, which was, however, a serious and continuous stain on his character exposing him to general censure. I say nothing of the notorious verses of Licinius Calvus:

'Whatever Bithynia had
and Caesar's sodomiser'.

I also pass over the attacks of Dolabella and the elder Curio, in which Dolabella calls him 'the queen's rival, inner partner of the royal bed', and Curio 'Nicomedes' brothel and Bithynian bagnio'. **2** I ignore the edicts of Bibulus in which he published his colleague as 'queen of Bithynia, who previously desired a king, and now a kingdom' ... **4** Finally, at Caesar's Gallic triumph his soldiers, amongst other songs, such as are usually sung in jest as they follow the chariot, declaimed this one which became notorious:

'Caesar mastered Gaul, and Nicomedes Caesar:
look, Caesar now celebrates his triumph, who mastered Gaul,
but Nicomedes celebrates no triumph, though he mastered Caesar.'

7.61 To Juventius

Catullus 99

Compare poems 24, 48, 81 written to young boys, esp. poem 48 (to Juventius), with 7 (to Lesbia: doc. 7.47).

    I stole a sweet kiss while you played, honey-sweet Juventius,
    One sweeter than sweet ambrosia.
    But I did not take it unpunished — for more than an hour,
    I remember, I hung at the top of the gallows
5   While I justified myself to you, though with all my tears
    I couldn't lessen your anger the tiniest bit;
    No sooner was it done than, your lips rinsed,
    With plenty of water, you wiped it away with all your fingers
    So no contagion from my lips might remain,
10   As though it were the foul spit of a polluted whore.
    Worse, you handed me in my misery over to vengeful love

And have not failed to torment me in every way,
So that that sweet kiss was now changed for me from ambrosia
And became more bitter than bitter hellebore.
15   Since you lay down such punishments for my unhappy love,
I'll never after this steal any kisses again.

PROSTITUTES

There was no stigma attached to frequenting prostitutes of either sex; indeed, visiting a prostitute could be seen to divert males' sexual drives away from citizen women (Val. Max. 7.3.10). In Plautus' *Curculio*, the slave Palinurus tells his young master: no one stops a man from using the public street, as long as he doesn't make his way through enclosed property — so, as long as you steer clear of wives, widows, virgins, and free-born young men and boys, make love to anyone you like (*Curc.* 32–7). They could be visited by people of any rank: Gell. 4.14.1–6 (citing Ateius Capito) records that in 151 BC the curule aedile Aulus Hostilius Mancinus (*MRR* I.455) brought a suit against a prostitute called Manilia, because he was driven away from her apartment at night by stones; her defence was that he was drunk and that she was protecting herself; she appealed to the tribunes who forbade the case to be put to the people because of Mancinus' inappropriate behaviour.

Women prostitutes were supposed to wear a coloured (masculine) toga to distinguish them from respectable citizen women who wore the stola, but often wore more spectacular clothing; on togate prostitutes: Stone 1994: 13 with n. 7; Sebesta 1994: 50; McGinn 1998: 156–71.

Prostitutes could be independent, paying rent for a room; or an employee of a brothel or tavern; or of course a slave. More reputable girls would live with their mother or a procuress, or set up their own establishment. Prostitutes had to be registered with the aediles. Charges for sexual services at Pompeii ranged between 2 and 20 or more asses, presumably depending on the services rendered; according to Lucilius charges could be miniscule (doc. 7.62). While prostitutes were generally slaves or freedpersons, prostitution must often have been the only resort of poverty-stricken free women, especially in times of crisis: Evans 1991: 137–42. Higher-class professionals, however, could become wealthy: Sulla's initial wealth was said to have derived from a bequest by a prostitute: doc. 11.1.

Like actors and gladiators, male and female prostitutes were viewed as 'untouchable'; all of these were debarred from public life and could not stand for office. They could also be ill-treated with impunity: Cicero, in his defence of a client for raping an actress in a country-town (actresses were generally considered synonymous with prostitutes), states that the defendant had 'acted in accordance with a well-established tradition at stage shows' (*Planc.* 30).

A number of republican actresses are known by name; Antiodemis (*Anth. Pal.* 9.567: second century BC); Arbuscula (Cic. *Att.* 4.15.6); Bacchis (*Att.* 15.17.3); Dionysia (Cic. *Rosc. Am.* 23); Emphasis (*CIL* I² 1359); Eucharis (*CIL* I² 1214); Galeria Coppiola, Sammula and Lucceia (Pliny *Nat. Hist.* 7.158–9); Tertia (*Verr.* 2.3.78); Volumnia Cytheris (Cic. *Att.* 10.10.5, 10.16.5, 15.22, *Phil.* 2.58–62, 69). Eucharis and Volumnia Cytheris were freedwomen; Tertia, one of Verres' mistresses, was a free-born Sicilian actress, daughter of Isidorus the ballet-dancer, whom Verres 'married' to one of his own minions; the status of the rest of these is unknown, but they may well have been slaves; Garton 1964; 1972: 231–83; Evans 1991: 131–3, 216–17.

Prostitutes could be publicly shown off as acquisitions: Volumnia Cytheris, mistress of Mark Anthony, was present at a dinner party: *Att.* 9.26. In extreme situations they could achieve public recognition: Hispala Fecenia, a prostitute and freed slave, was responsible for the exposure of the Bacchanalia in 186 and granted the right to marry a free person: doc. 7.63; McGinn 1998: 87–90; Hillard 1993: 45; for prostitution: Balsdon 1974: 224–34; Gardner 1986: 132–4; Edwards 1997; Dixon 2001: 115–16; for prostitutes' participation in the Floralia and other cult activities: McGinn 1998: 24–6; doc. 7.79; on their civic disabilities: McGinn 21–69; on terminology for prostitutes: Adams 1983.

7.62 An old professional

Lucilius *Satires* 9.1.359–60

(*ROL* III.112.) Book 9 of Lucilius' satires was probably written towards the end of his life; he died c. 102. In 26.640–1 (a satire perhaps on the troubles of married life or a love affair) Lucilius speaks of some woman 'who hopes that she will de-goblet, de-silver, de-shawl, and de-mirror me of an ivory mirror'.

> If she's nothing to look at and if she was once a prostitute and whore,
> A cent (an *as*) is all it takes and she's yours.

7.63 Hispala Faecenia

Livy *History of Rome* 39.9.5–7

For the Bacchanalia, see doc. 3.63. As a woman *sui iuris* after the death of her patron, Hispala needed a tutor to perform any legal act, such as making a will: doc. 7.5. It appears, since Hispala maintained Aebutius, who was of equestrian rank, that she continued as a prostitute even after meeting him. After suppression of the rites, as a reward for their information, the senate passed a decree that both Hispala and Aebutius should be given 100,000 asses out of the treasury, Aebutius should be exempt from military service, and Hispala given the right to give and alienate property, marry outside her gens, chose her own tutor, and marry a man of free birth (Livy 39.19.3–6). The passage clearly implies that marriage of a freeborn person with a prostitute was otherwise banned: see Smethurst 1950: 81–2; Balsdon 1974: 37–43; cf. McGinn 1998: 91–94.

5 There was a noted prostitute, a freedwoman called Hispala Faecenia, not worthy of the profession to which she had grown accustomed while just a slave, who made her living in the same way even after she had been manumitted. **6** She had commenced a sexual relationship with Aebutius, a young man in the neighbourhood, which was in no way damaging to his property or reputation: this was because she had loved him and sought him out of her own accord, and, since his family made quite insufficient provision for him, he was supported through the generosity of the prostitute. **7** Even more, matters actually reached the point that, under the influence of their relationship, when she found herself in manu to no one after her patron's death, she applied to the tribunes and praetor for a guardian and made her will, naming Aebutius as her sole heir.

7.64 A powerful courtesan in Rome

Plutarch *Life of Lucullus* 6.2–5

L Licinius Lucullus was Sulla's lieutenant; P. Cornelius Cethegus was a popular politician powerful during the 70s: Cic. *Brut.* 178. Lucullus, cos. 74, wanted the province of Cilicia in order to conduct the war against Mithridates: docs 11.10–11, 12.10. Another manipulative concubine was Chelidon ('swallow'), mistress of Verres while he was praetor urbanus in 74 (Cic. *Verr.* 2.1.104, 120, 136–40, 2.24, 2.39, 2.116, 3.78, 5.34, 38).

2 A certain woman, called Praecia, one of those renowned for beauty and wantonness was at that time in Rome, who in other respects was in no way better than a courtesan, but who used her associates and companions to further the ambitions of her friends, thus adding to her other attractions the reputation of being a good and effective friend, and acquiring the greatest influence. **3** And when she won over Cethegus too, who was then at the peak of his reputation and in control of the city, and gained him as her lover, political power passed totally into her hands; no public measure was passed unless Cethegus approved it, and he did nothing except at Praecia's bidding. **4** So Lucullus won her over by presents and flattery — it was no doubt a great prize for a woman so arrogant and ostentatious to be seen sharing Lucullus' ambitions — and he immediately had Cethegus praising him and soliciting Cilicia for him. **5** But, once he had obtained this, he no longer needed to appeal to the assistance of Praecia or Cethegus, but everyone was unanimous in entrusting him with the Mithridatic war, on the grounds that no one else was better qualified to bring it to an end.

7.65 The longevity of women — and actresses

Pliny *Natural History* 7.158

Pliny (7.156–7) notes that Marcus Perperna lived to 98 years of age and Gorgias to 108, while Marcus Valerius Corvus (reputedly cos. 348, 346, 343, 335, 300, 299) made 100 years. Sixty year olds were no longer able to vote and were freed from public duties, but retained legal control over their familia; on respect for old age: Val. Max. 2.1.9. On life expectancies, see Parkin 1992: 92–106; on the elderly in antiquity, Finley 1981; Harlow & Laurence 2002: 117–31.

Among women, Livia, wife of Rutilius lived more than 97 years, Statilia, a lady of noble family under the emperor Claudius 99, Terentia, wife of Cicero 103, Clodia, wife of Ofilius, 115, and she also bore 15 children. The mime Lucceia gave a recitation on the stage at the age of 100. Galeria Coppiola, the actress of interludes, was brought back to the stage in the consulship of Gaius Poppaeus and Quintus Sulpicius (AD 9) at the votive games given for the recovery of the god Augustus in her 104th year; she had been brought out at her first appearance by Marcus Pomponius, aedile of the plebs, in the consulship of Gaius Marius and Gnaeus Carbo 91 years before (82 BC), and as an old woman was brought back to the stage as a curiosity by Pompey the Great at the dedication of his great theatre.

WOMEN AS OWNERS AND CONSUMERS

Terentia owned woodland and leased public land (*Att.* 2.45, 2.15.4); in fact one of Cicero's criticisms leading to their divorce was that she failed to keep her property intact as he requested: *Fam.* 14.1.5; Dixon 2001: 89–112; Verboven 2001; cf. doc. 7.40. Sassia of Larinum put her freedman doctor into business with a loan of capital: Cic. *Cluent.* 178 (cf. doc. 6.39). Servilia, Caesar's lover and Brutus' mother, profited from the sale of Pompeians' confiscated estates; *Att.* 14.21.3 (see doc. 7.45). At the other end of the social scale, Cicero (*Rosc. Am.* 23) states that the female dancer Dionysia could earn 200,000 sesterces; cf. Gell. 1.5.3 where she is known as a notorious dancing-girl.

Women sometimes adopted a public profile; Val. Max. 8.3.2 records that Gaia Afrania, wife of the senator Licinius Bucco who died in 48, often represented herself in court and became a notable example of the yapping woman, while Hortensia, daughter of the great orator Hortensius, spoke publicly in 42 BC in favour of removing the taxes on the womenfolk of the proscribed (App. *BC* 4.32). Women could testify in court: Julius Caesar's sister Julia and mother appeared in court to give witness regarding Pompeia's adultery with Clodius (Suet. *Jul.* 74.2; cf. doc. 7.85); Clodia appeared as a witness against Caelius (doc. 7.52). They also had more informal ways of networking: Dixon 1983 discusses the ways in which aristocratic women could exert political and social influence through patronage favours and marriage networks (questioned by Hillard 1993). When Roscius, for example, was proscribed he fled to Rome to the house of Caecilia, daughter of Metellus Baliaricus (cos. 123), who found Cicero to defend him: *Rosc. Am.* 27, 147, 149; doc. 2.51.

Not all noble women had an affluent life: one of Lucius Aemilius Paullus' daughters (let us hope not Tertia: doc. 3.40) married into surprisingly poverty-stricken conditions — into the household of the Aelii Tuberones, 16 of them living in one small house and living off one small farm, all together with their wives and children: Plut. *Aem.* 5.4–5, cf. Val. Max. 4.4.8–9. A noble girl's expectations of married life might well have made it difficult for her to cope with so many in-laws in such cramped conditions; doubtless she appreciated Aemilia's ornaments (doc. 7.70).

Livy's account of the speech of the chief centurion Spurius Ligustinus in 173 (Livy 42.34; doc. 5.9) tells us that Spurius was on campaign on an annual basis for 22 years, while he and his wife had eight children and worked a small farm-holding; for rural women, see Scheidel 1995, 1996; Treggiari 1976 (for the occupations of slave women in domestic service); cf. Rawson 2003: 206–7.

Upper-class women possessed jewellery and money in their own right even in the early Republic: when Rome was threatened by the Gauls in 390, the women of the city, according to Livy, offered to make up the ransom sum: they were therefore granted the right to be honoured by eulogies at their funeral: Livy 5.50. In 215, taxes were imposed on wealthy widows to provide for military pay while the lex Oppia restricted their ornaments and forbade them to ride in carriages: Livy 34.3–5. In 207, to expiate unfavourable omens and a lightning-strike on the temple of Juno on the Aventine, the augurs declared that married women had to make an offering to placate the goddess; all those resident within the tenth milestone were summoned by the aediles and 25 were chosen to receive contributions from the women's dowries, presumably golden ornaments, from which they made a golden bowl as an offering: Livy 27.37.7–10; doc. 7.83.

Livy (34.7.8) quotes Valerius speaking in favour of the repeal of the lex Oppia: 'women cannot claim magistracies, priesthoods, triumphs, military decorations, awards or the spoils of war. Cosmetics and adornments are women's decorations. They delight in these and boast of them and this is what our ancestors called the women's sphere'; see Wyke 1994 on the rhetoric of adornment in sustaining a gender hierarchy; for women as symbols of decadence: Wyke 1994; Dixon 2001: 56–65; cf. Bauman 1992: 31–4.

7.66 A toilet casket

ILS 8562

(*CIL* I² 561; *ILLRP* 1197; *ROL* IV.198.) A large bronze casket (the Ficoroni cista) with an inscribed lid, found in a tomb at Praeneste (Palestrina), dated to the late fourth century BC, c. 315; Fantham 1994: 223 (with fig. 7.4) notes that this is unmistakable evidence that Roman women in the fourth century BC possessed and could commission precious and sophisticated works. Its lid carries statues of Dionysus and two satyrs and its athletic scenes are taken from the *Argonautica* of Apollonius Rhodius. Under one of the legs the name Macolnia is also inscribed: Starr 1980: 312; Dohrn 1972; Cornell 1995: 390 with fig. 30.

Dindia Macolnia gave this to her daughter.
Novius Plautius made me at Rome.

7.67 Women lobby for luxury goods

Livy *History of Rome* 34.2.8–3.1

Following the battle of Cannae, the Oppian law, proposed by the tribune Gaius Oppius in 215, restricted women's use of luxury items such as jewellery and expensive clothing: they were forbidden to have, or perhaps wear, more than one semiuncia (half-ounce) of gold, wear a garment of different colours (presumably purple is especially indicated), or ride in a carriage within one mile of Rome, except for religious purposes; Livy 34.1–8; cf. Val. Max. 9.1.3; Gell. 10.23, 17.6; Tac. *Ann.* 3.33–4; *MRR* I.255. In 195, two tribunes, Marcus Fundanius and Lucius Valerius, proposed to repeal this law and, at the news that this repeal might be vetoed, women turned out in force, in the streets and forum, to persuade the men to vote for its repeal. Cato the Elder is here portrayed as showing his disapproval of he women's conduct; as censor in 184 he taxed luxuries including women's clothes, jewellery and vehicles: Livy 39.44.1–3; Plut. *Cato Mai.* 18.2. While Livy presents the law as one of those designed to appropriate private funds for public use, this does not appear to have been the case: later, in 210, senators surrendered their valuable metals, keeping an uncia of gold for each wife and daughter, while in 207 women collected contributions to present a golden bowl to Juno: Livy 26.35.5–8, 27.37.8 (doc. 7.83). With women's increased role in religious activities in Rome during the Second Punic War, greater display in women's rites may have become customary (as in Aemilia's ritual vessels and carriages: doc. 7.70) and the law was intended to curb this in a time of national emergency: Culham 1982 for the law as a sumptuary one, not a confiscatory measure inspired by the war; cf. Treggiari 1991: 212–14; Evans 1991: 52–3; Wyke 1994: 139–40.

2.8 'Indeed, it was not without some embarrassment that I made my way a short time ago to the forum through a throng of women. If respect for the dignity and modesty of them as individuals had not held me back, so they should not be seen to be rebuked by a consul, I would have said: **9** "What kind of behaviour is this, running around in public and blocking the streets and talking to other women's husbands? Could not each of you have asked your own husband the same thing at home? **10** Are you more persuasive in public than in private, and with other women's husbands rather than with your own? And yet, even at home, if modesty kept matrons within their proper limits, it's not your place to concern yourselves about what laws should be passed or repealed here."

11 'Our ancestors allowed no woman to transact business, even private business, without a guardian in control, and wanted them to be under the control of their fathers, brothers and husbands. We, in heaven's name!, now allow them to get involved in politics and to mingle with us in the forum and to attend formal and informal assemblies (*comitia* and *contiones*) . . . **14** What they want is complete freedom — or, to speak the truth, total licence! **3.1** And if they win in this, what will they not attempt?'

7.68 The extravagances of early second-century Roman women

Plautus *Pot of Gold* 505–22

Megadorus (a bachelor) is here speaking to his potential father-in-law Euclio, imagining the extravagances that a rich wife demands as a normal part of her lifestyle. Compare doc. 7.55 for women's extravagant tastes; for wives in Plautus, see Rei 1998.

505 Wherever you go nowadays, you see more wagons in front of city homes
     than you do in the country when you go to a farm.

But even this is a fine sight compared to when they come round for their money.
There stands the fuller, the dyer, the goldsmith, the wool weaver;
Salesmen of flounces, lady's underwear,
510 Veils, in purple dye, in yellow dye,
Muffs, balsam-scented shoes,
Retailers of linen, shoemakers,
Squatting cobblers, slipper-makers,
Sandal-makers, mallow-dyers,
515 Dealers in breast-bands, and corset-makers alongside them.
Now, you may think you've paid them all off: along with more demands come
Three hundred more, who stand like doorguards in your atrium —
weavers, fringe-makers, casket-makers.
520 You bring them in and pay them off. Now, you think, I've paid them all,
When in come saffron-dyers
And all sorts of other pests who are always demanding something.

7.69 The lex Voconia

Cicero *Republic* 3.17

Cf. Gell. 17.6.1 (for Cato's support for the law); Cic. *Verr*. 2.1.43, 110. The Voconian law in 169, proposed by the tribune Voconius Saxa, limited women's rights of inheritance, preventing men in the highest property class from making a daughter their heir or from leaving her more than half their fortune: in other words, no woman could be left more than half an estate by someone in the first census class. Cicero's *Republic* is set as a dialogue between Scipio Aemilianus, Laelius, and some of their friends in c. 129; it was actually written 54–51 (Atticus read it in 51: Cic. *Att*. 5.12.2). The daughter of the wealthy Publius Crassus Mucianus Dives, Licinia, was married to Gaius Gracchus; Crassus Mucianus presumably died intestate and therefore his daughter could inherit as an only child (cf. docs 5.44, 8.33). When there were sons there was a tendency to institute them as heirs and give the women a legacy. It was however possible to leave the estate to a male person with a trust to convey it to the deceased's daughter: Cic. *Fin*. 2.17.55; Crook 1967: 122; see Pomeroy 1975: 162–3; Hallett 1984: 93–6; Gardner 1986: 170–8; Dixon 1985; Crook 1986: 66–7, 71–2; Ruggini 1989: 607–8, for the law and the ways it was evaded.

But if I wished to describe the conceptions of justice, and the principles, customs and habits which have existed, I could show you not merely differences in all the different nations, but that there have been a thousand changes in a single city, even in our own in regard to these matters. For example, our friend Manilius here, being an interpreter of the law, would give you different advice about the rights of women in regard to legacies and inheritances from that which he used to give in his youth before the passing of the Voconian law. In fact that law, passed for men's advantage, is full of injustice to women. For why should a woman not have money of her own? Why may a Vestal Virgin have an heir, while her mother may not? Why on the other hand, if it was necessary to limit the amount of property a woman could own, should the daughter of Publius Crassus, if she were her father's only child, be permitted by law to have a hundred million sesterces, while mine is not even allowed three million?

7.70 Noblewomen and their cultic paraphernalia

Polybius *Histories* 31.26.1–8, 27.1–6

Clearly older women were allowed not only to appear in public at religious festivals but to use these occasions to display their wealth, and thus their husband's affluence and status. Aemilia was the wife of Scipio Africanus and grandmother by adoption of Publius Scipio Aemilianus, Polybius' friend; as sister of his natural father, Lucius Aemilius Paullus, she was also Aemilianus' aunt; she died in 162. The elder Scipio had died in 183, apparently leaving in his will his wife and sons as heirs. His daughters did not inherit equally with their mother and brothers but took 50 talents each into their marriages. The 25 talents paid to the daughters at his death is described as the second instalment of their dowry (perhaps Scipio had laid down that the remainder of the dowry be paid at Aemilia's death, with Aemilia having the use of it during her lifetime). Dowries were generally paid in three instalments over a period of three years: see Astin 1967: 36; Pomeroy 1975: 222–4; Hallett 1984: 44–6; Dixon 1985a: esp. 150–56; Gardner 1986: 100–1; Crook 1986: 70–1; for this passage, Walbank III.503–5.

Aemilia appears to have left as much money at her death (seven years after the lex Voconia) as her brother Aemilius Paullus two years later (Polyb. 31.26–7, cf. 18.35, 31.22, 28; Val. Max. 6.7.1). Paullus left some 60 talents to his two (adopted out) sons, but they had to pay back out of this his second wife's dowry of 25 talents and (according to Polybius) had to sell off property to pay the debt after funding his funeral games.

Papiria had been living in relative poverty since her divorce: when asked by his friends why he had divorced his virtuous, rich and lovely wife, Paullus is said to have touched his shoe and replied that it was new and beautiful but only he knew where it pinched (Plut. *Mor.* 141a). When Papiria died, Scipio transferred the ceremonial ornaments not to Aemilia's two daughters (the Corneliae) but to his own two sisters (the Aemiliae: wives of Q. Aelius Tubero and M. Porcius Cato, son of Cato the Elder): Polyb. 31.28.8–9. His giving property belonging to Aemilia, Cornelia's mother, to his own mother and sisters may well have caused tensions with Cornelia (mother of the Gracchi and his mother-in-law).

26.1 The first occasion (on which Scipio Aemilianus displayed generosity in money matters) was when the mother of his adoptive father died, the sister of his own father Lucius (Aemilius), and wife of his grandfather by adoption, the great Scipio. **2** He inherited from her a large fortune and his handling of it was to give the first proof of his principles. **3** For the lady, whose name was Aemilia, used to display immense magnificence whenever she left her house to take part in women's ceremonies, having shared the life and fortune of Scipio (Africanus) at the height of his success; **4** apart from her own attire and the decorations of her carriage, all the baskets, cups and other sacrificial vessels were made of silver or gold, and were carried in her train in such illustrious processions, **5** while her retinue of maids and menservants was proportionately large. **6** Immediately after Aemilia's funeral, he gave all this equipment to his mother (Papiria), who had been separated from Lucius for many years, and whose means were insufficient to maintain an appearance suitable for her birth. **7** Before this she had stayed away from these solemn processions, but now, when an important public sacrifice took place, she drove out in Aemilia's splendid equipage and when, in addition, the muleteers and pair and carriage were the same, **8** the women who saw it were astonished at Scipio's kindness and generosity and lifted up their hands praying for every blessing on him . . . **27.1** After this he had to pay the daughters of the great Scipio, the sisters of his adoptive father (the Corneliae), the second half of their dowries. **2** Their father had agreed to give each of the daughters 50 talents, **3** and their mother had given half of this to their husbands immediately on their marriage, but left the other half owing when she died. **4** As a result Scipio had to pay this debt to his father's sisters. **5** By Roman law the part of the dowry still owing had to be paid within three years, with personal property being handed over within ten months according to Roman custom, **6** but Scipio straightaway instructed his banker to pay each of them in ten months the whole 25 talents.

7.71 An expensive lampstand

Pliny *Natural History* 34.11–12

In his discussion of bronzeware, Pliny discourses on the construction and cost of Corinthian lampstands, which could clearly cost immense sums in the Republic. The funerary inscription of the lucky slave hunchback below (Clesippus Geganius), which dates to the first half of the first century BC, is given in *ILS* 1924 (*CIL* I² 1004).

At the sale of such a lampstand, on the instructions of Theon the auctioneer, a fuller named Clesippus, a hunchback of hideous appearance, was thrown in. It was bought by Gegania for 50,000 sesterces. She threw a party to display her purchases, and for the entertainment of her guests she had the man appear with no clothes on; struck with outrageous passion for him, she admitted him to her bed, and later made him her heir. He thus became extremely rich and worshipped the lampstand as a divinity — thus attaching this story to Corinthian lampstands generally — though his character was vindicated by his erecting a noble tomb to perpetuate the memory of Gegania's shame throughout the world.

7.72 A business-like woman

ILS 3423

(*CIL* I² 981; *ILLRP* 126; *ROL* IV.90.) This inscription on a stone tablet was found at Rome, dated to before 80 BC.

Publicia, daughter of Lucius, wife of Gnaeus Cornelius son of Aulus, built a temple and folding-doors for Hercules and had it adorned, and restored an altar sacred to Hercules. She superintended the performance of all these works out of her own and her husband's estate.

7.73 Forewomen of Minturnae

CIL I² 2685

(*ILLRP* 737; *ROL* IV.110.) In the early first century BC 'forepersons' of religious colleges at Minturnae, to the north-west of the ager Campanus, dedicated 29 slabs to serve as altars (destroyed by fire, c. 50 BC). A number of these were dedicated by women forepersons (magistrae); there were colleges of men and women but none were mixed. Tertia Domatia is clearly free-born, unlike the other dedicants of these altars. Each vicus, or 'quarter', probably elected annually a college of twelve forepersons for each cult, who may have had other duties concerned with the maintenance of the relevant cross-roads or street-corner or with the celebration of the Compitalia festival.

In the year of office of . . . . Members of the Board of Two. These forewomen present this as an offering to Venus: [T]ertia D[o]matia, daughter of Spurius; Alfia Flora, freedwoman of a matron; Cahia Astaphium, freedwoman of a matron; Dosithea, slave of Numerius Calidius; and others. . . .

7.74 Cicero's friend Caerellia

(a) Cicero *Letters to his Friends* 13.72.1–2

Cicero talks of Caerellia's estates, investments and possessions in Asia, writing to P. Servilius Vatia Isauricus, governor of Asia, in 46. He borrowed money off her, which Atticus thought 'undignified' (*Att.* 12.52.3); in 45 she copied out his *de finibus* from a copy she borrowed from Atticus (*Att.* 13.21a.2, 13.22); in 44 she came to him as an 'envoy', perhaps from the family of Publilia, Cicero's second wife (*Att.* 14.19.4); at *Att.* 15.26.4 she was apparently co-heir with Cicero to a property in Rome worth 380,000 sesterces.

1 Regarding the estate, investments, and possessions in Asia of my very close friend Caerellia, I recommended them to your notice as carefully as I could when I was with you in your garden; and you, in accordance with your usual practice and your continual, immense services to me, most generously promised that you would do all that was in your power. I expect that you remember it; I know you generally do. However, Caerellia's agents have written that, due to the size of your province, and your multi-tudinous business, you have had to be reminded over and over again. **2** So I beg you to remember that you told me that you would do everything your honour permitted with all liberality. Indeed, I think you have an great opportunity of assisting Caerellia (though it is a matter for you to consider and decide), following the senate's decree which was passed about the heirs of C. Vennonius. You will employ your own wisdom in inter-preting that decree. For I know that the authority of that class has always been of great weight with you. Concerning what still has to be done, I would like you to believe that in whatever ways you show kindness to Caerellia you will be doing me the greatest possible favour.

(b) Dio Roman History 46.18.1–4

Quintus Fufius Calenus (cos. 47) used Caerellia — whose friendship with Cicero must have been widely known — as ammunition against him in 43 in his defence of Mark Anthony; his other vicious jibes included Cicero's incest with his daughter, prostitution of his wife, and his son's constant inebriation (46.18.6) — which gives a clear idea of the very personal and vitriolic nature of Roman oratory.

1 This is what, Cicero or Cicerculus or Ciceracius or Ciceriscus or Graeculus or whatever you like being called, the uneducated, the naked, the perfumed man (Anthony) achieved; **2** and none of it was done by you — the clever, the wise, the user of much more lamp-oil than wine, the one who lets his clothing drag round his ankles, not, by heaven, like the dancers do who instruct us in the intricacies of arguments by their gestures, but just to conceal the ugliness of your legs! **3** Oh no, it's not from modesty that you act like this, you who spoke at such length about Anthony's lifestyle! Who is there who doesn't notice those delicate mantles you wear? Who is there who doesn't smell your grey hair, so very carefully arranged? Who does not know that you divorced your first wife, who had given you two children, and married instead in your old age a young girl, just so you could pay your debts out of her property? **4** And yet you didn't even hang onto her either, in order to have the liberty to consort with Caerellia, with whom you had an affair, though she was as much older than you as the girl you married was younger, and despite this you still write such letters to her as a babbling jester might write to a woman of seventy of whom he was enamoured.

WOMEN AND THE GODS

While, in Greek religion, goddesses tended to have women priests, in Rome goddesses had male priests: there were male flamines for the goddesses Ceres, Flora, Furrina, and Pomona. This necessarily deprived women of religious roles which they otherwise might have played. Though sacrifices were made in women's rites (such as at the festival of Fortuna Muliebris: doc. 7.82); men would have performed these sacrifices for them and, in most sacrifices, women had no role: the presiding magistrates and priests were male. Women and girls, in fact, were not allowed to be present for certain rituals (Festus 72). The exception to this rule were the Vestal Virgins, who attended various sacrifices and also had an important role in preparing the sacrificial flour (the mola salsa: see below), but this in effect denied other women even this supporting role. Their status as Vestals was not as women, but as females whose sexuality was denied (because of the cultural construction of the definition of gender at Rome, and in the ancient world generally). Historically, other women supported the state in times of crisis through their worship but in passive ways: taking part in supplicationes (doc. 7.83), praying and entreating divinities, and making offerings, often involving the use of splendid cultic paraphernalia (doc. 7.70).

In the domestic religious sphere, women might be expected to have some say. But here the construction of religion was also patriarchal. Cato explicitly comments that the slave woman housekeeper is to perform no religious rites (*Agr.* 143.1: doc. 5.31), perhaps because a foreign slave housekeeper may have been accustomed to performing un-Roman rites. But Cato points out some minor rites the slave woman housekeeper is to perform: on the Kalends, Ides and Nones of the month she was to place a wreath at the hearth (143.2; cf. 2.1 where the master worships the Lar of the household immediately coming to his farm).

For women in Roman religion, see Balsdon 1974: 235–51; Pomeroy 1975: 206–17; Harmon 1978: 1466–68; Stehle 1989: 152–6; Scheid 1992; Saller 1998: 87–9; women priests: Vanggaard 1988: 30–1.

WOMEN'S FESTIVALS

Women of Republican Rome participated in several festivals; if Ovid had treated the last six months of the year in his *Fasti* more would presumably be known about these. Most is known about rites concerning women's role as child-bearers and mothers, though little is articulated in the sources except for what is known about the Lupercalia (doc. 7.76). But women did have various festivals which primarily concerned them, and even rituals from which men were excluded; the exclusion of men is most explicit for the Bona Dea (docs 7.84–5), but is implied for the Pudicitia (doc. 7.75), Veneralia (doc. 7.79), Matralia (doc. 7.81) and Fortuna Muliebris (doc. 7.82), festivals in which the sources mention women's but not men's participation. These festivals during the year show women participating in rites especially relevant to child-birth and pregnancy, and, in addition to these festivals, the temples of these deities would also have been open for women to visit at other times of the year. The festival calendar indicates a regular occurrence of festivals for women: 15 February, 1 and 17 March, 1 and 23 April, 11 June and 6 July. The degree of participation, however, is difficult to determine; it is not known how many matrons turned up to these festivals or whether spatial considerations were a constraint.

Nevertheless, while the state religion was largely dominated by men, women did have opportunities to worship, and that their festivals were important is underlined by the fact that they are actually recorded in the — male — sources.

7.75 The Pudicitia

Livy *History of Rome* 10.23.1–10

Livy has the Pudicitia, which celebrated the chastity of Roman women, 'passing into oblivion', but Festus in the late second century AD knew of it (270, 271; drawing on Verrius of c. 55 BC–AD 20); Palmer 1974; Pomeroy 1975: 208; Scheid 1992: 390; Bauman 1992: 15–16; Richardson *Top. Dict.* 322. L. Volumnius Flamma was consul in 296 (also cos. 307) and proconsul in 295: *MRR* I.176, 178. His wife, Verginia, had clearly been married without manus, as she retained her patrician status: Linderski 1986: 259; cf. doc. 7.10.

1 In that year (295 BC) there were many portents, to avert which the senate decreed supplications for two days; **2** wine and incense were provided at public expense; crowds, both of men and women, were to offer prayers. **3** The supplication was made memorable by a quarrel which arose between matrons in the temple of Patrician Chastity, which stands in the cattle-market by the round temple of Hercules. **4** The matrons had excluded from their ceremonies Verginia, Aulus' daughter, a patrician girl married to a plebeian, the consul Lucius Volumnius, because she had married outside her patrician rank. A short altercation followed, which, due to the sex's hasty temper, blazed up into a passionate dispute, **5** Verginia boasting, with reason, that she had entered the temple of Patrician Chastity both as a patrician and as a chaste woman, who was the wife of the man to whom she had been married as a virgin, and that she was ashamed neither of her husband nor of his honours and achievements.

6 She then followed up her proud speech with a deed which did her credit: in the Vicus Longus, where she lived, she shut off a part of her house, which was spacious enough for a shrine of reasonable size, and erected an altar there. She summoned the plebeian matrons and, after complaining of the insult by the patrician women, said, **7** 'I dedicate this altar to Plebeian Chastity, and exhort you that, just as the men in this city compete for the prize of courage, **8** you as matrons do the same with regard to chastity, and strive that this altar may, if possible, be said to be tended more reverently than that one, and by women who are more virtuous.' **9** This altar was tended with nearly the same rites as the more ancient one, so that no women except one of proven chastity, who had been married to only one man, should have the right to sacrifice. **10** Later on the cult was cheapened by polluted participants, not only matrons but women of every status, and eventually passed into oblivion.

7.76 The Lupercalia (15 February)

See also Ovid *Fasti* 2.267–304, 5.99–102; Livy 1.5.1–2; Varro *Lat. Lang.* 5.85, 6.34; Dion. Hal. 1.32.3, 1.80.1; Plut. *Rom. Quest.* 68, *Rom.* 21.4–10; Val. Max. 2.3.9.
The exact ritual purpose of the Lupercalia, celebrated on 15 February, is not entirely clear, but most scholars agree that it was a ceremony concerned both with the purification of the city and with women's fertility. The festival started with the sacrifice of goats and a dog at the Lupercal, a cave at the base of the Palatine hill, where the she-wolf had suckled Romulus and Remus. The

foreheads of two patrician youths were smeared with the blood on the sacrificial knife; the blood-stain on their heads was immediately wiped off with milk: the youths then had to laugh. The goat skins were cut into strips: semi-naked young men (both aristocrats and equestrians), known as the Luperci, who had feasted and drunk wine heavily, ran through the streets of Rome, striking anyone they could, but particularly women, with these strips as part of a fertility ritual, to promote conception and ease of child-birth. Some sources have the youths clothed with a loin cloth, others, girt with strips of the goat-skin (the former is preferable given imperial depictions of the rite). It was at the Lupercalia in 44 BC that Antony as one of the Luperci offered a diadem to Julius Caesar: Plut. *Caes.* 61 below, *Ant.* 12.1; doc. 13.55; Cicero refers to him as, 'nude, perfumed, drunk' (*nudus, unctus, ebrius*): *Phil.* 3.12, cf. 2.85–7; *Cael.* 26 (for Caelius as one of the Luperci). Pope Gelasius I in AD 495 banned Christian participation in the Lupercalia: it was one of the most tenacious of the pagan rites. See Ogilvie 1969: 77–8, 1970: 51–3; Dumézil 1970: 349–50; Harmon 1978: 1441–46; Scullard 1981: 76–8; Hopkins 1991: 479–83; Wiseman 1995; Ziolkowski 1998/9: 194–210; North 2000: 47, 50; Turcan 2000: 47–8; Harlow & Laurence 2002: 74–5. The scene is immortalised in Shakespeare's *Julius Caesar*, Act 1, Scene 1.

(a) Varro *On the Latin Language* 6.13

The Lupercalia is so called because the Luperci sacrifice at the Lupercal. When the rex sacrorum announces the monthly festivals on the Nones of February, he calls this day 'februatus': for the Sabines call a purification 'februm', and this word is not unknown in our rites, for a goat hide, with a thong of which young women are flogged at the Lupercal, the men of old called a 'februs', and the Lupercalia was called Februatio (festival of purification), as I have shown in my *Books of Antiquities*.

(b) Plutarch *Life of Caesar* 61.1–3

1 It was the festival of the Lupercalia, regarding which many writers say that in olden days it was celebrated by shepherds, and also connected in some way with the Arcadian festival of Lycaean Zeus. **2** Many of the well-born youths and magistrates run through the city naked, striking those they encounter with rough thongs to invoke sport and laughter; **3** many noble women deliberately get in their way and put out their hands, like school children, for the blows, believing that this assists the pregnant in childbirth and the childless in conceiving.

7.77 The Matronalia (1 March)

Ovid *Fasti* 3.241–58

Cf. Varro *Lat. Lang.* 5.49, 74; Juv. 9.51–3; Pliny *Nat. Hist.* 16.235; Festus 131. The Matronalia marked the anniversary of the temple of Juno Lucina. The emphasis of these rites was on aid in pregnancy; on this day, husbands prayed for their wives and gave them presents, and the rites of the Salii were also celebrated (doc. 3.11). Here Mars (Juno's son) answers a question of Ovid's. The Matronalia should not be confused with the Matralia (June 11). See Dumézil 1970: 294–5; Scullard 1981: 86–7; Turcan 2000: 34; temple: Richardson *Top. Dict.* 214–15.

'Now the field is fertile, now is the time for breeding stock,
Now the bird on the branch prepares a house and home:
It is proper that Latin mothers should celebrate the fertile season,
For in their child-birth they engage in conflict and prayer.
245   Add that, where the Roman king kept watch,

On the hill which now bears the name of Esquiline,
A temple to Juno was founded by Latin married women
At public expense on, if I remember correctly, this very day.
Why should I make a long story of it and weary your mind with various reasons?
250 What you seek, look — it stands there before your eyes.
My mother loves brides: a crowd of mothers throngs my temple:
So pious a reason particularly becomes us both.'
Bring the goddess flowers: flowering plants
Delight this goddess: wreathe your heads with fresh flowers;
255 Say, 'You have given us, Lucina, the light of life'.
Say, 'You are there to help those who pray in childbirth'.
But whoever is pregnant, let her pray with loosened hair,
So the goddess may gently loose her childbirth.

7.78 The Liberalia (17 March)

Varro *On the Latin Language* 6.14

This festival celebrated Liber Pater, an Italian god of fertility and of wine. Ceres, Liber and Libera had a joint temple founded in 493 BC on the Aventine. That old women rather than matrons serve as priestesses both reflects the limited opportunities for unchaperoned public appearances by Roman matrons and the lack of priestly roles for women. Augustine (*Civ. Dei* 7.21), following Varro, mentions that in certain parts of Italy a phallus borne through the fields on a cart was brought into town to the accompaniment of crude songs, but this is not known for Rome. Liber shared Ceres' games (*ludi Ceriales*) on March 19. It was also on this day that Roman boys who had attained puberty donned the *toga virilis* (Ovid *Fasti* 3.771–2). See Dumézil 1970: 377–8; Scullard 1981: 91–2; Turcan 2000: 21.

The Liberalia is so called because on that day, throughout the whole city, old women sit crowned with wreaths of ivy, as priestesses of Liber, with cakes and a brazier on which they offer them up on behalf of those who buy them.

7.79 The Veneralia (1 April): matrons and prostitutes at the baths

Ovid *Fasti* 4.133–9, 145–50

The festival of the Veneralia honoured Fortuna Virilis (Virile Fortune). Those who 'do not wear the fillets and long robe' are women who are not matrons, i.e., prostitutes; the place of 'warm water' is the baths. Presumably men were not present at the baths when this festival was celebrated. See Pomeroy 1975: 208; Harmon 1978: 1459–67; Scullard 1981: 96–7; Scheid 1992: 387–8.

With due religious observances you worship the goddess, Latin matrons old and
     young,
And you, who do not wear the fillets and long robe.
135 Remove the golden necklaces from the marble neck,
Remove the rich adornments: the goddess must be completely bathed.
Return the golden necklaces to her neck, now dried:
She must now be given other flowers, now the blooming rose.
She herself commands you too to bathe under the green myrtle . . .

145 Now learn why to Fortuna Virilis you offer
 Incense in the place which is damp with warm water.
 All women remove their coverings when they enter that place
 And it sees every blemish of their naked bodies;
 Fortuna Virilis undertakes to conceal this and hide it from men
150 And for this service asks only a little incense.

7.80 The Vinalia (23 April)

Ovid *Fasti* 4.863–72

Cf. Plut *Rom. Quest.* 45; Pliny *Nat. Hist.* 18.287; the Praeneste calendar (*Inscript. Ital.* XIII.2: 126–33). The Vinalia was celebrated both on 23 April and 19 August. Ovid describes the festival of 23 April, when an offering of new wine was made to Jupiter, and emphasises the role played by prostitutes. The Praeneste calendar (AD 6–9) notes 24 April as a holiday for prostitutes. The temple next to the Colline Gate, taking its name from the Sicilian hill (Eryx), was the aedes of Venus Erycina, vowed by L. Porcius Licinus (cos. 184) during wars in Sicily and opened in 181 BC (Richardson *Top. Dict.* 408). See Scullard 1981: 106–08; Holleman 1989; Palmer 1997: 66–7; Turcan 2000: 43.

 I have spoken of Pales, and now I will speak of the Vinalia;
 One day, however, separates the two festivals.
865 Girls of the streets, celebrate the divine majesty of Venus:
 Venus is very appropriate for those who earn their wages as prostitutes.
 Offer incense and pray for beauty and popularity,
 Pray for charm and witty speech,
 Give the mistress the wild thyme she loves and her own myrtle
870 And chains of rushes concealed in bunched roses.
 It is now the proper time to frequent her temple
 Near the Colline Gate, which takes its name from the Sicilian hill.

7.81 The Matralia (11 June)

Ovid *Fasti* 6.475–80

Cf. Varro *Lat. Lang.* 5.106 (for the crusty golden cakes the women baked in heated earthenware); Plut. *Rom. Quest.* 16–17. The Mater Matuta was honoured in her temple in the Forum Boarium at this festival (Ovid's 'Theban goddess' is Ino, who is not, however, the equivalent of Mater Matuta). 11 June was the day her temple was dedicated; there had been a temple on the site, according to tradition, since Servius Tullius, and restored after the siege of Veii (Richardson *Top. Dict.* 246). The Matralia was celebrated only by matrons still in their first marriage (*univirae*). Slave-women were not permitted in the temple, but during the festival one was brought in, beaten, and expelled, to underline their exclusion. Women prayed not for blessings on their own children but for those of their sisters. On the same day they went to pray at the adjacent temple of Fortuna, built on the same podium (Ovid *Fasti* 6.621–2). See Dumézil 1970: 50–55, 337–9; Pomeroy 1975: 207; Scullard 1981: 150–1; Bettini 1991: 77–87; Scheid 1992: 386–7; Turcan 2000: 34.

 Go, good mothers (the Matralia is your festival),
 Offer the Theban goddess her yellow cakes.
 Adjoining the bridges and great Circus is a famous

Space, which takes its name from the ox statue there:
Here, on this day, they say Servius dedicated to Mother Matuta
A temple with his own sceptre-bearing hands.

7.82 Fortuna Muliebris: the Fortune of Women (6 July)

Dionysius of Halicarnassus *Roman Antiquities* 8.39.1, 8.55.3

Cf. Livy 2.40.1–12; Plut. *Cor.* 37; Val. Max. 1.8.4, 5.1.2. The traditional (but almost certainly fictitious) aetiology of this cult is that the successful general Coriolanus, exiled from Rome, led a Volscian army against it in 493 (or 488) BC; Roman appeals to his patriotism fell on deaf ears. Roman matrons gathered at the house of his mother and wife and convinced them to visit Coriolanus in his camp; accompanied by large numbers of matrons, his wife and mother persuaded him to lead the army away. The senate in gratitude voted to grant the women any wish: the temple and a cult statue of Fortuna Muliebris were the result, built on the site of the confrontation with Coriolanus, four miles south of Rome on the Via Latina. The temple was vowed on 1 December. Dionysius refers to the appointment of a woman priest, and matrons presiding over sacrifices: whether this was the case in the later Republic is unclear. The women dedicated a second cult statue, which spoke twice: 'You have dedicated me, matrons, in accordance with the sacred law of the city' (8.56.3–4). The women then decided that only *univirae* (women who had only married once) were to participate in the cult. This cult of Fortuna Muliebris is clearly for matrons; men do not seem to have participated. Slightly different details are recorded by Livy and Dionysius. See Balsdon 1974: 29–30; Ogilvie 1970: 334–6; Pomeroy 1975: 208; Scullard 1981: 160–1; Scheid 1992: 388–90; *BNP* 1.297; Turcan 2000: 75; doc. 6.17 for the festival of Juno Caprotina.

39.1 As the danger was now close at hand, their wives threw to the winds the propriety of staying at home and ran with lamentations to the shrines of the gods, prostrating themselves before the statues; and every sacred place was filled with the wailing and supplication of women, especially the temple of Jupiter Capitolinus . . . (A noble woman, Valeria, persuades the women to supplicate Coriolanus' wife and mother to entreat him to make peace. The women succeed and the senate and people grant them praise and an eternal remembrance.) **55.3** The women deliberated and decided to request a gift which would not cause jealousy, but to ask the senate for permission to found a temple to the Fortune of women (Fortuna Muliebris) on the place where they had made their prayers on their city's behalf, and for them to assemble there every year and sacrifice to her on the day that they had ended the war. The senate and people decreed, however, that a precinct should be purchased from public monies and dedicated to the goddess, and that a temple and altar be built in it, in whatever way the pontiffs might prescribe, and that sacrifices should be conducted at the public expense, with a woman commencing the rites, whomever the women themselves should decide upon as the celebrant.

7.83 The supplicatio of 207 BC

Livy *History of Rome* 27.37.7–15

The women of Rome are here expiating various prodigies, including the birth of an hermaphrodite child. This involvement of women in *supplicationes* was a feature of Roman history: Scheid 1992: 394–5; for the events of 207, see docs 4.49–50.

7 The pontiffs also decreed that thrice nine virgins should go through the city singing a hymn. While they were learning the hymn, composed by the poet Livius (Andronicus), in the temple of Jupiter Stator, the temple of Juno the Queen on the Aventine was struck by lightning; **8** as the haruspices' interpretation was that this portent concerned the matrons and that the goddess should be appeased by a gift, **9** an edict of the curule aediles summoned to the Capitol all matrons who resided in the city of Rome or within ten miles of the city, and these chose from amongst themselves twenty-five, to whom they should bring a donation from their dowries. **10** From these donations a golden basin was made as a gift and carried to the Aventine, and after proper purification the matrons offered a sacrifice.

11 A day was immediately named by the decemvirs for another sacrifice to the same goddess, the procedure for which was as follows: two white cows were led from the temple of Apollo through the Porta Carmentalis into the city; **12** after them were carried two cypress-wood statues of Juno the Queen; then came twenty-seven virgins, dressed in long robes, singing the hymn to Juno the Queen, **13** which at that time perhaps seemed praiseworthy to their uncultivated minds, but which now would seem rough and uncouth, if recited. The group of virgins were followed by the decemvirs, crowned with garlands of laurel and wearing the toga praetexta. **14** From the gate they came along the Vicus Iugarius into the forum. The procession stopped in the forum, and the virgins, passing a rope from hand to hand, moved forwards, accompanying the sound of their voices by beating time with their feet. **15** Then, via the Vicus Tuscus and the Velabrum, through the Forum Boarium, they continued to the Clivus Publicius and the temple of Juno the Queen. There the two victims were sacrificed by the decemvirs and the cypress-wood statues carried into the temple.

THE BONA DEA (3 DECEMBER)

Bona Dea was the 'Good Goddess'; she had two rites, on 1 May, and more importantly, on 3 December. Men were not permitted to know her real name, and simply knew her as 'Bona Dea' (Cic. *Har. Resp.* 37). Her December nocturnal rites were secret, as were the May rites held during the day. Such a nocturnal ceremony was unusual for the Romans (see doc. 3.63). Cicero in his ideal state wished to ban nocturnal sacrifices except for those offered 'on behalf of the people' (*Laws* 2.21), like the Bona Dea rites. The nocturnal festival was celebrated in the house of the consul (Cicero in 63) or the praetor (Julius Caesar in 62).

Cicero describes the sacrifice performed at the December Bona Dea festival as 'ancient and secret', taking place in the absence of men and performed by the Vestals 'on behalf of the Roman people' (as does Asc. 43); Cicero is discussing Clodius' profanation of the rites (Cic. *Har. Resp.* 37–8). The sacrifice (which was accompanied by a libation to the goddess) was a young sow, and the conclusion must be that, in the absence of men, the Vestals dispatched it. The stomach was burnt for Bona Dea. With the Vestals were Roman matrons, wearing purple headbands: presumably they were aristocrats, meeting in the magistrate's house with the aristocratic Vestals. Plutarch refers to 'fun and games' and the playing of music; Clodius, who profaned the rites with his presence, entered disguised as a lute-girl, who presumably would have been a slave (*Caes.* 9.8, 10.1). When Clodius' presence at the Bona Dea was discovered, Aurelia, Caesar's mother, stopped the sacred rites and hid the ritual objects, whatever they were (Plut. *Caes.* 10.3).

Wine was not permitted into the rite of 1 May under its own name; it was disguised by being called 'milk' (Macrob. *Sat.* 1.12.15); on 3 December the goddess received a libation; Juvenal in an incredible description accuses the women at the Bona Dea of drunkenness and orgiastic behaviour (6.315–40), but underlying his description is the probable fact that women did drink wine as part of the ceremony. Given its secrecy, absence of men, and connection with the good of the state, Bona Dea was presumably a fertility goddess of women whose role was extended to include the prosperity of the state. See Juv. 2.83–90, 6.314–41; Macrob. 1.12.20–1, 27; Versnel 1992, esp. 32–3, 1993: 229–35, 261–75; Pomeroy 1975: 210; Harmon 1978: 1467–8; Scullard 1981: 116–17, 199–201; Brouwer 1989; Scheid 1992: 391–3; *BNP* 1.129–30, 138; Staples 1998: 13–51; Turcan 2000: 80; Wilfang 2001: 250–3.

7.84 Terentia and the Catilinarian conspiracy, 63 BC

Plutarch *Life of Cicero* 19.4–5, 20.1–3

Terentia's half-sister Fabia was a Vestal Virgin, accused and acquitted of incest with Catiline in 73: MRR II.114. This incident took place on 4 December, the day before the debate in the senate on the fate of the Catilinarian conspirators.

19.4 As it was now evening and the people were gathered waiting, Cicero went out and told the citizens what he had done, and with their escort went to the house of a friend and neighbour, since his own was occupied by the women who were celebrating the secret rites of the goddess whom the Romans call 'Bona Dea' and the Greeks 'Gynaeceia' (Women's). **5** Every year a sacrifice is made to her in the consul's house by his wife or mother, with the Vestal Virgins present. On entering the house, Cicero with only a few people present, deliberated with himself what he should do with the conspirators... **20.1** While Cicero was making up his mind what to do, a sign was given to the women as they were sacrificing. For the altar, on which the fire seemed to have totally died down, sent out from the ash and burnt bark an immense, brilliant flame. **2** The other women were terrified by this, but the sacred virgins instructed Terentia, Cicero's wife, to go with all speed to her husband and tell him to carry out his resolutions for his country's good, as the goddess was giving him a great light on his road to safety and glory. **3** So Terentia, who was generally not of a mild and retiring disposition, but an ambitious woman and, as Cicero himself states, more inclined to share in his political concerns than to share her domestic concerns with him, told him this and urged him to take action against the conspirators.

7.85 Clodius and the Bona Dea, 62 BC

Plutarch *Life of Caesar* 9.1–10.9

Cf. Cic. *Har. Resp.* 37–8; *Att.* 1.12.3, 1.13.3; Plut. *Cic.* 28–9; Suet. *Jul.* 6.2, 74.2; Dio 37.45.2. Caesar was praetor and the rites were held in his house in 62 BC. Clodius' intrusion was raised in the senate, and referred to the Vestals and the pontifices, who decreed that it was 'nefas' (sacrilege); the rites had to be celebrated anew. The consuls introduced a bill for a trial for sacrilege. Clodius was tried, and Cicero disproved his alibi, but the bribed jurors acquitted him. In revenge, Clodius eventually succeeded in having Cicero banished; for this incident and Clodius' trial, see docs 12.52–4; Balsdon 1966; Lenaghan 1969: 114–17; Wiseman 1974: 159–69; Epstein 1986; Mulroy 1988: 165–78; Tatum 1990, 1999: 62–86; *BNP* 1.129–30; Leach 2001; Alexander *Trials* no. 236.

9.1 There were no disturbances in Caesar's praetorship, although he met with a disgraceful misfortune in his own household. **2** Publius Clodius was a patrician by birth, distinguished for both his wealth and eloquence, but second to none of the noted profligates of the time in insolence and audacity. **3** He was in love with Caesar's wife, Pompeia, and she was not unwilling. But strict watch was kept on the women's apartments, and Caesar's mother, Aurelia, a discreet woman, kept her eye on her daughter-in-law and made any meeting difficult and risky. **4** The Romans have a goddess whom they call 'Good', whom the Greeks call 'Gynaeceia' . . . **6** It is not lawful for a man to be present, or even in the house, while the rites are being celebrated; the woman are said to perform by themselves rites during their worship which are Orphic in nature. **7** So, when it is time for the festival, the husband, who is either consul or praetor, and every other male, leaves the house, while the wife takes it over and sets it in order. **8** The most important ceremonies are celebrated at night, when the all-night celebrations are mingled with fun and games, and with much music, too, as a feature.

10.1 As Pompeia was at that time conducting the festival, Clodius, who had as yet no beard, and so thought he would pass unnoticed, put on the dress and accessories of a lute-girl, and went there in the guise of a young woman. **2** Finding the door open, he was brought in without any difficulty by the maid, who was in the know. She ran on to tell Pompeia, but, as there was a long wait, Clodius had not the patience to remain where he had been left and wandered around in the large house, trying to avoid the lights, when an attendant of Aurelia's encountered him and asked him to play with her as one woman would another. When he refused, she dragged him forward and asked who he was and where he came from. **3** Clodius replied that he was waiting for Pompeia's maid Abra (this was her name), and was detected by his voice, whereupon the attendant sprang away with a scream to the lights and the crowds, crying out that she had caught a man. The women were terrified, and Aurelia put a stop to the rites of the goddess and covered up the ritual objects, ordering the doors to be closed and going around the house with torches looking for Clodius. **4** He was found to have taken refuge in the room of the girl who had let him in, and when they saw who he was the women drove him out of doors. **5** At once, that same night, the women went and told their husbands, and in the morning the report was all over the city that Clodius had committed sacrilege and should be punished for his crimes, not only against those he had directly offended, but against the city and the gods as well. **6** One of the tribunes therefore prosecuted Clodius for impiety, and the most powerful senators leagued against him, giving evidence about his adultery with his sister, who was married to Lucullus, and other dreadful acts of licentiousness. **7** The people opposed their efforts and defended Clodius, and were of great assistance to him with the jurors, who were terrified and afraid of the mob. **8** Caesar immediately divorced Pompeia, but when summoned as a witness at the trial said he knew nothing of the matters with which Clodius was charged. **9** As his statement appeared strange, the prosecutor asked him, 'Why then did you divorce your wife?' 'Because,' he replied,' I thought that my wife should not even be suspected.'

THE VESTAL VIRGINS

In ancient Rome, the Vestal Virgins were six women devoted since childhood exclusively to the service of the goddess Vesta, who presided over the hearth in Roman homes. Their main role, besides officiating at various state religious ceremonies, was to keep alight the sacred fire of Vesta in her round temple in the forum, and guard the 'sacred things', including the ancient palladium, the image of Minerva rescued from Troy when the Greeks sacked it, referred to by Livy as the 'pledge of Roman imperium' (26.27.14; doc. 2.29). According to tradition, the Vestals were established by Numa (docs 3.6, 7.89). Vesta's festival, the Vestalia, was celebrated on 9 June.

In return for giving up the prospect of marriage for thirty years, or for life, the Vestals were allowed various rights denied to other Roman women. Unlike all other Roman women, who had a legal male guardian, the Vestals left their father's potestas and were free of male control (XII Tables: doc. 1.34; docs 7.86, 88). But privileges meant responsibilities: if the sacred fire went out, the Vestal responsible would be flogged (doc. 7.88; Val. Max. 1.1.6). Losing their virginity was punished with death: if unchaste Vestals performed the rites they were considered to be bringing down the anger of the gods on the state as a whole; the men involved were scourged (in one case to death) and then executed (doc. 7.87). Accusations against and condemnation of Vestals for unchastity often occurred within the context of spectacular military disasters. After the worst defeat in Roman history, at Cannae in 216 BC, Vestals were accused of unchastity and put to death (doc. 4.38), as they were also in 113 BC (doc. 7.91). An elaborate procedure was used for the punishment of the Vestal Virgin, which ensured that the state itself could not stand accused of having killed someone (the Vestal) who had been dedicated to the gods (doc. 7.88).

Vestal Virgins were present and participated at various rites (for a description of the ten main rites, see Wildfang 2001), such as the Argei (doc. 3.7) and the Bona Dea (doc. 7.84–5). In addition, the preparation of enough mola salsa for Rome's official sacrifices must have been laborious. (Vestals ground the first ears of grain for the season and baked this with salt to make mola salsa, salted flour (meal): doc. 3.30).

The Vestals lived in the heart of the Roman state, in the Roman forum itself, where they had a special building, the *atrium Vestae* (Nash 1.154–9; Richardson *Top. Dict.* 42–4; Scott 1993). Vesta's temple, where the Vestals had to keep the sacred fire burning, was also in the forum (Nash 2.505–9; Richardson 412). They were the only women to have a permanent physical presence in the domain of the forum, and the only women who could address the senate. Both of these facts underline the anomaly of their position. Statues show that their hair was arranged as brides on their day of marriage, but they dressed as Roman matrons, that is, as women who were not eligible to be sought as brides. They had to be circumspect of dress so as not to arouse the sexual interest and attentions of men (doc. 7.89). Their religious status underlined the status of women in general, which was one of exclusion from direct participation in many of the state cults of the gods.

For the Vestal Virgins, see Balsdon 1974: 235–43; Ogilvie 1969: 90–1; Dumézil 1970: 585–7; Scullard 1981: 149–50; Pomeroy 1975: 210–14; Beard 1980, 1990: 22–5; 1995; Goodrich 1989: 270–87; Bauman 1992: 52–8; Scheid 1992: 381–4; *BNP* 1.51–4; Staples 1998; Wildfang 2001; for the Roman construction of Vestal Virginity: Beard 1980, 1995; Staples 135–56; as human sacrifices: Eckstein 1982.

7.86 A Vestal's Life

Dionysius of Halicarnassus *Roman Antiquities* 2.67.1–2

Gell. 1.12.1–19 has a long discussion on how a Vestal Virgin was chosen, noting that she must be physically without defect, and her parents must not have been slaves or had a lowly occupation. At 1.12.14 he quotes Fabius Pictor for the ritual words used by the pontifex maximus when accepting a Vestal: 'I accept you, Amata, as one who has fulfilled the legal requirements, as a priestess of Vesta, to perform the sacred rites which it is lawful for a priestess of Vesta to perform on behalf of the Roman people, the Quirites.' At 3.67.2 Dionysius records that Tarquinius Priscus added two Vestals to the initial four, and that the number of Vestals up to Dionysius' own day had remained six.

1 The Vestal Virgins live in the sanctuary of the goddess, which no one who wishes can be prevented from entering during the day, though it is not lawful for any man to stay there at night. **2** They were required to remain undefiled by marriage for thirty years, offering sacrifices and performing other religious rites in accordance with the law. During the first ten years they had to learn these rites, during the second ten to perform them, and during the remaining ten to teach others. When the period of thirty years had been completed, there was nothing which prevented those who so wished from putting aside the headbands and other insignia of their priesthood and marrying. And some, though only a few, have done so, but the ends of their lives were unenviable and not at all happy, and in consequence taking their misfortunes as ominous, the rest remain virgins in service to the goddess until their deaths, when another is again appointed by the pontiffs to fill the vacancy.

7.87 A Vestal's death, 481 BC

Dionysius of Halicarnassus *Roman Antiquities* 8.89.3–5

Livy 2.42.10–11. Cf. the similar description of a violation of vestal purity in Dion. Hal. 9.40.3–4 (in 471 BC), where he records the additional detail that the Vestal was scourged.

3 In Rome many portentous signs, in the form of unusual voices and visions, occurred as evidence of divine wrath. **4** The augurs and expounders of religious matters shared their experiences and proclaimed that some of the gods were wrathful because they were not receiving their customary honours, since their rites were not being conducted in a pure and holy manner. A great inquiry was then held by everyone, and eventually the pontiffs received information that one of the virgins who guarded the sacred fire, whose name was Opimia, had lost her virginity and was polluting the rites. **5** By tortures and other proofs the pontiffs discovered that the information was correct, and they took the headbands from her head, and, carrying her in procession through the Forum, buried her alive inside the city walls. The two men who were convicted of seducing her were flogged in public and then immediately executed. After this, the sacrifices and the auguries became favourable, as if the gods had remitted their anger against them.

7.88 Plutarch on the Vestal Virgins

Plutarch *Life of Numa* 9.8–10.13

After the Gallic victory at the battle of the Allia, traditionally dated to 390 BC, the Vestals removed the fire of Vesta and other sacred objects in their care from Rome: for these objects, thought by some to include the palladium brought from Troy by Aeneas, the Samothracian images, or two small jars (one open and one sealed), see Plut. *Cam.* 20.5–8.

9.8 The chief of the pontiffs (the pontifex maximus) had the duty of expounding and interpreting, or rather presiding over sacred ceremonies, not only being in charge of public rites, but overseeing private sacrifices too, and ensuring that established custom was not transgressed, as well as giving instructions as to whatever was necessary for the worship or propitiation of the gods. **9** He was also the overseer of the holy virgins, who are called Vestals. **10** To Numa is attributed the consecration of the Vestal Virgins and the care and worship of the perpetual fire which they guard, either because he considered the essence of fire to be pure and uncorrupted and so entrusted it to chaste and undefiled persons, or because he saw fire as barren and unfruitful and so analogous to virginity. **11** Yet, wherever fire is unquenched in Greece, as at Delphi and Athens, not virgins but women past the age of marriage have care of it . . . **15** Some consider that nothing other than the perpetual fire is guarded by the holy virgins; others say that certain sacred objects are kept in concealment by them, which no one else may see: what may be learnt and told about these things I have written in my *Life of Camillus*.

10.1 Initially, they say, Gegania and Verenia were consecrated by Numa, and then Canuleia and Tarpeia; and two others were later added by Servius, making up the number which has continued to this day . . . **5** He granted them great privileges, for example the right to make a will while their father was still alive and the power to manage their other affairs without a guardian, like mothers of three children. **6** When they appear in public, the fasces are carried in front of them, and if they meet someone being led to execution, he is spared — the Vestal has to swear that the encounter was involuntary and accidental, not contrived. If anyone passes underneath the litter on which they are being carried he is put to death. **7** For other offences the Vestals' punishment is flogging, the pontifex maximus carrying it out, with the offender sometimes naked, in a dark place, with a curtain pulled between them; **8** but if one has broken her vow of chastity, she is buried alive near the gate called the Colline; there a little mound of earth lies within the city, extending for some distance: in the Latin language it is called *choma*, 'agger'. **9** A small underground room has been constructed there, with steps leading down from above. In it is placed a bed with coverings and a lighted lamp, and small portions of the necessities of life, such as bread, water in a bowl, milk, and oil, as though they are absolving themselves from killing by hunger a person consecrated to the highest religious duties. **10** The offender is placed on a litter, which they throw coverings over, and tie down with cords, so that no cry she makes can be heard, and take her through the forum. **11** Everyone stands aside in silence and escorts it noiselessly with dreadful gloom: no other sight is more frightful, and the city observes no more awful day than this. **12** When the litter has been carried to the spot, the attendants undo the cords, and then the high priest, uttering certain silent prayers and raising his hands to the gods before the act, brings her out still covered and places her upon the steps that lead down to the room. **13** He then averts his face with the other priests; when she has descended, the ladder is drawn up and the room's entrance is concealed with a quantity of earth heaped up over it, so as to make it level with the rest of the mound. This is the punishment for those who break their vow of virginity.

7.89 A Vestal's punishment

Livy *History of Rome* 8.15.7–8

Livy dates this incident to 337 BC. Minucia was not allowed to free her slaves because slaves could be tortured to give evidence, but free people could not. On her punishment, Ennius wrote, 'Since no law ever demanded anything more horrible' (*Annals* 474).

In that year the Vestal Minucia, suspected initially because of her dress, which was more elegant than was fitting, was then accused before the pontiffs on the evidence of a slave, and was ordered by their decree to abstain from performing sacrifices and to retain her slaves in her own power. After her conviction, she was buried alive near the Colline Gate on the right of the paved road in the Polluted Field — a place named, I believe, for her unchastity.

7.90 A Vestal's miraculous powers

Pliny the Elder *Natural History* 28.12–13

Cf. Val. Max. 8.1; for the devotio rituals of the Decii, see doc. 3.16; for runaway slaves: docs 6.40–2.

12 As an important example of ritual there has survived that used by the Decii, father and son, to devote themselves; also extant is the Vestal Tuccia's plea of innocence when accused of unchastity, when she carried water in a sieve in the year 609 of the city (145 BC). **13** We believe today that our Vestals are able, with a prayer, to root runaway slaves to the spot, providing that they have not yet left the city.

COINAGE AND THE VESTAL VIRGINS

7.91 Condemnation of Vestals in 113 BC

Crawford *RRC* 428.1–2

(Grueber I.3871; Sydenham *CRR* 917–18; Harlan *RRM* 23.2–3 (53 BC); Hill *MAR* 23; date: Crawford: 55 BC; Harlan: 53 BC.) Denarius of 55 or 53 BC. Compare a similar coin: Crawford *RRC* 413.

This denarius was minted by Q. Cassius Longinus and commemorated his great-grandfather L. Cassius Longinus Ravilla. In 114 BC, the virgin daughter of a Roman eques was struck dead by a lightning bolt, her dress was wrenched away from her groin, exposing her vagina; her tongue protruded from her mouth. The omen was interpreted to mean that the Vestals had broken their vows. A slave accused his master of making love to the Vestal Aemilia, and another two Vestals were implicated with their lovers; the three were tried for incest. Aemilia was condemned but the other two acquitted by the pontiffs; the convicted Vestal Aemilia is not the same as in doc. 7.92. The plebs suspected a 'cover-up' and a tribune successfully carried a plebiscite naming L. Cassius Longinus Ravilla as prosecutor (*quaesitor*) and establishing a *quaestio extraordinaria* (special court), as he was well-known for his severity. The two Vestals previously acquitted, Licinia and Marcia, were also condemned to death in 113, as well as several equites. The curule seat shown on the coin is a reference to Ravilla's official position as *quaesitor*. The Sibylline books were consulted and two Gauls and two Greeks were buried alive, just as in 216 when two Vestals were found guilty of unchastity (Livy 22.57: doc. 4.38; cf. Plut. *Marcell.* 3.6–7). Condemnation of Vestals in 114–13 BC: Fenestella F11 (*HRR* II.82); Cic. *Brut.* 160, *Nat. Deor.* 3.74; Livy *Per.* 63; Asc. 45–6; Plut. *Rom. Quest.* 83; Oros. 5.15.22; Obsequens 37; Dio 26 F87; Val. Max. 3.7.9, 6.8.1; Porphyr. in Hor. *Sat.* 1.6.30; Zon. 7.8; *MRR* I.534, 537; Alexander *Trials* nos 38–44; McDougall 1992.

Obverse: Head of the goddess Vesta.
Reverse: Temple of Vesta (which was in the forum). Within the temple of Vesta there is a curule chair. On the left of the temple, a voting urn, and on the temple's right a voting tablet inscribed with the letters, A and C, for absolvo (I acquit) and condemno

(I condemn). The coin shows the temple's circular construction, as well as a statue, presumably Vesta, on the roof (not to be confused with the ancient statue within the temple itself).

7.92 The Vestal Virgin Aemilia honoured for her virtue

Crawford *RRC* 419.3

(Grueber I.3650–2; Sydenham *CRR* 833–4; Carson *PCRR* 172; Harlan *RRM* 5.4–5.) This is a denarius of 61 BC minted by the moneyer M. Aemilius Lepidus (c) in 61 BC. The reverse shows the *Basilica Aemilia et Fulvia*, a two-story portico constructed in the forum in 179 BC by M. Aemilius Lepidus (a), cos. 187, with his fellow censor M. Fulvius Nobilior; it provided shop-space for the north side of the forum (Varro *Lat. Lang.* 6.4; Livy 40.46.16, cf. 51.2–3; *MRR* I.392; Richardson *Top. Dict.* 55; Claridge 1998: 67). The denarius commemorates the decoration of the hall with shields by the moneyer M. Lepidus' father, Marcus Aemilius Lepidus (b), as consul in 78 BC.

On the obverse, and obviously representing one of the individuals on the shields, is a woman attired as a Vestal Virgin, whom scholars identify as the Vestal Aemilia who is reported to have rekindled the fire in the temple of Vesta (which had gone out) by throwing one of her loveliest garments onto it (Val. Max. 1.1.7). Lepidus (c) the moneyer was clearly attempting to overcome the burden of his father's seditious consulship of 78 by recalling both his more distant ancestor, the consul of 187, and Aemilia's virtue. Another of his coins stressed the deeds of his consular ancestor (Harlan *RMM* 5.1–2).

Obverse: Head of a veiled woman, wearing laurel wreath.
Reverse: Basilica Aemilia and Fulvia, two storied, with legend *Aimilia* above building (ignoring the Fulvia); portrait shields are attached to the columns; on the left the letters *REF* (*refecta*, 'rebuilt'), and on the right *SC* ('by decree of the senate'). The legend M(arcus) Lepidus underneath the building.

7.93 Home is where the hearth is

Cicero *On his House* 109

On the sanctity of the Roman home, Saller 1984: 354 notes that the demolition of the house was a symbolic destruction of the offender and all his family. When Cicero was exiled, his house on the Palatine was destroyed by Clodius by decree and replaced by a monument to Liberty; Cicero was recalled in 57, arriving in September, and made a case before the pontiffs that the consecration was null and void; his house was rebuilt. See docs 12.53–4, 58–60; Lacey 1986: 125–6; Treggiari 2002: 74–108.

What is more holy, what more protected by every kind of sanctity than the home of every individual citizen? There are his altars, his hearths, his household gods, his sacred rites, observances, rituals: it is a sanctuary so holy in the eyes of all that it is sacrilege to drag a person from it.

8

Tiberius and Gaius Gracchus

Land and its distribution and redistribution was an issue in late republican politics from the time of the Gracchi down to Caesar, with Saturninus, Drusus (the younger), Sulla and Caesar all concerned with land redistribution (Stockton 1979: 16). It is not an understatement to say that the demise of the Republic began with the Gracchi, plebeians with impeccable family backgrounds whose ancestors had been conspicuous in their military service (docs 8.1, 5.53). They attempted to deal with pressing economic and social problems — and failed. In 133 the violence that was to mark the late Republic (133–44 BC) began, when members of the senate shattered the concordia of the state by murdering Tiberius Gracchus. It was acknowledged by Appian — and accepted by modern historians — that the period of the Gracchi saw the beginning of the decline of the Republic: Tiberius' tribunate is the point at which Appian began his *Civil Wars*, part of his history of Rome (doc. 8.4).

Scholars are less agreed on the precise nature of the problems facing Rome which Tiberius as tribune in 133 and then his brother Gaius as tribune in 123 and 122 sought to overcome, and what their motives were. But the overall aim presented by the sources for Tiberius is that he wanted to settle Roman citizens on ager publicus (public land) so that they would become eligible for military service (docs 8.6, 9). Whether he did this from pure altruism, to 'get even' with the senate, to pursue gloria and advance his political career, or a combination of these motives, is up to the reader to decide. But it is clear that he did not, in proposing his law, deliberately seek to alienate the senate or to destroy its power. However, their obstruction of the workings of the land commission led him to a decision, the use of funds from Pergamum, which would interfere in senatorial prerogatives. Events led on from there to a disastrous conclusion (doc. 8.15).

Roman conquests of the third and second centuries, during which farmers were often away from their farms serving in the army, combined with the increase in the number of slaves, had resulted in much of the land of peasant farmers being concentrated in the hands of the few, and being worked by slaves. These were not yet latifundia, huge farms (such as could be found in Sicily at this time) but rather the rich tended to own a 'patchwork' of smaller estates run as independent units (cf. White 1967; Rathbone 1981: 21 on Etruria). To be eligible for military service, citizens had to belong to one of the property classes. When they lost their farms, and perhaps the use of ager publicus through the encroachments of the rich, they were no longer eligible for service in the army. A property census rating of 11,000 sesterces was necessary for military service;

with small farmers replaced by slaves, it became difficult to raise recruits, and slaves themselves were a danger (docs 1.19, 8.6). During the tribunate of Tiberius the slave revolt in Sicily (135–132 BC) was in full swing (doc. 6.43).

Both Appian and Plutarch agree that Tiberius' main concern was with increasing the number of soldiers by distributing the ager publicus. Rome owned large amounts of ager publicus, particularly in southern Italy from confiscations from communities that had gone over to Hannibal in 216 or soon after (see doc. 4.42). By 167 a law limited possession of ager publicus to 500 iugera per individual, but the senators resented this law and like the much earlier fourth-century Licinio-Sextian law which disallowed private possession of ager publicus (doc. 1.47) it seems to have been largely ignored. Certainly by Tiberius' time much of this land was treated as private property, and this was the cause of his conflict with the rich. But it was when Tiberius proposed that the plebeian assembly legislate on the bequest of Attalus III's kingdom of Pergamum to Rome, interfering in the senate's traditional prerogatives of foreign affairs and finance, that his opponents had a basis for blocking his measures, further aggravated by his decision to stand for a second time as tribune when the opposition to him became clear (doc. 8.15). The charge made against him, that he was aiming at kingship, was clearly not credible in anyone's eyes but was a deliberate attack on Tiberius.

The urban and rural poor alike were interested in Tiberius' proposed agrarian law and flocked to the assembly to support it, while the rich, who had much to lose, opposed it. Tiberius' tribunate marks the beginning of the trend toward violence in republican politics: there had been the occasional imprisonment of consuls by tribunes, but no political assassinations. The murder of Tiberius with 300 supporters (doc. 8.15), and his brother Gaius with 3,000 (doc. 8.32), even if these numbers were exaggerated, marked not a single aberration in the history of the Republic, but was a signal of what was to come — bloody proscriptions, civil wars and devastation on a scale unheard of in Italy. The tribunates of the Gracchi did not automatically lead to the destruction of the Republic, nor can they even be said to have set the process in train. Rather, the Gracchi and the problems which they sought to overcome, and the ways in which they reacted to opposition, which provoked the senate to respond with force, exposed fundamental flaws in the Roman political apparatus and demonstrated its inability to deal peacefully with these problems.

While Tiberius started out with several influential supporters in the senate, including his father-in-law Appius Claudius Pulcher (cos. 143) and princeps senatus (doc. 8.11), it was the assembly which became his, and Gaius', mainstay, though it was not as loyal as might have been expected. Gaius discovered this in 122 when the assembly was won over by Drusus' proposals to support his opponents. The Gracchi created a power-base independent of the senate and, particularly in Gaius' case, of family connections. Marius and Sulla did not follow in the footsteps of the Gracchi or appreciate the lesson that the senate was not absolute, but they also exposed the same fundamental political problem of who ruled Rome, senate or people. Nevertheless the Gracchi hardly caused the collapse of the Republic and the view that 'they precipitated the revolution that overthrew the Republic' (Scullard *GN* 38) is simplistic in the extreme. Rome was 'quiet' for two decades after Gaius' murder, and the forces that brought down the Republic had other origins than the problems Tiberius and Gaius sought to address.

Tiberius' younger brother, Gaius, born 154, also had influential friends and connections. He was married to Licinia, daughter of P. Licinius Crassus Dives Mucianus (cos. 131). He served in Numantia with Scipio Aemilianus, his cousin and brother-in-law, and was elected to serve on Tiberius' land-commission in 133. He clearly followed the policies of his brother, and was a highly accomplished orator (docs 8.26–7). He was elected tribune for 123, though returned fourth out of ten, showing that he was not immediately popular, and re-elected for 122. His tribunates were to see a vast legislative programme, with his first aims being to put fresh life into his brother's agrarian reform (docs 8.28–9) and to seek justice — though limited — against Tiberius' murderers (doc. 8.29). His legislation cannot always be firmly dated to one tribunate or other, but it generally either benefited the people or the equites, such as the reforms of the extortion court and tax collection both of which benefited the equites (doc. 8.28), and he may have been concerned not so much to court their support, as to show that the people were an important source of authority: the laws about these two matters emanated from the people's assembly and challenged senatorial control of foreign affairs and state finance. The extortion court ties in with his attacks on the corruption of Roman officials (docs 8.22–4). His road-building and granary projects (doc. 8.28) probably also benefited the equites, as well as the people. Like Tiberius, he resorted to a make-shift bodyguard when his fortunes were reversed, and, like Tiberius, died violently along with his supporters (docs 8.30–3). The success of his legislation is uncertain, and Appian judged his agrarian law a failure (doc. 8.35), but the lex agraria of 111 BC conferred ownership of the land on those to whom the Gracchan land commission had apportioned it (doc. 8.36). Cicero's verdict on the Gracchi was negative (doc. 8.37) except when circumstances demanded it (doc. 8.39), while Sallust who favoured the populares was supportive and pointed out that the senate's use of force endangered the state (doc. 8.40).

Ancient sources: there were several contemporary writers on the Gracchi: Calpurnius Piso (cos. 133; *HRR* I² 120–38), C. Fannius (cos. 122 and son-in-law of Laelius: *HRR* I² 139–41) and Sempronius Asellio (military tribune in 133; *HRR* I² 179–84), all holding office in the crucial period; none of their works survive intact. Sempronius' history probably began in 146 and he dealt with events at least down to Drusus' assassination; apparently L. Cornelius Sisenna's history was a continuation of Asellio's from this point (*HRR* I² 276–97). Posidonius (c. 135–51: *FGrH* 87), an eastern Greek, wrote a world history from 146 BC down to the mid-80s; it no longer survives but his material on the slave revolts was used heavily by Diodorus (see chapter 6). Both Tiberius and Gaius Gracchus were excellent orators, and fragments of Gaius' speeches survive (*ORF*⁴ 174–98; docs 8.22–4). Cicero provides valuable references to the Gracchi, and his study of oratory would have included the Gracchi. Of historians proper, Livy, Plutarch and Appian are the most important, but Livy's relevant books survive only in the abbreviated form of the fourth-century AD Summaries (the *Periochae*) of Books 58, 60, 61. Plutarch's *Life of Tiberius Gracchus* and *Life of Gaius Gracchus* are invaluable, closely following the Roman annalistic tradition, and his main source is the same as used by Appian: Book 1.9.35–26.113 of Appian's *Civil Wars* deals with the Gracchi. He made use of the hostile account of C. Fannius (one fragment of a speech made by him survives: doc. 8.28), as well as the political pamphlet which Gaius had written about his brother. The historical record for the Gracchi is, then, quite considerable, and Appian and Plutarch are largely reliable witnesses to it (Astin 1967: 332–4; Scullard *GN* 386). Diodorus 34/5.24–7 provides judgmental comments of little value. In this chapter, the sources are taken as an essentially correct view of the period. Modern critics can and do disagree, but the sources must form the backbone of any historical reconstruction of this controversial period. The evidence of epigraphy is invaluable: mainly the surviving boundary-stones set up by the agrarian commission, the lex Acilia, and the lex agraria of 111 BC. For the sources, see *GN* 375–6, cf. 203; Bernstein 1978: 231–46; Lintott 1994: 54–5.

For initial reading on the Gracchi: Smith 1955: 75–85; Marsh 1963: 32–49; Scullard *GN* 22–41; Lintott 1994; Shotter 1994: 17–28; the ager publicus: Badian 1969: 209–14; Stockton 1979: 206–16. The evidence for the tribunates of the Gracchi: *MRR* I.493–4 (Ti. Gracchus, tr. pl. 133), 513–14, 517–18 (C. Gracchus, tr. pl. 123, 122).

FAMILY BACKGROUND

8.1 The father and mother of the Gracchi

Plutarch Life of *Tiberius Gracchus* 1.1–7

Cornelia was the daughter of *the* great Scipio Africanus, who defeated Hannibal at Zama in 202 BC. The younger Scipio, Scipio Aemilianus, Tiberius' and Gaius' brother-in-law, was the son of L. Aemilius Paullus and adopted by P. Cornelius Scipio (the son of the hero of the Second Punic War: doc. 2.25). He was responsible for the destruction of Carthage in 146 BC. Sempronia, sister of the Gracchi, married the younger Scipio but the marriage was not a success (doc. 8.21). The family connections between the Gracchi and Scipiones are interesting, especially as Scipio Aemilianus was certainly no supporter of Tiberius.

The father of the Gracchi was Ti. Sempronius Gracchus the Elder. Praetor and proconsul in Spain 180–178, he defeated the Celtiberians there and was awarded a triumph. He secured the consulship for 177, was awarded another triumph, for subduing the Sardi of Sardinia (see doc. 5.53), was censor in 169 and consul again in 163: *MRR* I.388, 397–8, 423–4. His uncle, also a Ti. Sempronius Gracchus, had been consul in 215 and 213. The great-grandfather of the Gracchi brothers had also been involved in Sardinia, at that time Carthaginian, and as consul in 238 had captured it for the Romans (his grandson continued the pacification of the province), which the Carthaginians bitterly resented. The family, though plebeian, was therefore distinguished, and aristocratic. For these achievements, family background, connections with other families, and the marriage of Cornelia: Earl 1963: 9–10, 49–70; Boren 1968: 23–35; Gruen 1968: 51–3; Bernstein 1978: 19–50; Stockton 1979: 23–4.

1: Both Agis IV and Cleomenes were Spartan kings. Agis, reigning c. 244–240, attempted to redistribute Spartan land because of a shortage of citizens but was executed. Cleomenes, reigning c. 235–222, redistributed the land and revived the Lycurgan system of training, but was defeated by Antigonus III of Macedon in 222, fled to Egypt and committed suicide in 220 BC. Their attempts to build up the number of citizens by land redistribution failed and their fates are a fitting parallel to the Gracchi brothers (cf. doc. 8.41). Plutarch wrote the *Lives of Agis and Cleomenes* like his *Lives of Tiberius and Gaius Gracchus* as one work, but scholars have traditionally split these into four individual *Lives* with their own separate chapter breaks. **6**: Plutarch here tells an implausible tale of the elder Tiberius finding two serpents on his bed; whichever he killed first would mean the death of that spouse; he chose to kill the male serpent. **7**: The Ptolemy referred to at 1.7 may have been Ptolemy VIII Euergetes II (doc. 5.38).

1 Now that I have completed the first part of my account (the *Lives* of Agis and Cleomenes), I have to turn to the equally unfortunate story of the Roman pair Tiberius and Gaius Gracchus, whom I have chosen as their parallel. **2** They were the sons of Tiberius Gracchus, who was more renowned for his personal excellence than for having been censor and twice consul, and having celebrated two triumphs. **3** It was for this reason that he was thought worthy to marry Cornelia, daughter of that Scipio who conquered Hannibal, after Scipio's death, even though they were not friendly and were on different sides in politics . . . **5** Tiberius died shortly afterwards (c. 150 BC), leaving Cornelia with 12 children by him. **6** Cornelia took charge of both the children and the household, and showed herself to be so discreet, devoted to her children and high-minded that Tiberius was considered to have made no bad decision in choosing to die instead of such a wife; **7** for when King Ptolemy asked her to share his crown and marry him she refused. While a widow she lost all her other children except for a daughter who married Scipio (Africanus) the younger, and two sons, Tiberius and Gaius, concerning whom this *Life* is written, whom she brought up so zealously that, although it is admitted that they were the most naturally gifted of all Romans, their virtues were thought to be owed more to their education than to nature.

8.2 Cornelia's pride in her children

Valerius Maximus *Memorable Deeds and Sayings (On Poverty)*
4.4 preface

Cornelia's marriage occurred sometime between 175 and 165. She was the second daughter of P. Cornelius Scipio Africanus, and, when her brother adopted Scipio Aemilianus (who was her cousin), he also became Cornelia's nephew. Sempronia, the other surviving child beside the two sons, was older than the boys, and married Scipio Aemilianus; all these connections did not stop Aemilianus from repudiating Tiberius' treaty with the Numantines (doc. 8.7, cf. 8.20). For Cornelia: Boren 1968: 29, 34; Stockton 1979: 22–6, 116–17; Bauman 1992: 42–3; for her betrothal, doc. 7.8. Pliny saw a statue of Cornelia (Pliny *Nat. Hist.* 34.31), which is referred to by Plutarch (doc. 8.29), and of which the base actually survives (*ILLRP* 336). Scipio Aemilianus, on the death of his adoptive grandmother Aemilia (Scipio Africanus' wife), gave her possessions not to her granddaughters (the Corneliae), but to his own two sisters (the Aemiliae); see doc. 7.70. The date of the *Collecta* of Pomponius Rufus is not known.

That children are a mother's greatest adornments we find as follows in Book . . . of Pomponius Rufus' anthology: when a Campanian lady was a guest in her house and showed off her jewellery, the very finest there was at the time, Cornelia, the mother of the Gracchi, detained her in conversation until her children returned home from school, and then said, 'These are *my* jewels'.

8.3 Plutarch's comparison of the two brothers

Plutarch *Life of Gaius Gracchus* 2.2–5, 3.1–2

For Gaius needing a pitch-pipe to guide him while speaking, see doc. 8.27. The dolphins were presumably furniture ornaments.

2.2 First of all Tiberius was mild and sedate in his facial appearance, glance and demeanour, while Gaius was eager and vehement, so when they spoke to the people Tiberius did so decorously, remaining on the same spot, while Gaius was the first Roman to walk up and down on the rostra and pull his toga off his shoulder while he was speaking, like Cleon the Athenian is said to have been the first demagogue to pull at his garment and strike his thigh. **3** Gaius' oratory was awe-inspiring and passionate to the point of exaggeration, while Tiberius' was more pleasant and productive rather of pity in the hearer. His style was pure and accurately cultivated, while Gaius' was persuasive and glamorous. **4** It was the same with regard to their way of life and eating-habits, for Tiberius' was inexpensive and simple, while Gaius', though moderate and austere when compared with that of others, was extravagant and epicurean in comparison with his brother: evidence for this is Drusus' charge that he bought silver dolphins at a cost of 1,250 drachmas a pound. **5** The same distinction was apparent in their characters as in their oratory, with Tiberius being reasonable and mild, and Gaius harsh and hot-tempered, in consequence being often, against his judgement, carried away by anger while speaking, while his voice would become high-pitched, and he would become abusive and confuse his argument. . . .

3.1 These were the differences between them, but with regard to courage in the face of the enemy, justice towards subjects, diligence in government, and restraint in their pleasures they were indistinguishable. Tiberius was the elder by nine years; **2** and this meant that their careers were divided by a period of time, which was an important element in weakening their actions, as they did not come to prominence together or wield power at the same time, for their power would have been immense and unsurpassable had both worked together.

8.4 Tiberius Gracchus as the beginning of civil strife in Rome

Appian *Civil Wars* 1.2 (4–5)

This passage is from the beginning of Appian's *Civil Wars*, and he sees the period of the Gracchi as the beginning of violent conflict in the Republic. Scholars follow him in dating the beginning of the disintegration of the Republic from the time of the Gracchi. For Appian, Cn. Marcius Coriolanus' alliance with the Volsci against Rome (c. 490) is the only precedent: cf. doc. 7.82.

4 And this is the only occurrence of armed conflict that one might find in the ancient struggles, and this was brought about by an exile (Coriolanus), but the sword was never brought into the assembly, nor was there any civil killing, until Tiberius Gracchus proposed laws as tribune. **5** He was the first to lose his life in internal strife, and with him many others, who were gathered on the Capitol round the temple, were also slain. Nor did the internal strife come to an end with this dreadful deed . . .

THE TRIBUNATE OF TIBERIUS GRACCHUS (133 BC)

Tiberius came to the tribunate after creditable military service, and could ordinarily have expected to go further with his political career. He served in the Third Punic War, as quaestor under his relative P. Cornelius Scipio Aemilianus, who sacked Carthage in 146 BC. He was quaestor in Spain in 137 BC and extricated the army of Hostilius Mancinus from disaster by negotiating a treaty (*MRR* I.485; see docs 8.8, 5.48). On his way to Numantia Tiberius had observed the number of slave-operated farms and was concerned at the lack of free-born peasants. Fearing that the slaves would multiply and the peasants (and hence army recruitment) decrease, he decided to distribute the ager publicus amongst Roman citizens and increase the population liable for military service. Boren sees the 140s as a period of prosperity and public spending at Rome, followed by an economic 'downturn' in the 130s (Boren 1968: 41–5, 1969: 54–66; cf. Boren 1958; Scullard 1960: 73; Gruen 1968: 47–8), but the sources concentrate on the agrarian and military nature of the crisis, and Boren incorrectly employs modern economic models and concepts.

8.5 Slaves prejudice citizen livelihoods

Appian *Civil Wars* 1.7 (26–31)

While there were large estates in Sicily with hundreds of slaves, the pattern in Italy was different. The land of the wealthy tended to be held in numerous small estates, usually of about 200 iugera, even in the case of wealthy landowners who preferred to own and manage separately numerous small properties (Brunt *IM* 330–1, 352, 365; Stockton 1979: 14–15; cf. Cornell 1995: 393–4; doc. 2.15 for an estate of Cato the Elder). Many of these estates worked by slaves must have included ager publicus.

The Romans had acquired a great deal of land in their conquest of Italy, some of which was distributed, but most was not: this became public land, ager publicus, leased out for a tax or toll. The idea was to allow the Italian allies the use of this land, 'in order to increase the Italian population' (App. 1.18), which provided infantry and cavalry when called upon by the Romans to do so. But the rich took up the land, and farmed it using slaves, who could not be called up for military service, and encroached on the farms of the free peasantry. The Italian population decreased and the slave population grew. This passage clearly refers to the period of the third and second centuries BC which saw the influx of huge numbers of slaves into Rome who formed the backbone of the estates of the landed gentry (as is clear from Cato's *On Farming*: see doc. 6.32).

26 As the Romans subdued Italy in war bit by bit, they used to seize a part of the Italians' lands and build towns there, or choose colonists of their own to occupy towns which were already there. **27** Their intention was to use these as garrison-towns, while on each occasion they immediately distributed to the colonists the cultivated part of the land acquired by conquest, or sold or leased it; as for the part which was then lying idle because of the war — which tended to be the greater proportion — as they did not have the time as yet to divide it up, they used to proclaim that, in the meantime, those who wished to work it might do so in return for a tax on the crops every year, a tenth of the grain and a fifth of the fruit. It was laid down that those who farmed animals should pay tolls on both the larger and smaller stock animals. **28** They did all this in order to increase the Italian population, which they considered very tough, so that they would have home-grown allies. But the very opposite occurred. **29** For the rich took over most of the unassigned land and, being confident in time that no one would ever dispossess them, absorbed small plots adjoining theirs and those of their poor neighbours, purchasing some through persuasion and taking others by force, and ended up farming great plains rather than individual properties, using purchased slaves as farm-workers and herdsmen, as free men might be diverted from farm-work into the army. In addition the ownership of slaves brought them great gain from their abundance of children, who multiplied free from danger because they were not liable for military service. **30** In this way powerful men became extremely rich and slaves as a class multiplied throughout the country, while the Italian population dwindled, worn down by poverty, taxes, and military service. **31** If they had any respite from these, they had to spend their time in idleness, because the land was held by the rich, who used slaves as their farm-workers instead of free men.

8.6 Concerns about military recruitment

Appian *Civil Wars* 1.8–9 (32–7)

Already in the fourth century BC the Licinio-Sextian legislation of 367 (doc. 1.47) attempted to prevent the ager publicus from coming into private ownership. In addition, at some stage either in 367 or after, a provision was enacted that no-one was to hold more than 500 iugera of this ager publicus (c. 300 hectares or c. 150 acres). Varro (*Rust.* 1.2.9) wrote that C. Licinius Stolo in 367 was responsible for this limitation (the so-called Licinio-Sextian law).

But this attribution of the limit cannot be right. As Lintott 1994: 55 notes, the points made by Appian about the growth in the number of slave-worked estates can only apply to the third century at the earliest, and best suit the second century when there were huge numbers of slaves in Italy, when the wide use of slaves in agriculture and pastoralism in Sicily and southern Italy (and the revolt of those slaves) is well-known. Cato in 167 BC in his speech in defence of the Rhodians for their part in the Third Macedonian War refers to a law which displeased the senatorial class, because it restricted the amount of ager publicus that one could possess to 500 iugera (*ORF*⁴ F167); this is clearly the same as the law referred to by Appian below. In addition, in 173 BC, the consul L. Postumius restricted encroachment on the ager publicus of Campania (Livy 42.1.6, 19.1). A law in the early second century BC would also better fit the context of the Hannibalic War, when a large amount of land was confiscated from rebel communities. In addition, there was the recent (but undated) attempt of Laelius, consul in 140 and associate of Scipio Aemilianus, to reform the abuse of the ager publicus; he desisted when his proposed reform aroused senatorial opposition and for this he earned the nickname 'Sapiens' (Wise). (Plut. *Ti. Gracchus* 8.3 is the only source for this; cf. Scullard 1960: 62–5; Astin 1967: 194; Boren 1968: 50; Brunt 1971: 66; Bernstein 1978: 98; Stockton 1979: 33; Adshead 1981: 123–4). Laelius assisted in the senatorial persecutions of Tiberius' supporters in 132, and was opposed to the proposal of the tribune C. Papirius Carbo (in 131 or 130) which permitted tribunes to be re-elected.

Tiberius in 133 was addressing a problem that had been noted several decades before, as the previous laws on the limitation of holdings of ager publicus had been easily circumvented. Tiberius was to go further and attempt to put the ager publicus into the hands of small-scale peasant farmers, drawn from the Roman citizen class. There was no food shortage at Rome; rather it was a question of who was producing food — slaves as opposed to free citizens.

For the revolts of the large numbers of slaves employed in agriculture in Sicily, see docs 6.31–6 (note too the slave revolts in Italy itself in 198, 196 and 185). While slaves could be called up for military service in emergencies (doc. 6.1) this was not considered an ideal situation. Note also the revolt of 4,000 slaves at Minturnae in Italy at the same time as the revolts in Sicily (Lintott 1994: 55).

The main problem with Appian's account is that he views Tiberius as motivated by a pan-Italic ideal to restore the Italians to the land, whereas it is clear that the land was to be distributed to Roman citizens to farm, who would then provide the soldiers (assidui) Rome needed. Rural citizens were the backbone of the Roman army; the city of Rome itself provided few soldiers (Brunt 1988: 253–4).

For the background to both the land situation and Tiberius' law: Cowell 1962: 82–4; Earl 1963: 16–29 (unconvincingly critical of the picture drawn by Appian and Plutarch); Astin 1967: 191–8; Boren 1968: 46–9; Brunt 1971: 77–8; Badian 1972: 682–90; Bernstein 1978: 71–101; Stockton 1979: 14–18; Scullard *GN* 18–21; Shochat 1980: 77–85; Lintott 1994: 53–9; for the Italians and the ager publicus: Richardson 1980. Not all accept Tiberius' argument based on a manpower shortage for the army: see esp. Rich 1983, cf. Morley 2001: 60. However, Tiberius wanted to distribute the ager publicus, providing for small allotments for citizen farmers, and despite his death (and his brother's) this did happen. It is clear from the ancient sources that a shortfall of soldiers motivated him, and Tiberius' arguments about this should not be casually dismissed simply as 'propaganda'.

32 On this account, the people were concerned in case they should no longer have a good supply of allies from Italy and that their government might be at risk due to so great a number of slaves; and, since they could come up with no solution, **33** as it was neither easy nor at all fair to take away from so many men so much property that they had held for so long, including their own plantations, buildings and equipment, they finally and with difficulty passed a law introduced by the tribunes that nobody should occupy more than 500 iugera of this land or pasture more than 100 large stock (cattle) or 500 smaller stock (sheep). To enforce this they determined that there should be a number of free men, whose job it was to keep a watch and report what happened. **34** Having enshrined these measures in a law, they took an oath over and above it and set penalties for breaking it, believing that the rest of the land would soon be distributed in small lots among the poor; but there was no concern for the laws or oaths, and those who seemed to respect them made the land over dishonestly to their relations, while the majority completely ignored them, **35** until Tiberius Sempronius Gracchus, a distinguished and most ambitious man, an extremely powerful speaker and well-known to everyone for these reasons, spoke eloquently as tribune about the Italian people and the way that, though they were very good at warfare and related to the Romans, they were slowly declining into penury and depopulation with no hope of a solution. **36** He criticised the slave body, as being of no use for military service and never faithful to its masters, bringing forward as an example of this the disaster owners in Sicily had recently suffered at the hands of their slaves, whose numbers had swelled from agriculture, and the fact that the Romans' war against them was neither easy nor short, but long drawn out and full of dangers of all kinds. **37** When he had said this he proposed the renewal of the law that no one should hold more than the 500 iugera (of public land). But he added to the ancient law that their sons might hold half that amount; three elected men, changed annually, should divide the remainder of the land among the poor.

8.7 Plutarch on Tiberius' motives (1)

Plutarch *Life of Tiberius Gracchus* 5.1–6, 7.1–7

Appian in the previous passage has Tiberius as 'most ambitious' (1.9.35) but has him principally concerned with the decline in the number of free-hold peasants and hence of available soldiers. Here, Plutarch discusses the effect on Tiberius of the repudiation of his treaty with the Numantines. Numantia was a Celtiberian city in Spain, which the Romans were steadily conquering. Numantia had withstood six Roman attempts to take it, in 195, 153, 152, 140, 139–8, and the incident here in 137, when Tiberius by his treaty saved 20,000 Roman citizens; it was only captured in 133 by Scipio Aemilianus (docs 5.48–50). For the Numantine treaty and its role in motivating Tiberius: Earl 1963: 67; Boren 1968: 37–40; Bernstein 1978: 117–18; Stockton 1979: 29; Shochat 1980: 66–7.

5.1 After the war against Carthage, Tiberius was elected quaestor, and it fell to him to serve in a campaign against Numantia under the consul Gaius (Hostilius) Mancinus

(137 BC), who was not a bad man, but more unfortunate than any other Roman as a general. **2** Nevertheless, amid unexpected misfortunes and adverse encounters, not only did Tiberius' intelligence and courage shine out all the more brightly, but also, which was remarkable, his respect and honour towards his commander, who, under the misfortunes of the campaign, even forgot that he was general. **3** After being defeated in major battles, Mancinus tried to break camp, withdrawing the army during the night; the Numantines noticed this and immediately seized the camp, attacking the men as they fled, and killed the rearguard. They then encircled the whole force and drove them to difficult terrain with no chance of escape. Mancinus, who had given up hope of forcing his way to safety, sent heralds to propose a truce and peace-terms. **4** The Numantines declared that they had no confidence in anyone except Tiberius, and ordered that he be sent to them. **5** They came to this decision both because of the young man himself (for he had an excellent reputation among their troops), and because they remembered his father Tiberius, who had fought against the Spaniards and subdued many of them, but made a peace with the Numantines, which he had always ensured that the people kept scrupulously and justly. **6** So Tiberius was sent to negotiate with the enemy, and, after persuading them to accept some terms, and accepting others himself, he arranged a truce and unarguably saved the lives of 20,000 Roman citizens, without counting slaves and camp followers. . . .

7.1 When he returned to Rome, the whole transaction was being criticised and denounced as a terrible disgrace to Rome, although the relatives and friends of the soldiers, who formed a large part of the people, came running to Tiberius, blaming the disgrace of what had happened on his commander, and declaring that it was through Tiberius that so many citizens' lives had been saved. **2** Those, however, who were unhappy at what had been done urged that they should imitate the actions of their forefathers, who had thrown naked to the enemy the very generals who had been content to be released by the Samnites, and similarly throw out those who had had a part and share in the treaty, such as the quaestors and military tribunes, placing on their shoulders the perjury and repudiation of the agreement. **3** It was on this occasion that the people particularly demonstrated their good will and affection towards Tiberius. **4** For they voted that the consul should be handed over to the Numantines stripped and in chains, but spared all the others for Tiberius' sake. **5** It appears that Scipio (Aemilianus), at that time the greatest and most powerful man at Rome, also helped; but none the less he was criticised because he had not saved Mancinus and had not insisted that the treaty, negotiated by his relative and friend Tiberius, should be kept. **6** It seems most likely that the difference between the two men arose through the ambition of Tiberius and from the friends and sophists who encouraged him; but this difference led to no irremediable break. **7** My own view is that Tiberius would never have met with his misfortunes if Scipio (Aemilianus) Africanus had been at Rome during his political career; but he was already at Numantia and waging war there when Tiberius undertook his programme of proposed reforms.

8.8 Cicero blames the senate

Cicero *On the Responses of the Soothsayers* 43

Cicero, like Plutarch, sees the resentment (*dolor*) of Tiberius as crucial to his decision in 133 to press for reform of the ager publicus. This gives Tiberius only a negative motive, and allows no place for altruistic aims, to ensure that Rome had enough troops for her many wars. Cicero is clearly a hostile witness here and reflects the senatorial element that opposed Tiberius. Tiberius' reform is seen as a departure from senatorial authority, but he was not completely without senatorial support in his legislation: his father-in-law Appius Claudius Pulcher was actually princeps senatus, and he had the support of one of the consuls for 133, P. Mucius Scaevola, as well as the consul's brother P. Licinius Crassus Dives Mucianus, father-in-law of Gaius Sempronius Gracchus, and brother-in-law of Appius Claudius Pulcher (Plut. *Ti. Gracchus* 9.1); the latter two were eminent legal figures. Cicero's characterisation presents Tiberius' tribunate as a deliberate attack on senatorial authority, but it was not his intention in putting forward the lex Sempronia agraria to 'wage war' on the senate.

Tiberius Gracchus had been involved in concluding a treaty with the Numantines when he was serving as quaestor to the consul Gaius Mancinus. The unpopularity he gained from this and the inflexibility of the senate in refusing to ratify it inspired Tiberius with resentment and fear, and these forced that brave and distinguished man to break away from the authority of the senate.

8.9 Plutarch on Tiberius' motives (2)

Plutarch *Life of Tiberius Gracchus* 8.6–10

In addition to the Numantia issue, Plutarch adduces several other motives for Tiberius. Cornelia's special care over the education of her sons is commented upon by Plutarch (also at 1.3, 8.3, 17.3, 20.3; cf. doc. 8.12); for Diophanes of Miletus, the orator, and Blossius, the Stoic philosopher, see Stockton 1979: 25, 38. Whether Stoic philosophy influenced either brother is debated. The presence of Greek tutors in an aristocratic household was not in itself unusual. The extent to which Cornelia was an influence on her sons is unclear. She did persuade Gaius to desist from his attack on Octavius (doc. 8.29), and there were two opinions of her attitude to his activities: that she supported them and that she opposed them (Plut. *C. Gracchus* 13.1). There is no reason to assume that she was not ambitious for her sons and after her husband's death, as the sources indicate, her energies went into their upbringing (doc. 7.22).

Tiberius' observation of the slave-run estates in Etruria that dominated the countryside was a chief consideration in his decision to distribute the ager publicus to Roman citizens who would then be liable for military service. It is also clear from doc. 8.11 that there were soldiers who had no land. In this way, Tiberius was in the position of later generals, who had to provide land for their veterans. Scullard 1960: 64, 73 points to the large numbers of troops demobilised after the various campaigns of the 150s and the Third Punic War. Nagle 1976 argues that archaeological surveys of Etruria indicate that there were large numbers of small estates in this area; however, this overlooks the fact that the holdings of the wealthy were made up of numerous small holdings, like Cato the Elder's. Tiberius clearly did see evidence of the disappearance of the farmers eligible for service as assidui (soldiers), and identified a crucial socio-economic problem which he then set out to solve (Earl 1963: 21 dismisses the Etruria observations as a fabrication of Gaius'; see also Harris 1971: 203–6; Rich 1983).

6 As soon as Tiberius became tribune he put his plans straight into action, under the encouragement, as most report, of Diophanes the orator and Blossius the philosopher.

Diophanes was an exile from Mytilene, while Blossius was a native Italian from Cumae and had been a close friend of Antipater of Tarsus at Rome, who had honoured him by dedicating to him some of his philosophical treatises. **7** But some also put the blame on his mother Cornelia, since she often reproached her sons because the Romans still referred to her as the mother-in-law of Scipio, and not yet as the mother of the Gracchi. **8** Others say that a certain Spurius Postumius was responsible. He was the same age as Tiberius, and a rival of his for reputation as an advocate, and, when Tiberius returned from the campaign and found Postumius had far surpassed him in reputation and influence and was widely admired, he decided, it seems, to outdo him by undertaking a bold political programme which would give rise to widespread expectations. **9** But his brother Gaius has written in a certain pamphlet that, as Tiberius was travelling through Etruria on his way to Numantia, he observed the depopulated nature of the country, and that the farmers and herders were imported barbarian slaves, and that it was then that he first thought of the programme which was to bring countless ills on the two brothers. **10** But it was the people themselves who most of all kindled his energy and ambitions, who called on him by means of graffiti on porticoes, house walls and monuments to recover the public land for the poor.

8.10 The reaction of the wealthy to Tiberius' proposals

Appian *Civil Wars* 1.10 (38–42)

The reaction of those who had made use of the ager publicus is in many ways understandable. There had been an unstated understanding that the ager publicus could be farmed, and Tiberius had made no provision for reimbursement or compensation of any kind. But while Cicero has the 'honest men' ('boni') opposing the law because it would dispossess the rich and rob the state of those who defended it (*Sest.* 103), Tiberius' provision that the wealthy retain 500 iugera, and more depending on children, was very generous, especially as the lots distributed to the poor were a maximum of 30 iugera. The reaction of the wealthy: Earl 1963: 41–78; Stockton 1979: 10–11.

38 What particularly upset the wealthy was that they were no longer able to ignore the law, as they had before, because of the commissioners, nor could they buy the land from those to whom it was allocated, because Gracchus had foreseen this and forbidden it to be sold. **39** They banded together in groups and aired their grievances, accusing the poor of robbing them of their work of many years, their plantations and houses, while some had paid their neighbours for the land, and would lose their money with the land, while others had ancestral tombs on land that had been allotted to them in the division of their fathers' properties; others had spent their wives' dowries on their estates, or given the land as dowries to their daughters; some could show debts contracted to money-lenders with their land as surety, and there was widespread lamentation and anger. **40** On the other hand, the poor complained in their turn that they had been reduced from comfort to utter poverty and from there to childlessness, since they were not able to bring up their children. They enumerated how many campaigns they had served for the acquisition of this land, and were angry at the suggestion that they might be deprived of their part of the common land, while they abused their opponents for choosing to use slaves instead of free men, citizens and soldiers, since slaves were always an untrustworthy and hostile race and for that reason of no use in the army. **41** While the two sides were making such complaints and mutual recriminations, another large group of those who lived in the colonies or free towns, or who were in some way or other concerned with this land and had similar fears, flooded in (to Rome) and took the part of one side or the other. **42** Taking heart because of their numbers, they grew exasperated and kindled numerous conflicts while they waited for the voting on the law, with one party determined by any means to prevent its being enacted, the other to have it passed at all costs.

8.11 Tiberius' rhetoric

Plutarch *Life of Tiberius Gracchus* 9.1–6

(*ORF*[4] F149.) Tiberius had supporters in the senate, drawn largely from his family connections. However, he did not rely on these supporters, but rather on the backing of the people's assembly. Here he refers to landless soldiers, who had perhaps lost their farms while on long service, especially during the protracted wars in Spain. Crassus (P. Licinius Crassus, cos. 131) was pontifex maximus from 132 (Nasica was pontifex maximus in 133); Mucius Scaevola was consul in 133: *MRR* I.492, 499.

1 He did not draft the law on his own, but followed the advice of the citizens who were most eminent in merit and reputation, among whom were Crassus the pontifex maximus, Mucius Scaevola the jurist, who was then consul, and Appius Claudius, Tiberius' father-in-law. **2** And it did seem that no law against such injustice and greed had ever been put in more mild and gentle terms . . . **3** Despite the restitution being so conciliatory, the people were content to leave the past alone as long as the injustice would come to an end for the future, but the wealthy and landowners hated the law out of greed and the lawgiver out of rage and contentiousness and tried to turn the people against it on the grounds that Tiberius was introducing a redistribution of land to overthrow the state and stir up a revolution. **4** They had no success; Tiberius was striving for a policy which was just and good in itself, and employing oratory which would have adorned a less worthy subject. He was formidable and insuperable when, with the people crowding around the rostra on which he was mounted, he would speak on behalf of the poor: **5** 'The wild beasts that dwell in Italy have their homes, with each having a lair and a hiding-place, but the men who fight and die on behalf of Italy have a share of air and light — and nothing else. Without houses or homes they wander aimlessly with their children and wives, and their generals deceive them when they urge the soldiers on the battlefield to drive off the enemy to protect their tombs and temples; **6** not one of these Romans has a family altar, not one an ancestral tomb; instead, they fight and die to protect the luxury and wealth of others. They are called masters of the earth, yet have not a single clod of earth that is their own.'

8.12 Tiberius Gracchus as public figure

Cicero *Brutus* 103–4

In this essay on rhetoric, Cicero again sees the *invidia* (animosity) over the repudiation of the Numantine treaty as being a major stimulus for Tiberius' legislation. He pays tribute to Cornelia's education of her sons and to their Greek teachers (cf. doc. 7.22); Menelaus of Marathus (with others) is mentioned as Gaius' teacher in *Brut.* 100. Cicero also speaks of the Gracchi as characterised in their speeches to the people by a much easier and freer style of speaking, though down to their day the art of eloquence had not yet reached 'perfection' (333). Cicero is incorrect in stating that Tiberius was 'put to death by the state itself' (103); he was murdered by senators who took the law into their own hands. C. Papirius Carbo (cos. 120) was a member of Tiberius' land commission; he committed suicide in 119 after being prosecuted by Lucius Licinius Crassus (cos. 95).

103 If only Tiberius Gracchus and Gaius Carbo's attitude towards conducting the affairs of state properly had equalled their genius for speaking well! — indeed, no one would have surpassed them in reputation (gloria). Gracchus, as a result of the tempestuous violence of his tribunate, to which he proceeded enraged with the 'honest men' (the boni) over the animosity aroused by (the repudiation of) the Numantine treaty, was put to death by the state itself; Carbo, as a result of his constant irresponsibility in popular politics, only saved himself from the condemnation of a jury by a death at his own hands. But each was a top-class orator **104** — and I can state this with our fathers' memory of their speeches as my evidence; for we possess speeches of both Carbo and Gracchus in which the language does not yet achieve brilliance, but which are to the point and skilful in the extreme. Through the diligence of his mother Cornelia, Gracchus had been educated from boyhood and was thoroughly versed in Greek literature. For he had always had excellent teachers from Greece, one of whom, from his youth, being Diophanes of Mytilene, who was considered to be the most eloquent speaker in Greece at that time. But Gracchus' time for developing and displaying his talent was short-lived.

8.13 The passing of the agrarian reform and Octavius' deposition

Appian *Civil Wars* 1.11–13 (43–57)

Tiberius' proposal is made clear by Appian at doc. 8.6: to renew the law that no one should hold more than the 500 iugera, but adding that their children might each hold half that amount, and that a commission of three men divide the remaining land among the poor. Appian again here points to the idea of manpower; that Tiberius would build up the free population of Italy. Appian has 500 iugera and half again for each son, with no limit on the number of sons. Badian 1972: 702 points out that the Greek word here 'paides' is usually translated as 'sons' but actually means children, so that both sons and daughters could each have 250 iugera retained in their names. Tiberius wanted to restrict the ager publicus in the hands of the wealthy but the number of children of the wealthy was important too. The amount — 500 iugera — is still very generous. That paides — children — would include daughters makes sense given the fact that land was important for dowries, as Appian mentions.

The opposition of the tribune Marcus Octavius to the agrarian proposal was clearly unexpected by Tiberius. It was also, in a sense, unprecedented in that other pieces of legislation opposed by the nobility had been passed without the imposition of a tribunician veto. But in this case there was much more at stake than might have been the case in the past, namely the value and use of this land. The lex Hortensia of 287 (doc. 1.67) had provided that plebiscites were to be binding on the whole people, and no tribunician veto had been imposed between then and 133 BC. A tribunician veto in 188 had been withdrawn, as it was argued that the people should make the decision. Octavius in opposing the clear wishes of the assembly went against established practice. Tiberius' deposition of a tribune was unprecedented, but so was Octavius' veto in defiance of what the people wanted. At the debate in the senate concerning Tiberius' proposal to use the legacy of

Attalus, T. Annius Luscus (cos. 153) argued that Tiberius had committed an act of sacrilege by deposing Octavius, whose person, as tribune, was sacred and inviolable; he challenged Tiberius to a wager over the matter (Plut. *Ti. Gracchus* 14.5–9: *ORF*[4] F4). Whether Octavius' opposition stemmed from senatorial prompting (as per Brunt 1971: 79) is unclear, but possible. Appian 1.14.60 calls the replacement tribune Mummius; Plutarch has Mucius (doc. 8.14; seee *MRR* I.493). For the veto: see esp. Badian 1972: 697–9 (followed here); the deposition of Octavius: Cowell 1962: 91; Earl 1963: 79–87; Astin 1967: 205–10; Boren 1968: 57–9; Gruen 1968: 55; Brunt 1971: 79–80; Badian 1972: 706–12; Bernstein 1978: 160–97.

Tiberius had taken his proposal straight to the comitia plebis tributa (tribal assembly), responsible for electing tribunes and aediles, and for passing plebiscites, in which the urban population was confined to four of the thirty-five tribes, and the rural population to the others. He had not taken the legislation before the senate, then was to do this when it was suggested that he do so for the sake of arbitration (App. 1.12.50). The ager publicus clearly lay within the sphere of competence of the assembly. While it might be said that Tiberius' 'bypassing' of the senate was 'a breach of tradition' (Boren 1968: 56), there is no real ground for such an assertion, and there is no evidence that the senate was annoyed at any breach of tradition or protocol that occurred with the land legislation: see Astin 1967; 201–2; Stockton 1979: 62–3; esp. Badian 1972: 695–7; cf. Taylor 1962. There was also precedent in the example of Flaminius who as tribune in 232 had proposed and the assembly carried a law concerning land distribution that the senate largely opposed, including his own father. He distributed to poor Roman citizens the ager Gallicus, confiscated half a century earlier, in northern Italy. This area in fact became a major source of army recruits and Tiberius' plan was similar in conception (Badian 696). It was the legacy of Attalus that provoked the real breach, even if in murdering Tiberius and 300 of his supporters many senators were motivated by a desire to retain the ager publicus in their possession.

The provisions of the lex Sempronia agraria are known only from the summaries of the literary sources: ager publicus was to be distributed to Roman citizens; a minimum of 500 iugera could be retained with the maximum amount dependant on the number of children; the lex agraria of 111 indicates that the maximum size of any distributed plot was 30 iugera (see doc. 8.36); a commission of three was established to distribute this land (Tiberius, Gaius and Appius Claudius; see docs 8.16–18). For the agrarian law, see Earl 1963: 16–40; Boren 1968: 46–53; Brunt 1971: 78; Nagle 1971: 112–19; Badian 1972: 701–6; Scullard *GN* 25–8; Bernstein 1978: 123–59; Stockton 1979: 41–60; Shochat 1980: 85–89; Gargola 1995: 148–55; Tiberius' supporters: see esp. Nagle 1970. Tribunes had been active since the lex Hortensia (287 BC), though not directly challenging the senate's authority: Williams 2004.

43 Gracchus' intention in proposing the bill was not to effect a plentiful supply of money but of men, and being particularly enthused by the useful nature of the work, believing that Italy could experience nothing greater or more glorious, he paid no consideration to the attendant difficulties. **44** When it was the time for voting, he brought forward many other arguments at length and inquired of them whether it was not just that the common property should be divided in common and whether a citizen was not always more a legitimate concern of theirs than a slave, a soldier more useful than one who had no part in warfare, and a man who shared in the common property more devoted to the public welfare than one who did not. **45** Without spending much time on this comparison as being demeaning, he went straight on to a consideration of their country's hopes and fears, pointing out that they held most of their territory through conquest in war and hoped to possess the remainder of the inhabited world, and that now was the critical moment, as to whether they would have plenty of men and obtain the rest or lose what they had to their enemies through weakness and jealousy. **46** After exaggerating the glory and prosperity of the one, and the danger and fear of the other, he told the wealthy to consider all this, and to give this land as a gift, if necessary, from themselves to those who would bring up children to bring these hopes about. They should not, by disputing about trifles, overlook the larger picture, especially as they were getting sufficient compensation for the work they had put in, with each of them getting, without payment and for all time, undisputed possession of 500 iugera, and also half of this again for each of their children, should they have any. **47** After making a long speech along these lines and stirring up the poor and those others who were motivated by reason rather than the desire for gain, Gracchus ordered the clerk to read out the proposed law.

48 Marcus Octavius, however, another tribune, who had been induced by those in occupation of the lands to interpose his veto — for among the Romans the veto is always the more powerful — ordered the clerk to be silent. **49** Gracchus thereupon severely censured him and adjourned the meeting to the next assembly day. He stationed beside himself a sufficient guard, as if he were going to force Octavius against his will, and ordered the clerk with threats to read the bill out to the people. He began to read, but on Octavius' forbidding it fell silent. **50** The tribunes began to abuse each other, and the people were in considerable uproar, when the leading citizens asked the tribunes to submit the matter under debate to the senate, and Gracchus seized on the suggestion, as he believed that his law would be acceptable to all well-disposed people, and hurried to the senate-house. **51** But since he had few supporters there and was insulted by the rich, he ran back to the forum and said that at the next meeting of the assembly he would put a vote both about the proposed law and about Octavius' magistracy, to decide whether a tribune who acted against the interests of the people should continue to hold office. **52** And this he did; for when Octavius, not at all browbeaten, again interposed his veto, Gracchus put the vote about him first.

When the first tribe voted to depose Octavius from his magistracy, Gracchus turned to him and begged him to change his mind. As he would not be persuaded, he put the vote to the other tribes. **53** There were 35 tribes at that time, and, after the first 17 angrily concurred with the motion, Gracchus, as the eighteenth was about to give the decisive vote, again, in the sight of the people, urgently begged Octavius, whose position was now critical, not to render null and void a work that was extremely fair and useful to all Italy, nor to overturn the people's earnest wish, especially since it was only right for him as tribune to give in to their desires, and not to seek to have his office taken away by the people's condemnation. **54** After saying this and calling on the gods to witness that it was not willingly that he was dishonouring a colleague, as Octavius did not give in, he went on taking the votes. Octavius immediately became a private citizen and went off unnoticed.

55 Quintus Mummius was elected tribune in his place, and the agrarian law was passed. The first commissioners elected to allocate the land were Gracchus himself, the law's proposer, his brother of the same name (Gaius), and his father-in-law Appius Claudius, as the people were still very afraid that the law might not be put into effect, unless Gracchus and his whole family began the work. **56** Gracchus was highly thought of by the people because of this law, and was escorted home as if he were the founder not of a single city or race, but of all the nations in Italy. **57** After this the victors returned to their fields, from where they had come for this purpose, while the losers who remained in the city took it badly, saying that once Gracchus was a private citizen again he would be sorry that he had insulted the sacred and inviolable tribunate, and had given Italy such an occasion for conflict.

8.14 Tiberius mortally offends the senate

Plutarch *Life of Tiberius Gracchus* 13.2–14.3

The senate cannot have been unduly upset at Tiberius' act in taking agrarian legislation direct to the comitia tributa. Moreover, there were clearly several in the senate who supported the law, including a consul, and the princeps senatus (doc. 8.11). However the loss of so much ager publicus was obviously a blow to many of the wealthy senators and they attempted to frustrate the land commission through allocating it a paltry allowance. Tiberius added to senatorial resentment by interference in what was clearly a senatorial prerogative when he proposed to make use of the money available from the bequest of Attalus III of Pergamum (doc. 5.44): this gave rise to violent opposition. The money would be given to those citizens who settled the land to help them equip their farms. Tiberius heard of the bequest before the senate because the envoy from Pergamum, Eudemus, stayed at his house because of a prior connection with Tiberius' father. The charge of aiming at kingship was clearly without foundation. P. Cornelius Scipio Nasica (cos. 138), who was responsible for the violence leading to Tiberius' murder, was the pontifex maximus and Tiberius' cousin. For the attitude of the senate as a whole to the legislation (supporters and opponents): Briscoe 1974; Bernstein 1978: 102–22; senatorial reaction to Tiberius' plan for the Attalus legacy: Boren 1961, 1968: 60–1; Earl 1963: 92–5; Brunt 1965: 191–2; Nagle 1971: 119–27; Badian 1972: 712–16; Bernstein 1978: 207–11; Stockton 1979: 67–70.

13.2 Tiberius succeeded in carrying all these measures peaceably and without opposition, and in addition had a replacement tribune elected, not a man from a distinguished family, but Mucius, a client of his. The wealthy, angered at all of this and afraid of Tiberius' increasing power, kept insulting him in the senate, **3** and when, as was the custom, he requested a tent at the public expense for his work in dividing up the land, they did not grant it, though others had often received one for less important duties, and assigned him an expense allowance of nine obols a day on the proposal of Publius Nasica, who had utterly given himself up to hatred of Tiberius; for he possessed a very great deal of public land, and bitterly resented being obliged to give it up. **4** This enraged the people still more; and when a certain friend of Tiberius' died suddenly, with malignant eruptions apparent all over the corpse, they cried out that he had been poisoned . . . **6** Whereupon, Tiberius incited the people still further by going into mourning and bringing his children before the people and begging them to take care of them and of their mother, as if he had given himself up for lost.

14.1 When Attalus Philometor died and Eudemus of Pergamum brought his will to Rome, in which the king had named the Roman people as his heir, Tiberius immediately, to win popularity, proposed a law that the king's money be given to those citizens who had been allocated land, to use for equipping and cultivating their farms. **2** As regarded the cities which were part of Attalus' kingdom Tiberius said that it was not a matter to be decided by the senate, but that he himself would propose a motion to the people. **3** By this he gave extreme offence to the senate, and when Pompeius got up to speak he declared that he was Tiberius' neighbour and so knew that Eudemus of Pergamum had given him a diadem and purple robe out of the royal treasure, as the future king of Rome.

8.15 Tiberius' death

Appian *Civil Wars* 1.14–17 (58–72)

There are two accounts of Tiberius' attempt to gain re-election to the tribunate, in Appian and Plutarch, who includes the improbable detail of Tiberius asking for a diadem. The charge of aiming at kingship could not have been taken seriously but was one more way in which the senators opposed to Tiberius vented their displeasure. In Appian's account a tussle — hardly murderous — began in the comitia, in which some of the senators became involved.

Tiberius sought re-election to safeguard himself, as his enemies were threatening to prosecute him once his tribunate was over (Plut. *Ti. Gracchus* 16.1; App. 1.13), but this decision to stand again was also an object of attack, and Tiberius' methods caused all of the tribunes, with the exception of his nominated replacement for Octavius, to desert his cause. Tiberius had occupied the Capitol, driven the rich from the assembly, and the tribunes had fled. This was unprecedented and there was no political machinery to deal with the situation. The deadlock was only broken with violence.

In Plutarch's account, the senate deliberated but the consul did not take action (the consul P. Mucius Scaevola was in fact a supporter of Gracchus and preferred a constitutional approach: Plut. *Ti. Gracchus* 19.3). Nasica took the matter into his own hands and Gracchus and his supporters were bludgeoned to death with bench legs, staves and clubs. The concordia of the Republic was shattered, but it must be noted that it was Tiberius who commandeered the assembly place, and his supporters had armed themselves with clubs, prepared to use violence if necessary. When respect for the senate overcame them, the clubs were used not by them, but against them. Election day and the murder of Tiberius: Earl 1963: 103–9, 117–18; Astin 1967: 217–26; Boren 1968: 66–70; Gruen 1968: 58–9; Badian 1972: 716–26; Nippel 1984: 25–7; Lintott 1999: 209–10; Linderski 2002; Scaevola: Gruen 1965.

58 It was now summer, and the tribunician elections were at hand; as the day for voting approached, it was very clear that the rich had been earnestly supporting the election of those especially hostile to Gracchus. He was afraid as the danger came closer that he might not be tribune for the following year, and he summoned the people from the fields to the election. **59** As they were busy with the harvest, he was compelled by the nearness of the day appointed for voting to have recourse to the plebeians in the city, and he went round to them all individually asking them to elect him tribune for the next year, since he was at risk on their account. **60** When the voting took place, the first two tribes voted for Gracchus, but the rich objected that it was not legal for the same man to hold the office twice in succession and the tribune Rubrius, who had been chosen by lot to preside over the assembly, was in doubt as to the matter . . . **62** As there was much argument over this question, and Gracchus was losing, he postponed the election till the next day, and in total despair dressed himself in black, though still in office, and for the rest of the day led his son around the forum, introducing him to everyone and committing him to their care, as if his destruction at the hands of his enemies was close at hand.

63 On reflection, the poor were seized with great sorrow, both for themselves, believing that they would no longer be treated equally as citizens under the laws, but would be compelled to work for the rich, and for Gracchus himself, who was in such fear and suffering on their account, and they all escorted him to his house that evening with lamentation, bidding him to take courage for the next day. **64** With renewed confidence, Gracchus assembled his supporters before dawn and told them the signal, should fighting be necessary. He then occupied the temple on the Capitoline Hill, where the voting was to take place, and the middle of the assembly. **65** Obstructed by the tribunes and the rich, who would not allow the votes to be taken on this issue, he gave the signal. A sudden shout arose from those in the know, and violence broke out, with some of Gracchus' supporters protecting him like body-guards, and others girding up their togas, grabbing the rods and staves in the hands of the lictors, and breaking them into pieces. They then drove the rich from the assembly, **66** with such uproar and wounds, that the tribunes fled from their central position in fear, and the priests closed the temple. Many ran away in confused flight spreading false rumours, some that Gracchus had deposed the other tribunes from their office (this was believed because they could not be seen), others that he had declared himself tribune for the next year without an election.

67 While this was going on, the senate met in the temple of Fides. It seems amazing to me that it did not occur to them at that juncture to appoint a dictator, though they had often been protected in such dangers by the rule of one man, but an action which had been so useful in earlier times did not occur to the people, either then or later. **68** After taking their decisions, they made their way up to the Capitol. The first, who led the way, was the pontifex maximus, Cornelius Scipio Nasica; he cried in a loud voice, 'Those who wish to save their country, follow me!' . . . **69** When he reached the temple and advanced on Gracchus' men, they gave way, out of respect for such a distinguished man, and because they saw the senate accompanying him; but the senators grabbed the clubs from Gracchus' men, and smashed the benches and other pieces of equipment which had been provided for the assembly, and began to strike the Gracchans, pursuing them and driving them over the cliff. **70** In this uproar, many of Gracchus' men died, including Gracchus himself who was pressed up against the temple and slain at the door near the statues of the kings. All these bodies were thrown at night into the river Tiber.

71 In this way Gracchus, son of the Gracchus who was twice consul and of Cornelia, daughter of the Scipio who had taken its supremacy away from Carthage, was killed on the Capitol while still in office as tribune, as a result of an excellent proposition which, however, he pursued too violently. This was the first occasion on which a heinous crime of this sort took place in the assembly, and similar incidents were to be encountered on a regular basis from thenceforth. **72** The city was divided on the issue of Gracchus' death into grief and delight, with some people lamenting for both themselves and for him, as well as for the current state of affairs, for they considered that the state was no longer in existence and that it had been replaced by force and violence, while the others felt that all their wishes had been granted.

BOUNDARY-STONES OF THE GRACCHAN PERIOD

Despite Tiberius' murder, the activities of the land commission proceeded. The senate wanted to conciliate the people and the distribution of land went ahead, with the senate proposing that a new commissioner be chosen in place of Tiberius (Plut. *Ti. Gracchus* 21.1), implying that their opposition was not to Tiberius' agrarian legislation. Several boundary stones set up by the commissioners have survived, from Campania, the territory of the Hirpini, Lucania, and Picenum, and archaeology indicates centuriation (division into centuries or blocks) in this period in Apulia (Nagle 1970: 385; Scullard *GN* 384–5; Gargola 1995: 157–8).

Tiberius was replaced by P. Licinius Crassus Dives Mucianus, Scaevola's brother, and Gaius' father-in-law, who was elected consul for 131 (this election by the comitia centuriata, always dominated by the wealthiest citizens, is interesting); Crassus was killed in that year by Aristonicus who was leading an uprising against Rome in Pergamum (doc. 10.1). Claudius Pulcher also died, probably in 130. C. Papirius Carbo and M. Fulvius Flaccus joined Gaius on the commission. Fulvius was a supporter of Tiberius (Plut. *Ti. Gracchus* 18.2–3), and as consul in 125 he offered the allies citizenship in return for allowing the commission to distribute the ager publicus (Appian 1.21.87: doc. 8.28). The proposal fell through when he was sent to Transalpine Gaul to deal with the Celts threatening Marseilles (he celebrated a triumph in 123). The Latin colony of Fregellae revolted when the citizenship proposal died, and the town was destroyed by Opimius as praetor. This citizenship proposal was to be revived by Gaius.

The land to be distributed to citizens was generally accurately surveyed, marked off in large blocks (centuries) and then divided into individual plots, with fixed widths for roads. The process was overseen by the commission, whose names are recorded on most surviving stones. The lex agraria of 111 BC refers to a maximum distribution of 30 iugera. The lots allocated by the Gracchi will have been this size or smaller (doc. 8.36(14)). As those currently making use of the ager publicus could retain a minimum of 500 iugera and more depending on children, the wealthy who were in possession were clearly not disadvantaged by Tiberius' law. Colonists had earlier in the second century been allocated small plots of five to ten iugera (see Evans 1980: 161). For the commission established by Tiberius, see Earl 1963: 91–2; Nagle 1970: 385–94; Adshead 1981: 126–7; Scullard *GN* 29–31; Lintott 1994: 73; Gargola 1995: 155–63, 167–74.

8.16 Re-establishment of Gracchan boundary-stones of 132 BC

ILS 26

(*CIL* I² 719; *ILLRP* 474; *ROL* IV.174.) A small pillar found between Pisaurum and Fanum, dating to 82/81 BC; see Scullard *GN* 384 n.19.

Marcus Terentius Varro Lucullus, son of Marcus, acting as praetor, **5** by a resolution of the senate superintended the re-establishment of boundary-stones where Publius Licinius, Appius Claudius, and Gaius Gracchus, Board of Three for adjudging and assigning lands, established them.

8.17 Land-surveying boundaries, 131 BC

CIL I² 639

(*ILLRP* 470; *ROL* IV.168.) A pillar marking the corner of a century, found at Atina in Lucania, dated to 131 BC.

(On shaft) Gaius Sempronius Gracchus, son of Tiberius; Appius Claudius, son of Gaius; Publius Licinius, son of Publius; Board of Three for adjudging and assigning lands. Seventh hinge-baulk.

8.18 Land-surveying boundaries, 123 BC

ILS 25

(*CIL* I² 644; *ILLRP* 473; *ROL* IV.172.) A pillar marking an angle at the boundary of the estate of an established occupier, found at Rocca San Felice, dated to 123 BC.

(On shaft) Marcus Fulvius Flaccus, son of Marcus; Gaius Sempronius Gracchus, son of Tiberius; Gaius Papirius Carbo, son of Gaius; Board of Three for adjudging and assigning lands.

(On top) To established occupier; allowed free of charges.

THE UNDERMINING OF TIBERIUS' LEGISLATION

8.19 The land commission after Tiberius' death

Appian *Civil Wars* 1.18 (73–7)

Tiberius' death did not end the matter, and actions against his supporters continued. Nasica, however, was very unpopular and something of an embarrassment, and was sent off to Pergamum to organise the province, as Tiberius' law about Pergamum was disavowed by the senate. Nasica died there (Plut. *Ti. Gracchus* 21.4–7; cf. doc. 5.44). The consuls for 132 (P. Rupilius and P. Popillius Laenas) established a senatorial court (which Scaevola in 133 had not), which had Diophanes executed, and Blossius exiled (see doc. 8.9). Some supporters were executed, others banished without a trial: Cic. *Off.* 2.76; Plut. *Ti. Gracchus* 20.3–7; Gruen 1968: 60–1; Badian 1972: 727 ('the fierce inquisition started' in 132). Scipio Aemilianus made it clear that he disapproved of Tiberius' actions and thought his death justified, for which sentiments he lost popularity with the people (Plut. *Ti. Gracchus* 21.7).

73 After Gracchus was killed and Appius Claudius died, Fulvius Flaccus and Papirius Carbo were appointed as commissioners in their place, together with the younger Gracchus, to divide the land. Since those who possessed land neglected to register it, the commissioners proclaimed that informers should testify against them. **74** There was soon a huge number of difficult law-suits; for whenever a field which adjoined this land was sold or divided among the allies, it all had to be accurately investigated because of the measurement of this field, as to how it was sold or divided, though not all the owners still had their contracts or allotment deeds; even those which were found were ambiguous. **75** When the land was resurveyed, some owners were transferred from orchards and farm-buildings to bare ground, others from cultivated to uncultivated land or to swamps or marshes, since the survey had never been done accurately in the beginning as the land was won in battle. **76** The original proclamation, that anyone who wished might farm the unallocated land, had encouraged many to work land adjoining their own and blur the status of both; the passing of time had also confused everything. **77** And so the injustice done by the rich, though great, was hard to identify. There was nothing but a complete resettlement, with everyone being transferred from their own and settled on other people's property.

8.20 Scipio Aemilianus opposes Tiberius' judiciary law

Macrobius *Saturnalia* 3.14.6–7

(*ORF*[4] F30; Courtney *ALP* 122–4.) While the machinations of family groups in the Republic have been overrated by scholars emphasising prosopographical information and long-standing political alliances between families (Earl 1963, criticised by Brunt 1965: 191), it is clear that the Scipionic 'group' was opposed to the Gracchi (despite being related).

Tiberius put forward a judiciary law as a sequel to his agrarian legislation, giving the land-commissioners powers of adjudication (Livy *Per.* 58; Gruen 1968: 58). This was unpalatable to the allies who found an advocate in Scipio Aemilianus, and Appian *BC* 1.19.78 mentions Scipio's attack on this law in a speech to the senate in 129 BC: it presumably dealt with the harmful effects of bringing luxury to Rome as a result of the annexation of Pergamum and its revenues. Scipio was successful, and the jurisdiction over the land distribution was given to C. Sempronius Tuditanus (cos. 129) and not the land commissioners; he promptly left for Illyria. When Carbo as tribune proposed a law that a man could be elected tribune as often as he chose, Scipio argued against this in a speech in which he stated that in his view Tiberius Gracchus had been justly killed (Livy *Per.* 59).

6 However, we certainly know that the sons and — though it is a dreadful thing to say — the unmarried daughters of noble families as well regarded the practice of dancing as one of their accomplishments, our witness being Scipio Africanus Aemilianus, who states as follows in his speech against the judiciary law of Tiberius Gracchus: **7** 'They are taught disreputable feats, and, in the company of male dancers (cinaeduli) and zither and lute they go to a school for actors, they learn to sing songs which our ancestors considered disgraceful in the free-born — free-born girls and boys go, I say, to a dancing school and mix with male dancers. When someone told me this I could not bring myself to believe that men of noble birth taught their children such things: but when I was taken to the dancing school, I saw, on my oath, more than 50 boys and girls in that school and among them — and this more than anything else made me pity the state — a boy wearing the amulet of a freeborn child, the son of a candidate for office, a boy not less than twelve years old, dancing with castanets a dance which even a shameless little slave could not decently perform.'

8.21 Scipio Aemilianus and the allies, 129 BC

Appian *Civil Wars* 1.19–20 (78–85)

While Scipio Aemilianus did not attempt to interfere in the agrarian legislation, he successfully proposed that the land commission not deal with cases of disputes between the commissioners and allies as to what constituted ager publicus, as the allies did not have confidence in the commission.

Much of the ager publicus throughout Italy was near communities originally conquered by the Romans. When the Romans did not take positive steps to use this land, large numbers of allies will have continued farming it, and will have invested in this land, and presumably come to feel that it was their own. The first complaint from the allies comes in 129, so it is possible that the commissioners commenced work distributing the ager publicus in Roman territory and then moved onto allied territory. When Scipio was found dead, suspicions were raised about the causes, since he had taken the side of the allies against the activities of the land commission; cf. Livy *Per.* 59. Scipio and the allies: Astin 1967: 238–40; Gargola 1995: 161; cf. Stockton 1979: 11.

78 The Italians were unable to tolerate this situation, especially the pressures arising from the law-suits brought against them, and chose Cornelius Scipio, the destroyer of Carthage, to be their defender against these injustices. **79** As they had been his eager supporters in his wars he was reluctant to ignore their request, and in the senate, while he did not openly criticise Gracchus' law because of the people, he spoke against the hardship it caused and proposed that the law-suits should no longer be adjudicated by the commissioners, since the litigants had no confidence in them, but be settled by others. **80** As his suggestion seemed reasonable, the proposal was adopted, and Tuditanus the consul was appointed to judge the cases. But when he had begun on the task and saw its difficulties, he went off to fight the Illyrians, making this an excuse for not serving as judge, while the land-commissioners stayed idle, since no one brought them cases for judgement. **81** As a result Scipio became a target for the hatred and anger of the people, because they saw the man for love of whom and on whose behalf they had often opposed the nobility and aroused their enmity, and whom they had twice elected consul, though illegally, now acting in the interests of the Italians in opposition to their own. **82** When Scipio's enemies noticed this, they cried out that he was completely determined to abolish Gracchus' law, and to this end was going to bring about widespread slaughter and armed strife.

83 When the people heard this they took fright, until Scipio, after putting a writing tablet beside him, on which he intended during the night to write the speech he was going to make to the people, was found dead without a wound — perhaps the deed of Cornelia, mother of the Gracchi, so that Gracchus' law might not be abolished, aided and abetted by her daughter Sempronia, who was married to Scipio in a mutually loveless relationship because she was deformed and childless, or, perhaps, as some believe, he committed suicide because he saw that he would not be able to fulfil what he had promised. **84** Some say that slaves under torture stated that strangers, who were brought through the back door of the house at night, suffocated him, and that those who knew of it shrank from revealing it because the people were still angry with him and pleased at his death. **85** So Scipio died and was not thought worthy of a public funeral, though he had made great contributions to Rome's supremacy; in this way present anger outweighs past gratitude. And this event, important as it was, took place as if an unimportant incident in the strife brought about by Gracchus.

THE CAREER OF GAIUS GRACCHUS

Gaius had served in Numantia under Scipio Aemilianus, his cousin and brother-in-law. In 126 Gaius was a supporter of M. Fulvius Flaccus, Tiberius' friend, and he had been on the land commission from 130 BC. Fulvius proposed awarding the Italians citizenship, which would make them eligible for possession of the Roman ager publicus. He was elected as consul for 125 on this platform, but the senate duly sent him to protect Massilia against the Salluvii to the north; he was awarded a triumph in 123. Gaius served as quaestor in Sardinia from 125 (see doc. 8.22), where his family had been active in subduing the island (see docs 8.1, 5.53). His career began ordinarily enough, but the senate's desire to keep him in Sardinia (doc. 8.22; cf. 8.28: Appian 1.21.88), combined with a natural desire to avenge his brother, encouraged him to stand for the tribunate for 123, ten years after his brother's tribunate; he held a second in 122. As tribune Gaius passed numerous laws (Stockton 1979: 114–61 provides a detailed treatment). His was the most comprehensive legislative programme ever undertaken by a tribune; it could even be described as a 'presidential' tribunate. His great oratory, personal popularity (at least in 123), and the sheer volume of his legislation shows that he had a particular 'vision' for Rome. He was much more 'reformist' than his brother, and his real challenge to the senate was not so much that he deliberately undermined its authority but that he took the initiative on so many issues and that he made his proposals before the assembly of the people which made them sovereign in these issues.

For Appian he was anti-senatorial (1.21.89: doc. 8.28), for Plutarch his laws were designed 'to please the people and undermine the senate' (doc. 8.29), Diodorus has him dividing the state in two so as to win supreme power for himself (34/5.25.1), and Cicero has him more loyal to his brother than his country (doc. 8.26). It is clear that he did not want to overthrow the senate or even curtail most of its powers, though he did act in the interests of the people, and subjected the senate to new controls. He achieved a degree of long-term success in his proposals: the work of the land commission was finally wound down in 111, and those who were settled on the land would no doubt have felt grateful to the Gracchi. Gaius' provisions about grain were also of benefit to thousands of poorer citizens and his reforms concerning the law-courts were far reaching and fundamental, and helped improve senatorial provincial administration.

8.22 Gaius' defence on returning from Sardinia in 124 BC

Aulus Gellius *Attic Nights* 15.12.1–4

(*ORF*[4] FF26–8; Courtney *ALP* 124–6; Plut. *C. Gracchus* 2.10.) Gaius went to Sardinia as quaestor in 126 for 125; he returned to Rome in 124, before his consul (L. Aurelius Orestes, cos. 126), with no successor having been appointed because the nobiles wanted to keep Gaius out of Rome. The censors wanted to deprive him of his horse, but he defended himself before them and the people on the charge of leaving his province early, and of having played a part in the revolt of Fregellae (Plut. *C. Gracchus* 3.1). Plut. 2.9–10 gives a partial summary of the first speech. Gracchus was elected tribune for 123. He criticised the behaviour of Roman officials in their provinces, perhaps an indirect attack on Orestes (see also doc. 8.23). Gaius' early career: Cowell 1962: 95; Boren 1968: 85–9; Stockton 1979: 97–8; Lintott 1994: 75–7.

1 When Gaius Gracchus returned from Sardinia, he made a speech to the people in the assembly in the following words: **2** 'My conduct in my province,' he said, 'was such as I thought would be to your benefit, not such as would contribute to my own ambition. My establishment had no cook-shop, nor any slave boys of outstanding appearance, and at any entertainment of mine your sons were treated with less temptations than at military headquarters.' **3** Later on, he states: 'My conduct in my province was such that no one could say with truth that I received an *as,* or more than that, as a present, or that anyone was put to any expense on my account. I spent two years in my province; if any prostitute entered my house or any slave boy was solicited on my behalf, then consider me the most worthless and iniquitous of mankind. Since I conducted myself with such continence towards their slaves, then you are able to judge on what terms I lived with your sons.' **4** After an interval he continues: 'Accordingly, citizens, when I set out for Rome I brought back empty from the province the money-belts which I took there full of money. Others have brought home overflowing with money the amphorae which they had taken out full of wine.'

8.23 Gaius on the veniality of contemporary politicians

Aulus Gellius *Attic Nights* 11.10.2–6

(*ORF*[4] F44; Courtney *ALP* 126–8.) Manius Aquillius (cos. 129) working with a commission appointed by the senate, organised the province of Asia; part of Phrygia was awarded to Mithridates V of Pontus for his help against the rebellion of Aristonicus (cf. doc. 5.44); Nicomedes of Bithynia wanted the land instead and opposed the bill ratifying this, as did Gaius (it became part of the province of Asia in 116 BC). Gaius' comments about bribery were to be reflected in Sallust's comments about Jugurtha (docs 9.3, 9.7). Aquillius was prosecuted in the mid-nineties for extortion in Asia but was acquitted despite being guilty.

2 Fellow-citizens, if you wish to be advised wisely and honestly, when you consider the matter carefully you will find that none of us presents himself here without a price. All of us who make speeches are after something, and no one appears before you with any purpose other than to carry something away. **3** I myself, who am advising you to increase your taxes, by which you will be more easily able to administer your government and communal interests, do not come forward for free; but I ask you not for money, but for your good opinion and respect. **4** Those who come forward to dissuade you from accepting this law are not seeking respect from you, but money from Nicomedes; those who advise you to accept it, these too are seeking not your good opinion, but a reward and increase in their possessions; those, however, of the same rank and status who are silent, these are the most grasping, for they take money from everyone and deceive you all. **5** Because you think that they distance themselves from such matters, you give them your good opinion; **6** but the embassies from the kings, since they think that they are silent for their sake, present them with lavish and immense sums of money. In the same way, in the land of Greece, at a time when a Greek tragic actor was boasting that he had been given a silver talent for one play, Demades, the most eloquent man of his country, is said to have replied to him: 'Does it appear wonderful to you that you have made a talent by speaking? I received ten talents from the king for my silence.' In the same way, these men are now receiving an immense price for keeping quiet.

8.24 Gaius Gracchus on Roman magistrates

Aulus Gellius *Attic Nights* 10.3.2–5

(*ORF*[4] FF48–9; Courtney *ALP* 128–30.) This speech may have been delivered in the context of his proposal to award citizenship to the Italians during his second tribunate in 122 (though Stockton 1979: 120 sees it as early in the first). But the incident in (5) also shows that his target was the misconduct of Roman officials in general, as doc. 8.23 also indicates. The three towns mentioned in the first anecdote are on the Via Latina. Venusia is in Apulia.

2 I recently read the speech of (Gaius) Gracchus *On the Promulgation of Laws*, in which he complains with all the passion he can command that Marcus Marius and other respectable men of the Italian municipalities were unlawfully beaten with rods by magistrates of the Roman people.

3 These are his words on the subject: 'Recently a consul came to Teanum Sidicinum (in Campania). His wife said that she wished to bathe in the men's baths. The Sidicinian quaestor, Marcus Marius, was given the job of seeing that those who were washing in the baths were driven out. The wife reports to her husband that the baths were not handed over to her quickly enough and that they were not sufficiently clean. On that account a stake was set up in the forum and Marcus Marius, the most illustrious man in his city, led to it. His clothes were removed and he was beaten with rods. The people of Cales, when they heard this, passed an edict that no one should wash in the baths when a Roman magistrate was in the town. At Ferentinum our magistrate ordered the quaestors to be arrested for the same reason: one threw himself from the wall, the other was taken and beaten with rods.'

5 Gracchus in another place also speaks as follows: 'I will give you a single example of the degree of passion and lack of self-control possessed by our young men. Within these last few years a young man was sent from the province of Asia on behalf of his governor, not having to that time held a magistracy. He was carried in a litter. A ploughman, one of the Venusian peasants, encountered him and as a joke, since he was unaware who was being carried, asked whether they were carrying a corpse. When the young man heard this, he ordered the litter to be put down, and ordered him to be beaten with the straps with which the litter was tied together until he expired.'

8.25 Cornelia's advice to her son Gaius, 124 BC

Cornelius Nepos *On the Latin Historians* F59

(Courtney *ALP* 135–9.) Cornelia's letters were preserved after she died; here she writes to her son Gaius. Cornelius Nepos was a republican biographer: doc. 14.14. Cic. *Brut.* 211 refers to her letters as extant (see doc. 7.22); cf. Plut. *C. Gracchus* 13. Nepos might be quoting from an historian, or had perhaps had access to a collection of her letters. The setting is 124 BC, when Gaius was a candidate for his first tribunate. Cornelia had retired to Misenum after the death of Tiberius (Oros. 5.12.9; cf. Plut *C. Gracchus* 19). The historicity of these letters is sometimes doubted, but Nepos is close enough in time to Cornelia for them perhaps to be genuine, especially given Cicero's knowledge of the letters: cf. Horsfall 1987; Hemelrijk 1999: 64–8, 193–7; Plant 2004: 101–3. Note Plutarch's suggestion (doc. 8.29) that Cornelia was directly responsible for Gaius' withdrawing some of his legislation.

You will say that it is a noble deed to avenge oneself on enemies. To no one does this seem finer and more noble than to me, as long no harm is done to the state. But since that is not possible, it will be far better that our enemies should not perish and remain as they are now, rather than that the state be overthrown and perish.

I would swear a solemn oath that, except for those who killed Tiberius Gracchus, no enemy has given me as much trouble and hardship as you have in this affair — you who should have taken the part of all those children I used to have and should have seen to it that I had as little anxiety as possible in my old age. Whatever you were doing, your main object should have been to please me, and you should consider it criminal to do anything important against my will, especially since I only have a short time to live. Can you not do your duty even for that short time without going against my will and overthrowing the state? Where will it ultimately end? Will our family ever leave off its madness? Will a limit ever be put to it? Will we ever stop taking and giving offence? Will we ever feel great shame at creating uproar and disturbance in the state? Well, if that is not a possibility, stand for the tribunate when I am dead; feel free to do as you please when I will not know about it. When I am dead, you will sacrifice to me and call upon the spirit of your parent. At that time will you not be ashamed to summon the spirits of those whom you abandoned and deserted when they were alive and with you? If only heavenly Jupiter would not permit you to continue on this path or such insanity to enter your mind! And if you carry on, I fear that, through your own fault, you will have to suffer such hardship through your whole life that you yourself will not at any time be able to be satisfied with your conduct.

8.26 The most talented orator of the earlier period

Cicero *Brutus* 125–6

Cicero here discusses Gaius as an orator, but his prejudiced views of his political activities are in evidence. Many of the substantial fragments of Gaius' speeches are cited by Gellius: see Gell. 11.13.1–10 on Gaius' oratory. On this judgement of Gaius as orator, see Tac. *Dial.* 18.2.

125 Now, however, there comes a man of outstanding ability, extreme dedication and education from his boyhood, Gaius Gracchus. Do not imagine, Brutus, that anyone was ever more fully or more richly qualified for oratory.

I think exactly the same, he replied, and he is almost the only one of our earlier speakers that I read.

Yes, I certainly think that you should read him, Brutus. For with his early death the Roman state and Latin literature incurred a great loss. **126** If only he had chosen to display as much loyalty to his country as to his brother! How easily with such talent, if he had lived longer, would he have rivalled the reputation of his father or grandfather! Indeed, I believe that in eloquence he would have had no equal. He is lofty in diction, wise in ideas, impressive in his whole style. His works have not received the final touch; much is begun admirably, but clearly has not received the final polish. Indeed, he is an orator to be read by our youth, Brutus, if anyone is; for he cannot only sharpen, but nourish their talents.

8.27 Gaius' oratorical devices

Aulus Gellius *Attic Nights* 1.11.16

Cf. Cic. *de orat.* 3.225. Gell. 1.11.10–16 states that an oratorical pipe was played for Gaius when he addressed the people, to give him the proper pitch, and that some, as in Cicero's account, believed the musician stood behind him to modulate his delivery. Gellius however believes 'more reliable authorities' that the musician was in the audience, his purpose being to restrain Gracchus' energy as orator. The evidence of these documents suggests that Gaius was perhaps the greatest orator Rome had produced.

So this same Gracchus, Catulus, as you can hear from your client Licinius, an educated man who was Gracchus' amanuensis, used to have a experienced musician with an ivory pitch-pipe standing concealed behind him when he was addressing the assembly, who could quickly blow a note to rouse him up if lethargic, or restrain him from over-vehemence.

8.28 Gaius' legislative programme

Appian *Civil Wars* 1.21–3 (86–101)

The chronology of Gaius' reforms is difficult to ascertain (*MRR* I.513–4, 517–18). Appian and Plutarch date the grain, land and military laws to 123. The laws concerning the equites, lawcourts, and colonies clearly belong to the second tribunate of 122, as do those for roads. The citizenship proposal must belong to 122 as it is then that Drusus managed to win some of Gaius' limelight and derail the proposal; for chronology, see Stockton 1979: 226–39; for Gaius' legislative programme, Livy *Per.* 60; Vell. 2.6; Diod. 34/5.24–7; *MRR* I.513–14; Cowell 1962: 95–105; Boren 1968: 84–129; Gruen 1968: 79–105; Stockton 1979: 115–205; Scullard *GN* 32–5; Lintott 1994: 77–86.

1.21.86 *Land legislation*. Cf. Plut. *C. Gracchus* 5.1; Livy *Per.* 60. Gaius' first aim was to re-establish his brother's land legislation dividing the ager publicus amongst Roman citizens. The lex agraria of 111 (doc. 8.36), however, makes reference to Gaius' law, so it did not simply re-enact Tiberius' but was a law in its own right.

1.21.89 *The grain distribution* (the lex frumentaria). Cf. Plut. *C. Gracchus* 5.2; Livy *Per.* 60; *MRR* I.514. Appian incorrectly has a free grain distribution. The state bought up large quantities of grain, had granaries built at Rome for storing it, and offered it for sale at six and a third asses for a modius of grain, slightly below the usual market rate. As well as subsidising grain, the measure was designed to ensure that there was always an adequate supply of grain to hand: see Boren 1968: 91–3, 1969: 65; Stockton 126–9; Garnsey & Rathbone 1985. Gaius' re-organisation of tax collection in Asia was initiated to pay for this and his other measures.

1.21.90 *Re-election to the tribunate*. Gaius was easily elected because of a lack of a tenth candidate. It is possible that the tenth place had been left deliberately vacant for him. Fulvius Flaccus, the Gracchan land commissioner and consul of 125, was elected in 123 as a tribune for 122, and so went 'backwards' in the normal cursus honorum. He was to die with Gaius: see *MRR* I.517; Hall 1977.

1.22.91 *The extortion law*. Belonging to early in the second tribunate, this dealt with the recovery of money which Roman magistrates illegally extracted during their tenure of office from Latins, allies and foreigners subject to Rome. (It is sometimes referred to as the *lex Acilia repetendarum*, as Cicero (*Verr.* 1.51, 2.1.26) refers to such a law.) The accounts of Plut. *C. Gracchus* 5.3 and Livy *Per.* 60 that Gaius enrolled equites in the senate is a confusion with the fact that he gave the equites judicial rights and responsibilities that had hitherto been the province of the senate (Stockton 1979: 143–5). He might have been aiming to reduce the senate's political power, or more probably to provide a 'check' on its activities as well as ensure that provincial administration would be more effective and honest. Appian makes it clear that Gaius had reasonable grounds for acting: legitimate complaints against Aurelius Cotta, Salinator and Aquillius had come to nothing (92). The new system worked well on the whole, convicting about 50 per cent of those prosecuted (Lintott 1994: 82), but the equites tarnished their reputation in 92 BC when a court convicted the innocent P. Rutilius Rufus, who had restricted the activities of the publicani (Badian 1972a: 91; cf. Lintott 1994: 82); his nephew M. Livius Drusus in 91 BC as tribune attempted a reform of the courts (doc. 10.6).

Gaius' extortion law brought the equites political significance. Sulla clearly saw the equites' control of the courts as detrimental to the traditional prestige and power of the senate, and transferred the courts away from them (doc. 11.29). For the equites, see esp. Hill 1952; Henderson 1969; Brunt 1988a; for the *lex de repetundis* and the extortion court, see Hardy 1911: 1–34; Hill 1952: 108–11; Sherwin-White 1952, 1972, 1982; Boren 1968: 108–9; Balsdon 1969; Mattingly 1969, 1970, 1987 (arguing against identifying the Tabula Bembina extortion law with that of Gaius Gracchus, unfortunately incorrectly: Balsdon 1969: 108–12; Sherwin-White 1972); Brunt 1971: 87; Stockton 1979: 138–53, 230–6; Lintott 1981: 177–85, 1994: 5, 51–2, 81–2 (cf. 1982); cf. Henderson 1951.

1.21.86, 23.99–101 *The citizenship issue*. During the Second Punic War, after Cannae (216 BC), the issue of granting citizenship to leaders in the Latin communities had been raised but rejected by everyone in the senate except the proposer (cf. doc. 4.40). In the second century BC the Romans had become much more restrictive of Roman citizenship. Flaccus' failure had led to the revolt of Fregellae, and Gaius' attempt was to fail as was that of the younger Livius Drusus in 91 BC, son of the tribune who vetoed citizenship legislation in 122 (one of the many ironies of history): docs 10.5–9.

The Latins were to be offered full citizenship. The reward of citizenship for these loyal Latin communities must have been long overdue, especially due to their linguistic and cultural affinities with the Romans (cf. doc. 1.62). The Italians were offered voting rights but not full citizenship, so Gaius' proposal was not as radical as that of Flaccus. But the senatorial reaction was adverse, and it is this issue that sparks off the conflict between Gaius and the senate, and led (almost inevitably) to his death. Citizenship: Sherwin-White 1973: 136–7; Stockton 1979: 156–61.

The election of Lucius Opimius, the destroyer of Fregellae after it had revolted, as consul for 121 was a signal that there was opposition to the enfranchisement of the Latin allies. Opimius had been defeated for 122 through Gaius' support of another candidate, Gaius Fannius (cos. 122). However, Fannius — presumably unexpectedly for Gaius — joined Drusus in opposing the citizenship law. Fannius, as consul, was responsible for carrying out the senate's order that all non-voters were to leave Rome (the other consul, Cn. Domitius Ahenobarbus, was campaigning in Gaul); Fannius had argued in a speech against citizenship for the allies; only one fragment survives and clearly plays on the selfish feelings of the Romans: *ORF*[4] F3 (cf. Cic. *Brut.* 99): 'You think, I suppose, that if you give citizenship to the Latins, you are going to have a place, as you do now, in the assembly in which you are standing, and take part in the games and festivals? Don't you know that they will take over everything?' With Drusus' veto, the legislation was dead. For Fannius: Plut. *C. Gracchus* 8.1–3; Stockton 1979: 177–8; Scullard *GN* 36; Lintott 1994: 83.

1.23.98 *Colonies.* See for Gaius' colonies: App. 1.23.98 (doc. 8.28); Plut. *C. Gracchus* 6.3 (doc. 8.29); the colony Junonia on the site of Carthage: App. 1.24.102–6 (doc. 8.30). Livy *Per.* 60 assigns the colonies in Italy and Carthage to the second tribunate of 122. Land, colonies, roads: Cowell 1962: 96–7; Boren 1968: 101–4; Stockton 1979: 131–7; Lintott 1994: 78; doc. 4.62.

1.23.101 *M. Livius Drusus* was one of the tribunes for 122. He proposed twelve colonies in a successful attempt to outbid Gaius, and so the people 'despised Gracchus' proposed laws'. These twelve colonies never came to anything. He also introduced laws that the Latins on military service not be flogged, and removed the small rent payable by those on ager publicus. The people may have felt that Drusus' measures for the Latins were sufficient, and his proposed colonies detracted from Gaius' colonial programme. For Drusus, see Plut. *C. Gracchus* 9; *MRR* I.517; Stockton 1979: 176–8; Scullard *GN* 35–6; Lintott 1994: 83.

Lex de provinciis consularibus. This law is not mentioned by Appian or Plutarch but by Cicero and Sallust (see Stockton 129 n.34). The two provinces to which the consuls were to be assigned were to be decided by the senate before the election of the consuls themselves (Sall. *BJ* 27.3; Cic. *Dom.* 24, *Balb.* 61, *Fam.* 1.7.20, *Prov. Cons.* 3, 17; *MRR* I.514). In force until the *lex Pompeia* of 52 BC, the law confirmed that it was the senate which allocated the provincial commands, but removed personal considerations from the allocation of provinces (Badian *FC* 177–8; Stockton 129–31; Lintott 1994: 79–80).

The province of Asia. This measure, beneficial to the equites, but not described by Appian or Plutarch, arranged for tax-collection in the province of Asia (Attalus of Pergamum's bequest organised by Manius Aquillius). Gaius needed to ensure that the state had sufficient finance for the subsidy of grain, as well as his road and colony projects, and the land commission's activities. This *lex de provincia Asia* was passed by the people's assembly. The province was very wealthy, and proved an immense source of revenue for Rome; of Rome's 50 million denarii in public revenues, most of it came from Asia (Badian 1972a: 63–4). Gaius provided that the censors would, every five years, farm out by auction the right to collect taxes in the province. *Societates publicanorum*, companies of *publicani*, bid for the contracts. The state would receive the revenues annually from the publicani who then had to arrange collection themselves in Asia. Publicani already handled the collection of other taxes, and had financed the Second Punic War (docs 4.40, 60; Badian 1972a: 17); for Gaius and the publicani, see Badian 1972a: 63–4, 89; Stockton 1979: 153–6; Lintott 1994: 79.

86 The occupiers of the land still put off its division on all kinds of pretexts for a considerable time. Some people even proposed that all the Italian allies, who were making the most resistance about the land, should be enrolled as Roman citizens, since in return for this greater favour they would no longer make difficulties about the land. **87** The Italians welcomed this proposal, since they preferred Roman citizenship to the possession of the fields. Fulvius Flaccus, who was both consul and land-commissioner, supported them in this to the utmost. The senate, however, was angry at the thought of making their subjects equal citizens with themselves.

88 And so this undertaking was abandoned, and the people, who had been in hopes of land for so long, lost heart. While they were in this condition, Gaius Gracchus, who had gained their favour as a land-commissioner, stood for the tribunate — he was the younger brother of Gracchus the law-maker, and had stayed out of politics for some time after his brother's death; but, as many of the senators treated him with scorn, he stood for the tribunate. **89** After an electoral triumph, he immediately started devising plans against the senate, proposing that a monthly distribution of grain be made to each citizen at the public expense, which was quite unprecedented. **90** Thus by one political ploy, in which Fulvius Flaccus co-operated, he quickly won over the people. Straight afterwards he was elected tribune for the next year as well; for a law permitted the people to choose a tribune from the body of citizens, if there were not enough candidates for the office.

91 In this way Gaius Gracchus was tribune for the second time; already having the people in his pay, as it were, he now began to win over by a similar political ploy the so-called equites, who hold the middle status between senate and people. **92** He transferred the lawcourts, whose reputation had been lost because of bribery, from the senators to the equites, reproaching the former in particular because Aurelius Cotta, Salinator, and third in the list Manius Aquillius, who conquered Asia — all notorious bribe-takers — were acquitted by the judges, although ambassadors sent to complain about them were still in Rome going around making impassioned accusations against them. The senate was ashamed of such conduct and gave in to the law; and the people ratified it. **93** In this way the lawcourts were transferred to the equites from the senate; it is said that just after the law was passed, Gracchus stated that he had overthrown the power of the senate completely, and the train of events made his remark appear more and more significant. **94** For their role in passing judgement on all Romans and Italians, even on the senators themselves, to an unlimited degree, in cases which involved property, civil rights, and exile, exalted the equites to the status of being, as it were, their rulers, while it put the senators on the level of subjects. **95** Since the equites leagued with the tribunes in elections, and in return got from them whatever they wanted, they were a cause of great anxiety to the senators; soon it happened that the control of government was reversed, with the senate only retaining the dignity, while the equites held the power. **96** Indeed, they went so far that they not only possessed the power, but also insulted the senators beyond what was right. They started taking bribes, and, when they had had a taste of the enormous profits, they used them even more wickedly and immoderately than the senators had done. **97** They set suborned accusers on the wealthy and completely did away with suits involving bribery, partly by agreement amongst themselves and partly by force, so that the practice of this kind of inquiry completely disappeared and the judiciary law gave rise to another long-standing factional struggle, of no less impact than the earlier ones.

98 Gracchus also constructed lengthy roads throughout Italy, and got the support of a large number of contractors and workers, who were ready to do whatever he told them. He also proposed the foundation of numerous colonies. **99** He called on the Latins to demand full citizen rights, as the senate could not decently refuse them to men of the same race; to the other allies, who were not permitted to vote in Roman elections, he proposed to give the right to vote, so that he might have their support too in voting for his laws. **100** The senate was greatly concerned at this and ordered the consuls to proclaim that: 'No one who does not have a vote shall stay in the city or approach within 40 stades of it while the voting on these proposals is taking place.' **101** It also persuaded Livius Drusus, another tribune, to veto Gracchus' proposed laws, without stating his reasons to the people; it was not necessary that a vetoing tribune give his reasons. They also gave him the opportunity to conciliate the people by proposing twelve colonies; the people were so very pleased with this that it despised Gracchus' proposed laws.

8.29 Plutarch on Gaius' legislation

Plutarch *Life of Gaius Gracchus* 4.1–4. 5.1–3, 6.1–5

Gaius at first proposed two laws in 123 BC, designed to address his brother's death (Plut. *C. Gracchus* 4; Appian does not discuss these). The first (the *lex de abactis*) was that magistrates deposed by the people could not hold office again, which was aimed against Octavius who as tribune had obstructed Tiberius in 133. However, Cornelia, Gaius' mother, intervened and Gaius withdrew the proposal, Cornelia's intercession perhaps being a deliberate ploy to contrast the magnanimity of Gaius against the ruthlessness of Tiberius' enemies (Boren 1968: 93; Stockton 1979: 117). The second law (*lex ne de capite civis romani iniussu populi iudicetur*) stated that only the Roman people could authorise a death sentence against a Roman citizen; anyone who did so would be liable to the death penalty (this strengthened existing 'provocatio' legislation and was retroactive). P. Popillius Laenas as consul in 132, who had presided over the execution of many of Tiberius' supporters, went into self-exile when the law was passed (he returned in 121 when a law passed by one of the tribunes L. Calpurnius Bestia allowed for this: Boren 1968: 93; Stockton 1979: 117–21; Lintott 1999: 163–4; *MRR* I.525 n.3).

5.1: The military law (*lex militaris*; not mentioned by Appian) sits oddly with the broad programme until it is remembered that Gaius was acting in the interests of the people in general and that the tribunes had, historically, often acted in the interests of the citizen soldiers (Diod. 34/5.25.1 criticised the law as relaxing the 'ancient discipline' but the measures were simply fair; *MRR* I.514; Boren 1968: 94; Stockton 1979: 137). Clearly there were still problems with military recruitment.

4.1 After stirring up the people with such rhetoric — and he had a powerful voice and was a very forceful speaker — he proposed two laws, one stating that if the people had deposed any magistrate from office he was not allowed to hold office a second time; the other, that if any magistrate banished a citizen without trial he could be prosecuted by the people. **2** The first of these laws had the clear object of disqualifying Marcus Octavius, who had been deposed from the tribunate by Tiberius, while the second attacked Popillius: for as praetor he had banished Tiberius' friends. **3** Popillius did not stand trial and fled from Italy; Gaius himself withdrew the first law, stating that he had spared Octavius at his mother Cornelia's request. **4** The people were pleased that the motion was withdrawn, since they honoured Cornelia no less for her sons than for her father, and they later erected a bronze statue of her with the inscription, 'Cornelia, mother of the Gracchi'. . . .

5.1 Of the laws which he proposed to please the people and undermine the senate, one concerned the allotment of land, dividing the public land among the poor; another dealt with the army, laying down that clothing be supplied at public expense, with nothing being subtracted from soldiers' pay for this purpose, and no one younger than seventeen years of age being conscripted; **2** another concerned the allies, giving the Italians voting rights equal to those of citizens; a grain law lowered the market-price for the poor; while, through a jury law, he most severely undermined the power of the senate. **3** They alone had judged law suits, and by this had been formidable both to the people and to the equites; but Gracchus chose an additional 300 equites to add to the 300 senators, and juries were drawn from these 600. . . .

6.1 When the people not only passed this law, but granted him the power to select the judges from the equites, a kind of kingly power was invested in him, so that even the senate accepted his advice. His advice was always in favour of measures which did the senate credit; **2** an example of this is the very fair and honourable decision concerning the grain sent by Fabius (Q. Fabius Maximus Allobrogicus, cos. 121), the propraetor, from Spain, when Gracchus persuaded the senate to sell the grain and return the money to the cities, as well as to censure Fabius for having made Rome's rule oppressive and burdensome to her subjects; this added greatly to his reputation and gained him goodwill in the provinces. **3** He also proposed laws to send out colonies, to construct roads, and to establish granaries, making himself the director and organiser for all these undertakings and was never worn out by any of these numerous and weighty projects — rather, he carried out each one with amazing speed and application, as though it were his only concern, so that even those who most hated and feared him were thunderstruck at the way everything was accomplished and brought to completion. **4** The people were amazed at the mere sight of him, when they saw him attended by a mob of contractors, craftsmen, ambassadors, magistrates, soldiers, scholars — all of whom he handled with ease, still maintaining his dignity in his courtesy, and giving each his proper consideration. He thus showed up as malicious slanderers those who called him terrifying or utterly arrogant or violent. **5** In this way he was more effective as a popular leader when he associated with others and dealt with business than in his speeches from the rostra.

8.30 Gaius loses popular support

Appian *Civil Wars* 1.24 (102–6)

Because of Drusus' legislation in 122 BC, Gaius lost some of his popularity, and set off to establish a colony at Carthage, destroyed in 146 (doc. 4.62). The law (the *lex Rubria*) establishing the new colony (called Junonia) had been proposed by Rubrius, a fellow tribune. This was the first attempt to send a Roman colony outside of Italy itself. It marked — despite opposition — what would be the first in a long series of overseas colonies which would contribute to the romanisation of the western Mediterranean. (The lex Rubria was repealed after Gaius' death, but the settlers remained, and a land commission including Carbo was busy there after Gaius' death: *ILLRP* 475.) In 122, Gaius stood for a third tribunate, but despite winning a large number of votes was not elected (Plutarch *C. Gracchus* 12.7 reports a belief that the results were tampered with). The senate now had the initiative: the Latin citizenship proposal had been vetoed, and in 121 one of the tribunes, Minucius Rufus, proposed the repeal of the legislation founding Junonia. The dagger-carrying plebs were to signal a fresh outbreak of violence. The omens (certainly, as Gaius accused, invented) indicate the aristocracy's control of religion: see Rawson 1991: 153; docs 3.72–3 (for the political uses of religion).

102 After the failure of this attempt to win popular favour, Gracchus sailed to Africa together with Fulvius Flaccus, who, after his consulship, had been chosen tribune for the same reasons as Gracchus. A colony in Africa had been voted for on account of its reputation for fertility, and these men had been specifically chosen as its founders so the senate might have a brief rest from popular politics in their absence. **103** They laid out the colony's city on the spot where Carthage had once stood, without considering that when Scipio destroyed it he had laid curses on the site that it stay sheep pasture for ever more. **104** They assigned 6,000 colonists, instead of the smaller number given in the law, hoping in this way to gain the support of the people. When they returned to Rome, they summoned the 6,000 from all of Italy. **105** The officials who were still in Africa, laying out the site of the city, sent word that wolves had torn up and scattered the boundary markers of Gracchus and Fulvius, and the soothsayers considered the colony ill-omened. The senate therefore summoned the assembly, in which it was proposed to repeal the law about this colony; **106** when Gracchus and Fulvius saw they were failing in this matter as well, they were enraged and declared that the senate had lied about the wolves. The boldest of the plebs joined them, carrying daggers on their way to the Capitol, where the assembly about the colony was to be held.

8.31 Gaius reminds the people of his family connections, 122 BC

Gaius Gracchus Oratorum Romanorum Fragmenta[4] F47

(Courtney *ALP* 128–9.) This fragment of a speech appears to belong to a period when Gaius felt insecure and began to lose popularity, presumably later in his second tribunate in 122 (against Stockton 1979: 120–2). On Gaius' son, see Plut. *C. Gracchus* 15.2; Astin 1967: 319–20.

If I had wanted to speak to you and to ask you, as a member of an eminent family and one who had lost my brother on your account, and seeing that there is no descendant of the families of Publius Africanus and Tiberius Gracchus left apart from myself and my young son, that you would permit me to lead a quiet life uninvolved in politics for the present, so that my family might not utterly die out but that some offshoot of my family might survive, I believe you would have granted my request not unwillingly.

8.32 Gaius' death

Appian Civil Wars 1.25–6 (107–20)

The outbreak of violence was sparked off by an unpremeditated act of violence on the part of a Gracchan supporter. The senate, or at least part of it as in 132, was all too willing to resort to violence. Plut. *C. Gracchus* 13.1 explicitly notes that L. Opimius had secured the consulship for 121 through the support of Gaius' enemies.

Antyllus in Plut. *C. Gracchus* 13.3 (who incorrectly has Antyllius) was an attendant of the consul Opimius. Plut. 14.3 has the senate pass a decree that Opimius — as consul — save the state and overcome the tyrants. Such a decree, passed here for the first time, empowering the consuls to save the Republic is sometimes known as a *senatus consultum ultimum* (Scullard *GN* 36–7; Stockton 1979: 197; doc. 1.69). Beheading was common Roman practice for traitors (cf. doc. 4.44); strangulation was usually reserved for common criminals, and the choice of this method of execution by Opimius seems deliberate. Gaius' death and Opimius' role: Cowell 1962: 100–1; Brunt 1971: 90; Lintott 1972: 260–1, 1999: 210; Scullard *GN* 37; Stockton 1979: 195–200; Kyle 1998: 219–20; Keaveney 2003.

107 The people had already assembled, and Fulvius was beginning to speak about the matters in hand, when Gracchus came up to the Capitol accompanied by a body-guard of his supporters. **108** Troubled by his conscience over his portentous plans, he turned aside from the assembly's meeting-place, went into the portico, and walked around waiting on what was to happen. **109** A plebeian called Antyllus, who was making a sacrifice in the portico, saw him in this state of disturbance, and, putting his hand on him, either because he knew or suspected something or was motivated to speak by some other reason, begged him to spare his country. **110** Gracchus, even more disturbed, and alarmed like a criminal caught in the act, looked sharply at him; one of those who accompanied him, although there had been no signal or order given, supposed merely from Gracchus' fierceness towards Antyllus that the time had come, and, thinking that he would do Gracchus a favour by being the first to act, drew his dagger and killed Antyllus. **111** A cry went up, the dead body was seen in the middle of the crowd, and everyone rushed from the temple in fear of a similar fate.

Gracchus went into the assembly wishing to excuse himself from what had happened, **112** but no one would even listen to him and everyone turned from him as if he were polluted. He and Flaccus had no idea what to do, as through this premature act they had lost the opportunity to carry out their wishes, and they hurried to their homes, their supporters with them. The rest of the crowd occupied the forum after midnight as if in expectation of some disaster. **113** Opimius, the consul who was present in the city, ordered some armed men to gather at the Capitol at dawn, and summoned the senate through heralds, while he waited on what was to happen in the temple of the Dioscuri in the centre of the city.

114 Matters were like this when the senate summoned Gracchus and Flaccus from their homes to the senate-house to defend themselves, but they ran out with their weapons to the Aventine hill, hoping that, if they took it first, the senate would make some terms with them. **115** As they ran through the city, they offered the slaves freedom, but none of them listened to them. With the men that they had, however, they seized the temple of Diana, and sent Flaccus' son Quintus to the senate, requesting some form of agreement and harmonious co-existence. They were told to lay down their arms, come to the senate-house and state their wishes, or not to send any more messengers. **116** When they sent Quintus a second time, the consul Opimius arrested him, since he had been warned he was no longer an ambassador, and sent his armed men against Gracchus' supporters.

117 Gracchus fled across the river by the wooden bridge (the Pons Sublicius) to a grove, accompanied by a single slave, and being on the point of arrest presented his throat to the slave; **118** Flaccus took refuge in the workshop of an acquaintance, and as his pursuers did not know the house they threatened to burn the whole row. The man who had given him shelter shrank from pointing out the suppliant, but told another man to give him away. Flaccus was seized and killed. **119** The heads of Gracchus and Flaccus were taken to Opimius and he gave those who brought them the equivalent weight in gold; the plebs plundered their houses and Opimius arrested their sympathisers, threw them in prison, and ordered them to be strangled. **120** However, he allowed Quintus, Flaccus' son, to die as he chose. He then purified the city from the killings, and the senate ordered a temple of Concord to be erected in the forum.

8.33 Plutarch on the aftermath of Gaius' death

Plutarch *Life of Gaius Gracchus* 17.5–9

This is apparently the first time a reward was paid for a head; cf. Sulla's proscriptions (docs 11.19–23). Cornelia's house at Misenum was later occupied by Marius, Lucullus and Tiberius (Plut. *Mar.* 34.3–4: Cornelia paid 75,000 drachmas for it). Licinia was the daughter of the wealthy P. Licinius Crassus Dives Mucianus, member of the land-commission, and consul in 131, who was killed in Asia (cf. doc. 7.69). According to Plutarch, 3,000 died. This might be an exaggeration, but this was a much bloodier incident than the murder of Tiberius and his supporters, and the reprisals more widespread.

17.5 Gaius' head was brought by Septimulius to Opimius stuck on the point of his spear and when it was placed on the scales it weighed seventeen and two-thirds pounds, for Septimulius had acted not only abominably, but criminally, having removed the brain and poured in molten lead. The men who brought in Fulvius' head — they were of less importance — got nothing. **6** The bodies of these two and of the others who were killed, 3,000 in all, were thrown into the river, and their property was confiscated by the state; their wives were forbidden to go into mourning, and Licinia, Gaius' wife, was deprived of her dowry. **7** The most inhuman treatment was that of Fulvius' younger son, who had neither used violence nor been amongst whose who fought, but whom they had arrested when he came to propose a truce before the battle, and whom they killed after the fighting was over. **8** But what annoyed the people more than this or any of the other events was the erection by Opimius of a temple of Concord; for he appeared to be priding himself and exultant, and even in some way to be celebrating a triumph over the killing of so many citizens. **9** As a consequence some people during the night carved this verse under the inscription on the temple: 'This temple of Concord was made by an act of Discord.'

18.1 Opimius was the first person to use dictatorial powers during his consulship and to have 3,000 citizens put to death without a trial, among them Gaius Gracchus and Fulvius Flaccus, one of whom was an ex-consul and had celebrated a triumph and the other the most eminent man of his time in merit and reputation. Nor did he avoid fraud, but, when he was sent as envoy to Jugurtha the Numidian, took bribes from him (116 BC); **2** and after being convicted of the most heinous charge of bribery (109 BC), he grew old in disgrace, hated and insulted by the people, who were humbled and downcast by these events, though they soon made clear how much they wanted and missed the Gracchi. **3** For they set up statues of them in a prominent place, and they consecrated the sites where they were killed, and offered them the first-fruits of all the seasons, while many people sacrificed to them on a daily basis and worshipped them as if they were visiting the gods' shrines.

19.1 Furthermore Cornelia is said to have borne this further disaster nobly and magnanimously, and to have said regarding the sacred sites where the killings had taken place that the dead had worthy tombs. **2** She went to live at the place called Misenum, and made no change in her customary way of life. She had many friends and showed great hospitality to guests, and Greeks and scholars were her constant visitors, while all the kings received and sent presents to her. **3** She would please her visitors and friends greatly by recounting tales of the career and lifestyle of her father (Scipio) Africanus, but what they admired most was when she recalled without grief or tears the fates and achievements of her sons, relating them to anyone who asked as if she was speaking of men of olden days. **4** From this some people thought that she had lost her mind from old age or the weight of her troubles, and that she was insensible of her misfortunes, but it was these who were truly insensible of how much a noble disposition, and good ancestry and upbringing, can shield men against grief, and of how fate, while it may often defeat virtue's attempts to ward off misfortunes, cannot take away the power to bear this with equanimity.

8.34 Gracchan anti-senatorial reprisals

Cicero *Brutus* 128

Senatorial commanders and ambassadors were condemned by the Mamilian commission, established by the tribune C. Mamilius Limetanus in 109 to look into the Jugurthine affair: many senators were accused of taking bribes. Cicero here characterises the jurors (who were equites) as 'Gracchan judges' (Gracchani), clearly associating the popularist cause with the Gracchi; for Mamilius, see doc. 9.7. P. Scipio Nasica (cos. 111) was the son of the Nasica involved in killing Tiberius, and held the consulship with Lucius Calpurnius Bestia, who as tribune had legislation passed recalling Nasica (Bestia was also at some stage a member of the Gracchan land commission and distributed land in Africa: *ILS* 28 (*CIL* I² 696; *ILLRP* 475); Scullard *GN* 393–4 n.5). Cicero obviously has fellow-feeling with Opimius. Opimius was acquitted in 120 of killing Gaius, but convicted of bribery in 109 over his involvement in Numidia.

Publius Scipio Nasica's colleague in his consulship, Lucius Bestia, made a good beginning to his tribunate, for, through the measure which bears his name, he recalled Publius Popillius (Laenas), who had been banished by the violence of Gaius Gracchus, and was a keen-witted man and not ineloquent, though the end of his consulship was a sad one. For, under that hateful Mamilian law, Gaius Galba, an ex-quaestor and priest, and four ex-consuls, Lucius Bestia (cos. 111), Gaius Cato (cos. 114), Spurius Albinus (cos. 110), and that most pre-eminent citizen Lucius Opimius (cos. 121), the killer of Gracchus, who was acquitted by the people even though he had made a stand against the people's wishes, were got rid of by Gracchan jurors.

FAILURE OF THE GRACCHAN REFORMS

8.35 Modification of the agrarian legislation

Appian *Civil Wars* 1.27 (121–3)

Appian mentions three laws passed after Gaius' assassination: 1: those who had received land allotments could sell them; 2: Thorius' law that distribution of the ager publicus was to cease; 3. rent payable on ager publicus was abolished. Clearly the ager publicus distributed to individual farmers was inalienable under Tiberius' legislation to prevent the situation which arose at Appian 1.27.121, after a law was passed allowing sale, probably in 121 BC. Spurius Thorius introduced a second law, probably in 111 BC, bringing the issue of ager publicus to a close, ending the distribution of the land, and confirming the ownership of the allotments that had been distributed, as well as the ownership by those — the wealthy — who were occupying large amounts of the land.

The Roman census, which counted the number of Roman citizens (regardless of wealth) every five years, is sometimes invoked in the context of the success or failure of the Gracchan law reforms. In 164/3 BC there were 337,022 and in 136/5 317,933 Roman citizens. Certainly Tiberius, as he journeyed through Etruria, was struck by the number of farms worked by slaves as opposed to free men. Moreover, he was aware of the difficulties the state had had in recruiting soldiers, especially for the Spanish wars. He also knew of landless soldiers, who could easily have lost their farms while on protracted overseas service, particularly in Spain. The census figure for 125/4, apparently 294,336, shows that the decline had continued. But the crucial point was not merely the number of citizens, but how many could serve in the army as *assidui*. (There would *not* be more citizens created through the process of land distribution itself for many years, until farmers established themselves and could meet the minimum property qualification, and had children, who would be registered at 17 years.) Citizens who lost their farms and became impoverished might easily fall below the minimum property qualification for army service, which had in fact been reduced (it was to be abolished altogether by Marius). See esp. Brunt *IM* 75–80 (13–14 for the census figures themselves); also Earl 1963: 26; Astin 1967: 334–8; Stockton 1979: 49–50; Shochat 1980: 9–45 (fundamentally flawed); Lintott 1994: 57–8; for the lex Thoria, Badian 1964: 235–42.

The colony at Carthage continued, the work of the land-commission went on until 111 BC, and nearly all of Gaius' legislation remained 'on the books'. His activities as tribune pointed to the people as a repository of power; the senate was unable to deal with him except through violence.

121 In this way the strife caused by the second Gracchus came to an end. Not long afterwards, a law was passed which permitted the occupiers to sell the land under dispute; for even this had been forbidden by the law of the elder Gracchus. The rich immediately started buying from the poor, or forcibly seized the land on a number of pretexts. **122** So, for the poor, their condition became even worse than before, until Spurius Thorius, a tribune, introduced a law that the allocation of the land was no longer to be continued, and that the land would belong to those who occupied it, who should pay rent for it to the people, and that this money was to be distributed. This distribution gave some relief to the poor, but was of no help in increasing the population. **123** Gracchus' law, which was excellent and extremely useful if it could have been put into practice, was once and for all undermined by such devices, and shortly afterwards another tribune abolished the rent, and the people lost absolutely everything.

8.36 The lex agraria, 111 BC

CIL I² 585 (selections)

(*ROL* IV.372–436.) This agrarian law was engraved on the reverse side of the bronze tablet which held the earlier *lex Acilia de repetundis*; the whole tablet is known as the *tabula Bembina*, discovered at Urbino. This lex agraria is to be identified with the agrarian law introduced by Thorius.

The effect of this law was to bring to an end the activities of the agrarian commission. All the ager publicus, except the land which Tiberius' or Gaius' legislation had made exempt (1, 4), which had been allotted or retained by the possessor up to the limit allowed under the Gracchan legislation, was confirmed as private, as were the buildings upon it (7), and the land entered in the censors' lists as private (8). No-one was to interfere with this right of private ownership over this land (9), and no motions about these lands or buildings were to be made (9–10). Ownership was guaranteed, but the Gracchan limits were to be observed (13–14). There is disagreement amongst scholars whether this law abolished the rent on this land, but Appian states that rent was abolished later (the third law he mentions), and this law here does refer to rent, as in (14–15) where pasturing of less than a certain number of cattle does not incur rent. The references to ager publicus exempted by the Gracchi (1, 4, 7) are mainly to the ager Campanus, the Campanian land. Most of the ager publicus must have been distributed by this stage.

For the date of 111 BC: Hardy 1911: 35; cf. Badian 1969: 212 (dating the third law to 109–108 BC); for the law, see Hardy 1911: 35–90; Gruen 1968: 101–2; Badian 1964, 1969: 17–20; Scullard *GN* 43, 394; Lintott 1992, 1994: 63; Crawford *Statutes* no. 2.

1 [. . . tribunes of the plebs duly brought a bill before the plebs and the plebs duly voted in the forum on the . . . day of; the . . . tribe voted first; the fir]st to vote in the name of his tribe was Quintus Fabius, son of Quintus.

Regarding the state land in the country of Italy belonging to the Roman people in the consulship of Publius Mucius and Lucius Calpurn[ius (133 BC), not including the land which by a clause under the law or plebiscite introduced by Gaius Sempronius, son of Tiberius, tribune of the plebs, was exempted from division . . . **2** whatever land or ground out of that land or ground any long-standing occupier by law or plebiscite] took or kept for himself, provided that its size not be greater than the amount one man was allowed by law or plebiscite to tak[e or retain for himself.

Regarding the state land in the country of Italy belonging to the Roman people in the consulship of Publius Mucius and Lucius Calpurnius, not including the land which by a clause under the law or plebiscite introduced by Gaius Sempronius, son of Tiberius, tribune of the plebs, was exempted from division . . . **3** whatever land or ground] out of that land or ground a member of the Board of Three has granted or assigned by law or plebiscite to any Roman citizen selected, provided that it is not included in that land or ground beyo[nd . . .

4 Regarding the state land in the country of Italy belonging to the Roman people in the consulship of Publius Mucius and Lucius Calpurnius, not including the land which by a clause under the law or plebiscite introduced by Gaius Sempronius, son of Tiberius, tribune of the plebs, was exempted from division, whatever land or ground out of that land or ground was granted, given in exchange or co]nfirmed [by a member of the Board of Three to any person who exchanged public land for private.]. . . .

7 All land, ground or building which is recorded ab[ove . . . not including such land as has been ex]empt[ed by a clause above, is to be private . . ., **8** and there is to be right of purchase and sal]e [of that land, ground or building] in the same way as for other private grounds, land or buildings; and a censor, whoever is in office, shall cause that land, ground or building, which h[as been made private by this law, to be entered in the censor's lists in the same way as other private lands, grounds or buildings. . . .]; **9** and no one shall so act as to prevent any person to whom under law or plebiscite that land, ground, building or holding belongs or shall belong [from using, enjoying, holding or possessing] that land, gr[ound, building or holding . . . n]or is anyone to [bring a motion before] the sen[ate] in relation to this matter . . . **10** [nor is any person by virtue of a magistracy or imper]ium to express an opinion or bring a motion by which any of those to whom under law or plebiscite any such land, ground, building or holding belong[s or shall belong] . . . shall be prevented from [using, enjoying, holding or possessi]ng [that land, ground, building or holding], or by which possession shall be taken away against his will, or, if he be dec[eased, against the will of his heirs] . . . .

13 Regarding the state land in the country of Italy belonging to the Roman people in the consulship of Publius Mucius and Lucius Calpurnius, not including the land which by a clause under the law or plebi[scite introduced by Gaius Sempronius, son of Tiberius, tribune of the plebs, was exempted from division . . . and not inc]luding that land, which a long-standing occupier took or retained for himself by law or plebi[scite, provided that its size not be greater than the amount one man was allowed to take or retain for himself, if any person at any time when this law shall be introduced **14** shall have entered into that land for the purpose of culti]vation and possess or hold not more than 30 iugera of that land, that land is to be private.

Any person who shall send to pasture on common pasture land not more than ten head of larger cattle, and [any of their young less than a year old . . . or who shall] send to pasture [there not more than] . . . head of smaller cattle, and any of their young less than a year [old, that person shall not owe impost or pasture-tax for those cattle **15** to either people or tax-farmer and shall not be required to make any return or payment] in relation to this matter.

LATER VIEWS OF THE GRACCHI

8.37 Cicero on agrarian legislation

Cicero *On Duties* 2.73–85

In this essay dedicated to his son Marcus in 44 BC, Cicero is giving his clear opinion about agrarian and debt laws and expressing the optimates' concern about the distribution of public land. At 2.43 he states that Tiberius and Gaius 'were not approved of by the 'boni' when they were alive, and now they are dead they are numbered among those who were killed justifiably'; 1.76 he praises the actions of Scipio Nasica. At 2.72 he criticises Gaius Gracchus' largesse of grain for exhausting the treasury, but this must be an exaggeration as it was only a partial subsidy, and he probably confuses Gaius' measure with later grain distribution laws.

73 A person who holds public office must make it his first duty to see that each man keeps what belongs to him and that private citizens suffer no loss of property through an act of government . . . It was for this reason in particular that governments and states were instituted: so that each man might keep what belonged to him. For although men banded together under nature's guidance, it was in hope of keeping their possessions safe that they sought the protection of cities. . . . **78** Indeed, men who wish to be populares and who for that reason either try to bring in some agrarian reform so that the occupants may be driven out of their residences, or think that money which has been loaned should be made over to the borrowers, are undermining the foundations of the state, for they are disrupting, firstly, public harmony (*concordia*), which cannot exist when money is taken away from some people and made over to others, and, secondly, justice, which is completely done away with if each man is not allowed to keep what belongs to him . . .**79** How can it be just that a man who has never had any property should now hold land which had been occupied for many years or even generations, while the man who had had it should lose it? **80** It was by reason of this kind of wrong-doing that the Spartans banished their ephor Lysander and put to death their king Agis, which had never before happened in Sparta, and from that time on immense conflicts occurred and tyrants rose up, the optimates were driven out, and the excellently constituted state fell apart; nor indeed did it fall on its own, but, through the contagious nature of the evils which started in Sparta and then spread more widely, it overturned the rest of Greece too. What can we say of our own Gracchi, the sons of that eminent Tiberius Gracchus and grandsons of Africanus, but that it was strife over agrarian reform that destroyed them? . . . **85** And so men whose job it is to look after the state must refrain from that kind of generosity which takes property from some people to give it to others, and they should take especial care that each man keeps what belongs to him through the just administration of the law and courts and that the poorer classes should not be oppressed because of their humble status, while envy should not prevent the wealthy from holding onto or recovering what belongs to them.

8.38 Cicero on optimates and the Gracchi

Cicero *In Defence of Sestius* 96–7, 103

In this defence of Sestius (tr. pl. 57) delivered in 56 BC, Cicero is dividing senators into two groups.

96 There have always been two groups of men in this state who have been eager to participate in government and thus to distinguish themselves. Of these groups one wished to be and to be thought to be, populares, 'popular'; the other, optimates, 'best'. Those who wanted everything they did and said to be agreeable to the masses were considered populares, but those who so acted that their policies won the approval of all the best citizens were considered optimates . . . **97** All are optimates who are neither criminal, nor disgraceful in disposition, nor insane, nor embarrassed by troubles in their family. It follows, therefore, that these men, whom you have called a 'breed', are honest, of sound mind, and have their domestic circumstances comfortably organised . . .

103 Tiberius Gracchus proposed an agrarian law. The people were pleased: it looked as if the situation of the poorer classes would be relieved. The optimates, however, opposed it because they saw that it would give rise to dissension, and they also thought that, if the wealthy were evicted from land they had long occupied, the state would be stripped of its champions. Gaius Gracchus proposed a grain law. The people were delighted, as it provided plenty of food with no need to work. The 'good men' fought against it because they thought the masses would be drawn away from hard work towards idleness and they saw that the treasury would be drained.

8.39 Cicero praises the Gracchi

Cicero *On the Agrarian Law* 2.10

Cicero's speech against the Rullan land bill, as consul in 63, was delivered before the people. This may account for his pro-Gracchan sentiments here: while admitting that the Gracchan land legislation was good, this particular proposal — the Rullan — according to Cicero was not: see Bell 1997. Elsewhere Cicero shows no sympathy for the Gracchi (docs 8.34, 37, 38). Cicero here refers to the ager publicus as being 'privately owned', but it was so only in the sense that the wealthy occupied it.

For — I will speak frankly, Romans — I cannot disparage agrarian laws in themselves. I recall that those two most distinguished and most gifted men, the greatest friends of the Roman people, Tiberius and Gaius Gracchus, settled the plebs on public land, which had previously been privately owned. I am not one of those consuls who, like the majority, think it wrong to praise the Gracchi, whose advice, wisdom and laws, I see, have regulated many aspects of the administration.

8.40 Sallust on the Gracchi

Sallust *Jugurthine War* 42.1–4

Sallust, a supporter of Marius and a critic of the optimates, provides a positive assessment of the Gracchi to contrast with Cicero's views. At 41.2 he noted the unity of Rome that held until the destruction of Carthage in 146 BC, after which the people and the nobles went their separate ways, with a small group of oligarchs controlling the treasury, provinces, magistracies, and triumphs. The people's share was only military service and poverty; their farms could be snatched by powerful neighbours while they were away: Brunt 1971: 92. A triumvir: one of the three men on the land commission.

1 So when Tiberius and Gaius Gracchus, whose ancestors had done much in the Punic and other wars to increase Rome's power, tried to defend the liberty of the plebs and expose the crimes of the few, the guilty nobility were shocked and opposed the Gracchi's proceedings, using now the allies and Latins and now the Roman equites, whom hope of an alliance had detached from their support of the plebs. First they butchered Tiberius, and then Gaius a few years later, because he was engaging in the same issues, the one a tribune, the other a triumvir for founding colonies, along with Marcus Fulvius Flaccus. **2** Certainly the Gracchi's desire for victory had led them to behave with insufficient moderation. **3** But a good man should prefer to be beaten than to defeat injustice by doing wrong. **4** As it was, the nobility used their victory arbitrarily and killed or banished a number of people, which added more to their fears during the rest of their lives than to their powers. This is what generally destroys great states, when each side will do anything possible to overcome the other and then avenge themselves harshly on their defeated opponents.

8.41 Plutarch on the Gracchi as reformers

Plutarch *Agis and Cleomenes and the Gracchi Compared* 1.1–2, 5.4–6

Plutarch's *Life* of the Gracchi was paired with that of Agis IV and Cleomenes III of Sparta, who both tried to reform Sparta in the face of domestic crisis.

1.1 Now that this biography is also finished, it remains for me to take a survey of all the lives in parallel. As for the Gracchi, not even those who totally abuse and hate them on other grounds have dared to deny that, of all Romans, they were the best equipped by nature for the practice of virtue and enjoyed an excellent upbringing and education; **2** the natural gifts of Agis and Cleomenes appear to have been more formidable than theirs, in so far as, though they did not receive correct training and were brought up in customs and ways of life by which their elders had long since been corrupted, they made themselves leaders in economy and moderation. . . . **5.4** Those who criticise their characters blame the two Greeks for having been despotic and aggressive from the beginning, and the two Romans for having naturally been immoderately ambitious, though their enemies had nothing else to charge them with; in fact, they agree that it was because they were roused by the conflict with their opponents and by passions not natural to them, as if by blasts of wind, that they launched the state into such a dangerous crisis. **5** For what could have been more fair or just than their original proposals — had not the wealthy, in their attempts to obstruct the law by violence and factionalism, involved both of them in conflict, Tiberius through fear for his life and Gaius in his attempt to avenge his brother who had been killed without justice, without a decree of the senate, and even without the approval of a magistrate? **6** So, from what has been said, you will perceive the difference between them; but if I am to state my view of them separately, I should say that Tiberius was the most pre-eminent of them all in excellence, that Agis as a young man made the least mistakes, and that in achievements and courage Gaius was far behind Cleomenes.

9

Marius

Following Gaius Gracchus' death, the senatorial oligarchy re-established its influence, until increasing dissatisfaction with bribery, corruption and military incompetence brought change. One of the tribunes for 120 BC, P. Decius Subulo, prosecuted Opimius before the assembly for executing Roman citizens without a trial, which Gaius' *lex Sempronia* had prohibited. Opimius argued that he had carried out the senatorial decree calling upon him as consul to take measures to defend the state. He was acquitted, and P. Popillius Laenas, who had organised the witch-hunts of 132, returned from exile (*MRR* I.524; docs 8.19, 8.29). The senate's triumph seemed complete.

The next major phase in Roman politics came with the Jugurthine War. Sallust's *Jugurthine War* (*BJ*) 5 sees it as the first time a challenge was made to 'the arrogance of the nobility', and as the beginning of a struggle which ended with the civil war between Pompey and Caesar. It was the Jugurthine War, or rather the senate's poor handling of this, that gave Marius his chance to run for the consulship.

Marius' background was that of an equestrian from Arpinum. While he had not had the benefit of a thorough Greek education (docs 9.1–2), he clearly was not from an impoverished or obscure family. Arpinum possessed Roman citizenship, and Marius began his adult life with a military career typical of Roman equites. His military competence stood out and he was elected to a military tribunate on the basis of his service in Spain (doc. 9.4), and also held the quaestorship. But his early political career was chequered. His tribunate of 119 was gained with the support of L. Caecilius Metellus (cos. 119), whom Marius in his tribunate threatened with violence over opposition to his voting law (docs 9.4, 36). Only with difficulty did he later obtain a praetorship after missing out on an aedileship (see doc. 9.4), though his marriage to Julia connected him with an aristocratic Roman family (doc. 9.5). Sallust overlooks these electoral difficulties in his presentation of Marius (doc. 9.6).

By 109 he was in favour again with the Metelli and accompanied Q. Caecilius Metellus (cos. 109) to Numidia, clearly on the basis of his military skills. The death of the king of Numidia, Micipsa, in 118 had left two sons (Hiempsal and Adherbal) and their cousin Jugurtha as heirs to the Numidian throne. Jugurtha had Hiempsal killed and defeated Adherbal, who fled to Rome. Opimius was sent to divide the kingdom, but Jugurtha continued to attack Adherbal and ignored the Romans, killing Adherbal and his Italian supporters in 112. Bestia (cos. 111) and Albinus (cos. 110) were sent out to Numidia, but both were incompetent against Jugurtha. Widespread bribery by

Jugurtha of senators at Rome was suspected and clearly did occur. At about the same time, in 113 the army of Gnaeus Papirius Carbo (cos. 113) was destroyed by the Cimbri.

This military incompetence and the failure to defeat Jugurtha led to widespread dissatisfaction at Rome, and Mamilius' law as tribune in 109 BC established a *quaestio extraordinaria* to deal with those accused of having been bribed by Jugurtha, or who had otherwise aided him: Opimius, Albinus and Bestia were all convicted (doc. 9.7).

In Numidia, Metellus initially refused to let Marius return to Rome in 108 to campaign for the consulship of 107; Marius gained the support of Italian businessmen in Africa and the Roman troops, who wrote home supporting his consular candidacy. Metellus finally allowed him to go to Rome (doc. 9.9), and he was elected, probably because of dissatisfaction with the general performance of the nobility on the military front, and also because he had promised an end to the war, claiming that Metellus was protracting the war; the support of the equites must have been crucial (docs 9.7–9). The senate had already reassigned Numidia to Metellus, but one of the tribunes proposed a bill to grant the command to Marius. Metellus was furious, but was granted a triumph and the title 'Numidicus'.

Marius wanted more troops than the senate had authorised, so he changed the recruitment procedure, including members of the *capite censi*, the landless poor, in his army (docs 9.10–11). The Gracchi's concern with military recruitment in attempting to restore small landholders is relevant here. Marius recruited from even the poorest, and so created a client army dependant on its general for land at the end of its period of service.

Sulla acted as Marius' quaestor in Numidia. They clearly worked well together and Sulla was to be Marius' legate in the German wars. At this stage there was no animosity between them (doc. 9.12), and it was only in 88 BC that real rivalry between the two manifested itself. In Numidia as consul, Marius took several years to defeat Jugurtha and, when he was on the point of doing so, Bocchus, ruler of Mauretania, surrendered the king to Sulla (docs 9.13, 11.50).

Reforms to the army itself followed with the campaigns against the Germanic tribes, the Teutones and Cimbri (docs 9.23–6), with Roman fears of these migrating hordes leading to an unprecedented five consecutive consulships for Marius (104–100 BC). There had been a series of disasters against the Germans (doc. 9.14) and, with panic in Italy (doc. 9.16), Marius was a logical choice; the generals who had failed were prosecuted (doc. 9.19). The first years were quiet and Marius reformed the army (docs 9.21–2), but great victories were then won against the Germans in 102 and 101 and Italy was safe (docs 9.23, 9.26, 9.37). Marius had the support of populares and optimates alike (docs 9.24–5).

Marius in 104 had had the support of a tribune for 103, L. Appuleius Saturninus, in seeking the consulship. Saturninus' tribunate in 103 was not altogether remarkable. In 100 he was tribune for a second time, due to the murder of the tribune Nonius, whom Saturninus replaced. His land legislation, passed for Marius' veterans during 100, violently and against the omens, aroused opposition and led to Metellus going into exile. A grain law is also usually dated to this year (doc. 9.38).

Saturninus was elected for a third tribunate with the impostor L. Equitius, who claimed to be a son of Tiberius Gracchus. Saturninus, with Glaucia, who was hoping for the consulship, organised the killing of one of the consular candidates for 99, Memmius, to ensure the election of Glaucia, who was praetor in 100 (and so ineligible for election as he was holding a magistracy and so could not seek election to another). The senate acted and an emergency decree was passed, with the consuls (C. Marius and L. Valerius) empowered to 'preserve the imperium and majesty of the Roman people' (doc. 9.30). Marius as consul presided over the distribution of weapons. The senate and equites acted together and arms were given to the plebs. Saturninus and his supporters were besieged on the Capitol, and the water pipes cut off until they surrendered. Saturninus and his supporters were then held in the senate house, but the crowd broke in and stoned them; Glaucia was dragged from his house and his neck broken.

Saturninus, Glaucia and Equitius were thus all killed on the first day of the tribunate, 10 December 100. Marius apparently tried to save their lives but was unable to oppose the angry mob. His attitude towards Saturninus was unclear, but he had obtained his land grants for his veterans and as consul clearly felt his interests lay more with the senate.

Plutarch has Marius fall into obscurity for the 90s; this may be an exaggeration but certainly there was little scope for his military talents in this period. He was involved in the Social War (docs 10.14, 18, 23). One last consulship awaited Marius. The command against Mithridates was awarded to Sulla as consul for 88, but Marius intrigued with the tribune P. Sulpicius Rufus to replace Sulla in the command (doc. 9.32). Sulla did not accept this, marched on Rome, had Sulpicius killed and Marius exiled, and left for the east (doc. 9.33). Marius returned to Rome amidst bloodshed (doc. 9.34), and was elected to a final consulship for 86, but died after a few days in office on 13 January.

Any assessment of Marius' career must reflect not so much on his victory against Jugurtha — which may well have been Metellus' if he had been allowed to retain his command — but on Marius' five consecutive consulships and the victories against the Germans for which he was largely responsible. His reforms of the army were to play a crucial role from 88 to 44 BC, with generals able to rely on the support of their armies in their struggle for pre-eminence. Sulla was to reap the first benefits of the dependent relationship between a general and his client army.

Ancient sources: the main sources are Sallust's *Jugurthine War* which deals only with Marius' career in that conflict, and the unsatisfactory *Marius* of Plutarch.

Sallust's *Jugurthine War* (references to this work are abbreviated as *BJ*, *Bellum Jugurthinum*) deals with Marius' campaigns in Africa. His portrait of Marius and Sulla in their early political careers is favourable but he condemned Sulla's later career: Marius: *BJ* 84.2, 86, Sulla: *BJ* 95–6 (docs 9.10, 12). Metellus' leadership of the army is reported favourably (*BJ* 45.1–3), but his aristocratic *superbia* (arrogance) — which leads him to treat Marius' consulship aspirations with scorn — is also noted (doc. 9.6). Sallust's treatment of Marius is often seen as extremely favourable, with Marius as the ultimate *popularis* (note Marius' denunciations of the aristocracy: *BJ* 85: doc. 9.2), but the portrait is not totally flattering, and Sallust can be critical (doc. 9.6); Syme, however, overemphasises its negative aspects (1964: 159–4).

Sallust clearly realises the significance of the support of the equites in obtaining for Marius the consulship and command which was absolutely crucial for his future political career and without which he might have remained a minor politician (*BJ* 64.5–6), but neglects the details of Marius' early chequered career.

Plutarch *Marius*, esp. 7–12; *Sulla* 3–4, 6.1–2, 7–10: Plutarch used the writings of the philosopher Posidonius who wrote a universal history from 146 down to the 80s for Marius; Posidonius was a contemporary and actually spoke to Marius in his last days (*FGH* 87 FF37, 60). Posidonius dealt with the Cimbri (Strabo 7.2.2 = *FGrH* 87 F31) and Plutarch presumably used him for Marius' northern campaigns. Otherwise, Plutarch mentions Sulla, Rufus and Catulus as sources and probably used Sisenna and Scaurus, none of whom presented a favourable portrait, as well as Sallust. Sulla in his *Memoirs* denigrated Marius' achievements, while other contemporary writers, who would have been read by both Sallust and Plutarch, were hostile to him: the princeps senatus M. Aemilius Scaurus (cos. 115), P. Rutilius Rufus (cos. 105) and Q. Lutatius Catulus (cos. 102), while L. Cornelius Sisenna's account of Sulla can hardly have favoured Marius (*HRR* I^2 276–97). Plutarch's *Marius* is far from satisfactory as an historical account, not merely because of its hostility to Marius and its moralising nature, but because it fails to attach any significance to Marius' army reforms, and its lack of understanding of the political situation of the time is made clear at *Mar.* 8.5–9.4 where Plutarch fails to consider how Marius wrested the war against Jugurtha from Metellus.

Cicero is generally favourable to Marius (though he calls him 'omnium perfidiosissimus', 'more untrustworthy than anyone else': *Nat. Deor.* 3.80): both were novi homines, from the same town (Arpinum) and in fact related. But Cicero might have had ulterior motives: Marius had been involved in the violent deaths of Saturninus and Glaucia and their supporters, just as Cicero himself had put citizens to death without a trial: see Carney 1960. Cicero refers to an account of Marius' campaign against the Cimbri written by Archias the poet which won Marius' approval (Cic. *Arch.* 19–20), but the accounts of those hostile to him were too strong.

Licinianus 13–14 is important for Mallius (cos. 105) and the disastrous defeat by the Cimbri in 105 BC. Appian *BC* 1.28–32.125–45 (Appian's *Celtica* 13, now only fragmentary, presumably dealt with Marius' campaigns) is quite brief and a narrative with no interpretative material. For an inscription dealing with Marius' career, see doc. 9.35.

There are two biographies of Marius: Carney 1961 and Evans 1994. For the sources: Carney 1961: 2–7, 29 n.148; Brunt 1971: 96–104; Scullard *GN* 392–3; Evans 1994: 5–17. For initial reading on Marius: Carney 1961; Badian 1963/4, *FC* 227–51; Shotter 1994: 29–37; Lintott 1994a: 86–92; Evans 1994. A bust presumed to be that of Marius is in the Staatliche Antikensammlungen und Glyphotek, Munich (Evans 1994 frontispiece).

MARIUS' EARLY CAREER

9.1 Marius the man

Plutarch *Life of Marius* 2.1–2

Plutarch's *Marius* is less than satisfactory, and this passage gives a good indication of the moralising in which it indulges. Val. Max. 2.5.6, 4.4.8 speaks of monuments to Marius in Rome. Gaius Marius lacked the third nomen which many Romans possessed (Plut. *Mar.* 1), but this was not yet as unusual as Plutarch believes (Evans 1994: 20). Like Cato the Elder (doc. 5.58) Marius could of course speak Greek, but would not use it for important official occasions; cf. docs 9.2, 5.57.

1 As for Marius' appearance, I have seen a stone statue of him at Ravenna in Gaul, which fits well with the roughness and harshness supposed to have been characteristic of him. He was naturally brave and war-like, his education having been in the military rather than the civil sphere, and when in power he was unable to control his anger. **2** It is said that he never learnt Greek literature and never used the Greek language on any important occasion, on the grounds that it was ridiculous to study a literature whose teachers were subjects; and after his second triumph (in 101 BC), when at the consecration of a temple he put on some Greek performances, he just went into the theatre and sat down before immediately leaving. Plato often used to say to the philosopher Xenocrates, whose character seemed to have been rather too uncouth, 'My dear Xenocrates, sacrifice to the Graces' — and if anyone had persuaded Marius to sacrifice to the Greek Graces and Muses he would not have brought his career, so distinguished in military commands and public magistracies, to an end so unsightly, and would not have run aground upon an extremely blood-thirsty and cruel old age under the force of his anger, untimely ambition and uncontrollable arrogance.

9.2 Marius' self-portrait

Sallust *Jugurthine War* 85.31–5

Sallust has Marius after his election to the consulship of 107 BC encouraging the people to enlist for the war in Numidia, with much abuse of the *nobiles* as arrogant, decadent and idle. The speech is deliberately laconic and non-rhetorical (or at least not sophisticated) and Marius stresses both his readiness to endure the same hardships as his troops and the ways, as a novus homo, in which he differs from the nobility (as in having no ancestral *imagines*, which he mentions several times). For his education, see Plut. *Mar.* 3.1; Carney 1961: 11–14; Badian 1963/4: 143; Evans 1994: 21–3. His scorn for Greek education was meant to display his derision for the Roman nobility.

31 My words are not carefully chosen; I care little for that. Merit demonstrates itself sufficiently on its own. It is they (the *nobiles*) who need skill to cover up their shameful deeds with rhetoric. **32** Nor have I studied Greek literature; I had little interest in studying this, as it had not improved the characters of its teachers. **33** But I have learnt the best lessons by far for the good of the state: to smite the enemy, mount guard, fear nothing except disgrace, suffer heat and cold alike, sleep on the ground, and endure at the same time lack of food and hard work. **34** With these lessons I shall encourage my soldiers, and I shall not subject them to short rations while living sumptuously myself, or win my glory through their hard work. **35** This is the profitable way, this is the way for a citizen to lead his fellows.

9.3 Intrigue and corruption in Rome, c. 134

Sallust *Jugurthine War* 8.1–2

Jugurtha, nephew of Micipsa, sent to Spain by his uncle in 134, became intimate with Publius Scipio Aemilianus, under whom he served at Numantia (docs 5.49–50). Jugurtha employed wholesale bribery to get his own way at Rome (see doc. 9.7). Sallust comments on Metellus (43.5) that he possessed a mind above riches, for it had been the greed of Roman magistrates which had before that ruined Rome's prospects in Numidia and aided the enemy. At 41.6–8 Sallust speaks of the treasury, provinces, public offices, glory and triumphs being in the hands of a few men, giving rise to greed and violence. Both the *novi homines* and the *nobiles*, according to Sallust, were out for enrichment.

1 At that time in our army there were a great many new men and nobles, to whom riches meant more than virtue and integrity, who were party intriguers at home, influential with Rome's allies, and notorious rather than respected, who fired Jugurtha's ambitious spirit by promising that should king Micipsa die he alone would wield power in Numidia, since his merits were pre-eminent, while everything at Rome could be bought for money. **2** When Numantia had been destroyed, Publius Scipio decided to disband his auxiliary troops and return home. After making gifts to Jugurtha and commending him highly before the assembled soldiers, Scipio took him into his tent and there privately advised him to cultivate the friendship of the Roman people in general rather than that of individuals, and not to form the habit of offering bribes — it was dangerous to buy from the few what belonged to the many. If Jugurtha would continue in his good conduct, glory and a kingdom would come to him of their own accord, but if he acted too hastily his own money would bring about his downfall.

9.4 Marius' early career and changing fortunes

Valerius Maximus *Memorable Deeds and Sayings*
(On Fortune) 6.9.14

Arpinum in central Italy was a Volscian town where both Marius and Cicero were born, Marius probably in 157 BC. From the late fourth century it had *civitas sine suffragio* (citizenship without the right to vote), and from 188 full Roman citizenship (Livy 38.36.7–9). Marius was a *novus homo* in every sense, and this could account for the difficulty he had in entering Roman politics. But as Evans 1994: 24–6 shows, there were numerous *novi homines* who held lesser magistracies and consulships in the second century (cf. Wiseman 1971: 3), but there had not been a *novus homo* consul since 132 BC (see docs 9.9, 2.39–40). Marius was of equestrian rank, and Plutarch *Mar.* 3.1 incorrectly writes of the poverty of his background, though he was clearly not closely connected with the aristocracy of Arpinum, the Gratidii and the Tullii Cicerones (family and social background: Carney 1961: 8–14; Badian 1963/4: 142; Shotter 1994: 30). Plutarch's comments about the obscurity of his birth simply hide the fact that very little is known about Marius' early career. There is also no evidence that Marius was ever a publicanus. To enter political office required capital: there was the expense of the games that custom required, as well as the cost of electoral bribery (and despite his acquittal on a charge of bribery in the election for the praetorship in 115, Marius had clearly, like many politicians, engaged in this).

P. Cornelius Scipio Aemilianus gained a second consulship in 134 to finish the protracted war in Spain, and enlisted 500 friends and clients as volunteers, giving him an overall army of 4,000 (App. *Iber.* 84.366; Astin 1967: 136; Gabba 1976: 11). There was a patron-client link between the Marii and the Cornelii which could explain Marius' presence (Carney 1961: 15; Wiseman 1971: 121). However, while Plut. *Mar.* 3.2 has this campaign as Marius' first military service, this would have been when Marius was 23, a late start, so it has been suggested that Marius served in Spain for several years before Scipio's arrival, perhaps from 140 BC when he was about 17, commencing a typical career with military service (Evans 1994: 26–7). Marius under Scipio Aemilianus served alongside other figures who would be important: Gaius Gracchus, P. Rutilius Rufus (cos. 105), and Jugurtha (see doc. 5.50). As a member of the equestrian order he would have served in the cavalry.

At Numantia, he came to Scipio's attention, by fighting one of the enemy single-handedly, killing him in Scipio's presence, and accepting Scipio's tighter discipline for the army. Plutarch has a nice story about Scipio noting Marius' potential (Plut. *Mar.* 3.4; this is perhaps simply a topos, but does indicate that Marius performed in an exemplary fashion in Spain). It was this military ability which saw him elected by the assembly as a military tribune (presumably soon after his return from Spain when his deeds will have been recent and known to the assembly, perhaps around 130 or a few years later). A quaestorship, perhaps in 121, meant that he saw further military service (where he served as military tribune and quaestor is unknown). His career had well and truly begun, but there were to be checks. His career in Spain: Carney 1961: 15; Badian 1963/4: 144; Evans 1994: 27–9; cf. Astin 1967: 153–5, 182–3, 264.

Plutarch states that when Marius stood for election as a plebeian tribune in 119 he had the support of Caecilius Metellus, there being a patron-client relationship between the Metelli and the Marii (Plut. *Mar.* 4.1; Badian *FC* 194–5). How this came about is not known. But his activities as tribune seriously upset his relationship with the Metelli. He had a law (*lex Maria*) passed to ensure that those about to cast their votes could not be intimidated (see doc. 9.36). The consul L. Aurelius Cotta opposed this, and Marius was summoned to the senate house; Cotta asked the other consul Metellus for his opinion and when he also voiced opposition, Marius threatened to have him thrown in prison. Metellus appealed to the other tribunes but none supported him. The senate gave in, but Marius had broken faith (*fides*) with the Metelli. However, he was found connected with the Metelli again in the Numidian campaign (but again was to break with them). His successful opposition later in his tribunate to a law for grain distribution to the people might indicate a *rapprochement* with the senate or be a sign of political independence without fixed allegiances (Plut. *Mar.* 4.6–7; tribunate: Plut. *Mar.* 4; Cic. *Laws* 3.39: 'the Marian law even made the voting bridges narrow' (cf. doc. 9.36); Badian 1963/4: 145; Scullard *GN* 44–5; Evans 1994: 38).

The attempt perhaps in 118 to secure election to a curule aedileship and then soon after to an ordinary plebeian aedileship failed, an unprecedented double defeat. Cic. *Planc.* 51; Plut. *Mar.* 5.1–3 (cf. *Mor.* 202b) have the double repulse occurring on the same day, but this is unlikely, given the time elections took: see Evans 1994: 46. He stood in 116 for a praetorship for 115, and was last on the list of those elected, narrowly escaping conviction (a tied vote) on a charge of *ambitus*, that of bribing the voters (Plut. *Mar.* 5). Cic. (*Off.* 3.79) considers that at this point he had no chance of achieving candidacy for the consulship.

Next comes Gaius Marius, Fortune's great contest: for with extreme bravery he stood up to all her blows by his strength both of body and mind. Judged unworthy of the honours of Arpinum, he dared to stand for the quaestorship at Rome. Then, by his patience under repulses, he rather broke into the senate than entered it. In his candidature for the tribunate and aedileship too he experienced a similar electoral disgrace, and as a candidate for the praetorship clung to the last place, which, however, he won not without danger, for, accused of bribery, he obtained an acquittal from the jurors with the greatest difficulty. From that Marius, so lowly at Arpinum, so obscure at Rome, so disdained as a candidate for office, emerged the Marius who conquered Africa, who drove king Jugurtha before his chariot, who annihilated the armies of the Teutones and Cimbri, whose two trophies are seen in the city, whose seven consulships are read in the Fasti, and whose fate it was to be made consul after exile and to hold a proscription after having been proscribed. What could be more fickle or changeable than his position? If you were to put him amongst the wretched, he would be found the most wretched of all, if amongst the fortunate, the most fortunate.

9.5 Marriage to Julia

Plutarch *Life of Marius* 6.3–4

After his urban praetorship of 115, Marius went to Further Spain (Hispania Ulterior: Plut. *Mar.* 6.1) as governor. Plutarch states that after this he returned to Rome without wealth or rhetorical skill (Plut. *Mar.* 6.3), but he had almost certainly enriched himself there both in 134–33 and in 114, and was probably amongst those Romans exploiting the silver mines in Spain (see doc. 6.23; Diod. 34.38; Carney 1961: 23; Evans 1994: 57).

Soon after his return to Spain, Marius married Julia (as his second wife), with a son born in 109 or 108. Though this branch of the Julii had not had a consul for many decades, the marriage brought him into the Roman aristocracy. From the point of view of the Julii, Marius was wealthy and with good connections amongst the equites (Carney 1961: 23; Badian 1963/4: 146, 1972: 50–1; Evans 1994: 10, 61). Julia was to be the aunt of Julius Caesar, born 100 BC; Marius was therefore Caesar's uncle by marriage.

3 When he returned to political life he lacked both wealth and rhetorical skill, which the most prestigious men of that time used in their control of the people. 4 His steadfast spirit, persistence in hard work, and plain life-style gained him popularity with the citizens and he approached more closely to power through his reputation, so he was able to make a brilliant marriage to Julia, from the distinguished family of the Julii Caesares, who was the aunt of that Caesar who was later to become the greatest man in Rome and who, to some extent, imitated Marius because of this family relationship, as I have written in my *Life* of him.

MARIUS IN AFRICA

9.6 Gaius Marius — Sallust's view

Sallust *Jugurthine War* 63.1–64.6

Events in Rome were ominous. The Caecilii Metelli were prominent within the state (Scullard *GN* 44), with various consulships (123, 119, 117, 115, 113, 109 (the last)), and had assisted Marius to his tribunate. It was one of the Caecilii Metelli, Quintus Caecilius Metellus, who as consul in 109 BC took Marius to Africa with him, presumably both because of past links (though note the events of 119 BC) and because of Marius' military abilities. It was Numidia that gave Marius his great opportunity. In 113 BC three Vestal Virgins were condemned to death for unchastity, and two Greeks and two Gauls buried alive in the Forum, presumably due to the pressures felt by the Romans at this time (docs 7.91, 4.38).

The war in Africa. Masinissa as king of Numidia had been a loyal ally of Rome and friend of both the elder and younger Scipiones Africani, patrons of the Numidian royal house. When Masinissa died in 148, Micipsa gained the throne, and on his death in 118 BC bequeathed the kingdom to his two sons (Hiempsal and Adherbal), and to Jugurtha, his nephew (and a grandson of Masinissa), who had served with Scipio Aemilianus at Numantia: it seems in fact as if Jugurtha may even have been the senior partner in the inheritance. Hiempsal and Adherbal refused to recognise Jugurtha, who had Hiempsal assassinated, while Adherbal fled to Rome. See further comments at doc. 9.6.

63.5: Sallust here ignores Marius' problems in attaining the aedileship and praetorship (Paul 1984: 170).

63.7 The term *novus homo* (also as *homo novus*) strictly applied to a consul from an equestrian family (Wiseman 1971: 1, cf. 1–12 in general; Paul 1984: 17; docs 2.39–40), but in general was also used more broadly to include men of senatorial background who were the first to attain the consulship in their family. Cicero uses the term for those equestrians who were the first to hold political office and so enter the senate (Gelzer 1969: 34), as well as for equestrians who attained the consulship (Paul 17). The overall sense is of 'outsiders' (equestrians) entering the political system. In Sallust's *Jugurthine War* the novus homo is always contrasted with the nobilis. Marius in his speech at Rome contrasts his *virtus* (good qualities) as a homo novus with the inherited advantages of the nobiles (*BJ* 85; doc. 9.2). Marius as a novus homo who became a consul was unusual, but his career up to and including 108 BC was not in fact exceptional.

64.4: Sallust's comment that Metellus' insult (also at Plut. *Mar.* 8.6) 'kindled . . . Marius' desire for the office he aspired to' cannot mean that this insult was what provoked Marius to aspire to the consulship: this had presumably been in his mind for some time. He had fulfilled the requisite offices, and to hold an important military command he would need to be a consul. Marius therefore began asking Metellus to allow him to return to Rome to stand for the consulship of 107 BC. Marius was 49, and the minimum age for a consulship was 42 or 43. Metellus' son, Metellus (Pius), would at the earliest be expected to attain a consulship at the age of 42 in 86 BC when Marius would be seventy years old (the son became praetor in 89 for which the minimum age was thirty-nine). The younger Metellus actually reached the consulship in 80 (by which time Marius had held seven consulships and was dead: *MRR* II.79).

64.5 Marius' laxness can be compared with the favourable picture of Sulla's relations with the soldiery (*BJ* 95–6: doc. 9.12). But Plut. *Mar.* 7 has Marius popular with the troops for sharing their hardships and living like them, so that they wrote home that he must be made consul to end the war. Marius gained support by promising a quick victory to traders at Utica, and also the equites, both those in the army and those engaged in trade, who wrote home criticising Metellus' campaigning, urging that Marius be given command. Sallust seems to invent a lax Marius, and paints an unfavourable picture of him here, motivated by *ambitio*. On Marius and the support of the equites for the consulship and Numidian command, see also *BJ* 65.5, cf. 73.3; Plut *Mar.* 7.3–6; Vell. 2.11; Diod. 34/35.38; Dio 26 F89.3; Hill 1952: 120–1; Carney 1961: 26–8; Badian *FC* 192–6; Lintott 1994a: 91; Evans 1994: 63–8.

63.1 At about the same time it happened that, when Gaius Marius was offering a sacrifice to the gods at Utica, the haruspex (soothsayer) declared that it portended a great and wonderful future; accordingly, whatever he had in mind he should rely on the gods and carry it out, and make trial of his fortune as often as possible, since everything would turn out successfully. **2** Even before this Marius had been driven by an intense desire for the consulship, for acquiring which he had all the qualifications in abundance, except the antiquity of his family: a capacity for hard work, integrity, great military skill, and a spirit mighty in warfare, temperate in private life, unaffected by passionate desire for wealth, and covetous only of glory. **3** He had been born and spent his boyhood at Arpinum, and when he first reached the age of military service he trained himself in the performance of military duties, not in Grecian eloquence or the niceties of city life; engaged thus in wholesome occupations his unspoiled character quickly matured. **4** As a result, when he was a candidate before the people for the rank of military tribune for the first time, even though the majority did not know him by sight, he was known by his deeds and elected by all the tribes. **5** Then from that office he won one after another, always conducting himself in such a way that he seemed worthy of a higher position. **6** However, although he had shown himself so exceptional a man up to that point — for later on he was driven headlong by ambition — he still did not dare attempt the consulship. For even at that time, although the plebs could bestow the other magistracies, the nobility passed the consulship from hand to hand amongst themselves. **7** No 'new man' was so distinguished or his achievements so splendid that he was considered worthy of that honour and he was looked on as if he were unclean.

64.1 Therefore, when Marius saw that the words of the soothsayer pointed in the same direction as that in which his heart's desire was urging him, he asked Metellus to grant him leave of absence to stand for office. Although Metellus possessed in abundance courage, the love of glory and other qualities desired by good men, he also had a proud, disdainful spirit, a common weakness in the nobility. **2** At first, therefore, he was disturbed by the unusual situation, expressed his amazement at Marius' intention, and advised him, as if motivated by friendship, not to attempt so irregular a proceeding or entertain ideas above his station: all things are not to be desired by all men, said Metellus, and Marius should be content with his own lot; and finally he should beware of asking from the Roman people something which they would be justified in refusing.

3 After he had made this and similar comments and Marius' determination remained unshaken, he finally replied that as soon as public business permitted him he would do what Marius requested. **4** Later, when Marius often made the same request, he is said to have replied, 'Don't be in such a hurry to go to Rome — you'll be old enough to stand for the consulship when my son does'. The son, at that point, was serving there on his father's staff and was about twenty years of age. This kindled both Marius' desire for the office he aspired to and his hatred towards Metellus. **5** As a result he allowed himself to be motivated by desire and anger, the worst of all counsellors, abstained from no word or deed that might be of any use in gaining him popularity, and was less of a disciplinarian than before with the soldiers under his command in the winter-quarters, while in discussing the war with the businessmen, of whom there was a large community at Utica, he made simultaneous accusations and boasts: if half the army, he proclaimed, would be entrusted to him, in a few days he would have Jugurtha in chains; his commander was deliberately dragging things out, because, as a man of vain and despotic pride, he was too fond of power. **6** All these comments seemed all the more reliable to his listeners, because their businesses had been ruined by the lengthy duration of the war and because nothing moves fast enough for eager men.

9.7 The lex Mamilia assists Marius' ambitions

Sallust *Jugurthine War* 40.2–3, 75.4–5

Jugurtha through bribery had been able to keep the Romans at bay: after the murder of Hiempsal, when Adherbal went to Rome, Jugurtha sent envoys to Rome who bribed senators to take up his cause and who duly urged leniency against him (*BJ* 13.6–8). In the senate house, after Adherbal and Jugurtha's envoys had spoken, the bribed said everything they could in Jugurtha's support, but a few senators carried the day, amongst them the otherwise corruptible Aemilius Scaurus (cos. 115 and princeps senatus), who according to Sallust recommended supporting Adherbal and punishing the death of Hiempsal because Jugurtha's bribery was so blatant it would arouse popular resentment (*invidia*: *BJ* 15.5). Opimius (cos. 121 and chief figure in Gaius Gracchus' death: docs 8.33–4) was sent out at the head of a commission of ten: he had opposed Jugurtha, but in Numidia was won over 'by many gifts and promises' as were most of the others on the commission, and awarded Jugurtha the better half of Numidia (*BJ* 16; under the *lex Mamilia* Opimius would be convicted of treasonable activity with Jugurtha). Jugurtha, encouraged by what bribery could accomplish (*BJ* 20.1), in 112 attacked Adherbal; the senate sent an embassy of three young men, and Jugurtha briefly broke off the war (*BJ* 21.4–22.5). When they left, he attacked Cirta, Adherbal's capital; Adherbal sent a letter to Rome. Here Jugurtha's paid partisans in the senate attempted to forestall any action but another embassy was sent, due particularly to the influence of the princeps senatus Scaurus, but was unsuccessful (*BJ* 25).

The Italians besieged with Adherbal recommended surrender; he did so and was murdered, while the Italians were slaughtered (26). When news reached Rome, Jugurtha's bribed senators interrupted the discussions in the senate, wasted time, and tried to minimise the enormity of what had happened. But C. Memmius, tr. pl. 111 BC (*MRR* I.541), 'opposed to the power of the nobility', attacked the bribery and the senate's actions before the people, and the senate, fearing the people, assigned Numidia as one of the consular provinces, and preparations for war began (*BJ* 27). L. Calpurnius Bestia (cos. 111) was sent out with an army, and had initial successes, but was bribed by Jugurtha, and granted him a lenient peace; Scaurus, hitherto so opposed to Jugurtha, and who had accompanied Bestia as legate, was also won over by a massive bribe (*BJ* 29). Memmius launched another attack on the nobiles, pressed the case for war, and had Jugurtha summoned to Rome, but another tribune (bribed by Jugurtha) vetoed an interrogation before the people in the comitia tributa. Jugurtha took the opportunity of being in Rome to assassinate a pretender to the throne (*BJ* 30–5). As he left Rome, Sallust has Jugurtha refer to Rome as a city for sale (*BJ* 35.10; Livy *Per.* 64; cf. *BJ* 8.1, 20.1: 'at Rome everything could be bought', 'omnia Romae venalia esse'). Such bribery by foreigners of senators had been a practice since at least 169 (see Paul 1984: 261–3).

Spurius Postumius Albinus as consul for 110 prosecuted the war against Jugurtha; returning to Rome to hold elections, he left his brother Aulus in command: Jugurtha easily defeated him and the Romans surrendered and passed under the yoke (*BJ* 36–9). In 110, the comitia centuriata chose Metellus as one of the two consuls for 109, and awarded him Numidia as his province.

Mamilius' law of 109 BC. G. Mamilius Limetanus (tr. pl. 109; *MRR* I.546) proposed proceedings against those bribed by Jugurtha, or who had otherwise aided him (Sallust *BJ* 40); a *quaestio extraordinaria* was established, and several prominent senators were successfully prosecuted, including Opimius (Alexander *Trials* nos 52–7). There was widespread dissatisfaction with the nobiles, perhaps due to the events of 122 and bitterness over the senate's treatment of Gaius Gracchus and his supporters. Cicero refers to the jurors as 'Gracchani': the equites who were empowered by Gaius to serve as jurors (doc. 8.34). Sallust *BJ* 40.4 has Aemilius Scaurus naming himself as one of the three commissioners (*quaesitores*), for which note Sumner 1976; Paul 1984: 120–1; Alexander *Trials* 27. Sallust's comment that Jugurtha bribed Scaurus (29.2) might seem shaky given this. For the Mamilian commission (*quaestio*): Hill 1952: 119–21; Smith 1955: 97; Gruen 1968: 142–50; Gelzer 1969: 133; Badian 1972: 83, 85; Lintott 1994a: 89, 90.

Marius wanted not only to be consul but to be the commander in Africa. Canvassing for the consulship was an easier task than it might have been in that he represented himself as the one who could win the war. Metellus' conduct of the war in 109 and 108 was acceptable, as he was making good progress, and Marius' criticisms were not justified: he himself would take a few years to defeat Jugurtha, and only then through treachery organised by his quaestor Sulla. **75.4:** Gauda: *BJ* 65: a grandson of Masinissa with the Roman army; Marius promised him the Numidian throne. For the Jugurthine War: Last 1932: 113–39; Raven 1993: 49–53; Lintott 1994: 27–31; commentary of Paul 1984.

40.2 Measures to oppose the bill (of Mamilius) were taken both by those conscious of their guilt and by others afraid of the dangers arising from factional ill-will, and, since they were unable to resist it openly without admitting their approval of these and similar actions, they did so secretly through their friends and especially through men of Latin and Italian allied towns. **3** But the people passed the bill with incredible eagerness and decisiveness rather out of hatred for the nobility, against whom these measures were being directed, than out of concern for the state — so high were party passions running.

75.4 In this way Marius induced Gauda and the Roman equites, both those in the army and the businessmen, some by his personal influence, but most of them by the hope of peace, to write to their connections in Rome criticising Metellus' conduct of the war and demanding Marius as commander. **5** Accordingly many people canvassed for Marius' candidature for the consulship in a show of support that was highly flattering. Moreover, at that time the plebs, with the nobles frustrated by the law of Mamilius, were trying to promote *novi homines* (new men). Thus everything worked in Marius' favour.

9.8 One novus homo on another

Cicero *On Duties* 3.79

Cicero here is talking about the wrongs that stem from overreaching ambition. Generally he is quite pro-Marius as a fellow-townsman from Arpinum, and because of family links with the Marii: Carney 1960: 4; Badian 1963/4: 143; Evans 1994: 9; Everitt 2001: 19, 32. On novi homines (new men), see docs 2.39–40.

Gaius Marius had long lacked the hope of a consulship and had now been out of office for six years following his praetorship, nor did he seem to have any chance of even being a candidate for the consulship, when he was sent by Quintus Metellus, one of our most outstanding men and citizens, whose legate he was, to Rome. There he accused Metellus before the Roman people of protracting the war; if they would make him consul, he promised, he would in a short time deliver Jugurtha alive or dead into the power of the Roman people. And so he was elected consul, it is true, but he had forsaken good faith and justice in that by bringing a false charge he had subjected one of the best and most respectable citizens, although he was his legate and on a mission for him, to the people's ill-will.

9.9 Marius gets his heart's desire

Sallust *Jugurthine War* 73.1–7

Marius' election to the consulship of 107: Vell. 2.11.2; Plut. *Mar.* 8.6–9; Evans 1994: 57–68; *MRR* I.550. **73.1** Bomilcar was executed by Jugurtha for complicity in an attempt to assassinate him. **73.2** Plutarch has Metellus giving Marius leave to go twelve days before the elections in 108 for 107 BC; consular elections took place in October or November. **73.3** refers to the letters sent home by soldiers and equites with the army supporting Marius for the consulship and Numidian command.

73.7 Although many *novi homines* had held lesser offices and some had gone on to hold the consulship in the second century, there had not been a *novus homo* since Q. Pompeius was consul in 141, or perhaps P. Rupilius in 132 (Paul 1984: 191; doc. 2.39). The senate had made its decision

458

about the allocation of provinces, with Numidia again allotted to Metellus (*BJ* 62.10). The comitia centuriata elected Marius consul, and in this assembly the support of the equites will have been crucial (see Vell. 2.11.2); a plebiscite of the people gave him Numidia as his province: Sall. *BJ* 84.1. There was precedent in this in the people's appointment of Scipio Aemilianus to Africa in 147 (Astin 1967: 61–3; Lintott 1994a: 91; but Scipio's case was much more extraordinary in that Scipio had not been even a consul: docs 4.46–7). But Scipio had been a 'once-off' affair, whereas Marius' appointment to Numidia commenced a series of commands granted by the people to various commanders (Lintott 1994a: 91).

1 When Metellus learned from deserters of the fate of Bomilcar and the discovery of the plot, he again hastened to make all his preparations as if starting a completely new war. **2** As Marius kept on importuning him about his leave of absence, he sent him home, thinking that a subordinate who was simultaneously discontented and at odds with his commander would be of little value. **3** At Rome as well, the plebs, on hearing the letters which had been sent regarding Metellus and Marius, readily accepted what was said about both. **4** The commander's noble birth, which had previously been counted as an honour, became a source of ill-will, while in Marius' case his humble origins added to his popularity. In both cases, however, factional zeal had more weight than the good or bad qualities of the men involved. **5** Furthermore seditious magistrates (tribunes) whipped up the mob, in every assembly charging Metellus with treason and exaggerating Marius' virtues. **6** At length the plebs were so inflamed that all the craftsmen and farmers, those whose prosperity and credit depended on the work of their own hands, left their work to attend Marius considering their own necessities of life less important than his success. **7** And so the nobles were beaten, and after many years the consulship was granted to a *novus homo*. Afterwards, when the people were asked by the tribune of the plebs, Titus Manlius Mancinus, in a packed assembly whom they wished to lead the war against Jugurtha, they appointed Marius. Shortly before this the senate had assigned Numidia to Metellus: their decision was rendered null and void.

9.10 Marius takes command and enrols the *capite censi*

Sallust *Jugurthine War* 84.1–2, 86.1–4

Cf. Gell. 16.10.1; Plut. *Mar.* 9.1; Marius' later army reforms: docs 9.22–3. The Roman army was made up of soldiers whose ownership of property was felt to bind them to the interests of the state and its defence.

The senate hoped that the people would be disinclined for military service and Marius would lose support and/or troops, but he roused them in a stirring speech. Livy 1.43 states that Servius Tullius established classes based on property qualifications (cf. doc. 1.19); the *capite censi* were without property and exempt from military service, only entered on censors' list regarding their person (*caput*). Marius, by enrolling these, the *proletarii*, thereby created the beginning of the 'client army' and made generals dependent on the senate or tribunes to have land-grants made to landless soldiers. This consequence was not apparent at the time (Sallust 86.3 does not support the idea; see Gabba 1976: 14; Badian 1984: 197; Shotter 1994: 31–2; Evans 1994: 75–6). The property qualification had been lowered previously (Gabba 1976: 2–12), but Marius now did away with it entirely. Marius' motive in abolishing the property qualification can only have been due to a manpower shortage, owing to losses the Romans had sustained in recent years (Gabba 1976: 13–14). The numbers so enrolled need not have been large (Brunt *IM* 430 suggests 5,000) but the principle had been established. Marius ended up taking more troops than the senate had authorised: *BJ* 86.4. For the definition of *capite censi*, see doc. 9.11.

It is frequently stated that Marius created an army of landless professional soldiers who relied on their commanders for land. He did in fact provide land distributions for his soldiers (see below). However, soldiers transferring their loyalty to a commander from the state is in fact first seen with Sulla, who was the first to exploit his army as a body of *de facto* clients reliant on him for land settlement. Certainly Marius did not attempt to transfer his newly enrolled troops' loyalty from the state to himself.

For his speech attacking the senate (doc. 9.2), and the question of its authenticity (unlikely, according to most modern historians): *BJ* 85; Plut. *Mar.* 9.2–4; Syme 1964: 169; Paul 1984: 207–14; Evans 1994: 71–4.

84.1 Marius, as I said above, had been elected consul with the enthusiastic support of the plebs; while he had already been hostile to the nobles before this point, after the people assigned him the province of Numidia he threatened them with persistence and boldness, attacking now individuals, now the entire class, asserting that he had defeated them and taken the consulship as spoils, as well as other remarks intended to glorify himself and cause them annoyance. **2** Meanwhile he gave priority to preparations for the war, demanding reinforcements to bring the legions up to strength, summoning auxiliaries from foreign nations and kings, and in addition calling up the bravest members of the Latins and allies, most of whom he knew from military service, and a few only by reputation, while by personal solicitations he also induced veterans who had finished their service to join his force.

86.1 After Marius had made a speech in these terms and seen that it aroused the spirits of the plebs, he made haste to load his ships with provisions, money, arms and other useful items and ordered his legate Aulus Manlius to set sail with these. **2** Meanwhile he himself enrolled soldiers, not according to ancestral custom by property classes, but taking any man who volunteered, mostly the *capite censi*. **3** Some stated that he did this through lack of good men, others to win popularity, as it was from that class he had gained his status and rank — and to someone seeking power the poorest man is the most useful, for he is not concerned about his property, not having any, and considers anything respectable for which he receives pay. **4** As a result Marius set sail for Africa with a much greater force than had been authorised, and arrived at Utica in a few days. The army was handed over to him by the legate Publius Rutilius. **5** Metellus had avoided meeting Marius, so that he might not see what he had been unable to bear even hearing about.

9.11 Marius removes property qualifications for army service

Aulus Gellius *Attic Nights* 16.10.10–11, 14

10 Those of the Roman plebs who were the humblest and poorest, and who reported no more than 1,500 asses at the census, were called proletarii, while those who were assessed as having no property at all or next to none, were termed *capite censi*, 'counted by head', and the lowest rating of the *capite censi* was 375 asses. **11** But since property and money were seen as being a hostage or pledge to the state, and since there was in them a sort of guarantee and basis for patriotism, neither the proletarii nor the *capite censi* were enlisted as soldiers, unless in an extreme emergency, because they had little or no property or money . . . **14** Gaius Marius is said to have been the first man to have enrolled the *capite censi*, according to some in the war against the Cimbri at a time of great crisis for the state, or more probably, as Sallust says, in the Jugurthine War, an act unheard of before that time.

9.12 Sulla enters military life

Sallust *Jugurthine War* 95.1–96.3

Despite Marius' complaints that Metellus was being too slow in prosecuting the war, and promises of a decisive victory if he himself were elected consul, the war against Jugurtha continued after Marius' consulship expired; he continued the war as proconsul. Jugurtha was captured in 105, and Marius returned to Rome and celebrated his triumph on 1 January 104 BC (Sall. *BJ* 114; Livy *Per.* 67; *CIL* I² 1, p. 176), before turning his attention to the Germans. 3,007 pounds of gold, 5,775 pounds of uncoined silver and 287,000 drachmas in coins were said to have been carried in the triumphal procession: Plut. *Mar.* 12.6.

Sulla was chosen by Marius as his quaestor for 107 BC (*MRR* I.551), and would also serve under him in 104 as legate (when he captured Copillus, chief of the Tectosages: Plut. *Sull.* 4.1) and in 103 as military tribune (*MRR* I.561, 564). His military abilities were made clear in Numidia, and the two men obviously worked well together at this stage in their career; for Sulla's background: see doc. 11.1; Sisenna: *HRR* I² 276–97.

95.1 In the meantime the quaestor Lucius Sulla arrived in camp with a large force of cavalry, which he had been left behind to raise from Latium and the allies. **2** Since the event has brought that great man to my attention, it seems appropriate to say a few words about his character and style of life. For I shall not speak elsewhere about matters pertaining to Sulla, and Lucius Sisenna, who has given the best and most careful account of him, does not seem to me to have spoken with sufficient frankness.

3 Sulla, then, was a noble of patrician descent, but his family was by this point buried in almost total oblivion due to the worthlessness of his ancestors. He was well educated alike in Greek and Latin literature, and was of great mental capacity, devoted to pleasure, but more devoted to glory, spending his leisure time in extravagant living — though his enjoyments never interfered with his duties, except that he could have behaved more honourably as a husband. He was eloquent, clever, and good at making friends; his mind was incredibly deep in its ability to disguise his plans; and he was generous with many things, especially money. **4** He was the most fortunate of all men prior to the civil war, but his good fortune was never greater than his assiduous efforts, and many have doubted whether his courage or good luck were the greater. As to what he did afterwards, I am unsure whether one should speak of it more with shame or with disgust.

96.1 After Sulla, as I have said above, reached Africa and Marius' camp with his cavalry, although he was without training and experience in war, he became in a short time the most skilful soldier in the whole army. **2** In addition he spoke in a friendly manner to the soldiers, and granted favours to many at their request and to others of his own accord, though he was unwilling to accept favours himself and paid them back more promptly than a debt of money. He never asked anyone for repayment, but rather worked hard to have as many people as possible in his debt; **3** he would exchange jokes or serious conversation with the humblest, and spent much time with the men at their work, on the march and on guard duty, but in the meantime did not try, like those whom corrupt ambition motivates, to harm the reputation of the consul or any other respectable man. His only concern was to make sure that no one was before him in counsel or action, and that he surpassed nearly everyone. Such character and behaviour endeared him in a short time to Marius and the soldiers.

9.13 Rivalry between Sulla and Marius

Plutarch *Life of Marius* 10.3–9

For Jugurtha's capture: Sall. *BJ* 102, 105–13. Plutarch dates the enmity between Marius and Sulla to the incident involving Bocchus. But the deadly rivalry between the two men was as yet many years away. While Jugurtha's capture brought the campaign to an end, Marius was extremely close to victory over Jugurtha at this point, which influenced Bocchus' decision, as he had himself been severely defeated (Sall. *BJ* 101–2); Sulla negotiated Jugurtha's betrayal but Marius will not — rightly — have seen this as crucial in bringing the war to a conclusion; for Bocchus: cf. *BJ* 19.7.

Plutarch has Sulla through antipathy to Marius in 102 attaching himself to Quintus Lutatius Catulus, consul in 102 (Marius' fourth consulship): Plut. *Mar.* 4.5 citing Sulla (*HRR* I² 196). But Marius and Catulus were working closely together and Plutarch is clearly being disingenuous here (cf. Cagniart 1989). For a coin showing Bocchus delivering Jugurtha to Sulla: doc. 11.46. Jugurtha appeared in Marius' triumph in 104 BC, and was killed in the state prison: Livy *Per.* 67, cf. Plut. *Mar.* 12.3–5; doc. 12.22 (the prison).

3 The king of the natives in the interior was Bocchus, Jugurtha's son-in-law . . . **4** He sent for Lucius Sulla, Marius' quaestor, who had been useful to Bocchus during the campaign. **5** Sulla trusted him and made the journey up country to see him, but the native changed his mind and regretted his action, deliberating for several days the options of handing Jugurtha over or detaining Sulla. **6** Finally he carried out his original betrayal, and surrendered Jugurtha alive to Sulla. **7** This was the first seed of their incurable and savage conflict which came close to destroying Rome. **8** For there were many who wanted to give the credit to Sulla, out of jealousy of Marius, while Sulla himself used to wear a signet-ring he had had made, engraved with Jugurtha being surrendered to him by Bocchus. **9** He used this ring constantly, irritating Marius who was an ambitious man, disinclined to share glory with anyone else, and given to quarrels. He was led on by Marius' enemies who attributed the first and greatest achievements of the war to Metellus and its final stages and conclusion to Sulla, in an attempt to put an end to the people's admiration of and total devotion to Marius.

MARIUS AND THE GERMANS

The Romans suffered several defeats at the hands of the Germans in the last decade of the second century; there was also a particularly spectacular debacle when the Tigurini, a group of the Helvetii (Celts) in 107 killed Marius' fellow consul L. Cassius Longinus in battle and sent the Romans under the yoke (Livy *Per.* 65; *MRR* I.550; Harlan *RRM* pp. 160–1). The military incompetence of Caepio and the Germanic defeat of the Romans by the Cimbri in 105 BC were also catastrophic. Marius was elected to a second consulship to deal with the German tribes; then to a third, fourth, fifth and sixth. The people awarded him the command against the Germans, bypassing the senate. Marius spent 104 and 103 in military preparations (Plut. *Mar.* 14.1; Livy *Per.* 67); the Germans provided him with a breathing space by going to Spain (the Cimbri) and northern Gaul (the Teutones). Saturninus had supported Marius' election as consul for 103. In 102 the tribes were active again but divided their forces and Marius won his great victory over the Teutones at Aquae

Sextiae in Transalpine Gaul, while in 101 the Cimbri were defeated by the combined armies of Marius and Catulus at Vercellae in Cisalpine Gaul, north of the Po river. Marius was elected to his sixth consulship for 100 BC. His reiterated consulships: Evans 1994: 78–92; the Germans: Burns 2003: 66–87.

9.14 Disasters in Gaul

Livy *Periochae* 65, 67

Q. Servilius Caepio (cos. 106) had not co-operated in 105 BC with Cn. Mallius Maximus (cos. 105). At Arausio, now Orange (France), there was a disastrous defeat for the Romans. This propelled Marius to his second consulship, for 104, to deal with the crisis: Sall. *BJ* 104.4. In 105 Caepio's imperium was cancelled; and Longinus' law in 104 as tribune expelled from the senate anyone whose imperium had been abrogated (doc. 9.19). C. Norbanus prosecuted Caepio over the treasure which had been captured at Tolosa (modern Toulouse) in 106, and which had disappeared before it arrived in Rome (doc. 9.18); the outcome is unknown. But Caepio was also prosecuted over his role in the Arausio disaster, convicted, and went into exile at Smyrna in Asia Minor (Alexander *Trials* no. 66); for Caepio and Norbanus, see esp. Badian 1964a; Silanus: *MRR* I.545.

67: for Aurelius Scaurus, consul-suffect in 108 BC and legate in 105 BC (*MRR* I.548, 557), see also Licinianus 11; he is not to be confused with M. Aemilius Scaurus, the princeps senatus. Antias: *HRR* 1² 274 F63. Marius and his triumphal clothes: he went straight from his triumph to the Capitol where he had convened a meeting of the senate, but changed into an ordinary toga when he saw that he was giving offence: see doc. 9.35. The Gnaeus Manlius here is Cn. Mallius Maximus, cos. 105 (Paul 1984: 257). He like Caepio was prosecuted and convicted (exiled) for his role in the defeat at Arausio (Alexander *Trials* no. 64).

65 The consul Marcus Junius Silanus (cos. 109) lost a battle against the Cimbri (108 BC). The senate refused the request of envoys from the Cimbri for a dwelling-place and land on which they might settle. The proconsul Marcus Minucius (cos. 110) fought successfully against the Thracians (109/08). The consul Lucius Cassius was slaughtered with his army in the territory of the Nitiobroges by the Tigurine Gauls, who had left that state (107). The soldiers who were left after this slaughter made a treaty with the enemy that they be released unharmed after giving up hostages and half of all their possessions . . .

67 Marcus Aurelius Scaurus, a consular legate, was taken prisoner by the Cimbri when his army was routed; when he was summoned to their council he tried to deter them from crossing the Alps to enter Italy on the grounds that the Romans could not be defeated and was killed by Boiorix, a savage youth (105). The consul Gnaeus Manlius and proconsul Quintus Servilius Caepio were defeated in battle by these same enemies at Arausio, both their camps were plundered, and 80,000 soldiers and 40,000 servants and camp-followers killed, according to Antias. Caepio, through whose rashness the disaster had been incurred, was condemned and his property confiscated by the state, for the first time since King Tarquin, and his imperium was taken away (104). In the triumph of Gaius Marius Jugurtha with his two sons was led before his chariot and killed in prison (104). Marius came into the senate in his triumphal clothes, which no one had previously done; because of anxiety about the war against the Cimbri, his consulship was renewed for several years. The second and third times he was elected consul in his absence, and he won a fourth consulship by pretending not to campaign for it.

9.15 Panic in Italy

Licinianus 13–14

Cf. Licinianus 11. Following the massive defeat at the hands of the Cimbri (doc. 9.14). Saturninus established the *quaestio* before which Mallius and Caepio were prosecuted: Alexander *Trials* no 64 n.2, 66; cf. *MRR* I.563.

Gnaeus Mallius was exiled by the people from Rome on the same charge as Caepio through the bill brought in by Lucius Saturninus (103 BC). The consul Rutilius, Mallius' colleague, was left in sole charge of the state. And so, with fear of the advancing Cimbri shaking the whole country, he made all men of military age take an oath that they would not leave Italy, and messengers were sent through all Italy's coasts and ports to proclaim that no one less than 35 years of age should be taken on board a ship . . . (105 BC)

9.16 The man of the hour

Sallust *Jugurthine War* 114.1–4

The defeats of Carbo near Noreia in 113, Silanus in 109, Cassius Longinus in 107, and Cn. Mallius Maximus and Caepio in 105 by the Germanic tribes invading Gaul roused fear at Rome. 'Italy was overwhelmed with danger from the west, while for the first time the city needed a great general and sought the services of a person who would bring them safely out of such a tumultuous war' (Plut. *Mar.* 11.1). Marius was elected consul in 104 although *in absentia* (absent from Rome), violating the *lex Villia annalis* (180 BC) with its stipulation of a ten-year gap between consulships; however, this would pale compared to his successive run of consulships II–VI, 104–100 BC. The Gauls mentioned in the passage below are actually the Cimbri, a Germanic tribe, and the defeat was at Arausio in October 105. Gnaeus Manlius is Cn. Mallius Maximus, cos. 105 (see above).

1 At the same time the Gauls inflicted a defeat upon our commanders Quintus Caepio and Gnaeus Manlius, 2 which made all Italy tremble with fear. The Romans of the time and from then even down to our own day believed that everything else would fall before their valour, but that a war against the Gauls was a struggle for survival, not for glory. 3 But when it was announced that the war in Numidia was over and that Jugurtha was being brought to Rome in chains, Marius was elected consul in his absence and Gaul was assigned to him as his province. On the first day of January (104 BC) he held a triumph in great state as consul. At that time the hope and welfare of the state depended on him.

9.17 The Germanic tribes seek land

Florus *Epitome of Roman History* 1.38 (3.1–6)

1 The Cimbri, Teutones, and Tigurini, refugees from the extremities of Gaul as the Ocean had inundated their lands, started to look throughout the world for new places where they could settle, and, 2 being excluded from Gaul and Spain, migrated into Italy and sent representatives to Silanus' camp and then to the Senate requesting that the people of Mars grant them some land, as if for payment for military service, and employ their hands and weapons for any purposes it might wish. 3 But what land could the

Roman people give them when it was on the point of conflict over agrarian legislation? And so, rebuffed, they began seeking by force what they had failed to gain by entreaties. **4** Silanus was unable to withstand the barbarians' first onslaught, nor Manilius their second, nor Caepio their third: all were routed and their camps despoiled. **5** Rome would have been finished, if Marius had not belonged to that age. Even he did not dare to met them at once, but kept his soldiers in camp until the invincible frenzy, which the barbarians possess instead of courage, had worn off. **6** The barbarians, therefore, withdrew, mocking our men and advising them — such was their confidence that they would capture Rome — to give them any message they had for their wives.

9.18 The Tolosa treasure disappears

Orosius *History in Answer to the Pagans* 5.15.25

See also Cic. *Nat. Deor.* 3.74; *Vir. Illustr.* 73.5 (Saturninus' plan to use the treasure to finance his legislative programme of colonies for Marius' veterans); Dio 27.90; Strabo 4.1.13. The outcome of Caepio's trial over the Tolosa treasure is unknown (Alexander *Trials* no. 65); he went into exile at Smyrna after being prosecuted over the Arausio debacle (see doc. 9.14).

The proconsul Caepio captured a Gallic town called Tolosa and removed 100,000 pounds of gold and 110,000 pounds of silver from the temple of Apollo. He sent this off with guards to Massilia (Marseilles), a city on good terms with the Roman people, and, after those to whom he had entrusted its protection and conveyance had been — as some state — secretly killed, he is said to have criminally stolen the whole of it. This resulted in a large-scale enquiry being held at Rome.

9.19 Prosecution of generals who failed against the Cimbri

Asconius *Commentaries on Cicero* 78, 80

Longinus was tribuned in 104 BC (*MRR* I.559). Caepio had been deprived of his imperium and Longinus' law was chiefly aimed at him; his legislation reflects popular dissatisfaction not just with Caepio but with the general conduct of the wars against the Gallic and German tribes. Domitius: Cn. Domitius Ahenobarbus, who was to be consul in 96. Not co-opted to take his father's place as pontiff, he unsuccessfully accused Aemilius Scaurus (cos. 115) of failing to carry out his priestly duties correctly (Alexander *Trials* no. 68), and introduced the *lex Domitia*: see doc. 11.28. Marcus Junius Silanus (cos. 109) was acquitted, probably in 104 (Alexander no. 63). Silanus is also known for abrogating laws which had reduced the length of military service: Asc. 68; *MRR* I.545.

78 Lucius Cassius Longinus, son of Lucius, as tribune of the plebs in the consulship of Gaius Marius and Gaius Flavius, carried a number of laws aimed at reducing the power of the nobles, amongst which was the one that anyone condemned by the people or stripped of his office by them should not remain a member of the senate. This stemmed from his conflict with Quintus Servilius (Caepio), consul two years earlier, who had been stripped of his office by the people after his failure against the Cimbri (105 BC).

80 Marcus Silanus had been consul five years before Domitius' tribunate and had also failed against the Cimbri (109 BC); on these grounds Domitius prosecuted him before the people. The charge against him was that he had conducted his campaign against the Cimbri without the authority of the people, and that this had been the origin of the disasters which the people had suffered in the war against them; he also produced a document about this. But Silanus was acquitted decisively, as only two tribes, Sergia and Quirina, voted for conviction.

9.20 A rare triumph

ILS 8887

(*CIL* I² 2662; *ILLRP* 337; *ROL* IV.132.) Marcus Minucius Rufus (cos. 110), triumphed over the Scordisci and Triballi in 109 as proconsul in Macedonia, with further successes later (doc. 9.20); he celebrated a triumph at Rome in 106 BC; this inscription comes from the pedestal of a statue at Delphi. The Roman military record as a whole in this period, however, consisted mostly of a series of defeats, as the above passages show.

Marcus Minucius Rufus, son of Quintus, imperator. The people of Delphi dedicated (this statue) on account of his valour in defeating the Galli, Scordisti, Bessi and the rest of the Thracians.

ARMY REFORMS

Marius had not actually reformed the army for his Numidian campaign of 107 BC by abolishing the property qualification. But reforms to the legion took place at about this time, though not all are necessarily to be attributed to Marius. These reforms improved the efficiency of the Roman soldier and legion. Many Roman armies had been serving for long periods, as in Spain, but Marius' recruitment of the *capite censi* certainly hastened the development of standing professional armies in which experience and expertise were retained from year to year. For the army before Marius, see docs 5.11–21.

9.21 Publius Rutilius Rufus introduces gladiatorial training

Valerius Maximus *Memorable Deeds and Sayings* *(On Ancient Institutions)* 2.3.2

This is not attested elsewhere, and whether the Roman army was trained with gladiatorial techniques as a matter of course is uncertain. However, it is also possible that this was a reform of Marius which, through hostility to him, was instead attributed to Rutilius (cos. 105): Carney 1961: 3 (cf. Front. *Strat.* 4.2.2).

Practice in handling weapons was given to the soldiers by Gnaeus Mallius' colleague as consul, Publius Rutilius (105 BC): for, following the example of no previous general, he called in gladiatorial instructors from the troop of Gaius Aurelius Scaurus, and implanted in the legions a more skilful technique of avoiding and giving blows, and mingled valour with skill and skill in turn with valour to make the former stronger by the force of the latter and the latter more cautious by the knowledge of the former.

9.22 Marius' 'mules' and weapons reform

Plutarch *Life of Marius* 13.1–3

Cf. Festus 267, 345. When Marius was appointed consul for the second time, for 104 BC, he instituted army reforms centred largely around his 'mules'.

One reform was that of the eagles: prior to Marius, each legion had five standards (boar, eagle, wolf, horse, minotaur: Dusanic & Petkovic 2003). Marius replaced these with a single eagle standard (aquila: Pliny *Nat Hist*. 10.5). The eagles were the numina ('spirits' or 'divinities') of the legions (Tac. *Ann*. 2.17.2), but this aspect need not have been a Marian reform as Pliny (*Nat Hist*. 13.23) states that it was not known who started the worship of the standards. Certainly in the imperial period there was a well-developed cult of the legionary eagle. For the eagle standards in the Republic: Keppie 1984: 67–8; an illustration of an eagle: Goldsworthy 2000: 97; eagle standard on a denarius of 81 BC: Crawford *RRC* 372.2 (cf. *RCC* 365; Reece *RC* no 88).

It is not certain whether Marius introduced the cohortal legion, changing the basic unit of the legion from the maniple to the cohort, but it seems clear that this occurred about the turn of the century, perhaps gradually. The legion had traditionally (since the fourth century) been made up of 30 maniples, with each maniple having two centuries (each commanded by a centurion). Now each legion consisted of ten cohorts, a cohort having three maniples each of two centuries, with each century having 80 men. The change from 30 maniples to 10 cohorts embracing the maniples made the passing of orders easier. In each century there were six ranks of thirteen men, with the commanding centurion in front, and his second-in-command, the *optio*, at the rear. The new cohortal arrangement was much more flexible than the old system based on maniples with different types of troops placed in fixed battle positions. Individual cohorts could be placed anywhere within the battle formation: see Parker 1958: 28; Bell 1965: 404–19; Gabba 1976: 13–19; Keppie 1984: 57–68; Gilliver 1999: 18–19; Hanson 1995: 52; Goldsworthy 1996: 33–8; cf. Watson 1987: 85–7. That the soldiers carried their own baggage was significant as it gave greater mobility to the army with less reliance on the baggage train. The old system described by Polybius and Livy based on the velites and three lines of soldiers organised according to age and weaponry was done away with (docs 5.11, 5.15).

1 During the campaign he kept training the army *en route*, practising the men in all kinds of running and long marches, and compelling every man to carry his own baggage and prepare his own meals, hence the later expression 'Marius' mules' for those who enjoyed hard work and followed orders cheerfully and in silence. **2** However, others think there was a different origin for the expression. They say that when Scipio was besieging Numantia and wanted to inspect not only the weapons and horses, but also the mules and wagons to see whether the men were keeping them in proper condition and ready for action, Marius brought out his horse which was beautifully kept and a mule very different from all the others in condition, sleekness and strength; **3** the general was so pleased with Marius' animals and so often mentioned them, that those who wanted to make a joke would praise any persevering, patient and hardworking soldier by calling him one of Marius' mules.

9.23 Marius' campaign preparations against Teutones and Cimbri

Plutarch *Life of Marius* 15.1–4, 25.2–3

The years 104 and then 103, despite the fears of the Roman people, were quiet. Saturninus was tribune in 103 and called for Marius to be elected to a fourth consulship for 102, his colleague being the nobilis Q. Lutatius Catulus. Prior to the defeat of the Cimbri in 102 Marius altered the construction of the javelin (pilum). The pilum broke and so could not be hurled back by the enemy; if it struck an enemy's shield, it would droop downwards, making the shield heavy and useless to the enemy or, if more successfully thrown, would go on to pierce the soldier behind the shield. It was about two metres long, had a range of 30 metres, and was thrown in unison at the approaching enemy at a given signal. For the pilum (plural: pila): Bishop & Coulston 1993: 48, 53 & no. 50; Goldsworthy 1996: 183, 197–201, 229–30, 2000: 44, 53, 97, 125 (illustration: 44).

In 102, Marius won a decisive victory over Germanic tribes, the Ambrones and Teutones, in southern Gaul at Aquae Sextiae (now Aix-en-Provence). Marius as consul again the following year, with Catulus as proconsul, defeated King Boiorix of the Cimbri, another Germanic tribe, with a combined Roman army of 52,300, at Vercellae in Cisalpine Gaul (northern Italy). After the defeat, Catulus and his men tried to claim the victory as theirs, but at Rome it was Marius who was seen as the saviour of the city. But Marius shared the triumph (for the victories of 102 and 101) with Catulus (Plut. *Mar.* 19–27, cf. 14–18; *CIL* I^2 1, p. 177). His various reforms and his decisive generalship had clearly paid dividends. With the German threat over Italy was safe. Marius' campaigns against the Germans: Last 1932: 139–51; Carney 1961: 35–9; Scullard *GN* 55–8, cf. 53–6; Lintott 1994a: 96; Evans 1994: 81–92; Burns 2003: 66–76.

15.1 When Marius learnt that the enemy was nearby, he swiftly crossed the Alps, and, after constructing a camp by the river Rhone, he brought into it abundant provisions so that he should never be forced to give battle to the army's disadvantage because of his lack of supplies. **2** He made the transportation of supplies by sea to the army, which had been slow and expensive prior to this, easy and swift. **3** For the mouths of the Rhone, where it met the sea, had been silted up with a great deal of mud and obstructed with sand and deep clay brought in by the tide, and this made it difficult, laborious and slow for the transport ships to sail in. **4** As the troops were at leisure, Marius brought them here and dug a great canal, diverting a large part of the river into this and bringing it round to a suitable part of the coast where the river-mouth was deep and navigable for large ships, as well as being smooth and calm for entering the sea. This canal still bears his name today.

25.2 It is said that in preparation for the battle with the Cimbri the innovation to the javelin (*pilum*) was first made by Marius. **3** Previously the shaft was fastened into the iron head with two nails of iron, but Marius now, leaving one of the nails where it was, removed the other and put in instead an easily-breakable wooden pin so that when the javelin struck the enemy's shield it would not stay upright, but, with the wooden pin broken, would droop from the iron head and drag the spear downwards, due to the spear's crooked shape.

9.24 The optimates may not like Marius but can't do without him

Cicero *On the Consular Provinces* 19

A speech made before the consular elections in 56, perhaps in late June 56, regarding the allocation of provinces for 54 for the consuls of 55 (Pompey and Crassus were to be elected: doc. 12.70), in accordance with Gaius Gracchus' law (doc. 8.28). Cicero is arguing that personal hatreds (i.e., against Caesar) should not outweigh the needs of the state and argues for the replacement of Gabinius and Piso.

Who ever had more enemies than Gaius Marius? Lucius Crassus and Marcus Scaurus were antagonistic to him, all the Metelli were his enemies. Yet not only did they not attempt to have that enemy of theirs recalled from Gaul, but, in view of the importance of the Gallic war, they assigned him the province as an extraordinary command.

9.25 The nobility support Marius

Dio *Roman History* 27 F94.1

According to Dio, the election of Marius to his fifth consulship (101 BC) may have had senatorial support as well as that of the people.

In the barbarians' defeat, even though casualties in the battle had been heavy, a few were saved. Accordingly, Marius, to encourage and reward these at the same time, sold them all the booty very cheaply so it would not appear as if he had bestowed favours on any individual. By doing this Marius, although he had previously been well-regarded only by the populace, because he came from that class and had been brought to power by it, now also won the support of the nobles by whom he had been hated, so that he was praised equally by everybody and received the consulship for the following year, to enable him to finish off his campaign, from an enthusiastic and unanimous electorate.

9.26 Marius' German victories, 102–101 BC

Livy *Periochae* 68

The consul Gaius Marius defended his camp, which was assaulted with the greatest force by the Teutones and Ambrones. He then destroyed these same enemies in two battles near Aquae Sextiae, in which it is recorded that 200,000 of the enemy were killed and 90,000 captured. Marius was elected consul for the fifth time (in 102 for 101), in his absence. He postponed the triumph offered to him until he should conquer the Cimbri as well. The Cimbri drove back from the Alps and put to flight the proconsul Catulus, who was trying to block the Alpine passes and had left a fort on high ground at the river Atesis garrisoned with a cohort. This cohort, however, got itself out of difficulty by its own bravery and caught up with the fleeing proconsul and the army. The Cimbri had now crossed into Italy and were defeated in battle by the combined armies of the same Catulus and Gaius Marius. In this battle it is recorded that 140,000 of the enemy were killed and 60,000 captured. Marius was welcomed with the unanimous consent of the whole state, but instead of the two triumphs which were offered him he was satisfied with one. The leading men of the state, who for some time had had a grudge against him as a 'new man' elevated to positions of such importance, were now admitting that the state had been saved by him.

9.27 Marius' willingness to break the rules and reward good service

Cicero *In Defence of Balbus* 46–9

Cf. Val. Max. 5.2.8; Plut. *Mar.* 28.3. Lucius Cornelius Balbus, from southern Spain, served with the Romans in the war against Sertorius (79–72 BC). With Pompey's support he was granted citizenship in 72, ratified, with similar grants, by the *lex Gellia Cornelia* of 72, and was taken to Spain by Caesar in 61 as his chief engineer. Balbus was prosecuted in 56 for illegally claiming citizenship, under the *lex Papia* of 64 (Alexander *Trials* no. 276). Cicero, who was one of Balbus' advocates (along with Crassus and Pompey), cites Marius as a precedent. Marius had granted citizenship to two allied cohorts at Vercellae (in 101 BC); Plut. *Mar.* 28.3 states that 1,000 men were involved. The *lex Licinia Mucia* of 95 BC (doc. 10.2) essentially started the Social War by expelling Latins and Italians from Rome and scrutinising all those claiming citizenship. For Camerinum, an Umbrian town, see Livy 9.36.7; the treaty dated to 310 BC. See Badian 1970/1: 402–3; Brunt 1982, 1988d: 279; Mouritsen 1998: 90–1.

46 Can we therefore submit for your approval, as an authority for a precedent and for the action which is criticised by you, Gaius Marius? Do you ask for anyone more venerable, more steadfast, more pre-eminent in courage, wisdom and integrity? Good! He bestowed citizenship upon Marcus Annius Appius of Iguvium, an extremely courageous man endowed with the highest merits, while he also bestowed citizenship upon two whole cohorts from Camerinum, although he was aware that the treaty with the Camertes was one of the most inviolable and just of all treaties . . .

48 Accordingly, when a few years after this grant of citizenship the matter of citizenship was intensively investigated under the Licinian and Mucian law, who was there from the allied states, which had been granted citizenship, who was brought to trial? Titus Matrinius of Spoletium, from a Latin colony which was especially strong and illustrious, was the only one of those to whom Gaius Marius had granted citizenship who had to defend himself. His prosecutor, that eloquent man Lucius Antistius, did not say that the people of Spoletium had not approved it . . . , but since the colonies under the Appuleian law had not been founded — the law which Saturninus had brought in for Gaius Marius, allowing him to create three Roman citizens in each colony — he maintained that this grant should be invalid, as the measure itself had been repealed. **49** That prosecution has no resemblance to this case; but Gaius Marius possessed such prestige, that without employing Lucius Crassus, his relative by marriage, a man of amazing eloquence, he undertook the defence of that case and won it in a few words through the weight of his own personality. Who could there be, jurors, who would want to deprive our generals of the power to select the most courageous in war, in the battle-line and in the army, or our allies and federates of the hope of rewards in the defence of our state? But, if the countenance of Gaius Marius, if his voice, if the commanding flash of his eyes, if his recent triumphs, if his bodily presence had such power, let his prestige, let his achievements, let his memory, let the everlasting name of the bravest and most illustrious hero have the same power now!

9.28 Tribunician murder and Saturninus' land law

Appian *Civil Wars* 1.28–29, 31 (126–32, 138–40)

For L. Appuleius Saturninus, see also Livy *Per.* 69; Plut. *Mar.* 29–30; Val. Max. 9.7.1, 3; Florus 2.4.1–6; Last & Gardner 1932: 164–72; Smith 1955: 99–101; Gruen 1968: 168–83; Sherwin-White 1969: 2–5; Badian 1984; Lintott 1994a: 97–102; Evans 1994: 116–27; *MRR* I.563, 575–6, II.1. Saturninus was quaestor at Ostia (quaestor Ostiensis), perhaps in 105 or 104, but was replaced by the senate with M. Aemilius Scaurus; Saturninus became a popularis because of this treatment (Cic. *Har. Resp.* 43, *Sest.* 39; *MRR* I.560).

As tribune in 103 Saturninus successfully proposed a law to settle Marius' veterans of the Numidian campaign in Africa (*Vir. Illustr.* 73; *Inscript. Ital.* XIII.3, no. 7: a colony at Cercina, an island off the coast of Tunis, Africa; Julius Caesar's father served on the land commission);

Brunt *IM* 577–80; Scullard *GN* 400; Badian *FC* 199–200; Lintott 1994: 30; cf. Cic. *Balb.* 48. Land for the *capite censi* serving with Marius is not mentioned by Sallust or Plutarch in the context of the recruiting for Numidia for 107, but had now emerged as an issue, and caused great conflict in Saturninus' second tribunate in 100. Saturninus' support was important, according to Plut. *Mar.* 14.12–13, for Marius gaining his fourth consulship (102 BC).

In 100, in Marius' sixth consulship, Saturninus as tribune successfully proposed that Marius' veterans from the campaigns of 102–101 be settled in Transalpine Gaul. As with the legislation of 103, many of Marius' veterans were from the *capite censi* and were rewarded with land grants. The main point is that under Marius land grants for veterans became essential, and Sulla, Pompey and Caesar all had to address this issue. Saturninus, as a popularis, would find land distribution an attractive measure, given the optimates' opposition to this policy. See also *Vir. Illustr.* 73 (colonies were to be founded in Sicily, Achaea and Macedon: none in fact were); Plut. *Crass.* 2.10; Pliny *Nat Hist.* 3.80 (a colony in Corsica); Brunt 1988d: 278–80 (for the possibility that there were Marian colonies in Italy); Evans 1994: 117–23.

Saturninus in 103 or 100 passed the *lex Appuleia de maiestate* to deal with the crime of treason, maiestas, against the Roman people (this is often identified with the *lex latina tabulae Bantinae*, a law on a bronze tablet from Bantia in Lucania: Crawford *Statutes* 7). The juries were to be equestrian.

In 100 Saturninus passed a grain law (*lex frumentaria*; see *Rhet. ad Herenn.* 1.21; some scholars prefer a 103 dating). It perhaps restored Gaius Gracchus' original grain law, modified by M. Octavius (tr. pl. sometime between 122 and 104 (*MRR* II.471); note Marius' opposition to a grain law while tribune). The price for grain would be 6 1/3 asses a modius, subsidised as in Gaius' law by the state, but under Saturninus' provision was to be cheaper by 1/3 a modius. This law was opposed by the quaestor for 100, Q. Servilius Caepio, a relative of the Q. Servilius Caepio (cos. 106); for his opposition (which turned violent: *Rhet. ad Herenn.* 1.21), on the grounds of the burden to the treasury, he was prosecuted under the *lex Appuleia de maiestate* but was acquitted (*MRR* I.576; Alexander *Trials* no. 88). However, Caepio and a colleague minted coins in 100 BC, 'For the purchase of wheat by senatorial decree': doc. 9.38.

126: The Metellus here is the consul of 109 BC; his colleague as censor was Q. Caecilius Metellus Caprarius (his cousin). Glaucia: C. Servilius Glaucia, tribune, perhaps in 101 (or as early as 105 or 104), and praetor in 100 BC. He proposed and had carried a repetundae law (*lex Servilia Glauciae*) restoring the juries of the extortion courts to the equites (Q. Servilius Caepio as consul in 106 had introduced a mixed jury of senators and equites). See *MRR* I.571–2. **128**: Nonius (actually Aulus Nunnius) was elected tribune, murdered, and Saturninus took his place. **130**: 'Cimbri, a Celtic race': they were actually Germanic. **140**: Metellus went into exile on Rhodes, and Marius had him banned from 'fire and water' (Livy *Per.* 65; Cic. *Sest.* 101). But a vote of the comitia tributa secured his return in 99 BC, against Marius' wishes (cf. doc. 9.29).

126 The censor, Quintus Caecilius Metellus, tried to demote Glaucia, a senator, and Appuleius Saturninus, who had already been tribune, for their disgraceful life-styles, but did not succeed; for his colleague would not agree. **127** Shortly afterwards Appuleius, to revenge himself on Metellus, stood for another tribunate, using the opportunity of Glaucia's being praetor and presiding over the tribunician elections. Nonius, a man of distinguished birth, who employed blunt speech against Appuleius and reproached Glaucia severely, was elected tribune. **128** Glaucia and Appuleius, fearing lest he should take revenge on them once he was tribune, attacked him in an uproar with a mob of men as he was leaving the assembly and killed him after he had fled into a tavern. As this murder appeared pitiful and awful, Glaucia's supporters, before the people had assembled, elected Appuleius tribune at dawn. **129** In this way the murder of Nonius was hushed up because of Appuleius' tribunate, as people were afraid that he might convict them.

Metellus was also banished by them with the help of Gaius Marius, who was then holding his sixth consulship and was Metellus' secret enemy. Thus they all co-operated with each other. **130** Appuleius introduced a law to divide all the land that the Cimbri, a Celtic race, had seized in what the Romans now call Gaul. Marius had recently driven them out and made the land which had been theirs into Roman territory. **131** The law also provided that, if the people should ratify the law, the senate should swear within five days that it would obey the law, and that anyone who did not swear should no longer belong to the senate and pay the people a fine of twenty talents. Their motive was to revenge themselves on whose who were displeased with it, especially Metellus, who was not going to give in to the oath because of his high spirit. **132** This then was the proposed law, and Appuleius appointed the day for voting and sent out men to inform people in the country, in whom he had special confidence since they had served under Marius. The people were dissatisfied, however, because the Italians gained more than they did under the law. . . .

138 Metellus alone did not swear, but persisted fearlessly in his decision. Appuleius immediately sent his attendant for him and tried to drag him from the senate house. **139** When the other tribunes defended him, Glaucia and Appuleius rushed to the country people and told them that the land would not be theirs nor the law enacted unless Metellus were banished. They proposed a decree of exile against him and instructed the consuls to proclaim that no one was to share fire, water or shelter with him; and they appointed a day for the enactment of this decree. **140** The city people were terribly angry and attended Metellus constantly, daggers and all. Metellus thanked them and praised them for their determination, but said he could not allow any danger to happen to the country on his account. After this statement he left the city, and Appuleius had the decree ratified and Marius had its contents proclaimed.

9.29 Marius changes sides

Livy *Periochae* 69

Livy here records the story that Marius had secured his sixth consulship (for 100 BC) with bribes. Plutarch writes that Rutilius' account was that Marius had distributed money as bribes to secure the election of Valerius Flaccus as his consular colleague for 100 BC, to prevent Metellus being elected (Plut. *Mar.* 28.7–8; Rutilius: *HRR* I² 188 F4; Carney 1961: 40); for Memmius, see doc. 9.30. The slave war referred to here was the second great uprising in Sicily: cf. doc. 6.44. Manius Aquillius had been consul with Marius in 101. Marius took measures unwillingly against his former ally Saturninus.

Lucius Appuleius Saturninus, who had the support of Gaius Marius, and whose rival Aulus Nunnius was killed by the soldiers, was elected tribune of the plebs by violence, and conducted his tribunate no less violently than his campaign for office; after he had passed a land law by violence, he indicted Metellus Numidicus because he had not sworn to support it. Metellus was defended by the better citizens (the *boni*), but to avoid being the occasion for strife, he went into voluntary exile at Rhodes, and there found diversion in hearing and reading distinguished philosophers. With him gone, Gaius Marius, the man responsible for the civil strife, who had bought his sixth consulship with money distributed among the tribes, banned Metellus from fire and water.

The same Appuleius Saturninus, tribune of the plebs, killed Gaius Memmius, a candidate for the consulship, because he was afraid of him as an opponent of his proceedings. The senate was aroused at these deeds, and Gaius Marius too, a man of varying and change-able nature whose policy followed the dictates of fortune, had come over to its side. Saturninus, together with the praetor Glaucia and other associates in the same madness, was put down by armed force and killed in a sort of war. Quintus Caecilius Metellus was brought back from exile to the great applause of the whole state. The proconsul Manius Aquillius ended a slave war which had arisen in Sicily.

9.30 The senatus consultum 'ultimum'

Cicero *In Defence of Gaius Rabirius for Treason* 20–1

Cicero here gives the terms of the *senatus consultum ultimum* (SCU) passed to suppress Saturninus; cf. Val. Max. 3.2.18; for the SCU, see doc. 1.59. Cicero is defending, in 63, the senator Rabirius (and hence senatorial government) on a charge of *perduellio*, treason, for having murdered Saturninus 36 years earlier in a riot. The attack on Rabirius was orchestrated by Caesar and the *populares*; Caesar was one of two men on the board of two (*duoviri*) that convicted him (the other was L. Julius Caesar). Cicero defended him, against Labienus for the prosecution, when appealing against the conviction. The appeal was successful (Alexander *Trials* no. 220; cf. Tyrrell 1973).

Saturninus was elected in 100 to a third tribunate for 99 and Glaucia was seeking the consulship for 99. Marcus Antonius was chosen as one of the consuls; Glaucia and Memmius were rivals for the second position and Glaucia and Saturninus had Memmius beaten to death with clubs in the comitia centuriata (see doc. 9.29). A reaction set in against Saturninus: the next day the people gathered, determined to kill Saturninus, who seized the Capitol, with the praetor Glaucia, and the quaestor for 99, Gaius Saufeius. The ex-prisoner Gracchus (i.e., Equitius) had pretended to be Ti. Gracchus' son (Val. Max. 9.7.2), and was elected tribune with Saturninus for 99 and was killed with him on the first day of his office, 10 December 100 (*MRR* II.1).

20 A decree of the senate was passed that the consuls, Gaius Marius and Lucius Valerius, should summon those tribunes of the plebs and praetors whom they thought fit and take steps to preserve the imperium and majesty of the Roman people. They summoned all the tribunes of the plebs except Saturninus and all the praetors except Glaucia, and they ordered those who desired the safety of the state to take arms and follow them. Everyone obeyed; weapons from public buildings and armouries were issued to the Roman people with Gaius Marius, as consul, in charge of the distribution. I will, at this point, leave aside other matters, Labienus, to put a question to you personally. When Saturninus was in armed occupation of the Capitol, and with him Gaius Glaucia, Gaius Saufeius, and even that ex-prisoner Gracchus (i.e., Equitius); I will add, since you insist on it, that Quintus Labienus, your father's brother, was there too; while in the forum were Gaius Marius and Lucius Valerius Flaccus, the consuls, and with them the entire senate — and such a senate as even you are accustomed to praise to help in your detraction of the senate of today; there was also the equestrian order — and what equites they were, immortal gods! who in our fathers' time played a great part in government, including charge of the entire dignity of the law-courts — who had taken up arms alongside all men of all classes who believed that their own safety was tied in with the safety of the state; I ask you again personally, Labienus, what was Gaius Rabirius to do?

21 When, acting on a decree of the Senate, the consuls had issued a call to arms, when Marcus Aemilius (Scaurus), the princeps senatus, had armed himself and taken up his stand in the assembly, who, though he could hardly walk, thought that his lameness would be no hindrance in pursuit but only in flight, when even Q. Scaevola (the augur), worn out by old age, dreadfully ill, infirm, crippled and feeble in every limb, leaned on his spear, displaying both his mental vigour and bodily weakness and strength of spirit, when Lucius Metellus, Servius Galba, Gaius Serranus, Publius Rutilius, Gaius Fimbria, Quintus Catulus, and all the other ex-consuls of the time had taken up arms for the common safety; when all the praetors and everyone of high birth and military age were hastening to help, such as Gnaeus and Lucius Domitius, Lucius Crassus, Quintus Mucius, Gaius Claudius, Marcus Drusus; when all the Octavii, Metelli, Julii, Cassii, Catones, Pompeii . . . and in fact every man of pre-eminence was with the consuls — what then was Gaius Rabirius to do?

9.31 The sedition of Saturninus, Glaucia and Equitius, 100 BC

Appian *Civil Wars* 1.32–3 (141–6)

Plut. *Mar.* 30.4 has Saturninus and his supporters slaughtered as they made their way down into the forum. Marius' association with Saturninus, despite presiding as consul over the actions taken against the tribune, tarnished his career. Plutarch has Marius disliked at this point by both the nobles and people, reporting that he did not stand for the next censorship although he had been expected to do (*Mar.* 30.5), and refers to a lack of visitors and crowds around his doors, probably a reference to the fact that few paid him court and to a paucity of clients; Plutarch also has Marius neglected, as a military leader in peacetime (*Mar.* 32.1–2). Scholars argue that this disgrace is overemphasised, noting that Marius was elected augur while absent after his sixth consulship (Cic. *Letter to Brutus* 1.5.3), but do agree that his influence did quickly wane in the absence of a role which he could fill, as Plutarch states: Evans 1994: 128.

Glaucia was praetor in 100 and so could not legally seek election to the consulship for 99 as he was holding a magistracy. His involvement in the murder of Aulus Nunnius and senatorial distaste for his character (App. 1.28.126: doc. 9.28) told against him. **143**: Saufeius had been elected as quaestor for 99, and entered office on 5 December 100. He was thus in office at the time of the civil dissensions that took place on 10 December (the first day of Saturninus' third tribunate), in which he, Saufeius, lost his life (*MRR* II.2–3). For the death of Saturninus, see Badian 1984. Saturninus' legislation was declared invalid by the senate after his murder.

141 In this way Metellus, a most well-respected man, went into exile, and Appuleius (Saturninus) was tribune for the third time. One of his colleagues (Equitius) was considered to be a runaway slave, who claimed that the elder Gracchus was his father. The mob supported him in the election because they missed Gracchus so much. **142** When the consular elections came round, Marcus Antonius was indisputably elected to one of the consulships, while the other was contested between Glaucia and Memmius. As Memmius was by far the more illustrious, Glaucia and Saturninus were anxious about the result and sent some men with clubs to attack him at the election itself, who struck Memmius in the middle of the assembly and cut him down in the sight of everyone. **143** The assembly broke up in turmoil, with neither laws nor law-courts nor any shame remaining; the people were enraged and on the following day rushed in anger to kill Appuleius. He had, however, gathered another mob from the country and with Glaucia and Gaius Saufeius, the quaestor, seized the Capitol. **144** When the senate voted for their destruction, Marius was vexed, but nevertheless reluctantly issued arms to some people; and, while he was delaying matters, some other people cut off the water which ran to the temple. Saufeius, dying of thirst, suggested burning the temple, but Glaucia and Appuleius, in hopes that Marius would assist them, surrendered themselves, followed by Saufeius. **145** With everybody at once demanding that he put them to death, Marius locked them up in the senate house as if he intended to deal with them more legally. The people thought this just a pretext, took the tiles from the senate house roof, and battered Appuleius and his companions to death, including a quaestor and a tribune and a praetor, still wearing their official insignia. **146** A great crowd of others were killed in the sedition, including another tribune, supposedly the son of Gracchus, on his first day as tribune, while freedom, democracy, laws, reputation, and magisterial rank were no longer of any use, as even the tribunate, which had been created to hinder wrong-doers and protect the plebs, and was sacred and inviolable, was now committing and suffering such outrages.

9.32 Marius makes a bid for the command against Mithridates

Appian *Civil Wars* 1.55–6 (240–50)

Doc. 11.5 continues this extract from Appian. In 100 Marius had opposed the recall of Metellus, and he preferred to set sail for Asia rather than see Metellus return. Plutarch has Marius realising that his prowess lay in the military rather than the political scene (*Mar.* 31.3). In the Social War, which broke out in 91, Marius played a limited but important role (*Mar.* 33; doc. 10.18). Immediately after the Social War, conflict between Marius and Sulla led to the outbreak of civil war for the first time at Rome. Sulla, largely on the strength of his Social War successes, was elected to a consulship for 88 (he was to have a second consulship in 80). As consul, he was to have the command against Mithridates, but in 88 Marius manoeuvred to deprive Sulla of the command. Sulla did not accept this situation, and led his army against Rome and exiled Marius (doc. 11.5). So commenced the Marius-Sulla civil war.

Publius Sulpicius Rufus (tr. pl. 88) was one of the young men, along with Drusus, associated with the orator L. Licinius Crassus, cos. 95 (Cic. *de orat.* 1.25; Keaveney 1979: 454). He prosecuted Norbanus in 95 BC, and participated in the Social War (doc. 10.15), but the major event of his career was this tribunate of 88 BC, which sought to address the problem of the distribution of the newly enfranchised Latin and Italian citizens in the tribes (see docs 10.17, 21). His proposal to distribute them amongst all of the tribes rather than eight aroused fierce opposition, because the Italians would potentially outnumber the Romans at voting time in the people's assembly (though how many of the new citizens could be expected to attend Rome for voting is unclear). The law about citizenship was passed, and Appian has the newly distributed voters passing the law to give the command against Mithridates to Marius. Sulpicius had an armed band of equites whom he referred to as his 'anti-senate' (Plut. *Mar.* 35.2: 600 armed men; *Sull.* 8.3: 3,000). Marius supported him in return for the Mithridatic command and Sulpicius passed a law granting it to Marius. In addition, Sulpicius had those exiled under the *lex Varia* recalled (see doc. 10.9), and passed a law to limit the debts of senators to only 2,000 denarii (*MRR* II.41).

Sulpicius' opposition in late 89 to the consular candidacy of Gaius Julius Caesar Strabo for 88 BC (he had not been praetor), who also wanted the command against Mithridates, led to violence: Lintott 1971: 446–9. In 88 the consuls declared a suspension of public business (*iustitium*) when further violence erupted over the citizenship issue. The two consuls were attacked by Sulpicius' supporters; they fled, but Sulpicius had the son of the consul Q. Pompeius Rufus killed, with Sulla fleeing to the house of Marius. Sulla in his *Memoirs* (*HRR* I² 200), according to

Plut. *Mar*. 35.2–4, denied this: he went to have discussions with Marius. Sulla then cancelled the suspension of business, and Sulpicius had his laws passed. The strong optimate opposition to Sulpicius' enfranchisement proposal had led him into an alliance with Marius. Cicero notes that Sulpicius went from being an optimate opposed to Caesar Strabo's irregular consular candidacy to a popularis (Cic. *Har. Resp*. 43, cf. *Brut*. 201–5).

The revoking of Sulla's command (cf. doc. 11.5) led to Sulla's march on Rome, after which Sulla had Sulpicius executed and his laws revoked. (His slave who betrayed him was given his freedom in return for the information as to Sulpicius' whereabouts, but was thrown from the Tarpeian rock in punishment for betraying his master: Livy *Per*. 77; Plut. *Sull*. 10.1.) Sulla enacted some laws in the tribal assembly, but these were repealed when Marius and Cinna gained control of the city; these laws foreshadowed some of the reforms Sulla passed as dictator (App. *BC* 1.59.266–8, 73.339; Keaveney 1983: 71–4).

For Sulpicius: Livy *Per*. 77; Plut. *Mar*. 35.1–6, *Sulla* 8, 10.1; *MRR* II.41–2; Carney 1961: 54–5; Badian 1969a: 481–9, *FC* 230–4; Lintott 1971; Mitchell 1975; Keaveney 1979, 1982: 58–9; Keaveney 1983: 53–71; Scullard *GN* 68–70. Norbanus: Badian 1964a. Marius' desire for the command: see also Plut. *Mar*. 34; Luce 1970; Keaveney 1982: 61; Evans 1994: 132–6.

240 Up till now the murders and seditions had remained internal and not widespread; but after this the party leaders attacked each other with great armies according to the rules of war, and the country was the prize which lay between them. The beginning and origins of these took place immediately after the Social War, in the following way.

241 When Mithridates, king of Pontus and other nations, invaded Bithynia and Phrygia and the part of Asia which neighbours these, as I recounted in my previous book (*Roman History* 12), the consul Sulla was chosen as governor of Asia and commander of the Mithridatic War (he was still at Rome). **242** Marius, thinking it would be an easy and very profitable war, wanted the command, and with many promises got the tribune Publius Sulpicius to work with him to obtain it. He also led the new Italian citizens, who had little influence in elections, to hope to be distributed among all the tribes, suggesting nothing openly about the benefits to himself in that he would be able to use them as loyal adherents in everything. **243** Sulpicius at once introduced a bill for this purpose; if this were enacted, Marius and Sulpicius would have achieved everything they wanted, since the new citizens would far outnumber the old. **244** The older citizens, however, saw this and fought with the new citizens with all their strength. They used clubs and stones against each other and the evil continually increased until the consuls, afraid as the day for voting approached, proclaimed a vacation of several days, as was usual on the occasion of festivals, in order to delay the voting and the evil . . . (the son of the consul Quintus Pompeius, Sulla's son-in-law, is killed by the Sulpicians). **248** Sulla cancelled the vacation and hurriedly left for Capua where his army was, as if to cross from Capua to Asia for the war against Mithridates, for he was not yet aware of what was being done in opposition to him. **249** Sulpicius, with the vacation cancelled and Sulla out of the city, enacted the law and Marius, for whose sake all this had taken place, was immediately elected commander of the war against Mithridates instead of Sulla. **250** When Sulla learnt this he resolved that the matter should be decided by war and summoned his army to an assembly . . .

9.33 Marius banished from Rome by Sulla

Appian Civil Wars 1.60 (269–71)

After Sulla took Rome by force, Marius was banished and barely escaped. Sulpicius was not so lucky, and was put to death.

269 This was the first army of citizens to invade Rome as an enemy country. **270** From now on seditions were only to be decided by armies, and there were frequent attacks on Rome and battles for the walls and all other warlike activities, with no longer any sense of shame, whether for the laws, institutions or country, to restrain violence. **271** On this occasion Sulpicius, who still held the office of tribune, together with Marius who had been consul six times, and his son Marius, Publius Cethegus, Junius Brutus, Gnaeus and Quintus Granius, Publius Albinovanus, Marcus Laetorius and others with them, about twelve in number, were banished from Rome on the grounds that they had aroused sedition, fought against the consuls, and proclaimed freedom for slaves to incite them to rebellion, and were voted to be enemies of the Romans, while anyone who met them was permitted to kill them with impunity or bring them before the consuls; their goods had been confiscated.

9.34 Marius' atrocities on his return in 87 BC

Plutarch Life of Marius 43.4–8, 44.9, 46.6–9

Cf. Livy *Per.* 80; Vell. 2.21.1–23.1; App. *BC* 1.71–5.294–315; Diod. 38/39.4.1–3. Sulla, deprived of his command, fled but returned with six legions, and attacked and won Rome (doc. 11.5). Marius escaped from Rome with difficulty, almost meeting his death at Minturnae, but made it to Africa (Carney 1961: 57–9, 1961a), where many of his veterans were settled; he returned with Cinna to take revenge after Sulla had left for Asia Minor.

Cinna had been elected consul for 87 — he was hardly Sulla' choice; the other consul for 88, Q. Pompeius Rufus, was killed at the instigation of Cn. Pompeius Strabo's soldiers when sent to take over command of them. When Sulla departed for Asia Minor, Cinna agitated for the distribution of the new citizens in all the tribes (he was opposed by the other consul for 87, Gnaeus Octavius: doc. 10.26); violence erupted between the old and new citizens at Rome, involving the deaths of many of the new citizens. Octavius (illegally) deprived Cinna of his consulship (replacing him with L. Cornelius Merula, the flamen dialis, which meant in effect that Octavius was sole consul). Fleeing to Campania, Cinna won over the army there, and was joined by Sertorius and Cn. Carbo (who was to be consul with Cinna in 85 and 84 BC), while Marius and his son returned from Africa. The senatorial forces were led by Octavius (cos. 87), P. Licinus Crassus (cos. 97), Caecilius Metellus Pius (later to be consul in 80 and active against Sertorius in Spain) and Cn. Pompeius Strabo (cos. 89). Cinna captured and pillaged Ostia; Pompeius died, whereupon Metellus retreated; Octavius vacillated. The senate negotiated with Cinna — recognising him as consul — and he and Marius entered Rome. Crassus committed suicide and Octavius was murdered just before Marius entered the city. Sulla's measures taken after his successful march on Rome were annulled (Plut. *Mar.* 41–43; App. *BC* 1.64–70; Vell. 2.20; Livy *Per.* 79–80). Initially Marius insisted that he could not enter Rome because he had been banished. In the bloodshed that followed, both equites and senators were killed; the latter had their decapitated heads put on public display (App. *BC* 1.71.331). Cicero *de orat.* 3.8 lists the following important victims: Q. Catulus, M. Antonius, C. Julius and his brother Lucius, P. Crassus, the flamen dialis (Merula), C. Carbo. Marius did not live long into his seventh consulship (*MRR* II.53). Carney 1961: 60–70; Katz 1976; Fantham 1987.

The younger Marius was consul in 82 BC. With his death, Sulla's triumph would be complete; cf. App. *BC* 1.87.394–400.

43.4 The people was summoned into the forum, but before three or four tribes had given their votes Marius left off the pretence, giving up his sophistic definition of himself as an exile and entering the city with his bodyguard, a picked band of slaves who had joined him and whom he called 'Bardyiae'. **5** These killed many on his command, many simply at his nod, and finally Ancharius, a senator and ex-praetor, who met Marius and was not spoken to, was cut down with their swords in front of him. **6** After this, whenever anyone greeted Marius and was not addressed or replied to, they took this as a sign to slaughter him immediately in the street, so that even each of his friends was full of terror and fear whenever he approached to speak to Marius. **7** When many had been killed, Cinna's desire for bloodshed was satiated, but Marius' rage and thirst for blood kept increasing day by day and he removed anyone whom he had any grudge against. **8** Every road and every city was full of men who were fleeing and men hunting down those who were escaping or in hiding. . . . **44.9** Despite the headless bodies thrown into the street and trampled on, there was no pity, only general fear and terror at the sight. The people found the brutality of the so-called Bardyiae particularly hard to endure. **10** For they slaughtered householders in their houses, dishonoured their children, and raped their wives, and were unbridled in their plundering and bloodletting until Cinna and Sertorius' parties got together and took action against them when they were asleep in their camp, shooting them all down with javelins . . .

46.6 Marius died 17 days after becoming consul for the seventh time; and immediately in Rome there was a great feeling of delight and confidence, in that they were rid of a savage tyrant. **7** But in a few days they realised that they had exchanged an old master for a new one in his prime; Marius the son now revealed such savagery and bitterness in killing the noblest and most respected men . . . **9** Finally (in 82 BC) he was trapped in Praeneste by Sulla and, after many vain attempts to save his life, when the city was captured and escape impossible, he killed himself.

9.35 Marius' career inscription

ILS 59

(*Inscript. Ital.* 13.3.83; *CIL* 1² 1, p. 195; a copy at Arpinum: *CIL* X.5782; Evans 1994: 1–5, 32). Marius' career inscription, now lost, but reconstructed by Mommsen from fragments and Renaissance transcriptions, was one of the elogia of illustrious Romans erected in the Forum of Augustus. Triumphal robe: doc. 9.14; Plut. *Mar.* 12.7.

Gaius Marius, son of Gaius, seven times consul, praetor, tribune of the plebs, quaestor, augur, military tribune, contrary to the rule concerning the allocation of provinces waged war against Jugurtha king of Numidia as consul, captured him, and, when celebrating a triumph in his second consulship, ordered him to be led before his chariot. He was made consul for the third time in his absence and in his fourth consulship destroyed an army of the Teutones. In his fifth consulship he routed the Cimbri. He again celebrated a triumph over these and the Teutones. In his sixth consulship he freed the state when it was in chaos from the seditions of a tribune of the plebs and a praetor, who had armed themselves and occupied the Capitol. At more than 70 years of age, he was expelled from his country by civil strife and was restored by force and made consul for a seventh time. From the spoils of the Cimbri and Teutones he built a shrine to Honour and Virtue. In triumphal robe and patrician shoes [he entered the senate].

COINAGE

9.36 Marius' voting reform as tribune

Crawford *RRC* 292.1

A denarius (silver) coin of 119 (Foss), 113 or 112 (Crawford), or c. 105 BC (Carson). Grueber II.526; Sydenham *CRR* 548; Reece *RC* no. 43; Carson *PCRR* no. 110; Foss no. 3; Taylor 1966: 38 nos 4–5, 39 (interpreting the coin incorrectly).

Obverse: Bust of the goddess Roma.
Reverse: A voting scene in the comitium. A voter on the left hand side of the coin, just entering onto the voting bridge (pons), receives a voting tablet (tabella) from an attendant below, shown behind the pons, while at the end of the bridge another voter is depositing his voting tablet into a ballot-box (cista). A voting tablet is itself shown in the upper right, perhaps with the traces of the letter 'P' signifying, again perhaps, one of the tribes (either Pupinia or Papiria). Two parallel horizontal lines on the coin probably represent a marked-off voting area. The name of the moneyer, P. (Licinius) Nerva, appears prominently.

9.37 Triumph over the Germans

Crawford *RRC* 322.1

A denarius of 102 BC (Grueber I.1581, 1591; Sydenham *CRR* 589; Foss no. 4). A priest of the 'Great Mother', identified with Cybele, had foretold the victories over the Germans, and so Cybele's presence on this coin and the chariot are taken as referring to his victories (Plut. *Mar.* 17.9–11; cf. Diod. 36.13). The Syrian prophetess, called Martha, accompanied Marius on campaign: Plut. 17.1–5; cf. doc. 9.6.

Obverse: Bust of the goddess Cybele.
Reverse: The deity Victory in a biga (two-horse chariot).

9.38 Saturninus' grain bill

Crawford *RRC* 330.1

A denarius of 100 BC (Sydenham *CRR* 603; Carson *PCRR* no. 121; Foss 9; Grueber I.1125; *MRR* I.576). This coin is presumably a reference to the grain law of Saturninus, passed in 100 BC. Caepio had opposed the law with violence, but apparently saw no difficulty in then advertising his role in putting the law into effect. Struck by L. Calpurnius Piso and Q. Servilius Caepio.

Obverse: Head of Saturn, with the names 'Piso' and 'Caepio' and the abbreviation 'Q', indicating that they are quaestors.

Reverse: Two figures sitting on a bench, facing left; an ear of grain on either side of the coin, with the inscription 'AD.FRU.EMV.EX.S.C.: 'for the purchase of grain by decree of the senate.'

10

The 'Social' War

The Social War between Rome and the Italian allies broke out in 91 BC and was largely over by 89 BC, though resistance to Rome continued (doc. 10.28). The Italian allies (the *socii*, hence the name given to the war) desired Roman citizenship with the various benefits which this conferred. The Romans refused to enfranchise them, and war broke out. The seriousness of the situation then caused the Romans to enfranchise the Latins, and those Italian allies who had not revolted (doc. 10.17).

The Romans had over a period of centuries granted Roman citizenship to individuals in Latin and also allied Italian communities, but there was opposition at Rome to the enfranchisement of the Latins and a proposal about this had been rejected by the senate even in the emergencies of the Second Punic War (see doc. 4.40). The issue of citizenship for the allies became important in the last decades of the second century BC. According to Velleius Paterculus (2.2.2) Tiberius Gracchus promised citizenship to the whole of Italy: 'in the consulship of Publius Mucius Scaevola and Lucius Calpurnius (133 BC), 162 years ago, he split away from the senatorial party and promised citizenship to all of Italy'. This is debated, for it is not mentioned by Plutarch or Appian, and Tiberius in fact did not promise the allies citizenship but actually exacerbated relations with them. Cicero *Rep.* 3.41 notes, 'Tiberius Gracchus kept faith with the citizens, but disregarded the treaty rights of our allies and the Latins'. This presumably refers to the distribution of ager publicus to Roman citizens; Scipio Aemilianus therefore stepped in to defend the allies against the appropriation of ager publicus in their territories (doc. 8.21). Tiberius did not raise the idea of citizenship for the allies, and it probably was not an issue in 133 BC.

The question of citizenship was first raised in the 120s. A law was passed in 126 by the tribune M. Junius Pennus to prevent non-citizens from living in Rome and to expel those already doing so. In 125 BC, M. Fulvius Flaccus (a friend of Gaius Gracchus and member of the Gracchan agrarian commission) as consul proposed that all Italian communities should receive full franchise or the right of appeal against Roman magistrates, the *ius provocationis*, but the proposal was opposed by the senate (doc. 10.6). Fregellae revolted and was razed to the ground by Opimius (cf. doc. 8.28). This revolt could be taken as an indication that there was some desire amongst the Latin allies for citizenship. But the fact that only Fregellae revolted could point to specific local grievances on its part, and the character of its population had in fact changed and it was now more Oscan, i.e., Italian, in character.

The Italians had been allies of Rome for two centuries and contributed heavily to the success against Hannibal and in Rome's extensive second-century wars. A law granting Roman citizenship to magistrates in Latin colonies might have been passed at about the time of the revolt of Fregellae as a 'half-way' measure.

The next major move in this matter came with Gaius Gracchus: allies of Latin status were to be given full franchise and other allies were to be raised to Latin status (this was defeated by the senate through the counter-proposals of the tribune Livius Drusus: doc. 8.28). This proposal and Livius Drusus' counter colony measures were largely responsible for Gaius' loss of support amongst the body of Roman citizens (docs 8.28, 30). Saturninus in 100 BC, some twenty-five years later, raised Italian hopes by offering franchise to a select number of Marius' allied veterans, but the law was declared invalid by the senate after his murder. To what extent Gaius and Saturninus had in mind a Latin and Italian interest in citizenship is unclear, and it may well have been the case that they stimulated hopes for citizenship. Roman opposition to an extension of citizenship is clear from the lex Licinia Mucia of 95 which set up a *quaestio* on all aliens claiming to be citizens (doc. 10.2).

But by 91 BC there was clearly an overwhelming desire amongst Latins and Italians for Roman citizenship, and the Social War broke out on this very issue. The tribunate of the younger Livius Drusus in 91 brought this to the forefront of Roman politics (docs 10.4–9). He was — one of the peculiar twists of history that sometimes occur — the son of the tribune Livius Drusus who had opposed Gaius Gracchus in 122 BC. His proposal to give citizenship to the Italians was part of a broader programme (doc. 10.6), aimed at giving senators a role in the juries, dominated exclusively by the equites under Gaius Gracchus' legislation (doc. 8.28). This proposal may also have been influenced by the unfair conviction by an equestrian jury of his uncle Rutilius Rufus for extortion in Asia (doc. 10.5). But Drusus' citizenship proposal lost him support, and he was assassinated in his own home (doc. 10.9). The 'oath' which the Italians were supposed to have sworn to Drusus (doc. 10.8) is clearly an invention of Drusus' enemies, and was meant to create an impression that Drusus was aiming at a huge Italian clientela which would overshadow the smaller clientela relationships that Romans serving abroad had established.

Drusus' murder, like that of the tribunes Tiberius and Gaius Gracchus, Fulvius Flaccus, and Saturninus, was a forerunner of the internal violence about to descend upon Rome with Sulla's march in 88 (doc. 11.5). Drusus' attempted reforms and his association with the leader of the Marsi (Q. Poppaedius Silo: doc. 10.4, cf. 10.7, 10.18) led to a law in the next year (90 BC), successfully proposed by the tribune Varius, to try anyone suspected of collusion with the allies. When the allies revolted in 91 in frustration, the initial Roman response had been to deny them citizenship (doc. 10.11). Then, in an acknowledgement of the seriousness of the situation (freedmen were enrolled as soldiers) and of the fairness of the Italian demands, citizenship was offered to the Latins and the Italian communities that had not revolted (doc. 10.17). The rebels who surrendered (and so became *dediticii*) were enfranchised later, possibly in 87. The allies' demands could be seen as fair: 'every year and in every war they were providing . . . cavalry and infantry' (doc. 10.13); they fought as Cicero observed, 'to be received' into the Roman state (doc. 10.14).

After Poppaedius had led an abortive march on Rome (doc. 10.7), actual war between Rome and the Italian allies broke out in 91. Numerous allied communities rebelled, particularly the Marsi and the Samnites (docs 10.10–11). The revolt began at Asculum (doc. 10.10), and quickly spread. The rebels established a capital city, at Corfinium, renamed Italia, with a constitution along Roman lines, and minted their own coins (doc. 10.12). They had initial successes against the Romans, but the Latin allies remained loyal, as did the Etruscans and Umbrians (doc. 10.17) and Marius, Sulla and Gnaeus Pompeius Strabo served as legates under the consuls (docs 10.18–20).

As noted, citizenship was extended to the Latins and loyal Italians. The law enacting this, the lex Julia, was passed in 90 BC (doc. 10.21). The Latin and Italian communities were enfranchised and their citizens became Roman; their communities were given the status of *municipia*, and were governed by four officials, as at Tarentum in southern Italy (doc. 10.22). The Italians' distribution among the tribes was not effected immediately: P. Sulpicius Rufus' attempt to have them distributed fairly among all 35 tribes was rescinded by Sulla, but by the censorship of 70 BC some form of distribution had finally taken place and the censors counted 910,000 Roman citizens (doc. 10.24; *MRR* II.127). All of Italy south of the river Po (Cisalpine Gaul was north of the Po) now had Roman citizenship, and became one political unit.

Ancient sources: these are largely the narratives of Appian *Civil Wars* 1.34–53.150–231, and Diodorus 37.1–25 (fragments), as well as Velleius Paterculus 2.13–17 and Livy *Periochae* 70–6. Plutarch deals with Marius and Sulla's involvement: *Mar.* 33, *Sulla* 6 (*HRR* I² 197–8 F8); see also *Cato Min.* 2; *Cic.* 3.2 (Cicero saw service under Sulla in the Social War); *Luc.* 1–2; *Sert.* 4.2; Florus 2.6. Many scattered passages refer to the Social War itself: see the list at *CAH* IX¹ 919, including Licinianus 32. The history of Sisenna had a detailed treatment of the Social Wars (*HRR* I² 276–93 FF1–124), and Sulla wrote of his own role (*HRR* I² 197–9 FF8–10). Inscriptions are also important (docs 10.16, 22, 23, 25). Coins were minted by the Italian allies and are important for an understanding of their perspective (docs 10.29–31).

For the Social War, see esp. Badian 1969: 29–34, *FC* 227–51; Gabba 1976: 70–130, 1994; Keaveney 1987: 115–61, 189–93.

THE RESTRICTION OF ROMAN CITIZENSHIP

10.1 An embarrassing consulship

Valerius Maximus *Memorable Deeds and Sayings (Of those born in a humble situation who became illustrious)* 3.4.5

Perperna was consul in 130 (*MRR* I.501–2); he died in 129 before celebrating a triumph for his victory over and capture of Aristonicus in Asia Minor, the pretender to the throne of Pergamum who led a revolt against Rome (doc. 5.44). Perperna also played a leading role in crushing the First Sicilian slave revolt. Perperna's lack of legitimate Roman citizenship was only discovered when Perperna's father was named in a list of people whose return was demanded by their native cities. Valerius here has probably confused the Papian (in the 60s) and Pennan laws (126 BC). The Crassian 'carnage' refers to the defeat and death of P. Licinius Crassus Dives Mucianus (cos. 131) in Asia in 130 by Aristonicus. The incident typifies the phenomenon of non-citizens posing as such, and the aspirations of at least the elite of some of Rome's allies to become Roman citizens and enter into the political life of Rome. Perperna was Etruscan; the family was romanised but did not have Roman citizenship. Perperna: Brunt 1988a: 99–100, 129; Wiseman 1971: 3 n.1; Harris 1971: 198, 226, 332–3 (doubting the story); Münzer 1999: 91–3 for his Etruscan origins.

No small embarrassment to the consulship is Marcus Perperna, seeing that he was consul before he was a citizen, though in the conduct of war he was a far more useful general to the state than Varro: for he captured King Aristonicus and avenged the Crassian carnage, but, while his life triumphed, his death was condemned under the Papian law. For his father had taken on the rights of a Roman citizen with no justification, and the Sabelli forced him after a trial to return to his former residence. So Marcus Perperna's shadowy name, false consulship, misty command, and fleeting triumph resided unlawfully in an alien city.

10.2 The lex Licinia Mucia of 95 BC

Cicero *On Duties* 3.47

Cicero is here discussing the Athenians' fifth-century decree that the Aeginetans should have their thumbs cut off to restrict their naval power. The tribune L. Junius Pennus in 126 BC set up a commission to examine the rights of allies to be in Rome and to eject those there illegally. The Papian law, which Cicero refers to here, was passed in 65 against the illegal assumption of citizenship. For the lex Licinia Mucia, passed by the two consuls of 95, Q. Mucius Scaevola (see below) and L. Licinius Crassus, see doc. 9.27 where one of Marius' grants of citizenship was challenged under this law. Pennus' law of 126 indicates the Roman closed attitude to citizenship and desire to restrict this; the law may well have been motivated by Fulvius Flaccus' proposals canvassed in 126 while seeking the consulship of 125: Salmon 1962: 114; Badian 1970/1: 406; Brunt 1988a: 99–100.

They also do wrong who prohibit foreigners from enjoying the use of a city and exclude them from it, as Pennus did in our forefathers' time, and Papius recently. It is of course right that a non-citizen not be allowed to exercise citizen rights; the law on this was brought in by those extremely wise consuls Crassus and Scaevola. However, to prohibit foreigners from enjoying the use of a city is certainly barbarous.

10.3 The consequences of the lex Licinia Mucia

Asconius *Commentaries on Cicero* 67–8 (= Cicero *pro Cornelio*)

See Marshall 1985: 239–41.

67 'With regard to the lex Licinia Mucia, concerning the reduction of citizen numbers, I consider that all are agreed that, although it was passed by two consuls who were the wisest of all we have known, it was not only ineffective but seriously harmful for the state.'

Cicero is referring to the orator Lucius Licinius Crassus and Quintus Mucius Scaevola, the pontifex maximus, orator and jurist. In their consulship, they brought in the law to which Cicero is referring, which restored the allies to their own states. For **68** the peoples of Italy desperately wanted Roman citizenship, and because of this a large number of them were passing themselves off as Roman citizens; accordingly it seemed necessary to pass a law to restore everyone to the jurisdiction of their own states. But this law so alienated the leaders of the peoples of Italy that it may have been the main cause of the Italian war which broke out three years later.

MARCUS LIVIUS DRUSUS

Marcus Livius Drusus was tribune in 91 BC. Pliny *Nat. Hist.* 25.52 calls him 'the most well-known popular tribune of all; the people stood up and cheered him above anyone else. The optimates blamed him for the Marsic war' (i.e., the Social War). The Marsi of central Italy, who spoke Oscan, were prominent amongst the rebels and the Romans called the war after them: Diod. 37.1. Drusus attempted to deal with several problems: senatorial dissatisfaction at the control of the law-courts by the equites was his primary aim, but also, linked with the need for support for this, colonies for the landless poor, and a grain law presumably concerned with cheap distribution. Like his father, he was using the tribunate to advance the interests of the aristocracy, and the sources are clear that his first concern was with restoring senatorial power in the courts (Livy *Per.* 70, Vell. 13.1; App. *BC* 1.35.157–8; Diod. 37.10.1). Drusus was the grandfather of Livia Drusilla, the emperor Tiberius' mother, and wife of Augustus.

For Drusus, see *MRR* II.21–2; Hill 1952: 132–8, 141–2; Salmon 1962: 114–15; Gruen 1968: 206–14; Badian 1969: 29–34, *FC* 215–19; Gabba 1976: 70–3, 131–5, 1994: 111–13; Sherwin-White 1973: 139–40; Brunt 1988a: 100–3, 106–7, 1988b: 154; Scullard *GN* 62–4; Mouritsen 1998: 109–27; for Servilius Caepio (docs 9.14, 18), who organised the equites against Drusus: Badian 1964a: 40–41, 1969: 29–34.

10.4 Drusus' Italian friends

Plutarch *Life of Cato the Younger* 2.1–4

Cf. *Vir. Illustr.* 80. Cato the Younger and his siblings, including his older half-brother Caepio, were brought up in the home of their uncle Livius Drusus, tribune in 91. Poppaedius, when visiting, supposedly held Cato out of the window and shook him to try to get him to agree to support the Italians: Cato would have been four years old in 91. Poppaedius led the Marsi, part of the northern group of Italian peoples that rebelled; his forces ambushed and killed Caepio, Drusus' brother-in-law, in 90 BC (this is not the Q. Servilius Caepio who was consul in 106 BC, but a relative).

1 While Cato was still a child, the Romans' allies were trying to acquire Roman citizenship; and one of them, Pompaedius (Poppaedius) Silo, a man of great experience in war and of the highest reputation, a friend of Drusus', was spending several days at his house, during which time he came to be friendly with the children. 'Come,' he said to them, 'Ask your uncle to help us in our struggle for citizenship.' **2** Caepio agreed with a smile, but, when Cato made no reply, and gazed at the strangers with a stubborn, fierce glare, Pompaedius said to him, 'And you, young man, what do you say? Are you not able to join your uncle in helping the strangers like your brother?' **3** When he said nothing, but appeared through his silence and facial expression to refuse the request, Pompaedius lifted him through a window as if he would let him go, and ordered him to agree or he would drop him . . . **4** When Cato had put up with this treatment for some time without fright or fear, Pompaedius put him down, saying quietly to his friends, 'What a piece of luck for Italy that he is a child! If he were a man, I do not think we would get a single vote among the people.'

10.5 Drusus makes enemies

Livy *Periochae* 70–1

The 'largesse' at (70) were agrarian laws and the grain-distribution (see 71). Livy (cf. Asc. 21) gives the motive for Drusus' judicial reform as the condemnation of Drusus' uncle, Rutilius (cos. 105) in a court manned with equites as jurors. The publicani were the tax-collectors.

Quintus Mucius Scaevola (not Gaius as here), cos. 95, as proconsul of Asia (probably in 94 BC) with Publius Rutilius Rufus as his legate re-organised the province of Asia. Mucius left after nine months but Rutilius remained and incurred the hatred of the publicani for curbing their activities. As a result, in 92 he was prosecuted on a charge of *repetundae* (extortion) and although innocent was found guilty (Gaius Gracchus had legislated that the juries be drawn from amongst the equites, giving them control of the courts, docs 8.28–9). He showed his contempt for this conviction by going into exile in Asia Minor, amongst the people he was supposed to have misgoverned; all the cities of the province sent embassies to him (Val. Max. 2.10.5). For Rutilius' trial: Vell. 2.13; Cic. *Brut.* 115, *Font.* 38; *ORF*[4] Rutilius FF3–6; according to Dio F97 Marius played a role in the prosecution; Alexander *Trials* no. 94; Badian 1964: 107–9; cf. Kallet-Marx 1990; Badian 1972: 91–2.

70 Publius Rutilius, a man of the greatest integrity, was hated by the equestrian order, because as legate of the proconsul Gaius Mucius he had protected Asia against the wrongs of the publicani, and, since the law-courts were in their power, Rutilius was condemned for extortion and sent into exile (92 BC) . . . The senate refused to bear the equestrian order's lack of restraint in running the courts, and began to make every effort to transfer the courts to themselves, with their cause supported by Marcus Livius Drusus, tribune of the plebs, who roused the plebs with the ruinous hope of largesse in order to strengthen his position . . .

71 In order to gain greater strength in his attempt to support the senate's cause, Marcus Livius Drusus, tribune of the plebs, tried to win over the allies and the peoples of Italy with the hope of Roman citizenship; with their help he passed agrarian and corn laws by violence, and also brought in a law on the courts, that control of the courts should be shared equally by the senate and the equestrian order. But when, at last, it was not possible to give the allies the citizenship they had been promised, the Italians were furious and began to stir up a revolt. Their gatherings and conspiracies, and the speeches of their leading men in counsels are recorded. Because of these events Livius Drusus was hated even by the senate as being responsible for promoting rebellion among the allies, and he was killed in his own home by a person unknown.

10.6 The pro-Italian legislation of Drusus, 91 BC

Appian *Civil Wars* 1.34–5 (152–61)

Cf. Vell. 2.13–15. To gain support for the jury law, Drusus sought popular support through a law for colonies in Italy and Sicily: 'which had been voted long before' (156): these were presumably the colonies legislated for in his father's tribunate (see doc. 8.28) but which had never been carried out (Vell. 2.13.2 sees the popular measures as aimed at gaining support for the judicial one). This proposal, however, raised the opposition of the allies (doc. 10.9), because the colonies in Italy would require ager publicus which they held (they had managed to retain possession of this due to the intervention of Scipio Aemilianus: doc. 8.21). Livy (doc. 10.5) has Drusus proposing citizenship to the allies so as to gain support, but if Drusus had hoped that the promise of citizenship would counter the opposition to his colonies, he was wrong in the case of the Umbrians and Etruscans who preferred the land to citizenship and came to Rome to protest (doc. 10.9 below). Fulvius had raised similar hopes in 125 BC, and the presence of Pompaedius Silo in Drusus' house (doc. 10.4) shows that at least some of the allies wanted citizenship; for Fulvius' death, see doc. 8.32.

Drusus was clearly motivated by the desire to reform the courts; not only because his uncle had been a victim, but also because this was a long-standing senatorial grievance. Gaius Gracchus had given the juries to the equites; in 106 Q. Servilius Caepio as consul successfully proposed a law that the senate share the juries with the equites; but C. Servilius Glaucia (murdered with Saturninus: doc. 9.31) in either 101 or 100 restored the courts solely to equestrian control with his *lex Servilia repetundarum* (Gruen 1968: 166–7; Brunt 1988b: 155). Drusus' proposal to share the courts again reflected Caepio's measure, as well as the fact that there were not enough senators to man the juries.

Q. Servilius Caepio (a relative of the Q. Servilius Caepio, cos. 106), the brother-in-law of Drusus, but who became the personal enemy of Drusus, led the attack against Drusus (Hill 1952: 135 n.2 for sources). The equites were 'primarily angry' (App. 1.35.161) that they would become liable to accusations of bribery (cf. Cic. *Rab. Post.* 16). Drusus had his measure passed in the assembly with violence, but senatorial opposition to the inclusion of equites in the senatorial order and the enfranchisement of the Italians was led by one of the consuls for 91, L. Marcius Philippus. He had all Drusus' laws annulled after the death of one of Drusus' main senatorial supporters, the outstanding orator L. Licinius Crassus, who had opposed Philippus in the senate. Philippus had all of the laws annulled by a single decree of the senate as having been passed despite inauspicious omens (Asc. 69).

Drusus was aiming to appease the equites by including some of their number in the senate, but some may have been annoyed at missing out, and the law about bribery outweighed any advantage to be gained from this. Similarly, for the senate, regaining a share in the courts was outweighed by having to 'share' the senate with equites. Drusus' jury law was annulled, but Sulla took up his idea of enrolling equites in the senate: Badian 1972: 95; Brunt 1988b: 154. In 89 BC, a tribune (M. Plautius Silvanus) had a law passed in the assembly that the senators and equites would serve together on juries (Asc. 79; *MRR* II.34; Hill 1952: 137 n.7).

For the court proposal, see esp. Hill 1952: 132–8; see also Gruen 1968: 207–10; Weinrib 1970; Hands 1972; Brunt 1988b: 154–6, 1988c: 206–10; cf. Griffin 1973. There is no evidence that Drusus debased the coinage (Pliny *Nat. Hist.* 33.46; accepted by Hill 1952: 138 as one ground of the equites' opposition to Drusus).

152 Fulvius Flaccus in his consulship (125 BC) was the first and foremost to openly arouse in the Italians the desire for Roman citizenship — that they should be partners in the empire instead of subjects. When he introduced the idea and strongly persisted in it, he was sent off because of this on some military command by the senate. **153** During this, his consulship came to an end, but he later obtained the tribunate and managed to have the younger Gracchus as his colleague, who helped him to bring in other measures in the Italians' favour. **154** When they were both killed, as I narrated earlier, Italy was aroused even more; for they did not think it right that they be considered subjects instead of partners, or that Flaccus and Gracchus should have suffered such misfortunes while working on their behalf.

155 After them the tribune Livius Drusus, a man of most distinguished family, promised the Italians, at their own request, that he would introduce another law to grant them citizenship; they especially desired this because, at a stroke, they would become rulers instead of subjects. **156** In order to gain the people's support for this measure he tried to win them over with many colonies in Italy and Sicily, which had been voted long before, but not yet been carried out. **157** He attempted to reconcile by an impartial law the senate and the equites, who had serious differences with each other at that time over the law courts. As he was unable to transfer the courts back to the senate openly, he devised the following compromise: **158** as there were now hardly 300 senators due to the conflicts, he introduced a law that an equal number, chosen according to merit, should be added to their number from the equites, and that the courts of justice should for the future be made up from the entire body. He added a clause that they should make investigations into cases of bribery, as accusations of that kind were almost unknown, because bribery was such a common practice.

159 This was his plan for a compromise, but it turned out quite the opposite to what he expected. The senators were furious that so large a number should be added to their body all at once and be transferred from the equites to the highest rank, considering that it was not unlikely that they would form their own separate senatorial party and contend against the former senators more strongly than ever. **160** The equites for their part suspected that, by this treatment, the law-courts would for the future be transferred from the equites to the senate on its own, and, as they had acquired a taste for the immense wealth and power, they did not bear this suspicion without grief. **161** The majority of them, too, were worried and suspicious of each other, as to who seemed the more worthy to be enrolled in the 300; and jealousy towards their betters infected the remainder. The equites were primarily angry at the charge of bribery being revived, which they thought they had already firmly and completely suppressed on their own account.

10.7 A pre-emptive strike planned

Diodorus Siculus *Library of History* 37.13.1

Q. Poppaedius Silo (Pompaedius) was dissuaded from this attack on the way to Rome in 91, by Domitius, perhaps Gnaeus Domitius Ahenobarbus (cos. 96). Presumably the investigations they feared were connected with the lex Licinia Mucia and the problems Drusus was having in passing his legislation. This was the Poppaedius who had stayed in Drusus' house.

The Marsic leader, Pompaedius, commenced a great and hazardous enterprise. He assembled 10,000 men from those who feared the investigations, and led them against Rome with swords hidden under their clothes. His intention was to surround the senate with armed men and demand citizenship, or, if he failed, to destroy Rome's rule with fire and sword.

10.8 The 'oath' of the Italians to Drusus

Diodorus Siculus *Library of History* 37.11.1

This oath, supposedly sworn by Drusus' Italian supporters, was circulated by Drusus' enemy L. Philippus (see doc. 10.6 above) and was presumably composed to discredit Drusus on the grounds that it would have given Drusus unrivalled clientela and power in Italy: Sherwin-White 1973: 154–5; see docs 2.55–7.

I swear by Jupiter Capitolinus, and Roman Vesta, and Rome's ancestral god Mars, and Sun the Founder (i.e., Sol Indigetes), and Earth the benefactress of animals and plants, and also by the demi-gods who founded Rome and the heroes who have increased her empire, that the enemy and friend of Drusus shall be my enemy and friend, and I shall not spare my property nor the lives of my children and parents, unless it benefit Drusus and those who swear this oath. And if I become a citizen by Drusus' law, I will consider Rome my country and Drusus my greatest benefactor. And I will transmit this oath to as many of my countrymen as I can. May all good things come to me if I keep the oath, and the opposite if I break it.

10.9 Drusus' assassination

Appian *Civil Wars* 1.36–7 (162–5)

The Umbrians and Etruscans were clearly opposed to Drusus' agrarian legislation, due to the fact that these communities (most particularly the aristocracies there) had large amounts of ager publicus they were not willing to trade for citizenship: Salmon 1962: 114–15; Gruen 1968: 207; Badian 1969: 31–2, *FC* 218, 221; cf. Sherwin-White 1973: 136.

The tribune, Quintus Varius (90 BC; *MRR* II.26–7): for the lex Varia, see also App. 1.37.166–8; Asc. 22; Cic. *Brut.* 205, 304; Val. Max. 8.6.4. According to Appian, the equites, by prosecuting key senators, were seeking to become more powerful in the state. Marcus Aemilius Scaurus (cos. 115) was summoned to appear before the assembly under the terms of the law but was acquitted. Mummius was successfully prosecuted and retired to Delos; and Gaius Aurelius Cotta and Lucius Calpurnius Bestia went into exile before their cases were decided. Varius was condemned under his own law the following year; see Alexander *Trials* nos 100–6, 108–10.

162 And so it happened that the senate and equites, despite their differences, were united in their hatred of Drusus, and only the people were happy with their colonies. Even the Italians, on whose especial behalf Drusus was devising these measures, had concerns about the law on colonies, worried that the Roman public land, which was still undistributed, and which they were still farming, some in open violation and others clandestinely, would immediately be taken away from them, and that they might also be disturbed in their own lands. **163** The Etruscans and the Umbrians shared the Italians' fears, and, when they were, as was believed, summoned to the city by the consuls to overthrow Drusus, which was their true aim, though the pretext was to make their complaints, they opposed the law publicly and remained for the day of voting. **164** Aware of this, Drusus did not go out frequently, but regularly transacted his business in the poorly-lit atrium of his house, when one evening, as he was sending the crowd away, he suddenly cried out that he was wounded, and fell down while still saying the words. A shoemaker's knife was found thrust into his thigh.

165 In this way Drusus too was killed while tribune. The equites, to make his policy grounds for accusation against their enemies, persuaded Quintus Varius, a tribune, to introduce a law to prosecute anyone who helped the Italians acquire citizenship, whether openly or secretly, hoping that they might bring all the senators under a dreadful accusation and themselves sit in judgement on them, and with them out of the way be even more powerful in their rule of Rome.

THE SOCIAL WAR

The allies had not been interested in citizenship when Gaius Gracchus had proposed this, but by 91 a consciousness of the importance of citizenship may have come about due to the activities of the Gracchan land commission, against which Scipio Aemilianus had defended them in 129. There had also been grants of citizenship to allies, such as Marius' grant to two cohorts of Camertes who had fought with special bravery against the Cimbri (Val. Max. 5.2.8; Cic. *Balb.* 46; doc. 9.27), and the aristocracies in allied communities were presumably aware that Latin aristocrats possessed Roman citizenship. The extent to which Gaius and Fulvius may have acted as a stimulus to Italian aspirations for citizenship is not clear. Badian sees the allies as 'tired of being used as pawns in the game of domestic Roman politics', but this seems less convincing as a reason (1969: 30). The allies wanted citizenship because they desired to be on an equal footing with the Romans, for whom they had fought in so many wars, and also to be protected from the arbitrariness of the imperium of Roman magistrates (e.g., doc. 8.24). The issue of the ager publicus, revisited by Drusus in 91, was also a reminder of Roman dominance of the allies, and also of the steady encroachment of Romans on Italian land and Roman expansionism (so Nagle 1973, esp. 368). That the Italians were anxious that the Roman equites would overtake them in the business opportunities provided by the Roman empire and were worried about the increasing power of the equites at Rome via the courts (Salmon 1962: 112–13) does not have evidence to support it (cf. Sherwin-White 1973: 135).

After the Social War the allied aristocracies, now that they had acquired citizenship, entered the political life of Rome in full, surely reflecting the aspirations they had in 91 which drove them to revolt when these aspirations were crushed. The fact that most of the allies would never be able to exercise their voting rights as citizens effectively at Rome was irrelevant: in fact the distribution of the allies into a limited number of new tribes initially raised no problems, precisely because it was presumably not voting rights in the people's assembly which would most benefit them. On the question of the number of new tribes (noting that Velleius gives eight, while Appian 1.49.214–15, cf. 53.231 could be interpreted as ten): Lewis 1968; Harris 1971: 236–50; Gabba 1994: 123.

The Latin communities remained loyal because their aristocracies had the citizenship and provided no leadership for their communities' demands for citizenship (Venusia was the only exception to Latin loyalty; perhaps, as at Fregellae, there had been a shift in the ethnic composition of the town: Gabba 1994; 115). In the Italian allied communities the aristocracies wanted the citizenship and led their communities into war against Rome in order to obtain this. See Salmon: 1958, 1962; Nagle 1973; Sherwin-White 1973: 134–49, 214–18; Scullard *GN* 65–8; Gabba 1994: 104–28; for allied aims and the background to their citizenship demands: Salmon 1962: 108–9; Badian 1969: 30; Sherwin-White 1973: 134–9, cf. 139–44; Gabba 1976: 74, 1994: 104–15; Brunt 1988a; Mouritsen 1998: 129–51. With Drusus' assassination, his proposal for the enfranchisement of the Italians came to nothing.

10.10 Secession

Livy *Periochae* 72

Livy lists those of the Italian allies who revolted; they fell into two main groups of peoples: the Marsi and the Samnites (see also docs 10.11–12; Salmon 1958; 159–61, 172–7 on the different lists of rebels in the sources). The rebels as a whole were from central and southern Italy. Missing from this list are the Latin allies: their aristocracies were already in possession of Roman citizenship, and their communities were to be awarded citizenship for both remaining loyal and fighting the Italian rebels. Etruria and Umbria also remained loyal (Harris 1971: 212–29). The war which ran from 91 to 89, the main confrontation being in 91–90, began in Asculum. Servilius was actually a praetor or propraetor who attempted to threaten the Asculans and so the revolt started prematurely (*MRR* II.20).

The commencement of the war was occasioned by the Picentes, when the proconsul Quintus Servilius was killed in the town of Asculum along with all the Roman citizens who were in the town. The Roman people adopted military dress.

10.11 Full-scale war

Appian *Civil Wars* 1.38–9 (169–77)

An Italian embassy to Rome was rebuffed: the last chance for peace was wasted (Gabba 1994: 115) and a significant number of allies rebelled.

169 When the Italians learnt of the murder of Drusus and of the pretext for banishing the others (for supporting the Italians), they considered that they could no longer endure that those bringing measures on their behalf should suffer in such a way, and, seeing no other chance of their acquiring the citizenship, they decided to rebel against the Romans and make war against them with all their power. **170** They sent envoys to each other in secret, formed a league, and exchanged hostages as a pledge of loyalty.

For a considerable time the Romans remained unaware of this because of their lawsuits and internal strife in Rome; when they did find out, they sent men around to the cities, who knew them well, to discover secretly what was happening. **171** One of these saw a youth from Asculum being taken as a hostage to another city and informed Servilius, who was proconsul in that region. **172** There were, it appears, at that time, magistrates governing parts of Italy as pro-consuls . . . **173** Servilius hastened to Asculum, and delivered a threatening speech to the people who were celebrating a festival, whereupon they, supposing that the plot had been discovered, killed him. Fonteius, his legate, was also killed (for this is what they call those of senatorial rank who accompany provincial governors as assistants). **174** With these killed, there was no mercy shown to any of the other Romans, and the people of Asculum fell on them all and stabbed them, and plundered their belongings.

175 Once the revolt had started, all the peoples bordering Asculum joined in — the Marsi, Paeligni, Vestini, and Marrucini, who were followed by the Picentes, Frentani, Hirpini, Pompeiani, Venusini, Apulians, Lucanians and Samnites, peoples who had been hostile to Rome in earlier times, and all the other peoples between the River Liris (now, I think, the Liternus), and the end of the Adriatic, both maritime and inland. **176** They sent ambassadors to Rome to complain that, though they had helped the Romans in every way to build up their empire, they had not thought their helpers worthy of citizenship. The senate sternly replied that, if they repented of what they had done, they could send envoys, otherwise not. **177** In despair of any other remedy, they went on with their preparations; and, in addition to the soldiers stationed as garrisons at each city, there was a communal force amounting to some 100,000 cavalry and infantry. The Romans sent against them a force of equal size, made up of Roman citizens and of the Italian peoples who were still their allies.

10.12 The Italian constitution

Diodorus Siculus *Library of History* 37.2.4–7

The Italians' constitution was not a true federalist structure but rather a government modelled on Roman lines for the conduct of the war: Sherwin-White 1973: 137–8. Silver coins were issued. One of these that survives has Pompaedius Silo's name on it, with the reverse showing a sacrificial pig with four warriors on either side, obviously the rebels, swearing an oath over the pig. By minting such coins, which are on the same standard as the Roman silver denarius, the rebels challenged Rome's monopoly on the issuing of silver coinage (coins: Salmon 1958: 162–3; docs 10.29–31).

4 At war with the Romans were the Samnites, the Asculans, the Lucanians, the Picentes, the people of Nola, and other cities and nations; their most notable and largest city was Corfinium, recently established as the Italians' federal capital, where they had set up, among all the other things which strengthen a large city and government, a good-sized forum and a senate-house, and abundant supplies of everything needed for a war, including a large amount of money and a plentiful supply of provisions. **5** They also set up a joint senate of 500 men, from whom men worthy to rule the country and able to devise measures for the common safety would be selected, and they entrusted the management of the war to these, though they gave the senators full powers to make decisions. They ruled that two consuls and twelve praetors should be elected every year. **6** The men put into power as consuls were Quintus Pompaedius Silo, a Marsian by birth and the outstanding man of his nation, and secondly Gaius Aponius Motylus, of the Samnite race, who was also a man pre-eminent in reputation and achievements in his nation. They divided the whole of Italy into two parts, and assigned them as consular provinces and districts. **7** To Pompaedius they assigned the region from what is called Cercola to the Adriatic sea, the section towards the west and north, and granted him six praetors; the rest of Italy, that towards the east and south, they assigned to Gaius Motylus, providing him also with six praetors. When in this way they had organised their government skilfully, and for the most part in imitation of the long-standing Roman model, they then devoted themselves even more earnestly to the war which was to come, after naming their federal capital Italia (Italica).

BROTHERS-IN-ARMS

10.13 The Italians' grievances

Velleius Paterculus *Roman History* 2.15.1–2

Velleius succinctly states why the allies deserved citizenship: they fought for a state but had no share in its citizenship. Even though Velleius' ancestors fought on the Roman side (see doc. 10.18), he recognised that the allied cause was not unjust.

1 One hundred and twenty years ago, in the consulship of Lucius Caesar and Publius Rutilius (90 BC), the whole of Italy took up arms against the Romans. The revolt began with the people of Asculum, who had killed the praetor Servilius and his deputy Fonteius, and was next taken up by the Marsi and made its way into all districts of Italy. **2** The fate of the Italians was as cruel as their cause was just, for they were seeking citizenship in the state whose power they were defending by their arms: every year and in every war they were providing a double number of men, both of cavalry and of infantry, and yet were not admitted to citizen rights in the state which through them had reached so high a position that it was able to look down upon men of the same race and blood as foreigners and aliens.

10.14 The allies' aims

Cicero *Philippics* 12.27

Gnaeus Pompeius Strabo was consul in 89 BC and Cicero served under him in 90–89; see Sherwin-White 1973: 146. Cf. Plut. *Mar* 33.4: 'it is said that Poppaedius Silo, the leader of the Marsi (doc. 10.4), the most respected and influential of the enemy, said to Marius, "If you are a great general, Marius, come down and fight it out." Marius replied, "Well, if you are a great general, make me fight it out whether I want to or not"'; cf. Goldsworthy 1996: 145.

I can remember conferences with both the most bitter enemies and the most deeply rebellious citizens. The consul Gnaeus Pompeius, son of Sextus, held a conference in my presence, when I was a new recruit in his army, with the Marsian leader, Publius Vettius Scato, between the two camps. I recall the consul's brother, Sextus Pompeius, a learned and wise man, coming to this conference from Rome. Scato greeted him and asked, 'How shall I address you?' 'As a guest if I had the choice,' said Pompeius, 'but as an enemy by necessity.' It was a fair conference: no fear, no underlying suspicion, not even a lot of hatred. For the allies were not seeking to rob us of our state, but themselves to be received into it.

10.15 Heroic suicide at Asculum

Appian *Civil Wars* 1.48 (207–10)

Vidacilius, Lafrenius and Vettius had defeated Pompeius, but later Sulpicius defeated Lafrenius, who was killed in the battle; Lafrenius' troops fled to Asculum (see 10.11). Vidacilius then went to Asculum's assistance; the city was besieged by the Romans for some time and it fell in November 89 BC, after Vidacilius' suicide: he must have realised that the allied cause was lost: App. 1.47.204–6; Vell. 2.21.

207 Asculum was the home town of Vidacilius, and, fearing for its safety, he hurried there taking eight cohorts. . . . **208** he forced his way into the town through the middle of the enemy with what forces he could get, and reproached the citizens for their cowardice and disobedience. **209** As he gave up hope that the town could be saved, he killed all his enemies, who had been in conflict with him and who through jealousy had recently prevented the people from carrying out his orders; he then built a pyre in the temple, placed a couch on the fire, and held a feast with his friends. At the height of the drinking, he swallowed poison and, throwing himself onto the pyre, told his friends to set light to it. **210** So perished Vidacilius, a man who was proud to die for his country.

10.16 Inscriptions found on sling-shots

CIL I² 848, 857–61, 875, 877

(*ILLRP* 1089, 1092–4, 1099, 1100; *ROL* IV.212.) Lead sling-shots found at Corropoli (848) and Asculum, dated to 90–89 BC (see *CIL* I² 848–884). Pompeius is Pompeius Strabo, sent to besiege Asculum in 91, though he was first confined in Firmum by the Italian praetor Lafrenius. In 860 there is a pun on *pica* (magpie) and Picentes; woodpecker, *picus* (the bird connected with Picenum) may have been intended. In 877, the allusion is perhaps to the Samnite bull, stamped on coins struck by the Samnite leader Papius Mutilus.

848   (a) The Italians (b) Titus Lafrenius, praetor.
857   Hit Pompeius!
858   Bring safety for Pompeius (right to left).
859   For the Asculans!
860   Hit a magpie!
861   Runaways, you are doomed!
875   Evil's coming to you, evil one!
877   (a) Swallow the bull and go to hell! (b) But you'll vomit up the lot!

10.17 The senate learns the value of compromise

Appian *Civil Wars* 1.49 (211–15)

Umbria and Etruria, hearing of the scale of the revolt, were on the brink of joining. Rome found itself so short of troops that it enrolled freedmen, which it had not done even in the blackest days after Cannae (but see doc. 6.1). The Roman reliance on its allies for infantry and cavalry is made clear here (see doc. 10.13).

211 While these events were taking place on the Adriatic side of Italy, the inhabitants of Etruria and Umbria and other neighbouring peoples on the other side of Rome heard of them and were all roused to revolt. **212** The senate was afraid that they might be surrounded by war and unable to protect themselves, and garrisoned the coast from Cumae to the city with freedmen, who were then for the first time enrolled in the army because of the lack of troops. They also decreed that those of the Italians who had kept to their alliance should become citizens, which they practically all desired more than anything. **213** They sent the news round the Etruscans, who gladly accepted the citizenship. By this gift, the senate made the faithful more faithful, made sure of those who were indecisive, and undermined those at war through the hope of similar treatment. **214** The Romans did not enrol these new citizens in the 35 existing tribes, in case they outvoted the old citizens in the elections, but enrolled them in 10 new tribes, which voted last. **215** So it often happened that their vote was useless, since a majority was obtained from the 35 tribes that voted first. Either this was not noticed initially, or the Italians were pleased even with this, but when observed later it caused another political conflict.

10.18 The bitter outcomes of the conflict

Velleius Paterculus *Roman History* 2.15.3–16.4

Velleius stresses the roles of three Roman commanders in particular: Pompeius, Sulla, and Marius. Plutarch has Sulla and Marius on the verge of violent conflict before the outbreak of this war over the dedication by Bocchus, when named 'ally of the Romans', of a statue group at Rome showing Jugurtha surrendering to Sulla (Plut. *Mar.* 32.4–6, *Sulla* 6.1–2; Mackay 2000: 162–8). This may have annoyed Marius but it is an exaggeration to see a civil war between the two men postponed by the Social War. For details of the course of the Social War, see Appian and Diodorus (introduction above); Gabba 1994: 115–23. Marius' role in the Social War was initially much more limited than might have been expected given his previous consulships and successes; he had not recovered from the Saturninus affair and, despite the loss of two Roman consuls and the seriousness of the situation, Rome did not at first rely on Marius. The list of Roman legates (legati), appointed to the consuls for 90 (L. Julius Caesar and P. Rutilius Lupus) as given by Appian includes Gnaeus Pompey, Sulla, and Marius (App. 1.40.179; cf. *MRR* II.28–32). Marius served as legate under P. Rutilius Lupus (cos. 90); when Rutilius was killed, after having neglected Marius' advice, the senate appointed Marius and Q. Servilius Caepio to the command (*MRR* II.28); Poppaedius set a trap for Caepio and, when he was killed in an ambush, Marius was given full command of the consul's army. Sulla and Marius then together in a battle defeated the Marsi, who suffered 6,000 dead (Livy *Per.* 73–4; App. 1.43.191–46.203). Marius then gave up his command due to ill-health (*Mar.* 33.3); there is no need to dispute ill-health as the reason, contra Carey 1961: 52. Vell. 2.16.4 connects Marius with Sulla and Pompeius Strabo as the Roman commanders who defeated the allies. The link between Sulla and Marius in 90 BC should be noted. For Marius in the Social war: Carney 1961: 51–4; Evans 1994: 131; Sulla: see doc. 10.19; Gnaeus Pompeius: Seager 2002: 21–2.

Compare Velleius' list of Italian leaders with App. 1.40.181. Two are of particular interest: Papius Mutilus and Q. Poppaedius Silo, chosen as the two consuls of the new confederacy. Gaius Papius Mutilus, leader of the Samnite rebels, successfully invaded Campania. Attacking L. Julius Caesar (cos. 90) he was beaten by him in 90, and Sulla in 89 inflicted a comprehensive defeat on him. Wounded, he might have survived the Social War (App. 1.42, 1.51.224). Q. Poppaedius Silo (docs 10.4, 10.7, 10.29) led the Marsi rebels in northern Italy. He unsuccessfully tried to negotiate with Marius (Diod. 37.15.1–3). He had some military successes, with his killing of Caepio in 90 BC (App. 1.44; Livy *Per.* 73). In 89 BC one of the consuls of that year, L. Porcius Cato, with an ill-disciplined army, attacked the Marsi with some initial success but was defeated and killed by Poppaedius' forces (Livy *Per.* 75; App. 1.50.217; Vell. 2.16.4; Cato's army: Sisenna *HRR* I² 284 F52; Dio 31 F100; *MRR* II.32). Then, however, Cn. Pompeius Strabo defeated Poppaedius; he abandoned Corfinium and retook Bovianum for the Italians, but in 88 was defeated and killed by the army of Q. Caecilius Metellus Pius (Livy *Per.* 76; App. 1.53.230; Obsequens 56; Diod. 37.2.10–11, for the Italians' appeal for help to Mithridates). The Marsi were practically a spent force, and the war more or less over; for the Social War: Keaveney 1992a: 115–61. **2.16.3**: Q. Hortensius *Annals*: *HRR* II.9 F1.

15.3 The war wiped out more than 300,000 of the youth of Italy. The most distinguished Roman commanders in the war were Gnaeus Pompeius, father of Pompey the Great, Gaius Marius, whom I have already mentioned, Lucius Sulla, who had held the praetorship in the previous year, and Quintus Metellus, son of Metellus Numidicus... **16.1** The most celebrated Italian leaders were Silo Popaedius, Herius Asinius, Insteius Cato, Gaius Pontidius, Telesinus Pontius, Marius Egnatius, and Papius Mutilus. **2** Nor should I, through modesty, deprive my own family of glory, especially when I am recording the truth, for much is due to the memory of my great-grandfather, Minatius Magius of Aeculanum, grandson of Decius Magius leader of the Campanians, a man of great renown and loyalty, who showed such loyalty to the Romans in this war that, with a legion which he had himself enlisted among the Hirpini, he took Herculaneum along with Titus Didius, besieged Pompeii with Lucius Sulla, and occupied Compsa. **3** Others have recorded his services, but the longest and clearest account is that of Quintus Hortensius in his *Annals*. The Roman people made full repayment for his loyalty by a grant of citizenship to him and by making his sons praetors at a time when they only elected six. **4** So changeable and savage was the fortune of the Italian war that in two successive years two Roman consuls, Rutilius (Publius Rutilius Lupus, cos. 90) and then Cato Porcius (Lucius Porcius Cato, cos. 89), were killed by the enemy, the armies of the Roman people were routed in many places, and the Romans were compelled to adopt military dress and retain it for a long time. The Italians chose Corfinium as their capital and named it Italica. Then gradually the strength of the Romans was augmented by admitting to citizenship those who had not taken up arms or who had been quick to lay them down again, and Pompeius, Sulla, and Marius restored the wavering and sinking power of the Roman people.

THE EMERGENCE OF LUCIUS CORNELIUS SULLA

10.19 Sulla's victories, 89 BC

Livy *Periochae* 75

Cf. App. *BC* 1.50–2.216–25; *MRR* II.36; Keaveney 1982: 47–52. Sulla's victories against the allies ensured a consulship when he stood in 89 for 88 BC. Q. Pompeius Rufus (not to be confused with Gnaeus Pompeius Strabo (cos. 89 BC) who was the father of Pompey the Great) was also awarded a consulship for 88. Pompeius Rufus' son married Sulla's daughter.

The Romans were successful against the allies for a variety of reasons. The superior generalship of Pompeius Strabo and Sulla was crucial. That the Latins and many Italian communities remained loyal and supplied Rome with troops was also an important factor; troops also came from allies outside of Italy such as the Spanish horsemen to whom Pompeius Strabo awarded citizenship (doc. 10.23).

Lucius Cornelius Sulla, as legate, defeated the Samnites in battle and stormed two of their camps. Gnaeus Pompeius received the surrender of the Vestini . . . Lucius Sulla overcame the Hirpini, routed the Samnites in several battles and received the surrender of several peoples. After achievements rarely equalled by anyone else before becoming consul, Sulla set out for Rome to stand for the consulship.

10.20 Sulla receives his rewards, 88 BC

Velleius Paterculus *Roman History* 2.17.1–3

For Sulla's praetorship, see doc. 11.2.

1 With the Italian war ended for the most part, except for the remnants of revolt which continued at Nola, the Romans, who were exhausted, agreed to grant citizenship to the conquered and humiliated rather than giving it to them as a whole at a time when their own strength was still unimpaired. **2** Quintus Pompeius (Rufus) and Lucius Cornelius

Sulla entered upon the consulship, Sulla being a man who, up to the end of his victory, cannot be sufficiently praised, and who, after his victory, cannot be adequately censured. He was born from a noble family, the sixth in descent from Cornelius Rufinus who had been one of the famous leaders in the war against Pyrrhus, and, as his family's splendour had waned, for a long time he behaved as if he had no thought of standing for the consulship. **3** Then, after his praetorship, when he had gained renown in the Italian war, as he had earlier in his Gallic command under Marius in which he routed the most pre-eminent leaders of the enemy, he stood for the consulship, encouraged by his success, and was elected by the vote of almost all the citizens. But he did not achieve this honour until his forty-ninth year.

ITALIAN CITIZENSHIP

10.21 Rome makes the offer — at last!

Cicero *In Defence of Balbus* 21

Cf. Vell. 2.16.4 (doc. 10.18); App. *BC* 1.49.212–14; Livy *Per.* 80, 84. The lex Julia of October 90 offered full citizenship to all Latins, and to the allied communities, *municipia* (not individuals), that had not revolted, as well as to those who had surrendered (the *dediticii*) or were willing to do so within a given time. Two other laws were also part of the process (the lex Plautia Papiria (doc. 10.24), and the lex Calpurnia, more obscure in nature). The allied communities that continued fighting were finally enfranchised in 87 BC. By the end of 89 most of the Italians had surrendered, but the Samnites, Lucanians and Nola had not. Those of the Samnites still fighting in 87 refused citizenship

The question of distribution in the tribes was more difficult. The new citizens were restricted to a specific number of eight new tribes (doc. 10.26). This meant that, when voting took place in the tribal assembly (the comitia tributa, where voting took place by tribes), the influence of the new citizens was limited (cf. doc. 8.13: the deposition of Octavius in 133 occurred after 18 of the 35 tribes had voted). The Romans would thus safeguard the people's assembly from being swamped with new voters. How many of the new citizens realistically expected to vote is unclear, given their distance from Rome, but there were disputes over this tribal distribution: doc. 10.26.

Consequences: the enfranchisement of all the communities south of the Po river in Italy led to the romanisation of the peninsula; Italy north of the Po received Roman citizenship and was incorporated into Italy by 42 BC (Sherwin-White 1973: 159). Latin soon became the accepted language and, although many communities retained their ethnic identity in the short term, within two generations Italy was Roman. The citizenship was awarded to communities as a whole: citizens belonged to a particular *municipium* but were also citizens of Rome (Cic. *Laws* 2.2.5: Sherwin-White 154). The aristocracies of these communities entered into the political life of Rome. The wealthy new citizens, if they visited Rome, could vote in the comitia centuriata, where voting took place according to wealth classification, and here the Romans did not feel the danger of being swamped as they did in connection with the tribal assembly.

For the lex Julia and enfranchisement of the Latins and Italians: Taylor 1960: 101–17; Harris 1971: 230–6; Sherwin-White 150–3; Gabba 1976: 89–96, 1994: 123.

Finally came the Julian law, by which citizenship was given to allies and Latins, laying down that communities that had not ratified the offer should not have the citizenship. As a consequence, there was a serious dispute among the citizens of Heraclea and Naples, since a large proportion of the people in those two cities preferred to keep the freedom enjoyed under their treaty of alliance to Roman citizenship.

10.22 Franchise and constitution given to Tarentum (after 90 BC)

ILS 6086

(*CIL* I^2 590; *FIRA* i^2 18; Bruns 27; *ROL* IV.438–44; Sherwin-White 1973: 160, 359.) Following the grant of Roman citizenship by the lex Julia to the Italians not in arms in 90 (doc. 10.21), the municipium of Tarentum was granted this constitution (it may not have been immediately: spelling and style suggest a later date). It was engraved on a bronze tablet found at Tarentum. Curiae survived in Italian towns as voting units, when superseded at Rome (except in the curia curiata). The Board of Four consisted of the duoviri (Board of Two) and two aediles.

Ninth table of the law:

. . .] not shall he be allowed to be . . . nor shall anyo[ne] st[e]al by fraud or mis-[a]ppropriate any money, public, sacred or concerned with religion, belonging to that municipium, nor act in such a way whereby any of the above might ensue; nor shall he with evil intent lessen funds through mishandling public accounts or public fraud. Whoever should act thus, shall be fined four times the amount involv[ed], **5** and be condemned to pay that sum to the mu[n]icipium, and the demand and exaction of that sum shall be the responsibility of whoever shall be at that time a magistrate in the municipium.

The Board of Four including the aediles who shall be the first to serve under this law, whoever of them shall have come to Tarentum, shall, within the next twenty days after his first coming to Tarentum after the passing of this law, take steps to stand as surety for himself and present bondsmen and their estates (as sureties) to the Board of Four, **10** sufficient that any money, whether publi[c, sa]cred or concerned with religion, belonging to that municipium, which should come into his hands during his term of office, shall be properly secured to the municipium of Tarentum and he shall g[i]ve an account of that matter in whatever way the senate shall decide. And that member of the Board of Four to whom surety shall be given shall ac[c]ept it and shall have it recorded in the [p]ublic reco[rds] (tabulae); and whoever shall hold a public assembly (comitia) to propose for election the members of the Board of Two and a[ed]iles, **15** he shall, before a majority of the curiae shall return any of those who are seeking office at that assembly, accept bondsmen from the candidates sufficient that an[y] money, whether public, sacred or concerned with religion, belonging to that municipium, which should come [into] their hands during his term of office, shal[l be] prope[rl]y secured to the municipium of Tarentum and he shall give an accou[n]t of that matter **20** in whatever way the senate shall de[ci]de, and he shall have [i]t recorded in the public [reco]rds. With regard to those to [who]m [pub]lic busi[ness] in the m[unicipi]um shall be given by a vote of the senate, or who shall have performed public business, and who shall have [pai]d or exacted publi[c] money, he to whom that business shall have been given, or who has perform[ed] public business, or paid or exacted public money, shall give and present in good faith an account of that matter to the senate within the next ten d[ay]s **25** following the decisi[o]n of the senate of the municipium.

Anyone who is or shall be a decurion (member of the senate) of the municipium of Tarentum, or shall have voted [in] the senate in the municipium of Tarent[um], shall possess [in] good faith in the town of Tarentum or within the boundaries of that muni[cipium] a house (aedificium), which shall be roofed with not les[s] than 1,500 tiles. Whoever of the above who does not possess such a house of his own, **30** or who shall have bought a house or received one by formal purchase in such a way that he would fraudulently e[vade] this law, shall be condemned to pay the municipium of Tarentum money amounting to 5,000 sesterces for each year of the offence.

No one in the town which be[lo]ngs to that municipium shall take the roof off a house or dem[olish] or destroy one, unless he is going to restore it to a state no worse (than before) or unless by a vote of the senate. If anyone acts in opposition to this, he shall be condemned to pay the municipium **35** mon[e]y equa[l] in value to that of the house, and anyone [wh]o wish[e]s may bring an acti[on] for the payment of that sum. The magistrate who exacts the sum shall pay one-half into the [p]ublic treasury and spend one-half on the g[a]mes which he will put o[n] publicly during his term of office, or if he wishes to spend the money on a public monument to himself he shall be permitted, and shall be pe[rmitt]ed to do so at no liability (to penalty) to himself.

If any member of the Board of Four, whether a member of the Board of Two or an aedile, shall be minded publicly, for the sake of the municipium, **40** to make, lay, alter, build or pave within those boundaries belongi[ng] to that municipium, he shall be permitted to do so, provided that it shall be done without injury (to any person).

Anyone who does not owe money to the municipium of Tarent[um], and who is a citizen of the municipium and has not in the six years [p]revious to his wish to leave (the municipium) been a member of the Board of Two or a[edile, who wishes to leave the municipium of Tarentum, shall be permitted to do so at no liability (to penalty) to himself. . . .]

10.23 Spanish horsemen given citizenship under the lex Julia

ILS 8888

(*CIL* I² 709; *CIL* VI.37045; *Inscrip. Ital.* XIII.1 pp 85, 563; *ILLRP* 515; Diehl 267; *ROL* IV.272–4; *ARS* 60; Rawson 1978: no. 1; Gordon 1983: no. 15; see Sherwin-White 1973: 150; Mattingly 1975; Badian *FC* 257.) Gnaeus Pompeius Strabo (cos. 89) here grants citizenship to Spanish horsemen 'for valour'; the date is 17 November of either 90 or 89, while at Asculum (Picenum). This inscription was found on fragments of a bronze tablet at Rome and demonstrates that individual commanders could award citizenship for service in the field. A turma (squadron of horse) was one-tenth of an ala: first 30 and then 32 men. The Salluitan squadron was from Salduba, Spain (Iberia); from their names some of the Iberians were clearly partly romanised. Along with their names are those of 60 members of Pompeius Strabo's *consilium* (advisory council), including his son Pompey, Lepidus (cos. 78) and Catiline (Lucius Sergius, son of Lucius, of the tribe Tromentina).

According to Asconius 3, Pompeius Strabo also established colonies across the Po (Gallia Transpadana) in 89 by giving Latin rights to existing inhabitants, by which magistrates could acquire Roman citizenship (Taylor 1960: 123–31). Note too Marius' grant of citizenship to two cohorts of Camertes (doc. 9.27). Sextus Julius Caesar (cos. 91) sent his Numidian troops back to Africa because they were deserting, but he also had 10,000 infantry from Cisalpine Gaul (App. *BC* 1.42.188–9).

(a) GNAEUS POMPEIUS, SON OF SEXTUS, IMPERATOR, ON ACCOUNT OF THEIR VALOUR [made] Spanish horsemen [Roman] citizens [in cam]p at Asculum on 17 November according to the lex Julia. At the council (*consilium*)

[were] . . . Lucius Gellius, son of Lucius, of the Tromentine tribe, Gnaeus Octavius, son of Quintus . . . (there follows the names of some 60 staff officers).

(b)   THE SALLUITAN SQUADRON

(col. 1)	(col. 2)
Sanibelser, son of Adingibas	*Ilerdans*
Illurtibas, son of Bilustibas	Ootacilius, son of Suisetarten
Estopeles, son of Ordennas	Gnaeus Cornelius, son of Nesille
Tersinno, son of Austinco	Publius Fabius, son of Enasagin
(. . . others . . .)	*Begensians*
	Turtumelis, son of Atanscer
	Segiensians
	Sosinaden, son of Sosinasa
	(. . . others . . .)

(col. 4) Gnaeus Pompeius, son of Sextus, imperator, in camp at Asculum, presented the Salluitan squadron on account of their valour with a helmet horn, plate, collar, armlet, chest-plates, and a double ration of corn.

10.24 The Lex Plautia Papiria, 89 BC

Cicero In Defence of Archias 6–7

M. Plautius Silvanus and C. Papirius Carbo as tribunes in 89 passed the lex Plautia Papiria (MRR II.34), which gave citizenship to any individual who belonged to an Italian city which had a treaty with Rome, who was permanently resident in Italy, and reported himself to a praetor within 60 days of the passing of the law. It benefited those who belonged to communities which received citizenship under the lex Julia but who themselves were not living in their communities of origin when the lex Julia was passed. The poet Archias, a protégé of the Luculli, was attacked as a non-citizen by the Pompeians and defended by Cicero in 62. Although censors (L. Julius Caesar and P. Licinius Crassus) were appointed in 89, Cicero (11) states that in that year 'no census of any part of the population took place'. Progress at registering the new citizens was slow, but the census of 70–69 recorded some 900,000 citizens (see Brunt *IM* 94–9). For the lex Plautia Papiria: Taylor 1960: 101; Sherwin-White 1973: 152. The various states of Italy were transformed into *municipia*, and the municipium became the main political organisational unit of Roman Italy. Metellus Pius was praetor in 89: *MRR* II.33.

6 After a long period of time, after going to Sicily with Marcus Lucullus and returning with him from that province, Archias went to Heraclea; this city had been granted full civic privileges by the terms of its treaty with Rome and Archias wanted to be enrolled among its citizens. His own merits would have sufficiently recommended him, even without the prestige and influence there of Lucullus, and his request was granted by the people. **7** Roman citizenship was granted by the law of Silvanus and Carbo, which extended citizenship to 'all who have been registered in allied communities, if they were resident in Italy at the time of the passing of this law, and if they have reported themselves to the praetor within sixty days'. Archias had resided at Rome for many years, and had reported himself to the praetor Quintus Metellus, his great friend.

10.25 Sailors discharged with honour, 78 BC

CIL I² 588

(*ILLRP* 513; Bruns 176; *ARS* 71; *ROL* IV.444–50.) A decree of the senate in 78 BC concerning Asclepiades of Clazomenae, Polystratus of Carystus and Meniscus of Miletus in Asia Minor, on a bilingual tablet of bronze found at Rome. From the 'Italian War' on the three men had loyally served the Republic, and now these Greek naval captains from Asia Minor and Euboea are honourably discharged. The 'Italian War' is presumably the Social War (or possibly Sulla's war in Italy of 83–82: see Magie 1950: 236, 1113). The Romans are generous in granting various privileges to the men, ensuring that they suffer no material loss because of their absence, but not the right to vote: see esp. Marshall 1968. Roman citizenship, despite its extension to Italy, was not about to be distributed more widely. The inscription is heavily restored from the Greek version and the restorations are not marked here.

In the consulship of Quintus Lutatius Catulus, son of Quintus, and Marcus Aemilius Lepidus, son of Quintus, grandson of Marcus, and the urban praetorship and praetorship 'for aliens' of Lucius Cornelius Sisenna (i.e., he was praetor urbanus and praetor peregrinus), son of . . . in the month of May.

Quintus Lutatius Catulus, son of Quintus, consul, consulted the senate in the meeting-place (the curia) on 22 May. Present as witnesses were Lucius Faberius, son of Lucius, of the Sergian tribe, Gaius . . . son of Lucius, of the Poblilian tribe, Quintus Petillius, son of Titus, of the Sergian tribe.

With regard to the matter on which Quintus Lutatius, son of Quintus, consul reported, that Asclepiades, son of Philinus, of Clazomenae, Polystratus, son of Polyarces, of Carystus, and Meniscus, son of Irenaeus, of Miletus, who had been known as Meniscus son of Thargelius, served on our ships as captains at the beginning of the Italic war, that they served our state valiantly and loyally, and that he wished them to be discharged to their homes by senatorial decree, should it seem right to the senate that such honour be accorded them in return for their successful campaigns and valiant deeds on behalf of our state: on this matter the senators resolved the following:

'That Asclepiades, son of Philinus, of Clazomenae, Polystratus, son of Polyarces, of Carystus, and Meniscus, son of Irenaeus, of Miletus, who had been known as Meniscus son of Thargelius, be called upright men and our friends; that the senate and Roman people considered that they had served our state valiantly and loyally; on account of which the senate resolved that they, their children, and their descendants be free and exempt from all things (i.e., dues) in their own countries; that if any taxes have been exacted from their properties after they had left in the service of our state, that these be returned and restored to them, and, if any fields, houses or property of theirs have been sold after they left their homes in the service of our state, that all of these be restored in their entirety; and, if any deadline has expired after they left their homes in the service of our state, that that fact should not injure them, and that for that reason they should be owed no less, and that they shall be permitted no less to claim and exact such a debt, and they may have, possess and enjoy any inheritances which have come to them or their children; . . . .

That any judgements which have been made against them in their absence after they had left their homes shall be rendered void and judgements be made afresh in their entirety by decree of the senate. If their states publicly owe any moneys, they shall not be required to contribute towards these moneys. If any of our magistrates lease out Asia and Euboea, or impose tax on Asia or Euboea, they shall take care that these men shall not be required to pay anything. Also the consuls Quintus Lutatius and Marcus Aemilius, either or both as they should see fit, shall take care that they be entered in the official list of friends; and that they be permitted to erect a bronze tablet to Friendship on the Capitol and make a sacrifice; and that they instruct the city quaestor to send a gift according to official regulations and to make arrangements for their quarters and entertainment (as for foreign ambassadors). And that, if they should wish to send ambassadors about their affairs to the senate or to come as ambassadors, they, their children and their descendants shall be permitted to send ambassadors or come themselves. And that the consuls Quintus Lutatius and Marcus Aemilius, either or both as they should see fit, shall send a letter to our magistrates, who hold the provinces of Asia and Macedonia, and to their magistrates that the senate wishes and thinks right that these things be done in such as way as seems to them advantageous to our state and to their own dignity. Passed.

10.26 The dangers of pro-Italian legislation, 88 BC

Velleius Paterculus *Roman History* 2.20.2–3

For P. Sulpicius Rufus, tr. pl. 88, and his pro-Italian and pro-Marian legislation (such as the transfer of the Mithridatic command), see doc. 9.32. His proposal to distribute Italians among all the tribes caused riots from the existing citizens. Similarly the consul Cinna was driven out in 87 for the same reasons. The Italian rebels who did surrender (i.e., became *dediticii*) probably gained citizenship in 87 or perhaps 84, at the instigation of Cinna (Livy *Per.* 80, 84; App. *BC* 1.68.310; Licinianus 20–1), but some held out until 80 BC (see doc. 10.28).

2 Cinna was no more restrained than Marius or Sulpicius. Though the citizenship had been given to Italy in such a way that the new citizens were to be distributed among eight tribes so that their power and numbers might not weaken the position of the old citizens and the beneficiaries should not receive more power than the benefactors, Cinna promised to distribute them among all the tribes. For this purpose he had brought together into the city a vast crowd from all over Italy. **3** Because of this he was driven out by the strength of his colleague (Gnaeus Octavius) and the optimates and set out for Campania, while his consulship was taken away by the authority of the senate and Lucius Cornelius Merula, the flamen Dialis, was appointed in his place.

10.27 Cinna courts the Italians, 87 BC

Licinianus 20–1

Cinna and Marius took Rome in 87 and were proclaimed consuls for 86. Q. Caecilius Metellus Pius was attempting to crush the Samnite resistance; he recognised Cinna as consul, but, as a result of the Marian take-over, went into exile in Africa (App. *BC* 1.68.309, 80.365; Plut. *Mar.* 43.1; Diod. 38/39.2.1).

Legates were sent by Metellus to consult the senate about the attitude of the Samnites, who were refusing to make peace unless they and all deserters were granted citizenship and their property returned. The senate refused . . . when Cinna learnt of this through Flavius Fimbria he acceded to all their requests and added them to his troops . . . Citizenship was granted to all who had surrendered who had promised many thousands of soldiers, but who sent scarcely sixteen cohorts.

10.28 The dogged nature of Italian resistance, 82 BC

Velleius Paterculus *Roman History* 2.27.1–3

Most of the fighting in the Social War was over by 87 BC, and the Roman war against Mithridates proceeded despite the remnants of Italian opposition. When Cinna marched against Rome in 87 BC, the consuls recalled Q. Caecilius Metellus from fighting the Samnites in the last stages of the Social War: he would not agree to the Samnites' demands, but Cinna and Marius did (App. *BC* 1.68.309–12; Licinianus 23; Livy *Per*. 80; Badian 1958: 297). Sulla on his return from the east in 82 recognised the grants of citizenship to the Italian communities (Livy *Per*. 86), but the Samnites held out against Sulla, and a great battle was fought outside Rome at the Colline Gate. This defeat of the Samnite opposition to Rome in 82 BC was not the last and the Samnites held out at Nola until 80 BC (Licinianus 32); their defeat led to the incorporation of the Samnites into the Roman state, after centuries of opposition to Rome. Sulla and the Samnites: Salmon 1964, 1967: 340–87.

1 In the consulship of Carbo and Marius (the Younger), 109 years ago, Pontius Telesinus, a Samnite leader, who was brave in spirit and deeds and who deeply loathed the very name of Rome, collected about 40,000 of the bravest and most unyielding youth who still retained arms, and on 1 November fought with Sulla near the Colline Gate a battle which was so critical as to bring both Sulla and the city into the greatest danger. **2** Rome had not faced a greater danger when the camp of Hannibal was visible within the third milestone than on this day when Telesinus flew around the ranks of his army exclaiming that 'The Romans' last day is at hand!' and shouting that the city should be overthrown and destroyed, adding that, 'The wolves who stole Italian liberty will never disappear until the woods in which they are accustomed to take refuge are cut down!' **3** It was only after the first hour of the night that the Roman army was able to take breath and the enemy withdrew. On the next day Telesinus was found half-dead, with the expression rather of a conqueror than a dying man. His head was cut off and Sulla ordered it to be fixed on a spear and carried around Praeneste.

COINAGE IN THE SOCIAL WAR, 91–88 BC

No Roman coins specifically address the Social War. Coins of the allies were sometimes modelled on Roman coins, as in the case of the oath scenes, and have themes relating to the war. The allies minted on the Roman denarius standard, and paid their soldiers in it: they had been paid in denarii by the Roman authorities in their military service abroad (Harl *CRE* 50). The allies' coins had Latin legends as well as Oscan, the language of the southern belligerents. To meet the costs of paying Roman soldiers the Roman moneyers D. Silanus and L. Calpurnius Piso Frugi of 91–90 BC minted 'tens of millions' of denarii (Harl 50). With a quarter of a million of Italian and Roman soldiers mobilised, the coins were needed.

10.29 Allied soldiers swear an oath

Grueber II.323–324.10, 327, 329.

A denarius (Sydenham *CRR* 619–21, 634; Carson *PCRR* 124; Foss 22; *Historia Nummorum* 408). The coins discussed in docs 10.29–30 (*Historia Nummorum* 407 and 408) 'form the largest single block of the [allied] Social War coinage' (*Historia Nummorum* p. 55); Salmon 1958: 162–3; Crawford *CMRR* fig. 68. The allied soldiers swear an oath to the cause of allied liberty (the number eight could indicate the number of groups engaged in war against the Romans when the coin was minted or simply be used to fill up the coin; some coins with a similar scene have two, four or six soldiers). Grueber II.329 (Sydenham 634) has the name of the allied general Q. Silo (Q. Poppaedius Silo: docs 10.4, 10.7, 10.18) on the reverse, under the oath-taking scene. The name of the allied Samnite leader Gaius Papius Mutilus (docs 10.16, 18) appears on coins, some with a similar oath scene: Grueber II.330.31–333.42 (Sydenham 635–41).

Obverse: Head of the goddess Italia with wreath, facing left, with legend 'Italia' on right rim of coin.
Reverse: Eight warriors, four on either side of a pig which is held by an attendant; the eight warriors point their swords at the pig; behind the attendant, a standard.

10.30 Italian warrior and bull

Grueber II.327.19–329.30

A denarius (Sydenham *CRR* 627; Carson *PCRR* 128; Foss 24; Harl *CRE* 50, no. 39; *Historia Nummorum* 407). The bull stands for Italia and the allied cause: see coin at doc. 10.31; cf. Dench 1995: 212–15.

Obverse: Head of the goddess Italia.
Reverse: A standing warrior, with spear and sword, and reclining bull. Warrior's left foot is set upon a Roman standard.

10.31 The Italian bull gores the Roman wolf

Grueber II.327.18

A denarius (Sydenham *CRR* 628; Carson *PCRR* 125; Foss 26; *Historia Nummorum* 420). The god Bacchus was identified with the Italian deity Liber Pater.

Obverse: Head of the god Bacchus.
Reverse: A bull tramples a wolf, goring it with a horn; underneath, an Oscan inscription: Vitelliu (Italia).

11

Lucius Cornelius Sulla 'Felix'

Sulla first became prominent when he served with Marius in Africa in 107–105 (as quaestor in 107, then as proquaestor) and specifically when he arranged for the surrender of Jugurtha by Bocchus in 105 (docs 9.13, 11.50); his career until then had been unremarkable. His background was obscure and his family had not been prominent for some generations, though details concerning Sulla's poverty are probably exaggerated to highlight his subsequent rise to the position of Rome's most powerful man (docs 9.12, 11.1). He next worked with Marius in the northern campaigns in 104–103 (see Plut. *Sull.* 4, where the account of opposition between the two at this stage is clearly a later invention of Sulla's which Plutarch found in Sulla's *Memoirs*), and was obviously trusted by Marius on the strength of his African credentials. In fact it was only the issue of who was to hold the command against the King of Pontus, Mithridates, that led to the struggle between them, unless Plutarch's story about Marius' anger directed against Sulla on the occasion of King Bocchus' erection of a statue group showing Jugurtha being surrendered by Bocchus to Sulla is to be accepted (Plut. *Mar.* 32.4–6, *Sull.* 6.1–2). Little is known of Sulla's career in the 90s (doc. 11.2) but he was praetor in 93 and in 92 he was in Cilicia *pro consule*, and returned to Rome in time for the breaking out of the Social War, in which he played a prominent role in Campania and Samnium (docs 10.18–20). His election to the consulship for 88 BC would have been on the strength of these military successes.

The consulship brought with it the province of Asia and command against Mithridates, who was expanding his kingdom into Asia Minor, where at his instigation 80,000 Italians were massacred (doc. 11.4). At this point events took a turn that had serious ramifications — the tribune Sulpicius' agitation to have the newly enfranchised Italians distributed amongst all the tribes. In return for Marius' support for his enfranchisement proposal Sulpicius then had legislation passed that the command against Mithridates be transferred to Marius, who saw the war against Mithridates as 'an easy and very profitable' one (doc. 9.32). But so too did Sulla, who had left to join his army at Capua and who clearly saw this command as a crucial stage in his career. Marius obviously had not thought out the consequences of his attempt to take the command against Mithridates. After all, Marius had done the same to Metellus, depriving him of his command, and actually with Metellus in the field of operations (doc. 9.10).

In 88 BC, much depended on Sulla. And he decided — rightly or wrongly — that he was not going to be deprived of his command, and that the way to do this was to march upon Rome. His officers had some scruples but his soldiers (and his fellow consul) did not: the war promised plunder and they were worried Marius would use troops other than themselves (doc. 11.5). This march on Rome and its capture by a magistrate with imperium was extraordinary. The murder of a tribune, Sulpicius, and the mob-violence that followed were in themselves disastrous, but were not unprecedented (as in the cases of Tiberius and Gaius Gracchus, Drusus and Saturninus). Sulla introduced some political reforms and then set off for the east. Cinna, consul in 87, was driven from Rome by his fellow consul Octavius, deprived of office, and declared an enemy. Cinna decided not to accept this but raised an army, and was joined by Marius who, after initial fighting, had fled the city at Sulla's entry. With others he had been declared a public enemy, to be killed with impunity (doc. 9.33). Marius fought his way into the city, and the violence now rose to an unprecedented level as he settled old scores; he was elected for a seventh consulship for 86 (with Cinna, consul for the second time in 86, and consul again in 85 and 84) but died within a few days of taking office. There was now peace at Rome. But Sulla, despite being declared a *hostis* (and technically therefore without imperium), had gone to his province and commenced the war against Mithridates until arranging a peace treaty that enabled him to return to Rome in 83, after decisive victories at Chaeronea and Orchomenus in Greece (docs 11.7–10).

Cinna (cos. 87–84 BC) had unprecedented influence at Rome, but little is known of his policies. Significantly, the enfranchised Italians seem to have been finally distributed amongst all the tribes. When Valerius Flaccus was elected as consul in 86 BC to replace Marius and was sent out to Asia Minor (see doc. 11.7), he took an offer to Sulla that if he would submit to the senate he would cease to be a public enemy (Memnon *FGrH* 434 F24). Whether this was a senatorial initiative or simply a Cinnan one is unclear. Sulla dealt first with Mithridates, then with Fimbria who as legate led a mutiny against Flaccus in which the latter was killed and took over his army (doc. 11.8; there are two individuals called L. Valerius Flaccus' in this period: one took over Marius' consulship in 86 and was killed by Fimbria in Asia Minor, the other was the *princeps senatus* who led the senate in a policy of reconciliation towards Sulla and had been Marius' colleague in the his sixth consulship of 100).

Sulla, possibly in late 85, wrote to the senate reminding them of his past victories and his present successes against Mithridates, the fact that those exiled by Cinna had fled to him, and that he was returning to Rome to take vengeance (doc. 11.13). The princeps senatus (L. Valerius Flaccus) successfully proposed the sending of emissaries to Sulla, and the senate ordered Cinna and Carbo (consuls for 85) to stop recruiting an army until Sulla replied. Cinna and Carbo, however, declared themselves consuls again for 84 and Cinna raised an army against Sulla, but was murdered by his own troops; Carbo continued to oppose Sulla (doc. 11.12; App. *BC* 1.77).

Sulla returned to Italy. The consuls for 83 BC, C. Norbanus and L. Cornelius Scipio, were overcome, and many desertions took place to the Sullan camp; civil war broke out. The optimates largely supported Sulla and joined him, and amongst them were Crassus and Pompey (docs 11.14–15). The younger Marius and the Samnites held out, but were dealt with at Praeneste (doc. 9.34) and at the Battle of the Colline Gate (doc. 10.28). Sulla now turned his attention to Rome and his enemies, and there occurred the infamous proscriptions, in which hundreds — perhaps thousands — perished in addition to the thousands who had lost their lives in the civil war (docs 11.19–23). Sulla's reform programme of 88 was revived, with special attention paid to strengthening the senate and disempowering the tribunate which had challenged optimate control (docs 11.26–38). Sulla voluntarily laid down his dictatorship sometime in 80 BC, when he held his second consulship. With his death in 79 some ill-feeling was expressed about his reforms; though they survived his death, changes weakened their effect, and in 70 Crassus and Pompey, who had benefited under him, restored the tribunate (doc. 12.4). But his judicial and administrative reforms remained in force (docs 11.39–40).

Pompey first emerges at this point as an important figure, raising (as a private citizen: *privatus*) three legions for Sulla, and then being sent to deal with the Marians in Africa and Sicily. He managed to extract the concession of a triumph from Sulla, and ensured against the wishes of Lepidus that Sulla had a state funeral (docs 11.17–18, 44), but his political stance changed in the 70s.

Opinions concerning Sulla vary. Keaveney 1983: 195 can write, 'Sulla is a Roman magistrate legally elected who exercises his powers in accordance with the constraints his office places on him', while according to Ridley (2000: 211), 'by the extraordinary means of nomination by an interrex, Sulla was appointed to the even more extraordinarily monstrous office which he had created, a dictatorship the duration of which depended on his judgement or whim'. Badian's works tend to be very critical: Badian 1964 (cf. Balsdon 1965: 230–1), 1976, while Keaveney, especially 1982, is too apologetic. Recent works on aspects of the regime are more balanced: Dowling 2000; Mackay 2000. What is clear is that Sulla showed what was possible for a promagistrate invested with imperium and an army: this army returned with Sulla to Italy to do his bidding; 'his army was devoted to him, well-trained and immense, and elated by its successes' (App. *BC* 1.76.347'). In addition, for the first time, there had been a major civil war at Rome, as opposed to the civil dissensions and bloodshed centred around the tribunate.

Ancient sources: Appian 1.55–106.240–443, provides the basic narrative framework, and as for other periods, such as the Gracchi, is crucial given the loss of Livy, which survives for this period only in the form of summaries (*Periochae*).

Livy *Periochae* 77–90 preserves a chronological framework and important, though brief, details of the dictator's constitutional reforms. Sulla is in fact presented as preferring peace to civil war (doc. 11.14). Livy is decidedly anti-Marian; his criticisms of Sulla come with the capture of Rome and the proscriptions.

Plutarch's *Sulla* is unfortunately, but not surprisingly, almost totally lacking in detail about Sulla's constitutional reforms. But for details of the Mithridatic Wars, the overall narrative, and various other points, he is important. Other *Lives* provide details: *Marius* 10, 26, 35, 41, 45; *Pompey* 5–16; *Crassus* 6; *Caesar* 1. Plutarch has made use of Sulla's *Memoirs* and despite clear criticism of Sulla's proscriptions, his account with its hostile portrait of Sulpicius Rufus (*Sull*. 8) and Cinna and Carbo (*Sull*. 22.1) must owe something to Sulla's own narrative.

Cicero *pro Roscio Amerino* (esp. 2–3, 6, 125–6) delivered in Sulla's lifetime is an important source dealing with the proscriptions, but he was careful not to attack Sulla himself, arguing that abuses such as the confiscation of the elder Roscius' property were not countenanced by Sulla. Cicero in several works condemns the confiscation of the property of the proscribed, but is less concerned with the proscriptions themselves, for he too, in 63 BC, put men to death without a trial; see especially Dowling 2000: 306–13.

Sulla himself wrote his *Memoirs* (*Commentarii*: *HRR* I² 195–204), which were edited by L. Licinius Lucullus (cos. 74). Lucullus was the only officer, as quaestor in Sulla's army, to support Sulla's march on Rome in 88 (*MRR* II.52n.5 with Appian 253: doc. 11.5). The memoirs have not survived but Plutarch refers to them, and his sources and those of Appian will have made use of them. In these memoirs, Sulla denigrated Marius' achievements against the Cimbri, attributing the victory to himself (see also docs 9.23, 26). He emphasised his own *virtus* (courage) as a general and his *felicitas*, the good fortune bestowed upon him by the gods. For his memoirs and their propaganda value: Ramage 1991: 95–9.

Also important was the history (*Historiae*) written by L. Cornelius Sisenna (praetor 78) and used by Appian and Livy. Sisenna's account focussed on the Social War and Sullan period (see *HRR* I² 276–97), and his history probably commenced where that of Sempronius Asellio ended; Sallust seems then to have started his writing from the end of Sisenna's history. Sallust refers to Sisenna's work and appears to criticise Sisenna for not being critical enough of Sulla (*BJ* 95); see Rawson 1991.

Sallust presents Sulla as possessing the various qualities of a good soldier in the Jugurthine War, but views him as cruel and tyrannical in his dictatorship; for Sallust, his dictatorship is the beginning of the final collapse of the Republic, which for Sallust had begun with the sack of Carthage in 146 BC: Sall. *Cat.* 5, *BJ* 95–6 (doc. 9.12), *Hist.* 1.34–53.

In addition, there are Licinianus and the fragments of Diodorus 38–39. Consult also the list of sources at *CAH*¹ IX.920–21 (cf. 883), including several references to relevant passages in Cicero.

The main modern bibliography for Sulla is Keaveney's 1982 monograph; see also: Last & Gardner 1932; Munro 1932; Smith 1955: 95–107; Badian *FC* 228–51, 1964, 1969: 34–9, 1976; Baker 1967; Stockton 1966; Brunt 1971: 104–11; Scullard *GN* 61–84; Meier 1995: 74–100; Seager 1994; Shotter 1994: 38–50.

11.1 Sulla as a young man about town

Plutarch *Life of Sulla* 1.1–2.8

Cf. Sallust's description: doc. 9.12. Sulla's consular ancestor was P. Cornelius Rufinus, who had in fact been consul twice (290, 277 BC: *MRR* I.183–4, 194), and dictator; this was the height of the family's fortunes until Sulla himself. A coin (denarius) of the moneyer Q. Pompeius Rufus (2), in the 50s BC, shows a portrait of each of his grandfathers: Sulla, his maternal grandfather on the obverse, and his paternal grandfather Q. Pompeius Rufus (1), consul with Sulla in 88 BC (*MRR* II.39–40), on the reverse; each is identified with an inscription (*Sulla cos.*, *Rufus cos.*). Both portraits look alike and represent Sulla and Pompeius as typical Roman nobles: aquiline nose, prominent Adam's apple, tufted hair, and vertical curved lines in their cheeks (Grueber I.3883; Sydenham *CRR* 908; Crawford *RRC* 434.1 (54 BC); Carson *PCRR* 194; Harlan *RRM* 9.1–2 (58 BC)). Another denarius minted by Pompeius Rufus (2) has Sulla's and Pompeius' curule chairs as consuls depicted on either side of the coin (Grueber I.3885; Sydenham *CRR* 909; Crawford *RRC* 434.2; Harlan *RRM* 9.1–2; Jones 1990: 283–4). Family: Badian 1976: 37–8; Keaveney 1982: 6–8; Reams 1984; Hillard 1991. For statues of Sulla: see docs 11.31, 11.48. Sulla when he died was still in love with Metrobius the actor (doc. 11.39; cf. docs 7.57–61).

1.1 Lucius Cornelius Sulla came of a patrician, or as one might say, noble family. It is said that one of his ancestors, Rufinus, held the consulship, though his disgrace is better known than his holding this honour. For it was discovered that he had obtained more than ten pounds of silver plate, which was against the law, and for this reason he was expelled from the senate. **2** After him the family continued in its lowly position and Sulla's own family was poor. . . .

7 This is what is recorded of Sulla's fortunes in his youth. **2.1** What his personal appearance was like can be seen from his statues, but his facial complexion made the terribly sharp and dominating blueness of his eyes even more formidable, **2** for the pale skin was blotched here and there with angry patches of red; it was because of this, it is said, that he got his name describing his skin, and one of those insulting him at Athens made up a mocking verse which went: 'Sulla is a mulberry sprinkled with barley.'

3 It is not out of place to use this kind of evidence for Sulla, whom they say was by nature a lover of jokes, as a result of which, while he was still young and unknown, he used to spend his time living dissolutely with actors and comedians, **4** and, when he held supreme power, collected around him the most outrageous personages of stage and theatre, with whom he would drink and crack jokes all day, so that he appeared to be acting in a manner very ill-suited to his age and lowered the reputation of his magistracy by dismissing those who wanted his attention . . . **6** He was in love with Metrobius, an actor, while he was still young, and remained so. **7** Another experience of his was when he began by falling in love with a well-off prostitute called Nicopolis, who, as she got used to his society and to the charm he had as a youth, ended up falling in love with him and left him as her heir at her death. **8** He also inherited from his step-mother, who loved him as though he were her own son; and from these legacies he was moderately well-off.

11.2 Sulla's political career after Numidia and Gaul

Plutarch *Life of Sulla* 5.1–4

Sulla's political career actually took a long time to develop. He did not become consul until he was 48 or 49 years of age, and on the strength of his Social War victories (not 'suo anno'). Sulla had been unsuccessful in standing for the praetorship in 98 BC, but through bribery succeeded in becoming praetor urbanus in 93, not having held the aedileship. In 92 he was in Cilicia *pro consule* (with the military powers of consul; Keaveney 1995). On his return the incident over Bocchus' dedication of statues supposedly occurred (see doc. 10.18). Sulla was then involved in the Social War; for his career before his consulship of 88: *MRR* II.14, 18; Badian 1976: 40–5; Sumner 1978; Keaveney 1982: 6–55; Brennan 1992.

1 Sulla, thinking that his reputation in war should serve him well in politics, left the army and went straight into public life, but when he stood as a candidate for the praetorship he was proved wrong. **2** He assigns the reason for this to the plebs; for he says that they knew of his friendship with Bocchus and looked forward, if he served as aedile before becoming praetor, to some splendid hunts and wild animal combats from Libya and so they appointed other candidates as praetors to force him to become aedile. **3** It appears, however, from later events that Sulla is not giving the real reason for his failure. **4** For in the next year he achieved the praetorship after winning over the people, partly by flattery and partly also by money.

MITHRIDATES VI OF PONTUS

Mithridates VI (also spelt as Mithradates) was king of Pontus (120–63 BC), and an enemy of Rome for the forty years before his death. Pontus takes its name from the Black Sea (Pontus Euxinus), and its territory consisted of the southern coast (map at Hind 1994: 134, cf. 129–40). After murdering his mother and brother, Mithridates effected the conquest of the Crimea and northern shore of the Black Sea, and conquered Cappadocia and Bithynia while Rome was engaged in the Social War. In Asia, he conquered the Greek cities and massacred the Italian residents (doc. 11.4). Greece, in particular Athens, came over to him. Defeated but not destroyed by Sulla, who was anxious to return home upon Cinna's death in 84, Mithridates engaged the Romans in a further two wars, being finally dealt with by Pompey. For Rome's wars against him: Appian *BC* 1.76.347, *Mithr.*; Plut. *Sull.* 11–21; Cic. *Flacc.* 57–61, *Mur.* 31–4, *Man.* esp. 4–13; Hind 1994: 130; for Mithridates: Lintott 1976; Scullard *GN* 72–6; Sherwin-White 1977a: 70–5; McGing 1986; Hind 1994.

11.3 Mithridates

Appian Mithridatic Wars 20–1 (76–81)

See also Livy *Per.* 77–8. Mithridates and Tigranes, king of Armenia, had divided Cappadocia between them, but the senate sent Sulla to Cilicia to put Ariobarzanes I on the throne (Badian 1964a; Ariobarzanes: Sherwin-White 1977; Sullivan 1980: 125–68). In 91 BC Mithridates conquered Bithynia, driving out Nicomedes IV, who had previously been an ally of Rome, and Tigranes drove Ariobarzanes out of Cappadocia. Manius Aquillius (cos. 101, with Marius) restored Nicomedes and Ariobarzanes in 90 BC and Mithridates and Tigranes withdrew. Aquillius had Nicomedes attack Mithridates, who unsuccessfully protested; Mithridates retaliated by deposing Ariobarzanes (again), sparking off the First Mithridatic War (89–85), and capturing and killing Aquillius: Hind 1994: 143–4.

76 After having conquered the whole kingdom of Nicomedes by this one assault, Mithridates took it over and organised the cities. He then invaded Phrygia, and stayed at the inn where Alexander had lodged, thinking it a good omen that Mithridates should be quartered where once Alexander had stayed. **77** He then overran the rest of Phrygia, as well as Mysia and the areas of Asia which the Romans had recently acquired, sending his officers to the neighbouring provinces and subjugating Lycia, Pamphylia and the country as far as Ionia . . . **80** Shortly afterwards he captured Manius Aquillius, who was primarily responsible for this embassy and the war, and led him around bound on a donkey, proclaiming to all who saw him that he was Manius, and finally poured molten gold down his mouth at Pergamum, as a criticism of the Roman's taking of bribes. **81** He appointed satraps over the different peoples and proceeded to Magnesia, Ephesus and Mitylene, all of which gladly welcomed him, while the Ephesians destroyed their Roman statues, for which they were punished not long afterwards.

11.4 The First Mithridatic War: massacre in Asia, 88 BC

Appian *Mithridatic Wars* 22–3 (85–7, 91–2)

Mithridates aimed at extending his empire, and the conquest of the Greek cities of Asia Minor and his invasion of Greece points to great ambition and perhaps the desire to create a hellenistic-style kingdom. 80,000 Italians were supposedly killed in Asia Minor in 88. The Greek cities were ready to go over to Mithridates presumably due to the tax-collecting activities of the publicani: Keaveney 1982: 78–9; Mithridates' conquest of Asia: Hind 1994: 144–9.

85 The conflict in Rome delayed Sulla for some time, as I have written in my *Civil Wars*; in the meantime Mithridates built a large number of ships to attack Rhodes, and wrote in secret to all satraps and city governors that, on the thirtieth day, they should all attack the Romans and Italians in their towns, the men, their women and children and their freedmen of Italian birth, kill them and throw out their bodies unburied, and share their possessions with King Mithridates. **86** He proclaimed punishment to anyone who buried them or concealed them, and rewards to informers and those who killed anyone in hiding, as well as freedom to slaves who did this to their masters, and remission of half their debt to debtors who did this to their creditors. **87** These orders Mithridates sent in secret to all the cities at the same time . . .

91 These were the dreadful fates met by the Italians and Romans in Asia, men, children and women all together, and their freedmen and slaves who were of Italian blood. From this it was extremely clear that the actions of the inhabitants of Asia were motivated not only by fear of Mithridates, but also by hatred of the Romans. **92** But they paid a double penalty, at the hands of Mithridates himself, who not long afterwards broke his word and ill-treated them, and later at the hands of Cornelius Sulla.

THE ORIGINS OF THE CIVIL WAR

11.5 Sulla is robbed (almost) of his great chance

Appian *Civil Wars* 1.57–9 (250–3, 258–68)

This passage follows on from doc. 9.32. Sulla did not accept the deprivation of his command. He fled from Rome, going to Nola, where his army was preparing to cross to Asia for the war against Mithridates; he proceeded to march on Rome, the first Roman to do so. It is important to note that his senior officers deserted him: they would not march on the city (his quaestor and relative L. Licinius Lucullus was the only exception), though he was joined by the other consul Q. Pompeius Rufus. With six legions he quickly overcame the unprepared Marius and Sulpicius; Sulpicius' measures were annulled because they had been passed by violence (App. *BC* 1.59.268, Cic. *Phil.* 8.7), and he was murdered; Marius fled. Sulla's soldiers had followed him, bound first to him rather than to the state: the first-fruits of the Marian army reforms and the recruitment of the *proletarii* had come to fruition (Badian 1976: 48). Support for Sulla's actions in the city was non-existent: he had done the unthinkable by marching on Rome itself.

He then introduced several reforms. The Italians were no longer distributed amongst all the tribes (which explains the Italian opposition in 83–82 to Sulla at Praeneste and elsewhere), no proposal was to go before the people before it had been to the senate, voting was not to be by tribes but by centuries in the comitia centuriata, so giving voting power — as Appian noted — to the wealthy and conservatives. Three hundred men were enrolled in the senate as its numbers had become depleted (App. *BC* 1.59.242–5): the overall thrust was to restore the senate as opposed to the people. This legislation was all annulled when Sulla left Rome, but foreshadowed that when he was dictator.

Cinna was elected as consul for 87, probably not to Sulla's liking; he swore an oath to support Sulla, but once Sulla had left Rome he instigated a prosecution through the tribune M. Virgilius; Sulla nevertheless left Italy and did not submit to a trial (Plut *Sull.* 10.6–8; Dio F102.1; Katz 1976: 546–9; for the election of 88 for 87: Katz 1976). Marius returned in an orgy of revenge after Sulla had gone to the east (doc. 9.34); Sulla (but not yet his army) was voted a public enemy, a *hostis* (App. *BC* 1.73.340).

For Sulla's march on Rome and his constitutional measures of 88: Carney 1961: 54–6; Katz 1975; Levick 1982; Keaveney 1982: 56–77, 1983a: 71–4; Seager 1994: 172–3; for Sulpicius, esp. Badian *FC* 230–6.

250 When Sulla learnt this, he resolved that the matter should be decided by war and summoned his army to an assembly. The army was eager for the campaign against Mithridates, because it would be profitable, and they thought that Marius would enlist for it other soldiers than themselves. **251** Sulla spoke of the way he had been insulted by Sulpicius and Marius, and, without clearly alluding to anything else (for he did not as yet dare to mention this kind of war), he urged them to be ready to carry out his orders. **252** They understood what he meant, and, as they were afraid on their own account in case they should lose the chance to go on the campaign, they laid bare Sulla's intention and told him to lead them to Rome with all confidence. **253** Sulla was delighted and took six legions there straightaway. All his senior officers, however, except one quaestor, fled to the city, because they could not undertake to lead an army against their country; envoys who met him on the road asked him why he was marching with armed forces against his country. His reply was: 'To liberate her from her tyrants.'. . .

258 Marius and Sulpicius went to meet them (Sulla and Pompeius Rufus, the consuls) near the Esquiline forum with as many men as they had been able to arm. **259** And here a battle took place between the enemies, the first in Rome no longer under a factional banner, but unambiguously under trumpets and standards according to the rules of war; to such a degree of evil had the irresponsibility of factionalism now progressed . . . **261** Sulla called for fresh troops from his camp and sent others around by the Suburran road to outflank the enemy in the rear. **262** The Marians fought feebly against the new arrivals and, fearing that they might be surrounded, summoned the other citizens who were still fighting from their houses and proclaimed freedom to the slaves if they would share their dangers. **263** When no one came forward they despaired and fled at once from the city, along with the nobles who had co-operated with them. . . .

265 At dawn Sulla and Pompeius summoned the people to an assembly and lamented over the government's having so long been in the hands of demagogues, stating that what they had done had been out of necessity. **266** They proposed that nothing should be brought before the people which had not already been discussed by the senate, as had been done in earlier times but long since abandoned, and that voting should be not by tribes but by centuries, as King Tullius had laid down, thinking that through these two measures, with no law being brought before the people until it had gone to the senate and voting not being in the hands of the poor and audacious but rather in those of the wealthy and prudent, no opportunity would be given for sedition to arise. **267** They diminished the power of the tribunes in many other ways, as it had become extremely tyrannical, and enrolled all at once 300 of the best citizens into the senate, which had been reduced to a very small number and become despised for that reason. **268** All the measures enacted by Sulpicius after the vacation from business had been proclaimed by the consuls were cancelled as not legal.

SULLA AND MITHRIDATES

See Appian *Mithr.* 22–63.83–263; Livy *Per.* 78, 81–3; Plut. *Sull.* 11–25. Sulla arrived in Greece in 87 BC, with five legions. Mithridates' general Archelaus had taken most of central Greece. Sulla sailed from Italy to Epirus, and marched to Athens, which he besieged but mercifully spared in 86 BC. In two battles in Greece, in 86 at Chaeronea and Orchomenus, Sulla defeated Archelaus. Going to Asia Minor, he made peace with Mithridates, in order to return to Rome now that Cinna was dead (84 BC), instead of destroying Mithridates' power. Keaveney 1982: 105 (who takes a favourable attitude to Sulla) argues, however, that Sulla made peace because he was aware of the extent of Mithridates' resources and wanted to avoid a costly war for Rome. Mithridates' campaigns in Asia and Greece: Rostovtzeff 1932: 234–54; Hind 1994: 149–61; Sulla's campaign: Keaveney 1982: 80–109; Rostovtzeff 244–54.

11.6 Dedication to Sulla, 87 BC

CIL I² 712

(*ILLRP* 350; *ROL* IV.136.) On the pedestal of a statue at Delos, dated to 87 BC. This inscription recognises Sulla as proconsul, which as a *hostis* he technically was not. The collegia are presumably business corporations, perhaps connected with the slave-trade of which Delos was an important centre (cf. doc. 6.13), prior to its being sacked in 88 BC by one of Mithridates' generals.

Lucius Cornelius Sulla, son of Lucius, proconsul. From the money which the collegia contributed by general subscription.

11.7 Sulla's victories in Greece

Livy *Periochae* 81–3

Lucius Valerius Flaccus replaced Marius as consul upon his death in 86. He was given Asia as his province and the command against Mithridates, but was killed by his legate Gaius Flavius Fimbria in 85 (*MRR* II.53, 59; Cinna accepted Fimbria as commander). Fimbria played a major role in dealing with Mithridates, winning several battles, and finally a great victory over four generals at the river Rhyndacus. His success might have continued, but Sulla, hearing of Cinna's murder in 84 (Livy *Per.* 83 (doc. 11.12); Plut. *Pomp.* 5.1–3; App. *BC* 1.78.355–8), was eager for a peace. After Rhyndacus, Mithridates' son fled to his father at Pergamum, with Fimbria in pursuit, and Mithridates fled to the nearby port of Pitane, where Fimbria besieged him. But although Lucullus had a fleet nearby he refused to help, and Mithridates escaped, soon to conclude a peace with Sulla.

81 Lucius Sulla besieged Athens (87 BC), which Archelaus, Mithridates' commander, had occupied, and captured it after great difficulty (86 BC), leaving the town its liberty and property. Magnesia, the only city in Asia which had remained loyal, was defended against Mithridates with the greatest courage . . . **82** (86 BC) Sulla defeated in battle the king's forces, which had seized Macedonia and entered Thessaly, with 100,000 of the enemy killed and their camp captured as well. When the war then recommenced, he again routed and destroyed the king's army. Archelaus surrendered himself and the royal fleet to Sulla. Lucius Valerius Flaccus, the consul, Cinna's colleague, was sent to replace Sulla, but, hated by his army because of his greed, he was killed by his own legate Gaius Fimbria, a man of the utmost daring, and his command transferred to Fimbria. The storming of cities in Asia by Mithridates and the brutal plundering of the province . . . is also narrated. **83** Flavius Fimbria routed in battle several of Mithridates' commanders and captured the city of Pergamum, all but capturing the king during the siege. He stormed the city of Ilium, which was waiting to hand itself over to Sulla, destroyed it, and recovered a large part of Asia . . . After crossing to Asia, Sulla made peace with Mithridates on condition that he evacuate the following provinces — Asia, Bithynia, and Cappadocia. Fimbria was abandoned by his army, which crossed to Sulla; he stabbed himself, and offered his throat to his slave telling him to kill him.

11.8 Sulla makes terms with Mithridates — and the province

Plutarch *Life of Sulla* 22.8–25.5

After his successes against Archelaus in Greece, Sulla concluded the 'Peace of Dardanus' with Mithridates in 85 BC, named after their meeting-place near Troy. Sulla's own troops were disappointed at the peace with Mithridates, hoping for plunder. He then attacked Fimbria, whom he clearly saw as a rival and enemy, arguing that Flaccus' army, which Fimbria had taken over, was intended to be used against him. But a fragment of Memnon of Heraclea in the Pontus, writing a history of Heraclea in the second century AD, preserves the detail that the senate in dispatching the army wanted Sulla to co-operate with Flaccus or to defeat Mithridates first (*FGrH* 434 F24; Badian 1964: 224). Peace terms: Keaveney 1982: 103–5; Hind 1994: 161–2. For Fimbria: Livy *Per.* 83; App. *Mithr.* 59–60.241–9; Plut. *Sull.* 24.7–25.3, *Luc.* 3; Vell. 2.24.1; Diod. 38/39.8.1–4; Dio F104; Rostovtzeff 1932: 256–9; Lintott 1971; Hind 1994: 160.

22.8 After this Archelaus (Mithridates' general) knelt down and begged Sulla to put an end to the war and to make peace with Mithridates. **9** Sulla granted his request and the terms were that Mithridates was to give up Asia and Paphlagonia, restore Bithynia to Nicomedes and Cappadocia to Ariobarzanes, pay the Romans 2,000 talents and give them 70 bronze-armoured ships together with their equipment; **10** Sulla was to guarantee to Mithridates the rest of his empire and have him voted an ally of Rome. (Mithridates tries to renege on the terms, but is concerned about Fimbria, who after killing Flaccus marches against him) . . .

24.7 Sulla realised that his soldiers were aggrieved at the cessation of hostilities (for they considered it dreadful that they should see this most hostile of kings, who had had 150,000 Romans in Asia massacred on the same day, sailing away with the wealth and spoils of Asia, which he had continuously plundered and taxed for four years). He defended himself to them by saying that, if Fimbria and Mithridates had both joined forces, he could not possibly have fought them together. . . . **25.1** He set out from there against Fimbria who was encamped near Thyateira, and, after making camp nearby, started encircling his camp with a ditch. **2** But Fimbria's soldiers came out from their camp unarmed, welcomed Sulla's men and willingly helped them out with their work. **3** Fimbria saw them changing sides and, fearing that Sulla would not be open to reconciliation, he committed suicide in his camp.

4 Sulla now imposed on Asia as a whole a penalty of 20,000 talents, while he ruined private families by the brutal behaviour and arrogance of the troops quartered on them. **5** Orders were given that every host should give his lodger four tetradrachms a day and should provide an evening meal for him and as many friends as he liked to invite, while an officer should receive fifty drachmas a day and two suits of clothes, one to wear at home and one to wear to the forum.

11.9 Sulla's punishes the provincials of Asia

Appian *Mithridatic Wars* 61–3 (250–2, 259–61)

The misery of the Greek cities which had led most of them to welcome Mithridates now resumed with the Sullan arrangements for the province.

250 After having settled Asia, Sulla granted freedom to the Ilians, Chians, Lycians, Rhodians, Magnesia and some others, either rewarding them for their allegiance, or compensating for what they had suffered from their goodwill towards him, and inscribed them as friends of the Romans, sending his army around to all the rest. **251** He also proclaimed that slaves, to whom Mithridates had given freedom, were to return immediately to their masters. As many disobeyed, and some cities revolted, there were numerous massacres of both free men and slaves on various excuses, the walls of many towns were razed, they were plundered and their inhabitants enslaved. . . . **252** After this a proclamation was circulated that the high-ranking citizens from each city were to meet Sulla at Ephesus on a stated day. When they had assembled, he addressed them from the platform as follows: . . .

259 To spare even now the Greek race, name and reputation throughout Asia, and for the sake of the good name which is so dear to the Romans, I will only impose on you five years' of taxes to be paid immediately, together with whatever the war has cost me, and anything else to be spent in restoring the province. **260** I will assign these to each of you city by city and will lay down the deadline for payments, and those who do not keep to this I will punish as enemies.

After this speech, Sulla divided up the fine between the envoys and sent men for the money. **261** The cities were desperate, and borrowed at high rates of interest, mortgaging to the lenders their theatres, gymnasia, walls, harbours and every piece of public property, under pressure from the soldiers who urged them on with insults. In this way the money was collected and brought to Sulla and Asia had nothing but misery.

11.10 The after-effects of Sulla's taxation of Asia

Plutarch *Life of Lucullus* 4.1, 20.1–6

In 84 BC, as proquaestor, Lucullus was responsible for carrying out Sulla's measures. As consul in 74 he acquired the command against Mithridates and once in Asia attempted to ameliorate Sulla's impositions. Plutarch (*Luc.* 23.1) records that the cities celebrated festivals called Lucullea to honour him. However, his organisation of Asia provoked hostility from those at Rome who had lost financially in the process and he was eventually superseded by Pompey (docs 12.10–11). For Lucullus in Asia, see Keaveney 1992: 75–128.

4.1 After peace had been made, Mithridates sailed away into the Black Sea, and Sulla fined Asia 20,000 talents, commissioning Lucullus to collect this money and coin it, and it seemed to the cities to be some abatement of Sulla's harshness when Lucullus showed himself not only honest and just, but even mild in his performance of so heavy and disagreeable a duty . . .

20.1 Lucullus now turned his attention to the cities in Asia, in order that, while he was at leisure from warfare, he might contribute in some way to justice and law, from a long lack of which unspeakable and incredible misfortunes gripped the province, which was ravaged and enslaved by the tax-gatherers and money-lenders, with families forced to sell their handsome sons and virgin daughters, and cities their votive offerings, pictures and sacred statues. **2** At last men had to surrender to their creditors and become their slaves, but what preceded this was far worse — tortures of rope, barriers, and horses, of standing under the open sky in the heat of summer, and in winter being thrust into mud or ice — so that slavery seemed in contrast to be a removal of burdens and peace. **3** Such were the evils which Lucullus found in the cities and in a short time he freed the oppressed from them all.

First he ordered that the rate of interest (per month) should be reckoned at 1 per cent and no more; secondly he cut off any interest that exceeded the principal; third and most important of all, he laid down that the lender should receive no more than the fourth part of his debtor's income, and any lender who added interest to principal lost the lot. As a result, in less than four years all debts were paid off, and the properties restored to their owners free of encumbrances. **4** This public debt arose from the 20,000 talents which Sulla had fined Asia; twice the amount had been paid back to the money-lenders, by whose reckoning of the interest the debt amounted to 120,000 talents. **5** These men consequently made an outcry against Lucullus at Rome as to the terrible hardships they had suffered, and bribed some of the tribunes to work against him, as they were men of great influence who had many politicians under obligations to them. **6** Lucullus, however, was not only beloved by the peoples whom he had well treated, but other provinces also longed to have him, and congratulated those who were lucky enough to have such a governor.

11.11 Lucullus in Asia

CIL I² 714

(*ILLRP* 362; *ROL* IV.134.) This inscription on two fragments of a statue pedestal was found at Delos, presumably dedicated by grateful businessmen.

[Lucius Licinius] Lucullus, [son of Lucius], proquaestor. Set up by the [Athe]nian p[eople], men from Italy, and Gree[k bu]sinessmen on the island.

EVENTS IN ROME

11.12 Waiting for Sulla, 85–84 BC

Livy *Periochae* 83–4

There was clearly a party in the senate that favoured an accommodation with Sulla; their spokesman was L. Valerius Flaccus, princeps senatus since 86 BC. Cn. Papirius Carbo (cos. 85, 84) had less authority in the senate and less overall power than the more ruthless Cinna, but he, along with the consuls for 83, L. Cornelius Scipio Asiaticus and Gaius Norbanus, rallied opposition to Sulla; Carbo was consul for a third time, with the younger Marius, in 82 BC. The younger Marius was possibly Marius' adopted son; he had not yet been praetor. The provision that all armies be disbanded was aimed against Sulla, whose power resided solely with his troops. Carbo was unable to rally the senate in unison against Sulla, and many joined Sulla on his return, because he represented the optimates, while the Marians were connected with the populares and the tribunician violence of Sulpicius. Pompey, Crassus, Q. Metellus Pius, and perhaps Cicero, were among those that joined Sulla.

The right to vote granted to new citizens referred to here (84) may mean that enfranchisement of the Italians was finally put into place, or that the new citizens were finally distributed throughout all 35 tribes. L. Valerius Flaccus became princeps senatus in 86 BC (he is not to be confused with the L. Valerius Flaccus murdered by Fimbria (above), or the L. Valerius Flaccus defended by Cicero) and had been consul with Marius in 100 BC. Flaccus was later to be instrumental in the appointment of Sulla as dictator, and was made his master of horse (magister equitum). The usual term for a dictatorship was six months.

83 When Lucius Cinna and Gnaeus Papirius Carbo, who had made themselves consuls for a two-year period, were preparing for war against Sulla, it was brought about by Lucius Valerius Flaccus, the princeps senatus, who made a speech in the senate, and by the others who were desirous of concord, that envoys be sent to Sulla to discuss peace. Cinna was killed (84 BC) by his own army, when he was trying to force it to embark to fight Sulla against its will. Carbo remained as sole consul . . .

84 Sulla replied to the envoys who had been sent by the senate that he would place himself in the power of the senate, if the citizens, who had taken refuge with him after being driven out by Cinna, were reinstated. Although this condition seemed just to the senate, Carbo and his party prevented it from taking effect as they thought war would be of more service to them. The same Carbo wished to demand hostages from all the towns and colonies in Italy, to compel their loyalty against Sulla, but this was prevented by a unanimous decision of the senate. By decree of the senate, the right to vote was granted to new citizens. Quintus Metellus Pius, who had taken the side of the optimates, started stirring up war in Africa, but was beaten by the praetor Gaius Fabius (84 BC), and a decree of the senate that all armies everywhere should be disbanded was passed due to the party of Carbo and the Marians. Freedmen were distributed through the 35 tribes. It also contains the preparations for the war which was being aroused against Sulla.

11.13 Sulla invades Italy, 83 BC

Appian *Civil Wars* 1.76–7, 79 (347–8, 350–1, 363)

Sulla's decision to march on Italy was partly determined by the murder of Cinna by his troops in 84; Cinna had dominated Roman politics since 87. This period, 87–84 BC, is known as the 'Cinnan period' (*Cinnanum tempus*). There was a reform of the coinage, perhaps reasserting the exchange rates of bronze and silver (the praetor Marius Gratidianus pre-empted his fellow praetor and the tribunes by issuing the edict in his own name (*MRR* II.57, 60); see also doc. 11.19 below for Gratidianus). There was peace in Italy (Cic. *Brut.* 308: 'three years without fighting', *triennium sine armis*), but the threat of Sulla's return hung over Rome. For Cinna, see Bennet 1923; Last & Gardner 1932: 264–9; Bulst 1964; Gruen 1968: 229–47; Frier 1971; Scullard *GN* 70–2; Seager 1994: 173–87; Lovano 2002.

In his letter to the senate, Sulla stressed his military achievements. The exiles who returned with him to Italy were displayed to great effect in Sulla's triumph, calling upon his as 'saviour' and 'father': Plut. *Sull.* 34.1–2.

347 Sulla now hurried on his return to deal with his enemies, having quickly put an end to the war with Mithridates, as I related earlier. In less than three years he had killed 160,000 men, recovered Greece, Macedonia, Ionia, Asia and many other nations for the Romans that Mithridates had seized, taken the king's fleet away from him, and from such a great area restricted him just to his ancestral kingdom. He returned with an army which was well-disposed to him, well-trained, immense, and inspired by his successes. **348** He commanded a vast number of ships, money, and equipment suited to all contingencies, and was an object of fear to his enemies: indeed Carbo and Cinna were so afraid of him that they sent throughout Italy to gather money, troops and supplies … **350** Sulla wrote spiritedly to the senate, relating what he had achieved in Libya against Jugurtha the Numidian while still a quaestor, and against the Cimbri as a legate, and as praetor in Cilicia, and as consul, boasting of his recent achievements against Mithridates and listing for them the many nations whom he had recovered en masse from Mithridates for the Romans. He particularly stressed that those who had been banished from Rome by Cinna had fled to him and that he had received them in their desperate condition and assisted them in their misfortunes. **351** In return for this, he said, his enemies had declared him a public enemy and razed his house and killed off his friends, and his wife and children had with difficulty escaped to him …

363 Bringing with him five legions of troops from Italy and 6,000 cavalry, together with other troops from the Peloponnese and Macedon, altogether some 40,000 men, Sulla sailed from the Piraeus to Patrae and from Patrae on to Brindisi (Brundisium) in 1,600 ships. The Brundisians received him without a fight, in return for which he later gave them exemption from taxation, which the town still enjoys.

11.14 Sulla's return welcomed

Livy *Periochae* 85

Clearly Sulla with his five legions was in a superior military position to the 'Marians' (a convenient term for the supporters of Marius, Cinna, and then Carbo and the younger Marius). As in the case of Cinna's murder, Sulla's military achievements were a decisive factor in encouraging desertions from his opponents. From Brundisium Sulla marched to Campania, where he defeated the consuls

C. Norbanus and L. Cornelius Scipio Asiaticus (83 BC), while in 82 Carbo and the younger Marius recruited in Etruria and Cisalpine Gaul. The decision to release Scipio may have been motivated by a desire to win some popular goodwill for Sulla.

Sulla crossed to Italy with his army and sent envoys to discuss peace terms. When these were treated with violence by the consul Gaius Norbanus, he conquered this same Norbanus in battle. And when he was about to assault the camp of the other consul, Lucius Scipio, with whom he had done everything possible to come to terms, but unsuccessfully, the consul's entire army, invited by soldiers sent by Sulla, carried their standards over to Sulla. Although Scipio might have been killed, he was released. Gnaeus Pompey (the Great: cos. 70, 55, 52), son of that Gnaeus Pompeius (Strabo: cos. 89) who had taken Asculum, enlisted an army of volunteers and came with three legions to Sulla, to whom all the nobles were making their way, and as a result of this migration to his camp Rome was deserted.

11.15 Sulla gathers his supporters

Appian *Civil Wars* 1.80 (365–8)

For the civil war between the Marians and Sulla (83–82 BC), see App. *BC* 1.84–94; Plut. *Sull.* 27–9; Diod. 38/39.6. Note Pompey's rise, recruiting as a private citizen and without authority from the state three entire legions from Picenum (recruitment of legions and early aid to Sulla: Keaveney 1982: 111–22; Badian *FC* 252–84; Seager 2002: 25–9). Pompey's father had been equivocal as to where he placed his loyalties, but eventually fought against Cinna and Marius, though he was negotiating with Cinna when his own death intervened. (Vell. 2.21.4 has Pompeius Strabo dying of disease; other sources of lightning: Last & Gardner 1932: 264 n.1; Hillard 1996.) Q. Caecilius Metellus Pius (praetor in 89), defeater of Poppaedius in the Social War, had gone to Africa after Cinna took charge of Rome. With Sulla's return to Italy, Metellus joined him and subdued northern Italy for the Sullan cause. He was rewarded with a consulship for 80 and the position of pontifex maximus. Crassus joined Sulla with an army of 2,500, probably including clients, raised in Spain, where he had been in hiding from the Marians (Plut. *Crass.* 6.1). For Sulla's supporters, see Keaveney 1984.

365 Caecilius Metellus Pius met him . . . and spontaneously offered himself as an ally along with the force he had with him, being still a proconsul — for those who have been selected for this rank retain it until they return to Rome. **366** After Metellus came Gnaeus Pompey, who not long after was called Magnus ('the Great'), the son of that Pompeius (Strabo) who had been killed by lightning and who was not considered to have been a friend of Sulla's, but the son removed this suspicion, arriving with a legion which he had collected in Picenum on the basis of his father's reputation, which was still high there. **367** Shortly afterwards he raised two more legions and became the most useful of all Sulla's lieutenants; consequently, though he was still very young, Sulla treated him with honour and he was the only man, they say, that Sulla rose to greet when he approached. **368** When the war was nearly over Sulla sent him to Libya to drive out Carbo's supporters and replace Hiempsal on his throne, as he had been overthrown by the Numidians.

11.16 The Marian last stand, 82 BC

Livy *Periochae* 86–8

In 82, Sulla and the younger Marius fought at Sacriportus, near Praeneste, to which the latter retreated after a heavy defeat (doc. 9.34). In a series of battles in 82, Metellus, Pompey and Crassus along with Sulla crushed Carbo and Norbanus. The final — and spectacular — battle occurred at the Colline Gate, outside Rome on 1 November 82 BC, where Sulla and Crassus clashed with the Marian allies, the Samnites and Lucanians (doc. 10.27). Here Sulla's left wing got into difficulties, and was pressed against the city walls, but Crassus on the right overcame the enemy wing and Sulla prevailed; the Samnites and Lucanians not killed in battle were later massacred. The younger Marius, hearing the news at Praeneste, killed himself; the siege of that city by Q. Lucretius Afella ended with a massacre of the inhabitants. (Sulla celebrated the fall of the city by establishing annual games in the circus on the day, the *ludi victoriae Sullanae*, still celebrated in Velleius Paterculus' day: Vell. 2.27.6.) According to Velleius the younger Marius was 26 years (2.26.1), 27 years according to Appian (1.87.394). The Marians were pursued into Sicily and Africa by Pompey (Keaveney 1982c: 123–30; Badian *FC* 270–1). Details of the campaigns of 83–82: App. *BC* 1.79–94.360–439; cf. Strabo 5.4.11; Diod. 38/39.15; Last & Gardner 1932: 272–6; Scullard *GN* 77–8; Keaveney 1982: 129–47; Seager 1994: 187–96.

After the suicide of the younger Marius and the fall of Praeneste, Sulla took the name Felix ('Fortunate' or 'Lucky'): Vell. 2.27.5, but according to Plut. *Sull.* 34.3 it was after his triumph over Mithridates in January 81 BC. Appian *BC* 1.97.452 has it before the triumph in the context of the voting of the equestrian statue of Sulla (see docs 11.26, 11.48). The fall of Praeneste, which marked the climax of Sulla's victories in Italy, should be preferred.

Appian *BC* 1.97.452 refers to a document in which the senate decreed Sulla be called Epaphroditus, a surname he had used during the Mithridatic War, stressing his relationship with Aphrodite, the Greek equivalent of Venus (cf. doc. 11.35). The precise meaning of 'Epaphroditus' is uncertain but for Sulla it clearly meant 'beloved of Aphrodite'; for Sulla as Felix and Epaphroditus, see Plut. *Sull.* 34.1–4; Balsdon 1951; Badian 1969: 35; Keaveney 1982: 83, 1983b: 60–6; Ramage 1991: 100–2; Seager 1994: 199. He also considered Apollo an important deity, and carried a statuette of the god, to which he prayed before battle (as at the Colline Gate when matters became desperate): Plut. *Sull.* 29.11–13; Front. *Strat.* 1.11.11; Val. Max. 1.2.3; Keaveney 1983b: 56–60.

86 Gaius Marius, son of Gaius Marius, was made consul unconstitutionally, though not yet 20 years old . . . Sulla made terms with the peoples of Italy, to prevent them being afraid of him as a threat to their citizenship and recently granted right to vote . . . The praetor Lucius Damasippus, on the decision of Gaius Marius the consul, assembled the senate and slaughtered all the nobles in Rome. Among their number was Quintus Mucius Scaevola, the pontifex maximus, who was killed as he fled in the fore-court of the temple of Vesta . . .

87 Sulla besieged Gaius Marius, whose army he had routed and destroyed at Sacriportus, in the town of Praeneste, and recovered Rome from the hands of his enemies. When Marius tried to break out, Sulla drove him back . . .

88 Sulla slaughtered Carbo's army at Clusium, Faventia and Fidentia and drove him out of Italy; he fought it out with the Samnites, who alone of the Italian peoples had not yet put down their arms, near the city of Rome in front of the Colline Gate . . .

11.17 Pompey wants his quid pro quo

Plutarch *Life of Pompey* 13.1–9

See also Plut. *Pomp*. 11, 14. In 82 the young Pompey was given a senatorial grant of extraordinary propraetorian imperium and six legions by Sulla and sent first to Sicily to deal with Carbo whom he killed, and then to Africa in 81 where he defeated and killed Cn. Domitius Ahenobarbus (Cinna's son-in-law; *MRR* II.69), and Iarbas, the pretender to the Numidian throne, restoring Hiempsal. Sulla then requested that Pompey dismiss five of his six legions and return to Rome as a private citizen, but Pompey declined, on the pretext that his army would not permit him to do so. With his legions camped outside Rome he gained a triumph from Sulla and an unwilling senate (cf. doc. 11.18), and Sulla called him Magnus ('the Great'); Pompey did not immediately use Magnus as a cognomen (i.e., as a surname). That Pompey could extort such a concession as a triumph from Sulla indicated the extent to which Sulla's reforms could not contain the force of personalities and their armies within a strait-jacket of laws. Pompey in Sicily and Africa: Livy *Per*. 89; App. *BC* 1.95.440; Diod. 38/9.9–10, 20; Keaveney 1982c: 131; Hillman 1997; Seager 2002: 27–8; triumph: Badian 1955, 1961, *FC* 270–2; Twyman 1979; Seager 28.

1 When he returned to Utica (81 BC), Pompey received letters from Sulla ordering him to discharge all the rest of his troops and remain there with one legion to await his successor. **2** At this Pompey was aggrieved and upset, but hid his feelings, while his army was openly indignant, and, when he requested them to return to Italy before him, they shouted out against Sulla and declared that they would never desert him and refused to allow him to trust the tyrant. **3** Pompey first tried to calm the men down and comfort them, but, as he was unable to convince them, he came down from the platform and went away to his tent in tears, while they seized him and set him on the platform again; **4** this took up a great part of the day, with the soldiers telling him to remain and stay in command, and Pompey asking them to obey orders and not mutiny, until, after they continued to harangue him and shout, he swore that he would kill himself if they forced him, and in this way, with reluctance, they put a stop to it. **5** The first report that Sulla had was that Pompey had revolted... **6** but when he learned the truth of the matter and saw everyone rushing out to welcome Pompey and show their goodwill by escorting him to Rome, he sought to go one better: **7** he went out to meet him and, after greeting him in the warmest manner possible, addressed him in a loud voice as 'Magnus' and told everybody else there to do the same; 'Magnus' means great. **8** Others say that Pompey was first given this title by the whole army in Africa, but that it gained strength and force when Sulla confirmed it. **9** Pompey himself was the last person to use it and only a long time afterwards, when he was sent to Spain as a proconsul against Sertorius (77 BC), did he begin to sign himself in his letters and decrees as 'Pompeius Magnus'; for it was no longer likely to cause jealousy and had become a matter of course.

11.18 The young Pompey's triumph, 81 BC

Licinianus 31

See also Plut. *Pomp*. 14.1–8. Pompey had not been a praetor or a consul and so could not technically hold a triumph; as Plut. points out (*Pomp*. 14.1) the younger Scipio had not been able to triumph for his successes in Spain for the same reason. Sulla had initially opposed Pompey's request because Pompey had not held either office. Thereupon Pompey made his celebrated remark that people worship the rising not the setting sun. Sulla, according to Plutarch, thunderstruck at this remark, granted the triumph. Sulla gave ground, not simply because of Pompey's assistance — the crucial three legions he raised at Picenum, and his solid service in Africa — but also because a marriage alliance was arranged between them, with Pompey divorcing his wife to marry Sulla's stepdaughter Aemilia, already married and pregnant (leading to the sorry saga related at Plut. *Pomp.* 9). So Pompey, at the age of 24 (Livy *Per.* 89), while still an eques, celebrated a triumph on 12 March 81 for his successes in Africa.

Sulla had already in January 81 celebrated his triumph over Mithridates, while C. Valerius Flaccus celebrated one for his victories in Spain and Gaul, and L. Murena for Asia. Sulla did not celebrate a triumph for his conquest of Rome and Italy as Romans did not triumph over fellow citizens. The names of towns in Greece and Asia Minor he had captured were displayed in his triumph but not those of towns in Italy (Val. Max. 2.8.7). The triumph: 'L. Cornelius Sulla Felix, son of Lucius, grandson of Publius, dictator, celebrated a triumph over King Mithridates VI on 28–29 January (81 BC)' (*Fasti Triumphales, CIL* 1.1² p. 178: cf. Plut. *Sull.* 34; Pliny *Nat. Hist.* 33.16; App. *BC* 1.101.473; Val. Max. 2.8.7). Sulla's triumph: Plut. *Sull.* 34.1–5; Sumi 2002: 416–18. Connected with the triumph was his dedication of 10 per cent of the spoils from Mithridates to Hercules, a custom of Roman generals: Plut. *Sull.* 35.1; Sumi 419–21. Pompey's triumph: *CIL* I.1² p. 178; Plut. *Pomp.* 14, *Crass.* 7.1; Val. Max. 8 15 8; Keaveney 1982: 195, 1983: 188–9. Career of Pompey to Sulla's death: Last & Gardner 1932: 277–80; Leach 1978: 1–33; Greenhalgh 1980: 1–29; Keaveney 1982c; Seager 1994: 190–1, 196, 2002: 25–9.

At the age of 25, while still a Roman eques, which was totally unprecedented, Pompey as propraetor celebrated a triumph from Africa, on 12 March. On this day, it is said, the Roman people saw elephants in his triumph. But when he entered the city the triumphal gate was smaller than the four elephants yoked to his chariot, although he made the attempt twice.

SULLA'S PROSCRIPTIONS

Sulla and his generals had conquered Italy, 'with battle, fire and murder' (App. *BC* 1.95.440) and widespread proscriptions followed Sulla's gaining control of Rome. Proscription meant that those whose names were on the lists were liable to be put to death, with no judicial procedure involved (doc. 11.20). The victims were senators and equites who had supported the Marians and opposed Sulla. Their property was confiscated, leading to numerous abuses in which Sulla's associates added names to the lists of the proscribed in order to gain their property. The sons and grandsons of the proscribed could not hold political office until Caesar as dictator allowed this (docs 11.22, 13.54). Those who appealed directly to Sulla were spared (Cic. *Sull.* 72), but most did not have the chance or opportunity.

Cicero cites a sentence of the proscription law, passed to validate the proscriptions that had been carried out, which was to be in effect until 1 June 81 BC. It was proposed by the interrex Lucius Valerius Flaccus: Cic. *Rosc. Am.* 126 (*ARS* 64; Crawford *Statutes* 49): '(he is to see) that the goods be sold of those persons who have been proscribed or of those persons who have been killed inside the enemy's lines.'

Proscriptions: docs 11.19–23; Keaveney 1982: 167 n.18: Sall. *Orat. Lep.* 6; Cic. *Sest.* 7, *Laws* 2.56; Dion. Hal. 8.80.2; Suet. *Jul.* 11; App. *BC* 1.91.422; Plut. *Sull.* 31; Quint. *Inst. Or.* 11.1.85; Sen. *de Ira* 2.34.3; Dio 37.25.3; Diod. 38/39. 17–19; *MRR* II.69; Last & Gardner 1932: 276–7; Keaveney 1982: 148–68; Seager 1994: 197–8.

11.19 Sulla's brutality

Livy *Periochae* 88

Marius' ashes were disinterred and scattered into the Anio river (Pliny *Nat. Hist.* 7.187). Marcus Marius Gratidianus, twice praetor (cf. doc. 11.13), son of a sister (Maria) of Marius and adopted by Marius' brother Marcus, was killed by Catiline, his brother-in-law, at the tomb of Quintus Lutatius Catulus whom Gratidianus had prosecuted, leading Catulus to commit suicide (Catulus had defeated the Cimbri, and shared a triumph with Marius in 101, but then turned against Marius: App. *BC* 1.74.341–2; Plut. *Mar.* 44.8; Diod. 38.2–3; Cic. *de orat.* 3.9, *Tusc. Disp.* 5.56, *Nat. Deor.* 3.80). Catulus' son instigated the murder of Gratidianus: Sall. *Hist.* I.44; Plut *Sull.* 32.3–4; Gruen 1968: 233; Marshall 1985; McGushin 1992: 105–6; Evans 1994: 9, 147.

The Villa Publica was the rendezvous for military recruits, and the location for the holding of the census, in the Campus Martius. The survivors from the battle of the Colline Gate were gathered there. Plutarch has 6,000 deaths (and the executions in the circus) with Sulla summoning the senate to the temple of Bellona: he rose to speak as the execution of the survivors began: Plut. *Sull.* 30.3–4 (see Dowling 2000: 303). Plut. *Sull.* 32.1 gives the number of Praenestians killed as 12,000.

With the state restored, Sulla polluted a most glorious victory by cruelty such as no man had ever shown before. He slaughtered 8,000 men, who had surrendered, in the Villa Publica; he set up a proscription list, and filled the city and all Italy with slaughter, and among these killings ordered all the people of Praeneste, who were unarmed, to be cut down, and had Marius (Marcus Marius Gratidianus), a man of senatorial rank, killed after having his legs and arms broken, his ears cut off and his eyes gouged out.

11.20 Sulla's 'iron fist'

Appian *Civil Wars* 1.95–6 (440–8)

Carbo (cos. 82) was executed, Norbanus (cos. 83) committed suicide, and their supporters both in Rome and in the Italian communities were all punished with death. **440**: Carbo who in his third consulship had fled to Africa was proscribed, and humiliated and executed by Pompey (Plut. *Pomp.* 10.1–6; Val. Max. 9.3.2; Carbo had defended him in a law-suit in 86 or 85: Alexander *Trials* no. 120). Norbanus had fled to Rhodes and was tracked down there by Sulla's agents and committed suicide (App. *BC* 1.91.422). **442**: The estimates of the proscribed vary. Appian gives 'some 40 senators and 1,600 equites' as proscribed, with the names of further senators added to these; Plutarch (doc. 11.21) has 80 individuals proscribed, with two further lists of 220 names; Orosius (doc. 11.23) puts the figure as high as 9,000; Valerius Maximus (9.2.1) gives a total of 4,700 for all the proscribed. **448**: Sulla's violence was also visited on the Italians, and land confiscated from them was awarded to his veterans: Keaveney 1982: 181–6; McGushin 1992: 105–6.

440 Pompey was sent to Libya against Carbo and to Sicily against Carbo's friends there; **441** Sulla himself summoned the Romans to an assembly and made a speech boasting about his achievements and making a number of menacing statements to inspire terror, ending up with saying that he would bring about some changes beneficial to the people if they would obey him, but that he would spare none of his enemies, and that he would deal with them with the utmost severity, and take vengeance with all his might on praetors, quaestors, military tribunes and anybody else who had co-operated with his enemies, after the day on which the consul Scipio did not adhere to the agreements made with him. **442** After saying this, he immediately published a proscription list of some 40 senators and 1,600 equites. He was apparently the first man to draw up a list of those whom he punished with death, to offer prizes to killers and rewards to informers, and to lay down punishments for those who hid the proscribed. **443** Not long afterwards he added the names of other senators to these. Some of these were captured unawares and killed where they were caught, in their houses, the streets, or shrines; some were borne through mid-air to Sulla and thrown at his feet; others were dragged and trampled on, with all the observers so terrified that they were unable to utter a word against these injustices. **444** Exile was the fate of some and confiscation of their possessions that of others. Investigators searched everywhere for those who had escaped from the city and whomever they caught they killed.

445 There was also much slaughter, banishment and confiscation among the Italians who had obeyed Carbo or Norbanus or Marius or any of their subordinates. **446** There were vicious judgements against them throughout all Italy and various charges — of taking command, of army service, of contributing money or other services, even of giving counsel against Sulla. Hospitality, friendship, lending money — for both borrower and lender — were all crimes, and one might be arrested for willingness to help someone or even for being his companion on a journey. These accusations particularly targeted the rich. **447** When accusations against an individual failed, Sulla took vengeance on cities and punished these instead, destroying citadels, razing walls, imposing general fines, or crushing them with severe taxes; **448** and among most of them he settled his ex-troops to hold Italy by means of garrisons, while he took away their land and houses and shared them amongst his men, by which he made these well-disposed to him even after he was dead; as these could not possess their holdings securely unless Sulla's measures were secure, they fought on his behalf even after he had died.

11.21 The proscription lists

Plutarch *Life of Sulla* 31.1–9

The proscription lists had been preceded by butchery on a scale unprecedented at Rome, even during Marius' bloody return to Rome. Whether the speech was made by Fufidius or Caecilius Metellus, and whether at Sulla's prompting or not, is of little concern. Orosius (doc. 11.23) has L. Fursidius; Florus 2.9.25 has Fufidius advising Sulla to leave some people alive so he would have someone to give orders to. The lists were published widely, as the men could be hunted down wherever they went. Those who aided the proscribed risked death in their own turn. Another victim of Sulla's, though not proscribed, was Q. Lucretius Afella (*MRR* II.72), who had besieged and taken Praeneste. He decided to stand for the consulship and, when Sulla failed to persuade him not to stand, he was executed by a centurion (Livy *Per.* 89; Plut. *Sull.* 33.5–6; App. *BC* 1.101.471; Keaveney 2003).

1 Sulla now devoted himself to butchery, and the city was filled with murders without number or limit, with many people being killed out of private enmity, with whom Sulla had no concerns, but permitted it as a favour to his supporters, **2** until one of the young men, Gaius (Caecilius) Metellus, ventured in the senate to ask Sulla what end there would be to these evils . . . **3** Sulla replied that he did not know yet whom he would spare, and Metellus answered, 'Then tell us whom you intend to punish'. Sulla said that he would do this. **4** Some say this last speech was made not by Metellus, but by one of Sulla's associates called Fufidius.

5 Sulla at once published a list condemning 80 men, without consulting any of the magistrates; everybody was indignant, but the next day but one he proscribed another 220, and on the third day again no fewer. **6** He made a speech to the people on the subject and told them that he had proscribed as many men as he could remember, but that he would proscribe later any who had now slipped his mind . . . **8** What seemed most unjust of all, Sulla deprived the sons and grandsons of the proscribed of their civil rights and confiscated all their property. **9** The lists were published not only in Rome, but in every city of Italy.

11.22 The 'sins of the fathers'

Velleius Paterculus *Roman History* 2.28.4

Nor was his ferocity directed only towards those who had borne arms against him, but towards many of the innocent. Furthermore, the goods of the proscribed were sold and their children were not only deprived of their fathers' property, but also prohibited from the right of standing for magistracies, and, at one and the same time, the greatest injustice of all, the sons of senators had both to bear the burdens of their rank and lose its privileges.

11.23 'Butchery was unrestrained'

Orosius *History in Answer to the Pagans* 5.21.1–5

1 Shortly after Sulla had entered Rome as conqueror, he violated religion and good faith by killing 3,000 unarmed and unsuspecting men who had surrendered through intermediaries. After this, an immense number of people were also killed — I will not say of innocent men, but even some of Sulla's own supporters — who are reported to have numbered more than 9,000. Murders took place unrestrained throughout the city, with assassins roaming far and wide motivated by anger or plunder. **2** With everyone openly murmuring what each individually feared for himself, Q. Catulus at last asked Sulla openly, 'Whom are we going to live with if we kill armed men in war and unarmed men in peace?' **3** Sulla then, at the suggestion of the first centurion L. Fursidius, was the first to bring in his infamous proscription list. The first proscription was of 80 people, who included four ex-consuls: Carbo, Marius, Norbanus and Scipio, and with them Sertorius, the greatest cause of fear at that time. **4** A second was then brought out with 500 names — Lollius was reading this, quite unconcerned and aware of no wrong-doing, when he suddenly came upon his own name, and while he was making in agitation for the forum, his head covered, he was murdered. **5** But confidence and an end to wickedness was not provided even by these lists, for some were murdered after being proscribed, while others were proscribed after they had been murdered.

11.24 Making a quick profit

Plutarch *Life of Cicero* 3.4–6

Many enriched themselves through the proscriptions. Plutarch has the anecdote of the apolitical Q. Aurelius, who saw his name on the list of the proscribed and commented that he was being pursued by his Alban estate; he had not gone far when he was slain by someone who had been hunting for him (Plut. *Sull.* 31.11–12). Crassus in particular benefited from acquiring at low prices the property of the proscribed (Plut. *Crass.* 6.8). In 89 Cicero had done military service under Sulla against the Marsi (Cic. *Div.* 1.72, 2.65). Sextius Roscius of Ameria in southern Umbria was murdered and two of his relatives in conjunction with Chrysogonus had his name included amongst the proscribed, in order to acquire the property cheaply. Cicero spoke for the son, Sextus Roscius (*pro Sexto Roscio Amerino*); for Sextus Roscius of Ameria and Chrysogonus, see Badian *FC* 249–51; Stockton 1966: 263–4; Keaveney 1982: 155; Seager 1994: 205–6; cf. doc. 2.51.

4 At this time Chrysogonus, Sulla's freedman, put up for auction the estate of a man who, so it was said, had been on one of Sulla's proscription lists and been killed. Chrysogonus bought it himself for 2,000 drachmas. 5 At this Roscius, the son and heir of the deceased, was indignant and made it known that the real value of the estate was 250 talents. Sulla was furious at being found out and, after Chrysogonus fabricated a case, charged Roscius with parricide. No lawyer could be found to defend him, but everyone kept clear, fearing Sulla's severity . . . 6 Cicero undertook the defence of Roscius and succeeded to everyone's admiration, but as he was afraid of Sulla he went overseas to Greece (79–77 BC), after spreading the word that it was for the sake of his health.

11.25 Cicero defies Sulla's freedman

Cicero *In Defence of Sextus Roscius of Ameria* 21

Although the proscription was no longer mentioned, and even those who were previously afraid returned, believing that they were now out of danger, the name of Sextus Roscius (the father), a very great supporter of the nobility, was entered on the proscription lists; the purchaser was Chrysogonus; three estates, perhaps the most notable, were given to Capito (Titus Roscius Capito) as his own property, which he still possesses to this day; as for the rest of the property this Titus Roscius, as he says himself, seized it in Chrysogonus' name. This property, worth 6,000,000 sesterces, was purchased for 2,000 sesterces. All this, I am sure, jurors, was done without Sulla's knowledge.

THE DICTATORSHIP AND CONSTITUTIONAL REFORMS

When Sulla entered Rome in 82 his imperium technically lapsed (from the point of view of his opponents it had lapsed when he was declared a *hostis* by Cinna). The senate proceeded to confirm all his acts as consul (88 BC) and proconsul (87–82 BC) and voted him an equestrian statue to be erected before the rostra. This was the first occasion such an honour had been voted; the inscription read, converting Appian's Greek into a Roman legend, 'Cornelio Sullae Imperatori Felici': App. *BC* 1.97.451; cf. Cic. *Phil.* 9.13.

As both the consuls for 82 had been proscribed and were dead (Carbo, and the younger Marius at his own hand), Sulla ordered the senate to appoint an interrex, and it chose the princeps senatus, L. Valerius Flaccus (cos. 100). Sulla wrote to Flaccus that it was his opinion that a dictator be appointed to restore Rome and Italy, and that that dictator should be — himself. Flaccus introduced the lex Valeria to the comitia, which elected Sulla dictator 'legibus scribundis et reipublicae constituendae' ('to make laws and reform the constitution'). The office of dictator had not been in use since the Hannibalic wars, 120 years ago. Sulla now had supreme authority unchecked by any veto and with no fixed term (doc. 11.26). Although there was an election, Plutarch was correct to write that Sulla, 'appointed himself dictator' (doc. 11.27). He had Flaccus appointed his master of horse (magister equitum: Cic. *Att*. 9.15.2). As dictator he carried out various reforms (docs 11.27–9, 31), extended the pomerium of Rome (Gell. 13.14.4; Tac. *Ann*. 12.23; Sen. *Brev. Vit*. 13.8; Sumi 2000: 426; doc. 1.3), and had a modest building programme in Rome and Italy (Ramage 1991: 113–14). Sulla as dictator: *MRR* II.66–7, 74–6; Last & Gardner 1932: 282–308; Badian 1976: 56–9; Scullard *GN* 80–3; Keaveney 1982: 161–203; Seager 1994: 197–207.

11.26 Unlimited dictatorship

Appian *Civil Wars* 1.98–9 (456–62)

459: It was actually 120 years since the last dictatorship. **462**: Appian states that the dictatorship of Sulla was 'unlimited' compared to the previous short dictatorships of fixed periods, but Appian (459) also indicates, as did events, that Sulla did not seek a lifelong dictatorship (unlike Julius Caesar).

456 Sulla became *de facto* king, or tyrant, not through election but by power and force, but as he needed the pretence of being elected he contrived this as follows . . . **457** If by some chance there should not be a consul, an interrex was appointed to hold a consular election. **458** Sulla made use of this custom. As there were no consuls, since Carbo had died in Sicily and Marius (the Younger) at Praeneste, he went out of the city and ordered the senate to choose an interrex.

459 They selected Valerius Flaccus, expecting that he would soon hold a consular election; but Sulla wrote to Flaccus instructing him to present his view to the people that Sulla considered it expedient that for the present there be in the city the position which they call the dictatorship, a custom which had ceased for 400 years; he ordered them that their appointee should not rule for a fixed period, but until he should have stabilised the city and Italy and the whole government, which had been shaken by seditions and wars. **460** That his intention in this proposal referred to Sulla himself was not at all doubtful; and Sulla did not hide it, revealing at the end of his letter that in his own opinion he could be particularly useful to the city in that role.

461 This was Sulla's message, and, while the Romans were unwilling, they were no longer electing people according to law and considered that this action was no longer within their power, so in the general confusion they welcomed the charade of an election as a show and pretence of freedom, and elected Sulla to be their tyrant and master for as long as he chose. **462** In earlier days the rule of dictators had been autocratic, but limited to a short period of time; now for the first time it became unlimited and so a complete tyranny. However, they added for the sake of appearances the condition that they appointed him dictator to enact whatever laws he might think fit and to restore the constitution.

11.27 Sulla's powers

Plutarch *Life of Sulla* 33.1–2

1 He appointed himself dictator, reviving this type of magistracy after 120 years. **2** He was voted immunity for all his past actions, and for the future the power of life and death, confiscation, founding colonies or cities, sacking cities, and the making and deposing of kings as he chose.

11.28 Sulla's 'reforms'

Livy *Periochae* 89

Fasces: Appian *BC* 1.100.465 (doc. 11.29) has the 24 fasces being a custom of the kings, while the summariser of Livy here has such a thing never happening before, which seems to be a mistake, as it was customary for dictators to have 24 fasces carried by 24 attendants (lictors) before them (Polyb. 3.87; Plut. *Fab.* 4.3; Dion. Hal. 9.24; Keaveney 1983: 193 n.58). *Tribunes*: see docs 11.30, 32.

Senate: Sulla first brought the senate up to its traditional number of 300 members by enrolling those with distinguished military service. To increase the size of the senate further — to 600 members — he drew upon the equites, who could provide men of sufficient wealth to join this body (see also App. *BC* 1.100.468): Sulla chose them from 'the best of the equites'. Italians will have been included; see Sall. *Cat.* 37.6: 'common soldiers'; Dion. Hal. 5.77.5 (Badian 1969: 38; Gabba 1976: 144; Keaveney 1982: 174–5). This was not to emasculate the equestrian order by drawing their wealthiest and most powerful men into the senate but, in order to increase the size of the senate on the scale Sulla wished, he had to draw on this class (Seager 1994: 200–1). The new senators presumably felt obligations to Sulla as they were appointed by him. The actual jurors were selected from the senate by vote of the tribes: App. 468; see Hill 1932.

Priesthoods: Sulla increased the numbers of priests, augurs, and officials in charge of the Sibylline Books to 15. The *lex Domitia* of 104 had provided that 17 of the 35 tribes in the tribal assembly elect the priests of Rome's four main collegia of priests (*MRR* I.559). Sulla rescinded the law, clearly seeing it as a popularist measure, and returned to the traditional procedure whereby existing members co-opted others when vacancies occurred; the *lex Domitia* was reintroduced by T. Labienus as tribune in 63 BC: Dio 37.37.

Religious policy: The Sibylline Books kept in the temple of Jupiter on the Capitol had perished when that temple burned in 83 BC. Sulla began the rebuilding of the temple and also the reconstituting of the collection by seeking oracles throughout the known world.

Sulla was made dictator, and appeared in public with 24 fasces, which had never happened before. He strengthened the constitution of the state by new laws, weakened the power of the tribunes of the plebs, and took from them all power of introducing legislation. He added to the colleges of pontiffs and augurs so there were fifteen members in each college; he recruited the senate from the equestrian order; he took away from the sons of the proscribed the right to stand for magistracies, and he sold off their goods, of which he seized the largest part for himself. The proceeds were 350,000,000 sesterces.

11.29 Lawcourts returned to the senate

Velleius Paterculus *Roman History* 2.32.3

With the senate increased to 600 members, the juries could be transferred to that body and adequately manned by it; in fact the increase in the senate's numbers beyond 300 may well have been motivated by Sulla's wish to give the senate exclusive judicial control. Gaius Gracchus had given the equites sole control of the courts, but the most recent law concerning the juries, the *lex Plautia iudiciaria* of 89 (*MRR* II.34), had legislated that the jurors be drawn from 15 men from each of the tribes, with all classes of citizens eligible. Sulla now granted the senate a monopoly of jury membership: see Gruen 1968: 255–78.

In addition, Sulla re-organised the law-courts (*quaestiones*). There were to be seven quaestiones: murder and poisoning (de sicariis et veneficiis), extortion (de repetundis), peculation (de peculatu), assault (de iniuria), treason (de maiestate), electoral bribery (de ambitu), and forgery (of coins or wills, or using incorrect weights: de falsis). These remained the seven main quaestiones for the rest of the Republic and the early Imperial period. (Some of these quaestiones already existed, those concerned with extortion, treason, murder and electoral bribery.)

Sulla's treason law (*lex Cornelia maiestatis*, incorporating the earlier *lex Porcia* of about 100 BC) dealt mainly with promagistrates in their provinces, and controlled their imperium: they could not start wars, march with their troops outside their province, or leave their province without senatorial authorisation. Sulla's own actions are relevant here, and he clearly aimed to prevent another Sulla using his armies outside his allocated province. But a law in itself would not be enough to stop Julius Caesar in 49 BC. The increase in number of the praetors to eight, or possibly ten (Pomponius *Dig.* 1.2.2.32), provided the magistrates to preside over the courts. In addition, after their term of office was over, they with the two retiring consuls comprised ten promagistrates to govern Rome's provinces (Sicily, Sardinia and Corsica, the two Spains, Africa, Macedonia, Asia, Cilicia, Gallia Narbonensis, and perhaps Cisalpine Gaul if it was a province at this stage). It was under the *lex Cornelia de sicariis et veneficiis* that Cicero brought his case in 80 BC for the younger Roscius (the *pro Sexto Roscio Amerino*): Crawford *Statutes* 50.

The right of acting as jurors, which Gaius Gracchus had taken from the Senate and given to the equites, Sulla gave back to the Senate.

11.30 Balance of constitutional power returned to the senate

Appian *Civil Wars* 1.100 (465–70)

465: the election of consuls for 81 BC was part of Sulla's overall plan to restore the constitution and establish normality. **466**: this refers to the *cursus honorum*, a strict progression of office, from quaestor to praetor to consul, which had held since the *lex Villia Annalis* of 180 BC and which was now reinforced by Sulla. The number of quaestors was increased to twenty and they automatically became members of Sulla's larger senate; previously most became senators, but not all, as the senate's traditional membership of 300 could not absorb them all (quaestors were elected by the tribal assembly). This automatic entry meant that the censors no longer decided which of them could enter the senate (Cic. *Laws* 3.27); quaestors: see Gruen 1968: 258–64, cf. 124; Scullard *GN* 83; Keaveney 1982: 176–7; Cloud 1994: 512–26. Age criteria were also put in place: possibly 29 years in the year of election for the quaestorship, with 39 for the praetorship, and 42 years for the consulship (Keaveney 1982: 173–4; Seager 1994: 201). This aimed to prevent extra-ordinary careers. The holding of the aedileship was not a requisite part of the Sullan cursus honorum (nor had it ever been an essential stage): however, one of the duties of the aediles was the organising of games (ludi Romani and ludi Megalenses by the curule aediles, and the ludi Ceriales and ludi Plebeii by the plebeian aediles) which could make an aedile popular and bring him to the attention of the voters for subsequent elections (cf. doc. 2.71 for Caesar's games as aedile).

Sulla himself had been consul in 88, and was to be elected again for 80, laying down the dictatorship in 81. He therefore broke the provisions of his own law requiring a ten year lapse before holding the same office for a second time; possibly he had a special dispensation from the senate.

467: for the tribunate, see also docs 11.29, 11.32: Livy (doc. 11.28) notes that Sulla took from the tribunes 'all power of introducing legislation'. The tribunate therefore lost its legislative character, which was one of its main features; all legislative proposals now had to go first before the senate, greatly decreasing the popular element in the constitution; the tribunician power of veto was taken away or severely restricted. App. *BC* 467 (cf. Asc. 78) adds that those elected to the tribunate could hold no further office. These features of Sulla's legislation were a clear emasculation of the office. From the optimate point of view, the tribunate had been a source of civil strife since Tiberius Gracchus, followed by Gaius Gracchus, Saturninus, and Livius Drusus; Sulla himself had suffered from Sulpicius. Curtailing the power and prestige of the tribunate strengthened the power of the senate, and ensured that there was no legislation introduced which was inimical to senatorial interests. According to Caesar *BC* 1.5, 1.7, Sulla took the rest of their prerogatives away from the tribunes, but left their power of veto, and tribunes could still exercise their right to protect the safety and property of plebeians (Cic. *Laws* 3.22). Tribunician powers were fully restored in 70 BC (doc. 12.4). **468**: see doc. 11.28 for the equites enrolled into the senate.

469: The enfranchisement of the 'youngest and the strongest' of the slaves perhaps points to the intended use of these freedmen as intimidators in the voting process and as voters, but no evidence points to any specific role for them. But they and the 12,000 Sullan veterans who had received land and money were formidable support for Sulla, as Appian notes (App. 1.104.489). The 10,000 freed, enfranchised slaves were known as the Cornelii: App. 1.100.469, 104.489; Lintott 1999: 80–1. Compare the freed slaves of Marius, the Bardyiae (doc. 9.34); for a dedication by the freed slaves, see doc. 11.31.

470 (cf. 448: doc. 11.20) According to Appian, Sulla distributed land to 23 legions, to provide him with support throughout Italy. Etruria and Umbria had been particularly opposed to him and may have provided the bulk of the land. See Brunt *IM* 300–12; Keaveney 1982: 183–6, 1982b: 511–37. The issue of providing land to other veterans was to become important later on.

465 However, in a pretence of maintaining the country's constitution, he allowed them to appoint consuls, and Marcus Tullius (Decula) and (Gnaeus) Cornelius Dolabella were elected (for 81 BC); but like a king, Sulla was dictator over the consuls; for 24 axes were carried in front of him, the same number carried before the kings of olden days, and he also had a large bodyguard. **466** He repealed laws and added others; and he forbade anyone to become praetor before he had been quaestor, and to be consul before he had been praetor, and he prohibited anyone from holding the same office for a second time until ten years had passed. **467** He reduced the power of the tribunes to such an extent that it seemed to be insignificant, and passed a law preventing a tribune from going on to hold any other office — for which reason all those of reputation or family who used to seek the office avoided it for the future . . . **468** To the senate itself, which had been greatly reduced in number by the seditions and wars, he added about 300 of the best equites, allowing the tribes to vote on each of them. **469** He freed more than 10,000 slaves of proscribed persons, choosing the youngest and the strongest, made them Roman citizens, and added them to the people, calling them Cornelii after himself, thus ensuring that he could make use of 10,000 of the plebeians who were ready to carry out his orders. **470** With the intention of doing the same throughout Italy, he distributed to the 23 legions who had served under him a large amount of land in the different communities, as I have already related, some of which was still unallocated, and some of which he took away from the communities as a penalty.

11.31 Dedication to Sulla from some grateful freedmen

ILS 881

(*CIL* I² 722; *ILLRP* 353; *ROL* IV.136; cf. Gordon 1983 no. 16.) This inscription dates to 82–79 BC and is inscribed on a pedestal, presumably surmounted with a statue of Sulla. Seven Latin inscriptions survive for Sulla from Italy, probably part of statue bases honouring him: Ramage 1991: 110. One of the districts (*vici*) of Rome dedicated a statue of him: *CIL* I² 721 (*ILS* 872; *ILLRP* 352). Statues of Sulla at Rome: Suet. *Jul.* 75.4; Dio 42.18.2, 43.49.1.

To Lucius Cornelius Sulla Felix, dictator, son of Lucius, from his freedmen (*leiberteini*).

11.32 Sulla and the tribunate

Cicero *On the Laws* 3.20–2

Cicero's brother Quintus is speaking here (Marcus follows with a more balanced view). The repeal of Sulla's laws concerning the tribunate began in 75 (*MRR* II.96: Aurelius Cotta as consul) and was completed by Pompey as consul in 70 (docs 12.4–5), who restored the power of the tribunes, which Sulla had left as 'a shadow without substance': Vell. 2.30.4. Cicero here refers to their continued right of protecting plebeians and their property, the *ius auxilii*. For Clodius, see docs 12.52–4.

20 Indeed, was it not the overthrow of Gaius Gracchus and the daggers, which he himself said had been cast into the forum so that citizens could use them to stab each other, that totally altered the stability of the state? Why should I go on to mention Saturninus, Sulpicius and the rest, whom the state was unable to remove without a sword? . . . **22** And what ruin and destruction did he (Clodius) bring about, ruin such as could only have been brought about by the frenzy of a foul beast without reason or hope inflamed by the frenzy of a mob! Consequently, I greatly approve of Sulla's laws on this subject, who removed from the tribunes of the plebs the power of doing wrong through their legislation, but left them their right of assistance (*ius auxilii*). And as for our friend Pompey, though in all other matters I always praise him in the highest possible terms, I am silent about the power of the tribunes; for I should not criticise him and am unable to praise him.

LEGISLATION

From Appian it is clear that Sulla had a comprehensive legislative programme (doc. 11.30). The increase in the number of senators, the diminution in the powers of the tribunes, the transfer of the courts to the senate, and the enforcement of the *lex Villia Annalis*, clearly strengthened the position of the senate while weakening the popularist element. In addition, Sulla abolished the position of princeps senatus, presumably so that no individual senator had undue influence.

11.33 The institution of twenty quaestors

Crawford *Statutes* 14

(*CIL* I² 587; Bruns 89; *ARS* 69; *ROL* IV.302–11.) Cf. Tac. *Ann.* 11.22.6 ('Sulla increased the number of quaestors to 20 to enlarge the senate, to which Sulla had transferred the courts'). This is a fragment of Sulla's quaestorship law of 81 BC on a bronze tablet which was to be set up on a wall by the temple of Saturn, the storehouse of state records. This fragment makes arrangements for the appointment and employment of extra *viatores* (messengers, or official summoners) and *praecones* (heralds) to assist the elected quaestors. These viatores and praecones hold their posts for annual terms. Note the reference to voting by tribes: Sulla nearly always used the comitia centuriata for the passing of legislation (doc. 11.5). *Decuria* = panel, group. *Eighth tabula*: not the eighth part or section of the law but simply indicating the positioning of this tablet with respect to the other tablets on which the law was engraved. Quaestors came into office in December.

[Lucius Cornelius, son of Lucius, dictator . . . duly proposed to the people, and the people duly resolved in the forum . . . on the day of . . . tribe] voted first; for his tribe [the first to vote was . . .]

Eighth tabula of the law: Concerning the Twenty Quaestors. . . .

7 The consuls now in office shall, before the first day of next December, select from those who are Roman citizens one viator (messenger) who shall attend as messenger in that group which is or will be **10** required to attend on the quaestors at the treasury on and after the fifth day of next December. And the same consuls shall, before the first day of next December, select from those who are Roman citizens one praeco (crier) who shall attend as crier in that group which is or will be required to attend on the quaestors at the treasury on and after the fifth day of next December . . . .

32 And they shall select all those messengers and criers, whom they shall consider to be worthy of that rank. For whichever group each messenger shall have been selected in this way, **35** he is to be a messenger in that group just as others in that group are to be messengers. And for whichever group each crier shall have been selected in this way, he is to be a crier in that group just as others in that group are to be criers. And law and statute in all matters are to apply to those messengers and to a quaestor concerning those messengers, **40** just as if those messengers had been formerly selected for or substituted as one of three messengers for that group, for which group any of them shall have been selected as messenger under this law. And law and statute in all matters are to apply to those criers and to a quaestor concerning those criers, just as if those criers **45** had been formerly selected for or substituted as one of three criers for that group, for which group any of them shall have been selected as crier under this law.

Whichever of the quaestors shall be obliged by law or plebiscite to select or substitute messengers, those quaestors **50** shall select or substitute four messengers according to the law and statute by which those now in office have selected or substituted three messengers; and whichever of the quaestors shall be obliged by law or plebiscite to select or substitute criers, those quaestors shall select or substitute four criers according to the law and statute **55** by which those now in office have selected or substituted three criers . . .

11.34 Lex Cornelia de sicariis et veneficiis

Crawford *Statutes* 50

This remained in force as the statute for murder (except for parricide) into the Principate. Rives 2003: 317–22. The angle brackets in the text give Crawford's proposed readings.

1 The praetor or judge of the investigation, to whom the investigation concerning murderers shall have fallen by lot, in respect of what <has or shall have> occurred in the city of Rome <or> within one mile, with <those> jurors who shall have fallen by lot to him according to this statute, is to make investigation concerning the capital crime of that person who <has been or> shall have been armed with a weapon for the purpose of killing a man or perpetrating a theft, or <has or> shall have killed a man, or by whose malice aforethought that <has been or> shall have been done.

5 The <praetor or> judge of the investigation <. . .> with those jurors who shall have fallen to him <by lot according to this statute is to make investigation concerning the capital crime of that person> who, for the purpose of killing a man, has or shall have prepared or <has or> shall have sold or <has or> shall have bought or <has or> shall have had or <has or> shall have administered a poisonous drug.

6 <The praetor or judge of the investigation . . .> is to make investigation concerning the capital crime of the person who <has or shall have been> military tribune in the first four legions <. . .>, quaestor, tribune of the plebs <. . .>, or has or shall have given his opinion in the senate, whoever of them has or shall have conspired, or has or shall have combined, or has or shall have plotted, <. . .> or <has or> shall have given false witness with malice aforethought, <. . .> in order that someone might be condemned on a capital charge in a public court.

11.35 Sulla renews a grant of autonomy to Stratonicea, 81 BC

RDGE 18, lines 1–22, 49–131

(*ARS* 68; *OGIS* 441.) This is a decree of the senate, proposed by Sulla as dictator, renewing an earlier grant of autonomy to the city of Stratonicea, recognising the arrangements Sulla had made concerning the city when he was in the east; it had supported the Romans in the Mithridatic War. The stimulus for the decree is unknown; perhaps the city's privileges were being threatened by Roman magistrates and it sought reassurances from the senate; more probably, it was part of a general ratification of Sulla's arrangements in the east (compare *ARS* 67). The people of Stratonicea had asked permission to dedicate to the senate a golden crown worth 200 talents. Restorations are not included.

Lucius Cornelius Sulla Felix (Epaphroditus), son of Lucius, dictator, to the magistrates, council and people of Stratonicea, greetings; we are aware that you, through your ancestors, have always done your duty towards our empire and that on every occasion you have sincerely preserved your loyalty to us; and that in the war against Mithridates you were the first of those in Asia to oppose him, and for that reason most eagerly took upon yourselves many dangers of all kinds on behalf of our state . . . **10** both public and private, on account of your friendship, good will and gratitude towards us, and on the occasion of the war sent envoys to the other cities of Asia and to the cities of Greece . . .

Lucius Cornelius Sulla Felix, dictator, to the magistrates, council and people of Stratonicea, greetings. I have handed over to your envoys the following resolution by the senate:

Lucius Cornelius Sulla Felix, son of Lucius, dictator, consulted the senate on 27 March **20** in the comitium; Gaius Fannius son of Gaius . . . Gaius Fundanius son of Gaius . . . were present at the writing (of the decree) . . .

49. . . . [And Lucius Cornelius Sulla Felix, dictator, decreed . . .] that they make use of the same laws and customs as they did before, and that whatever decrees they made because of the war which they declared against King Mithridates, that all these remain in force; that they keep possession of Pedasus, Themessus, Ceramus, and the lands, villages, harbours, and revenues of the cities which the commander Lucius Cornelius Sulla assigned and granted them as a mark of their excellence; that the shrine of Hecate, most manifest and greatest goddess, which has long been revered . . . and the precinct be inviolate; **60** that, regarding what they lost in the war, the senate give instructions to the magistrate setting out for Asia to give care and attention to ensuring that their actual property be restored to them, that they recover their prisoners of war, and that concerning everything else they receive their due; and that any envoys who come to Rome from Stratonicea be granted by the magistrates audience with the senate out of turn.

Concerning this matter it was resolved (by the senate) as follows:

It was resolved to reply in a friendly manner in their presence to the envoys of Stratonicea in the senate, to renew good will, friendship, and alliance with them, and **70** to address the envoys as good and honourable men and our friends and allies from a good and honourable people, our friend and ally. And concerning the matters on which the envoys and Lucius Cornelius Sulla Felix, dictator, spoke, that it was well known to the Romans from the letters sent by the governors of Asia and Greece and by the legates who had been in those provinces that the Stratoniceans had always consistently preserved their friendship, loyalty and good will toward the Roman people in time of war and peace, **80** and had always taken care to protect with enthusiasm the interests of the Roman people with soldiers, grain, and great expenditures . . . (and) because of their high sense of honour had waged war alongside them and had most bravely opposed the generals and armies of King Mithridates on behalf of the cities of Asia and Greece.

Concerning these matters it was decreed as follows: that the senate is pleased to remember good and just men and to provide that Lucius Cornelius Sulla Felix, **90** dictator, should instruct the proquaestor to give them gifts of hospitality according to the ordinance; and that they should make use of the same laws and customs as they did before; and that whatever laws and decrees they passed because of this war against Mithridates, that all these remain in force for them; and that whatever states, revenues, lands, villages and harbours the commander Lucius Cornelius Sulla assigned and granted them in consultation with his council as a mark of their excellence, they be permitted to keep possession of these; and that the Roman people . . .; **100** and that Lucius Cornelius Sulla Felix, dictator, if he wishes, take note of the states, villages, lands, and harbours which he as commander assigned to Stratonicea, and allocate the tax which each is to pay to Stratonicea; and, if he so allocates, that he send letters to those states which he assigned to Stratonicea, for them to pay a tax of so much to Stratonicea; **110** and that those who may at any time be governors of the provinces of Asia and Greece see to it and ensure that these things are carried out in this way: that the shrine of Hecate be inviolate; that whatever proconsul may govern the province of Asia take note of the properties the Stratoniceans are missing, who seized these, and who are in possession of them, so that he may ensure that these are given back and restored; that they are able to recover their prisoners of war, and that in all other **120** matters they receive their due, as he considers most in keeping with the interests of the state and with his own good faith. Resolved.

And with regard to the crown sent to the senate by the people, that the people be permitted to dedicate it wherever Lucius Cornelius Sulla Felix, dictator, considers it appropriate, and that, if they wish, they be allowed to offer sacrifice on the Capitol. And to the envoys who come from Stratonicea **130** to Rome that they be granted by the magistrates audience with the senate out of turn. Resolved.

11.36 Tax-exemption for sanctuaries

RDGE 23 lines 5–69 (73 BC)

(*SIG*[3] 747; Bruns 180; *IG* VII.413; *ARS* 74.) A dispute arose between the sanctuary of Amphiaraus at Oropus (north of Athens) and tax-collectors (publicani) in 73 BC. The sanctuary claimed that Sulla had exempted it from taxation. The case was investigated by the consuls for 73, M. Terentius Varro Lucullus and G. Cassius Longinus, who confirmed the tax exemption. They note here that a decree of general tax exemption had been passed recognising exemptions awarded by the senate, Roman generals and Sulla, and more specifically that the senate had in Sulla's consulship (80 BC) confirmed by decree his tax exemption for Amphiaraus. A board of 16 senators had been chosen by the consuls to assist them to come to a decision. It was a nice touch when the tax farmers suggested that Amphiaraus was not a god (technically he was a hero, a demi-god) and therefore not exempt from taxation. Amphiaraus was a healing deity and Sulla's vow will have concerned some medical ailment. Oropus made an offering to Amphiaraus and Hygiea (Health) for Metella, Sulla's wife (*IG* VII.264, 372). Sulla and the publicani: Badian 1972: 95; Brunt 1990.

5 October 14 in the Basilica Porcia. Present on our council were . . . (16 names)

Concerning the matters on which Hermodorus, son of Olympichus, priest of Amphiaraus, who was previously named ally by the senate, and Alexidemus, son of Theodorus, and Demaenetus, son of Theoteles, envoys of the Oropians, spoke: that since in the law on tax farming those **20** lands were exempted which Lucius Sulla granted for the sake of preserving the sacred precincts of the immortal gods, and that these revenues which are under dispute were assigned by Lucius Sulla to the god Amphiaraus, so that no revenue should be paid to the tax farmer for these lands.

And concerning the matters on which Lucius Domitius Ahenobarbus spoke on behalf of the tax farmers, that in the law on tax farming those lands were exempted which Lucius Sulla granted for the sake of preserving the sacred precincts of the immortal gods, but that Amphiaraus, to whom these lands are said to have been granted, is not a god, so that the tax farmers should be permitted to collect taxes on these lands.

On the advice of our council we declared our resolve: we shall lay before the senate our findings, **30** which we have recorded also in the minutes:

'Concerning the territory of Oropus, about which there was a dispute with the tax farmers, this had been exempted by the law on tax farming, so that the tax farmer may not collect taxes on it. We investigated in accordance with the decree of the senate.

'In the law on tax farming it appears to have been exempted as follows: "excluding those, which in accordance with a decree of the senate, a commander or commanders of ours, for the sake of honouring the immortal gods and preserving sacred precincts, granted and left them to enjoy, and excluding those which the commander Lucius Cornelius Sulla on the advice of his council, for the sake of the **40** immortal gods and the preservation of sacred precincts, granted to them to enjoy, which same the senate ratified and which was not subsequently made invalid by a decree of the senate."

'Lucius Cornelius Sulla appears to have made this decision on the advice of his council: "For the sake of repaying a vow I assign to the sanctuary of Amphiaraus land extending 1,000 feet in every direction, so that this land too may be inviolable." Similarly for the god Amphiaraus he seems to have consecrated all the revenues of the city, the territory and the harbours of the Oropians to the games and sacrifices which the Oropians perform for the god Amphiaraus, and likewise also to all those which they may perform in the future for the victory and empire of the Roman people, **50** with the exception of the lands of Hermodorus, son of Olympichus, priest of Amphiaraus, who has remained a consistent friend of the Roman people.

'Concerning this matter a decree of the senate appears to have been passed in the consulship of Lucius Sulla Felix and Quintus Metellus Pius (80 BC), which decree the senate worded as follows: "Whatever Lucius Cornelius Sulla on the advice of his council assigned or granted to the god Amphiaraus and to his sanctuary, these same the senate considered to have been given and granted to this god."

'In (Sulla's) council were present the same people as in the first record of deliberations, fourteenth page.'

The following decree of the senate was passed: **60** October 16 in the comitium. Present at the writing were (3 names) . . . Concerning the matters which the consuls Marcus Lucullus and Gaius Cassius investigated and reported that they had investigated concerning the territory of Oropus and the tax farmers, that the territory of the Oropians appeared to have been exempted by the law on tax farming, and that it did not seem right that the tax farmers should collect taxes on it, it was so decreed, as they deemed best in keeping with the interests of the state and with their own good faith.

11.37 Sumptuary legislation, 81 BC

(a) Gellius *Attic Nights* 2.24.11

There had been previous sumptuary legislation: the *lex Licinia sumptuaria*, passed soon after 143 BC (it had allowed 100 asses to be spent on certain days, 200 for weddings, and 30 asses on normal days, though it allowed unlimited amounts of the products of earth, vine and orchard), superseded the *lex Fannia* of 161 BC, which had set monetary limits on how much could be spent on a dinner (doc. 5.56; cf. docs 2.22–4, 13.54). Sulla's motivation here is unclear and he himself was no stranger to drinking and gluttony (even after passing this law: Plut. *Sull.* 35.3, 36.1). He also seems to have abolished the grain distribution (Licinianus 34; Sall. *Hist.* 1.55.11). See Plut. *Sull.* 38.3 for the extravagance at Sulla's funeral.

Afterwards, Lucius Sulla as dictator, at a time when these laws were consigned to forgetfulness through dust and old age, and numerous people with ample patrimonies were squandering and dissipating both family and fortune into whirlpools of dinners and banquets, brought a law before the people in which it was stated that on the Kalends, Ides and Nones, on days of games and on certain solemn festivals it was proper and legal to spend 300 sesterces on a dinner, but on other days no more than 30.

(b) Macrobius *Saturnalia* 3.17.11–12

11 These laws were followed by the Cornelian law, another sumptuary law, which was brought in by Cornelius Sulla as dictator, which did not restrict the magnificence of banquets or set a limit on gourmandising, but it lowered the prices of things. Ye gods! What foods they were, the choice and almost unheard of kinds of delicacies! What fish and titbits it names, and yet lays down cheaper prices for them! I would venture to say that the cheapening of foodstuffs encouraged people into the preparation of an abundance of dishes and allowed even the less well-off to cater to their gluttony. **12** I will say clearly what I think. A person seems to me to be extravagant and prodigal beyond all others, at whose banquet such dishes are served up, even if they cost him nothing. And so it is clear that this age of ours is much more disposed to practise complete self-control in this matter, since most of the delicacies included in the Sullan law as being generally well-known, none of us knows even by name.

11.38 Privileges granted to actors in Asia

RDGE 49

In the winter of 85/4 BC Sulla had billeted troops in the towns which had supported Mithridates and imposed an indemnity of 20,000 talents (docs 11.9–10). The actors' guild in the region appealed, and Sulla confirmed a pre-existing agreement exempting them from such obligations, in fact from all 'public and military service'. In 81 Sulla allowed the actors to erect a marble stele recording this. Teso and Pergamum were the centres of the two guilds mentioned; Sulla's earlier letter is partly preserved here, but the senate's decree is lost. For Sulla and the theatre, see Garton 1964: 137–56. For a similar grant by Lucius Mummius in Greece in the second century BC, see *IG* VII.2, 413. Sulla had a strong personal friendship with the actors Metrobius and Roscius, and after he retired spent his last days in the company of actors, dancers and harpists (doc. 11.39; Macrob. 3.14.13). A citharist is a harp player.

With good fortune!
   A Lucius Cornelius Sulla Felix, son of Lucius, dictator, to the magistrates, council and people of Cos, greetings; to the citharist Alexander of Laodicea, a good and honourable man and our friend, envoy of the joint association of the theatrical artists of Ionia and the Hellespont and the theatrical artists of Dionysus our Leader, I have granted permission to erect a stele in your most prominent place **10** on which will be inscribed the privileges I have given to the artists; as, following his embassy to Rome, the senate passed a decree approving of this, I therefore wish you to ensure that a most prominent place be provided, where the stele concerning the artists may be erected. I attach below copies of my letter (to the artists) and of the decree of the senate . . .
   B . . . together with the good will you bear us, I therefore wish you to know that, on my council's advice, I have proclaimed my decision that you shall keep whatever privileges, offices, and exemptions from public service our senate, consuls, and proconsuls have given and granted you as a mark of honour to Dionysus, the Muses and your association; and that, just as before, you shall be exempt from all public service

and military service, **10** you shall not pay any tax or contribution, you shall not be troubled by anyone for supplies or lodging, and you shall not be forced to have anyone billeted on you . . .

SULLA IN RETIREMENT

It is not exactly known when Sulla laid down his dictatorship; presumably he held it down to the moment of his retirement in 79 BC, that is, he remained dictator during his term as consul in 80, retiring into private life in 79 BC (Scullard *GN* 83–4). Plut. *Sull.* 34.6 indicates that Sulla laid his dictatorship down prior to the election of the consuls for 78, i.e., at some time before July 79: Sulla then gave back to the people the right to elect consuls, and went about the forum as an ordinary citizen (cf. App. *BC* 1.103.484). Appian 478 has Sulla dictator while in his second consulship in 80, drawing an analogy with the emperors who with their supreme authority nevertheless held the consulship: 'although dictator, Sulla held a second consulship', but has him refusing a consulship for 79, and laying down the dictatorship. This suggests that he resigned from the dictatorship after his consulship in 80 BC expired. In 79 BC, he allowed the consular elections for 78 to run their course to the extent that he permitted the election of Lepidus as consul, though — according to Plutarch — reproving Pompey for supporting this candidate, who received more votes than Catulus, and cutting Pompey out of his will (Plut. *Sull.* 34.7–9, *Pomp.* 15; Keaveney 1982c: 135). Syme points out that as far as is known there were only two consular candidates anyway and that, 'Stories that exemplify the prescience of Sulla may well excite distrust' (1964: 185). See also Last & Gardner 1932: 309–12; Badian 1970: 8–14, 1976: 8–9; Twyman 1976; Scullard *GN* 83–4; Keaveney 1982: 198, 1983: 191–8; Seager 1994: 205.

11.39 Sulla's love life

Plutarch *Life of Sulla* 36.1–4

Cf. Plut. *Sull.* 33.3: 'good-looking women, female impersonators, actors, freedmen of the worst possible type, were given by him (from his confiscations) the territories of nations and the revenues of cities'. Valeria made a pass at Sulla at an exhibition of gladiators, and they soon married: *Sull.* 35.5–11. Sulla had divorced and sent away his previous wife Metella on the advice of the priests when she became fatally ill, so that his house would not become polluted (he was augur: for which see Keaveney 1982a: 150–4). But he gave her a magnificent funeral, disobeying his own sumptuary legislation (*Sull.* 35.2–4).

1 Nevertheless, even though he had Valeria at home, he still associated with women who were actresses or cithara-players and with musicians from the theatre, who used to lie drinking on couches all day long. **2** Those who were at this time most influential with him were Roscius the comedian, Sorex the leading comic actor, and Metrobius the female impersonator, who was now past his prime, but Sulla throughout everything insisted that he was in love with him. **3** By living in this way he aggravated a disease which had not originally been serious, and for a long time he was not aware that he had ulcers in the intestines, which resulted in the whole flesh being corrupted and turning into worms, so that although a number of people spent day and night removing them it was nothing compared with the way they multiplied: all his clothing, baths, washing-water, and food were overrun with that flux and corruption, so greatly did it keep breaking out. **4** To counter it, he frequently immersed himself in water to wash off and cleanse his body. But it was of no benefit: the transformation quickly overcame him, and the immensity of their number prevented all attempts at purgation.

SULLA'S ABDICATION, 79 BC

11.40 Why abdicate?

Appian *Civil Wars* 1.103–4 (478, 480–3, 487–9)

Why Sulla stepped down from the dictatorship and retired has unnecessarily worried both ancient writers (see Appian immediately below) and modern scholars. Sulla held the consulship for 80 BC with Q. Caecilius Metellus Pius, his supporter. Having passed numerous laws and reorganised the courts, he must have felt that he had carried out what he had been appointed as dictator to achieve: he had 'stabilised the city and Italy and the whole government' (doc. 11.26). Despite the proscriptions and his own illegal acts, what is clear is that he wanted to restore senatorial government, and this he had done in his dictatorship. To hold consular elections was to emphasise the return to normality which he had restored.

Sulla clearly felt confident in his 10,000 freedmen and his veterans, as Appian notes, but presumably also in the senators who owed their places to him and those who had supported him, such as Crassus and Pompey. And despite Appian's lists of crimes, the fact was that his enemies were proscribed and dead, so he had nothing to fear. The constitutional element in him — despite his illegalities — was clearly strong and the thought of a lifelong dictatorship may not have even have occurred to him. Caesar was to comment that Sulla did not know his political 'ABC': Suet. *Jul*. 77. A view which sees him forced into retirement by the senate rests largely on the (unfounded) assumption that Sulla would not have willingly given up power.

478 The following year (80 BC) Sulla, although dictator, consented to become consul for the second time with Metellus Pius to provide a pretence and facade of democratic government . . . **480** The next year (79 BC) the people, to flatter Sulla, chose him again as consul, but he refused it and appointed Servilius (Vatia) Isauricus and (Appius) Claudius Pulcher, and of his own accord willingly laid down supreme power although no one was troubling him.

481 This act of Sulla's seems amazing to me, that he should have been the first and only person up to that time to lay down such immense power with no one compelling him to do so, not to sons (like Ptolemy in Egypt and Ariobarzanes in Cappadocia and Seleucus in Syria), but to the very people who were the subjects of his tyranny; **482** and it is incredible that, after recklessly forcing his way to power, once he was in possession of it he should have laid it down. It is also strange beyond everything that he was not afraid, though in this war more than 100,000 young men had died and of his enemies he had removed 90 senators, 15 consuls, and 2,600 equites, including those who were banished; **483** the property of these men had been confiscated and the bodies of many thrown out without burial, yet Sulla, worried neither by those at home nor by the banished, nor by the cities whose citadels, walls, land, houses, money and privileges he had done away with, proclaimed himself a private citizen . . .

487 In my view Sulla — in every respect the same strong and powerful man — set his heart on becoming a tyrant when a private citizen and a private citizen when a tyrant, and after that on spending his time in rural isolation. **488** For he went off to his own estate at Cumae in Italy and there occupied himself in solitude with the sea and hunting, not because he wanted to avoid private life in Rome, nor because he was too frail to do what he wished — **489** he was still at a robust time of life and sound in health, and throughout Italy there were 120,000 men who had recently served under him and had received large grants of money and plenty of land from him, while in the city there were 10,000 Cornelii, besides the rest of his party, devoted to him and still formidable to everyone else, all of whom relied on Sulla for their immunity for the acts they had committed in co-operation with him. But my view is that, tired of war, tired of power and tired of Rome, he fell in love with the countryside.

11.41 Dedication to his sister

CIL I² 2646

(*ROL* IV.88.) On the fragment of an architrave found at Verona.

[Lucius Cornelius Su]lla, [son of Lucius], built this in the name of his [s]ister [Cornelia].

LATER VIEWS OF SULLA

11.42 Pliny the Elder's view of Sulla

Pliny *Natural History* 7.137–8

According to Plutarch (*Sull.* 37.3), Sulla dreamed that his dead son invited him to come and live with him and his mother Metella in happiness. The temple of Jupiter Capitolinus which had burnt down in 83 was rebuilt and dedicated in 69 BC by Q. Lutatius Catulus, cos. 78 (*ILRRP* 367–8), the instigator of Marius Gratidianus' death: doc. 11.19. Despite the survival of Sulla's *Memoirs*, the fact that many of his political reforms were overturned and his initial rule so bloody ensured that his memory aroused many criticisms.

137 The only person to have assumed the surname 'Fortunate' is Lucius Sulla, who actually won the title by shedding the blood of fellow-citizens and making war on his native country. And what proofs of good fortune inspired him? Was it his ability to proscribe and slaughter so many thousands of his fellow-citizens? What a corrupt interpretation of the word! How unfortunate he was to be in the future! Were they at their deaths not more fortunate then, whom today we pity, while there is no one who does not hate Sulla? **138** Come now, was not the end of his life more cruel than the calamity of all the proscribed, when his body ate itself away and gave birth to its own torments? Although he kept up a good pretence, and although we believe from that last dream, when he was almost on the point of death, that he alone was able to conquer hatred by glory, nevertheless he admitted that his happiness was lacking one thing — that he had not dedicated the Capitol.

11.43 Dionysius on Sulla's dictatorship

Dionysius of Halicarnassus *Roman Antiquities* 5.77.4–6

Dionysius is discussing the first dictatorship at Rome, that of Titus Larcius Flavus (cf. Livy 2.18.4–8; doc. 1.14); Spurius Cassius was his master of horse. The sentiments are very much like those of Pliny; see Dowling 2000: 323–4. Sallust, too, criticises Sulla for bringing everything to a bad end and demoralising the army (*Cat.* 11.4–6).

4 But in our fathers' time, a full 400 years after Titus Larcius' dictatorship, the institution was discredited and became hateful to all men under Lucius Cornelius Sulla, the first and only dictator who exercised his power as dictator cruelly and severely; as a result the Romans then noticed for the first time what they had previously been unaware of, that the rule of a dictator is a tyranny. **5** For Sulla made up the senate from just about anybody, reduced the power of the tribunate to the minimum, depopulated whole cities, abolished some kingdoms and created others, and committed many other arbitrary actions, which it would be a lengthy task to recount; and of the citizens, besides those who died in battle, he killed not less than 40,000 after they had surrendered to him, and some of these after first torturing them. **6** Whether all these acts of his were necessary or beneficial to the state it is not now the time to inquire; what I have tried to show is that on their account the name of dictator was loathed and appeared terrible.

11.44 Sulla on himself

Plutarch *Life of Sulla* 38.6

Sulla died in 78, at the relatively young age of only sixty years. Lepidus, cos. 78, with some support, wanted to deprive Sulla of funeral honours, but the other consul, Q. Lutatius Catulus (*MRR* II.85) and Pompey ensured that there was a sumptuous state funeral, and the women at Rome gave huge quantities of spices; the senate, equites, his legions and the plebeians all participated; for the funeral: Appian *BC* 1.105–6.493–500; Plut. *Sull.* 38; Sumi 2002: 420–1.

His monument is in the Campus Martius; it is said that the inscription on it is one that he wrote for himself. The purport of it is that none of his friends had outdone him in doing good and none of his enemies in doing harm.

COINAGE 87–81 BC

Sulla's name appeared on four issues of coins (Crawford *RRC* 359, 367, 368, 381): see Crawford 1964; Keaveney 1982a: 154–61; Ramage 1991: 102–6; Mackay 2000: 198–206. While there are some difficulties of interpretation regarding these coins, they were clearly meant to serve Sulla's interests and propaganda purposes, as on the coins appear Roma, Venus, the palm branch of victory, the triumphal chariot, trophies, and symbols of Sulla's position as augur. More than anyone previously, Sulla used coinage to convey specific messages, in which he was followed by Pompey, Caesar and the emperors.

11.45 Cinna and grain distribution

Crawford *RRC* 351.1

A denarius, 86 BC (Grueber I.2463; Sydenham *CRR* 717; Foss no. 14). This coin probably refers to a free distribution of grain (Foss; Lovano 2002: 76).

Obverse: Bust of Ceres, goddess of agricultural growth.
Reverse: Ear of wheat. Two male figures sitting on a bench (*subsellium*), facing right, with an ear of grain on the far right.

11.46 Sulla triumphant

Crawford *RRC* 367

This coin is an aureus (gold coin) of c. 82 BC (Grueber II.461 no. 5; Sydenham *CRR* 756; Sutherland no. 76; Carson *PCRR* no. 141; Foss no. 15; Keaveney 1982a: 160; Crawford *CMRR* fig. 72; Ramage 1991: 103). The coin hails Sulla as imperator, and the following coin (doc. 11.47) has him as imperator for a second time. This coin type forms the bulk of Sulla's coinage.

Obverse: Bust of the goddess Roma.
Reverse: Sulla, wearing toga, in triumphal quadriga (four-horse chariot), facing right; Victory flies above him, facing left, and carrying a victory wreath; inscription: L. Sull[a] Im[perator]. Sulla carries in his right hand a laurel branch (Grueber, Sydenham), or a caduceus, herald's staff (Crawford); a laurel branch of victory is the best interpretation. He holds the reins in his left hand.

11.47 Sulla and Venus

Crawford *RRC* 359.1

An aureus of c. 84–83 BC, minted by Sulla outside Italy (Carson *PCRR* no. 142; Foss no. 16; Ramage 1991: 102–3; Keaveney 1982a: 160; Crawford *CMRR* fig. 72; Mackay 2000: 198–206, cf. 177–93). The jug and lituus refer to Sulla's role as augur. Which two acclamations as imperator are being referred to is debated: Cilicia and Chaeronea, or Chaeronea and the Colline Gate (see Mackey 2000: 177–206 for the arguments). As the Colline Gate battle involved a victory over citizens, a coin representing two major events of his career, Cilicia and his victory over Mithridates, is to be preferred.

Obverse: Head of the goddess Venus, with diadem, facing right, with standing Cupid (holding a palm-branch, the sign of victory) facing left; inscription: Sulla.
Reverse: Jug and lituus (augur's staff; the jug and lituus were symbols of the augurate), with a trophy on either side; inscription: Imper[ator] iterum (a second time).

11.48 Sulla's equestrian statue

Crawford *RRC* 381

An aureus of c. 80 BC (Grueber II.463 no. 16; Sydenham *CRR* 762; Sutherland no. 77; Crawford *RRC* 381.1; Carson *PCRR* no. 143; Foss no. 20; Hill *MAR* no. 112; Gordon 1983: no. 16; Ramage 1991: 104, 110).

Obverse: Bust of the goddess Roma.
Reverse: Equestrian statue of Sulla, facing left, right hand raised; inscription: L. Sull(a) Fe[li(x) Dic(tator)].

11.49 Establishment of Sulla's colonies (?)

Crawford *RRC* 381

A denarius of 81 BC (Grueber I.2844; Sydenham *CRR* 744; Foss 19). This coin is sometimes taken to be related to Sulla's military colonies, but note Crawford: 'I do not believe that there is any reference to Sulla's colonies or to his enlargement of the pomerium' (cf. doc. 1.3).

Obverse: Bust of the goddess Ceres.
Reverse: Ploughman, holding a staff, with pair of oxen, facing left.

11.50 The coinage of Sulla's son

Crawford *RRC* 426.1

A denarius (Grueber I.3824; Sydenham *CRR* 879; Carson *PCRR* 186; Harlan *RRM* 16.1–2). Sulla's son Faustus Cornelius Sulla issued silver denarii c. 60 BC (perhaps in 63 BC) commemorating the surrender of Jugurtha by Bocchus to Sulla. The coin may represent the signet ring which Sulla had cut to commemorate the occasion (Plut. *Mar.* 10.8–9: doc. 9.13).

Obverse: Bust of the goddess Diana wearing diadem.
Reverse: Sulla seated, facing left; Bocchus kneels before him, handing an olive branch (vertical) to Sulla. Jugurtha, facing left and with his hands bound, kneels behind the seated Sulla.

12

The Collapse of the Republic

Pompey's career to 78 BC had been extraordinary, for he thrived under Sulla, though he disregarded Sulla's constitution both in Sulla's lifetime and after his death, while he was nevertheless the defender of the Sullan senate against both Lepidus and then Sertorius: on Sulla's death in 78 Pompey had ensured he had a magnificent funeral (doc. 11.44). Cicero in the 70s was pursuing his oratorical training and gain-ing increasing experience in the law-courts (doc. 2.62), while Caesar, who was to be quaestor in 69, avoided embroilment with Lepidus (doc. 12.2), whose insurrection almost immediately followed Sulla's death in 78 BC. As consul for that year, Lepidus may have desired to emulate Sulla and seize control of the state. In 79 Pompey had not opposed the election of Lepidus as consul for 78, although Sulla apparently objected to his candidature (doc. 11.39). Lepidus' revolt was put down by Catulus (cos. 78) with Pompey's involvement (doc. 12.2). Pompey then refused to disband his army, and was granted imperium to go to Spain in 77 to help Caecilius Metellus Pius (cos. 80) against Sertorius; after initial setbacks, and lack of support from Rome, Pompey sent a letter to the senate in 75 BC requesting reinforcements (doc. 12.3). After Sertorius' assassination by Perperna, who had brought remnants of Lepidus' army to join Sertorius, Pompey defeated and killed Perperna and organised Spain into provinces. The senate's ability to deal with the revolts of Lepidus and Sertorius (and Spartacus' slave revolt), indicates the success of Sulla's constitutional reform: the senate as a united body opposed both men, and successfully.

Pompey was recalled by the senate in 71 to assist Crassus in suppressing Spartacus' uprising (doc. 6.45), and was awarded a triumph. He then successfully stood for the consulship of 70 with Crassus as his fellow consul: Pompey had at this stage held no other civic magistracies. The two apparently disagreed at the beginning of their consulship, but did restore tribunician powers, reform the law-courts, and during their consulship the census of Roman citizens was taken (docs 12.4–7).

The last time a tribune and the popular assembly had conferred a military command was in the case of Sulpicius Rufus in 88 BC, who transferred Sulla's command against Mithridates to Marius (doc. 9.32). In 67 and 66 BC Pompey benefited directly from the restoration of the tribunate through the lex Gabinia (67) and then the lex Manilia (66). These commands gave him imperium on an unrivalled scale; despite the senate's opposition to the lex Gabinia Pompey received a three-year command and in fact was to deal with the pirates infesting the Mediterranean in a few months (docs 12.8–9). In the following year, through the lex Manilia, Pompey was awarded Lucullus' command in the east against Mithridates, where Lucullus had had some spectacular success: the campaign had, however, dragged on, Clodius Pulcher had encouraged Lucullus' troops to mutiny, and the publicani were unhappy with Lucullus' favourable treatment of the provincials (docs 11.10, 12.10). Cicero spoke in favour of Pompey receiving the command and Lucullus, deprived of his command, became Pompey's implacable enemy as a result. Pompey defeated Mithridates in the same year, and spent until 62 reorganising the east (docs 12.11–12).

In Pompey's absence, Cicero had held the praetorship in 66 and reached the consulship in 63. In this year the Catilinarian Conspiracy broke out, and, despite Cicero's palpable desire to emphasise the enormity of Catiline's threat to the state, it does seem in fact to have been a serious threat (docs 12.14–23). Cicero with the authority of the senate put five of the chief conspirators to death: Caesar had spoken against this in the senate, but Cato the Younger had successfully urged their execution. As the conspirators were Roman citizens they should have been tried and Cicero would pay dearly for this with exile in 58–57 BC. In 62 BC, the scandal of Clodius' profanation of the rites of the Bona Dea occurred: he was put on trial, and Cicero disproved his alibi, incurring Clodius' political enmity as a result (docs 7.85, 12.36, 46, 54).

Pompey had enjoyed great successes in the east (docs 12.27–30) and his return was viewed with apprehension, but he disbanded his troops when he landed at Brundisium in 62 BC. There was tension between both himself and Cicero, who felt slighted that Pompey was not effusive enough over Cicero's role in squashing Catiline (docs 12.30–2). Pompey's victories were duly celebrated in his (third) triumph in 61 (docs 12.28, 2.55). He sought ratification for his re-organisation in the east and land for his veterans. But he had miscalculated: the senate obstructed both measures (doc. 12.34). Another issue developed: the equites had bid too much for their contract to collect taxes and wanted the contract re-negotiated; Crassus supported them in this. The senate, principally led by Cato, refused. The proposal that equites be liable to prosecution for accepting bribes in judicial cases also caused friction between senate and equites (doc. 12.33). These two issues played a role in the next major development at Rome, with far reaching consequences: the events of the consulship of Caesar (59 BC). He had used massive bribery to gain election as pontifex maximus in 63 BC against more senior senatorial contenders (doc. 3.20), as praetor-elect for 62 had opposed in 63 the execution of Catiline's chief supporters (doc. 12.21), and had been successful as governor in Further Spain (61 BC), where he had earned a triumph, planning to celebrate this on his return to Rome in 60. He requested that he be allowed to stand in absentia (a magistrate with imperium could not enter the pomerium of the city and he had to retain his imperium in order to celebrate his triumph); on Cato's urging the senate refused to grant this permission (doc. 12.37).

The election of Caesar as consul brought three men together in what is often known as 'the First Triumvirate': Caesar, Crassus and Pompey; the initiative came from Caesar, the most junior of the three. Cicero was offered a close relationship with the three but true to his republican ideals refused (doc. 12.38), as he later did a place on Caesar's land commission (doc. 12.44). He would also turn down a position on Caesar's staff in Gaul in 58 which might have saved him from exile. Pompey married Caesar's daughter Julia to cement the alliance (docs 12.39, 43). During his consulship Caesar effected the ratification of Pompey's eastern settlements (acta) and land for his veterans, while the publicani received relief from their contract (docs 12.41–3). He was able to act unopposed: Caesar's fellow-consul was M. Calpurnius Bibulus, Cato's son-in-law, who with Cato opposed Caesar's agricultural legislation. Violence in the forum led to Bibulus spending the remainder of the year in his house proclaiming unfavourable omens, and was inactive to the extent that jokes apparently circulated about the 'Consulship of Julius and Caesar' (doc. 12.41).

Fearing that Caesar might achieve the consulship, the senate had assigned the 'woods and pastures' as the consular provinces for the consuls of 59 (doc. 12.41). Caesar therefore ensured that he was awarded the governorship of the two Gauls and Illyricum (north-east of the Adriatic) for five years. Opposition to the triumvirate grew in 59, led largely by the younger Curio, who however was to be tribune of the plebs in 50 BC and, as such, a chief supporter of Caesar (docs 12.48–50, 13.14–16). Cicero complained about 'certain political matters' in 59 (doc. 12.46) and in his opinion this led to the adoption of Clodius by a plebeian; Clodius was duly elected to the tribunate for 58 and carried out an extensive legislative programme; he also attacked Cicero, who went into exile (docs 12.52–4), arranged for Cato to go on an official mission to Cyprus (docs 12.55–7), and began attacks on Pompey, who as a consequence then supported the moves for Cicero's recall. Cicero describes his triumphant return to Italy and Rome (docs 12.58–60), where he proposed that Pompey be given powers to deal with Rome's grain crisis (docs 12.61–3).

Caesar had meanwhile been busy conquering, pillaging and massacring in Gaul (docs 12.64–6), gaining enormous amounts of wealth with which to pursue his political aims at Rome. Cicero was soon speaking with his customary freedom, attacking Caesar in the hope of separating Pompey from Caesar. This, along with growing antagonism between Crassus and Pompey, resulted in a re-alliance of the triumvirs, with Caesar meeting Crassus at Ravenna and then Pompey at Luca in April 56 (docs 12.67–70). It was agreed that Crassus and Pompey should share the consulship again for 55, and be granted five-year provincial commands to follow, while Caesar's command in Gaul would also be extended for another five years. Cicero was 'brought to heel' and as part of his 'palinode' in 56 opposed the proposal to deprive Caesar of his command (doc. 12.71), while he was also forced to defend old enemies at the behest of the triumvirs (doc. 12.75).

This rapprochement was undercut by the death of Julia in childbirth (Pompey turned down another marriage alliance with Caesar), and Crassus' death in Parthia (docs 12.77–82). Caesar meanwhile continued amassing wealth from his conquests in Gaul and Britain (docs 12.83–9). In his absence, on-going factional violence in Rome between Clodius and Milo was to set the stage for Pompey's sole consulship in 52, his acceptance by the optimates, and the outbreak of civil war, which it could be argued was brought about by senators whose main aim was Caesar's downfall. Tacitus (doc. 12.1) associates Pompey with Marius and Sulla as individuals who were part of the process of the transformation from political liberty to the 'sole dominion' of Augustus. Like the other four major protagonists in this period Pompey was to meet a violent death: Crassus was killed in battle, Pompey was murdered, Cato committed suicide, Caesar was assassinated and Cicero was proscribed.

The main studies for individuals in the period 78–44 BC are: *Caesar*: Fuller 1965; Balsdon 1967, Yavetz 1983; Bradford 1984; Southern 2001; esp. Gelzer 1968; Meier 1995; his Tenth Legion: Dando-Collins 2002; *Cicero*: Smith 1966; Stockton 1971; Rawson 1975; Lacey 1978; Mitchell 1979, 1991; Habicht 1990; Fuhrmann 1992; Everitt 2001; *Clodius*: Tatum 1999; *Crassus*: Adcock 1966; Marshall 1976; Ward 1977; Gruen 1977; *Pompey*: Leach 1978; Greenhalgh 1980, 1981; Seager 2002; Southern 2002.

Portrait busts: the best known portrait bust of Pompey is in the Ny Carlsberg Glyptothek, Copenhagen; it is Augustan in date, usually said to be a copy of a contemporary portrait (Rawson 1975: plate 2; Leach 1978: plates 2–3; Greenhalgh 1980: plate 1; Meier 1995: plate 8; Everitt 2001: plates; Southern 2001: 20; cover of Seager 2002; Southern 2002: plate 6; other busts: Toynbee 1978: plates 18–21). There are numerous busts of Caesar: Toynbee plates 33–7; Rawson plate 6; Meier plates 1–4; Everitt: plates; Southern 2001: 10, 53, 59; Southern 2000 plates 11, 13. For a coin portrait of Caesar, see doc. 13.74. There is a possible portrait bust of Crassus: Meier plate 9. For busts of Cicero: Toynbee plates 22–3; Rawson plates 1, 5; Meier plate 13; Everitt plates; Southern 2001: 37. There is a magnificent bronze portrait bust of Cato the Younger from North Africa: Toynbee plates 38–9 (also with a stone bust); Rawson plate 4; Meier plate 11; Everitt plates; Southern 2002: plate 8. Mark Antony is best known from the exquisitely crafted green slate bust produced in Egypt, but there are less flattering portraits of him (Toynbee plates 51–2; Meier plate 18; Everitt: plates; Rawson plate 7; Southern 2001: 78, 112).

For the period 78–44 BC, see Syme 1939: 28–96; Cowell 1962: 130–68; Brunt 1971: 112–47, 1988; Scullard *GN* 85–153; Seager 1994; Rawson 1994; Sherwin-White 1994; Shotter 1994: 51–87; Wiseman 1994, 1994a; Gruen 1995; cf. Crook, Lintott & Rawson 1994. Chapters Twelve and Thirteen cannot assess why the Republic collapsed (or was transformed), but aim to provide some of the main passages and interpretative comment needed for the study of the period.

Ancient sources (for 78–44 BC): for this period there is a degree of contemporary information unrivalled for any other period in Roman history due to the writings of Cicero and Caesar. In addition, the biographies of Plutarch and the histories written in the imperial age are important as they provide the overall chronological framework within which Cicero's more detailed information can be placed.

Caesar's *Gallic War* is an account of his campaigns in Gaul; it is in seven books with an eighth by Hirtius continuing the account. Caesar's *Civil War* provides his perspective on events: needless to say, this is hardly objective. Caesar presents himself and his actions in the way he wants these to be viewed and interpreted. However, along with Cicero's letters, Caesar's *Civil War* provides a personal and contemporary perspective on the conflict. The *Alexandrian War*, *Spanish War* and *African War* dealing with these campaigns are not by Caesar, but they provide detailed accounts, starting with Caesar's arrival in Alexandria in 48 BC and concluding with his return to Rome in 45 BC.

Cicero delivered various speeches in this period, not all of which survive; there are fifty-seven speeches in all for the period 81–43 BC: those delivered by his opponents do not survive. He could clearly be tendentious, and he cannot be accepted as giving the 'whole truth and nothing but the truth'. There is also the commentary of Asconius on five of these speeches. Particularly important is Asconius' commentary on Cicero's

Milo (doc. 13.1), which shows that Cicero in defending Milo on the charge of killing Clodius was not being completely accurate. Cicero's correspondence is also crucial. He wrote letters to his close friend Atticus (*Att.*), to his brother Quintus (*Quint.*), to Brutus, and to others (*Fam.*), and amongst the collection of letters to friends are some written to him. Some 912 letters survive. These letters, usually dated, provide detailed information about the unfolding of events, though many contain contemporary allusions which are difficult to understand.

Another contemporary source is Sallust. He wrote two important historical monographs, one concerning the war against Jugurtha (see chapter nine) and the other concerning the conspiracy of Catiline (docs 12.14–16, 19–23). In addition, his *Historiae* (*Histories*) dealt with the period from 78 BC (perhaps continuing the history of Sisenna, but 78, Sulla's death, marked a logical place to begin). The last dated fragment (in Book Five) refers to 67 BC but his intention must have been to continue his account beyond that date. An important fragment is Pompey's dispatch from Spain to the senate (doc. 12.3). As in his two historical monographs there is an overriding emphasis on attacking the nobiles and emphasising the decline of Rome.

Lucan (AD 39–65) wrote the Pharsalia (*de bello civili*), a poetic epic which commences with Caesar crossing the Rubicon and ends with Caesar in Alexandria (48–47 BC) but is unfinished. He almost certainly drew on Livy's lost books for this period.

There are also the historians of the imperial period. None of Livy's books on this period survive, but are summarised in *Periochae* 90–116. Velleius Paterculus in Book 2.29–58 deals with this period in a brief but important continuous chronological treatment; there is a reasonably long section on Caesar (2.41–59). Appian *Civil Wars* 1.107–121, 2.1–117 is also very important in presenting a chronological framework. As in other parts of his *Civil Wars* he uses sources now lost. For Lucullus' and Pompey's campaigns against Mithridates, his *Mithridatica* 67–121 is vital. Dio, books 36–44, also covers this period.

There are various biographies for the period. The beginning of Suetonius' biography of Caesar, the *Divus Julius*, is lost and in its current state the *Life* commences in Caesar's sixteenth year. His approach, after sketching the details of Caesar's life, is (as in the other biographies) to develop themes rather than to use a chronological approach. He is certainly interested in the personal characteristics of his subject, but the account is reliable. Plutarch wrote several biographies of the individuals involved in this period: Antony, Brutus, Caesar, Cato the Younger, Cicero, Crassus, Lucullus, Pompey, and Sertorius. The number of relevant biographies indicates the importance of the period. They are of mixed quality and offer his usual moral observations. But he drew heavily on lost historians and in many of the *Lives* there is a wealth of detail about individual historical events (such as the account of Cato in Africa). In the *Lives* of those involved in the events of 52–44 BC, however, there is a frustrating lack of detail about the main events.

12.1 Tacitus on republican history

Tacitus *Histories* 2.38

Tacitus alludes to the tribunes Ti. and G. Gracchus, Saturninus and Drusus. Otho was hailed emperor by the praetorians in AD 69 but committed suicide when his troops were defeated; Vitellius was proclaimed emperor by his troops in 69; his forces were defeated by those of Vespasian and he was killed by the mob in December 69.

The old lust for power, long ingrained in mankind, came to maturity and erupted as the empire became great; for equality was easily maintained while Rome's power was moderate. But when, with the conquest of the world and the destruction of rival cities or kings, there was the freedom to desire the secure enjoyment of wealth, the struggles between senators and people first blazed up. At one time the tribunes stirred up trouble, at another the consuls were in control, and the city and forum saw the first attempts at civil war; then Gaius Marius, from the lowest ranks of the plebs, and Lucius Sulla, the most ruthless of the nobles, conquered liberty by arms and turned it into tyranny. After them came Gnaeus Pompey, who was no better, though cleverer at concealing his aims, and from then there was no other aim but autocracy. Legions of Roman citizens did not shrink from fighting at Pharsalus or Philippi, and it was even less likely that the armies of Otho and Vitellius would have made or abandoned war of their own accord: the same divine wrath, the same human madness, the same criminal purposes drove them to conflict.

THE AFTERMATH OF SULLA

12.2 The revolt of Lepidus, 78–77 BC

Appian *Civil Wars* 1.107 (501–4)

M. Aemilius Lepidus (cos. 78) had supported Sulla and benefited financially from the proscriptions; though Sulla (according to Plutarch) did not support him as a consular candidate (doc. 11.39), he was elected. Lepidus' measures undermined Sulla's settlement: exiles were to be recalled, confiscated land was to be returned to its original owners, and grain distributions resumed (Licinianus 34; Livy *Per.* 90). An uprising broke out in Etruria on Sulla's death and Lepidus and the other consul of 78, Q. Lutatius Catulus, were authorised to suppress it; Lepidus decided to support the rebels. The senate nevertheless assigned him Transalpine Gaul for 77, presumably hoping to get him out of the way, and made the two consuls swear not to fight.

When the senate recalled him to Rome to hold the consular elections, he marched on the city in 77 and demanded both a second consulship and the restoration of tribunician powers; when the tribunes had asked this of the consuls in 78, Lepidus had refused (Licinianus 33–5; Sall. *Hist.* 1.77.14). Caesar, though invited, did not join the revolt (Suet. *Jul.* 3; Plut. *Caes.* 1.1). A *SCU* was passed on the motion of L. Marcius Philippus (cos. 91), and Pompey was appointed to support Catulus in squashing the revolt. Lepidus retreated to Etruria and then to Sardinia, where he died. The remnants of his army, under Perperna (M. Perperna Veiento), joined Sertorius in Spain. Lepidus' legate M. Junius Brutus (the father of Brutus, Caesar's assassin), was killed by Pompey after he had surrendered.

Lepidus: Licinianus 33–4; App. *BC* 1.105.491, 107.501–4; Sall. *Hist.* 1.54–83 (55: speech of Lepidus; 77: speech of Philippus); Plut. *Pomp.* 15–16, *Sull.* 34.7–9; *MRR* II.85; Last & Gardner

1932: 314–17; Hayne 1972; Leach 1978: 42–3; Scullard *GN* 85–6; Badian *FC* 275–6; Spann 1987: 75–7; Seager 1994: 208–9, 2002: 30–2; esp. Gruen 1995: 12–17); Hillman 1998; cf. Smith 1960: 4–10.

501 This was the end of Sulla, and as soon as the consuls returned from the funeral they began engaging in a heated quarrel, while the citizens started to side with one or the other. Lepidus, who wanted the support of the Italians, stated that he would return the land taken from them by Sulla. **502** As the senate was afraid of both parties, it made them take an oath that they would not resort to war. When Lepidus was assigned Transalpine Gaul by lot, he did not return to the assembly because in the following year he would be free from his oath not to make war on the Sullans, as it was considered that the oath was only binding during the year of office. **503** As his plans did not escape observation, he was summoned by the senate, and as he well knew the reasons for the summons he came with his entire army, with the intention of bringing it into the city with him. When this was prevented he ordered his men to take up arms, and Catulus on the other side did the same. **504** A battle took place not far from the Campus Martius in which Lepidus was beaten, and with no further attempt at resistance he sailed off to Sardinia, where he died of a consumption. His army gradually melted away, with the greater part of it taken by Perperna to Sertorius in Spain.

12.3 Pompey's letter to the senate, 75 BC

Sallust *Histories* 2.98 [82]

Quintus Sertorius (c. 126–73 BC) was an eques from Nursia, a Sabine city. He served against the Cimbri under Q. Servilius Caepio and Marius, and under T. Didius in Spain as military tribune from 97–93, and was awarded a corona (Plut *Sert*. 2–3; *MRR* II.7–8). As quaestor in 90 (*MRR* II.27) he saw service in the Social War which made him popular. In either 89 or 88 he stood for the tribunate but Sulla effectively prevented his election, so he turned to Cinna (*Sert*. 4). As praetor (in 83) he was allotted Roman Spain, and went there when it was clear that Sulla would be victorious (Plut. *Sert*. 6; App. *BC* 1.86.392–3; *Iber*. 101.438–41; Livy *Per*. 90–1; cf. Sall. *Hist*. 1.81–6; Spann 1987: 1–39; Strisino 2002).

Initially driven out of Spain by the proconsul C. Annius, Sertorius returned at the invitation of the Lusitanians in 80, defeating a series of Roman commanders sent against him; by 77 he controlled most of Roman Spain, where he set up a Roman-style senate and government (Sall. *Hist*. 1.94–103; Plut. *Sert*. 7–12; *MRR* II.70, 77, 81). The consuls of 77 declined to go to Spain, and Pompey, who had after Lepidus' defeat again refused to disband his army, was sent with proconsular imperium to assist Q. Caecilius Metellus Pius (cos. 80) against Sertorius and Perperna (Cic. *Man*. 62; Hillman 1998; Seager 2002: 32).

After various successes by the Roman generals, including an indecisive engagement at Sucro in 75 BC, Sertorius counter-attacked, in 75 cutting off their supplies (Sall. *Hist*. 2.29–33, 59; Livy *Per*. 91–3; Plut. *Pomp*. 16–19, *Sert*. 18–22; App. *BC* 1.108–112.449–69; *MRR* II.90, 94, 98–9, 104; Spann 1987: 40–120). Pompey, still an eques, wrote the following letter to the senate for reinforcements: there is no reason to doubt that Sallust's version is based on Pompey's original letter. For the letter: Spann 120–22; Hillman 1990: 446–9; McGushin 1992: 242–7; Gruen 1995: 19–20.

In 72 Perperna assassinated Sertorius (doc. 12.4), and in the same year was defeated and executed by Pompey (Sall. *Hist*. 3.84–7; Livy *Per*. 96; App. *BC* 1.113–15. 525–38, *Iber*. 101.438–41; Plut. *Pomp*. 20–1, *Sert*. 25–7; *MRR* II.118). Val. Max. 6.2.8: Helvius Mancia, taunted by Pompey, described him as *adulescentulus carnifex* (youthful butcher) due to his murder of Cn.

Domitius Ahenobarbus, M. Brutus, Cn. Carbo and Perperna. In 70, an amnesty was granted under a *lex Plautia* to those who had supported Lepidus and Sertorius (Sall. *Hist.* 3.37). For Sertorius: Plut. *Sert.* (with Konrad 1994); Last & Gardner 1932b: 318–26; Scullard *GN* 85–9; Leach 1978: 44–54; Greenhalgh 1980: 40–57; Badian *FC* 277–81; Spann 1987; Seager 1994: 215–21, 2002: 32–5; Gruen 1995: 19–20; Konrad 1995.

1 'If I had undertaken such hardships and dangers in a war against you, my country and my country's gods — and frequently from my early youth the most abominable enemies have been routed under my leadership and your safety assured — you could have taken no worse measures against me in my absence than you are doing at present, Fathers of the Senate, for after dispatching me, despite my youth, to a most savage war, you have destroyed me, together with an excellent army, as far as you could, by starvation, the most wretched of all deaths. **2** Is it with such expectations that the Roman people sends its sons to war? Are these the rewards for wounds and blood so often shed on the state's behalf? Wearied by writing letters and sending legates I have exhausted all my own resources and even my hopes, and in the meantime you have given me barely a year's expenses over a three-year period. **3** By the immortal gods! Do you think I can perform the function of a treasury or maintain an army without provisions and pay?

4 'I admit that I entered this war with more zeal than prudence, for within 40 days of receiving the mere title of general from you I had raised and prepared an army and driven the enemy, who were already at the throat of Italy, from the Alps into Spain; through those mountains I opened up another route than that of Hannibal, and one more convenient for us. **5** I recovered Gaul, the Pyrenees, Lacetania, and the Indigetes, and withstood with newly-enrolled soldiers and far inferior numbers the first attack of the conqueror Sertorius, and spent the winter in camp surrounded by the most savage enemy, not in the towns or in pursuit of my own popularity.

6 'Why, then, should I enumerate the battles or winter campaigns, the towns destroyed or recovered? Actions speak louder than words: the capture of the enemy's camp at Sucro, the battle at the river Turia, and the destruction of the enemy leader Gaius Herennius, together with his army and the city of Valentia, are known to you well enough; in return for which, grateful senators, you have given me want and hunger. As a result, the condition of my army and the enemy's is the same; for neither is given pay, **7** and both can march as victor into Italy. **8** I warn you of this and beg you to give it your attention, rather than compelling me to take care of the army's necessities in a private capacity. **9** Whatever of Hither Spain is not held by the enemy has been ravaged either by ourselves or by Sertorius to the point of utter devastation except for the coastal cities, so that it is actually an expense and burden on us; last year Gaul provided Metellus' army with pay and provisions, and now it can scarcely keep itself because of a bad harvest; I have exhausted not only my property but even my credit. **10** You are all that is left — unless you come to our aid, the army, albeit against my will and with advance warning on my part, will cross over into Italy, and with it all the war in Spain.'

This letter was read in the senate at the beginning of the following year (74 BC). But the consuls distributed between themselves the provinces decreed by the senate, Cotta taking Hither Gaul and Octavius Cilicia. Then the next consuls (for 74 BC), Lucius Lucullus and Marcus Cotta, greatly disturbed by Pompey's letters and messages, both for the sake of the state and because if the army was led into Italy they would have neither glory or status, provided him with money and reinforcements by every means possible, with the nobility especially exerting themselves, the majority of whom were already giving him their support and backing up their words with deeds.

THE CONSULSHIP OF 70 BC

Pompey returned to Italy in 71 BC at the request of the senate to assist in the crushing of the revolt of Spartacus, who had defeated the two consuls of 72 (L. Gellius Publicola & Cn. Cornelius Lentulus Clodianus), each separately and then with their armies combined (*MRR* II.116). Crassus was appointed proconsul against Spartacus and in six months in 72–71 BC defeated the slave rebels (Sallust *Hist.* 4.20–41; Livy *Per.* 96–7; App. *BC* 1.118–121; Plut. *Crass.* 10–11, *Pomp.* 21.1–3; *MRR* II.118, 123). Pompey returned in time to kill 5,000 fugitives from Crassus' last engagement against the slaves, and wrote to the senate that he (Pompey) had finished the war (see doc. 6.43). Crassus nevertheless asked for Pompey to stand for the consulship with him and they kept their armies under arms outside Rome, awaiting their triumph (Pompey for his victory in Spain) and ovatio (Crassus), and were elected to the consulship *in absentia*. Plutarch has Pompey and Crassus differing on issues throughout the consulship, and being reconciled at its end; Appian has them reconciled at the beginning of the consulship (App. *BC* 1.121 (doc. 12.5); Plut. *Crass.* 12, *Pomp.* 23; Appian's less dramatic account is to be preferred).

Restoration of tribunician powers: Sulla had stripped the tribunate of its powers (doc. 11.30). Lepidus had proposed to restore these in 78 BC (doc. 12.2), and there had been various other attempts opposed by the senate, such as L. Licinius Macer's in 73 (apparently with Pompey's support, Sallust *Hist.* 3.48), through the seventies. In 75 BC, the prohibition from holding further office was removed. The full restoration of the tribunate came with Pompey and Crassus in 70 BC (the sources give Pompey most of the credit). This was an important qualification of the Sullan constitution. Tribunician reform in 70 BC: Cic. *Verr.* 1.44–5; Plut. *Pomp.* 22.4 (other sources: *MRR* II.126); Stockton 1973: 209–10; McDermott 1977a; Leach 1978: 60–1; Greenhalgh 1980: 67; Marshall & Beness 1987: esp. 373–8; Seager 1994: 224, 227, 2002: 37; Gruen 1995: 23–8.

However in 70 BC Pompey failed to gain land for the veterans who had served with him in Spain. The *lex Plotia agraria*, proposed in 70 BC, was never put into effect (*MRR* II.128; Smith 1957; Marshall 1972; Seager 1994: 227, 2002: 39). At the end of 70, neither Pompey nor Crassus took up a provincial command (Plut. *Pomp.* 23.3–4; Badian *FC* 284).

12.4 From Spartacus to the consulship, 72–70 BC

Livy *Periochae* 96–97

96 (72 BC) The praetor, Quintus Arrius, killed Crixus, leader of the runaways, along with 20,000 men. The consul Gnaeus Lentulus lost a battle to Spartacus. The consul Lucius Gellius and the praetor Quintus Arrius were defeated in battle by the same man. Sertorius was murdered at a banquet by Marcus Perperna, Manius Antonius and other conspirators, in his eighth year as leader, a great commander and more often than not the victor over two generals, Pompey and Metellus, but towards the end cruel and spendthrift. The command of his faction was transferred to Marcus (Perperna), whom Gnaeus Pompey conquered, captured and killed; Pompey recovered Spain in about the tenth year after the war had started. The proconsul Gaius Cassius and praetor Gnaeus Manlius lost a battle to Spartacus, and the war was entrusted to the praetor Marcus Crassus.

97 (72–70 BC) The praetor Marcus Crassus first won a battle against part of the runaways, composed of Gauls and Germans, with 35,000 of the enemy's soldiers killed, including their leaders Castus and Gannicus. He then fought the matter out with Spartacus, who was killed with 60,000 of his men. The praetor Marcus Antonius undertook a campaign with little success against the Cretans and closed it with his death. The proconsul Marcus Lucullus subdued the Thracians. Lucius Lucullus won a battle against Mithridates in Pontus, with more than 60,000 of the enemy's soldiers killed. Marcus Crassus and Gnaeus Pompey were made consuls (Pompey by senatorial decree, while a Roman eques and before he had held the quaestorship) and restored the power of the tribunes. The courts were also transferred by the praetor Marcus Aurelius Cotta to the Roman equites. Mithridates was forced by the hopelessness of his circumstances to take refuge with Tigranes, king of Armenia.

12.5 Pompey 'neither praetor nor quaestor'

Appian *Civil Wars* 1.121 (560–1)

The senate passed a law to exempt Pompey from the Sullan *lex annalis*, the provisions of which prescribed that the quaestorship and praetorship be held prior to the consulship, with a minimum age (42) for election to the consulship (Cic *Man.* 62; Livy *Per.* 97; cf. Plut. *Pomp.* 22.5–9: his discharge as an eques).

560 Crassus accomplished this (the defeat of Spartacus) in six months, and as a result was immediately at loggerheads with Pompey over which of them deserved the greatest prestige. He did not disband his army, for neither had Pompey. Both were candidates for the consulship, but while Crassus had held the praetorship in accordance with Sulla's legislation, Pompey had held neither praetorship nor quaestorship, and was only 34 years old. He had, however, promised the tribunes that he would restore their magistracy to much of its traditional power. **561** Once elected consuls, they still did not disband their armies, keeping them close to the city. Each made an excuse: Pompey that he was waiting for the return of Metellus for his Spanish triumph, Crassus that Pompey should be the first to do so.

12.6 The law courts in 70 BC

Cicero *Against Verres* 1.37–40

See also doc. 12.4. Sulla had handed the courts over to the senators, overturning Gaius Gracchus' reform (docs 11.29, 8.28). Lucius Aurelius Cotta as praetor in 70 BC (brother of the Cottas who were consuls in 75 and 74 BC) introduced a law (the *lex Aurelia*) to give membership of the juries to three groups: the senators, the equites, and the tribuni aerarii ('treasury officials'), who belonged to the same census qualification as the equites. Pompey as consul-elect had noted the corruption of the courts according to Cicero (*Verr.* 1.45), but his role in the actual reform is not attested. This was the last time during the Republic that membership of the courts was an issue: MRR II.127; Ward 1970: 67–71; Stockton 1973: 216–18; Marshall 1975; Brunt 1980: 284–6; Seager 1994: 225–6, 2002: 37–8; Gruen 1995: 29–36; cf. McDermott 1977.

37 I shall not only remind you, but deal with, corroborating every detail, the entire account of judicial wickedness and corruption, which has occurred during the ten years since the courts have been transferred to the senate. **38** The Roman people will learn from me, jurors, how it was that for nearly 50 successive years, while the equestrian order made the decisions in the courts, not even the slightest suspicion of receiving money as a bribe fell upon a single Roman eques when acting as a juror; how it was that, when the courts were transferred to the senatorial order, and the power of the people over you as individuals had been removed, Quintus Calidius declared, after his conviction, that someone of praetorian rank should not in all fairness be convicted for less than 3,000,000 sesterces; how it was that, when Publius Septimius, the senator, was convicted, with Quintus Hortensius as praetor in charge of the extortion court, the penalty was specifically calculated with regard to the fact that he had taken a bribe when acting as juror; **39** how it was that in the cases of the senators Gaius Herennius and Gaius Popilius, who were both convicted of embezzlement, and in that of Marcus Atilius, who was convicted of treason, it was clearly established that they had taken bribes as jurors; how it was that senators were found, when Gaius Verres as city praetor was appointing jurors, who would vote against a defendant, whom they were convicting, without knowing anything about the case; how it was that a senator was found who, when acting as juror, in the same case took money from the defendant to bribe the other jurors, and from the prosecutor to convict the defendant. **40** And now, in what terms can I bewail that humiliating and calamitous blot on the whole order, the fact that in this country, when the senatorial order served in the courts, the voting-tablets of jurors under oath were marked with different colours? I promise you that I shall deal with all these facts with diligence and severity.

12.7 Enrolment of the Italians as Roman citizens

The effects of the enfranchisement of the Italians can be seen, with nearly one million Roman citizens registered in 70 BC (see *MRR* II.127; Brunt *IM* 97; Leach 1978: 61). The censors, Gnaeus Lentulus and Lucius Gellius, were the first elected since 86 BC. Cicero in delivering his oration against Verres notes that the census coincided with elections and ludi (games).

(a) Livy *Periochae* 98

The censors, Gnaeus Lentulus and Lucius Gellius, conducted a harsh censorship, with 64 members removed from the senate. When they closed the lustrum, 900,000 citizens were registered.

(b) Cicero Against Verres 1.54

I will not allow the case to be decided only when this concourse from all over Italy, which has gathered from all parts at one and the same time for the elections, games and census, shall have left Rome.

POMPEY'S EXTRAORDINARY COMMANDS

12.8 The lex Gabinia, 67 BC

Cicero *On the Appointment of Gnaeus Pompey* (Man.) 52–3

Aulus Gabinius (tr. pl. 67, cos. 58) legislated that the consul M'. Acilius Glabrio be given command over Bithynia and Pontus and part of Lucullus' army, signalling the beginning of the end of Lucullus' eastern command, and prohibited loans to foreign envoys present at Rome (for both: *MRR* II.142–3; Williams 1984). He also proposed the *lex Gabinia*, which gave Pompey extensive control of the Roman Mediterranean world to deal with the pirates who threatened Roman commerce and Rome's food supply. Previous commands against the pirates had been held by M. Antonius (cos. 99) in 101 and 100 (Plut. *Pomp.* 24.10; *MRR* I.572, 576) and by his son as praetor in 74 BC (doc. 12.4; *MRR* II.101–2). Cicero here, in speaking in 66 BC on the proposal to grant Pompey the command against Mithridates, refers to the *lex Gabinia* and Hortensius' opposition to it.

Pompey had taken no command after his consulship of 70, preferring to withdraw from public life, appearing only when accompanied by great crowds (Plut. *Pomp.* 23.3–4). He was presumably awaiting another opportunity for military service. However, the senate (with the exception of Caesar) opposed the granting of such wide-ranging powers, including one of the consuls, C. Calpurnius Piso, Catulus (cos. 78), Hortensius (cos. 69), and two tribunes, Trebellius and Roscius. When Roscius tried to indicate in the assembly that the command should be shared, the people shouted so angrily that a raven flying over the assembly was stunned and fell into the crowd (Plut. *Pomp.* 25.12).

Gabinius initially proposed the appointment of a consular, without mentioning Pompey, whom the people turned to when the law was passed, granting him greater forces than the law had proposed (Plut. *Pomp.* 26.2–3; Dio 36.25–6). On the day Pompey was chosen, the price of grain plummeted (Cic. *Man.* 44; Plut. *Pomp.* 26.4, 27.2). He had imperium for three years over the Mediterranean and 400 stades inland (50 miles or 80 kilometres), 500 ships (200 were originally proposed), and 15 legates who had been praetors and were now invested with propraetorian imperium (Plut. *Pomp.* 25.6; *Pomp.* 26.3 (24 legates); App. *Mith.* 94 (also 24); *MRR* II.148–9 lists 15 known legates). Piso's attempts to frustrate the preparations by interfering with Pompey's equipment and discharging the crews of his ships were countered by a show of popular support for Pompey; Pompey prevented Gabinius from passing a law to depose Piso from his consulship (Plut. *Pomp.* 27.1–4). The whole campaign lasted three months ('in 40 days he had expelled them from the entire sea': Livy *Per.* 99).

Lex Gabinia and the pirates: Sall. *Hist.* 5.21–4; Livy *Per.* 99; Plut. *Pomp.* 24–9; App. *Mith.* 94; Dio 36.20–7; *MRR* II.144–5; Leach 1978: 66–74; Greenhalgh 1980: 73–100; Wiseman 1994: 331–5; Souza 1999: 149–78; Seager 2002: 43–9; Rauh 2003: 173–4.

52 So what does Hortensius say? That if supreme command is to be bestowed on one man, Pompey is the best choice by far, but that supreme command should not be granted to one man. That argument is now out of date, proved wrong far more by events than by words. For it was you yourself, Quintus Hortensius, who, to the very best of your abilities and with your unique eloquence, gave a lengthy, authoritative and brilliant speech in the senate against that courageous man, Aulus Gabinius, after he had proposed a measure concerning the appointment of a single commander against the pirates, while from this very spot you likewise made a lengthy speech against the same proposal. **53** Well, by the immortal gods, if your judgement had had more weight with the Roman people than their own safety and their real interests, would we today possess this our present glory and world-wide empire? Or did you think our empire existed, at a time when envoys, quaestors and praetors of the Roman people were being taken prisoner, when we were prevented from private and public communication with all our provinces, when all seas were so closed to us that we were even unable to engage in either private or public business overseas?

12.9 Pompey and the pirates, 67 BC

Plutarch *Life of Pompey* 25.1–26.4

25.1 The pirates' power had spread throughout the whole of our Mediterranean sea, rendering it unnavigable and impassable to all trade. **2** It was this which primarily induced the Romans, who were suffering from a shortage of food supplies and anticipating a great scarcity, to send Pompey out to clear the sea of pirates. **3** Gabinius, one of Pompey's intimate friends, proposed a law giving him not command of the sea, but complete autocracy and unlimited power over all men. **4** The law gave him command over the sea up to the pillars of Hercules (Gibraltar), and over all the mainland up to 400 stades from the sea. **5** Not many places within the Roman world were outside these limits, and the greatest nations and most powerful kings were included within them. **6** In addition, he was given power to select 15 legates from the senate to be assigned specific tasks, to take as much money from the treasury and taxation officials as he wished, and to command 200 ships, with full authority over the number and levying of soldiers and crews of rowers.

7 When these provisions were read out, the people received them with great enthusiasm, though the most important and influential members of the senate thought this undefined and limitless power too great for envy, but still something to be feared. **8** They therefore opposed the law, except for Caesar; he supported the law, not in the least because of any concern he felt for Pompey, but because from the beginning he was trying to gain the favour of the people and win their support. **9** All the rest violently attacked Pompey, and when one of the consuls (Gaius Calpurnius Piso) told him that if he wanted to be a second Romulus he would not escape Romulus' fate, he only narrowly escaped being torn to pieces. **10** When (Quintus Lutatius) Catulus came forward to speak against the law, the people respected him enough to keep quiet for a time, but when after speaking at length in generous praise of Pompey he advised them to spare such a man and not to keep on exposing him to continuous dangers and wars and asked, 'Whom else will you have, if you lose him?' with one voice they all shouted out, 'You!' **11** So Catulus, as he couldn't convince them, retired, and when Roscius came forward to speak no one would listen to him . . . **26.1** When Pompey heard that the law had been passed, he entered the city by night, to avoid the envy that would be caused by the people rushing to meet him. **2** He appeared at daybreak and conducted a sacrifice; and at an assembly held for him he arranged that he was given many other powers besides those already voted, almost doubling his forces. **3** Five hundred ships were manned for him, and 120,000 infantry and 500 cavalry raised. Twenty-four men who had held commands or served as praetor were chosen by him from the senate, and he was also given two quaestors. **4** The fact that the price of foodstuffs fell straightaway allowed the people in their delight to say that the very name of Pompey had put an end to the war.

12.10 Lucullus' victory over Mithridates and Tigranes, 69 BC

Plutarch *Life of Lucullus* 28.7–9

There was a desultory Second Mithridatic War (83–81 BC), fought by L. Licinius Murena, who was defeated by Mithridates: Sherwin-White 1994: 229–33. The Third Mithridatic War (73–66) was more serious, at first prosecuted by L. Licinius Lucullus, and then Pompey (Glabrio as proconsul in Pontus and Bithynia in 66 BC achieved nothing). Lucullus (cos. 74) had served under Sulla (cf. doc. 11.5). He obtained the province of Cilicia and Asia by intrigue (doc. 7.64) and in 73 drove Mithridates from Asia and Bithynia, and invaded Pontus, driving Mithridates from there in 72; in 71 he organised tax-relief in Asia (doc. 11.10). In 69 BC he scored a spectacular success against Tigranes II of Armenia, Mithridates' son-in-law, and sacked Armenia's capital Tigranocerta, but Tigranes and Mithridates eluded him and the war dragged on.

In the battle of 69 BC, Tigranes had 20,000 bowmen, 55,000 horsemen, 150,000 infantry, 35,000 engineers and more; Lucullus had a total of 16,000 infantry plus about 1,000 others (Plut. *Luc.* 26.5–6, 27.2); 100,000 enemy infantry and most of the cavalry perished; the Romans lost five men. 'The sun never beheld such a battle as this' (*Luc.* 28.8). But his army, encouraged by Publius Clodius Pulcher, his brother-in-law, mutinied in Armenia in the winter of 68–67, his arrangements for the provincials did not benefit Roman businessmen, and at Rome he was accused of lengthening the war for his own gloria. Gabinius partly dismantled his command and the *lex Manilia* of 66 BC replaced him with Pompey; Lucullus did not celebrate his triumph until 63 (doc. 2.34). Back in Rome, he divorced his wife Clodia for adultery: the women slaves under torture named her brother Clodius (Plut. *Luc.* 34, 38.1; doc. 7.85; Keaveney 1992: 242 n.13). Pompey clearly built on Lucullus' achievements and Lucullus opposed the ratification of his eastern acta (doc. 12.27). For Lucullus in 74–66 BC, see esp. Plut. *Luc.*; *MRR* II.101, 111, 146; Hillman 1991; Keaveney 1992: 75–128; Sherwin-White 1994: 239–48; Wylie 1994; Bellemore 1996; Clodius: Mulroy 1988: 157–65; Tatum 1991, 1999: 44–9; cf. Glew 1981.

7 It is said that over 100,000 of Tigranes' infantry were killed and only a few of all his cavalry escaped. Only 100 of the Romans were wounded, and five were killed. **8** Antiochus the philosopher mentions this battle in his treatise *Concerning Gods* and says that the sun never beheld such a battle as this. And Strabo, another philosopher, in his *Historical Commentaries* says that the Romans themselves were ashamed and laughed at one another for needing arms against such slaves. Livy has also stated that the Romans had never been so numerically inferior when they faced an enemy; for the victors were hardly even a twentieth part of the conquered, but less. **9** The Roman generals who were most skilful and experienced in war praised Lucullus for this in particular, that he outgeneralled two kings who were most pre-eminent and powerful by two very opposite tactics, speed and slowness. For he used up Mithridates, who was at the height of his power, by long delays; but crushed Tigranes by his speed, being one of the few generals ever to use delay for success and boldness for safety.

12.11 Pompey and Mithridates

Plutarch *Life of Pompey* 30.1–2

Manilius, as tribune for 66 BC, proposed a law to distribute freedmen into the tribes of their patrons; he tried to rush his bill through, violence broke out and the senate annulled the law (*MRR* II.153; Wiseman 1994: 338). His second measure gave command of the war against Mithridates to Pompey, with the provinces of Cilicia, Bithynia and Pontus, and the imperium he had already been granted under the *lex Gabinia*. There was opposition from Hortensius and Catulus, but supporters of the law included four consulars.

Pompey quickly defeated Mithridates and received the submission of Tigranes in 66; he campaigned in the Caucasus region in 66–65; and annexed Syria in 64 and Judaea in 63. Jerusalem was captured and some of the Temple treasures removed, and Pompey entered and so desecrated the Holy of Holies in the Temple (sources: Seager 2002: 210 n. 72; Smallwood 1976: 27 n. 21). Mithridates, after a long flight, committed suicide in 63.

Pompey organised Bithynia-Pontus as a province; the province of Cilicia was enlarged, Syria (including Judaea) became a province. Several client kingdoms liable to pay tribute to Rome were created, including Armenia, Galatia, Palestine, Cappadocia, and Commagene. Pompey said he had 'found Asia the remotest of the provinces and made her a central possession of his country'. He had established for himself an enormous client base and resources (Pliny *Nat. Hist.* 7.99 = doc. 12.28, cf. doc. 2.55; Flor. 1.40.31), but his arrangements would not be accepted without question in Rome.

The *lex Manilia* and Pompey in the east: Cic. *Man.*; Livy *Per.* 100; Plut. *Pomp.* 30–4; App. *Mith.* 97–103; Dio 36.45–54; *MRR* II.153; Jameson 1970; Leach 1978: 75–101; Greenhalgh 1980: 101–67; Sherwin-White 1994: 248–65; Seager 2002: 49–62. Cicero and the *lex Manilia*: Smith 1966: 77–81; Rawson 1975: 52–3; Lacey 1978: 24–5; Mitchell 1979: 153–6; Habicht 1990: 27–8; Jerusalem: Smallwood 1976: 16–30.

1 When it was reported at Rome that the war against the pirates was over and that Pompey, being at leisure, was visiting the Eastern cities, one of the tribunes, Manlius (Manilius), proposed a law that Pompey should be given all the territory and forces under the command of Lucullus, with the addition of Bithynia as well, which was under the command of Glabrio, to make war on the kings Mithridates and Tigranes, keeping also the naval forces and command of the sea he had originally been granted. 2 This meant that the entire Roman empire was placed in the hands of one man, for the only provinces which could be thought to be outside his control by the earlier law, Phrygia, Lycaonia, Galatia, Cappadocia, Cilicia, Upper Colchis and Armenia, were now added to it, along with the armies and troops which Lucullus had used in his conquest of Mithridates and Tigranes.

12.12 The lex Manilia, 66 BC

Cicero *On the Appointment of Gnaeus Pompey* (Man.) 27–8

Cicero as praetor in 66 BC was enthusiastic in this speech on the appointment of Pompey and praised Pompey's defeat of the pirates (they had served together in the Social War: doc. 10.14). In the *Philippics* many years later Cicero ascribed the Gabinian and Manilian laws to 'turbulent tribunes', as if he had not spoken in support of the *lex Manilia* (*Phil.* 11.18). This passage sums up Pompey's career and also makes clear that Cicero was a supporter of Pompey at this stage; cf. Dio 36.43; Plut. *Cic.* 9; Asc. 60, 64–6.

27 If only, Quirites, you had so large a supply of brave and honest men as to make this a difficult decision of yours regarding who, in your view, should be put in total authority over such important matters and so great a war! But as the case stands, as Gnaeus Pompey is unique as one whose merit has surpassed not only the glory of the men of today, but even the memory of olden days, what consideration is there that could make anyone hesitate at this point? 28 For my point of view is that a very great commander must have these four qualities — knowledge of warfare, courage, reputation and luck. Who, therefore, has there ever been or ought to have been more knowledgeable than Pompey here? — who left school and boyhood studies for his father's army and the study of warfare in a dangerous campaign with the fiercest of enemies; who, in his earliest youth, served in the army of a very great commander, while at the approach of manhood he was himself the commander of a huge army; who has engaged more often with the nation's enemy, than any other man has disputed with his own, who has fought

more wars than others have read of, who has held more offices than other men have longed for; whose youth was instructed in the knowledge of warfare not by the teachings of others, but by his own commands, not by defeats, but by victories, not by campaigns, but by triumphs? To sum up, what kind of warfare can there be in which the fate of his country has not exercised his talents? The Civil, African, Transalpine, Spanish, Slave, and Naval wars, various and dissimilar types of wars and of opponents, not only waged by himself without aid, but even carried through to a successful conclusion, make it clear that there is nothing in the military sphere which is outside Pompey's experience.

THE CATILINARIAN CONSPIRACY AND CICERO'S CONSULSHIP

The main issue of 63 BC was the conspiracy of Catiline. At the beginning of the year P. Servilius Rullus as tribune proposed a land law to establish a commission of ten men for five years to settle colonies in Italy and the provinces, with the land purchased with public money. Cicero successfully opposed the bill; agrarian legislation continued to arouse conservative opposition, but the public monies and powers involved clearly helped to determine Cicero's response (*Leg. Agr.* 1–3; doc. 12.13; *MRR* II.168; Smith 1966: 99–101; Sumner 1966; Ward 1972: 250–8; Rawson 1975: 64–6; Lacey 1978: 32–3; Wiseman 1994: 349–51; Habicht 1990: 29–30; Drummond 1999, 2000).

Cicero as quaestor in Sicily in 75 BC had organised for grain to be sent to Rome to alleviate a shortage, but made his mark chiefly in his prosecution of Verres in 70. In 66 as praetor he defended Manilius in a case of extortion (Ward 1970a; Ramsey 1980). With Catiline and C. Antonius Hibrida he was a candidate in 64 for the consulship of 63; Sallust (doc. 2.39) suggests that Catiline's candidature benefited Cicero, who was elected with Antonius. Catiline, praetor in 68 BC, was propraetor in Africa in 67–66 BC. His extortion there was such that his candidature for a consulship for 65 was denied on that ground, and he could not stand for 64 as he was awaiting trial; the senators on the jury voted for conviction, the equites for acquittal: he was acquitted (*MRR* II.151, 155; Alexander *Trials* no. 212).

In 66 P. Cornelius Sulla and P. Autronius Paetus had been elected as consuls for 65 but were convicted of bribery (under the *lex Calpurnia*); a 'young noble' Cn. Piso planned to assassinate their replacements L. Aurelius Cotta and L. Manlius Torquatus in December 66, with the assistance of Catiline. Piso had planned to seize the two Spains; he went there and was murdered by the provincials. This 'first (Catilinarian) conspiracy' (Sall. *BC* 19.5) does not warrant the title and Catiline's involvement may largely have been a product of Cicero's imagination. Involvement of Crassus and/or Caesar in the plot (Asconius, Suetonius) is also implausible; for the 'first conspiracy': Sall. *BC* 18; Cic. *Cat.* I.15, *Mur.* 81; Asc. 82–3; Suet. *Jul.* 9; Syme 1964: 89–96; Seager 1964; Gruen 1969a; cf. Sumner 1965; *MRR* II.157. Catiline finally stood for the consulship in 64, for 63 BC.

After being rebuffed for a consulship for a second time in 63 (for 62), Catiline's conspiracy emerged as a threat to the state; his main supporters were Lentulus, Cethegus, Statilius, and Gabinius (not the tr. pl. 67), who with Caeparius were to be executed by Cicero. P. Cornelius Lentulus Sura (cos. 71) had been expelled by the senate in 70, but elected praetor again for 63; he had established links with Sulla's veterans in Etruria, who were not prospering.

Fulvia, through Q. Curius, made known the details of Catiline's plot and an *SCU* was passed when news arrived that Catiline's forces planned to march on Rome (doc. 12.17). Nevertheless, Catiline attended the senate on 8 November 63, where Cicero delivered the *In Catilinam I* against him; Catiline fled, leaving his fellow conspirators in Rome, who planned to assassinate Cicero while Catiline organised his army in Etruria.

Cicero delivered four speeches against Catiline, the *In Catilinam* I–IV; see also Cic. *Mur.*; Plut. *Cic.* 10–23, *Crass.* 13, *Caes.* 7–8, *Cato Min.* 22–4 (with Pelling 1985); Dio 37.29–42; App. *BC* 2.2–7.4–25; see also docs 7.44, 7.84. Modern works: Yavetz 1963; Syme 1964: 60–137;

Smith 1966: 105–31; Brunt 1971: 74–92; Marshall 1974; Rawson 1975: 60–87; Phillips 1976 (correctly arguing against Waters 1970 and Seager 1973); Lacey 1978: 27–41; Scullard *GN* 108–10; Lewis 1988; Habicht 1990: 31–3; Lintott 1999: 76–7, 212; Wiseman 1994: 346–58; Gruen 1995: 416–33; Meier 1995: 163–77; Bauman 1996: 45–9; Stone 1999; Levene 2000; Everitt 2001: 82–107; cf. Harrison 1997: 74.

12.13 Cicero on agrarian legislation

Cicero *On the Agrarian Law* 1.21–3

This speech was delivered to the senate on the first day of Cicero's consulship (1 January) against the tribune Rullus, who had proposed to sell all state lands (with some exceptions) to purchase land for distribution in Italy. Those 'feared more than Rullus' are Crassus and Caesar. For Cicero's speech on this occasion, cf. doc. 2.40.

21 I am speaking now of the danger to our safety and freedom. **22** For what in the state, or in your independence and prestige, do you think will be left for you untouched, once Rullus — and those whom you fear far more than Rullus — with his band of needy and rascally settlers, with all his forces, with all his silver and gold has occupied Capua and the surrounding cities? Such plans, conscript fathers, I will vehemently and fiercely resist, nor shall I, while I am consul, permit men to bring forward the designs they have long been formulating against the state. **23** You were greatly in error, Rullus, you and some of your colleagues, when you hoped that by opposing a consul who was popular in real truth, not just in show, you could make yourself look popular in overthrowing the government.

12.14 Sallust on Catiline

Sallust *Conspiracy of Catiline* 5.1–8

Unsavoury details of Catiline's early career are also sketched at 15.1–2; Cic. *Cat.* 1.4 (cf. 26), and are known also from Asconius' comments on Cicero's (otherwise lost) *In toga candida*, delivered in 64 BC in the senate when Cicero was seeking the consulship for 63 BC (Asc. 87, 91). In 73 Catiline was acquitted of involvement with the Vestal Virgin Fabia, half-sister of Cicero's wife Terentia: Sall. *BC* 15.1–2 (who also accuses him of having murdered his step-son; see Syme 1964: 65, 84–6). Catiline decapitated the body of M. Marius Gratidianus in the Sullan excesses and bore the head through Rome (cf. doc. 11.19); in 64 BC he was charged with the murder of those proscribed by Sulla but acquitted (Alexander *Trials* no. 217). For his supporters, including it was said Crassus, see Sall. *BC* 17.1–7, cf. 48.4. He promised the abolition of debts, proscription of the rich, and for his supporters offices, priesthoods, and plunder (*BC* 21.2).

1 Lucius Catiline was of noble birth and possessed great vigour of both mind and body, but an evil and depraved nature. **2** From his youth he delighted in civil wars, murder, robbery and political strife and in these he spent his early manhood. **3** His body was able to endure hunger, cold and want of sleep to an incredible degree. **4** His mind was daring, crafty, untrustworthy, capable of any pretence or dissimulation, covetous of other men's property, prodigal with his own, violent in its passions; he possessed more than enough eloquence, but insufficient wisdom. **5** His insatiable mind always desired things which were excessive, incredible, out of his reach.

6 After the dictatorship of Lucius Sulla, he had been seized with the overpowering desire to take over the government, with little consideration of the means by which he should achieve it, provided that he acquire sovereignty on his own account. **7** His headstrong spirit was tormented more and more every day by poverty and by the consciousness of guilt, both of which he had aggravated by those practices I mentioned earlier. **8** He was further incited by the corruption of a society troubled by two great and opposing evils, extravagance and avarice.

12.15 Fulvia helps to reveal Catiline's plans

Sallust *Conspiracy of Catiline* 23.1–4

Fulvia's role may not have been as significant as Sallust suggests, but clearly the boni saw Cicero's candidature as more acceptable than Catiline's: see doc. 2.39.

1 Among the conspirators was Quintus Curius, a man not of low birth but steeped in disgrace and crime, whom the censors had expelled from the senate because of his immorality. **2** This man was just as reckless as he was untrustworthy; he could neither keep quiet about what he had heard, nor even hide his own heinous deeds; he was absolutely heedless as to what he said or did. **3** He was engaged in an intrigue of long-standing with Fulvia, a well-born woman, and when he started to fall out of favour with her, because poverty forced him to be less generous, he quickly started boasting and promising her 'seas and mountains' and occasionally threatening her with a weapon, unless she submitted to him, and generally behaved more savagely than before. **4** Fulvia, however, when she learned the reason for Curius' arrogance, had no intention of covering up such danger to the state, but without mentioning her source recounted to a number of people what she had heard about Catiline's conspiracy.

12.16 Catiline plans his conspiracy

Sallust *Conspiracy of Catiline* 26.1–27.2

According to Sallust Catiline's failure in the consular elections in 64 BC led him to plot his revolution in detail, but he also stood in 63 for the consulship of 62. Sulla's veterans were mainly settled in Etruria and were motivated to support Catiline by the hope of plunder and booty. They had clearly not made good soldier-settlers. Note that at §26, Antonius had been granted Cisalpine Gaul as his province, but Cicero let him have Macedonia, a more attractive option, and declined a province for himself. While Antonius was suspected of Catilinarian sympathies (*MRR* II.166), in October he was given the command against the rebels in Etruria.

26.1 After these preparations, Catiline none the less stood for the consulship for the next year (62 BC), hoping that should he be elected he could easily do what he liked with Antonius. In the meantime he was not idle, but kept working on all kinds of plots against Cicero, **2** who, however, was not lacking in the guile and astuteness to evade them. **3** For at the very start of his consulship, by numerous promises made through Fulvia, Cicero had persuaded Quintus Curius, whom I mentioned a short while ago, to lay bare Catiline's plots to him. **4** He had also persuaded his colleague Antonius not to harbour designs against the state by agreeing to let him have his province; he had also secretly stationed around himself bodyguards of friends and clients. **5** When election day came and Catiline was successful neither in his candidature nor in the plots he had made against the consuls in the Campus Martius, he decided on war and resorting to extreme measures, since his undercover attempts had met with failure and dishonour. **27.1** He therefore dispatched Gaius Manlius to Faesulae and that area of Etruria, a certain Septimius of Camerinum to the Picene district, Gaius Julius to Apulia, and others to any other places he believed might suit his purpose. **2** In the meantime he was busy with many plans at once: laying traps for the consul, preparing to set fires, stationing armed men in strategic places, and himself went armed, ordering the others to do the same, and urging them to be always alert and ready.

12.17 Cicero foils Catiline's consular aspirations

Cicero *In Defence of Murena* 52–3

In September 63 BC, on Cicero's motion, the consular elections were postponed to discuss the situation in the senate on the next day, when Cicero accused Catiline of a plot against the state; Catiline responded defiantly (Cic. *Mur.* 51). At the consular elections on the following day D. Junius Silanus and L. Licinius Murena were elected. At *Cat.* 1.11 Cicero accused Catiline of wanting to kill him (Cicero) and Catiline's rivals for the consulship on the day of the elections. Catiline now equipped armed followers throughout Italy. But it was only when Cicero informed the senate on October 21 that Manlius was to march on Rome on October 27, with Catiline to begin a revolt the next day, that the senate reacted. On 22 October an *SCU* was passed. On 6 November Catiline organised the assassination of Cicero, which was foiled when the would-be assassins were denied access to Cicero's house. On 8 November Cicero made the first of his four speeches against Catiline. Catiline was present in the senate, believing that there was some support there for his plans. Catiline left Rome that night, joining Manlius in Etruria, and on 9 November Cicero delivered his *In Catilinam II* before the people. At this stage Murena, consul-elect for 62, was accused of bribery by the unsuccessful Ser. Sulpicius Rufus (cos. 51) and M. Porcius Cato (the Younger) as tribune-elect for 62 (*MRR* II.174). Cicero delivered the *pro Murena* in his defence, arguing that if Murena were to be convicted Catiline would be elected in his place, with all the attendant dangers that would bring.

52 Impelled by his actions, and by the awareness that Catiline was bringing men who were already members of the conspiracy into the Campus Martius armed with swords, I entered the Campus with an unshakeable bodyguard of the very bravest men and wearing that broad and conspicuous breastplate, not so it should protect me — for I was aware that Catiline generally aimed not at the side or the stomach but at the head and neck — but so that all the 'honest men' should notice it and, when they saw their consul in such a fearful danger, rush to his aid and defence, as indeed they did. And so, Servius, when they thought that you were rather lethargic in your candidature and saw Catiline inflamed with hope and desire, all those who wanted to eject this pest from the state at once went over to Murena. **53** Indeed, a great change of support can happen suddenly at consular elections, particularly when the trend is towards a respectable man who is distinguished in his candidature by numerous other advantages.

THE COLLAPSE OF THE REPUBLIC

12.18 Cicero's portrait of Catiline

Cicero *Against Catiline* 2.7–9

This speech was delivered before the people on 9 November, after Catiline had left Rome, and demonstrates the latitude of expression allowed orators (cf. doc. 7.74b). Compare the characterisation of Catiline's followers at Sall. *Cat.* 14.1–7 (Paul 1985).

7 Of what imaginable or conceivable wickedness and criminality has he not been the instigator? In all of Italy can any poisoner, gladiator, robber, assassin, parricide, forger of wills, cheat, glutton, spendthrift, adulterer, woman of notoriety, corrupter of youth, corrupted youth, or desperate character be found who does not admit that they have lived on the most intimate terms with Catiline? What murder has been committed through all these years without his involvement? What abominable act of lechery has been accomplished, if not through his agency? **8** Who, indeed, has ever presented such great allurements for young men as this fellow? He has made love to some of them in the most disgusting fashion, while he has most disgracefully allowed others to make love to him, promising some the satisfaction of their wanton passions, others the murder of their parents — and in this he not only encouraged them, but even gave them a hand. And now how swiftly he has assembled an immense number of desperate men, not only from the city, but also from the country! There was no one overwhelmed by debt, whether from Rome or any corner of the whole of Italy, that he did not admit into this incredible league of crime. **9** And note his various interests in a wide range of activities: there is no one in a gladiatorial school a little too inclined towards crime who does not claim he is Catiline's intimate friend, no one on the stage too inconsequential or good-for-nothing who does not affirm that he has been almost his sworn companion.... **10** And if these comrades of his will go after him, if these dissolute swarms of desperate men will leave the city, how happy we shall be, how fortunate the state, how illustrious the praise for my consulship! For the wanton behaviour of these men is no longer moderate — their temerity has become inhuman and unendurable! They think of nothing but murder, arson and robbery. They have squandered their patrimonies, they have mortgaged their properties; their money has run out long ago, and now their credit is beginning to fail — and yet the wanton tastes they had in abundance still remain. If they, in their drinking and gambling, only desired revels and prostitutes, they would indeed be hopeless cases, but we could at least put up with them; but who can bear that idle fellows should be setting an ambush for the bravest of men, idiots for the prudent, drunkards for the sober, the somnolent for the watchful? These, I tell you, reclining at their banquets, embracing their prostitutes, drowsy with wine, stuffed with food, garlanded with wreathes, smothered with unguents, and weakened by vice, belch forth in their talk the slaughter of good men and the conflagration of the city!

12.19 Cicero aided by the Allobroges

Sallust *Conspiracy of Catiline* 43.1–2, 44.1–3

The Allobroges of Transalpine Gaul, oppressed by their governor and Roman money-lenders, had sent ambassadors to Rome. Lentulus, who was in charge of the conspiracy at Rome, approached them and attempted to draw them into the conspiracy, naming the conspirators and divulging their plans. Initially tempted, the Allobroges eventually decided that the rewards of informing the senate would be more beneficial. They passed the information on to Q. Fabius Sanga, their patron at Rome, who informed Cicero (Sall. *BC* 40–1), who arranged that when the conspirators were arrested the Allobroges would give evidence against them.

43.1 At Rome Lentulus and the others who were leading the conspiracy, who had organised what seemed to them a huge body of troops, had arranged that when Catiline reached the locality of Faesulae with his army the tribune Lucius Bestia should call a public meeting (contio) and by vilifying the actions of Cicero throw the blame for a catastrophic war on that best of consuls; that was to act as the signal for the rest of the large body of conspirators each to carry out his own duties on the following night. **2** Their responsibilities are said to have been divided up in this way: Statilius and Gabinius with a large gang were to start fires at 12 strategic sites in the city, while the resulting confusion would make it easier to gain access to the consul and the others against whom their conspiracy was directed; Cethegus was to station himself outside Cicero's door and use violence against him, while others were assigned their own targets; the sons of various families, mostly of the nobility, were to kill their fathers; lastly, taking advantage of the disorder caused by the slaughter and arson, they were all to rush to join Catiline . . . **44.1** The Allobroges, on Cicero's instructions, were introduced to the others by Gabinius. They demanded that Lentulus, Cethegus, Statilius and Cassius too give them an oath, which they would send sealed to their countrymen, as otherwise they would be reluctant to be drawn into so grave an affair. **2** The others gave it without suspicion, though Cassius promised to come to Gaul himself soon and left Rome before the envoys. **3** Lentulus sent a certain Titus Volturcius from Croton with them, so that before they proceeded homewards the Allobroges might confirm the alliance by exchanging pledges with Catiline.

12.20 An unprovoked attack on Caesar

Sallust *Conspiracy of Catiline* 49.1–4

Cicero made arrangements for the conspirators to be arrested at the Mulvian bridge, in the early hours of the morning of 3 December. On that day, Cicero delivered his *Against Catilinam III* before the people, coupling himself with Pompey: Pompey had expanded the empire, Cicero had saved the home and seat of that empire (3.26). In the senate on 4 December, Crassus was implicated in the plot by one of the conspirators, but on the motion of Cicero the senate voted that the information was false (Sall. *BC* 48; Marshall 1974; Phillips 1976: 447). Sallust reports that he himself heard Crassus complain that Cicero was behind the allegation, with the purpose of preventing Crassus from defending the accused (*BC* 48.9; Plut. *Crass.* 13.3–4, *Cic.* 14.2–3; Parrish 1973 for Crassus in 63–62). Enemies of Caesar, such as Catulus (cf. doc. 3.20), also tried unsuccessfully to implicate him: however, his attempt to save the lives of the conspirators (*BC* 51.1–43; doc. 12.21) did not compromise him. For Caesar's career to 63: Taylor 1941, 1957; for the prosecution of Rabirius in 63 by the tribune Labienus at Caesar's instigation (to show his popularist sympathies) for involvement in the killing of Saturninus on 10 December 100, see doc. 9.30; Tyrrell 1973; Alexander *Trials* no. 220; for his election as pontifex maximus; doc. 3.20.

1 At the same time Quintus Catulus (cos. 78) and Gaius Piso (cos. 67) in vain tried by entreaties, influence and bribes to persuade Cicero to have a false accusation brought against Gaius (Julius) Caesar either through the Allobroges or some other witness. **2** For both were bitter personal enemies of Caesar; Piso, when on trial for extortion, had been charged by him with unjustly executing a man from Transpadane Gaul, while Catulus' hatred arose out of his candidature for the pontificate, because he had reached a ripe old age and attained the highest offices but was beaten by Caesar, while still a young man. **3** Moreover, it seemed an opportune time as Caesar, through his pre-eminent generosity in private life and lavish entertainments in office, was heavily in debt. **4** But they were unable to incite the consul to so monstrous a crime . . .

12.21 Caesar on the fate of the conspirators

Sallust *Conspiracy of Catiline* 51.43

Cicero was unsure of how to deal with the conspirators (Sall. *BC* 46), and Plutarch has Cicero's wife Terentia bringing him news of a good omen that decided him (doc. 7.84). The senate on 5 December voted that the conspirators were guilty of treason. The consul elect, Junius Silanus, called upon to speak first, argued that they be executed, as did subsequent speakers, but he changed his mind after Caesar, as praetor-elect, spoke. Caesar argued for confiscating their property and sentencing them to life-long imprisonment in Italian cities; Cato then successfully argued for their execution, emerging as a leader of the optimates on this issue. As tribune for 62 he arranged that the senate subsidise grain for the people, to the cost of 1,250 talents (Plut. *Cat.* 26.1, *Caes.* 8.5; *MRR* II.175), not as Plutarch suggests to counter the popularity of Caesar, but probably as a response to Catiline's conspiracy. On Cato's motion, Cicero was acclaimed *pater patriae*, Father of his Country.

The debate in the senate: Sall. *BC* 50–3; Plut. *Cic.* 20.4–21, *Caes.* 7.7–8.5, *Cato Min.* 22.4–23; Sallust's defence of Cicero's decision: Stone 1999: 58–60; Cato and Caesar: Taylor: 1949: 124–5; Syme 1964: 103–20; Meier 1995: 170–5.

'Am I then advising that the prisoners be allowed to leave and augment Catiline's army? Certainly not! My view is this, that their properties should be confiscated and that they should be kept imprisoned in the strongest municipia, and that no one in future should refer the matter to the senate or bring it before the people; should anyone act against this, they should be considered by the senate as conspiring against the state and public safety.'

12.22 The public prison (carcer)

Sallust *Conspiracy of Catiline* 55.2–6

On the night of 5 December the principal conspirators met their deaths. Cicero announced to the crowd in the forum, 'They have lived' (Plut. *Cic.* 22.4). The prison (Rome's only public one) was located on the west side of the comitium; it was of stone and had two levels, one underground of seven metres diameter reached only through an opening in the ceiling. It was a place of execution, primarily for non-citizens; defeated enemy leaders would be incarcerated here after being paraded in the triumph, and then usually immediately strangled. Jugurtha, however, languished here for some time before his execution. The carcer survives. Murderers and traitors could be thrown to their deaths from the Tarpeian Rock (Saxum Tarpeium), a cliff of the Capitoline (Richardson *Top. Dict.* 377–8; Simone 1999), though 'capital' punishment, for aristocrats, usually meant exile and loss of civic rights (doc. 1.21). See, for the carcer, Livy 1.33.8; Pliny *Nat. Hist.* 7.212; Val. Max. 9.12.6; Vell. 2.7.2; Festus 325; Frank 1924: 39–47; Nash 1.206–8; Mulryne 1977: 14–15; Richardson *Top. Dict.* 71; Kyle 1998: 217–18.

2 Cicero himself, after setting guards, led Lentulus to the prison; the praetors did the same for the others. **3** In the prison there is a place which is called the Tullianum, when you have gone up a little way towards the left, about twelve feet below ground. **4** Walls enclose it on all sides and it has a vaulted stone roof: its neglected condition, darkness and stench make it hideous and terrifying to behold. **5** After Lentulus was let down into this place, the executioners carried out their orders and strangled him with a noose. **6** Thus that patrician, from the illustrious family of the Cornelii, who had held consular authority at Rome, met an end befitting his character and actions. Cethegus, Statilius, Gabinius and Caeparius suffered the same punishment.

12.23 Catiline's stand

Sallust *Conspiracy of Catiline* 60.7–61.9

Public opinion was divided on events and Cicero had a foretaste of the recriminations that would lead to his exile in 58 BC. When he went to make his speech on leaving office on 31 December, two tribunes, Q. Caecilius Metellus Nepos and L. Calpurnius Bestia, vetoed it (*MRR* II.174). News of the execution of the conspirators led many in Catiline's force to desert. He attempted to escape with the remainder, by forced marches, to Cisalpine Gaul, but Q. Caecilius Metellus Celer (proconsul of Cisalpine Gaul in 62) blocked his escape with three legions. On the approach of C. Antonius, Catiline decided to meet him in battle.

60.7 When Catiline saw his troops routed and that he was left with just a few men, he rushed, mindful of his family and former rank, into the thickest of the enemy and was pierced through and through as he fought. **61.1** Once the battle was over, you could clearly perceive the audacity and resolution possessed by Catiline's army. **2** For almost every man covered with his lifeless body the position he had taken when alive at the start of the fighting. **3** True, a few in the centre, whom the praetorian cohort had dispersed, were lying a little way away from the rest, but all their wounds were in front. **4** Catiline, indeed, was found far in advance of his men among the corpses of his enemies, still breathing slightly and retaining on his face the ferocity of spirit he had possessed in his lifetime. **5** Finally, out of the entire army no free-born citizen was captured either during the battle or in flight; **6** all of them put the same value on their own lives as on those of the enemy. **7** The army of the Roman people had won a victory that was neither a cause for rejoicing nor bloodless. All the best fighting men had either fallen in battle or had come away with serious wounds. **8** Indeed, many, who had left the camp to view the battlefield or to look for booty, when they turned over the enemy's corpses found now a friend, now a guest, now a relative; similarly some recognised their personal enemies. **9** And so the entire army was moved with joy and sorrow, mourning and rejoicing.

12.24 Pliny on Cicero

Pliny *Natural History* 7.116–17

Pliny is here reviewing Romans of intellectual eminence, such as Ennius, Virgil, and Varro. L. Roscius Otho in 67 (as tr. pl.) reserved 14 rows in the theatre for the equites (*MRR* II.145); always unpopular, this led to rioting in 63.

116 But on what grounds could I be silent about you, Marcus Tullius? By what distinctive mark can I make known your supreme eminence? By what, in preference to the most abundant testimony of the decree of that whole nation, selecting out of your whole life just the achievements of your consulship? **117** Your oratory induced the tribes to reject the agrarian law — their own livelihood; your persuasion induced them to excuse Roscius, the proposer of the law about the theatre, and to endure with equanimity being marked out by a distinction of seats; your plea made the children of the proscribed ashamed of standing for office; your genius turned Catiline to flight; you proscribed Mark Antony. Hail, you who were the first to be titled Father of your Country (*pater patriae*), first winner of a civilian triumph and crown of honour for oratory, and parent of eloquence and of Latin letters, and — as your former enemy, the dictator Caesar, wrote of you — winner of a laurel crown greater than that of any triumph, since it is much more important to have advanced the frontiers of the Roman mind than those of Rome's empire.

12.25 The human side of Cicero

Macrobius *Saturnalia* 2.1.10–13, 3.2, 3.5

Vatinius (tr. pl. in 59: *MRR* II.286) was elected consul with Q. Fufius Calenus in September 47 for the remainder of that year. For Cicero's biting wit, see also Plut. *Cic.* 25–7; doc. 13.53.

1.10 First I would like to remind you of two very eloquent men of olden times, the comic poet Plautus and the orator Tullius (Cicero), who were both outstanding in the wittiness of their jokes . . . **12** What Cicero could do in this way is well-known to anyone who has taken the trouble to read the collection his freedman (Tiro) made of his patron's jokes, which some ascribe to Cicero himself. Similarly, who does not know that his enemies used to call him that 'consular buffoon'? — as Vatinius actually does in his own speech. **13** Indeed, would it not take too long, I would remind you of the cases in which, in his defence of the most guilty clients, he won victory by a joke; for example, when he was defending Lucius Flaccus, accused of extortion, and got him off clearly proved charges through an opportune witticism . . .
    3.2 When Marcus Cicero was dining with Damasippus, who produced a mediocre wine with the words, 'Try this Falernian — it's 40 years old,' Cicero replied, 'It carries its age well.' . . . **5** The consulship of Vatinius, which only lasted a few days, gave Cicero plenty of opportunities for exercising his sense of humour in some widely publicised sayings: 'A great portent has occurred in Vatinius' term of office,' he said, 'because in his consulship there has been neither winter, spring, summer, or autumn.' And when Vatinius asked him why it had been too much trouble for Cicero to visit him when he was ill, he replied, 'I intended to come when you were consul, but night overtook me'. However, Cicero was thought to have been getting his revenge here, recalling the retort made by Vatinius to his boast that he had returned from exile carried in triumph on the shoulders of the people: 'Then where did you get those varicose veins?'

12.26 Cicero's poem on his consulship

Cicero *On Divination* 1.20–1

(F 10.) Prophecies of disaster made in 65 were supposedly fulfilled during Cicero's consulship; here Quintus quotes his brother's poem *On My Consulship* to prove the value of divination (the Muse Urania is speaking); cf. doc. 12.31. Cic. *Att.* 1.19.10: Cicero also wrote a summary of his consulship in Greek which he sent to Atticus for comment.

> Then who, perusing the records and volumes of the diviners' art,
> Failed to bring to light the mournful prophecies written by the Etruscans?
> All seers uttered warnings to beware the destruction and ruin
> Plotted against the nation by men of aristocratic birth
> Or proclaimed the overthrow of law in continual prophecies,
> And ordered that the temples of the gods and city
> Be snatched from the flames and frightful butchery and slaughter be feared;
> And these would be fixed and resolved by inexorable destiny
> Unless first, high on a column, with handsome form,
> A sacred statue of Jupiter faced to the east;
> Then would the people and revered senate be able to discern
> Hidden plans, if, turned to the rising sun,
> It should behold from its station the seats of the senators and people.
> This statue was long postponed with many delays
> Till with you as consul it was placed at last in its lofty position,
> And just at the moment of time fixed and predicted
> Jupiter exhibited his sceptre on his elevated column
> And the destruction prepared for our fatherland by flame and sword
> Was revealed to senate and people by Allobrogian voices.

POMPEY'S RETURN FROM THE EAST

In 63 BC, the tribunes proposed various honours for Pompey as conqueror of the east (Vell. 2.40), and Cicero organised a vote of thanksgiving. In January 62 Nepos as tribune (cf. doc. 12.23) proposed two measures: that Pompey be recalled to deal with Catiline and his army, and that Pompey be allowed to stand for the consulship *in absentia*. Cato as tribune opposed both measures, while Caesar as praetor supported them; violence broke out, the senate passed an *SCU* and Nepos fled to Pompey (Nepos, however, as consul in 57 was to support Cicero's recall from exile). Caesar was suspended from his office by the senate but later re-instated. He was then accused before Novius Niger (*quaesitor* appointed to investigate the Catilinarian conspiracy) of being an accomplice of Catiline, but successfully rebutted the charge, and the accuser Vettius had his goods confiscated, was beaten up in front of the rostra, and imprisoned: Plut. *Cic.* 23, *Cato Min.* 26–9, Suet. *Jul.* 16–18; Dio 37.38.2, 37.41–3; other refs: *MRR* II.173–4; Wiseman 1994: 358–6; for the 'Vettius Affair' in 59, see doc. 12.51.

In 62 Clodius apparently violated the rites of the Bona Dea on 3 December and Caesar, in whose house the rites had been conducted as praetor, divorced his wife Pompeia: see doc. 7.85. Clodius was acquitted, but Cicero had disproved his alibi and Clodius became his inveterate enemy. Caesar then left for Further Spain, his propraetorian province for 61.

Towards the end of 62 BC Pompey, after a public dispatch (Cic. *Fam.* 5.7; doc. 12.30), arrived in Italy; he celebrated his triumph in 61 (doc. 12.28) and disbanded his army. Pompey desired ratification of his eastern acta, as well as land for his veterans (doc. 12.34). He met with considerable opposition from the senate and one of the consuls for 60, Metellus Celer. By the end of 60, Pompey had failed to achieve both aims and the stage was set for his co-operation with Caesar.

12.27 Pompey's golden crown

Velleius Paterculus *Roman History* 2.40.4–5

Cf. Dio 37.21.3–4 (Caesar supported these honours, Cato opposed them); Dion. Hal. 3.62.2. T. Ampius Balbus and T. Labienus were tribunes in 63 BC (*MRR* II.167–8). Both Lucullus (cos. 74) and Metellus Creticus (cos. 69) had reason to feel that Pompey had robbed them of their 'gloria'.

4 In Gnaeus Pompey's absence, Titus Ampius and Titus Labienus, tribunes of the plebs, proposed a law that Pompey should be allowed at the Circus games to wear a golden crown (corona aurea) and the full dress of triumphators, and at the theatre the toga praetexta and the golden crown. But he did not venture on this privilege more than once, and this indeed was too often. For Fortune raised this man to the summit by such great leaps, triumphing first over Africa, then over Europe, and then over Asia, and the divisions of the world became so many monuments of his victory. Greatness never lacks jealousy. **5** Both Lucullus, and Metellus Creticus who remembered the affront he had received — indeed his complaint was not unjust, for Pompey had robbed him of the captive generals who were to adorn his triumph — opposed him, along with a section of the optimates, who tried to prevent Pompey's promises to the cities and the rewards for good service to him being carried out according to his wishes.

12.28 Pompey's victories

Pliny *Natural History* 7.96–9

Cf. Pliny *Nat. Hist.* 7.93–5, 37.11–18. Pompey in Pliny's view was equal to not only Alexander but even (nearly) Hercules. Pompey's triumph lasted for two days, 28–29 September 61 BC: Plut. *Pomp.* 44–5; Dio 37.21; App. *Mith.* 116–17.565–78; *MRR* II.181; Greenhalgh 1980: 168–76; Meier 1995: 178–9; Seager 2002: 79–80; cf. doc. 2.55 for Pompey's clientela.

96 Well then, after the recovery of Sicily, he first, as one of Sulla's supporters, rose up as the state's champion, and, after the subjugation of the whole of Africa and its reduction to Roman domination, and with the title Magnus acquired as one of the spoils, though an equestrian — a thing which no one had ever done before — rode in a triumphal chariot and immediately afterwards crossed over to the West, and after erecting trophies in the Pyrenees added to his victories the subjection to Roman domination of 876 towns from the Alps to the borders of Further Spain and, with greater magnanimity, refrained from mentioning Sertorius. After extinguishing the civil war which was on the point of stirring up all our foreign relations he again led triumphal chariots into Rome as an equestrian, having twice been *imperator* before serving as a common soldier. **97** Following this, he was sent to every sea and then to the East and brought back unending titles for his country, in the manner of those who conquer in the sacred contests (i.e., panhellenic games) — for these are not crowned themselves, but crown their country; accordingly he bestowed these honours on the city in the shrine of Minerva that he dedicated from the proceeds of the spoils:

Gnaeus Pompeius Magnus, *imperator*, after ending a thirty years' war, scattering, routing, killing and receiving the surrender of 12,183,000 persons, sinking or capturing 846 ships, receiving the surrender of 1,538 towns and forts, and subduing the lands from the Maeotians to the Red Sea, duly fulfils his vow to Minerva.

98 This is his summary of his deeds in the East. The announcement of the triumph which he held on 28 September in the consulship of Marcus Piso and Marcus Messalla (61 BC) was as follows:

After liberating the sea coast from pirates and restoring the command of the sea to the Roman people, he celebrated a triumph over Asia, Pontus, Armenia, Paphlagonia, Cappadocia, Cilicia, Syria, the Scythians, Jews and Albanians, Iberia, the island of Crete, the Basternae, and in addition to these over King Mithridates and Tigranes. **99** The greatest achievement in these glorious exploits was (as he himself said in the assembly when he was speaking of his successes) to have found Asia the remotest of the provinces and to have made her a central possession of his country. If, on the other side, anyone wants to survey in a similar fashion the achievements of Caesar, who showed himself greater than Pompey, he would truly have to enumerate the whole world, which, it will be agreed, would be a task without end.

12.29 Pompey's dedication to Minerva

Diodorus Siculus *Library of History* 40.4
(Const. Porph. *Excerpta* 4, 405–6)

Pompey had his achievements in Asia inscribed and set up as a dedication; a copy of the inscription follows:

Pompey the Great, son of Gnaeus, Imperator, liberated the coastline of the inhabited world and the islands this side of Ocean from the war against the pirates, having also saved from siege the kingdom of Ariobazanes (king of Cappadocia), Galatia and the lands and provinces beyond it, Asia, and Bithynia; he protected Paphlagonia and Pontus, Armenia and (Scythian) Achaea, as well as Iberia, Colchis, Mesopotamia, Sophene and Gordyene; he subdued Darius, king of the Medes, Artoles, king of the Iberians, Aristobulus, king of the Jews, Aretas, king of the Nabataean Arabs, Syria bordering on Cilicia, Judaea, Arabia, the province of Cyrene, the Achaeans, the Iozugi, the Soani, the Heniochi, all the other tribes along the coastline between Colchis and the Maeotic Sea, with their kings, nine in number, and all the nations dwelling between the Pontic and the Red Seas; he extended the frontiers of the empire to the limits of the earth; and protected, and in some cases increased, the revenues of the Roman people.

After confiscating the statues and the other images of the gods, as well as the other valuables taken from the enemy, he has dedicated to the goddess 12,060 pieces of gold, and 307 talents of silver.

12.30 Cicero writes to Pompey, April 62 BC

Cicero *Letters to his Friends* 5.7

Pompey's reply to Cicero's letter informing him of his role in suppressing Catiline's conspiracy did not mention Cicero's actions and Cicero here shows his disappointment; he is tactful, however, as he clearly desires to be politically close to Pompey ('public interest will unite and bind us together'). The identity of these 'old enemies, now your new friends' who were disappointed by Pompey's public dispatch is disputed by modern historians: perhaps Sullan discontents and Catiline's supporters who might have hoped for something from a powerful, unscrupulous Pompey: see Shackleton Bailey 1977: I.280–1; Seager 2002: 75. Cicero's 'own great goodwill' was manifested in his support for the *lex Manilia* with its retrospective approval of the *lex Gabinia*, and in moving as consul a ten-day supplicatio (thanksgiving) for Pompey on the news of Mithridates' death and another on receipt of Pompey's dispatch (Cic. *Prov.* 27).

1 From Marcus Tullius Cicero, son of Marcus, to Gnaeus Pompeius Magnus, son of Gnaeus, Imperator, greetings. I hope all is well with you and your army, as it is with me. I received immeasurable pleasure, like everyone else, from your public dispatch; for you display such a hope of peace as I, relying on you alone, have always been promising everyone. But I must tell you that your letter dealt a severe blow to your old enemies, now your new friends, who despond, cast down from their high hopes.

2 Although the letter you sent to me displays only slight indication of your regard for me, I must tell you that it was most welcome to me anyway. For in nothing do I generally take such pleasure as in the consciousness of my services to others; if these do not receive a mutual response, I am quite content that the balance of the service lies with me. I do not doubt that, if my own great goodwill towards you has not sufficiently attached you to me, the public interest will unite and bind us together.

3 So that you are not unaware of what I missed in your letter, I will write plainly, just as is demanded both by my character and our friendship. My achievements were such that I expected some congratulatory comment in your letter for the sake of both our close relationship and the commonwealth; I suppose that you left it out for fear of giving anyone offence. But I must tell you that what I did for the country's safety is approved by the judgement and testimony of the whole world; when you arrive back, you will recognise that I acted with such policy and magnanimity as to make you well content to have me as your political ally and friend, a not much lesser Laelius to a much greater Africanus.

12.31 Cicero compares himself and Pompey

Cicero *On Duties* 1.77–8

Here, writing in 44 BC, Cicero quotes from his own poem on his consulship, and praises himself by quoting Pompey's opinion of him.

77 The truth, however, is in the verse which, I am told, the dishonest and envious attack, 'Arms, yield to the toga, victory laurels, to civic praise'. Not to mention other examples, did not arms yield to the toga when I was piloting the state? For never was the state in more serious danger or greater peace. So, as a result of my advice and diligence, the weapons, of their own accord, fell suddenly from the hands of the most desperate citizens. What achievement in war was ever so great? What triumph can be compared to it? **78** For I may boast to you, son Marcus, as to you belong the inheritance of this glory and the necessity of imitating my deeds. Indeed it was to me that Gnaeus Pompey, a man overwhelmed with praises for his exploits in war, paid this compliment in the hearing of many when he said that his third triumph would have been won in vain unless by my services to the state he were to have somewhere to celebrate it.

12.32 Relations cool between Cicero and Pompey, January 61 BC

Cicero *Letters to Atticus* 1.13.4

The 'dear friend' here is Pompey. Cicero's opinion will largely have been motivated by Pompey's tardiness in praising Cicero's role in the suppression of the Catilinarian conspiracy: Shackleton Bailey 1965: I.305; Seager 2002: 77.

Your dear friend (do you know whom I'm talking about? The person about whom you wrote to me that he began to praise once he no longer dared to find fault) declares his great regard, his esteem, his affection for me, with praise on the surface, though underneath, but, still visible, lies his jealousy. Without courtesy, sincerity, political influence, integrity, courage, or plain speaking — but I'll write in more detail at another time, as I don't yet know enough on the subject and I dare not entrust a letter on such important matters to any sort of unknown chap.

12.33 The equites ask for remission of their tax contract

Cicero *Letters to Atticus* 1.17.8–9 (December 61)

Cf. *Att.* 2.1.8 (doc. 12.36). After the Catilinarian conspiracy in which the equites and senators had united against Catiline, Cicero had worked out his political idea of the *concordia ordinum* ('concord of the orders') in 62 BC; the conspiracy had created a unity of all 'honest' men (*coniunctio omnium bonorum*: *Att.* 1.16.6). In 61 BC, two issues affected this, as Cicero describes, dispute over the law courts and the tax contract in Asia. The request of the equites, championed by Crassus (censor in 65: *MRR* II.157), who had overbid on the tax contract in Asia, was in Cicero's estimation simply 'disgraceful': Balsdon 1962: 135–7; Smith 1966: 138; Badian 1972: 111–12; Rawson 1975: 100–1; Marshall 1976: 96–7; Ward 1977: 211; Lacey 1978: 53; Leach 1978: 118–20; Greenhalgh 1980: 188–97; Scullard *GN* 112–13; Habicht 1990: 43; Sherwin-White 1994: 365.

8 We are living in a commonwealth which is feeble, unhappy, and unstable. I suppose you have heard that our friends, the equites, have almost broken with the senate; for a start, they took great exception to the pronouncement under senatorial decree of a bill authorising investigation in the case of jurors who had taken bribes. While this was being voted on, I happened to be away, and, realising that the equestrian order was very annoyed though they said nothing publicly, I criticised the senate using, as I felt, the whole weight of my reputation, giving an extremely authoritative and eloquent speech in a rather disreputable cause. **9** Now, here come further pretensions of the equites, which are almost unendurable! — and I have not only borne with these but even given them my support. Those who bought the taxes of Asia from the censors complained in the senate that they had been induced by their cupidity to make too high a bid; they asked that their contract be cancelled. I was their chief supporter, or rather first but one, for it was Crassus who urged them to make this bold demand. The whole thing is invidious — the demand is disgraceful, a confession of reckless conduct! There was terrible risk that, if they were made no concessions, they would openly break with the senate. Here, again, it was I in particular who came to their assistance, and ensured that they found the senate fully attended and feeling generous, and on the Kalends of December and the following day I spoke at length about the dignity and concord of the orders (*concordia ordinum*). The business has still not yet been settled, but the senate's wishes are obvious. The only one who spoke against it was Metellus, the consul-elect; our hero Cato was going to speak, but lost his chance as the day was not long enough.

12.34 Pompey's setbacks in 60 BC

Dio Cassius *Roman History* 37.49.1–50.6

Pompey on his return to Italy divorced his wife Mucia, whose behaviour in his absence had caused comment. To overcome Cato's general opposition, Pompey proposed — through an intermediary — marriage to the elder of Cato's nieces, and the hand of the younger for his son. Cato, aware of Pompey's motives, rejected this proposal (Plut. *Pomp.* 44, *Cato Min.* 30). Unfortunately, Mucia was half-sister to Metellus Celer, who, with L. Afranius, was to be one of the consuls for 60 and Celer would prove more than uncooperative: *MRR* II.182–3.

Afranius, a novus homo from Picenum, was a legate of Pompey's in Spain (against Sertorius): Cicero had a low opinion of him (Cic. *Att.* 1.18.5, 1.19.4, 20.5; cf. Dio 37.49.3). According to Cicero, Pompey employed *divisores*, bribery agents, to secure Afranius' election, though he does not believe that Piso, cos. 61, was also involved. However, Cato and Domitius had two decrees passed: that magistrates' houses could be searched and that it was an offence to have *divisores* in one's house (*Att.* 1.16.12; cf. Plut. *Pomp.* 44.4). Cato, however, in 60 would employ bribery to ensure that Bibulus, his son-in-law, was elected consul for 59.

Pompey wanted land for his veterans, and employed the tribune L. Flavius to secure this (*MRR* II.184). Ager publicus was to be used as well as land purchased with the eastern revenues and was to be made available not just to veterans but also to other citizens, in order to win their support. Cicero supported the law, with qualifications ensuring that private property would not be affected: Cic. *Att.* 1.18.6, 1.19.4, 2.1.6–8; Dio 37.49–50. Metellus opposed the measure and Cicero has the senate against it 'suspecting some new power for Pompey' (*Att.* 1.19.4); it had gone 'quite cold' by mid-60 (doc. 12.36).

Metellus' opposition to the agrarian law and the ratification of Pompey's acta was such that he was dragged off to prison by Flavius (*Att.* 2.1.8: doc. 12.36); when Metellus summoned the senators there, ordering a hole cut in the wall to admit them, Pompey gave in and ordered Flavius to release Metellus. At the end of 60, his veterans were without land and his acta unratified; according to Dio, he regretted disbanding his legions (Dio 37.50). Land grants and acta: App. *BC* 2.9.31–4; Scullard *GN* 112–13; Sherwin-White 1994: 365; Seager 2002: 81–2.

49.1 Pompey arrived in Italy at this time and had Lucius Afranius and Metellus Celer appointed consuls, hoping vainly that through them he would be able to achieve all that he wanted. **2** He particularly wanted some land to be granted to his soldiers and all his settlements to be ratified, but at the time he failed to achieve either of these. For the optimates, who even before this had not been on good terms with him, prevented a vote being taken; **3** and, as for the consuls themselves, Afranius (who knew more about dancing than about business) was of no assistance at all, and Metellus, angry that Pompey had divorced his sister, although he had children by her, opposed him violently in everything . . . **5** And since Pompey had annulled some of Lucullus' acts, Lucullus demanded that an investigation be made in the senate into the acts of both of them, so it could ratify whichever one's they approved of. **50.1** Cato and Metellus and all the others of the same mind strongly supported him. Accordingly, when the tribune (Lucius Flavius), who was proposing that land be granted to Pompey's men, added to this measure the proposal that land be granted to all the citizens as well, so that they would more readily vote for this and ratify Pompey's acts, Metellus met every point with such opposition that, when the tribune had him thrown into prison, he then desired the senate to assemble there . . . **5** So, when Pompey could effect nothing because of Metellus and the others, he said they were jealous of him and that he would reveal this to the people, but as he was afraid that they too might fail him and cause him greater shame, he withdrew his demands. **6** In this way he realised that he possessed no real power, but just the name and envy arising from his former authority, while in reality he received no profit from this, and repented of having dismissed his legions and having put himself in his enemies' power.

12.35 Cicero's stance in 60 BC

Cicero *Letters to Atticus* 1.19.4–7 (15 March 60)

Flavius' agrarian legislation, discussed here by Cicero who supported it while ensuring occupiers of the land were not disadvantaged, was thwarted by Metellus Celer (cos. 60) and other optimates (*MRR* II.183, 184). Herennius: *MRR* II.184; Clodius: docs 12.52–4. 5: Herennius' attempts to transfer Clodius to the plebs were vetoed by the other tribunes.

4 Affairs in the city are as follows. The agrarian law is being enthusiastically pushed by the tribune Flavius, with Pompey's support, though there is nothing 'popular' about it but the proposer. From this law, with the approval of an assembly, I tried to remove everything that disadvantaged private interests; I wanted to remove from its control such land as was state land in the consulship of Publius Mucius and Lucius Calpurnius (133 BC), confirm the holdings of Sulla's settlers, and leave the people of Volaterra and Arretinum, whose land was confiscated but not allocated, in possession of their land; I did not reject one motion, that the land should be bought out of the money from abroad, received from the new taxes over a five-year period. The entire proposal for land distribution is being opposed by the senate, which suspects that some new power for Pompey is sought: in truth, he has set his heart on the bill being passed. To the great gratitude of all those who are to receive the land, I am ensuring that the possessions of all private owners be confirmed; after all, this is my army, as you are well aware, the well-to-do. However, for the people and Pompey I am meeting their wishes (as I also wish to do) through purchase, which if carefully organised I believe could drain off the dregs of the city and repopulate Italy's desolation. But the whole affair has gone cold with the interposition of war. Metellus is certainly a good consul and a good friend of mine. The other one (L. Afranius) is such a nonentity that he doesn't know what he's purchased.

   5 That is all about politics, unless you think it relates to politics that a certain Herennius, a tribune and tribesman of yours, and a totally worthless and needy chap, has begun making regular attempts to have Publius Clodius transferred to the plebs. He gets a lot of vetoes. This is all, I believe, about the commonwealth. **6** However, since the great Nones of December (63 BC), when I reached extraordinary and undying glory, joined with the ill-will and hostility of many, I have not ceased to involve myself in politics with that same greatness of mind, or to maintain the prestige I then won and undertook; but when I afterwards noted the light-mindedness and weakness of the courts, through Clodius' acquittal, and then saw how easily our friends, the tax-farmers, were separated from the senate, although not estranged from myself, and moreover how some wealthy men, I mean the fish-lovers (*piscinarii*), friends of yours, were not able to hide their jealousy of me, I thought I should look for greater resources and more stable protection. **7** And so, I drew Pompey, who had kept quiet for too long about my achievements, into choosing to give me in the senate, not once but on a number of occasions and at length, the credit for saving our empire and the world. That was not of such importance to me (for my achievements are neither so unknown as to need witnesses nor so doubtful as to need praise) as to the state, as there were some scoundrels who considered that some disagreement out of all this discord might arise between Pompey and myself. I have united myself with him in so close a relationship that both of us can feel safer as individuals and politically stronger by our alliance.

12.36 Cicero tries to influence Pompey and Caesar, June 60 BC

Cicero *Letters to Atticus* 2.1.6–8

The agrarian law is that of Flavius (tr. pl. 60); Atticus had clearly criticised Cicero's dealings with Pompey. Clodius had according to his enemies heavily bribed the jurors in his Bona Dea trial. Cicero (*Att.* 1.16.5, 11) refers to a certain *Calvus ex Nanneianis* as distributing the money to the jurors. Identification of Crassus as this person has been the traditional explanation (esp. Ward 1977: 208, 227–30; cf. Marshall 1976: 98), but the poet C. Licinius Calvus (see doc. 7.34) has also been a candidate (esp. Tatum 1999: 82–5). Senators were covered by provisions concerning judicial bribery but the equites were exempt from these (Cic. *Cluent.* 145–8, *Rab. Post.* 16–18). Cato duly proposed a law (*lex de iudiciis*) in the senate to investigate jurors who had taken bribes, which was strongly opposed by the equites, and dropped (cf. *Att.* 1.17.8 (doc. 12.33), 1.18.3). Cicero saw the bribery law as dissolving the *concordia ordinum* (*Att.* 1.18.3). Cato also opposed the equites' demand for tax relief. For the law-court issue: Smith 1966: 138; Marshall 1976: 98; Ward 1977: 210; Lacey 1978: 49; Sherwin-White 1994: 365; Gruen 1995: 241.

Caesar had achieved successes in Further Spain (Hispania Ulterior) which he was governing in 60 (*MRR* II.184). In his hope that Caesar might become more 'constitutionally-minded', Cicero is alluding to his hopes that he could influence Caesar, in the same sense as Cicero felt he could influence Pompey for the good of the state (*Att.* 1.20.2); Pompey and Cicero were moving closer together, with Pompey's public acknowledgement (at last) in the senate in 60 of Cicero's achievements of 63: *Att.* 1.19.7: doc. 12.35 (March 60 BC).

6 You mention the agrarian law — it seems to have gone quite cold. And in a gentle sort of fashion you criticise me for my friendly relations with Pompey, though I wouldn't want you to think that I have become allied with him for my own protection; but circumstances were so constituted that any disagreement that arose between us would inevitably have occasioned major conflicts in the state. If I have in this way foreseen and taken measures against this, it is not that I have departed from my constitutionalist policy, but that he is now more constitutionally-minded and has relaxed somewhat from his attempts to win popular favour. As for my achievements, which many had tried to stir him up to attack, you should be aware that he commends them far more flatteringly than his own, proclaiming that he served the state well, but that I saved it. I do not know how much his doing this is of benefit to me, but it is certainly advantageous for the state. And what if I can even make Caesar, who is certainly at the moment sailing with a favourable wind, more constitutionally-minded? **7** Would that harm the state so much? Even if no one bore me any ill will, if everyone was well disposed to me, as would be reasonable, none the less medicines for healing the corrupt parts of the state ought to be tried instead of cutting them out. But now, when the equites, whom I stationed on the Capitoline slope with you as their standard-bearer and chief, have abandoned the senate, with our leaders thinking that they've reached the summit of human fortune if they have bearded mullet in their fishponds which will swim up to their hands, and neglecting all other business, don't you think that I have done enough good if I succeed in stopping those who have the power from wanting to do harm?

8 Regarding our friend Cato you do not feel for him more warmly than I do, but despite all his principles and integrity he is sometimes a nuisance politically; he voices his opinion as if he were in Plato's *Republic*, not in the sewers of Romulus' city. What can be more proper than that any juror who takes a bribe be brought to trial? Cato brought this motion and the senate agreed: the equites declare war on the senate-house — not on me, for I disagreed. What could be more shameless than tax-farmers reneging on their contract? Yet the loss was worth incurring to keep the order on our side. Cato opposed and carried his point. And so, a consul is confined in prison, and one riot follows another, while not one of those who used to back me or the consuls who succeeded me in the defence of the state is of any assistance. 'So then,' you ask, 'shall we keep these as mercenaries?' Why not, if we are unable to do so in any other way? Or should we act as the servants of our freedmen and even our slaves? But, as you would say, enough serious talk.

12.37 Caesar foregoes his triumph

Appian *Civil Wars* 2.8 (26–30)

By the time Caesar returned to Rome in mid-60 BC, Pompey's agrarian law was more or less dead, his acta had not been ratified, and his friendship with Cicero had brought no dividends. The senate, particularly Cato, had been hostile to Pompey and Cato took the lead in opposing Caesar's request to stand for the consulship *in absentia* in order to hold his triumph — which the senate had voted. Caesar therefore had to disband his army and forego the triumph in order to stand for the consulship. There were two other candidates: Lucius Lucceius and Marcus Calpurnius Bibulus. Caesar and Lucceius made a pact that Lucceius should promise to distribute money to the centuries in their joint names; the optimates reacted by distributing bribes to aid Bibulus' election; Cato stated that the largesse was distributed for the good of the Republic (Suet. *Jul.* 19.1). Caesar and Bibulus were elected (*MRR* II.187–8); cf. Plut. *Caes.* 13; App. *BC* 2.9; Sherwin-White 1994: 365–6.

26 After being selected as praetor for Spain, Caesar was detained in Rome by his creditors, as he owed much more than he was able to pay off because of his expenses connected with holding office. He was reported to have said that he needed 25,000,000 sesterces in order to have nothing. **27** However, he settled with those who were importuning him, as far as he could, and went to Spain, where he paid no attention to administering the cities, arbitrating on legal cases and all other matters of that kind, as he thought these of no use in furthering his plans, but raised an army and attacked the remainder of the Spanish tribes one after another, until he had made the entire country of Spain pay tribute to the Romans. He also sent a large amount of money to Rome to the public treasury. **28** As a result, the senate granted him a triumph, and he made arrangements outside the walls for a magnificent triumphal procession during the days in which candidates for the consulship were being invited to stand and had to be present in person — anyone who entered the city was not allowed to leave again to celebrate his triumph. **29** He was extremely eager to attain the magistracy, and as his procession was not yet ready he sent to the senate requesting that he be allowed to work through his friends and stand in his absence, knowing that it was illegal, but that it had been done by others. **30** Cato spoke in opposition, and spent the final day for the presentation of candidates in making speeches. Caesar, therefore, ignored his triumph, presented himself as a candidate and waited for the election.

12.38 Caesar makes overtures to Cicero, December 60 BC

Cicero Letters to Atticus 2.3.3–4

Cicero had supported Pompey's agrarian law, but decided to oppose Caesar's (which had the same purpose as Pompey's: to provide land for Pompey's veterans). The quotation from book 3 is from Cicero's poem on his consulship, for which see doc. 12.26; 'one omen best': spoken by Hector in Homer *Iliad* 12.243.

3 The matter needs careful consideration. Either I strongly oppose the agrarian law, which will involve something of a struggle, though a praiseworthy one, or I keep quiet, which is almost the same as leaving for Solonium or Antium, or I even give it my assistance, as they say Caesar unhesitatingly expects me to do. Cornelius, Balbus I mean, came to visit me, Caesar's friend. He declared that Caesar will follow my advice and Pompey's in everything and will work to unite Crassus and Pompey. **4** This would mean my intimate association with Pompey, and even with Caesar, should I wish, reconciliation with my enemies, peace with the populace, relaxation in my old age. But I'm affected by that conclusion of mine in Book Three:

> 'Meanwhile the paths, which from your earliest youth
> And which as consul, with courage and spirit, you sought,
> Keep to these and increase your prestige and good men's praise.'

Calliope herself dictated this to me in that book in which there are many aristocratic sentiments, so I do not think I ought to hesitate; may I always feel: 'one omen best — to fight for your country'.

THE FIRST TRIUMVIRATE

Pompey needed ratification of his eastern acta and land for the veterans of his eastern campaigns, Crassus wanted financial relief for the equites (and probably greater prestige), and Caesar needed the consulship followed by a lucrative province. Caesar played the key role in bringing Crassus and Pompey together in this relationship now known as the 'First Triumvirate' (doc. 12.39) to pursue various ends. Overtures were made to Cicero but he would not join the three. Cato had played a key role in obstructing Pompey over the land and acta issues, Crassus over the equites' tax request, and Caesar over his request to celebrate his triumph and be allowed to stand for the consulship in absentia. This association allowed the three men involved to achieve their political ends. It distanced Pompey from the optimates (for several years) and from Cicero, who had hoped to draw him towards the boni. For Caesar, his consulship of 59 involving violence and exciting optimate opposition and hatred for the years ahead had long-term repercussions, with the threat of prosecution over his activities in 59 becoming the key theme of his political career. The association lasted until Julia, Caesar's daughter, died in 54 and Crassus was killed in Parthia in 53. Pompey and Caesar remained on good terms, but Pompey's political position shifted and his appointment with the optimates' blessing as sole consul in 52 marks the beginning of the real change in his relationship with Caesar.

For the formation of the first triumvirate: Cic. *Att.* 2.3.3–4 (doc. 12.38); Vell. 2.44.1; Suet. *Jul.* 19.2; Plut. *Caes.* 13, *Pomp.* 47, *Cato Min.* 31; Dio 38.54, 56–7; Syme 1939: 34–6; Smith 1966: 140–2; Gelzer 1968: 68–9; Marshall 1976: 91–104; Ward 1977: 214–16; Leach 1978: 121–2; Greenhalgh 1980: 198–203; Scullard *GN* 112–14; Shotter 1994: 66–9; Gruen 1995: 86–90; Meier 1995: 190–203; Seager 2002: 83–4.

12.39 The 'first triumvirate'

Velleius Paterculus *Compendium of History* 2.44.1–3

Modern scholars have referred to this alliance as the 'First Triumvirate' but this is not an ancient term. Cic. *Att.* 2.13.2 refers to a *regnum* (kingship). Varro wrote a work entitled *Tricaranus* ('The Three Headed Monster': App. *BC* 2.9.33), and given his supportive attitude to Cicero in late 59 (*Att.* 2.25.1) this work could date to 59 BC. Velleius uses the term *societas* (partnership), and Livy *Per.* 103, *conspiratio* (secret agreement); cf. Lucan 1.86–7; see Ridley 1999. Cicero refers to Pompey's marriage to Julia as recent in a letter of May 59 (*Att.* 2.17.1). It cemented the relationship between Pompey and Caesar and was a key factor in the alliance between the two men until her death.

1 It was in Caesar's consulship that the partnership in political control between him and Gnaeus Pompey and Marcus Crassus was formed, which was to be so destructive to the city, the world, and no less, at different periods, to the men themselves. Pompey's reason for supporting this plan was **2** so that his settlements in the overseas provinces, which, as I have said already, many were opposing, should finally be ratified by Caesar as consul; Caesar's was because he realised that, in making this concession to Pompey's prestige, he would increase his own, and by putting onto Pompey the ill-will arising from their joint political control he would strengthen his own power; Crassus' was so that he might achieve, through the influence of Pompey and the power of Caesar, the pre-eminent place which he had not been able to reach on his own. **3** In addition, a marriage connection was made between Caesar and Pompey, in that Gnaeus Magnus married Julia, Gaius Caesar's daughter.

12.40 Relations between Crassus and Pompey

Plutarch *Life of Crassus* 7.1–4

Crassus and Pompey were very different political figures but their various needs would be met by their association with Caesar. They had held a joint consulship in 70 BC (docs 12.4–5).

1 Crassus was annoyed by Pompey's success in his campaigns, by the fact that he celebrated a triumph before becoming a senator, and by his being called Magnus, which means 'Great', by his fellow-citizens. When on one occasion someone said, 'Pompey the Great is coming,' Crassus laughed and asked 'As great as what?' **2** Accordingly he gave up all attempts to equal Pompey in military achievements and threw himself into politics, and through his hard work, advocacy in the courts, loans of money and his help in canvassing and supporting candidates for office obtained influence and prestige rivalling that won by Pompey from his many great military expeditions. **3** They both had their own special position: when Pompey was away he had the greater reputation and influence in the city due to his campaigns, but when he was at home he was often less important than Crassus, because, owing to the arrogance and pretence of his way of life, he would avoid crowds, retire from the forum and assist only a few of those who asked him, and then with no great eagerness, so as to retain his influence the more unimpaired for use on his own behalf. **4** Crassus, on the other hand, was continually ready to be of use, never aloof or difficult to get hold of, and was always actively involved in whatever was going on, and so, by his kindness to everyone, gained the advantage over Pompey with his haughty reserve. Both men, it is said, were similarly gifted with dignity of appearance, persuasiveness of speech and grace of countenance.

CAESAR'S CONSULSHIP

Caesar's consulship was marked by a legislative programme 'more fitting for a radical tribune than a consul' (doc. 12.43). Caesar carried through the wishes of Pompey and Crassus, after which his own agenda emerged: a military command in the west, sponsored by P. Vatinius, the main supporter of the triumvirs on the tribunician bench. In addition, Caesar's extortion law (*lex de repetundis*) remained an important law for provincial government in the imperial period (*MRR* II.188). Cicero refused to accept Caesar's overtures and did not support his land legislation or accept any of his invitations to official posts (doc. 12.44, 12.54, cf. 12.38). His opposition seems to have been a decisive factor in the adoption of Clodius as a plebeian, which paved the way for Clodius' tribunate of 58 and Cicero's exile (docs 12.52–4). The triumvirate became unpopular throughout the course of the year (docs 12.48–50), with Curio prominent amongst the critics, and Cicero complains about the general loss of liberty (doc. 12.49).

The sources for this period are not as satisfactory as they might be: there are several letters of Cicero from 59, but the later sources diverge on details. For 59 BC, see docs 12.41–51; *MRR* II.187–8; Fuller 1965: 67–73; Smith 1966: 140–2; Balsdon 1967: 54–65; Taylor 1968; Leach 1978: 123–30; Mitchell 1991: 98–113; Wiseman 1994a: 368–75; Ryan 1996; Gelzer 1968: 71–101; Gruen 1995: 90–7; Meier 1995: 204–23; Southern 2001: 49–61; Seager 2002: 86–100.

12.41 'In the consulship of Julius and Caesar', 59 BC

Suetonius *Life of the Deified Julius* 19.2–20.2

The senate, fearing that another military command would increase Caesar's popularity, assigned as provinces to the consuls of 59 the 'woods and pastures' (Suet. *Jul.* 19.2: *silvae callesque*). Bibulus' opposition to Caesar and his legislation took the form of *obnuntiatio* (declaration of unfavourable omens) at meetings of the assembly: cf. doc. 3.72. Caesar did not allow this to interfere with his legislative programme and Bibulus' consulship was therefore ineffective, his main achievement being to postpone the consular elections for 58 (*Att.* 2.20.6, 2.21.5, cf. 2.23.3).

19.2 Caesar was therefore made consul with Bibulus. For the same reason, the optimates took care that the provinces assigned the consuls-elect would be of the most trivial importance; that is, woods and pastures . . . **20.1** After taking office, Caesar's first enactment was that the daily proceedings of both the senate and the people should be collected and published. He also revived an ancient custom that, in the months when he did not have the fasces, a state officer should walk in front of him while the lictors followed behind. He proposed an agrarian bill, and used force to drive his colleague from the forum when he pronounced that the omens were unfavourable, and, when his colleague made a complaint in the senate on the following day, no one could be found who was bold enough to bring a motion or express their opinion about such a disruption, although decrees had often been passed regarding lighter disturbances. Bibulus was driven to such a degree of desperation that, until the end of his magistracy, he stayed at home, merely issuing edicts that the omens were unfavourable. **2** From that time on, Caesar handled all matters of state on his own and on his own judgement, so that some humorists, when they were acting as witnesses to documents, wrote as a joke not 'done in the consulship of Caesar and Bibulus' but 'in the consulship of Julius and Caesar', putting the same man down twice by name and surname, while the following verses were soon widely circulated:

> 'A deed took place recently, not in Bibulus' year but Caesar's —
> For I don't remember anything happening in Bibulus' consulship!'

12.42 Caesar's agrarian legislation

Dio *Roman History* 38.1.1–7, 7.4–6

Caesar as consul effectively carried land legislation, though the tribune Flavius had failed the previous year. Caesar had prepared his legislation carefully and there could be no real cause for disputing it. He established a committee of twenty, which Cicero, despite his opposition to the legislation, was to be invited to join (doc. 12.44). Campania was state property (confiscated in 211 from Capua after its defection to Hannibal and recapture by Rome) and was important as a source of revenue: docs 4.42, 44. Caesar left it out of his initial legislation but in May the Campanian land (*ager Campanus*) was added to the legislation for distribution to 20,000 citizens. Cicero's hopes that this distribution of the Campanian land would incense the boni seem to have been misplaced (*Att.* 2.16.1); he had spoken against the distribution of the ager Campanus in 63 when it was proposed in Rullus' land legislation. For this land legislation, see also Cic. *Att.* 2.3.3, 2.16.1–2 (doc. 12.45), 2.17.1, 2.19.3 (Pompey in Capua, presumably overseeing the distribution of the ager Campanus), *Quint.* 5.1, 10.1–2; cf. [Caes.] *Alex.* 68.1; Livy *Per.* 103; Vell. 2.44.4–5; Suet. *Jul.* 20; Plut. *Pomp.* 47–8, *Caes.* 14, *Cato Min.* 31–3; App. *BC* 2.10–14.34–42; *MRR* II.187–8; Crawford 1989.

7.4: Caesar finally dealt with the request of the equites in 61 BC for a reduction in the price contracted for the taxes for Asia Minor, organising this through the assembly, and giving them a one-third reduction, more than they expected (see also doc. 12.45; Cic. *Planc.* 35; Suet. *Jul.* 20.3; App. *BC* 2.13.46–8; Val. Max. 2.10.7; Dio 38.7.5). Pompey's eastern acta were also ratified in the assembly (Vell. 2.44.2; Plut. *Pomp.* 48.4; Dio 38.7.5; cf. Suet. *Jul.* 20.4; Plut. *Cato Min.* 31.1; Murphy 1993).

1.1 The next year Caesar wanted to grant favours to the whole people in order to make them even more firmly attached to his side. As he also wished to appear to be supporting the optimates, to avoid incurring their enmity he told them frequently that he would not propose any measure that was not in their interests; **2** indeed, he framed a law about the land, which he wished to distribute to the whole populace, in such a way that not the slightest fault could be found with it, though he pretended that he would not introduce it if they did not wish for it. No one was able to criticise him in any way over this law, for the swollen city mob, **3** which was primarily responsible for the constant disturbances, would be channelled into work and agriculture, and most of Italy, which was now desolate, would be recolonised, so that not only those who had endured the hardships of campaign, but all the others too would have sufficient means to live on, while this would involve no expense for the city or loss to the optimates, many of whom would acquire both dignity and office. **4** He wished to allocate all the public land except for Campania (which he advised them to keep separate as state property because of its excellence), and told them to purchase the rest, not from anyone who was unwilling nor for a price desired by the land commissioners, but firstly from those willing to sell and secondly for the same price as that assessed in the tax registers. **5** He stated that they had a large amount of surplus money from the booty taken by Pompey and from the tributes and taxes recently established, and that they should, in so far as it had been acquired through the dangers faced by citizens, spend it on these same persons. **6** In addition, he proposed that there should be not just a few land commissioners, so as to appear like an oligarchy, nor should they be people who had to give an account of their conduct in office, which might displease someone, but firstly there should be twenty so the honour should be shared, and secondly they should be the most suitable men, except for himself. **7** For he insisted on this at the beginning, so he might not be thought to be proposing a measure to his own advantage; he himself was satisfied, so he said, with planning and proposing the measure, though he was clearly doing a favour to Pompey, Crassus and the rest. . . .

7.4 In this way Caesar won the support of the populace, while he gained that of the equites by releasing them from one-third of the taxes for which they had contracted; they were responsible for all tax collection and, though they had often asked the senate for some satisfaction, they had not been successful because Cato and others opposed it. **5** When Caesar had won over this class, encountering no protests, he first ratified all Pompey's settlements, with no opposition from Lucullus or anyone else, and then enacted many other measures without resistance. **6** Not even Cato objected, although, when he was praetor a little while later, he would never mention the title of Caesar's laws, because they were called 'Julian'; for although he followed them in allocating the courts, he most ridiculously concealed their name.

12.43 Caesar's methods as consul

Plutarch *Life of Caesar* 14.1–13

When Caesar's land legislation was opposed in the senate, he took it to the comitia tributa. Bibulus (with the assistance of three of the tribunes, Q. Ancharius, Cn. Domitius Calvinus (cos. 53), and C. Fannius), unsuccessfully opposed it. The legislation (the *lex Julia agraria*) was passed with violence: Pompey and Crassus appeared on the rostrum with Caesar, and Pompey 'filled the forum with armed men': cf. Plut. *Pomp.* 47; Dio 38.5.4. Bibulus came into the assembly with Cato and Lucullus and his fasces and insignia were broken, and tribunes wounded; Cato was almost hauled off to prison. On the next day Bibulus attempted to have the law annulled in the senate but it would not act. He then kept to his house observing the omens for the remainder of his consulship, through edicts declaring them unfavourable, so that technically the assembly could not meet (the *obnuntiatio*) and Caesar's legislative activities were therefore invalid. Even the announcement of a magistrate that they were observing the sky was enough to render an assembly invalid (it was unique, however, to observe the omens from home).

The plebeians swore to observe the agrarian law, and a clause was added by Caesar that the senate do the same. Cato, Metellus Celer and Favonius refused to take the oath until the last moment open for them to do so, with Cicero persuading Cato of the necessity: they would otherwise have gone into exile. For the land legislation, oath and omens: Cic. *Dom.* 39, *Har. Resp.* 48, *Att.* 2.18.2; App. *BC* 2.10–12.34–42; Plut. *Pomp.* 48.5; Suet. *Jul.* 20.1; Dio 38.6.1–7.2; *MRR* II.187. Bibulus' observation of the omens: Taylor 1949: 95; Gelzer 1968: 73–4; Meier 1995: 212–13; Lintott 1999: 135.

1 So Caesar, supported and defended by the friendship of Crassus and Pompey, put himself forward for the consulship; **2** once he was triumphantly elected with Calpurnius Bibulus and had entered upon his office, he immediately proposed laws more fitting for a radical tribune than a consul, bringing forward measures for the allocation and distribution of land. **3** When the respectable elements in the senate opposed him, this gave him just the pretext he needed and, protesting loudly that he was being driven to the assembly against his will, and forced by the insolence and intransigence of the senate to pay court to it, he hurried there. **4** After placing Crassus on one side of himself and Pompey on the other, he asked them if they approved of his laws. When they declared that they did, he called on them to assist him against those who were threatening to oppose him with swords. **5** They promised to do this, and Pompey added that he would meet swords with a sword and shield too. **6** The nobility were irritated by this rash and childish speech, unworthy of his own dignity and unsuited to the respect due to the senate, but the people were delighted.

7 Caesar went on to obtain an even greater claim to Pompey's influence, as he had a daughter, Julia, engaged to Servilius Caepio, whom he now engaged to Pompey, saying that he would give Servilius Pompey's daughter, though she too was not unengaged, but had been promised to Faustus, son of Sulla. **8** And shortly afterwards Caesar married Calpurnia, Piso's daughter, and had Piso made consul for the following year, at which Cato protested violently, crying out that it was unendurable to have the government prostituted by marriage alliances and men promoting each other to provinces, armies and offices by the means of women.

9 As Caesar's colleague Bibulus achieved nothing in his efforts to obstruct Caesar's laws, and was often in danger, with Cato, of being killed in the forum, he shut himself up at home for the rest of his term. **10** Straight after his marriage, Pompey filled the forum with armed men and assisted the people in ratifying the legislation and granting Caesar Gaul on both sides of the Alps for five years, along with Illyricum and four legions. **11** When Cato tried to speak against these measures, Caesar had him led off to prison, imagining that he would appeal to the tribunes; **12** but when he walked off without a word and Caesar saw that not only were the nobles displeased, but that the people out of respect for Cato's excellent qualities were following him in silence with downcast faces, he secretly asked one of the tribunes to have him released. **13** Of the rest of the senators, only a very few used to attend Caesar's meetings in the senate; the rest showed their disapproval by staying away.

12.44 Cicero turns down Caesar's offers

Cicero *On the Consular Provinces* 40–1

There was to be a board of twenty on the land commission (doc. 12.42; *Att.* 2.6.2), and Cicero was invited to join it (*Att.* 9.2a.1; Vell. 2.45.2); Cicero in this passage (and at *Att.* 2.7.4) refers to a Board of Five, presumably a sub-committee of the twenty; M. Valerius Messalla, pontifex maximus and consul in 61, was a member of this sub-committee (*ILS* 46). Cicero had refused Caesar's overtures for him to join the triumvirate in December 60 (doc. 12.38), and now refused to join the Five. Cicero attributed Caesar's hostility to him as arising out of his refusal to serve on the commission (*Att.* 9.2a.1). Cicero also refused the position of Caesar's legate in Gaul (*Att.* 2.18.3, 2.19.5), and in April 59 the offer of an ambassadorship to Egypt in case the optimates thought he had received it as a bribe to change his views on the triumvirate (*Att.* 2.5.1, 2.18.3).

40 I think it relevant here, to prevent my being frequently interrupted by some people or condemned in the thoughts of those who are silent, to explain briefly the nature of my relations with Caesar. In the first place I will make no mention of that time when we were all young men and were very intimate with him — myself, my brother and my cousin Gaius Varro. After I became deeply involved in politics, my opinions differed from his but, despite our differences, we still remained united by friendship. **41** As consul he brought in measures in which he wanted me to participate; while I did not approve of these, I had, however, to feel pleased with his opinion of me. He asked me to be one of the Commission of Five; he wanted me to be one of the three consulars most closely allied to himself; he offered me any ambassadorial role I wished, with whatever privileges I might choose. I rejected all these offers, not because I was ungrateful, but because I remained true to my own convictions.

12.45 Cicero on Caesar's consulship, late April/early May 59 BC

Cicero *Letters to Atticus* 2.16.2

The three tribunes who opposed Caesar's land legislation were entitled to veto the legislation but did not have the chance to do so, due to the violent nature of the assembly: Pompey was not to be drawn on the issue of the veto. Seager 2002: 95 notes that 'Cicero displays Pompey taking refuge in sophistries'; his quotation is from a play by the Greek tragedian Sophocles. The Alexandrian king was Ptolemy XII Auletes, confirmed in his rule of Egypt by legislation passed by Caesar and recognised as 'king and ally' of the Roman people at the cost of 6,000 talents (Suet. *Jul.* 54.3; *MRR* II.188).

I have absolutely no idea what our friend Gnaeus (Pompey) is planning at the moment,

'For he no longer blows on little pipes,
But with wild gusts without a mouthband'

since it's been possible to bring him even to these lengths. Until now he has quibbled, saying that he approves of Caesar's laws but that Caesar himself has to be responsible for his own actions; that he was in favour of the agrarian bill, but whether vetoes were possible or not was in no way his concern; that he was in favour of finally settling the case of the Alexandrian king, but whether Bibulus had been observing the sky was not for him to inquire into; regarding the tax-farmers he had wanted to do that order a favour, but wasn't able to foretell what might happen if Bibulus went down to the forum on that occasion.

12.46 Cicero's 'complaint about certain political matters'

Cicero *On his House* 41

Publius Clodius Pulcher had been quaestor in Sicily in 61–60 BC. His attempted transfer to the plebeians from the patrician class in 60, so he could stand for the tribunate, had been proposed by the tribune C. Herennius but vetoed by other tribunes, and opposed by his brother-in-law Metellus Celer as consul (doc. 12.35; *Att.* 1.18.4–5, 2.1.5; Dio 37.51.1). While the sources concentrate on Clodius' desire for revenge on Cicero for his prosecution over the Bona Dea scandal, his legislative programme was clearly his main motivation in aspiring to plebeian status and aspects of it had presumably been worked out in 60–59 BC.

Caesar as pontifex maximus presided over Clodius' *transitio ad plebem* in March 59 in the form of an adoption by one Fonteius, a twenty-year-old plebeian who then emancipated Clodius. His change of name from Claudius had already occurred: Clodius was referred to several times by Cicero as Clodius in 61 (Riggsby 2002: 117).

Cicero claimed that it was something which he himself had said in his defence of his colleague Antonius Hibrida (cos. 63), who was being prosecuted for extortion as proconsul in Macedonia (62–61 BC), that led Caesar to engineer the adoption of Clodius. Criticism of the triumvirs had clearly not been well-received by the three (doc. 12.50) and Cicero may not be exaggerating his own role in the transfer; Velleius certainly takes Cicero's continuing opposition as the reason (doc. 12.54)

For Cicero's speech in the case of Antonius, the adoption, and Cicero's later complaints that the transfer was illegal (and hence Clodius' legislation invalid): see doc. 12.47; cf. Cic. *Att.* 8.3.3, Cic. *Dom.* 34–42, *Prov.* 42, 45–6; Suet. *Jul.* 20.4; Plut. *Caes.* 14.16–17, *Cato Min.* 33.6; App. *BC* 2.14.52–3; Dio 38.10.1, 38.12 (doc. 12.52), 39.11.2, 39.21.4; cf. *Att.* 2.9.1. Cicero himself admitted that many of the leading citizens of the state (*principes civitatis*) saw nothing illegal in the adoption (*Dom.* 42). See Smith 1966: 148–9; Gelzer 1968: 77–8; Habicht 1990: 46–7; Tatum 1999: 104–11; Seager 2002: 91–2; Meier 1995: 214–15.

It was perhaps at the sixth hour of the day that, in a case in which I was defending Gaius Antonius, my colleague, I made a complaint about certain political matters which seemed to me to impact on my poor client's case. Scoundrels reported this to certain worthy gentlemen in terms very different from those I had actually used. At the ninth hour of that very same day your adoption occurred.

12.47 'This loathsome and monstrous beast'

Cicero *In Defence of Sestius* 15–16

Caesar and Pompey presided over the adoption as a means of silencing Cicero, who immediately retired to his country estates (Cic. *Att.* 2.4–17); Caesar convened the comitia curiata as pontifex maximus. Cicero here claims that Pompey bound Clodius not to harm Cicero's interests, and in a letter in July 59 (*Att.* 2.19.4, cf. 2.21.6, 2.22.2, 2.25.5) writes that Pompey was deceiving himself in giving Cicero assurances that Clodius wouldn't 'say a word' against him, while Clodius let everyone else hear his threats (*Att.* 2.23.3). Cicero later claimed Pompey 'showed more concern for restoring me (from exile) than for keeping me here' (*Att.* 8.3.3: doc. 13.35).

15 Gnaeus Pompey, a most illustrious man and one who had been extremely friendly to me at a time when many people were showing me hostility, had bound Clodius by every kind of pledge, agreement and sacred oath not to act against me in any way during his tribunate . . . **16** This loathsome and monstrous beast, though bound by the auspices, tied down by ancestral custom, fettered by sacred law, was suddenly freed by a consul through a law in the comitia curiata, either, as I believe, because he was prevailed on by entreaties, or, as many people considered, because he was angry with me, but certainly unaware of and not foreseeing the great crimes and evils which were hanging over our heads.

12.48 'Publius is our only hope' (c. 28 April 59)

Cicero *Letters to Atticus* 2.15.1–2

When Caesar's first agrarian law had not found enough land, he included the ager Campanus. Bibulus delayed the elections for the consulship of 58 in an attempt to undermine the triumvirate, but two associates of the triumvirs were to be finally elected in October: Gabinius (who had proposed the *lex Gabinia*) and L. Calpurnius Piso Caesoninus (Caesar's father-in-law). Publius is Clodius. Cicero in 59 was apprehensive about Clodius and his hostility towards him, but was concerned with two possibilities, a challenge in court or the threat of violence (*Att.* 2.5.3, 2.7.2, 2.9.3, 2.19.1, 4, 2.20.2, 2.21.6, 2.22.1–2, 2.23.3, 2.24.5, *Quint.* 1.2.16). Cicero earlier in April had met Curio on the Appian Way who told him that Clodius was standing for the tribunate as the enemy of Caesar (*inimicissimus Caesaris*: *Att.* 2.12). Cicero was hopeful that this would change the current political situation.

1 One thing I can't understand is how a scheme can be devised to provide enough land without anyone objecting. **2** Bibulus has shown great nobility of mind in delaying the (consular) elections, but what does it achieve except an expression of his personal opinion without any solution for the state's problems? No doubt about it, Publius is our only hope. Alright, let him become tribune, if for no other reason than to bring you back from Epirus more quickly. I don't see how you could bear to miss him, especially if he wants to pick a quarrel with me. But if anything of that kind happens, I'm sure you will fly back. Even if it doesn't, whether he wrecks or revitalises the state, I anticipate a splendid show, as long as I can watch it with you sitting beside me!

12.49 Curio's opposition to 'our masters', June 59

Cicero *Letters to Atticus* 2.18.1

In *Att.* 2.17.1 Cicero writes that it was generally agreed that Pompey was working for tyranny and that this explained his marriage to Julia, and support of the Campanian land legislation. Here Cicero laments the servitude of the times (cf. doc. 12.50). Curio the Younger (Gaius Scribonius Curio) was the son of the consul of 76; despite his opposition to the triumvirs in 59 (cf. *Att.* 2.8.1, 2.12.2), as tribune in 50 he became Caesar's man.

We are mastered on all sides, and no longer object to being in servitude, but fear death and exile as worse evils, though they are much less serious. This is the present state of affairs, lamented by one universal groan, but alleviated by no one's actions or words. The aim of our masters, I suspect, is to leave nothing for anyone else to bestow. The only one to speak or oppose them openly is young Curio. He gets great rounds of applause, a most prestigious amount of greetings in the forum, and a multitude of other signs of goodwill from the 'honest' men.

12.50 The unpopularity of the triumvirate, mid-July 59

Cicero *Letters to Atticus* 2.19.2–3

Pompey was at Capua, possibly overseeing the distribution of the ager Campanus there. The ringmaster (*dominus*) at the gladiatorial show is unknown, perhaps Gabinius as a candidate for the consulship for 58 (Shackleton Bailey 1965: I.389). The displeasure of the triumvirs was made clear in threatening the repeal of the Roscian Law and the grain law. The Roscian law passed in 67 reserved the first 14 rows of seats in the theatre for the equites (*MRR* II.145; cf. doc. 12.25). The grain law could be the *lex Terentia Cassia* (73 BC) dealing with the price of grain from Sicily. The threatened rescindments would punish the equites and the plebs. For the unpopularity of the triumvirate: Rawson 1975: 110; Meier 1995: 217–18. **2**: for the quotation from Ennius on Fabius Maximus 'Cunctator', see doc. 4.34.

2 You should be aware that there has never been anything so infamous, humiliating, and uniformly hateful to all types, classes and ages of men as this current state of affairs — more, I assure you, than I wished, let alone what I expected. Those 'popular' politicians have now taught even mild-tempered people to hiss. Bibulus is in heaven, I don't know why, but he is praised as though 'one man alone by his delays restored for us the state (Ennius)'. My very dear Pompey has brought about his own ruin, which is a great grief to me. They hold no one by good will; I am afraid that they may find it necessary to employ fear. For my part, however, I neither fight with their party on account of my friendship with him, nor do I assent to it or I should be condemning all that I did earlier. I take a middle path. **3** The feeling of the people has been evident at the great theatre and shows. For, at the gladiators, both the ringmaster and his friends were greeted with hissing, and at the Games of Apollo (ludi Apollinares) the tragic actor Diphilus impudently attacked our dear Pompey: 'To our misery you are Great' — he had to encore this numerous times. 'The time will come when you will deeply rue that same manliness' — he spoke that to the applause of the entire theatre, and the rest the same. Actually these verses are such as to seem to have been written for the occasion by an enemy of Pompey. 'If neither laws nor customs can compel' and the rest were recited to immense noise and shouting. When Caesar arrived, applause died. The younger Curio followed him, and got the kind of applause that Pompey used to receive in the time when all was well with the state. Caesar took it badly. A letter is said to be flying to Pompey at Capua. They are at loggerheads with the equites who stood up to applaud Curio, they are at war with everyone; they threaten the Roscian law, even the grain law. Matters are certainly in a bad way. I would actually have preferred their undertaking to pass in silence, but I fear that that may not be possible. People won't endure it, though it seems it must be endured. But now there is just one universal cry, though united by hatred rather than the ability to oppose them.

12.51 The Vettius affair

Cicero *Letters to Atticus* 2.24.2–3

Written probably in August 59, and certainly before the consular elections in October. L. Vettius in 62 had accused Caesar of complicity in the Catilinarian conspiracy. In 59 he confessed before the senate that he was plotting to kill Pompey, and that the younger Curio was associated with him in the plot. Vatinius and Caesar brought Vettius to the forum, where at a contio he implicated, amongst others, Cicero, Lucullus, Domitius and Cicero's son-in-law Piso. Cicero believes that Vettius promised Caesar that he would bring the younger Curio under suspicion. Vettius was imprisoned and died in prison, strangled or poisoned, according to the sources, on the orders of the very men who put him up to the incident. Caesar was able to exploit the affair to strengthen his relationship with Pompey and keep him apart from the optimates.

Cicero anticipated Vettius asking to turn informer and that prosecutions would be instituted on his information; see Cic. *Att.* 2.24.2–4, *Vat.* 24–6, Cic. *Sest.* 132; Suet. *Jul.* 20.5; Plut. *Luc.* 42.7–8; App. *BC* 2.12.43–5; Dio 38.9.2–4; Taylor 1950, 1954; Seager 1965: 525–9, 2002: 98–9; Marshall 1976: 107; 1987: 121–4; Ward 1977: 236–42; Leach 1978: 127–8; Greenhalgh 1980: 223–6; Wiseman 1994a: 375.

2 That chap Vettius, my old informer, clearly promised Caesar that he would find a way to bring the younger Curio under suspicion of some crime. So he wormed his way into the young man's friendship and became a close associate of his, as events make clear. He finally brought things to the point where he told him that he had decided with the help of his slaves to make an attack on Pompey and kill him. Curio carried this information to his father, and he to Pompey. **3** The affair was brought to the senate's attention. When Vettius was brought in, he denied that he had ever been friendly with Curio, at least not for a long time; he then requested a public guarantee of safety. This was shouted down. Nevertheless he related that a band of young men existed, with Curio as leader, which initially included Paulus, Caepio (that is Brutus), and Lentulus, the flamen's son, his father being aware of this; later on Gaius Septimius, Bibulus' clerk, had brought Vettius a dagger from Bibulus. This was totally laughed down — as though Vettius could not have had a dagger unless the consul gave him one! His story was all the more disbelieved, because on the 13th Bibulus himself had informed Pompey to watch out for a plot, for which Pompey had thanked him. When the younger Curio was brought in, he replied to Vettius' statements, and Vettius was particularly criticised for stating that the plan of the young men had been to attack Pompey during Gabinius' gladiatorial show in the forum, and that Paullus was one of the leaders, as it was well known that he was then in Macedonia. A senatorial decree was passed that Vettius, since he had admitted to having a weapon, should be put in chains and any person who let him go would be acting against the interests of the state. The general view is that the original idea was for Vettius to have been arrested in the forum with his dagger, together with his slaves with their weapons, and that he would then have asked to turn informer. And that's what would have happened if the Curios had not taken the affair to Pompey beforehand.

CLODIUS AND CICERO

In assisting Clodius' transfer to the plebs, Pompey and Caesar must have realised that he would stand for the tribunate (cf. docs. 12.47–8). But it appears that they did not want him to stand for 58 BC. In April, Clodius was promised an embassy to Egypt (it actually went to someone else), and offered another to Tigranes (possibly to have him out of Rome for the tribunician elections in July). He did not take it up and did not receive a place on the agrarian commission of twenty. Cicero in April sees Pompey and Caesar as keeping Clodius' tribunate in reserve for the time when it will suit them, and hears hints from Curio that there might be a falling out amongst the triumvirs and their associates (*Att.* 2.4.2, 2.7.2–3). However, there was no substantial rift between Pompey, Caesar and Clodius at this stage. Clodius supported the legislation of Vatinius as tribune in 59 arranging the special five-year command for Caesar (App. *BC* 2.14.53) but this law, though early in the year, cannot be precisely dated.

12.52 Clodius' reforms as tribune

Dio *Roman History* 38.12.5–13.1, 13.6

Clodius was elected as tribune for 58 and was to pursue an extensive legislative programme (Cic. *Dom.* 129, *Prov.* 46; Plut. *Cic.* 30.1). His legislation was introduced on 1 January 58 and became law on 4 January.

The distribution of grain free of charge: Sulla had abolished Gaius Gracchus' grain law, and the *lex Terentia Cassia* of 73 BC had revived it in some form; Cato as tribune in 62 persuaded the senate to provide cheap grain for the poor and landless to ensure their support during the Catilinarian crisis (Plut. *Cato Min.* 26.1, *Caes.* 6–7). Cicero emphasises the cost of Clodius' law to the treasury: *Sest.* 55, *Dom.* 25, *Asc.* 8; Meijer 1983: 159–61. *Restoration of the collegia* ('guilds'): many collegia were abolished in 64 by the senate, as was the associated Compitalia (festival of the cross-roads) which was also now revived. Collegia included those born free, freedmen, and slaves, and their size ranged from 100 to 1000 members. They provided funeral funds for members and celebrated dinners and festivals together, and could play an important role in elections; Clodius' measure had clear *popularis* overtones: Cic. *Sest.* 34, 55, *Att.* 3.15.4, *Piso* 8–9; Asc. 7–8; for collegia: Lintott 1967: 160–3; Treggiari 1969: 168–77; Nippel 1984: 28–9; Tatum 1999: 25–6. *Censorship*: censors had the right to revise the roll of senators and to expel members; Clodius' law meant that the senator involved had to be present, allowing the senator the right of defending himself (Cic. *Sest.* 55, *Pis.* 9–10; *Prov.* 46; Asc. 8; Dio 40.57.1). This measure was clearly designed to seek senatorial support.

Other measures: Gabinius and Piso had become consuls for 58 and both supported Clodius: Gabinius was given command of Cilicia (later changed to Syria) and Piso of Macedonia (Cic. *Sest.* 24–5, *Dom.* 70; cf. *Prov.* 1–2; *MRR* II.193). Cicero saw Clodius as buying the acquiescence of the consuls. *Obnuntiatio*: Clodius abolished the *auspicia* for assemblies, permitting assemblies to meet on *dies fasti* (see doc. 3.28), obviously in reaction to Bibulus' activities in 59 BC (references at *MRR* II.196). Clodius' legislation: Weinstock 1937; Balsdon 1957: 15–16; Rundell 1979: 309–18; Mitchell 1986; Tatum 1990a, 1990b, 1993, 1999: 117–35; cf. Cerutti 1998. Clodius was in no way a puppet or agent of the triumvirs: he was independent from the beginning of his tribunate and by its end had attacked and alienated Pompey, and to a lesser extent Caesar. His aim, judging from his legislation, was to be a popular tribune and he pursued his own interests; see Gruen 1966; Tatum 1999: 114–75. For his scriba (scribe) and chief supporter, Sextus Cloelius, see esp. Asc. 33 (doc. 13.1); Damon 1992.

12.5 Cicero irritated numerous people with his speeches, and those whom he helped were not so much won over to his side as those who were injured were alienated . . . **6** he also made himself some very bitter enemies by always trying to get the better of even the most powerful men and by always employing an uncontrolled and excessive freedom of speech towards everyone alike in his pursuit of a reputation for intellect and eloquence above anyone else's, even in preference to being thought a worthy citizen. **7** As a result of this, and because he was the greatest boaster alive and considered no one his equal, but in speeches and life alike despised everyone and thought no one on the same footing as himself, he was a trial and a burden to others and was accordingly envied and hated even by those who were otherwise in sympathy with him. **13.1** So Clodius hoped that he could soon deal with him if he first won over the senate, equites and people, and straightway started distributing free grain (for now Gabinius and Piso had become consuls he introduced a bill for its being handed out to the poor), and revived the associations called *collegia* in Latin, which had existed in ancient times but been disbanded for some time; he also forbade the censors to remove anyone from any order or censure anyone, without his being tried and convicted before both censors . . . **6** Clodius also, afraid that if he indicted Cicero some people might use this method of postponing or delaying the trial, introduced a measure that none of the magistrates might observe signs from the heaven on days on which the people had to vote on anything.

12.53 Cicero leaves town

Dio *Roman History* 38.17.1–6

After Clodius had passed his main legislation, he turned on Cicero, who had preferred to stay in Rome rather than join Caesar's staff (*Att.* 2.18.3, 2.19.5, *Prov.* 42, cf. Plut. *Cic.* 30.3–4). When Clodius had a law passed forbidding fire and water to anyone who had put citizens to death without a trial, Cicero went around the city in mourning clothes (the *toga pulla*) and with his hair uncut; 20,000 equites imitated him and supplicated the citizenry on Cicero's behalf. The senate met to decree that the people should also go into mourning, but Gabinius and Piso as consuls opposed this, and Clodius had armed men stationed around the senate house (the law allocating the consuls' provinces was passed on the same day as that concerning the execution of citizens without a trial).

Pompey avoided meeting Cicero and told a delegation of senators that he would act only if the senate passed a *senatus consultum*, when he would take up arms against the armed tribune (Cic. *Piso* 77). Cicero therefore went into voluntary exile, and Clodius immediately passed a law which both mentioned Cicero explicitly by name and forbade any further discussion of the matter (Cic. *Att.* 3.12.1, 3.15.6). Cicero's house was demolished, and a shrine to Libertas (Liberty) erected on the site by Clodius: in 57 the site was returned to Cicero and compensation paid for the house, and for two villas destroyed by Clodius (Cic. *Dom.* 102–22; *Att.* 4.2.2–5; Plut. *Cic.* 33.1; Dio 38.17.6; Berg 1997).

Caesar was outside the city walls awaiting departure for Gaul and told Clodius, who sought his opinion in a contio at the Circus Flaminius, that he disapproved of the execution of the conspirators but did not believe in retroactive legislation. That was all the support he gave Cicero, and he left for Gaul soon after Cicero went into exile, after the praetors for 58 BC, L. Domitius Ahenobarbus and C. Memmius, had unsuccessfully attacked Caesar's legislation in the senate (Suet. *Jul.* 23.1, *Nero* 2.2). Cicero's exile: Cic. *Att.* 3.4, 3.12, 3.15.5 (*Att.* 3.1–27 are from the period of exile, March 58 to September 57), *Dom.* 47, 50, 54–5, 62, 83, 110, *Sest.* 25, 53–4, 65, 69, *Piso* 14, 16, 30, 72, 77, *Planc.* 96–7, *Red. Sen.* 4, 8, 13, 17; Livy *Per.* 103; Asc. 46; Vell. 2.45 (doc. 12.54); Plut. *Cic.* 30–2, *Pomp.* 48.9, *Caes.* 14.7, *Cato Min.* 35.1; App. *BC* 2.15.54–8; Dio 38.14–17.

1 However Caesar (who was outside the walls as he had already taken charge of his army, so Clodius assembled the populace there to allow him to arbitrate on the proposal) condemned the illegality of the actions taken regarding Lentulus, **2** but did not approve the proposed punishment; he stated that everyone knew what he had thought about events at the time (for he had voted to spare their lives), but it was not appropriate for such a retrospective law to be drawn up now. **3** This was Caesar's view, and Crassus gave some support to Cicero through his son, but sided himself with the populace. Pompey kept promising Cicero help, but by making various excuses at different times and deliberately leaving town on frequent trips, did nothing to assist him. **4** When Cicero perceived this, he was afraid and again attempted to carry weapons (among other things openly castigating Pompey), but was prevented from doing this by Cato and Hortensius in case a civil war should eventuate, and departed unwillingly with the disgrace and

THE COLLAPSE OF THE REPUBLIC

dishonour of having chosen to go into exile. **5** Before he left, he went up to the Capitol and dedicated a small statue of Minerva, whom he called 'Protectress'. He slipped away to Sicily, for he had been governor there and had great hopes of honourable treatment from its towns and citizens. **6** On his departure the law came into force, not only with no opposition, but once he was out of the way with the support among others of those who had seemed to be Cicero's chief adherents. His property was confiscated, and his house destroyed, as though an enemy's, and its site dedicated for a temple to Liberty. A decree of exile was passed against Cicero himself, and his stay in Sicily was prohibited; he was banished 3,750 stades from Rome, and it was proclaimed that should he ever be found inside this limit both he and those who received him could be killed with impunity.

12.54 Clodius' hatred for Cicero

Velleius Paterculus *Compendium of History* 2.45.1–2

For Clodius' profanation of the rites of the Bona Dea, see doc. 7.85; Cicero disproved his alibi, but he was acquitted. For Caesar's invitation to Cicero to join the land-commission, see doc. 12.44.

1 At about the same time Publius Clodius, a man of noble family, a skilful speaker and man of audacity, who knew no limits in speech or action except his own wishes, passionate in the execution of his evil schemes, notorious too for his affair with his sister, and who had been brought to trial for his profanation of the Roman people's most sacred rites, since he felt a violent hatred for Marcus Cicero (for what friendship could there be between men so different?) and had had himself transferred from the patricians to the plebs, proposed a law as tribune that whoever had put a Roman citizen to death without a trial should be forbidden fire and water (i.e., exiled): although Cicero was not expressly named, he alone was the target. **2** And so this man, who had deserved the best from the state, won the calamity of exile as his reward for saving his country. Caesar and Pompey were not free from the suspicion of having been involved in Cicero's downfall. Cicero seemed to have brought this on himself by having refused to be one of the commission of 20 men in charge of distributing the land in Campania.

CATO THE YOUNGER IN CYPRUS

Prior to Cicero's exile Clodius had proposed that Cyprus, the property of Ptolemy, the brother of Ptolemy XII Auletes of Egypt (recognised by Rome in 59 BC), be annexed. A little later (the chronology is imprecise), Clodius moved a second law to send Cato to Cyprus to administer the annexation of the island and to re-instate exiles at Byzantium (docs 12.56(b), 57). Earlier in his tribunate he recognised the Galatian tetrarch Brogitarus as ruler of a kingdom in Phrygia centred on Pessinus (apparently in return for a large amount of money: Cic. *Sest.* 56, *Har. Resp.* 27–9).

The revenues from Cyprus would offset the cost of his grain law. Cicero states that Clodius chose Cato because he wanted both Cicero and Cato out of the way (doc. 12.56a), but Plutarch's comment that Cicero's exile would only be effected with Cato's absence is incorrect (doc. 12.57). Cato in fact had counselled Cicero to acquiesce in going into exile, to avoid a civil war (Cic. *Red. Sen.* 6; Plut. *Cato Min.* 35.1; Dio 38.17.4), and had not objected to Clodius' legislative programme.

Clodius presumably foresaw that once Cato, who 'had always spoken unrestrainedly against extraordinary commands' (*Sest.* 60), had received an extraordinary command from a tribune in the popular assembly he would now be intrinsically bound up with Clodius' programme. Clodius at a contio read out a letter from Caesar congratulating him on the fact that Cato could never again speak against extraordinary commands: Cicero states that Caesar either did not send it or did not intend it read out in public (*Dom.* 22). When Cicero returned from exile he went up to the Capitol with his supporters and destroyed the records of Clodius' tribunate, arguing in the senate for the illegality of Clodius' transfer to the plebs and so for the measures of his tribunate. Cato spoke in opposition, that Clodius' transference to the plebs was not illegal, and that his own acts in Cyprus and Byzantium would be nullified if Clodius' acts were rescinded; Cato and Cicero were on bad terms for some time after this (Plut. *Cic.* 34, *Cato Min.* 40). For Cato in Cyprus, and Cicero and Cato, see esp. Rundell 1979: 315–18; references at *MRR* II.198; Oost 1955; Badian 1965; Mitchell 1991: 132–3; Wiseman 1994a: 384; Tatum 1999: 150–1, 155–6; Seager 2002: 103.

12.55 Cato the Younger in Cyprus

Cicero *In Defence of Sestius* 59–63

The commission to Cyprus was clearly a prestigious one, despite Cicero's denigration of it (*Sest.* 60), and Cato went to Cyprus willingly as *quaestor pro praetore*. Ptolemy committed suicide in Cyprus, and Cato realised nearly 7,000 talents, receiving a triumphant reception on his return to Rome (Plut. *Cato Min.* 36, 39). Clodius, as it turned out, had picked the best man for the job. There can never have been any intention that Cato would disgrace himself. **63:** Cato, along with other senators, had not attended senate meetings called by Caesar as consul in protest against the violence of Caesar's methods.

59 That unfortunate king of Cyprus, who had always been our friend, our ally, about whom no damaging suspicion had ever been brought to the attention of the senate or our commanders, saw himself with his own eyes, as they say, being auctioned off with every scrap of food and clothing . . . **60** Their aim in this business was to put a blot on the reputation of Marcus Cato, being unaware of what strength lies in seriousness of character, in integrity, in greatness of soul, and, lastly, in that excellence which remains calm in tempestuous storms, which shines in darkness, which, even when shaken, remains unmoved and steadfast in its proper place, and which always gleams with its true light and is never diminished by other people's baseness. Their intention was not to honour Marcus Cato, but to exile him, not to entrust that task to him, but to impose it on him, for they openly stated in the assembly (contio) that they had torn out Marcus Cato's tongue, which had always spoken unrestrainedly against extraordinary commands . . . **61** When I was consul, at which time he was tribune-elect of the plebs, he put his life in hazard; he expressed that opinion, for the unpopularity of which, he saw, he would have to take responsibility at the risk of his life; he spoke with vehemence, he acted with spirit; he expressed clearly what he felt; he was leader, instigator, prime mover of those measures — not that he did not see the danger to himself, but in such a storm threatening the state he thought that he should consider nothing but the danger to his country . . .

62 If he had refused the command, do you doubt that violence would have been done to him, since all the measures of that year would have seemed in the process of being overthrown by that one man? . . . **63** For could a man who had failed to attend senate meetings in the previous year — though if he had attended, he could at least have seen me as one of the supporters of his political opinions — could he have calmly remained in Rome, once I had been banished and in my name the entire senate and his own stance been condemned?

12.56 Cato and Cicero as exiles

Cicero paints Cato as an exile (cf. Vell. 2.45.4) like himself, believing that his own exile redounded to his credit because it came about through his role in suppressing the Catilinarian conspiracy. While deploring Caesar's refusal to interfere with his exile, Cicero here in (c), in April 49 BC, puts the blame on Pompey.

(a) Cicero *On his House* 65

So the hated Marcus Cato is banished to Cyprus, as if in receipt of a favour. Scoundrels were unable to endure the sight of two people, and these were driven out, one by being granted a distinction which was the deepest insult, the other by a disaster which redounded very much to his credit.

(b) Cicero *In Defence of Sestius* 56

Exiles who had been convicted were brought back from Byzantium at a time when citizens who had not been convicted were driven out of Rome.

(c) Cicero *Letters to Atticus* 10.4.3 (14 April 49 BC)

The one (Caesar), who once would not even raise me up when I prostrated myself at his feet, declared that he could do nothing against the other's (Pompey's) wishes.

12.57 Cato neutralised?

Plutarch *Life of Cato the Younger* 34.3–7

3 Clodius could not expect to overthrow Cicero with Cato in Rome, but as he was plotting for this more than anything else, when he entered on the tribunate he summoned Cato and told him that, as he considered him the man of most integrity among all the Romans, he was ready to prove this by his actions. **4** Though many were requesting the command concerning Cyprus and Ptolemy and begging to be sent, he considered only Cato worthy of it and offered him this favour with pleasure. **5** When Cato protested that the affair was a trick and insult, not a favour, Clodius replied with arrogance and contempt, 'Well, if you do not consider it a favour, you will go on it as a disfavour,' and he immediately went before the people and had a law passed sending Cato on the mission. **6** And when he set out, Clodius gave him not a ship, nor a soldier, nor an assistant, only two secretaries, one of whom was a thief and total rascal, and the other one of Clodius' clients. **7** And as if he had imposed just a small task on him with Cyprus and Ptolemy, he also instructed him to restore the exiles of Byzantium, as he wished Cato to be out of the way for as long as possible, while he was tribune.

CICERO'S TRIUMPHANT RETURN

With Cicero exiled and Caesar absent, Clodius saw himself as Pompey's equal (App. *BC* 2.15.58) and with the people 'devoted to him' began attacking Pompey's acta (Plut. *Pomp.* 48.10). Clodius' arrangements for Cyprus had interfered with Pompey's eastern settlement but were perhaps at that stage not the cause of any friction. However, Clodius freed Tigranes, the son of the king of Armenia, held hostage for Pompey in the house of L. Flavius (doc. 12.58). A skirmish on the Appian Way in which Pompey's adherents attempted to regain the hostage resulted in the death of Papirius, one of Pompey's followers. A riot broke out at Rome and Gabinius' fasces as consul were smashed, his followers wounded, and Clodius consecrated his property to the gods. The other consul, Piso, supported Clodius and was himself wounded. On 11 August, a slave of Clodius was apprehended with a dagger outside the senate and confessed to attempted murder: Pompey thereafter 'shunned the forum, shunned the senate, shunned the public' (Cic. *Mil.* 18), and retired to his house (Tigranes' affair: Cic. *Dom.* 66–7, 124, *Piso* 27–8, *Mil.* 18, 37; Plut. *Pomp.* 48.10–49.2; Dio 38.30.1–4; Asc. 47). Clodius also brought Bibulus into the assembly to affirm that he had been observing the heavens when Caesar's legislation was passed, therefore technically invalidating it (Cicero on his return from exile argued that Clodius thereby overlooked that the measures of his own tribunate were tied to Caesar's *acta* which included the transition of Clodius to the plebeians: *Dom.* 40, *Har. Resp.* 48–9).

Pompey in reaction to Clodius' attacks considered how to bring the senate over to his side. Culleo (Q. Terentius Culleo, tr. pl. 58: *MRR* II.197) advised him to divorce Julia and exchange Caesar's friendship for that of the senate, but he was genuinely fond of her and refused (Plut. *Pomp.* 48.8, 49.4). Instead he sought to recall Cicero to help him against Clodius, hoping that Cicero would not speak against the triumvirate (App. *BC* 2.16.59; Dio 39.6.1). Already in 58 (unsuccessful) moves had been made by two tribunes (Ninnius and Culleo) to recall Cicero from exile (*MRR* II.196–7) and on 29 October eight tribunes supported his recall but the tribunician veto was applied.

Cicero's recall from exile was effected in 57 through the agency of eight of the tribunes, with two tribunes once again opposed (Serranus and Numerius Rufus). Sestius was the most important of these and visited Caesar in Gaul, who was lukewarm but did not oppose the recall. Another of the tribunes, T. Annius Milo, began to employ gangs against Clodius to counter the latter's use of violence. Recall: esp. Cic. *Sest.* 72–8, also *Att.* 3.20.3, 3.23; *Red. Sen.*, esp. 4, 6, 8, 12, 21–2, 26–7, *Red. Quir.*, *Dom.* 70, *Piso* 35, *Fam.* 1.9.16; Asc. 11; Plut. *Cic.* 33, *Pomp.* 49.1–6; Dio 39.7.6–8; *MRR* II.200–2; exile and recall: Seager 1965; Smith 1966: 153–83; Rawson 1975: 106–21; Lacey 1978: 52–77; Greenhalgh 1981: 1–20; Scullard *GN* 116–17; Habicht 1990: 48–50; Mitchell 1991: 134–57; Fuhrmann 1992: 89–96; Wiseman 1994a: 386, 389; Tatum 1999: 176–85; Seager 2002: 101–9.

12.58 Pompey recalls Cicero to deal with Clodius

Dio Roman History 38.30.1–4, 39.6.1–8.3

On 1 January 57 a senatorial resolution concerning Cicero's recall was frustrated by a tribune, and on 23 January a tribunician bill put to the assembly ended in bloodshed (Cic. *Sest.* 75 for date), when Clodius' brother Appius Claudius supplied gladiators he had on hand for funeral games (Dio 39.7.2); several people were killed and others wounded. This was probably the occasion when Cicero's brother Quintus who had come to the assembly to plead for his brother's return was driven from the rostra and forced to take shelter behind the bodies of freedmen and slaves killed in the fighting (doc. 2.3; cf. Plut. *Cic.* 33.4). For the rest of the year there were clashes between Milo and Clodius and their followers; Milo also made use of gladiators. Q. Caecilius Metellus Nepos, originally opposed to Cicero's recall, changed sides and supported his fellow consul P. Cornelius Lentulus Spinther.

The senate decreed in July that a law about Cicero's recall be brought before the comitia centuriata (doc. 12.59); of the magistrates only the praetor Appius Claudius Pulcher (Clodius' brother) and two tribunes (Serranus and Rufus) were opposed. The senate — attended by 417 members — was unanimous except for one vote — that of Clodius, who spoke against Cicero when the bill was put to the comitia centuriata on 4 August 57, but it was duly passed. Cicero was to see this vote as vindication of his actions while consul in 63 (*Red. Sen.* 27, *Red. Quir.* 17, *Dom.* 75, 87, 90, *Piso* 35, *Sest.* 109, 128). There is a lacuna (gap) in the manuscript at 39.6.2.

38.30.1 Cicero was not in exile for long, but was recalled by Pompey, the very man who had been mainly responsible for his banishment. The reason for this was that Clodius had been bribed to seize and release Tigranes the Younger, **2** who was still imprisoned at the home of Lucius Flavius, and when Pompey and Gabinius were annoyed at this he treated them with contempt, inflicted blows and wounds on their followers, and broke the consul's fasces and confiscated his property. **3** Pompey, enraged at this, especially because of the way Clodius was using against him the authority which he had himself restored to the tribunes, determined to recall Cicero and immediately began to work through Ninnius for his restoration . . .

39.6.1 While this was happening in Gaul, Pompey had meanwhile put Cicero's return to the vote. The man he had used Clodius to drive out, he now brought back to help him against that very same person! — so swiftly does human nature sometimes alter, with men receiving the very opposite treatment from those people from whom they expect assistance or injury. **2** He was supported by some of the praetors and tribunes, including Titus Annius Milo, who brought the proposal before the populace. Spinther the consul, was acting partly as a favour to Pompey, and partly to take vengeance on Clodius for a private enmity . . . (the sentence breaks off here). **3** Clodius, on his side, was supported by various magistrates, including his brother Appius Claudius, a praetor, and the consul Nepos who had a private reason for disliking Cicero. **7.1** So these men caused even more disorder than before, now they had the consuls as leaders, as did the other people in the city as they took one side or the other. Consequently, many other forms of anarchy took place, **2** including that of Clodius who, during the voting, as he knew the people were going to recall Cicero, got hold of the gladiators that his brother had organised for the funeral games of Marcus, his relative, and charged into the gathering, wounding many and killing many others. **3** As a result the proposal was not passed and Clodius was feared by all, both as the associate of gladiators and for other reasons. He then stood for the aedileship, hoping to avoid paying the penalty for his violence if he were elected . . . **8.1** Milo's contesting this caused great disturbance, and in the end he also gathered some gladiators and others with the same aims as himself and kept coming to blows with Clodius, with killings occurring through practically the whole city. **2** Nepos was afraid of his colleague and of Pompey and the other leading men and changed his stance, so the senate decreed on Spinther's motion that Cicero be recalled. The populace, on the motion of both consuls, passed the measure. **3** Clodius of course spoke against it, but with Milo as his opponent could commit no violence, and Pompey among others spoke in support of the law so that that side was much the stronger.

12.59 Cicero's account of his return

Cicero *Letters to Atticus* 4.1.4–5

Written about 10 September 57 BC. The speech referred to here is the *Red. Sen.* ('I expressed my thanks to the senators'), and there was also the speech to the Roman people (*Red. Quir.*), delivered 5 and 7 September respectively. Cicero refers to his *nomenclator*: the slave employed by wealthy Romans to remember the names of associates, voters and clients. The Porta Capena was a gate in Rome's Servian Wall through which the Via Appia passed (Richardson *Top. Dict.* 301). Cicero arrived in Rome on 4 September, deliberately timing his arrival to coincide with the celebration of the Ludi Romani, and the next day, the Nones, he delivered his speech to the senate, in which he prided himself on the general support for his recall (cf. doc. 1.8).

4 I set out from Dyrrachium on 4 August, the very same day the law about me was voted upon. I arrived at Brundisium on the Nones of August. My dear little Tullia was there to meet me, and it was her birthday . . . On 11 August, while I was at Brundisium, I learnt from a letter from my brother Quintus that the law had been passed in the comitia centuriata to astounding demonstrations of enthusiasm from all ages and ranks and with an incredible assemblage of people from Italy. I then set out, after receiving the most distinguished attention from the people of Brundisium, and, as I journeyed, deputations gathered from all sides with their congratulations. **5** My arrival at Rome was such that there was no man of any rank known to my nomenclator who did not come to meet me, except for enemies who were unable to conceal or deny that they were my enemies. When I arrived at the Porta Capena, the temples' steps were crowded with ordinary citizens, and their welcome was marked by immense applause, while similar crowds and applause accompanied me right up to the Capitol — in the forum and on the Capitol itself the number of people was astonishing. In the senate, on the following day, the Nones of September, I expressed my thanks to the senators.

12.60 Cicero's view of Clodius

Cicero *On the Responses of the Soothsayers* 57–9

This speech was delivered in 56 BC. A strange noise had been heard near Rome and the haruspices (soothsayers) had given broad interpretations of why the noise had occurred: rites, sacred sites, assassinations, violated oaths, and impiety. Cicero argued in this speech that all of these stemmed from individual actions by Clodius. By being adopted by Fonteius, Clodius had according to Cicero extinguished the rites of the Claudii Pulchi: this was not true as Fonteius emancipated Clodius and he never ceased being a Claudian (Clodius also had two brothers). The Aelian and Fufian laws, of the mid-second century, regulated the use of obnuntiatio. Clodius' law to allow senators to defend themselves against expulsion from the senate is construed by Cicero as an abolition of the censorship: see doc. 12.52. The 'generals' refers to Clodius' tampering with the loyalty of Lucullus' army in Asia Minor.

57 By taking the name of Fonteius, Clodius has consigned the name, religion, memory and family of his parents to oblivion; by his inexpiable crime, he has overthrown the gods' fires, their thrones, tables, concealed and inmost hearths, and secret rites forbidden not only to the sight but even to the hearing of men; he has set on fire the shrine of those very goddesses whose aid is used in combating fires elsewhere. **58** And what can I say about his dealings with his country? Firstly, by violence, weapons and threats he drove from the city, from all the protection of his country, a citizen whom you have consistently proclaimed to be that country's saviour: next, after achieving the downfall of one whom I have always stated to be the senate's partner and whom he kept stating was its leader, he overthrew the senate itself, the originator of the state's well-being and policy, by violence, massacre and fire; he abolished two laws, the Aelian and Fufian, which were of the greatest benefit to the state; he did away with the censorship; he removed the right of veto; he annulled the auspices; he furnished consuls, who were his partners in crime, with funds, provinces and an army; those who were kings he sold, those who were not he named so; he drove Gnaeus Pompey from his house by armed violence; he overturned generals' monuments; he demolished his enemies' houses; he inscribed his own name on your monuments. The crimes he committed against his country are endless. And what of the individual citizens he has put to death? The allies he has severed from us? The generals he has betrayed? The armies where he has stirred up trouble? **59** Still worse, how grievous are those crimes he has committed against himself, against his own family! Who has ever treated an enemy camp worse than he has all the parts of his body? What ship on the public river has ever been so open to all traffic than his youth has been? What wastrel has ever wallowed so unrestrictedly with prostitutes as he has with his sisters? And last of all, what Charybdis so monstrous has the creative talent of poets been able to paint, which could gulp down oceans so great as the plunder of Byzantines and Brogitaruses he has swallowed up? Or what Scylla ever had dogs so conspicuous and famished as those you see him using, wretches like Gellius, Clodius and Titius, to devour the very rostra themselves.

POMPEY'S GRAIN COMMAND, 57 BC

Cicero became reconciled with Pompey (Dio 39.9.1), reconciled Pompey with the senate (Plut. *Pomp.* 48.5), and showed his gratitude to Pompey by acting on his behalf to help secure an extraordinary command for him (the *cura annonae*) to deal with the grain shortage. After Cicero's return on 4 September, the plebs had blamed him, because of the large numbers of Italians who had come to Rome to welcome him, for a shortage of grain in Rome, and he describes violence in the forum and on the Capitol; *Dom.* 13 adds that he stayed home on 7 September, when the consul Metellus Nepos was stoned and stabbed by two of Clodius' supporters. On the next day, at a meeting of the senate which most of the consulars avoided because of the violence of the day before, Cicero proposed powers for Pompey to deal with the grain shortage. Cicero elsewhere mentions a nocturnal rally organised by Clodius, presumably outside Cicero's house, at which Clodius' supporters demanded grain from Cicero (*Dom.* 14). On 9 September, the senate was well attended and approved the grain law.

The tribune Messius, who had earlier unsuccessfully moved a law for Cicero's recall (Cic. *Red. Sen.* 21; *MRR* II.202), attempted to secure wider powers for Pompey than those being proposed by the consuls and Pompey may have been behind this. The consuls' proposal was the one ratified; nevertheless it gave him broad powers and he was granted 15 legates, the only known ones being Cicero and his brother Quintus (*MRR* II.205). Pompey divided the Mediterranean world up between them and himself visited Sicily, Sardinia and Africa, collecting grain for Rome (Plut. *Pomp.* 50.1, *Mor.* 240C). He is known as active in this capacity for the years 57–54 (there is no evidence for 53). See Cic. *Dom.* 5–16, 25–6 (11: blaming the crisis on a shortage in the grain-growing provinces, and hoarding; 25: blaming Clodius' free grain distributions); Livy *Per.* 104; Asc. 38; Dio 39.9, 16.2; cf. Cic. *Fam.* 5.17.2; *MRR* II.203–4, 211; Leach 1978: 134–6; Meijer 1983: 161; Habicht 1990: 50–1; Lintott 1999: 10, 214; Tatum 1999: 182–3, 186–7; Seager 2002: 107–9.

12.61 Cicero proposes Pompey's command

Cicero *Letters to Atticus* 4.1.6–7

This passage follows on from above doc. 12.59; cf. Cic. *Dom.* 25–6. The 'one praetor and two tribunes' referred to here are Appius Claudius and the two tribunes opposed to Cicero's recall. Cicero was waiting for the pontiffs to rule whether Clodius' consecration of his house was valid, and so kept out of the issue as to whether Pompey should have wider powers than those proposed by the consuls. Messalla and Afranius were supporters of Pompey.

6 Two days after that (Cicero's return on 4 September), when the price of grain was extremely high and people had gathered first at the theatre and then at the senate, shouting, on Clodius' instigation, that the shortage of grain was my doing, the senate held meetings during those days about the grain supply and Pompey was called on to superintend it, not only by the populace but also by the honest men (boni). As he himself wanted it and the crowd called on me by name to make the proposal, I did so in an elaborate speech. In the absence of all the consulars, except Messalla and Afranius, on the pretext that they thought it was not safe for them to voice an opinion, a senatorial decree ratified my proposal that Pompey should be asked to take on the commission, and a law was brought in to that effect. The decree was immediately read out and the people applauded in the new absurd fashion when my name was mentioned. I then addressed the meeting, with the consent of all the magistrates present except for one praetor and two tribunes.

7 On the following day the senate was crowded, with all the consulars there. Nothing Pompey requested was refused. When he asked for 15 legates, he named me first and said that I should be his second self in all matters. The consuls drew up a law which gave Pompey total control over grain supplies throughout the world for a five-year period; Messius proposed another one, which gave him control over all moneys and added on a fleet, army and authority in the provinces overriding that of their governors. Our consular law now appears quite moderate, Messius' one is felt unendurable. According to himself Pompey prefers the first, according to his friends the second. The consulars, led by Favonius, are furious. I keep quiet, all the more because the pontiffs have not yet given any reply about my house. If they declare it no longer sacred, I have an outstanding site, and the consuls, by senatorial decree, will make an estimate of the value of the building; if not, they will demolish it, let out a contract in their own name, and make an estimate for the whole.

12.62 A secret agenda behind Pompey's command?

Plutarch *Life of Pompey* 49.4–8

4 Pompey was won over by the arguments of those who thought that he ought to bring back Cicero, Clodius' greatest enemy and a great favourite with the senate, **5** and he escorted Cicero's brother, who was petitioning on his behalf, with a large force into the forum, where people were wounded and some killed, though he got the better of Clodius. **6** The law was passed, and Cicero returned and immediately reconciled Pompey to the senate, and, by his advocacy for the grain law, made him once again almost total master of all the Romans' possessions by land and sea. **7** For all harbours, trading centres, crop distributions — in a word, all goods carried by sea, or produced on land — were put under his control. **8** Clodius attacked it on the grounds that the law had not been proposed because of the scarcity of grain, but that the scarcity of grain had been contrived so that the law might be proposed and Pompey's power, which was, as it were, withering away as a result of his depressed spirits, might be revitalised and restored by a new office.

12.63 Rioting at the theatre and on the Capitol

Dio *Roman History* 39.9.1–3

1 Cicero set aside the hatred he felt for Pompey as a result of his exile, and was reconciled to him, paying him back at once for his good services. **2** A severe famine had broken out in the city, and the whole populace rushed into the theatre . . . and then to the Capitol where the senators were meeting, and threatened at first to slaughter them with their own hands, and then to burn them alive, along with the temples, **3** but Cicero persuaded them to appoint Pompey as superintendent of the grain supply, and also to give him for this purpose proconsular imperium for five years both within Italy and outside of it. So now, as earlier in the matter of the pirates, Pompey was again to rule the whole world then under the power of Rome.

CAESAR IN GAUL

12.64 The Gallic scare, 60 BC (written 15 March)

Cicero *Letters to Atticus* 1.19.2–3

Cf. *Att.* 1.20.5. Events in 60 shifted the focus of attention towards Gaul. A revolt of the Allobroges in Transalpine Gaul in 62, oppressed by debt (cf. doc. 12.19), was crushed in 61 by Pomptinus, governor of Transalpine Gaul (*MRR* II.176). In 60 BC, the Helvetii defeated the Aedui, the sole 'brothers' which the Romans had in non-Roman Gaul, and planned a large-scale migration into Gaul. The senate reacted by altering the provinces allocated to the consuls, arranging that they govern the Gauls (Cisalpine and Transalpine). The tribune Flavius threatened to rescind the command, and may have succeeded in doing so, but Metellus Celer died (April 59) without going to his province. The threat in Gaul did not eventuate. The Sequani, chief rivals with the Aedui in central Gaul, had invited Ariovistus, a German king, to aid them against the Aedui, whom he defeated; he was proclaimed a 'Friend of the Roman People' and given gifts; the leader of the Helvetii died. Caesar as proconsul was allocated the governorship of Cisalpine Gaul and Illyricum for five years under the *lex Vatinia*; the senate was to add Transalpine Gaul. When he arrived in Gaul in 58, things were at first peaceful.

Cicero refers to three ambassadors chosen to persuade Gallic tribes not to link up with the Helvetii, who were planning their migration into Gaul. The description of Lentulus as 'perfume on lentils' reflects his inadequacy for the task (Shackleton Bailey 1965: I.335). Caesar in Gaul: the basic narrative is, of course, Caesar's own commentaries, the *BG*; see also Livy *Per.* 103–8; Suet. *Jul.* 25; Plut. *Caes.* 17–27; Dio 38.31–50, 39.40–6, 50–3, 40.4–12.1, 31–41; *MRR* II.197, 203, 211, 219, 224, 230, 237; Fuller 1965: 97–165; Balsdon 1967: 65–104; Scullard *GN* 126–34; Bradford 1984: 59–128; Wiseman 1994a: 381–8, 408–17 (with map of Gallic peoples, p. 382); Meier 1995: 224–330; Southern 2001: 62–94; Dando-Collins 2002: 13–63; Burns 2003: 88–139.

2 In politics the most important issue at present is the scare of a Gallic war. The Aedui, our brothers, have recently suffered a defeat and there is no doubt that the Helvetii are in arms and making raids into the province. The senate has decreed that the consuls should draw lots for the two Gauls, a levy be held, all exemptions from service be cancelled, and ambassadors with full powers be sent to address the communities of Gaul and attempt to stop them uniting with the Helvetii. The ambassadors are Quintus Metellus Creticus and Lucius Flaccus and, 'perfume on lentils', Lentulus, son of Clodianus. **3** While I am on the topic, I cannot omit mentioning that, when the first lot drawn from among the consulars was mine, a crowded senate unanimously proclaimed that I ought to be kept in Rome. The same thing happened to Pompey after me, so that it appeared as if we two were being kept as guarantees for the Republic's safety. Why, anyway, should I wait for flattering comments on myself from other people, when I am so good at it myself?

12.65 Genocide in Gaul

Caesar *Gallic War* 1.29.1–3

On 28 March 58 BC, the Helvetii (based in what is modern Switzerland) and other tribes began a mass migration. Caesar succeeded in initially blocking them by destroying the bridge across the Rhone, but they crossed the river through the territory of the Sequani. They were not in the Roman province but Caesar pursued them. He had five legions, including two raised by recruitment in Cisalpine Gaul (bringing the total number of legions in Gaul to six). He then went to Bibracte in Aedui territory to resupply; the Helvetii turned to the pursuit and met Caesar in battle. He defeated them, and forced them to re-settle the lands they had abandoned. Ariovistus, having previously defeated the Aedui, had settled in Gaul, to the discomfiture not just of the Aedui but of the Sequani who had invited him in. With the Helvetii defeated, the Aedui and Sequani asked Caesar to expel him; he drove Ariovistus and his Germans from Gaul: Caes. *BG* 1; Cic. *Prov.* 33; Plut. *Caes.* 18–20; Dio 38.31–50; *MRR* II.197; cf. Powell 1998; Ramage 2001.

1 In the camp of the Helvetii were found records written in Greek which were brought to Caesar, which included a detailed list stating what number of them had left their homes, how many were able to bear arms and a separate list of children, old men and women. **2** The total of all of these amounted to 263,000 Helvetii, 36,000 Tulingi, 14,000 Latobrigi, 23,000 Rauraci, and 32,000 Boii; of these there were about 92,000 able to bear arms. **3** The grand total was 368,000. A census was held of those who returned home, at Caesar's order, and the number was found to be 110,000.

12.66 Caesar and the Nervii, 57 BC

Caesar *Gallic War* 2.15, 27–8

In 57 BC, Caesar conquered most of Gaul and was voted, on the proposal of Cicero, an unprecedented fifteen-day supplicatio for his victories (Pompey had been awarded a ten-day supplicatio: doc. 12.30). Most of the year was spent campaigning against the Belgic tribes in north-west Gaul. Caesar's campaigns in 56 brought the rest of Gaul under Roman authority; in particular he campaigned against the tribes of the Atlantic coast, especially the Veneti. The following year (55) saw German tribes advance into Gaul across the Rhine; Caesar defeated them and made a show of force across the Rhine into German territory. This year and the next (54) he went to Britain, but in 54 there was an uprising in northern Gaul amongst the Treviri and the Eburones which continued into 53, when Caesar marched across the Rhine again. The following year, 52 BC, saw the revolt of Vercingetorix (doc. 12.89). The passage below concerns his campaign against the Nervii in 57, one of the Belgae; he almost lost against them at the river Sambre.

15.2 Caesar came to the borders of the Ambiani, who surrendered themselves and their belongings to him without delay. **3** Their nearest neighbours were the Nervii; when Caesar inquired about their character and lifestyle, he was informed as follows: **4** traders had no access to them; they allowed no wine or any other luxuries to be imported, because they believed that such things enfeebled their spirits and diminished their courage. **5** They were fierce men of great courage, who reproached and accused the rest of the Belgians for surrendering to the Roman people and renouncing their ancestral courage; **6** they proclaimed that they would send no envoys nor accept any peace terms . . .

27.3 The enemy, even when all hope of safety was lost, displayed immense courage; when their first ranks had fallen, the next stood on them as they lay there and fought from their bodies; **4** when these were thrown down and the corpses heaped up, the remainder, as if from a mound, threw their missiles at our men and intercepted and returned our javelins. **5** It was clear, therefore, that they were to be judged men of immense courage, who had dared to cross a very broad river, climb huge banks, and advance over very unfavourable terrain; the greatness of their spirit made such immense difficulties easy. **28.1** With the battle over and the nation and name of the Nervii almost brought to extermination, the elders, whom I said earlier were hiding with the children and women in the creeks and marshes, believed, when the outcome was reported, that there was nothing to hinder the conquerors, **2** nothing to save the conquered, and sent, with the consent of all the survivors, envoys to Caesar and surrendered to him, stating, in relating the disaster which had befallen their state, that they had been reduced from 600 senators to three, and from 60,000 men who could bear arms, to 500. **3** To show compassion to these wretched suppliants, Caesar was careful to leave them unharmed, ordering them to keep their lands and towns and commanding their neighbours to restrain themselves and their associates from any injuries or crimes against them.

THE CONFERENCE AT LUCA, 56 BC, AND ITS OUTCOMES

12.67 Pompey's unpopularity

Cicero *Letters to his Brother Quintus* 2.3.2–4 (12–15 February 56)

On 7 February 56 Milo was tried in the forum, prosecuted by Clodius for the violence in 57. Pompey's speech in Milo's favour was interrupted by Clodius' gang (*operae Clodianae*) and when Clodius spoke he too was heckled and insulted by obscene verses about his relationship with his sister: for the identity of Clodius' sisters: McDermott 1970; Hillard 1973; docs 7.47–52, cf. 12.60 for further insults. Pompey told Cicero that he was suspicious of a plot against his life, and of Crassus' support for C. Porcius Cato (not Cato the Younger) a tribune who supported Clodius. Pompey was also suspicious that Crassus was financing Clodius.

Ptolemy XII Auletes, having paid 6,000 talents in 59 to be recognised as king of Egypt, was deposed by the Egyptians and his daughter Berenice took the throne. Ptolemy took refuge in

Pompey's Alban villa. Cicero with Hortensius and Lucullus proposed that Lentulus Spinther (cos. 57) restore Ptolemy when he became proconsul of Cilicia in 56, with force if necessary. However, a Sibylline oracle that the Romans not assist the king of Egypt 'with a multitude' (i.e., an army) was circulated by the tribune C. Cato, and Marcellinus as consul upheld that force not be used. It was also proposed by Crassus that a commission of three chosen from those already holding imperium (and therefore as Cicero *Fam.* 1.1.3 notes not excluding Pompey) effect the king's restoration. Bibulus proposed that it be three *privati* instead. Hortensius then proposed that Lentulus restore Ptolemy, but without force; Cicero supported this. Volcatius (cos. 66), with the backing of the tribune P. Rutilius Lupus (*MRR* II.209), proposed that Pompey carry out the restoration, at which Servilius Isauricus (cos. 79) proposed that the king not be restored at all. In the end the senate decided — in agreement with the oracle — that it would be dangerous to the Republic for Ptolemy to be restored 'with a multitude'; there was a debate as to whether Pompey or Lentulus should restore him. Pompey's friends (familiares) made it clear that Pompey wanted the commission (Cic. *Quint.* 2.2.3). The debate lasted throughout 13 January and was continued on 14 and 15 January: the senate could not meet after 15 January as the rest of the month was made up of comitial (assembly) days.

The matter then came before the assembly, inconclusively, with Marcellinus blocking meetings by pronouncing various festivals and supplications for the comitial days when the assembly would have met, even ordaining that the Latin Festival had to be repeated, winning Cicero's approval: Cic. *Quint.* 2.5.2. Finally the senate (the date of the relevant meeting is unknown: cf. Cic. *Fam.* 1.7.4) in fact voted not to restore Ptolemy at all, but this decision was vetoed. Pompey's opponents in the senate had nevertheless won out, and he was not chosen to restore Ptolemy. (Ptolemy was in fact to be restored by Gabinius (cos. 58) as proconsul of Syria in 55 BC without authorisation from Rome but with encouragement from Pompey; Ptolemy promised Gabinius 10,000 talents: 240 million sesterces.) Pompey was unpopular both with the plebs and the boni (Cic. *Quint.* 2.5.3, cf. 2.6.4). The question of Ptolemy's restoration: Cic. *Quint.* 2.2.3, 2.3.1, 3, 2.5.2–3, *Fam* 1.1, 1.2.1–2, 1.5a.2, 1.7.4; Plut. *Pomp.* 49.6; Dio 39.16.1; Wiseman 1994a: 391–2; Leach 1978: 137–9; Greenhalgh 1981: 28–33; Seager 2002: 111–15.

2 Milo's trial took place on 7 February. Pompey spoke, or rather attempted to, for as soon as he stood up Clodius' gang put up a great clamour and kept interrupting him throughout his speech, not only with shouting, but with loud insults and abuse. As he came to a conclusion (and I must say that he showed courage, and was not put off, but said all he had to and occasionally even won silence by the force of his personality) — when he concluded, Clodius got up. Our side made such a noise (for we wanted to return the favour) that it affected his thoughts, tongue and countenance. That was finished by the eighth hour, as Pompey had spoken till just after the sixth hour, when all sorts of abuse and lastly some extremely obscene verses were thrown at Clodius and Clodia. Pale and furious Clodius started asking his supporters in the middle of the shouting who was it who was starving the people to death; his gang replied, 'Pompey!' Who wanted to go to Alexandria? They replied 'Pompey!' Whom do you want to go? 'Crassus!' (he was there in support of Milo but with little good-will) . . . **4** So I think great things are afoot. Pompey is aware, and passes the information on to me, that there is a plot on hand against his life, that Gaius Cato is being backed by Crassus and supplying Clodius with money; and that both are being supported by Crassus and Curio, Bibulus and his other critics; he says he has to keep well on guard not to be got the better of, with the crowd who attend public meetings just about alienated from him, the nobility hostile, the senate against him, and the youth misconducting themselves. So he is getting prepared and collecting men from the countryside, while Clodius is strengthening his gangs, and getting them ready for the festival of the Quirinalia. With a view to the same occasion we are far superior with Milo's personal forces, but a large band is expected from Picenum and Gaul to help us stand up to Cato's bills about Milo and Lentulus.

12.68 Cicero on Luca (to Lentulus Spinther, December 54)

Cicero *Letters to Friends* 1.9.7–9, 11–12

In December 54 Cicero wrote to Lentulus in his province of Cilicia (where he was proconsul); in this letter he explains how he came, as he says, 'to include Caesar' (1.9.12) in his policy: friendly relations with him were necessary because of Caesar's connections with Pompey, with whose interests Cicero states he had always associated himself. He also mentions the promises made by Pompey to Caesar, and by Quintus, Cicero's brother, to Pompey: that Cicero would, in effect, 'behave himself'. The letter is a justification for Cicero's activities after Luca (Shackleton Bailey 1977: I.307).

Caesar's activities as consul had come under scrutiny in 58, when L. Domitius Ahenobarbus (cos. 54) as praetor had unsuccessfully attacked Caesar's legislation; Ahenobarbus was now threatening to renew these attacks (*MRR* II.194; Suet. *Jul.* 24.1). On 5 April 56 BC the issue of the Campanian land was hotly debated in the senate, exacerbated by the shortage of funds and the high price of grain: Pompey had just been awarded 40 million sesterces as grain commissioner, and was planning a trip to Sardinia (Cic. *Quint.* 2.6.1: 9 April 56). Cicero at this senate meeting successfully proposed that the issue of the Campanian land 'should be referred to a full senate on the Ides of May', which was an attack on Caesar's land legislation; his speech to this effect 'caused a sensation', 'not only where I had intended (presumably Caesar), but even with people I had never imagined (Pompey)'. A few weeks previously Cicero had subjected Vatinius (tr. pl. 59) to a hostile cross-examination as a witness in the prosecution of Sestius (the *In Vatinium*, of 10 February 56) in which he had spoken 'regarding the use of violence, the auspices and the grants of kingdoms': Vatinius as tribune in 59 had been a major ally of the triumvirs and had passed legislation granting Caesar his commands. Both of these attacks angered Caesar. (After Luca, Cicero would have to defend Vatinius, in August 54, at a trial for bribery: Caesar was to be particularly insistent that Cicero appear in Vatinius' defence: *Fam.* 1.9.19.) The Campanian land was indeed debated by the senate on 15 and 16 May but Cicero did not attend (*Quint.* 2.9.2).

Pompey left on his trip to Sardinia, but went via Luca. Caesar had already seen Crassus at Ravenna, where Caesar 'complained a great deal' about Cicero's planned debate. Cicero (*Fam.* 1.9.9) makes it quite clear that Caesar met with Crassus at Ravenna, and with Pompey at Luca. Later sources, Plutarch, Suetonius and Appian have a three-man meeting at Luca, but Cicero is clearly correct (Jackson 1978). Pompey's thinly veiled accusation in the senate that Crassus was trying to kill him indicated that all was not well between him and Crassus, but Caesar was able to organise a reconciliation between them.

For Ravenna and Luca: Appian (below); Suet. *Jul.* 24.1; Plut. *Pomp.* 51.1–4, *Caes.* 21, *Cato Min.* 41.1–2, *Crass.* 14.5–7; cf. Dio 39.27–8; Lazenby 1959; Gruen 1969; Mitchell 1969 (arguing against Cicero wishing to attack Caesar's Campanian land legislation in 56); Smith 1966: 184–7; Luibheid 1970; Rawson 1975: 128–31; Marshall 1976: 127–30; Ward 1977: 261–6; Jackson 1978; Lacey 1978: 77–9; Leach 1978: 143–4; Greenhalgh 1981: 38–41; Habicht 1990: 50–3; Mitchell 1991: 175–82; Shotter 1994: 72–3; Wiseman 1994a: 394; Tatum 1999: 213–15, 218–22; Seager 2002: 110–19.

7 My entire cross-examination was in fact nothing but a criticism of Vatinius' tribunate. In it I spoke throughout with the greatest independence and spirit regarding the use of violence, the auspices and the grants of kingdoms, and not only indeed in this case but consistently and frequently in the senate. **8** In the consulship of (Cn. Cornelius Lentulus) Marcellinus and (L. Marcius) Philippus, on the Nones of April, the senate adopted my proposal that the matter of the Campanian land should be referred to a full senate on the Ides of May. Could I have done more to invade the citadel of that clique or been more forgetful of my past difficulties or more mindful of my past career? My speech caused a sensation, not only where I had intended, but even with people I had never imagined. **9** After the senate had passed a decree on my motion, Pompey, without showing me any sign of being angry, left for Sardinia and Africa and en route joined Caesar at Luca. There Caesar complained a great deal about my motion (he had been stirred up against me by Crassus whom he had seen beforehand at Ravenna). Pompey was said to be extremely upset; although I heard this from other people, I learnt this primarily from my brother. Pompey met him in Sardinia a few days after he had left Luca. 'You're the man I want,' he said. 'Nothing could be more fortunate than our meeting. If you don't speak seriously to your brother Marcus, you're going to have to pay up on that pledge you made me on his behalf.' In short, he made a serious complaint, mentioned what he had done for me, recalled the talks he had had so frequently with my brother himself about Caesar's legislation and what my brother had pledged to him about me, and called my brother himself to witness that his actions over my return had had Caesar's approval. He asked that he commend Caesar's cause and prestige to me, requesting that I should not attack them if I was unwilling or unable to defend them . . .

11 If I had seen the state in the control of reprobates and villains, as we know happened in Cinna's time and some other periods, no rewards (which have not the slightest weight with me) or dangers (which can influence even the bravest men), would have made me join their side, however great their services to me. However, the chief man in the state was Gnaeus Pompey, who had won this power and glory through services to the state of the greatest importance and the most outstanding military achievements, and whose successful reputation I had promoted from my youth, while in my praetorship and consulship I had visibly supported it. For his part he had himself assisted me with his authority and by voicing his opinion in the senate and by plans and hard work in conjunction with you. He had only one enemy in Rome who was also mine, so I did not think that I need be afraid of the reputation of inconsistency if, in sometimes voicing my opinion, I had changed direction a little and shown my desire to enhance the reputation of a great man who had performed many services on my behalf.

12 In this policy I had to include Caesar, as you will see, since his interest and prestige were bound up with Pompey's. The long-standing friendship, which you are aware existed between Caesar and my brother and myself, was here of great value, as was Caesar's courtesy and generosity which we soon clearly observed in his letters and his services to us. Concern for the state also influenced me strongly, as it seemed to me that it did not desire a conflict with these men, especially after Caesar's immense achievements, and strongly objected to one. But what had most influence on my decision were the promises on my behalf which Pompey had given to Caesar and my brother to Pompey.

12.69 Caesar's clientela at Luca

Appian *Civil Wars* 2.17 (61–3)

Pompey and Crassus were to be consuls for 55 BC (*MRR* II.214–15) and to have respectively Spain and Syria as their provinces for five years; Caesar was to be proconsul in Gaul and Illyricum for another five years, and to appoint ten legates (*MRR* II.211).

While the story of the 120 lictors and 200 senators at Luca might be an exaggeration (cf. doc. 2.57), clearly various magistrates did make their way to Luca, and amongst them, specifically named as present, were Appius Claudius Pulcher, cos. 54 (Clodius' brother) and Metellus Nepos, cos. 57 (Plut. *Caes.* 21.2; cf. Suet. *Jul.* 24.1). The second double consulship of Pompey and Crassus was supported by Clodius and to cement their alliance Pompey's son married Appius' daughter (Tatum 1991a).

Appius Claudius' and Clodius' brother Gaius was praetor in 56; Clodius himself was aedile (*MRR* II.208). What Clodius stood to gain is unclear: perhaps it was simply a case of family advancement to the consulship (Tatum 1999: 214). Clodius made a public speech to win Pompey's approval, and inveighed against the opposition of Marcellinus (cos. 56) to the candidature of Pompey and Crassus (Dio 39.29.1; Tatum 1999: 215). He did not, however, desist from his hatred of Cicero (as Cic. *Har. Resp.* indicates). Appian on Caesar and the Celts [Gauls]: *Gallic History* FF xv–xxi.

61 Caesar, who had achieved numerous brilliant successes in Gaul and Britain, which I have recounted in my book on the Celts, returned loaded with wealth to Cisalpine Gaul on the river Po to allow his army a short rest from constant warfare. **62** From here he dispatched large amounts of money to many people in Rome, and those who were the magistrates for that year and others who had achieved distinction as governors or generals went in turn to meet him; so many of them were there that 120 lictors could be seen around him at a time and more than 200 senators, some of them thanking him for what they had already received, and others hoping to get money from him or trying to gain some other benefit from the same source. Caesar could now manage anything as a consequence of his huge army, the immensity of his wealth, and his eagerness to oblige everyone. **63** Pompey and Crassus, his partners in the regime, also came at his invitation. In their deliberations it was resolved that Pompey and Crassus should hold the consulship again, and that Caesar's governorship over his provinces should be extended for another five years.

12.70 The re-election of Pompey and Crassus

Dio *Roman History* 39.31.1–2

Pompey and Crassus, despite deciding to become consuls, still had to be elected in the comitia centuriata. When initially asked by the consul Marcellinus if they would stand, both were evasive, but declared their candidature after the date for nominations closed. They then prevented Marcellinus from holding elections, employing Clodius' loyal supporter C. Cato as tribune to interpose his veto; the elections were finally held early in 55 after an interregnum (Livy *Per.* 105; Dio 39.27). C. Porcius Cato would later be tried for delaying the elections, but acquitted.

L. Domitius Ahenobarbus also stood as a candidate for the consulship, encouraged by his brother-in-law M. Porcius Cato, but withdrew when his slave was killed, and he, Cato and other supporters wounded. Ahenobarbus would be consul in 54. Publius Crassus, Crassus' son, brought soldiers from Caesar to assist in the election of his father and Pompey. See Plut. *Crass.* 15.6, 51.4–52.2, *Cato Min.* 41.6–42.1; App. *BC* 2.17; Dio 39.27–31 (incorrectly seeing Pompey and Crassus as in rivalry with Caesar).

1 After this Pompey and Crassus were appointed consuls following an interregnum, since none of those who had previously announced their candidature put up any opposition, though Lucius Domitius, who had canvassed right up to the very last day, set off from his house for the assembly in the dark, but, when the slave carrying the light in front of him was murdered, took fright and proceeded no further. **2** Accordingly, as no one opposed their magistracy, and what is more as Publius Crassus, who was Marcus' son and at that point one of Caesar's officers, brought soldiers into Rome to ensure this, they were elected without difficulty.

12.71 Cicero on Caesar's command

Cicero *On the Consular Provinces* 19, 29, 34–5

Cicero delivered this speech following the conference of Luca, after Pompey's talk to Cicero's brother Quintus (doc. 12.68) had forced Cicero to adopt a more moderate political line and desist from attacking the Campanian land legislation of 59 BC. The debate in June 56 concerned the assignation of four provinces: the two Gauls, Macedonia, and Syria. Cicero successfully spoke against the proposal to deprive Caesar of the command of one or both of the provinces of Gaul (with one or both to be assigned to the consuls to be elected for 55) with fulsome praise of Caesar and his conquests. This speech, *On the Consular Provinces*, might be Cicero's 'palinode' to which he refers at Cic. *Att.* 4.5.1 (doc. 12.72), but not all agree: Syme 1939: 37. He stresses that it is for the good of the state that Caesar remain in control of Gaul (esp. 34–5) and reviews his relationship with Caesar (40–44), blaming himself for his own exile and expressing gratitude that Caesar had acquiesced in his recall. Cicero described his own predicament to Atticus in April 55 as one of being seen as a madman (insanus) if he said what he should or of being a slave (servus) if he said what he was constrained to say (*Att.* 4.6.2). He nevertheless used this speech to continue his feud with Piso and Gabinius, arguing that their provinces, Macedonia and Syria, be reassigned because of their incompetence (1–18). Gabinius, as proconsul in Syria 57–55 with unlimited imperium under Clodius' law, certainly did not deserve these reproaches and continued as proconsul to the end of 55; in this period he was an able governor, putting down uprisings in Judaea and dealing with pirates (Sherwin-White 1994: 271–3; *MRR* II.203, 210–11, 218).

19 A vitally important war has been fought in Gaul; mighty races have been subdued by Caesar, but they are not yet bound to us by laws, by established rights, by a sufficiently stable peace. We see that the war is nearly at an end, and, to speak truth, almost completed, but it is only on condition that the same man who began the war follows it up to the end that we may presently see it brought to a final conclusion, and, if he is succeeded, there is a danger that we may hear of the remnants of that important war being revived and renewed.

28 Recently the matter of pay for his army was referred to us; not only did I vote for it, but I even worked hard to persuade you to do so too; I gave lengthy replies to those who disagreed; I was part of the committee that drafted the resolution. At that point, too, I conceded more to the man than to any kind of necessity. For my view was that even without this monetary assistance he was able to maintain his army by booty already won and conclude the war; but I did not think that the honour and glory of a triumph should be diminished by any parsimony on our part. We passed a resolution about ten legates, whom some totally refused to grant, while others asked for precedents, others wanted to postpone the discussion, and others wanted to grant them but omitting any flattering terms; I spoke on this matter too in such a way that everyone could understand that I did what I felt was in the interests of the state all the more lavishly due to the prestige of Caesar himself. **29** But, now it is a matter of allocating provinces, I am interrupted, though I expressed my views on those other questions to a silent audience. In the former cases honours for Caesar were at issue, but now my only concern is military considerations and the highest benefits to the state. For why should Caesar wish to remain in his province, unless to hand over to the state the work he has on hand completely finished?

34 One or two summers more, with fear or hope, punishment or rewards, arms or laws, can bind the whole of Gaul to us with ever-lasting chains. But, if the work of conquest is abandoned prematurely and without finishing touches, although the power of our enemies has been truncated, it will at some point come to life again and result in the renewal of the war. **35** And so let Gaul stay under the protection of the person to whose loyalty, courage and good fortune it has been entrusted. For if he, who has already been adorned with Fortune's richest gifts, were unwilling to risk tempting that goddess too often, if he were in haste to return to his country, his household gods, the honour which he sees waiting for him at Rome, his delightful children, his illustrious son-in-law, if he were longing to ride to the Capitol in triumph with that distinguished mark of honour, if, finally, he feared some set-back, which could not add to his glory as much as it could take away, it would however still be incumbent on us to wish that all those tasks should be completed by the same man by whom they have been so nearly brought to an end. But, as what he has achieved at this point is enough for his own glory, but not enough for the state, and as he prefers to postpone his enjoyment of the fruits of his labours rather than not fulfil the duty he has undertaken for the commonwealth, we ought neither to recall a general who is so dedicated to successful service of the state, nor to disturb and impede the whole policy relating to the war in Gaul which is now so nearly finalised.

12.72 Cicero's 'palinode'

Cicero *Letters to Atticus* 4.5.1–2 (June 56)

Cicero refers in this letter to his palinode, in which he said goodbye to 'principles, truth and honour' in his support of the triumvirate.

1 I feel my palinode was something which doesn't do me credit. But farewell to principles, truth and honour! . . . **2** The truth is I wanted to forge an unbreakable connection for myself with this new alliance to make it totally impossible for me to slip back to those people who, even when they should feel sorry for me, won't stop being jealous of me . . . Since those who have no power do not wish to be my friends, let me try to make myself liked by those who do possess power.

THE EVENTS OF 55 BC

12.73 The second consulship of Crassus and Pompey

Plutarch *Life of Pompey* 52.3–5

C. Trebonius, tribune in 55 BC, passed the *lex Trebonia* to provide for two five-year proconsular commands: Syria and the provinces of Spain (Ulterior and Citerior), with the governors to make peace and war as they saw fit. Spain still provided scope for military activity, while Syria was the gateway to Parthia. Syria went to Crassus, Spain to Pompey. Pompey, contrary to Plutarch, did not obtain Libya (Africa) as part of his command. Two tribunes, P. Aquillius Gallus and C. Ateius Capito, as well as M. Porcius Cato, opposed the *lex Trebonia* without success (*MRR* II.216) and Livy *Per.* 105 has Cato removed from the rostra by force; Plut. *Cato Min.* 43 and Dio 39.33–6 write of bloodshed and a few deaths, with Aquillius prevented by an armed guard from leaving the senate. See also: Cic. *Att.* 4.9.1; Plut. *Pomp.* 52, *Crass.* 15; Vell. 2.46.2; *MRR* II.217. Pompey and Crassus successfully proposed in the assembly an extension of Caesar's command for five years. The proposals in the senate to make one or both of the Gauls a consular province for 54 (so depriving his Caesar of command) came to nothing. The cost of the additional four legions raised by Caesar for Gaul without senatorial approval were to be met by the state and he was allowed to appoint ten legates: Cicero supported these measures.

Bribery had been used to ensure the election of Vatinius to the praetorship for 55, rather than M. Porcius Cato; Plut. *Cato Min.* 42.5 (doc. 3.72) has the better citizens ejected and prevented from voting; cf. Val. Max 7.5.6; Plut. *Pomp.* 53.4; Dio 39.32 (violence at the elections of the curule aediles, with Pompey splattered with blood, at the sight of which Julia fainted and miscarried); for Pompey's theatre: docs 2.68–9; Dio 39.38.1–6.

3 By such means they made their way into office, and even then did not behave any more appropriately. First, while the people were in the act of voting for Cato's election to the praetorship, Pompey dissolved the assembly on the grounds of inauspicious omens, and they proclaimed Vatinius praetor instead of Cato, after bribing the tribes. 4 They then, by means of Trebonius, a tribune, brought in laws which, according to their agreement, continued Caesar's command for a second term of five years, and gave Crassus Syria and the expedition against the Parthians, and Pompey himself the whole of Libya, both Spanish provinces and four legions, two of which he lent to Caesar at his request for the war in Gaul. 5 While Crassus went out to his province at the end of his consulship, Pompey opened his theatre and put on gymnastic and musical contests at its dedication, as well as wild beast combats, in which 500 lions were killed and above all an elephant fight, a most astounding spectacle.

12.74 Jobs for the boys

Dio *Roman History* 39.33.1–34.1

Dio incorrectly gives Caesar's extension of command as three years, not five. The picture of Caesar's supporters does not tally with the accounts of Plutarch and Appian above who record pre-arranged deals for 55 BC to benefit all three men. Favonius (praetor in 49) was a supporter of Cato and opponent of the triumvirate.

1 With the magistrates appointed, Pompey and Crassus started working to achieve their aims. They did not speak on their own behalf either in the senate or the assembly, but

seriously pretended that there was nothing else they desired; **2** however, one of the tribunes, Gaius Trebonius, put forward a proposal that one of them should be given Syria and the neighbouring regions as his province, and the other the two Spains (where there had been recent disturbances), both for a five-year period, and that they were to have the use of as many troops as they wished, both citizens and allies, and the power to make war or peace with whomever they chose. **3** Many people disapproved of this, especially Caesar's friends, because, after attaining their own aims, Pompey and Crassus were bound to prevent Caesar from holding power for much longer, and some of them therefore prepared themselves to oppose the proposal. The consuls were then afraid that they might fail to achieve their object, and gained their support by extending Caesar's command too for another three years, to give the correct figure. **4** They did not, however, bring anything before the people on his behalf until their own position was secured. Caesar's supporters were in this way won over and stayed quiet, and most of the others were too subdued by fear to say anything, satisfied, by so doing, to preserve their lives. **34.1** On the other hand, Cato and Favonius opposed all their projects, with two tribunes and some others working with them, but, as they were a few struggling against a large number of opponents, they spoke out in vain.

12.75 Cicero defends his enemies in court

Cicero also worked for Pompey and Caesar in other trials in 56–54 BC. Caesar asked him to defend Cornelius Balbus, a Spaniard granted citizenship by Pompey; this is the *pro Balbo* (Brunt 1982). Pompey requested defences of Caninius Gallus, who as tribune in 56 had proposed that Pompey restore Ptolemy Auletes (*MRR* II.209), and Aemilius Scaurus for misconduct as a candidate in the consular elections for 53; he seems to have been Pompey's preferred choice for consul; Caninius was convicted, the other two acquitted (Alexander *Trials* nos 276, 280, 295; Bucher 1995). (This is not the Caninius who was suffect consul in 45.) Particularly galling for Cicero were the defences he made at Pompey's request of both Vatinius (whom he had previously attacked in his *In Vatinium*) and Gabinius. Vatinius was prosecuted for misconduct in his election to the praetorship for 55; with Cicero defending him, he was acquitted (Alexander *Trials* no. 292; see comment at doc. 12.68); for Gabinius, see below, doc. 12.76. One consolation in 53 (or perhaps 52) was his election to the augurate, on the proposal of Pompey and Hortensius (cos. 69), which position he had long desired: in 59 he had said that it was the one offer that might have tempted him to support the triumvirate (*Att.* 2.26.2: 59 BC; augurate: *Fam.* 15.4.13, *Phil.* 2.4; *MRR* II.233).

(a) Cicero *Letters to his Friends* 7.1.4 (to M. Marius, (?) September 55)

I was weary of it (forensic oratory) even at the time when youth and ambition led me on, and when I could indeed turn down a case I did not wish to defend, but now life is just not worth living. I have no reward to expect for my hard work, and I am sometimes obliged to defend persons who have deserved none too well of me at the entreaty of those who have deserved well.

(b) Cicero *Letters to his Brother Quintus* 3.5.4 (October or November 54)

Some of my enemies I have not attacked, others I have actually defended. Not only my mind, but even my hatred, are not free.

THE DEATH OF JULIA AND THE EVENTS OF 54 BC

In December (probably) of 55 BC, Domitius Ahenobarbus was elected to the consulship and Cato to the praetorship for 54, both of which had been prevented earlier by Pompey and Crassus (cf. doc. 3.72). Clodius' brother Appius Claudius Pulcher was the other consul elected for 54, with Pompey and Caesar's support (Cic. *Scaur.* 31, *Fam.* 1.9.4; *MRR* II.221). The enmity between Cicero and Clodius remained. Ahenobarbus as consul renewed his attacks on Caesar's legislation of 59 (Suet. *Jul.* 24.1, *Nero* 2.2), again unsuccessfully.

In 54 BC Messalla Rufus and Aemilius Scaurus were prosecuted under the *lex Tullia de ambitu* for misconduct during 54 in their campaigns for the consulship of 53 but the outcome is uncertain (Alexander *Trials* nos 299–300). In 52 Scaurus was prosecuted again for the same offence and convicted: Pompey's law *de ambitu* probably stimulated the retrial (Alexander no. 319).

Gabinius on 23 October was acquitted of *maiestas* (treason) for his restoration of Ptolemy without the authorisation of the senate, but one hour later was convicted of extortion in his province of Syria, where he had upset the publicani (Cic. *Att.* 4.18.4, *Quint.* 2.12.2; Alexander nos 296–7; Fantham 1975). Gabinius as consul in 58 had ignored Cicero's plea to prevent Clodius exiling him, and Cicero had attacked his proconsulship in Syria. Cicero wrote to Quintus (3.1.15) in September 54 that Pompey was pressuring him for a reconciliation with Gabinius but that he would never give in. Nevertheless he appeared as a witness for his defence in the trial for *maiestas*, and defended him in the trial for extortion.

12.76 Electoral scandal in 54 BC

Cicero *Letters to Atticus* 4.17 & Letters to his Brother Quintus 3.3.2–3

In the course of 54 evidence of an electoral scandal broke: Memmius, one of the candidates for 53, revealed with Pompey's connivance, but to Caesar's annoyance, that he and a fellow candidate, Cn. Domitius Calvinus (tr. pl. 59; not to be confused with Domitius Ahenobarbus, cos. 54), had made a pact with the consuls in office in 54 BC. The elections for 53 were therefore continually postponed by *obnuntiatio* to the great pleasure of the boni, suspicious that the consuls had sold out to the candidates. All four candidates were to be prosecuted for bribery. See also Cic. *Att.* 4.15.7 (incidentally mentioning at §6 the loud applause he himself received when he entered the theatre), *Fam.* 1.9.25, *Quint.* 3.1.16, 3.2.3; cf. Plut. *Cato Min.* 44.2–7 (the tribunician candidates for 53 arrange with Cato to avoid bribery in the tribunician elections).

This election scandal delayed the election of consuls for 53 until July 53; Calvinus and Messalla Rufus were elected and then took office (Dio 40.45.1). Elections for 53: Gruen 1969b, 1995: 148–9, 331–2; Mitchell 1991: 193–4; Lintott 1999: 214–15.

(a) *Letters to Atticus* 4.17.2–3, 5 (1 October 54)

2 The consuls are embroiled in a dreadful scandal because Gaius Memmius, one of the candidates, read out in the senate an agreement which he and his fellow competitor Domitius made with the consuls, that they would both give the consuls 4,000,000 sesterces, if they were elected, unless they had found three augurs who would state that they had been present when a lex curiata was passed, which had not been passed, and two consulars, who would state that they had been present at a decree arranging for the consular provinces, even though the senate had not met. This agreement, as was stated, was not an oral one, but with names and details in many people's notebooks, and was produced by Memmius at Pompey's instigation with the names erased. This meant nothing to Appius; he hasn't lost anything. His colleague is ruined and totally finished. **3** Memmius' chances, now the coalition is dissolved against the wishes of Calvinus, have gone cold, all the more because we now understand that his revelation has seriously displeased Caesar. Our friend Messalla and his fellow competitor Domitius have treated the populace very liberally, and hence are very popular. They were sure to become consuls . . . **5** Three of the candidates are expected to face prosecution, Domitius by Memmius, Messalla by Quintus Pompeius Rufus, Scaurus by Triarius or Lucius Caesar. 'What can you say on their behalf?' you may ask. I'll be damned if I know!

(b) *Letters to his Brother Quintus* 3.3.2–3 (21 October 54 BC)

2 Now hear what has been going on in politics. Day after day election days are cancelled by the declaration of inauspicious omens to the great joy of all honest men, as the consuls are extremely unpopular due to the suspicion of their having arranged to take bribes from the candidates. All four consular candidates have been charged. Their cases are difficult, but I shall do my best to save our friend Messalla, which involves the safety of the others too. Publius Sulla has charged Gabinius with bribery, with his step-son Memmius, his brother Caecilius and his son Sulla as co-prosecutors. Lucius Torquatus put in a rival claim to prosecute, but to everyone's delight failed to get it. **3** You will be interested to know what is going on with Gabinius: we shall know about the treason in three days' time; in that trial he is disadvantaged by the dislike felt for him by all classes, and is greatly damaged by the witnesses, while his case is handled by unenthusiastic prosecutors. The jury is a diverse one, the president Alfius is reliable and solid, and Pompey urgently trying to influence the jurors. What will happen I don't know, but I see no place for him in the community, am very unworried by the thought of his ruin, and perfectly at ease as to how things will turn out.

12.77 Julia buried in the Campus Martius

Plutarch *Life of Caesar* 23.5–7

Plutarch could well be judging by later events in seeing people 'disturbed' at this break in the relationship with Caesar; Appian *BC* 2.19.68 has a similar account. While Pompey did not renew the marriage alliance with Caesar after the death of Julia, no real break between the two men can be dated to this point. The link between Pompey and Caesar was weakened, but it was Pompey's sole consulship of 52 and his reconciliation with the senate that saw the beginning of the breakdown in the relationship. Pompey planned to bury Julia at his Alban villa, but the crowds carried the body to the Campus Martius; Ahenobarbus (cos. 54) opposed her burial there as sacrilegious, but to no effect (Dio 39.64; App. *BC* 2.64; Plut. *Pomp.* 53.6). Caesar was in Britain and received the letters advising him of her death on his return; he staged a gladiatorial show in her honour in 46: doc. 2.74.

5 (On returning to Gaul from Britain) Caesar found letters from his friends in Rome which were about to be sent across to him, informing him of his daughter's death. She had died in child-birth at Pompey's house. **6** Both Pompey and Caesar were greatly distressed at this, and their friends were very disturbed as the relationship which preserved the otherwise troubled state in peace and harmony was now dissolved. And the baby also died, only a few days after its mother. **7** As for Julia, the people took her body and carried her, in spite of the tribunes, to the Campus Martius, where her funeral was held and where she lies buried.

12.78 Caesar attempts to arrange a marriage alliance

Suetonius *Life of the Deified Julius* 27.1

Pompey in fact married Cornelia, daughter of Q. Metellus Scipio, soon after entering his sole consulship in 52 (Plut. *Pomp.* 55.1–3; cf. doc. 7.44). Cornelia's husband had been the younger Crassus, killed in Parthia on his father's staff. Metellus as one of the candidates for the consulship of 52 was involved in electoral bribery and civic disturbances. He was prosecuted but Pompey called the jurors to his house and asked for their support: the prosecutor abandoned the case when he saw Scipio escorted from the forum by the jurors. Pompey chose him as his colleague in July (Plut. *Pomp.* 55.7–8, cf. *Cato Min.* 48.7–8; App. *BC* 2.24.93–4 (cf. doc. 13.6); Dio 40.51.3, 53.1–2; *MRR* II.234; Seager 2002: 137).

To maintain his relationship and good-will with Pompey, Caesar offered him as his wife Octavia, his sister's grand-daughter, who was married to Gaius Marcellus (cos. 50), and for himself asked for Pompey's daughter in marriage, who was betrothed to Faustus Sulla.

12.79 Cicero feels for Caesar

Cicero *Letters to his Brother Quintus* 3.1.17, 3.6.3
(September and November, 54)

For Cicero's affection for his own daughter Tullia, see docs 7.26–7.

3.1.17 While I was still folding up this letter, letter-carriers arrived from you on the 20th (September), the twenty-seventh day after you sent it. How worried I was! And how distressed I was by Caesar's charming letter! The more charming it was, the more distress I felt for the misfortune which has befallen him.

    3.6.3 I got great pleasure in learning from your letter of the courage and dignity with which Caesar conducts himself in his immense sorrow.

CRASSUS IN PARTHIA

12.80 Crassus' Parthian aims

Plutarch *Life of Crassus* 15.7–16.3

Crassus and Pompey received provinces by the *lex Trebonia*, rather than by lot (doc. 12.74). While Pompey remained in Rome and administered Spain through legates, Crassus set out for Syria in November 55, with Ateius the tribune cursing him at the city gate as he left. The *lex Trebonia* had not specifically provided for a war against Parthia, but Crassus in Rome had soon made his hopes for military glory against Parthia clear. Arriving in Syria in 54 BC he carried out punitive raids into Mesopotamia, and seized the Temple treasures of Jerusalem. In 53 he invaded Parthia but at the river Balik the Parthians defeated the Romans, decapitating Crassus' son, P. Licinius Crassus, and displaying the head, fixed to a spear, to Crassus. The survivors retreated to Carrhae where on 9 June the Parthians completed their task. Crassus was killed in flight and some 30,000 of the Roman army had lost their lives. It was one of the most spectacular defeats the Roman army had ever experienced. Crassus' defeat was not due to lack of military experience or ineptitude but rather to the tactics employed against him. The Parthians were said to have poured molten gold down Crassus' throat: *MRR* II.230, 231; Plut. *Crass.* 16–30; App. *BC* 2.18.66; Dio 40.17–27; Joseph. *Ant.* 14.105–9, *BJ* 1.179; Marshall 1976: 139–61; Wardman 1977: 280–8; Scullard *GN* 123–5; Wiseman 1994a: 402–3.

15.7 When the lots were cast, Crassus received Syria and Pompey the Spanish provinces. **16.1** Everyone was pleased with the way the lot turned out. Most people did not want Pompey to be far from Rome, and Pompey, who loved his wife, intended to spend most of his time there, while as soon as the lot took place Crassus showed by his delight that he considered that no more glorious piece of good fortune than this had ever happened to him, and could hardly keep quiet among strangers and in public, while to his intimate friends he made many empty, childish boasts unsuited to his age and temperament, since before this he had been anything but boastful or pompous. **2** Now, however, frantic with excitement and out of his senses he did not intend Syria or the Parthians to be the limit of his success, but wanted to make Lucullus' campaigns against Tigranes and Pompey's against Mithridates look like child's play, in his hopes seeing himself reaching as far as Bactria and India and the Outer Sea. And yet in the decree passed concerning his command there was no mention of a Parthian war. **3** But everyone knew that Crassus was obsessed with this idea and Caesar wrote to him from Gaul approving the project and encouraging him to start the war.

12.81 Cicero on Marcus Licinius Crassus

Cicero *On Duties* 1.25, 3.75

At *Off.* 1.109 Cicero links Crassus with Sulla as examples of those who would stoop to anything to achieve their aims.

1.25 In those with greater ambitions, the love of riches leads them to strive for power and patronage, as in the case of Marcus Crassus, who recently stated that no amount of money was enough for the man who wished to be the leading citizen in the state, unless he could keep an army on the income from it.

3.75 But if you were to give Marcus Crassus the power to get himself named as an heir, though he was not truly an heir, by snapping his fingers, believe me, he would dance in the forum.

12.82 The death of Crassus

Ovid *Fasti* 6.463–8

Of course, grief is sometimes mixed with joy,
lest festivals prove an unmixed delight for the people:
Crassus at the Euphrates lost his eagles, his son, and his soldiers,
And was himself the last to perish.
'Parthian, why do you rejoice?' said the goddess. 'You shall return the standards,
while there will be an avenger who shall take vengeance for the death of Crassus.'

CAESAR AND BRITAIN

In 55 and again in 54 BC Caesar invaded Britain. His declared motive was the assistance given by the British to the Gauls (*BG* 4.20); there was also the allure of another conquest, and presumably the desire for booty (and pearls: Suet. *Jul.* 47). There were no territorial gains from either expedition, and no garrisoning force was left behind; it is hardly likely that any of the tribute imposed was paid. Actual conquest only began in the reign of the emperor Claudius. Caesar on his return had to deal with an uprising in north Gaul (*BG* 5.24–58; Cic. *Fam.* 7.10.2). For his campaigns in Britain, carried out with the Seventh and Tenth Legions, see Caes. *BG* 4.20–38, 5.7–23; Plut. *Caes.* 23.2–4; Suet. *Jul.* 25; App. *Gallic History* i.5, xix; Dio 39.50–3, 40.1–4; *MRR* II.219, 224; Fuller 1965: 115–16, 121–6; Balsdon 1967: 82–5; Gelzer 1968: 130–1, 142; Bradford 1984: 94–107; Wiseman 1994a: 400–2; Meier 1995: 280–2, 292–3; Southern 2001: 74–7; Dando-Collins 2002: 30–49.

12.83 Caesar's first expedition to Britain, 55 BC

Dio Cassius *Roman History* 39.50.1–53.2

50.1 Caesar was at this time the first Roman to cross the Rhine, and afterwards, in the consulship of Pompey and Crassus, he crossed over to Britain . . . **51.1** Caesar wanted to cross to this country at this time, because the rest of Gaul was at peace and he had won over the Morini. He made the crossing with his infantry by the best possible route, but did not land at the most suitable spot, as the Britons, who had learnt of his voyage, had seized all the landing-places facing the mainland. **2** He therefore sailed around a certain projecting promontory and along the other side of it, where he disembarked in the shallows, overcoming those who engaged with him and gaining a foothold before more help could arrive, afterwards driving back these attackers too. **2** Only a few of the barbarians were killed (being chariot-drivers and cavalry they easily escaped the Romans, whose cavalry had not yet arrived), but panic-stricken at the reports about the Romans which had come from the mainland, and at the fact that they had dared to cross at all and been able to set foot in their country, they sent some of the Morini, friends of theirs, to Caesar to treat for peace. When he requested hostages, they were at that point willing to give them to him, **52.1** but when the Romans meanwhile faced problems because of a storm which damaged the fleet they had there and the one which was joining them, they changed their minds and, while they did not attack them openly (for the camp was heavily defended), they captured some men who had been sent out to forage for supplies in the belief that the country was friendly, and killed them all, except a few, for Caesar swiftly came to their rescue, after which they attacked the Romans' defences. They achieved nothing, but suffered reverses, though they would not make peace terms until they had been defeated a number of times. **3** Caesar would not have considered coming to terms with them, except that the winter was approaching and he did not possess a sufficient force to continue to make war at that time of year, as the force which was coming to back him up had been damaged and the Gauls had revolted as a result of his absence, so he reluctantly made peace with the Britons, this time demanding numerous hostages, but only getting a few.

53.1 He sailed back to the mainland and put an end to the uprisings, having gained nothing from Britain either for himself or for Rome, except the prestige of having made an expedition against the Britons. He took great pride in this and the Romans at home extolled this achievement to a marvellous degree. Because they saw that what had formerly been unknown was now familiar, and the formerly unheard of accessible, they considered the hopes for the future aroused by these deeds as actual facts, and rejoiced at all their anticipated future gains as if they already possessed them. Because of this they voted the celebration of a thanksgiving (supplicatio) lasting twenty days.

12.84 Cicero to his brother in Britain

Cicero *Letters to his Brother Quintus* 2.16.4–5

Written in late August 54, from Rome to Quintus who was serving as Caesar's legate. Cicero wrote a literary account of Caesar's expedition to Britain: Gelzer 1967: 139; at *Quint.* 3.5.4 he expresses himself as not sufficiently stimulated to write a poem on the British tides. Cicero had also written a poem, 'On my vicissitudes', and was hoping for further favourable comments from Caesar.

4 I come now to what should perhaps have been first. How happy I was to get your letter from Britain! I dreaded the Ocean, I dreaded the island coastline; not that I am making light of what is still to come, but there is more to hope than fear, and I am more troubled by anticipation than by anxiety. I see that you have some really splendid literary material — places, nature, topography, customs, peoples, fighting, and of course the general himself! I shall be pleased to help you, as you request, in any way you like and I shall send you the verses you ask for (an owl to Athens!)

5 But look here, you seem to be keeping something from me. Brother, what does Caesar think of my poem? He wrote to me earlier that he had read the first book and had never read anything better than the first part, even in Greek; the rest to a certain point he thought more slipshod (the word he used). Tell me the truth: is it the content or the style he doesn't like? Don't worry at all — I won't think a whit less of myself. Just tell me the truth frankly and, as you always do, like a brother.

12.85 Mail from Britain

Cicero *Letters to Atticus* 4.18.5 (October or November 54)

In a letter to Trebatius, *Fam.* 7.7.1, Cicero wrote in June 54, 'I hear there is no gold or silver in Britain; in that case I suggest you get a war-chariot and hurry back to us as soon as possible'.

From my brother Quintus and from Caesar I received letters on 24 October sent from the shores of nearer Britain on 25 September. Britain has been subdued, hostages taken, no booty, but tribute has been imposed and they are bringing the army back from Britain.

12.86 Why Quintus joined Caesar in Gaul and Britain

Cicero *Letters to his Brother Quintus* 3.6.1 (November 54)

Quintus had clearly been bemoaning conditions in Gaul; Marcus reminds him of the advantages which will accrue to both of them from Caesar's patronage and support.

Marcus to his brother Quintus, greetings. I have nothing to reply to your earlier letter, which is full of irritation and complaining (you write that you gave another too in the same vein to Labeo the day before, which hasn't arrived yet) — your more recent letter removed all my annoyance. I only advise and beg you to remember amid these annoyances and labours and deprivations our reason for your going there. We were not, after all, looking out for slight or trivial benefits. What was it that we thought worth buying at the cost of our separation? We were in search of solid support from the good will of a great and extremely powerful man for every aspect of our public standing. We are relying more on hope than on money; if that is lost, the rest will have been accumulated just to be thrown away. So, if you keep on carrying your mind back to the purpose behind our former decision and hope, you will find it easier to put up with those military labours and the other annoyances.

12.87 Caesar's engineer, Mamurra

Cf. Catullus 43 (doc. 7.49); *Att.* 7.7.6; Suet. *Jul.* 73 (Caesar invited Catullus to dinner after he had apologised for attacking Caesar and Mamurra); Fordyce 1961: 159–60; Quinn 1972: 41–5, 267–8; Wiseman 1985a: 103, 105; Wray 2001: 71–5. Poem 29 was written before Julia's death and after the first invasion of Britain, with Catullus seeing Pompey and Caesar (here called 'Romulus') as associates. Mamurra was of an equestrian family and had served with Pompey against Mithridates, and with Caesar in Spain in 61, and was Caesar's engineer in Gaul. He had made an immense fortune and indulged in luxurious living: Catullus' bile against him may have been because of his resentment of Mamurra's success; he must have been capable to have been serving with Caesar in Gaul. For Mamurra's rapacity and luxury, see *Att.* 7.7.6; note Pliny *Nat. Hist.* 36.48 for his covering of the walls of his house with marble veneer; for Caesar and Catullus: Gelzer 1967: 134; Quinn 44–5, 269–74; for *cinaedi* (sodomites), see docs 7.57–60.

(a) Catullus 29

Who can see it, who can endure it,
Unless a shameless, greedy gambler,
That Mamurra owns the wealth that once belonged to long-haired Gaul
and Britain at the end of the world?
5   Romulus, you sodomite, can you put up with the sight?
And shall that arrogant, overbearing chap
Now wander through everyone's bedrooms
Like a white dove or an Adonis?
Romulus, you sodomite, can you put up with the sight,
10   You shameless, greedy gambler?
Surely this isn't why, O egregious one,
You went to the furthest island in the west,
So this worn-out prick owned by you two
Could squander two or three hundred times its worth?
15   What is this but perverse generosity?
Hasn't he finished off or got through enough?
First he went through his inherited property,
Then the plunder from Pontus, then thirdly
Spain's, as the gold-bearing Tagus river knows:

20   Now fears are felt for Gaul and Britain.
      Why on earth do you coddle him? What can he do
      But eat up rich inheritances?
      Surely this wasn't why you, the city's wealthiest men —
      Father-in-law, son-in-law — have ruined the entire world?

(b) Catullus 57

      They suit one another well, those shameless sodomites (*cinaedi*),
      Mamurra that pathic and Caesar.
      And no wonder! Identical stains,
      Picked up by one in the city, by the other at Formiae,
5   Mark them, which cannot be washed away,
      Equally diseased, just like twins,
      Both learned scholars on one little bed,
      Neither a more voracious adulterer than the other,
      Friendly rivals even of young girls.
      Yes, they suit one another well, those shameless sodomites.

12.88 Caesar on Britain

Caesar *Gallic War* 5.12.1–6, 14.1–5

12.1 The interior of Britain is inhabited by natives who state that according to their tradition they are indigenous to the island, **2** the coastal region by people who crossed over from Belgium for the purposes of plunder or warfare, who after the invasion settled there and began to cultivate the land. Nearly all of these are called by the names of the states from which they came before their journey to Britain. **3** There is a vast population and very numerous farm buildings similar to those in Gaul, with an immense number of cattle. **4** They use either bronze or gold coins or, instead of coins, iron rods of a standard weight. **5** Tin is found in the midland regions of Britain, iron in the coastal regions, but of the latter the supply is small; they use imported bronze. There is timber of all kinds as in Gaul, except for beech and fir. **6** They consider it wrong to eat hare, chicken and goose, but keep these for diversion and pleasure. The climate is more temperate than that of Gaul, with milder cold seasons . . . **14.1** Of all the inhabitants, the most civilised by far are those who live in Kent, a completely coastal region, whose lifestyle differs little from that of the Gauls. Most of the inland dwellers do not plant corn, **2** but live on milk and meat and dress in skins. Indeed, all the Britons dye themselves with woad, which produces a blue colour, and gives them a more frightful appearance in battle; **3** they wear their hair long and shave their whole body except for the head and upper lip. **4** Ten or twelve men have wives in common, especially brothers with brothers and fathers with sons; **5** but the offspring are considered to belong to the family to which the girl was first taken in marriage.

12.89 Vercingetorix

Caesar *Gallic War* 7.1.1–8, 3.1–4.2

Caesar's campaigns had until now been against a disunited Gaul, which he and his legates had conquered piecemeal. In the winter at the beginning of 52 BC, the Gauls united in one great revolt against the Romans, led by Vercingetorix, in which even the Aedui joined. As Caesar notes, one of their motives was the fate of Acco, chief of the Suessiones, who had been executed by Caesar in the traditional Roman way (flogging to death) as the ring-leader of the revolt in 53 (*BG* 6.4, 6.44). Caesar deals with this revolt in *BG* 7, probably the most dramatic and exciting part of the *BG*. After various incidents, including Caesar's capture of Avaricum (the main town of the Bituriges) and his massacre of its inhabitants (despite which the Aedui soon defected), Caesar besieged Vercingetorix in Alesia. He in turn was surrounded by a besieging Gallic force, and had to build two walls, one around Alesia, and one on the outside of his position against the besieging Gauls. Their attack failed and Alesia surrendered. Vercingetorix surrendered personally to Caesar, and was to appear in his triumph, and then be executed. A twenty-day supplicatio was decreed by the senate. But Caesar had to fight some last battles. He made a demonstration of force against the Bituriges, and then the Carnutes. It was against the Bellovaci in the north-west, however, that the last real fighting took place, followed by a final battle in the south-west of Gaul at Uxellodunum. After its surrender, he cut off the hands of the defenders (*BG* 8.1–48; hands: 44; *BG* 8 is the continuation of Caesar's *BG* by Hirtius, cos. 43). In 51, Gaul was pacified and subdued. Caesar made administrative arrangements and now he could turn his attention elsewhere.

1.1 When Gaul was quiet, Caesar, as he had decided, sets out for Italy to hold the assizes. There he learns of the murder of Clodius and, on being informed of the senate's decree that all younger men should be called up and sworn in, he resolves to hold a levy throughout his province. **2** These events are quickly reported to Transalpine Gaul. The Gauls invent and add to the rumours, a matter which the situation seemed to demand, that Caesar was detained by disturbances at Rome and, because of such great discord, was unable to join his army. **3** Excited by this opportunity, those who even before this were bemoaning their subjection to the rule of the Roman people begin to make war plans with greater freedom and audacity. **4** Assemblies were summoned by arrangement between the Gallic chiefs in wooded and remote areas and they complain of the death of Acco; they point out that his fate could next fall upon them; **5** they pity the misfortune suffered by the whole of Gaul; with all kinds of promises and rewards they call upon men to begin the war and champion the freedom of Gaul at the risk of their lives. **6** First of all, they say, they must find a way, before their secret plans become generally known, to cut Caesar off from his army. **7** That was easy, because the legions would not dare to leave their winter quarters in their commander's absence, nor could the commander reach his legions without an escort. **8** Finally, it was better to die in battle than to fail to win back their former prestige in warfare and the liberty handed down by their forefathers . . . **3.1** When the day comes, the Carnutes, under the leadership of two desperate men, Cotuatus and Conconnetodumnus, rush at a given signal against Cenabum, put to death the Roman citizens who had settled there for trading purposes, amongst them Gaius Fufius Cita, a respected Roman eques who by Caesar's order was in charge of the corn supply, and seize their possessions. **2** The report is swiftly carried to all the states of Gaul — for whenever any more important or glorious event occurs, they proclaim it loudly through the fields and localities; others then take it up and hand it on to their neighbours, as happens on this occasion. **3** For the deeds done at Cenabum at sunrise were heard before the end of the first watch on the borders of the Arverni, a distance of some 160 miles.

4.1 In a similar way there, Vercingetorix, son of Celtillus, an Arvernian, a youth of the highest influence, whose father had held the chieftainship of the whole of Gaul, and consequently, because he aimed at kingship, had been put to death by the state, summons his dependants and easily inflames their spirits. **2** As soon as his plan is known there is a general rush to arms.

13

Civil War and Dictatorship

The 'First Triumvirate' had survived in 56 BC, much to Cicero's disappointment, but events soon paved the way for the break-down of the alliance. The deaths of Julia and Crassus left only two partners, who were no longer joined by family ties, and Pompey gradually began to align himself with the optimates. During Caesar's absence in Gaul, factional violence led by Milo and Clodius reached such heights that the consular elections in 54 were so delayed that the consuls for 53 did not enter office until July, and elections for 52 were continually postponed, with bribery rampant. As a result there was increasing talk of making Pompey dictator, until a confrontation between Milo and Clodius on the Appian Way on 18 January 52 resulted in Clodius' murder and riots in Rome in which the senate-house was burned down (docs 13.1–2). In consequence Pompey was made sole consul for 52, a position the optimates, led by Cato, were more willing to allow him than a dictatorship (docs. 13.3–4). Later he took his new father-in-law, Q. Caecilius Metellus Pius Scipio (one of the declared candidates for 52) as colleague in the consulship for the last five months of the year (doc. 13.6). Milo was convicted and Pompey took the opportunity to introduce more stringent anti-violence and anti-bribery laws (doc. 13.5). He was granted a further five-year governorship in Spain and his increased influence and favour with the optimates widened the breach with Caesar, whose supporters wished to ensure that he could safely hold a second consulship, which he wanted after his Gallic command (doc.13.7). In contrast, the 'hard-line' optimates, like Cato the Younger, wanted to see Caesar brought to trial for his actions as consul in 59 before he should be elected to such a second consulship, and attempted to replace him in Gaul with a successor: this issue and the resulting on-going debate were to lead directly to civil war.

The Marcelli (consuls in 51, 50 and 49) were to be particularly opposed to Caesar and senatorial hostility towards him continued to grow during 51. Pompey was pressured into requesting from Caesar a legion he had lent him to deal with a crisis in Gaul (docs 13.9–10) and, though this legion and another of Caesar's own were withdrawn in 50 to deal with the Parthian crisis, they in fact remained in Italy under Pompey's command, a situation which then seemed to present a threat to Caesar (docs 13.10, 13, 21). On 29 September 51 the senate passed a resolution (doc. 13.12) that the question of Caesar's successor should take precedence over all other government business from 1 March 50. However, Caesar, with the immense wealth gained in Gaul, was not without supporters, most notably one of the consuls for 50, L. Aemilius Lepidus Paullus, who presented obstacles to this discussion, and the tribune C. Scribonius Curio, one of Caesar's most notable critics in 59, now won over to his side by payment of his immense debts, who demanded joint disarmament by both Caesar and Pompey (docs 13.14–16).

During 50 Pompey moved inexorably closer to the optimates and himself supported attempts to terminate Caesar's command. The breach between the two had widened to such an extent by August that to Cicero's friend and correspondent, M. Caelius Rufus, war appeared inevitable (docs 13.16–18). Nevertheless, war was only the direct choice of a few 'die-hard' optimates, for when Curio managed on 1 December 50 to divide the senate on a vote for joint disarmament, only 22 senators voted against, while 370 were in favour of Pompey laying down his command as well as Caesar, in order to avoid civil war. At this point C. Claudius Marcellus as consul entrusted the safety of the state to Pompey (docs 13.22–4). When in January two of the tribunes for 49, M. Antony and Q. Cassius Longinus, attempted to veto the *senatus consultum ultimum* outlawing Caesar, they were obstructed and fled to Caesar at Ravenna (docs 13.24–5). On the night of 10 January 49 Caesar crossed the river Rubicon into Italy, making civil war inevitable, justifying himself on the grounds that his command had been terminated unfairly and insultingly (docs 13.26–7). Suetonius, however, considers that his main motive was to escape the prosecution by his enemies for his acts in 59, which Cato had been continually threatening (doc. 13.28).

To the surprise of Cicero, at least, Pompey decided to abandon Rome, and withdrew first to Brundisium and then to western Greece, where Cicero was to join him, despite overtures from Caesar. Caesar pursued Pompey down the Italian peninsula and then returned to Rome before proceeding to Spain (Pompey's province), where he dealt with Pompeian opposition (docs 13.29–38). Now, as later, Caesar was to deal with his defeated opponents with clemency. After returning from Spain, Caesar held the dictatorship for eleven days to preside over the consular elections; after himself being elected for 48, he followed Pompey to Greece (doc. 13.42). Pompey's supporters were riven with jealousy of each other and hatred of Caesar, and his forces were inadequately trained (doc. 13.43). After an initial defeat in an attempt to blockade the army at Dyrrachium, Caesar overwhelmingly overcame the Pompeian forces at Pharsalus in August 48 (docs 13.43–4). Pompey fled and was to be killed in Egypt, by advisors of the Egyptian king, to Caesar's great regret (docs 13.46, 52). After a stay in Egypt with Cleopatra, Caesar had to engage in further military campaigns in Asia (against Pharnaces: doc. 13.48), in Africa (against Metellus Scipio, Cato and other Pompeians) and finally in Spain (against Pompey's sons). With this final victory at Munda in Spain in 45 his victory was complete.

From 46 in particular Caesar began an intensive programme of political reform (colonies, debt relief, and grain distribution: doc. 13.54). Despite his clemency, and his practice of placing defeated opponents in key positions (docs 13.51–2, cf. 13.57), he was unpopular with the optimates because of his neglect of republican values and his increasing autocracy (docs 13.50, 53). He received numerous unprecedented honours from the senate and people (doc. 13.55). The granting of a perpetual dictatorship in February 44 BC led to a conspiracy of more than 60 senators to murder him before he left for his Parthian campaign on 18 March (docs 13.61–2); Caesar was assassinated on the Ides (15th) of March 44. The conspirators, however, did not take advantage of their position, as Cicero laments (docs 13.67–9), and Caesar's popularity and the unpopularity of the 'tyrannicides' was enhanced by the generosity of Caesar's will (doc. 13.63) in which he adopted his great-nephew Octavian, who was to complete the demise of the republic. It could be argued that it was the intransigence of the senatorial aristocracy towards Caesar (particularly of the twenty-two optimates – amongst whom Cato was conspicuous – voting against peace on 1 December 50 BC), Pompey's attitude, and Caesar's own personality and the legacy of his own actions in his consulship of 59 BC, that led to the events of 50 and the outbreak of the war between Caesar and Pompey.

For the ancient sources and background reading for this period, see the introduction to chapter 12.

ANARCHY IN ROME

Cn. Domitius Calvinus and M. Valerius Messalla Rufus had finally entered office as consuls in July 53, but three of the consular candidates for 52 caused various disruptions for the rest of the year: Q. Caecilius Metellus Pius Scipio (who was to become Pompey's father-in-law in July 52), T. Annius Milo, and P. Plautius Hypsaeus. In addition, Clodius was a candidate for a praetorship. Not only did wide-spread bribery take place on an unprecedented scale, but these candidates had armed gangs in their employ, and the consul Calvinus was wounded in one incident.

Milo had spent extravagantly on ludi in 53 to ensure election; he had put on immensely expensive games and squandered three patrimonies in so doing (Cic. *Mil.* 95; Asc. 31; cf. Cic. *Quint.* 3.7.2). He also, following Clodius' murder and his own return to Rome, as part of his campaign for a consulship, distributed 1,000 asses to each voter (Asc. 33). When he went into exile, his debts, according to Pliny the Elder, amounted to 70,000,000 sesterces (*Nat. Hist.* 36.104). Clodius, on the other hand, could expect election to the praetorship given his popularity with the plebs and sections of the senate and the support of Pompey, and he naturally supported Milo's rivals Scipio and Hypsaeus (Cic. *Milo* 25, 89). These two were also Pompey's choice: he did not support Milo, as his own rapprochement with Clodius now made Milo dispensable (*Quint.* 3.6.6). The year 53 ended without elections having been held (Dio 40.46.3), and the increasing anarchy was giving rise to calls that Pompey assume the dictatorship, a possibility Cicero had noted as early as November 54: Dio 40.45–6; App. *BC* 2.20; Plut. *Pomp.* 54.5; Cic. *Quint.* 3.6.6; disorders in 53: Cic. *Quint.* 3.3.6, *Mil.* 26; Livy *Per.* 107; Dio 40.46.3–48.1, 40.53; Plut. *Cato Min.* 47.1, *Pomp.* 54.3; Lintott 1999: 215.

Increasing conflict in Rome between the rival gangs of Clodius and Milo, the murder of Clodius on the Appian Way on 18 January 52 BC, and the subsequent riots in the city, led directly to Pompey's election as sole consul for 52.

13.1 The murder of Clodius, 18 January 52 BC

Asconius *Commentaries on Cicero* 30–6

Marcus Lepidus (*MRR* II.236; Welch 1995) is M. Aemilius Lepidus (cos. 46 and 42, praetor 49) and member of the second triumvirate; he was the son of the consul of 78 who led a revolt against the state (doc. 12.2). While he was interrex (he took up office on 20 January), an attack on his house was carried out by the gangs of Clodius and he was trapped there for five days (Cic. *Mil.* 13; Asc. 33, 36, 43). The interrex under whom the elections were actually held was Ser. Sulpicius Rufus, cos. 51 (*MRR* II.236). Pompey was proconsul by virtue of his governorship of Spain which he was governing by legates and assumed the sole consulship on the 24th of the intercalary month before March.

The tribune Q. Pompeius Rufus (tr. pl. 52) was successfully prosecuted at the end of his term by M. Caelius Rufus (tr. pl. 52) under the *lex Pompeia de vi* (the Pompeian law on violence) for his role in the disturbances after Clodius' death, including the burning of the senate house, and went into exile; another tribune of that year, T. Munatius Plancus Byrsa, was also successfully prosecuted for the same offence by Cicero (*MRR* II.236; Alexander *Trials* nos 327–28). This law specifically mentioned the murder on the Appian Way (see also Cic. *Mil.* 15, 70. 79; Asc. 36; App. *BC* 2.23). This M. Caelius Rufus is Cicero's correspondent: cf. doc. 13.12. For Asconius' account, which relies on 'official records' (*acta*), and is to be preferred to Cicero's partisan speech, see Marshall 1985: 159–213.

The murder of Clodius and its aftermath: Cic. *Mil.* 12–13, 61, 67, 70, 91; Dio 40.48.1–49.5; App. *BC* 2.21.75–8; Caes. *BG* 7.1.1; Livy *Per.* 107; Wiseman 1994a: 407–8; Tatum 1999: 239–42; Seager 2002: 133–4; Southern 2002: 114–15.

30 Titus Annius Milo, Publius Plautius Hypsaeus, and Quintus Metellus Scipio were candidates for the consulship, supporting their candidature not only by lavish and open bribery, but also by gangs of armed men. There was a bitter feud between Milo and Clodius, because Milo was a close friend of Cicero's and as tribune had worked strenuously to have Cicero recalled, while Publius Clodius still remained violently hostile to him after his recall, and therefore enthusiastically supported Hypsaeus and Scipio against Milo. Milo and Clodius frequently came to blows with each other in Rome, at the head of their own gangs: they were both equal in recklessness, but Milo was on the side of the optimates. Moreover, while Milo was standing for the consulship, Clodius was a candidate, in the same year, for the praetorship, which he realised would be crippled with Milo as consul. The consular elections had been long delayed and could not be completed because of these **31** desperate squabbles between the candidates, and for this reason in January there were still no consuls or praetors, and the election-day was being put off by the same means as before; Milo in fact wanted the elections to be completed as soon as possible and was confident both of the support of the 'honest' men, since he was opposing Clodius, and of the people because of the largesse he had widely distributed and his immense expenditure on theatrical performances and gladiatorial shows, on which Cicero informs us he spent three patrimonies, while his opponents preferred to postpone them, and so Pompey, Scipio's son-in-law, and the tribune Titus Munatius, had not allowed a proposal to be put to the senate for an assembly of patricians to choose an interrex, the traditional procedure in such a situation being to appoint an interrex. On 18 January (for I consider it best to follow the official records and this very speech which agrees with the official records, rather than Fenestella who gives the date of 19 January) Milo set out for Lanuvium, his home town where he was dictator, to appoint a flamen on the following day. At about the ninth hour, he was encountered by Clodius, a little past Bovillae, the spot being close to a shrine of the Bona Dea; Clodius was returning from Aricia, where he had been addressing the town officials. Clodius was riding on horseback; he was accompanied by some 30 slaves, the usual practice when making a journey at that time, who were lightly equipped and armed with swords. Moreover Clodius had three friends with him, of whom one was a Roman eques called Gaius Causinius Schola, and two well-known plebeians, Publius Pomponius and Gaius Clodius. Milo was travelling in a carriage, with his wife Fausta, daughter of the dictator Lucius Sulla, and a relation called Marcus Fufius. Accompanying them **32** was a large band of slaves, including some gladiators, amongst whom were the two well-known figures Eudamus and Birria. They were at the far end of the column, moving more slowly, and began a brawl with the slaves of Publius Clodius. When Clodius looked back threateningly at this uproar, Birria threw a spear through his shoulder. With the fight in progress, more of Milo's men hurried up. The wounded Clodius was conveyed into a near-by tavern in Bovillae.

When Milo heard that Clodius had been wounded, he decided that it would be more dangerous for himself to leave him alive, while his death would be a great relief, even if he had to undergo a penalty, and ordered him to be turned out of the tavern. The leader of Milo's slaves was Marcus Saufeius. Clodius, who was hiding, was then dragged out and finished off with a number of wounds. His body was left in the road, because Clodius' slaves were either dead or in hiding with serious injuries . . . To Clodius' house hurried the tribunes Titus Munatius Plancus, brother of the orator Lucius Plancus, and Quintus Pompeius Rufus, grandson of the dictator Sulla through his daughter. 33 At their urging, the ignorant mob carried the body to the forum, naked and trampled, on the couch as it had been laid, so that the wounds could be seen, and placed it on the rostra. There Plancus and Pompeius, who supported Milo's opponents, held a public meeting and whipped up hostility to Milo. Under the leadership of the clerk Sextus Cloelius the people carried the body of Publius Clodius into the senate-house and cremated it there, using benches, tribunals, tables and secretaries' notebooks; the senate-house itself caught fire and the Basilica Porcia next door to it was also damaged. The crowd of Clodius' supporters also attacked the house of Marcus Lepidus, the interrex (for he had been appointed to this office) and that of Milo, who was absent, but was driven back with arrows. Then they seized the axes from the grove of Libitina and carried them to Scipio's house and Hypsaeus' and finally to Pompey's gardens, calling on him now as consul, now as dictator.

The conflagration of the senate-house gave rise to a good deal more anger among citizens than the murder of Clodius. And so Milo, who was thought to have gone into voluntary exile, reassured by his opponents' unpopularity, returned to Rome on the night of the burning of the senate-house. Undeterred, he still campaigned for the consulship; he even openly gave each man 1,000 asses according to tribe. Some days later the tribune Marcus Caelius held a public meeting on his behalf and Cicero himself pleaded his case to the people. Both stated that Milo had been ambushed by Clodius.

In the meantime, one interrex after another was appointed, because consular elections could not be held 34 on account of the disturbances caused by the candidates and the same armed bands. So, as a first step, a senatorial decree was passed that the interrex, tribunes and Gnaeus Pompey, who was proconsul and near the city, should see to it that the state suffered no harm, and that Pompey should hold a levy throughout Italy . . . 35 During all this, as the feeling was increasing that Gnaeus Pompey should be appointed dictator as the only way to solve the state's problems, 36 it seemed safer to the optimates that he should be created consul without a colleague, and, when the matter had been debated in the senate, in a senatorial decree on the motion of Marcus Bibulus, Pompey was appointed consul by the interrex Servius Sulpicius on the 24th of the intercalary month and took up office immediately. Three days later he moved new laws, two promulgated by senatorial decree, one on violence, which specifically mentioned the murder on the Appian Way, the burning of the senate-house and the attack on the house of the interrex Marcus Lepidus, and the other on bribery, in which the penalties were intensified and the court procedure made shorter.

POMPEY AS SOLE CONSUL, 52 BC

Asconius notes that there were calls for Pompey to be made dictator after Clodius' murder. A military levy was held throughout Italy. The level of violence and corruption in 53 and 52 BC had become unacceptable, even by Roman standards. With the calls for Pompey to be made dictator growing, Cato and his supporters felt that it would be better if Pompey had a more regular office, and Bibulus therefore proposed that he be made sole consul. It is this appointment of Pompey as sole consul, at the proposal and support of the optimates, which marks the change in the relationship between Pompey and Caesar which up to now, despite some retrospective comments by the sources, had been amicable. That the proposal came from Bibulus, Caesar's thwarted consular colleague of 59, is not without significance. Unfortunately there are few letters of Cicero from 52. Pompey's third consulship and his legislation: Plut. *Cato Min.* 47.3–48, *Pomp.* 54.5–55; Dio 40.50–8; App. *BC* 2.23–5; Taylor 1949: 148–52; *MRR* II.233–4; Leach 1978: 150–60; Greenhalgh 1981: 81–93; Scullard *GN* 120; Wiseman 1994a: 410, 413; Gruen 1995: 153–5, 233–9, 337–50; Seager 2002: 133–40; Southern 2002: 115–17; for Bibulus as princeps senatus, see Ryan 1996.

13.2 Cicero blames Clodius for his encounter with Milo

Cicero *In Defence of Milo* 27

Meanwhile, as Clodius was aware — nor was it difficult to be aware of it — that Milo, as chief magistrate (dictator) at Lanuvium, had, under the obligation of sacred and civil law, to take a journey to Lanuvium to proclaim the appointment of a flamen, he suddenly left Rome the day before so he might, as was clear from the event, lay an ambush for Milo in front of his estate.

13.3 The optimates turn to Pompey

Dio *Roman History* 40.50.3–5

Cicero had desired to detach Pompey from Caesar: his attempt to do this in 56 had helped lead to the conference at Luca and his own compromised support of the triumvirate. Pompey, as Plutarch, Dio and Appian attest, was invited by the senate to become sole consul and was increasingly reconciled with the optimates. He now emerges as the supporter of law and order, and so sided with the boni. However, his attempts to influence the trials of his father-in-law, Metellus Scipio (who became his consular colleague in July 52: Plut. *Pomp.* 55.7–8, cf. *Cato Min.* 48.7–8; App. *BC* 2.24.93–4; Dio 40.51.3, 53.1–2; *MRR* II.234; Seager 2002: 137), and of the tribune T. Munatius Plancus Byrsa, attempts criticised by Cato, show that he was not in any sense a tool of the senate. Cato also made it clear that he did not want Pompey's gratitude for his support of the grant of the third consulship: his support was not for Pompey as such but for the state (Plut. *Pomp.* 54.7–9; cf. doc. 13.5; Gruen 1995: 153–4). But Pompey's good relationship with the senate was established and would develop.

3 The city was in a state of suspense over who were to be its magistrates, with some people saying that Pompey should be elected dictator, others that Caesar should be consul . . . **4** As they were afraid of both men, the rest of the senate, as well as Bibulus who was the first to be asked for his opinion, anticipated the populace's enthusiasm by giving Pompey the consulship, so he would not be named dictator, and as sole consul, so that Caesar might not be his colleague. **5** This novel action was without precedent, yet they appeared to have made the right decision; as Pompey was less supportive of the populace than Caesar, they hoped to detach him from them completely and make him one of their own. And this worked out: elated at this new and unexpected honour, he no longer made any plans to please the people, but tried to carry out in every respect the wishes of the senate.

13.4 Bibulus and Cato support Pompey

Plutarch *Life of Pompey* 54.5–8

5 When, later on, Rome was again without consuls and more people now brought up more vigorously the question of a dictatorship, Cato and his party were afraid that they would be forced to give way and so decided to let Pompey have some sort of legal magistracy to prevent his holding the absolute authority of a dictatorship. **6** In fact Bibulus, Pompey's enemy, was the first to propose in the senate that Pompey should be elected sole consul, arguing that in this way Rome would either be saved from its current chaos or at least be enslaved to its best citizen. **7** The proposal appeared incredible, bearing in mind its advocate, and Cato got up, giving rise to the belief that he would oppose it, but, when everyone fell silent, declared that he would not personally have proposed the measure, but that as it had been proposed by someone else he recommended that they adopt it, as he preferred any government to no government, and thought that Pompey would govern better than anyone else in times of such chaos. **8** The senate accepted the measure and decreed that Pompey, if elected consul, should govern without a colleague, but that if he himself should want a colleague, he could choose whomever he thought suitable at the end of two months of office.

13.5 Milo's conviction

Dio *Roman History* 40.54.1–2

Pompey as sole consul introduced various measures. Asconius (doc. 13.1) notes two of these: one law on violence and another on electoral bribery. Milo was charged with murder and other offences on 26 March 52 BC and was tried on 4–7 April. Pompey had previously indicated that he would not support Milo: he had spoken before the people the day after Clodius' body was brought to Rome, and had attacked Milo; three tribunes asked Pompey if he knew that Milo had been plotting to kill Clodius, and Pompey had answered in the affirmative. Pompey then refused to grant Milo an interview on 22 January. Pompey stayed at home thereafter, heavily guarded, and on one occasion dismissed a senate meeting, fearing Milo's arrival (Asc. 36).

Milo was defended at his trial under the *lex Pompeia de vi* by Cicero and M. Claudius Marcellus (cos. 51); the prosecution was carried out by Mark Antony and Appius Claudius Pulcher; Clodius' wife Fulvia was amongst those called as witnesses: she had done her part to inflame the crowd when Clodius' body had been brought into the forum and won the sympathy of the crowd in court. Milo was condemned to exile for the murder. Under Pompey's second law, the *lex Pompeia de ambitu* (for electoral bribery), Milo was tried and convicted for offences in the consular campaign for 52. He was tried and convicted for this again under the *lex Licinia de sodaliciis* and also again tried and convicted (this time in absentia) for Clodius' murder under the *lex Plautia de vi*.

The *lex Pompeia de ambitu* was a retrospective piece of legislation, covering events back to Pompey's first consulship, i.e., 70 BC. This led Caesar's supporters, according to Appian, to be suspicious that Caesar was being targeted (*BC* 2.23.87–8). Laws about vis (violence) and ambitus existed already (Milo was prosecuted under both the existing and new Pompeian laws), but Pompey's laws provided for quicker procedures and harsher penalties (exile for both crimes).

Pompey had soldiers posted in the forum and the outcome of the trial was not in doubt. The presence of the soldiers affected Cicero's delivery and his defence of Milo was poor. Cicero sent Milo in exile at Massilia (Marseilles) the polished oration which he had not delivered: Milo sarcastically commented that if Cicero had in fact delivered this speech he, Milo, would never have tasted the delights of the sea-food at Massilia.

Others were also prosecuted. Scipio's case was aborted, but others were not so lucky. Pompey, breaking his own recent law, attempted but was foiled by Cato, who was one of the jurors, to deliver in court an encomium in 51 on Plancus (Plut. *Cato Min.* 48.9–10). The tribune is mentioned in Asconius (doc. 13.1) as active in the disturbances after Clodius' murder, including the burning of the senate house, after which he was successfully prosecuted by Cicero under Pompey's law against violence (*MRR* II.235; Alexander *Trials* no. 327).

Hypsaeus (who had been acquitted in 54 of causing disruptions in the elections for aedile for 54), the second of the two consular candidates supported by Pompey in 53 (the first being Metellus Scipio) was now abandoned by Pompey despite Hypsaeus' personal appeal and was condemned (Plut. *Pomp.* 55.10–11).

Other trials under the *lex Pompeia de vi* resulted in the acquittal of M. Saufeius (who organised Milo's slaves) for involvement in the murder of Clodius, but Sextus Cloelius was convicted for bringing Clodius' body into the curia (Alexander *Trials* nos 313–15). Messalla Rufus, cos. 53, was acquitted in a case under the *lex Pompeia de ambitu* by three votes, one from each of the voting orders, for his conduct during the consular campaign for 53 (*Trials* 329).

Milo's trials: Cic. *Mil.*; Asc. 30–56; Livy *Per.* 107; Plut. *Cic.* 35; App. *BC* 2.22, 24; Dio 40.54; Alexander *Trials* no. 309–12 (with references to the sources); Huzar 1978: 37–8; Ruebel 1979; Lintott 1974: 73–5; Gruen 1995: 337–44; Seager 2002: 134–6; Cicero's involvement: Smith 1966: 197; Rawson 1975: 137–9; Lacey 1978: 89–90; Mitchell 1991: 200–1.

1 The courts met peacefully as a result of these measures and many were convicted on a variety of charges, including Milo amongst others for the murder of Clodius, even though he had Cicero speaking for the defence. **2** For when the orator saw the unprecedented sight of Pompey and the soldiers in the court he was so panic-stricken and overwhelmed with fear that he said nothing of the speech he had prepared, but merely with difficulty uttered a few words that died away and gladly retired. The speech now extant, which purports to have been delivered on Milo's behalf at the time, was written later at leisure, when he had recovered his confidence.

13.6 Scipio as Pompey's fellow-consul

Appian *Civil Wars* 2.24–5 (92, 95)

Appian (doc. 13.7) has those exiled from convictions under Pompey's laws about violence and ambitus going to Caesar. Scipio as consul: *MRR* II.234–5.

92 All those condemned were exiled and Gabinius was fined in addition to being exiled. The senate praised these proceedings loudly, voted Pompey two more legions, and extended the term of his provincial government . . . **95** Pompey, as if he had corrected all the problems which had necessitated one-man rule, made Scipio his consular colleague for the rest of the year. But even after this, when others had been appointed to the office, Pompey none the less remained the overseer and ruler and main power in Rome; for he possessed the senate's goodwill, particularly due to their jealousy of Caesar, who had not consulted them at all during his consulship, and because Pompey had swiftly helped the state recover from its illness and not annoyed or offended any of them during his magistracy.

13.7 Caesar plans a second consulship

Appian *Civil Wars* 2.25 (96–7)

The tribunes for 52 BC had planned to make Caesar Pompey's consular colleague in 52 BC, but Caesar preferred that he be allowed to stand in absentia for a later consulship: all ten tribunes passed a law allowing him to do so. Pompey supported the law, but soon after had a law passed that candidates for office had to announce their candidature in person in Rome. Caesar's friends at Rome were angry at this development. Pompey, however, after his own law had been inscribed in bronze and deposited in the treasury, exempted Caesar from it. Scholars assume that Pompey surely was not guilty simply of an oversight here (Seager 2002: 139, 234). It is possible, however, that Pompey had seen the tribunician law as qualifying his own later one and that no attack on Caesar was meant (Gruen 1995: 456–7). Cicero stresses that the tribunician law did have Pompey's support, as Appian also notes. Caesar would be eligible to stand for a consulship for 48, and hence needed his command to run to the end of 49, to stand in absentia for the consular elections in summer 49, and step immediately into a consulship without any intervening period as a private citizen.

For himself, Pompey took another five-year command in Spain, governing it through legates. In addition, in the previous year the senate had resolved that there should be a five-year gap between holding an office and taking up a provincial command and Pompey now had this made into law (*lex Pompeia de provinciis*). Until five years had elapsed and magistrates currently in office could take up these governorships, governors were to be chosen by lot from consulars and praetorians who had not previously held a province. Under this law Cicero was chosen by lot as governor (proconsul) of Cilicia, and left Rome in May 51 to take up his post (Mitchell 1991: 205 for references); see Cic. *Att.* 7.1.4, 7.3.4, 7.6.2, *Fam.* 6.6.5, 16.12.3; Suet. *Jul.* 26.1, 28.2; App. *BC* 2.25; Dio 40.51.2, 56; Plut. *Pomp.* 56.1–2; Caes. *BC* 1.32.3; *MRR* II.234, 236.

96 Those who were exiled went to Caesar in droves, warning him to watch out for Pompey, as Pompey's law on bribery was aimed at him in particular, but Caesar encouraged them and spoke favourably of Pompey, and persuaded the tribunes to introduce a law to allow him to stand for the consulship a second time in his absence. Pompey was still consul when this was ratified and made no objection to it. **97** As Caesar suspected that the senate would oppose this and was afraid that he might become a private citizen and vulnerable to his enemies, he worked towards keeping his power until elected consul, and requested the senate to allow him a little more time in his current governorship of Gaul or of part of it. When Marcellus (cos. 51), who succeeded Pompey as consul, prevented this, Caesar is recorded as replying to the person who informed him, with his hand on his sword-hilt, 'This shall give it to me.'

CIVIL WAR

M. Claudius Marcellus and Servius Sulpicius Rufus were elected consuls for 51 BC. (M. Claudius Marcellus was consul in 51, another Marcellus, C. Claudius Marcellus (his first cousin) was consul for 50 BC, and another Marcellus, also a C. Claudius Marcellus (brother of Marcus), for 49: all three were opposed to Caesar.)

It is unclear when Caesar's command in Gaul was due to expire but early in 51 BC M. Claudius Marcellus began moves against Caesar. He proposed that a successor to Caesar be appointed before Caesar's tenure as proconsul of Gaul had expired, arguing that the war in Gaul was over, and that Caesar not be allowed to stand in absentia for the consulship. Marcellus also argued that Pompey's additional clause exempting Caesar from the decree requiring candidates for the consulship to be present was not valid as it had been added by Pompey and was not part of the decree itself. Caesar used the tribunes to veto Marcellus' proposals; the other consul, Ser. Sulpicius Rufus, also acted in Caesar's interests to resist Marcellus (Hirtius [Caes.] *BG* 8.50; Suet. *Jul.* 28.2–3; Dio 40.59; cf. *Fam.* 4.1.1, 4.2.2, 4.3.1 (letters to Ser. Sulpicius Rufus, cos. 51), 8.1.2, 8.2.2, 8.5.3). Marcellus showed his personal hostility to Caesar by having one of the citizens of Novum Comum scourged (docs 13.8–9).

Pompey did not support Marcellus, in particular opposing his plan to terminate Caesar's command. At a senate meeting in the temple of Apollo on 22 July 51, the issue of pay for Pompey's troops was discussed, and a question came up about the legion which he had lent Caesar at the beginning of 53 (Pompey had lent a legion to Caesar to compensate for the disaster suffered by Caesar's two generals, Titurius and Cotta: App. *BC* 2.29.115: doc. 13.23). Pompey was compelled to say that he would withdraw this legion but would not, despite pressure, say when. The question of Caesar's command also came up at this meeting, and it was decided to hold a debate later, on 13 August, which was postponed until 1 September; legion: [Cic.] *Fam.* 8.4.4 (doc. 13.10); Caes. *BG* 6.1.2; App. *BC* 2.26.100; Plut. *Pomp.* 52.4; Dio 40.65.1. Cato as a consular candidate for 51 had promised to have Caesar recalled from Gaul and prosecuted, but he was not elected.

On 1 September 51 Pompey in the senate argued that no decree could be passed about the Gallic provinces, but Metellus Scipio (Pompey's father-in-law) proposed the motion that the Gallic provinces should be discussed (before any other item of business) in the senate on 1 March 50 BC (Cael. in [Cic.] *Fam.* 8.9.5). Later, on 29 September 51, Pompey indicated that a debate about the consular provinces could take place in March 50 (docs 13.12, 13.35; see also Plut. *Caes.* 29; App. *BC* 2.26.99).

These attempts to have Caesar recalled were the first steps to civil war; the main sources for the lead-up to war: App. *BC* 2.25–31; Plut. *Pomp.* 56–9, *Caes.* 28–30; Dio 40.59–66; [Cic.] *Fam.* 8.8 (senatorial decrees at 8.8.5–8). At *Att.* 7.3.4, 7.6.2, Cicero argues for giving in to Caesar's demands and for peace at any price; see too *Fam.* 16.12.3 (doc. 13.30) for Caesar's terms. Events of 51: Syme 1939: 40; Wiseman 1994a: 415; Gruen 1995: 460–3; Meier 1995: 351–2; Seager 2002: 140–3.

13.8 Marcellus has a Transpadane Gaul flogged

Cicero *Letters to Atticus* 5.11.2 (6 July 51)

'Our friend' here is Pompey: he was patron of the Transpadani. The colony had been founded under legislation authored by Vatinius as tribune in 59 BC (*MRR* II.190). Marcellus was showing his opposition to Caesar's activities during his consulship of 59.

Marcellus behaved with cruelty over the man from Comum. Even though he may not have held a magistracy, he was still a Transpadane; so I imagine Marcellus has irritated our friend no less than Caesar. But that's his business.

13.9 Growing senatorial hostility to Caesar, 51 BC

Appian *Civil Wars* 2.26 (98–100)

Novum Comum: doc. 13.8; Cic. *Att.* 5.2.3; Plut. *Caes.* 29.2. Marcellus refused to accept as legal Caesar's grant by a lex Vatinia in 59 of Latin rights to Comum.

98 Caesar founded the town of Novum Comum at the foot of the Alps and granted it Latin rights, one of which was that whoever held the magistracies each year should become Roman citizens; for this is a condition of Latin status. Marcellus (cos. 51) had one of the men of Novum Comum, who had been a magistrate and who was accordingly considered a Roman, beaten with rods for some reason, in defiance of Caesar, something which does not happen to Romans. Marcellus in his anger revealed his true purpose that the blows should be the mark of the alien — he instructed the man to carry them to Caesar and show them to him. **99** As well as insulting Caesar in this manner, he also proposed to send successors to take over his provinces, before the appointed time; but Pompey prevented this with a specious pretence of good will, saying that they should not insult a distinguished man who had been so very useful to his country in a dispute over a short period of time, while he made it clear that Caesar's command must be terminated immediately it expired. **100** For this reason Caesar's greatest enemies were elected consuls for the following year (50 BC), Aemilius Paullus and Claudius Marcellus, cousin of the Marcellus already mentioned, while Curio was made tribune, who was Caesar's bitter enemy and very popular with the people and a very skilled speaker. Of these Caesar was unable to win over Claudius by money, but bought Paullus' neutrality for 1,500 talents, and the cooperation of Curio with an even larger sum, as he knew he was encumbered by numerous debts.

13.10 Pressure is put on Pompey

Caelius in [Cicero] *Letters to Friends* 8.4.4

Cf. doc. 13.12. Written by M. Caelius Rufus to Cicero in Cilicia on 1 August 51. Caelius, tr. pl. 52 and aedile in 50, kept up a regular correspondence with Cicero while the latter was in Cilicia and these letters provide an invaluable source for the events of 51 and 50; Cicero's letters to Curio: *Fam.* 2.1–6 (53 BC), 2.7 (December 51). The temple of Apollo was outside the pomerium in the Campus Martius and therefore Pompey, who was invested with imperium, could be present at the meeting. The consuls-elect for 50 were L. Aemilius Lepidus Paullus and C. Claudius Marcellus.

In politics we had ceased to expect anything new; but when the senate met in the temple of Apollo on 22 July (51 BC) and the question was put about pay for Pompey's troops, the matter of the legion which Pompey had lent to Caesar was brought up, whom it belonged to and how long Pompey would let it stay in Gaul. Pompey was compelled to state that he would remove the legion, but not straightaway in response to the remarks and outcry from his detractors. Then there was a question put about the replacement of Gaius Caesar, regarding which (that is, on the question of the provinces) it was agreed that Pompey should return to the city as quickly as possible so that a debate on the replacement of governors could be held with him present — Pompey was on the point of going to his army at Ariminum and left at once. I think the debate will take place on the Ides [13th] of August. Either a decision will be reached or it will be disgracefully vetoed — for during the discussion Pompey made the comment that everyone ought to pay attention to the senate's dictates. I, however, am looking forward to nothing so much as Paullus, as consul-elect, being the first to give his views on the issue.

13.11 Marcellus tries to end Caesar's command prematurely

[Caesar] *Gallic War* 8.53.1–2

The law of Pompey and Crassus was the lex Licinia Pompeia in 55 BC, extending Caesar's command for another five years in Gaul.

1 In the previous year (51 BC), in an attack on Caesar's position, Marcellus, contrary to a law of Pompey and Crassus, had brought prematurely before the senate a motion on Caesar's provinces. Opinions were voiced, and when Marcellus, who wanted any position for himself which could be gained from the ill-will felt towards Caesar, called for a division, the crowded senate crossed over in support of the 'No' side. **2** This did not alter the resolution of Caesar's enemies, but incited them to come up with more compelling reasons, which could be used to force the senate to approve what they themselves had resolved.

13.12 Pompey's views on the termination of Caesar's command

Caelius in [Cicero] *Letters to Friends* 8.8.4–5, 9

In this letter from M. Caelius Rufus to Cicero in early October 51 BC, Caelius gives an account of the senatorial proceedings of 29 September 51, in the temple of Apollo, and quotes decrees of the senate (8.8.5–8). Marcellus addressed the senate on the issue of the consular provinces, and the senate resolved, with Pompey's agreement, that the consuls elected for 50 (Paullus and C. Marcellus) would on 1 March in their year of office (50) bring the matter before the senate and after doing so were to bring no other matter to the senate until this issue was resolved. Another decree of the same day, that no one with the power of veto prevent the discussion about the provinces taking place on that day, was vetoed by four tribunes (but the resolution itself about the provinces was not); a decree concerning the discharge of individual soldiers from Caesar's army was also vetoed by two of these four tribunes, including C. Vibius Pansa (who would be cos. 43). As noted, Pompey in September 51 made it clear that on the Kalends of March 50, the matter of Caesar's command should be discussed. Caelius wrote to Cicero on 2 September 51 that Pompey was openly against Caesar being elected consul while retaining his province and army (*Fam.* 8.9.5). This letter with its reference to 'having trouble with Caesar' is the first real indication of a rift between Pompey and Caesar.

4 Finally, after frequent postponements and much serious discussion, it became clear that Gnaeus Pompey wanted him (Caesar) to leave his command after the Kalends of March. The senate approved and I send you a copy of the decree and recorded resolutions. **5** 'On this day, 29 September, in the temple of Apollo, . . . In as much as M. Marcellus, consul, did address the senate on the matter of the consular provinces, it was resolved: that L. Paullus and C. Marcellus, consuls, on entering their office, should on or after the Kalends of March in their year of office (50 BC) refer the question of the consular provinces to the senate, and that from the Kalends of March they should bring no business before the senate, either previously or in conjunction; moreover for the same purpose they might hold a meeting of the senate on comitial (assembly) days and pass decrees . . . '

9 Furthermore the confidence of the public has been greatly enhanced by some comments made by Gnaeus Pompey, in which he remarked that before the Kalends of March he could not justly make any decision about Caesar's provinces, but after the Kalends of March he would have no hesitation. When he was asked what would happen if any vetoes were interposed at that stage, he said that it was of no importance whether Gaius Caesar was not going to follow the senate's decree or if he was getting someone ready to prevent the senate from passing a decree. 'And what,' asked someone else, 'if he wants to be consul and keep his army?' Pompey replied mildly: 'What if my son wants to take his stick to me?' As a consequence of these remarks people think that Pompey is having trouble with Caesar.

13.13 Parthian problems

Caelius in [Cicero] *Letters to Friends* 8.10.2–3 (17 November 51)

Crassus' defeat in Parthia had been salvaged to an extent by his quaestor Cassius (C. Cassius Longinus, one of the conspirators on the Ides of March, 44 BC), who had regrouped the survivors in Syria. In September 51 the Parthians crossed the Euphrates towards Roman Syria, and Caelius in November wrote that Pompey, Caesar or the consuls were possible choices to deal with the problem (Cic. *Fam.* 8.10.2). Pompey saw himself as the natural choice (*Att.* 6.1.14; cf. Hillman 1996), but for the moment Cassius, then Cicero and Bibulus as governors in 51–50 of Cilicia and Syria respectively, dealt with the situation (Cic. *Att.* 5.21.2, *Fam.* 2.10.2; Dio 40.28–9; *MRR* II.242–3, 250–1). The two legions raised from Pompey and Caesar's troops to fight the Parthians were not dispatched, but in late 50 were incorporated into Pompey's forces for the war against Caesar.

2 The reports about the Parthian crossing have given rise to a lot of talk. One view is that Pompey should be sent, another that Pompey ought not to be taken away from Rome, another that Caesar should go with his army, another the consuls, but no one wants *privati* sent by senatorial decree. Moreover the consuls, who are afraid that the senate may not approve their military appointment and that the job might go shamefully over their heads to someone else, are unwilling to have senate meetings at all, to the point where they appear to be neglecting government. But whether due to negligence or inertia or the fear I suggested, it is respectably obscured under the belief that they are men of moderation who have no wish for a province . . . **3** It's now the end of the year — I am writing this letter on 17 November. I can clearly see that nothing can be done before the Kalends of January. You know (M. Claudius) Marcellus, how slow and ineffectual he is, and Servius (Sulpicius Rufus) too, a real procrastinator. What do you think of their behaviour, what do you see as their ability to get something done which they are not interested in, when they are dealing so feebly with something they do want as to make it look as if they are not interested? When the new magistrates come in, if there is going to be a Parthian war, that issue will take up the first months, but if there's not going to be a war there, or if it's small enough for you two (Cicero and Bibulus) or your successors to cope with with a few reinforcements, I can see Curio being active in two directions, first taking something away from Caesar, then giving something to Pompey, any little gift, however trifling. Paullus, too, is talking unjustifiably about a province. Our friend Furnius (tr. pl. 50) is ready to put up resistance to his greed.

THE EVENTS OF 50 BC

One of the tribunes elected in 51 for 50, Servaeus, was convicted of electoral bribery under the *lex Pompeia de ambitu* and C. Scribonius Curio was elected in his place (*MRR* II.249; Alexander *Trials* no. 332). The hope was expressed that Curio, opposed to the triumvirate in 59 (docs 12.49–50), would support the boni and the senate as tribune in 50, and he was viewed as a friend of the optimates (Caelius in [Cic.] *Fam.* 8.4.2, 8.8.10, 8.10.3; cf. [Cic.] *Fam.* 8.5.2–3). Curio was popular with the plebs due to his magnificent games and had married Fulvia, Clodius' widow (references at *CAH* IX[1] 418 n.191); for Curio's games: Pliny *Nat. Hist.* 36.116–20; cf. Cic. *Fam.* 2.3; Dio 40.60.2; App. *BC* 2.26.

In 50 Curio advocated a legislative programme, which included a measure on the Campanian land, apparently involving buying up land from existing occupants (Caelius in [Cic.] *Fam.* 8.10.4). He had been massively in debt, but was relieved of his financial embarrassments by Caesar and served his interests, though at first he concealed his change of alliance, moving formally over to Caesar in February 50 when his own request for a month to be intercalated was refused: Plut. *Pomp.* 58.2, *Caes.* 29.3, *Ant.* 5.2; App. *BC* 2.26.101; Dio 40.60.2; *MRR* II.249.

The consuls elected for 50 BC were one of M. Marcellus' cousins, C. Claudius Marcellus, and L. Aemilius Lepidus Paullus (*MRR* II.247). Already in 51 Caelius seems to reflect rumours that Paullus as consul-elect had been bribed by Caesar (*Fam.* 8.4.4: doc. 13.10). Paullus was the son of the M. Lepidus, cos. 78, who had led a revolt, and in 50 Paullus did support Caesar, who had helped him financially to complete his rebuilding of the Basilica Aemilia in the forum at the cost of 1,500 talents (9 million denarii: *Att.* 4.16.8; Plut. *Caes.* 29.3, *Pomp.* 58.2; App. *BC* 2.26.101; *MRR* II.247). Vettius in 59 BC had implicated Paullus in the plot to assassinate Pompey (doc. 12.51).

The debate about consular provinces was due to take place on 1 March 50, but the matter was apparently postponed, and Paullus clearly played a key role in whatever happened, being presiding consul (Caelius in [Cic.] *Fam.* 8.11.1). The motion is next heard of being put when Marcellus was presiding consul in April; Paullus stayed silent, indicating his opposition (App. *BC* 2.27). Caelius in a letter of April notes that Pompey had now decided, along with the senate, that Caesar was to step down from his command on or before 13 November (the Ides of November) 50: [Cic.] *Fam.* 8.11.3: doc. 13.16.

Censors were elected for 50 BC: Appius Claudius Pulcher (cos. 54), Clodius' brother, returning from his proconsulship in Cilicia (Cicero was his successor) and L. Calpurnius Piso Caesoninus (cos. 58). Despite his own extortion in his province, Appius expelled senators for possession of art collections, even attempting to expel Curio. The expelled senators went to Caesar. Appius and his harrying of art collectors: Caelius in [Cic.] *Fam.* 8.14.4, 8.12.1–3, 8.17.1; Plut. *Pomp.* 58; Dio 40.63–4; cf. Cic. *Att.* 6.9.5; *MRR* II.247–8.

13.14 Curio changes sides

Caelius in [Cicero] *Letters to Friends* 8.6.3–5 (February 50 BC)

Cicero in his province had heard of disturbances in Curio's tribunate: 'tumultuosae contiones' (Cic. *Fam.* 2.12.1, June 50). On Curio's road bill: App. *BC* 2.27 (he planned to be superintendent for 5 years — Appian sees this bill and the expected optimate opposition to it as a deliberate move to excuse his change of allegiance from Pompey). In 50 Caelius was curule aedile: *MRR* II.248. For the panthers, see doc. 2.72.

3 We have really industrious consuls! — up till now they'd not managed to get a single decree through the senate except about the (date of the) Latin Festival. **4** Our friend Curio's tribunate is a total frost. I just can't tell you how dormant everything is here. If it weren't for my battle (as aedile) with shopkeepers and water-pipe inspectors, the whole city would be fast asleep . . . **5** Regarding my remark above about Curio's frozen inactivity, he's now warmed up — and being enthusiastically torn to pieces! Most irresponsibly, because he didn't get his own way about intercalation, he's gone over to the populace and begun talking in support of Caesar. He's declared a road bill, rather like Rullus' agrarian bill, and a food bill, which instructs the aediles to make distributions. He'd not started any of this when I wrote the first part of my letter . . . You'll be in disgrace if I don't have any Greek panthers.

13.15 Joint disarmament

Appian *Civil Wars* 2.27 (103–5)

Modern scholars disagree on the exact date when Caesar's second term as governor of Gaul was due to expire, and whether the dates set for the discussion of termination of his command (1 March 50) and later for the actual termination of his command (13 November 50) were reasonable: Pompey thought the 13 November date 'fair' and accused Curio of simply making trouble (doc. 13.16). (This scholarly issue is known as the *Rechtsfrage*, the 'legal question' of when Caesar was to lay down his governorship.) Caesar (doc. 13.27) states that the *SCU* of 7 January 49 deprived him of six months of his command (i.e., it was due to expire in mid-49). However, Pompey's insistence in 51 that Caesar's command not be debated until 1 March 50, could be taken to indicate in fact that Caesar's five year command as arranged by Crassus and Pompey in their consulship (55 BC) under the *lex Pompeia Licinia*, as an extension of the five-year command awarded in 59, was due in fact to expire on or soon after that March date in 50, five years later (as argued by Stockton 1975; Meier 1995: 327–8; cf. Jameson 1970a: 1 March 49 BC). On the other hand, Pompey later insisted that 13 November 50 BC be the absolute terminal point for Caesar's command. This date might not be of any significance in itself for when Caesar assumed command, but could simply have been in the nature of a 'deadline'.

Caesar in fact had in early 51 unsuccessfully asked for an extension of his command from the senate until he should be elected to the consulship (Plut. *Caes.* 29.1, *Pomp.* 58.3: doc. 13.22; App. *BC* 2.25.97), clearly aiming to bridge any gap between the end of his governorship and taking up a consulship in 48, the first year he could hold a second consulship, as he himself notes (doc. 13.42). Pompey was anxious, however, that there *should* be such a gap (docs 13.16, 13.18).

If Caesar planned to stand in summer 49 for the consulship of 48, there would therefore be ample time for him to be prosecuted for his activities as consul in 59 BC if he stood down on 13 November 50. In this case, Caesar would need to rely on Pompey in any confrontation with Cato and other optimates, or face prosecution and its serious consequences for his career.

Curio proposed early in the year that both Caesar and Pompey lay down their arms. On 1 December 50 Curio again proposed, this time successfully, that *both* Pompey and Caesar lay down their arms: it produced a dramatic vote in favour of peace (doc. 13.23).

103 Matters turned out as Curio had anticipated, and he had an excuse for taking an opposing line. Claudius proposed the sending of successors to Caesar to take over his provinces, for his term was coming to an end. Paullus kept silent. **104** Curio, who was believed to disagree with both, supported Claudius' motion but added that Pompey ought to lay down his provinces and army like Caesar, for in this way Rome's government would be free and without fear on all sides. **105** Many argued with this as unfair, as Pompey's term had not yet ended, at which Curio showed himself more openly and decidedly against sending successors to Caesar, unless the same applied to Pompey — as they were suspicious of each other, he stated, the city could enjoy no definite peace unless they all became private citizens. He said this because he was aware that Pompey would not lay down his command and saw that the people were now angry with Pompey over his prosecutions for bribery.

13.16 Curio opposes Pompey

Caelius in [Cicero] *Letters to Friends* 8.11.3 (April 50 BC)

Caelius here indicates that Pompey expressed his unwillingness in early 50 BC regarding Caesar being elected consul while still in control of Gaul and his army. This highlights Caesar's predicament as, clearly, he did not wish there to be an opportunity for his enemies to prosecute him for the events of 59. Pompey was presumably envisaging that Caesar would stand for the consulship of 48 BC. Another Marcellus was elected for 49, the brother of the Marcellus who had been consul in 51.

As for politics, all dispute is centred on just one issue, that of the provinces. The current state of play is that Pompey appears to be supporting the senate on Caesar having to lay down his command on the Ides of November (50 BC). Curio would put up with any-thing rather than allow that, and has put aside the rest of his programme. Moreover our friends, whom you know well, don't dare to take the matter to outright conflict. This is how the scene for the whole issue is set: Pompey acts as if he is not attacking Caesar but settling the issue so as to be fair to him; he says Curio is deliberately stirring up trouble. Yet he strongly disapproves and clearly is afraid of Caesar becoming consul-elect before he has handed over his army and province. He is getting fairly rough treatment from Curio and the whole of his third consulship is being subjected to criticism. I can tell you this: if they use every means to restrain Curio, Caesar will protect his veto-giver; if, as seems likely, they are too scared, Caesar will stay as long as he likes.

13.17 Pompey's illness encourages him to confront Caesar

Appian *Civil Wars* 2.28 (107–11)

Pompey in his attitude towards Caesar may have been encouraged by the support he received throughout Italy when he fell ill. See also Cic. *Att.* 8.16.1, 9.5.3 (prayers and municipal decrees for Pompey); Vell. 2.28.2; Plut. *Pomp.* 57: at. 57.9, Pompey states, 'In whatever part of Italy I stamp my foot on the ground, armies of infantry and cavalry will spring up'.

107 While sick in Italy, Pompey wrote a disingenuous letter to the senate praising Caesar's achievements and narrating his own from the beginning — that he had not sought his third consulship or the provinces and army which followed, but had been granted them after he had been called on to cure the state. Regarding the powers he had unwillingly accepted, he said, 'I will willingly lay them down for those who wish to take them back and will not wait for the designated date on which they expire.' **108** The disingenuousness of his letter created an impression of sincerity for Pompey and prejudice towards Caesar, as not going to give up his command even at the fixed time.

When he reached the city, Pompey made similar statements to the senators and then promised to lay down his command. **109** As a friend and kinsman of Caesar, he said that Caesar would very gladly do the same, for he had had a lengthy and difficult campaign against very warlike peoples, had added a great deal of territory to his country, and would now come back to his honours, sacrifices and relaxations. He said this so that Caesar would immediately be assigned successors, while he had only made a promise. **110** Curio exposed his deviousness, stating that promises were not enough and that he should immediately lay down his command and Caesar not disarm until Pompey was a privatus. Because of their private enmity, it would not be advantageous either for Caesar or for the Romans that such great power be held by one man, but that each of them should have power against the other, in case either should use violence against Rome. **111** With no further attempt at concealment, he ceaselessly attacked Pompey as aiming at tyranny and stated that, if he did not lay down his command now through his fear of Caesar, he would never do so. He proposed that, if they did not obey, both should be voted public enemies and an army be raised against them, for by doing this he concealed that he had been bought by Caesar.

13.18 Caelius forecasts war

Caelius in [Cicero] *Letters to Friends* 8.14.2–4 (c. 8 August 50)

2 On important political matters, I have often written to you that I cannot see peace lasting another year; and the closer the inevitable conflict approaches, the plainer the danger seems. The question on which the great powers will come into conflict is that Gnaeus Pompey is determined not to allow Gaius Caesar to become consul unless he gives up his army and provinces, while Caesar is sure he cannot be safe if he leaves his army; he has, however, proposed that both should give up their armies. This is what their love-affair and scandalous alliance have come to — not sliding into secret disparagement, but breaking out into war! For my own position, I cannot decide what course to take; I don't doubt the same question is going to trouble you too. I have obligations and friendly relations with the men on one side; on the other side I love the cause, and hate the people . . . **3** In the present conflict I see that Gnaeus Pompey will have on his side the senate and those who sit on juries, while all who live in fear and gloomy expectations for the future will join Caesar; his army is without comparison. At all events, there is still enough time to weigh up their respective forces and choose which side to join . . .

4 To sum up, what do I think will happen? If one or the other does not go to the Parthian war, I see great dissension ahead, to be settled by steel and force. Both are well prepared with resolution and troops. If only it could happen without personal risk, Fortune would be preparing a great and entertaining show for your benefit.

13.19 Cato responds to Cicero's wish for a supplicatio

Cato in [Cicero] *Letters to Friends* 15.5 (late April 50 BC)

In this very characteristic letter — brief, to the point and surely heavily ironic — in reply to one of Cicero's, Cato explains why he voted against the successful motion of mid-April for a *supplicatio* in Cicero's honour for his defeat of brigands on Mount Amanus: *MRR* II.251. Bibulus, hopeless governor of Syria, was Cato's son-in-law and Cato got him a twenty-day supplicatio (*Att.* 7.2.6–7). Caelius discusses the arrangements in the senate for Cicero's supplicatio (Cic. *Fam.* 8.11.1–2) and Caesar had also written congratulating Cicero and commenting gleefully on Cato's attitude (Cic. *Att.* 7.1.7, 7.2.7). For a similar request to C. Marcellus, as consul-elect for 50, see doc. 2.44.

1 That which the public interest and our friendship encourage me to do, I do willingly, that is, rejoice that the courage, integrity and diligence, which it is well known were displayed by you as a civilian in a grave crisis at home, are being put to good use with equal assiduity by you as a soldier. As a result, that which I was able to do according to my own judgement, that is praise by both vote and speech the fact that the province was protected by your integrity and judgement, that the kingdom of Ariobarzanes, and the king himself, were saved, and that the hearts of our allies were brought back to an enthusiastic acceptance of our rule, this I did.

2 As to the supplicatio being decreed, if you, in a matter in which the safety of the state was secured, not in any way by chance but by your own judgement and moderation, would prefer that we should thank the immortal gods rather than give the credit to you, I rejoice at it. But if you think a supplicatio automatically leads to a triumph, and this is the reason you prefer chance to get the praise rather than yourself, I should say that a triumph does not always follow a supplicatio, and that it is far more glorious than a triumph to have the senate resolve that a province was secured and preserved by the clemency and integrity of its governor rather than by the force of soldiers and the goodwill of the gods; that was my view when I gave my vote.

3 I have written to you at length against my usual practice to make you believe (as I very much wish you to do) that I am making every effort to convince you both that I supported the course that I thought most conducive to your honour, and that I rejoice that your own preference was adopted. Goodbye, retain your affection for me, and, following the road you have begun, continue to demonstrate to the allies and the state your responsibility and diligence.

13.20 Cicero on his return to Italy

Cicero *Letters to Atticus* 7.7.4–7 (?19 December 50)

Cicero had been a reluctant governor: *Att.* 5.2.1 mentions that before leaving Italy he had received a visit from Hortensius and had specifically asked him not to allow his term of office in Cilicia to be extended (Cicero made the same request of Curio: Cic. *Fam.* 2.7.4). He returned to Rome in January 49. See *Fam.* 2.10.2–3, cf. 8.5.1, in which Caelius hopes Cicero has enough trouble in Cilicia to win 'some laurel' (i.e., be awarded a triumph). His hopes were in vain (cf. *Att.* 6.8.5, 9.7.5; Plut. *Cic.* 37.1); for the issue of a triumph, Wistrand 1979a: 3–60 (Cato's letter: 23–5).

6: Caesar was planning to be a candidate for the consulship of 48. His tribunes for 49 were Mark Antony and Q. Cassius Longinus (not to be confused with the later conspirator, C. Cassius Longinus, also tribune that year). Pompey's 'council' was made up of his close associates. The phrase referring to an adoption of a 'man from Gades' refers to the adoption of Balbus (earlier Caesar's engineer) by the wealthy Theophanes of Mytilene; for Mamurra, see doc. 12.87.

4 Regarding my triumph, unless Caesar attempts something underhand through his tribunes, all seems to be plain sailing; but calmest of all is my own mind which takes the whole thing in a spirit of acquiescence, all the more because I hear from a number of people that it has been decided by Pompey and his council to send me to Sicily because I have imperium. That's just stupid! Neither the senate nor the people has authorised me to hold imperium in Sicily, and, if the state refers this to Pompey, why send me rather than a private individual? And so, if this imperium is going to be troublesome, I'll make use of the first gate I see. **5** You state that the anticipation of my arrival is astounding, but that none of the honest, or reasonably honest, men have doubts about what I will do. I don't understand whom you mean by 'honest men'. I know of none, that is if we are looking for classes of good men. There are some honest men individually, but in political conflicts you need to look for classes and species. Do you consider the senate 'honest', when it is their doing that the provinces have no governors? — Curio would never have held out, if discussion had begun with him, but the senate refused to support the proposal and as a consequence there are no governors to succeed Caesar. What of the tax-farmers, who are never reliable and are now Caesar's greatest friends, or the money-lenders, or the farmers, who desire peace above anything else? — unless you think they are afraid of living under an autocracy, but they would never have worried about that, as long as they were left in peace.

6 You may ask whether I approve of accepting the candidature of a man who retains his army after the legal date has passed. I disapprove even of his candidature in absence, but once that was granted, the other was granted with it. Do I approve of his ten years' command and the way it was put in place? I then approve of my exile, of the loss of the Campanian lands, of a patrician being adopted by a plebeian, and of a man from Gades by someone from Mytilene, and of the wealth of Labienus and Mamurra and Balbus' gardens and estate at Tusculum. The source of all these evils is the same. We should have opposed him when he was weak and it was easy; now we are facing eleven legions, all the cavalry he might want, the Transpadane Gauls, the urban populace, so many tribunes, our desperate young men, and a leader of such prestige and daring. We must either fight it out with him, or allow his candidature according to law. 'Fight,' you'll say, 'rather than be a slave.' **7** For what? If you're defeated, proscription; if you win, you'll still be a slave. . . . I can see clearly what would be best in these terrible circumstances: no one can be certain what will happen if it comes to war, but we all assume that, if the honest men are defeated, he'll be no more merciful than Cinna in slaughtering the leading men and no more moderate than Sulla in robbing the wealthy . . .

13.21 Caesar loses two legions in 50 BC

[Caesar] *Gallic War* 8.54.1–55.2

In 50 the senate decreed that two legions be prepared for the Parthian campaign; the question of Caesar's return of a legion loaned by Pompey had already been the subject of senatorial discussion in August 51: doc. 13.10; see also Caes. *BC* 1.32.6; Dio 41.65.

54.1 The senate then decreed that one legion was to be sent by Gnaeus Pompey, and a second by Gaius Caesar for the Parthian campaign, and it was quite clear that the two legions were to be taken off only one man. **2** For Gnaeus Pompey gave up the First Legion, which he had sent to Caesar as it was raised by a levy in Caesar's province, as if one of his own. **3** Caesar, however, although there was no doubt at all about the intentions of his enemies, returned the legion to Pompey and from his own troops ordered the Fifteenth, which he had kept in Nearer Gaul, to be handed over in accordance with the senate's decree . . . **5** He himself set out for Italy. **55.1** When he arrived, he learnt that through the agency of the consul Gaius Marcellus the two legions he had sent back, which in accordance with the senate's decree should have been led off for the Parthian campaign, had been handed over to Gnaeus Pompey and kept in Italy. **2** Although this action left no doubt in anyone's mind what was in train against Caesar, Caesar still decided to put up with everything as long as some hope was left to him of the issue being resolved constitutionally rather than through military conflict.

13.22 Caesar's friends — and enemies, 50 BC

Plutarch *Life of Pompey* 58.1–9.2

Plutarch here summarises the events of 50 BC. Curio's support came from Piso, Caesar's father-in-law, and his friend Mark Antony (tr. pl. 49): cf. Plut. *Ant.* 5. Curio's suggestion that both men lay down their command was considered by many in the senate as unfair, as Pompey's command had three years yet to run (doc. 13.15). But the mood for peace was clear: only 22 senators sided with Marcellus and the rest with Curio. Marcellus therefore went to Pompey's Alban villa and entrusted him with the two legions that were stationed in Italy in preparation for the aborted Parthian campaign (*Att.* 7.5.4; Dio 64.4; doc. 13.21). Marcellus' commission to Pompey appears to have taken place towards the end of 50.

58.1 Caesar, too, was now becoming more actively involved in public affairs, and no longer stayed at a distance from Italy's borders, but was always sending his soldiers to Rome to vote in elections and using money to win over and bribe numerous magistrates. **2** Among these were the consul Paullus, who changed sides for 1,500 talents, and the tribune Curio, who was relieved from irretrievable debt by Caesar, plus Mark Antony, who out of friendship for Curio had become involved in his debts. **3** It was actually said of one of Caesar's centurions, who had come back to Rome and was standing near the senate-house, when he heard that the senate would not give Caesar a prolongation of command, that he clapped his hand on his sword and said, 'But this will give it to him.' **4** And all of Caesar's actions and preparations had this end in view. Nevertheless Curio's demands and requests on Caesar's behalf seemed very fair. **5** He demanded one of two alternatives: either that Pompey as well should be required to disband his army, or that Caesar should not — on the grounds that whether they became private citizens on equal terms, or remained rivals with their present forces, they would cause no disturbance, but whoever made one of the two weak doubled the power he feared. **6** When Marcellus, the consul, replied to this by calling Caesar a robber, and urging that he be voted a public enemy if he did not lay down his arms, Curio, supported by Antony and (L. Calpurnius) Piso, got his way in having the matter put to the senate's vote. **7** He proposed that those who wanted only Caesar to lay down his arms and Pompey to retain his command move to one side; the majority did so. **8** When he a second time made the proposal that all those who wanted both men to lay down their arms and neither retain command move to one side, only 22 sided with Pompey and all the rest with Curio. **9** He felt that he had won and rushed joyfully to the assembly which welcomed him with applause and pelted him with garlands and flowers. Pompey was not in the senate, as commanders of armies are not allowed into the city.

10 Marcellus, however, got up and said he was not going to sit there listening to speeches, but, as he could see the imminent arrival of ten legions marching over the Alps, he was personally going to dispatch someone to oppose them in his country's defence. **59.1** At this everyone put on mourning as if for a national disaster, while Marcellus, with the senators following him, marched through the forum on his way to see Pompey and standing in front of him declared, 'I order you, Pompey, to come to your country's aid, to make use of the forces already prepared for action and to levy others.' **2** Lentulus (L. Cornelius Lentulus Crus) too, one of the two consuls elected for the following year (49 BC), said the same. But when Pompey began to raise troops, some refused to obey the order and others showed up only reluctantly and without enthusiasm, while most people demanded a settlement.

13.23 Pompey 'the better republican'

Appian *Civil Wars* 2.29–31 (112–23)

Curio had early in 50 proposed that both Pompey and Caesar lay down their commands simultaneously (docs 13.15–18, 13.22). On 1 December 50, Curio in the senate again made this proposal. C. Claudius Marcellus as consul divided it into two separate motions, one to send out successors to Caesar (which passed) and one to deprive Pompey of his command, which was not carried, which was exactly what Marcellus had intended. But Curio re-introduced his motion, and the senate voted 370 to 22 to preserve the peace by decreeing that both Pompey and Caesar were to lay down their arms. Marcellus then took matters into his own hands and entrusted the state to Pompey, supported by the consul-elect for 49, his cousin. Pompey's words as recorded and interpreted by Appian may indicate some disingenuousness: clearly he had made up his mind for war, accepting Marcellus' commission readily enough, and took command of the two legions which had been set aside for the Parthian campaign. Curio's tribunate ended with the new tribunes taking up office on 10 December, and he left to join Caesar at Ravenna. See Hirtius in [Caesar] *BG* 8.52.5; Plut. *Pomp.* 58.4–59.1 (doc. 13.22); Dio 40.64–6; for Curio's peace proposals in 50: Taylor 1949: 158–9; Lacey 1961; Greenhalgh 1981: 109–24; Wiseman 1994a: 42; Meier 1995: 340–3; Gruen 1995: 470–90; Seager 2002: 147.

112 Pompey was enraged with him (Curio) and threatened him, immediately withdrawing to the suburbs in indignation. The senate was now suspicious of both men, but considered Pompey the better republican, while they hated Caesar for behaving towards them with contempt during his consulship; some of them considered that it was really not safe to remove Pompey's power until Caesar should have laid down his, since he was outside the city and possessed of more sweeping ambitions than Pompey. **113** Curio gave the opposite viewpoint, that they needed Caesar against Pompey, or that everyone should be disbanded together. As he did not carry his point, he dismissed the senate with the whole affair still unresolved — tribunes are able to do this. Pompey thus had cause to regret restoring the tribunate to its former powers after it had been reduced to insignificance by Sulla. **114** Despite being dismissed, however, they voted on just one issue, that Caesar and Pompey should each send one legion of soldiers to Syria to defend it after the disaster incurred by Crassus. **115** Pompey was devious and demanded back the legion which he had recently lent to Caesar to compensate for the disaster suffered by Caesar's two generals, Titurius and Cotta. Caesar made each man a present of 250 drachmas and sent the legion to Rome with another of his own. As the anticipated emergency in Syria did not eventuate, these legions spent the winter at Capua, **116** while the people sent by Pompey to Caesar spread many reports hostile to Caesar and assured Pompey that Caesar's army was worn out by long, hard service and longing for home, and that it would defect to him as soon as it crossed the Alps. **117** Though they gave these reports, either from ignorance or because they had been bribed, every soldier enthusiastically supported and laboured for Caesar from being used to serving in his campaigns and from the rewards accorded by war to the victors and all the other things they received from Caesar — for he gave lavishly, to ensure their support for his plans — and, though they were well aware of these, they stood by him nonetheless. **118** Pompey, however, relied on this information and did not collect either an army or equipment appropriate for so great an enterprise. The senate asked each man for his opinion, and Claudius (Marcellus) cunningly divided the question into two and asked for their views separately, whether successors to Caesar should be sent and whether Pompey should be deprived of his command. The majority voted against the latter motion, but in favour of successors for Caesar. **119** Curio then put it to the vote whether both should lay down their commands: 22 senators voted against, and 370 went back to Curio's view to avoid civil war, whereupon Claudius dismissed the senate, with the cry; 'Have it your own way — with Caesar as your master!'

120 When a false report suddenly came to hand that Caesar had crossed the Alps and was marching against the city, there was immense confusion and fear on all sides, and Claudius proposed that the army at Capua should go to engage Caesar as an enemy. When Curio opposed him on the grounds that the report was false, he declared: **121** 'If I am hindered by a vote from taking steps for the public safety, I shall do so on my own authority as consul.' With these words, he ran from the senate to the suburbs with his colleague, where he presented a sword to Pompey, saying, 'My colleague and I instruct you to march against Caesar on your country's behalf, and we give you for this purpose the army now at Capua or in any other region of Italy and whatever troops in addition you should yourself wish to levy.' **122** Pompey undertook to obey the consuls' orders, but added, 'If there is no better way,' whether being disingenuous or still making a pretence of decency. **123** Curio had no authority outside the city (for tribunes are not allowed to go outside the walls), but publicly lamented what had occurred and demanded that the consuls should proclaim that no one had to obey Pompey's levy. He was unsuccessful, and as his period of office was coming to an end and he was afraid for himself, as well as having given up any hope of being able to assist Caesar any longer, he left in haste to join him.

THE FLIGHT OF THE TRIBUNES

In 50 BC the consuls elected for 49 BC were C. Claudius Marcellus, brother of the consul of 51 BC, and L. Cornelius Lentulus Crus (*MRR* II.256); both were opposed to Caesar. Caesar's candidate, Servius Galba, was defeated. Antony, however, was elected to the college of augurs on the death of Hortensius (*MRR* II.254), and was also elected as one of the tribunes for 49 (*MRR* II.258). He had served with Gabinius in Syria, participating in his expedition to Egypt in 55. Antony's grandfather was a Sullan executed by Marius (Plut. *Ant.* 1, 3, 5). Caesar used the rights of the tribunes as a major pretext for war (cf. doc. 1.22). On 21 December Antony as tribune attacked Pompey's entire career and spoke for those condemned under the laws of 52 (Cic. *Att.* 7.8.5). On 1 January 49 matters came to a head with a dispatch from Caesar read to the senate.

13.24 Caesar's view of events in January 49

Caesar *Civil War* 1.1.1–5.5

Caesar's *Civil War* (*BC*) commences with a reference to a dispatch with which Caesar obviously considers his readers to be familiar. This was brought by Curio from Caesar at Ravenna and read out in the senate, despite opposition. Caesar proposed that both Pompey and himself give up their armies; if Pompey would not, neither would Caesar and he would defend his position with arms. Cicero on 4 January returned to Rome, and worked to no avail for peace. On 7 January the optimates, especially Lentulus and Cato, successfully had an *SCU* passed and warned that Pompey should not be deceived by offers from Caesar: Plut. *Caes.* 31, *Pomp.* 59, *Ant.* 5; App. *BC* 2.32–3; Cic. *Att.* 9.11a.2; references at *MRR* II.251. Cicero's earlier conversations with Pompey in December 50 BC in fact indicated to him that Pompey had no desire for peace (*Att.* 7.4.2, 7.8).

Caesar's offers, Pompey's reaction, Cicero's attempts for peace, and the flight of the tribunes on 7 January: doc. 13.25; Dio 41.1.13.4; App. *BC* 2.32–33.124–33; Plut. *Pomp.* 59, *Caes.* 31; Syme 1939: 42–3; Fritz 1942; Pocock 1959; Gelzer 1968: 190–3; Rawson 1975: 188–9; Lacey 1978: 108; Leach 1978: 171–2; Huzar 1978: 47–9; Greenhalgh 1981: 129–32; Habicht 1990: 62; Mitchell 1991: 245–8; Fuhrmann 1992: 132–4; Wiseman 1994a: 421–2; Meier 1995: 343–46; Gruen 1995: 489–90; Southern 2001: 98–101; Seager 2002: 148–51.

1.1 When the consuls had been handed Caesar's dispatch, permission was obtained from them with difficulty, and after a great struggle on the part of the tribunes, that it be read in the senate; they could not, however, gain permission for a motion to be brought before the senate regarding the dispatch. The consuls propose a motion concerning the Republic. **2** The consul, Lucius Lentulus, urges on the senate, promising that he will not fail the Republic if they are prepared to speak their views boldly and resolutely; **3** but, if they consider Caesar and try to win his favour, as they have done on earlier occasions, he will consider his own interests and not submit to the senate's authority: he, too, could take refuge in Caesar's favour and friendship. (Q. Caecilius Metellus Pius) Scipio voices the same view: **4** that Pompey is of a mind not to fail the Republic, if the senate supports him; if it delays and acts in a more conciliatory fashion, the senate will vainly request his assistance, should it choose to do so at a later date.

2.1 This speech of Scipio's, as the senate was meeting in the city and Pompey was close by, appeared to come from Pompey's own mouth. **2** Some had voiced more moderate views, such as, initially, Marcus Marcellus, who gave a speech to the effect that the matter should not be referred to the senate until levies had been held throughout Italy and armies enlisted, under whose protection the senate could venture, safely and freely, to make whatever decrees it wished; **3** and such as Marcus Calidius, who gave his view that Pompey should set out for his provinces, so that there should be no reason for hostilities: Caesar was afraid, he said, now two legions had been extorted from him, that it might appear that Pompey was holding them back and keeping them near the city to use them against him; such as Marcus Rufus, too, who supported Calidius' view with a few minor changes. **4** All these were vehemently and abusively attacked by the consul Lucius Lentulus. **5** Lentulus totally refused to put Calidius' motion. Marcellus, frightened by the abuse, abandoned his proposal. **6** And so most of them were forced by the language of the consul, fear at the presence of the army, and the threats of Pompey's friends, against their will and under pressure, to support Scipio's proposal: that Caesar should disband his army before a certain date; if he did not do this, he should be considered to be planning acts against the Republic. **7** Marcus Antonius and Quintus Cassius, tribunes, interpose their veto. The question of their veto is at once brought to the senate. **8** Violent opinions are voiced, and the more violent and fierce the speech, the more loudly the speaker is applauded by Caesar's enemies.

3.1 When the senate was dismissed in the evening, all its members are summoned out by Pompey. Pompey praises the brave and encourages them for the future, and reproaches and rouses the unenergetic. **2** Many from the old armies of Pompey are called up from all sides with hope of rewards and promotions, and many are summoned from the two legions handed over by Caesar. **3** The city and comitium itself are full of tribunes, centurions, volunteers . . . **4.4** Pompey himself, urged on by Caesar's enemies, and by his wish to have no one his equal in prestige (dignitas), had completely turned away from Caesar's friendship and become reconciled with their common enemies . . . **5.3** That final and ultimate decree of the senate is resorted to, which had never previously been called upon, except when the city was on the point of destruction and when, through the temerity of evil-doers, everyone despaired of safety: the consuls, praetors, tribunes and any men of proconsular rank near the city are to take measures that the Republic suffer no harm. **4** This resolution is recorded by the senate's decree on 7 January. And so, on the first five days on which the senate could meet from the day Lentulus took up his consulship, excepting two election days (i.e., up to 7 January), the most severe and harsh decrees are passed regarding Caesar's command and those most important persons, the tribunes of the plebs. **5** The tribunes immediately flee from the city and take themselves to Caesar. At that time he was at Ravenna and awaiting replies to his very moderate requests, in case men's sense of justice might be able to bring matters to a peaceful conclusion.

13.25 Cicero on the flight of the tribunes

Cicero Letters to his Friends 16.11.2–3 (12 January 49)

The tribunes fled to Caesar at Ravenna, where he made their treatment a pretext for war (Caes. *BC* 1.7, 22; doc. 1.22; App. *BC* 2.33.133: Curio and Cassius 'immediately made their way secretly to Caesar that night using a hired cart and wearing slaves' clothing'). Caesar's view that his proposals were moderate is not one shared by Cicero, who saw them as threatening and belligerent. Cicero is writing here to Tiro.

2 True that our friend Caesar has sent a sharp, threatening letter to the senate and continues to declare that he will keep his army and province against the senate's wishes, and my friend Curio is encouraging him. Our friend Antony and Quintus Cassius, without being forcibly expelled, left to join Caesar together with Curio, after the senate had given the consuls, praetors, tribunes and us proconsuls, the duty of seeing to it that the state took no harm. **3** Never has the state been in greater danger, never have wicked citizens had a leader more ready for action. True that on our side too preparations are very earnestly underway. This is happening through the authority and enthusiasm of our friend Pompey, who has begun, rather late, to be afraid of Caesar.

13.26 Crossing the Rubicon: 'the die is cast'

Appian *Civil Wars* 2.34 (134–40)

News of the senatus consultum of 7 January reached Caesar by 10 January and he made the momentous decision to defend his position with arms, just as his enemies in the senate had taken up arms against him. On the night of 10–11 January he crossed the Rubicon, bringing his troops into Italy. Ariminum, the first town in Italy proper, was taken. Caesar took his enemies unawares, and unprepared. The phrase, 'Let the die be cast!', is from a play of the Greek playwright, Menander. According to Plut. *Pomp.* 60.4, Caesar spoke this in Greek; cf. *Caes.* 32.8; Suet. *Jul.* 31.2. In Italy, the senate's concerns belonged to another world: on 1 March 49 Cicero wrote to Atticus that in Campania the inhabitants were thinking only of their fields and investments (*Att.* 8.13.2).

134 Although the war had now started on both sides, being already openly declared, the senate considered that Caesar's army would take some time in arriving from Gaul and that he would not rush into such a venture with only a few men, and so ordered Pompey to raise 130,000 men from Italy, particularly veterans who would have experience of war, and to enlist as many brave men as possible from neighbouring provinces. **135** They voted him for the war the entire public treasury straightaway and their private fortunes in addition, if needed for the soldiers' pay. In their anger and partisanship, they sent round to the allies for additional funds, with the greatest possible haste. **136** Caesar had sent for his own army, but being used to depend on the surprise caused by his speed and the terror caused by his audacity, rather than on the immensity of his preparations, he decided, with his 5,000 men, to be the first to attack in this great war and to seize the strategic positions in Italy before the enemy. **137** Caesar, therefore, sent the centurions, with a few of their most courageous soldiers, dressed in civilian clothes, to enter Ariminum and take the city by surprise; this is the first town in Italy after you leave Cisalpine Gaul. **138** As evening approached, Caesar withdrew from a drinking-party, on the grounds that he was not feeling well, leaving his friends to continue feasting, and, mounting his chariot, drove towards Ariminum, with his cavalry following at a distance. **139** On his journey he came to the Rubicon river, which forms Italy's frontier, where he stopped and, gazing at the stream, revolved in his mind a consideration of each of the evils that would result, if he crossed this river in arms. **140** He recovered himself and said to those with him, 'My friends, my not crossing will bring about evils for me — my crossing will for all mankind.' With these words, he crossed with a rush like one possessed, uttering this well-known phrase, 'Let the die be cast!'

13.27 Caesar's justification

Caesar *Civil War* 1.8.1–11.4

The proposal of Pompey's father-in-law, Metellus Scipio, in the senate on 1 January that Caesar dismiss his army (Caes. *BC* 1.2.6: doc. 13.24) and so become a private citizen would have meant the loss of Caesar's imperium and that he would be open to prosecution by his enemies. This was a situation he wished to avoid, and he complained (whether justly or not) in his *Civil Wars* that he had been deprived of six months of command. At Ariminum, Caesar received the praetor Roscius and Lucius Caesar (son of one of Caesar's legates: *MRR* II.267) as public envoys, but with a personal communication from Pompey (Fritz 1941; Shackleton Bailey 1960; *MRR* II.265).

Caesar replied with his own proposals for peace which Roscius and Lucius Caesar presented Pompey with on 23 January at Capua; Pompey replied in turn but Caesar argues here that he could not accept Pompey's conditions. Preparations for war continued.

To Caesar his right to stand in absentia for the consulship while retaining his Gallic command was the crucial issue, as well as the taking up of arms against him. The historian Asinius Pollio recorded the words of Caesar when he saw the carnage after the battle of Pharsalus (doc. 13.28), 'they wanted it like this; with all my great achievements, I Gaius Caesar would have been condemned, if I had not looked to my army for help' (Suet. *Jul*. 30.4 (doc. 13.28) = *HRR* II.68 Γ2; cf. Plut. *Caes*. 46.1–2). Caesar in his speech to his troops in January 49 exhorted them to defend his *dignitas*, and Cicero has Caesar claiming that he invaded Italy because of his *dignitas* (*Att*. 7.11.1; Caesar *BC* 1.7.7). Caesar has a veteran say before Pharsalus that in this battle Caesar's *dignitas* and the soldier's *libertas* (freedom) would be recovered: *BC* 3.91. Defending the rights of the tribunes, as noted above, was also a motive Caesar stressed (doc. 13.24).

Discussions of his motives for crossing the Rubicon and choosing war: Shackleton Bailey 1965: I.38–40 (against Pollio); Gelzer 1968: 190–2; Ehrhardt 1995; Gruen 1995: 494; cf. Balsdon 1967: 119–20; Scullard *GN* 122; Yavetz 1983: 10–11; Wiseman 1994a: 423; Rawson 1994: 424–9; Meier 1995: 364–7; Southern 2001: 101; Seager 2002: 150.

8.1 After learning the wishes of the soldiers he sets out for Ariminum with the Thirteenth Legion and there meets the tribunes who had fled to join him; he summons the remaining legions from their winter-quarters and orders them to follow him. **2** To Ariminum comes the young man Lucius Caesar, whose father was one of his legates. When their first greetings were over, he reveals the reason for his coming, that he has instructions for him from Pompey on a private matter: **3** he says that Pompey wants to clear himself in Caesar's eyes, and that Caesar should not take as an attack on himself what he had done for the sake of Rome. He had always put the good of Rome before private friendships. Caesar, considering his high position, should also for the benefit of Rome give up his partisanship and grievances and not be so bitterly angry with his enemies as to harm the state in his desire to harm them. **4** He adds a few remarks of the same kind together with excuses for Pompey. The praetor Roscius puts before Caesar nearly the same proposals in the same words, explaining that they came from Pompey.

9.1 Although these proceedings appeared to do nothing towards alleviating the wrongs that had been committed, now, however, that he had obtained suitable men to convey his wishes to Pompey he asks of both, as they had brought him Pompey's instructions, that they not object to taking his terms in reply back to Pompey, in case they might be able, by a little trouble, to put a stop to serious conflict and free all Italy from fear. **2** As for himself, he said, his prestige (*dignitas*) had always been of prime importance to him, and preferable to life itself. He had been grieved that a kindness bestowed on him by the Roman people should be insultingly wrested from him by his enemies, and that he should be dragged back to the city deprived of six months of command, when the people had decreed that he could be a candidate in absentia at the next elections. **3** However, for Rome's sake he had endured with equanimity the loss of this privilege: when he sent a dispatch to the senate suggesting that everyone should give up their armies, he had not even been granted that. **4** Levies were being held throughout Italy, two legions, taken from him on the pretence of a Parthian war, were being kept back, the state was in arms. What was the aim of all this but his destruction? **5** He was, however, prepared to agree to anything and to put up with anything for the sake of Rome. Let Pompey set out for his provinces, let them both disband their armies, let everyone in Italy lay down arms, let the state be freed from fear, and let free elections and the control of the whole state be entrusted to the senate and Roman people. **6** That this might be done more easily and on definite conditions and be ratified by an oath, either let Pompey come nearer or allow him to approach Pompey: in this way all conflict would be settled through discussion.

10.1 After accepting the commission Roscius arrives at Capua with Lucius Caesar where he finds Pompey and the consuls; he reports Caesar's demands. **2** After deliberation they reply and send them back to him with instructions, of which the gist was as follows: **3** Caesar should return to Gaul, leave Ariminum and disband his army; if he did so, Pompey would go to the Spanish provinces. **4** Meanwhile, until a pledge be received that Caesar would do as he promised, the consuls and Pompey would not pause in levying troops. **11.1** It was an unfair condition to demand that Caesar should leave Ariminum and return to his province, while he himself (Pompey) kept not only his provinces but someone else's legions; to desire Caesar to disband his army, while he was holding levies; **2** to promise to go to his province and not to fix a deadline by which he must go, so that even if he set out when Caesar's consulship had finished, he would still appear guiltless of breaking his oath; **3** furthermore, failure to make an opportunity for a conference or promise to approach Caesar meant that all hopes of peace should be abandoned. **4** Accordingly, he sends Mark Antony from Ariminum to Arretium with five cohorts; he himself stays at Ariminum with two cohorts and arranges the holding of a levy there; he occupies Pisaurum, Fanum, and Ancona, each with one cohort.

13.28 Suetonius on Caesar's motives

Suetonius *Life of the Deified Julius* 30.1–4

1 But when the senate would not interfere and his enemies declared that they would come to no compromise over matters affecting the state, he crossed into Cisalpine Gaul, held the assizes, and stopped at Ravenna, intending to resort to war should the senate take more serious action against the tribunes of the plebs who used their vetoes on his behalf. **2** This was his excuse for civil war, but it is thought that he had other reasons. Gnaeus Pompey used to state that, because Caesar's private wealth was not sufficient to finish the works he had undertaken, or to fulfil on his return the expectations he had raised in the populace, he wanted general mayhem and anarchy. **3** Others say that he was afraid of being called to account for what he had done in his first consulship contrary to the auspices, laws and vetoes, for Marcus Cato habitually proclaimed, and on oath, that he would prosecute Caesar the instant he dismissed his army. It was also publicly said that, if he returned as a privatus, he would have to defend his case before jurors surrounded by armed men, as Milo did. **4** Asinius Pollio renders this more probable, when he states that Caesar at Pharsalus looked on his enemies as they lay dead on the battlefield or fled, with these actual words, 'They wanted it like this; with all my great achievements, I Gaius Caesar would have been condemned, if I had not looked to my army for help.'

13.29 Pompey abandons Rome

Cicero *Letters to Atticus* 7.11.3–4 and 7.13.1 (? 21 and 23 January 49)

Caesar had the Thirteenth Legion with him at Ravenna (doc. 13.27) and eight legions in Gaul, of which two were on their way to him. Pompey had seven legions in Spain and three in Italy. Two of his legions, at Capua, the First and the Fifteenth, were made up of Caesar's veterans. He controlled Rome and had the backing of the senate. After taking Ariminum, Caesar occupied various towns, and reached Ancona. As Appian noted he acted with speed and employed surprise. Pompey, hearing of Caesar's advance, abandoned Rome on 17 January, and retired to Capua, ordering the consuls and the senate to join him there, unless they wanted to be declared enemies of the state. Pompey had boasted in 50 BC, after the whole of Italy had joined in spontaneous thanksgiving for his recovery from illness, that he had only to stamp his feet in Italy and infantry and cavalry would spring from the soil (doc. 13.17). But when news reached Rome that Caesar had crossed the Rubicon, Pompey's lack of military preparedness caused criticism, and Favonius ordered Pompey to stamp on the ground (Plut. *Pomp.* 57.8, 60.7; cf. App. *BC* 2.37.146).

Domitius Ahenobarbus, appointed proconsul for Transalpine Gaul as Caesar's successor, defended Corfinium against Pompey's urgings and was defeated; Caesar released the captured senators and equestrians (Burns 1966). Pompey made his way to Brundisium on the south-east coast, and on 17 March, despite Caesar's attempted blockade, he sailed to Epirus, and established his forces at Dyrrachium. Caesar then went to Rome for two weeks, having a meeting with Cicero on the way at Formiae (see doc. 13.37). At Rome, Caesar made it clear he was no Sulla or Marius, but when debarred from the treasury by one of the tribunes, took the money by force (App. *BC* 2.41.163–4; Plut. *Caes.* 35).

For the civil war, see esp. Caesar *BC*, Plut. *Pomp.* 60–73, *Caes.* 34–56, *Cato Min.* 52–72; App. *BC* 2.35–100; Dio 41.10–43.12; Fritz 1942; Fuller 1965: 180–298; Balsdon 1967: 120–51; Greenhalgh 1981: 133–255; Wylie 1992: 557–65; Rawson 1994: 424–37; Meier 1995: 367–429; Southern 2001: 95–140; Seager 2002: 152–68; Southern 2002: 125–41.

11.3 Let's return to our friend. What do you think, for heaven's sake, of Pompey's plan? I mean why has he abandoned Rome? I'm totally at a loss. At that point nothing seemed more stupid. Abandoning Rome? Wouldn't you have done the same if the Gauls were on their way? 'The state isn't made up of house walls,' he might say. But it is of altars and hearths . . . **4** The complaints from the public are amazing (as to Rome I don't know, but you will tell me) at the city being without magistrates, without the senate. What's more, the idea of Pompey as a run-away affects people amazingly. And so, the situation is completely changed. They now think there should be no concessions to Caesar. You will have to explain to me what all this means.

13.1 But you see what kind of a war it is: a civil war, true, but one originating not from conflict from among the citizens, but from the recklessness of one desperate citizen. He, however, is strong in his army, has won many to his side by hopes and promises, and has coveted every man's entire possessions. The city has been delivered to him, without protection, full of resources. What might you not fear from a man who considers our temples and homes not as his native land but as plunder? But what he will do or how, without senate or magistrates, I have no idea; he certainly won't be able to maintain any pretence of behaving constitutionally.

13.30 Caesar's terms

Cicero *Letters to his Friends* 16.12.2–4 (27 January 49)

According to Cicero in this letter to Tiro, Caesar offered the following terms after the flight of Pompey and the boni from Rome.

2 As Caesar, driven by some insanity and unmindful of his name and honours, has seized Ariminum, Pisaurum, Ancona, and Arretium, we have abandoned Rome — how wisely or courageously there is no point in arguing. **3** You see our situation. True he is offering terms, that Pompey go to Spain, that the levies which have been raised and our forces be disbanded, while for his part he will hand over Transalpine Gaul to Domitius and Cisalpine Gaul to Considius Nonianus (who have been allocated them); he will come to Rome to canvass for the consulship and no longer wants his candidature to be accepted *in absentia*; he will canvass for three market-days in person. We have accepted his terms, as long as he withdraws his troops from the places he has occupied, so a senate meeting can be held in Rome to discuss these terms without fear. **4** If he does this, there is hope of peace, though not an honourable one (for the terms are imposed on us), but anything is better than to be in our current situation.

13.31 Pompey marshals his forces

Appian *Civil Wars* 2.38 (152)

Cicero disapproved of the departure from Italy but Pompey had a precedent in the example of Sulla, who had returned from the east to triumph over his enemies and capture Rome. Pompey had considerable resources in the east. His clients, gained during the Mithridatic war (cf. doc. 2.55), sent troops, and he collected a fleet from the east. At Pharsalus, Pompey's auxiliaries spoke many languages (App. *BC* 2.75.314; kings, princes and eastern states assisting Pompey listed at 2.71.300). Cicero criticised Pompey's plan to 'incite foreign kings, to lead foreign races in arms to Italy' (Att. 8.11.2). In Cicero's view, Pompey was eager to rule like a Sulla (*Att.* 9.7.3; 8.11.2: both Caesar and Pompey 'wish to reign'). In 9.10.2 he pictures Pompey as thinking, 'What Sulla could do, I can' (cf. 9.14.2, 10.7.1): Pompey was surely regarding Sulla as an example of what was militarily achievable (Seager 2002: 161). For Pompey's forces and resources at the beginning of the war, see Caesar *BC* 3.3–5.

Pompey hastened from Capua to Nuceria, and from Nuceria to Brundisium to cross the Adriatic to Epirus and there finish his preparations for war. He wrote to all the provinces and to their kings, cities, governors and leaders to send him assistance for the war as speedily as possible. While they were all doing this, Pompey's own army was in Spain and ready to set out to any place where it might be needed.

13.32 Cicero agonises as to whether to join Pompey

Cicero *Letters to Atticus* 8.3.1–4 (18–19 February 49)

Cf. *Att.* 8.11.3–4. Cicero on 22 January 49 expressed to Atticus his doubts about whom to join in the conflict but even here his preference for Pompey comes through (*Att.* 7.12.2–3), and he was to join Pompey, even after personal solicitation from Caesar (docs 13.36–7). His friend and correspondent Caelius had no qualms; in August 50 he told Cicero that he would join the stronger side, and when war broke out he joined Caesar ([Cic.] *Fam.* 8.14.3 (doc. 13.18); *Att.* 7.3.6; Brunt 1986).

1 Troubled as I am by most serious and unhappy events, and not having the opportunity to consult with you in person, I would still like your advice. The whole matter at issue is this: if Pompey leaves Italy — which I think he will — what do you think I should do? You may be able to advise me more easily, if I briefly set out what comes to my mind in favour of each side.

2 As well as the greatest obligations which I owe to Pompey regarding my restoration and the friendship I have with him, the state's cause itself leads me to feel that my policy should be joined to his policy and my fortune to his. There is something else: if I remain and abandon that band of most upright and distinguished citizens, I have to fall into the power of one man. While he demonstrates in many ways that he is my friend (and you are aware that I endeavoured long ago to make him such, because I suspected that this storm was imminent), two things, however, have to be considered — how much confidence can be placed in him, and, however definitely he is a friend of mine, whether the role of a brave man and good citizen should be to stay in the city, in which he has held the highest offices and commands, has achieved great things, and been endowed with the most glorious priestly office, with reduced status, and with danger to be undergone, together, perhaps, with some dishonour, should Pompey ever restore the constitution. So much on this side.

3 Now see what lies on the other. Our friend Pompey has done nothing which has not lacked wisdom and courage, and, I should add, nothing which hasn't been contrary to my advice and influence. I say nothing of the past, how he promoted, aggrandised and armed Caesar against the state, supported his laws passed by violence and contrary to the auspices, added on Transalpine Gaul, became his son-in-law, acted as augur at Publius Clodius' adoption, showed more concern for restoring me than for keeping me here, extended Caesar's command, consistently supported him during his absence, exerted himself, even in his third consulship after he had taken on the role of defender of the state, to see that the ten tribunes brought in their law that Caesar could stand in absentia, which he confirmed in some way by a law of his own, opposed the consul Marcus Marcellus, when he was trying to end Caesar's command in Gaul on the Kalends of March — saying nothing of all this, what could be more disgraceful or more confused than this departure from Rome, or rather this shameful flight in which we are now engaged? What terms would not have been accepted in preference to abandoning our country? The terms were bad, I admit, but what could be worse than this?

4 Alright, he will restore the constitution. When? What provision has been made for such hope? Hasn't Picenum been lost? Hasn't the road to Rome been opened? Has not all money, public and private, been handed over to the enemy? What's more, there is no party, no strength, no base to draw those who wish to defend the constitution. Apulia was chosen, the least populated part of Italy and the most distant from the onset of this war, perhaps in despair as on the coast and opportune for flight.

13.33 Pompey summons Cicero

Pompey in [Cicero] *Letters to Atticus* 8.11c (20 February 49)

Cicero in fact procrastinated about joining Pompey in Apulia, and did not sail with him to Dyrrachium in Epirus. His leaving Italy was then delayed by Caesar's control of the peninsula and he only sailed to Dyrrachium in June.

Greetings. I read your letter with pleasure; I recognised your former qualities still active for the public welfare. The consuls have joined the army I command in Apulia. I urge you very strongly, in view of your unrivalled and constant concern for our country, to join us so that we may work together to bring aid and assistance to our afflicted country. I suggest that you travel by the Appian Way and come quickly to Brundisium.

13.34 Caesar to Oppius and Cornelius Balbus

Caesar in [Cicero] *Letters to Atticus* 9.7c (c. 5 March 49)

This letter was written on the march through Italy. Caesar's policy of clemency contrasted strongly with Pompey's policy that senators who did not join him would be enemies of the state, or the talk in Pompey's camp of proscriptions and confiscations of property (doc. 13.43). The Spanish-born L. Cornelius Balbus, cos. 40, had earlier been Caesar's officer of engineers (*praefectus fabrum*) and was one of his main supporters in the civil war, along with C. Oppius, an eques.

1 I am extremely pleased that you express in your letter how strongly you approve of the events at Corfinium. I will willingly follow your advice, all the more willingly because I had of my own accord decided to show as much clemency as possible and work hard towards a reconciliation with Pompey. Let us try to see whether in this way we can regain everyone's good will and enjoy a long-lasting victory, since all others by their cruelty have been unable to escape hatred or to make their victory last, except for only Lucius Sulla, whom I am not going to imitate. Let this be the new type of conquest, to defend ourselves with clemency and generosity. Regarding how this can be done, I have a few ideas and many more can be found. I ask you to turn your thoughts to such matters. **2** I captured Numerius Magius, Pompey's prefect. Of course I followed my usual practice and released him at once. Two prefects of engineers of Pompey's have now come into my power and been released by me. If they wish to show their gratitude, they should urge Pompey to prefer to be my friend rather than the friend of those who have always been his and my bitter enemies, whose intrigues have brought Rome to its present condition.

13.35 Cicero's debts to Caesar

Cicero *Letters to Atticus* 5.6.2 (?19 May 51), 7.8.5
(25/26 December 50)

Cicero's debt to Caesar is mentioned as 800,000 sesterces (200,000 denarii; *Att.* 5.5.2: 15 May 51; see Gelzer 1968: 137). Despite Cicero's constant criticisms of Caesar in his letters, he had had little compunction in borrowing money from him. Caesar's successes in Gaul had enabled him to give financial support to numerous senators (cf. docs 12.68–9).

5.6.2 But I shall keep persisting in one matter, as long as I think you are in Rome, and that is in asking you about Caesar's loan, that you leave it settled.

7.8.5 But what annoys me most is that Caesar's money must be repaid and the provision for my triumph be used for that purpose; it has an ugly look to be in debt to a political opponent. But this and much else when we are together.

13.36 Caesar to Cicero

Caesar in [Cicero] *Letters to Atticus* 9.6a (c. 5 March 49)

Written by Caesar on the way to Brundisium. Caesar was to see Cicero at his estate at Formiae (doc. 13.37). C. Furnius (tr. pl. 50) may have become praetor in 42 BC: *MRR* II.359.

Although I have just seen our friend Furnius and was unable to speak or hear his news at my leisure, since I am hurrying and on the march with my legions already sent on ahead, I could not, however, omit writing to you and sending him to express my thanks, as I have often done and expect to do even more often: you have done me such services. I especially request you, since I expect to come soon to Rome, that I may see you there so I can make use of your advice, influence, prestige and help in everything. I must return to my purpose: you will overlook my haste and the brevity of this letter. You will learn all the rest from Furnius.

13.37 Caesar visits Cicero, March 49

Cicero *Letters to Atticus* 9.18.1 (28 March 49)

Ten days after Pompey fled from Italy, Caesar called on Cicero, who was therefore courted by both of the protagonists in this conflict. Caesar wanted Cicero to attend the senate at Rome, but Cicero insisted on his own freedom of speech or non-attendance. Caesar was displeased at his non-attendance (*Att.* 10.8.3), and advised him to stay out of the conflict (*Att.* 10.8b). Antony, in charge of Italy, refused to allow him to leave Italy (esp. *Att.* 10.8a), but Cicero managed to join Pompey's forces at Dyrrachium in June (cf. *Att.* 10.18). He may have been critical of Pompey and his decision to quit Italy, but Cicero's loyalties lay with those who most closely represented the forces of the Republic (cf. Cic. *Phil.* 3.36–8). On board ship bound for Dyrrachium he wrote to Terentia that, 'I shall at last with my peers be fighting to defend the Republic' (*Fam.* 14.7.2, cf. *Fam.* 2.16.3). Caesar's visit: Smith 1966: 220–1; Rawson 1975: 194–5, 1994: 429; Lacey 1978: 112; Wistrand 1979a: 110–24; Habicht 1990: 64; Mitchell 1991: 258; Fuhrmann 1992: 137–8; Meier 1995: 378.

On both points I took your advice; my words were such that he thought well of me rather than thanked me, and I was adamant on the matter of not going to Rome. But we were mistaken in thinking him compliant — I have never seen anyone less so. He said that in my judgement I was convicting him, that the rest would be slower to come, if I did not. I replied that their case was not the same as my own. After a long discussion, 'Come on, then, and work for peace.' 'At my own discretion?' I asked. 'Would I dictate to you?' he replied. 'Well,' I said, 'I shall work along the lines that the senate does not approve of an expedition to the Spanish provinces nor of armies being transported to Greece, and,' I went on, 'I shall have a lot to say commiserating with Gnaeus.' His response to that was, 'But I don't want those sorts of things said.' 'That's what I thought,'

I replied, 'but that is why I do not want to be there, as I must either make those kind of remarks or not come to Rome — with much else, which I could not keep quiet about, were I there.' The conclusion was that he asked me to think things over, as if looking for a way to end the conversation. I could not refuse. That's how we parted. I believe, therefore, that he is not pleased with me. But I was pleased with myself, a feeling I have not had for some time.

13.38 Caesar's actions after Pompey's flight from Brundisium

Caesar *Civil War* 1.32.1–33.4

32.1 After carrying out these arrangements Caesar withdraws his soldiers into the nearest towns so they might for the remainder of the time have some rest from labour; he himself sets out for Rome. **2** Having summoned the senate he reminds them of the injuries done him by his personal enemies. He declares that he had not sought any extraordinary position, but, in waiting for the proper time for his consulship, had been content with the privileges open to all citizens. **3** A proposal had been brought forward by the ten tribunes and passed, though his enemies spoke against it, and Cato in particular bitterly opposed it, using his old delaying tactics of making the discussion drag on for days, that he should be allowed to stand for the consulship in absence, Pompey himself being consul at the time; if Pompey disapproved, why had he allowed it to be passed? If he approved, why did he prevent him from making use of the people's kindness? **4** He points out his own patience, when of his own accord he suggested that the armies be disbanded, although this would have meant a sacrifice for himself of prestige and position. **5** He comments on the vindictiveness of his enemies who, what they demanded in the other case, refused in his, and preferred total upheaval to giving up their imperium and armies. **6** He relates the way they wronged him in taking away his legions, their cruelty and insolence in impinging upon the rights of the tribunes; he reminds them of the terms he proposed, the meetings requested and refused. **7** Under these circumstances he urges and desires them to take up the government and administer it alongside himself. If fear makes them shun this, he will not put the burden on them, but administer the state on his own. **8** Envoys should be sent to Pompey regarding a settlement, nor was he frightened by what Pompey had said a little earlier in the senate, that the prestige of those to whom envoys are sent is enhanced, while fear is attributed to those who send them. **9** Such considerations seemed to belong to a weak and feeble spirit. His wish was, just as he had striven to outdo others in achievements, to surpass them too in justice and equity.

33.1 The senate approves the proposal to send envoys, but no one who could be sent was found, everyone refusing the duty of the embassy, primarily through fear. **2** For Pompey, on leaving the city, had said in the senate that he would take the same view of those who remained in Rome and those who were in Caesar's camp. **3** So three days were spent in discussion and excuses. Moreover Lucius Metellus, a tribune, is put up by Caesar's enemies to thwart this proposal and prevent everything else he might propose to enact. **4** When his aim was understood, with several days already having been wasted, Caesar, in order to avoid spending any more time, having failed to achieve the business he had intended to transact, leaves the city and goes to Further Gaul.

13.39 The battle for autocracy

Cicero *Letters to Atticus* 10.7.1 (?22 April 49)

The Republic is not the question at issue. The struggle is over who is to be autocrat, in which the king who has been expelled is the more moderate, honourable and blameless, and unless he is the winner the name of the Roman people must inevitably be wiped out, but, if he is the winner, his victory will follow Sulla's practice and example. So, in this conflict, you should support neither openly and adapt yourself to events. But my case is different, because I am tied by an obligation and cannot be ungrateful.

13.40 Pompey endures no equal

Velleius Paterculus *Compendium of History* 2.33.3

Cf. Caesar *BC* 1.4 (doc. 13.24): the trouble with Pompey was that he didn't want anyone to rival him in prestige (cf. Lucan *Phars.* 1.125–6; Florus 2.13.14).

From the time Pompey first went into public life, he could endure no equal at all, and in those affairs, in which he ought to have been first, he desired to be the only one. No one craved all other things less, or glory more than he did; he was unrestrained in grasping at magistracies, though extremely diffident once in office, while he entered into them with the greatest eagerness, only to lay them down without concern, and, although he appropriated of his own free-will whatever he desired, he would resign it at the wish of other people.

13.41 Cicero compares himself to Pompey and Caesar

Cicero *Letters to Atticus* 10.4.4 (14 April 49)

I do not rank the achievements of these top commanders above my own, nor even their very fortune, though they seem to be at the peak of prosperity, and my fortune appears more turbulent. For can anyone be fortunate and happy, who has either abandoned his country or oppressed it?

13.42 Caesar's first dictatorship, 49 BC

Caesar *Civil War* 3.1.1–2.2

After swiftly overrunning Italy, Caesar then proceeded to Spain, on the way leaving Trebonius (tr. pl. 55) to besiege Massilia. Trebonius had proposed the lex Trebonia (doc. 12.73), and had been Caesar's legate in Gaul (54–50 BC). Ahenobarbus, released from Corfinium, raised fresh forces and held out in Massilia, escaping to Pompey when Trebonius took the city: *MRR* II.261–2. In Spain, Caesar defeated Pompey's legates Afranius (cos. 60) and Petreius, not without difficulties, and returned to Rome (Caes. *BC* 1.34–87; App. *BC* 2.42–3; Dio 41.19.1–24.3; *MRR* II.266, 268). Consular elections could not be held in Rome as the consuls for 49 were not present and Caesar's attempt to have the praetor M. Aemilius Lepidus (cos. 46, 42; brother of Lepidus, cos. 50, and younger son of Lepidus, cos. 78) preside was unsuccessful. While at Massilia Caesar was named dictator after a law to this effect was passed by the praetor Lepidus, and on returning to Rome in 49 presided over the consular elections in which he himself was elected consul for 48

(*MRR* II.272). He resigned the dictatorship, after eleven days, and made his way to northern Greece (leaving Lepidus in charge of Rome). Bibulus had been given the Pompeian naval command and unsuccessfully tried to prevent Caesar crossing to Epirus. Caesar then unsuccessfully besieged Pompey at Dyrrachium but defeated him at Pharsalus on 9 August 48 BC. His legislation during this short period as dictator included debt relief, the restoration of exiles and sons of the proscribed, and he ensured the celebration of the Latin Festival.

Caesar was made dictator for the first time in 49 BC, again in late 48 for a year, for a third time in 46 for a period of ten years, for annual terms, and the fourth dictatorship of 45 was converted into a life-time dictatorship in February 44 BC. He held the consulship in 48, 46, 45 and 44.

1.1 Caesar as dictator held the elections and Julius Caesar and Publius Servilius (Isauricus) were made consuls, for this year (48 BC) was the first in which Caesar was legally able to become consul. **2** Once this was done, as credit throughout Italy was fairly tight and debts were not being repaid, he decided that arbitrators should be appointed to make assessments of property and possessions at pre-war values, and that the creditors should be paid at these rates. **3** He thought that this was the best way to remove or lessen the fear of the abolition of debts, which often accompanies wars or civil strife, and to preserve the debtors' honour. **4** Furthermore, in motions brought before the people by praetors and tribunes, he restored to their former status several persons, who, in the period when Pompey had kept troops in the city as a bodyguard, had been convicted of bribery under the Pompeian law, in whose trials, which were completed in a single day, one set of jurors had heard the evidence, and another given their votes . . . **2.1** He allowed 11 days for these measures and for holding the Latin festival and all the elections, and then resigned the dictatorship, left the city and went to Brundisium. **2** He had ordered 12 legions and all the cavalry to meet there. However, he found only enough ships to transport scarcely 15,000 legionaries and 500 cavalry. This one thing, shortage of ships, prevented Caesar from quickly concluding the war.

13.43 Cicero regrets deciding to join Pompey

Cicero *Letters to Friends* 7.3.1–3

In this letter written in mid-April 46 to M. Marius (an old friend, probably one of the Marii of Arpinum), Cicero recalls his views of Pompey's followers at Dyrrachium (cf. Plut. *Cic.* 38; *Att.* 11.4). Caesar's opinion was along the same lines (doc. 13.44). At (2) note the phrase, 'nothing good except the cause': Pompey's followers in fact were not the *boni*, the 'honest men' (the 'good') after all in Cicero's eyes, and the only thing good was the cause itself, not its adherents. The 'certain engagement' that according to Cicero gave Pompey false confidence was his defeat of Caesar at Dyrrachium in July (Caes. *BC* 3.63–72; Plut. *Caes.* 39, *Pomp.* 65.7–8). Caesar's opinion was similar to Cicero's: Pompey should not have drawn any conclusions from this defeat (*BC* 3.72). Caesar lifted the siege, moved his troops, and Pompey pursued him: the 'pitched battle' that resulted was Pharsalus.

1 Since I very frequently ponder the general miseries in which we have lived for so many years and, as I see it, will continue to live, I have been in the habit of bringing to mind the last time we were together; I even remember the actual day. It was on 12 May in the year Lentulus and Marcellus were consuls (49 BC) and I had come down that evening to my Pompeian place and you were there to see me, very worried in your mind.

You were worried by considerations of my duty on the one hand and my danger on the other; if I stayed in Italy, you feared I would be failing in my duty; if I left for the war you were concerned about the danger to me. On that occasion you doubtless saw that I, too, was in such confusion that I could not decide what was best for me to do. But I preferred to give in to honour and reputation rather than to weigh up chances of personal safety.

2 I came to repent of my action, not so much on the grounds of danger to myself as on those of the many evils with which I was struck when I arrived (at Dyrrachium): first of all that the troops were neither numerous nor warlike; secondly that, apart from the commander and a few others (I mean among the chief figures), all the rest were greedy for plunder in the war itself and so bloodthirsty in the way they talked that I shuddered at the thought of their victory; finally, the most distinguished among them were deep in debt. In short — nothing good except the cause. After seeing all this, I despaired of victory and began trying to persuade them to make peace, of which I had always been a supporter; then, when Pompey was strongly opposed to that view, I set to persuading them to delay the war. Sometimes he approved of this and seemed to be going to follow this policy, and perhaps he would have done, if he had not started, after a certain engagement, having confidence in his troops. From that time, that pre-eminent man was no longer a general. With an inexperienced and hastily collected army he fought a pitched battle against the toughest of legions. He was defeated, even his camp was lost, and he fled shamefully and alone. **3** As far as I was concerned that was the end of the war, and I could not see how we, who had been no match for the enemy with our forces intact, would be superior with our forces shattered.

13.44 Caesar on those in Pompey's camp

Caesar *Civil War* 3.82.2–83.4

Caesar here particularly criticises Domitius, Scipio and Lentulus Spinther. L. Domitius Ahenobarbus as consul in 54 had opposed the triumvirate; he was to command Pompey's left wing at Pharsalus and was killed in the battle; Q. Caecilius Metellus Pius Scipio (cos. 52, Pompey's father-in-law), had been responsible for the proposal at the beginning of 49 that Caesar disarm; he escaped from Pharsalus to Africa and died at Thapsus; P. Cornelius Lentulus Spinther was the consul in 57 who had promoted Cicero's recall and was the older brother of Lentulus Crus, cos. 49, one of the Pompeians released by Caesar after Corfinium who rejoined Pompey. He died shortly after Pharsalus.

82.2 With this addition to Pompey's forces and the uniting of two great armies, the former view of everyone was confirmed and their hope of victory increased, so that whatever interval lay before them seemed only a delay in their return to Italy, and, whenever Pompey acted with some slowness or deliberation, they proclaimed that it was the business of only a day, but that he was making the most of his command and behaving to men of consular and praetorian rank as though they were slaves. **3** They were already openly fighting over rewards and priesthoods and allocating the consulship for years ahead, while others were demanding the houses and other property of those who were in Caesar's camp . . . **83.1** Domitius, Scipio and Lentulus Spinther were already in daily contention for Caesar's priesthood, and openly sinking to the worst invective in their speech, as Lentulus paraded the distinction of his age, Domitius boasted his influence with the people and prestige, and Scipio trusted in his kinship with Pompey . . . **4** In short, all were concerned about potential honours for themselves or monetary rewards or prosecuting private enmities, and they did not reflect on the ways in which they could conquer the opposition, but how they ought to use their victory.

13.45 Dolabella tries to entice Cicero away from Pompey

[Cicero] *Letters to Friends* 9.9.2–3 (?May 48)

This letter was written from Caesar's camp outside Dyrrachium by Dolabella (tr. pl. 47), one of Caesar's legates (*MRR* II.281), to his father-in-law Cicero (Dolabella was married to Cicero's daughter Tullia). Dolabella recognises Cicero's adherence to Pompey and the optimates, but argues that it is time for him to abandon this political position. It is usually thought that Caesar was instrumental in having this letter written. Dolabella commanded a fleet for Caesar in 49 but was defeated and won no military distinction fighting in northern Greece in 49–48; for the letter, see Rawson 1975: 201; Habicht 1990: 65; Fuhrmann 1992: 140–1.

2 You can see Gnaeus Pompey's position — he is defended neither by the glory of his name and achievements, nor by his status as patron of kings and nations, which he used frequently to boast about, and does not have the chance which the most lowly people have, of being able to flee with honour. Driven out of Italy, Spain lost, his veteran army taken, and now finally blockaded, which I don't think has ever happened before to any of our generals! And so, use your common sense to consider what he can hope for or what good you can do him; you will then find it easiest to make the decision which would be most advantageous for you. But I beg you that, if he does get out of his current predicament and takes refuge with his fleet, you consider your own interests and be, at long last, your own friend, rather than anyone else's. You have now done enough for duty and friendship, you have done enough for your party and the kind of state of which you approved. **3** It is now time to take our stand where the state is at present, rather than, by longing after its old form, to find ourselves nowhere.

13.46 The death of Pompey the Great

Plutarch *Life of Pompey* 79.1–80.3

After his defeat at Dyrrachium, Caesar marched into Thessaly and Pompey followed; a battle took place at Pharsalus in August 48, in which Pompey and his forces were thoroughly routed. Pompey was on the left wing with the two legions Caesar had handed over for the Parthian war; Caesar placed himself opposite. Domitius Calvinus (cos. 53; he had opposed Caesar as tr. pl. in 59 BC) commanded Caesar's centre. Antony commanded Caesar's left wing. Pompey's father-in-law, Q. Caecilius Metellus Scipio, led Pompey's centre. Caesar's troops stampeded Pompey's cavalry (led initially with success by Labienus) and he called up his reserves against Pompey's tiring troops, and drove them into Pompey's camp. Pompey and his forces fled and Pompey, via Lesbos where his wife Cornelia joined him, made for Egypt. The advisors (Achillas, Potheinus and Theodotus) of the young king Ptolemy XIII decided to kill Pompey rather than earn Caesar's hostility by receiving him. Achillas took Septimius and sailed out to Pompey's trireme. Septimius had been Pompey's military tribune in 67 BC and was serving in Egypt in this capacity from 55 to 48 (*MRR* II.147, 278). Philip who cremated the remains of the corpse was Pompey's freedman. Lucan describes the scene in his *Civil Wars* 8.472–691 (with Malamud 2003). Pompey's remains were later retrieved and buried by Cornelia at his Alban villa; Caesar arrived in Egypt three days after Pompey's death, on 2 October, and was presented with his head and signet ring; he had Achillas and Potheinus executed. Theodotus escaped but either Brutus later had him slowly tortured to death (Plut. *Pomp.* 80.7–10) or Cassius had him crucified (Appian *BC* 2.90.377). Pompey's sons and Cato went to Cyrenaica in Africa; Lentulus Crus, cos. 49, was killed in Egypt the day after Pompey.

Pharsalus and Pompey's death in Egypt: Caes. *BC* 3.88–97; Lucan 7.214–872, bk. 8 passim; Plut. *Pomp.* 69, *Caes.* 42–6; Dio 41.57; App. *BC* 2.84–6; *MRR* II.272–84; Fuller 1965: 231–9; Balsdon 1967: 135–7; Gelzer 1968: 236–41; Leach 1978: 200–9; Greenhalgh 1981: 231–65; Meier 1995: 397–400; Leigh 1997: 77–157 (Lucan on Pompey); Southern 2001: 116–18; Seager 2002: 166–8; Southern 2002: 138–40.

79.1 As it was a long distance to land from the trireme, and none of those in the boat with him had a friendly word for him, he looked at Septimius and asked, 'Surely I am not mistaken? Were you a comrade-in-arms of mine?' He only nodded his head, without saying anything or showing any friendliness. **2** As there was deep silence again, Pompey took a small roll containing a speech written by him in Greek, which he had prepared for his address to Ptolemy, and started to read it. **3** As they approached the shore, Cornelia, along with his friends, watched from the trireme with great anxiety as to what would happen, and began to take courage when she saw many of the royal entourage at the landing place as if to give him an honourable reception. **4** But at this point, while Pompey was holding Philip's hand so he could stand up more easily, Septimius first ran him through with his sword, and then Salvius next and Achillas drew their daggers and stabbed him. **5** Pompey drew his toga over his face with both hands, without saying or doing anything unworthy of himself, only groaning and enduring their blows, having lived one year less than sixty and ending his life only one day after his birthday.

80.1 When the people on the ships saw the murder, they gave such a cry of lamentation that they could be heard from the shore and fled, quickly weighing anchor. A strong wind assisted them as they ran out to sea, so that the Egyptians, though they wanted to pursue them, turned back. **2** But they cut off Pompey's head, and threw the rest of his body naked from the boat and left it there for anyone who wanted to see such a sight. **3** But Philip remained by him, until they had had their fill of gazing at it; he then washed the body in sea-water, and wrapped it in one of his own tunics as he had no other, and looked along the shore until he found the remains of a small fishing-boat, old but sufficient for a funeral pyre for a body which was naked and not intact.

13.47 Cicero on Pompey's death

Cicero *Letters to Atticus* 11.6.5 (27 November 48)

I never had any doubt regarding Pompey's fate. The hopelessness of his situation was such that all rulers and peoples were totally convinced of it, so that, wherever he went, I thought this would happen. I cannot help grieving over his wretched fate; I knew him to be a man of integrity, clean living, and good character.

13.48 'Veni, vidi, vici', 47 BC

Plutarch *Life of Caesar* 49.10–50.4

Caesar arrived in Alexandria three days after Pompey's murder, where he later dallied with Cleopatra (who evaded the forces of her rival brother who held Alexandria by arriving at the palace in a 'bed-sack', a type of sack in which slaves kept the bed-clothes when not in use: Plut. *Caes.* 49.1). Caesar supported her in the Egyptian power struggle and was besieged in the royal palace by the population, but rescued by the arrival of forces from Mithridates of Pergamon; during the conflict Ptolemy XIII drowned. Caesar's son by Cleopatra, Caesarion (Ptolemy XV), was born in 47 BC. Caesar stayed in Egypt for a few weeks more, then moved north to deal with Pharnaces, king of the Crimea and son of the Mithridates whom Pompey had defeated. He defeated Pharnaces on 2 August 47 at Zela. The Domitius here is Cn. Domitius Calvinus (cos. 53) put in command of Asia Minor after Pharsalus (*MRR* II.277). Cleopatra: Bradford 1971; Grant 1972; Whitehorne 1994: 186–96; Southern 1999; Chaveau 2002.

49.10 Leaving as ruler of Egypt Cleopatra, who a little while afterwards had a son by him called Caesarion by the Alexandrians, he set out for Syria. **50.1** After leaving Syria, he learnt while crossing Asia that Domitius had been defeated by Pharnaces, son of Mithridates, and had fled from Pontus with a few troops, while Pharnaces was making full use of his victory to occupy Bithynia and Cappadocia, attempting to take over the country called Lesser Armenia, and stirring up revolt among all the kings and tetrarchs there. **2** Accordingly Caesar immediately marched against him with three legions, fought a great battle against him near the city of Zela, and drove him in flight from Pontus, while utterly destroying his army. **3** When he reported how swift and speedy this battle had been in writing to one of his friends, Amantius, at Rome, he used just three words, 'Came, saw, conquered!' **4** In Latin, the words have the same inflectional ending and thus an impressive brevity.

13.49 Cicero regrets his position

Cicero *Letters to Atticus* 11.9.1 (3 January 47)

After Pharsalus, Cicero sailed to Corcyra where he refused Cato's suggestion that he take command of the Pompeian forces there; according to Plutarch, Pompey's two sons (Gnaeus and Sextus) threatened him with violence and nearly death (Plut. *Cic.* 39.2, *Cato Min.* 55.6). He returned from Dyrrachium to Italy. Dolabella had written to Cicero that he would intercede with Caesar on his behalf if Cicero were to retire from the conflict when Pompey was defeated (doc. 13.45), but when Cicero arrived at Brundisium, Antony informed him that Caesar was reviewing on an individual basis the cases of those who had supported Pompey and wished to return to Italy (*Att.* 11.7.2; *MRR* II.278). Cicero's lack of caution in returning to Italy became clearer when Pompey's defeat did not mean that Caesar emerged as victor: the war was continued by Pompey's sons and supporters and Caesar's dominance was by no means wholly secure until after the defeat of the Pompeians in Spain at Munda.

Caesar sent Cicero a letter in August 47 during his campaign against Pharnaces (*Fam.* 14.23); Cicero was 'pardoned' in September and arrived in Rome in October. A series of letters to Atticus survives from Brundisium bemoaning his situation: *Att.* 11.5–25 (November 48 to September 47); for Cicero's return to Italy: Wistrand 1979a: 167–202; Habicht 1990: 66–7.

As you write, I did indeed act incautiously and more hastily than I should have, and I have no hope, now that I am being kept back by the exemptions in the edicts. If these had not been effected by your zeal and good will, I would have been able to retire to a place of solitude. Now even that is forbidden. But why should I be pleased to have come before the beginning of the tribunate, if I am not pleased to have come at all? What am I to hope for from a person who was never my friend, now I am legally ruined and crushed? Every day Balbus' letters to me grow less warm, and perhaps many letters from many writers are going to Caesar against me. I am destroyed by my own fault; nothing in my wretched state is owing to chance — it can all be laid on my shoulders. When I saw what kind of war it was, with total lack of preparation and weakness against an excellently prepared opposition, I decided what to do and determined on a plan which was not so much courageous, but permissible, especially in my case.

CAESAR'S DICTATORSHIP

Caesar was named dictator for the second time, for twelve months, shortly after Pharsalus by his fellow consul for 48 BC, P. Servilius Isauricus. In Italy, M. Caelius Rufus as praetor (*peregrinus*) pushed for debt cancellation and suspension of rent payments; he was removed from office by Servilius, and joined in a revolt in southern Italy with Milo who had returned from exile; both were killed by soldiers sent against them (*MRR* II.273).

Antony, master of the horse in late 48 and 47 (and so second-in-command to the dictator), temporarily lost Caesar's support in 47 due to his mishandling of the situation in Italy (*MRR* II.287). Dolabella as tribune for 47 had agitated for a cancellation of debts which led to disorders and bloodshed at Rome; Antony had difficulty in restoring order in Rome, and in dealing with mutinous soldiers in Campania. After his defeat of Pharnaces in 47, Caesar returned to Rome in September 47; he dealt with the debt-problem and mutiny (Chrissanthos 2001). The troops had marched on Rome; Caesar went out to them and their loyalty was restored through their devotion to him and his threat to discharge them. He made it clear that Antony — whose public drunkenness, debaucheries, involvement with the actress Cytheris, and luxurious way of life during this period (vomiting into his tunic at an assembly in the forum after an all-night eating and drinking binge) — had lost his favour, though he was restored to this after Caesar's return from Munda. Dolabella was forgiven, served under Caesar in Africa and Spain, and was chosen by Caesar to replace him as consul for 44 BC when he went to Parthia (Plut. *Ant.* 9–10; App. *BC* 2.92–4; *MRR* II.286–7, 311, 317); he had divorced Cicero's daughter Tullia, though she was pregnant, in (November?) 46 without repaying her dowry (cf. doc. 7.26).

Caesar went to Africa in December 47, and defeated the Pompeians led by Metellus Scipio (cos. 52) at Thapsus on 6 April 46 (Scipio committed suicide; *MRR* II.297). Cato committed suicide a few days later at Utica, which its residents refused to defend against Caesar. Cato preferred to die than to receive a pardon from Caesar (Plut. *Cato Min.* 66); Cicero (*Off.* 1.112) describes Cato as preferring to die rather than look on the face of a tyrant (i.e., Caesar). Probably in late April 46, Caesar (also consul for the third time in 46) was made dictator for the third time, now for ten years in succession (Dio 43.14.3). The events in Africa are dealt with by *The African War*, included amongst Caesar's works but clearly not by him.

Caesar returned to Rome and celebrated four triumphs (for Gaul, Egypt, Pontus and Africa) in 46 BC after Thapsus (doc. 2.35). He built a temple to Venus Genetrix ('Ancestress': see Weinstock 1971: 80–7), vowed at Pharsalus, and began the Forum Julium. Gladiatorial and naval contests were held in honour of his daughter Julia (doc. 2.74). Made consul for the fourth time for 45, he proceeded to Spain, making the journey from Rome in 27 days: App. *BC* 2.103.426–9; Plut. *Caes.* 56.1–2; Dio 43.31.2–32.2.

Pompey's son Gnaeus had previously left Africa for Spain, and after Thapsus his younger brother Sextus joined him there; Caesar defeated them at Munda in March 45 BC. Gnaeus was later captured and killed; Sextus continued the revolt in Further Spain and survived Caesar's death. [Caesar's] *Spanish War* deals with this campaign. Labienus, who had also fought at

Thapsus, was killed at Munda. A triumph for Munda was celebrated in October 45: unlike Caesar's previous four, this one celebrated a defeat over Romans, incurring the displeasure of the public (Plut. *Caes*. 56.7–9; *MRR* II.305).

13.50 Cicero to L. Papirius Paetus

Cicero *Letters to Friends* 9.15.3–4 (?first intercalary month, 46 BC)

One of several amusing letters written by Cicero to his wealthy friend Paetus at Naples: see *Fam.* 9.15–26. Q. Lutatius Catulus was consul in 78 and acknowledged leader of the optimates from then until defeated by Caesar for the position of pontifex maximus in 63 (doc. 3.20).

3 You speak to me of Catulus and those times. What is the resemblance? Then, indeed, I did not like to be away too long from protecting the state; for I was sitting in the stern in charge of the helm. But now I hardly even have a place in the hold! **4** Do you think there will be any less decrees of the senate if I am in Naples? When I am in Rome and often in the forum, decrees of the senate are written at the home of your admirer, my intimate acquaintance; indeed, when it occurs to him, I am put down as present at their drawing up, and I hear of a senatorial decree, said to have been passed on my motion, reaching Armenia and Syria, before I hear so much as a mention of the matter itself. And I don't want you to think that I am joking. I should tell you that letters have been brought to me from kings at the ends of the earth, in which they thank me for proposing the motion to give them the title of kings, when I was not only unaware of their royal appellation, but even of their very existence.

13.51 Caesar's pardons

Cicero *In Defence of Marcellus* 13, 15

M. Claudius Marcellus (cos. 51), best known for scourging a magistrate of Novum Comum (docs 13.8–9) and for attempting to have Caesar replaced in Gaul before his term expired on the grounds that Gaul was pacified, resided at Mytilene after Pharsalus. In 46, the senate requested that M. Marcellus be pardoned; his cousin, C. Claudius Marcellus (cos. 50, and already pardoned), according to Cicero fell at Caesar's feet. Cicero, called upon to speak, delivered the *pro Marcello*. In this speech Cicero praises Caesar, urges him to restore a proper constitution, and notes that the city has not seen the naked sword and that only in battle has the state lost men. There are clear hopes here that some form of restitution of the *res publica* will be possible (Dyer 1990). By 44, Cicero was less optimistic (doc 13.53). As for (M. Claudius) Marcellus himself, he was stabbed at the Piraeus by a friend in May 45 and died (*Fam.* 4.12.1–3; see also Cic. *Fam.* 4.4.3–4, 4.7–12, *Att.* 13.10). For Marcellus' letter to Cicero after his pardon, and Cicero's reply, see *Fam.* 4.11, 4.10. Caesar's clemency (clementia) was an important piece of propaganda in the civil wars, but may genuinely have been intended to avoid bloodshed and discourage resistance.

13 Note, conscript fathers, the far-reaching effects of Caesar's decision: all of us who went to war impelled by some wretched and calamitous fate which attends the state, though we can be charged with culpability on the grounds of human error, have assuredly been acquitted of criminality. When Caesar preserved Marcus Marcellus for the state at your intercession, and when he restored me both to myself and to the state without any intercession, and all these other renowned men too, to themselves and to their country, whose number and eminence you can see at this very meeting, he did not bring enemies into the senate, but decided that most people had been induced by ignorance and false and groundless fears to go to war, not by greed or bloodthirstiness . . . **15** No critic of events will be so unjust as to question Caesar's wishes with regard to war, since he has without loss of time decided on the restitution of those who advocated peace, though showing more resentment to the rest. That was perhaps less to be wondered at when the outcome and fortune of war was undecided and doubtful, but when a victor treats the advocates of peace with respect, he is surely proclaiming that he would have preferred not to fight at all rather than to win.

13.52 Caesar fails to bear grudges

Cicero *Letters to Friends* 6.6.8, 10 (?October 46)

Written to A. Caecina, a Pompeian from Etruria exiled after Pharsalus, who had written a 'libellous' book against Caesar (Suet. *Jul.* 75.5); to counteract this he later produced a book of *Remonstrances*, dwelling on Caesar's clemency. He had surrendered to Caesar in 46 and was in Sicily awaiting permission to return to Italy.

8 In Caesar we see a mild and merciful disposition, just as you portrayed in your outstanding book of *Remonstrances*. He is also amazingly impressed by remarkable talents, such as your own, and moreover gives way to widely-held opinions, as long as these are fair and inspired by duty, and not petty or self-interested . . . **10** No one is so hostile to the cause, which Pompey embraced with more enthusiasm than preparation, as to dare to speak of us as bad citizens or reprobates. In this respect I always have to admire Caesar's sense of responsibility, fairness and wisdom. He never mentions Pompey except in the most respectful terms. Perhaps he acted with harshness towards Pompey on numerous occasions — but those were the acts of war and victory, not of Caesar himself. Look how he has welcomed us! He made Cassius his legate, put Brutus in charge of Gaul, and Sulpicius (cos. 51) of Greece, while Marcellus, with whom he was particularly angry, has been restored in the most honourable way.

13.53 Cicero to Manius Curius

Cicero *Letters to Friends* 7.30.1–2 (beginning of 44 BC)

In 45, Caesar was sole consul (his fourth consulship) until the beginning of October; he then resigned and was replaced by Q. Fabius Maximus and C. Trebonius; when Fabius Maximus died on the last day of the year, Caesar replaced him with C. Caninius Rebilus (see *MRR* II.305). Cicero quipped that no one had breakfast in Caninius' consulship (cf. his comments on Vatinius: doc. 12.15). Caesar's third dictatorship ended in April 45, and his fourth dictatorship immediately followed, but sometime in February 44 he became dictator for life; in 44 he was also consul, with Antony as his colleague. Cicero is here writing to a friend of his, a businessman in Patrae (western Greece). Caesar's administrative activities 49–44 BC, and the dictatorship for life: *MRR* II.305–6; Syme 1939: 52–60; Fuller 1965: 298–302; Balsdon 1967: 150–78; Gelzer 1968: 272–322; Sumner 1971; Scullard *GN* 143–53; Rawson 1994: 438–67; Shotter 1994: 79–87; Meier 1995: 461–79; Southern 2001: 141–8; cf. Collins 1955; Ehrenberg 1964.

1 It is unbelievable how disgraced I feel in living in today's Rome. You show yourself to have been far more farsighted about events when you took flight from here. Although things here are still disagreeable when you hear them, nevertheless to hear them is more bearable than to see them. You at least were not in the Campus when the elections to the quaestorship started at the second hour. An official seat had been put out for Quintus Maximus, whom these men used to call consul; at the report of his death, the seat was taken away. He (Caesar), however, having taken the auspices for a comitia tributa, held a centuriate assembly, and at the seventh hour proclaimed a consul elected, to remain in office until the Kalends of January — the morning of the following day. So I can tell you that in the consulship of Caninius no one had any breakfast! However, no crime was committed in his consulship; his vigilance was amazing — **2** he did not close an eye in the whole of his magistracy! You'll find all this laughable; that's because you are not here. If you were to see it, you couldn't keep from tears. What if I told you the rest? There are countless examples in the same vein.

13.54 Caesar's legislation as dictator

Suetonius *Life of the Deified Julius* 41.1–43.2

Caesar introduced many measures which cannot all be dated; his main reforms concerned the calendar, grain distribution, and debt relief, which date to 46. Sumptuary legislation was also introduced to limit personal expenditure and extravagance. The various vacancies in the senate caused by the civil war were filled. Not all approved of new senators from Gaul: there was a popular song that they had changed their trousers for togas (Suet. *Jul.* 80.2). Elections continued but in a controlled manner. Caesar clearly did not have a 'blueprint' for reform but carried out what he considered were necessary measures. In addition to those described in this passage, Caesar's plans included constructing a temple to Mars, a theatre, a highway from the Adriatic, a canal through the Isthmus, libraries, restructure of the law code, draining the Pomptine marshes, and waging war against the Dacians and Parthians.

For Caesar's reforms, see Cic. *Off.* 2. 84 (debt legislation); Suet. *Caes.* 40–4; Plut. *Caes.* 59; Appian *BC* 2.102; Dio 43.25–6, 47–53; *MRR* II.293–4; Gelzer 1967: 310–14; Balsdon 1967: 152–5; Rawson 1994: 453–8; Meier 1995: 446–7; building plans: Suet. *Caes.* 44.1; calendar: doc. 3.29; the senate, see esp. Syme 1979.

41.1 He filled the vacancies in the senate, enrolled more patricians, and increased the number of praetors, aediles, and quaestors, as well as that of the minor officials; he also reinstated those who had been stripped of their privileges by action of the censors or had been condemned for bribery by a jury. **2** He shared elections with the people on the basis that, except for the candidates for the consulship, the people should choose half the magistrates and he should personally nominate the other half. These he announced by circulating brief notes around the tribes: 'Caesar the Dictator to tribe such-and-such. I recommend to you so-and-so to hold their magistracies by your votes.' He even admitted to office the sons of those who had been proscribed. He restored the right of jury service to two classes, the equites and senators, disqualifying the third class, the tribunii aerarii. **3** He registered the people for the corn dole by a new method and locale, street by street, using the owners of apartment buildings, and reduced the number of those who received free grain from 320,000 to 150,000; so that new meetings did not have to be called in the future to enrol people he laid down that the places of those who died were to be filled by lot every year by the praetors from those who were not registered. **42.1** Since 80,000 citizens had been assigned to overseas colonies, he enacted a law to rebuild the population of the depleted city that no citizen older than twenty or younger than forty years of age, unless he was serving in the army, should absent himself from Italy for more than three years in succession; that no senator's son should go overseas except as one of a magistrate's household or staff; and that graziers should have among their herdsmen at least one-third who were free-born. He also granted citizenship to all medical practitioners and teachers of liberal arts at Rome to induce them to stay in the city and encourage others to settle there. **2** Regarding debts he disappointed those who wanted them cancelled, which was frequently called for, but finally decreed that debtors should satisfy their creditors through a valuation of their property at the price they had purchased it for before the civil war, with whatever interest they had paid in cash or pledged in writing being deducted from the total; by this arrangement about a quarter of the loan was wiped out. **3** He dissolved all guilds except those founded in ancient times. He increased penalties for crimes; and, since the wealthy had less compunction about committing crimes because they were merely exiled with their property intact, he punished murders of fellow-citizens, as Cicero records, by the confiscation of their entire property, and the rest by the confiscation of half of it.

43.1 He administered justice with great conscientiousness and severity. He even removed those convicted of extortion from the senatorial order. He annulled the marriage of an ex-praetor who had married a woman the day after her divorce from her husband, although there was no suspicion of adultery. He imposed duties on foreign goods. He forbade the use of litters and the wearing of scarlet robes or pearls to everyone except those of a certain standing and age and on specific days. **2** He particularly enforced his law against luxury by placing watchmen in parts of the market to seize and bring him delicacies which were on sale in violation of his prohibition, while he sometimes sent his lictors and soldiers to take from a dining-room items, even after they had been served, which his watchmen had failed to confiscate.

13.55 Caesar's unconstitutional honours

Suetonius *Life of the Deified Julius* 76, 78.1–80.1

The honours for Caesar began in earnest from 20 April 45 BC with the news that Caesar had prevailed at Munda. He had now overcome all his enemies (the continued existence of Sextus Pompeius hardly counted). A supplicatio of an unprecedented fifty days was voted. He was granted the right to wear a laurel wreath, apparently particularly pleasing to him due to his increasing thinness of hair. *Imperator* was granted to him as a hereditary title; he was awarded the name *Liberator*. He was to manage the army and public finances, and to have a public palace. Annual races were to be held in the Circus on 21 April in his honour. The month Quintilis in which Caesar was born was renamed July. He was named 'Father of his Country' (45 BC, *parens patriae*: Weinstock 1971: 201–5). The senate and people decreed all these.

Rex ('king'): The Romans had overthrown the Etruscan kings in 509 BC and republican sentiment detested the notion of monarchy. Prior to February 44, when he was made perpetual dictator, Caesar was still within republican norms: his power was conferred by the senate and the third dictatorship of 46 was of ten years' duration, held in annual terms (though traditionally a dictatorship lasted six months). A command against Parthia was voted to Caesar, who appointed officials, named in advance, to hold office during his planned absence of three years in Parthia. Sixteen legions and 10,000 cavalry were prepared. A rumour circulated that Parthia could only be conquered by a king and it was suggested that Caesar be known as king of those subject to Rome. There are different interpretations of the diadem and Lupercalia incident. It is possible that Caesar was testing public opinion, to see what the reaction would be to his becoming king, or that the incident at the Lupercalia was meant as a public demonstration that he intended to reject kingship: Antony's offer could hardly have been spontaneous. His planned departure on 18 March roused the conspirators to act on 15 March. Parthia: Suet. *Jul.* 44.3; Plut. *Caes.* 58.6; Appian *BC* 2.110; Dio 43.51; *MRR* II.317 on the arrangements for while he was away, with Dolabella to take his place as consul for 44 (an arrangement Antony, as the other consul for 44, opposed); Lupercalia incident and aiming for kingship: Dumézil 1970: 349–50; Weinstock 1971: 331–40.

God: In the Hellenistic and Roman East Caesar, like Hellenistic kings and other Roman generals, had already been accorded divine status. Then, in 46 BC after the victory at Thapsus in Africa, a statue of him was erected in Rome standing on a globe with an inscription that he was a 'demi-god'. After Munda, temples were dedicated to him, and one jointly to Caesar and Clemency; statues of him were to be placed in all the temples in Rome; and a statue of him was placed in the temple of Quirinus and inscribed, 'To the Unconquered God'. Antony was a member of the college of the recently established Luperci Juliani (it was probably in this capacity that he participated in the Lupercalia: doc. 7.76) and was appointed as the first flamen of Caesar, though he did not take up this appointment until 40 BC. Caesar was allowed triumphal dress (and so appear as Jupiter) for all public occasions; like the gods, he had a couch (pulvinar) on which his image was placed; his house was to have a pediment, like a temple. Whether he had become a god or not by 15 March 44 BC is unclear: formal deification in fact came after his death. But he was in 45 and 44 clearly approaching divine status, even if outright worship was not yet practised. Sulla, Pompey and Caesar all claimed special relationships with Venus, who had an intimate connection with Rome, though Caesar with his emphasis on Venus Genetrix ('Ancestress', mother of Aeneas) alone claimed divine ancestry. All three had some sort of veneration in the east: Caesar alone of the three brought this into Rome itself. For the tribunes Caesetius Flavus and Epidius Marullus, see *MRR* II.323.

For Caesar's divine status: *SIG*³ 760; honours, civic and divine: Suet. *Jul.* 45; App. *BC* 2.106; Dio 43.42.2–43.1, esp. 44.4–7; Cic. *Phil.* 2.110–11; Taylor 1931: 58–77; Syme 1939: 55; Fuller 1965: 298–302; Gelzer 1968: 307–10, 315–16; Weinstock 1971: passim, note 281–6; North 1975; Rawson 1994: 458–67; Meier 1995: 466–79; *BNP* I.140–9; Gradel 2002: 54–61.

76.1 Not only did he accept excessive honours: a continuous consulship, a perpetual dictatorship, the censorship of morals, as well as the praenomen 'Imperator' and the cognomen 'Father of his Country', a statue among those of the kings, and a raised seat in the orchestra, but he also allowed honours too great for the mortal condition to be bestowed on him: a golden seat in the senate-house and on the tribunal, a chariot (for carrying divine images) and litter in the circus procession, temples, altars, statues next to those of the gods, a couch , a flamen, a college of the Luperci, and the naming of a month after him; indeed, there were no honours that he did not receive or grant at will. **2** His third and fourth consulships he held in name only, satisfied with the power of the dictatorship, which was voted him at the same time as the consulships, and in both years he substituted two consuls for himself for the three final months, in the meantime holding no elections except for tribunes and plebeian aediles and designating prefects instead of praetors to administer the city's affairs in his absence. When a consul died suddenly on the day before the Kalends of January, he gave the vacant magistracy for a few hours to someone who asked him for it. **3** With the same licence and disdain for ancestral custom, he appointed magistrates for several years ahead, bestowed decorations of consular rank on ten ex-praetors, and admitted to the senate men who had been granted citizenship and even some half-barbarous Gauls. In addition, he placed his personal slaves in charge of the mint and public revenues. He entrusted the supervision and command of the three legions he had left at Alexandria to his favourite Rufio, son of one of his freedmen . . .

78.1 However, the incident that particularly aroused deadly hatred against him was when all the conscript fathers approached him with numerous high honours that they had voted him, and he received them before the temple of Venus Genetrix, without rising from his seat. Some people believe that he was held back by Cornelius Balbus, when he attempted to rise; others, that he made no such attempt at all, but instead glared at Gaius Trebatius when he advised him to stand up. **2** This action of his seemed the more intolerable, as when, in one of his triumphs, he rode past the tribunician benches, he was so furious that one of the college, Pontius Aquila (tr. pl. 45), did not stand up, that he cried out, 'Go on then, Aquila, make me restore the Republic, tribune!' and for several successive days would not promise anything to anyone except with the rider, 'That is, if Pontius Aquila will permit it.'

79.1 To this insult, which so obviously showed his disdain for the senate, he added a deed of far greater arrogance, for, at the Latin festival, as he was returning to Rome, amongst the extravagant and unheard-of acclamations of the populace, someone in the crowd placed a laurel wreath on his statue, with a white fillet tied to it, and when the tribunes Epidius Marullus and Caesetius Flavus (tr. pl. 44 BC) ordered that the fillet be removed from the wreath and the man taken off to prison, Caesar sharply reprimanded them and deposed them from office, grieved either that the suggestion of monarchy had been so unenthusiastically received, or, as he stated, because he had been deprived of the prestige of refusing it. **2** From then on, however, he was unable to dispel the ill-repute of having aspired to the title of king, although, when the plebs greeted him as king, he replied that his name was Caesar and not Rex (King), and when, at the Lupercalia, the consul Antony attempted a number of times to place a diadem on his head, he refused to accept it and sent it to the Capitol as an offering to Jupiter Optimus Maximus. **3** Indeed, the rumour had even spread widely that he was going to move to Alexandria or Troy, taking the wealth of the state with him, and leaving Italy exhausted by levies and his friends in charge of Rome, while at the next meeting of the senate Lucius Cotta was going to announce the view of the Fifteen in charge of the Sibylline Books, that, since it was written in the books of fate that the Parthians could only be conquered by a king, Caesar should be given the title of king. **80.1** It was for this reason that the conspirators hurried on their plans, to avoid having to assent to this.

CAESAR'S PERSONALITY

13.56 Caesar's appearance

Suetonius *Life of the Deified Julius* 45.1–3

For portrait busts of Caesar, see the introduction to chapter 12.

45.1 Caesar is said to have been tall, with a fair complexion, shapely limbs, a rather full face, and keen black eyes, and to have had sound health, except that towards the end of his life he was subject to sudden fainting fits as well as nightmares. He also had two attacks of epilepsy while on campaign. **2** He was fastidious in the care of his person, and so not only kept his hair carefully trimmed and shaved, but even had his body hair plucked — some people accuse him of that at any rate — while he was extremely vexed by the disfiguring effect of his baldness, since he found it exposed him to the ridicule of his opponents. As a result he used to comb his receding hair forward from the crown of his head and, of all the honours voted him by the senate and people, there was none that pleased him more or that he made use of more gladly than the privilege of wearing a laurel wreath on all occasions. **3** They say, too, that his dress was unusual: his purple-striped tunic had fringed sleeves down to the wrist and he always wore a belt over it, though it was rather loosely fastened. This, it is said, was the reason for Sulla's frequent warning to the optimates to beware of the 'ill-girt boy'.

13.57 Caesar versus Cato: a value judgement

Sallust *Conspiracy of Catiline* 53.6–54.6

Sallust's comparison of the virtues of both Caesar and Cato was written c. 42 BC. He may have been intending a tacit criticism of both by 'extreme good qualities' in the first line — both overdid their excellences (Caesar his liberality, and Cato his 'justice'). However, they are his heroes in the *Conspiracy of Catiline* rather than Cicero, and their speeches play a prominent part in the work. Cato's principles could be flexible where necessary: note his bribery on behalf of Bibulus, his son-in-law: doc. 12.37. On Sallust's aim here, see Stone 1999.

53.6 Now within my living memory there have been two men of extreme good qualities but very different characters, Marcus Cato and Gaius Caesar. Since the subject has come up, it is not my intention to pass them by in silence, but to disclose the nature and character of each, as far as my ability permits. **54.1** Well, their descent, age and eloquence were very similar, their greatness of spirit equal, and likewise their glory, but in other respects they were different. **2** Caesar was considered great in kindnesses and liberality, Cato in the integrity of his life. The former became noted for his clemency and compassion, while severity added to the latter's dignity. **3** Caesar won glory by giving, helping and pardoning, Cato by making no gifts. In the one there was a refuge for the wretched, in the other the destruction of evildoers. The former's good-nature, the latter's firmness were the subjects of praise. **4** Finally, Caesar had trained himself to work hard, to stay vigilant; intent on his friends' affairs, to neglect his own, to refuse nothing worth giving; for himself he longed for great imperium, an army, a new war in which his virtue could shine forth. **5** But Cato's pursuit was moderation, what was fitting, and most of all gravity. **6** He did not try to rival the rich in richness, nor the ambitious in politics, but the active man in virtue, the moderate in modesty, the blameless in self-control; he preferred rather to be than to seem good; thus the less he sought glory, the more it followed him.

13.58 Catullus on Caesar

Catullus 93

Suet. *Jul.* 73: Caesar invited Catullus to dinner after the latter had apologised for invective against Caesar and Mamurra: cf. doc. 12.87. Cremutius in Tacitus (*Ann.* 4.34) comments on the fact that the poems of M. Furius Bibaculus and Catullus were full of insults against the Caesars, but that Julius and Augustus ignored them.

I have no very great desire, Caesar, to try to please you,
or even to know whether you are white or black.

13.59 Caesar's literary abilities

Suetonius *Life of the Deified Julius* 56.1–7

Pliny *Ep.* 5.3.5 mentions light-hearted poetry written by Caesar (not highly commended by Tac. *Dial.* 21.6); according to Plut. *Caes.* 2 Caesar wrote and recited poems while held by the Cilician pirates. His oratory was highly praised by Cicero (doc. 2.63), and he wrote a treatise on *Analogy*. Of his works, the three books on the *Civil War* and seven books on the *Gallic War* (the eighth was written by Hirtius) survive; see doc. 14.6.

1 He left memoirs of his deeds in the *Gallic War* and the *Civil War* against Pompey. The author of the accounts of the Alexandrian, African and Spanish campaigns is unknown: some think it was Oppius; others Hirtius, who also completed the last book of the *Gallic War* which Caesar left unfinished. Regarding Caesar's memoirs, Cicero, also in the *Brutus*, comments: **2** 'He wrote memoirs which should be highly praised; they are simply, straightforwardly, and gracefully composed, with all the clothing of rhetorical ornamentation removed; but while his aim was to provide material for others who wanted to write history to draw upon, he has perhaps gratified several fools, who may choose to touch up his writings with curling-tongs, but has deterred all sensible men from writing on it.' **3** Concerning these memoirs, Hirtius (*BG* 8, pref. 5–6) stresses that: 'These memoirs are so highly regarded in all men's judgement that he seems to have deprived writers of an opportunity rather than offered them one, while our admiration for this is greater than that of others, for they know how beautifully and faultlessly he wrote, while we also know how easily and rapidly he completed the task.' **4** Asinius Pollio considers that the memoirs were composed with insufficient care and accuracy, since in many cases Caesar put too much trust in reports given by others of their deeds and records his own actions incorrectly, either deliberately or through forgetfulness; and he believes that Caesar intended to revise and correct his work.

5 He also left a two-volume work *On Analogy*, two more volumes *In Answer to Cato*, and a poem entitled *The Journey*. Of these, he wrote the first while crossing the Alps when returning to his army after holding assizes in Cisalpine Gaul, the second at roughly the time of the battle of Munda; and the last during the 24 days he was travelling between Rome and Further Spain. **6** Some letters of his to the senate are also extant, and he appears to have been the first to convert them to pages and the form of a note-book, while, previously, consuls and generals sent their reports written right across the sheet. Some letters of his to Cicero are also extant, as well as others to his close friends on personal matters, in which, if anything had to be conveyed confidentially, he wrote in cipher, that is with the order of the letters changed, so that no word can be understood: if anyone wishes to decipher these and find out their meaning, he has to change the fourth letter of the alphabet, that is, D, for A and so on with the rest. **7** Certain writings of his boyhood and early youth are mentioned, such as *Praises of Hercules* and a tragedy *Oedipus* and *Collected Sayings*; but Augustus forbade the publication of all these minor works in a very brief and frank letter sent to Pompeius Macer, whom he had chosen to organise his libraries.

13.60 Caesar's outstanding intellect

Pliny *Natural History* 7.91–4

91 The most outstanding example of mental vigour I consider to be the dictator Caesar; I am not now thinking of courage and perseverance, nor of an elevation of mind able to embrace all that the heavens contain, but of native vigour and quickness winged as if with fire. We are told that he was accustomed to read or write and dictate or listen simultaneously, and to dictate to his secretaries four letters at the same time on matters of great importance, **92** or, if not otherwise occupied, seven. He also fought fifty pitched battles and was the only one to beat Marcus Marcellus (cos. 222), who fought thirty-nine — for I would not count it to his glory that in addition to victories over fellow-citizens he killed 1,192,000 persons in his battles, a huge, if unavoidable, injury to the human race, as he himself admitted it to be by not publishing the number slaughtered in the civil wars.

93 It would be fairer to credit Pompey the Great with the 846 ships he captured from the pirates: unique to Caesar, in addition to what was mentioned above, was the distinction of his clemency in which he surpassed all others — even to the point of regretting it later; he also presented an example of magnanimity with which no other can be compared. **94** To count under this label the spectacles that he put on and the wealth he poured out, or the magnificence of his public works, would condone extravagance, but it demonstrated the genuine and unparalleled elevation of an unsurpassed mind that, when Pompey the Great's letter cases were captured at Pharsalus and Scipio's at Thapsus, he showed the highest integrity and burnt them instead of reading them.

THE IDES OF MARCH

Caesar's honours ended in his being made perpetual dictator (*dictator perpetuo*) in February 44, which was to be the climax of his career. Many of those he had pardoned were not reconciled to his prominence. But in becoming dictator for life it was made wholly transparent that he had no intention of restoring the Republic: this was one man rule (Plut. *Caes.* 57.1).

Marcus Junius Brutus was won over to the cause by Gaius Cassius Longinus, though probably predisposed to it. Brutus and Cassius, both pardoned by Caesar after Pharsalus (doc. 13.52), were the most prominent assassins ('tyrannicides'); all told more than sixty senators were involved (only Dio has Brutus as the instigator of the conspiracy). Cassius had been quaestor under Crassus in Syria; he survived Carrhae and organised the defence of Syria, where he served as proquaestor in 52–51, inflicting a major defeat on the Parthians in 51. Tribune in 49 (not to be confused with the tribune of the same year Q. Cassius Longinus who was a Caesarian) he was an adherent of Pompey's and commanded a fleet near Sicily, but after Pharsalus surrendered it to Caesar in the Hellespont, and was pardoned, serving with him as a legatus against Pharnaces. Other assassins included Decimus Brutus whom Caesar had chosen as consul for 42, and Trebonius (tr. pl. 55, cos. suff. 45). The assassination took place on the Ides (15) of March, 44 BC. Caesar went to the senate house on the Ides despite ill-omens, a dream of Calpurnia (his wife) and an illness: all perhaps post-eventum inventions of the sources. On the way he was handed a scroll with details of the plot but did not read it (perhaps another invented detail). His assassination heralded the return of civil war.

For the Ides of March, see also Cic. *Div.* 2.23, docs. 13.66–70; Suet. *Jul.* 80.4–82; Plut. *Brut.* 17, *Caes.* 62–6; App. *BC* 2.111–17; Dio 44.12–22; Smith 1957a; Balsdon 1958, 1967: 167–71; Fuller 1965: 302–7; Gelzer 1968: 324–9; Horsfall 1974; Clarke 1981: 33–42; Meier 1995: 479–86; Morgan 1997; Sedley 1997; Southern 2001: 147–8.

13.61 Caesar's assassination

Plutarch *Life of Caesar* 66.4–14

4 Now Antony, who was a close friend of Caesar's and physically fit, was detained outside (the senate-house) by Brutus Albinus (Trebonius in Plut. *Brutus* 17.1) who deliberately engaged him in a lengthy conversation. **5** Caesar went on in and the senate rose in his honour, while some of Brutus' partisans went and stood behind his seat, while others went to meet him as though they were going to support the petition being made by Tillius Cimber on behalf of his brother in exile, and they joined him in his entreaties, accompanying Caesar as far as his seat. **6** When, after sitting down, Caesar continued to reject the requests and started to grow angry with one or another as they importuned him more urgently, Tillius grasped his toga with both hands and pulled it down from his neck — the signal for the attack. **7** It was Casca who gave the first blow with his dagger, in the neck, a wound which was neither mortal or even deep, probably because he was nervous at the beginning of such a bold venture, and Caesar, as he turned, was therefore able to grab the knife and hold on to it. **8** At nearly the same moment both cried out, the victim in Latin, 'You villain, Casca, what are you doing?', the aggressor to his brother in Greek, 'Brother, help!' **9** This was how it began, while those who were not in the plot were thunderstruck and terrified at what was being done, not daring to flee or go to Caesar's help, or even to utter a word. **10** All of those who had prepared themselves for the murder produced their naked daggers, and Caesar was encompassed by them all, wherever he turned confronting blows and dagger aimed at his face and eyes, driven here and there like a wild beast and entangled in the hands of them all — **11** for they all had to participate in the sacrifice and taste his blood. It was for this reason that Brutus too gave him one blow in the groin. **12** And some say that Caesar fought back against all the others, darting this way and that and crying out, but, when he saw that Brutus had drawn his dagger, he covered his head with his toga and sank down, either by chance or because he had been pushed there by his murderers, against the pedestal on which the statue of Pompey stood. **13** The pedestal was drenched with blood, so as to appear that Pompey himself was presiding over this vengeance on his enemy, lying at his feet and struggling convulsively under numerous wounds. **14** He is said to have received twenty-three, and many of the conspirators were wounded by each other as they tried to direct so many blows into one body.

13.62 'Et tu, Brute?'

Suetonius *Life of the Deified Julius* 82.1–2

Brutus was, according to some sources, the descendant of L. Junius Brutus, who played the pivotal role in the expulsion of the Tarquins from Rome and in 509 BC became one of the first two consuls. His statue, with a naked sword, stood on the Capitol. Plutarch notes that Marcus Brutus' enemies denied this family connection because L. Brutus had killed his own sons when they took part in a plot to restore the Tarquins, and therefore could have had no descendants (doc. 7.14). But for Brutus himself the connection was apparently real and a motivating force. Graffiti wishing that L. Brutus was alive were scrawled on Caesar's statue; on Brutus' praetorian tribunal and chair was written, 'You sleep, Brutus' and 'You're not Brutus' (Suet. *Jul.* 80.3; Plut. *Caes.* 62.4, *Brut.* 9.6–9). His mother Servilia was Cato's sister and Brutus married Cato's daughter Porcia (after Cato's suicide at Utica). Brutus' father had taken part in the revolt of Lepidus and controlled Cisalpine Gaul. He surrendered to Pompey there but Pompey had him executed the next day (Plut. *Pomp.* 16.4–9): this was one of the murders that gave Pompey his reputation as the *adulescentulus carnifex*: cf. doc. 12.3. Caesar was rumoured to be Brutus' father through an early liaison of Caesar's with Servilia, Brutus' mother, who sent him an intimate letter during the Catilinarian debate which Cato insisted on seeing: Cato silently read the note and passed it back to Caesar with the words, ' Take it, you drunk' (Plut. *Cato Min.* 24; *Brut.* 5; cf. doc. 7.45). Brutus joined Pompey's forces in the civil war as representing the res publica (commonwealth) but requested Caesar's pardon after Pharsalus and was made governor of Cisalpine Gaul in 46, urban praetor for 44 BC and designated as consul for 41. He was approached by Cassius a little before the Ides of March and reminded of his famous ancestor. Brutus enjoyed Caesar's favour, but his adherence to republican ideals led him to be the unofficial leader of the assassination attempt; for Brutus, see Plut. *Brut.* 1–17, esp. 1, 4, 5, 14–17; *MRR* I.1–2, II.302; App. *BC* 2.111–22; Dio 44.13–19; Africa 1978; Clarke 1981: 9–47; Wistrand 1981.

1 As he took his seat, the conspirators gathered round him as if to pay their respects, and straightaway Tillius Cimber, who had taken the lead, came closer as if to ask a question. When Caesar shook his head and put him off to another time, he seized his toga by both shoulders. Then as Caesar cried out, 'This is violence,' one of the Cascas wounded him from behind just below the throat. **2** Caesar seized Casca's arm and ran it through with his stylus, but, as he tried to leap up, he was stopped by another wound; when he saw that on every side he was confronted by drawn daggers, he covered his head with his toga and at the same time drew its fold down to his feet with his left hand to fall more decently with the lower part of his body also covered. Like this he was stabbed with twenty-three blows, without uttering a word, except for a groan at the first stroke, though some have recorded that when Marcus Brutus came at him he said (in Greek), 'You, too, my child?'

13.63 Caesar's will

Suetonius *Life of the Deified Julius* 83.2

Cf. Dio 44.35.2; App. *BC* 2.143.596–8; Plut. *Caes.* 68. The reading of Caesar's will with its bequest to the people of Rome incited popular opposition to the tyrannicides. The will was ratified by the senate on 18 March. Octavian, Caesar's great-nephew and the future princeps Augustus had been made pontifex and urban prefect in 47, served with Caesar in 45 in Spain, and was adopted as Caesar's heir in his will in September 45, and designated master of horse in 44. He was to exploit his relationship with Caesar, and emerged as sole ruler of the Roman empire in 31 after a series of civil wars, defeating Antony and Cleopatra at Actium (both committed suicide in 30). Octavia, Octavian's sister, was married to Antony in 40 and, divorced by him in 32, raised his children by both Fulvia and Cleopatra, as well as her own by her first marriage to C. Claudius Marcellus, cos. 50 (inveterately opposed to Caesar but pardoned by him), who died in 40 BC. Fulvia, married to Clodius Pulcher (tr. pl. 58), had a daughter who was Octavian's first wife. Fulvia was then briefly married to Curio (tr. pl. 50) and, after his death in Africa, to Antony.

At his funeral in the Campus Martius, the senatorial decree granting Caesar divine and human honours was read out and Antony made a short speech; the crowd then (unsuccessfully) attacked the houses of Brutus and Cassius; Caesar's funeral: Suet. *Jul.* 84–5. Those who had been 'liberated' by Caesar's murder did not appreciate the liberators.

In his last will he named as his three heirs his sisters' grandsons, Gaius Octavius to three-quarters of the property and Lucius Pinarius and Quintus Pedius to the remaining quarter; at the very end he also adopted Gaius Octavius, who was to take his name, into his family; and he named several of his assassins amongst the guardians of his son, if one should be born to him, Decimus Brutus even among the heirs in the second degree. To the people he bequeathed for their public use his gardens near the Tiber and 300 sesterces to each man.

13.64 Omens of Caesar's assassination

Cicero *On Divination* 1.118–19

For the omens preceding Caesar's death, see Val. Max. 1.6.13; Pliny *Nat. Hist.* 11.71; for the soothsayer (haruspex) Spurinna, see Suet. *Jul.* 81 (doc. 3.41).

118 If we concede the proposition that there is a divine power which pervades men's lives, it is not difficult to apprehend the principle which directs those signs which we see come to pass. For it is possible that, in the choice of a sacrificial victim, there is some intelligent force which guides us, which is diffused through the whole world, or that when you are about to make the sacrifice a change takes place in the vitals so that something is either taken away or added; for in a moment nature adds or changes or diminishes many things. **119** The clearest proof, which shows that this cannot be doubted, is what happened just before Caesar's death. When he was offering sacrifices on that day on which he first sat on a golden throne and showed himself in a purple robe, no heart was found in the vitals of the fat ox. Now do you think that any animal that has blood can exist without a heart? Caesar was not perturbed by the strangeness of this occurrence, even though Spurinna said that he should beware lest both thought and life desert him; for, he said, both of these stemmed from the heart. On the following day there was no head on the liver of the sacrificial beast. These omens were foretold to Caesar by the immortal gods so he might foresee his death, not so that he might be on his guard against it. So when those organs without which the victim could not have lived are not found in the vitals, we should understand that the absent organs disappeared at the moment of sacrifice.

13.65 The fates of Pompey, Crassus and Caesar

Cicero *On Divination* 2.22–3

Cicero here argues against his brother Quintus that divination is of no use if events are ruled by Fate, and that in this case knowledge of the future is a disadvantage.

22 Leaving aside the men of earlier days, do you think that it would have been of any advantage to Marcus Crassus, when he was at the peak of his wealth and fortune, to know that he was going to perish beyond the Euphrates in shame and dishonour after the death of his son Publius and the destruction of his army? Or do you think that Gnaeus Pompey would have found happiness in his three consulships, in his three triumphs and in the fame of his pre-eminent achievements if he had known that, after losing his army, he would be slaughtered in a lonely Egyptian spot, and that there would follow, after his death, events which we cannot speak of without tears?

23 What indeed do we think of Caesar's case? If he had foreseen that in the senate, which he for the most part had chosen himself, in Pompey's hall, in front of the statue of Pompey himself, with so many of his own centurions looking on, he would be slaughtered by the most noble citizens, some of whom owed everything they possessed to him, and so little honoured that not only none of his friends would approach his corpse, but not even any of his servants, in what torment of mind would he have spent his life?

CICERO ON THE ASSASSINATION AND ITS AFTERMATH

Cicero had largely occupied himself with philosophy in the years immediately prior to Caesar's assassination; the Ides of March called him back to the service of the Republic. Cicero, whose name Brutus invoked on 15 March after the assassination, unsuccessfully urged the conspirators, who had seized the Capitol, to convene the senate (doc. 13.69). In the event, Antony seized the initiative and on 18 March summoned the senate and had Caesar's acta and his will confirmed. An uneasy truce was arranged between him and the assassins. The senate gave Brutus and Cassius the task of buying corn in Asia (Brutus) and Sicily (Cassius); they would then be granted provinces. But when Brutus and Cassius left Rome and Italy in August 44, Brutus went to Greece, Cassius to Asia Minor, and they took over Asia Minor for the Republican cause. They received from the senate *imperium maius* in the east largely due to Cicero's efforts and his opposition to Antony, but in 43 BC the tyrannicides were outlawed by a law of Q. Pedius, Octavian's uncle. Brutus and Cassius met the forces of Antony and Octavian in Philippi in Macedonia in 42. Cassius committed suicide at Philippi when defeated by Antony; Brutus defeated Octavian. In the further battle there, Brutus was defeated, deserted by his army, and committed suicide.

Cicero from September 44 to April 43 spoke against Antony in the senate (delivering the *Philippics*). Octavian and Antony were soon rivals; Octavian with the consul Hirtius defeated Antony twice in early 43. However, a meeting between Antony, Lepidus and Octavian led to the formation of the 'second triumvirate' in late 43. Lepidus had been Caesar's fellow consul in 46, as a reward for military successes in Further Spain while proconsul in Hither Spain against Pompeian forces for which he was awarded a triumph. He was master of horse in the same year and again in 45 and 44; for Lepidus' career to 44 BC, see Weigell 1992: 20–40; Welch 1995; for his coins as moneyer, see doc. 7.92.

Proscriptions were carried out; Cicero's name was put on the list by Antony and Octavian opposed this at first but yielded. On 7 December 43 Cicero met his death; Antony had his head and hands nailed to the rostra (Plut. *Cic.* 47–9). The events of 44–43, esp. Cicero's role: Suet. *Aug.* 8–12; Plut. *Cic.* 46–9; Appian *BC* 4.19–20; Dio 47.8.3–4; Smith 1966: 236–58; Lacey 1978: 141–69; Huzar 1978: 81–92; Clarke 1981: 46–78; Mitchell 1991: 289–324; Rawson 1975: 260–95, 1994: 468–87.

13.66 Cicero on the Ides of March

Cicero *Letters to Atticus* 14.4.2 (10 April 44)

The Ides of March are our consolation. Our heroes achieved all that rested with themselves gloriously and magnificently; what remains needs money and men, none of which we have.

13.67 The tyrannicides lose popularity

Cicero *Letters to Atticus* 14.5.2 (11 April 44)

Those who ought to be guarded by all mankind, not only for their protection but also for their glorification, are praised and loved, but that is all, and are confined within their houses.

13.68 Caesar's acts are ratified

Cicero *Letters to Atticus* 14.9.2 (17 April 44)

The tyranny lives on, the tyrant is dead! We rejoice at the death of a murdered man whose acts we defend!

13.69 The assassination proves ineffectual

Cicero *Letters to Atticus* 14.10.1 (19 April 44)

Cf. *Att.* 14.12.1 (22 April) where Cicero states that the Ides had brought nothing but satisfaction for their hatred and grief; at 14.12.2 he discusses Octavian's respectful behaviour towards him.

And so, was this what my — and your — dear Brutus worked for, that he should stay at Lanuvium, that Trebonius should set out on by-ways for his province, that everything done, written, said, promised and planned by Caesar should have more weight than if he himself were alive? Do you remember me crying out on that first day on the Capitol that the senate should be summoned to the Capitol by the praetors? Immortal gods! What could have been effected then to the rejoicing of all good men — even the reasonably good — with the power of the bandits broken! You blame the Liberalia (17 March). What could have been done then? We were long done for by that point. Do you remember how you cried out that the cause was lost if he had a state funeral? But he was even cremated in the forum and given a pathetic eulogy, and slaves and paupers were sent against our houses with torches. Then what? That they dare to say, 'Are you opposing Caesar's wishes?' This and the like I am unable to endure. So I am planning a trip to 'land beyond land'; your land, however, is out of the gale.

13.70 Matius' letter to Cicero

Matius in [Cicero] *Letters to Friends* 11.28.2–4 (?October 44 BC)

This letter of Gaius Matius is written in reply to a letter from Cicero (*Fam.* 11.27). Matius had served in Gaul with Caesar, and was his friend and influential with him; he had spoken to Caesar in Cicero's favour in 49 and 48. Cicero had been informed by Trebatius that Matius was annoyed that Cicero had criticised him for supporting the passing of a law (identity unknown), and for helping to organise Octavian's celebrations on 20–30 July 44 of the *ludi victoriae Caesaris*, established in 46 for Caesar's victory at Pharsalus, and of funeral games for Caesar (see *Att.* 15.2, cf. 14.1; Stockton 1969: 196–200; Shackleton Bailey 1977: II.486–7; Weinstock 1971: 368; Morgan 1997: 39). Matius and Trebatius in Gaul: Cic. *Fam.* 7.15 (53 BC). Cicero's protestations of friendship with Matius in *Fam.* 11.27 are undermined by his negative comments at *Att.* 14.2.

2 I am well aware of the criticisms people have made against me following Caesar's death. They count it as a failing that I should find it difficult to bear the death of a friend and that I am angry that the man I loved should have been killed; for they say that country should be ranked before friendship, just as if they have already demonstrated that his death benefited the state. But I shall not argue like a debater: I admit that I have not yet arrived at that stage of philosophy. In the civil conflict I followed not Caesar, but a friend, whom, although I did not approve of his actions, I did not desert. I never approved of civil war or even of the cause of the conflict, which I did my very best to quench in its infancy. And so, in my friend's victory, I was allured by the delights of neither office nor money, rewards which others, whose influence with him was less than mine, took unfair advantage of. My property was even lessened by one of Caesar's laws, thanks to which many who rejoice at Caesar's death continue to live in Rome. I exerted myself to ensure that our conquered fellow-citizens be treated with forbearance, as if to save my own life.

3 Can I, then, who wanted everyone unharmed, not be angry at the killing of the man who brought it about, especially when the same men were responsible for both his unpopularity and his death? 'You will pay, then,' they insist, 'since you dare to disapprove of our action!' What unheard-of arrogance! Some may take pride in an act, while others are not even allowed to grieve with impunity! Even slaves have always had the freedom to hope or fear, to rejoice or grieve of their own free will, not that of someone else; this freedom those 'authors of our liberty', as these people like to call themselves, are now trying to use fear to wrest from us. **4** They will get nowhere. I will never deviate from duty or compassion through any threats of danger. For I never considered an honourable death a thing to be avoided, and often would even have desired it.

13.71 The end of the Republic

Tacitus *Annals* 1.1

Tacitus in this passage is showing that periods of temporary 'rule' by such as Sulla and Caesar were the logical prelude to the autocracy of principate (cf. doc. 12.1).

At the beginning of Rome's existence as a city it was ruled by kings; Lucius Junius Brutus then instituted the consulship together with political liberty. Dictatorships were assumed for short periods of time; the powers of decemvirs did not last more than two years, while the consular authority of military tribunes was short-lived. The autocracies of both Cinna and Sulla were brief; the predominance of Pompey and Crassus was quickly superseded by that of Caesar, and the armed might of Lepidus and Antony by that of Augustus, who took the whole state, exhausted by civil discord, under his sole dominion.

COINAGE

13.72 Caesar's victory over the Gauls

Crawford *RRC* 452.2

An aureus (gold coin); 48–47 BC (Grueber I.505; Sydenham *CRR* 1009; Reece *RC* 101).

Obverse: Female head (a goddess, perhaps Pietas?), facing right, and wearing a diadem and an oak wreath.
Reverse: A trophy of arms, made up of Gallic weapons, helmet, shield and armour. Legend: Caesar.

13.73 Caesar and Venus

Crawford *RRC* 458.1

A denarius, c. 47 BC (Grueber II.469; Sydenham *CCR* 1013; Carson *PCRR* 222; Reece *RC* 102).

Obverse: Bust of Venus, wearing diadem.
Reverse: Aeneas, holding the palladium (see docs 2.29, 7.88) and carrying his father on his flight from Troy. Anchises and Venus were the parents of Aeneas, legendary founder of the Julian family. The coin is usually dated generally to after the defeat of Pompey at Pharsalus (Carson), or to 47–46 BC (Crawford).

13.74 Caesar as Perpetual Dictator

Crawford *RRC* 480.7a

A denarius of February-March 44 BC (Grueber I.549; Sydenham *CCR* 1062; Carson *PCRR* 246).

Obverse: Head of Caesar with veil (face visible); legend: *Caesar Dict. Perpetuo* (Caesar, Perpetual Dictator). The veil presents Caesar as pontifex maximus, showing the official importance he attached to this position.
Reverse: Standing Venus, facing left, with a sceptre in her right hand and a Victory deity in the palm of her left hand.

13.75 Assassination of Caesar

Crawford *RRC* 508.3

A denarius of 43–42 BC (Grueber II.480; Sydenham *CRR* 1301; Carson *PCRR* 274; Meier 1995: pl. 26; Southern 2001: 148). The assassination of Caesar is represented as emancipation.

Obverse: Head of Brutus; this is the only contemporary portrait of him. Legend: *Brut. Imp.* (Brutus imperator).
Reverse: A freedom cap, as worn by emancipated slaves, between two daggers. Legend: *Eid. Mar.* (*Eidibus Martiis*: on the Ides of March).

14

The Ancient Sources

There are various ancient sources of evidence for the history of the Roman Republic. This collection has, for obvious reasons, concentrated on literary sources, whether the works of historical writers such as Polybius, Livy, Sallust and Appian, or of biographers, notably Suetonius and Plutarch. There are also valuable excerpts from works now lost given in the writings of antiquarians and scholars (Varro, Dionysius of Halicarnassus, Pliny the Elder, Aulus Gellius and Macrobius), while useful light on issues in political and social history can be cast by poets: Ennius, Lucilius, Catullus and the comic dramatists. There are, of course, in addition, speeches delivered in the law-courts, notably by one of the most prolific of Roman writers and orators, Cicero, although it is important to be aware that Cicero's speeches only give one side of the case, and that a very biased one. Similarly with his *Letters* the reader should be aware that they are private communications which convey much contemporary gossip information on family matters and often contradict his public statements. However, this collection has also attempted to provide access to other sources, most importantly information recorded on stone (epigraphy), as well as to historians whose work only survives in 'fragments', phrases, sentences or paragraphs quoted or paraphrased by other ancient historians or commentators. Relevant archaeological and numismatic evidence (evidence from artefacts, excavations and coins) has been referred to wherever possible. The notes below are intended as a general introduction to Roman historiography (historical writing), whether in Latin or Greek, and are aimed at helping the reader to understand the aims and methodology of the ancient authors.

General bibliography: Dorey 1966, 1967; McDonald 1975; Gabba 1981, 1983; Fornara 1983; Moxon 1986; Lintott 1994; Grant 1995; Comber 1997; Kraus and Woodman 1997; Marincola 1997; Mellor 1998, 1999; Kraus 1999; Clarke 1999; for non-literary evidence: Astin 1989: 13–16; Ogilvie & Drummond 1989: 11–24; Snodgrass 1983 (archaeology); Crawford 1983 (numismatics).

14.1 Epigraphy

See: Millar 1983; Gordon 1983; Wiseman 1986; Ogilvie & Drummond 1989: 11–14; Keppie 1991; Cooley 2000, 2000a; Bodel 2001.

Epigraphy is the study of texts which have been inscribed, generally on stone or bronze, or on some less durable material such as pottery. There are often problems of dating with inscriptions, and many are partially damaged and hence difficult to read or interpret. Such texts are often 'impersonal' texts, such as state decrees, treaties, or laws (docs 3.64, 5.22, for example), but inscriptions can also be personal, as when they record a funerary epitaph (the largest group of Latin inscriptions, in which the deceased or their relatives reveal important information about the family and about the members' perceptions of each other and their domestic role); they can also record a dedication or personal gift: see docs 7.23–5, 31–3, 37, 66. Inscriptions can also detail the achievements of individuals, particularly generals or public benefactors, whether commissioned by themselves, or by communities in their honour: in either case the account is not necessarily objective (docs 4.10, 5.32, 41–2, 12.18), though epigraphy can act as a valuable supplement to literary sources.

14.2 The Roman Annalistic tradition

See: Frier 1979: esp. 83–105, 255–84; Culham 1989; Ogilvie & Drummond 1989: 5–9; Rawson 1991b: 1–15; Forsythe 1994; Bucher 1995; Cornell 1995: 12–16.

The pontifex maximus used to keep an annual record called the *annales maximi*, which was posted on a whitened board outside the Regia, his official residence; it contained the names of magistrates and of important events such as triumphs, treaties, wars, the building of temples, eclipses, plagues, earthquakes and portents. It was continued until the pontificate of P. Mucius Scaevola (pontifex maximus 130–115 BC) and was a valuable source for historians of early Rome, comprising some 80 books by that time. While some of the earlier books were fabricated on legendary characters and themes, the records from 400 BC (an eclipse of the sun on 21 June 400: Cic. *Rep.* 1.25) seem to have been genuine, though their content was of course limited. Cato the Elder, in his *Origines* (*HRR* I² 77), stated: 'I do not choose to copy out what is on the pontifex maximus' tablet: how many times grain became dear, how many times the sun and moon were obscured or eclipsed'. The pontiffs also kept the *libri pontificales*, which contained instructions for cult formulae and rituals, and recorded the dedication dates of temples, while the *libri lintei* ('Linen Books') were preserved in the temple of Juno Moneta, and apparently contained lists of magistrates and other historical information. Early historians also had access to lists of republican consuls (or other chief magistrates), called *fasti*, which were kept as records for chronological purposes, since these magistrates gave their name to the year.

HISTORIANS AND ANNALISTS

14.3 Fabius Pictor and the early historians

See: *HRR* I² 5–39; *FGrH* 809; Badian 1966; Mattingly 1976; Wiseman 1979: 9–26; Cornell 1986, 1986a; Forsythe 1994, 2000: 1–11; Momigliano 1990; Rawson 1991a: 245–71.

Quintus Fabius Pictor, who wrote in Greek, was the first Roman historian and went on an embassy to Delphi during the Second Punic War. He makes use of the history of

Timaeus of Tauromenium (c. 350–260) whom Polybius criticises in book 12 of his *Histories* for factual errors and inappropriate methodology.

Polybius makes use of Fabius, though aware of his pro-Roman bias (as in his belief that the Barcid family was responsible for the outbreak of the Second Punic War): see docs 4.5, 4.25, 4.36 for Polybius' comments on Fabius Pictor and Philinus of Acragas in Sicily. It is not clear whether Livy knew Fabius' work at first-hand.

Fabius dwelt at length on the legendary foundation of Rome: *SEG* 26.1123, F2, col. A (from Taormina, second century BC), 'Quintus Fabius, called Pictorinus, a Roman son of Gaius, who related the arrival of Heracles in Italy and the return of Lanoeus, an ally of Aeneas and Ascanius; much later there were Romulus and Remus and the foundation of Rome by Romulus, who was the first to be king.'

L. Cincius Alimentus, another pioneer historian, was a contemporary of Fabius Pictor and was at one stage Hannibal's prisoner; praetor in 210, he also wrote in Greek, as did the philhellene A. Postumius Albinus, whose history was published before Cato's death in 149. Latin writers included M. Porcius Cato (cos. 195), L. Cassius Hemina (first half of the 2nd century BC), L. Calpurnius Piso Frugi (cos. 133 BC), C. Sempronius Tuditanus (cos. 129), L. Coelius Antipater (c. 120 BC), Q. Claudius Quadrigarius (a contemporary of Sulla), C. Licinius Macer (tr. pl. 73 BC), and Valerius Antias (first century BC). The documentary sources from which they drew their information could include the *annales maximi* and pontifical records, the *libri lintei*, public records from the state archives, and private family records and oral traditions, as well as the writings of earlier annalists.

14.4 Cato the Elder

See: *HRR* I² 55–97; Rawson 1985, 1989: 451–63; Gruen 1992: 52–83; Dalby 1998; Forsythe 2000: 3–5.

Cato was consul in 195 BC (when he served in Spain: doc. 5.45) and censor in 184 (doc. 1.17). His *Origines* (*Beginnings*), which he started in 168, was the first full-scale history in Latin, dealing with the origins of various peoples in Italy (from Aeneas to 149 BC). He claimed Greek descent for the settlers of Italy and drew heavily on Fabius Pictor. He was also the pre-eminent orator of his time, with more than 150 speeches known to Cicero: for his style, see Cicero *Brutus* 65–9; Sallust *Histories* 1 F1 calls him 'disertissimus', 'most eloquent'. Cato was also the author of a work on morals, one of advice to his son, a book of sayings, one on priestly law, and a manual on soldiering.

With regard to his history, Dionysius of Halicarnassus 1.11.1 classes him amongst the most learned of Roman historians, and (1.74.2) praises his care in the collection of data. Cornelius Nepos (*Cato* 3.2–4) relates that the first of the seven books of the *Origines* contained the deeds of the kings of the Roman people, the second and third the origin of each of the Italian states, the fourth book the narrative of the first Punic war, and the fifth that of the second. He dealt 'with the other wars' in the same way down to the praetorship of Servius Sulpicius Galba, who robbed the Lusitanians (doc. 5.47). His comment on Cato as an historian is that, 'He displays great industry and diligence, but no learning' (3.4).

In his *Origines*, Cato stressed the collective role of the Roman people, rather than individual 'heroes'. Pliny *Nat. Hist.* 8.5 states that Cato removed the names of military commanders, but recorded that the elephant in the Carthaginian army that was the bravest in battle was called the Syrian and that it had one broken tusk. Aulus Gellius *Attic Nights* 3.7.18–19 (*HRR* I² 80–1) cites Cato on the military tribune Caedicius in the First Punic War in Sicily, who engaged the Carthaginians with 400 men, allowing the rest of the army to retreat. Cato compared him with the Spartan king Leonidas who 'was honoured by all Greece with especial glory and gratitude through monuments of the most illustrious renown', whereas Cato in contrast makes clear that this military tribune just acted as a normal Roman.

Docs 2.15–17, 6.31–3 come from Cato's *de agri cultura* (*On Farming*) of c. 160 BC, which gives detailed, practical advice on the running of a villa estate and on the treatment of slaves on such a property; docs 3.21, 3.26, 3.32–3 refer to religious rites appropriate on such a farm, while docs 2.17 and 3.68 prescribe medical treatments. At doc. 5.59 Cato gives advice 'to his son' or to a more general readership; at docs 5.54–55 he is cited by Diodorus Siculus and Polybius regarding his criticism of 'modern' luxurious tastes.

Gellius cites Cato's speeches on several occasions: doc. 5.36 (in support of the Rhodians), 7.11 (in support of the Voconian law), 7.18 (on the relationship between adultery and alcohol in women). Livy puts a speech into his mouth against the repeal of the Oppian law (doc. 7.67), but this should not be taken as reflecting anything actually said on the occasion by Cato.

14.5 Polybius of Megalopolis

See: Walbank 1967–79, 1972, 2002; Derow 1979, 1994; Richardson 1979; Sacks 1981; Astin 1989: 3–7; Davidson 1991; Eckstein 1992, 1997.

Polybius, born c. 200 (died c. 118 BC), was a prominent Achaean, from the region in the north-east of the Peloponnese, who served as hipparch of the Achaean confederacy in 170/69. After Rome's victory at Pydna in 168 he was deported to Italy with 1,000 other Achaeans, and only released in 150. After being lucky enough to become a close friend of Scipio Aemilianus (Polyb. 31.23.1–25.1) he was allowed to stay in Rome during this period and went to Spain and Africa with Scipio. He assisted in the Roman settlement of Greece after 146, where many statues were erected in his honour: Pausanias *Description of Greece* 8.37.2 quotes an inscription at Lycosoura: 'Greece would never have come to grief, had she obeyed Polybius in all things, and having come to grief, she found succour through him alone.'

The greater part of his history, which was in 40 books, is lost; only books 1–5 are complete. The work was concerned with events from 220 to 167 BC in particular: later Polybius continued the history in a further ten books down to 146 (*Hist.* 3.4); unfortunately the Penguin translation is not complete and omits many significant passages. Polybius wrote what he titled 'pragmatike historia', pragmatic history, or military and political history with a practical, didactic bias. His work is a systematic historical treatise ('pragmateia') covering world history, not just isolated events or geographical areas

(1.4.1–7), and he stresses the importance of accurate research and information, rather than history's use as entertainment.

As an Achaean he has certain pro-Achaean and anti-Aeolian biases, and he idealises the character of his friend Scipio Aemilianus and the rest of his family (such as Scipio's father, L. Aemilius Paullus). He has an intimate knowledge of the Scipiones and Aemilii and discusses the character of Scipio Africanus at doc. 4.51 (cf. doc 6.8; *Hist.* 10.2.2–13), and that of Scipio Aemilianus at docs 5.55, 7.70.

As a Greek living in aristocratic circles in Rome, Polybius gives a detailed view as an outsider of Roman institutions and customs, providing information so central to Roman life that the Roman accounts do not mention them; especially important are docs 1.58 on the Roman constitution; 3.73–4 on Roman religious and funerary practices; 7.70 on women's festival paraphernalia.

He is given to cite treaties verbatim, or at least closely paraphrase them: for treaties in the Punic Wars, see docs 4.1–3, 17, 45, 58; for those relevant to the conquest of the Mediterranean: docs 5.23, 27, 29–30, 37; at doc. 4.19 he shows his use of official figures for troop numbers prior to the Second Punic War.

At *Hist.*1.1.5–6 he gives his reasons for writing: 'for who is there so indifferent or frivolous that he does not wish to know by what means and under what system of government nearly the whole inhabited world has in less than 53 years been subjugated and fallen under a single rule, that of the Romans — an entirely unprecedented state of affairs — or who is so dedicated to other spectacles or studies as to consider anything more important than this knowledge?'

He is concerned to explicate his use of sources and methodology: docs 4.1–5, 21, 31; he gives his reasons for concentrating on the First Punic War: doc. 4.5; uses logic to back up his statements: doc. 4.8; shows an interest in underlying causation: docs 4.21, 23–4 (the Second Punic War); is fair in assigning responsibility: doc. 4.27; and personally tests the truth of statements (crossing the Alps in Hannibal's footsteps): doc. 4.31; at *Hist.* 31.22.8–11 he makes it clear that he expects his most interested readers to be Romans who can check most of his facts.

On the importance of truth he states, *Hist.* 12.11a, that the greatest fault in history is falsehood, and that (12.12.3) just as a living creature when deprived of its eyes is totally incapacitated, so, when history is deprived of truth, nothing is left but an unprofitable tale (cf. doc. 4.5). He sees dramatisation of history as a serious fault; *Hist.* 2.56: 'it is not a historian's business to startle his readers with sensational descriptions, nor should he try, as the tragic poets do, to represent speeches which might have been delivered . . . it is his task first and foremost to record with fidelity what actually happened and was said, however commonplace this might be'.

14.6 Julius Caesar (cos. 59, 48, 46–44)

See: Adcock 1956; Collins 1972; Raditsa 1973; Batstone 1991; Meier 1995: 254–64; Welch & Powell 1998; Ramage 2001, 2002.

Caesar's *Gallic War* is an account of his campaigns in Gaul in seven books with an eighth continuing the account by Aulus Hirtius (cos. 43), one of Caesar's officers.

Caesar's narrative is impersonal (written in the third person) and dispassionate, while intended to keep himself before the eyes of the Roman world during his absence in Gaul, and he provides information on Gallic and British customs, as well as military campaigns (see docs 3.44, 12.88). The title *Commentarii* (*Notebooks*) which he gave to his work on the *Gallic War* implies that they were later to be written up in a more sophisticated style. Caesar also wrote three books on the *Civil War*, which give his perspective on events. Needless to say, they are not entirely objective, particularly with regard to his motive for invading Italy (see esp. docs 13.24, 13.27, 13.42 13.44), and his justification of events differs from the account of Cicero's letters and Asinius Pollio's quotation of Caesar's words after the battle of Pharsalus: 'They wanted it like this; with all my great achievements, I Gaius Caesar would have been condemned, if I had not looked to my army for help' (Suet. *Jul.* 30.4: doc. 13.28). The *Alexandrian War*, *Spanish War* and *African War* dealing with the campaigns in 48–45 are not by Caesar (Hirtius may have written the *Alexandrian War*: Suet. *Jul.* 56.1).

Caesar was also the author of light-hearted poetry (Pliny *Letters* 5.3.5), and Plutarch *Caes.* 2 records that while a captive of the Cilician pirates (cf. doc. 6.13) he wrote and recited poetry. In oratory Caesar believed in the use of analogy (on which he wrote a treatise) and on the use of ordinary, not high-flown, words: Gell. 1.10.4. His oratory was highly praised by Cicero (doc. 2.63). His brief letters to Oppius and Cornelius Balbus and to Cicero (docs 13.37, 13.39) show his command of terse, lucid expression while in action. For his literary talents, see doc. 13.59, where Suetonius cites Asinius Pollio as believing that Caesar intended to revise and correct his work.

14.7 Sallust

See: Paul 1984, McGushin 1994 (commentaries); Syme 1964; Dorey 1966: 30–47; Earl 1991; Levene 1992; Kraus & Woodman 1997: 10–50; Stone 1999; Kraus 1999.

Gaius Sallustius Crispus (c. 86–35) was tribune in 52 and expelled from the senate in 50; as tribune he opposed Cicero and Milo and was supposed to have had an affair with Milo's wife. He commanded a legion for Caesar in 49 and was praetor in 46 and governor of Africa. After being accused of extortion he withdrew from politics to write history. He was very wealthy: the *horti Sallustiani* (Sallustian gardens) belonged to him. He was said to have married Cicero's divorced wife Terentia (Jerome *adversus Jovinianum* 1).

His *Bellum Catilinae* (*Catiline's War*, or *Catilinarian Conspiracy*), written c. 42, deals with the career of Catiline and events in Cicero's consulship (63 BC) and afterwards (docs 12.14–16, 19–23, 2.39). In this work he stresses Rome's moral decline and polarises the figures of Caesar and Cato the Younger, his 'heroes', as *exempla* of moral excellence (doc. 13.57). Cicero must have been one of his main sources, but he also spoke directly to participants: at *BC* 48.9 he personally overheard Crassus, blaming Cicero for trying to implicate him in the conspiracy. His reasons for writing on Catiline he gives as follows (*BC* 3.2, 4.3–4): 'For myself, although the narrator and doer of deeds win by no means equal renown, I still consider the writing of history as one of the most difficult of undertakings; in the first place, because your words have to be equal to the deeds narrated; and in the second place because most people will think your criticisms of misdeeds to be inspired by malice and jealousy; when you commemorate the great merit and reputation of good men, people will happily accept the things they think they could easily do themselves, but dismiss anything beyond this as fictitious — if not untrue . . . So I shall give a brief account of the conspiracy of Catiline as truthfully as I can; for I consider that villainy to have been especially memorable due to the unprecedented nature of the crime itself and the danger to which it gave rise.'

His second work, the *Jugurthine War*, was written c. 41/40, and concerns Jugurtha's war with Rome under the command of Metellus Numidicus and Marius (docs 9.2, 6–7, 9–10); Sulla is also given considerable space (doc. 9.12). Sallust is here emphasising again the decline of Rome, particularly within the nobility and its values, and the war is a good subject through which to show a brilliant novus homo (Marius) contrasted with the corrupt and incompetent nobility. Sallust's rationale for writing is as follows (*BJ* 4.1, 5.1–2): 'But among intellectual pursuits, one of the most important is the recording of historical events . . . I am going to write of the war which the Roman people waged with Jugurtha, king of the Numidians, first because it was a long and bloody conflict, with victory alternating between the two sides, and secondly because it was then for the first time that resistance was made to the arrogance of the nobles — a struggle which was to throw everything, divine and human, into confusion and reach such a frenzied pitch that civil strife was only ended by a war and the devastation of Italy.' Sallust comments (*BJ* 17.7) that, regarding the original inhabitants of Africa, his account varies from tradition but was translated for him from the Punic books said to have been written by King Hiempsal. His main sources were probably the autobiographies of Aemilius Scaurus (cos. 115), Rutilius Rufus (cos. 105), and Sulla.

Sallust also wrote a history beginning in 78, the death of Sulla, which is extant only in fragments: one important fragment from this work is Pompey's dispatch from Spain to the senate (doc. 12.3). The *Histories* were perhaps a continuation of the work of L. Cornelius Sisenna, praetor in 78. Sallust criticises him for speaking of Sulla with 'insufficient frankness': *Jug.* 95.2 (doc. 9.12); Cicero speaks of him highly (*Brut.* 228). An invective against Cicero and two letters to Caesar attributed to Sallust appear not to be genuine.

Sallust was a Caesarian, and Suetonius (*Gramm.* 15) records that he was satirised for his criticisms of Pompey; his *Histories* tend to be critical of Pompey. He was a popularis earlier in his career, and his sympathies tend that way: his view of the Gracchi (doc. 8.40) is very positive and in marked contrast to Cicero's negative portrayals. While, however, his criticisms are primarily reserved for the corrupt nobility (docs 9.3, 9.7), he is also critical of irresponsible tribunes in 110 BC (*BJ* 37.1).

14.8 Diodorus Siculus

See: Rawson 1985: 223–7; Sachs 1990, 1994.

Diodorus of Agyrium in Sicily (hence 'Siculus', the Sicilian), wrote a *Bibliotheke* (*Library of History*) in 40 books, covering universal history from the earliest times down to 60 BC. It was probably completed in Rome in 30 BC. At 40.8 he states that, 'The subject matter is contained in forty books, and in the first six I have recorded the events and legends prior to the Trojan War; I have not given dates in these with any precision since no chronological record for them was at hand . . .' Only books 1–5 and 11–20 (covering the period 480–302 BC) survive, with others preserved in fragments. For the Roman period he follows the narrative of Polybius, and then Posidonius (from 146 BC). His account of the second-century Sicilian slave rebellions, which depends greatly on Posidonius (c. 135–51 BC), is the main source for these revolts (see doc. 6.43, and 6.26 for conditions in the Spanish silver mines, for which he cites Posidonius). His narrative also helps to shed light on the events leading up to the Social War, in particular the tribunate of M. Livius Drusus and the oath supposedly taken in his name by the Italians (docs 10.7–8, cf. 10.12). He also records the divine vengeance taken on a mocker of the Great Mother's priest (doc. 3.61).

14.9 Livy

See: Ogilvie 1970; Oakley 1997 (commentaries); Walsh 1955, 1961; Luce 1977; Seager 1977; Wiseman 1979: 3–56; Astin 1989: 8–11; Henderson 1989; Cornell 1995: 1–16; Miles 1995; Jaeger 1997, 1999; Kraus & Woodman 1997: 51–81; Feldherr 1998; Mellor 1999: 48–75; Forsythe 1999; Chaplin 2000; Ridley 2000.

Titus Livius (59 BC–AD 17) came from the city of Patavium (Padua) and was criticised for his Patavinitas (Paduanism) by Asinius Pollio. He wrote an annalistic history, his *ad urbe condita* (*From the Foundation of the City*), which dealt with the period from the foundation of the city to 9 BC. The work consisted of 142 books, of which only books 1–10 and 21–45 survive (with some additional fragments), though there is an *Epitome* (summary) for books 37–40 and 48–55 and a series of fourth-century AD summaries (the *Periochae*) for all books except books 136 and 137. Some of these summaries do not entirely reflect the contents of the extant books, and they may have been made from an earlier *précis*, not directly from Livy's work.

Livy's history is based on literary sources, particularly in books 31–145 on the work of Polybius, with some additions from later writers such as Valerius Antias and Claudius Quadrigarius, now lost. While he cites other authors, it appears that often, though not always, his references to second-century writers such as Calpurnius Piso and Fabius Pictor may have been derived at second hand from first-century authors. His use of Polybius is so close that gaps in Polybius' narrative can be supplied from Livy's account (as in doc. 5.27: the peace treaty with the Aetolian League, 189 BC). At doc. 4.42 he prefers not to refer there to an early Latin demand for one of the magistracies because 'Coelius and other writers' have with some reason omitted it. He therefore does not set it down as certain. Similarly in doc. 7.42 he affects to disbelieve the account of aristocratic women as mass poisoners in 331 BC as not all accounts mention it, though he still proceeds to give a narrative of events. However, he can show some critical awareness, as with the false genealogies, created for the aggrandisement of various families, which have falsified the historical record (doc. 2.28).

Livy had access to earlier histories, the researches of antiquarians (such as Varro) and original records (inscriptions, paintings, documents, lists of consuls, and records of priesthoods). He made little use of non-literary sources, and has been criticised for not directly consulting the 'linen rolls' (*libri lintei*) which contained the lists of magistrates when his sources were at variance (4.23.1–3): 'I find in Licinius Macer that the same consuls were re-elected the following year (434 BC) . . . Valerius Antias and Quintus Tubero state that Marcus Manlius and Quintus Sulpicius were the consuls for that year. But despite such a great discrepancy, both Tubero and Macer give the Linen Rolls as their authority; neither conceals the fact that older writers had recorded that there were military tribunes in office for that year. Licinius prefers to follow the Linen Rolls without hesitation; Tubero is uncertain of the truth. Along with all the other matters buried in antiquity, this also should remain undecided.' At 6.1.1–3, Livy explains that for the history of Early Rome (books 1–5) sources were few and far between, with only the commentaries of the pontiffs and other public and private records available — and that these were nearly all lost when the city was fired by the Gauls (c. 390 BC), while he admits (pref. 6) that 'events belonging to the time before the city was founded or was about to be founded, with their adornment of poetic legends rather than irrefutable historical record, it is my intention neither to affirm or deny'.

Livy shows awareness of alternative versions, as on casualty numbers at Cynoscephalae in 197 (33.10.7–10); similarly Cornell 1995: 356 points out that at 10.17.11–12 he is aware of four different accounts of a campaign in 296 BC. He is, however, often inclined to let the reader decide on the truth of variant versions. In his account of events in 362, when Marcus Curtius devoted himself to death after an earthquake in Rome, Livy states that the Lacus Curtius could have been named for him, or for Mettius Curtius, a soldier of Titus Tatius in the time of Romulus (7.6.5–6). Here he seems to suggest that the Lacus Curtius was named after M. Curtius (though in 1.13.5 he seems to accept that it was named after Mettius Curtius). He states, 'I would have spared no effort had there been any way a researcher could reach the truth; as it is, tradition must be adhered to where antiquity makes certainty impossible, and the name of the pool is better known from this more recent legend'. In contrast, Varro *On the Latin Language* 5.148–50, shows himself aware of three different versions of the story and cites four authors as his authorities: Procilius (tr. pl. 56 BC?), L. Calpurnius Piso Frugi (cos. 133), Q. Lutatius Catulus (cos. 102), and an unknown Cornelius.

Livy's objectivity is praised in Tacitus (*Ann.* 4.34): Aulus Cremutius Cordus, who was prosecuted in AD 25 for praising Brutus and calling Cassius 'last of the Romans' in his *History*, mentions Livy as an exemplum; foreseeing condemnation Cremutius starved himself to death stating, 'I am charged with having praised Brutus and Cassius, of whose deeds many have written and no one without respect. Titus Livius, outstanding for eloquence and objectivity, praised Pompey to such a degree that Augustus called him a Pompeian: but their friendship did not suffer.'

Livy sees a grave moral decline in his own time, compared with the virtues that enabled Rome to defeat Hannibal, and his aim in his writing is ostensibly a moral one (pref. 9–10): 'These are the points to which I would like all my readers to direct their attention — the lifestyle and behaviour of our ancestors, the men and the means by which in both politics and war the empire was first acquired and then increased; then let him see how, as the old teaching gradually lapsed, morals at first declined and then sank lower and lower and finally began the headlong plunge, bringing us to the present day, when we can tolerate neither our vices or their remedies. What especially makes the study of history salutary and profitable is that you behold instances of all kinds of human experiences set forth on a conspicuous monument; from this you may find for yourself and your state things to imitate, as well as things — rotten in the conception and outcome — to avoid.' He is above all a conservative: Seager 1977 notes Livy's 'uniform and extreme' hostility to all popular politicians and his favourable view of a unified senate responding to provocation.

Livy is an invaluable source on early Rome: see doc. 1.11 on the first consuls; 1.15 on the censorship; 1.24 on the first secession; 1.29 on the decemvirate; 1.45–55, 2.41 on the conflict of the orders; 1.60–7, 69–71, 2.33, 5.2–3, 5.8, 6.7 on the struggle for Italy; 2.9 on public works; 5.11 on the early Roman army; and 7.15 on magisterial duty vis-à-vis family life. For religious rituals and practices in early Rome, see docs 3.6, 3.12–14, 3.16, 3.31, 3.54–55, 3.70, 7.75, and 7.83; he is especially detailed on augury and portents: 3.39, 3.48, 3.50; for the importation of foreign cults, see docs 3.57, 3.59, 3.36. At doc. 3.23 he gives the formula for the declaration of war established by the fourth king of Rome, Ancus Marcius, in a form which, though it may be an antiquarian reconstruction, he seems to consider an accurate transcription of an ancient formula.

Livy (books 21–30) is an essential source for the Second Punic War, especially doc. 4.20 on Roman manpower in 217 BC. Livy is a patriotic writer and his account is intended to put Roman actions in the best, and Hannibal's in the worst, possible light: see docs 4.22, 4.25, 4.28–9, though at doc. 4.54 he admits to praise for Hannibal at Zama. He gives useful information on war loans by businessmen: docs 4.40, 4.60. Books 31–45 of his *History* deal with Rome's conquest of the Greek East, down to 167 BC (see docs 5.33, 5.52–3) and doc. 5.9 on the centurion Spurius Ligustinus gives valuable information regarding the number of campaigns in which a centurion in 171 could have been engaged.

His speeches are rhetorical additions to his *History*, often intended to drive home his message of moral decline: the call for the repeal of the Oppian law is, for example, a good chance for him to put a suitably moralising speech into the mouth of Cato the Elder (doc. 7.67).

Livy's fame was certainly well-established by AD 79: Pliny the Younger, luckily for himself, preferred not to accompany his uncle to observe the eruption of Vesuvius, staying behind to read a volume of Livy, and he records the anecdote of the 'man from Cadiz' who 'was so excited by the famous name of Livy that he came from his far corner of the earth to have a look at him and then went home again' (*Letters* 6.20, 2.3).

14.10 Velleius Paterculus

See: Woodman 1975; Starr 1981; Syme 1984: 3.1090–1104; Kraus & Woodman 1997: 82–4.

Velleius was born c. 20 BC and, after a successful military career, was a candidate for the praetorship of AD 15. At doc. 10.18 he relates that his great-grandfather, Minatius Magius of Acculanum, served in the Social War; the Roman people granted him citizenship as a reward and made his sons praetors. In his brief work he covers the period from mythological times down to AD 29; most of book 1 is lost. As a senator and official, he took part in or witnessed many events that he described; despite his summary treatment of a lengthy period, and flattering portrait of the emperor Tiberius, he is still the only source for certain historical details (such as for the Social War in which he had a family interest) and is the only Latin historical writer on Roman affairs to have survived between Livy and Tacitus.

14.11 Appian of Alexandria

See: Gowing 1992; Bucher 2002.

Appian was an Egyptian Greek who lived in the mid-second century AD (he died in the 160s) and wrote a history of Rome to the conquest of Egypt in 30 BC. At *BC* pref. 15 he describes himself as, 'having reached the highest place in my own country and acted as advocate at Rome in front of the emperors, until they considered me worthy of being made a procurator'. Appian was a friend of the orator M. Cornelius Fronto, whose letter to Antoninus Pius, requesting the appointment of Appian as procurator, survives (Fronto *Letter to Antoninus* 9).

He comments at *BC* 1.6, that, 'I have written and compiled this work, which is valuable for those who wish to see men's immeasurable ambition, their terrible love of power, their untiring perseverance, and the forms taken by innumerable evils'. In his preface, Appian states that he will deal with the Romans' history in terms of their dealings with various peoples and regions. The first three books cover Rome's expansion into Italy, and the following books will cover Rome's enemies arranged chronologically. He will end with the civil wars, the annexation of Egypt, and the establishment of the monarchy. Of his 24 books, only the preface and books 6–9 (Spanish, Hannibalic, Punic and Macedonian Wars) and 11–17 (Syrian, Mithridatic and Civil Wars) survive intact.

He uses reliable sources, such as Polybius, Asinius Pollio and Caesar, and the work of Hieronymus of Cardia (323–c.272). He may also be following the narrative of Posidonius, who continued Polybius. He often conflates events when summarising in his attempt to cover 1,000 years of history, but provides a useful chronological framework within which to fit other sources. His work is especially valuable as many of the sources he employed are now lost.

Appian begins his *Civil Wars* with the tribunate of Tiberius Gracchus. Appian's *Celtica* 13, now only fragmentary, presumably dealt with Marius' campaigns; see also 9.28, 9.31–3 on Saturninus and Glaucia and events late in Marius' career. His work is an important narrative for Drusus and the Social War, as well as for Sulla, and he also provides an invaluable framework for the fall of the Republic in chapters 12 and 13. At docs 4.13, 4.15, 4.62 he provides crucial information on the Punic Wars, esp. on the sack of Carthage; docs 5.45, 47, 49–50 are essential for the Roman conquest of Spain; 6.45 is a valuable source on the revolt of Spartacus (cf. 6.23 on the plebs at Rome).

14.12 Cassius Dio

See: Millar 1964; Gowing 1992.

Cassius Dio, a Greek from Bithynia, was prominent in Roman politics in the early third century AD and suffect-consul c. AD 204. His history of Rome, in 80 books, from its beginnings to AD 229 is generally well-preserved for the period 69 BC to AD 46. His work was inspired, he tells the reader, by a dream of the goddess Fortune, which came to him after the emperor Severus had approved a short book concerning the dreams and omens relating to Severus' accession (73.23.3–5): 'I then felt the wish to compose an account of everything else that concerned the Romans; consequently I resolved not to leave the first account separate but to include it in the current history, in order that I might compose and leave behind me in a single treatise a narrative of everything from the beginning down to a point to be determined by Fortune . . . She, it appears, is fated to be the guardian of the course of my life and in consequence I have dedicated myself to her. I took ten years to collect the material for all Roman history from its beginning down to the death of Severus, and I spent twelve more years in the composition of the work; as for later events, they shall be recorded down to whatever point may be possible.'

Except for his own time, Dio uses literary sources, which are often impossible to identify, but he does comment at 53.19 that it is easier to find sources for the period prior to 27 BC because everything was reported to the senate and people and historians generally had access to material. He is a very valuable source for the period following Pompey and Crassus' first consulship, though, as a monarchist, he sees all participants in the first-century BC conflicts as aiming at autocracy. Inaccuracies (as at doc. 12.74) may be due to his working from notes which he made during his initial ten years of study.

CICERO

14.13 Marcus Tullius Cicero

See: Dorey 1965; Rawson 1975, 1991: 58–79; Mitchell 1979, 1991; MacKendrick 1995; Kirby 1997; Powell 1998; Powell & Patterson 2004.

Marcus Tullius Cicero (106–43 BC) is one of the most important sources for first-century BC Roman history. He was not, of course, an historian, but as consul in 63 was deeply involved in politics down to the fall of the Republic and his speeches and letters provide very important information on the society and politics of the period. In his voluminous letters, to friends (16 books), to Atticus (16 books), to his brother Quintus, and to Brutus, Cicero expresses privately his personal feelings and doubts on politics and society at Rome, often on a daily basis, alongside more official letters of business and patronage. Much of what he reports in his personal letters is often trivial gossip, with news on trials and politics mixed up with reports on his personal health and current literary pursuits (see for example doc. 12.84). While he may have considered publishing a small selection of these letters (*Att.* 16.5.5), the *Letters to Friends* were not published until after his death by his freedman Tiro (see doc. 6.47), and the others considerably later, and due to their private and personal nature they often present Cicero in a very 'unheroic' light; he is very much aware of his own status and importance (see, for example, docs 2.44, 12.30, 12.32, 12.59, 12.64) and can be beset by indecision as to the political course to take (docs 12.38, 12.68, 13.35), while in some letters he gives his real views on a situation, which contradict the stance he has maintained in public (docs 12.33, 12.35, 12.72, 12.75, 13.53).

Some 58 speeches of Cicero survive, his first major trial being the defence of Roscius of Ameria for parricide in 80 BC (docs 2.51, 11.25). In his 'courtroom' speeches (generally for the defence, except for the prosecution of Verres: doc. 5.65) he is of course giving a partisan viewpoint intended to convince a jury of his client's innocence. In addition, the speeches, often delivered mostly *ex tempore*, were actually polished up after the event for publication, although the actual content (as opposed to the style) presumably could not be altered to any great extent from what was actually delivered. Asconius states that Cicero's speech on behalf of Milo in 52 was extremely weak and hesitant, due to the threat of violence, and so the speech that is extant bears no relation to that actually given at the trial (doc. 13.5); similarly the second series of speeches again Verres, though they were prepared, were not delivered in court, because Verres went into exile after the first. Cicero discusses his forensic training and early experience in doc. 2.62, and gives general advice in his *On Duties* on the rationale for undertaking prosecution or defence (doc. 2.60). His attack on Catiline before the people (*In Catilinam II*: doc. 12.18) delivered on 9 November 63 is a grand set-piece of insult and abuse, which bears little relation to the actual past deeds of Catiline and his supporters — nor was it meant to; Cicero was drumming up opposition to the revolt in any way possible and using every possible form of vilification to achieve his aim. Furthermore his views, as on the Gracchi, can vary, depending on his audience (docs 8.37–9).

Cicero was also a philosopher and particularly relevant to the study of the history of this period is his *Republic*, a dialogue between Scipio Aemilianus and his friends, on the ideal state (cf. doc. 1.4). At *On Divination* 2.6–7 he explains why he turned to the study of philosophy: 'The state's serious crisis was the cause of my expounding philosophy, since during the civil war I was able neither to protect the state as I was accustomed to do, nor to remain inactive, nor to find anything that I preferred to do that was worthy of me. Therefore my fellow-citizens will pardon me — rather they will be grateful to me — because, when the state was in the power of one man, I neither hid myself, deserted my post, was cast down, nor behaved like one enraged at the man or the times . . . Accordingly it was in my books that I delivered my opinion to the senate, or harangued the people, believing that I had exchanged care of the state for philosophy.'

His contribution to the theory of Latin rhetoric comprises his *de Oratore*, *Orator* and *Brutus* (see docs 2.62, 7.22, 8.12, 26, 34), while his *de Inventione* is a treatise expounding certain rhetorical techniques. He was also a poet, writing, among other things, a poem on his consulship (doc. 12.26, cf. 12.31, 12.84).

BIOGRAPHERS

14.14 Cornelius Nepos

See: Jenkinson 1967; Wiseman 1979: 154–66; Geiger 1985; Dionisotti 1988; Millar 1988; Titchener 2003.

Nepos (c. 110–24 BC) is the first Latin biographer whose work survives. Originally from Cisalpine Gaul, he lived in Rome from about 65 BC and was a correspondent of Cicero and a personal friend of Atticus. Catullus dedicated a book of his poems to him (poem 1). He wrote some 16 books *On Famous Men*, grouped according to categories (such as generals, kings and historians), and, like Plutarch later, he compared Greeks with Romans. Of this work his *Lives of Famous Foreign Generals*, which is extant, includes Hamilcar and Hannibal, though they were apparently not included in the first edition which appeared c. 34 BC, only in the second (c. 27 BC). Of the lives of historians those of M. Porcius Cato and Atticus are extant. He also wrote a universal history, a geography, and several books of anecdotes, plus a longer life of Cicero (Gell. 15.28.2). The *Lives* are not intended for a scholarly readership, and are both entertaining and moralising, while he does not always use first-hand sources, especially for his Greek subjects. He provides a useful comparison of Roman with Athenian women (doc. 7.28) and in one of the fragments of his work on Latin historians, quotes a letter purporting to be from Cornelia to her son Gaius Gracchus (doc. 8.25).

14.15 Suetonius

See: Townend 1967; Baldwin 1983; Wallace-Hadrill 1983, 1995.

Gaius Suetonius Tranquillus was born c. AD 70 and of equestrian rank. He was known by Pliny the Younger, who mentions him in his *Letters* and probably went with him to Bithynia c. 110 when Pliny governed that province. A high-ranking bureaucrat, he wrote numerous categories of biographies of literary figures (grammarians, rhetoricians, poets, historians and so on), of which those on grammarians and rhetoricians are extant (see docs 2.61, 6.18, 6.53, and 6.54 for his *Life of Terence*). His best-known work is the *Lives of the Caesars*, the biographies of the 12 emperors from Julius Caesar to Domitian; these survive except for the first chapters of the *Life of the Deified Julius*. He avoids a chronological structure, instead presenting the achievements and characters of these emperors under a series of topics, illustrated with anecdotes from their lives. He obviously had access to archival material in his *Life* of Julius Caesar which is one of the longest and most detailed, and frequently quotes from documents or cites earlier authors. Passages from Suetonius' *Life* of Caesar have been extensively used in chapters 12 and 13.

14.16 Plutarch

See: Gossage 1967; Jones 1971; Russell 1972; Pelling 1979, 1980; Astin 1989: 8; Hillard 1987; Swain 1990; Edwards 1991; Stadter 1992; Lamberton 2002.

Plutarch of Chaeronea (c. AD 50–120) is best known as a biographer, despite his many works on rhetoric and moral philosophy. He was also the author of antiquarian works, 'Greek Questions' and 'Roman Questions' (see docs. 2.36, 5.60), concerned primarily with traditional religious practices. He travelled widely, to Egypt as well as Italy and Rome, and was a priest at Delphi for 30 years. For the study of Roman history, his most important work is his 23 pairs of *Parallel Lives*, 19 of which have comparisons.

The comparisons (omitted in the Penguin translation) are an important part of the text, though Plutarch's deliberate pairing of *Lives* can lead to distortion in focus and misleading overviews and generalisations. Often Plutarch leaves his final conclusion and summing-up of the biography until the comparison, as in doc. 8.41 (the Gracchi compared to Agis IV and Cleomenes III of Sparta).

Plutarch is unashamedly a biographer, not an historian, and concerned primarily with the revelation of character through action and demonstrating *exempla* of virtues and vices in his study of great political and military figures. In his work he conflates information from different sources and concentrates on anecdote rather than 'fact'. For Plutarch's source methodology, see Plutarch *Life of Numa* 1.1–7, where he admits that there is a 'vigorous debate about the time at which King Numa lived' and proceeds to cite various views on the subject. After noting that the chronological problems are insurmountable, he then proceeds anyway with Numa's life (1.6–7): 'So it is difficult to be accurate about the chronology, and especially that based on the names of Olympic victors, the list of which is said to have been published at a late date by Hippias of Elis who had no authoritative basis for his work; I shall, therefore, start from a suitable point and recount the facts which I have found most worthy of mention in Numa's life.'

Plutarch sees character as determining destiny; for him characters are an unchanging constant in any biography, determining vice or virtue, and not swayed by or developing through events. This leads to sweeping statements and judgements of earlier motives extrapolated from later actions. Plutarch, for example, sees Caesar as unnaturally ambitious and as planning world domination from his earliest youth, not driven to it by the opposition of the optimates (*Life of Caesar* 58.2): 'As Caesar was naturally possessed of ambition and the ability to succeed, his numerous achievements did not make him stop and enjoy what he had laboured for, but instead inspired him with confidence for future deeds and gave rise to plans for greater successes and a passion for new glory, as though he had used up his earlier stock. What he felt was exactly like competitive rivalry with himself, as if he were someone else, and a desire that his future achievements should surpass his old ones . . .' The same methodology can be seen in other descriptions, such as that of Marius (doc. 9.1), Crassus (doc. 2.21), or the young Pompey (doc. 11.17), where he presents his 'heroes' as stereotypes of their most marked characteristics. Similarly, rather than seeing rivalry as gradually developing between colleagues, he tends to predate hostility to an early point in their careers: see especially doc. 9.13 (Marius and Sulla), 12.5, 12.40, 12.80 (Pompey and Crassus), 12.77 (Pompey and Caesar).

Plutarch has a great love of anecdote believing it to reveal character ('Those who are sketching, as it were, a portrait of a soul ought not to leave out even tiny marks of character': *Life of Cato the Younger* 24.1). On these grounds he leaves Caesar and Cato squared off in the senate-house over the Catilinarian issue to give the history of Caesar's love affair with Cato's sister Servilia, the immorality of Cato's womenfolk, and Cato's own divorce and remarriage to Marcia (whom in the meantime he had permitted to marry Hortensius, his best friend, on Hortensius' request: *Life of Cato the Younger* 24.1–25.4, 25.8–13). For some of his most memorable anecdotes, see docs 2.14, 2.58, 4.61, 5.58, 6.34, 7.20–1, 7.58 (Cato the Elder), 2.22, 2.59, 7.64 (Lucullus), 9.1, 7.59

(Marius), 11.1 (Sulla), 2.21, 12.80 (Crassus), 10.4 (Cato the Younger) and 8.33 (the death of Gaius Gracchus).

Plutarch provides detailed descriptions of incidents, which flesh out the more prosaic accounts in other sources: note particularly the *Lives* of Fabius Maximus and Marcellus for the Second Punic War (docs 4.47–8, 4.52), and his *Life* of the Gracchi (especially docs 8.1, 8.3, 8.9, 8.29, 8.33), as well as his account of the death of Pompey (doc. 13.46). As a Greek, and because of his interest in Roman religious practices, he also gives valuable information on the lifestyle and punishments of the Vestal Virgins and on the Bona Dea cult (docs 7.88, 7.85).

He sees Fortune as playing an important role in men's lives and makes moralising judgements on that basis. On Crassus' death in Parthia, he states (*Life of Pompey* 53.9–10): 'How small a thing is Fortune when compared with human nature! For she cannot satisfy its desires, since the entire extent of the empire and huge immensity of space was not enough for two men, who had heard and read that the gods,

> "divided everything in existence into three parts and each received his share",
> yet did not consider Rome's dominion sufficient for themselves, though there
> were only two of them.'

ANTIQUARIANS AND SCHOLARS

14.17 M. Terentius Varro

See: Rawson 1985.

Varro (116–27 BC) studied at Rome with L. Aelius 'Stilo', the great Roman scholar born c. 150 BC who was responsible for a commentary on the XII Tables, and then at Athens. Although a Pompeian, who served with Pompey in Spain and against the pirates as well as on Caesar's twenty-person land commission in 59, Caesar commissioned him in 45 to organise Rome's first public library (Suet. *Jul.* 44.2). His 41 books of *Human and Divine Antiquities* no longer survive, but books 5–10 of his 25-book *de lingua Latina* (*On the Latin Language*) are partly extant; books 5–25 were dedicated to Cicero and probably published in 43 BC, and parenthetically provide valuable information on customs and traditions in their discussion of grammar and language: see, for example, doc. 3.15, which in providing the etymology of 'pomerium' also describes the Etruscan ritual for founding a town (cf. docs 3.17: on priesthoods; 1.13: on the magistracies; 3.2 on early deities). At docs 3.22 and 3.47 he quotes from the *Censors' Records* and the augural books to illustrate his analysis of the terms *inlicium* and *templum*. His *de re rustica* (*On Farming*) written for his wife in 37 BC is also extant: see doc. 6.35. He was Rome's greatest scholar and a prolific writer: Gellius records that he had written 490 books by the age of 78 years (Gell. 3.10.17).

14.18 Dionysius of Halicarnassus

Hill 1961; Balsdon 1971; Schultze 1986: 121–42; Gabba 1991; Fox 1993.

Dionysius of Halicarnassus came to Rome in 30 BC, where he taught rhetoric and published his 20 books of *Roman Antiquities* (down to the beginning of the first Punic War) 22 years after Augustus' assumption of power. The first 11 books (to 441 BC) survive. As a Greek he describes much in Roman society of which we would otherwise know little and is a very useful source for the constitution and customs of early Rome. He attempts to prove that Rome was essentially in origin a Greek city, as at 7.70.1–71.1: 'I promised at the end of my first book, which I wrote and published concerning the Romans' background, that I would confirm this theory with innumerable proofs, by bringing in ancient customs, laws and practices, which they preserve down to my own time, just as they received them from their forefathers; for I do not believe that it is sufficient for those who write the ancient history of other countries to recount it in a trustworthy fashion as they received it from the country's inhabitants, but consider that it also needs numerous and indisputable pieces of supporting evidence, if it is going to appear reliable . . . I shall use Quintus Fabius as my authority, without needing any further confirmation; for he is the most ancient of all Roman historians, and provides proof not only from what he has heard from others, but also from his own knowledge.' His work has been extensively employed in chapters 1 and 2.

While his work is full of lengthy rhetorical and moralising speeches, he is however concerned with questions of accuracy and authenticity and attempts to make sense of the quasi-legendary material with which he is working, as with the family relationships of the Tarquinii (4.6.1): 'These children were not his sons but his grandsons. Due to their total lack of thought and laziness, the authors have published this historical account of them without having examined any of the impossibilities and irrationalities which undermine it, each of which I will try to make clear in a few words . . .'. At 1.7.2–3 he lists as his sources, 'men of the greatest learning' with whom he associated, and histories written by the approved Roman authorities: Cato, Fabius Maximus, Valerius Antias, Licinius Macer, the 'Aelii, Gellii and Calpurnii' and 'many other renowned writers'.

14.19 Valerius Maximus

See: Maslakov 1984; Skidmore 1996.

Valerius Maximus composed his *Memorable Deeds and Sayings* in the reign of the emperor Tiberius (AD 14–37), and it was perhaps published shortly after AD 31. It comprises various series of short anecdotes, with both Roman and foreign examples, under a series of moral headings. Valerius uses his sources uncritically, borrowing from Livy and Cicero in particular; though entertaining (e.g., docs. 7.14, 7.41), his work is mainly valuable when he borrows from authors now lost.

14.20 Pliny the Elder

See: How 1985; French & Greenaway 1986; Wallace-Hadrill 1990; Beagon 1992; French 1994.

The antiquarian and miscellanist Pliny the Elder, who died at the eruption of Vesuvius on 24 August 79, is best known for his 37-book encyclopaedia, the *Natural History*, aimed at including all the knowledge of his time — astronomical, geographical, physiological, biological, botanical, metallurgical and so on. At pref. 17, Pliny states that he has collected 20,000 important facts through reading approximately 2,000 volumes, of which few were ever handled by scholars because of the recondite nature of their contents, written by 100 authors. The value of these 'facts' is considerably enhanced because he usually cites his source for each. Much of the information he imparts helps to add new dimensions to our knowledge of Roman life and customs: see especially docs 3.24, 7.90 (for religious rites), 1.27 (colossal art), 6.3, 6.12, 6.16 (on slaves), 7.65 (on life expectancies), and doc. 7.71 for the price of lampstands and a very lucky slave hunchback. The attentive reader will find numerous citations of Pliny's *Natural History* in the comments on documents, refining the detail of what is known more generally from other sources.

14.21 Aulus Gellius

See: Holford-Strevens 1988.

Gellius was born in the early second century AD and apparently spent much of his life at Rome. The 20 books of his *Attic Nights*, which probably were published c. AD 180, are particularly concerned with matters of Latin grammar and expression; the work is arranged in short chapters based on notes which he had made on various texts, referring to philosophy, history, religion, grammar and literary and textual criticism: the depth of his reading, especially in Latin, enables him to comment on numerous erudite works that are now lost. His preface states that he decided to write up these notes into a read-able form while in Attica (hence the title) and completed them later for the instruction and entertainment of his children (pref. 1): this need be no more than a literary device, as is the frequent dialogue-setting between Gellius and his teachers and friends. His discussion of literary usages often includes valuable citations, often quite lengthy, of passages of texts no longer extant. Some of the most notable of these are extracts from speeches of well-known political figures and orators, such as Gaius Gracchus, tr. pl. 123, 122 (docs 8.22–4, 8.27), Cato *On the Voconian law* and *On the Dowry* (docs 7.11, 18), and his support for the Rhodians in 167, taken from Tiro's criticism of this speech (doc. 5.36), and Scipio Aemilianus' attack as censor on P. Sulpicius Gallus and other effeminate men (doc. 7.57). He also gives definitions of ancient terms, such as pomerium, plebiscite, capite censi and the various assemblies (docs 1.3, 1.20, 1.57, 9.11), and cites the exact wording of military oaths dating from 190 BC, taken from Cincius' *On Military Science* (doc. 5.21), and the details of sumptuary legislation in 161 and 81 BC (docs 5.56, 11.37). One of his most important and lengthy citations is from Fabius Pictor *On the Pontifical Law* where he informs the reader of the taboos which hedged the flamen dialis (doc 3.19).

His love of reading shines through the fragmented structure of his miscellany (pref. 22–3): 'To this day I have already made twenty volumes of notes. Whatever longer life remains to me by the gods' will and leisure from managing my affairs and seeing to the education of my children, I shall spend all that remaining spare time in gathering brief and amusing memoranda of the same type. And so the number of books, with the help of the gods, will keep pace with the years of life itself, however few or many there may be, nor do I wish to be granted a life which will outlast my capacity to write and take notes.'

14.22 Macrobius

Ambrosius Theodosius Macrobius was a high-ranking senator in the fifth century AD. His *Saturnalia* is set in the form of a series of dialogues at the Saturnalia of, perhaps, AD 383, beginning the night before the festival (which commenced on 17 December) and lasting through the holiday. The guests include great pagan literary and political figures of the time who range through various matters, both serious (a great deal of space is given to the poet Virgil) and more trivial, such as food and drink. Like Gellius, Macrobius' main value for the Roman Republic is in his citation of works no longer extant: these include a speech of Scipio Aemilianus against Tiberius Gracchus' judiciary law (doc. 8.20), Sulla's sumptuary laws (doc. 11.37), the formula for an evocatio in 146 BC, calling the gods from Carthage (doc. 3.56), numerous witticisms of Cicero (doc. 12.25) and the menu of a pontifical banquet c. 69 BC (doc. 2.23).

POETS

14.23 Quintus Ennius

See: Jocelyn 1972: 987–1026 and 1967; Skutsch 1985; Rawson 1989: 444–8; Gruen 1990: 106–23; Coffey 1995: 24–32; Hinds 1998; Mellor 1999: 15–16; on the lowly status of poets c. 240–140 BC: MacMullen 1991: 422–4 with n. 12.

Born in 239 BC in southern Italy, Q. Ennius was brought by Cato the Elder to Rome in 204 from Sardinia, where he was serving with a Calabrian regiment (Nepos *Cato* 1.4). He was thus trilingual, in Oscan, Greek and Latin, and Gellius describes him as having three hearts: Gell. 17.17.1. He naturalised various Greek metres and considered himself a 'poeta', writing *poemata* not *carmina* (songs). At Rome he was on friendly terms with the Cornelii Scipiones, Sulpicii, Fulvii and Caecilii, and Fulvius Nobilior took Ennius to the East with him in 189 (for which he was criticised by Cato: Cicero *Tusc. Disp*. 1.3). Ennius chronicled the campaign and wrote a play, the *Ambracia*, on the capture of that town in Aetolia. He was given Roman citizenship in 184 by Nobilior's son. According to L. Aelius Stilo (Gell. 12.4.4), the friend portrayed in Ennius' portrait of Servilius Geminus (doc. 2.46) was Ennius himself: see Gruen 1990: 111–13.

He wrote at least 20 tragedies, many freely adapted from Greek works, 3 comedies, some 4, or more, books of satires (*saturae*), a gastronomic poem, an account of the gods (the *Epicharmus*), epigrams, and a prose work, the *Euhemerus*, on the gods as men of olden times. His best known work was however his *Annals*, originally in 15 books, to which three more were later added. In this work he attempted to improve on Naevius' *Song of the First Punic War* (doc. 4.18, cf. 4.57). Homer, seen by Ennius in a dream on Mount Helicon, was supposedly the source of his poetic inspiration for his *Annals*, and in the work Homer tells how his soul migrated into Ennius' body (1.4–15; Skutsch 70–1, as lines 2–11).

Ennius provides some useful maxims on Roman customs and tradition, all the more valuable because they are cited as significant in other later works: doc 1.9 (on custom); 1.10 (on kingship); doc. 2.46 (on friendship and the values of the *nobiles*); 5.60 (on Roman views of nudity). He also records details of traditional religious practices and beliefs: doc. 3.1 (the twelve Olympians in council), 3.5 (Numa and religious institutions), 3.45 (Romulus and divination). He was frequently cited on Hannibal and the Second Punic War (docs 4.30, 4.34, 4.37) while his epigram on Scipio Africanus (d. 184) accords Scipio semi-divine status (doc. 4.58).

On his satires, Ennius wrote:

> Greetings, poet Ennius, you who pledge mortal men
> In flaming verses from your inmost marrow (*Sat.* 6–7).

On himself (*Epigrams* 7–10), he wrote (for his *imago*, funerary mask):

> Look, O citizens, on the portrait of Ennius in his old age.
> It was he who depicted the greatest deeds of your ancestors.

And for his tomb:

> Let no one grace me with tears or make a funeral with weeping.
> Why? Because I wing my way alive from one man's mouth to another's.

14.24 Gaius Lucilius

See: Gratwick 1982: 156–71; Rudd 1986; Gruen 1992: esp. 272–317; Coffey 1995: 35–62.

Lucilius, born c. 180 BC (died 102/1), was of equestrian rank and the great-uncle of Pompey the Great (Vell. 2.29.2). He served with Scipio Aemilianus at Numantia (docs 5.49–50) and there are many allusions in his poetry to this campaign; he was on friendly terms with Scipio and C. Laelius. His work contains many personal attacks, perhaps modelled on the Greek poet Archilochus, on noted political figures and on moral decline; some 1,400 lines of his satires are extant. At *Satires* 26.1.632–4 he writes:

> . . . (I don't want) that by the very uneducated
> Or the extremely learned, I should be read; Manius Manilius
> Or Persius I don't want to read these lines, I want Junius Congus to.

Manilius was consul in 149, Persius a well-born orator; Congus clearly is the ideal reader: not overly well-informed but sufficiently educated to appreciate the work. Cicero *de orat.* 2.25, who has Laelius Decumus not Congus, gives as his reason that the one would understand nothing, and the other understand perhaps more than Lucilius did himself; cf. Pliny *Nat. Hist.* pref. 7.

He presents a satirical view of life in the second century: doc. 1.7 (on life in the forum); 4.55 (on Hannibal); 5.4 (on Rome's invincibility); 5.49 (Scipio's moral reforms of the army); 5.56 (on sumptuary legislation). He is particularly enlightening on social issues: 6.4–5 (the slaves owned (or not owned) by rich and poor in Rome); 6.19 (his own favourite slave); 6.30 (a prominent gladiatorial match); 6.40 (the runaway slave's dog-collar); 7.38 ('a 'good' wife); 7.56 (on the ways noble women are idealised as beautiful); and 7.62 (the charges for an aging prostitute).

14.25 Gaius Valerius Catullus

See: Quinn 1972; Lyne 1980: 19–61; Wiseman 1985; Newman 1991.

Catullus came from a wealthy family in Verona and as a young man served on the staff of C. Memmius, who was governor of Bithynia in 57–56 BC. He seems to have died in 54 BC, at the age of only 30 years: at least there is no mention of events after 55 in his work. He was the author of numerous works of invective against Caesar and his engineer Mamurra (docs 7.49, 12.87, 13.58), and was part of a cultivated literary circle which modelled itself on hellenistic culture. Much of his work (some 114 poems) is taken up with the theme of a love affair with 'Lesbia', perhaps a poetic construct rather than Clodia, the sister of the tribune Clodius with whom she has been identified (docs 7.47–9, 51), and he does address himself to other loves as well (see especially doc. 7.61). In doc. 7.46 he satirises conventional morals in Roman aristocratic society.

Glossary

Aedile: one of four lesser magistrates (two curule, two plebeian) elected in the comitia tributa. Their main duties concerned the infrastructure of the city of Rome as well as the organisation of public games (the ludi Romani and Megalensia by the curule aediles, the ludi Ceriales and Plebeii by the plebeian aediles). The aedileship was not an essential rung in the cursus honorum.

Ager publicus: land under Roman public ownership, generally confiscated during wars in Italy. It was leased out by the censors to occupiers for a minimal rent.

Ambitus: the act of acquiring support during candidature for office through illegal means, such as bribery.

Amicitia: an informal political alliance (literally 'friendship') in which amici ('friends') provided mutually beneficial services.

Apparitor: an official attendant to a magistrate.

As: the smallest bronze coin. Ten asses equalled a denarius, two and a half equalled a sesterce.

Assembly: see comitia.

Atrium: the main reception room of a Roman house, containing a rectangular opening in the roof below which was a pool (the impluvium).

Auctoritas: the ability to influence people and events through one's status (i.e., as a magistrate) or one's personal reputation.

Augur: a member of the priestly college of augures, concerned with divination. Augurs took the auspices prior to the undertaking of military campaigns and before public meetings. From 300 BC five of the nine augurs were plebeians.

Auspicium: the right to take auspices (to consult the will of the gods) before elections and other public business. Auspicium was possessed by both senior magistrates (greater auspices) and junior magistrates (lesser auspices).

Basilica: a large building for public use, which might contain law-courts, shops, banking institutions and offices.

Boni: the 'good' or 'honest' men, a term which by the first century BC had come to mean the conservative element in government; see optimates.

Bulla: a locket worn by freeborn boys prior to assuming the toga of manhood.

Campus Martius: the 'Field of Mars'; this lay outside the pomerium and was the assembly point for armies awaiting their commander's triumph, a training-ground, and the site of the comitia centuriata. The lustratio, the closing ceremony of the census, was performed there by the censors.

Capite censi: the 'head count', Roman citizens too poor to belong to one of the five economic classes in the comitia centuriata and below the minimum property qualification for army service, prior to the reforms of Marius.

Censor: the most senior of Roman magistrates, though without imperium; in the later republic two were elected every five years for a period of 18 months. Their duties included conducting a census of all citizens, letting out contracts for public works, and scrutinising the membership of the senate and equestrian class.

Census: a census was conducted every five years by the censors to update the list of Roman citizens, their family, and their property qualification.

Clientela: clientship or patronage. Clients were free men (including freedmen) who received the protection of a patron (often in legal matters), in return supporting him in political life and enhancing his prestige.

Cognomen (plural: cognomina): the final name of a Roman citizen, denoting the branch of the gens to which he belonged; cognomina were generally assigned on the basis of some defect — Cicero (wart), Brutus (stupid) — or were formally granted to commemorate a great military victory (Numidicus, Africanus, Dalmaticus). In aristocratic families more than one cognomen could be hereditary (e.g., the Cornelii *Scipiones Nasicae*). Adoptive sons took their adoptive father's name but could add an additional cognomen from their original nomen, such as Publius Cornelius Scipio who also took the name Aemilianus, because he was the son of L. Aemilius Paullus.

Collegia: societies, such as the priestly colleges, that of the tribunes of the plebs, or work-related organisations.

Comitia: an assembly, or formal gathering of the Roman people.

Comitia centuriata: a political assembly (initially a military assembly) in which the people were organised by classes on an economic basis, favouring the wealthy. It met on the Campus Martius, elected consuls, praetors and censors, heard treason trials, declared war and peace, and passed laws.

Comitia tributa: a political assembly organised on the basis of the 35 tribes (4 urban, the others rural), which elected curule aediles, quaestors and military tribunes and passed laws. It met initially in the comitium (to the north-east of the forum) and then in the forum itself.

Comitia curiata: the earliest assembly, whose functions were gradually subsumed by the comitia centuriata. By the late republic it primarily ratified the appointment of priests, adoptions, and wills.

Concilium plebis: a plebeian assembly, which elected tribunes of the plebs and plebeian aediles, enacted plebiscites, and held non-capital trials.

Consuls: the two senior magistrates, with imperium and auspicium. The consuls' primary duties were military and their imperium was senior to that of any other magistrate (except that of a dictator) or provincial governor.

Consul suffectus: a substitute consul (suffect-consul), appointed by the senate, who took over the office for part of the year in the event that a consul died in office.

Consularis: an ex-consul. Consulars had great prestige in the senate.

Contio (plural: contiones): a public meeting of an informal nature, which could be called by a tribune of the plebs or another magistrate, used for preliminary discussion of laws or other business.

Curia (hostilia): the senate house in the forum Romanum (or the senatorial body in a municipality). Curia also meant a tenth of each of the three earliest tribes in the time of the kings, and was the unit on which the comitia curiata was based.

Cursus honorum: the 'road of honour' or career path. It was necessary to serve as quaestor and praetor before running for the consulship, and the lex Villia annalis in 180 BC (updated by Sulla) prescribed set intervals between each magistracy and minimum ages for candidature.

Curule chair: the sella curulis, originally Etruscan, a backless stool made of ivory, reserved for consuls, praetors and curule aediles as a sign of rank.

Dedicitii: peoples who had unconditionally surrendered to Rome by making a deditio in fidem (surrendering to Rome's good faith).

Denarius: a silver coin, usually the largest denomination in the republic; 10 asses made a denarius (or four sesterces) and 6,250 denarii a silver talent. A denarius was roughy equivalent to the Greek drachma.

Dictator: an extraordinary magistrate who, prior to Sulla, held power for a fixed period of time (six months or less) either to command an army or hold elections. The dictator was preceded by 24 lictors and existing magistrates were subordinate to him. He appointed a master of horse (magister equitum) as his second-in-command.

Dignitas: a man's personal standing based on his achievements and reputation.

Drachma: a Greek coin roughly equivalent to the Roman denarius.

Equites (sing.: eques): the equites, or equestrian order, were originally the cavalry, and later the business class.

Emancipation: the act of freeing a son or daughter from dependence (patria potestas); the emancipated person became legally independent (sui iuris) of the father.

Fasces: a bundle of birch rods tied with leather thongs, carried by twelve lictors before the consuls (on alternate months); praetors were allowed six lictors. The fasces, which outside of Rome included an axe, symbolised the kings' and then the magistrates' power to punish citizens.

Fasti: the calendar listing festivals of the gods and days on which assemblies and business could or could not be held. Fasti consulares listed magistrates, fasti triumphales triumphs.

Flamen (plural: flamines): a member of the college of pontifices, a priest in charge of the worship of a particular deity, such as the flamen dialis (the priest of Jupiter).

Forum Romanum: a forum was an open-air meeting place. The main forum in Rome was the forum Romanum, the chief public square, where the comitia tributa was held (from 145 BC), the senate-house was sited, and most public business, like law-suits, took place.

Gens (plural: gentes): a clan whose members shared the same nomen or family name, such as Cornelius, Julius, Licinius, or Pompeius, and who could trace their descent back to a common ancestor. Groups within a gens could be distinguished by different cognomina: members of the gens Cornelius, for example, could be distinguished by cogomina such as (Cornelius) Cinna, Dolabella, Lentulus, Scipio, and Sulla.

Haruspices (sing.: haruspex): diviners or soothsayers, members of the Etruscan aristocracy, particularly concerned with examining the entrails of animals after sacrifice.

Hospitium: ritualised friendship, often hereditary, maintained particularly between Romans and non-Romans in Italy and elsewhere.

Ides: the thirteenth day of every month, except March, May, July and October when it fell on the fifteenth.

Imagines (sing.: imago): masks of ancestors kept in the atrium and carried in funeral processions. The rank of censor, consul, praetor or aedile conferred the right to keep such imagines.

Imperator: a commander-in-chief or general, especially one who had won a great victory and been hailed by his troops.

Imperium: supreme power, including command in war and the execution of law, possessed by senior magistrates for their year of office (or longer if prorogued). Imperium was symbolised by the fasces, carried by the lictors. Imperium pro praetore: the imperium possessed by a propraetor, prorogued after his year in office as praetor; imperium pro consule; the imperium possessed by a proconsul.

Interrex (plural: interreges): literally 'between the kings', a patrician member of the senate with full imperium appointed to conduct business for five days in cases where the consuls had been killed and elections had not yet been held.

Iugera (sing.: iugerum): a unit of land measurement, roughly equivalent to 5/8 of an acre or 1/4 of a hectare.

Kalends: the first day of the month.

Latifundia: estates in Sicily and Italy consisting of large areas of farming land, usually worked by slaves.

Legate: a senior member of a general's military staff who was of senatorial rank.

Lex (plural: leges): a law passed by one of the assemblies of the Roman people.

Lictors: Roman citizens who accompanied senior magistrates with imperium and carried the fasces.

Ludi: games put on at the state's expense and organised by the aediles, who often contributed to the expense to win popularity with the electorate.

Lustrum: the five-year period during which the censors technically served (though they were only actually in office for 18 months) and the purification ceremony (lustrum) with which one of the censors, chosen by lot, concluded the five-yearly census of the Roman people.

Magister equitum: the master of the horse, a dictator's second-in-command.

Manumission: the act of freeing a slave. Freed slaves (freedmen) automatically became citizens.

Manus: literally 'hand', the authority which a husband could possess over his wife if she was married 'in manu' (i.e., came into his authority); in this case she entered her husband's family. For women to be married 'in manu' was uncommon by the end of the republic.

Municipium: a township in Italy, or in the provinces, with its own magistrates and own citizen rights.

Nobilis (plural: nobiles): literally 'known men', members of the families which formed

GLOSSARY

the political elite of Rome, which came to mean that one of the family's ancestors had held the consulship. The nobiles tended, though not exclusively, to dominate the higher magistrates.

Nomen: family name of a citizen, such as Cornelius, Julius, or Tullius, denoting the gens to which he belonged. Daughters were called by the feminine form of the nomen: i.e., Cornelia, Julia, Tullia.

Nomenclator: a slave whose job was to remember the names of his master's associates, clients and voters.

Nones: the fifth day of every month, except March, May, July and October, when it was the seventh.

Novus homo (plural: novi homines): literally a 'new man', or non-nobilis, none of whose ancestors had held the consulship (such as Marius or Cicero), or perhaps even reached senatorial rank.

Nundina (plural: nundinae): a market-day; markets were held eight days apart; three market-days (at least seventeen days) had to pass before a bill which had been presented could be put to the vote.

Optimates: literally 'the best', another term for the boni or conservative element in government, contrasted in the first century BC with the populares.

Paterfamilias: the male head of the family, with potestas over all household members who had not been emancipated.

Patria potestas: literally 'power of the father', the power of the head of the family over all descendants (unless emancipated).

Patricians: the original Roman aristocracy which originated under the monarchy, hence a privileged group of senatorial families.

Plebeians: non-patricians, members of the plebs, the mass of Roman citizens, who had their own officials (tribunes of the plebs and plebeian aediles).

Pomerium: the religious boundary of Rome.

Pontiff (plural: pontifices): one of a college of priests who advised on sacred ceremonial. Their number was increased to eight in 300 BC and to 15 by Sulla. The pontifex maximus was the chief of these.

Populares (sing.: popularis): literally 'supporters of the people', politicians who proposed popular measures, generally bypassing the senate in doing so and going directly to the people.

Praenomen: a Roman man's first name. Only some 18 personal names were in use in the republic, such as Gaius, Lucius, Marcus, Publius.

Praetor: a senior magistrate, with imperium and auspicium; praetors were initially the senior magistrates and after the appointment of consuls a praetor could perform consular duties in the consuls' absence. They were generally in charge of the administration of law in Rome. From c. 244 BC there were two praetors, the praetor urbanus (for Rome) and a praetor peregrinus (for foreigners and non-citizens). Their number was increased to eight under Sulla.

Princeps senatus: the 'leader of the senate'; a patrician ex-consular or ex-censor who had the right to speak first on any motion in the senate. The position was for life.

Privatus: a private citizen, with no military rank.

GLOSSARY

Promagistrate: a magistrate (a proconsul or propraetor) whose command was prorogued (continued) into the following year.

Prorogation: the extension of a magistrate's imperium beyond the end of his year of office.

Publicani: tax-collectors, businessmen who bid for the right to collect taxes in the provinces.

Quaestio (plural: quaestiones): a tribunal of inquiry, or a standing court (quaestio perpetua: introduced in 149 BC).

Quaestor: a junior magistrate with fiscal responsibilities. Sulla raised their number to 20, set the minimum age qualification as 30 years and gave them automatic entry to the senate.

Quindecimviri sacris faciundis: the 15 keepers of the Sibylline Books (earlier the duumviri, two men, and then the decemviri, ten men).

Quirites: Roman citizens who were civilians; the ususal term by which citizens are addressed by orators.

Repetundae: literally '(money) to be recovered', or extortion by officials in authority, especially Roman governors in provinces.

Respublica: the state or government, originally res publica, 'the thing which unites the people', 'public affairs'.

Senate: a group of 100 unelected patricians under the monarchy, which became 300 in the republic, who acted as an advisory body to the magistrates. Their number was raised to 600 by Sulla and then to 900 by Julius Caesar.

Senatus consultum (plural: senatus consulta): a senatorial decree which went to one of the comitia for ratification; the 'senatus consultum ultimum' (SCU) was a suspension of the constitution and declaration of a state of emergency.

Sesterces (sing.: sesterce): Roman coins, each worth two and a half asses or a quarter of a denarius.

SPQR: the senate and people of Rome (senatus populusque Romanus).

Sui iuris: legally independent.

Suovetaurilia: the sacrifice of a pig, sheep and ox.

Toga: the formal dress of a male Roman citizen made of undyed wool; the toga praetexta, which had a purple border along one edge, was worn by officials and children. Candidates for office wore a whitened toga, the toga candida. People in mourning wore the toga pulla, made of dark wool.

Tribune of the plebs: ten plebeian officials created c. 494 to convene popular assemblies and represent the interests of the people. They took up office on 10 December.

Abbreviations and General Bibliography

Abbreviations of personal names

A.	Aulus
App.	Appius
C.	Gaius
Cn.	Gnaeus
D.	Decimus
L.	Lucius
M.	Marcus
M'.	Manius
P.	Publius
Q.	Quintus
Ser.	Servius
Sex.	Sextus
Sp.	Spurius
T.	Titus
Ti.	Tiberius

Abbreviations of ancient literary sources

Amm. Marc.	Ammianus Marcellinus *History*
App. *BC*	Appian *Bellum Civile* (*Civil Wars*)
App. *Hann.*	Appian *Hannibalic Wars*
App. *Iber.*	Appian *Iberike* (*The Spanish Wars*)
App. *Mac.*	Appian *The Macedonian Wars*
App. *Mith.*	Appian *The Mithridatic Wars*
App. *Pun.*	Appian *The Punic Wars*
App. *Syr.*	Appian *The Syrian Wars*
Arist. *Pol.*	Aristotle *Politics*
Arnob.	Arnobius *Adversus nationes* (*Against the Nations*)
Asc.	Asconius *Commentaries on Five Speeches of Cicero*
Athen.	Athenaeus *Deipnosophistae*
Aug. *Civ. Dei*	St Augustine *On the City of God*
Caes.	Caesar
Caes. *BC*	Julius Caesar *Bellum Civile* (*Civil War*)

Caes. *BG*	Julius Caesar *Bellum Gallicum* (*Gallic War*)
[Caes.] *Alex.*	[Caesar] *Bellum Alexandrum* (*Alexandrian War*)
Cat.	Catullus *Poems*
Cato *Agr.*	Cato the Elder *On Farming*
Cato F	Jordan, H. 1860, *M. Catonis praeter librum de re rustica quae exstant*, Leipzig.
Cato *de re militari*	Huschke, P.E. 1908, *Iurisprudentia Anteiustiniana*, Leipzig.
Cic.	Cicero
[Cic.]	A letter in *Letters to Friends* written to Cicero, not by him, or a work attributed to Cicero but not written by him.
Cic. *Amic.*	*De amicitia* (*On Friendship*)
Cic. *Arch.*	*Pro Archia* (*In Defence of Archias*)
Cic. *Att.*	*Epistulae ad Atticum* (*Letters to Atticus*)
Cic. *Balb.*	*Pro Balbo* (*In Defence of Balbus*)
Cic. *Brut.*	*Brutus*
Cic. *Caec.*	*Pro Caecina* (*In Defence of Caecina*)
Cic. *Caelio*	*Pro Caelio* (*In Defence of Caelius*)
Cic. *Cat.*	*In Catilinam I–IV* (*Against Catiline*)
Cic. *Cluent.*	*Pro Cluentio* (*In Defence of Cluentius*)
Cic. *De orat.*	*De oratore* (*On the Orator*)
Cic. *Div.*	*De divinatione* (*On Divination*)
Cic. *Dom.*	*De domo sua* (*On his House*)
Cic. *Fam.*	*Epistulae ad Familiares* (*Letters to Friends*)
Cic. *Fin.*	*De finibus* (*On Ends*)
Cic. *Flacc.*	*Pro Flacco* (*In Defence of Flaccus*)
Cic. *Font.*	*Pro Fonteio* (*In Defence of Fonteius*)
Cic. *Har. Resp.*	*De haruspicum responsis* (*Concerning the Responses of the Soothsayers*)
Cic. *Laws*	*De legibus* (*On the Laws*)
Cic. *Leg. Agr.*	*De lege agraria* (*On the Agrarian Law*)
Cic. *Letters to Brutus*	*Epistulae ad M. Brutum*
Cic. *Man.*	*Pro Lege Manilia* (*On the Command of Cn. Pompey, On the Manilian Law*)
Cic. *Mil.*	*Pro T. Annio Milone* (*In Defence of Titus Annius Milo*)
Cic. *Mur.*	*Pro Murena* (*In Defence of Murena*)
Cic. *Nat. Deor.*	*De natura deorum* (*On the Nature of the Gods*)
Cic. *Off.*	*De officiis* (*On Duties*)
Cic. *Orat.*	*Orator*
Cic. *Phil.*	*Philippicae* (*Philippics*)
Cic. *Piso*	*In Pisonem* (*Against Piso*)
Cic. *Planc.*	*Pro Cn. Plancio* (*In Defence of Gnaeus Plancio*)
Cic. *Prov.*	*De provinciis consularibus* (*On the Consular Provinces*)
Cic. *Quint.*	*Epistulae ad Quintem Fratrem* (*Letters to his Brother Quintus*)
Cic. *Rab. Perd.*	*Pro Rabirio perduellionis reo* (*In Defence of Rabirius on the Charge of Treason*)
Cic. *Rab. Post.*	*Pro C. Rabirio Postumo* (*In Defence of Gaius Rabirius Postumus*)
Cic. *Red. Quir.*	*Post Reditum ad Quirites* (*Speech to the People on his Return from Exile*)

Cic. *Red. Sen.*	*Post Reditum in Senatu* (*Speech to the Senate on his Return from Exile*)
Cic. *Rep.*	*De republica* (*On the Republic*)
Cic. *Rosc. Am.*	*Pro Roscio Amerino* (*In Defence of Roscius of Ameria*)
Cic. *Scaur.*	*Pro Scauro* (*In Defence of Scaurus*)
Cic. *Sen.*	*De senectute* (*On Old Age*)
Cic. *Sest.*	*Pro Sestio* (*In Defence of Sestius*)
Cic. *Sull.*	*Pro Sulla* (*In Defence of Sulla*)
Cic. *Top.*	*Topica*
Cic. *Tull.*	*Pro Tullio* (*In Defence of Tullius*)
Cic. *Tusc. Disp.*	*Tusculan Disputations*
Cic. *Vat.*	*In Vatinium* (*Against Vatinius*)
Cic. *Verr.*	*In Verrem* (*Against Verres, The Verrine Orations*)
CJ	*Codex Justinianus* (*The Lawcode of Justinian*)
Columella	Columella *de re rustica* (*On Farming*)
Const. Porph.	Constantine VII Porphyrogenitus
Dio	Cassius Dio *Roman History*
Diod.	Diodorus Siculus *Library of History*
Dion. Hal.	Dionysius of Halicarnassus *Roman Antiquities*
Enn. *Ann.*	Ennius *Annals*
Ep.	*Letter* (*Epistle*)
F	Fragment
FF	Fragments
Festus	Festus *Breviarium* (*Summary of Roman History*)
Flor.	Florus *Epitome of all the Wars over Seven Hundred Years* (*Epitome of Roman History*)
Front. *Strat.*	Frontinus *Strategemata*
Gaius *Dig.*	Gaius *Digest*
Gaius *Inst.*	Gaius *Institutiones* (*Institutions*)
Gell.	Aulus Gellius *Attic Nights*
Hor.	Horace
Hor. *Ep.*	Horace *Epistles*
Hor. *Odes*	Horace *Odes*
Hor. *Sat.*	Horace *Satires*
Hor. *Serm.*	Horace *Sermones*
Joseph. *Ant.*	Josephus *Antiquitates Judaicae* (*Jewish Antiquities*)
Joseph. *BJ*	Josephus *Bellum Judaicum* (*Jewish War*)
Justin	Justin *Epitome*
Juv.	Juvenal *Satires*
Livy	Livy *History of Rome*
Livy *Epit.*	Livy *Epitome*
Livy *Per.*	Livy *Periochae* (in Loeb Classical Library, *Livy*: vol. 14)

Lucan *Phars.*	Lucan *Pharsalia*
Lucretius	Lucretius *de rerum natura* (*On the Nature of the Universe*)
Macc.	Maccabees
Macrob.	Macrobius *Saturnalia*
Nepos	Cornelius Nepos
Nepos *Atticus*	*Life of Atticus*
Nepos *Cato*	*Life of Cato (the Elder)*
Nepos *Hannibal*	*Life of Hannibal*
Obsequens	Julius Obsequens *A Book of Prodigies* (in Loeb Classical Library, *Livy*: vol. 14)
Orosius	Orosius *Histories against the Pagans*
Ovid *Metam.*	Ovid *Metamorphoses*
Ovid *Trist.*	Ovid *Tristia*
Paus.	Pausanius *Description of Greece*
Plaut.	Plautus
Plaut. *Amph.*	*Amphitryo*
Plaut. *Aul.*	*Aulularia* (*The Pot of Gold*)
Plaut. *Bacch.*	*Bacchides* (*The Two Bacchises*)
Plaut. *Capt.*	*Captivi*
Plaut. *Curc.*	*Curculio*
Plaut. *Merc.*	*Mercator*
Plaut. *Mostell.*	*Mostellaria*
Plaut. *Poen.*	*Poenulus*
Pliny *Ep.*	Pliny the Younger *Letters*
Pliny *Nat. Hist.*	Pliny the Elder *Natural History*
Plut.	Plutarch
Plut. *Aem.*	*Life of Aemilius Paullus*
Plut. *Ant.*	*Life of Antony* (*M. Antonius*)
Plut. *Brut.*	*Life of Brutus*
Plut. *Caes.*	*Life of Julius Caesar*
Plut. *Cam.*	*Life of Camillus*
Plut. *Cato Mai.*	*Life of Cato Major* (*Cato the Elder*)
Plut. *Cato Min.*	*Life of Cato Minor* (*Cato the Younger*)
Plut. *Cic.*	*Life of Cicero*
Plut. *Cor.*	*Life of Coriolanus*
Plut. *Crass.*	*Life of Crassus*
Plut. *Fab.*	*Life of Fabius Maximus*
Plut. *Flam.*	*Life of Flamininus* (*T. Quinctius Flamininus*)
Plut. *C. Gracchus*	*Life of Gaius Gracchus*
Plut. *T. Gracchus*	*Life of Tiberius Gracchus*
Plut. *Luc.*	*Life of Lucullus*
Plut. *Mar.*	*Life of Marius*
Plut. *Marcell.*	*Life of Marcellus*
Plut. *Mor.*	*Moralia*
Plut. *Numa*	*Life of Numa*

Plut. *Pomp.*	*Life of Pompey*
Plut. *Pyrrh.*	*Life of Pyrrhus*
Plut. *Rom.*	*Life of Romulus*
Plut. *Rom. Quest.*	*Roman Questions* (*Moralia* 263–91; in Loeb Classical Library, *Plutarch*: vol. 4)
Plut. *Sert.*	*Life of Sertorius*
Plut. *Sull.*	*Life of Sulla*
Polyb.	Polybius *Histories*
Pomponius *Dig.*	Pomponius *Digest*
Porphyr. in Hor. *Sat.*	Porphyry *Commentary on Horace's Satires*
Quint. *Inst. Or.*	*Institutio Oratoria* (*Training in Oratory*)
Rhet. ad Herenn.	[Cicero] *Rhetorica ad Herennium*
Sall.	Sallust
Sall. *BJ*	*Bellum Jugurthinum* (*Jugurthine War*)
Sall. *Cat.*	*Bellum Catilinae* (*War Against Catiline, Conspiracy of Catiline*)
Sall. *Hist.*	*Historiae* (*Histories*)
Sen. *de Ira*	Seneca the Younger *de Ira* (*On Anger*)
Sen. *Brev. Vit.*	Seneca the Younger *De brevitate vitae* (*On the Brevity of Life*)
Serv. *Aen.*	Servius *On the Aeneid*
Sisenna	Sisenna in Peter *HRR* I² 276–97
Stobaeus	Stobaeus *Anthology*
Strabo	Strabo *Geography*
Suet.	Suetonius
Suet. *Aug.*	*Divus Augustus* (*Life of the Deified Augustus*)
Suet. *Claud.*	*Divus Claudius* (*Life of the Deified Claudius*)
Suet. *Jul.*	*Divus Julius* (*Life of the Deified Julius*)
Suet. *Gram.*	*de Grammaticis* (*On Grammarians*)
Suet. *Rhet.*	*de Rhetoribus* (*On Rhetoricians*)
Tac. *Ann.*	Tacitus *Annals*
Tac. *Dial.*	Tacitus *Dialogus de oratoribus* (*Dialogue on Orators*)
Tac. *Hist.*	Tacitus *Histories*
Tert. *Apol.*	Tertullian *Apologeticus*
Tert. *Nat.*	Tertullian *Ad nationes*
Ulpian *Tit.*	Ulpian (Domitius Ulpianus) *Tituli* (*Titles*)
Ulpian *Dig.*	Ulpian *Digest*
Val. Max.	Valerius Maximus *Memorable Deeds and Sayings*
Varro *Lat. Lang.*	Varro *de lingua Latina* (*On the Latin Language*)
Varro *Rust.*	Varro *de re rustica* (*On Farming*)
Vell.	Velleius Paterculus *Roman History*
Vir. Illustr.	*de viris illustribus* (*Deeds of Famous Men*); ascribed to but not by Sextus Aurelius Victor.
Zon.	Zonaras *Epitome of History*

Abbreviations of journals, editions of inscriptions, commentaries and frequently cited works

AC	*Antiquité Classique*
ActClass	*Acta Classica*
AHB	*Ancient History Bulletin*
AHR	*American Historical Review*
AJA	*American Journal of Archaeology*
AJAH	*American Journal of Ancient History*
AJPh	*American Journal of Philology*
Alexander *Trials*	Alexander, M.C. 1990, *Trials in the Late Roman Republic*, Toronto.
AncSoc	*Ancient Society*
AncW	*Ancient World*
ANRW	*Aufstieg und Niedergang der Römischen Welt*, Berlin.
ARS	Johnson, A.C. et al. 1961, *Ancient Roman Statutes. A Translation with Introduction, Commentary, Glossary, and Index*, Austin.
AS	*Anatolian Studies*
Badian *FC*	Badian, E. 1984, *Foreign Clientelae (264–70 BC)*, second edition, Oxford.
BICS	*Bulletin of the Institute of Classical Studies*
BNP	Beard, M., North, J., Price, S. 1998, *Religions of Rome*, vols 1–2, Cambridge.
Bruns	Bruns, C.G. 1919, *Fontes iuris Romani antiqui*, seventh edition, Tübingen.
Brunt *IM*	Brunt, P.A. 1971, *Italian Manpower 225 BC–AD 14*, Oxford.
Burnett *CRW*	Burnett, A. 1987, *Coinage in the Roman World*, London.
CAH	*The Cambridge Ancient History*
CAH VII[1]	Cook, S.A., Adcock, F.E., & Charlesworth, M.P. (eds) 1928, *CAH, Volume VII, The Hellenistic Monarchies and the Rise of Rome*, first edition, Cambridge.
CAH VII.2[2]	Astin, A.E., Drummond, A., Frederiksen, M.W., Ogilvie, R.M., & Walbank, F.W. (eds) 1989, *CAH, Volume VII, Part Two: The Rise of Rome to 220 BC*, second edition, Cambridge.
CAH VIII[1]	Cook, S.A., Adcock, F.E., & Charlesworth, M.P. (eds) 1930, *CAH, Volume VIII: Rome and the Mediterranean, 218–133 BC*, first edition, Cambridge.
CAH VIII[2]	Astin, A.E., Frederiksen, M.W., Ogilvie, R.M. & Walbank, F.W. (eds) 1989, *CAH, Volume VIII: Rome and the Mediterranean to 133 BC*, second edition, Cambridge.
CAH IX[1]	Crook, S.A., Adcock, F.E. & Charlesworth, M.P. (eds) 1932, *CAH, Volume IX. The Roman Republic 146–43 BC*, first edition, Cambridge.
CAH IX[2]	Crook, J.A., Lintott, A. & Rawson, E. (eds) 1994, *CAH, Volume IX. The Last Age of The Roman Republic 146–43 BC*, second edition, Cambridge.
Carson *PCRR*	Carson, R.A.G. 1978, *Principal Coins of the Romans Volume I. The Republic*, London.
CEA	*Cahiers des études anciennes*

CIL	*Corpus Inscriptionum Latinarum*
CIL I²	Mommsen, T. (ed.) 1893, 1918, *CIL, Volume I, Inscriptiones Latinae antiquissimae ad C. Caesaris mortem*, parts 1–2, second edition, Berlin.
CIL VI	Henzen, G. (ed.) 1876–1926, *CIL, Volume VI, Inscriptiones urbis Romae Latinae*, parts 1–6, Berlin.
CJ	*The Classical Journal*
ClAnt	*Californian Studies in Classical Antiquity*
C&M	*Classica et Mediaevalia*
Courtney *ALP*	Courtney, E. 1999, *Archaic Latin Prose*, Atlanta.
CPh	*Classical Philology*
CQ	*Classical Quarterly*
CR	*Classical Review*
Crawford *CMRR*	Crawford, M.H. 1985, *Coinage and Money under the Roman Republic*, London.
Crawford *RRC*	Crawford, M.H. 1974, *Roman Republican Coinage*, vols I–II, Cambridge.
Crawford *Statutes*	Crawford, M.H. (ed.) 1996, *Roman Statutes*, vols I–II, London.
CW	*Classical World*
DDA	*Dialoghi di Archaeologia*
Diehl	Diehl, E. 1930, *Altlateinische Inschriften*, third edition, Berlin.
EMC/CV	*Echos du Monde Classique / Classical Views*
FGrH	Jacoby, F. (1954–64) *Die Fragmente der griechischen Historiker*, with *Supplements*, Leiden.
FIRA	Riccobono, S. 1941, *Fontes iuris Romani antejustiniani*, part 1, second edition, Florence.
Foss	Foss, C. 1990, *Roman Historical Coins*, London.
G&R	*Greece and Rome*
Gordon 1983	Gordon, A.E. 1983, *Illustrated Introduction to Latin Epigraphy*, Berkeley.
Gordon *Album*	Gordon, A.E. 1958–65, *Album of Dated Latin Inscriptions*, vols 1–7, Berkeley.
GRBS	*Greek, Roman and Byzantine Studies*
Grueber	Grueber, H.A. 1910, *Coins of the Roman Republic in the British Museum*, vols I–III, London.
Harl *CRE*	Harl, K.W. 1996, *Coinage in the Roman Economy 300 BC–AD 700*, Baltimore.
Harlan *RRM*	Harlan, M. 1995, *Roman Republican Moneyers and their Coins, 63 BC–49 BC*, London.
Hill *MAR*	Hill, P.V. 1989, *The Monuments of Ancient Rome as Coin Types*, London.
Historia Nummorum	Burnett, A.M. (ed. et al.) 2001, *Historia Nummorum. Italy*, London.
HRR	Peter, H. 1906, 1914, *Historicorum Romanorum Reliquiae*, vol. 1, second edition (1914), vol. 2, first edition (1906), Stuttgart.
HSCPh	*Harvard Studies in Classical Philology*
Huschke	See: Abbreviations of ancient sources, Cato
IG	*Inscriptiones Graecae*

IG VII	Dittenberger, W. 1892, *IG VII. Inscriptiones Megaridis et Boeotiae*, Berlin.
ILLRP	Degrassi, A. 1963–65, *Inscriptiones Latinae Liberae Rei Publicae*, vol. 1, second edition (1965), vol 2, first edition (1963), Florence.
ILS	Dessau, H. 1892–1916, *Inscriptiones Latinae Selectae*, Berlin, vols I–III.
Inscr. Ital.	Degrassi, A. *Inscriptiones Italiae*, 1937–63, Rome.
JHS	*Journal of Hellenic Studies*
Jordan	See: Abbreviations of ancient sources, Cato
JRA	*Journal of Roman Archaeology*
JRMES	*Journal of Roman Military Equipment Studies*
JRS	*Journal of Roman Studies*
Lactor	*London Association of Classical Teachers — Original Records*
LCM	*Liverpool Classical Monthly*
LSAG²	Jeffrey, I. 1990, *Local Scripts of Archaic Greece*, second edition, Oxford.
MAAR	*Memoirs of the American Academy at Rome*
MH	*Museum Helveticum*
MRR	Broughton, T.R.S. 1951–60, *The Magistrates of the Roman Republic*, vols 1–3, New York.
Nash	Nash, E. 1968, *Pictorial Dictionary of Ancient Rome*, vols 1–2, second edition, London.
NC	*Numismatic Chronicle*
OGIS	Dittenberger, W. 1903–05, *Orientis Graeci Inscriptiones Selectae*, vols 1–2, Leipzig.
ORF	Malcovati, H. 1976, *Oratorum Romanorum Fragmenta. Liberae Rei Publicae*, fourth edition, Torino.
P&P	*Past and Present*
PBSR	*Papers of the British School at Rome*
PCRR	Carson, R.A.G. 1978, *Principal Coins of the Romans. Volume I. The Republic c. 290–31 BC*, London.
PCPhS	*Proceedings of the Cambridge Philological Society*
Platner-Ashby	Platner, S.B. & Ashby, T.A. 1926, *A Topographical Dictionary of Ancient Rome*, Oxford.
PP	*La parola del passato*
RDGE	Sherk, R.E. 1969, *Roman Documents from the Greek East*, Baltimore.
Reece *RC*	Reece, R. 1970, *Roman Coins*, London.
RIDA	*Revue internationale des droits de l'antiquité*
RhM	*Rheinisches Museum*
Richardson *Top. Dict.*	Richardson, L. 1992, *A New Topographical Dictionary of Ancient Rome*, Baltimore.
RSA	*Rivista storica dell'Antichità*
Scullard *GN*	Scullard, H.H. 1982, *From the Gracchi to Nero. A History of Rome from 133 BC to AD 68*, fifth edition, London.
SEG	*Supplementum Epigraphicum Graecum*
SIG³	Dittenberger, W. (1915–24) *Sylloge Inscriptionum Graecarum*, vols I–IV, Leipzig.

SO	*Symbolae Osloenses*
Steinby	Steinby, M. 1993–2000, *Lexicon Topographicum Urbis Romae*, vols I–IV, Rome.
Sutherland	Sutherland, C.H.V. 1974, *Roman Coins*, London.
Sutherland 1987	Sutherland, C.H.V. 1987, *Roman History and Coinage 44 BC–AD 69*, Oxford.
Sydenham *CRR*	Sydenham, E.A. 1952, *The Coinage of the Roman Republic*, London.
TAPhA	*Transactions of the American Philological Association*
Walbank	Walbank, F.W. 1967–79, *A Historical Commentary on Polybius*, vols I–III, Oxford.
ROL	Warmington, E.H. 1936–40, *Remains of Old Latin*, vols I–IV, London.
WS	*Wiener Studien*
ZPE	*Zeitschrift für Papyrologie und Epigraphik*
ZSS	*Zeitschrift der Savigny-Stiftung für Rechtsgeschichte (romanistische Abteilung)*

General and Background Reading on Roman History

Listed immediately below are works which serve as a useful introduction to Roman history; some deal also with the imperial period but cannot be excluded because of this. The books in this list generally do not appear in the chapter bibliographies which follow.

Adkins, L. & Adkins, R.A. 1994, *A Handbook to Life in Ancient Rome*, New York.
Alföldy, G. 1988, *The Social History of Rome*, Baltimore.
Balsdon, J.P.V.D. (ed.) 1965, *Roman Civilization* = 1965, *The Romans*, London.
Barrow, R.H. 1949, *The Romans*, Harmondsworth.
Beard, M. & Crawford, M.H. 1985, *Rome in the Late Republic*, London.
Bickermann, E.J. 1980, *Chronology of the Ancient World*, revised edition, London.
Blois, L. de & Spek, R.J. van der 1997, *An Introduction to the Ancient World*, London.
Boardman, J., Green, J. & Murray, O. 1986, *The Oxford History of the Classical World*, Oxford = 2001, *The Oxford History of the Roman World*.
Boren, H.C. 1977, *Roman Society. A Social, Economic, and Cultural History*, Lexington.
Carcopino, J. 1941, *Daily Life in Ancient Rome*, Harmondsworth.
Cary, M. & Scullard, H.H. 1976, *A History of Rome down to the Reign of Constantine*, third edition, London.
Christiansen, E. 1995, *A History of Rome*, Cambridge.
Cornell, T. & Matthews, J. 1982, *Atlas of the Roman World*, revised edition, Oxford.
Cornell, T.J. 1995, *The Beginnings of Rome. Italy and Rome from the Bronze Age to the Punic Wars (c. 1000–264 BC)*, London.
Crawford, M. 1992, *The Roman Republic*, second edition, London.
Dupont, F. 1992, *Daily Life in Ancient Rome*, Oxford.
Giardina, A. (ed.) 1993, *The Romans*, Chicago.
Glay, M. le, Voison, J.-L. & Bohec, Y. le 1996, *A History of Rome*, Cambridge MA.
Grant, M. 1978, *A History of Rome*, New York.
Grant, M. 1992, *Greeks and Romans. A Social History*, London.
Hornblower, S. & Spawforth, A. (eds) 1996, *The Oxford Classical Dictionary*, third edition, Oxford.

Jones, P. & Sidwell, K. 1997, *The World of Rome. An Introduction to Roman Culture*, Cambridge.

Kamm, A. 1995, *The Romans. An Introduction*, London.

Lintott, A. 2000, *The Roman Republic*, Stroud.

Marsh, F.B. 1963, *A History of the Roman World from 146 to 30 BC*, third edition revised by Scullard, H.H., London.

Matz, D. 1997, *An Ancient Roman Chronology, 264–27 BC*, North Carolina.

McDonald, A.H. 1966, *Republican Rome*, London.

Mommsen, T. 1868, *A History of Rome*, vols I–IV, London.

Ogilvie, R.M. 1976, *Early Rome and the Etruscans*, London.

Scarre, C. 1995, *The Penguin Historical Atlas of Ancient Rome*, Harmondsworth.

Scullard, H.H. 1980, *A History of the Roman World 753–146 BC*, fourth edition, London.

Scullard, H.H. 1982, *From the Gracchi to Nero*, fifth edition, London.

Starr, C. 1953, *The Emergence of Rome as Ruler of the Western World*, second edition, Ithaca.

Starr, C. 1990, *A History of the Ancient World*, Oxford.

Stobbart, J.C. 1961, *The Grandeur that was Rome*, fourth edition, revised by Maguiness, W.S. & Scullard, H.H., London.

Ward, A.M, Heichelheim, F.M. & Yeo, C.A. 1998, *A History of the Roman People*, third edition, New Jersey.

Source Books and Anthologies

Beard, M., North, J. & Price, S. 1998, *Religions of Rome, Volume 2: A Sourcebook*, Cambridge.

Carter, J.M. 1970, *Sallust: Fragments of the Histories and Pseudo-Sallust: Letters to Caesar*, *Lactor* 6, London.

Cherry, D. 2001, *The Roman World. A Sourcebook*, Malden MA.

Dudley, D.R. 1967, *Urbs Roma. A Source Book of Classical Texts on the City and its Monuments*, London.

Ferguson, J. 1980, *Greek and Roman Religion. A Source Book*, Park Ridge.

Gardner, J.F. & Wiedemann, T.E.J. 1991, *The Roman Household. A Sourcebook*, London.

Grant, F.C. 1957, *Ancient Roman Religion*, New York.

Humphrey, J.W., Oleson, J.P. & Sherwood, A.N. 1998, *Greek and Roman Technology: A Sourcebook*, London.

Jones, A.H.M. (ed.) 1968, *A History of Rome through the Fifth Century. Volume 1: The Republic*, New York.

Kaegi, W.E. & White, P. (eds) 1986, *Readings in Western Civilization. Volume 2: Rome. Late Republic and Principate*, Chicago.

Kagan, D. 1975, *Problems in Ancient History. Volume Two. The Roman World*, second edition, New York.

Lacey, W.K. & Wilson, B.W.J.G. 1970, *Res Publica. Roman Politics and Society According to Cicero*, Oxford.

Lefkowitz, M.R. & Fant, M.B. 1992, *Women's Life in Greece and Rome. A Source Book in Translation*, second edition, Baltimore.

Lewis, N. & Reinhold, M. (eds) 1990, *Roman Civilization. Selected Readings. Volume I: The Republic*, third edition, New York.

Lewis, N. 1985, *The Ides of March*, Sanibel & Toronto.

Lomas, K. 1996, *Roman Italy, 338 BC – AD 200. A Sourcebook*, London.

Luck, G. 1985, *Arcana Mundi. Magic and the Occult in the Greek and Roman World. A Collection of Ancient Texts*, Baltimore.

McDermott, W.C. & Caldwell, W.E. 1970, *Readings in the History of the Ancient World*, second edition, New York.

Meijer, F. & Nijf, O. van 1992, *Trade, Transport and Society in the Ancient World*, London.

Mellor, R. 1998, *The Historians of Ancient Rome. An Anthology of the Major Writings*, London.

Plant, I.M. 2004, *Women Writers of Ancient Greece and Rome. An Anthology*, London.

Rawson, B. 1978, *The Politics of Friendship: Pompey and Cicero*, Sydney.

Ridley, R.T. 1987, *History of Rome: a Documented Analysis*, Rome.

Sabben-Clare, J. 1971, *Caesar and Roman Politics 60–50 BC. Source Material in Translation*, Oxford.

Shaw, B.D. 2001, *Spartacus and the Slave Wars. A Brief History with Documents*, Boston.

Shelton, J. 1988, *As the Romans Did. A Sourcebook in Roman Social History*, New York.

Stockton, D.L. 1981, *From the Gracchi to Sulla. Sources for Roman History, 133–80 BC, Lactor 13*, London.

Thorpe, M.A. 1970, *Roman Politics, 80–44 BC, Lactor 7*, London.

Wiedemann. T.E.J. 1981, *Greek and Roman Slavery*, London.

Wilkinson, L.P. 1966, *Letters of Cicero: A Selection in Translation*, revised edition, London.

Yavetz, Z. 1988, *Slaves and Slavery in Ancient Rome*, New Brunswick.

Bibliographies to Chapters

The chapter bibliographies are not intended to be exhaustive but primarily list those works cited in the comments to documents.

Chapter One: Early Republican Rome 507–264 BC

Alföldi, A. 1965, *Early Rome and the Latins*, Ann Arbor.

Alonso-Núnez, J.M. 1999, 'The mixed constitution in Polybius' *Eranos* 97: 11–19.

Antaya, R. 1980, 'The etymology of pomerium' *AJPh* 101: 184–9.

Astin, A.E. 1958, 'The lex annalis before Sulla' *Latomus* 17: 49–64.

Astin, A.E. 1978, *Cato the Censor*, Oxford.

Astin, A.E. 1982, 'The censorship of the Roman republic: frequency and regularity' *Historia* 3: 174–87.

Badian, E. 1989, 'The *scribae* of the Roman Republic' *Klio* 71: 582–603.

Billows, R. 1989, 'Legal fiction and political reform at Rome in the early second century' *Phoenix* 43: 112–42.

Bloch, R. 1960, *The Origins of Rome*, London.

Brunt, P.A. 1971, *Social Conflicts in the Roman Republic*, London.

Brunt, P.A. 1988, *The Fall of the Roman Republic and Related Essays*, Oxford.

Brunt, P.A. 1988a, 'The equites in the Late Republic' in Brunt 1988: 144–93, revision of 1962, *Trade and Politics in the Ancient World* 1: 117–49 = Seager 1969: 83–115.

Brunt, P.A. 1988b, '*Libertas* in the Republic' in Brunt 1988: 281–350.

Brunt, P.A. 1988c, '*Amicitia in the Roman Republic*' in Brunt 1988: 351–81.

Brunt, P.A. 1988d, 'Clientela' in Brunt 1988: 382–442.

Brunt, P.A. 1988e, 'Factions' in Brunt 1988: 443–502.

Cornell, T.J. 1989, 'Rome and Latium to 390 BC' in *CAH* VII.2²: 243–308.

Cornell, T.J. 1989a, 'The recovery of Rome' in *CAH* VII.2²: 309–50.

Cornell, T.J. 1989b, 'The conquest of Italy' in *CAH* VII.2²: 351–419.

Cornell, T.J. 1995, *The Beginnings of Rome. Italy and Rome from the Bronze Age to the Punic Wars (c. 1000–264 BC)*, London.

Cornell, T.J. 2001, 'Cicero on the origins of Rome' in Powell, J.G.F. & North, J.A. (eds) *Cicero's Republic*, London: 41–56.

Cram, R.V. 1940, 'The Roman censors' *HSCPh* 51: 71–110.

Crook, J.A. 1967, *Law and Life of Rome*, London.

Crook, J.A. 1986, 'Women in Roman Succession' in Rawson, B. (ed.) *The Family in Ancient Rome. New Perspectives*, London: 59–82.

Deman, E.B. van 1922, 'The Sullan Forum' *JRS* 12: 1–31.

Develin, R. 1975, '*Comitia tributa plebis*' *Athenaeum* 53: 302–37.

Develin R. 1977, '*Comitia tributa* again' *Athenaeum* 55: 425–6.

Develin, R. 1985, *The Practice of Politics at Rome, 366–167 BC*, Brussels.

Develin R. 1986, 'The integration of plebeians into the political order after 366 BC' in Raaflaub, K.A. (ed.) *Social Struggles in Archaic Rome: New Perspectives on the Conflict of the Orders*, Berkeley: 327–52.

Drummond, A. 1989, 'Rome in the fifth century I: the social and economic framework' in *CAH* VII.2²: 113–71.

Drummond, A. 1989a, 'Rome in the fifth century II: the citizen community' in *CAH* VII.2²: 172–242.

Eder, W. 1986, 'The political significance of the codification of law in archaic societies: an unconventional hypothesis' in Raaflaub, K.A. (ed.) *Social Struggles in Archaic Rome: New Perspectives on the Conflict of the Orders*, Berkeley: 262–300.

Evans, R.J. 1990, 'Consuls with a delay between the praetorship and the consulship (180–49 BC)' *AHB* 4: 65–71.

Ferenczy, E. 1976, *From the Patrician State to the Patricio-Plebeian State*, Budapest.

Flower, H.I. 1996, *Ancestor Masks and Aristocratic Power in Roman Culture*, Oxford.

Franke, P.R. 1989, 'Pyrrhus' in *CAH* VII.2²: 456–85.

Gabba, E. 1991, *Dionysius and 'The History of Archaic Rome'*, Berkeley.

Grant, M. 1970, *The Roman Forum*, London.

Grieve, L.J. 1985, 'The reform of the *comitia centuriata*' *Historia* 34: 278–309.

Grimal, P. 1983, *Roman Cities*, Wisconsin.

Gruen, E.S. 1992, *Culture and National Identity in Republican Rome*, London.

Hall, U. 1964, 'Voting procedure in Roman assemblies' *Historia* 13: 267–306.

Hall, U. 1998, '"Species libertatis": voting procedure in the Late Roman Republic' in Austin, M. & Harries, J. et al. (eds) *Modus Operandi, Essays in Honour of Geoffrey Rickman*, London: 15–30.

Harris, W.V. 1990, 'On defining the political culture of the Roman republic: some comments on Rosenstein, Williamson, and North' *CPh* 85: 288–94.

Henderson, M.I. 1969, 'The establishment of the *equester ordo*' in Seager 1969: 69–80 = 1963, *JRS* 53: 61–72.

Heurgon, J. 1973, *The Rise of Rome to 264 BC*, Berkeley.

Hill, H. 1952, *The Roman Middle Class in the Republican Period*, Oxford.

Kunkel, W. 1973, *An Introduction to Roman Legal and Constitutional History*, second edition, Oxford.

Linderski, J. 1986, 'Religious aspects of the Conflict of the Orders: the case of *confarreatio*' in Raaflaub, K.A. (ed.) *Social Struggles in Archaic Rome: New Perspectives on the Conflict of the Orders*, Berkeley: 244–61.

Lintott, A.W. 1972, 'Provocatio, from the Struggle of the Orders to the Principate' *ANRW* I.2: 226–67.

Lintott, A. 1999, *The Constitution of the Roman Republic*, Oxford.

Lintott, A.W. 1999a, *Violence in Republican Rome*, revised edition, Oxford.

Loewenstein, K. 1973, *The Governance of Rome*, The Hague.

Lomas, K. 1993, *Rome and the Western Greeks 350 BC–AD 200*, London.

Mackie, N. 1992, '*Popularis* ideology and popular politics at Rome' *RhM* 135: 49–73.

MacMullen, R. 1980, 'How many Romans voted?' *Athenaeum* 58: 454–7.

Marshall, A.J. 1984, 'Symbols and showmanship in Roman public life: the fasces' *Phoenix* 38: 120–41.

McDonald, A.H. 1966, *Republican Rome*, London.

Meiggs, R. 1973, *Roman Ostia*, second edition, Oxford.

Millar, F. 1984, 'The political character of the classical Roman Republic, 200–151 BC' *JRS* 74: 1–19.

Millar, F. 1986, 'Politics, persuasion and the people before the Social War (150–90 BC)' *JRS* 76: 1–11.

Millar, F. 1989, 'Political power in mid-republican Rome: curia or comitium?' *JRS* 79: 138–50.

Millar, F. 1995, 'Popular politics at Rome in the late republic' in Malkin, I. & Rubinsohn, Z.W. (eds) *Leaders and Masses in the Roman World*, Leiden: 91–113.

Millar, F. 1998, *The Crowd in Rome in the Late Republic*, Michigan.

Millar, F. 2002, *The Roman Republic in Political Thought*, Hanover.

Mitchell, R.E. 1986, 'The definition of *patres* and *plebs*: an end to the Struggle of the Orders' in Raaflaub, K.A. (ed.) *Social Struggles in Archaic Rome: New Perspectives on the Conflict of the Orders*, Berkeley: 130–74.

Mitchell, R.E. 1990, *Patricians and Plebeians. The Origin of the Roman State*, Ithaca.

Momigliano, A. 1986, 'The rise of the *plebs* in the archaic age of Rome' in Raaflaub, K.A. (ed.) *Social Struggles in Archaic Rome: New Perspectives on the Conflict of the Orders*, Berkeley: 175–97.

Momigliano, A. 1989, 'The origins of Rome' in *CAH* VII.2²: 52–112.

Moore, T.J. 1993, 'Morality, history, and Livy's wronged women' *Eranos* 91: 38–46.

Mulryne, T.W. 1977, *The Roman Forum*, London.

Mouritsen, H. 2001, *Plebs and Politics in the Late Roman Republic*, Cambridge.

Münzer, F. 1999, *Roman Aristocratic Parties and Families*, Baltimore.

Nicolet, C. 1980, *The World of the Citizen in Republican Rome*, London.

North, J.A. 1990, 'Politics and aristocracy in the Roman republic' *CPh* 85: 277–87.

North, J.A. 1990a, 'Democratic politics in Republican Rome' *P&P* 126: 3–21.

Ogilvie, R.M. & Drummond, A. 1989, 'The sources for early Roman history' in *CAH* VII.2²: 1–29.

Palmer, R.E.A. 1970, *The Archaic Community of the Romans*, Cambridge.

Patterson, J.R. 1992, 'The city of Rome: from Republic to Empire' *JRS* 82: 186–215.

Patterson, J.R. 2000, 'Living and dying in the city of Rome: houses and tombs' in Coulson, J. & Dodge, H. (eds) *Ancient Rome. The Archaeology of the Eternal City*, Oxford: 259–89.

Patterson, J.R. 2000a, 'On the margins of the city of Rome' in Hope, V.M. & Marshall, E. (eds) *Death and Disease in the Ancient City*, London: 85–103.

Patterson, J.R. 2000b, *Political Life in the City of Rome*, Bristol.

Pina Polo, F. 1995, 'Procedures and functions of civil and military *contiones* in Rome' *Klio* 77: 203–16.

Pinsent, J. 1975, *Military Tribunes and Plebeian Consuls: the Fasti from 444V to 342V*, Wiesbaden.

Purcell, N. 1989, 'Rediscovering the Roman Forum' *JRA* 2: 156–66.

Purcell, N. 1995, 'Forum Romanum (The Republican Period)' in Steinby II.325–36.

Raaflaub, K.A. (ed) 1986, *Social Struggles in Archaic Rome: New Perspectives on the Conflict of the Orders*, Berkeley.

Raaflaub, K.A. 1986a, 'The Conflict of the Orders in Archaic Rome: a comprehensive and comparative approach' in Raaflaub, K.A. (ed.) *Social Struggles in Archaic Rome: New Perspectives on the Conflict of the Orders*, Berkeley: 1–51.

Rathbone, D. 1993, 'The *census* qualifications of the *assidui* and the *prima classis*' in Sancisi-Weerdenburg, H. et al. (ed.) *De Agricultura*, Amsterdam: 121–52.

Ross Holloway, R., 1994, *The Archaeology of Early Rome and Latium*, London.

Ryan, X. 1998, 'The biennium and the curule aedileship in the late Republic' *Latomus* 3: 3–14.

Salmon, E.T. 1967, *Samnium and the Samnites*, Cambridge.

Salmon, E.T. 1982, *The Making of Roman Italy*, London.

Sandberg, K.A.J. 2001, *Magistrates and Assemblies. A Study of Legislative Practice in Republican Rome*, Rome.

Scott, R.T. 1995, 'Domus publica' in Steinby II.165–6.

Scott, R.T. 1999, 'Regia' in Steinby IV.189–92.

Scullard, H.H. 1973, *Roman Politics, 220–150 BC*, second edition, Oxford.

Scullard, H.H. 1980, *A History of the Roman World*, 753 to 146 BC, fourth edition, London.

Seager, R. (ed.) 1969, *The Crisis of the Roman Republic. Studies in Political and Social History*, Cambridge.

Seager, R. 1972, 'Cicero and the word *popularis*' *CQ* 22: 328–38.

Seager, R. 1977, '*Populares* in Livy and the Livian tradition' *CQ* 27: 377–90.

Shatzman, I. 1975, *Senatorial Wealth and Roman Politics*, Brussels.

Sherwin-White, A.N. 1972, 'The Roman citizenship: a survey of its development into a world franchise' *ANRW* I.2: 23–58.

Skutsch, O. 1985, *The Annals of Q. Ennius*, Oxford.

Stambaugh, J.E. 1988, *The Ancient Roman City*, Baltimore.

Staveley, E.S. 1972, *Greek and Roman Voting and Elections*, London.

Staveley, E.S. 1989, 'Rome and Italy in the early third century' in *CAH* VII.2²: 420–55.

Stewart, R. 1998, *Public Office in Early Rome. Ritual Procedure and Political Practice*, Ann Arbor.

Tansey, P. 2000, 'The princeps senatus in the last decades of the Republic' *Chiron* 30: 15–30.

Taylor, L.R. 1966, *Roman Voting Assemblies from the Hannibalic Wars to the Dictatorship of Caesar*, Ann Arbor.

Toher, M. 1986, 'The Tenth Table and the Conflict of the Orders' in Raaflaub, K.A. (ed.) *Social Struggles in Archaic Rome: New Perspectives on the Conflict of the Orders*, Berkeley: 301–26.

Torelli, M. 1999, *Tota Italia. Essays in the Cultural Formation of Roman Italy*, Oxford.

Ungern-Sternberg, J. von, 1986, 'The formation of the "Annalistic Tradition": the example of the Decemvirate' in Raaflaub, K.A. (ed.) *Social Struggles in Archaic Rome: New Perspectives on the Conflict of the Orders*, Berkeley: 77–104.

Van Sickle, J. 1987, 'The elogia of the Cornelii Scipiones and the origin of epigram at Rome' *AJPh* 108: 41–55.

Vanderbroeck J.J. 1987, *Popular Leadership and Collective Behavior in the Late Roman Republic (ca. 80–50 BC)*, Amsterdam.

Walbank, F. 1972, *Polybius*, Berkeley.

Watson, A. 1975, *Rome of the XII Tables*, Princeton.

Westbrook, R. 1988, 'The nature and origins of the Twelve Tables' *ZSS* 105: 74–121.

Whittaker, C.R. 1994, *Frontiers of the Roman Empire*, Baltimore.

Wiseman, T.P. 1969, 'The census in the first century BC' *JRS* 59: 59–75.

Wiseman, T.P. 1970, 'The definition of "eques Romanus" in the Late Republic and Early Empire' *Historia* 19: 67–83.

Wiseman, T.P. 1971, *New Men in the Roman Senate, 139 BC–AD 14*, Oxford.

Wiseman, T.P. 1990, 'The central area of the Roman Forum' *JRA* 3: 245–7.

Yacobsen, A. 1992, '*Petitio et largitio*: popular participation in the centuriate assembly of the late republic' *JRS* 82: 32–52.

Yacobsen, A. 1995, 'Secret ballot and its effects in the late Roman republic' *Hermes* 123: 426–42.

Yacobsen, A. 1999, *Elections and Electioneering in Rome. A Study in the Political System of the Late Republic*, Stuttgart.

Chapter Two: The Public Face of Rome

Adcock, F.E. 1959, *Roman Political Ideas and Practice*, Ann Arbor.

Ashby, T. 1935, *The Aqueducts of Ancient Rome*, Oxford.

Astin, A.E. 1978, *Cato the Censor*, Oxford.

Auget, R. 1994, *Cruelty and Civilisation: the Roman Games*, second edition, London.

Badian, E. 1984, 'The house of the Servilii Gemini' *PBSR* 52: 49–71.

Baker, A. 2000, *The Gladiator*, London.

Balsdon, J.P.V.D. 1960, 'Panem et circenses' in Bibaw, J. (ed.) *Hommages à Marcel Renard*, vol. II, Brussels: 57–60.

Balsdon, J.P.V.D. 1969, *Life and Leisure in Ancient Rome*, London.

Barton, C.A. 1993, *The Sorrows of the Ancient Romans. The Gladiator and the Monster*, Princeton.

Barton, C.A. 2001, *Roman Honor: the Fire in the Bones*, Berkeley.

Beacham, R.C. 1999, *Spectacle Entertainments of Early Imperial Rome*, New Haven.

Bell, A.J. 1997, 'Cicero and the spectacle of power' *JRS* 87: 1–22.

Bettini, M. 1991, *Anthropology and Roman Culture. Kinship, Time, Images of the Soul*, Baltimore.

Blackman, D.R. 1979, 'The length of the four great aqueducts of Rome' *PBSR* 34: 12–18.

Blackman, D.R. & Hodge, A.T. 2001, *Frontinus' Legacy*, Ann Arbor.

Bomgardner, D.L. 2000, *The Story of the Roman Amphitheatre*, London.

Braund, D.C. 1984, *Rome and the Friendly King: the Character of the Client Kingship*, London.

Braund, D.C. 1989, 'Function and dysfunction: personal patronage in Roman imperialism' in Wallace-Hadrill, A. (ed.) *Patronage in the Ancient World*, London: 137–52.

Brennan, T.C. 1994, 'M'. Curius Dentatus and the praetor's right to triumph' *Historia* 43: 423–39.

Brennan, T.C. 1996, 'Triumphus in Monte Albano' in Wallace, R.W. & Harris, E.M. (eds) *Transitions to Empire*, Norman: 315–37.

Briscoe, J. 1992, 'Political groupings in the Middle Republic' in Deroux, C. (ed.) *Studies in Latin Literature and Roman History*, vol. VI, Brussels: 70–83.

Broughton, T.R.S. 1991, *Candidates Defeated in Roman Elections: Some Ancient Roman 'Also-Rans'*, Philadelphia.

Brunt, P.A. 1966, 'The Roman mob' *P&P* 35: 3–27.

Brunt, P.A, 1982, 'Nobilitas and Novitas' *JRS* 72: 1–17.

Brunt, P.A. 1988, *The Fall of the Roman Republic and Related Essays*, Oxford.

Brunt, P.A. 1988a, 'The equites in the Late Republic' in Brunt 1988: 144–93, revision of Seager 1969: 83–115 = 1962, *Trade and Politics in the Ancient World* 1: 117–49.

Brunt, P.A. 1988b, '*Libertas* in the Republic' in Brunt 1988: 281–350.

Brunt, P.A. 1988c, '*Amicitia in the Roman Republic*' in Brunt 1988: 351–81.

Brunt, P.A. 1988d, 'Clientela' in Brunt 1988: 382–442.

Brunt, P.A. 1988e, 'Factions' in Brunt 1988: 443–502.

Burckhardt, L.A. 1990, 'The political elite of the Roman Republic; comments on recent discussion of the concepts *nobilitas* and *homo novus*' *Historia* 39: 77–99.

Burton, P.J. 2003, '*Clientela* or *amicitia*? Modeling Roman international behavior in the Middle Republic (264–146 BC)' *Klio* 85: 333–69.

Cameron, A. 1976, *Circus Factions: Blues and Greens at Rome and Byzantium*, Oxford.

Carandini, A. 1988, *Schiavi in Italia: gli strumenti pensanti dei Romani fra tarda Repubblica e medio Impero*, Rome.

Cherry, D. 1993, 'Hunger at Rome in the late republic' *EMC/CV* 12: 433–50.

Chevallier, R. 1976, *Roman Roads*, London.

Clark, D.L. 1957, *Rhetoric in Greco-Roman Education*, Westport.

Clarke, M.L. 1996, *Rhetoric at Rome*, third edition, London.

Claridge, A. 1998, *Rome: An Archaeological Guide*, Oxford.

Cloud, D. 1994, 'The constitution and public criminal law' in *CAH* IX²: 491–530.

Coleman, K. 1990, 'Fatal charades: Roman executions staged as mythological enactments' *JRS* 80: 44–73.

Coleman, K. 1996, 'Ptolemy Philadelphus and the Roman amphitheater' in Slater, W.J. (ed.) *Roman Theater and Society*, Ann Arbor: 49–68.

Coleman, K. 2000, 'Entertaining Rome' in Coulston, J. & Dodge, H. (eds) *Ancient Rome. The Archaeology of the Eternal City*, Oxford: 210–58.

Coleman, K. 2003, 'Euergetism in its place. Where was the amphitheatre in Augustan Rome?' in Lomas, K. & Cornell, T. (eds) *Bread and Circuses. Euergetism and Municipal Patronage in Roman Italy*, London: 61–88.

Cornell, T.J. 1995, *The Beginnings of Rome. Italy and Rome from the Bronze Age to the Punic Wars (c. 1000–264 BC)*, London.

Connolly, P. & Dodge, H. 1998, *The Ancient City. Life in Classical Athens and Rome*, Oxford.

Craig, C.P. 1981, 'The *accusator* as *amicus*' *TAPhA* 111: 31–7.

Crawford, O.C. 1941, 'Laudatio funebris' *CJ* 37: 17–27.

Crook, J.A. 1967, *Law and Life of Rome*, London.

D'Arms, J.H. 1984, 'Control, companionship and clientela: some social functions of the Roman communal meal' *EMC/CV* 3: 327–48.

David, J.-M. 1996, *The Roman Conquest of Italy*, Oxford.

Develin, R. 1978, 'Tradition and the development of triumphal regulations in Rome' *Klio* 60: 429–38.

Develin, R. 1985, *The Practice of Politics at Rome, 366–167 BC*, Brussels.

Dixon, S. 1993, 'The meaning of gift and debt in the Roman elite' *EMC/CV* 12: 451–64.

Dodge, H. 2000, 'Greater than the pyramids: the water supply of ancient Rome' in Coulston, J. & Dodge, H. (eds) *Ancient Rome. The Archaeology of the Eternal City*, Oxford: 166–209.

Drummond, A. 1989, 'Early Roman clientes' in Wallace-Hadrill, A. (ed.) *Patronage in the Ancient World*, London: 89–116.

Dudley, D.R. 1967, *Urbs Roma. A Source Book of Classical Texts on the City and its Monuments*, London.

Earl, D. 1967, *The Moral and Political Tradition of Rome*, London.

Edlund, I.E.M. 1977, 'Invisible bonds: clients and patrons through the eyes of Polybios' *Klio* 59: 129–36.

Eisenstadt, S.N. & Roniger, L. 1984, *Patrons, Clients and Friends*, Cambridge.

Epstein, D.F. 1987, *Personal Enmity in Roman Politics 218–43 BC*, London.

Evans R.J. 1991, 'Candidates and competition in consular elections at Rome between 218 and 49 BC' *ActClass* 34: 111–36.

Evans, H.B. 1994, *Water Distribution in Ancient Rome*, Ann Arbor.

Eyben, E. 1993, *Restless Youth in Ancient Rome*, London.

Fantham, E. 1997, 'The contexts and occasions of Roman public rhetoric' in Dominik, W.J. (ed.) *Roman Eloquence. Rhetoric in Society and Literature*, London: 111–28.

Flower, H.I. 1996, *Ancestor Masks and Aristocratic Power in Roman Culture*, Oxford.

Flower, H.I. 2004, 'Spectacle and political culture in the Roman Republic' in Flower, H.I. (ed.) *The Cambridge Companion to the Roman Republic*, Cambridge: 322–43.

Frank, T. 1924, *Roman Buildings of the Republic*, Rome.

Franklin, J.L. 1980, *Pompeii, the Electoral Programmata, Campaigns and Politics, AD 71–79*, Rome.

Futrell, A. 1997, *Blood in the Arena. The Spectacle of Roman Power*, Austin.

Gelzer, M. 1969, *The Roman Nobility*, Oxford.

Gilula, D. 1981, 'Who's afraid of rope-walkers and gladiators? (Ter. *Hec.* 1–57)' *Athenaeum* 59: 29–37.

Gold, B.K. 1982, *Literary and Artistic Patronage in Ancient Rome*, Austin.

Gowers, E. 1993, *The Loaded Table*, Oxford.

Gowers, E. 1995, 'The anatomy of Rome from Capitol to Cloaca' *JRS* 85: 23–32.

Grimal, P. 1983, *Roman Cities*, Wisconsin.

Grant, M. 1967, *Gladiators*, London.

Gruen, E.S. 1968, *Roman Politics and the Criminal Courts, 149–78 BC*, Cambridge MA.

Gruen, E.S. 1986, *The Hellenistic World and the Coming of Rome*, Berkeley.

Gruen, E.S. 1990, *Studies in Greek Culture and Roman Policy*, Berkeley.

Gruen, E.S. 1992, *Culture and National Identity in Republican Rome*, London.

Gruen, E.S. 1996, 'The Roman oligarchy' in Linderski, J. (ed.) *Imperium sine fine: T.R.S. Broughton and the Roman Republic*, Stuttgart: 215–36.

Hagen, V.W. von 1966, *Roman Roads*, London.

Hall, U. 1964, 'Voting procedure in Roman assemblies' *Historia* 13: 267–306.

Higginbotham, J. 1997, *Piscinae: Artificial Fishponds in Roman Italy*, Chapel Hill.

Hindley, G. 1971, *A History of Roads*, London.

Holleran, C. 2003, 'The development of public entertainment venues in Rome and Italy' in Lomas, K. & Cornell, T. (eds) *Bread and Circuses. Euergetism and Municipal Patronage in Roman Italy*, London: 46–60.

Hopkins, K. 1983, *Death and Renewal*, Cambridge.

Horsfall, N. 2003, *The Culture of the Roman Plebs*, London.

Humphrey, J.H. 1986, *Roman Circuses. Arenas for Chariot Racing*, London.

Hyland, A. 1990, *Equus: the Horse in the Roman World*, London.

Jongman, W. 1988, *The Economy and Society of Pompeii*, Amsterdam.

Jongman, W. 2003, 'Slavery and the growth of Rome. The transformation of Italy in the second and first centuries BCE' in Edwards, C. & Woolf, G. (eds) *Rome the Cosmopolis*, Cambridge: 100–122.

Kaster, R.A. 1997, 'The shame of the Romans' *TAPhA* 127: 1–19.

Keaveney, A. 1992, *Lucullus, a Life*, London.

Kennedy, G.A. 1972, *The Art of Rhetoric in the Roman World*, Princeton.

Kirby, J.T. 1997, 'Ciceronian rhetoric: theory and practice' in Dominik, W.J. (ed.) *Roman Eloquence. Rhetoric in Society and Literature*, London: 13–31.

Kleijn, de G. 2001, *The Water Supply of Ancient Rome*, Amsterdam.

Köhne, E. & Ewigleben, C. (eds) 2000, *Gladiators and Caesars: the Power of the Spectacle in Ancient Rome*, London.

Konrad, C.I. 1996, 'Notes on Roman also-rans' in Linderski, J. (ed.) *Imperium sine fine, T.R.S. Broughton and the Roman Republic*, Stuttgart: 103–43.

Levick, B. 1982, 'Morals, politics and the fall of the Roman republic' *G&R* 29: 53–62.

Kyle, D.G. 1998, *Spectacles of Death in Ancient Rome*, London.

Lacey, W.K. 1978, *Cicero and the End of the Roman Republic*, London.

Laurence, R. 1994, 'Rumour and communication in Roman politics' *G&R* 41: 62–73.

Laurence, R. 1997, 'Writing the Roman metropolis' in Parkin, H. (ed.) *Roman Urbanism: Beyond the Consumer City*, London: 1–20.

Laurence, R. 1999, *The Roads of Roman Italy*, London.

Linderski, J. 1985, 'Buying the vote: electoral corruption in the late republic' *AncW* 11: 87–94.

Lintott, A. 1990, 'Electoral bribery in the Roman republic' *JRS* 80: 1–16.

Lintott, A. 1999, *Violence in Republican Rome*, revised edition, Oxford.

Lo Cascio, E. 1994, 'The size of the Roman population: Beloch and the meaning of the Augustan census figures' *JRS* 84: 23–40.

MacAdam, A. 1998, *Rome (Blue Guide)*, London.

Mackie, N. 1992, '*Popularis* ideology and popular politics at Rome' *RhM* 135: 49–73.

MacMullen, R. 1980, 'Roman elite motivation: three questions' *P&P* 88: 3–16.

Marchetti, S.C. 2004, '"I could not love Caesar more": Roman friendship and the beginning of the principate' *CJ* 99: 281–99.

Marshall, A.J. 1968, 'Friends of the Roman people' *AJPh* 87: 39–55.

Maxfield, V.A. 1981, *The Military Decorations of the Roman Army*, London.

Morgan, M.G. 1978, 'The introduction of the Aqua Marcia into Rome, 144–140 BC' *Philologus* 122: 25–58.

Morgan, M.G. 1990, 'Politics, religion and the games in Rome, 200–150 BC' *Philologus* 134: 14–36.

Mouratidis, J. 1996, 'On the origin of the gladiatorial games' *Nikephoros* 9: 111–34.

Mouritsen, H. 2001, *Plebs and Politics in the Late Roman Republic*, Cambridge.

Nevett, L. 1997, 'Perceptions of domestic space in Roman Italy' in Rawson, B. & Weaver, P. (eds) *The Roman Family in Italy. Status, Sentiment, Space*, Canberra: 281–98.

Nichols, J. 1980, 'Tabulae Patronatus: a study of the agreement between patron and client-community' *ANRW* II.13: 535–61.

Nicolet, C. 1980, *The World of the Citizen in Republican Rome*, London.

Nippel, W. 1995, *Public Order in Ancient Rome*, Cambridge.

O'Connor, C. 1993, *Roman Bridges*, Cambridge.

Patterson, J.R. 2000, *Political Life in the City of Rome*, Bristol.

Plass, P.C. 1995, *The Game of Death in Ancient Rome*, Madison.

Potter, D. 2001, 'Death as spectacle, and subsequent disposal' *JRA* 14: 478–84.

Rawson, B. 2003, *Children and Childhood in Roman Italy*, Oxford.

Rawson, E. 1975, *Cicero. A Portrait*, London.

Rawson, E. 1991, 'Chariot-racing in the Roman Republic' in Rawson, E. *Roman Culture and Society*, Oxford: 389–407 = 1981, *PBSR* 49: 1–16.

Rich, J. 1989, 'Patronage and international relations in the Roman Republic' in Wallace-Hadrill, A. (ed.) *Patronage in the Ancient World*, London: 117–36.

Richardson, J.S. 1971, 'The Commentariolum petitionis' *Historia* 20: 436–42.

Robinson, O.F. 1992, *Ancient Rome. City Planning and Administration*, London.

Rosenstein, N. 1990, 'War, failure and aristocratic competition' *CPh* 85: 255–65.

Rosenstein, N. 1990a, *Imperatores Victi*, Berkeley.

Rosenstein, N. 1993, 'Competition and crisis in mid-republican Rome' *Phoenix* 47: 313–38.

Rosenstein, N. 1992, '*Nobilitas* and the political implications of military defeat' *AHB* 6: 117–26.

Rossiter, J. 1978, *Roman Farm Buildings in Italy*, Oxford.

Scheidel, W. 2003, 'Germs for Rome' in Edwards, C. & Woolf, G. (eds) 2003, *Rome the Cosmopolis*, Cambridge: 158–76.

Scobie, A. 1986, 'Slum, sanitation and mortality in the Roman world' *Klio* 68: 399–433.

Scullard, H.H. 1964, 'The political career of a *novus homo*' in Dorey, T.A. (ed.) *Cicero. Studies in Latin Literature and its Influence*, London: 1–25.

Scullard, H.H. 1981, *Festivals and Ceremonies of the Roman Republic*, London.

Seager, R. (ed.) 1969, *The Crisis of the Roman Republic. Studies in Political and Social History*, Cambridge.

Seager, R. 1972, 'Factio: some observations' *JRS* 62: 53–8.

Seager, R. 1972a, 'Cicero and the word *popularis*' *CQ* 22: 328–38.

Seager, R. 1977, '*Populares* in Livy and the Livian tradition' *CQ* 27: 377–90.

Sear, F. 1989, *Roman Architecture*, revised edition, London.

Shackleton Bailey, D.R. 1986, '*Nobiles* and *novi* reconsidered' *AJPh* 107: 255–60.

Shatzman, I. 1975, *Senatorial Wealth and Roman Politics*, Brussels.

Silverman, S. 1965, 'Patronage and community-nation relationships in central Italy' *Ethnology* 4.2: 172–89.

Sitwell, N.H.H. 1981, *Roman Roads of Europe*, London.

Smith, R.E. 1966, *Cicero the Statesman*, Cambridge.

Stambaugh, J.E. 1988, *The Ancient Roman City*, Baltimore.

Stockton, D. 1971, *Cicero. A Political Biography*, Oxford.

Storey, G.R. 1997, 'The population of ancient Rome' *Antiquity* 71: 966–78.

Tatum, W.J. 1991, 'Military defeat and electoral success in republican Rome' *AHB* 5: 149–52.

Taylor, L.R. 1937, 'The opportunities for dramatic performances in the time of Plautus and Terence' *TAPhA* 68: 284–304.

Taylor, L.R. 1949, *Party Politics in the Age of Caesar*, Berkeley.

Taylor, L.R. 1960, *The Voting Districts of the Roman Republic*, Ann Arbor.

Toner, J.P. 1995, *Leisure and Ancient Rome*, Cambridge.

Ulrichs, R.B. 1994, *The Roman Orator and the Sacred Stage*, Brussels.

Vanderbroeck, P.J.J. 1986, 'Homo novus again' *Chiron* 16: 239–42.

Van Sickle, J. 1987, 'The elogia of the Cornelii Scipiones and the origin of epigram at Rome' *AJPh* 108: 41–55.

Versnel, H.S. 1970, *Triumphus*, Leiden.

Veyne, P. 1990, *Bread and Circuses*, Harmondsworth.

Vishnia, R.F. 1996, *State, Society and Popular Leaders in Mid-Republican Rome 241–167 BC*, London.

Wallace-Hadrill, A. 1988, 'The social structure of the Roman house' *PBSR* 56: 43–97.

Wallace-Hadrill, A. 1989, 'Patronage in Roman society: from republic to empire' in Wallace-Hadrill, A. (ed.) *Patronage in the Ancient World*, London: 63–87.

Wallinga, T. 1994, 'Ambitus in the Roman world' *RIDA* 41: 411–42.

Weinstock, S. 1971, *Divus Julius*, Oxford.

Welch, K. 1991, 'Roman amphitheatres revived' *JRA* 4: 272–81.

Welch, K. 1994, 'The Roman arena in late-Republican Italy: a new interpretation' *JRA* 7: 59–80.

Welch, K. 1998, 'Caesar and his officers in the Gallic War commentaries' in Welch, K. & Powell, A. (eds) *Julius Caesar as Artful Reporter: the War Commentaries as Political Instruments*, London: 85–110.

White, K.D. 1970, *Roman Farming*, London.

White, P. 1978, 'Amicitia and the profession of poetry in early imperial Rome' *JRS* 68: 74–92.

Wiedemann, T. 1992, *Emperors and Gladiators*, London.

Wiseman, T.P. 1971, *New men in the Roman senate, 139 BC–AD 14*, Oxford.

Wiseman, T.P. 1974, 'Legendary genealogies in Late-Republican Rome' *G&R* 21: 153–64.

Wiseman, T.P. 1985, *Roman Political Life 90 BC to AD 69*, Exeter.

Wiseman, T.P. 1987, *Roman Studies. Literary and Historical*, Liverpool: 126–56 = 1970, 'Roman republican road building' *PBSR* 38: 122–52.

Yacobsen, A. 1992, '*Petitio et largitio*: popular participation in the centuriate assembly of the late republic' *JRS* 82: 32–52.

Yacobsen, A. 1995, 'Secret ballot and its effects in the late Roman republic' *Hermes* 123: 426–42.

Yacobsen, A. 1999, *Elections and Electioneering in Rome. A Study in the Political System of the Late Republic*, Stuttgart.

Yavetz, Z. 1969, 'The living conditions of the urban plebs in Republican Rome' in Seager 1969 = 1958, *Latomus* 17: 500–17.
Yegül, F.K. 1992, *Baths and Bathing in Classical Antiquity*, Cambridge MA.

Chapter Three: Religion in the Roman Republic

Alföldi, A. 1965, *Early Rome and the Latins*, Ann Arbor.
Altheim, Γ. 1938, *A History of Roman Religion*, London.
Bailey, C. 1932, *Phases in the Religion of Ancient Rome*, Oxford.
Barton, T. 1994, 'Astrology and the state in Imperial Rome' in Thomas, N. & Humphrey, C. (eds) *Shamanism, History, and the State*, Ann Arbor: 146–63.
Barton, T. 1994a, *Ancient Astrology*, London.
Bauman, R.A. 1990, 'The suppression of the Bacchanals: five questions' *Historia* 39: 334–48.
Bauman, R.A. 1992, *Women and Politics in Ancient Rome*, London.
Beard, M. 1985, 'Writing and ritual: a study of diversity and expansion in the Arval Acta' *PBSR* 53: 114–62.
Beard, M. 1986, 'Cicero and divination: the formation of a Latin discourse' *JRS* 76: 33–46.
Beard, M. 1987, 'A complex of times: no more sheep on Romulus' birthday' *PCPhS* 213: 1–15.
Beard, M. 1988, 'Roman priesthoods' in Grant, M. & Kitzinger, R. (eds) *Civilization of the Ancient Mediterranean*, vol. II, New York: 933–9.
Beard, M. 1989, 'Acca Larentia gains a son: myths and priesthood at Rome' in MacKenzie, M.M. & Roueché, C. (eds) *Images of Authority: Papers Presented to Joyce Reynolds*, Cambridge: 41–61.
Beard, M. 1990, 'Priesthood in the Roman Republic' in Beard, M. & North, J. (eds) *Pagan Priests: Religion and Power in the Ancient World*, London: 19–48.
Beard, M. 1991, 'Writing and religion: *Ancient Literacy* and the function of the written word in Roman religion' in Beard, M. et al. (eds) *Literacy in the Roman World*, Ann Arbor: 35–58.
Beard, M. 1994, 'Religion' in *CAH* IX²: 729–68.
Beard, M. 1994a, 'The Roman and the foreign: the cult of the 'Great Mother' in imperial Rome' in Thomas, N. & Humphrey, C. (eds) *Shamanism. History and the State*, Ann Arbor: 164–90.
Beard, M. & Crawford, M. 1999, *Rome in the Late Republic*, second edition, London.
Bettini, M. 1991, *Anthropology and Roman Culture. Kinship, Time, Images of the Soul*, Baltimore.
Bispham, E. & Smith, C. 2000, *Religion in Archaic and Republican Rome and Italy*, Edinburgh.
Bloch, H. 1960, *The Origins of Rome*, London.
Boardman, J. (ed.) 1993, *The Oxford History of Classical Art*, Oxford.
Bodel, J. 1986 [1994], 'Graveyards and groves: a study of the lex Lucerina' *AJAH* 11: 1–133.
Bodel, J. 2000, 'Dealing with the dead: undertakers, executioners and potter's fields in ancient Rome' in Hope, V.M. & Marshall, E. (eds) *Death and Disease in the Ancient City*, London: 128–51.
Bremmer, J.N. 1987, 'Slow Cybele's arrival' in Bremmer, J.N. & Horsfall, N.M. (eds) *Roman Myth and Mythography*, London: 105–11.
Brunt, P.A. 1978, 'Laus imperii' in Garnsey, P.D.A. & Whittaker, C.R. (eds) *Imperialism in the Ancient World*, Cambridge: 159–91 = 1990, *Roman Imperial Themes*, Oxford: 288–323.
Burkert, W. 1987, *Ancient Mystery Cults*, Harvard.
Burton, P.J. 1996, 'The summoning of the Magna Mater to Rome' *Historia* 45: 36–63.
Cohee, P. 2001, 'Is an augur a sacerdos? (Cic. *Leg.* 2.20–21)' *Philologus* 145: 79–99.
Cornell, T.J. 1989, 'Rome and Latium to 390 BC' in *CAH* VII.2²: 243–308.
Cornell, T.J. 1995, *The Beginnings of Rome. Italy and Rome from the Bronze Age to the Punic Wars (c. 1000–264 BC)*, London.

Cowell, F.R. 1964, *Cicero and the Roman Republic*, third edition, Harmondsworth.

Cramer, F.H. 1951, 'Expulsion of astrologers from ancient Rome' *C&M* 12: 9–50.

Cramer, F.H. 1954, *Astrology in Roman Law and Politics*, Chicago.

Cumont, F. 1912, *Astrology and Religion among the Greeks and Romans*, New York.

Cumont, F. 1922, *Afterlife in Roman Paganism*, Yale.

Dumézil, G. 1970, *Archaic Roman Religion,* vols 1–2, Chicago.

Dupont, F. 1992, *Daily Life in Ancient Rome*, Oxford.

Edelstein, E.J. & Edelstein, L. 1945, *Asclepius. A Collection and Interpretation of the Testimonies*, vols 1–2, Baltimore.

Feeney, D. 1998, *Literature and Religion at Rome. Cultures, Contexts, and Beliefs*, Cambridge.

Ferguson, J. 1987, 'Classical religions' in Wacher, J. (ed.) *The Roman World*, vol. II, London: 749–64.

Flower, H.I. 1996, *Ancestor Masks and Aristocratic Power in Roman Culture*, Oxford.

Flower, H.I. 2004, 'Spectacle and political culture in the Roman Republic' in Flower, H.I. (ed.) *The Cambridge Companion to the Roman Republic*, Cambridge: 322–43.

Gabba, E. 1991, *Dionysius and 'The History of Archaic Rome'*, Berkeley.

Gager, J.G. 1992, *Curse Tablets and Binding Spells from the Ancient World*, New York.

Garlan, Y. 1975, *War in the Ancient World*, London.

Garnsey, P. 1984, 'Religious toleration in classical antiquity' in Sheils, W.J. (ed.) *Persecution and Toleration*, Oxford: 1–27.

Gasparro, G.S. 1985, *Soteriology and Mystic Aspects in the Cult of Cybele and Attis*, Leiden.

Glinister, F. 2000, 'Sacred rubbish' in Bispham, E. & Smith, C. 2000: 54–70.

Goar, R.J. 1972, *Cicero and the State Religion*, Amsterdam.

Goodman, M.D. & Holladay, A.J. 1986, 'Religious scruples in ancient warfare' *CQ* 36: 151–71.

Gordon, 1990, 'From Republic to Principate: priesthood, religion and ideology' in Beard, M. & North, J. (eds) *Pagan Priests: Religion and Power in the Ancient World*, London: 179–98.

Gordon, R. 1999, '"What's in a list?" Listing in Greek and Graeco-Roman malign magical texts' in Jordan, D.R., Montgomery, H. & Thomassen, E. (eds) *The World of Ancient Magic*, Bergen.

Graf, F. 2000, 'The rite of the Argei – once again' *MH* 57:94–103.

Green, S.J. 2000, 'Multiple interpretations of the opening and closing of the temple of Janus: a misunderstanding of Ovid *Fasti* 1.281' *Mnemosyne* 53: 302–09.

Gruen, E.S. 1990, *Studies in Greek Culture and Roman Policy*, Leiden.

Gruen, E.S. 1992, *Culture and National Identity in Republican Rome*, London.

Hallett, J.P. 1970, '"Over troubled waters": the meaning of the title *pontifex*' *TAPhA* 101: 219–27.

Harmon, D.P. 1978, 'The public festivals of Rome' *ANRW* II.16.2: 1440–68.

Harris, W.V. 1989, *Ancient Literacy*, Cambridge MA.

Hayne, L. 1992, 'Isis and Republican politics' *ActClass* 35: 143–9.

Henig, M. 1983, *A Handbook of Roman Art*, Cornell.

Heyob, S.K. 1975, *The Cult of Isis among Women*, Leiden.

Hope, V.M. 2000, 'Contempt and respect: the treatment of the corpse in ancient Rome' in Hope, V.M. & Marshall, E. (eds) *Death and Disease in the Ancient City*, London: 104–27.

Hopkins, K. 1991, 'From blessing to violence' in Molho A. et al. (eds) *City States in Classical Antiquity and Medieval Italy*, Stuttgart: 479–98.

Hopkins, K. 1999, *A World Full of Gods: Pagans, Jews and Christians in the Roman Empire*, London.

Hus, A. 1962, *Greek and Roman Religion*, London.

Jocelyn, H.D. 1966/7, 'The Roman nobility and the religion of the Republican state' *Journal of Religious History* 4: 89–104.

Jones, P. & Sidwell, K. 1997, *The World of Rome. An Introduction to Roman Culture*, Cambridge.

Jongman, W. 2003, 'Slavery and the growth of Rome. The transformation of Italy in the second and first centuries BCE' in Edwards, C. & Woolf, G. (eds) *Rome the Cosmopolis*, Cambridge: 100–122.

Kamm, A. 1995, *The Romans: an Introduction*, London.

Kraemer, R.S. 1992, *Her Share of the Blessings. Women's Religions Among Pagans, Jews, and Christians in the Greco-Roman World*, New York.

Kragelund, P. 2001, 'Dreams, religion and politics in Republican Rome' *Historia* 50: 53–95.

Kyle, D.G. 1998, *Spectacles of Death in Ancient Rome*, London.

Liebeschuetz, J.H.W.G. 1979, *Continuity and Change in Roman Religion*, Oxford.

Linderski, J. 1986, 'The augural law' *ANRW* II.16.3: 2146–2312.

Lindsay, H. 2000, 'Death-pollution and funerals in the city of Rome' in Hope, V.M. & Marshall, E. (eds) *Death and Disease in the Ancient City*, London: 152–73.

Lintott, A. 1999, *Violence in Republican Rome*, second edition, Oxford.

MacBain, B. 1982, *Prodigy and Expiation: a Study in Religion and Politics in Republican Rome*, Brussels.

Meier, C. 1995, *Caesar*, London.

Morris, I. 1992, *Death-ritual and Social Structure in Classical Antiquity*, Cambridge.

Nappa, C. 1999, 'Catullus 59: Rufa among the graves' *CPh* 94: 329–35.

Nicolet, C. 1980, *The World of the Citizen in Republican Rome*, London.

Nippel, W. 1984, 'Policing Rome' *JRS* 74: 20–9.

North, J.A. 1976, 'Conservatism and change in Roman religion' *PBSR* 44: 1–12.

North, J.A. 1979, 'Religious toleration in Republican Rome' *PCPhS* 205: 85–103.

North, J.A. 1980, 'Novelty and choice in Roman religion' *JRS* 70: 186–91.

North, J.A. 1986, 'Religion and politics, from Republic to Principate' *JRS* 76: 251–8.

North, J.A. 1988, 'Sacrifice and ritual: Rome' in Grant, M. & Kitzinger, R. (eds) *Civilization of the Ancient Mediterranean*, vol. II, New York: 981–6.

North, J.A. 1988a, 'The afterlife: Rome' in Grant, M. & Kitzinger, R. (eds) *Civilization of the Ancient Mediterranean*, vol. II, New York: 997–1007.

North, J.A. 1989, 'Religion in Republican Rome' in *CAH* VII.2^2: 573–624.

North, J.A. 1990, 'Diviners and divination at Rome' in Beard, M. & North, J. (eds) *Pagan Priests: Religion and Power in the Ancient World*, London: 51–71.

North, J.A. 1995, 'Religion and rusticity' in Cornell, T.J. & Lomas, K. (eds) *Urban Society in Roman Italy*, London: 135–150.

North, J.A. 1997, 'The religion of Rome from monarchy to principate' in Bentley, M. (ed.) *Companion to Historiography*, London: 57–68.

North, J.A. 2000, *Roman Religion*, Oxford.

North, J.A. 2000a, 'Prophet and text in the third century BC' in Bispham, E. & Smith, C. 2000: 92–107.

Noy, D. 2000, 'Building a Roman funeral pyre' *Antichthon* 34: 30–45.

Noy, D. 2000a, '"Half-burnt on an emergency pyre": Roman cremations which went wrong' *G&R* 47: 186–96.

Ochs, D.J. 1993, *Consolatory Rhetoric. Grief, Symbol, and Ritual in the Greco-Roman Era*, Columbia.

Ogilvie, R.M. 1969, *The Romans and their Gods*, London.

Ogilvie, R.M. 1970, *A Commentary on Livy Books 1–5*, revised edition, Oxford.

Orlin, E.M. 1997, *Temples, Religion and Politics in the Roman Republic*, Leiden.

Pallottino, M. 1975, *The Etruscans*, London.

Parke, H.W. 1988, *Sibyls and Sibylline Prophecy in Classical Antiquity*, London.

Penella, R.J. 1987, 'War, peace, and the *ius fetiale* in Livy 1' *CPh* 82: 233–7.

Rawson, E. 1985, *Intellectual Life in the Late Roman Republic*, London.

Rawson, E. 1991, 'Religion and politics in the late second century BC at Rome' in Rawson, E. *Roman Culture and Society*, Oxford: 149–68 = 1974, *Phoenix* 28: 193–212.

Rawson, E. 1991a, 'Prodigy lists and the use of the *annales maximi*' in Rawson, E. *Roman Culture and Society*, Oxford: 1–15 = 1971, *CQ* 21: 158–69.

Rawson, E. 1991b, 'Scipio, Laelius, Furius and the ancestral religion' in Rawson, E. *Roman Culture and Society*, Oxford: 80–101 = 1973, *JRS* 63: 161–74.

Rawson, E. 1992c, 'Caesar, Etruria, and the *Disciplina Etrusca*' in Rawson, E. *Roman Culture and Society*, Oxford: 289–323 = 1978, *JRS* 68: 132–52.

Rich, J.W. 1976, *Declaring War in the Roman Republic in the Period of Transmarine Expansion*, Brussels.

Rose, H.J. 1948, *Ancient Roman Religion*, second edition, London.

Roullet, A. 1972, *The Egyptian and Egyptianizing Monuments of Imperial Rome*, Leiden.

Rüpke, J. 2004, 'Roman religion' in Flower, H.I. (ed.) *The Cambridge Companion to the Roman Republic*, Cambridge: 179–95.

Salzman, M.R. 1990, *On Roman Time*, Berkeley.

Scafuro, A. 1989, 'Livy's comic narrative of the Bacchanalia' *Helios* 16: 119–42.

Scheid, J. 1992, 'The religious roles of Roman women' in Schmitt Pantel, P. (ed.) *A History of Women: Vol. I, From Ancient Goddesses to Christian Saints*, Cambridge MA: 377–408.

Scheid, J. 1992a, 'Myth, cult and reality in Ovid's *Fasti*' *PCPhS* 38: 118–31.

Scheid, J. 1993, 'The priest' in Giardini, A. (ed.) *The Romans*, Chicago: 55–84.

Scheid, J. 1995, '*Graeco ritu*: a typically Roman way of honoring the gods' *HSCPh* 97: 15–31.

Scheid, J. 2003, *An Introduction to Roman Religion*, Edinburgh.

Schofield, M. 1986, 'Cicero for and against divination' *JRS* 76: 47–65.

Scullard, H.H. 1973, *Roman Politics, 220–150 BC*, second edition, Oxford.

Scullard, H.H. 1980, *A History of the Roman World, 753 to 146 BC*, fourth edition, London.

Scullard, H.H. 1981, *Festivals and Ceremonies of the Roman Republic*, London.

Sharwood Smith, G.J. 1975, *Temples, Priests and Worship*, London.

Skutsch, O. 1985, *The Annals of Q. Ennius*, Oxford.

Solmsen, F. 1979, *Isis among the Greeks and Romans*, Cambridge MA.

Spaeth, B.S. 1996, *The Roman Goddess Ceres*, Austin.

Stambaugh, J.E. 1978, 'The functions of Roman temples' *ANRW* II.16.1: 554–608.

Stehle, E. 1989, 'Venus, Cybele, and the Sabine women: the Roman construction of female sexuality' *Helios* 16: 143–64.

Stone, S. 1994, 'The toga: from national to ceremonial costume' in Sebesta, J.L. & Bonfante, L. (eds) *The World of Roman Costume*, Wisconsin: 13–45.

Summers, K. 1996, 'Lucretius' Roman Cybele' in Lane, E.N. (ed.) *Cybele, Attis and Related Cults*, Leiden: 337–65.

Syme, R. 1982, *Some Arval Brethren*, Oxford.

Szemler, G.J. 1972, *The Priests of the Roman Republic*, Brussels.

Szemler, G.J. 1986, 'Priesthoods and priestly careers in ancient Rome' *ANRW* II.16.3: 2314–31.

Takács, S.A. 1995, *Isis and Sarapis in the Roman World*, Leiden.

Takács, S.A. 2000, 'Politics and religion in the Bacchanalian affair of 186 BCE' *HSCPh* 100: 301–10.

Taylor, L.R. 1949, *Party Politics in the Age of Caesar*, Berkeley.

Taylor, L.R. 1966, *Roman Voting Assemblies*, Ann Arbor.

Thomas, G. 1984, 'Magna Mater and Attis' *ANRW* II.17.3: 1500–35.

Torelli, M. 1982, *Typology and Structure of Roman Historical Reliefs*, Michigan.

Toynbee, A.J. 1965, *Hannibal's Legacy*, vols I–II, London.
Toynbee, J.M.C. 1971, *Death and Burial in the Roman World*, London.
Turcan, R. 1996, *The Cults of the Roman Empire*, Oxford.
Turcan, R. 2000, *The Gods of Ancient Rome*, Edinburgh.
Vaahtera, H.J. 2000, 'Roman religion and the Polybian politeia' in Bruun, C. (ed.) *The Roman Middle Republic. Politics, Religion, and Historiography*, c. 400–133 BC, Rome: 251–64.
Vaahtera, H.J. 2001, *Roman Augural Lore in Greek Historiography*, Stuttgart.
van der Meer, L.B. 1987, *The Bronze Liver of Piacenza*, Amsterdam.
Vanggaard, J.H. 1988, *The Flamen*, Copenhagen.
Vermaseren, M.J. 1977, *Cybele and Attis*, London.
Versnel, H.S. 1976, 'Two types of Roman *devotio*' *Mnemosyne* 29: 365–410.
Versnel, H.S. 1980, 'Self-sacrifice, compensation and the anonymous gods' in *Le sacrifice dans l'antiquité* (*Entretiens Hardt* 27), Geneva: 135–94.
Versnel, H.S. 1990, *Inconsistencies in Greek and Roman Religion I. Ter Unus. Isis, Dionysos, Hermes*, Leiden.
Versnel, H.S. 1993, *Inconsistencies in Greek and Roman Religion II. Transition and Reversal in Myth and Ritual*, Leiden.
Versnel, H.S. 1993a, 'Saturn and the Saturnalia. The question of origin' in Sancisi-Weerdenburg, H. et al. (eds) *De Agricultura*, Amsterdam: 98–120.
Wagenvoort, H. 1980, *Pietas. Selected Studies in Roman Religion*, Leiden.
Walsh, P.G. 1996, 'Making a drama out of a crisis: Livy on the Bacchanalia' *G&R* 43: 188–203.
Warde Fowler, W. 1911, *The Religious Experience of the Roman People from the Earliest Times to the Age of Augustus*, London.
Wardman, A. 1982, *Religion and Statecraft among the Romans*, London.
Watson, A. 1992, *The State, Law and Religion*, Athens.
Watson, A. 1993, *International Law in Archaic Rome. War and Religion*, Baltimore.
Wiedemann, T. 1986, 'The *fetiales*: a reconsideration' *CQ* 36: 478–490.
Wildfang, R.L. 2001, 'The Vestals and annual public rites' *CM* 52: 223–55.
Wiseman, T.P. 1979, *Clio's Cosmetics. Three Studies in Greco-Roman Literature*, Leicester.
Wiseman, T.P. 1994, 'The senate and the *populares*, 69–60 BC' in *CAH* IX[2]: 327–67.
Witt, R.E. 1997, *Isis in the Ancient World*, London (a republication of 1971, *Isis in the Greco-Roman World*, London).
Ziolkowski, A. 1992, *The Temples of Mid-Republican Rome and Their Historical and Topographical Context*, Rome.
Ziolkowski, A. 1998/9, 'Ritual cleaning-up of the city: from the Lupercalia to the Argei' *AncSoc* 29: 191–218.

Chapter Four: The Punic Wars: Rome against Carthage

Adcock, F. 1940, *The Roman Art of War under the Republic*, Cambridge MA.
Alonso-Núnez, J.M. 1999, 'The mixed constitution in Polybius' *Eranos* 97: 11–19.
Astin, A.E. 1967, 'Saguntum and the origins of the Second Punic War' *Latomus* 26: 577–96.
Astin, A.E. 1978, *Cato the Censor*, Oxford.
Bagnall, N. 1990, *The Punic Wars. Rome, Carthage and the Struggle for the Mediterranean*, London.
Bagnall, N. 2002, *The Punic Wars 264–146 BC*, Oxford.
Baker, G.P. 1929, *Hannibal*, New York.
Baronowski, D.W. 1993, 'Roman military forces in 225 BC (Polybius 2.23–4)' *Historia* 42: 181–202.

Baronowski, D.W. 1995, 'Polybius on the causes of the Third Punic War' *CPh* 90: 16–31.

Beard, M. 1994, 'Religion' in *CAH* IX[2]: 729–68.

Bernstein, A.H. 1994, 'The strategy of a warrior-state: Rome and the wars against Carthage, 264–201 BC' in Murray, W., Knox, M. & Bernstein, A. (eds) *The Making of Strategy: Rulers, States, and War*, Cambridge: 56–84.

Bradford, E. 1981, *Hannibal*, London.

Briscoe, J. 1989, 'The Second Punic War' in *CAH* VII.2[2]: 44–80.

Caven, B. 1980, *The Punic Wars*, London.

Cornell, T.J. 1996, 'Hannibal's legacy: the effects of the Hannibalic War on Italy' in Cornell, Rankov & Sabin 1996: 97–117.

Cornell, T.J., Rankov, B. & Sabin, P. (eds) 1996, *The Second Punic War. A Reappraisal*, London.

Cottrell, L. 1960, *Enemy of Rome*, London [a novel].

Curchin, L.A. 1991, *Roman Spain. Conquest and Assimilation*, London.

Daly, G. 2002, *Cannae. The Experience of Battle in the Second Punic War*, London.

de Beer, G. 1955, *Alps and Elephants*, London.

de Beer, G. 1967, *Hannibal's March*, London.

de Beer, G. 1969, *Hannibal. The Struggle for Power in the Mediterranean*, London.

Develin, R. 1980, 'The Roman command structure in Spain 218–199' *Klio* 62: 355–67.

Dorey, T.A. & Dudley, D.R. 1971, *Rome Against Carthage*, London.

Eckstein, A.M. 1982, 'Human sacrifice and fear of military disaster in Republican Rome' *AJAH* 7: 69–95.

Eckstein, A.M. 1987, *Senate and General: Individual Decision Making and Roman Foreign Relations 264–194*, Berkeley.

Edwards, J. 2001, 'The irony of Hannibal's elephants' *Latomus* 60: 900–5.

Erdkamp, P. 1992, 'Polybius, Livy and the "Fabian Strategy"' *AncSoc* 23: 127–47.

Errington, R.M. 1970, 'Rome and Spain before the Second Punic War' *Latomus* 29: 25–57.

Errington, R.M. 1972, *The Dawn of Empire. Rome's Rise to World Power*, Ithaca.

Erskine, A. 1993, 'Hannibal and the freedom of the Italians' *Hermes* 121: 58–62.

Flower, H.I. 2000, 'The tradition of the *spolia opima*: M. Claudius Marcellus and Augustus' *ClAnt* 19: 34–59.

Frank, T. 1928, 'Rome and Carthage: the First Punic War' in *CAH* VII[1]: 665–98.

Fuller, J.F.C. 1954, *The Decisive Battles of the Western World*, vol. 1, London.

Gilliver, C.M. 1999, *The Roman Art of War*, Stroud.

Goldsworthy, A. 2000, *The Punic Wars*, London.

Goldsworthy, A. 2000a, *Roman Warfare*, London.

Goldsworthy, A. 2001, *Cannae*, London.

Gruen, E. S. 1990, *Studies in Greek Culture and Roman Policy*, Berkeley.

Gruen, E.S. 1992, *Culture and National Identity in Republican Rome*, London.

Hallward, B.L. 1930, 'Hannibal's invasion of Italy' in *CAH* VIII[1]: 25–56.

Hallward, B.L. 1930a, 'The Roman defensive' in *CAH* VIII[1]: 57–82.

Hallward, B.L. 1930b, 'Scipio and victory' in *CAH* VIII[1]: 83–115.

Hallward, B.L. & Charlesworth, M.P. 1930, 'The fall of Carthage' in *CAH* VIII[1]: 466–84.

Hanson, V.D. 1995, 'From phalanx to legion 350–250 BC' in Parker, G. (ed.) *The Cambridge Illustrated History of Warfare. The Triumph of the West*, Cambridge: 32–49.

Harris, W.V. 1979, *War and Imperialism in Republican Rome, 327–70 BC*, Oxford.

Harris, W.V. 1989, 'Roman expansion in the West' in *CAH* VII.2[2]: 107–62.

Haywood, R.M. 1933, *Studies on Scipio Africanus*, Westport.

Hoyos, B.D. 1983, 'Hannibal: what kind of genius?' *G&R* 30: 171–80.

Hoyos, B.D. 1985, 'Treaties true and false: the error of Philinus of Agrigentum' *CQ* 35: 92–109.

Hoyos, D. 1989, 'A forgotten Roman historian: L. Arruntius and the "true" causes of the First Punic War' *Antichthon* 23: 51–66.

Hoyos, D. 1994, 'Barcid "proconsuls" and Punic politics, 237–218 BC' *RhM* 137: 246–74.

Hoyos, D. 2000, 'Hannibal's *bon mot*: authenticity and survival' *CQ* 50: 610–14.

Hoyos, D. 2003, *Hannibal's Dynasty. Power and Politics in the Western Mediterranean*, London.

Jocelyn, H.D. 1969, 'The poet Cn. Naevius, P. Cornelius Scipio and Q. Caecilius Metellus' *Antichthon* 3: 32–47.

Kagan, D. 1975, *Problems in Ancient History. Vol. Two. The Roman World*, second edition, New York.

Keay, S.J. 1988, *Roman Spain*, London.

Kern, P.B. 1999, *Ancient Siege Warfare*, Bloomington.

Khader, A. & Soren, D. (eds) 1987, *Carthage: A Mosaic of Ancient Tunisia*, New York.

Lancell, S. 1995, *Carthage. A History*, Oxford.

Lancell, S. 1998, *Hannibal*, Oxford.

Lazenby, J.F. 1978, *Hannibal's War: A Military History of the Second Punic War*, London.

Lazenby, J.F. 1996, *The First Punic War: A Military History*, London.

Lazenby, J.F. 1996a, 'Was Maharbal right?' in Cornell, Rankov & Sabin 1996: 39–47.

Lazenby, J.F. 2004, 'Rome and Carthage' in Flower, H.I. (ed.) *The Cambridge Companion to the Roman Republic*, Cambridge: 225–41.

Liddell Hart, B.H. 1926, *A Greater than Napolean: Scipio Africanus*, London.

Lintott, A.W. 1972, 'Imperial expansion and moral decline in the Roman Republic' *Historia* 21: 626–38.

Mellor, R. 1999, *The Roman Historians*, London.

Miles, R. 2003, 'Rivalling Rome: Carthage' in Edwards, C. & Woolf, G. (eds) *Rome the Cosmopolis*, Cambridge: 123–46.

Mix, E.R. 1970, *Marcus Atilius Regulus*, Paris.

Oakley, S.P. 1985, 'Single combat in the Roman Republic' *CQ* 35: 392–410.

Ogilvie, R.M. 1969, *The Romans and their Gods*, London.

Palmer, R.E.A. 1997, *Rome and Carthage at Peace*, Stuttgart.

Peddie, J. 1997, *Hannibal's War*, Stroud.

Picard, G.C. 1964, *Carthage*, London.

Picard, G.C. & Picard, C. 1961, *Daily Life in Carthage at the Time of Hannibal*, London.

Picard, G.C. & Picard, C. 1968, *The Life and Death of Carthage*, London.

Picard, G.C. & Picard, C. 1987, *Carthage*, second edition, London.

Proctor, D. 1971, *Hannibal's March in History*, Oxford.

Rankov, B. 1996, 'The Second Punic War at sea' in Cornell, Rankov & Sabin 1996: 49–57.

Raven, S. 1993, *Rome in Africa*, third edition, London.

Rawlings, L. 1996, 'Celts, Spaniards, and Samnites: warriors in a soldier's war' in Cornell, Rankov & Sabin 1996: 81–95.

Rawson, E. 1989, 'Roman tradition and the Greek world' in *CAH* VIII²: 422–76.

Rawson, E. 1991, 'Religion and politics in the late second century BC at Rome' in Rawson, E. *Roman Culture and Society*, Oxford: 149–68 = 1974, *Phoenix* 28: 193–212.

Rich, J. 1996, 'The origins of the Second Punic War' in Cornell, Rankov & Sabin 1996: 1–37.

Richardson, J.S. 1986, *Hispaniae. Spain and the Development of Roman Imperialism, 218–82 BC*, Cambridge.

Ridley, R.T. 1986, 'To be taken with a pinch of salt: the destruction of Carthage' *CPh* 81: 140–6.

Ridley, R.T. 2000, 'Livy and the Hannibalic war' in Bruun, C. (ed.) *The Roman Middle Republic. Politics, Religion, and Historiography c. 400–133 BC*, Rome: 13–40.

Rosenstein, N. 2002, 'Marriage and manpower in the Hannibalic War: *assidui, proletarii* and Livy 24.18.7–8' *Historia* 51: 163–91.

Roth, J.P. 1999, *The Logistics of the Roman Army at War (264 BC– AD 235)*, Leiden.

Sabin, P. 1996, 'The mechanics of battle in the Second Punic War' in Cornell, Rankov & Sabin 1996: 59–79.

Sabin, P. 2000, 'The face of Roman battle' *JRS* 90: 1–17.

Salmon, E. 1960, 'The strategy of the Second Punic War' *G&R* 7: 131–42.

Samuels, M. 1990, 'The reality of Cannae' *Militärgeschichtliche Mitteilungen* 47: 7–29.

Schulten, A. 1928, 'The Carthaginians in Spain' in *CAH* VII¹: 769–92.

Scullard, H.H. 1930, *Scipio Africanus in the Second Punic War*, Cambridge.

Scullard, H.H. 1948, 'Hannibal's elephants' *NC* 8: 158–68.

Scullard, H.H. 1970, *Scipio Africanus, Soldier and Politician*, London.

Scullard, H.H. 1973, *Roman Politics 220–150 BC*, second edition, Oxford.

Scullard, H.H. 1974, *The Elephant in the Greek and Roman World*, London.

Scullard, H.H. 1980, *A History of the Roman World, 753 to 146 BC*, fourth edition, London.

Scullard, H.H. 1989, 'Carthage and Rome' in *CAH* VII.2²: 486–569.

Scullard, H.H. 1989a, 'The Carthaginians in Spain' in *CAH* VIII²: 17–43.

Scullard, H.H. & Gowers, W. 1950, 'Hannibal's elephants again' *NC* 10: 271–83.

Shean, J.F. 1996, 'Hannibal's mules: the logistical limitations of Hannibal's army and the Battle of Cannae, 216 BC' *Historia* 45: 141–87.

Skutsch, O. 1985, *The Annals of Q. Ennius*, Oxford.

Smith, P.J. 1993, *Scipio Africanus and Rome's Invasion of Africa. A Historical Commentary on Titus Livius, Book XXIX*, Amsterdam.

Starr, C.G. 1953, *The Emergence of Rome as Ruler of the World*, Cornell.

Steinby, C. 2000, 'The Roman boarding-bridge in the First Punic War. A study of Roman tactics and strategy' *Arctos* 34: 193–210.

Sumner, G.V. 1968, 'Roman policy in Spain before the Hannibalic War' *HSCPh* 1968: 205–46.

Sumner, G.V. 1972, 'Rome, Spain, and the outbreak of the Second Punic War: some clarifications' *Latomus* 31: 469–80.

Tarn, W.W. 1907, 'The fleets of the First Punic War' *JHS* 27: 48–60.

Thiel, J.H. 1946, *Studies on the History of Roman Sea-Power in Republican Times*, Amsterdam.

Thiel, J.H. 1954, *A History of Roman Seapower Before the Second Punic War*, Amsterdam.

Torr, C. 1935, *Hannibal Crosses the Alps*, Cambridge.

Toynbee, A.J. 1965, *Hannibal's Legacy*, vols I–II, London.

Vishnia, R.F. 1996, *State, Society and Popular Leaders in Mid-Republican Rome 241–167 BC*, London.

Visonà, P. 1988, 'Passing the salt: on the destruction of Carthage again' *CPh* 83: 41–2.

Walbank, F.W. 1956, 'Some reflections on Hannibal's pass' *JRS* 46: 37–45.

Wallinga, H.T. 1956, *The Boarding-Bridge of the Romans*, Gravenhage.

Warmington, B.H. 1969, *Carthage*, second edition, London.

Warmington, B.H. 1988, 'The destruction of Carthage: a retractio' *CPh* 83: 308–10.

Watson, G.R. 1969, *The Roman Soldier*, London.

Wise, T. & Healy, M. 1999, *Hannibal's War with Rome. The Armies and Campaigns, 216 BC*, Oxford.

Chapter Five: Rome's Mediterranean Empire

Adams, C.E.P. 2001, 'Feeding the wolf: logistics and the Roman army' *JRA* 14: 465–72.

Adcock, F.E. 1940, *The Roman Art of War under the Republic*, Harvard.

Alston, R. 1994, 'Roman military pay from Caesar to Diocletian' *JRS* 94: 113–23.

Armstrong, D. & Walsh, J.J. 1986, '*SIG*³ 593: the letter of Flamininus to Chyretiae' *CPh* 81: 32–46.

Astin, A.E. 1967, *Scipio Aemilianus*, Oxford.

Astin, A.E. 1978, *Cato the Censor*, Oxford.

Astin, A.E. 1989, 'Roman government and politics, 200–134 BC' in *CAH* VIII²: 163–96.

Astin, A.E. 1989a, 'Sources' in *CAH* VIII²: 1–16.

Austin, N.J.E. & Rankov, N.B. 1995, *Exploratio. Military and Political Intelligence in the Roman World from the Second Punic War to the Battle of Adrianople*, London.

Badian, E. 1968, *Roman Imperialism in the Late Republic*, second edition, Ithaca.

Badian, E. 1970, *Titus Quinctius Flamininus: Philhellenism and Realpolitik*, Cincinnati.

Badian, E. 1972, *Publicans and Sinners*, Oxford.

Balsdon, J.P.V.D. 1967, 'T. Quinctius Flamininus' *Phoenix* 21: 177–90.

Balsdon, J.P.V.D. 1979, *Romans and Aliens*, London.

Bell, M.J.V. 1965, 'Tactical reform in the Roman Republican army' *Historia* 14: 404–22.

Bernstein, A.H. 1994, 'The strategy of a warrior-state: Rome and the wars against Carthage, 261–201 BC' in Murray, W., Knox, M. & Bernstein, A. (eds) *The Making of Strategy. Rulers, States, and War*, Cambridge: 56–84.

Bettini, M. 1991, *Anthropology and Roman Culture. Kinship, Time, Images of the Soul*, Baltimore.

Bishop, M.C. & Coulston, J.C.N. 1993, *Roman Military Equipment from the Punic Wars to the Fall of Rome*, London.

Boardman, J. 1993, *The Oxford History of Classical Art*, Oxford.

Bowra, C. M. 1957, 'Melinno's hymn to Rome' *JRS* 47: 21–8.

Bradley, K. 1994, *Slavery and Society at Rome*, Cambridge.

Braund, D. 1984, *Rome and the Friendly King; the Character of the Client Kingship*, London.

Buraselis, K. 1996, 'Vix aerarium sufficeret: Roman finances and the outbreak of the Second Macedonian War' *GRBS* 37: 149–72.

Campbell, B. 1987, 'Teach yourself how to be a general' *JRS* 77: 13–29.

Carrié, J.-M. 1993, 'The Soldier' in Giardina, A. (ed.) *The Romans*, Chicago: 100–37.

Connolly, P. 1975, *The Roman Army*, London.

Connolly, P. 1981, *Greece and Rome at War*, London.

Connolly, P. 1989, 'The early Roman army' in Hackett, J. (ed.) *Warfare in the Ancient World*, London: 136–48.

Connolly, P. 1989a, 'The Roman army in the age of Polybius' in Hackett, J. (ed.) *Warfare in the Ancient World*, London: 149–68.

Connolly, P. 1997, 'Pilum, gladius and pugio in the late Republic' *JRMES* 8: 41–57.

Cornell, T.J. 1995, 'Warfare and urbanization in Roman Italy' in Cornell, T.J. & Lomas, K. (eds) *Urban Society in Roman Italy*, London: 121–34.

Couston, J.C.N. 1998, 'How to arm a Roman soldier' in Austin, M., Harries, J. & Smith, C. (eds) *Modus Operandi. Essays in Honour of Geoffrey Rickman*, London: 167–90.

Crawford, M.H. 1977, 'Rome and the Greek world: economic relationship' *Economic History Review* 30: 42–52.

Crawford, M.H. 1978, 'Greek intellectuals and the Roman aristocracy in the first century BC' in Garnsey, P.D.A. & Whittaker, C.R. (eds) *Imperialism in the Ancient World*, Cambridge: 193–207, 330–8.

Curchin, L.A. 1991, *Roman Spain: Conquest and Assimilation*, Routledge.

Dando-Collins, S. 2002, *Caesar's Legion. The Epic Saga of Julius Caesar's Elite Tenth Legion and the Armies of Rome*, New York.

Derow, P.S. 1979, 'Polybius, Rome and the East' *JRS* 69: 1–15.

Derow, P.S. 1989, 'Rome, the fall of Macedon and the sack of Corinth' in *CAH* VIII²: 290–323.

Dubuisson, M. 1983, 'Les *opici*: Osques, Occidentaux ou Barbares?' *Latomus* 42: 522–45.

Dusanic, S. & Petkovic, Z. 2003, 'The five standards of the pre-Marian legion. A note on the early plebeian *militaria*' *Klio* 85: 42–56.

Eckstein, A.M. 1987, *Senate and General: Individual Decision Making and Roman Foreign Relations 264–194*, Berkeley.

Eckstein, A.M. 1995, 'Glabrio and the Aetolians: a note on deditio' *TAPhA* 125: 271–89.

Eckstein, A.M. 1999, 'Pharos and the question of Roman treaties of alliance in the Greek East in the third century BCE' *CPh* 94: 395–418.

Eckstein, A.M. 2002, 'Greek mediation in the first Macedonian War 209–205 BC' *Historia* 51: 268–97.

Erdkamp, P. 1998, *Hunger and the Sword. Warfare and Food Supply in Roman Republican Wars (264–30 BC)*, Amsterdam.

Errington, R.M. 1989, 'Rome and Greece to 205 BC' in *CAH* VIII²: 81–106.

Errington, R.M. 1989a, 'Rome against Philip and Antiochus' in *CAH* VIII²: 244–89.

Erskine, A. 1990, *The Hellenistic Stoa: Political Thought and Action*, London.

Erskine, A. 1994, 'The Romans as common benefactors' *Historia* 43: 70–87.

Evans, R.J. 1993, 'The structure and source of Livy 38.44.8–39.44.9' *Klio* 75: 180–7.

Fabricius, E. 1932, 'Some notes on Polybius' description of Roman camps' *JRS* 22: 78–87.

Flower, H.I. 2000, 'The tradition of the *spolia opima*: M. Claudius Marcellus and Augustus' *ClAnt* 19: 34–59.

Forbes, H. & Foxhall, L. 1982, 'Sitometreia' *Chiron* 12: 41–90.

Fuller, J.F.C. 1965, *Julius Caesar*, London.

Gabba, E. 1976, *Republican Rome, the Army and the Allies*, Oxford.

Gabba, E. 1989, 'Rome and Italy in the second century BC' in *CAH* VIII²: 197–243.

Garlan, Y. 1975, *War in the Ancient World*, London.

Gilliver, C.M. 1999, *The Roman Art of War*, Stroud.

Goldsworthy, A.K. 1996, *The Roman Army at War, 100 BC–AD 200*, Oxford.

Goldsworthy, A. 2000, *Roman Warfare*, London.

Graham, F. 1981, *Dictionary of Roman Military Terms*, Newcastle.

Grainger, J.D. 1995, 'The campaign of Cn. Manlius Vulso in Asia Minor' *AS* 45: 23–42.

Grant, M. 1974, *The Army of the Caesars*, London.

Gruen, E. S. 1982, 'Greek *pistis* and Roman fides' *Athenaeum* 60: 50–68.

Gruen, E. 1984, 'Material rewards and the drive for empire' in Harris, W.V. (ed.) *The Imperialism of Mid-Republican Rome*, Rome: 59–82.

Gruen, E. S. 1986, *The Hellenistic World and the Coming of Rome*, Berkeley.

Gruen, E.S. 1990, Review of J.-L. Feray, 1988, *Philhellénisme et impérialisme: aspects idéologiques de la conquête romaine du monde hellénistique, de la seconde guerre de Macédoine à la guerre contre Mithridate*, Rome, *CPh* 85: 324–9.

Gruen, E.S. 1990a, *Studies in Greek Culture and Roman Policy*, Berkeley.

Gruen, E.S. 1992, *Culture and National Identity in Republican Rome*, London.

Habicht, C. 1989, 'The Seleucids and their rivals' in *CAH* VIII²: 324–87.

Hammond, N.G.L. 1988, 'The campaign and the battle of Cynoscephalae in 197 BC' *JHS* 108: 60–82.

Hansen, E.V. 1971, *The Attalids of Pergamon*, second edition, Ithaca.

Hanson, V.D. 1995, 'From phalanx to legion 350–250 BC' in Parker, G. (ed.) *The Cambridge Illustrated History of Warfare. The Triumph of the West*, Cambridge: 32–49.

Hanson, V.D. 1995a, 'The Roman way of war 250 BC–AD 300' in Parker, G. (ed.) *The Cambridge Illustrated History of Warfare. The Triumph of the West*, Cambridge: 50–61.

Harris, W.V. 1979, *War and Imperialism in Republican Rome 327–70 BC*, Oxford.

Harris, W.V. 1984, 'The Italians and the empire' in Harris, W.V. (ed.) *The Imperialism of Mid-Republican Rome*, Rome: 89–109.

Harris, W.V. 1989, 'Roman expansion in the West' in *CAH* VIII²: 107–162.

Hassall, M., Crawford, M. & Reynolds, J. 1974, 'Rome and the eastern provinces at the end of the second century BC: the so-called "piracy law" and a new inscription from Cnidos' *JRS* 64: 195–220.

Hodge, P. 1977, *The Roman Army*, London.

Holden, M. 1973, *The Legions of Rome*, London.

Hopkins, K. 1978, *Conquerors and Slaves*, Cambridge.

Hyland, A. 1990, *Equus: the Horse in the Roman World*, London.

Jocelyn, H.D. 1969, 'The poet Cn. Naevius, P. Cornelius Scipio and Q. Caecilius Metellus' *Antichthon* 3: 39–41.

Kagan, D. 1975, *Problems in Ancient History. Vol. Two: The Roman World*, second edition, New York.

Kähler, H. 1965, *Der Fries vom Reiterdenkmal des Aemilius Paullus in Delphi*, Berlin.

Keaveney, A. 1998, 'Three Roman chronological problems (141–132 BC)' *Klio* 80: 66–90.

Keay, S. 2001, 'Romanization and the Hispaniae' in Keay, S. & Terrenato, N. (eds) *Italy and the West. Comparative Issues in Romanization*, Oxford: 115–44.

Keay, S.J. 1988, *Roman Spain*, London.

Keppie, L. 1983, *Colonisation and Veteran Settlement in Italy*, London.

Keppie, L. 1984, *The Making of the Roman Army*, London.

Keppie, L. 1989, 'The Roman army of the later Republic' in Hackett, J. (ed.) *Warfare in the Ancient World*, London: 169–91.

Krasilnikoff, J.A. 1996, 'Mercenary soldiering in the west and the development of the army of Rome' *Analecta Romana* 23: 7–20.

Levick, B. 1982, 'Morals, politics and the fall of the Roman republic' *G&R* 29: 53–62.

Linderski, J. 2001, 'Silver and gold of valor: the award of *armillae* and *torques*' *Latomus* 60: 3–15.

Lintott, A.W. 1972, 'Imperial expansion and moral decline in the Roman republic' *Historia* 21: 626–38.

Luttwak, E.N. 1976, *The Grand Strategy of the Roman Empire*, Baltimore.

MacMullen, R. 1982, 'Roman attitudes to Greek love' *Historia* 31: 484–502.

MacMullen, R. 1984, 'The legion as society' *Historia* 33: 440–56.

MacMullen, R. 1991, 'Hellenizing the Romans (2nd Century BC)' *Historia* 40: 419–38.

Magie, D. 1950, *Roman Rule in Asia Minor*, vols I–II, Princeton.

Maxfield, V.A. 1981, *The Military Decorations of the Roman Army*, London.

McColl, J.B. 2002, *The Cavalry of the Roman Republic*, London.

McDonald, A.H. 1967, 'The treaty of Apamea (188 BC)' *JRS* 57: 1–8.

McDonald, A.H. & Walbank, F.W. 1969, 'The treaty of Apamea (188 BC): the naval clauses' *JRS* 59: 30–9.

Mellor, R. 1975, *Thea Rome: the Worship of the Goddess Roma in the Greek World*, Göttingen.

Millar, F. 1984, 'The Mediterranean and the Roman revolution: politics, war and the economy' *P&P* 102: 1–24.

Miller, M.C.J. & de Voto, J.G. 1994, *Polybius and Pseudo-Hyginus: the Fortification of the Roman Camp*, Chicago.

Morel, J.-P. 1989, 'The transformation of Italy, 300–133 BC The evidence of archaeology' in *CAH* VIII²: 477–516.

Nicolet, C. 1980, *The World of the Citizen in Republican Rome*, London.

BIBLIOGRAPHIES TO CHAPTERS

North, J.A. 1981, 'The development of Roman imperialism' *JRS* 71: 1–9.

Oakley, S.P. 1985, 'Single combat in the Roman Republic' *CQ* 35: 392–410.

Parker, H.M.D. 1958, *The Roman Legions*, second edition, Cambridge.

Peddie, J. 1994, *The Roman War Machine*, Gloucestershire.

Plant, I.M. 2004, *Women Writers of Ancient Greece and Rome. An Anthology*, London.

Pollitt, J.J. 1978, 'The impact of Greek art on Rome' *TAPhA* 108: 155–74.

Potter, D. 2004, 'The Roman army and navy' in Flower, H.I. (ed.) *The Cambridge Companion to the Roman Republic*, Cambridge: 66–88.

Preston, R. 2001, 'Roman questions, Greek answers: Plutarch and the construction of identity' in Goldhill, S. (ed.) *Being Greek under Rome. Cultural Identity, the Second Sophistic and the Development of Empire*, Cambridge: 86–119.

Quesada Sanz, F. 1997, 'Gladius hispaniensis: an archaeological view from Iberia' *JRMES* 8: 250–70.

Rawson, B. 2003, *Children and Childhood in Roman Italy*, Oxford.

Rawson, E. 1989, 'Roman tradition and the Greek world' in *CAH* VIII²: 422–76.

Rawson, E. 1991, 'The literary sources for the pre-Marian army' *PBSR* 39: 13–31.

Reiter, W. 1988, *Aemilius Paullus, Conqueror of Greece*, London.

Rich, J.W. 1996, 'Augustus and the spolia opima' *Chiron* 26: 85–127.

Richardson, J.S. 1976, *Roman Provincial Administration*, Basingstoke.

Richardson, J.S. 1976a, 'The Spanish mines and the development of provincial taxation in the second century BC' *JRS* 66: 139–52.

Richardson, J.S. 1979, 'Polybius' view of the Roman empire' *PBSR* 34: 1–11.

Richardson, J.S. 1986, *Hispaniae: Spain and the Development of Roman Imperialism, 218–82 BC*, Cambridge.

Richardson, J.S. 2000, *Appian. Wars of the Romans in Iberia*, Warminster.

Rosenstein, N. 1990, *Imperatores Victi*, Berkeley.

Rosenstein, N. 1992, '*Nobilitas* and the political implications of military defeat' *AHB* 6: 117–26.

Roth, J.P. 1999, *The Logistics of the Roman Army at War (264 BC – AD 235)*, Leiden.

Sabin, P. 2000, 'The face of Roman battle' *JRS* 90: 1–17.

Saunders, C. 1944, 'The nature of Rome's early appraisal of Greek culture' *CPh* 39: 209–17.

Scullard, H.H. 1973, *Roman Politics, 220–150 BC*, second edition, Oxford.

Scullard, H. H. 1980, *A History of the Roman World, 753 to 146 BC*, fourth edition, London.

Shatzman, I. 1972, 'The Roman general's authority over booty' *Historia* 21: 177–205.

Sherwin-White, A.N. 1984, *Roman Foreign Policy in the East 168 BC to AD 1*, London.

Smith, R.E. 1958, *Service in the Post-Marian Army*, Manchester.

Starr, C.G. 1980, *The Beginnings of Imperial Rome: Rome in the Mid-Republic*, Ann Arbor.

Stephenson, I.P. 1997, 'Roman Republican training equipment: form, function and the mock battle' *JRMES* 8: 311–15.

Toynbee, A.J. 1965, *Hannibal's Legacy*, vols I–II, London.

Vishnia, R.F. 1996, *State, Society and Popular Leaders in Mid-Republican Rome 214–167 BC*, London.

Wallace-Hadrill, A. 1988, 'Greek knowledge, Roman power' *CPh* 83: 224–33.

Wallace-Hadrill, A. 1998, 'To be Roman, go Greek: thoughts on Hellenization at Rome' in Austin, M., Harries, J. & Smith, C. (eds) *Modus Operandi. Essays in Honour of Geoffrey Rickman*, London: 79–91.

Walsh, J.J. 1996, 'Flamininus and the propaganda of liberation' *Historia* 45: 344–63.

Wardman, A. 1976, *Rome's Debt to Greece*, London.

Warry, J. 1989, *Warfare in the Classical World*, London.

Watson, G.R. 1958, 'The pay of the Roman army: the Republic' *Historia* 7: 113–120.

Watson, G.R. 1969, *The Roman Soldier*, London.

Watson, G.R. 1987, 'The army of the Republic' in Wacher, J., (ed.) *The Roman World*, vol. I, London: 75–88.

Webster, G. 1985, *The Roman Imperial Army*, third edition, London.

Wilkes, J. 1972, *The Roman Army*, Cambridge.

Williams, C.A. 1999, *Roman Homosexuality. Ideologies of Masculinity in Classical Antiquity*, Oxford.

Wise, T. & Healey, M. 1999, *Hannibal's War with Rome*, Oxford.

Wiseman, T.P. 1966, 'The ambitions of Quintus Cicero' *JRS* 56: 108–15.

Yavetz, Z. 1962, 'The policy of C. Flaminius and the plebiscitum Claudianum' *Athenaeum* 40: 325–44.

Yavetz, Z. 1991, 'Towards a further step into the study of Roman imperialism' *CEA* 26: 3–22.

Zhmodikov, A. 2000, 'Roman Republican heavy infantrymen in battle (IV–II centuries BC)' *Historia* 49: 67–78.

Chapter Six: Slaves and Freedmen

Alföldy, G. 1988, *The Social History of Rome*, London.

Astin, A.E. 1978, *Cato the Censor*, Oxford.

Badian, E. 1982, 'Figuring out Roman slavery [Review of Hopkins 1978]' *JRS* 72: 165–69.

Baldwin, B. 1966/7, 'Two aspects of the Spartacus slave revolt' *CJ* 62: 289–94.

Balsdon, J.P.V.D. 1979, *Romans and Aliens*, London.

Bodor, A. 1981, 'The ethnic and social composition of the participants in the slave uprising led by Spartacus' in Danov, C.M. & Fol, A. (eds) *Spartacus: Symposium Rebus Spartaci Gestis Dedicatum*, Sofia: 85–94.

Bosworth, A.B. 1968, 'Review of Capozza, M. 1966, *Movimenta servili nel mondo Romano in età Repubblicana I*, Rome' *JRS* 58: 272–4.

Bradley, K.R. 1978, 'Slaves and the conspiracy of Catiline' *CPh* 73: 329–36.

Bradley, K.R. 1979, 'Holidays for slaves' *SO* 54: 111–18.

Bradley, K.R. 1983, 'Slave kingdoms and slave rebellions in ancient Sicily' *Historical Reflections/Réflexions Historiques* 10: 435–51.

Bradley, K.R. 1985, 'The early development of slavery at Rome' *Historical Reflections/Réflexions Historiques* 12: 1–8.

Bradley, K.R. 1987, *Slaves and Masters in the Roman Empire. A Study in Social Control*, New York.

Bradley, K.R. 1989, *Slavery and Rebellion in the Roman World, 140 BC – 70 BC*, Indiana.

Bradley, K. 1992, '"The regular, daily traffic in slaves": Roman history and contemporary history' *CJ* 87: 125–38.

Bradley, K.R. 1994, *Slavery and Society at Rome*, Cambridge.

Brunt, P.A. 1958, 'Review of Westermann 1958' *JRS* 48: 164–70.

Brunt, P.A. 1965, 'Work and Slavery' in Balsdon: 169–81 (see general bibliography).

Brunt, P.A. 1988, 'The army and the land in the Roman Revolution' in Brunt, P.A. *The Fall of the Roman Republic and Related Essays*, Oxford: 240–75; revision of 1962, *JRS* 52: 69–86.

Buckland, W.W. 1908, *The Roman Law of Slavery. The Condition of the Slave in Private Law from Augustus to Justinian*, Cambridge.

Burford, A. 1972, *Craftsmen in Greek and Roman Society*, London.

Carcopino, J. 1941, *Daily Life in Ancient Rome*, Harmondsworth.

Cornell, T. J. 1995, *The Beginnings of Rome. Italy and Rome from the Bronze Age to the Punic Wars (c. 1000–264 BC)*, London.

Crawford, M.H. 1977, 'Republican denarii in Romania: the suppression of piracy and the slave-trade' *JRS* 67: 117–24.

Dalby, A. 1998, *Cato. On Farming. De Agricultura*, Devon.

Daube, D. 1946, 'Two early patterns of manumission' *JRS* 36: 57–75.

Doi, M. 1984, 'On the negotiations between the Roman state and the Spartacus army' *Klio* 66: 170–4.

Dupont, F. 1992, *Daily Life in Ancient Rome*, Oxford.

Finley, M.I. 1968, *Ancient Sicily to the Arab Conquest*, London.

Finley, M.I. 1980, *Ancient Slavery and Modern Ideology*, Harmondsworth.

Finley, M.I. 1987, *Classical Slavery*, London.

Forbes, H. & Foxhall, L. 1982, 'Sitometreia' *Chiron* 12: 41–90.

Forrest, W.G. & Stinton 1962, 'The First Sicilian Slave War' *P&P* 22: 87–92.

Grant, M. 1992, *Greeks and Romans. A Social History*, London.

Green, P. 1961, 'The First Sicilian Slave War' *P&P* 20: 10–29.

Greenhalgh, P. 1980, *Pompey. The Roman Alexander*, London.

Gruen, E.S. 1992, *Culture and National Identity in Republican Rome*, Cornell.

Harris, W.V. 1980, 'Towards a study of the Roman slave trade' *MAAR* 36: 117–40.

Hopkins, K. 1978, *Conquerors and Slaves*, Cambridge.

Hughes, K. 1975, *Slavery*, London.

Jones, A.H.M. 1960, 'Slavery in the Ancient World' in Finley, M.I. (ed.) *Slavery in Classical Antiquity. Views and Controversies*, Cambridge: 1–15 = 1956, *The Economic History Review* 9: 185–99.

Jongman, W. 2003, 'Slavery and the growth of Rome. The transformation of Italy in the second and first centuries BCE' in Edwards, C. & Woolf, G. (eds) 2003, *Rome the Cosmopolis*, Cambridge: 100–22.

Kamienik, R. 1976, 'Gladiatorial games during the funeral of Crixus: contribution to the revolt of Spartacus' *Eos* 64: 83–90.

Korzheva, K.P. 1976, 'Spartacus' rebellion in Soviet historiography' *Soviet Studies in History* 15.1: 67–97.

Konstan, D. 1975, 'Marxism and Roman slavery' *Arethusa* 8: 145–69.

Laurence, R. 1999, *The Roads of Roman Italy*, London.

Libourel, J.M. 1973, 'Galley slaves in the Second Punic War' *CPh* 68: 116–19.

Lintott, A. 1994, 'The Roman empire and its problems in the late second century' in *CAH* IX[2]: 16–39.

Lintott, A. 1999, *Violence in Republican Rome*, second edition, Oxford.

Marshall, B. 1972, 'Crassus' ovation in 71 BC' *Historia* 21: 669–73.

Marshall, B. 1973, 'Crassus and the command against Spartacus' *Athenaeum* 51: 109–21.

Marshall, B.A. 1976, *Crassus. A Political Biography*, Amsterdam.

McCarthy, K. 2000, *Slaves, Masters, and the Art of Authority in Plautine Comedy*, Princeton.

McDermott, W.C. 1972, 'M. Cicero and M. Tiro' *Historia* 21: 259–86.

Millar, F. 1995, 'The Roman *libertus* and civic freedom' *Arethusa* 28: 99–105.

Parker, H. 1998, 'Loyal slaves and loyal wives; the crisis of the outsider-within and Roman *exemplum* literature' in Joshel, S.R. & Murnaghan, S. (eds) *Women and Slaves in Greco-Roman Culture*, London: 152–73.

Rathbone, D.W. 1981, 'The development of agriculture in the "ager Cosanus" during the Roman Republic: problems of evidence and interpretation' *JRS* 71: 11–23.

Rathbone, D.W. 1983, 'The slave mode of production in Italy' *JRS* 73: 160–8.

Raymer, A.J. 1940/1, 'Slavery – the Graeco-Roman defence' *G&R* 10: 17–21.

Rei, A. 1998, 'Villains, wives and slaves in the comedies of Plautus' in Joshel, S.R. & Murnaghan, S. (eds) *Women and Slaves in Greco-Roman Culture*, London: 92–108.

Richardson, J.S. 1976, 'The Spanish mines and the development of provincial taxation in the second century BC' *JRS* 66: 139–52.

Robinson, O.F. 1981, 'Slaves and the criminal law' *ZSS* 98: 213–54.

Robinson, O.F. 1995, *The Criminal Law of Ancient Rome*, London.

Rowland, R.J. 1970, 'Grain for slaves: a note on Cato, *de agri culturi*' *CW* 63: 229.

Rubinsohn, Z.W. 1971, 'Was the Bellum Sparticum a servile insurrection?' *Rivista di Filologia* 99: 290–9.

Rubinsohn, Z.W. 1982, 'Some remarks on the causes and repercussions of the so-called "Second Slave Revolt" in Sicily' *Athenaeum* 60: 436–51.

Seager, R. 1994, 'The rise of Pompey' in *CAH* IX²: 208–28.

Seager, R. 2002, *Pompey the Great. A Political Biography*, second edition, Oxford.

Shaw, B.D. 2001, *Spartacus and the Slave Wars. A Brief History with Documents*, Boston.

Taylor, L.R. 1961, 'Freedmen and freeborn in the epitaphs of imperial Rome' *AJPh* 82: 113–32.

Tellegen-Couperus, O. 1993, *A Short History of Roman Law*, London.

Thalmann, W.G. 1996, 'Versions of slavery in the *Captivi* of Plautus' *Ramus* 25: 112–49.

Thébert, Y. 1993, 'The slave' in Giardina, A. (ed.) *The Romans*, Chicago: 138–74.

Thompson, F.H. 2003, *The Archaeology of Greek and Roman Slavery*, London.

Toynbee, A.J. 1965, *Hannibal's Legacy*, vols I–II, Oxford.

Treggiari, S.M. 1969, *Roman Freedmen during the Late Republic*, Oxford.

Verbrugghe, G.P. 1972, 'Sicily 210–70 BC: Livy, Cicero and Diodorus' *TAPhA* 103: 535–59.

Verbrugghe, G.P. 1974, 'Slave rebellion or Sicily in revolt' *Kokalos* 20: 145–59.

Verbrugghe, G.P. 1975, 'Narrative pattern in Posidonius' *History*' *Historia* 24: 187–204.

Vogt, J. 1974, *Ancient Slavery and the Ideal of Man*, Oxford.

Ward, A.M. 1975, 'Caesar and the pirates' *CPh* 70: 267–8.

Ward, A.M. 1977, 'Caesar and the pirates, II. The elusive M. Iunius Iuncus and the year 75/4' *AJAH* 2: 26–36.

Ward, A.M. 1977a, *Marcus Crassus and the Late Roman Republic*, Columbia.

Watson, A. 1965, *The Law of Obligations in the Later Roman Republic*, Oxford.

Watson, A. 1967, *The Law of Persons in the Later Roman Republic*, Oxford.

Watson, A. 1975, *Rome of the XII Tables*, Princeton.

Watson, A. 1983, 'Roman slave law and Romanist ideology' *Phoenix* 37: 53–65.

Watson, A. 1987, *Roman Slave Law*, Baltimore.

Westermann, W.L. 1945, 'Slave maintenance and slave revolts' *CPh* 40: 1–10.

Westermann W.L. 1955, *The Slave Systems of Greek and Roman Antiquity*, Philadelphia.

Wiedemann, T.E.J. 1981, *Greek and Roman Slavery*, London.

Wiedemann, T.E.J. 1997, *Slavery: Greece and Rome*, revised edition, Oxford.

Wiedemann, T.E.J. 1985, 'The regularity of manumission at Rome' *CQ* 35: 162–75.

Yavetz, Z. 1988, *Slaves and Slavery in Ancient Rome*, New Brunswick.

Ziolkowski, A. 1986, 'The plundering of Epirus in 167 BC: economic considerations' *PBSR* 54: 69–80.

Chapter Seven: Women and the Family

Adams, J.N. 1982, *The Latin Sexual Vocabulary*, London.

Adams, J.N. 1983, 'Words for "prostitute" in Latin' *RhM* 126: 321–58.

Adcock, F.E. 1945, 'Women in Roman life and letters' *G&R* 14: 1–11.

Arieti, J.A. 2002, 'Rape and Livy's view of Roman history' in Deacy, S. & Pierce, K.F. (eds) *Rape in Antiquity. Sexual Violence in the Greek and Roman Worlds*, Chippenham: 209–29.

Astin, A.E. 1967, *Scipio Aemilianus*, Oxford.

Babcock, C.L. 1965. 'The early life of Fulvia' *AJPh* 86: 1–32.

Balsdon, J.P.V.D. 1959, 'Women in Republican Rome' *History Today* 9: 455–61.

Balsdon, J.P.V.D. 1966, 'Fabula Clodiana' *Historia* 15: 65–73.

Balsdon, J.P.V.D. 1974, *Roman Women. Their History and Habits*, revised edition, London.

Bannon, C. 1997, *The Brothers of Romulus: Fraternal Pietas in Roman Law, Literature and Society*, Princeton.

Barnard, S. 1990, 'Cornelia and the women of her family' *Latomus* 49: 383–92.

Bauman, R.A. 1992, *Women and Politics in Ancient Rome*, London.

Beard, M. 1980, 'The sexual status of vestal virgins' *JRS* 70: 12–27.

Beard, M. 1990, 'Priesthood in the Roman Republic' in Beard, M. & North, J. (eds) *Pagan Priests: Religion and Power in the Ancient World*, London: 19–48.

Beard, M. 1995, 'Re-reading (Vestal) virginity' in Hawley, R. & Levick, B. (eds) *Women in Antiquity: New Assessments*, London: 166–77.

Best, E.E. 1969/70, 'Cicero, Livy and educated Roman women' *CJ* 65: 199–204.

Bettini, M. 1991, *Anthropology and Roman Culture. Kinship, Time, Images of the Soul*, Baltimore.

Boswell, J.E. 1984, '*Expositio* and *oblatio*: the abandonment of children and the ancient and medieval family' *AHR* 89: 10–33.

Bradley, K.R. 1986, 'Wet-nursing at Rome: a study in social relations' in Rawson, B. (ed.) *The Family in Ancient Rome. New Perspectives*, London: 201–29.

Bradley, K.R. 1991, *Discovering the Roman Family*, Oxford.

Bradley, K.R. 1998, 'The Roman family at dinner' in Nielsen, I. & Nielsen, H.S. (eds) *Meals in a Social Context*, Aarhus: 36–55.

Brouwer H.H.J. 1989, *Bona Dea: the Sources and a Description of the Cult*, Leiden.

Cameron, A. & Kurht, A. (eds) 1983, *Images of Women in Antiquity*, London.

Cantarella, E. 1987, *Pandora's Daughters: the Role and Status of Women in Greek and Roman Antiquity*, Baltimore.

Carp, T. 1981, 'Two Matrons of the Late Republic' in Foley, H.P. (ed) *Reflections of Women in Antiquity*, New York: 343–54.

Champlin, E. 1991, *Final Judgements. Duty and Emotion in Roman Wills 200 BC–AD 250*, Berkeley.

Claridge, A. 1998, *Rome. An Oxford Archaeological Guide*, Oxford.

Clark, G. 1981, 'Roman women' *G&R* 28: 193–212.

Clark, P.A. 1991, 'Tullia and Crassipes' *Phoenix* 45: 28–38.

Clarke, J.R. 1998, *Looking at Lovemaking. Constructions of Sexuality in Roman Art 100 BC–AD 250*, Berkeley.

Collins, J.H. 1951/2, 'Tullia's engagement and marriage to Dolabella' *CJ* 47: 162–8.

Corbett, P. E. 1930, *The Roman Law of Marriage*, Oxford.

Corbier, M. 1991, 'Constructing kinship in Rome: marriage and divorce, filiation and adoption' in Kertzer, D.I. & Saller, R.P. (eds) *The Family in Italy from Antiquity to the Present*, New Haven: 127–46.

Corbier, M. 1991a, 'Family behaviour of the Roman aristocracy, second century BC–third century AD' in Pomeroy, S.B. (ed.) *Women's History and Ancient History*, Chapel Hill: 173–96.

Corbier, M. 2001, 'Child exposure and abandonment' in Dixon, S. (ed.) *Childhood, Class and Kin in the Roman World*, London: 52–73.

Cornell, T. J. 1995, *The Beginnings of Rome. Italy and Rome from the Bronze Age to the Punic Wars (c. 1000–264 BC)*, London.

Crawford, O.C. 1941, 'Laudatio funebris' *CJ* 37: 17–27.

Crook, J. 1967, 'Patria potestas' *CQ* 17: 113–22.

Crook, J.A. 1967a, *Law and Life of Rome*, London.

Crook, J.A. 1986, 'Women in Roman Succession' in Rawson, B. (ed.) *The Family in Ancient Rome. New Perspectives*, London: 59–82.

Culham, P. 1982, 'The *lex Oppia*' *Latomus* 41: 786–93.

Delia, D. 1991, 'Fulvia reconsidered' in Pomeroy, S.B. (ed.) *Women's History and Ancient History*, Chapel Hill: 197–217.

Dickison, S.K. 1973, 'Abortion in antiquity' *Arethusa* 6: 159–66.

Dixon, S. 1983, 'A family business: women's role in patronage and politics at Rome 80–44 BC' *C&M* 34: 91–112.

Dixon, S. 1984, 'Family finances: Tullia and Terentia' *Antichthon* 18: 78–107.

Dixon, S. 1985, 'Breaking the law to do the right thing: the gradual erosion of the Voconian law in ancient Rome' *Adelaide Law Review* 9: 519–34.

Dixon, S. 1985a, 'Polybius on Roman women and property' *AJPh* 196: 147–70.

Dixon, S. 1985b, 'The marriage alliance in the Roman elite' *Journal of Family History* 10: 353–78.

Dixon, S. 1986, 'Family finances: Terentia and Tullia' in Rawson, B. (ed.) *The Family in Ancient Rome. New Perspectives*, London: 93–120.

Dixon, S. 1988, *The Roman Mother*, London.

Dixon, S. 1992, *The Roman Family*, Baltimore.

Dixon, S. 1997 'Conflict in the Roman family' in Rawson, B. & Weaver, P. (eds) *The Roman Family in Italy. Status, Sentiment, Space*, Canberra: 149–67.

Dixon, S. 2001, *Reading Roman Women. Sources, Genres and Real Life*, London.

Dixon, S. (ed.) 2001a, *Childhood, Class and Kin in the Roman World*, London.

Dohrn, T. 1972, *Die Ficoronische Ciste*, Berlin.

Dorey, T.A. 1958, 'Cicero, Clodia and the *Pro Caelio*' *G&R* 27: 175–80.

Douglas, A.E. 1958, 'Roman cognomina' *G&R* 5: 62–6.

Dumézil, G. 1970, *Archaic Roman Religion,* vols 1–2, Chicago.

Eckstein, A.M. 1982, 'Human sacrifice and fear of military disaster in Republican Rome' *AJAH* 7: 69–95.

Edwards, C. 1997, 'Unspeakable professions: public performance and prostitution in Ancient Rome' in Hallett, J.P. & Skinner, M.B. (eds) *Roman Sexualities*, Princeton: 66–95.

Ellis, S.P. 2000, *Roman Housing*, London.

Engels, D. 1980, 'The problem of female infanticide in the Greco-Roman world' *CPh* 75: 112–20.

Engels, D. 1984, 'The use of historical demography in ancient history' *CQ* 34: 386–93.

Epstein, D.F. 1986, 'Cicero's testimony at the *Bona Dea* trial' *CPh* 81: 229–35.

Evans, J.K. 1991, *War, Women and Children in Ancient Rome*, London.

Eyben, E. 1980/1, 'Family planning in Graeco-Roman antiquity' *AncSoc* 11/12: 5–82.

Eyben, E. 1981, 'Was the Roman "youth" an "adult" socially?' *AC* 50: 328–50.

Eyben, E. 1993, *Restless Youth in Ancient Rome*, London.

Fantham, E. 1991, '*Stuprum*: public attitudes and penalties for sexual offences in Republican Rome' *EMC/CV* 10: 267–91.

Fantham, E. et al. (eds) 1994, *Women in the Classical World: Image and Text*, Oxford.

Finley, M.I. 1981, 'The elderly in classical antiquity' *G&R* 28: 156–71.

Forbis, E.P. 1990, 'Women's public image in Italian honorary inscriptions' *AJPh* 111: 493–512.

Gardner, J.F. 1985, 'The recovery of dowry in Roman law' *CQ* 35: 449–53.

Gardner, J.F. 1986, *Women in Roman Law and Society*, London.

Gardner, J.F. 1991, 'The purpose of the lex Fufia Caninia' *EMC/CV* 10: 21–39.

Gardner, J.F. 1995, 'Gender-role assumptions in Roman law, *EMC/CV* 14: 377–400.

Gardner, J.F. 1998, *Family and Familia in Roman Law and Life*, Oxford.

Gardner, J.F. 1999, 'Status, sentiment and strategy in Roman adoption' in Corbier, M. (ed.) *Adoption et fosterage*, Paris: 63–80.

Gardner, J.F. & Wiedemann, T. 1991, *The Roman Household: a Sourcebook*, London.

Garnsey, P. 1991, 'Child rearing in ancient Italy' in Kertzer, D.I. & Saller, R.P. (eds) *The Family in Italy from Antiquity to the Present*, New Haven: 48–65.

Garton, C. 1964, 'A Republican mime-actress' *CR* 14: 238–9.

Garton, C. 1972, *Personal Aspects of the Roman Theater*, Toronto.

George, M. 1997, 'Repopulating the Roman house' in Rawson, B. & Weaver, P. (eds) *The Roman Family in Italy. Status, Sentiment, Space*, Canberra: 299–320.

Golden, M. 1988, 'Did the ancients care when their children died?' *G&R* 35: 152–63.

Golden, M. 1992, 'Continuity, change and the study of ancient childhood' *EMC/CV* 11: 7–18.

Goodrich, N.L. 1989, *Priestesses,* New York.

Gordon, A.E. 1977, 'Who's who in the *Laudatio Turiae*' *Epigraphica* 39: 7–12.

Gratwick, A.S. 1991, 'Catullus 32' *CQ* 41: 547–51.

Gray-Fow, M.J.G. 1988, 'The wicked stepmother in Roman literature and history: an evaluation' *Latomus* 47: 741–57.

Hales, S. 2000, 'At home with Cicero' *G&R* 47: 44–55.

Haley, S.P. 1985, 'The five wives of Pompey the Great' *G&R* 32: 49–59.

Hallett, J.P. 1984, *Fathers and Daughters in Roman Society. Women and the Elite Family*, Princeton.

Hallett, J.P. & Skinner, M.B. (eds) 1997, *Roman Sexualities*, Princeton.

Harlow, M. & Laurence, R. 2002, *Growing Up and Growing Old in Ancient Rome. A Life Course Approach*, London.

Harmon, D.P. 1978, 'The public festivals of Rome' *ANRW* II.16.2: 1440–68.

Harris, W.V. 1982, 'The theoretical possibility of extensive infanticide in the Graeco-Roman world' *CQ* 32: 114–16.

Harris, W.V. 1986, 'The Roman father's power of life and death' in Bagnall, R.S. & Harris, W.V. (eds) *Studies in Roman Law*, Leiden: 81–95.

Harris, W.V. 1994, 'Child-exposure in the Roman Empire' *JRS* 84: 1–22.

Hawley, R. & Levick, P. (eds) 1995, *Women in Antiquity. New Assessments*, London.

Hemelrijk, E.A. 1999, *Matrona Docta. Educated Women in the Roman Elite from Cornelia to Julia Domna*, London.

Hemelrijk, E.A. 2004, 'Masculinity and femininity in the *Laudatio Turiae*' *CQ* 54: 185–97.

Hillard, T.W. 1989, 'Republican politics, women and the evidence' *Helios* 16: 165–82.

Hillard, T.W. 1993, 'On the stage, behind the curtain: images of politically active women in the Late Roman Republic' in Garlick, B., Dixon, S. & Allen, P. (eds) *Stereotypes of Women in Power. Historical Perspectives and Revisionist Views*, New York: 37–64.

Hinds, S. 1987, 'The poetess and the reader: further steps towards Sulpicia' *Hermathena* 143: 29–46.

Holleman, A.W. 1989, 'Q. Fabius' vow to Venus Erycina (217 BC) and its background' in Devijver, H. & Lipinski, E. (eds) *Studia Phoenicia X. Punic Wars*, Leuven: 223–8.

Holzberg, N. 2000, 'Lesbia, the poet, and the two faces of Sappho: "womanufacture" in Catullus' *PCPhS* 46: 28–44.

Hopkins, K. 1965, 'Contraception in the Roman Empire' *Comparative Studies in Society and History* 7: 124–51.

Hopkins, K. 1991, 'From violence to blessing: symbols and rituals in ancient Rome' in Molho, A. et al. (eds) *City States in Classical Antiquity and Medieval Italy*, Ann Arbor: 479–98.

Hopkins, M.K. 1964/5, 'The age of Roman girls at marriage' *Population Studies* 18: 309–27.

Horsfall, N. 1983, 'Some problems in the "Laudatio Turiae"' *BICS* 30: 85–98.

James, S.L. 2003, *Learned Girls and Male Persuasion: Gender and Reading in Roman Love Elegy*, Berkeley.

Joshel, S.R. & Murnaghan, S. (eds) 1998, *Women and Slaves in Greco-Roman Culture: Differential Equations*, London.

Keith, A.M. 2000, *Engendering Rome. Women in Latin Epic*, Cambridge.

Kertzer, D.I. & Saller, R.P. 1991, *The Family in Italy from Antiquity to the Present*, New Haven.

La Follette, L. 1994, 'The costume of the Roman bride' in Sebesta, J.L. & Bonfante, L. (eds) *The World of Roman Costume*, Wisconsin: 54–64.

Lacey, W.K. 1986, 'Patria Potestas' in Rawson, B. (ed.) *The Family in Ancient Rome. New Perspectives*, London: 121–44.

Larsson Lovén, L. & Strömberg, A. (eds) 1998, *Aspects of Women in Antiquity*, Jonsered.

Leach, E.W. 2001, 'Gendering Clodius' *CW* 94: 335–59.

Lefkowitz, M.R. & Fant, M.B. 1992, *Women's Life in Greece and Rome*, second edition, Baltimore.

Lenaghan, J.O. 1969, *A Commentary on Cicero's Oration De Haruspicum Responso*, Hague.

Lilja, S. 1982, 'Homosexuality in Plautus' plays' *Arctos* 16: 57–64.

Linderski, J. 1986, 'Religious aspects of the Conflict of the Orders: the case of *confarreatio*' in Raaflaub, K.A. (ed.) *Social Struggles in Archaic Rome: New Perspectives on the Conflict of the Orders*, Berkeley: 244–61.

Lowe, N.J. 1988, 'Sulpicia's syntax' *CQ* 38: 193–205.

MacMullen, R. 1980, 'Roman elite motivation: three questions' *P&P* 88: 3–16.

MacMullen, R. 1982, 'Roman attitudes to Greek love' *Historia* 31: 484–502.

MacMullen, R. 1991, 'Hellenizing the Romans (2nd Century BC)' *Historia* 40: 419–38.

Marchetti, S.C. 2004, '"I could not love Caesar more": Roman friendship and the beginning of the principate' *CJ* 99: 281–99.

Martin, D. 1996, 'The construction of the ancient family: methodological considerations' *JRS* 86: 40–60.

McDonnell, M. 1983, 'Divorce initiated by women in Rome' *AJAH* 8: 54–80.

McDonnell, M. 1987, 'The speech of Numidicus at Gellius *N.A.* 1.6' *AJPh* 108: 81–94.

McDougall, J.I. 1992, 'Cassius Ravilla and the trial of the Vestals' *AHB* 6: 10–17.

McGinn, T.A.J. 1998, *Prostitution, Sexuality and the Law in Ancient Rome*, Oxford.

Moore, T.J. 1993, 'Morality, history, and Livy's wronged women' *Eranos* 91: 38–46.

Mulroy, D. 1988, 'The early career of P. Clodius Pulcher: a re-examination of the charges of mutiny and sacrilege' *TAPhA* 118: 155–78.

North, J.A. 2000, *Roman Religion*, Oxford.

Ogilvie, R.M. 1969, *The Romans and their Gods*, London.

Ogilvie, R.M. 1970, *A Commentary on Livy Books 1–5*, revised edition, Oxford.

Palmer, R.E.A. 1974: 'Roman shrines of female chastity from the caste struggle to the Papacy of Innocent I' *RSA* 4: 113–59.

Palmer, R.E.A. 1997, *Rome and Carthage at Peace*, Stuttgart.

Papanghelis, T.D. 1991, 'Catullus and Callimachus on large women (a reconsideration of c. 86)' *Mnemosyne* 44: 372–86.

Parker, H.N. 1994, 'Sulpicia, the *Auctor de Sulpicia*, and the authorship of 3.9 and 3.11 of the *Corpus Tibullianum*' *Helios* 21.1: 39–62.

Parker, H.N. 1997, 'The teratogenic grid' in Hallett, J.P. & Skinner, M.B. (eds) *Roman Sexualities*, Princeton: 47–65.

Parker, H. 1998, 'Loyal slaves and loyal wives; the crisis of the outsider-within and Roman *exemplum* literature' in Joshel, S.R. & Murnaghan, S. (eds) *Women and Slaves in Greco-Roman Culture*, London: 152–73.

Parkin, T. 1992, *Demography and Roman Society*, Baltimore.

Parkin, T. 1997, 'Out of sight, out of mind: elderly members of the Roman family' in Rawson, B. & Weaver, P. (eds) *The Roman Family in Italy, Status, Sentiment, Space*, Canberra.

Plant, I.M. 2004, *Women Writers of Ancient Greece and Rome. An Anthology*, London.

Pomeroy, S.B. 1973, 'Selected bibliography on women in antiquity' *Arethusa* 6: 125–57.

Pomeroy, S.B. 1975, *Goddesses, Whores, Wives, and Slaves. Women in Classical Antiquity*, London.

Pomeroy, S.B. 1976, 'The relationship of the married woman to her blood relatives in Rome' *AncSoc* 7: 215–27.

Ramage, E.S. 1994, 'The so-called Laudatio Turiae as panegyric' *Athenaeum* 82: 341–70.

Rawson, B. 1974, 'Roman concubinage and other *de facto* marriages' *TAPhA* 104: 279–305.

Rawson, B. (ed.) 1986, *The Family in Ancient Rome. New Perspectives*, London.

Rawson B. 1986a, 'The Roman family' in Rawson, B. (ed.) *The Family in Ancient Rome. New Perspectives*, London: 1–57.

Rawson, B. (ed.) 1991, *Marriage, Divorce and Children in Ancient Rome*, Oxford.

Rawson, B. 2003, *Children and Childhood in Roman Italy*, Oxford.

Rawson, B. & Weaver, P. (eds) 1997, *The Roman Family in Italy. Status, Sentiment, Space*, Canberra.

Rei, A. 1998, 'Villains, wives and slaves in the comedies of Plautus' in Joshel, S.R. & Murnaghan, S. (eds) *Women and Slaves in Greco-Roman Culture*, London: 92–108.

Richlin, A. (ed.) 1992, *Pornography and Representation in Greece and Rome*, Oxford.

Richlin, A. 1992a, *The Garden of Priapus; Sexuality and Aggression in Roman Humor*, revised edition, New York.

Richlin, A. 1993, 'Not before homosexuality: the materiality of the *cinaedus* and the Roman law against love between men' *Journal of the History of Sexuality* 3.4: 523–73.

Riddle, J.M. 1992, *Contraception and Abortion from the Ancient World to the Renaissance*, Cambridge MA.

Rouselle, A. 1988, *Porneia: On Desire and the Body in Antiquity*, Oxford.

Rudd, N. 1986, *Themes in Roman Satire*, London.

Ruggini, L.C. 1989, 'Juridical status and historical role of women in Roman patriarchal society' *Klio* 71: 604–19.

Russell, B.F. 2003, 'Wine, women, and the polis: gender and the formation of the city-state in archaic Rome' *G&R* 50: 77–84.

Saller, R.P. 1984, '*Familia, domus* and the Roman concept of the family' *Phoenix* 38: 336–55.

Saller, R.P. 1986, '*Patria potestas* and the stereotype of the Roman family' *Continuity and Change* 1: 7–22.

Saller, R.P. 1987, 'Men's age at marriage and its consequences in the Roman family' *CPh* 82: 21–34.

Saller, R.P. 1991, 'Corporal punishment, authority and obedience in the Roman household' in Rawson, B. (ed.) *Marriage, Divorce and Children in Ancient Rome*, Oxford: 144–65.

Saller, R.P. 1991a, 'Roman heirship strategies in principle and in practice' in Kertzer, D.I. & Saller, R.P. (eds) *The Family in Italy from Antiquity to the Present*, New Haven: 26–47.

Saller, R.P. 1994, *Patriarchy, Property and Death in the Roman Family*, Cambridge.

Saller, R.P. 1998, 'Symbols of gender and status hierarchies in the Roman household' in Joshel, S.R. & Murnaghan, S. (eds) *Women and Slaves in Greco-Roman Culture. Differential Equations*, London: 85–91.

Saller, R.P. 1999, 'Pater familias, mater familias and the gendered semantics of the Roman household' *CPh* 94: 182–97.

Salway, B. 1994, 'What's in a name? A survey of Roman onomastic practice from c. 700 BC to AD 700' *JRS* 84: 124–45.

Santirocco, M. 1979, 'Sulpicia reconsidered' *CJ* 74: 229–39.

Scafuro, A. 1989, 'Livy's comic narrative of the Bacchanalia' *Helios* 16.2: 119–42.

Scheid, J. 1992, 'The religious roles of Roman women' in Schmitt Pantel, P. (ed.) *A History of Women: Vol. I, From Ancient Goddesses to Christian Saints*, Cambridge MA: 377 408.

Scheidel, W. 1995, 'The most silent women of Greece and Rome: rural labour and women's life in the ancient world (I)' *G&R* 42: 202–17.

Scheidel, W. 1996, 'The most silent women of Greece and Rome: rural labour and women's life in the ancient world (II)' *G&R* 43: 1–10.

Scott, R.T. 1993, 'Atrium vestae' in Steinby I.138–42.

Scullard, H.H. 1981, *Festivals and Ceremonies of the Roman Republic*, London.

Sebesta, J.L. 1994, 'Symbolism in the costume of the Roman woman' in Sebesta, J.L. & Bonfante, L. (eds) *The World of Roman Costume*, Wisconsin: 46–53.

Shaw, B.D. 1987, 'The age of Roman girls at marriage: some reconsiderations' *JRS* 77: 30–46.

Shaw, B.D. 2001, 'Raising and killing children: two Roman myths' *Mnemosyne* 54: 33–77.

Shaw, B.D. & Saller, R.P. 1984, 'Close-kin marriage in Roman society' *Man* 19: 432–44.

Skinner, M.B. 1983, 'Clodia Metelli' *TaPhA* 113: 273–87.

Smethurst, S.E. 1950, 'Women in Livy's history' *G&R* 19: 80–87.

Snyder, J.M. 1989, *The Woman and the Lyre: Women Writers in Classical Greece and Rome*, Carbondale.

Staples, A. 1998, *From Good Goddess to Vestal Virgin. Sex and Category in Roman Religion*, London.

Starr, C. G. 1980, *The Beginnings of Imperial Rome: Rome in the Mid-Republic*, Ann Arbor.

Stehle, E. 1989, 'Venus, Cybele, and the Sabine women: the Roman construction of female sexuality' *Helios* 16: 143–64.

Stone, S. 1994, 'The toga: from national to ceremonial costume' in Sebesta, J.L. & Bonfante, L. (eds) *The World of Roman Costume*, Wisconsin: 13–45.

Sullivan, J.P. 1984, 'The roots of anti-feminism in Greece and Rome' *Helix* 19/20: 71–84.

Tatum, W.J. 1990, 'Cicero and the *Bona Dea* scandal' *CPh* 85: 202–8.

Tatum, W.J. 1999, *The Patrician Tribune. Publius Clodius Pulcher*, Chapel Hill.

Thomsen, O. 2002, 'An introduction to the study of Catullus' wedding poems: the ritual drama of *Catullus 62*' *C&M* 53: 255–88.

Treggiari, S. 1976, 'Jobs for women' *AJAH* 1: 76–104.

Treggiari, S. 1991, *Roman Marriage. Iusti Coniuges from the time of Cicero to the Time of Ulpian*, Oxford.

Treggiari, S. 1991a, 'Ideals and practicalities in matchmaking in ancient Rome' in Kertzer, D.I. & Saller, R.P. (eds) *The Family in Italy from Antiquity to the Present*, New Haven: 91–108.

Treggiari, S. 1991b, 'Divorce Roman style: how easy and how frequent was it?' in Rawson, B. (ed.) *Marriage, Divorce and Children in Ancient Rome*, Oxford: 7–30.

Treggiari, S. 1994, 'Putting the bride to bed' *EMC/CV* 13: 311–31.

Treggiari, S. 1996, 'Women in Roman society' in Kleiner, D.E.E. & Matheson, S.B. (eds) *I Claudia, Women in Ancient Rome*, New Haven: 116–25.

Treggiari, S. 1999, 'The upper-class house as a symbol and focus of emotion in Cicero' *JRA* 12: 33–56.

Treggiari, S. 2002, *Roman Social History*, London.

Turcan, R. 2000, *The Gods of Ancient Rome*, Edinburgh.

Vanggaard, J.H. 1988, *The Flamen*, Copenhagen.

Verboven, K. 2001, 'A note on the Oppii from Velia and Cicero's divorce' *Latomus* 60: 314–20.

Versnel, H.S. 1992, 'The festival for Bona Dea and the Thesmophoria' *G&R* 39: 31–55.

Versnel, H.S. 1993, *Inconsistencies in Greek and Roman Religion II. Transition and Reversal in Myth and Ritual*, Leiden.

Wallace-Hadrill, A. 1996, 'Engendering the Roman house' in Kleiner, D.E.E. & Matheson, S.B. (eds) *I Claudia, Women in Ancient Rome*, New Haven: 104–15.

Watson, A. 1967, *The Law of Persons in the Later Roman Republic*, Oxford.

Watson, A. 1971, *Roman Private Law around 200 BC*, Edinburgh.

Watson, A. 1975, *Rome of the XII Tables*, Princeton.

Watts, W.J. 1973, 'Ovid, the law and Roman society on abortion' *ActClass* 16: 89–101.

Wildfang, R.L. 2001, 'The Vestals and annual public rites' *CM* 52: 223–55.

Williams, C.A. 1999, *Roman Homosexuality. Ideologies of Masculinity in Classical Antiquity*, Oxford.

Williams, G. 1958, 'Some aspects of Roman marriage ceremonies and ideals' *JRS* 48: 16–29.

Wiseman, T.P. 1974, *Cinna the Poet and other Essays*, New York: 159–69.

Wiseman, T.P. 1985, *Catullus and his World: a Reappraisal*, Cambridge.

Wiseman, T.P. 1995, 'The god of the Lupercal' *JRS* 85: 1–22.

Wistrand, E. 1976, *The So-called Laudatio Turiae*, Göteborg.

Wray, D. 2001, *Catullus and the Poetics of Roman Manhood*, Cambridge.

Wyke, M. 1994, 'Woman in the mirror: the rhetoric of adornment in the Roman world' in Archer, L.J. & Fischler, S. (eds) *Women in Ancient Societies. An Illusion of the Night*, London.

Ziolkowski, A. 1998/9, 'Ritual cleaning-up of the city: from the Lupercalia to the Argei' *AncSoc* 29: 191–218.

Chapter Eight: Tiberius and Gaius Gracchus

Adshead, K. 1981, 'Further inspiration for Tiberius Gracchus?' *Antichthon* 15: 118–28.

Astin, A.E. 1967, *Scipio Aemilianus*, Oxford.

Badian, E. 1964, 'The Lex Thoria: a reconsideration' in Badian, E. (ed.) *Studies in Greek and Roman History*, Oxford: 235–42.

Badian, E. 1969, 'From the Gracchi to Sulla (1940–1959)' in Seager 1969: 3–51 = 1962, *Historia* 11: 197–245.

Badian, E. 1972, 'Tiberius Gracchus and the beginning of the Roman Revolution' *ANRW* I.1: 668–731.

Badian, E. 1972a, *Publicans and Sinners. Private Enterprise in the Service of the Roman Republic*, Oxford.

Balsdon, J.P.V.D. 1969, 'The history of the extortion court at Rome, 123–70 BC' in Seager 1969: 132–48 = 1938, *PBSR* 14: 98–114.

Bauman, R.A. 1992, *Women and Politics in Ancient Rome*, London.

Bell, A.J. 1997, 'Cicero and the spectacle of power' *JRS* 87: 1–22.

Bernstein, A.H. 1978, *Tiberius Sempronius Gracchus: Tradition and Apostasy*, Ithaca.

Boren, H.C. 1958, 'Numismatic light on the Gracchan crisis' *AJPh* 79: 14–55.

Boren, H.C. 1961, 'Tiberius Gracchus: the opposition view' *AJPh* 82: 140–55.

Boren, H.C. 1968, *The Gracchi*, New York.

Boren, H.C. 1969, 'The urban side of the Gracchan economic crisis' in Seager, R. (ed.) *The Crisis of the Roman Republic*, Cambridge: 54–68 = 1957/8, *AHR* 6: 890–902.

Briscoe, J. 1974, 'Supporters and opponents of Tiberius Gracchus' *JRS* 64: 125–35.

Brunt, P.A. 1965, 'Review of Earl 1963' *Gnomon* 37: 189–92.

Brunt, P.A. 1971, *Social Conflicts in the Roman Republic*, London.

Brunt, P.A. 1988, 'The army and the land in the Roman Revolution' in Brunt, P.A. *The Fall of the Roman Republic and Related Essays*, Oxford: 240–75; revision of 1962, *JRS* 52: 69–86.

Brunt, P.A. 1988a, 'The equites in the Late Republic' in Brunt, P.A. *The Fall of the Roman Republic and Related Essays*, Oxford: 144–93, revision of 1962, *Trade and Politics in the Ancient World* 1: 117–49 = in Seager 1969: 83–115.

Cornell, T.J. 1995, *The Beginnings of Rome. Italy and Rome from the Bronze Age to the Punic Wars (c. 1000–264 BC)*, London.

Cowell, F.R. 1962, *The Revolutions of Ancient Rome*, London.

Earl, D.C. 1963, *Tiberius Gracchus: A Study in Politics*, Brussels.

Evans, J.K. 1980, '*Plebs rustica*. The peasantry of classical Italy' *AJAH* 5: 19–47, 134–73.

Gargola, D.J. 1995, *Lands, Laws and Gods: Magistrates and Ceremony in the Regulation of Public Lands in Republican Rome*, North Carolina.

Garnsey, P. & Rathbone, D. 1985, 'The background to the grain law of Gaius Gracchus' *JRS* 1985: 20–4.

Gruen, E.S. 1965, 'The political allegiance of P. Mucius Scaevola' *Athenaeum* 43: 321–32.

Gruen, E.S. 1968, *Roman Politics and the Criminal Courts, 149–78 BC*, Cambridge MA.

Hall, U. 1977, 'Notes on M. Fulvius Flaccus' *Athenaeum* 55: 280–8.

Hardy E.G. 1911, *Roman Laws and Charters*, Oxford.

Harris, W.V. 1971, *Rome in Etruria and Umbria*, Oxford.

Hemelrijk, E.A. 1999, *Matrona Docta: Educated Women in the Roman Elite from Cornelia to Julia Domna*, London.

Henderson, M.I. 1951, 'The process "de repetundis"' *JRS* 1951: 71–88.

Henderson, M.I. 1969, 'The establishment of the *equester ordo*' in Seager 1969: 69–80 = 1963, *JRS* 53: 61–72.

Hill, H. 1952, *The Roman Middle Class in the Republican Period*, Oxford.

Hopkins, K. 1978, *Conquerors and Slaves*, Cambridge.

Horsfall, N. 1987, 'The "letter of Cornelia": yet more problems' *Athenaeum* 65: 231–4.

Keaveney, A. 2003, 'The tragedy of Caius Gracchus: ancient melodrama or modern farce?' *Klio* 85: 22–332.

Kyle, D.G. 1998, *Spectacles of Death in Ancient Rome*, London.

Linderski, J. 2002, 'The pontiff and the tribune: the death of Tiberius Gracchus' *Athenaeum* 80: 339–66.

Lintott, A.W. 1972, 'Provocatio. From the Struggle of the Orders to the Principate' *ANRW* I.2: 226–67.

Lintott, A.W. 1981, 'The *leges de repetundis* and associate measures under the Republic' *ZSS* 98: 162–212.

Lintott, A.W. 1992, *Judicial Reform and Land Reform in the Roman Republic*, Cambridge.

Lintott, A.W. 1999, *Violence in Republican Rome*, second edition, Oxford.

Lintott, A.W. 1994, 'Political History, 146–95 BC' in *CAH* IX²: 40–77.

Marsh, F.B. 1963, *A History of the Roman World from 146 to 30 BC*, third edition, London.

Mattingly, H.B. 1969, 'The two republican laws of the tabula Bembina' *JRS* 59: 129–43.

Mattingly, H.B. 1970, 'The extortion law of the tabula Bembina' *JRS* 60: 154–68.

Mattingly, H.B. 1987, 'A new look at the lex repetundarum Bembina' *Philologus* 131: 71–81.

Morley, N. 2001, 'The transformation of Italy, 225–28 BC' *JRS* 91: 50–62.

Nagle, D.B. 1970, 'The failure of the Roman political process in 133 BC, Part I' *Athenaeum* 48: 372–94.

Nagle, D.B. 1971, 'The failure of the Roman political process in 133 BC, Part II' *Athenaeum* 49: 111–28.

Nagle, D.B. 1976, 'The Etruscan journey of Tiberius Gracchus' *Historia* 25: 487–89.

Nippel, W. 1984, 'Policing Rome' *JRS* 74: 20–9.

Plant, I.M. 2004, *Women Writers of Ancient Greece and Rome. An Anthology*, London.

Rathbone, D.W. 1981, 'The development of agriculture in the "ager Cosanus" during the Roman Republic: problems of evidence and interpretation' *JRS* 71: 11–23.

Rawson, E. 1991, 'Religion and politics in the late second century BC at Rome' in Rawson, E. *Roman Culture and Society*, Oxford: 149–68 = 1974, *Phoenix* 28: 193–212.

Rich, J.W. 1983, 'The supposed Roman manpower shortage of the later second century BC' *Historia* 32: 287–331.

Richardson, J.S. 1980, 'The ownership of Roman land: Tiberius Gracchus and the Italians' *JRS* 70: 1–11.

Riddle, J.M. 1970, *Tiberius Gracchus. Destroyer or Reformer of the Republic?*, Lexington, MA.

Scullard, H.H. 1960, 'Scipio Aemilianus and Roman politics' *JRS* 50: 59–74.

Seager, R. (ed.) 1969, *The Crisis of the Roman Republic*, Cambridge.

Sherwin-White, A.N. 1952, 'The extortion procedure again' *JRS* 42: 43–55.

Sherwin-White, A.N. 1972, 'The date of the lex repetundarum and its consequences' *JRS* 62: 83–99.

Sherwin-White, A.N. 1973, *The Roman Citizenship*, second edition, Oxford.

Sherwin-White, A.N. 1982, 'The lex repetundarum and the political ideas of Gaius Gracchus' *JRS* 72: 18–31.

Shochat, Y. 1980, *Recruitment and the Programme of Tiberius Gracchus*, Brussels.

Shotter, D. 1994, *The Fall of the Roman Republic*, London.

Smith, R.E. 1955, *The Failure of the Roman Republic*, Cambridge.

Stockton, D. 1979, *The Gracchi*, Oxford.

Taylor, L.R. 1962: 'The forerunners of the Gracchi' *JRS* 52: 19–27.

White, K.D. 1967, 'Latifundia. A critical review of the evidence on large estates in Italy and Sicily up to the end of the first century AD' *BICS* 14: 62–79.

Williams, P. 2004, 'The Roman tribunate in the 'Era of Quiescence' 287–133 BC' *Latomus* 63: 281–94.

Chapters Nine & Ten: Marius, and the Social War

Astin, A.E. 1967, *Scipio Aemilianus*, Oxford.

Badian, E. 1963/4, 'Marius and the nobles' *Durham University Journal* 25: 141–54.

Badian, E. 1964, 'Mam. Scaurus cites precedent' in Badian, E. (ed.) *Studies in Greek and Roman History*, Oxford: 105–111 = 1958, *CR*: 216–20.

Badian, E. 1964a, 'Caepio and Norbanus. Notes on the decade 100–90 BC' in *Studies in Greek and Roman History*, Oxford: 34–70 = 1957, *Historia* 6: 318–46.

Badian, E. 1969, 'From the Gracchi to Sulla (1940–1959)' in Seager 1969: 3–51 = 1962, *Historia* 11: 197–245.

Badian, E. 1969a, 'Quaestiones variae' *Historia* 18: 447–91.

Badian, E. 1970/1, 'Roman politics and the Italians' *DDA* IV–V: 373–409.

Badian, E. 1972, *Publicans and Sinners. Private Enterprise in the Service of the Roman Republic*, Oxford.

Badian, E. 1984, 'The death of Saturninus. Studies in chronology and prosopography' *Chiron* 14: 101–47.

Bell, M.J.V. 1965, 'Tactical reform in the Roman Republican army' *Historia* 14: 404–22.

Bishop, M.C. & Coulston, J.C. 1993, *Roman Military Equipment*, London.

Brunt, P.A. 1971, *Social Conflicts in the Roman Republic*, London.

Brunt, P.A. 1982, 'The legal issue in Cicero *pro Balbo*' *CQ* 32: 136–47.

Brunt, P.A. 1988, *The Fall of the Roman Republic and Related Essays*, Oxford

Brunt, P.A. 1988a, 'Italian aims at the time of the Social War' in Brunt 1988: 93–143; revision of 1965, *JRS* 55: 90–109.

Brunt, P.A. 1988b, 'The equites in the Late Republic' in Brunt 1988: 144–93; revision of 1962, *Trade and Politics in the Ancient World* 1: 117–49 = Seager 1969: 83–115.

Brunt, P.A. 1988c, 'Judiciary rights in the Republic' in Brunt 1988: 194–239.

Brunt, P.A. 1988d, 'The army and the land in the Roman Revolution' in Brunt 1988: 240–80; revision of 1962, *JRS* 52: 69–86.

Burns, T. S. 2003, *Rome and the Barbarians, 100 BC–AD 400*, Baltimore.

Cagniart, P.F. 1989, 'L. Cornelius Sulla's quarrel with C. Marius at the time of the Germaic invasions' *Athenaeum* 67: 139–49.

Carney, T.F. 1960, 'Cicero's picture of Marius' *WS* 73: 83–122.

Carney, T.F. 1961, *A Biography of C. Marius*, Assen.

Carney, T.F. 1961a, 'The flight and exile of Marius' *G&R* 8: 98–121.

Dench, E. 1995, *From Barbarians to New Men*, Oxford.

Dusanic, S. & Petkovic, Z. 2003, 'The five standards of the pre-Marian legion. A note on the early plebeian *militaria*' *Klio* 85: 42–56.

Evans, R.J. 1994, *Gaius Marius. A Political Biography*, Pretoria.

Everitt, A. 2001, *Cicero. A Turbulent Life*, London.

Fantham, E. 1987, 'Lucan, his scholia, and the victims of Marius' *AHB* 1: 89–96.

Gabba, E. 1976, *Republican Rome, the Army and the Allies*, Oxford.

Gabba, E. 1994, 'Rome and Italy: the Social War' in *CAH* IX[2]: 104–28.

Gelzer, M. 1969, *The Roman Nobility*, Oxford.

Gilliver, C.M. 1999, *The Roman Art of War*, Stroud.

Goldsworthy, A.K. 1996, *The Roman Army at War, 100 BC – AD 200*, Oxford.

Goldsworthy, A.K. 2000, *Roman Warfare*, London.

Griffin, M.T. 1973, 'The "leges iudiciariae" of the pre-Sullan era' *CQ* 23: 108–26.

Gruen, E.S. 1968, *Roman Politics and the Criminal Courts, 149–78 BC*, Cambridge MA.

Hands, A.R. 1972, 'Livius Drusus and the courts' *Phoenix* 26: 268–74.

Hanson, V.D. 1995, 'The Roman way of war, 250 BC–AD 300' in Parker, G. (ed.) *The Cambridge Illustrated History of Warfare. The Triumph of the West*, Cambridge: 50–61.

Harris, W.V. 1971, *Rome in Etruria and Umbria*, Oxford.

Hill, H. 1952, *The Roman Middle Class in the Republican Period*, Oxford.

Kallet-Marx, R. 1990, 'The trial of Rutilius Rufus' *Phoenix* 44: 122–39.

Katz, B.R. 1976, 'The siege of Rome in 87 BC' *CPh* 71: 328–36.

Keaveney, A. 1979, 'Sulla, Sulpicius and Caesar Strabo' *Latomus* 38: 451–60.

Keaveney, A. 1982, *Sulla: the Last Republican*, London.

Keaveney, A. 1982a, 'Sulla augur. Coins and the curiate law' *AJAH* 7: 150–71.

Keaveney, A. 1983, 'What happened in 88?' *Eirene* 20: 53–86.

Keaveney, A. 1987, *Rome and the Unification of Italy*, London.

Keaveney, A. 1992, *Lucullus. A Life*, London.

Keaveney, A. 1992a, *Rome and the Unification of Italy*, London.

Keppie, L. 1984, *The Making of the Roman Army*, London.

Last, H. & Gardner, R. 1932, 'The enfranchisement of Italy' in *CAH* IX[1]: 158–210.

Last, H. 1932, 'The wars of the age of Marius' in *CAH* IX[1]: 102–57.

Lewis, R.G. 1968, 'Appian *BC* I.49, 124: dekateuontes: Rome's new tribes 90–87 BC' *Athenaeum* 46: 273–91.

Lewis, R.G. 1971, 'A problem in the siege of Praeneste, 82 BC' *PBSR* 39: 32–9.

Lintott, A.W. 1971,'The tribunate of P. Sulpicius Rufus' *CQ* 21: 442–53.

Lintott, A.W. 1994, 'The Roman empire and its problems in the late second century' in *CAH* IX²: 16–39.

Lintott, A.W. 1994a, 'Political history, 146–95 BC' in *CAH* IX²: 40–103.

Luce, T.J. 1970, 'Marius and the Mithridatic command' *Historia* 19: 161–94.

Mackay, C.S. 2000, 'Sulla and the monuments: studies in his public persona' *Historia* 49: 161–210.

Magie, D. 1950, *Roman Rule in Asia Minor*, vols I–II, Princeton.

Marshall, A.J. 1968, 'Friends of the Roman people' *AJPh* 87: 39–55.

Marshall, B. 1985, *A Historical Commentary on Asconius*, Columbia.

Mattingly, H.B. 1975, 'The consilium of Cn. Pompeius Strabo' *Athenaeum* 53: 262–6.

Mitchell, T.N. 1975, 'The volte-face of P. Sulpicius Rufus in 88 BC' *CPh* 70: 197–204.

Mouritsen, H. 1998, *Italian Unification. A Study in Ancient and Modern Historiography*, London.

Münzer, F. 1999, *Roman Aristocratic Parties and Families*, Baltimore.

Nagle, D.B. 1973, 'An allied view of the Social War' *AJA* 77: 367–78.

Parker, H.M.D. 1958, *The Roman Legions*, second edition, Oxford.

Paul, G.M. 1984, *A Historical Commentary on Sallust's Bellum Jugurthinum*, Wiltshire.

Raven, S. 1993, *Rome in Africa*, third edition, London.

Rawson, B. 1978, *The Politics of Friendship: Pompey and Cicero*, Sydney.

Salmon, E.T. 1958, 'Notes on the Social War' *TAPhA* 87: 159–84.

Salmon, E.T. 1962, 'The cause of the Social War' *Phoenix* 16: 107–19.

Salmon, E.T. 1964, 'Sulla redux' *Athenaeum* 42: 60–79.

Salmon, E.T. 1967, *Samnium and the Samnites*, Cambridge.

Seager, R. (ed.) 1969, *The Crisis of the Roman Republic. Studies in Political and Social History*, Cambridge.

Seager, R. 2002, *Pompey the Great*, Oxford.

Sherwin-White, A.N. 1969, 'Violence in Roman Politics' in Seager 1969: 151–9 = 1956, *JRS* 46: 1–9.

Sherwin-White, A.N. 1973, *The Roman Citizenship*, second edition, Oxford.

Shotter, D. 1994, *The Fall of the Roman Republic*, London.

Smith, R.E. 1955, *The Failure of the Roman Republic*, Cambridge.

Sumner, G.V. 1976, 'Scaurus and the Mamilian Inquisition' *Phoenix* 30: 73–5.

Syme, R. 1964, *Sallust*, Berkeley.

Taylor, L.R. 1960, *The Voting Districts of the Roman Republic*, Rome.

Taylor, L.R. 1966, *Roman Voting Assemblies from the Hannibalic War to the Dictatorship of Caesar*, Ann Arbor.

Tyrrell, W.B. 1973, 'The trial of C. Rabirius in 63 BC' *Latomus* 32: 285–300.

Watson, G.R. 1987, 'The army of the Republic' in Wacher, J. (ed.) *The Roman World*, vol. I, London: 75–88.

Weinrib, E.J. 1970, 'The judiciary law of M. Livius Drusus (tr. pl. 91 BC)' *Historia* 19: 414–43.

Wiseman, T.P. 1971, *New Men in the Roman Senate 139 BC – AD 14*, Oxford.

Chapter Eleven: Lucius Cornelius Sulla 'Felix'

Badian, E. 1955, 'The date of Pompey's first triumph' *Hermes* 83: 107–18.

Badian, E. 1961, 'Servilius and Pompey's first triumph' *Hermes* 89: 254–6.

Badian, E. 1964, 'Waiting for Sulla' in Badian, E. (ed.) *Studies in Greek and Roman History*, Oxford: 206–34 = 1962, *JRS* 52: 47–61.

Badian, E. 1964a, 'Sulla's Cilician command' in Badian, E. (ed.) *Studies in Greek and Roman History*, Oxford: 157–78 = 1959, *Athenaeum* 37: 279–303.

Badian, E. 1969, 'From the Gracchi to Sulla' in Seager 1969: 34–39 = 1962, *Historia* 11: 197–245.

Badian, E. 1970, 'Additional notes on Roman magistrates' *Athenaeum* 48: 3–14.

Badian, E. 1972, *Publicans and Sinners. Private Enterprise in the Service of the Roman Republic*, Oxford.

Badian, E. 1976, *Lucius Sulla: the Deadly Reformer* in Dunstan, A.J. (ed.) *Essays on Roman Culture. The Todd Memorial Lectures*, Toronto: 35–74 = 1970, *Lucius Sulla: the Deadly Reformer*, Sydney.

Baker, G.P. 1967, *Sulla the Fortunate, the Great Dictator*, Rome.

Balsdon, J.P.V.D. 1951, 'Sulla Felix' *JRS* 41: 1–10.

Balsdon, J.P.V.D. 1965, 'Review of Badian, E. *Studies in Greek and Roman History*, Oxford' *JRS* 55: 229–32.

Bennet, H. 1923, *Cinna and his Times*, Menasha.

Brennan, T.C. 1992, 'Sulla's career in the nineties: some reconsiderations' *Chiron* 22: 103–58.

Brunt, P.A. 1971, *Social Conflicts in the Roman Republic*, London.

Brunt, P.A. 1990, 'Sulla and the Asian publicans' in Brunt, P.A. (ed.) *Roman Imperial Themes*, Oxford: 1–8 = 1956, *Latomus* 19: 17–25.

Bulst, S. 1964, '"*Cinnanum Tempus*": a reassessment of the "*Dominatio Cinnae*"' *Historia* 13: 307–37.

Carney, T.F. 1961, *A Biography of C. Marius*, Assen.

Cloud, D. 1994, 'The constitution and public criminal law' in *CAH* IX^2: 491–530.

Crawford, M.H. 1964, 'The coinage of the age of Sulla' *NC* 4: 141–58.

Dowling, M.B. 2000, 'The clemency of Sulla' *Historia* 49: 303–40.

Evans, R.J. 1994, *Gaius Marius. A Political Biography*, Pretoria.

Frier, B.W. 1971, 'Sulla's propaganda: the collapse of the Cinnan Republic' *AJPh* 92: 585–604.

Gabba, E. 1976, *Republican Rome, the Army and the Allies*, Oxford.

Garton, C. 1964, 'Sulla and the theatre' *Phoenix* 18: 137–56.

Greenhalgh, P. 1980, *Pompey. The Roman Alexander*, London.

Gruen, E.S. 1968, *Roman Politics and the Criminal Courts, 149–78 BC*, Cambridge MA.

Hill, H. 1932, 'Sulla's new senators in 81 BC' *CQ* 26: 170–7.

Hillard, T.W. 1991, 'Sulla's early fortunes and his reputation' *Antichthon* 25: 63–71.

Hillard, T. 1996, 'Death by lightning, Pompeius Strabo and the people' *RhM* 139: 135–45.

Hillman, T.P. 1996, 'Cinna, Strabo's army, and Strabo's death in 87 BC' *AC* 45: 81–9.

Hillman, T.P. 1997, 'Pompeius in Africa and Sulla's order to demobilize (Plutarch, *Pompeius* 13, 1–4)' *Latomus* 56: 94–106.

Hind, J. 1994, 'Mithridates' in *CAH* IX^2: 129–64.

Jones, J.M. 1990, *A Dictionary of Ancient Roman Coins*, London.

Katz, B.R. 1975, 'The first fruits of Sulla's march' *AC* 44: 100–25.

Katz, B.R. 1976, 'Studies on the period of Cinna and Sulla' *AC* 45: 497–549.

Keaveney, A. 1982, *Sulla: the Last Republican*, London.

Keaveney, A. 1982a, 'Sulla augur. Coins and the curiate law' *AJAH* 7: 150–71.

Keaveney, A. 1982b, 'Sulla and Italy' *Critica Storica* 19: 499–544.

Keaveney, A. 1982c, 'Young Pompey: 106–79 BC' *AC* 51: 111–39.

Keaveney, A. 1983, 'Studies in the *dominatio Sullae*' *Klio* 65: 185–208.

Keaveney, A. 1983a, 'What happened in 88?' *Eirene* 20: 53–86.

Keaveney, A. 1983b, 'Sulla and the gods' in Deroux, C. (ed.) *Studies in Latin Literature and Roman History*, Brussels: 44–79.

Keaveney, A. 1984, 'Who were the Sullani?' *Klio* 66: 114–50.

Keaveney, A. 1992, *Lucullus. A Life*, London.

Keaveney, A. 1995, 'Sulla's Cilician command: the evidence of Apollinaris Sidonius' *Historia* 44: 29–36.

Keaveney, A. 2003, 'The short career of Q. Lucretius Afella' *Eranos* 101: 84–93.

Last, H. & Gardner, R. 1932, 'Sulla' in *CAH* IX[1]: 261–312.

Leach, J. 1978, *Pompey the Great*, London.

Levick, B.M. 1982, 'Sulla's march on Rome in 88 BC' *Historia* 31: 503–8.

Lintott, A.W. 1971, 'The offices of C. Flavius Fimbria in 86–5 BC' *Historia* 20: 696–701.

Lintott, A.W. 1976, 'Mithridatica' *Historia* 25: 489–91.

Lintott, A.W. 1999, *Violence in Republican Rome*, second edition, Oxford.

Lovano, M. 2002, *The Age of Cinna: Crucible of Late Republican Rome*, Stuttgart.

Mackay, C.S. 2000, 'Sulla and the monuments: studies in his public persona' *Historia* 49: 161–210.

Marshall, B. 1985, 'Catilina and the execution of M. Marius Gratidianus' *CQ* 35: 124–33.

McGing, B. 1986, *The Foreign Policy of Mithridates VI Eupator, King of Pontus*, Leiden.

McGushin, P. 1992, *Sallust, The Histories*, vols I–II, Oxford.

Meier, C. 1995, *Caesar*, London.

Munro, M. 1932, 'Review of Carcopino, J. 1931, *Sylla ou le monarque manquée*' *JRS* 22: 239–41.

Ramage, E.S. 1991, 'Sulla's propaganda' *Klio* 73: 93–121.

Rawson, E. 1991, 'L. Cornelius Sisenna and the early first century BC' in Rawson, E. *Roman Culture and Society*, Oxford: 363–88 = 1979, *CQ* 29: 327–46.

Reams, L.E. 1984, 'Sulla's alleged early poverty and Roman rent' *AJAH* 9: 158–74.

Ridley, R.T. 2000, 'The dictator's mistake: Caesar's escape from Sulla' *Historia* 49: 211–29.

Rives, J. 2003, 'Magic in Roman law' *ClAnt* 22: 313–39.

Rostovtzeff, M. 1932, 'Pontus and its neighbours: the First Mithridatic War' in *CAH* IX[1]: 211–60.

Seager, R. (ed.) 1969, *The Crisis of the Roman Republic*, Cambridge.

Seager, R. 1994, 'Sulla' in *CAH* IX[2]: 165–207.

Seager, R. 2002, *Pompey the Great. A Political Biography*, second edition, Oxford.

Sherwin-White, A.N. 1977, 'Ariobarzanes, Mithridates, and Sulla' *CQ* 27: 173–83.

Sherwin-White, A.N. 1977a, 'Roman involvement in Anatolia, 167–88 BC' *JRS* 67: 63–75.

Shotter, D. 1994, *The Fall of the Roman Republic*, London.

Smith, R.E. 1955, *The Failure of the Roman Republic*, Cambridge.

Stockton, D. 1966, 'Sulla, le monarque malgré lui' in Kagan, D. (ed.) *Problems in Ancient History. Vol. Two: The Roman World*, first edition, London: 259–66.

Sullivan, R.D. 1980, 'The dynasty of Cappadocia' *ANRW* II.7.2: 1125–68.

Sumi, G.S. 2002, 'Spectacles and Sulla's public image' *Historia* 51: 414–32.

Sumner, G.V. 1978, 'Sulla's career in the nineties' *CPh* 56: 395–6.

Syme, R. 1964, *Sallust*, Berkeley.

Twyman, B.L. 1976, 'The date of Sulla's abdication and the chronology of the first book of Appian's Civil Wars' *Athenaeum* 54: 271–95.

Twyman, B.L. 1979, 'The date of Pompeius Magnus' first triumph' in Deroux, C. (ed.) *Studies in Latin Literature and Roman History*, vol. I, Brussels: 175–208.

Chapters Twelve & Thirteen: The Collapse of the Republic & Civil War and Dictatorship

Adcock, F.E. 1966, *Marcus Crassus, Millionaire*, Cambridge.

Africa, T. 1978, 'The mask of the assassin: a psychohistorical study of Marcus Junius Brutus' *Journal of Interdisciplinary History* 8: 599–626.

Astin, A.E. 1968, *Politics and Policies in the Roman Republic*, Belfast.

Badian, E. 1965, 'M. Porcius Cato and the annexation and early administration of Cyprus' *JRS* 55: 110–21.

Badian, E. 1972, *Publicans and Sinners*, Oxford.

Badian, E. 1989, 'The *scribae* of the Roman Republic' *Klio* 71: 582–603.

Badian, E. 1990, 'The consuls, 179–49 BC' *Chiron* 20: 371–413.

Balsdon, J.P.V.D. 1957, 'Roman history: 58–56 BC: three Ciceronian problems' *JRS* 47: 15–20.

Balsdon, J.P.V.D. 1957a, 'The veracity of Caesar' *G&R* 4: 19 28.

Balsdon, J.P.V.D. 1958, 'The Ides of March' *Historia* 7: 80–94.

Balsdon, J.P.V.D. 1962, 'Roman history, 65–50 BC: five problems' *JRS* 52: 134–41.

Balsdon, J.P.V.D. 1966, 'Fabula Clodiana' *Historia* 15: 65–73.

Balsdon, J.P.V.D. 1967, *Julius Caesar. A Political Biography* (= *Julius Caesar and Rome)*, London.

Batstone, W. 1991, 'A narrative gestalt and the force of Caesar's style' *Mnemosyne* 44: 126–36.

Bauman, R.A. 1996, *Crime and Punishment in Ancient Rome*, London.

Beard, M. 1994, 'Religion' in *CAH* IX^2: 729–68.

Bell, A.J. 1997, 'Cicero and the spectacle of power' *JRS* 87: 1–22.

Bellemore, J. 1996, 'The quaestorship of Cato and the tribunate of Memmius' *Historia* 45: 504–08.

Berg, B. 1997, 'Cicero's Palatine home and Clodius' shrine' in Deroux, C. (ed.) *Studies in Latin Literature and Roman History*, vol. VIII, Brussels: 122–43.

Bradford, E. 1971, *Cleopatra*, New York.

Bradford, E. 1984, *Julius Caesar. The Pursuit of Power*, London.

Brunt, P.A. 1971, *Social Conflicts in the Roman Republic*, London.

Brunt, P.A. 1980, 'Patronage and politics in the *Verrines*' *Chiron* 10: 273–89.

Brunt, P.A. 1982, 'The legal issue in Cicero, *pro Balbo*' *CQ* 32: 136–47.

Brunt, P.A. 1986, 'Cicero's *officium* in the Civil War' *JRS* 76: 12–32.

Brunt, P.A. 1988, 'The fall of the Roman Republic' in Brunt, P.A. *The Fall of the Roman Republic and Related Essays*, Oxford: 1–92.

Bucher, G.S. 1995, 'Appian *BC* 2.24 and the trial *de ambitu* of M. Aemilius Scaurus' *Historia* 44: 397–421.

Burns, A. 1966, 'Pompey's strategy and Domitius' stand at Corfinium' *Historia* 15: 74–95.

Burns, T.S. 2003, *Rome and the Barbarians, 100 BC–AD 400*, Baltimore.

Cagniart, P.F. 1995, 'Strategy and politics in Caesar's Spanish campaign, 49 BC: variation on a theme by Clausewitz' *AncW* 26: 29–44.

Cerutti, S.M. 1998, 'P. Clodius and the stairs of the temple of Castor' *Latomus* 57: 292–305.

Chauveau, M. 2002, *Cleopatra: Beyond the Myth*, Cornell.

Chrissanthos, S.G. 2001, 'Caesar and the mutiny of 47 BC' *JRS* 91: 63–75.

Clarke, M.L. 1981, *The Noblest Roman. Marcus Brutus and his Reputation*, London.

Collins, J.H. 1955, 'Caesar and the corruption of power' *Historia* 4: 445–65.

Collins, J.H. 1972, 'Caesar as political propagandist' *ANRW* I.1: 922–66.

Corbeill, A. 1996, *Controlling Laughter. Political Humour in the Late Roman Republic*, Princeton.

Cowell, F.R. 1962, *The Revolutions of Ancient Rome*, London.

Crawford, M.H. 1989, 'The lex Iulia Agraria' *Athenaeum* 67: 179–90.

Crook, J.A., Lintott, A. & Rawson, E. 1994, 'The fall of the Roman Republic' in *CAH* IX^2: 769–76.

Damon, C. 1992, 'Sex. Cloelius, *scriba*' *HSCPh* 94: 227–50.

Dando-Collins, S. 2002, *Caesar's Legion. The Epic Saga of Julius Caesar's Elite Tenth Legion and the Armies of Rome*, New York.

De Witt, N.J. 1942, 'The non-political nature of Caesar's commentaries' *TAPhA* 73: 341–52.

Drummond, A. 1999, 'Tribunes and tribunician programmes in 63 BC' *Athenaeum* 87: 121–67.

Drummond, A. 2000, 'Rullus and the Sullan possessores' *Klio* 82: 126–53.

Dyer, R.R. 1990, 'Rhetoric and intention in Cicero's *pro Marcello*' *JRS* 80: 17–30.

Ehrenberg, V. 1964, 'Caesar's final aims' *HSCPh* 68: 149–60.

Ehrhardt, C.T.H.R. 1995, 'Crossing the Rubicon' *Antichthon* 29: 30–41.

Epstein, D.F. 1986, 'Cicero's testimony at the *Bona Dea* trial' *CPh* 81: 229–35.

Everitt, A. 2001, *Cicero. A Turbulent Life*, London.

Fantham, E. 1975, 'The trials of Gabinius in 54 BC' *Historia* 24: 425–43.

Fordyce, C.J. 1961, *Catullus*, Oxford.

Frank, T. 1924, *Roman Buildings of the Republic*, Rome.

French, R. 1994, *Ancient Natural History. Histories of Nature*, London.

French, R. and Greenaway, F. (eds), 1996, *Science in the Early Roman Empire. Pliny the Elder, his Sources and his Influence*, London.

Fritz, K. von, 1941, 'The mission of L. Caesar and L. Roscius in January 49 BC' *TAPhA* 72: 125–56.

Fritz, K. von 1942, 'Pompey's policy before and after the outbreak of the civil war of 49 BC' *TAPhA* 73: 145–80.

Fuller, J.F.C. 1965, *Julius Caesar*, London.

Fuhrmann, M. 1992, *Cicero and the Roman Republic*, Oxford.

Gelzer, M. 1968, *Caesar. Politician and Statesman*, Oxford.

Glew, D.G. 1981, 'Between the wars: Mithridates Eupator and Rome, 85–73 BC' *Chiron* 11: 109–30.

Gradel, I. 2002, *Emperor Worship and Roman Religion*, Oxford.

Grant, M. 1972, *Cleopatra*, New York.

Greenhalgh, P. 1980, *Pompey. The Roman Alexander*, London.

Greenhalgh, P. 1981, *Pompey. The Republican Prince*, London.

Griffin, M. 1973, 'The tribune C. Cornelius' *JRS* 63: 196–213.

Gruen, E.S. 1966, 'P. Clodius: instrument or independent agent?' *Phoenix* 20: 120–30.

Gruen, E. 1969, 'Pompey, the Roman aristocracy, and the conference of Luca' *Historia* 18: 71–108.

Gruen, E.S. 1969a, 'Notes on the "First Catilinarian Conspiracy"' *CPh* 64: 20–4.

Gruen, E.S. 1969b, 'The consular elections for 53 BC' in Bibauw, J. (ed.) *Hommages à M. Renard*, vol. II, Brussels: 311–21.

Gruen, E.S. 1971, 'Pompey, Metellus Pius, and the trials of 70–69 BC: the perils of schematism' *AJPh* 92: 1–16.

Gruen, E.S. 1977, 'M. Licinius Crassus. A review article' *AJAH* 2: 117–28.

Gruen, E.S. 1995, *The Last Generation of the Roman Republic*, second edition, Berkeley.

Habicht, C. 1990, *Cicero the Politician*, Baltimore.

Harrison, S.J. 1997, 'The survival and supremacy of Rome: the unity of the shield of Aeneas' *JRS* 87: 70–6.

Hayne, L. 1972, 'M. Lepidus (cos. 78): a re-appraisal' *Historia* 21: 661–8.

Hickson-Hahn, F. 2000, 'Pompey's *supplicatio duplicata*: a novel form of thanksgiving' *Phoenix* 54: 244–54.

Hill, H. 1952, *The Roman Middle Class in the Republican Period*, Oxford.

Hillard, T.W. 1973, 'The sisters of Clodius again' *Latomus* 32: 505–14.

Hillman, T.P. 1990, 'Pompeius and the senate: 77–71' *Hermes* 118: 444–54.

Hillman, T.P. 1991, 'The alleged *inimicitiae* of Pompeius and Lucullus: 78–74' *CPh* 86: 315–8.

Hillman, T.P. 1996, 'Pompeius ad Parthos?' *Klio* 78: 380–99.

Hillman, T.P. 1998, 'Pompeius' imperium in the war with Lepidus' *Klio* 80: 91–110.

Hillman, T.P. 1998a, 'Notes on the trial of Pompeius at Plutarch, *Pomp.* 4.1–6' *RhM* 141: 176–93.

Holland, T. 2003, *Rubicon. The Triumph and Tragedy of the Roman Republic*, London.

Horsfall, N. 1974, 'The Ides of March: some new problems' *G&R* 21: 191–9.

Hoyos, D. 1979, 'Imperial Caesar?' *Ancient Society* 9: 134–57.

Huzar, E.G. 1978, *Mark Antony. A Biography*, Minneapolis.

Jackson, J. 1978, 'Cicero, *Fam.* 1.9.9, and the conference of Luca' *LCM* 3: 175–7.

Jameson, S. 1970, 'Pompey's imperium in 67: some constitutional fictions' *Historia* 19: 539–60.

Jameson, S. 1970a, 'The intended date of Caesar's return from Gaul' *Latomus* 29: 638–60.

Katz, B.R. 1977, 'Caesar Strabo's struggle for the consulship – and more' *RhM* 120: 45–65.

Keaveney, A. 1992, *Lucullus. A Life*, London.

Kelly, G.P. 2001, 'The attempted exile of L. Hostilius Tubulus' *Athenaeum* 89: 229–35.

Konrad, C.F. 1994, *Plutarch's Sertorius: A Historical Commentary*, Chapel Hill.

Konrad, C.F. 1995, 'A new chronology of the Sertorian War' *Athenaeum* 83: 157–87.

Kyle, D.G. 1998, *Spectacles of Death in Ancient Rome*, London.

Lacey, W.K. 1961, 'The tribunate of Curio' *Historia* 10: 318–29.

Lacey, W.K. 1974, 'Clodius and Cicero: a question of *dignitas*' *Antichthon* 8: 85–92.

Lacey, W.K. 1978, *Cicero and the End of the Roman Republic*, London.

Last, H. & Gardner, R. 1932, 'The breakdown of the Sullan system and the rise of Pompey' in *CAH* IX[1]: 313–49.

Lazenby, J.F. 1959, 'The conference of Luca and the Gallic War. A study in Roman politics 57–55 BC' *Latomus* 18: 67–76.

Leach, E.W. 2001, 'Gendering Clodius' *CW* 94: 335–59.

Leach, J. 1978, *Pompey the Great*, London.

Leigh, M. 1997, *Lucan. Spectacle and Engagement*, Oxford.

Levene, D.S. 2000, 'Sallust's Catiline and Cato the Censor' *CQ* 50: 170–91.

Lewis, R.G. 1988, 'Inscriptions of Amiternum and Catilina's last stand' *ZPE* 74: 31–42.

Linderski, J. 1972, 'The aedileship of Favonius, Curio the Younger and Cicero's election to the augurate' *HSCPh* 76: 181–200.

Lintott, A.W. 1967, 'P. Clodius Pulcher – felix Catilina?' *G&R* 14: 157–69.

Lintott, A.W. 1974, 'Cicero and Milo' *JRS* 64: 62–78.

Lintott, A.W. 1999, *Violence in Republican Rome*, second edition, Oxford.

Luibheid, C. 1970, 'The Luca conference' *CPh* 65: 88–94.

Malamud, M. 2003, 'Pompey's head and Cato's snakes' *CPh* 98: 31–44.

Marshall, A.M. 1999, 'Atticus and the eastern sojourn' *Latomus* 58: 56–68.

Marshall, B.A. 1972, 'The *lex Plotia agraria*' *Antichthon* 6: 43–52.

Marshall, B.A. 1974, 'Cicero and Sallust on Crassus and Catiline' *Latomus* 33: 804–13.

Marshall, B.A. 1975, 'Q. Cicero, Hortensius and the lex Aurelia' *RhM* 118: 136–52.

Marshall, B.A. 1976, *Crassus. A Political Biography*, Amsterdam.

Marshall, B.A. 1985, *A Historical Commentary on Asconius*, Missouri.

Marshall, B.A. 1987, 'Pompeius' fear of assassination' *Chiron* 17: 119–33.

Marshall, B.A. & Beness, L. 1987, 'Tribunician agitation and aristocratic reaction 80–71 BC' *Athenaeum* 65: 361–78.

McDermott, W.C. 1970, 'The sisters of P. Clodius' *Phoenix* 24: 39–47.

McDermott, W.C. 1972, 'M. Cicero and M. Tiro' *Historia* 21: 259–86.

McDermott, W.C. 1977, 'The Verrine jury' *RhM* 120: 64–75.

McDermott, W.C. 1977a, 'Lex de tribunicia potestate' *CPh* 72: 49–52.

McGushin, P. 1992, *Sallust. The Histories. Translated with Introduction and Commentary*, vols I–II, Oxford.

Meier, C. 1995, *Caesar. A Biography*, New York.

Meijer, F. 1993, 'Cicero and the costs of the Republican grain laws' in Sancisi-Weerdenburg, H. (ed. et al.) *De Agricultura*, Amsterdam: 153–63.

Millar, F. 1995, 'The last century of the Republic. Whose history?' *JRS* 85: 236–43.

Millar, F. 1998, *The Crowd in Rome in the Late Republic*, Michigan.

Mitchell, T.N. 1969, 'Cicero before Luca (September 57 – April 56 BC)' *TAPhA* 100: 295–320.

Mitchell, T.N. 1979, *Cicero. The Ascending Years*, New Haven.

Mitchell, T.N. 1986, 'The leges Clodiae and obnuntiatio' *CQ* 36: 172–6.

Mitchell, T.N. 1991, *Cicero. The Senior Statesman*, New Haven.

Morgan, L. 1997, '"Levi quidem de re ..." Julius Caesar as tyrant and pedant' *JRS* 87: 23–40.

Mouritsen, H. 2001, *Plebs and Politics in the Late Roman Republic*, Cambridge.

Mulroy, D. 1988, 'The early career of P. Clodius Pulcher: a re-examination of the charges of mutiny and sacrilege' *TAPhA* 118: 155–78.

Mulryne, T.W. 1977, *The Roman Forum*, London.

Murphy, J. 1993, 'Pompey's eastern acta' *AHB* 7: 136–42.

Nippel, W. 1984, 'Policing Rome' *JRS* 74: 20–9.

North, J.A. 1975, 'Praesens Divus [Review of Weinstock 1971]' *JRS* 65: 171–7.

Oost, S.I. 1955, 'Cato Uticensis and the annexation of Cyprus' *CPh* 50: 98–109.

Parrish, E.J. 1972, 'The senate on January 1, 62 BC' *CW* 65: 160–8.

Parrish, E.J. 1973, 'Crassus' new friends and Pompey's return' *Phoenix* 27: 357–80.

Paul, G.M. 1985, 'Sallust, *Catiline* 14.2' *Phoenix* 39: 158–61.

Pelling, C.B.R. 1985, 'Plutarch and Catiline' *Hermes* 113: 311–29.

Phillips, E.J. 1976, 'Catiline's Conspiracy' *Historia* 25: 441–8.

Pocock, L.G. 1959, 'What made Pompeius fight in 49 BC?' *G&R* 6: 68–81.

Powell, A. 1998, 'Julius Caesar and the presentation of massacre' in Welch, K. & Powell, A. (eds) *Julius Caesar as Artful Reporter: the War Commentaries as Political Instruments*, London: 111–38.

Powell, A. & Welch, K. (eds) 2002, *Sextus Pompeius*, London.

Quinn, K. 1972, *Catullus. An Interpretation*, London.

Raditsa, L. 1973, 'Julius Caesar and his writings' *ANRW* I.3: 417–56.

Ramage, E.S. 2001, 'The *bellum iustum* in Caesar's *de Bello Gallico*' *Athenaeum* 89: 145–70.

Ramage, E.S. 2002, 'The *Populus Romanus*, imperium, and Caesar's presence in the *De Bello Gallico*' *Athenaeum* 90: 125–46.

Ramsey, J.T. 1980, 'The prosecution of C. Manilius in 66 BC and Cicero's *Pro Manilio*' *Phoenix* 34: 323–36.

Ramsey, J.T. 2004, 'Did Julius Caesar temporarily banish Mark Antony from his inner circle?' *CQ* 54: 161–73.

Rauh, N.K. 2003, *Merchants, Sailors and Pirates in the Roman World*, Stroud.

Rawson, E. 1975, *Cicero. A Portrait*, London.

Rawson, E. 1991, 'Caesar's heritage: hellenistic kings and their Roman equals' in Rawson, E. *Roman Culture and Society*, Oxford: 169–88 = 1975, *JRS* 65: 148–59.

Rawson, E. 1994, 'Caesar: civil war and dictatorship' in *CAH* IX²: 424–67.

Ridley, R.T. 1999, 'What's in the name: the so-called first Triumvirate' *Arctos* 33: 133–44.

Riggsby, A.M. 2002, 'Clodius/Claudius' *Historia* 51: 117–23.

Ruebel, J.S. 1979, 'The trial of Milo in 52 BC: a chronological study' *TAPhA* 109: 231–49.

Rundell, W.M.F. 1979, 'Cicero and Clodius: the question of credibility' *Historia* 28: 301–28.

Ryan, F.X. 1996, 'Bibulus as President of the Senate' *Latomus* 55: 384–8.

Seager, R. 1964, 'The First Catilinarian Conspiracy' *Historia* 13: 338–47.

Seager, R. 1965, 'Clodius, Pompeius and the exile of Cicero' *Latomus* 24: 519–31.

Seager, R. (ed.) 1969, *The Crisis of the Roman Republic*, Cambridge.

Seager, R. 1973, 'Iusta Catilinae' *Historia* 22: 240–8.

Seager, R. 1994, 'The rise of Pompey' in *CAH* IX²: 208–28.

Seager, R. 2002, *Pompey the Great. A Political Biography*, second edition, Oxford.

Sedley, D. 1997, 'The ethics of Brutus and Cassius' *JRS* 87: 41–53.

Shackleton Bailey, D.R. 1960, 'The credentials of L. Caesar and L. Roscius' *JRS* 50: 80–3.

Shackleton Bailey, D.R. 1965–70, *Cicero's Letters to Atticus*, vols I-VII, Cambridge.

Shackleton Bailey, D.R. 1977, *Cicero: Epistulae ad Familiares*, vols I-II, Cambridge.

Sherwin-White, A.N. 1969, 'Violence in Roman politics' in Seager, R. (ed.) *The Crisis of the Roman Republic*, Cambridge: 151–9.

Sherwin-White, A.N. 1994, 'Lucullus, Pompey and the East' in *CAH* IX²: 229–73.

Shotter, D. 1994, *The Fall of the Roman Republic*, London.

Siani-Davies, M. 1996, 'Gaius Rabirius Postumus: a Roman financier and Caesar's political ally' *Arctos* 30: 207–40.

Simone, A.C. 1999, 'Saxum Tarpeium' in Steinby IV.237–8.

Smallwood, E.M. 1976, *The Jews under Roman Rule. From Pompey to Diocletian*, Leiden.

Smith, R.E. 1955, *The Failure of the Roman Republic*, Cambridge.

Smith, R.E. 1957, 'The *lex Plotia agraria* and Pompey's Spanish veterans' *CQ* 51: 82–5.

Smith, R.E. 1960, 'Pompey's conduct in 80 and 77 BC' *Phoenix* 14: 1–13.

Smith, R.E. 1966, *Cicero the Statesman*, Cambridge.

Southern, P. 1998, *Mark Antony*, Stroud.

Southern, P. 1999, *Cleopatra*, Stroud.

Southern, P. 2001, *Julius Caesar*, Stroud.

Southern, P. 2002, *Pompey*, Stroud.

Souza, P. de 1999, *Piracy in the Graeco-Roman World*, Cambridge.

Spann, P.O. 1987, *Quintus Sertorius and the Legacy of Sulla*, Fayetteville.

Squires, S. 1990, *Asconius Pedianus, Quintus. Commentaries on Five Speeches of Cicero*, Bristol.

Stockton, D. 1969, *Thirty-Five Letters of Cicero*, Oxford.

Stockton, D. 1971, *Cicero. A Political Biography*, Oxford.

Stockton, D. 1973, 'The first consulship of Pompey' *Historia* 22: 205–18.

Stockton, D. 1975, '"Quis iustius induit arma"' *Historia* 24: 232–59.

Stone, M. 1999, 'Tribute to a statesman: Cicero and Sallust' *Antichthon* 33: 48–76.

Strisino, J. 2002, 'Sulla and Scipio "Not to be trusted"? The reasons why Sertorius captured Suessa Aurunca' *Latomus* 61: 33–40.

Sumner, G.V. 1965, 'The consular elections of 66 BC' *Phoenix* 19: 226–31.

Sumner, G.V. 1966, 'Cicero, Pompeius, and Rullus' *TAPhA* 97: 569–82.

Sumner, G.V. 1971, 'The lex annalis under Caesar' *Phoenix* 25: 246–71, 357–71.

Sumner, G.V. 1977, 'The Pompeii in their families' *AJAH* 2: 8–25.

Syme, R. 1939, *The Roman Revolution*, Oxford.

Syme, R. 1964, *Sallust*, Berkeley.

Syme, R. 1979, 'Caesar, the senate, and Italy' in Badian, E. (ed.) *Ronald Syme. Roman Papers*, Oxford, vol. I: 88–119.

Syme, R. 1979a, 'A Roman post-mortem. An inquest on the fall of the Roman Republic' in Badian, E. (ed.) *Ronald Syme. Roman Papers*, Oxford, vol. I: 205–17.

Tanner, J. 2000, 'Portraits, power and patronage in the late Roman Republic' *JRS* 90: 18–50.

Tatum, W.J. 1990, 'Cicero and the *Bona Dea* scandal' *CPh* 85: 202–7.

Tatum, W.J. 1990a, 'Cicero's opposition to the *lex Clodia de collegiis*' *CQ* 40: 187–94.

Tatum, W.J. 1990b, 'The *lex Clodia de censoria notione*' *CPh* 85: 34–43.

Tatum, W.J. 1991, 'Lucullus and Clodius at Nisibis (Plutarch, *Lucullus* 33–34)' *Athenaeum* 79: 569–79.

Tatum, W.J. 1991a, 'The marriage of Pompey's son to the daughter of Ap. Claudius Pulcher' *Klio* 73: 122–29.

Tatum, W.J. 1993, 'The *Lex Papiria de dedicationibus*' *CPh* 88: 319–28.

Tatum, W.J. 1996, '*Hospitem* or *hostem*?' *RhM* 139: 358–60.

Tatum, W.J. 1999, *The Patrician Tribune. Publius Clodius Pulcher*, Chapel Hill.

Taylor, L.R. 1931, *The Divinity of the Roman Emperor*, Middletown.

Taylor, L.R. 1941, 'Caesar's early career' *CPh* 36: 113–32.

Taylor, L.R. 1949, *Party Politics in the Age of Caesar*, Berkeley.

Taylor, L.R. 1950, 'The date and the meaning of the Vettius affair' *Historia* 1: 45–51.

Taylor, L.R. 1954, 'On the date of *ad Atticum* 2.24' *CQ* 4: 181–2.

Taylor, L.R. 1957, 'The rise of Julius Caesar' *G&R* 4: 10–18.

Taylor, L.R. 1968, 'The dating of the major legislation and elections in Caesar's first consulship' *Historia* 17: 173–93.

Townend, G.B. 1987, 'C. Oppius on Julius Caesar' *AJPh* 108: 325–42.

Townend, G.B. 1983, 'A clue to Caesar's unfulfilled intentions' *Latomus* 42: 601–6.

Toynbee, J.M.C. 1978, *Roman Historical Portraits*, London.

Treggiari, S.M. 1969, *Roman Freedmen during the Late Republic*, Oxford.

Twyman, B. 1972, 'The Metelli, Pompeius and prosopography' *ANRW* I.1: 816–74.

Tyrrell, W.B. 1973, 'The trial of C. Rabirius in 63 BC' *Latomus* 32: 285–300.

Ward, A.M. 1968, 'Cicero's support of Pompey in the trials of M. Fonteius and P. Oppius' *Latomus* 27: 802–09.

Ward, A.M. 1970, 'Cicero and Pompey in 75 and 70 BC' *Latomus* 29: 58–71.

Ward, A.M. 1970a, 'Politics in the trials of Manilius and Cornelius' *TAPhA* 101: 545–56.

Ward, A.M. 1970b, 'The early relationships between Cicero and Pompey until 80 BC' *Phoenix* 24: 119–29.

Ward, A.M. 1972, 'Cicero's fight against Crassus and Caesar in 65 and 63 BC' *Historia* 21: 244–58.

Ward, A.M. 1977, *Marcus Crassus and the Late Roman Republic*, Columbia.

Waters, K.H. 1970, 'Cicero, Sallust, and Caesar' *Historia* 19: 195–215.

Weigel, R.D. 1992, *Lepidus. The Tarnished Triumvir*, London.

Weinstock, S. 1937, 'Clodius and the lex Aelia Fufia' *JRS* 27: 215–22.

Weinstock, S. 1971, *Divus Julius*, Oxford.

Welch, K.E. 1995, 'The career of M. Aemilius Lepidus' *Hermes* 123: 443–54.

White, P. 1997, 'Julius Caesar and the publication of *acta* in late Republican Rome' *Chiron* 27: 73–84.

Whitehorne, J. 1994, *Cleopatras*, London.

Williams, R.S. 1984, 'The appointment of Glabrio (*cos*. 67) to the eastern command' *Phoenix* 38: 221–34.

Wiseman, T.P. 1966, 'The ambitions of Quintus Cicero' *JRS* 56: 108–15.

Wiseman, T.P. (ed.) 1985, *Roman Political Life 90 BC – AD 69*, Exeter.

Wiseman, T.P. 1985a, *Catullus and his World*, Cambridge.

Wiseman, T.P. 1994, 'The senate and the *populares*, 69–60 BC' in *CAH* IX²: 327–67.

Wiseman, T.P. 1994a, 'Caesar, Pompey and Rome, 59–50 BC' in *CAH* IX²: 368–423.

Wistrand, E. 1979, *Caesar and Contemporary Roman Society*, Göteborg.

Wistrand, E. 1979a, *Cicero Imperator. Studies in Cicero's Correspondence 51–47 BC*, Göteburg.

Wistrand, E. 1981, *The Policy of Brutus the Tyrannicide*, Göteburg.

Wray, D. 2001, *Catullus and the Poetics of Roman Manhood*, Cambridge.

Wylie, G. 1992, 'The road to Pharsalus' *Latomus* 51: 552–65.

Wylie, G. 1994, 'Lucullus Daemoniac' *AC* 63: 109–19.

Yavetz, Z. 1963, 'The failure of Catiline's conspiracy' *Historia* 12: 485–99.
Yavetz, Z. 1983, *Julius Caesar and his Public Image*, London.

Chapter Fourteen: The Ancient Sources

Adcock, F. 1956, *Julius Caesar as Man of Letters*, Cambridge.
Astin, A.E. 1989, 'Sources' in *CAH* VIII²: 1–16.
Badian, E. 1966, 'The early historians' in Dorey, T.A. (ed.) *Latin Historians*, London: 1–38.
Baldwin, B. 1983, *Suetonius*, Amsterdam.
Balsdon, J.P.V.D. 1971, 'Dionysius on Romulus: a political pamphlet?' *JRS* 61: 18–27.
Beagon, M. 1992, *Roman Nature. The Thought of Pliny the Elder*, Oxford.
Bodel, J. (ed.) 2001, *Epigraphic Evidence: Ancient History from Inscriptions*, London.
Bucher, G.S. 1995, 'The annales maximi in the light of Roman methods of keeping records' *AJAH* 12: 2–61.
Bucher, G.S. 2002, 'The origins, program, and composition of Appian's *Roman History*' *TAPhA* 130: 411–58.
Chaplin, J.D. 2000, *Livy's Exemplary History*, Oxford.
Clarke, K. 1999, *Between Geography and History: Hellenistic Constructions of the Roman World*, Oxford.
Coffey, M. 1995, *Roman Satire*, second edition, London.
Collins, J.H. 1972, 'Caesar as a political propagandist' *ANRW* I.1: 922–66.
Comber, M. 1997, 'Re-reading the Roman historians' in Bentley, M. (ed.) *Companion to Historiography*, London: 43–56.
Cooley, A.E. 2000, 'Inscribing history at Rome' in Cooley, A.E. (ed.) *The Afterlife of Inscriptions*, London.
Cooley, A.E. 2000a, *The Epigraphic Landscape of Roman Italy*, London.
Cornell, T.J. 1986, 'The formation of the historical tradition of early Rome' in Moxon, I.S. et al. (eds) *Past Perspectives. Studies in Greek and Roman Historical Writing*, Cambridge: 67–86.
Cornell, T.J. 1986a, 'The value of the literary tradition concerning archaic Rome' in Raaflaub, K.A. (ed.) *Social Struggles in Archaic Rome: New Perspectives on the Conflict of the Orders*, Berkeley: 52–76.
Cornell, T.J. 1995, *The Beginnings of Rome. Italy and Rome from the Bronze Age to the Punic Wars (c. 1000–264 BC)*, London.
Crawford, M. 1983, 'Numismatics' in Crawford, M. (ed.) *Sources for Ancient History*, Cambridge: 183–233.
Culham, P. 1989, 'Archives and alternatives in Republican Rome' *CPh* 84: 100–15.
Dalby, A. 1998, *Cato: On Farming*, Totnes.
Davidson, J. 1991, 'The gaze in Polybius' *Histories*' *JRS* 81: 10–24.
Derow, P.S. 1979, 'Polybius, Rome and the East' *JRS* 69: 1–15.
Derow, P.S. 1994, 'Polybius and his predecessors' in Hornblower, S. (ed.) *Greek Historiography*, Oxford: 73–90.
Dionisotti, A. 1988, 'Nepos and the generals' *JRS* 78: 35–49.
Dorey, T.A. (ed) 1965, *Cicero*, London.
Dorey, T.A. (ed.) 1966, *Latin Historians*, London.
Dorey, T.A. (ed.) 1967, *Latin Biography*, London.
Earl, D.C. 1991, *The Political Thought of Sallust*, Cambridge.
Eckstein, A.M. 1992, 'Notes on the birth and death of Polybius' *AJPh* 113: 387–406.
Eckstein, A.M. 1997, 'Physis and Nomos: Polybius, the Romans and Cato the Elder' in Cartledge,

P., Garnsey, P. & Gruen, E. (eds) *Hellenistic Constructs. Essays in Culture, History and Historiography*, Berkeley: 175–98.

Edwards, M.J. 1991, *Plutarch. The Lives of Pompey, Caesar and Cicero*, Bristol.

Feldherr, A. 1998, *Spectacle and Society in Livy's History*, Berkeley.

Fornara, C.W. 1983, *The Nature of History in Ancient Greece and Rome*, Berkeley.

Forsythe, G. 1994, *The Historian L. Calpurnius Piso Frugi and the Roman Annalistic Tradition*, Lanham.

Forsythe, G. 1999, *Livy and Early Rome. A Study in Historical Method and Judgment*, Stuttgart.

Forsythe, G. 2000, 'The Roman historians of the second century BC' in Bruun, C. (ed.) *The Roman Middle Republic. Politics, Religion and Historiography, c. 400 –133 BC*, Rome: 1–11.

Fox, M. 1993, 'History and rhetoric in Dionysius of Halicarnassus' *JRS* 83: 31–47.

Frier, B.W. 1979, *Libri annales pontificum maximorum: the Origins of the Annalistic Tradition*, Rome.

Gabba, E. 1981, 'True history and false history in classical antiquity' *JRS* 71: 50–62.

Gabba, E. 1983, 'Literature' in Crawford, M. (ed.) *Sources for Ancient History*, Cambridge: 1–79.

Gabba, E. 1991, *Dionysius and 'The History of Archaic Rome'*, Berkeley.

Geiger, J. 1985, *Cornelius Nepos and Ancient Political Biography*, Stuttgart.

Gordon, A.E., 1983, *An Illustrated Introduction to Latin Epigraphy*, Berkeley.

Gossage, A.J. 1967, 'Plutarch' in Dorey, T.A. (ed.) *Latin Biography*, London: 45–78.

Gowing, A.M. 1992, *The Triumviral Narratives of Appian and Cassius Dio*, Ann Arbor.

Grant, M. 1995, *Greek and Roman Historians; Information and Misinformation*, London.

Gratwick, A.S. 1982, 'The satires of Ennius and Lucilius' in Kenney, E.J. & Clausen W.V. (eds) *The Cambridge History of Classical Literature. Volume 2: Latin Literature*, Cambridge: 156–71.

Gruen, E.S. 1990, *Studies in Greek Culture and Roman Policy*, Berkeley.

Gruen, E.S. 1992, *Culture and National Identity in Republican Rome*, London.

Henderson, J. 1989, 'Livy and the invention of History' in Cameron, A. (ed.) *History as Text: the Writing of Ancient History*, London: 64–85.

Hill, H. 1961, 'Dionysius and the origins of Rome' *JRS* 51: 88–93.

Hillard, T.W. 1987, 'Plutarch's late-republican Lives. Between the lines' *Antichthon* 21: 19–48.

Hinds, S. 1998, *Allusion and Intertext*, Cambridge.

Holford-Strevens, L.A. 1988, *Aulus Gellius*, London.

How, N. 1985, 'In defence of the encyclopedic mode: On Pliny's preface to the *Natural History*' *Latomus* 44: 561–76.

Jaeger, M. 1997, *Livy's Written Rome*, Ann Arbor.

Jaeger, M. 1999, 'Guiding metaphor and narrative point of view in Livy's *ab urbe condita*' in Kraus, C.S. (ed.) *The Limits of Historiography. Genre and Narrative in Ancient Historical Texts*, Leiden: 165–95.

Jenkinson, E. 1967, 'Nepos – an introduction to Latin biography' in Dorey, T.A. (ed.) *Latin Biography*, London: 1–16.

Jocelyn, H.D. 1967, *The Tragedies of Ennius*, Cambridge.

Jocelyn, H.D. 1972, 'The poems of Quintus Ennius' *ANRW* I.2: 987–1026.

Jones, C.P. 1971, *Plutarch and Rome*, Oxford.

Keppie, L. 1991, *Understanding Roman Inscriptions*, Baltimore.

Kirby, J.T. 1997, 'Ciceronian rhetoric: theory and practice' in Dominik, W.J. (ed.) *Roman Eloquence. Rhetoric in Society and Literature*, London: 13–31.

Kraus, C.S. (ed.) 1999, *The Limits of Historiography. Genre and Narrative in Ancient Historical Texts*, Leiden.

Kraus, C.S. 1999, 'Jugurthine disorder' in Kraus, C.S. (ed.) *The Limits of Historiography. Genre and Narrative in Ancient Historical Texts*, Leiden: 217–47.

Kraus, C.S. & Woodman, A.J. 1997, *Latin Historians*, Oxford.

Lamberton, R. 2002, *Plutarch*, Yale.

Levene, D.S. 1992, 'Sallust's *Jugurtha*: an historical fragment?' *JRS* 82: 53–70.

Lintott, A. 1994, 'The crisis of the Republic: sources and source-problems' in *CAH* IX²: 1–15.

Luce, T.J. 1977, *Livy, the Composition of his History*, Princeton.

Lyne, R.O.A.M. 1980, *The Latin Love-Poets, from Catullus to Horace*, Oxford.

MacKendrick, P. 1995, *The Speeches of Cicero. Context, Law, Rhetoric*, London.

MacMullen, R. 1991, 'Hellenizing the Romans (2nd Century BC)' *Historia* 40: 419–38.

Marincola, J. 1997, *Authority and Tradition in Ancient Historiography*, Cambridge.

Maslakov, G. 1984, 'Valerius Maximus and Roman historiography: a study of the exempla tradition' *ANRW* II.32.1: 437–96.

Mattingly, H.B. 1976, 'Q. Fabius Pictor, father of Roman history' *LCM* 1:3–7.

McDonald, A.H. 1975, 'Theme and style in Roman historiography' *JRS* 65: 1–10.

McGushin, P. 1994, *A Commentary on Sallust's Histories*, vols I–II, Oxford.

Meier, C. 1995, *Caesar, a Biography*, London.

Mellor, R. (ed.) 1998, *The Historians of Ancient Rome: an Anthology of the Major Writings*, London.

Mellor, R. 1999, *The Roman Historians*, London.

Miles, G. 1995, *Livy: Reconstructing Early Rome*, Ithaca.

Millar, F. 1983, 'Epigraphy' in Crawford, M. (ed.) *Sources for Ancient History*, Cambridge: 80–136.

Millar, F. 1988, 'Cornelius Nepos, "Atticus" and the Roman Revolution' *G&R* 35: 41–55.

Millar, F.G.B. 1964, *A Study of Cassius Dio*, Oxford.

Mitchell, T.N. 1979, *Cicero, the Ascending Years*, New Haven.

Mitchell, T.N. 1991, *Cicero, the Senior Statesman*, New Haven.

Momigliano, A. 1990, *The Classical Foundations of Modern Historiography*, Berkeley.

Moxon, I.S. et al. (eds) 1986, *Past Perspectives: Studies in Greek and Roman Historical Writing*, Cambridge.

Newman, J.K. 1991, *Roman Catullus and the Modification of the Alexandrian Sensibility*, Hildesheim.

Oakley, S.P. 1997, *A Commentary on Livy, Books VI–X*, vols I–II, Oxford.

Ogilvie, R.M. 1970, *A Commentary on Livy, Books 1–5*, revised edition, Oxford.

Ogilvie, R.M. & Drummond, A. 1989, 'The sources for early Roman history' in *CAH* VII.2²: 1–29.

Paul, G.M. 1984, *A Historical Commentary on Sallust's Bellum Jugurthinum*, Liverpool.

Pelling, C.B.R. 1979, 'Plutarch's method of work in the Roman *Lives*' *JHS* 99: 74–96.

Pelling, C.B.R. 1980, 'Plutarch's adaptation of his source-material' *JHS* 100: 127–40.

Powell, J. 1998, *Cicero the Philosopher*, Oxford.

Powell, J. & Patterson, J. (eds) 2004, *Cicero, the Advocate*, Oxford.

Quinn, K. 1972, *Catullus, an Interpretation*, London.

Raditsa, L. 1973, 'Julius Caesar and his writings' *ANRW* I.3: 417–56.

Ramage, E.S. 2001, 'The *bellum iustum* in Caesar's *de Bello Gallico*' *Athenaeum* 89: 145–70.

Ramage, E.S. 2002, 'The *Populus Romanus*, imperium, and Caesar's presence in the *De Bello Gallico*' *Athenaeum* 90: 125–46.

Rawson, E. 1975, *Cicero, a Portrait*, London.

Rawson, E. 1985, *Intellectual Life in the Late Roman Republic*, London.

Rawson, E. 1989, 'Roman tradition and the Greek world' in *CAH* VIII^2: 422–76.

Rawson, E. 1991, 'Cicero the historian and Cicero the antiquarian' in Rawson, E. *Roman Culture and Society*, Oxford: 58–79 = 1972, *JRS* 62: 33–45.

Rawson, E. 1991a, 'The first Latin annalists' in Rawson, E. *Roman Culture and Society*, Oxford: 245–71 = 1976, *Latomus* 35: 689–717.

Rawson, E. 1991b, 'Prodigy lists and the use of the *annales maximi*' in Rawson, E. *Roman Culture and Society*, Oxford: 1–15 = 1971, *CQ* 21: 158–69.

Richardson, J.S. 1979, 'Polybius' view of the Roman empire' *PBSR* 34: 1–11.

Ridley, R.T. 2000, 'Livy and the Hannibalic war' in Bruun, C. (ed.) *The Roman Middle Republic. Politics, Religion and Historiography, c. 400–133 BC*, Rome: 13–40.

Rudd, N. 1986, *Themes in Roman Satire*, London.

Russell, D.A. 1972, *Plutarch*, London.

Sachs, K.S. 1990, *Diodorus Siculus and the First Century*, Princeton.

Sachs, K.S. 1994, 'Diodorus and his sources' in Hornblower, S. (ed.) *Greek Historiography*, Oxford: 213–32.

Sacks, K.S. 1981, *Polybius on the Writing of History*, Berkeley.

Schultze, C. 1986, 'Dionysius of Halicarnassus and his audience' in Moxon, I.S. et al. (eds) *Past Perspectives: Studies in Greek and Roman Historical Writing*, Cambridge: 121–42.

Skutsch, O. 1985, *The Annals of Q. Ennius*, Oxford.

Seager, R. 1977, '*Populares* in Livy and the Livian tradition' *CQ* 27: 377–90.

Skidmore, C. 1996, *Practical Ethics for Roman Gentlemen: the Work of Valerius Maximus*, Exeter.

Snodgrass, A. 1983, 'Archaeology' in Crawford, M. (ed.) *Sources for Ancient History*, Cambridge: 137–84.

Stadter, P.A. (ed.) 1992, *Plutarch and the Historical Tradition*, London

Starr, R.J. 1981, 'The scope and genre of Velleius' *History*' *CQ* 31: 162–74.

Stone, M. 1999, 'Tribute to a statesman; Cicero and Sallust' *Antichthon* 33: 48–76.

Swain, S. 1990, 'Plutarch's *Lives* of Cicero, Cato, and Brutus' *Hermes* 118: 192–203.

Syme, R. 1984, 'Velleius Paterculus' in Badian, E. (ed.) *Ronald Syme. Roman Papers*, Oxford, vol. 3: 1090–1104.

Syme, R., 1964, *Sallust*, Berkeley.

Titchener, F. 2003, 'Cornelius Nepos and the biographical tradition' *G&R* 50: 85–99.

Townend, G.B. 1967, 'Suetonius and his influence' in Dorey, T.A. (ed.) *Latin Biography*, London: 79–112.

Walbank, F.W. 1967–79, *A Historical Commentary on Polybius*, vols I–III, Oxford.

Walbank, F.W. 1972, *Polybius*, Berkeley.

Walbank, F.W. 2002, *Polybius, Rome and the Hellenistic World: Essays and Reflections*, Cambridge.

Wallace-Hadrill, A. 1983, *Suetonius: the Scholar and his Caesars*, London.

Wallace-Hadrill, A. 1990, 'Pliny the Elder and Man's Unnatural History' *G&R* 37: 80–96.

Wallace-Hadrill, A. 1995, *Suetonius*, London.

Walsh, P.G. 1955, 'Livy's Preface and the distortion of history' *AJPh* 76: 369–83.

Walsh, P.G. 1961, *Livy, his Historical Aims and Methods*, Cambridge.

Welch, K. & Powell, A. (eds), 1998, *Julius Caesar as Artful Reporter: the War Commentaries as Political Instruments*, London.

Wiseman, T.P. 1979, *Clio's Cosmetics: Three Studies in Greco-Roman Literature*, Leicester.

Wiseman, T.P. 1985, *Catullus and his World*, Cambridge.

Wiseman, T.P. 1986, 'Monuments and the Roman annalists' in Moxon, I.S. et al. (eds) *Past Perspectives: Studies in Greek and Roman Historical Writing*, Cambridge: 87–100.

Woodman, A.J. 1975, 'Questions of date, genre and style in Velleius: some literary answers' *CQ* 25: 272–306.

Index of Ancient Sources

Numbers here refer to documents. Abbreviations used for authors and titles are given in square brackets: Appian [App.] *Civil Wars* [*BC*].

General Index

Numbers refer to documents and their introductions. For ancient authors, see also the index of ancient sources.

Censors' Records, 3.22, 3.47, 14.17
census, the, 1.15–17; census qualifications, 1.19; *see also* lustrum
Cethegus, *see* Cornelius Cethegus
Chalcis (Euboea), 5.26
Charops of Epirus, 5.33, 5.37
chickens, sacred, 3.50–2, 5.48
children, 1.33, 7.1–5, 7.12, 7.14–15, 13.12; *see also* bulla, education, family, women
Chilon (slave of Cato the Elder), 7.21
Chrysogonus (freedman of Sulla), 2.51, 6.13, 6.38, 11.24–5
Chyretiae (Thessaly), 5.25
Cicero, *see* Tullius Cicero
Cilicia, 5.68–70, 6.13, 11.13, 12.67, 13.7, 13.13, 13.19–20
Cimbri, the, 9.14–19, 9.23, 9.26, 9.28, 9.35, 11.13
Cincinnatus, *see* Quinctius Cincinnatus
Cincius Alimentus, L. (historian), 14.3
Cinna, *see* Cornelius Cinna
Civil War, the, 2.35, 2.56, 13.24–52
Claudia (epitaph of), 7.31
Claudia Quinta, 3.59, 7.30
Claudius Caecus, App. (cos. 307, 296; cen. 312), 1.53, 1.55, 1.73, 2.4, 2.5, 7.52
Claudius Caudex, App. (cos. 264), 4.7, 4.8
Claudius Crassinus Inregillensis Sabinus, App. (cos. 471, decemvir 451/450), 1.30
Claudius Marcellus, C. (cos. 50), 12.78, 13.9, 13.12, 13.15, 13.19, 13.22–3, 13.51, 13.63
Claudius Marcellus, C. (cos. 49), 13.24
Claudius Marcellus, M. (cos. 222, 214, 210, 208, suffect cos. 215), 4.46, 4.47, 4.60, 5.40, 13.60
Claudius Marcellus, M. (cos. 166, 155, 152), 5.47
Claudius Marcellus, M. (cos. 51), 13.5, 13.7–9, 13.11–13, 13.24, 13.32, 13.51–2
Claudius Pulcher, App. (cos. 143), 8.8, 8.11, 8.13, 8.16–17, 8.19
Claudius Pulcher, App. (cos. 54), 5.68, 6.53, 12.58, 12.69, 12.76
Claudius Pulcher, P. (cos. 249), 3.51, 6.49
Claudius Quadrigarius, Q. (historian), 14.3, 14.9
Cleomenes III of Sparta, 8.1, 8.41
Cleopatra VII (69–30), 13.48, 13.63

Clesippus Geganius (hunchback), 7.71
clientela, 2.49–57, 12.11, 12.69
Clodia (wife of L. Licinius Lucullus, sister of Clodius), 7.9, 12.10
Clodia Metelli (wife of Q. Metellus Celer, cos. 60; sister of Clodius), 7.47, 7.51–2, 12.67, 14.25
Clodius Pulcher, P. (tr. pl. 58), 2.3, 6.30, 7.36, 7.57, 7.85, 12.10, 12.35–6, 12.46–8, 12.52–62, 12.67, 12.69–70, 12.71, 12.89, 13.1–2, 13.5, 13.63, 14.25
Coelius Antipater, L. (historian), 14.3, 14.9
coinage, 3.79, 6.44, 7.91–2, 9.36–8, 10.12, 10.29–31, 11.1, 11.45–50, 13.72–5
collegia, 6.52, 7.73, 11.6, 11.38, 12.52, 13.54
colonies, 1.55, 1.64, 1.65, 1.67, 2.38, 8.5, 8.28–30, 9.18, 9.27, 9.28, 10.6, 10.9, 11.49, 12.13, 13.54
comitia centuriata, 1.19–21, 1.30, 11.5, 12.16–17, 12.58–9, 12.70, 13.53
comitia curiata, 1.20, 12.47, 12.76
comitia tributa, 1.20–1, 8.13, 8.15, 9.36, 10.17, 10.26, 11.12, 12.7, 13.53
concordia ordinum, the, 12.33, 12.36
confarreatio, 3.19, 7.10; *see also* marriage
Conflict of the Orders, the, 1.24–5, 1.28–57, 3.50, 7.75; *see also* decemvirate, Twelve Tables
consuls, duties of, 1.11, 1.13, 1.46–9, 1.58, 2.39, 2.40, 3.38, 12.42–3, 13.3–4, 13.6
Corinth, 1.4, 5.40–2
Coriolanus, *see* Marcius Coriolanus
Cornelia ('mother of the Gracchi'), 5.38, 7.8–9, 7.22, 7.29, 7.70, 8.1–2, 8.9, 8.12, 8.15, 8.21, 8.25, 8.29, 8.33, 14.14
Cornelia (daughter of Cinna, wife of Julius Caesar), 7.35
Cornelia (wife of P. Licinius Crassus and Pompey the Great), 7.44, 12.78, 13.46
Cornelius Balbus, L. (cos. 40), 3.41, 9.27, 10.21, 12.38, 12.75, 13.20, 13.34, 13.49, 13.55, 14.6
Cornelius Cethegus, P., 7.64
Cornelius Cinna, L. (cos. 87–84), 7.35, 9.34, 10.26–27, 11.5, 11.7, 11.12–13, 11.15, 12.68, 13.20, 13.71
Cornelius Dolabella, Cn. (cos. 81), 6.13
Cornelius Dolabella, P. (tr. pl. 47), 7.8, 7.26, 13.45, 13.49, 13.55

Fabius Pictor (antiquarian), 3.3, 3.19, 14.21

Fabius Pictor, Q. (historian), 4.5, 4.19, 4.21,
4.24, 4.38, 5.53, 14.3–4, 14.9

Fabius Vibulanus, Q. (cos. 467), 1.27, 1.43

family, the Roman, 7.1–85; *see also* adultery,
children, household, slaves, women

Fannius, C. (cos. 122), 8.28

farming, 2.15–16, 2.18, 2.24, 3.3, 3.26, 3.71,
6.31–2; *see also* ager publicus, Cato the
Elder

fasces, the, 1.11, 2.13, 2.57, 3.4, 8.15, 11.28,
12.41, 12.58, 12.69

fasti, the, 14.2

Fausta (daughter of Sulla), 13.1

Favonius, M. (aed. 53, praet. 49), 12.43,
12.61, 12.74, 13.29

Feriae Latinae, the, 3.9, 12.67, 13.14, 13.42,
13.55

festivals, 3.8–9, 3.21, 3.69–71, 5.33, 6.17,
7.39, 7.70, 7.75–84, 11.37; *see also*
aediles, games, Bona Dea, Feriae Latinae,
Fortuna Muliebris, Liberalia, Lupercalia,
Matralia, Matronalia, Melinno of Lesbos,
Pudicitia, Robigalia, Saturnalia,
supplicatio, Titeia, Veneralia, Vinalia

fetials, the, 3.12

Fimbria, *see* Flavius Fimbria

First Secession, the, *see* Conflict of the
Orders

'First Triumvirate', the, 12.38–89

fish-breeding, *see* piscinarii

Flaccus, *see* Fulvius Flaccus (cos. 125, tr. pl.
122) *or* Valerius Flaccus (cos. 100,
suffect cos. 86)

flamen dialis, 2.25, 3.17, 3.19

flamens, 2.23, 3.6, 3.17, 3.71, 7.10, 13.2,
13.55

Flamininus, *see* Quinctius Flamininus

Flaminius, C. (cos. 223, 217), 3.51, 4.32

flautists, 3.24, 3.70

Flavius Cn. (aed. 304), 1.54

Flavius, L. (tr. pl. 60), 12.34–6, 12.42, 12.58,
12.64

Flavius Fimbria, C. (cos. 104), 10.27, 11.7–8

foedus Cassianum, the, 1.26

Fonteius (adoptive father of Clodius), 12.46,
12.60

foreign cults, 3.55–65

Fortuna Muliebris, 7.82

forum Boarium, 1.2, 3.31, 4.38, 7.83

forum Julium, 2.74

forum Romanum, 1.2, 1.5–8, 2.3

freedmen, freedwomen, 1.36–7, 1.54, 6.2,
6.17, 6.18, 6.46–60, 7.13, 7.33, 7.50,
7.63, 7.73, 10.17, 11.12, 11.30–1, 11.40,
12.58, 13.46, 13.75; freedmen's 'liberty
cap', 1.59, 6.51, 13.75; *see also*
Chrysogonus, Publilius Syrus, Statius,
Terence, Tiro

Fufius Calenus, Q. (cos. 47), 7.74

Fulvia (informant of Cicero), 7.44, 12.15–16

Fulvia (wife of Clodius, Curio and Mark
Antony), 7.44, 13.63

Fulvius Flaccus, M. (cos. 125; tr. pl. 122),
1.59, 8.18, 8.19, 8.28, 8.30, 8.32–3, 8.40,
10.2, 10.6

Fulvius Nobilior, M. (cos. 189), 5.45, 5.52,
14.23

funerary practices, 1.42, 1.68, 2.74, 3.74–8,
12.77, 13.1, 13.46, 13.69, 14.23; funerary
eulogies, 2.28–9, 3.74, 7.23, 7.35, 7.37;
feasts, 2.74, 3.77; games, 2.3, 2.70,
2.73–4, 6.30; *see also* gladiators,
imagines

Furius Camillus, L. (cos. 338, 325), 1.64,
3.55

Furius Crassipes (second husband of Tullia),
7.26

Furnius, C. (tr. pl. 50, ?praet. 42), 13.13,
13.36

Gabinius, A. (tr. pl. 67, cos. 58), 12.8–10,
12.48, 12.50, 12.52–3, 12.58, 12.67,
12.71, 12.75–6

Galatia, 5.29

Galba, *see* Sulpicius Galba

Gallic sack of Rome, 1.2, 1.61, 3.16, 5.2,
5.10, 7.88, 14.9

Gallic War, the, 2.31, 2.47, 2.56–7, 5.17,
6.10–11, 12.43, 12.64–6, 12.71, 12.73–4,
12.80, 12.83–9, 13.7, 13.10, 13.21, 13.23,
13.72, 14.6; *see also* Britain, C. Julius
Caesar

Games, 2.8, 2.35, 2.37, 2.65–6, 2.68, 2.70–2,
3.24, 3.54, 3.59, 5.56, 11.30, 12.27,
12.50, 13.14, 13.70; *see also* aediles,
festivals

Gauda (grandson of Masinissa), 9.7

Tigranes II 'the Great', king of Armenia, 11.3, 12.4, 12.10–11

Tigranes the Younger, 12.58

Tillius Cimber, L. (?praet. 45, assassin of Caesar), 13.61–2

Timaeus of Tauromenium, 14.3

Tiro, M. Tullius (freedman of Cicero), 2.18, 5.36, 6.46–7, 7.40, 12.25, 13.25, 14.13, 14.21

Titeia, the, 5.26; *see also* T. Quinctius Flamininus

toga, 12.27, 3.74, 4.29, 4.61, 5.6, 13.61–2; of triumphator, 2.32, 13.55; of candidate, 2.36; mourning, 2.41, 12.53; cinctus gabinus, 316; praetexta, 3.62

Tolosa treasure, the, 9.14, 9.18

Torquatus, *see* Manlius Imperiosus Torquatus

torture, 4.13, 11.43; *see also* slaves

trade, 1.1, 1.4, 2.12, 2.19, 3.8, 4.1–3, 4.61, 12.8; *see also* piracy

traditional values, Roman, 1.9, 2.12–17, 2.20, 2.36, 5.58, 5.61–2, 7.20–1, 9.2, 12.23

Trasimene, battle of Lake, 3.51, 4.32, 4.34

treaties, 1.26–7, 1.63–4, 4.1–4, 4.17, 4.23, 4.27–8, 4.45, 4.58, 5.22–3, 5.27, 5.29–30, 5.39, 5.48, 8.7, 11.8, 14.1, 14.5

Trebonius, C. (tr. pl. 55, suffect cos. 45), 12.73–4, 13.42, 13.53, 13.61, 13.69

tribes of early Rome, 1.18, 1.54; *see also* comitia tributa

tribunes of the plebs, 1.13, 1.21–5, 1.45–6, 1.58, 9.31, 9.36, 11.28, 11.30, 11.32, 12.1, 12.5, 13.23–5, 13.28; *see also* Rome (early history of), P. Clodius Pulcher, M. Livius Drusus, C. Scribonius Curio, Ti. and C. Sempronius Gracchus, L. Appuleius Saturninus

tribunes, military, 1.13, 5.8, 5.9, 5.12–13, 5.16, 5.18–21, 5.33, 5.49, 14.4

tribute, 8.28, 11.8–10, 11.36, 12.11, 12.29, 12.35, 12.37, 12.42, 12.85

triumphs, 2.29, 2.32–5, 2.55, 2.69, 4.59, 5.8–10, 5.29, 5.40, 5.45, 5.50, 5.52–4, 6.45, 7.60, 8.1, 9.1, 9.12, 9.14, 9.20, 9.26, 9.35, 11.13, 11.17–18, 12.3, 12.5, 12.24, 12.27–9, 12.31, 12.37, 12.40, 12.71, 13.19–20, 13.35, 13.55, 13.65

Trojan legend, the, 2.29, 5.6, 7.88, 13.55, 13.73, 14.3, 14.8

Tuccia (Vestal Virgin), 7.90

Tuditanus, *see* Sempronius Tuditanus

Tullia (daughter of Cicero), 6.46, 7.7, 7.26–7, 7.36, 12.59, 13.45

Tullius Cicero, M. (cos. 63), 2.39–40, 9.4 (as a novus homo), 2.42–5 (on friendship), 2.51–4 (on patronage), 2.60 (on prosecution and defence), 2.61–2, 5.57, 6.53 (on his education as orator), 2.68, 2.72–3 (on public entertainment), 3.35, 3.37–8, 3.40, 3.44, 3.49, 3.51–2, 12.26 (on divination), 5.1 (on courage), 5.60, 5.62 (on Roman customs), 5.64–70, 6.48 (on provincial administration), 6.11, 6.38–9, 6.48 (on treatment of slaves), 6.42 (on a runaway slave), 6.46–7 (and Tiro), 7.26–7, 12.59 (affection for his daughter Tullia), 7.36, 7.40 (relationship with Terentia), 7.39 (on Pomponia), 7.44, 7.84, 12.13–24, 14.7 (role in the Catilinarian conspiracy), 7.69 (on inheritance law), 7.74 (and Caerellia), 7.85, 7.93, 11.32, 12.46–8, 12.52–60 (and Clodius), 7.93 (on his home), 8.8, 8.10, 8.12, 8.26, 8.34, 8.37–9, 11.32 (on the Gracchi), 9.8, 9.24, 9.27, 9.30 (on Marius), 10.14, 11.24 (army service), 11.12 (joins Sulla), 2.51, 11.24–5 (defence of Roscius of America), 2.40, 8.37–9, 12.13 (on agrarian legislation), 11.32, 12.8, 12.12, 12.20, 12.30–2, 12.34–6, 12.53, 12.56, 12.58, 13.32, 13.37, 13.47 (relationship with Pompey), 11.32 (on Sulla), 12.6 (on judicial corruption), 12.20 (praised by Pliny), 12.25, 13.53 (sense of humour), 12.26, 12.31, 12.38 (poem on his consulship), 12.33 (and the equites), 12.36, 12.38, 12.44–5, 12.66, 12.79, 12.84, 12.86 (relationship with Caesar), 12.49–50 (on the unpopularity of the 'triumvirate'), 12.53, 12.55–7 (and Cato the Younger), 12.58–60 (recall from exile), 12.61–3 (and Pompey's grain command), 12.67–9 (on the conference of Luca), 12.71–3 (on Caesar's Gallic command), 12.75 (defends his enemies in court), 13.5 (defence of Milo), 5.68–70, 13.7, 13.13, 13.19 (governorship of Cilicia), 13.32–3,

eBooks – at www.eBookstore.tandf.co.uk

A library at your fingertips!

eBooks are electronic versions of printed books. You can store them on your PC/laptop or browse them online.

They have advantages for anyone needing rapid access to a wide variety of published, copyright information.

eBooks can help your research by enabling you to bookmark chapters, annotate text and use instant searches to find specific words or phrases. Several eBook files would fit on even a small laptop or PDA.

NEW: Save money by eSubscribing: cheap, online access to any eBook for as long as you need it.

Annual subscription packages

We now offer special low-cost bulk subscriptions to packages of eBooks in certain subject areas. These are available to libraries or to individuals.

For more information please contact webmaster.ebooks@tandf.co.uk

We're continually developing the eBook concept, so keep up to date by visiting the website.

www.eBookstore.tandf.co.uk